Ultimate Study Guide: Foundations Microsoft Project 2013

Dale A. Howard
Gary L. Chefetz

Ultimate Study Guide: Foundations

Microsoft Project 2013

Publisher: Chefetz LLC dba MSProjectExperts
Authors: Dale A. Howard and Gary L. Chefetz
Cover Design: Emily Baker
Copy Editor: Rodney L. Walker

ISBN: 978-1-934240-27-4

Library of Congress Control Number: 2013937361

Published and distributed by Chefetz LLC dba MSProjectExperts, 90 John Street, Suite 404, New York, NY 10038. (646) 736-1688 http://www.msprojectexperts.com

MSProjectExperts publishes a complete series of role-based training/reference manuals for Microsoft's Enterprise Project Management software including Microsoft Project and Microsoft Project Server. Use our books for self-study or for classroom learning delivered by professional trainers and corporate training programs. To learn more about our books and courseware series for Administrators, Implementers, Project Managers, Resource Managers, Executives, Team Members, and Developers, or to obtain instructor companion products and materials, contact MSProjectExperts by phone (646) 736-1688 or by email info@msprojectexperts.com.

Contents

Introduction

Welcome to the *Ultimate Study Guide: Foundations Microsoft Project 2013,* a complete learning experience and reference manual for the Microsoft Project 2013 desktop application. Our goal in writing this book is to teach you how to use the software effectively.

We take a systematic approach to the topical ordering in this book, in which every module teaches you foundational skills by following the project life cycle. In these modules, you learn how to define a new project; plan your project with tasks, resources, and assignments, analyze the Critical Path, baseline your project, enter actual progress, analyze variance, revise your project, report about project progress, and then close the project.

Throughout each module, we provide a generous amount of information notes, warnings, and best practices. Information notes call your attention to important additional information about a subject. Warnings help you to avoid the most common problems experienced by others, while best practices provide tips for using the tool based on our field experience.

Microsoft Project 2013 offers a set of new and powerful features that make your job easier. I guarantee you will love the new dashboard reports feature that allows you to create reports that include Excel charts and Word tables. Download the sample files, work through the hands-on exercises and you will master it in no time."

Dale A. Howard, Microsoft Project MVP

Gary L. Chefetz, Microsoft Project MVP

MSProjectExperts

Download the Sample Files

Before working on any of the Hands On Exercises in this book, you must download and unzip the sample files required for each exercise. You can download these sample files from the following URL:

http://www.msprojectexperts.com/foundations2013

Module 01

Project Management Overview

Learning Objectives

After completing this module, you will be able to:

- Understand the PMI® definition of a project
- Comprehend the project management process as defined by PMI®

Inside Module 01

What is a Project?

According to *A Guide to the Project Management Body of Knowledge* (*PMBOK® Guide, 5th Edition* © 2013) from the Project Management Institute, a project is "A project is a temporary endeavor undertaken to create a unique product, service, or result." According to this definition, a project is:

- **Temporary** – Every project has a definite beginning and end.
- **Unique** – Every project is something your organization has not done before, or has not done in this manner.

Understanding the Project Management Process

Because Project 2013 is a project management tool, you use the software most effectively in the context of the normal project management process. Therefore, it is important to become acquainted with each of the phases of the project management process and with the activities that take place during each phase. According to the Project Management Institute, the project management process consists of five phases including: definition, planning, execution, control, and closure.

Initiation

The Initiation phase of a project authorizes the creation of the project and is a part of the project's scope management process. The Initiation phase of a project usually includes the creation of definition documents that may include one or more of the following:

- The **Project Charter** is a high-level document that recognizes the existence of the project. This document usually includes the product or service description, the analysis of the business need, and the authority to assign resources to the project. Developed by senior management and stakeholders, the Project Charter feeds the development of the Statement of Work document.
- The **Statement of Work** (SOW) document defines the project and the product or service produced by the project. Other names for this document are proposal, business plan, Scope of Work, or scoping document. The Statement of Work can include one or more of the following sections:
  - Executive Summary
  - Phases, Deliverables, and Activities (Tasks)
  - Sponsor Responsibilities (Rules of Engagement)
  - Assumptions and History
  - Acceptance Criteria
  - Change Control Policies and Procedures
- A **Work Breakdown Structure** (WBS) document breaks the project work into meaningful components using summary tasks and subtasks. You use summary tasks to represent the Phases and Deliverables in the project, and you use subtasks to show the activities team members must perform to complete a Phase or Deliverable section in the project. You see the Work Breakdown Structure of summary tasks and subtasks in Project 2013 on the left side of any task view, such as the *Gantt Chart* view.

Information: MSProjectExperts recommends that you carefully define your project and do not stop the Initiation process until you fully understand your project requirements. In a famous Dilbert™ cartoon, the pointy-haired boss asks Dilbert to start a project to create a new product for a customer. When Dilbert complains that he does not know the customer's product requirements, the pointy-haired boss replies, "start working on the project and we'll come up with the requirements later."

Planning

The Planning phase is typically when the project manager becomes directly involved with the project. This phase is of major importance to the potential success of any project. According to the *PMBOK® Guide,* the Planning phase can include any of the following processes:

- Scope Planning and Definition
- Activity Definition
- Activity Sequencing
- Activity Duration and Work Estimating
- Resource Planning
- Schedule Development
- Cost Planning and Budgeting
- Risk Management Planning
- Project Plan Development

Best Practice: MSProjectExperts strongly recommends that you perform risk management planning in every project. In the real world, remember that things go wrong, and you must plan for them.

Execution

The Execution phase of a project is the process of moving forward with the project by performing the activities (tasks) associated with the project. Execution also involves coordinating the resources to carry out the project plan. The Execution stage should include the following processes:

- **Saving a Project Baseline** – Prior to beginning work on the project, you must save a baseline for your project. Use the baseline to compare project progress with your original project estimates and then to analyze project variance. You should save the project baseline at the beginning of the project, and you should never change the original project baseline without good reason and without stakeholder agreement.

- **Tracking Project Progress** – Collecting actual project data is critical to controlling the project. Ideally, you should gather and update actual progress from your project team on a weekly basis, or at any other frequency tuned to your project lifecycle.

- **Analyzing Project Variance** – Throughout the life of the project, you must analyze project variance between the current project schedule and the original baseline schedule, and identify trouble spots in the project.
- **Revising the Project Plan** – Based on the results of variance analysis, you may need to make revisions to the project to stay within its predefined scope, schedule, and budget.
- **Reporting Project Progress** –Throughout the life of the project, you should seek to identify the reporting needs of all project participants, and then create custom views and reports in Project 2013 to meet these needs.

Monitoring and Controlling

During the Monitoring and Controlling phase of the project, various interested parties may request changes, including your customer, your project stakeholders, your project executives, your fellow project managers, and even your project team members. In the face of relentless change requests, you must maintain control over the project to ensure that your project meets its objectives. Some of the common aspects of project control are the following:

- **Change Control** –Change control is the process of managing changes to the predefined scope of the project.
- **Continued Communication** –A critical component of controlling any project is communication. You must keep communication lines open at all times with all project participants.

Best Practice: MSProjectExperts recommends that your organization define a formal change control process to manage project changes. Every project change can potentially increase the project cost and delay the project finish date. Without a change control process in place, you may not be able to reject changes that are not beneficial to the project's goals and objectives, needlessly driving up your project costs and delaying the completion of your project!

Closure

The Closure phase of the project formalizes the acceptance of the project and then closes the project. At the conclusion of project closure, release your resources from the project team to work on other projects. The Closure phase can include any of the following:

- **Project Closure Methodologies** are the processes through which you formally close your project. They must clearly define the "exit criteria" which are critical to measuring the success of your project.
- A **Lessons Learned** meeting (aka "post mortem" meeting) is a wise practice to evaluate the successes and failures during the project life cycle. From this meeting, you should document the lessons learned and then use this information when you plan future projects. The goal of every lessons learned meeting is to determine "how we can do better the next time."
- Use a **Template Creation** process to create project templates from successful projects for similar project types. It is part of your job as a project manager to define project types, build templates to meet other project needs, and modify templates to meet the unique needs of each project.

Once you understand the project management process, you are ready to begin learning how to use Project 2013. In the remainder of this book, I show you how to harness the power of the software by using best practices during each stage of the project management life cycle. During the Initiation stage, I show you how to define a new project using a six-step process. During the Planning stage, I show you how to conduct the task, resource, and assignment planning process. During the Execution stage, I show you how to view the Critical Path, baseline your project, enter task progress, perform variance analysis, and revise your project. During the Monitoring and Controlling stage, I show you how report on your project, and to handle change control issues. Finally, during the Closure stage, I show you how to save a completed project as a template and how to use the *Compare Projects* utility.

Module 02

Project 2013 Overview

Learning Objectives

After completing this module, you will be able to:

- Understand and use the new start experience
- Understand the purpose of the Global.mpt file in Project 2013
- Name the objects shown in the Project 2013 user interface
- Understand the features of the Ribbon
- Customize the Ribbon and the Quick Access Toolbar
- Access and use the Backstage
- Use navigation tricks to better navigate the Project 2013 environment
- Understand the symbols used in the Gantt Chart view
- Read and understand a Gantt chart
- Create and use a three-tiered timescale

Inside Module 02

Introducing a New Start Experience

Each time you launch Project 2013, the software displays the *Start* screen shown in Figure 2 - 1. Notice that this page contains a list of recently opened files in the *Recent* section of the sidepane on the left side of the page. In the main content area of the page, notice that the first four buttons offer you four methods for creating a new project: creating a new blank project, creating a new project from an existing project, creating a new project from an Excel workbook, and creating a new project from a *Tasks* list in SharePoint. In addition, notice that the main content area also shows you a selection of project templates available in the *Office.com* website, such as the *Software Development Plan* template. Notice finally that the top of the page offers you a *Search for online templates* field in which you can search for other project templates in the *Office.com* website.

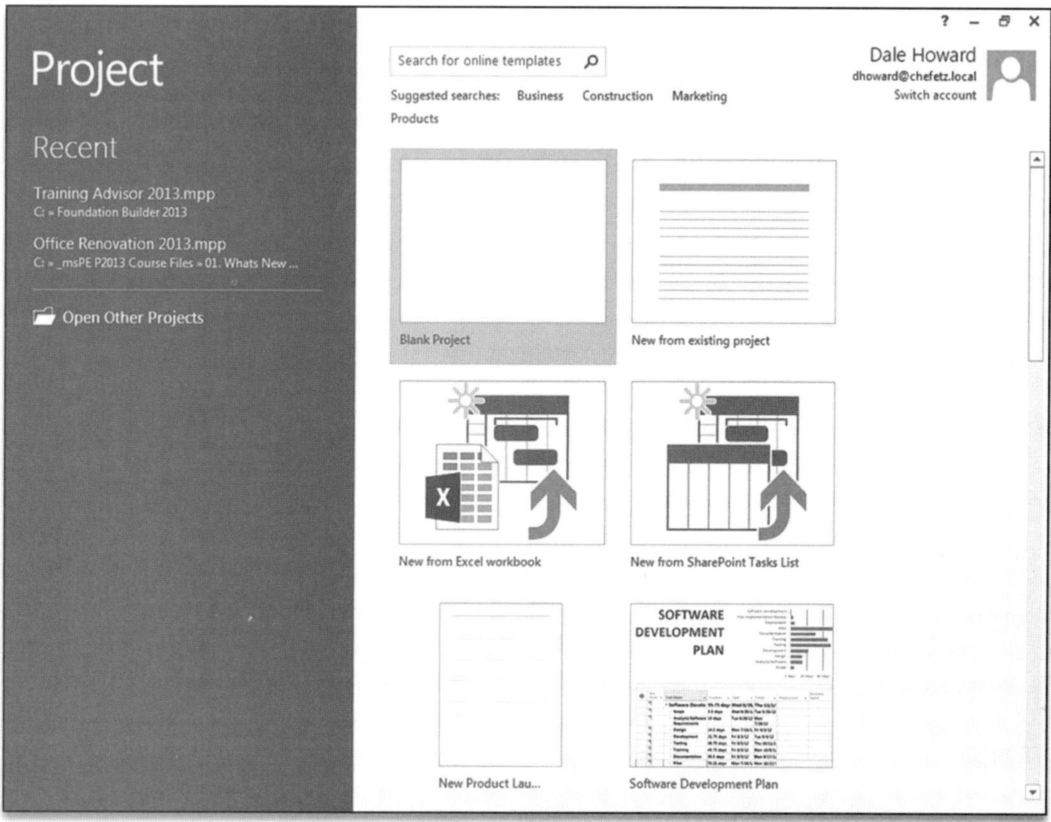

Figure 2 - 1: Start screen

Information: If you float your mouse pointer over the name of a recently used project in the *Recent* section of the sidepane, the software displays a floating tool tip that reveals the file path and the complete file name for the project. This functionality is new behavior when compared with a similar feature available in the *Backstage* in Project 2010.

To pin one of the recently used files shown in the *Recent* section of the page, float your mouse pointer over the file and then click the "pushpin" symbol at the right end of the file name. To open a recently used file, click the name of the file in the *Recent* section of the sidepane. To open any other project, click the *Open Other Files* link in the sidepane and then open the file using the commands available on the *Open* page of the *Backstage*.

To create a new project, click one of the buttons in the main content area of the page. To pin one of the Office.com templates so that Project 2013 always displays the template in the *Welcome to Office* page, float your mouse pointer over the template button and then click the "pushpin" symbol in the lower-right corner of the button.

To search for a project template in the *Office.com* website, enter your search term in the *Search online templates* field and then click the *Start searching* button at the right end of the field. During the search process, Project 2013 briefly displays a *SEARCHING THOUSANDS OF ONLINE TEMPLATES* message, and then reveals the search results on the *New* page of the *Backstage* as shown in Figure 2 - 2. Notice that using the search term *server* yielded two templates related to Project Server 2013. To further filter the list of templates, click one of the template categories shown in the *Category* list on the right side of the *New* page.

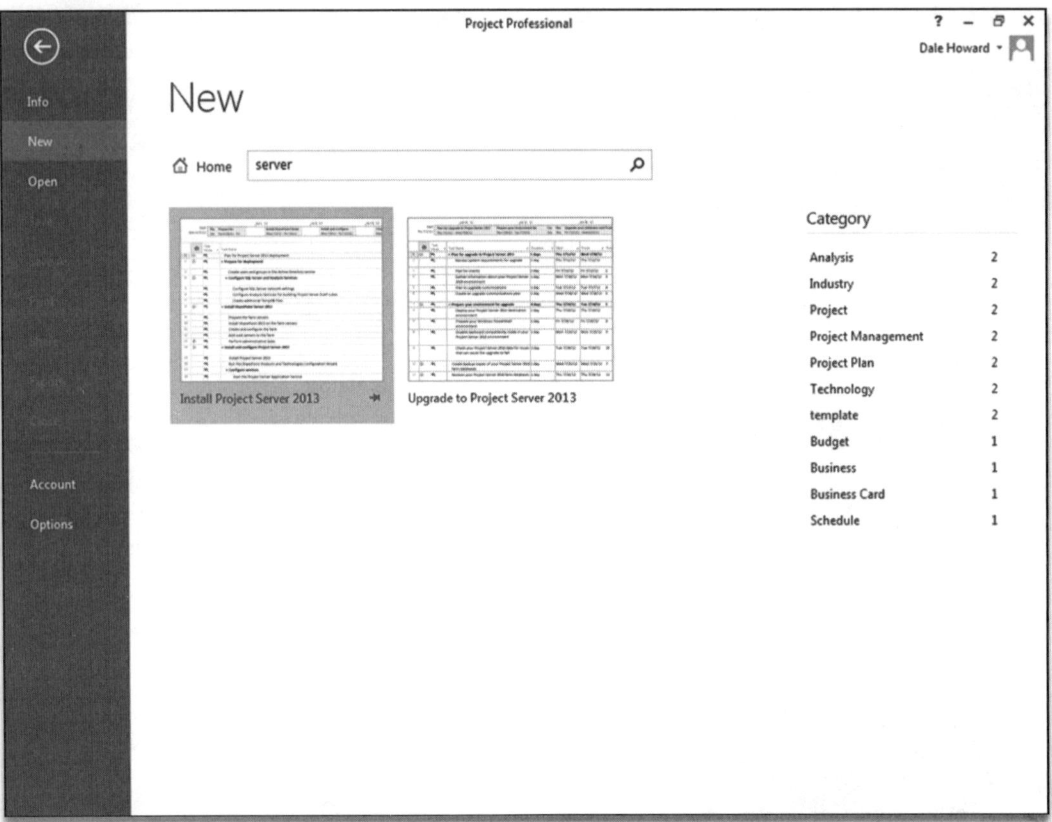

Figure 2 - 2: Search for an online template

To return to the *Welcome to Office* page, click the *Back* button (large left-arrow button) at the top of the sidepane in the *Backstage*. To exit the *Welcome to Office* page and navigate directly to the main user interface of Project 2013, press the **Escape** key on your computer keyboard. The software automatically opens a new blank project file named Project1.

Information: To prevent Project 2013 from displaying the *Welcome to Office* page, press the **Escape** key to exit the *Start* screen, click the *File* tab, and then click the *Options* button in the sidepane of the *Backstage*. On the *General* page of the *Project Options* dialog, **deselect** the *Show the start screen when this application starts* option and then click the *OK* button.

Introducing the Global.mpt File

Project 2013 uses the Global.mpt file as the template to create all new blank project files. When you launch the software, Project 2013 opens the Global.mpt file from your hard drive and loads it into memory in the background. This file contains all of the default objects that ship with Project 2013, including default views, tables, filters, groups, reports, and calendars. You can also use the Global.mpt file to store any custom personal objects you create, such as custom views, tables, filters, groups, reports, and calendars. Storing your custom personal objects in the Global.mpt file makes them available to all current and future projects.

Although you cannot view the Global.mpt file directly, you can view it indirectly. After pressing the **Escape** key to exit the *Start* screen shown previously in Figure 2 - 1, click the *File* tab and then click the *Info* tab in the *Backstage*. Click the *Organizer* button in the *Organize Global Template* section of the *Info* page and the software displays the *Organizer* dialog shown in Figure 2 - 3. The list on the left side of the dialog shows the default and custom objects stored in the Global.mpt file.

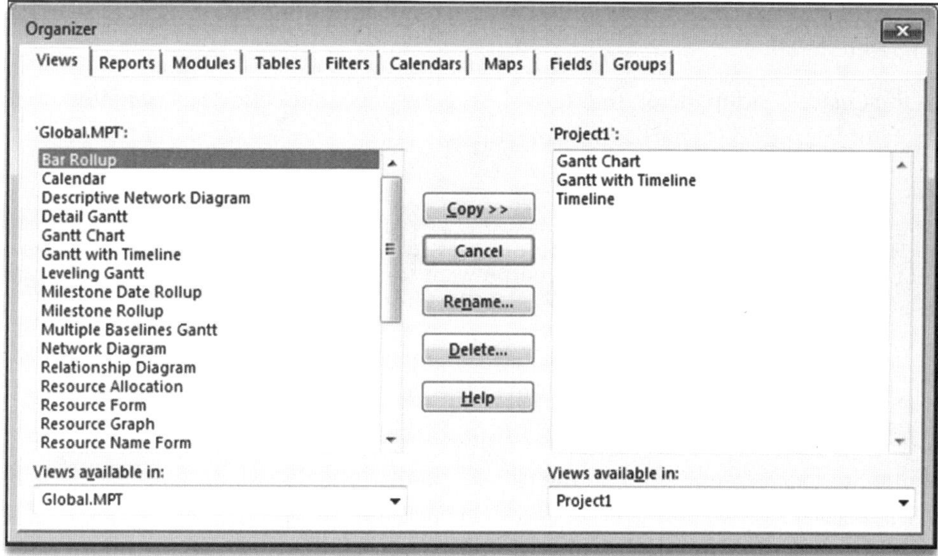

Figure 2 - 3: Organizer dialog shows the Global.mpt file

Click the *Cancel* button to close the *Organizer* dialog and then press the **Escape** key on your computer keyboard to exit the *Backstage*. Alternately, you can click the *Back* button (large left-arrow button) at the top of the sidepane in the *Backstage*.

Warning: You must have at least one project open in Project 2013 before you can access the *Organizer* dialog.

Hands On Exercise

Exercise 2 - 1

Explore the new Start experience in Project 2013.

1. Launch Project 2013.
2. Examine the new *Start* screen in the *Backstage*.
3. Click the *Open Other Projects* link at the bottom of the sidepane in the *Start* screen to display the *Open* page in the *Backstage*.
4. Click the *Back* button (large left-arrow button) in the upper left corner of the page.
5. In the *Search* section at the top of the *Start* screen, click the *Products* link to search for product-related templates.
6. In the *Category* sidepane on the right side of the page, click the *Marketing* item to limit the search for templates used to market new products.

Warning: If you complete steps #7-10 below, you prevent Project 2013 from displaying the *Start* screen every time you launch the software. If you **do not** want to see the *Start* screen every time you launch the software, then complete these four steps. If you **do** want to see the *Start* screen every time you launch the software, then click the *Open* button in the *Backstage* and skip ahead to step #12.

7. Click the *Options* button at the bottom of the sidepane in the *Backstage* to display the *Project Options* dialog.
8. In the *Start up options* section of the *General* page in the dialog, deselect the *Show the Start screen when this application starts* option, and then click the *OK* button.
9. Click the *Close* button (**X**) in the upper right corner of the Project 2013 application window to exit the software.
10. Launch Project 2013 again.

Notice that Project 2013 no longer displays the *Start* screen when you launch the software.

11. Click the *File* tab and then click the *Open* button on the left side of the *Backstage*, if necessary.
12. On the *Open* page of the *Backstage*, select the *Computer* option, and then click the *Browse* button.
13. In the *Open* dialog, navigate to the folder where you unzipped the sample files that accompany this book.
14. In the *Open* dialog, select the **Project Navigation 2013.mpp** sample file, and then click the *Open* button.
15. Leave this project open for the next Hands On exercise.

Exercise 2 - 2

Examine the Global.mpt file in Project 2013.

1. Return to the **Project Navigation 2013.mpp** sample file, if necessary.
2. Click the *File* tab and then click the *Info* tab.
3. On the *Info* page of the *Backstage*, click the *Organizer* button.
4. In the lower left corner of the *Organizer* dialog, notice that the software selects the *Global.MPT* item on the *Views available in* pick list by default.
5. Individually click each of the tabs at the top of the *Organizer* dialog to see all of the default objects included in the Global.mpt file, including the default views, tables, filters, groups, and reports.
6. Click the *Cancel* button to close the *Organizer* dialog.
7. Press the **Escape** key on your computer keyboard to exit the *Backstage* and return to the main Project 2013 user interface.
8. Click the *Save* button on the *Quick Access Toolbar*, but **do not** close the **Project Navigation 2013.mpp** sample file.

Understanding the User Interface

For those project managers who upgrade to Project 2013 from the 2010 version of the software, the user interface is very similar between the two versions. For users who upgrade from the 2007 version or earlier versions of the software, the most striking feature of Project 2013 is the user interface, which conforms to the standard of other applications in the Office 2013 suite, such as Word 2013, Excel 2013, or PowerPoint 2013. Figure 2 - 4 displays the Project 2013 user interface with the main features labeled.

You use these user interface features as follows:

- Use the *Ribbon* to access commands and buttons in Project 2013.
- Customize and use the *Quick Access Toolbar* to display frequently used commands and buttons.
- Use the *File* tab to access all file-related features, such as open, save, or print in the *Backstage*.
- Use the *Timeline* pane to create a report about the current task schedule of your project.
- Use the *Select All* button to select all items in the current view. You can also right-click on the *Select All* button and use the shortcut menu to select a different table.
- Use the *Timescale* to determine the current level of zoom applied to your project.
- Use the *Task Sheet* pane to list tasks or activities in your project
- Use the *Gantt Chart* pane to view a Gantt bar for every task in your project
- Use the *Default Task Mode* selector to specify the default *Task Mode* for new tasks you add to the project.
- Use the *Zoom* slider to quickly zoom the *Timescale*.
- Use the *Quick View* selector to apply four commonly used views and to access the most recent report.

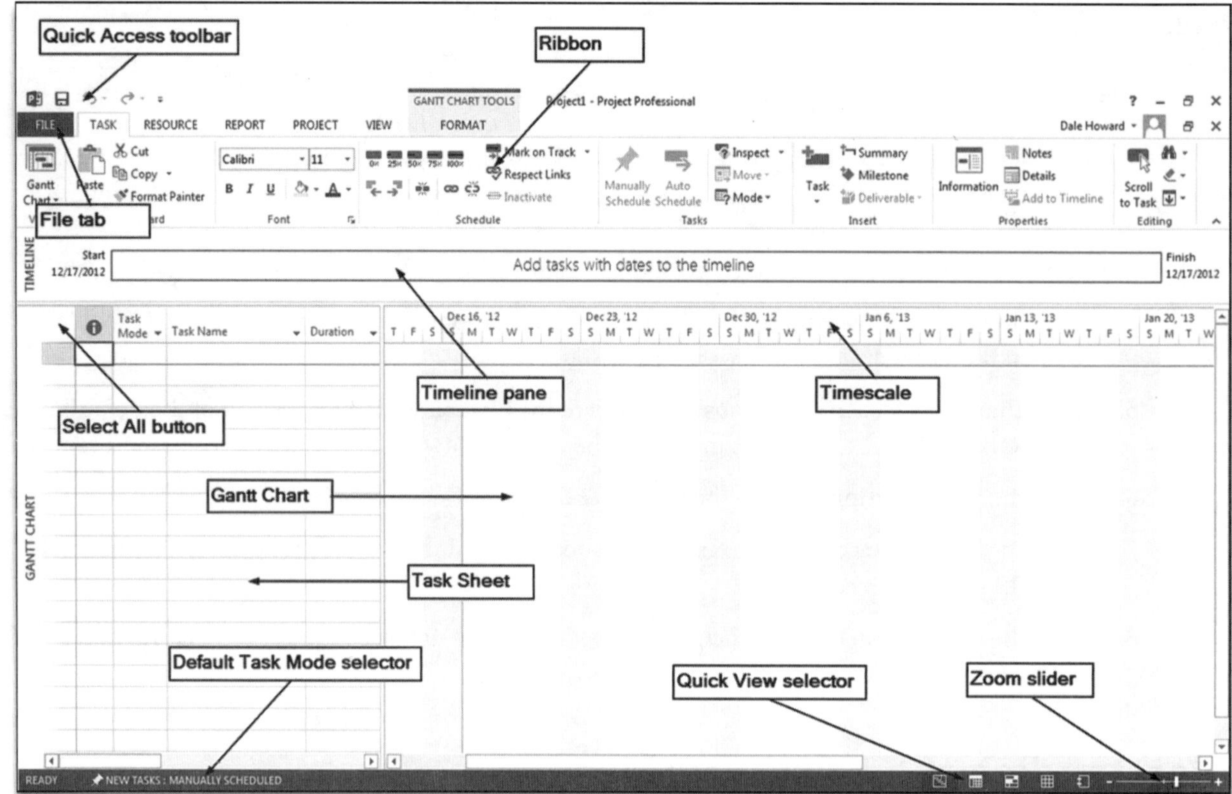

Figure 2 - 4: Features of the Project 2013 user interface

Understanding the Ribbon

Use the *Ribbon* to access commands and buttons in Project 2013. By default, the software includes six ribbons, including the *Task, Resource, Report, Project, View,* and *Format* ribbons. To display any ribbon, click the relevant tab at the top of the *Ribbon*. For example, click the *Task* tab to display the *Task* ribbon.

Using the Task Ribbon

Project 2013 displays the *Task* ribbon by default when you access the main user interface. The *Task* ribbon contains all of the commands and buttons you need for task planning. Figure 2 - 5 shows the *Task* ribbon.

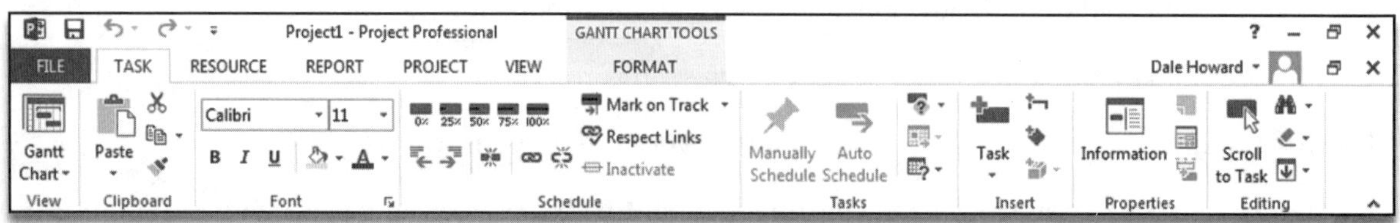

Figure 2 - 5: Task ribbon

The software organizes the commands and buttons on the *Task* ribbon into eight sections, which include the *View, Clipboard, Font, Schedule, Tasks, Insert, Properties,* and *Editing* sections. The *View* section of the *Task* ribbon contains a single button, the *Gantt Chart* pick list button. If you click the top half of this split button, Project 2013 displays the most recent view containing a Gantt chart on the right side of the view. If you click the bottom half of the button (the pick list arrow), the software displays a list of the most commonly used task and resource views, including any custom views you create.

The *Font* section offers you a complete set of buttons used to format the font. This section also includes the *Font Dialog Launcher* button, circled in the image shown in Figure 2 - 6.

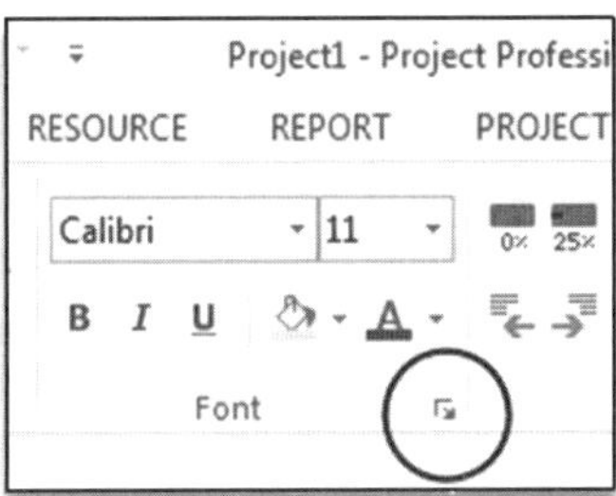

Figure 2 - 6: Font Dialog Launcher icon

When you click the *Font Dialog Launcher* button, Project 2013 displays the *Font* dialog shown in Figure 2 - 7. This dialog includes all of the commands available in the *Font* section of the *Task* ribbon.

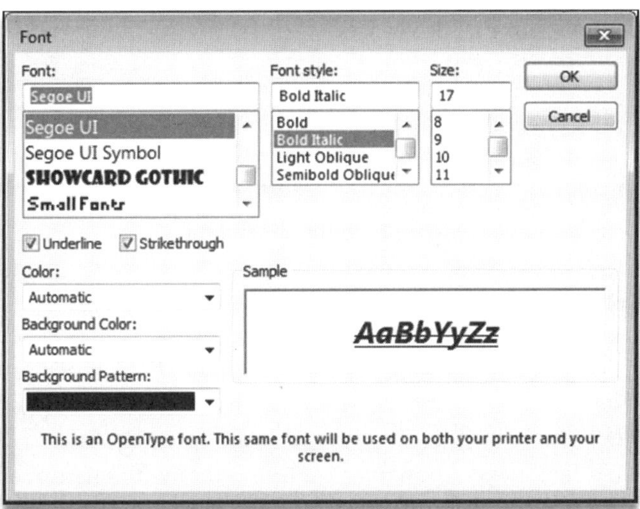

Figure 2 - 7: Font dialog

Using the Resource Ribbon

Click the *Resource* tab to display the *Resource* ribbon shown in Figure 2 - 8. The software divides the *Resource* ribbon into five sections, which include the *View, Assignments, Insert, Properties,* and *Level* sections. The *View* section of the *Resource* ribbon contains a single button, the *Team Planner* pick list button. If you click the top half of this split button, Project 2013 displays the *Team Planner* view. If you click the bottom half of the button (the pick list arrow), the software displays a list of the most commonly used task and resource views, including any custom views you create.

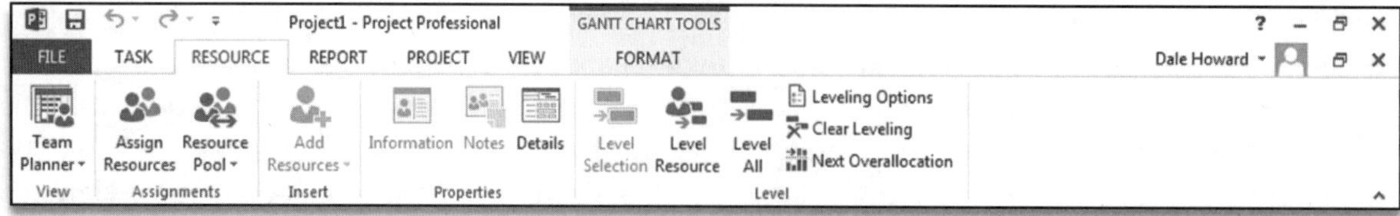

Figure 2 - 8: Resource ribbon

Warning: The **Professional** version of Project 2013 displays the *Team Planner* pick list button in the *View* section of the *Resource* ribbon. If you have the **Standard** version of the software, the *View* section displays the *Resource Sheet* pick list button instead. If you click the top half of this split button, the software displays the *Resource Sheet* view.

Use the *Resource* ribbon while displaying any resource view (such as the *Resource Sheet* view) to manage the resources in your project. The exception to this statement is the *Assign Resources* button, which you can use with any task view (such as the *Gantt Chart* view) to assign resources to tasks.

Using the Report Ribbon

Click the *Report* tab to display the *Report* ribbon shown in Figure 2 - 9. New to Project 2013, the *Report* ribbon provides access to the powerful new graphical dashboard reports. The software divides the *Report* ribbon into three sections, which include the *Project, View Reports,* and *Export* sections. Notice that the *View Reports* section contains eight pick list buttons that allow you to work with the new reporting feature.

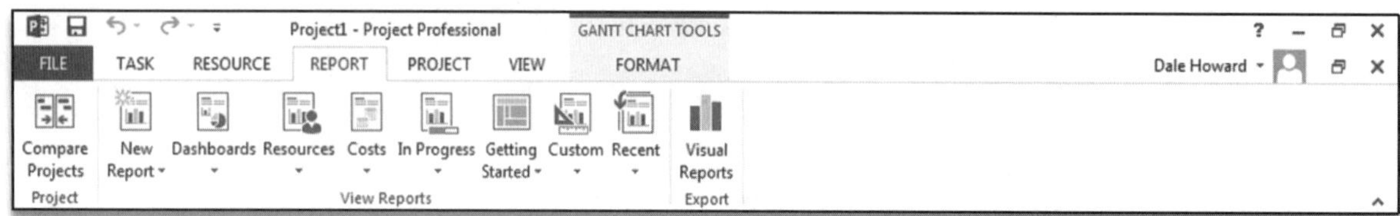

Figure 2 - 9: Report ribbon

Using the Project Ribbon

Click the *Project* tab to display the *Project* ribbon shown in Figure 2 - 10. The software divides the *Project* ribbon into six sections, including the *Insert, Apps, Properties, Schedule, Status,* and *Proofing* sections. New to Project 2013 is the *Apps* section which contains a single button, the *Apps for Office* pick list button. An Office App is a web page loaded inside of the software in a task pane, allowing you to interact with custom applications built for use with Project 2013. For example, an Office App might show you additional information about a selected task or resource, where the related data comes from an external source such as a SharePoint list, Project Server 2013, a web service, or another enterprise application.

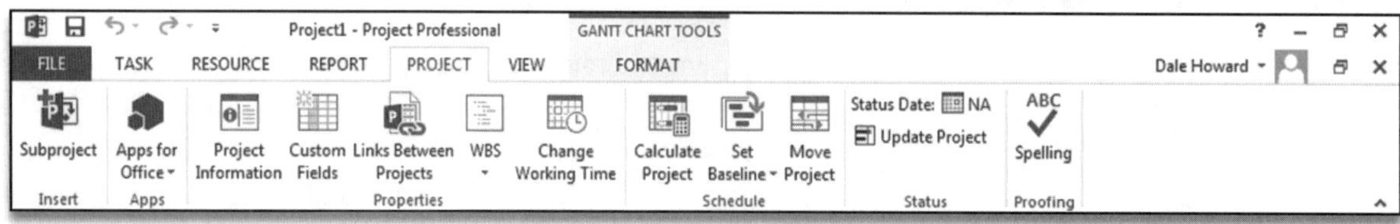

Figure 2 - 10: Project ribbon

Use the *Project* ribbon to specify high-level information about your project or to use an Office App with your project. For example, to save a baseline for your project, click the *Set Baseline* pick list button in the *Schedule* section of the *Project* ribbon.

Using the View Ribbon

Click the *View* tab to display the *View* ribbon shown in Figure 2 - 11. The software divides the *View* ribbon into seven sections, including the *Task Views, Resource Views, Data, Zoom, Split View, Window,* and *Macros* sections. The *Task Views* section includes five pick list buttons that allow you to display commonly used task views, such as the *Task Usage* view. The *Resource Views* section contains four pick list buttons that allow you to display commonly used resource views, such as the *Resource Sheet* view.

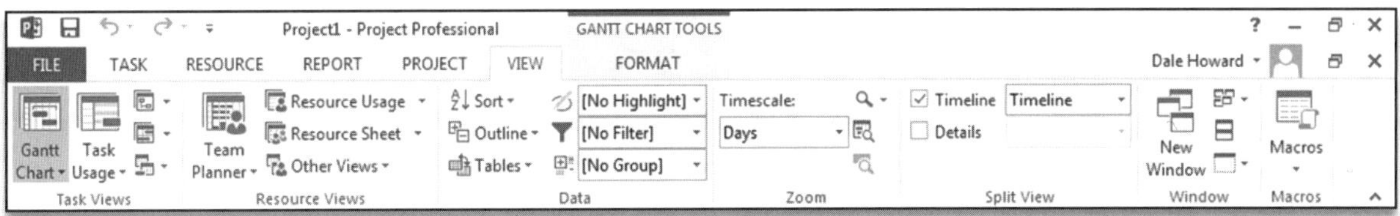

Figure 2 - 11: View ribbon

Use the *View* ribbon to apply default and custom views, tables, filters, and groups to your project. For example, you can use the *Timeline* and *Details* options in the *Split View* section of the *View* ribbon to display the *Timeline* pane above the *Gantt Chart* pane, or to display the *Task Form* pane below the *Gantt Chart* pane.

Using the Format Ribbon

You use the *Format* ribbon to customize a view. Before you click the *Format* tab, select a view to format (such as the *Gantt Chart* view), and then click the *Format* tab. Project 2013 displays the *Format* ribbon for the current view with commands and buttons specific to the current view. Figure 2 - 12 shows the *Format* ribbon for the *Gantt Chart* view. Notice in Figure 2 - 12 that the software indicates I am editing the *Gantt Chart* view by displaying the purple *Gantt Chart Tools* header above the *Format* tab.

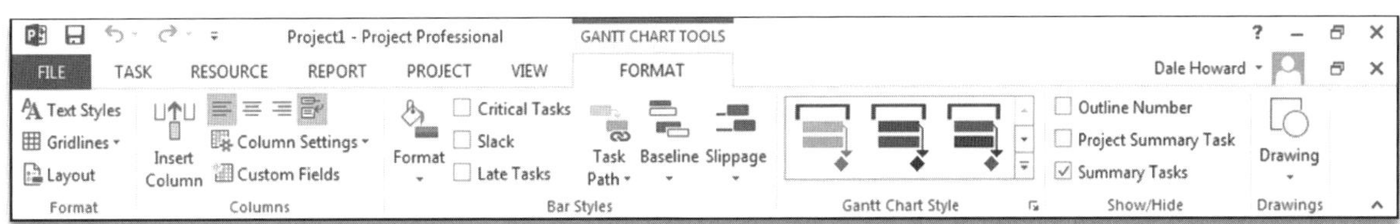

Figure 2 - 12: Format ribbon for the Gantt Chart view

The software divides the *Format* ribbon into sections relevant to the type of view currently displayed. For example, the *Format* ribbon for the *Gantt Chart* view contains six sections, including the *Format, Columns, Bar Styles, Gantt Chart Style, Show/Hide,* and *Drawings* sections.

Remember that the *Format* ribbon shows the appropriate formatting options for your current view. This means that the commands and buttons on the *Format* ribbon can vary widely depending on the formatting options available for the current view. For instance, Figure 2 - 13 shows the *Format* ribbon for the *Task Usage* view. Notice the set of options available in the *Details* section of the *Format* ribbon.

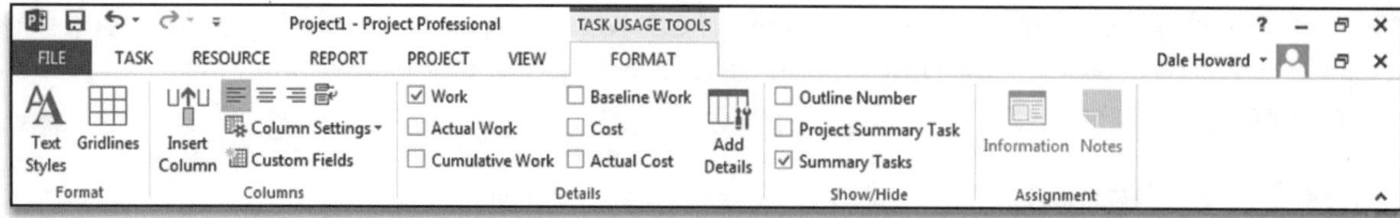

Figure 2 - 13: Format ribbon for the Task Usage view

Figure 2 - 14 shows the *Format* ribbon for the *Team Planner* view. Notice that the *Format* ribbon for this view includes a number of buttons and commands not available when formatting other views.

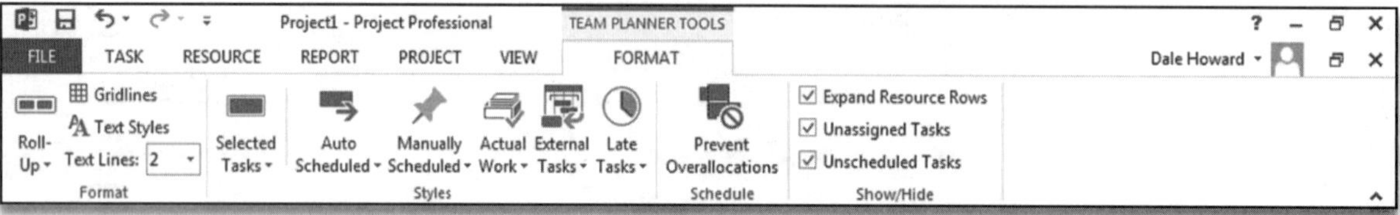

Figure 2 - 14: Format ribbon for the Team Planner view

Warning: Remember that if you use the **Standard** version of Project 2013, the software does not include the *Team Planner* view. This view is only available in the **Professional** version of the software.

Figure 2 - 15 shows the *Format* ribbon for the *Calendar* view. Notice that the *Format* ribbon shows very few options for formatting the *Calendar* view

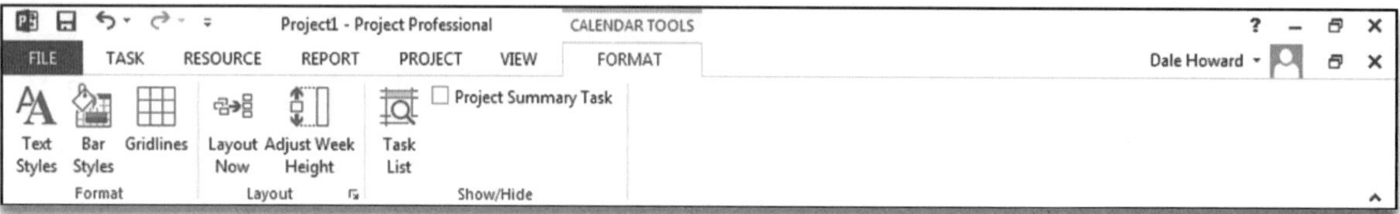

Figure 2 - 15: Format ribbon for the Calendar view

Information: I do not document the commands and buttons available on the *Format* ribbon for every view in Project 2013. Keep in mind that every view offers a unique set of options for formatting the view, plus one or more options in common with other views of that type.

Collapsing the Ribbon

Project 2013 allows you to collapse the ribbon to see more information in the current view. The software offers you three different methods to collapse and expand the ribbon. These methods include:

- Double-click any ribbon tab.
- Right-click any ribbon tab and either select or deselect the *Collapse the Ribbon* item on the shortcut menu.
- Click either the *Collapse the Ribbon* button or the *Pin the Ribbon* button at the far right edge of any applied *Ribbon*.

Information: If you like to use keyboard shortcuts, you can also collapse and expand the *Ribbon* by pressing the **Control + F1** keyboard shortcut on your computer keyboard.

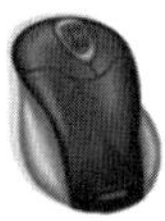

Hands On Exercise

Exercise 2 - 3

Study the ribbon in Project 2013.

1. Return to the **Project Navigation 2013.mpp** sample file, if necessary.
2. Click the *Task* tab to display the *Task* ribbon, if necessary.
3. Examine the buttons in each section of the *Task* ribbon.
4. In the lower right corner of the *Font* section of the *Task* ribbon, click the *Font Dialog Launcher* button.
5. Examine the options in the *Font* dialog and then click the *Cancel* button to close the dialog.
6. Individually click the *Resource*, *Report*, *Project*, *View*, and *Format* tabs and study the buttons on each of these ribbons.
7. Double-click the *Format* tab to collapse the ribbon.
8. Click the *Task* tab to expand the ribbon temporarily.
9. Right-click the *Task* tab and then **deselect** the *Collapse the Ribbon* item on the shortcut menu.

Customizing the User Interface

Project 2013 offers you two ways to customize the user interface by modifying the ribbon and the *Quick Access Toolbar*. I discuss each of these topics separately.

Customizing the Ribbon

You can customize the ribbon by adding custom ribbon tabs, custom ribbon groups, and buttons. To begin the process of customizing the ribbon, complete the following steps:

1. Right-click any ribbon tab, such as the *Task* tab, and then click the *Customize the Ribbon* item on the shortcut menu.

Project 2013 displays the *Project Options* dialog with the *Customize Ribbon* tab selected, as shown in Figure 2 - 16. Notice that the *Customize Ribbon* page of the *Project Options* dialog contains two sections:

- Use the *Choose commands from* section on the left side of the dialog to select the commands you want to add to the ribbon.
- Use the *Customize the Ribbon* section on the right side of the dialog to select the ribbon you want to customize.

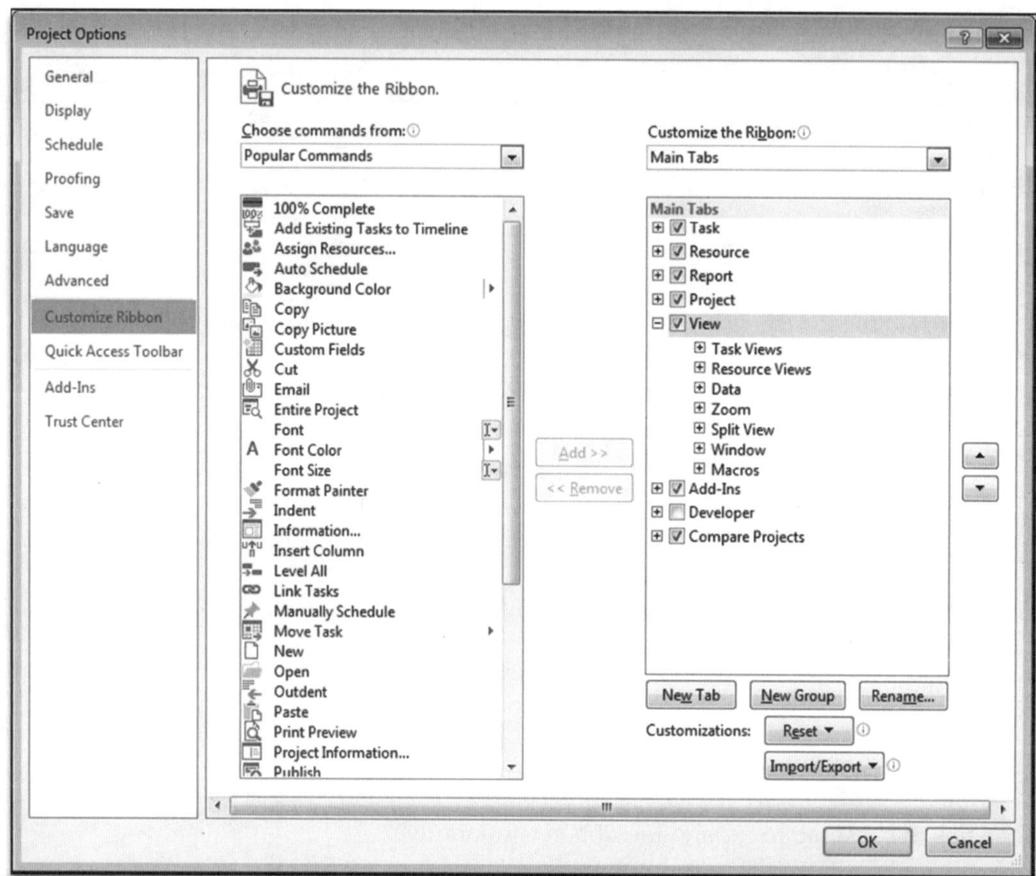

Figure 2 - 16: Project Options dialog, Customize Ribbon section

Information: You can also display the *Customize Ribbon* page of the *Project Options* dialog by clicking the *File* tab, clicking the *Options* button in the *Backstage*, and then clicking the *Customize Ribbon* tab in the *Project Options* dialog.

2. Click the *Choose commands from* pick list to choose the type of commands you want to add to the ribbon. The pick list offers you the following choices: *Popular Commands* (the default setting), *Commands Not in the Ribbon, All Commands, Macros, File Tab, All Tabs, Main Tabs, Tool Tabs,* and *Custom Tabs and Groups.*
3. Click the *Customize the Ribbon* pick list and select which ribbon tabs to display in the dialog. You have three choices: *Main Tabs* (the default setting), *Tool Tabs* (used for formatting views), and *All Tabs* (offers both the *Main Tabs* and the *Tool Tabs*).

After you select your options on the *Choose Commands From* pick list and the *Customize the Ribbon* pick list, you are ready to customize the ribbon. The software offers you multiple choices for customizing the ribbon:

- Display or hide a ribbon tab.
- Create a new ribbon tab.
- Create a ribbon group in a new or existing ribbon tab.
- Add or remove buttons on a default or custom ribbon tab.
- Rename a ribbon tab, a ribbon group, or a button.
- Move buttons, ribbon groups, and ribbon tabs on the ribbon.
- Reset the ribbon to its default settings.
- Import or export the customized ribbon and *Quick Access Toolbar* settings to a file.

Displaying/Hiding a Ribbon Tab

To display or hide any ribbon tab, select or deselect the option checkbox to the left of the ribbon tab in the *Customize the Ribbon* section of the *Project Options* dialog. For example, if you are a software developer, you might want to display and use the *Developer* ribbon so that you can create macros in the Office VBA programming language for Project 2013. To display the *Developer* ribbon, **select** the option checkbox for the *Developer* tab, and then click the *OK* button. Figure 2 - 17 shows the *Developer* ribbon after selecting the option to display it in the *Project Options* dialog.

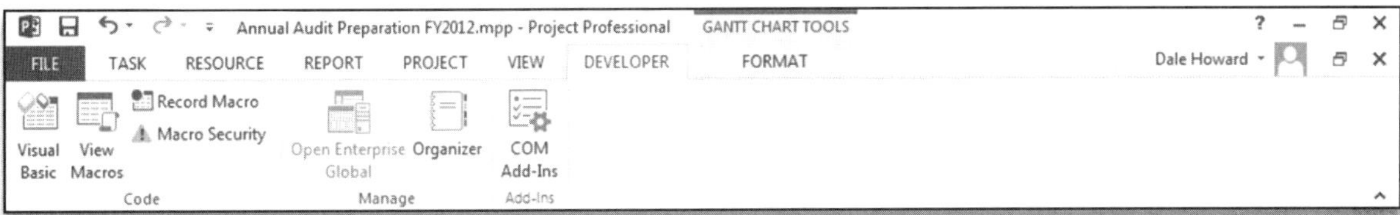

Figure 2 - 17: Developer ribbon

To hide any ribbon tab currently displayed, **deselect** the option checkbox for the ribbon tab in the *Project Options* dialog and then click the *OK* button.

Creating a New Ribbon Tab or Ribbon Group

To create a new ribbon tab, select an existing ribbon tab in the location where you want to insert the new ribbon tab, and then click the *New Tab* button. The software inserts a new ribbon tab named *New Tab* **below** the selected ribbon tab. Figure 2 - 18 shows a new ribbon tab I added below the *View* ribbon. Notice that the new ribbon tab also includes a custom ribbon group named *New Group*. Every default and custom ribbon tab must contain at least one ribbon group, but you can also create additional ribbon groups.

Project 2013 allows you to organize the ribbon buttons into groups, with a label displayed at the bottom of each group. You can add a custom ribbon group to any default or custom ribbon tab. To create a new custom ribbon group, select an existing ribbon tab or ribbon group, and then click the *New Group* button. The software adds the new custom ribbon group below the selected ribbon tab or ribbon group. You should create a custom ribbon group for every section of buttons you want to display on your custom ribbon tab.

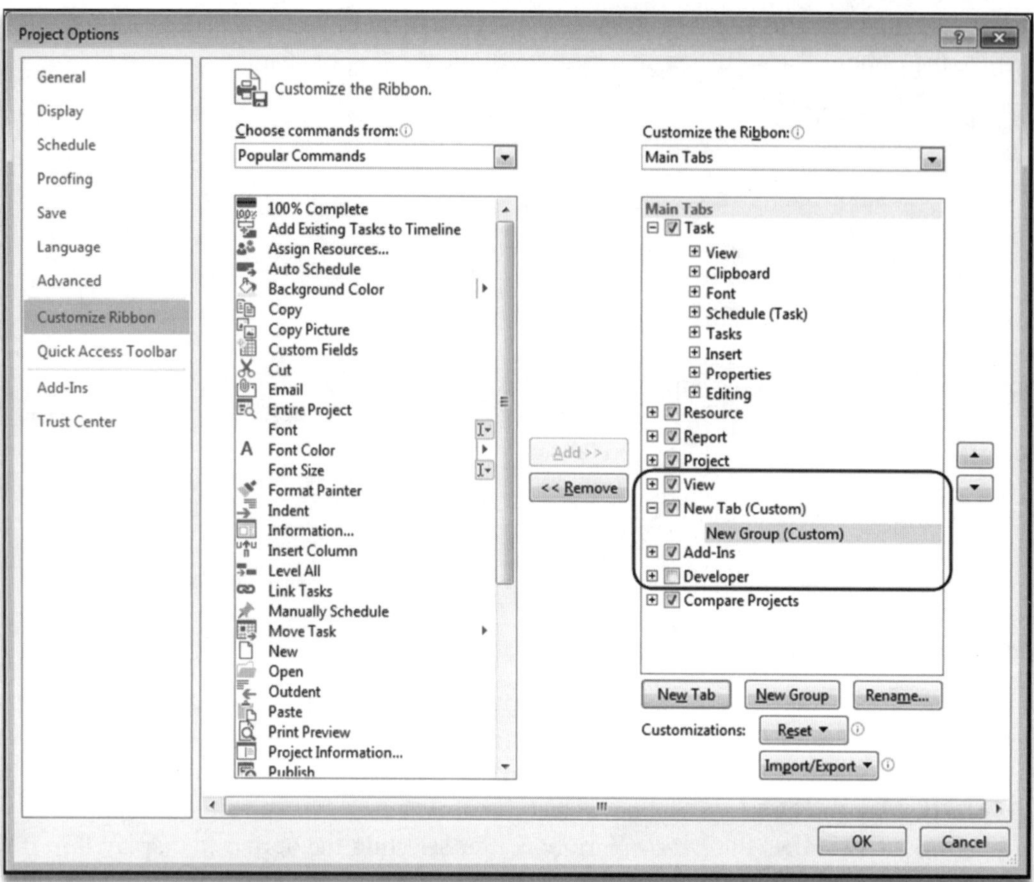

Figure 2 - 18: Project Options dialog, Customize Ribbon page after inserting a custom ribbon tab below the View tab

Information: To remove a custom ribbon group or ribbon tab, select the item in the list on the right and then click the *Remove* button. Be careful about removing any ribbon group on one of the default ribbon tabs, however, as the only way to restore it is to reset the entire ribbon back to its default settings using the *Reset* button.

Renaming a Ribbon Tab or Ribbon Group

After creating a new ribbon tab or ribbon group, you should immediately rename it. To rename a ribbon tab, click the name of the ribbon tab and then click the *Rename* button. Project 2013 displays the *Rename* dialog shown in Figure 2 - 19. Enter the name of the new ribbon tab in the *Display name* field and then click the *OK* button.

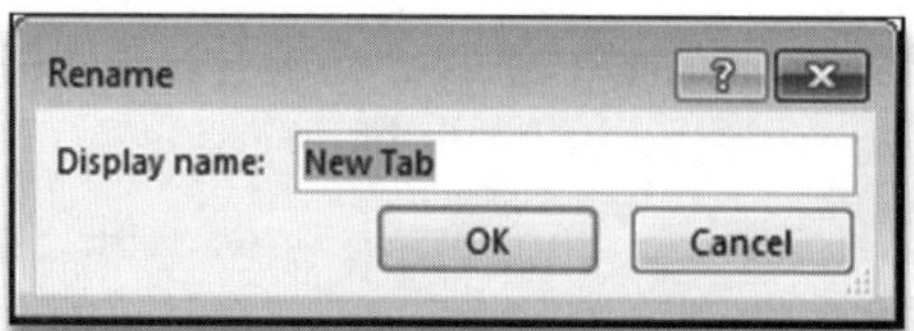

Figure 2 - 19: Rename dialog for a new custom ribbon tab

To rename a ribbon group, select the name of the ribbon group and then click the *Rename* button. Project 2013 displays the *Rename* dialog shown in Figure 2 - 20. Enter the name of the new ribbon group in the *Display name* field and then click the *OK* button.

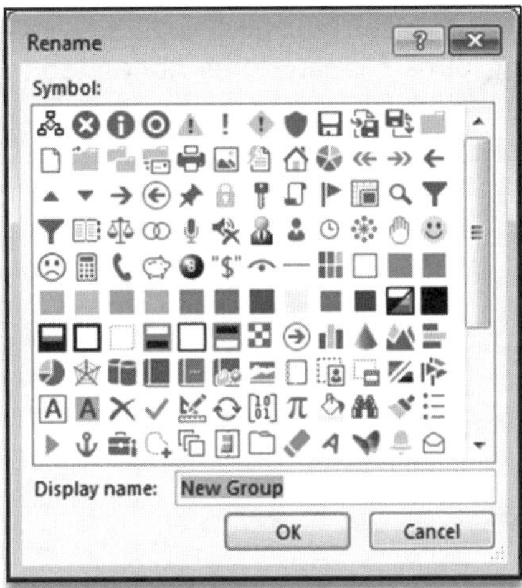

Figure 2 - 20: Rename dialog for a new custom ribbon group

Information: When you use the *Rename* dialog to rename a ribbon group, selecting a symbol in the *Symbol* list does not affect the ribbon group at all. Selecting a symbol in the *Symbol* list only applies to renaming buttons that you add to a custom ribbon group.

Adding, Removing, and Renaming Buttons on a Ribbon Tab

After creating a new custom ribbon tab and adding custom ribbon groups, you are ready to add buttons to your new custom ribbon tab. Before you add a button, be sure to click the *Choose commands from* pick list in the upper left side of the dialog and to select an option that displays the type of commands you want to add. For example, I normally select the *All Commands* item on the pick list to make sure I can see every available command. If you want to add buttons for any macros you record or write, you should select the *Macros* item on the *Choose commands from* pick list instead.

To add a button to a ribbon tab, select the button in the list of buttons on the left, select the ribbon group in the list on the right, and then click the *Add* button. Project 2013 adds the button to the selected ribbon group.

To rename a button, if necessary, click the name of the button and then click the *Rename* button. Project 2013 displays the *Rename* dialog shown previously in Figure 2 - 20. Enter the new name of the button in the *Display name* field, select a symbol for the button in the *Symbol* list, and then click the *OK* button.

Warning: You cannot add a button to any default ribbon tab unless you create a custom ribbon group on that ribbon tab. This means that you cannot add buttons to a default ribbon group on any default ribbon tab.

To remove a button on any ribbon tab, select the button in the list on the right and then click the *Remove* button. Remember that you can also remove a custom ribbon tab or custom ribbon group using the same process.

Moving Items in the Ribbon

Project 2013 allows you to move default and custom ribbon tabs, ribbon groups, and buttons into the order you want to display them. To move any of these, select the object you want to move and then click the *Move Up* and *Move Down* buttons (up-arrow and down-arrow buttons on the right side of the dialog). Figure 2 - 21 shows a new custom ribbon tab with multiple ribbon groups. I created this ribbon tab to help me perform the six steps needed to define a new project.

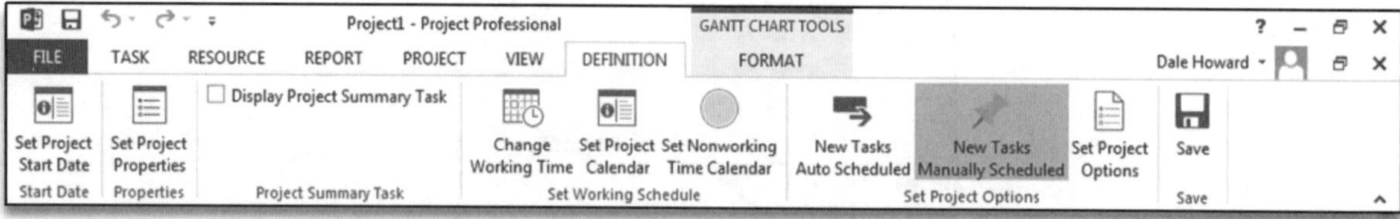

Figure 2 - 21: New custom ribbon tab

Hands On Exercise

Exercise 2 - 4

Customize the ribbon by adding a ribbon group and buttons to a default ribbon tab.

1. Return to the **Project Navigation 2013.mpp** sample file, if necessary.
2. Right-click on any ribbon tab, such as the *Task* tab, and then click the *Customize the Ribbon* item on the shortcut menu.
3. In the *Customize Ribbon* section of the *Project Options* dialog, click the *Choose commands from* pick list and select the *All Commands* item on the list.
4. In the *Customize Ribbon* section of the *Project Options* dialog, click the *Customize the Ribbon* pick list and select the *Tool Tabs* item on the list.
5. In the list of ribbon tabs on the right side of the dialog, scroll to the bottom of the list and expand the *Design* tab in the *Table Tools* section.
6. Select the *Table Styles* group for the *Design* tab and then click the *New Group* button.

Notice that Project 2013 added a new ribbon group named *New Group (Custom)* to the *Design* tab.

7. Select the *New Group (Custom)* item and then click the *Rename* button.
8. In the *Rename* dialog, enter *Table Text Formatting* in the *Display name* field, and then click the *OK* button.
9. With the *Table Text Formatting (Custom)* ribbon group still selected, individually select each of the following buttons and click the *Add* button to add them to the new ribbon group:
    - *Font* (the *Font* button with the pick list button on the right)

- *Font Size*
- *Bold*
- *Italic*
- *Underline*
- *Font Color*
- *Background Color*

10. Click the *OK* button to close the *Project Options* dialog.
11. Click the *Report* tab to display the *Report* ribbon.
12. In the *View Reports* section of the *Report* ribbon, click the *Dashboards* pick list button and select the *Project Overview* report.
13. In the lower left corner of the *Project Overview* report, click anywhere in the *Milestones Due* table.
14. Click the *Design* tab with the *Table Tools* applied.

Notice the new *Table Text Formatting* section and buttons you added to the *Design* ribbon with the *Table Tools* applied.

Resetting the Ribbon

Project 2013 allows you to reset the entire ribbon back to its default settings, or to reset any default ribbon tab to its default settings. To reset only a single ribbon tab, select the ribbon tab in the list on the right, click the *Reset* pick list button and choose the *Reset only selected Ribbon tab* item on the list. The software resets the selected ribbon tab immediately. To reset the entire ribbon, click the *Reset* pick list button and choose the *Reset all customizations* item on the list. The software displays the warning dialog shown in Figure 2 - 22. Click the *Yes* button to confirm the reset action.

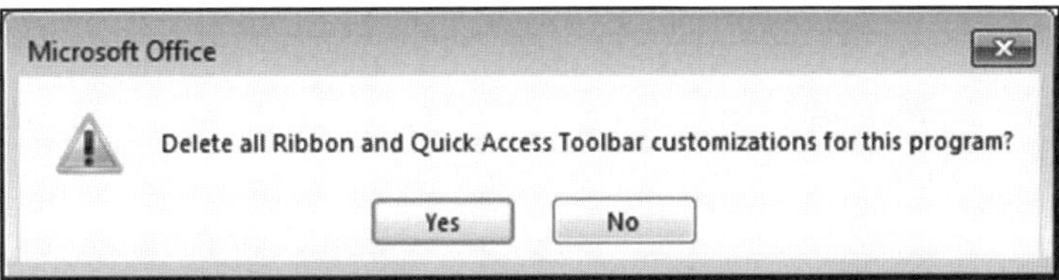

Figure 2 - 22: Warning dialog to reset all customizations to the Ribbon and Quick Access Toolbar

Warning: Notice in the dialog shown previously in Figure 2 - 22 that the software is about to reset all of the customizations to both the ribbon **and** the *Quick Access Toolbar*. If you do not want to reset customizations to the *Quick Access Toolbar*, then **do not** select the *Reset All Customizations* option. Instead, individually reset each customized ribbon tab by selecting the *Reset only selected Ribbon tab* item on the *Reset* pick list.

Customizing the Quick Access Toolbar

Like the ribbon, Project 2013 also allows you to customize the *Quick Access Toolbar*. By default, the *Quick Access Toolbar* appears above the ribbon, in the upper left corner of the application window. By default, the *Quick Access*

Toolbar contains only three buttons: the *Save, Undo,* and *Redo* buttons. You use the *Quick Access Toolbar* to provide quick access to the buttons you use most often. For example, many users like to add the *Open* and *Print* buttons to the *Quick Access Toolbar*. Project 2013 allows you to customize the *Quick Access Toolbar* in two ways:

- Add or remove buttons on the *Quick Access Toolbar*.
- Move the *Quick Access Toolbar* below the ribbon.

To rapidly customize the *Quick Access Toolbar*, click the *Customize Quick Access Toolbar* button (pick list arrow button) at the far right end of the toolbar. The software displays a pick list menu of commonly used buttons, such as the *New* and *Open* buttons, as shown in Figure 2 - 23. Individually select any of the buttons shown on the pick list menu to add them to the *Quick Access Toolbar*. Keep in mind that when you use this method, Project 2013 always adds the selected buttons to the right end of the *Quick Access Toolbar*.

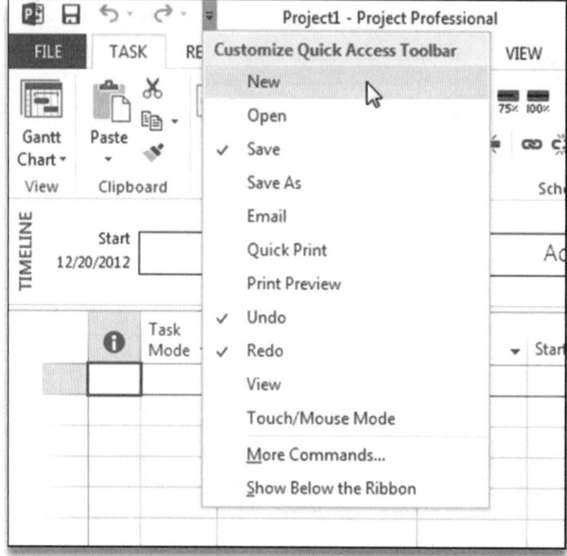

Figure 2 - 23: Customize Quick Access Toolbar menu

To display the *Quick Access Toolbar* below the ribbon so that you can see all of the buttons easily, click the *Customize Quick Access Toolbar* button again and then select the *Show Below the Ribbon* item on the pick list menu. Alternately, you can also right-click on any ribbon tab and select the *Show Quick Access Toolbar Below the Ribbon* item on the shortcut menu.

To take more control over the buttons you want to add and to control their location on the *Quick Access Toolbar*, right-click any ribbon tab and then select the *Customize Quick Access Toolbar* item on the shortcut menu. The software displays the *Project Options* dialog with the *Quick Access Toolbar* tab selected, as shown in Figure 2 - 24.

Information: Project 2013 offers you two additional methods for displaying the *Project Options* dialog with the *Quick Access Toolbar* tab selected. The first method is to click the *File* tab, click the *Options* button in the *Backstage*, and then click the *Quick Access Toolbar* tab in the *Project Options* dialog. The second method is to click the *Customize Quick Access Toolbar* button and then to click the *More Commands* item at the bottom of the pick list.

The process of customizing the *Quick Access Toolbar* is very similar to the process of customizing the ribbon. Click the *Choose commands from* pick list to choose the type of commands you want to add to the *Quick Access Toolbar*.

The pick list offers you quite a number of choices, including *Popular Commands* (the default setting), *Commands Not in the Ribbon, All Commands,* and *Macros,* plus the commands found on every available ribbon tab.

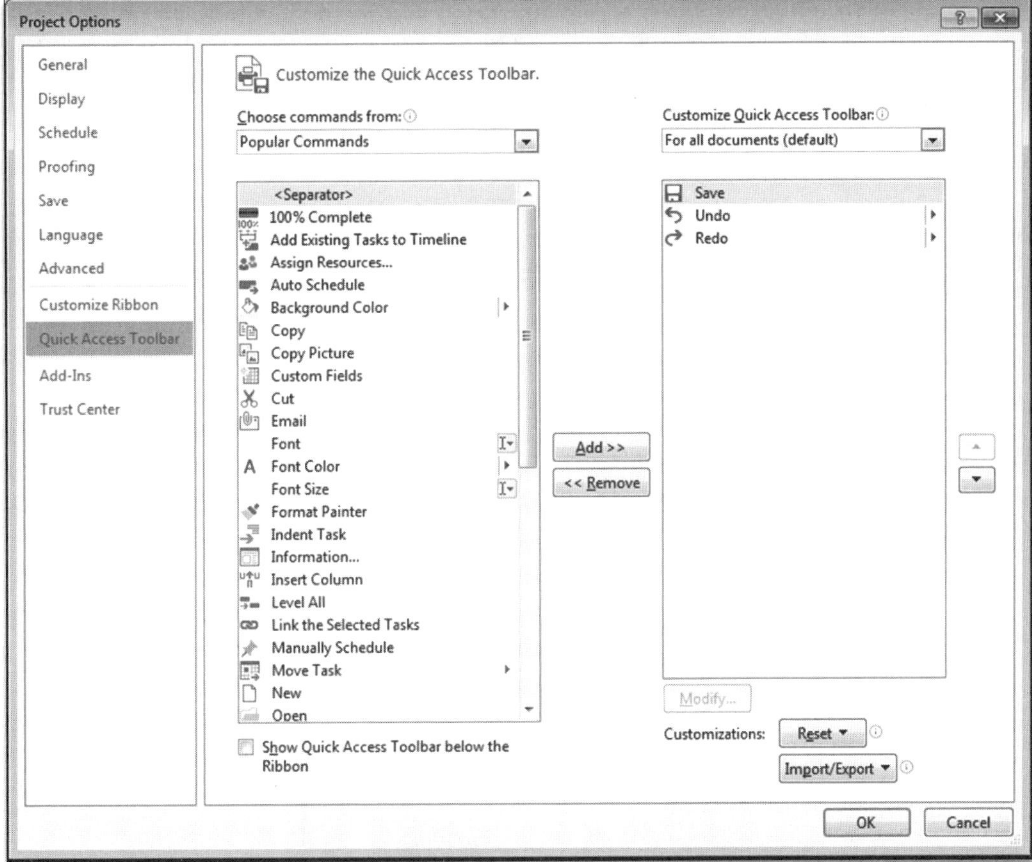

Figure 2 - 24: Project Options dialog, Quick Access Toolbar section

Click the *Customize Quick Access Toolbar* pick list and choose how to customize the *Quick Access Toolbar*. The choices on the pick list allow you to customize the *Quick Access Toolbar* for all projects or only for the active project. The second option means that you could theoretically have a different customized *Quick Access Toolbar* for every project you manage, based on your project management needs for each project.

After you select your options on the *Choose commands from* pick list and the *Customize Quick Access Toolbar* pick list, you are ready to customize the *Quick Access Toolbar*. The software offers you the following customization choices:

- Add/remove buttons and separators on the *Quick Access Toolbar*.
- Add a button for a macro and then modify the macro button.
- Change the display order of buttons on the *Quick Access Toolbar*.
- Reset the *Quick Access Toolbar* to its default settings.

Information: Project 2013 also allows you to display the *Quick Access Toolbar* below the ribbon by selecting the *Display Quick Access Toolbar below the Ribbon* checkbox in the lower left corner of the *Project Options* dialog.

Adding/Removing Buttons on the Quick Access Toolbar

To add a button to the *Quick Access Toolbar*, select the button in the list of buttons on the left. In the list of buttons on the right, select the button in the location where you want to add the new button, and then click the *Add* button. The software adds the new button **below** the selected button. To add a separator to organize the buttons into groups, select the *<Separator>* item at the top of the list on the left and click the *Add* button. You place separators in the list of buttons to add gridlines between the buttons and to separate the buttons into groups.

Information: To quickly add any button to the *Quick Access Toolbar*, you do not need to use the *Project Options* dialog at all. Instead, right-click on any button on the ribbon and then select the *Add to Quick Access Toolbar* item on the shortcut menu.

If you add a button for a macro to the *Quick Access Toolbar*, the software activates the *Modify* button in the lower right corner of the *Project Options* dialog. Click the *Modify* button to change the name of the button and to change the icon displayed for the button on the *Quick Access Toolbar*. The software displays the *Modify Button* dialog shown in Figure 2 - 25.

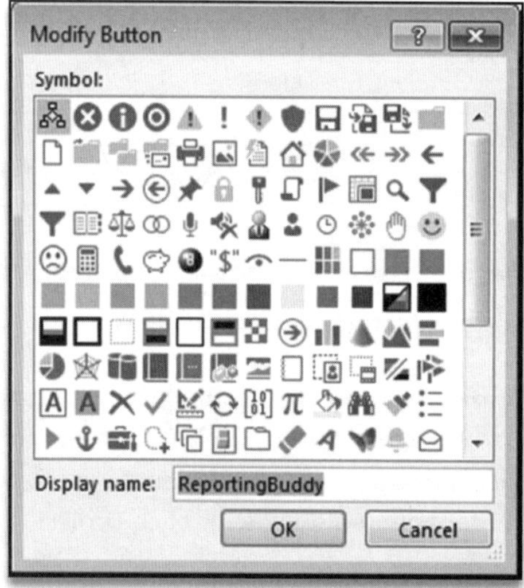

Figure 2 - 25: Modify Button dialog

To remove a button or separator on the *Quick Access Toolbar*, select the item in the list of buttons on the right side of the *Project Options* dialog, and then click the *Remove* button.

Moving Items in the Quick Access Toolbar

Project 2013 allows you to move the buttons and separators on the *Quick Access Toolbar* into the order you want to display them. To move a button or a separator, select the item you want to move and then click the *Move Up* and *Move Down* buttons (up-arrow and down-arrow buttons on the right side of the *Project Options* dialog). Figure 2 - 26 shows the custom setup of my *Quick Access Toolbar*. I included the buttons I most commonly use, and then I organized the buttons into groups of similar functionality using separators.

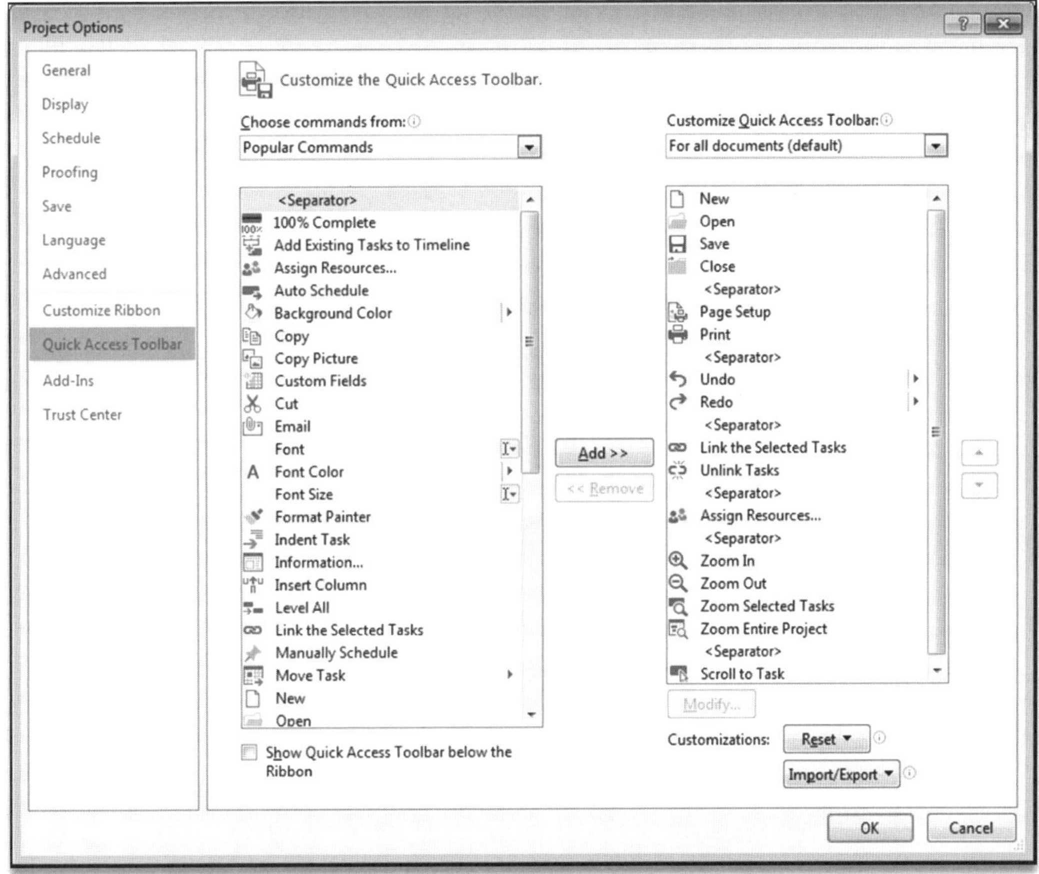

Figure 2 - 26: Project Options dialog, Quick Access Toolbar section after adding, moving, and renaming buttons

Information: If you create a customized *Quick Access Toolbar* for all documents and then create a different customized *Quick Access Toolbar* for a particular project, Project 2013 combines the two toolbars together whenever you open that particular project. The combined *Quick Access Toolbar* includes the buttons for all projects in the left half of the toolbar, with the buttons from the individual project in the right half of the toolbar.

Resetting the Quick Access Toolbar

Project 2013 allows you to reset only the *Quick Access Toolbar* to its default settings, or to reset both the *Quick Access Toolbar* and the ribbon to their default settings. To reset only the *Quick Access Toolbar,* click the *Reset* pick list button in the lower right corner of the *Project Options* dialog, and then select the *Reset only Quick Access Toolbar* item on the list. The software displays the *Reset Customizations* dialog shown in Figure 2 - 27. Click the *Yes* button to reset the *Quick Access Toolbar* to its default settings.

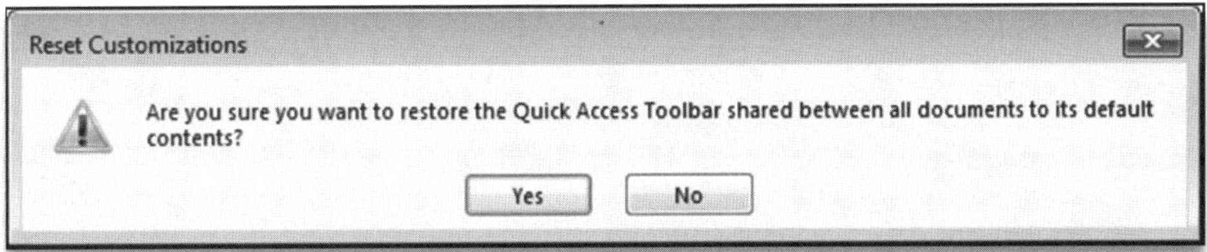

Figure 2 - 27: Reset Customizations dialog to reset the Quick Access Toolbar

To reset both the *Quick Access Toolbar* and ribbon, click the *Reset* pick list button and select the *Reset all customizations* item on the list. The software displays the confirmation dialog shown in Figure 2 - 28. Click the *Yes* button to confirm the reset action.

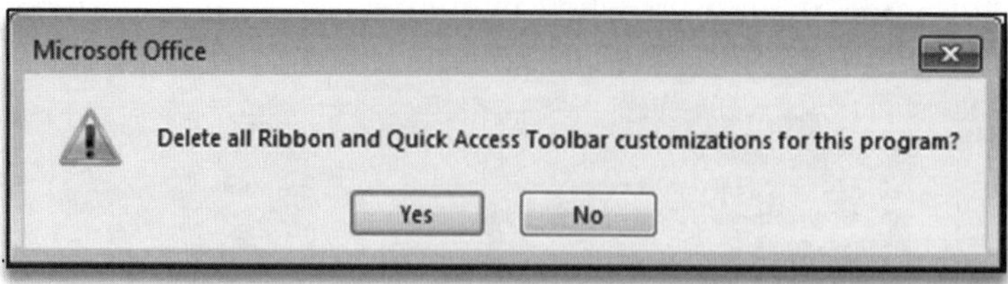

Figure 2 - 28: Confirmation dialog to reset the Ribbon and Quick Access Toolbar

Warning: Notice in the dialog shown previously in Figure 2 - 28 that the software is about to reset all of the customizations to both the *Quick Access Toolbar* **and** the ribbon. If you do not want to reset customizations to the ribbon, then **do not** select the *Reset All Customizations* option. Instead, click the *Reset* pick list button and select the *Reset Only Quick Access Toolbar* item on the list.

Hands On Exercise

Exercise 2 - 5

Customize the *Quick Access Toolbar* by adding tracking buttons.

1. Return to the **Project Navigation 2013.mpp** sample file, if necessary.
2. Right-click on any ribbon tab, such as the *Task* tab, and then select the *Customize Quick Access Toolbar* item on the shortcut menu.
3. In the *Quick Access Toolbar* section of the *Project Options* dialog, click the *Choose commands from* pick list and select the *All Commands* item on the list.
4. In the list of commands on the right side of the dialog, select the *Redo* command.
5. Individually select each of the following buttons and click the *Add* button to add them to the *Quick Access Toolbar*:
   - *0% Complete*
   - *25% Complete*
   - *50% Complete*
   - *75% Complete*
   - *100% Complete*
6. Click the *OK* button to close the *Project Options* dialog, and then examine the new buttons you added to the *Quick Access Toolbar*.

Importing/Exporting a Custom Ribbon and Quick Access Toolbar

Project 2013 allows you to back up your ribbon and *Quick Access Toolbar* customization settings by exporting them to a file. You can also give this file to other users who can import your customization settings into their own Project 2013 application. To export these settings to a file, click the *Import/Export* pick list button in the lower left corner of the *Project Options* dialog and then select the *Export all customizations* item on the pick list. The *Project Options* dialog includes the *Import/Export* pick list button on both the *Customize Ribbon* tab and the *Quick Access Toolbar* tab, by the way. The software displays the *File Save* dialog shown in Figure 2 - 29. In the *File Save* dialog, enter a name for the customization file in the *File name* field, select a destination for the file, and then click the *Save* button.

Information: Notice in in the *File Save* dialog shown in Figure 2 - 29 that ***.exportedUI** is the file extension for the exported customization file.

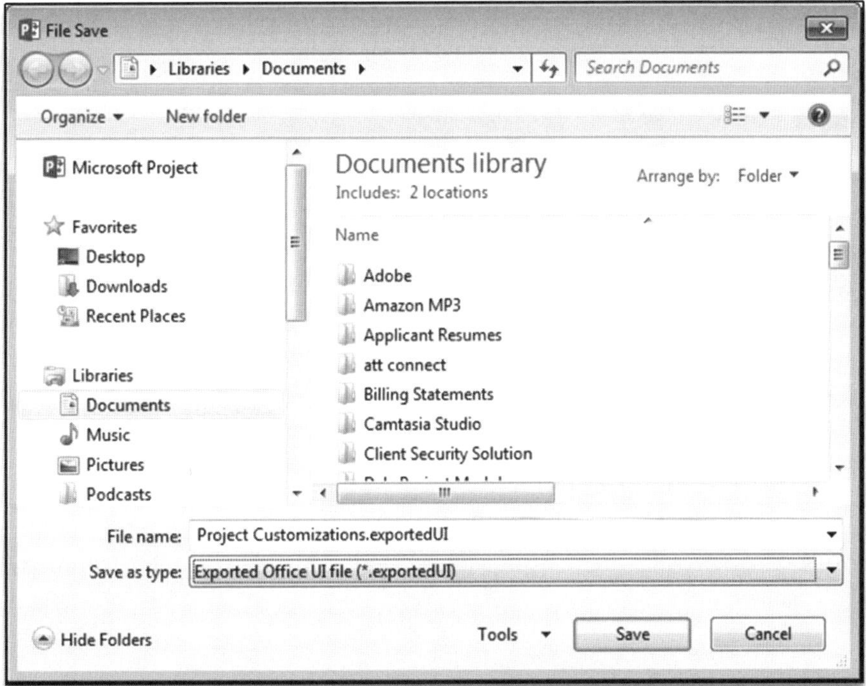

Figure 2 - 29: File Save dialog

To import the ribbon and *Quick Access Toolbar* customization settings from a file, click the *Import/Export* pick list button and select the *Import customization file* item on the pick list. The software displays the *File Open* dialog shown in Figure 2 - 30. In the *File Open* dialog, navigate to the location of the customization file and select it, and then click the *Open* button.

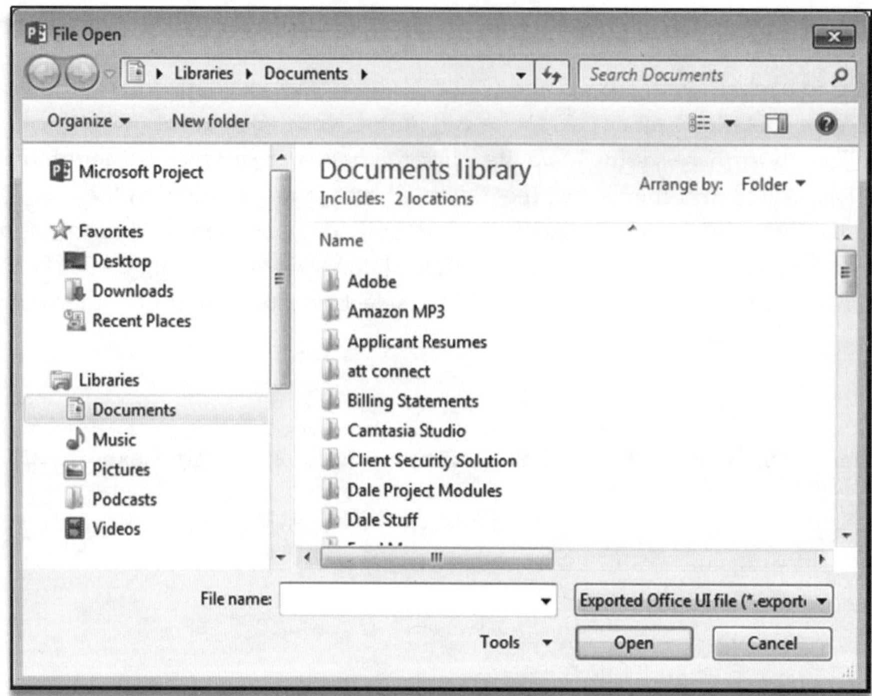

Figure 2 - 30: File Open dialog

The software displays the confirmation dialog shown in Figure 2 - 31. In the confirmation dialog, click the *Yes* button to import the customized *Ribbon* and *Quick Access Toolbar* settings, and replace your current *Ribbon* and *Quick Access Toolbar* settings. Click the *OK* button in the *Project Options* dialog to view your new customized ribbon and *Quick Access Toolbar*.

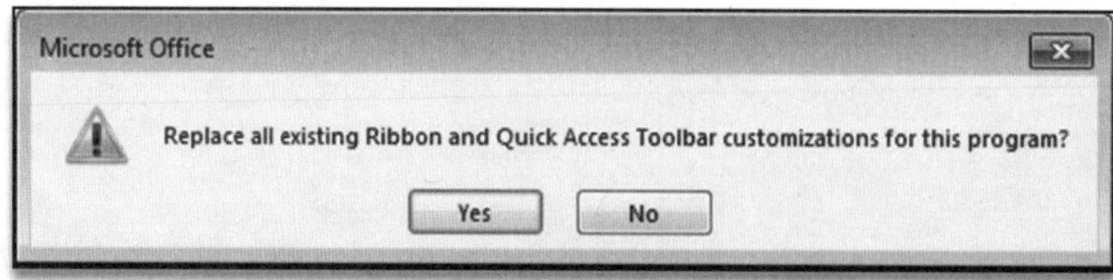

Figure 2 - 31: Warning dialog when importing Ribbon and Quick Access Toolbar customization settings

Hands On Exercise

Exercise 2 - 6

Export the *Ribbon* and *Quick Access Toolbar* customization settings to a file.

1. Return to the **Project Navigation 2013.mpp** sample file, if necessary.
2. Right-click any ribbon tab, such as the *Task* tab, and then select the *Customize the Ribbon* item on the shortcut menu.
3. In the *Project Options* dialog, click the *Import/Export* pick list button and select the *Export all customizations* item on the list.
4. In the *File Save* dialog, navigate to the folder where you unzipped the sample files that accompany this book.
5. In the *File Save* dialog, leave the default name **Project Customizations.exportedUI** in the *File name* field, and then click the *Save* button.
6. Click the *OK* button to close the *Project Options* dialog.

Exercise 2 - 7

Reset the customizations you made to the ribbon and the *Quick Access Toolbar.*

1. Right-click any ribbon tab, such as the *Task* tab, and then select the *Customize Quick Access Toolbar* item on the shortcut menu.
2. In the *Project Options* dialog, click the *Reset* pick list button and select the *Reset all customizations* item on the list.
3. When prompted in the confirmation dialog, click the *Yes* button to delete all customizations to the ribbon and the *Quick Access Toolbar.*

Notice in the list of commands on the right side of the dialog how Project 2013 removed all of your customization settings the *Quick Access Toolbar.*

4. Click the *OK* button to close the *Project Options* dialog.
5. Click the *Report* tab to display the *Report* ribbon.
6. In the *View Reports* section of the *Report* ribbon, click the *Dashboards* pick list button and select the *Project Overview* report.
7. In the lower left corner of the *Project Overview* report, click anywhere in the *Milestones Due* table.
8. Click the *Design* tab with the *Table Tools* applied.

Notice how resetting the ribbon removed the new *Table Text Formatting* section and buttons you added to the *Design* ribbon with the *Table Tools* applied.

Exercise 2 - 8

Import *Ribbon* and *Quick Access Toolbar* customization settings from a file.

Information: As a special gift to you, MSProjectExperts developed a number of best practice customization settings for the *Ribbon* and *Quick Access Toolbar*, and then saved these settings to a customization file. After you complete this exercise, I believe you will find your Project 2013 user interface to be much more user friendly.

1. Right-click any ribbon tab, such as the *Task* tab, and then select the *Customize Quick Access Toolbar* item on the shortcut menu.

2. Click the *Import/Export* pick list button and select the *Import customization file* item on the list.

3. In the *File Open* dialog, navigate to the folder where you unzipped the sample files that accompany this book.

4. In the *File Open* dialog, select the **Customized Ribbon and Quick Access Toolbar.exportedUI** sample file, and then click the *Open* button.

5. When prompted in the confirmation dialog, click the *Yes* button to replace all current customization to the ribbon and the *Quick Access Toolbar.*

6. In the lower left corner of the *Project Options* dialog, select the *Show Quick Access Toolbar below the Ribbon* option.

7. Click the *OK* button to close the *Project Options* dialog.

8. Examine the each of the commands added to the *Quick Access Toolbar.*

9. Click the *Definition* tab to display the new *Definition* ribbon.

10. Study the sections and commands in the *Definition* ribbon.

You can use the commands in the *Definition* ribbon to properly define every new project you start, whether you start the project from a blank file or from a template file.

11. Click the *Report* tab to display the *Report* ribbon.

12. In the *View Reports* section of the *Report* ribbon, click the *Dashboards* pick list button and select the *Project Overview* report.

13. In the lower left corner of the *Project Overview* report, click anywhere in the *Milestones Due* table.

14. Click the *Design* tab with the *Table Tools* applied.

Notice the *Table Text Formatting* section and buttons added from the customization file to the *Design* ribbon with the *Table Tools* applied.

Accessing and Using the Backstage

As I noted earlier in this module, click the *File* tab to access the most commonly used file commands, such as opening, saving, or printing a project file. If you click the *File* tab when you have no project currently open (or you have the default *Project1* file open), the software displays the *Backstage* with the *Open* page selected, as shown in Figure 2 - 32. Notice that the *Open* page includes a *Recent Projects* section to show the list of files you opened recently.

Information: If you open any project and then click the *File* tab, the software displays the *Backstage* with the *Info* page selected instead.

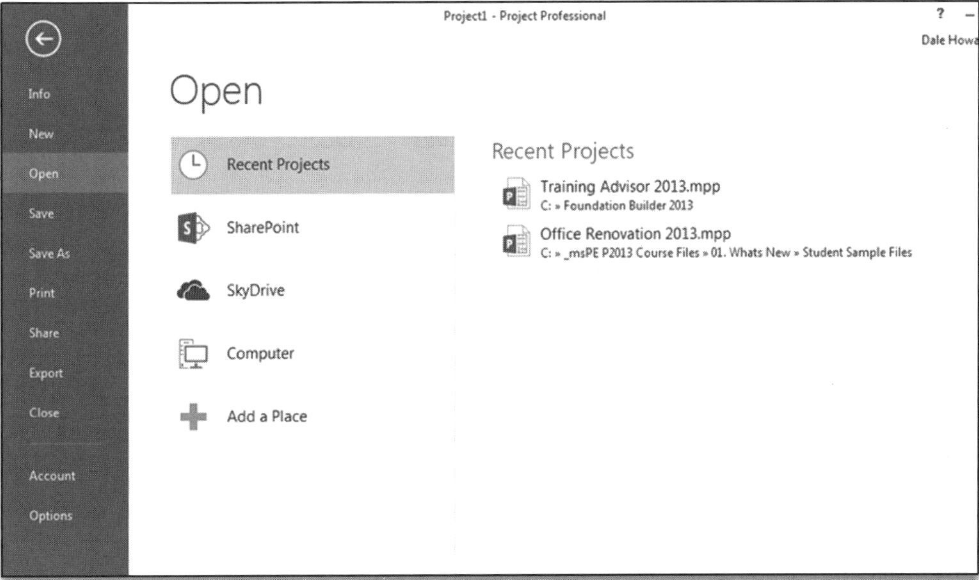

Figure 2 - 32: Open page in the Backstage

The sidepane on the left side of the *Backstage* contains both tabs and buttons, which allow you to use the file features in Project 2013. In the *Backstage*, you can perform any of the following actions:

- Click the *Info* tab to display the *Info* page for the active project. Use this page to see and edit high-level information about your active project, and to access to the *Organizer* dialog.
- Click the *New* tab to display the *New* page. Use this page to create a new project using several different methods.
- Click the *Open* tab to display the *Open* page. Use this page to open a recently used project or to browse to any folder and open other projects.
- Click the *Save* button to save the active project.
- Click the *Save As* tab to display the *Save As* page. Use this page to save the active project to a SkyDrive or Office 365 SharePoint folder, to synchronize the active project with a SharePoint Tasks list, or to browse to any folder and save the active project.

- Click the *Print* tab to display the *Print* page. Use this page to print the active project.
- Click the *Share* tab to display the *Share* page. Use this page to synchronize the active project with a SharePoint Tasks list or to e-mail a copy of the active project to a fellow user.
- Click the *Export* tab to display the *Export* page. Use this page to save the active project using an alternate file type, such as a Project 2007 file, or to save the active project as a PDF document.
- Click the *Close* button to close the active project.
- Click the *Account* tab to display the *Account* page. Use this page to sign into a Windows Live SkyDrive account or an Office 365 SharePoint account, or to view the activation status of your copy of Project 2013.
- Click the *Options* button to display the *Project Options* dialog.

Using the Info Page

To specify information about the active project, click the *Info* tab in the *Backstage*. Project 2013 displays the *Info* page for the project, as shown in Figure 2 - 33. Notice the following about the *Info* page:

- The software displays the name and file path for the active project in the upper left corner of the page.
- The software displays statistics and properties for the active project on the right side of the page.
- The software allows you to create and manage Project Server 2013 login accounts. This feature is only available in the **Professional** version of Project 2013.
- The software allows you to access the *Organizer* dialog.

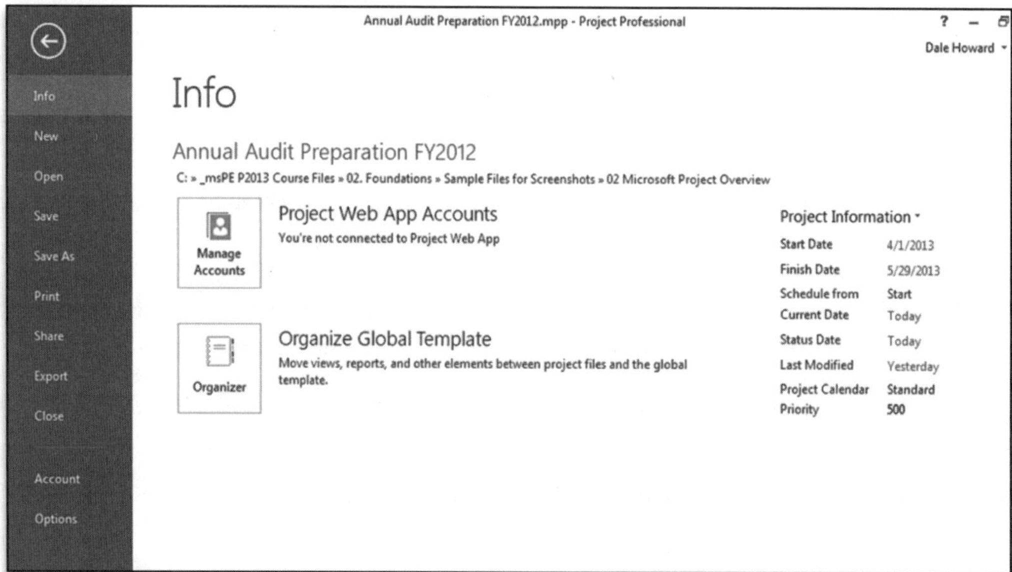

Figure 2 - 33: Info page for the selected project

Information: If you click the file path in the upper left corner of the *Info* page, Project 2013 displays a menu with two available options. If you select the *Copy link to clipboard* item, the software copies the file path to the Windows Clipboard, suppressing spaces in the path name with the **%20** character string. If you select the *Open file location* item, the software launches the Windows Explorer and navigates to the folder where the file resides.

When you click the *Manage Accounts* button, the software displays the *Project Web App Accounts* dialog shown in Figure 2 - 34. Again, keep in mind that this feature is only available in the **Professional** version of Project 2013, and you use this feature to specify login information for your organization's Project Server 2013 instances. Notice that the dialog shown in Figure 2 - 34 contains two login accounts. I use the *Computer* account to launch Project 2013 in desktop only mode, and I use the *Project Server 2103 Internal* account to log in to our organization's internal Project Server 2013 instance.

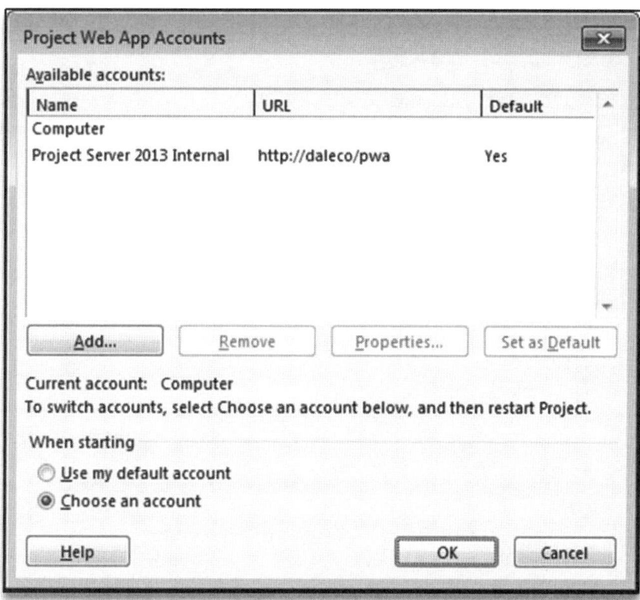

Figure 2 - 34: Project Web App Accounts dialog

When you click the *Organizer* button on the *Info* page of the *Backstage*, the software displays the *Organizer* dialog shown previously in Figure 2 - 3. You use the *Organizer* dialog to manage default and custom objects in Project 2013, such as views, tables, filters, groups, reports, and calendars.

When you click the *Project Information* pick list in the upper right corner of the *Info* page, the software displays the pick list shown in Figure 2 - 35. On the pick list, select the *Advanced Properties* item to display the *Properties* dialog, in which you can enter custom properties for the selected project.

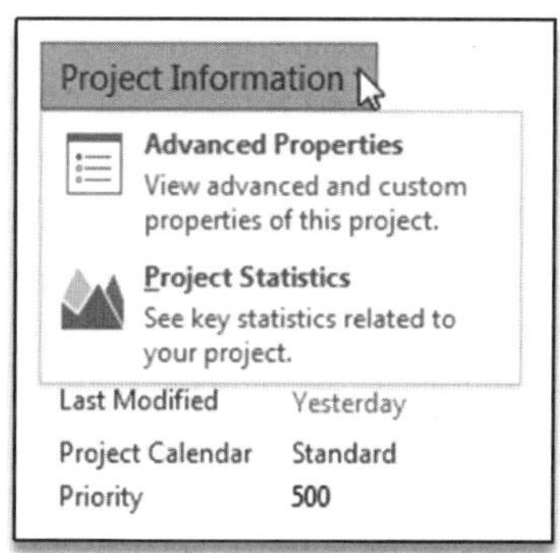

Figure 2 - 35: Project Information pick list in the Backstage

Select the *Advanced Properties* item on the list to display the *Properties* dialog shown in Figure 2 - 36. Use this dialog to enter high-level properties about the project, such as a *Title* for the project and *Comments* about the project.

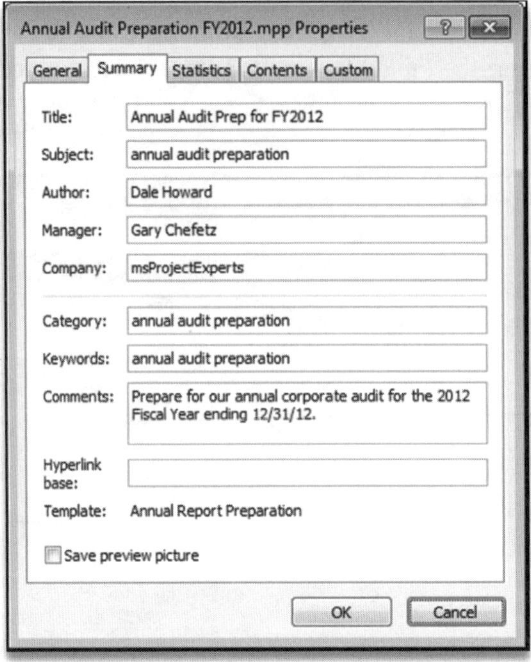

Figure 2 - 36: Properties dialog

Select the *Project Statistics* item on the list to display the *Project Statistics* dialog shown in Figure 2 - 37. Use this dialog to view the statistics about the current schedule of the project compared to the original baseline schedule.

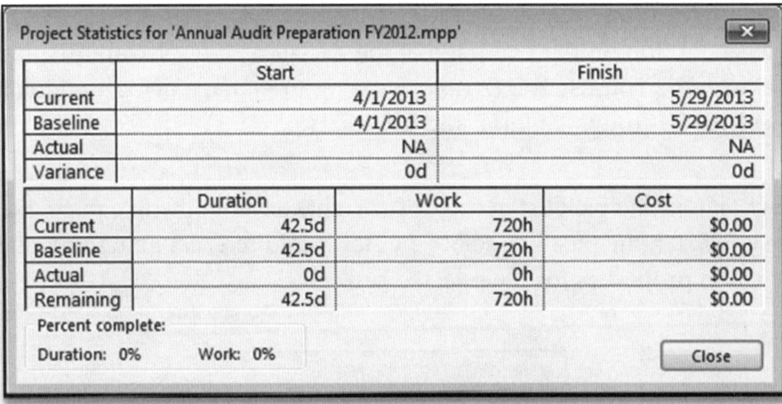

	Start	Finish
Current	4/1/2013	5/29/2013
Baseline	4/1/2013	5/29/2013
Actual	NA	NA
Variance	0d	0d

	Duration	Work	Cost
Current	42.5d	720h	$0.00
Baseline	42.5d	720h	$0.00
Actual	0d	0h	$0.00
Remaining	42.5d	720h	$0.00

Figure 2 - 37: Project Statistics dialog

Using the New Page

To create a new project, click the *New* tab in the *Backstage*. Project 2013 displays the *New* page shown in Figure 2 - 38. Notice that the *New* page appears very similar to the *Start* screen shown previously in Figure 2 - 1. Notice that the *New* page includes the following types of templates for you to use to create a new project:

- **Blank Project** – Use this template to create a new blank project.
- **New from existing** – Use this template to create a new project that is a copy of an existing project.

- **New from Excel workbook** – Use this template to create a new project from a Microsoft Excel workbook using the *Import/Export Wizard*.
- **New from SharePoint Tasks List** – Use this template to create a new project from a *Tasks* list in a SharePoint site. Before you can use this feature, your SharePoint administrator must create a SharePoint site containing a *Tasks* list.

In addition to the four types of templates listed previously, the *New* page also offers a selection of Project 2013 templates available in the *Office.com* website. Microsoft allows you to download and use any of these templates free of charge. Notice that each Office.com template button includes a preview picture of the file created from that template type. To create a new project, click one of the Office.com template buttons and create the new project.

Information: To pin one of the *Office.com* templates so that Project 2013 always displays the template at the top of the *Start* screen and the *New* page in the *Backstage*, float your mouse pointer over the template icon and then click the *Pin to list* button (pushpin button) in the lower-right corner of the icon. To unpin a pinned template, float your mouse pointer over the pinned template icon and then click the *Unpin from list* button (pushpin button) in the lower-right corner of the icon.

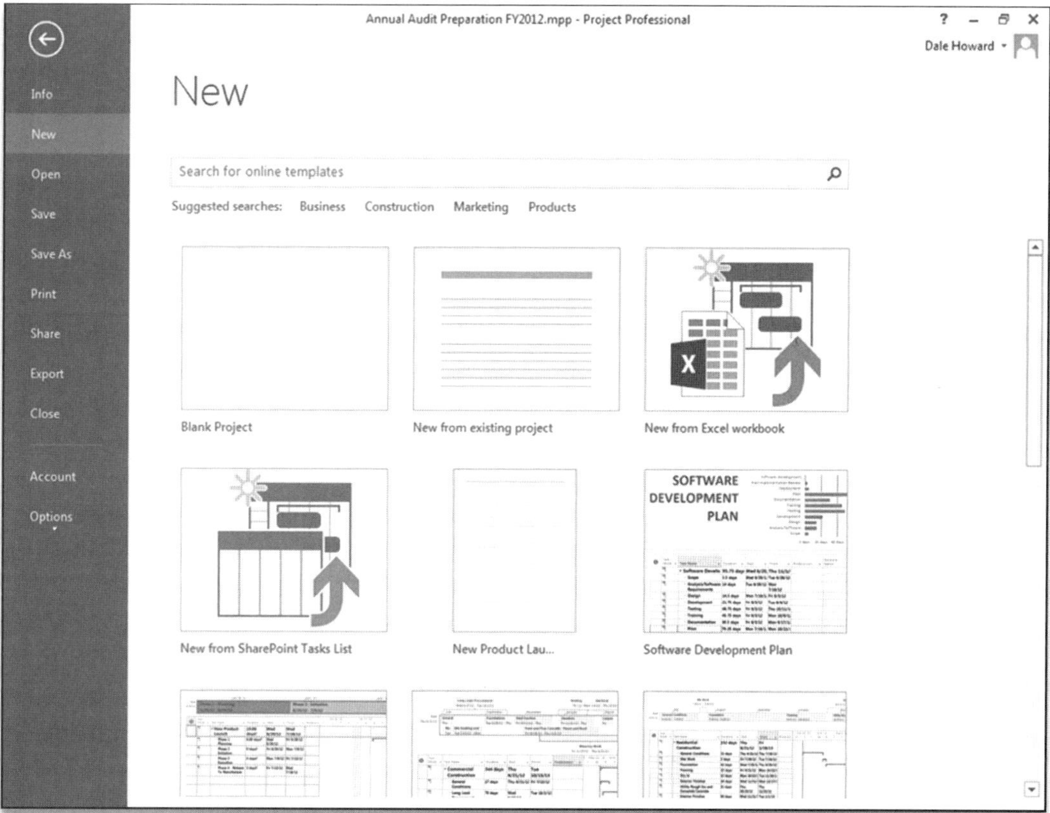

Figure 2 - 38: New page in the Backstage

If the *New* page does not display the type of template you want to use to create a new project, you can use the search features on this page to locate an appropriate template in the *Office.com* website. To search for a project template, enter your search term in the *Search for online templates* field and then click the *Start searching* button at the right end of the field. Alternately, you can click one of the links in the *Suggested searches* line, such as the *Marketing* link. During the search process, Project 2013 briefly displays a *SEARCHING THOUSANDS OF ONLINE*

TEMPLATES message, and then reveals the search results on the *New* page as shown in Figure 2 - 39. Notice that using the search term *Products* yielded three project templates.

In addition, notice that the top of the *New* page offers you a *Search for online templates* field in which you can search for other project templates in the *Office.com* website, along with four links on the *Suggested searches* line to allow you to search for commonly used templates such as business or construction templates.

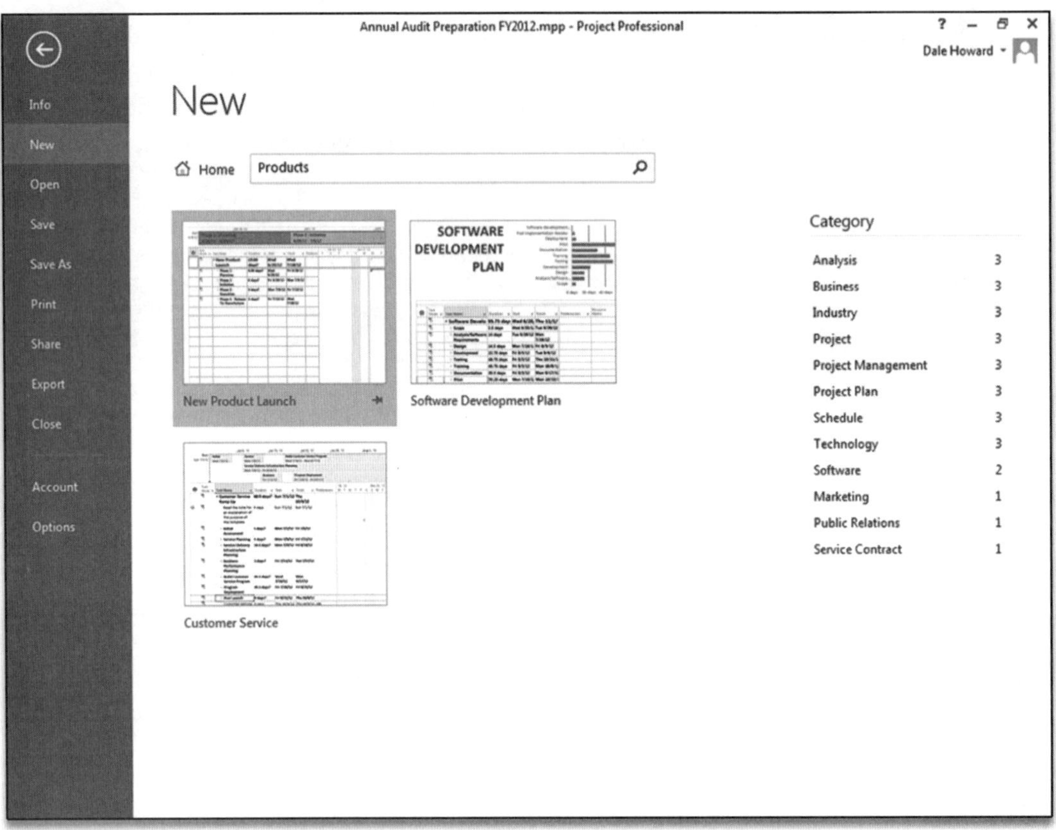

Figure 2 - 39: Search for a template in Office.com

After the software displays your search results, the *Category* sidepane on the right side of the page displays sub-categories of templates available in the *Office.com* website. For example, notice the *Category* list reveals that two of the three *Products* templates shown previously in Figure 2 - 39 are also *Software* templates. To further filter the list of templates, click one of the template sub-categories shown in the *Category* list. Project 2013 shows you all of the templates that match the category you selected in the *Search for online templates* field or in the *Suggested searches* line, and the sub-category you selected in the *Category* list. For example, if I click the *Software* item in the *Category* list, the software displays only the *New Product Launch* and *Software Development Plan* templates, indicating that they are both *Products* templates and *Software* templates. After conducting a search for templates in the *Office.com* website, you can return to the unfiltered *New* page by clicking the *Home* button to the left of the *Search for online templates* field.

To create a new project from one of the *Office.com* templates, click the name of the template you want to use. Project 2013 displays a preview dialog for the selected template similar to the one shown in Figure 2 - 40. Notice that the preview dialog shown displays a preview of the *New Business Plan* template, which includes a pre-built *Timeline* report at the top of the template. The preview dialog also includes additional information about the template, including the name of the template creator (in this case, Microsoft), a description of when and how to use the template, and the rating of the template by members of the user community. For some of the templates, the preview dialog also displays the download size of the template.

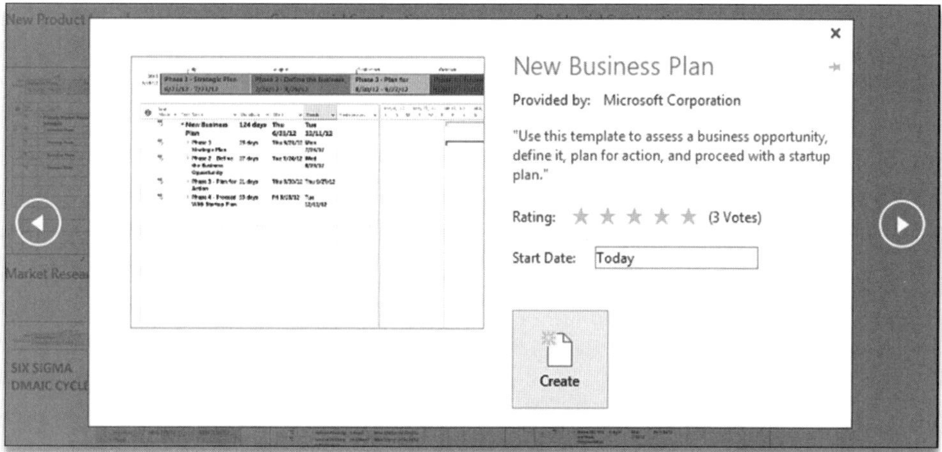

Figure 2 - 40: New Business Plan template preview dialog

To create a new project from the selected template, enter the *Start* date of the project in the *Start Date* field and then click the *Create* button. Project 2013 downloads a copy of the template, saves it in the default *Templates* folder on your computer's hard drive, and then creates a new project from the selected template, ready for you to use to plan and manage your project.

Information: To navigate in the preview dialog to the previous template or the next template on the *New* page, click the *Previous* or *Next* buttons (big white arrow buttons) on either side of the preview dialog.

Accessing Templates Stored in Your Templates Folder

Because of new functionality in Office 2013, the *New* page in the *Backstage* **does not** automatically allow you to create a new project from any template stored in your default *Templates* folder. This includes templates that you download from the *Office.com* website and templates that you create personally and save in your *Templates* folder. If you want to create a new project from any template stored in your *Templates* folder, you must complete the following steps first:

1. Click the *File* tab and then click the *Options* button in the *Backstage*.

2. Click the *Save* tab in the *Project Options* dialog. The software displays the *Save* page of the *Project Options* dialog shown in Figure 2 - 41.

3. In the *Default personal templates location* field in the *Save templates* section of the dialog, manually enter the path for your default *Templates* folder based on the example below, or use the *Browse* button to navigate to your default *Templates* folder.

C:\Users\YourUserID\AppData\Roaming\Microsoft\Templates

4. Click the *OK* button.

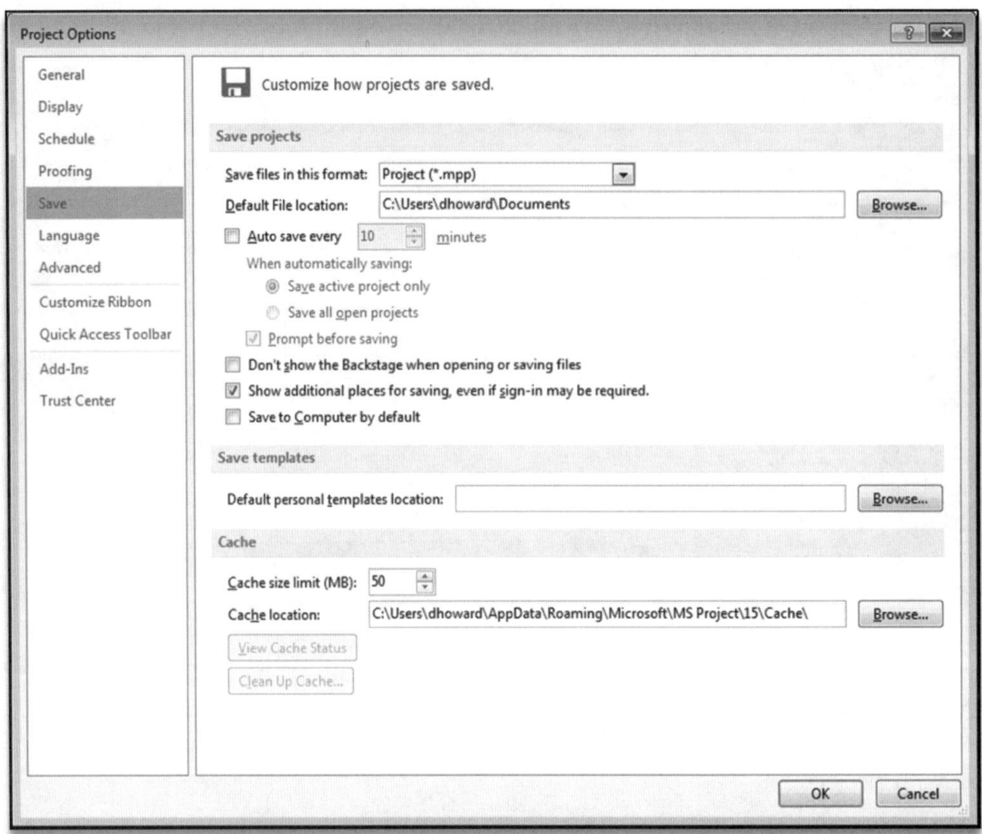

Figure 2 - 41: Project Options dialog, Save page

Warning: If you want to use templates in the default *Templates* folder with any of your other Office 2013 applications, you must repeat the same process detailed above **in each of these applications individually**. There is no way currently to specify the default *Templates* folder for all of the Office 2013 applications simultaneously.

The next time you navigate to the *Start* screen or to the *New* page in the *Backstage*, Project 2013 displays two new links in the upper left corner of the page: the *FEATURED* link and the *PERSONAL* link. When selected, the *FEATURED* link displays *Office.com* templates plus the four default template types. Click the *PERSONAL* link to view project templates stored in your default *Templates* folder, as shown in Figure 2 - 42. Notice that I have four templates available for use in my default *Templates* folder, all downloaded from the *Office.com* website.

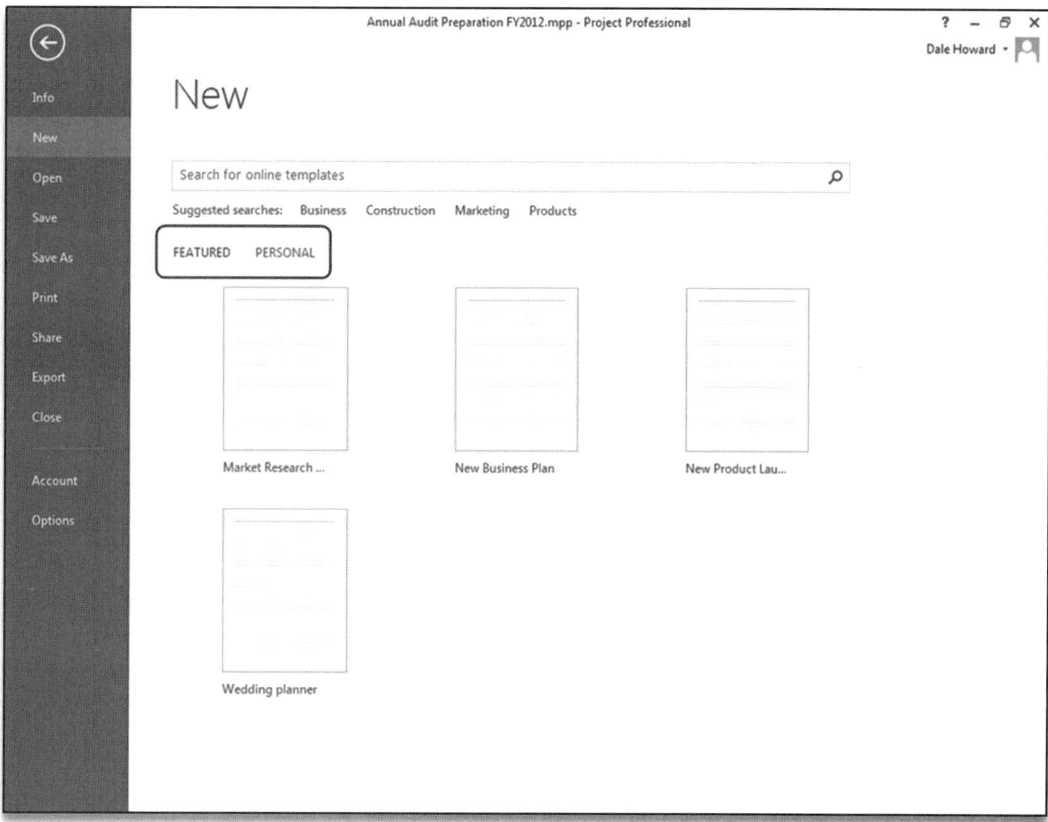

Figure 2 - 42: New page shows templates in the default Templates folder

To create a new project from a personal template stored in your default *Templates* folder, click the *PERSONAL* link on the *New* page of the *Backstage* and then click the icon for the template you want to use. Project 2013 displays the dialog shown in Figure 2 - 43. Notice that the dialog does not contain a preview image of the template, nor does it provide any other information about the template. In this dialog, enter a date in the *Start Date* field and then click the *Create* button. The software creates the new project as a copy of the template you selected.

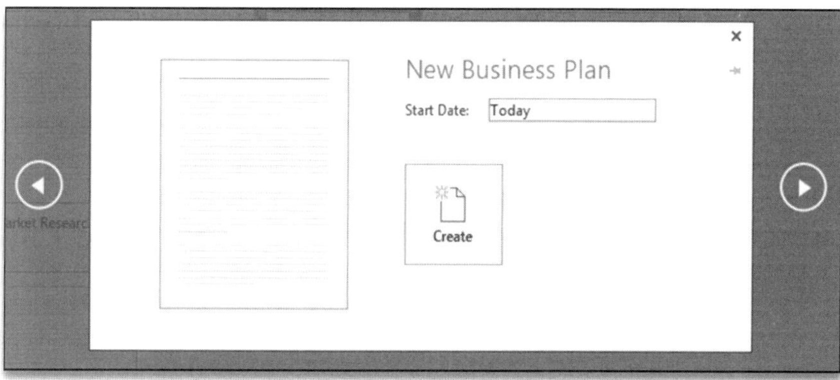

Figure 2 - 43: Preview dialog for a personal template

Information: To navigate in the dialog to the previous template or the next template in the *PERSONAL* section of the *New* page, click the *Previous* or *Next* buttons (big white arrow buttons) on either side of the dialog.

Hands On Exercise

Exercise 2 - 9

Explore the *New* and *Info* pages in the *Backstage*.

1. Click the *File* tab and then click the *Close* button to close the **Project Navigation 2013.mpp** sample file.
2. If prompted in a confirmation dialog to save the changes to the **Project Navigation 2013.mpp** sample, click the *Yes* button.

If Project 2013 displays the *New* page in the *Backstage*, skip step #3 and continue with step #4. Otherwise, continue this exercise with step #3.

3. Click the *File* tab and then click the *New* tab in the *Backstage*.
4. In the *Suggested searches* section at the top of the *New* page, click the *Marketing* link to search for marketing-related templates.
5. Select the icon for the *New Business Plan* template.

Notice the relevant information about this template in the upper right corner of the dialog, including the creator of the template and recommendations on using the template.

6. In the *New Business Plan* dialog, enter **February 2, 2015** in the *Start Date* field and then click the *Create* button.
7. Click the *File* tab and then click the *Info* tab in the *Backstage*, if necessary.

In the *Project Information* section on the right side of the *Info* page, notice the relevant information about this project, including the current *Start Date* and *Finish Date* for the project.

8. Click the *Project Information* pick list and then click the *Advanced Properties* item on the pick list.
9. In the *Properties* dialog, enter *Office Apps Startup* in the *Title* field.
10. In the *Properties* dialog, enter your name in the *Author* and *Manager* fields, enter the name of your organization in the *Company* field, and then click the *OK* button.
11. Press the **Escape** key on your computer keyboard to return to the main Project 2013 user interface.

Notice that Project 2013 displays in the Project Summary Task (Row 0 or Task 0) the *Title* information you entered in the *Properties* dialog.

12. Click the *File* tab and then click the *Close* button in the *Backstage*.
13. When prompted in a dialog to save your new project, click the *No* button.
14. Press the **Escape** key on your computer keyboard to exit the *New* page in the *Backstage* and return to the main Project 2013 user interface.

Exercise 2 - 10

Customize Project 2013 to give you access to your personal templates.

1. Click the *File* tab and then click the *Options* button in the *Backstage*.
2. In the *Project Options* dialog, click the *Save* tab.
3. In the *Default personal templates location* field in the *Save templates* section of the dialog, manually enter the path for your default *Templates* folder based on the example below, or use the *Browse* button to navigate to your default *Templates* folder.

C:\Users\YourUserID\AppData\Roaming\Microsoft\Templates

Information: If you are not certain about your Windows network user ID, contact your network administrator for this information. You cannot complete the preceding step unless you enter a valid Windows network user ID.

4. Click the *OK* button.
5. Click the *File* tab and then click the *New* tab in the *Backstage*.

At the top of the *New* page in the *Backstage*, notice the *FEATURED* and *PERSONAL* links. Notice also that the software selects the *FEATURED* link by default, which shows you the templates available from the Office.com website.

6. Click the *PERSONAL* link at the top of the *New* page.

Notice the button for the *New Business Plan* template, from which you created a new project in Exercise 2 - 9. Remember that the *PERSONAL* page displays templates you downloaded from Office.com, or new templates you created and saved in your default *Templates* folder.

7. Click the button for the *New Business Plan* template.

Notice that the upper right corner of the *New Business Plan* dialog contains none of the relevant information about the template that you saw previously in the *New Business Plan* dialog in Exercise 2 - 9. You only see information in this dialog for templates you download from the *Office.com* website.

8. In the *New Business Plan* dialog, enter **February 2, 2015** in the *Start Date* field and then click the *Create* button.
9. Leave this project open for the next Hands On exercise.

Using the Save As Page

To save a new project, click the *Save As* tab in the *Backstage*. Project 2013 displays the *Save As* page shown in Figure 2 - 44. Use the *Save As* page to synchronize a project with a *Tasks* list in SharePoint, to save your project files in a Windows Live SkyDrive folder or in an Office 365 SharePoint folder, or to save your project files to your computer.

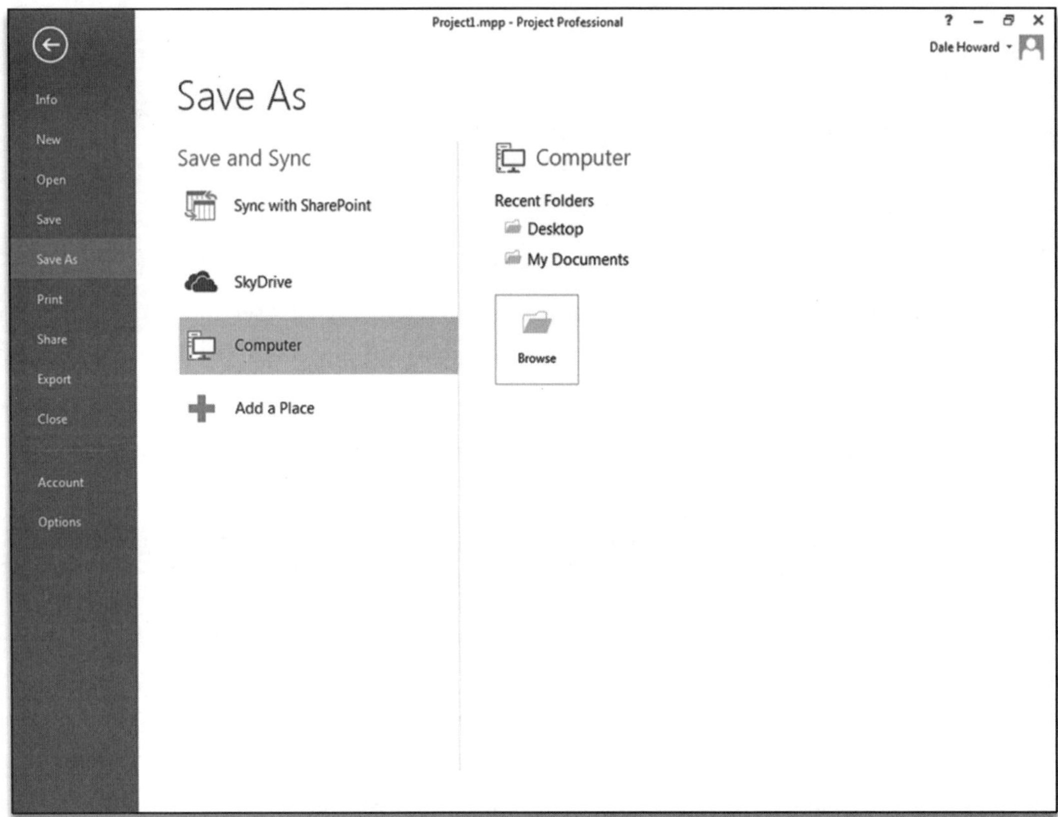

Figure 2 - 44: Save As page in the Backstage

Saving a Project to a Windows Live SkyDrive Folder

To save your project in a Windows Live SkyDrive folder, select the *SkyDrive* option in the *Save and Sync* section of the *Save As* page. Project 2013 updates the *Save As* page with a *SkyDrive* section, as shown in Figure 2 - 45. On this page, you see a new feature that allows you to save your projects to a Windows Live SkyDrive folder. SkyDrive is a cloud-based file storage system offered by Microsoft, by the way.

Before you can use the SkyDrive feature, however, you must have a valid Windows Live ID, and you must log in to Windows Live to access your SkyDrive file storage system. If you do not have a Windows Live ID, click the *Learn more* link to learn more about Windows Live SkyDrive, and then click the *Sign up* link to create a new Windows Live ID.

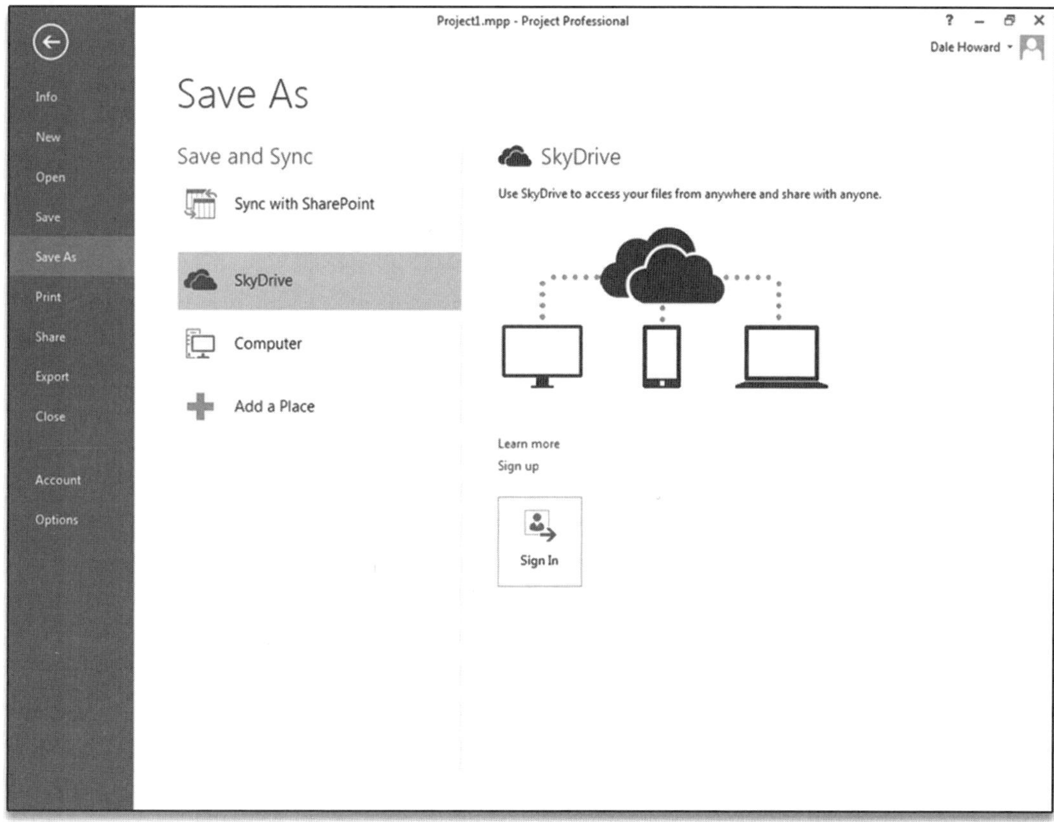

Figure 2 - 45: Save As page with the SkyDrive options enabled

Once you have a Windows Live ID, click the *Sign In* button on the *Save As* page of the *Backstage*. The software displays the *Add a service* dialog shown in Figure 2 - 46. Enter your Windows Live e-mail address in the *Add a service* dialog and then click the *Next* button.

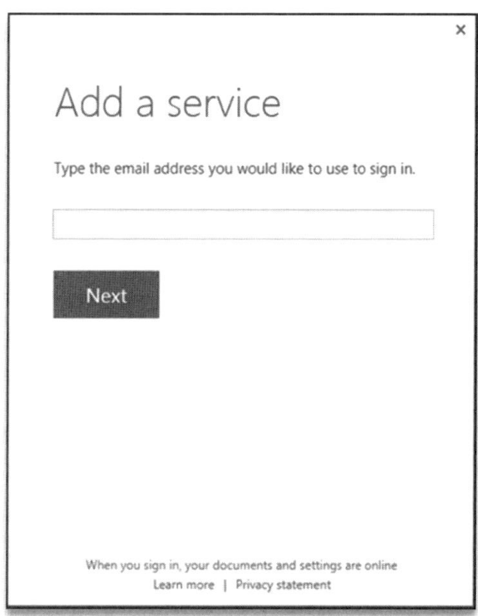

Figure 2 - 46: Add a service dialog

The software displays the *Sign in* dialog with your Windows Live e-mail address entered in the *Microsoft account* field shown in Figure 2 - 47. Enter your password in the *Password* field and then click the *Sign in* button.

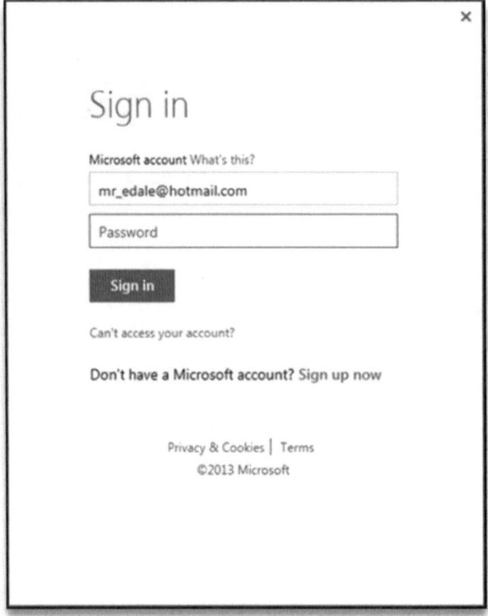

Figure 2 - 47: Sign in dialog

After you successfully log in to Windows Live using your Windows Live ID, the software refreshes the *Save As* page to show your SkyDrive account., as shown in Figure 2 - 48. Notice that the software displays the name of your SkyDrive account at the top of the page.

Information: When you log in to Windows Live to access a SkyDrive location in Project 2013, the software automatically logs you into Windows Live in all of the other applications in the Office 2013 family of software tools, including Word 2013, Excel 2013, and PowerPoint 2103.

Notice that the *Dale Howard's SkyDrive* section of the page includes the *Get SkyDrive for Windows and take your files with you anywhere* section at the bottom. If you click the *Learn More* link, the software launches your Internet Explorer and navigates to the *Microsoft SkyDrive* web page. On this page, you can learn how to download and use the free SkyDrive desktop app for Windows from Microsoft. To hide the *Get SkyDrive for Windows and take your files with you anywhere* section in the *Save As* page, click the *Don't show this message again* (**X**) button at the right end of the section.

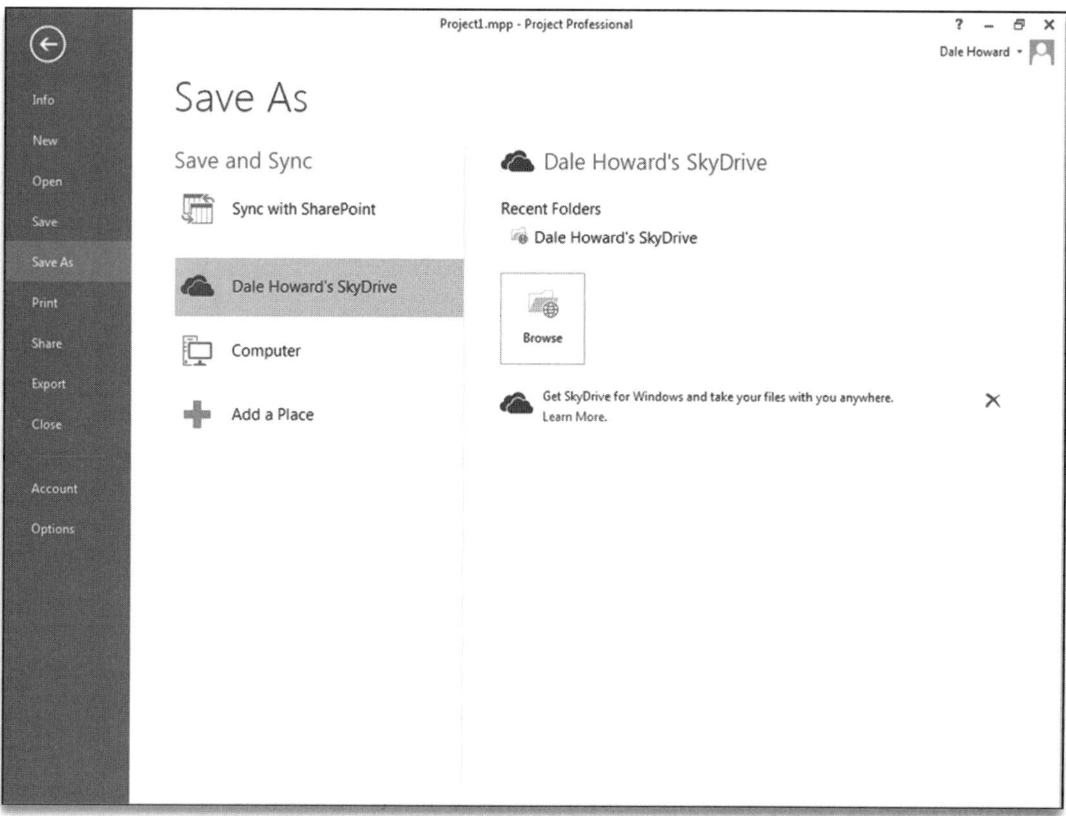

Figure 2 - 48: Save As page after logging into SkyDrive

To save the active file to a SkyDrive folder, click the *Browse* button. Project 2013 displays the *Save As* dialog, revealing the available folders in your SkyDrive location. Notice in Figure 2 - 49 that the *Save As* dialog shows three default SkyDrive folders: *Documents, Pictures,* and *Public*. Select a SkyDrive folder and then click the *Save* button to save your project file in the SkyDrive folder.

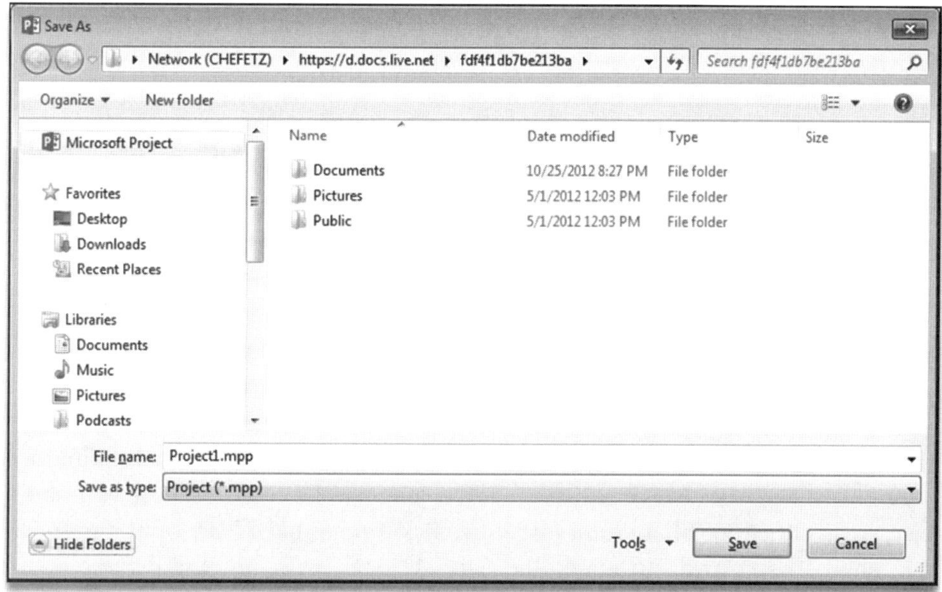

Figure 2 - 49: Save As dialog shows SkyDrive folders

Saving a Project to your Computer

To save the current project file to a folder on your computer, click the *Computer* option in the *Save and Sync* section of the *Save As* page. The software displays a *Save As* page similar to the one shown previously in Figure 2 - 44. The *Computer* section of the *Save As* page shows the list of recently used folders in which you saved project files. Select one of the recently used folders or click the *Browse* button to display a *Save As* dialog similar to the one shown previously in Figure 2 - 49. In the *Save As* dialog, navigate to the folder where you want to save your project, enter a name for the project in the *File name* field, and then click the *Save* button.

By the way, the *Save As* dialog offers you a number of additional ways to navigate to a folder and to save an existing project, including each of the following:

- Click one of the folders shown in the "breadcrumb" bar at the top of the dialog.
- Click the *Previous Locations* pick list button at the right end of the "breadcrumb" bar.
- Enter a search term in the *Search* field in the upper right corner of the dialog.
- Click the *New Folder* button at the top of the dialog and then create a new folder.
- Select a folder in either the *Favorites* list or the *Libraries* list on the left side of the dialog.
- Select a computer drive and folder in the *Computer* list on the left side of the dialog.
- Click the *Save as type* pick list at the bottom of the dialog, and choose an alternate file type to save, such as an Excel file.
- Click the *Tools* pick list button at the bottom of the dialog and select the *Map Network Drive* option to map a network drive and assign it a drive letter.

Information: After you save the project initially, you can click the *Save* button to save the latest changes to the project.

Saving a Project to an Office 365 SharePoint Folder

A new feature in Project 2013 allows you to save your project files in an Office 365 SharePoint location. To use this feature, however, you must already have an existing Office 365 SharePoint account. If you have an account, you can save your project in an Office 365 SharePoint folder by clicking the *Add a Place* option in the *Save and Sync* section of the *Save As* page. The software updates the *Save As* page with an *Add a Place* section, as shown in Figure 2 - 50.

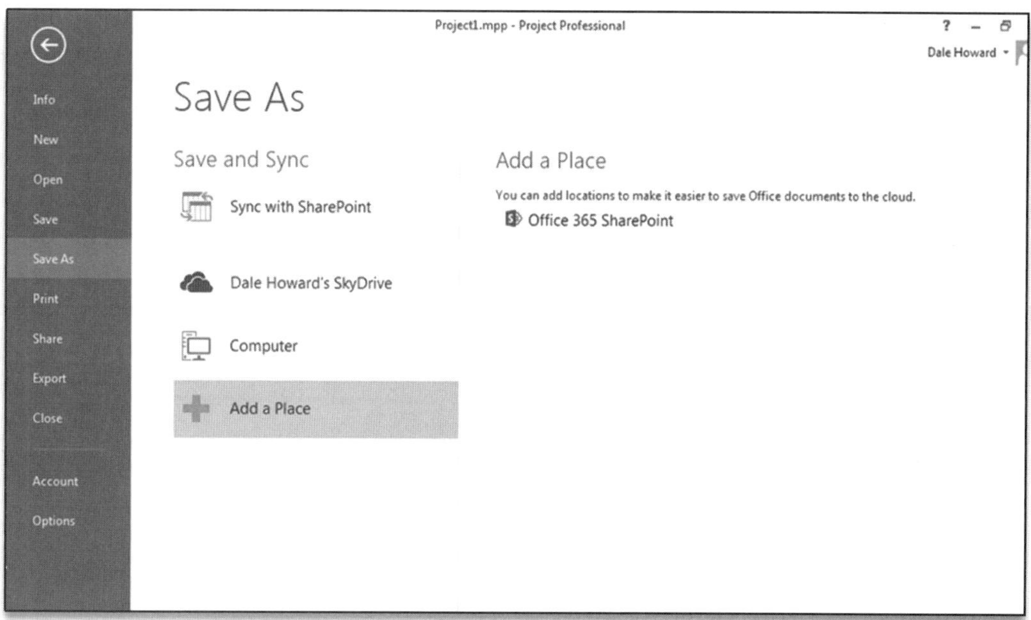

Figure 2 - 50: Save as Page shows the Add a Place section

If you click the *Office 365 SharePoint* link, Project 2013 displays the *Add a service* dialog shown previously in Figure 2 - 46. Enter your Office 365 SharePoint e-mail address in the *Add a service* dialog and then click the *Next* button. The software displays the *Sign in* dialog with your Office 365 SharePoint e-mail address entered in the *User ID* field, as shown in Figure 2 - 51. Enter your password in the *Password* field, leave the *Keep me signed in* option selected, and then click the *Sign in* button.

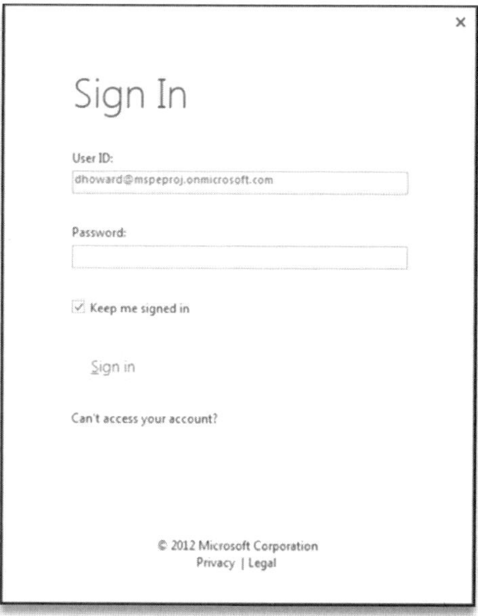

Figure 2 - 51: Sign in dialog

After you successfully log in to Office 365 SharePoint, the software refreshes the *Save As* page as shown in Figure 2 - 52. Notice that Project 2013 displays the name of the Office 365 SharePoint location at the top of the page and shows a new Team Site in the *Recent Folders* list.

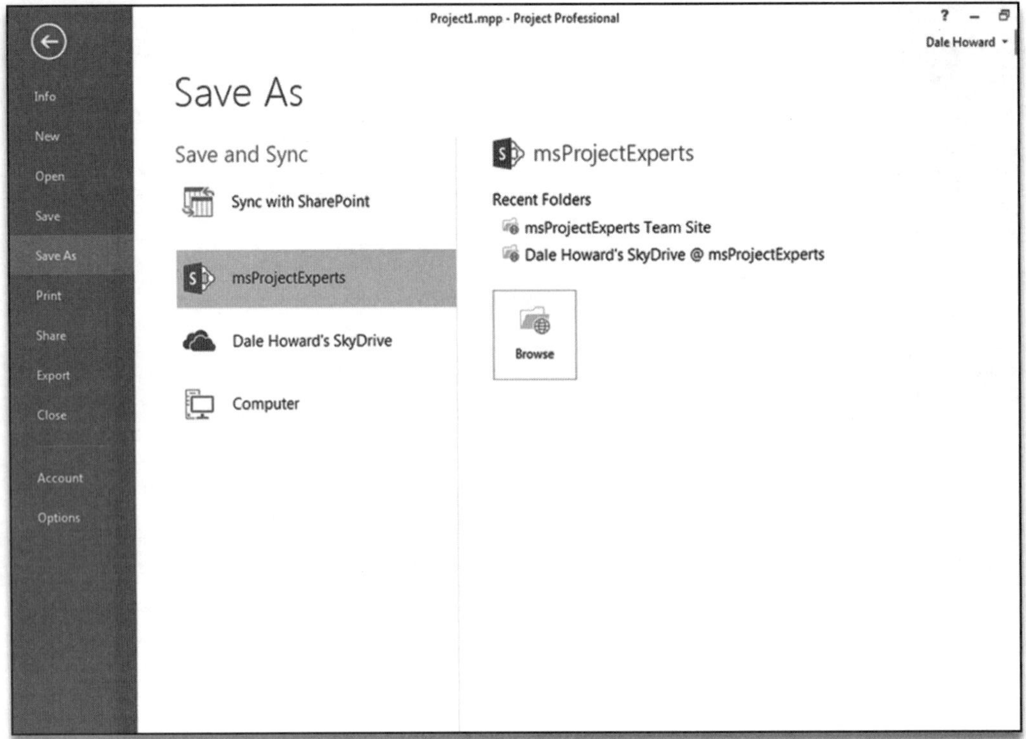

Figure 2 - 52: Save As page after logging into Office 365 SharePoint

To save the current project in the Office 365 SharePoint location, click the *Team Site* link in the *Recent Folders* section or click the *Browse* button. In the *Save As* dialog shown in Figure 2 - 53, double-click the *Documents* folder or navigate to the folder where you want to save your project, enter a name for your project, and then click the *Save* button.

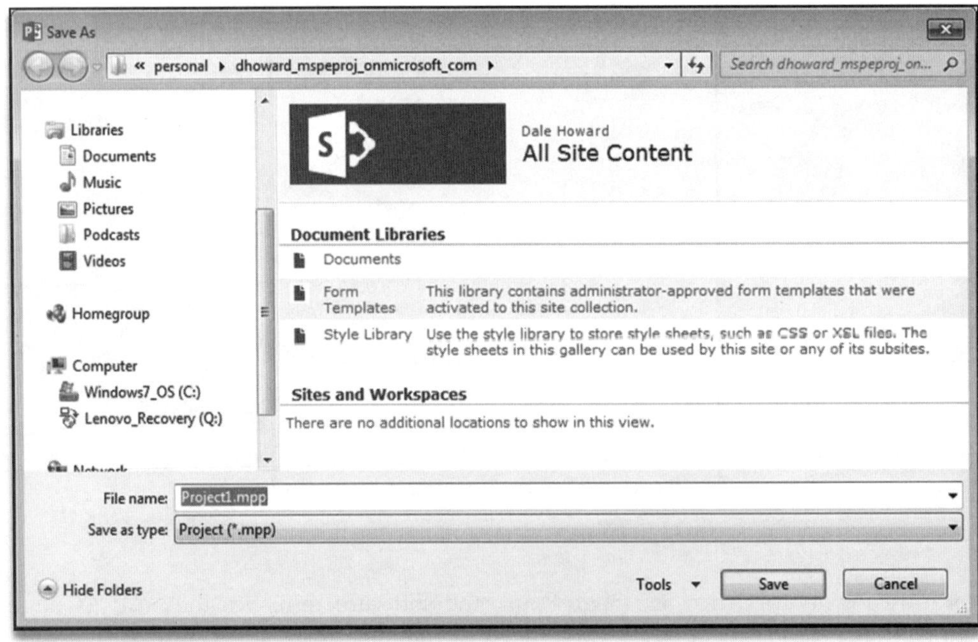

Figure 2 - 53 : Save As dialog shows Office 365 SharePoint folders

Hands On Exercise

Exercise 2 - 11

Save a project file to your computer.

1. With the **New Business Plan.mpp** project file still open, click the *File* tab and then click the *Save As* tab in the *Backstage.*
2. On the *Save As* page in the *Backstage,* click the *Computer* option and then click the *Browse* button.
3. In the *Save As* dialog, navigate to the folder where you unzipped the sample files that accompany this book.
4. In the *Save As* dialog, manually enter **Launch an Office Apps Development Startup** in the *File name* field and then click the *Save* button.
5. Click the *File* tab, click the *Save As* tab again, and then select the *Computer* option again, if necessary.

In the *Recent Folders* list on the right side of the *Save As* page, notice the name of the folder where you unzipped the sample files that accompany this book.

6. Press the **Escape** key on your computer keyboard to exit the *Save As* page in the *Backstage* and return to the main Project 2013 user interface.
7. Leave this project open for the next Hands On exercise.

Exercise 2 - 12

Save a project file to a cloud-based file storage location.

Warning: To complete this Hands On Exercise, you must have a valid user account for either Windows Live or Office 365 SharePoint. If you do not have a user account for either of these cloud-based storage systems, then you must skip this exercise. If you have a user account for Windows Live or Office 365 SharePoint, then complete the relevant steps in this exercise.

1. With the **Launch an Office Apps Development Startup.mpp** project file still open, click the *File* tab and then click the *Save As* tab in the *Backstage.*
2. On the *Save As* page in the *Backstage,* select the *SkyDrive* option and then click the *Sign In* button.
3. In the *Sign in to Office* dialog, click the *Sign In* button.
4. In the *Sign in* dialog, enter your Windows Live user ID and password, and then click the *Sign in* button.

Notice that Project 2013 refreshes the *Save As* page in the *Backstage* to show you information about your Windows Live SkyDrive location.

5. On the *Save As* page in the *Backstage*, click the *Browse* button.

6. In the *Save As* dialog, double-click the *Documents* folder in your Windows Live SkyDrive location.

7. In the *Save As* dialog, enter the name **Launch an Office Apps Development Startup - SkyDrive.mpp** in the *File name* field and then click the *Save* button.

8. Click the *File* tab and then click the *Save As* tab in the *Backstage*.

9. On the *Save As* page in the *Backstage*, select the *Add a Place* option.

10. In the *Add a Place* section on the right side of the *Save As* page, select the *Office 365 SharePoint* option.

11. In the *Sign in* dialog, enter your Office 365 SharePoint user ID and password, and then click the *Sign in* button.

Notice that Project 2013 refreshes the *Save As* page in the *Backstage* to show you information about your Office 365 SharePoint location.

12. On the *Save As* page in the *Backstage*, click the *Browse* button.

13. In the *Save As* dialog, double-click the *Documents* folder in your Office 365 SharePoint location.

14. In the *Save As* dialog, enter the name **Launch an Office Apps Development Startup – Office 365.mpp** in the *File name* field and then click the *Save* button.

15. Click the *File* tab and then click the *Close* button in the *Backstage*.

16. Press the **Escape** key on your computer keyboard to exit the *New* page in the *Backstage* and return to the main Project 2013 user interface.

Using the Open Page

To open an existing project, click the *Open* tab in the *Backstage*. If you previously signed into a Windows Live SkyDrive location or an Office 365 SharePoint location, Project 2013 displays an *Open* page similar to the one shown in Figure 2 - 54. Notice in my example that the software selects the *Recent Projects* option by default, but also shows links for my Office 365 SharePoint location (*msProjectExperts*) and my Windows Live SkyDrive location (*Dale Howard's SkyDrive*).

To open a recently used project, click the name of the project in the *Recent Projects* section of the *Open* page. To pin any recently opened project to the top of the *Recent Projects* list, float your mouse pointer over the file, and then click the *Pin this document to the Recent Projects list* button (pushpin button) at the right end of the file name. To unpin a pinned document, float your mouse pointer over the file, and then click the *Unpin this document from the Recent Projects list* button (pushpin button) at the right end of the file name.

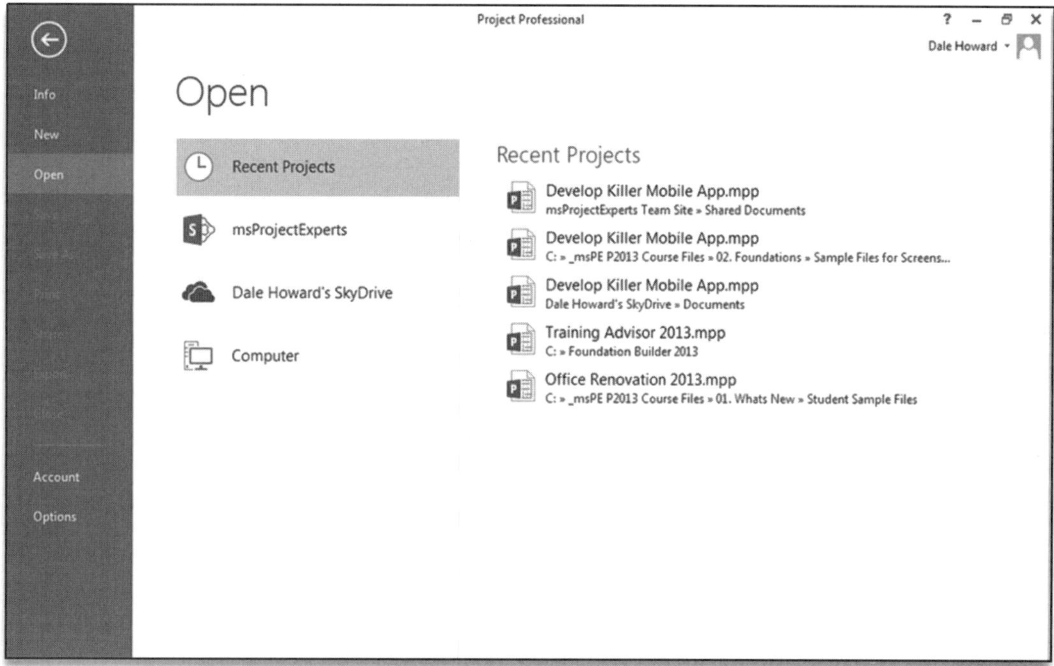

Figure 2 - 54: Open page in the Backstage, Recent Projects selected

To open a file from an Office 365 SharePoint folder, click the name of your Office 365 SharePoint location in the *Open* page. Project 2013 updates the *Open* page as shown in Figure 2 - 55. Notice that the *Recent Folders* section includes folders in the Office 365 SharePoint location for msProjectExperts. To open a file from the Office 365 SharePoint location, click the name of the recently used folder or click the *Browse* button, and then open the file using the *Open* dialog.

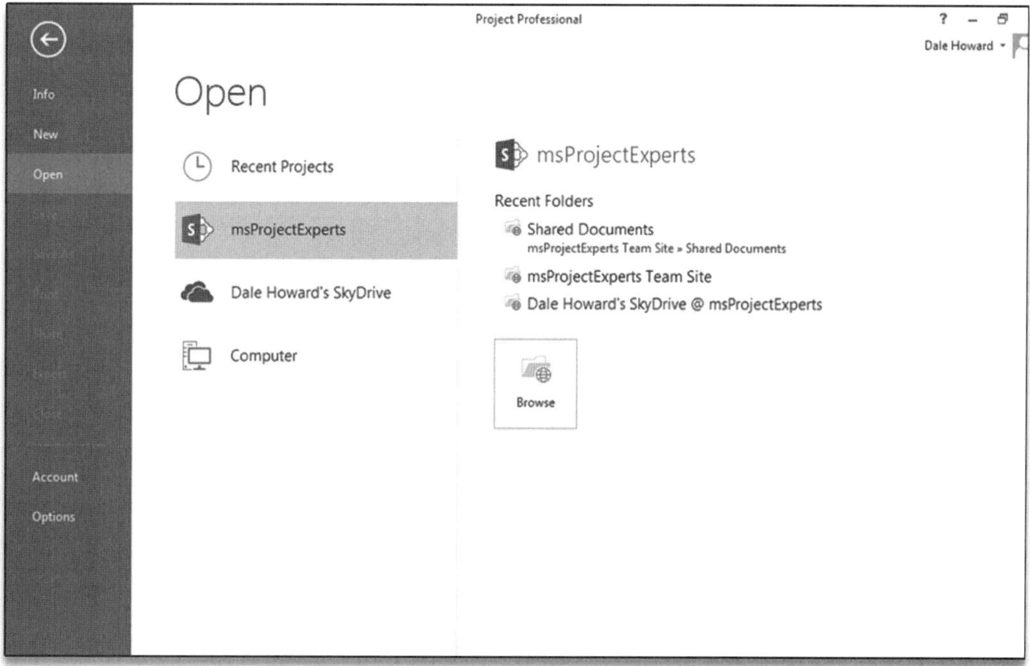

Figure 2 - 55: Open a project from an Office 365 SharePoint location

To open a file from a SkyDrive folder, click the *SkyDrive* option in the *Open* page. Project 2013 updates the *Open* page as shown in Figure 2 - 56. Notice that *Recent Folders* section shows one recently used SkyDrive folder. To open a file from a SkyDrive folder, click the name of the recently used folder or click the *Browse* button, and then open the file using the *Open* dialog.

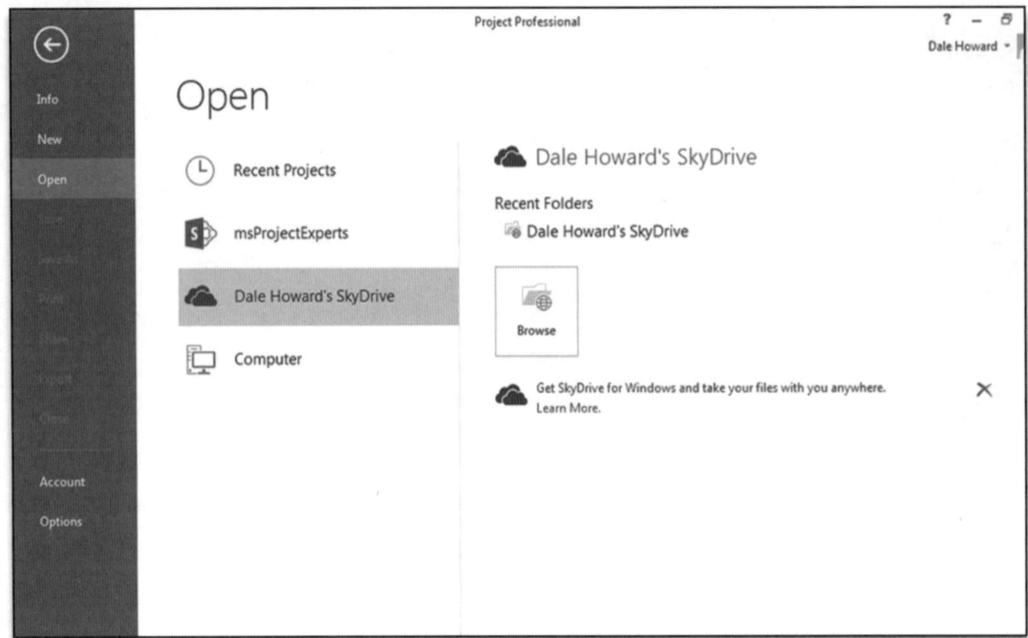

Figure 2 - 56: Open a file from a SkyDrive folder

To open a file from your computer, click the *Computer* option in the *Open* page. The software updates the *Open* page as shown in Figure 2 - 57. Notice that *Recent Folders* section shows a list of recently used folders on your computer. To open a file from your computer, click the name of the recently used folder or click the *Browse* button, and then open the file in the *Open* dialog.

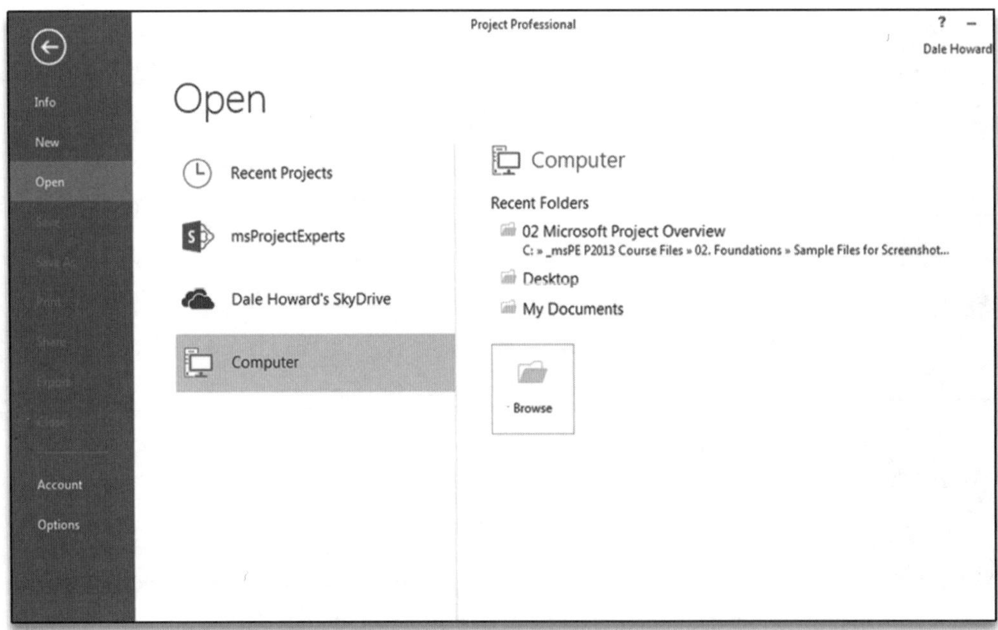

Figure 2 - 57: Open a file from your computer

When you click the *Browse* button in any section of the *Open* page, Project 2013 displays the *Open* dialog. Figure 2 - 58 shows the *Open* dialog, ready to open a project from an Office 365 SharePoint location.

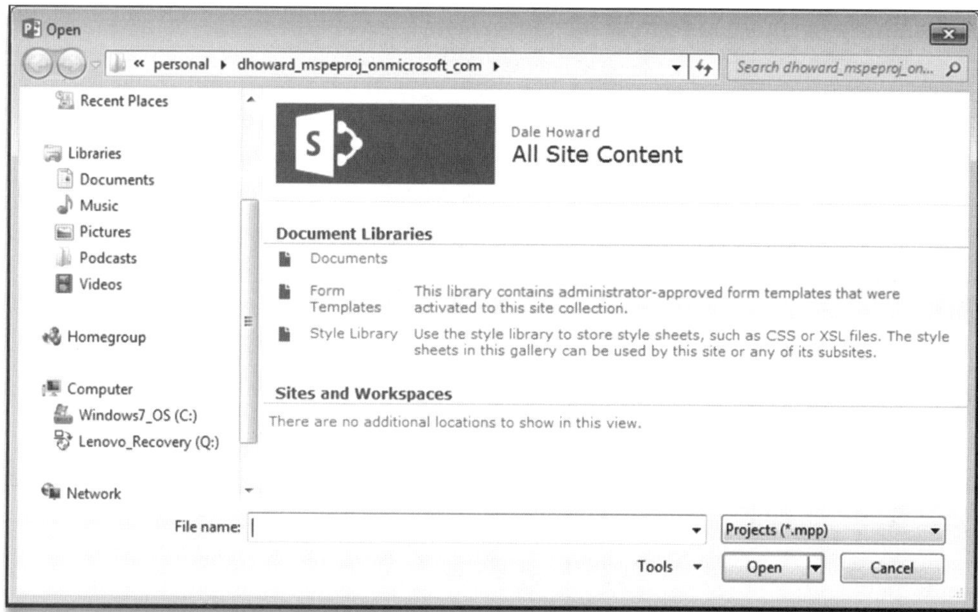

Figure 2 - 58: Open dialog

By the way, the *Open* dialog offers you a number of ways to locate and open an existing project, including the following:

- Click one of the folders shown in the "breadcrumb" bar at the top of the dialog.
- Click the *Previous Locations* pick list button at the right end of the "breadcrumb" bar.
- Enter a search term in the *Search* field in the upper right corner of the dialog.
- Select a link in the *Favorites* list or the *Libraries* list on the left side of the dialog.
- Select a computer drive in the *Computer* list on the left side of the dialog.
- Click the *Type* pick list in the lower right corner of the dialog, and choose an alternate file type to open, such as an Excel workbook file.
- Click the pick list button on the right edge of the *Open* button and select whether you want to open the selected file *Read/Write* or *Read-Only* mode, or to open a copy of the selected file.
- Click the *Tools* pick list button at the bottom of the dialog and select the *Map Network Drive* option to map a network drive and assign it a drive letter.

Using the Print Page

To print the active project, click the *Print* tab in the *Backstage*. The software displays the *Print* page shown in Figure 2 - 59. Using the *Print* page, you can control any of the following printing options:

- Specify the number of copies to print in the *Copies* field.
- Select an available printer in the *Printer* pick list.
- View the printer status in a tool tip by floating your mouse pointer over the *Printer Status* icon in the *Printer* section of the page.
- Set printer options by clicking the *Printer Properties* link.
- Specify the date range for printing project information by clicking the *Settings* pick list and choosing a pre-defined or custom date range.
- Manually enter a date range in the *Dates* fields.
- Specify the page range to print by selecting a value in the *Pages* fields.
- Specify the orientation of the printout on the *Print Orientation* pick list.
- Specify the paper size on the *Paper Size* pick list.
- Display the *Page Setup* dialog by clicking the *Page Setup* link.
- View the print preview of the project in the right side of the page.
- Zoom in to the print preview to see more details by clicking anywhere in the print preview.
- Navigate the pages in the print preview pane using the navigation buttons in the lower right corner of the page.
- Click the *Print* button to print the project file to the specified printer using your specified options.

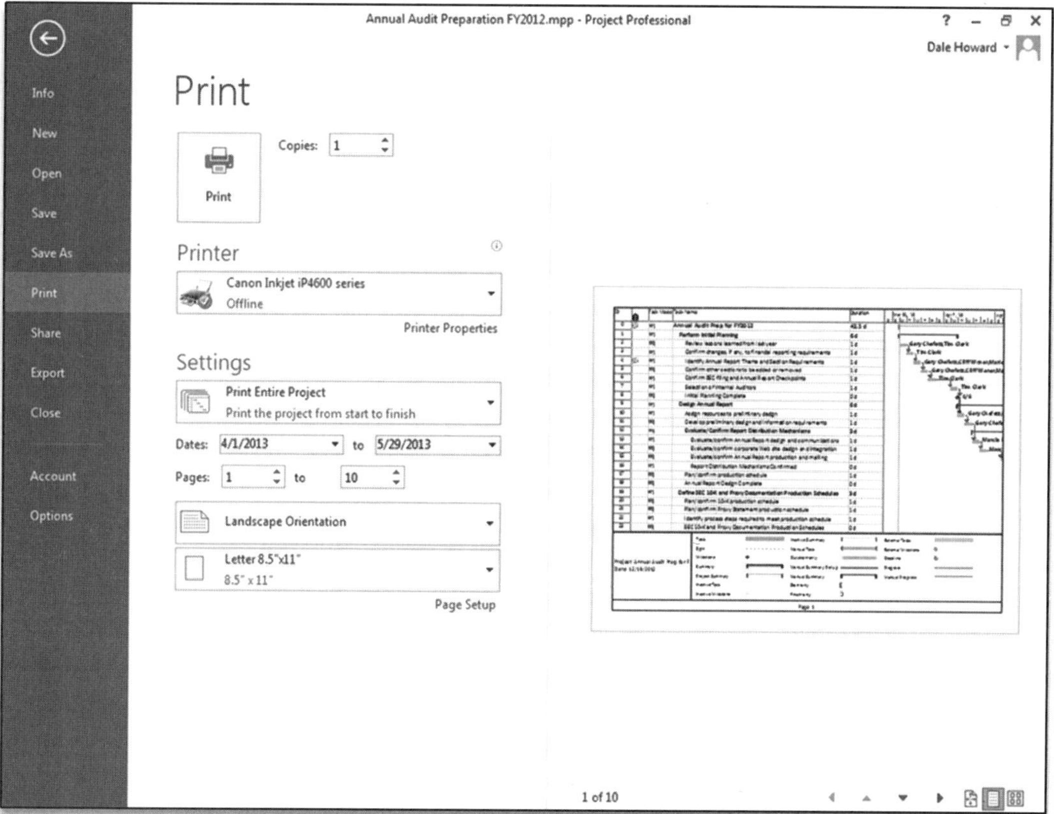

Figure 2 - 59: Print page in the Backstage

Hands On Exercise

Exercise 2 - 13

Pin a project file on the *Open* page of the *Backstage*, then open and print the project file.

1. Click the *File* tab and then click the *Open* tab in the *Backstage*, if necessary.

Notice that the *Recent Projects* section of the *Open* page contains the names of projects and templates you used recently.

2. In the *Recent Project* section of the *Open* page, float your mouse pointer over the **Project Navigation 2013.mpp** sample file and then click the "pushpin" symbol at the right end of the file name.

Notice that this action "pins" the selected project at the top of the *Recent Projects* list.

3. If you see a *SkyDrive* option on the *Open* page, click this option and study the information shown in the *SkyDrive* section of the *Open* page.

4. If you see an option for your organization's Office 365 SharePoint location on the *Open* page, click this option and study the information shown in this section of the *Open* page.

5. Click the *Computer* option.

6. In the *Recent Folders* section of the *Open* page, click the name of the folder where you unzipped the sample files that accompany this book.

7. In the *Open* dialog, select the **Project Navigation 2013.mpp** sample file, and then click the *Open* button.

8. Click the *File* tab and then click the *Print* tab in the *Backstage*.

9. Click successive times anywhere in the print preview on the right side of the *Print* page to zoom in and zoom out in the print preview pane.

10. In the *Settings* section of the *Print* page, click the *to* pick list, and select **April 30, 2014** on the pick list.

11. In the *Printer* section of the page, leave your default printer selected, and then click the *Print* button.

12. Press the **Escape** key on your computer keyboard to exit the *Print* page in the *Backstage* and return to the main Project 2013 user interface.

13. Save but **do not** close the **Project Navigation 2013.mpp** sample file.

Using the Share Page

Click the *Share* tab to access the new *Share* page in the *Backstage* shown in Figure 2 - 60. The *Share* page in Project 2013 replaces the *Save & Send* page found previously in the 2010 version of the software. The *Share* page offers only two options: the *Sync with SharePoint* and *Email* options.

Click the *Sync with SharePoint* option and then click the *Go to Save As* button in the *Sync with SharePoint Tasks List* section on the right side of the page. The software displays the *Save As* page in the *Backstage* and selects the *Sync with SharePoint* option, which you can synchronize your project file with a *Tasks* list in SharePoint.

Click the *Email* option and then click the *Send as Attachment* button in the *Email* section of the page. Project 2013 creates a new e-mail message in your default e-mail application, and then adds a copy of the active project as an attachment to the e-mail message.

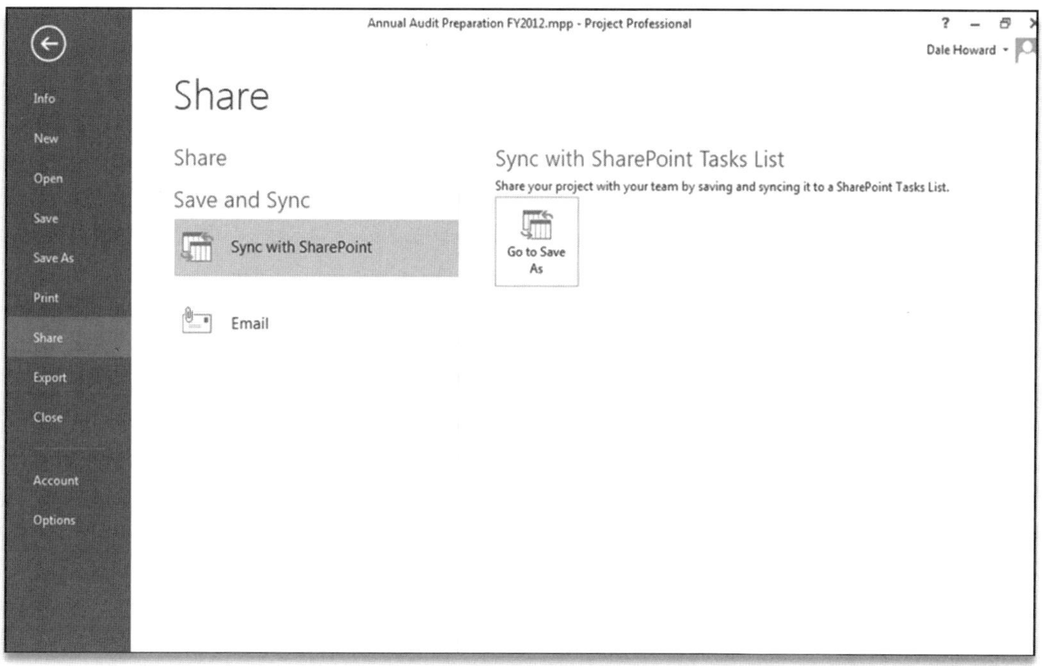

Figure 2 - 60: Share page in the Backstage

Using the Export Page

Click the *Export* tab to see the new *Export* page in the *Backstage* shown in Figure 2 - 61. Use the *Export* page to export a project file to a PDF file or XPS file, or to export the project file to another file format.

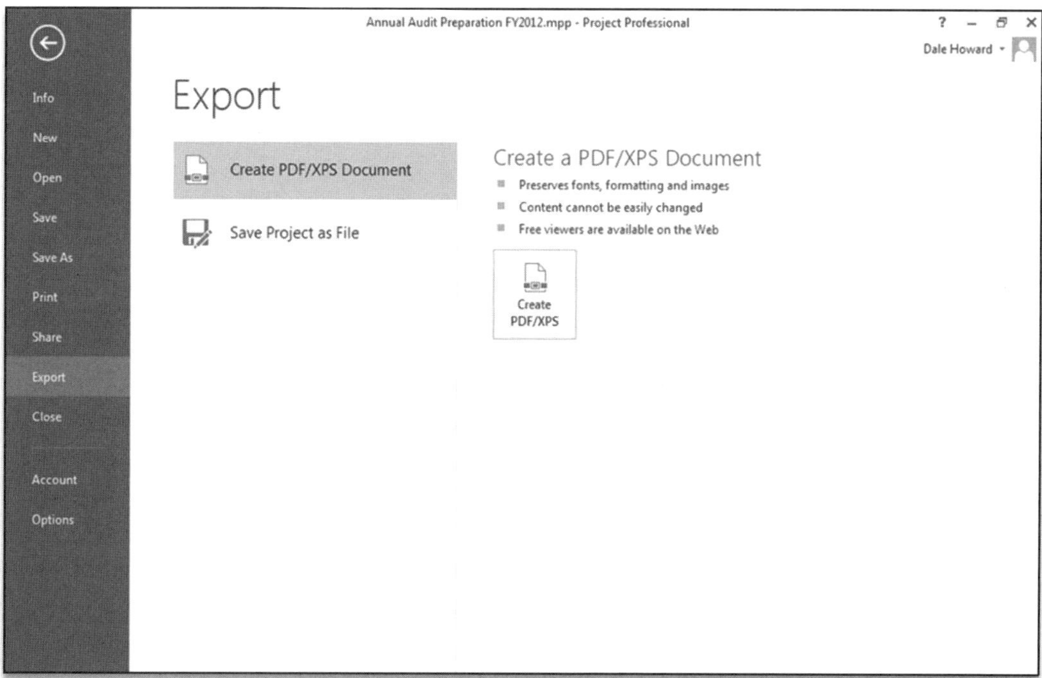

Figure 2 - 61: Export page in the Backstage

Exporting a Project File to a PDF or XPS Document

Best Practice: Before you export a project to either a PDF or XPS file, MsProjectExperts recommends as a best practice that you navigate to the *Print* page in the *Backstage* and set your print options. After setting your print options, study the print preview shown on the *Print* page to make sure the document will print correctly. If the project will print correctly, it will render correctly in a PDF or XPS file. This is because whenever you export a project to a PDF or XPS file, Project 2013 actually **prints** the project file to the selected file type.

To export a project file to a PDF file, click the *Create PDF/XPS Document* option in the *Export* page and then click the *Create PDF/XPS* button in the *Create a PDF/XPS Document* section of the page. Project 2013 displays the *Browse* dialog shown in Figure 2 - 62. Notice that the software selects the *PDF Files (*.pdf)* format by default on the *Save as type* pick list in the *Browse* dialog. In the *Browse* dialog, navigate to the folder where you want to export the project file. Optionally, you may also click the *Save as type* pick list and select the *XPS Files (*.xps)* format, if needed. Click the *OK* button to export the project file to a PDF or XPS document.

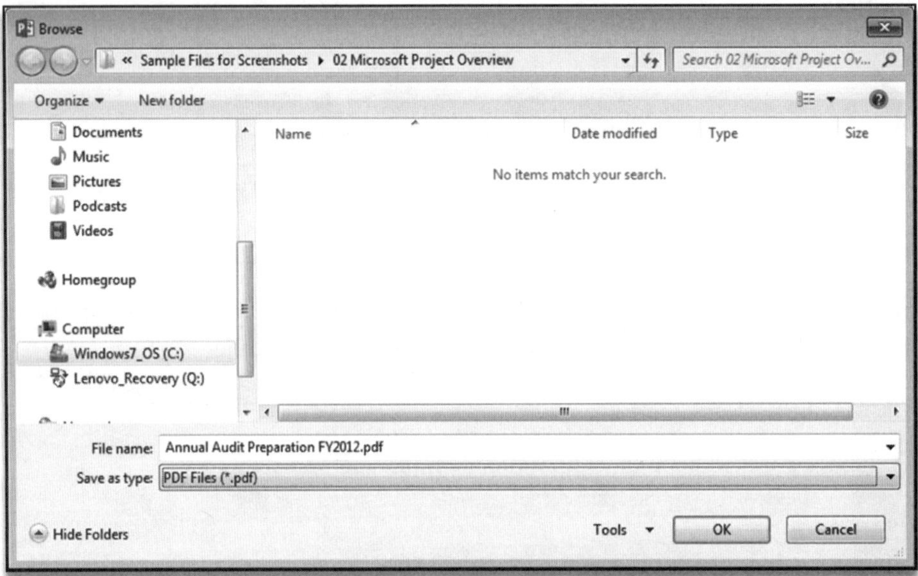

Figure 2 - 62: Browse dialog

Project 2013 displays the *Document Export Options* dialog shown in Figure 2 - 63. Select your desired options for exporting the project file to a PDF for XPS document and then click the *OK* button.

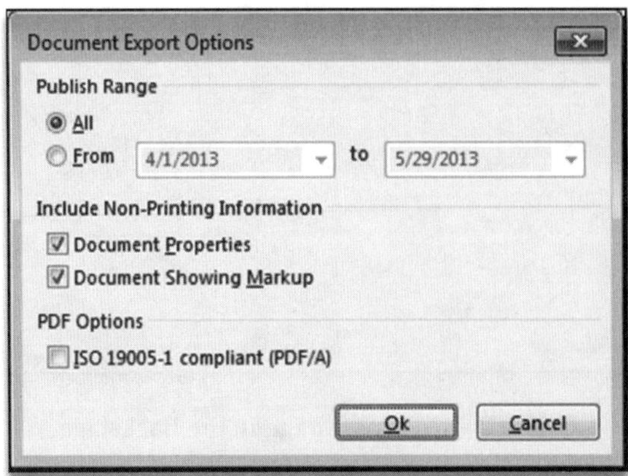

Figure 2 - 63: Document Export Options dialog

Exporting a Project File to an Alternate File Type

When you click the *Save Project as File* option in the *Export* page in the *Backstage,* Project 2013 updates the page as shown in Figure 2 - 64. Using the options in the *Save Project as File* section of the *Export* page, you can export your project file to the following file types:

- **Project** – This is the default Project 2013 file type, which is also compatible with Project 2010.
- **Project 2007 Project** – This file type provides backwards compatibility with Project 2007.
- **Project Template** – This file type allows you to save a project file as a Project 2013 project template, which is also compatible with Project 2010.
- **Project 2007 Template** – This file type allows you to save a project file as a Project 2007 project template.
- **Microsoft Excel Workbook** – This file type allows you to save a project file as an Excel 2013 workbook, which is also compatible with Excel 2007 and 2010.
- **XML Format** – Select this file type to save your project file as an Extensible Markup Language (XML) file.
- **Save as Another File type** – Select this option to save the project file using other available file types, such as a *Text* file.

By default, the software selects the *Project* file type initially. Select one of the six available file types in the *Save Project as File* section of the page, and then click the *Save As* button to save your file using the *Save As* dialog.

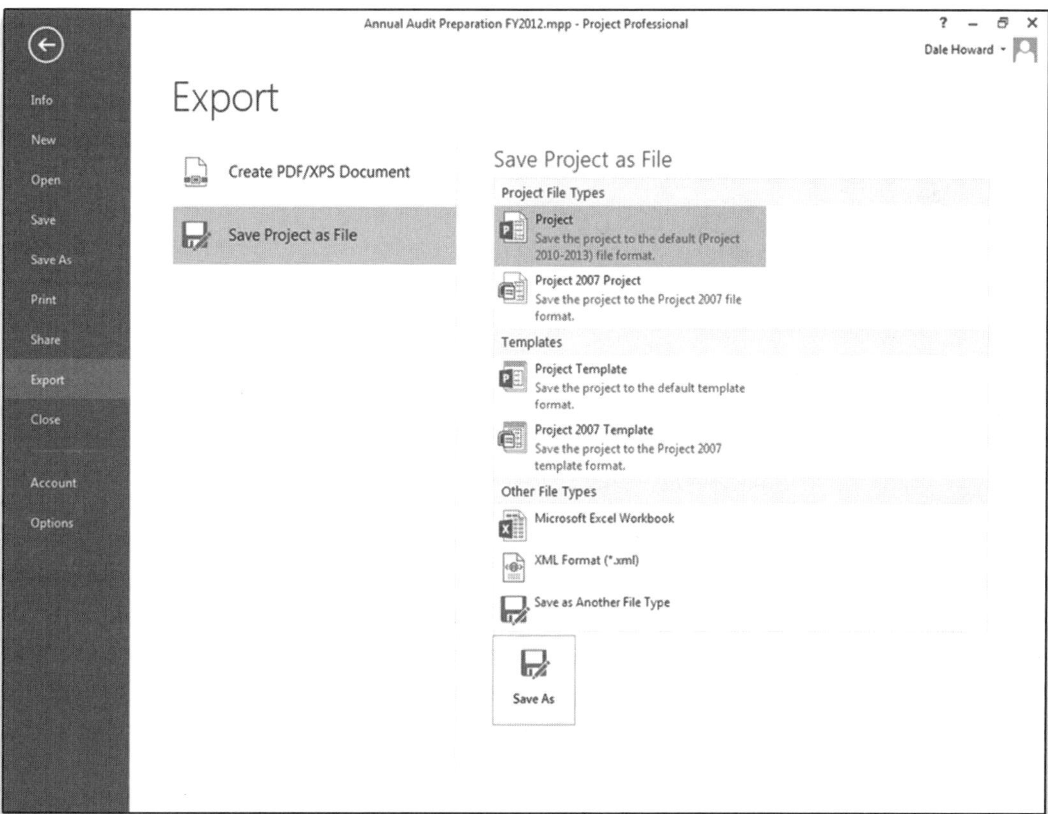

Figure 2 - 64: Export page, Save Project as File selected

In addition to the default list of file types, you can also select the *Save as Another File Type* option and then click the *Save As* button to display the *Save As* dialog. In this dialog, click the *Save as type* pick list where you can select one of the previous file types or one of these additional file types:

- **Project 2000-2003 Project** – This file type provides backwards compatibility with the 2000, 2002, and 2003 versions of Project.
- **PDF File** – Select this file type to save a project file as a Portable Document Format (PDF) file. Using the PDF file type allows you to share project information with users who do not have any version of Project installed on their workstations.
- **XPS File** – Select this file type to save a project file as an XML Paper Specification file. Using the XPS file type allows you to share project information with users who do not have any version of Project installed on their workstations.
- **Excel Binary Workbook** – Select this file type to save the project file as a Macro-Enabled Excel workbook file stored in Binary format rather than saving it in the XLSX format. Use this file format to save a very large Project file quickly and efficiently. This file type is compatible with Excel 2013, 2010, and 2007.
- **Excel 97-2003 Workbook** – Select this file type to save a project file as an Excel workbook using a format that allows Excel 97 through Excel 2003 to open the workbook directly without using a converter.
- **Text File** – Select this file type to save your project file as a *Tab Delimited* text file.
- **CSV File** – Select this file type to save your project file as a *Comma Delimited* text file.

Select one of the file types on the *Save as type* pick list and then click the *Save* button.

Information: You can also save a project file using an alternate file type by clicking the *File* tab and then clicking the *Save As* tab in the *Backstage*. On the *Save As* page, click the *Computer* option and then click the *Browse* button. In the *Save As* dialog, click the *Save as type* pick list, select an alternate file type, and then click the *Save* button.

Hands On Exercise

Exercise 2 - 14

Save a project file as a PDF document.

1. With the **Project Navigation 2013.mpp** file still open, click the *File* tab and then click the *Print* tab in the *Backstage*.
2. In the *Settings* section of the *Print* page, click the *to* pick list and select **August 21, 2014**.
3. Click the *Export* tab in the *Backstage*.

4. On the *Export* page of the *Backstage*, leave the *Create PDF/XPS Document* option selected, and then click the *Create PDF/XPS* button.
5. In the *Browse* dialog, navigate to the folder where you unzipped the sample files that accompany this book, and then click the *OK* button.
6. In the *Document Export Options* dialog, click the *Ok* button.
7. Launch your Windows Explorer application and navigate to the folder where you unzipped the sample files that accompany this book.
8. Double-click the **Project Navigation 2013.pdf** document.
9. In your Adobe Acrobat Reader application, scroll through and study the PDF document.
10. When finished, close your Adobe Acrobat Reader and Windows Explorer applications.
11. Save but do not close the **Project Navigation 2013.mpp** sample file.

Using the Account Page

Click the *Account* tab to display the *Account* page in the *Backstage*. If you did not log in to Windows Live SkyDrive account or an Office 365 SharePoint account on the *Save As* page, the *Account* page appears like the one shown in Figure 2 - 65. The *Account* page contains a *User Information* section on the left and a *Product Information* section on the right. Use the features in the *User Information* section to change the background pattern and theme colors used in Project 2013 or to connect your software to services such as Windows Live SkyDrive, Office 365 SharePoint, Flickr, YouTube, Facebook, LinkedIn, or Twitter. Use the features in the *Product Information* section to determine the activation status of your software or to learn more about your version of the software.

Information: If you previously logged in with a Windows Live SkyDrive account or with an Office 365 SharePoint account, you see the login status for these two items in the *Connected Services* list at the bottom of the *User Information* section of the *Account* page in the *Backstage*.

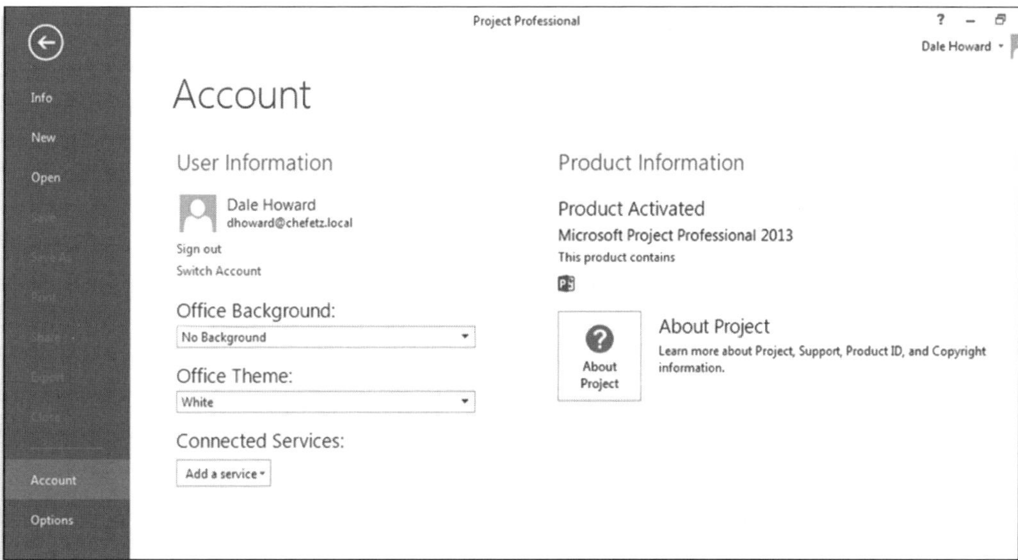

Figure 2 - 65: Account page in the Backstage without logging in to Windows Live or Office 365

Adding Connected Services to Project 2013

To log in to a Windows Live SkyDrive location, an Office 365 SharePoint location, or any other connected service, click the *Add a service* pick list button in the *Connected Services* section of the *Account* page. The software displays the *Add a service* pick list shown in Figure 2 - 66. Select the *Storage* item to log in to an Office 365 SharePoint location or a Windows Live SkyDrive location. Select the *Other Sites* item to log in using your *Windows Live Connect* information so that you can connect with services such as Flickr, LinkedIn, Facebook, Twitter, and YouTube. Select the *Office Store* item to log in to the Office Store website so that you can connect to Office Apps.

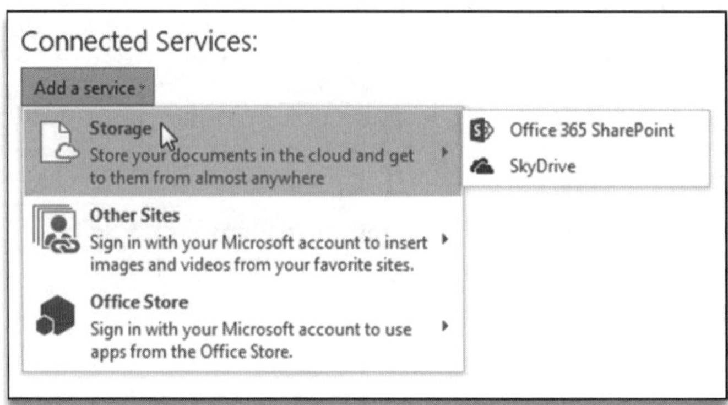

Figure 2 - 66: Add a service pick list

To log in to an Office 365 SharePoint location, click the *Add a service* pick list, select the *Storage* item, and then click the *Office 365 SharePoint* item on the flyout menu. Project 2013 displays the *Add a service* dialog shown previously in Figure 2 - 46. Remember that you must have an existing Office 365 account to use this feature. Enter your Office 365 SharePoint e-mail address in the *Add a service* dialog and then click the *Next* button. The software displays the *Sign in* dialog with your Office 365 SharePoint e-mail address entered in the *User ID* field, as shown previously in Figure 2 - 47. Enter your password in the *Password* field, leave the *Keep me signed in* option selected, and then click the *Sign in* button. The software displays the name of the Office 365 SharePoint site in the *Connected Services* list.

To log in to a Windows Live SkyDrive location, click the *Add a service* pick list, select the *Storage* item, and then click the *SkyDrive* item on the flyout menu. Project 2013 displays the *Add a service* dialog shown previously in Figure 2 - 46. Remember that you must already have an existing Windows Live ID to use this feature. Enter your Windows Live e-mail address in the *Add a service* dialog and then click the *Next* button. The software displays the *Sign in* dialog with your Windows Live e-mail address entered in the *Microsoft account* field, as shown previously in Figure 2 - 47. Enter your password in the *Password* field and then click the *Sign in* button. The software displays the name of the Windows Live SkyDrive location in the *Connected Services* list.

To log in to Windows Live Connect, click the *Add a service* pick list, select the *Other Sites* item, and then click the *Microsoft account* item on the flyout menu. Project 2013 displays the *Add a service* dialog shown previously in Figure 2 - 46. Keep in mind that you must have an existing Windows Live ID to use this feature. Enter your Windows Live e-mail address in the *Add a service* dialog and then click the *Next* button. The software displays the *Sign in* dialog with your Windows Live e-mail address entered in the *Microsoft account* field, as shown previously in Figure 2 - 47. Enter your password in the *Password* field and then click the *Sign in* button.

If you click the *Add a service* pick list shown in Figure 2 - 67, you see several new items on the pick list, including the *Images & Video* and *Sharing* items. The items on the *Images & Video* flyout menu connect you to Flickr or YouTube so that you can access your stored pictures and videos. The items on the *Sharing* flyout menu connect you to Facebook, LinkedIn, or Twitter so that you can share documents with other users. When you connect Project 2013 to any of these services, remember that you also connect every other Office 2013 application to these services. Using this connected functionality, you could embed a photo from Flickr in a presentation in PowerPoint 2013, for example.

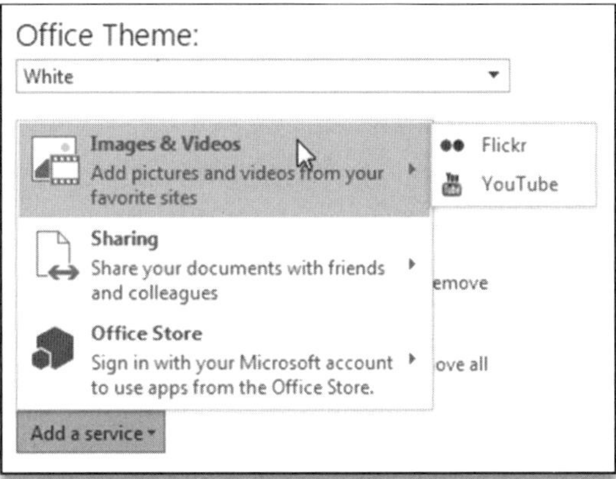

Figure 2 - 67: Add a service pick list shows two new services

To add the Flickr connected service, click the *Add a service* pick list, select the *Images & Videos* item, and then select the *Flickr* item on the flyout menu. The software displays the *All your photos in one place* dialog shown in Figure 2 - 68. To use this feature, you must have an existing Flickr account, or you can create a new Flickr account during the connection process. To connect Project 2013 and the rest of your Office 2013 software applications to Flickr, click the *Connect* button in the dialog.

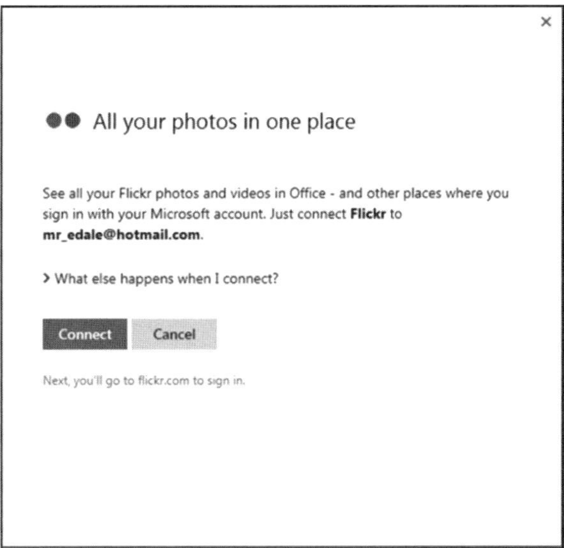

Figure 2 - 68: All your photos in one place dialog to add pictures and videos from Flickr

The software displays the *Yahoo!* dialog shown in Figure 2 - 69. If you do not already have a Yahoo user account, click the *Create New Account* button at the top of the dialog and create a new user account. Otherwise, enter your Yahoo user account and password in the dialog and click the *Sign In* button.

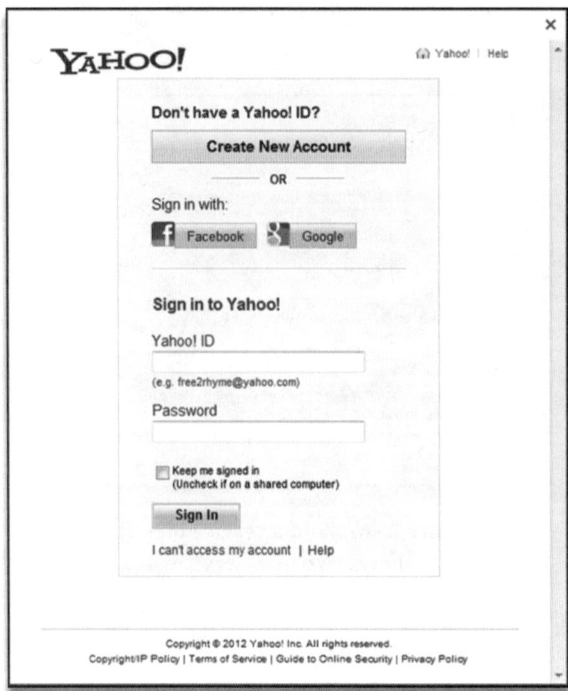

Figure 2 - 69: Sign in to Yahoo dialog

When the software completes the sign in process, you see the *Flickr* dialog shown in Figure 2 - 70. To change your Flickr connection settings, click the *connection settings* hyperlink in the dialog. Otherwise, click the *Done* button to close the dialog.

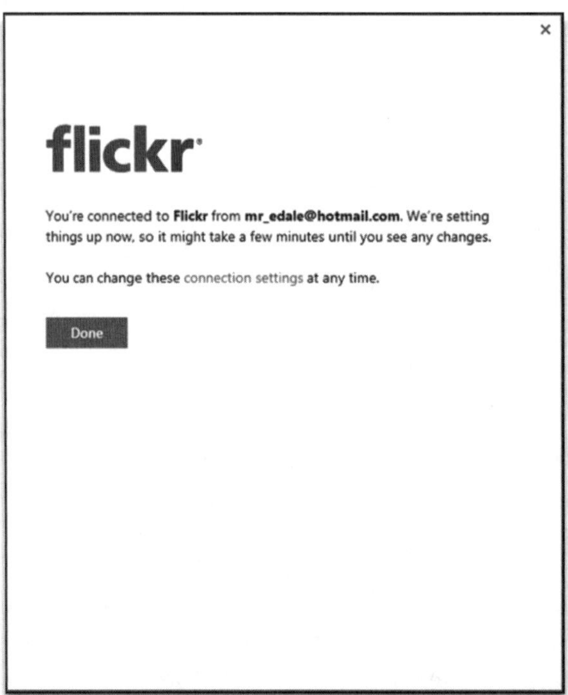

Figure 2 - 70: Flickr dialog

To add the YouTube connected service, click the *Add a service* pick list, select the *Images & Videos* item, and then click the *YouTube* item on the flyout menu. The software adds the YouTube service immediately and does not prompt you to log in to YouTube.

To add the Facebook connected service, click the *Add a service* pick list, select the *Sharing* item, and then click the *Facebook* item on the flyout menu. The software displays the *Share to Facebook* dialog shown in Figure 2 - 71. To use this feature, you must have an existing Facebook account, or you can create a new Facebook account during the connection process. To connect Project 2013 and the rest of your Office 2013 software applications to Facebook, click the *Connect* button and then log in to Facebook in the *Facebook* login dialog.

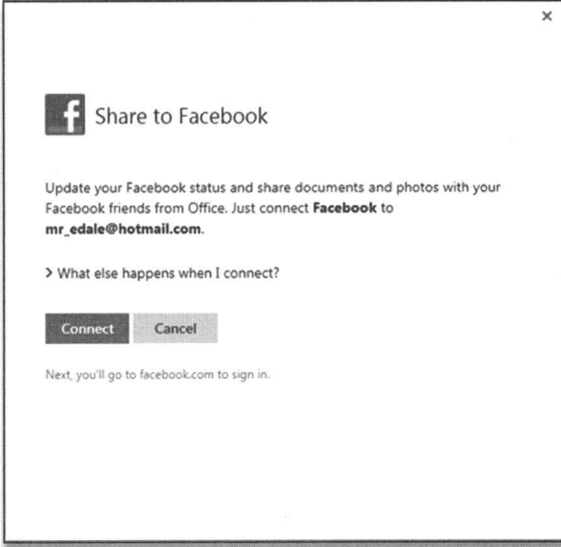

Figure 2 - 71: Share to Facebook dialog

To add the LinkedIn connected service, click the *Add a service* pick list, select the *Sharing* item, and then select the *LinkedIn* item on the flyout menu. The software displays the *Share to LinkedIn* dialog shown in Figure 2 - 72. To use this feature, you must have an existing LinkedIn account. To connect Project 2013 and the rest of your Office 2013 software applications to LinkedIn, click the *Connect* button and then sign in to LinkedIn in the *LinkedIn* dialog.

Figure 2 - 72: Share to LinkedIn dialog

To add the Twitter service, click the *Add a service* pick list, select the *Sharing* item, and then click the *Twitter* item on the flyout menu. The software displays the *Share on Twitter* dialog shown in Figure 2 - 73. To use this feature, you must have an existing Twitter account. To connect Project 2013 and the rest of your Office 2013 software applications to Twitter, click the *Connect* button and then sign in to Twitter in the next dialog.

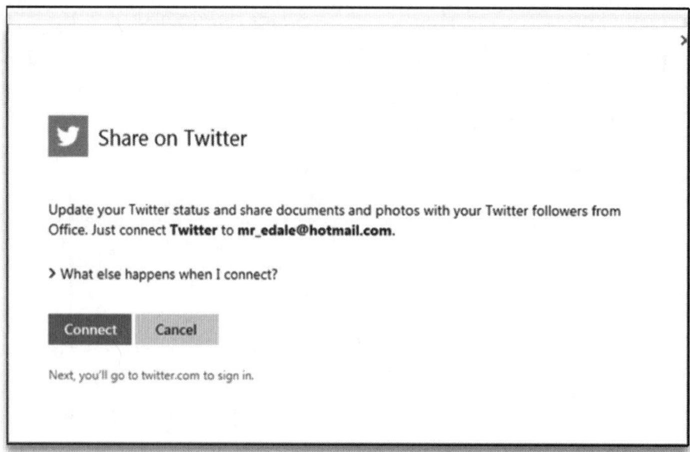

Figure 2 - 73: Share on Twitter dialog

To add the Office Store service, click the *Add a service* pick list, select the *Office Store* item, and then click the *Office Store* item on the flyout menu. The software displays the *Add a service* dialog shown previously in Figure 2 - 46. To connect Project 2013 and the rest of your Office 2013 software applications to the Office Store, you must have an existing Microsoft account. Enter your Windows Live e-mail address in the *Add a service* dialog and then click the *Next* button. The software displays the *Sign in* dialog with your Windows Live e-mail address entered in the *Microsoft account* field, as shown previously in Figure 2 - 47. Enter your Windows Live ID and password in the dialog and then click the *Sign in* button. The software displays the Office Store in the *Connected Services* list.

Figure 2 - 74 shows the *Account* page in the *Backstage* after adding several new services. Notice that the *Connected Services* list displays the Windows Live SkyDrive, Office 365 SharePoint, Office Store, Flickr, LinkedIn, and YouTube connected services.

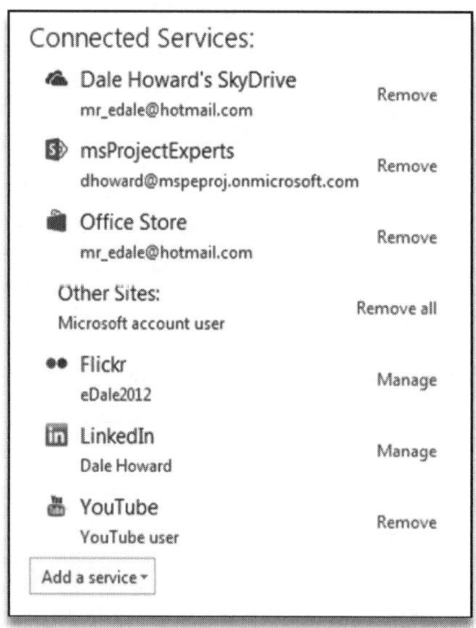

Figure 2 - 74: New services added to the Connected Services list

Changing the Office Background and Theme

To change the background pattern used in all of your Office 2013 applications, click the *Office Background* pick list shown in Figure 2 - 75. The software selects the *No Background* option by default, but offers you 14 background patterns from which to choose. To see a preview of each background pattern, float your mouse pointer over the name of a pattern in the *Background Pattern* pick list and then look at the pattern preview in the upper right corner of the *Account* page in the *Backstage*. When you select a background pattern on the *Office Background* pick list, the software applies a light gray pattern in the upper right corner of every application in the Office 2013 family of software tools.

To change the color theme used in all of your Office 2013 applications, click the *Office Theme* pick list. The software offers you three color themes from which to choose: *White* (the default), *Light Gray*, and *Dark Gray*. The color theme you select controls the colors of all items in the user interface of your Office 2013 applications, such as color of the buttons in the ribbon, the colors used in the *Backstage*, and the color of the background pattern.

Information: You can also specify the background pattern and the color theme you want to see in Office 2013 by clicking the *Options* button in the *Backstage* to navigate to the *General* page of the *Project Options* dialog. To specify the background pattern or color theme, select the *Always use these values regardless of sign in to Office* checkbox, select a background pattern in the *Office Background* pick list, and select a color theme in the *Office Theme* pick list. Click the *OK* button when finished.

Figure 2 - 75: Office Background pick list

Viewing Information about Your Project 2013 Software

The *Product Information* section of the *Account* page shows you the activation status of your copy of Project 2013. Notice in Figure 2 - 65, shown previously, that I properly activated my copy of the software. You can also click the *About Project* button to display the *About Microsoft Project* dialog shown in Figure 2 - 76. Using this dialog, you can determine the current version and ID number of your Project 2013 software, view the software license, gather troubleshooting information about your computer system, and learn how to contact Microsoft Support. Click the *OK* button to close the dialog when finished.

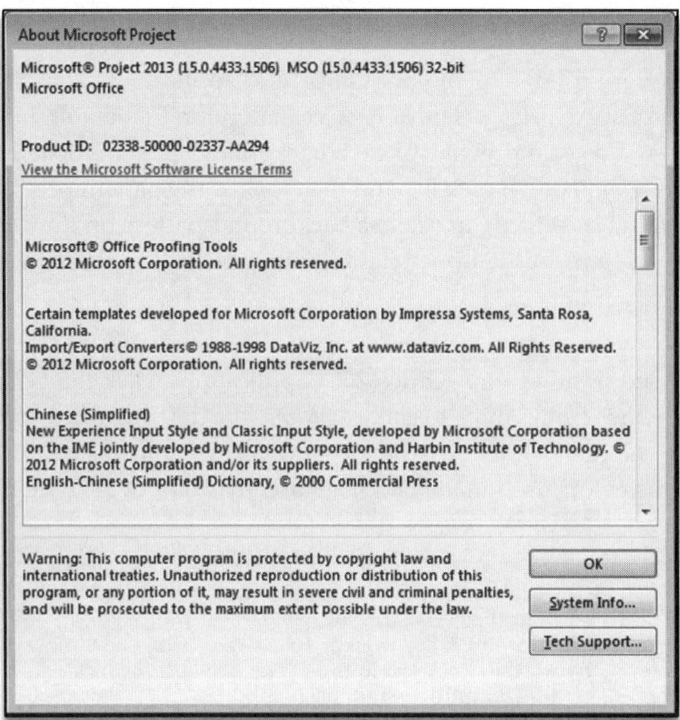

Figure 2 - 76: About Microsoft Project dialog

Hands On Exercise

Exercise 2 - 15

Connect your Project 2013 to other online services on the *Account* page in the *Backstage*.

Warning: To complete this Hands On Exercise, you must have a valid user account with Windows Live, and you must have a valid user account with at least one of the following online services: Flickr, YouTube, Facebook, LinkedIn, or Twitter. If you do not meet these requirements, you should skip this exercise. If you meet these requirements, then complete the relevant steps in this exercise.

1. Click the *File* tab and then click the *Account* tab in the *Backstage*.

In the *Connected Services* section of the *Account* page, notice your connections to Windows Live SkyDrive or Office 365 SharePoint, completed previously in Exercise 2 - 12.

2. In the *Connected Services* section of the *Account* page, click the *Add a service* pick list button, select the *Other Sites* item on the pick list, and then select the *Microsoft account* item on the flyout menu.

3. Enter your Windows Live e-mail address in the *Add a service* dialog and then click the *Next* button.
4. In the *Sign in* dialog, enter your password, and then click the *Sign in* button.
5. Click the *Add a service* pick list button again, select either the *Images & Videos* or the *Sharing* item on the pick list, and then select one of online services on the flyout menu, such as *Flickr, YouTube, Facebook, LinkedIn,* or *Twitter.*
6. In the *Share* dialog, click the *Connect* button.
7. If you see an additional dialog asking you to authorize Microsoft to use your account, complete all of the required steps in the dialog.
8. Press the **Escape** key on your computer keyboard to exit the *Account* page in the *Backstage* and return to the main Project 2013 user interface

Exercise 2 - 16

Explore other features on the *Account* page in the *Backstage.*

1. Click the *File* tab and then click the *Account* tab in the *Backstage,* if necessary.
2. Click the *Office Background* pick list and then click the *Circuit* item.

In the upper right corner of the *Backstage,* notice the background pattern applied to all of the applications in your Office 2013 suites of tools.

3. If you do not like the background pattern currently applied, click the *Office Background* pick list again and select a different background pattern, or select the *No Background* item instead.
4. Click the *Office Theme* pick list and then select the *Dark Gray* item.

Notice how the software applies theme color to the sidepane on the left side of the *Backstage* and to the background pattern in the upper right corner of the *Backstage.*

5. Click the *Office Theme* pick list again and then click the default *White* item.
6. In the *Product Information* section of the *Account* page, click the *About Project* button.
7. Examine the information shown in the *About Microsoft Project* dialog, and then click the *OK* button when finished.
8. Press the **Escape** key on your computer keyboard to exit the *Account* page in the *Backstage* and return to the main Project 2013 user interface.

Using the Options Button

To specify options settings in Project 2013, click the *Options* button in the *Backstage.* The software exits the *Backstage* and then displays the *Project Options* dialog shown in Figure 2 - 77. In the *Project Options* dialog, you can specify settings for the active project, for all future projects, as well as for the Project 2013 desktop application.

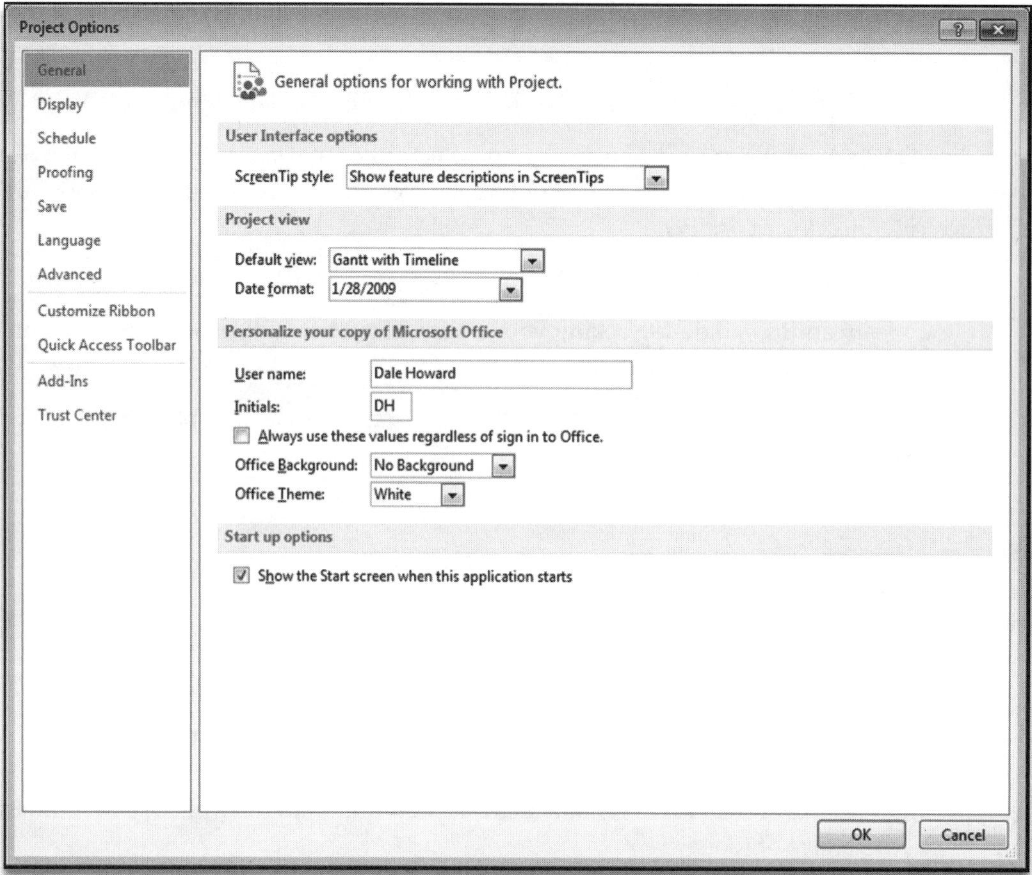

Figure 2 - 77: Project Options dialog

Notice that the *Project Options* dialog offers eleven sections in which to specify options settings. These sections include:

- The *General* section contains general settings for the Project 2013 application.

- The *Display* section contains settings that control how Project 2013 displays application content.

- The *Schedule* section contains settings that control scheduling, calendars, and calculations for the active project and for all future projects.

- The *Proofing* section contains settings that determine how the software proofs and corrects text in your project files.

- The *Save* section contains settings that control how and where the software saves your project files.

- The *Language* section contains settings that specify the language used by the software.

- The *Advanced* section contains advanced settings for the active project, for all future projects, and for the software. For example, the *Tasks are critical if slack is less than or equal to ____ days* option determines how Project 2013 determines the *Critical Path* in the active project.

- The *Customize Ribbon* section allows you to customize the ribbon by adding tabs, sections, and buttons.

- The *Quick Access Toolbar* section allows you to customize the *Quick Access Toolbar* by adding or removing buttons.

- The *Add-Ins* section allows you to view and manage Office Add-Ins for Project 2013.

- The *Trust Center* gives access to the settings that determine your level of security for VBA macros, trusted publishers, add-ins, Office Apps catalogs, legacy file formats, and privacy options.

I present an in-depth discussion of many of these *Backstage* features in succeeding modules in this book. To exit the *Backstage* without taking any other actions, click the *Back* button (large left-arrow button) in the upper left corner of the *Backstage* or press the **Escape** key on your computer keyboard.

Closing a Project File

To close the active project file, click the *Close* button in the *Backstage*. The software exits the *Backstage* and returns you to your Project 2013 application window.

Navigating in Project 2013

Project 2013 offers several features that help you to navigate in the active project. These options include using the scroll bars, using shortcut menus, using keyboard shortcuts, zooming the *Timescale*, using the *Scroll to Task* button, and using screen tips and tool tips. I discuss each of these navigation features individually.

Navigating to the Beginning of the Project

At the end of each workday, you may want to scroll back to the beginning of your project while in the *Gantt Chart* view before you save and close your project file. The fastest way to accomplish this is to use two keyboard shortcuts in a row. Press **Control + Home** to move the cursor to the first task in the task list, and then press **Alt + Home** to scroll the Gantt chart to the beginning of the first task's Gantt bar.

Using the Scroll Bars

Drag the vertical scroll box up and down in the scroll track to scroll to exact task ID numbers and task names. Drag the horizontal scroll box left and right in the scroll track to scroll to precise dates in any task view.

Using Shortcut Menus

When you right-click any object in the Project 2013 application window, the software displays a shortcut menu with *Mini Toolbar*. For example, Figure 2 - 78 shows the shortcut menu with the *Mini Toolbar* when I right-click a task.

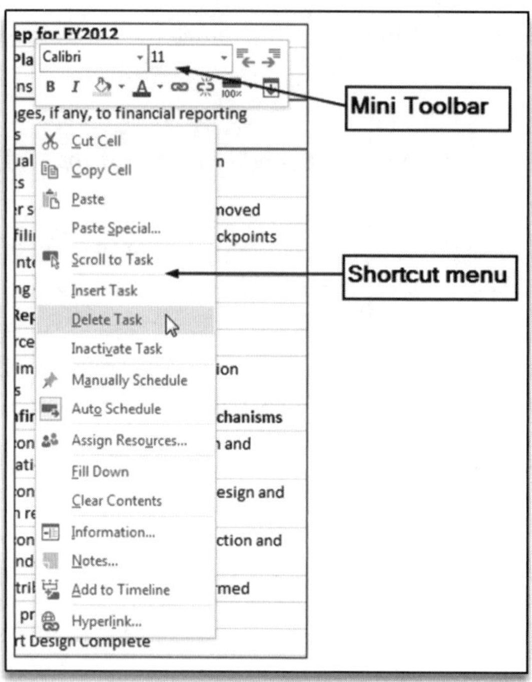

Figure 2 - 78: Mini Toolbar and shortcut menu for tasks

The shortcut menu offers shortcut options relevant to the type of object that you click. If you right-click task information, such as in the *Gantt Chart* view, you see a shortcut menu with task-related options that allow you to perform functions like adding a new task, deleting an existing task, or setting a task to *Manually Scheduled*. If you right-click resource information, such as in the *Resource Sheet* view, you see resource-related functions, such as adding a new resource or deleting an existing resource. Shortcut menus also have some options in common, such as being able to perform a cut, copy, paste, or paste special operation using the shortcut menu. If you right-click assignment information, such as in the *Task Usage* or *Resource Usage* view, the shortcut menu includes additional functions, such as inserting or deleting an assignment.

The *Mini Toolbar* offers you quick options for working the kind of data selected. If you right-click task information, such as in the *Gantt Chart* view, the *Mini Toolbar* offers you options such as formatting the font or linking tasks. If you right-click resource information, such as in the *Resource Sheet* view, the *Mini Toolbar* offers you options such as formatting the font and using the *Fill Down* feature.

If you right-click any graphical object in the *Gantt Chart* view, such as a Gantt bar, the software displays the shortcut menu and *Mini Toolbar* shown in Figure 2 - 79.

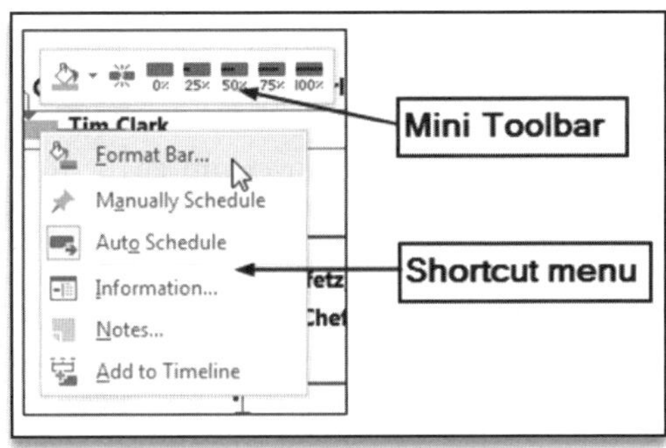

Figure 2 - 79: Mini Toolbar and shortcut menu for a Gantt bar

Using Built-In Keyboard Shortcuts

For users who prefer using the keyboard instead of the mouse, Project 2013 offers two types of keyboard shortcuts. The first type includes the same set of keyboard shortcuts found in previous versions of the software. You can continue to use keyboard shortcuts such as **Ctrl + S** to save a file and **Ctrl + C** to copy information to the Windows Clipboard. The second type includes keyboard shortcuts called *KeyTips* for use with the tabs on the ribbon and for the buttons on each ribbon and on the *Quick Access Toolbar*. To activate these keyboard shortcuts, press the **Alt** key on your computer keyboard. The software displays the *KeyTips* for each tab on the ribbon and for each button on the *Quick Access Toolbar*, as shown in Figure 2 - 80.

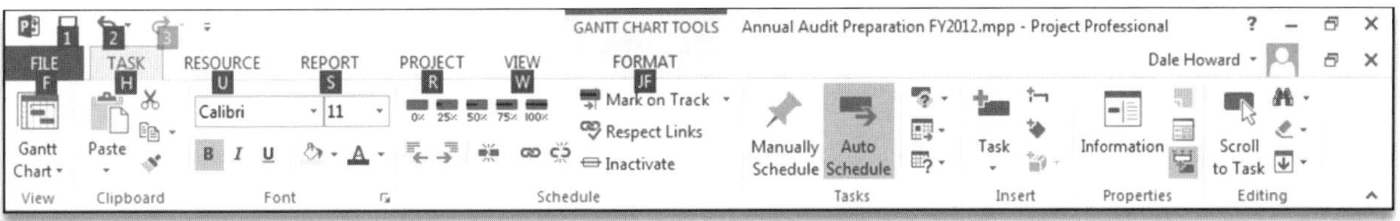

Figure 2 - 80: Ribbon with KeyTips for tabs

Notice in Figure 2 - 80 that **F** is the *KeyTip* for the *File* tab, **U** is the *KeyTip* for the *Resource* tab, and **2** is the *KeyTip* for the *Undo* button on the *Quick Access Toolbar*. With *KeyTips* activated, press the keyboard shortcut key for the *KeyTip* you want to use to select a ribbon tab or a button on the *Quick Access Toolbar*. When you press the shortcut key for a ribbon tab, the software displays the selected ribbon with the *KeyTips* activated for the buttons. For example, in Figure 2 - 81, I pressed the **R** key to display the *KeyTips* for the *Project* ribbon. To activate the *Project Information* button, I must press the **I** key on my computer keyboard.

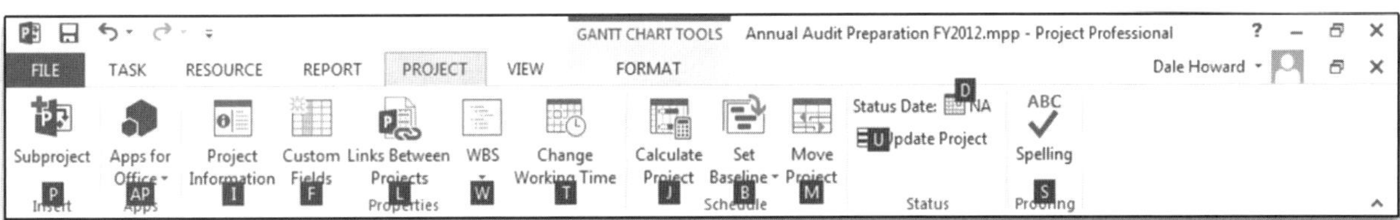

Figure 2 - 81: Project ribbon with KeyTips for buttons

Zooming the Timescale

Project 2013 shows the current level of zoom on the *Timescale* at the top each view that includes a *Gantt Chart* pane, such as the *Gantt Chart* view or the *Tracking Gantt* view, and at the top of views that contain a timephased grid, including the *Task Usage* and *Resource Usage* views. You describe the current level of zoom applied to your project by stating the time units displayed on the top half of the *Timescale*, adding the word "over" in the middle of your description, and then stating by the time units displayed on the bottom half of the *Timescale*. For example, the default level of zoom applied to the *Gantt Chart* view in every new project is *Weeks over Days*. Other commonly-used levels of zoom include *Months over Weeks* and *Quarters over Months*. A slightly unusual level of zoom is *Months over 3-Day Periods*, which approximates a *Months over Half Weeks* level of zoom.

The software offers you multiple ways to zoom the *Timescale* to display more or less detail in any view that includes a *Timescale*, such as the *Gantt Chart* view or the *Resource Usage* view. You find the zoom options in the *Zoom* section of the *View* ribbon and in the *Zoom Slider* in the lower right corner of the application window. Use the following features in the *Zoom* section of the *View* ribbon to zoom the *Timescale* in your project:

- Click the *Timescale* pick list and select a pre-formatted level of zoom, such as *Weeks*.
- Click the *Zoom* pick list and select either the *Zoom In* or *Zoom Out* item on the pick list. The software zooms to the next pre-formatted level of zoom. For example, if you have the *Weeks* level of zoom applied and then you click the *Zoom Out* item, Project 2013 applies the *Months* level of zoom.
- Click the *Zoom* pick list and select the *Zoom...* item on the pick list. In the *Zoom* dialog shown in Figure 2 - 82, select any default or custom zoom level and then click the *OK* button.
- Click the *Zoom Entire Project* button to apply a custom zoom level that displays every task's Gantt bar in the current width of the Gantt chart in any *Gantt Chart* view, or to display all *Work* and *Cost* values in the current width of the timephased grid in the *Task Usage* or *Resource Usage* view.
- Select two or more tasks and then click the *Zoom Selected Tasks* button to apply a custom zoom level that displays the selected task's Gantt bars in the current width of the Gantt chart in any *Gantt Chart* view, or to display all *Work* and *Cost* values for the selected tasks in the current width of the timephased grid in the *Task Usage* or *Resource Usage* view.

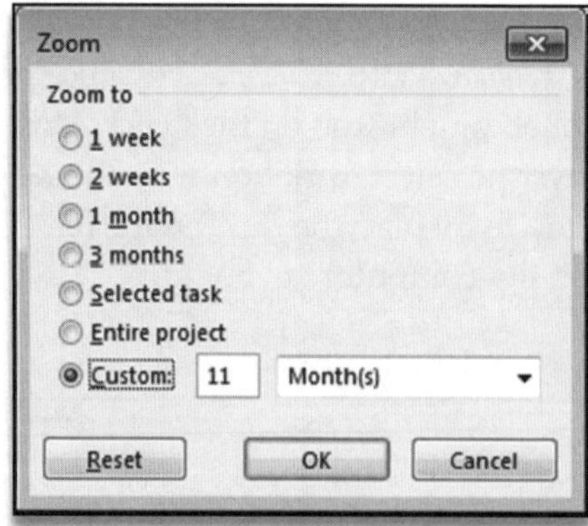

Figure 2 - 82: Zoom dialog

You can also click the *Zoom Out* and *Zoom In* buttons at either end of the *Zoom Slider* in the lower right corner of the Project 2013 application window. In addition, you can manually drag the slider bar in the *Zoom Slider* to the left and to the right to zoom out and zoom in.

Information: You can use the *Zoom Slider* in any view containing a Gantt chart, such as the *Gantt Chart* and *Tracking Gantt* views, along with the *Task Usage*, *Resource Usage*, and *Calendar* views.

Using the Scroll to Task Button

In any task view, such as the *Gantt Chart* view, select a task. In the *Editing* section of the *Task* ribbon, click the *Scroll to Task* button to bring the left end of the selected task's Gantt bar into view. In the *Task Usage* view, select a task name or a resource assignment and then click the *Scroll to Task* button to scroll the timephased *Work* or *Cost* information into view. In the *Resource Usage* view, select a resource name or a task assignment and then click the *Scroll to Task* button to scroll the timephased *Work* or *Cost* information into view.

Using Screen Tips and Tool Tips

You can display many helpful screen tips and tool tips in Project 2013 by floating your mouse pointer over many of the objects in the user interface. For example, float the mouse pointer over the *Select All* button, column headers, Gantt bars, and link lines between dependent tasks. Figure 2 - 83 shows the screen tip displayed while floating the mouse pointer over the *Task Mode* column header.

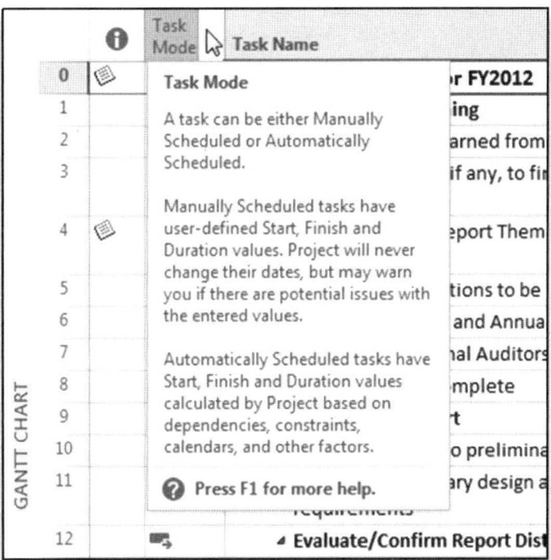

Figure 2 - 83: Screen tip for the Task Mode column

Information: To access a *Help* article about any column in Project 2013, float your mouse pointer over the column header and then press the **F1** function key on your computer keyboard.

Hands On Exercise

Exercise 2 - 17

Explore the navigation features in Project 2013.

1. Return to your **Project Navigation 2013.mpp** sample file, if necessary.
2. Right-click task ID #3, *Interview and select architect*, to display the shortcut menu and the *Mini Toolbar*.
3. In the *Mini Toolbar*, click the *Background Color* pick list button and choose the *Blue, Lighter 60%* color in the *Theme Colors* section of the palette.
4. Click anywhere outside of the selected task to see the blue cell background color.
5. Click the *Undo* button on the *Quick Access Toolbar* to remove the cell background color.

Notice in the *Timescale* that the current level of zoom applied to the *Gantt Chart* view is *Months over 3-Day Periods*. Remember that this level of zoom approximates *Months over Half-Weeks*.

6. Using the *Zoom In* or *Zoom Out* buttons on the *Quick Access Toolbar*, zoom the *Timescale* to the following levels:
   - *Months over Weeks*
   - *Quarters over Months*
   - *Years over Half Years*
   - *Hours over 15-Minute Periods*
   - *Weeks over Days*
7. On your computer keyboard, press **Control + Home** and **Alt + Home** to scroll back to the beginning of the project.
8. Select task IDs #21-38, from the *Strip walls* task to the *Carpentry Complete* milestone task, and then click the *Zoom Selected Tasks* button on the *Quick Access Toolbar*.

Notice how Project 2013 created a custom level of zoom to display the Gantt bars for all of the selected tasks using the current width of the *Gantt Chart* pane.

9. Click the *Zoom Entire Project* button on the *Quick Access Toolbar*.
10. Slowly scroll down the task list from the first task to the last task in the project, watching the Gantt bars in the *Gantt Chart* pane as you scroll.

Notice again how Project 2013 created a custom level of zoom to display the Gantt bars for all of the tasks in your project using the current width of the *Gantt Chart* pane.

11. Click the *Zoom In* button on your *Quick Access Toolbar* to return to the *Weeks over Days* level of zoom.
12. On your computer keyboard, press **Control + Home** and **Alt + Home** to scroll back to the beginning of the project.
13. Select task ID #60, *Construction Complete,* and then click the *Scroll to Task* button on your *Quick Access Toolbar.*

Notice how Project 2013 scrolls the *Gantt Chart* pane to the beginning of the Gantt bar for the selected task.

14. Select task ID #14, the *Pack rooms* task, and then click the *Scroll to Task* button on your *Quick Access Toolbar.*

Again notice how the software scrolls the *Gantt Chart* pane to the beginning of the Gantt bar for the selected task.

15. On your computer keyboard, press **Control + Home** and **Alt + Home** to scroll back to the beginning of the project.
16. Float your mouse pointer over the *Duration* column header and read the information about duration displayed in the tooltip.
17. While the software displays the *Duration* tooltip, press the **F1** function key on your computer keyboard.
18. Maximize the *Help* window and study the information about the *Duration* column, including how the software calculates the *Duration* value for tasks in your project.
19. Close the *Help* window when finished.
20. Save but **do not** close the **Project Navigation 2013.mpp** sample file.

Understanding the Planning Wizard

The *Planning Wizard* is an interactive help feature in Project 2013 that offers you guidance as you work on your project. The *Planning Wizard* offers guidance in three areas: using Project 2013, scheduling, and errors.

The software displays the *Planning Wizard* any time you take an action that causes it to activate in any of the preceding three categories. For example, entering the same *Duration* value on three successive tasks causes the software to display the *Planning Wizard* message about using Project 2013 shown in Figure 2 - 84. Notice the *Don't tell me about this again* checkbox option in the lower left corner of the dialog. If you select this option, Project 2013 no longer displays *Planning Wizard* messages in this situation again.

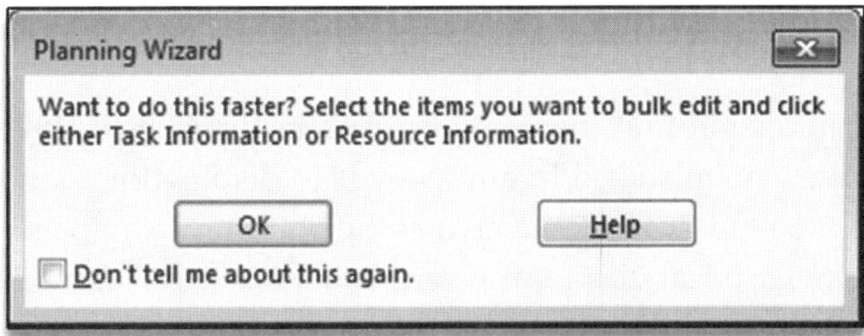

Figure 2 - 84: Planning Wizard

You control the function of the *Planning Wizard* through several settings in the *Project Options* dialog. Click the *File* tab and then click the *Options* button in the *Backstage* to display the *Project Options* dialog. Click the *Advanced* tab in the *Project Options* dialog and examine the options in the *Planning Wizard* section shown in Figure 2 - 85. By default, the software selects all of the options in the *Planning Wizard* section of the dialog. I recommend you leave these options selected to gain the most benefit from using the *Planning Wizard*. Click the OK button to close the *Project Options* dialog.

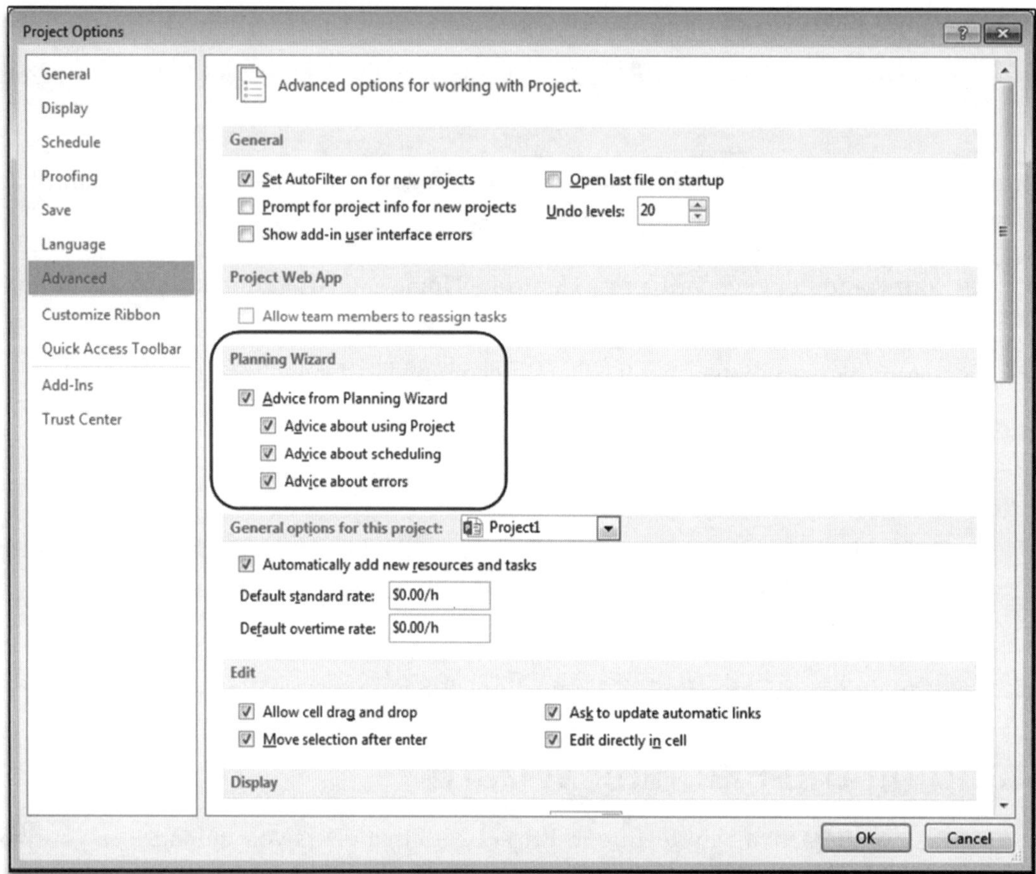

Figure 2 - 85: Project Options dialog
Planning Wizard options on the Advanced page

Understanding Gantt Chart Symbols

To a new user of Project 2013, understanding the symbols used in the *Gantt Chart* view can be a daunting task. The easiest way to learn about the symbols used in any view is to display the view in a project and then to print the project. In the printout, you can study the *Legend* area at the bottom of any page. The *Legend* displays a simple key for understanding the symbols used in view. For example, Figure 2 - 86 shows the *Legend* for the *Gantt Chart* view of a project.

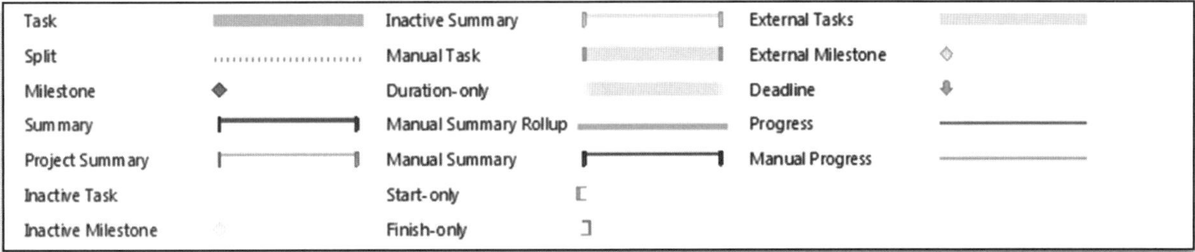

Figure 2 - 86: Legend for the Gantt Chart view

The only symbol the *Legend* does not explain is the arrow line drawn from one task to another, which is the link line symbol. This symbol represents the dependency relationship between the two tasks, and models the order in which team members perform the two dependent tasks.

Reading a Gantt Chart

Once you understand the symbols used in the *Gantt Chart* view, you can begin to read and understand the data presented in the view. For example, consider the *Gantt Chart* view for the very simple project shown in Figure 2 - 87. In this simple project, notice that the *Gantt Chart* view visually reveals the following:

- The project structure includes two phases named PHASE I and PHASE II. You can easily see that these two phases run parallel, meaning that the phases run concurrently.

- The Gantt bar for *PHASE I* summary task, represented by the black "upside down" Gantt bar, indicates that this phase runs from Monday, June 1, through Tuesday, June 23.

- The milestone symbol for the *Phase I Complete* task confirms that the finish date for this phase is Tuesday, June 23.

- The Gantt bar for *Phase II* summary task indicates that this phase runs from Monday, June 1 through Monday, June 22.

- The milestone symbol for the *Phase II Complete* task confirms that the finish date of this phase is Monday, June 22.

- The summary Gantt bar for the Project Summary Task (Row 0), represented by the gray "upside down" Gantt bar, indicates that the project runs from Monday, June 1, through Tuesday, June 23.

- The milestone symbol for the *Project Complete* task confirms that the scheduled finish date for the project is Tuesday, June 23.

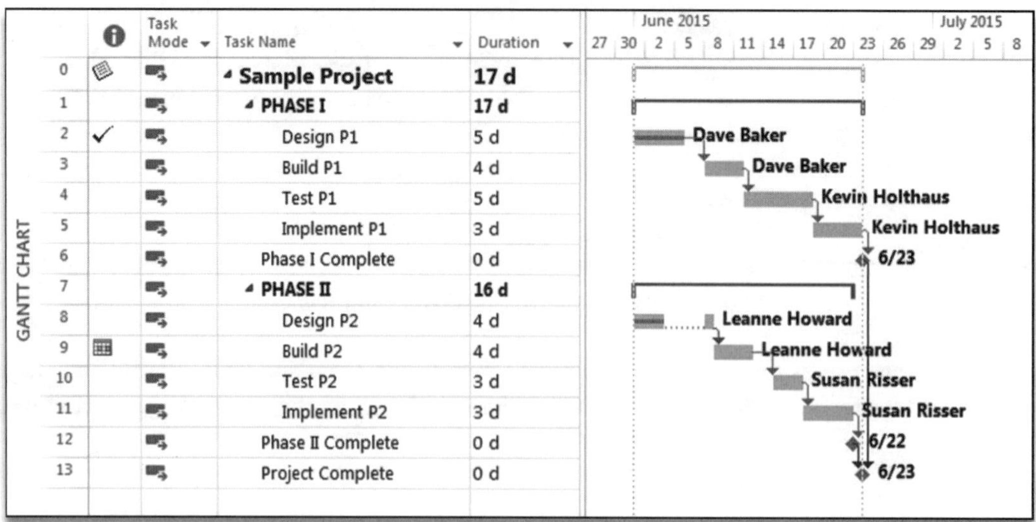

		Task Mode	Task Name	Duration
0			Sample Project	17 d
1			PHASE I	17 d
2	✓		Design P1	5 d
3			Build P1	4 d
4			Test P1	5 d
5			Implement P1	3 d
6			Phase I Complete	0 d
7			PHASE II	16 d
8			Design P2	4 d
9			Build P2	4 d
10			Test P2	3 d
11			Implement P2	3 d
12			Phase II Complete	0 d
13			Project Complete	0 d

Figure 2 - 87: Gantt Chart view for a simple project

The Gantt bar for each task reveals the current task schedule. For example, Project 2013 schedules the *Design P1* task from Monday, June 1, through Friday, June 5. The software schedules the *Build P1* task from Monday, June 8, through Thursday, June 11. Remember that you can float your mouse pointer over any Gantt bar to determine its current schedule using the information in the tooltip. Project 2013 determines the length of each Gantt bar based on the value shown for the task in the *Duration* column on the left side of the *Gantt Chart* view.

The progress bar (dark blue stripe) running completely through the Gantt bar for the *Design P1* task indicates that this task is 100% complete. The progress bar for the *Design P2* task runs only partially through its Gantt bar, indicating that this task is only partially complete. The task split symbol (...) in the middle of Gantt bar for the *Design P2* task indicates that the resource completed part of the task work the first week and will complete the remaining work on the task in the second week.

Information: Do not be alarmed by the task split task symbol (...) in the Gantt bar for the *Build P2* task. This symbol means that work started, stopped, and resumes at the current schedule date.

The link lines between the tasks in the *Gantt Chart* view indicate that all tasks must occur sequentially in the project. Notice also that I linked both the *Phase I Complete* and *Phase II Complete* milestone tasks to the *Project Complete milestone* task. This guarantees that the *Project Complete* milestone shows the correct finish date of the entire project.

Understanding Gantt-Optimized Scheduling Benefits

One of the unfortunate habits of many Project 2013 users (and of many users of previous versions, as well) is that they simply use the software to draw a *Gantt Chart* view of the project, and then do nothing more. It is a shame that people undervalue the best practice of using Gantt-optimized scheduling.

Refer back to Figure 2 - 87 and notice the "waterfall structure" of tasks in the PHASE I and PHASE II sections of the project. Whether you want to schedule a project that uses an "agile" methodology like SCRUM, or you want to schedule a project that uses a formal phase-gate structure, your goal is to build a waterfall structure when you use Gantt-optimized scheduling. The benefit is that this forces you to build a schedule structure that also optimizes readability and analysis. Most notably, a clean waterfall structure allows you to avoid going overboard on dependency relationships revealing the true work paths in your project or process model. Simplicity is easier to manage; less is more.

Best Practice: One of the reasons why Project 2013 users have a difficult time applying Gantt-optimized scheduling is because **business pressures** often force project managers to group tasks by organizational units, such as by who does the work. You should design your project Work Breakdown Structure to represent actual work paths and work flows. Designing a project schedule structure around organizational units is less productive compared to an integrated work path approach. In addition, MsProjectExperts recommends that you provide your users with an organizational-oriented project view to meet egocentric reporting demands.

Creating a Three-Tiered Timescale

By default, Project 2013 displays a two-tiered *Timescale*. However, with customization you can set up a three-tiered *Timescale*, which allows you to display different time units on each tier. For example, an organization might need to show the fiscal year on one tier and the calendar year on the other two tiers.

The default setting of the *Timescale* in Project 2013 shows only two tiers, formatted with weeks on the top tier and days on the bottom tier. To add a third tier to the *Timescale*, complete the following steps:

1. Double-click anywhere on the *Timescale*. The software displays the *Timescale* dialog shown in Figure 2 - 88.
2. In the *Timescale options* section of the dialog, click the *Show* pick list and select the *Three tiers (Top, Middle, Bottom)* item on the list.
3. Click the *Top Tier* tab.
4. Select your time *Units* and *Label* in the *Top Tier Formatting* section.
5. Click the *OK* button when finished.

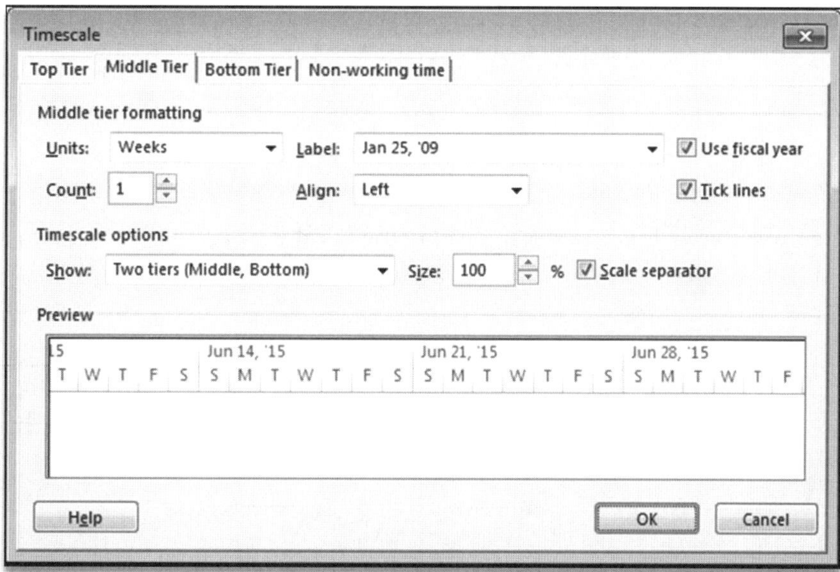

Figure 2 - 88: Timescale dialog

Displaying Fiscal Year in a Three-Tiered Timescale

If your company uses a fiscal year different from the calendar year, you can use the three-tiered *Timescale* to display the fiscal year against the calendar year. Complete these steps to add a third tier to display the fiscal year:

1. Click the *File* tab and then click the *Options* button in the *Backstage*.
2. In the *Project Options* dialog, click the *Schedule* tab.
3. In the *Calendar options for this project* section of the *Schedule* page, click the *Fiscal year starts in* pick list and choose the beginning month for your organization's fiscal year.
4. Optionally select the *Use starting year for FY number* checkbox if this is necessary to display your organization's fiscal year correctly.
5. Click the *OK* button to close the *Project Options* dialog.
6. Double-click anywhere in the *Timescale* to display the *Timescale* dialog.
7. In the *Timescale options* section of the dialog, click the *Show* pick list and select the *Three tiers (Top, Middle, Bottom)* item on the list.
8. On the *Top Tier* page, set the *Units* value to *Years*, and **select** the *Use fiscal year* option.
9. On the *Middle Tier* and *Bottom Tier* pages, select your desired *Units* options and then **deselect** the *Use fiscal year* option.
10. Click the *OK* button.

Figure 2 - 89 shows the three-tiered *Timescale* set to display the fiscal year on the top tier and the calendar year on the middle and bottom tiers. Notice in the top tier that the 2016 fiscal year begins in April 2015.

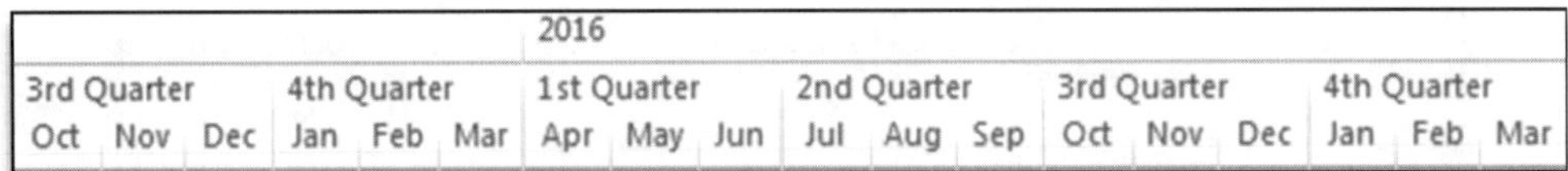

Figure 2 - 89: Three-Tiered Timescale

Information: The settings on the *Timescale* apply to only the current view in the active project. To apply the three-tiered *Timescale* to every future project, you should modify the *Timescale* settings for each project template that you use.

Hands On Exercise

Exercise 2 - 18

Display both the fiscal year and calendar year on a three-tiered timescale.

1. Return to your **Project Navigation 2013.mpp** sample file, if necessary.
2. Click the *File* tab and then click the *Options* button in the *Backstage.*
3. In the *Project Options* dialog, click the *Schedule* tab.
4. In the *Calendar options for this project* section of the *Schedule* page, click the *Fiscal year starts in* pick list and choose *April* as the beginning month of each fiscal year.
5. Click the *OK* button to close the *Project Options* dialog.
6. Double-click anywhere in the *Timescale* to display the *Timescale* dialog.
7. In the *Timescale* dialog, click the *Show* pick list in the *Timescale options* section, and then select the *Three tiers (Top, Middle, Bottom)* item from the list.
8. Click the *Top Tier* tab to display the *Top Tier* page in the dialog.
9. On the *Top Tier* page, set the *Units* value to *Years,* and leave the *Use fiscal year* option selected.
10. Click the *Middle Tier* tab to display the *Middle Tier* page in the dialog.
11. On the *Middle Tier* page, set the *Units* value to *Months,* set the *Label* value to *January 2009,* and **deselect** the *Use fiscal year* option.
12. Click the *Bottom Tier* tab to apply the *Bottom Tier* page in the dialog.
13. On the *Bottom Tier* page, set the *Units* value to *Weeks,* the *Label* value to *Jan 25, Feb 1 …,* and **deselect** the *Use fiscal year* option.
14. Click the *OK* button to close the *Timescale* dialog.
15. Examine the *Timescale* at the beginning of the project.

Notice how the top tier of the *Timescale* displays the fiscal year (2015), the middle tier displays the current month and calendar year (April 2014) and the bottom tier displays the current week.

16. Save and close the **Project Navigation 2013.mpp** sample file.

Module 03

Inside Project 2013

Learning Objectives

After completing this module, you will be able to:

- Understand the organization of data in the Project 2013 data model
- Describe how the Project 2013 data model affects views, tables, filters, and groups
- Use appropriate views, tables, filters, and groups to display the data you want to see
- Filter your project data by applying standard filters, highlight filters, and AutoFilters

Inside Module 03

Understanding the Project 2013 Data Model

Figure 3 - 1 displays the simplified Project 2013 data model as it affects views, tables, filters, and groups. Notice that Project 2013 recognizes two separate and distinct types of data: *Task* data and *Resource* data. Each type of data includes its own unique set of views, tables, filters, and groups.

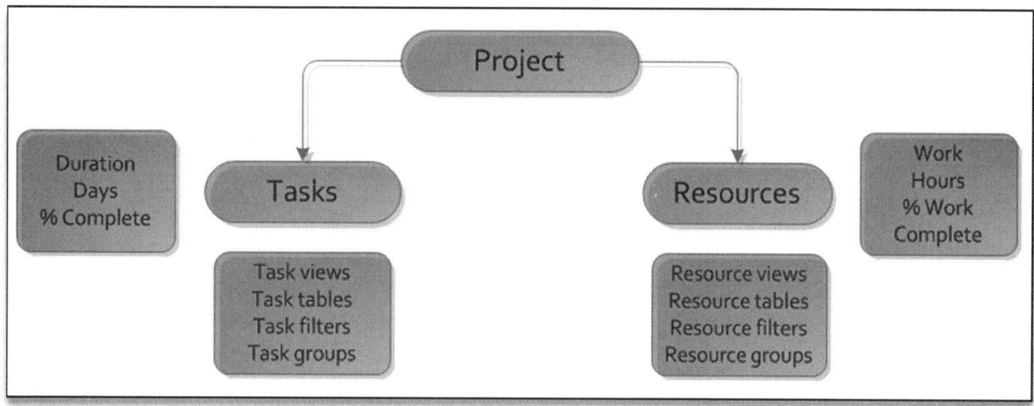

Figure 3 - 1: Simplified Project 2013 Data Model

Task data carries *Duration* values measured in days by default. Project 2013 measures the percentage of the *Duration* value completed to date using the *% Complete* field. *Resource* data carries *Work* (or effort) values, measured in hours by default. Project 2013 measures the percentage of work completed to date using the *% Work Complete* field.

Information: It might be less confusing to some of us if Microsoft renamed the *% Complete* field as the *% Duration Complete* field because this field actually measures the percentage of the *Duration* value consumed to date.

Understanding Views

Project 2013 includes 27 default views, of which 21 are task views and 6 are resource views. Software users often define views as "different ways of looking at my project data." Although this definition is correct, Project 2013 formally defines a view as:

View = Table + Filter + Group + Screen

In the Project 2013 definition of a view, the *Table* displays the columns you see on the left side of the view, the *Filter* displays the rows you see, the *Group* organizes the data rows into groups with similar attributes or characteristics, and the *Screen* determines what appears on the right side of the view. Specifically, the *Screen* determines whether you see some type of a Gantt chart, a timephased grid, or no screen at all on the right side of the view.

The *Gantt with Timeline* view is the default view Project 2013 displays when you launch the software. The *Gantt with Timeline* view is a combination view that consists of two separate views, each displayed in its own pane. The *Gantt with Timeline* view includes the *Timeline* view in the top pane and the *Gantt Chart* view in the bottom pane.

Warning: If you apply any other view after applying the *Gantt with Timeline* view, Project 2013 continues to display the *Timeline* view in the top pane. To close the *Timeline* pane, double-click the split bar at the bottom of the *Timeline* pane, or click the *View* tab and deselect the *Timeline* checkbox in the *Split View* section of the *View* ribbon.

To apply a view, use any of the following methods:

- Click the *Task* tab to display the *Task* ribbon. In the *View* section of the *Task* ribbon, click the *Gantt Chart* pick list button and select any view on the list. You can also select the *More Views* item at the bottom of the list. Figure 3 - 2 shows the views available on the *Gantt Chart* pick list in the *Views* section of the *Task* ribbon.

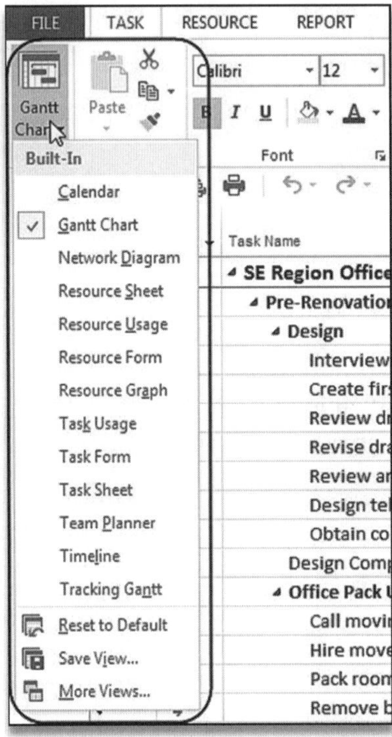

Figure 3 - 2: Gantt Chart pick list on the Task ribbon

- Click the *Resource* tab to display the *Resource* ribbon. In the *View* section of the *Resource* ribbon, click the *Team Planner* pick list button and select any view on the list. You can also select the *More Views* item at the bottom of the list.

Warning: The *Resource* ribbon displays the *Team Planner* pick list button only if you have the **Professional** version of Project 2013. If you have the **Standard** version of the software, the *Resource* ribbon displays the *Resource Sheet* pick list button instead.

- Click the *View* tab to display the *View* ribbon. Click any pick list button in the *Task Views* or *Resource Views* sections of the *View* ribbon and select a view on the list. On any view pick list, you can also select the *More Views* item at the bottom of the list.

- Right-click the *View Bar* and select a view on the shortcut menu. You can also select the *More Views* item near the bottom of the shortcut menu. The *View Bar* is the white bar that displays the name of the view on the left side of the Project 2013 application window.

Information: You can also expand the *View Bar* to show view buttons by right-clicking the *View Bar* and then selecting the *View Bar* item at the bottom of the shortcut menu.

When you select the *More Views* item at the bottom of any view pick list, Project 2013 displays the *More Views* dialog shown in Figure 3 - 3. This dialog displays every default and custom view. Select any view in the dialog and then click the *Apply* button.

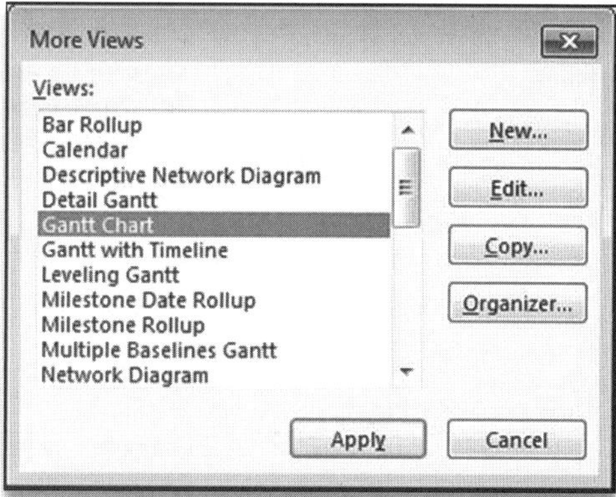

Figure 3 - 3: More Views dialog

Information: By default, the *Gantt with Timeline* view does not appear on any view pick list, and appears **only** in the *More Views* dialog. To change this setting, display the *More Views* dialog, select the *Gantt with Timeline* view in the dialog, and then click the *Edit* button. In the *View Definition* dialog, select the *Show on Menu* checkbox and then click the *OK* button. After making this selection, you can select the *Gantt with Timeline* view from any view pick list, such as on the *Gantt Chart* pick list button on the *Task* ribbon.

Best Practice: In the *More Views* dialog, Project 2013 allows you to edit any view by selecting it and then clicking the *Edit* button. Although the software allows you to do this, MsProjectExperts recommends that you **do not** modify any of the default views included with the software. Instead, if no default view meets your reporting needs, copy a default view and then modify the new view to meet your reporting needs.

Using Single Views and Combination Views

In Project 2013, a *Single* view is any view that displays in a single window. You commonly use *Single* views such as the *Gantt Chart* and *Resource Sheet* views.

In Project 2013, a *Combination* view is any view that contains two views, displayed in a split-screen format with each view in its own pane. The view in the secondary pane (usually the bottom pane) displays detailed information about the selected task, resource, or assignment in the view contained in the primary pane (usually the top pane). The most commonly used *Combination* views are the *Task Entry* view and the new *Gantt with Timeline* view.

Information: In the *Gantt with Timeline* view, the *Timeline* view is in the top pane, but it is actually the secondary pane. The *Gantt Chart* view is in the bottom pane, but it is the primary pane. This differs from all other combination views, such as the *Task Entry* view.

Figure 3 - 4 shows a *Single* view, the *Tracking Gantt* view. You use the *Tracking Gantt* view to analyze schedule variance during the *Executing* stage of your project.

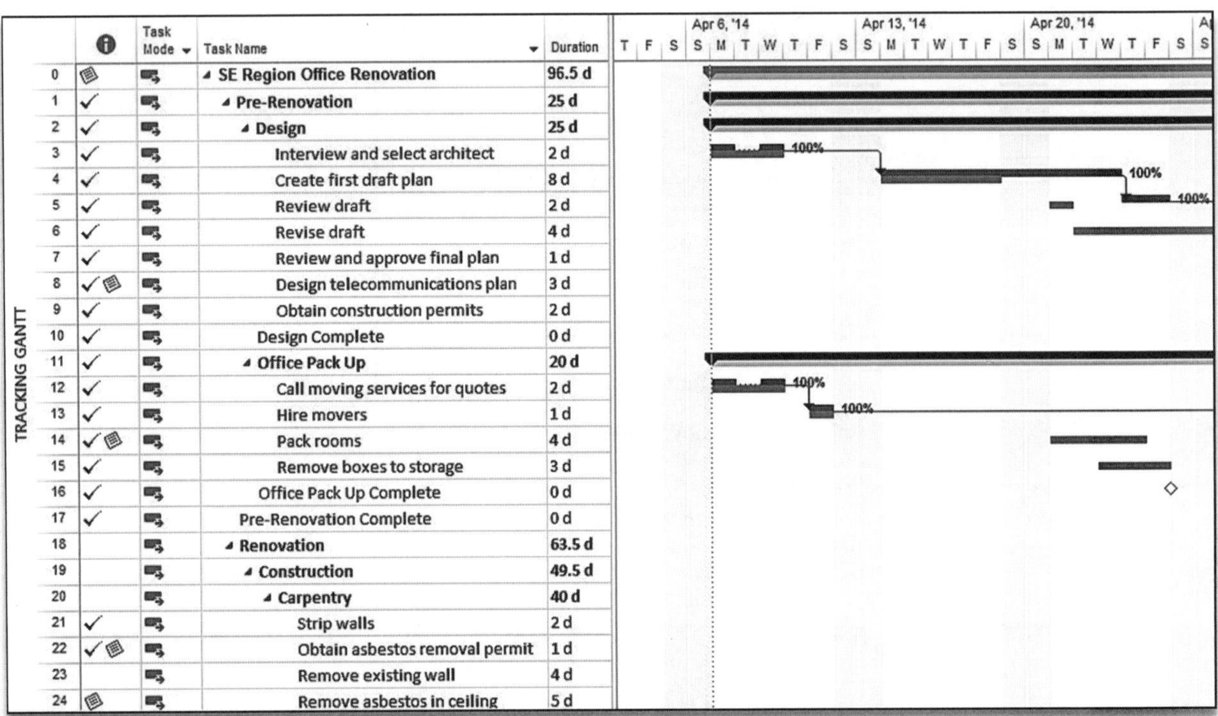

	Task Name	Duration
0	SE Region Office Renovation	96.5 d
1	Pre-Renovation	25 d
2	Design	25 d
3	Interview and select architect	2 d
4	Create first draft plan	8 d
5	Review draft	2 d
6	Revise draft	4 d
7	Review and approve final plan	1 d
8	Design telecommunications plan	3 d
9	Obtain construction permits	2 d
10	Design Complete	0 d
11	Office Pack Up	20 d
12	Call moving services for quotes	2 d
13	Hire movers	1 d
14	Pack rooms	4 d
15	Remove boxes to storage	3 d
16	Office Pack Up Complete	0 d
17	Pre-Renovation Complete	0 d
18	Renovation	63.5 d
19	Construction	49.5 d
20	Carpentry	40 d
21	Strip walls	2 d
22	Obtain asbestos removal permit	1 d
23	Remove existing wall	4 d
24	Remove asbestos in ceiling	5 d

Figure 3 - 4: Single view - Tracking Gantt view

Figure 3 - 5 shows a *Combination* view, the *Resource Allocation* view. The *Resource Allocation* view includes the *Resource Usage* view in the primary pane (top pane) and the *Leveling Gantt* view in the secondary pane (bottom pane). You can use the *Resource Allocation* view for leveling resource overallocations.

Warning: To exit a *Combination* view and apply any other view is not nearly as easy as you might think. You must first close the view shown in the secondary pane by double-clicking anywhere on the split bar that separates the primary pane from the secondary pane. After you close the view in the secondary pane, you can apply any other view.

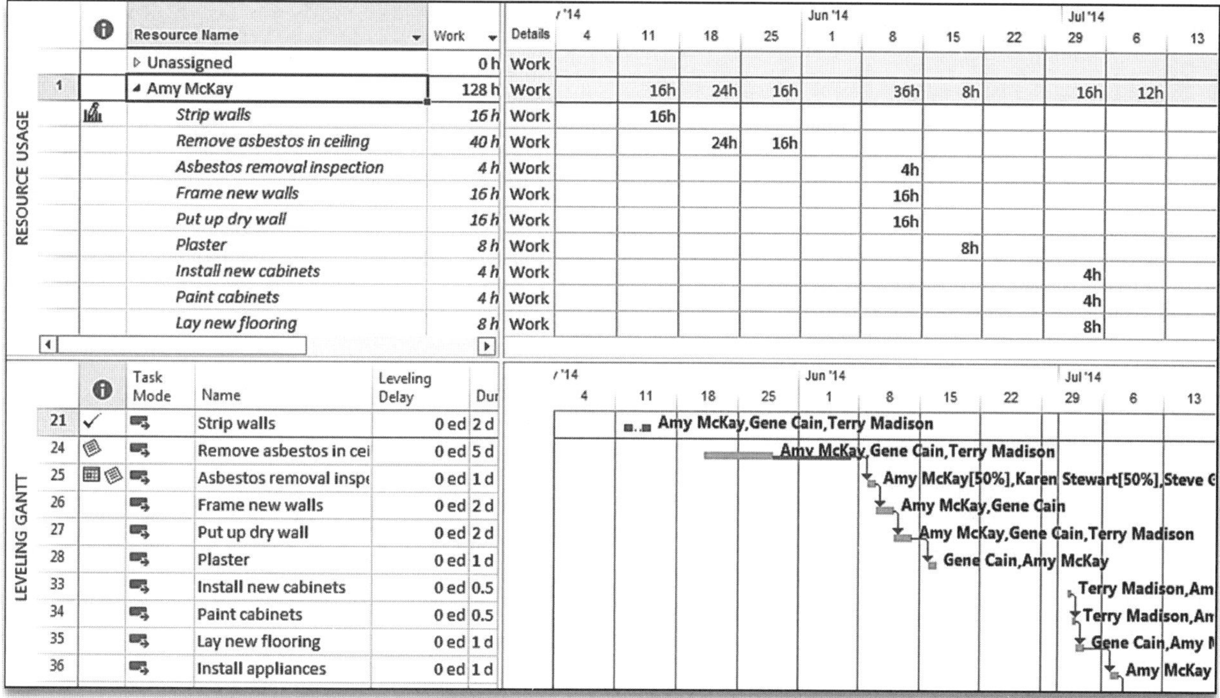

Figure 3 - 5: Combination view - Resource Allocation view

Hands On Exercise

Exercise 3 - 1

Apply task and resource views in Project 2013.

1. Open the **Project Navigation 2013.mpp** sample file.

2. Click the *Task* tab to display the *Task* ribbon, if necessary.

3. Using the *Gantt Chart* pick list button, individually apply and study each of the following task views:

    - *Calendar*
    - *Tracking Gantt*
    - *Task Usage*

4. Click the *Resource* tab to display the *Resource* ribbon.

5. Using the *Team Planner* pick list button, individually apply and study each of following resource views:

    - *Resource Sheet*
    - *Resource Usage*
    - *Team Planner*

6. Click the *View* tab to display the *View* ribbon.

7. In the *Resource Views* section of the *View* ribbon, click the *Other Views* pick list button and then select the *More Views* item in the list.

8. In the *More Views* dialog, select the *Task Entry* view and then click the *Apply* button.

9. In the upper pane (*Gantt Chart* view), select task ID #8, *Design telecommunications plan.*

10. In the lower pane (*Task Form* view), examine the assignment information for the resources assigned to this task.

11. In the *Split View* section of the *View* ribbon, **deselect** the *Details* checkbox to close the lower viewing pane.

12. In the *Task Views* section of the *View* ribbon, click the *Other Views* pick list button and then select the *Task Sheet* view.

13. In the *More Views* dialog, select the *Task Sheet* view and then click the *Apply* button.

Notice that the *Task Sheet* view contains the same columns included in the *Gantt Chart* view, but does not contain a Gantt chart on the right side of the view. The *Task Sheet* view is an ideal view to use when you need to print all of the columns included the *Gantt Chart* view, but you do not want to include a Gantt chart in the printout.

14. Save but **do not** close your **Project Navigation 2013.mpp** sample file.

Understanding Tables

Project 2013 includes 27 default tables, of which 17 are task tables and 10 are resource tables. By definition, a table is a collection of columns and the name of each table describes the type of columns in the collection. For example, the task *Cost* table contains columns showing the cost data associated with each task in the project. Because the software displays tables within views, you can only use task tables with task views and resource tables with resource views. To apply any table in the current view, use either of the following methods:

- Click the *View* tab to display the *View* ribbon. In the *Data* section of the *View* ribbon, click the *Tables* pick list button and select any table on the list. You can also select the *More Tables* item at the bottom of the list. Figure 3 - 6 shows the list of available tables on the *Tables* pick list in the *Data* section of the *View* ribbon.

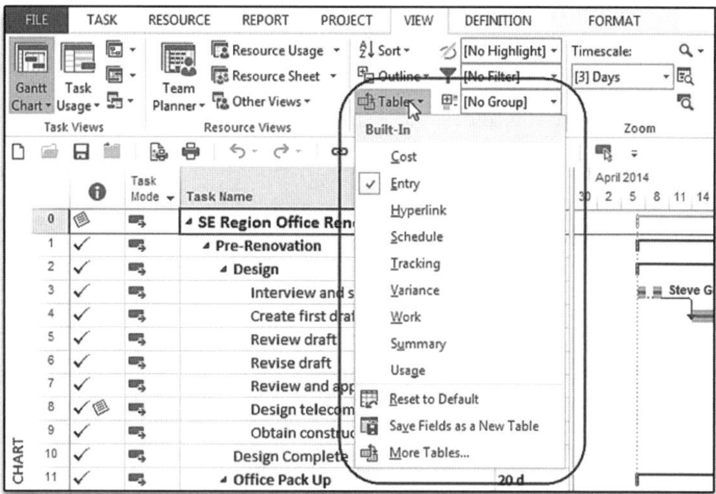

Figure 3 - 6: Tables pick list on the View ribbon

- Right-click the *Select All* button (blank button in the upper left corner of the *Task Sheet* or *Resource Sheet*) and then select any table on the shortcut menu. You can also select the *More Tables* item at the bottom of the shortcut menu.

When you select the *More Tables* item at the bottom of the *Tables* pick list or shortcut menu, Project 2013 displays the *More Tables* dialog shown in Figure 3 - 7. This dialog displays every default and custom table for the type of view applied currently. This means if you have a task view applied, the *More Tables* dialog displays the complete list of task tables. If you have a resource view applied, the *More Tables* dialog shows the complete list of resource tables. Select any table in the dialog and then click the *Apply* button.

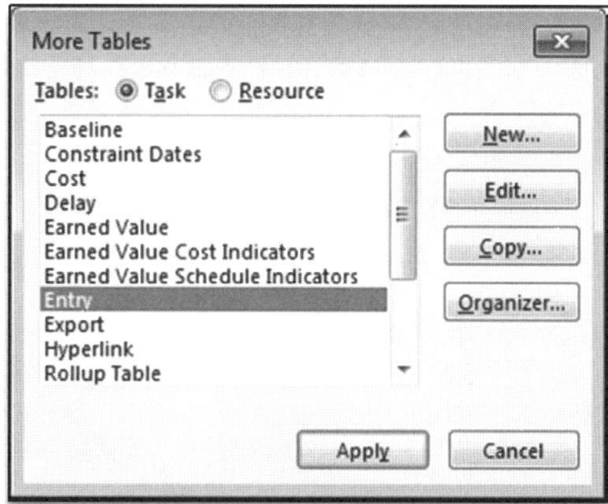

Figure 3 - 7: More Tables dialog

Warning: While in a task view, such as the *Gantt Chart* view, the *More Tables* dialog only allows you to apply task tables, such as the *Schedule* table. While in a resource view, such as the *Resource Sheet* view, the *More Tables* dialog only allows you to apply resource tables, such as the *Usage* table. Keep in mind that the Project 2013 data model governs this behavior.

Best Practice: In the *More Tables* dialog, Project 2013 allows you to edit any table by selecting it and then clicking the *Edit* button. Although the software allows you to do this, MsProjectExperts recommends that you do not modify any of the default tables included with the software. Instead, if no default table meets your reporting needs, copy a default table and then modify that new table to meet your reporting needs.

Figure 3 - 8 shows the task *Tracking* table applied in the *Task Sheet* view. Notice that this table contains many of the columns that you might use to manually enter task progress in your project, such as the *Actual Start, Actual Finish,* and *Actual Work* columns.

TASK SHEET

	Task Name	Act. Start	Act. Finish	% Comp.	Phys. %	Act. Dur.	Rem. Dur.	Act. Cost	Act. Work
0	**SE Region Office Renovation**	**4/7/2014**	**NA**	**36%**	**0%**	**34.5 d**	**62 d**	**$20,555**	**370 h**
1	**Pre-Renovation**	**4/7/2014**	**5/9/2014**	**100%**	**0%**	**25 d**	**0 d**	**$16,095**	**282 h**
2	**Design**	**4/7/2014**	**5/9/2014**	**100%**	**0%**	**25 d**	**0 d**	**$12,935**	**156 h**
3	Interview and select architect	4/7/2014	4/9/2014	100%	0%	2 d	0 d	$600	10 h
4	Create first draft plan	4/14/2014	4/23/2014	100%	0%	8 d	0 d	$2,340	52 h
5	Review draft	4/24/2014	4/25/2014	100%	0%	2 d	0 d	$540	10 h
6	Revise draft	4/28/2014	5/1/2014	100%	0%	4 d	0 d	$900	20 h
7	Review and approve final plan	5/2/2014	5/2/2014	100%	0%	1 d	0 d	$420	8 h
8	Design telecommunications plan	5/5/2014	5/7/2014	100%	0%	3 d	0 d	$3,625	48 h
9	Obtain construction permits	5/8/2014	5/9/2014	100%	0%	2 d	0 d	$4,510	8 h
10	Design Complete	5/9/2014	5/9/2014	100%	0%	0 d	0 d	$0	0 h
11	**Office Pack Up**	**4/7/2014**	**5/2/2014**	**100%**	**0%**	**20 d**	**0 d**	**$3,160**	**126 h**
12	Call moving services for quotes	4/7/2014	4/9/2014	100%	0%	2 d	0 d	$240	12 h
13	Hire movers	4/11/2014	4/11/2014	100%	0%	1 d	0 d	$120	2 h
14	Pack rooms	4/28/2014	5/1/2014	100%	0%	4 d	0 d	$1,600	64 h
15	Remove boxes to storage	4/30/2014	5/2/2014	100%	0%	3 d	0 d	$1,200	48 h
16	Office Pack Up Complete	5/2/2014	5/2/2014	100%	0%	0 d	0 d	$0	0 h
17	Pre-Renovation Complete	5/9/2014	5/9/2014	100%	0%	0 d	0 d	$0	0 h
18	**Renovation**	**5/12/2014**	**NA**	**8%**	**0%**	**5 d**	**58.5 d**	**$4,460**	**88 h**
19	**Construction**	**5/12/2014**	**NA**	**9%**	**0%**	**4.3 d**	**45.2 d**	**$4,460**	**88 h**
20	**Carpentry**	**5/12/2014**	**NA**	**15%**	**0%**	**6.06 d**	**33.94 d**	**$4,460**	**88 h**
21	Strip walls	5/12/2014	5/14/2014	100%	0%	2 d	0 d	$1,680	48 h
22	Obtain asbestos removal permit	5/13/2014	5/13/2014	100%	0%	1 d	0 d	$1,660	8 h
23	Remove existing wall	5/15/2014	NA	50%	0%	2 d	2 d	$1,120	32 h
24	Remove asbestos in ceiling	NA	NA	0%	0%	0 d	5 d	$0	0 h

Figure 3 - 8: Tracking table displayed in the Task Sheet view

Figure 3 - 9 shows the resource *Work* table applied in the *Resource Sheet* view. Notice that this table contains all of the columns that identify the work for each resource.

RESOURCE SHEET

	Resource Name	% Comp.	Work	Overtime	Baseline	Variance	Actual	Remaining	Add New Column
1	Amy McKay	13%	128 h	0 h	84 h	44 h	16 h	112 h	
2	Bob Siclari	0%	56 h	0 h	56 h	0 h	0 h	56 h	
3	Cher Zall	0%	24 h	0 h	24 h	0 h	0 h	24 h	
4	Gene Cain	14%	224 h	0 h	164 h	60 h	32 h	192 h	
5	Jerry King	100%	92 h	0 h	80 h	12 h	92 h	0 h	
6	Karen Stewart	0%	20 h	0 h	16 h	4 h	0 h	20 h	
7	Marcia Bickel	88%	32 h	0 h	24 h	8 h	28 h	4 h	
8	Mary Jo Peterson	0%	48 h	0 h	48 h	0 h	0 h	48 h	
9	Mover	47%	240 h	0 h	240 h	0 h	112 h	128 h	
10	Russ Powell	20%	120 h	0 h	120 h	0 h	24 h	96 h	
11	Steve Garcia	49%	70 h	0 h	66 h	4 h	34 h	36 h	
12	Terry Madison	28%	116 h	0 h	56 h	60 h	32 h	84 h	
13	Paint	0%	275 Gallons	0 h	275 Gallons	0 Gallons	0 Gallons	275 Gallons	
14	Project Budget								
15	Travel Expense	35%		0 h		0			

Figure 3 - 9: Work table displayed in the Resource Sheet view

Notice in the table shown previously in Figure 3 - 9 includes an extra column labeled *Add New Column* at the right end of the table. This extra column is a **virtual column** that appears by default in **every** table you apply in Project 2013. The *Add New Column* virtual column allows you to add a default column to the current table, or to create a custom column. I discuss how to use the *Add New Column* virtual column feature later in this book when I teach you how to create a custom view.

In the task *Tracking* table and in the resource *Work* table shown previously in Figures Figure 3 - 8 and Figure 3 - 9, the column labels on many of the columns do not show the **real name** of the column. Instead, they show a "nick-name" or label for the column to save column space. For example, the real name of the *Act. Start* column in the *Tracking* table is *Actual Start*. The real name of the *Variance* column in the resource *Work* table is *Work Variance*. To determine the real name of any column, float your mouse pointer over the column header and look for the text enclosed in the parentheses characters in the tooltip. When I float my mouse pointer over the *Variance* column, for example, notice that the tooltip shown in Figure 3 - 10 reveals the real name of the column, which is *Work Variance*.

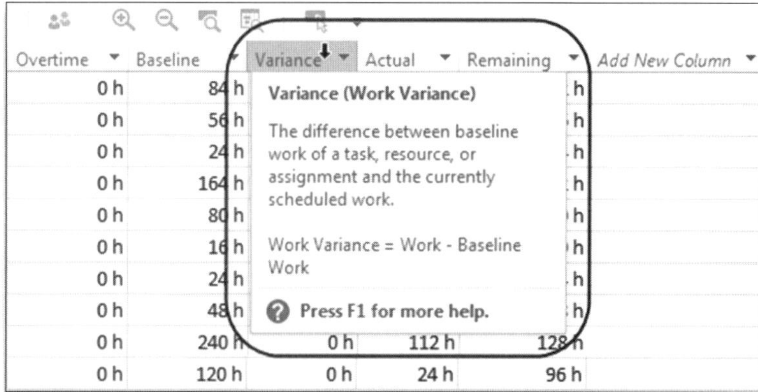

Figure 3 - 10: Tooltip shows the real name of the Variance column

Hands On Exercise

Exercise 3 - 2

Apply task and resource tables in Project 2013.

1. Return to the **Project Navigation 2010.mpp** sample file, if necessary.

Notice the *Add New Column* virtual column to the right of the *Resource Names* column. You can use this feature to quickly add a new column to any table.

2. Click the *View* tab to display the *View* ribbon, if necessary.
3. In the *Data* section of the *View* ribbon, click the *Tables* pick list and select the *Cost* table.
4. Examine all of the columns included in the *Cost* table.

Notice that every column in the *Cost* table displays task cost information.

5. Float your mouse pointer over the *Baseline* column header and read the text in the tooltip to determine the real name of this column.

Notice that the real name of *Baseline* column is actually *Baseline Cost*, while the "nickname" for this column is simply *Baseline*.

6. Right-click the *Select All* button and select the *Work* table.
7. Examine all of the columns included in the *Work* table.

Notice that every column in the *Work* table displays task work information.

8. Right-click the *Select All* button and select the *Schedule* table.
9. Examine all of the columns included in the *Schedule* table.

Notice that the last column in the *Schedule* table is *Total Slack*. Project 2013 calculates this column and uses the *Total Slack* information to determine whether each task is a Critical task. Critical tasks have a *Total Slack* value of *0 days*, while non-Critical tasks have a *Total Slack* value greater than *0 days*.

10. Right-click the *Select All* button again and select the *Entry* table.
11. Drag the split bar to the right edge of the *Duration* column.
12. Save and close your **Project Navigation 2013.mpp** sample file.

Understanding Filters

Project 2013 ships with 70 default filters, of which 45 are task filters, and 25 are resource filters. The software includes 11 new task filters but no new resource filters. The new task filters include:

- **Completed Milestones** – Use the *Completed Milestones* filter to display all completed milestone tasks in your projects.
- **Late Milestones** – Use the *Late Milestones* filter to display incomplete *Milestone* tasks that are late. By definition, a **late task** in Project 2013 is any task where the time-phased cumulative percent complete (represented by the black progress line in a Gantt bar) does not reach the *Status Date* you specify for the project. If you do not specify a *Status Date* for your project, then the software uses the *Current Date* to determine whether tasks are late. If any task is late, then the software displays a *Late* value in the *Status* field for that task.
- **Milestones Due This Month** – Use the *Milestones Due This Month* filter to display *Milestone* tasks with a *Finish* date occurring during the current month.
- **No Actuals** – Use the *No Actuals* filter to display tasks that contain no actual work to date.
- **No Resources Assigned** – Use the *No Resources Assigned* filter to display tasks without assigned resources. This filter is very useful when auditing your project to make sure you assigned at least one resource to every subtask in the project.

- **Overallocated Tasks** – Use the *Overallocated Tasks* filter to display tasks assigned to an overallocated resource.

Warning: Because of an unfixed bug in the release (RTM) version of Project 2013, the *Overallocated Tasks* filter **does not** display parallel tasks assigned to an overallocated resource. Instead, this filter only shows tasks in which two specific conditions cause the overallocation: when you assign a resource to the task with a *Units* value greater than the *Max. Units* value for the resource, and when you assign a resource to work on a task during a nonworking time period, such as a weekend. Because of these limitations, the *Overallocated Resource* filter is of very limited practical use.

- **Summary Task with Assigned Resources** – Use the *Summary Task with Assigned Resources* filter to display summary tasks to which you assigned resources. Because assigning resources to a summary task is very bad practice, this new filter is very useful when auditing your project to make sure you have no resources assigned to summary tasks
- **Tasks Due This Week** – Use the *Tasks Due This Week* filter to see any tasks with a *Finish* date during the current week.
- **Tasks Starting Soon** – Use the *Tasks Starting Soon* filter to see tasks starting in an upcoming time period.
- **Tasks with Durations < 8h** – Some organizations use a methodology that does not allow a project manager to specify a task *Duration* value less than *1 day*. If your organization uses a methodology such as this, use the *Tasks with Duration < 8h* filter to display tasks with a *Duration* value of less than *1 day*.
- **Upcoming Milestones** – Use the *Upcoming Milestones* filter to see all incomplete *Milestone* tasks in your project.

Understanding the New Date Filters

A new feature in Project 2013 is that the software uses the date in the *Current Date* field to calculate the dates of the first and last days of the current week, and to calculate the dates of the first and last days of the current month. The software specifically uses this information with the *Milestones Due This Month, Tasks Due This Week,* and *Tasks Starting Soon* filters. For example, for the *Milestones Due This Month* filter, the software captures the date in the *Current Date* field, calculates the date of the last day of the month, and then filters for any *Milestone* task with a *Finish* date less than the date of the last day of the month.

Filters allow you to display or highlight specific data rows according to your filter criteria. Because the software applies filters within views, you can only use task filters with task views and resource filters with resource views. The software offers you three ways to apply filters:

- Apply a filter as a **standard filter**.
- Apply a filter as a **highlight filter**.
- Use **AutoFilter**.

I discuss each of these methods individually.

Applying a Standard Filter

When you apply a filter as a **standard filter**, Project 2013 displays only the data rows that meet your filter criteria. To apply a standard filter, click the *View* tab to display the *View* ribbon. In the *Data* section of the *View* ribbon, click the *Filter* pick list and select a filter. You can also select the *More Filters* item near the bottom of the list. Figure 3 - 11 shows the list of filters on the *Filter* pick list.

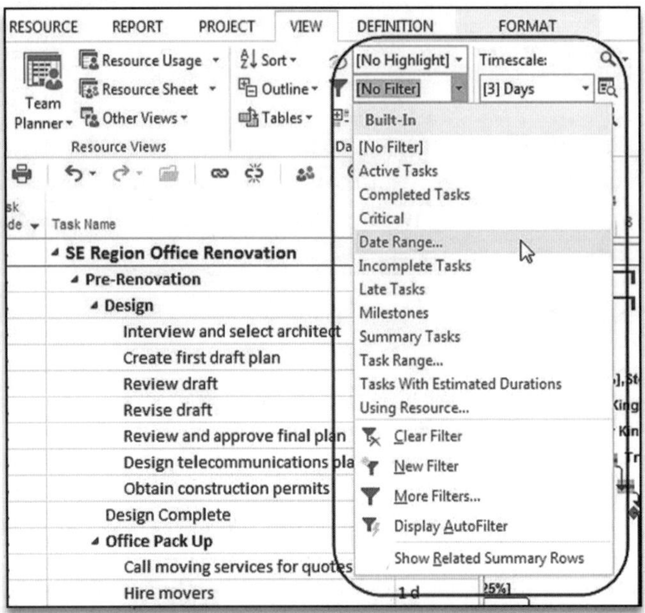

Figure 3 - 11: Apply a Standard Filter

Notice that the *Filter* pick list allows you to choose from a list of most commonly used filters, plus you can choose additional filtering options. These additional options include *Clear Filter* to remove filtering criteria, *New Filter* to create a new filter from scratch, *More Filters* to display the *More Filters* dialog, and *Display AutoFilter* to turn on the *AutoFilter* feature in the data grid.

Any filter name that ends with an ellipsis character (...) is an **interactive filter**. This means that when you select the filter, Project 2013 prompts you in one or more dialogs for your filter criteria, and then it applies the filter using the criteria you supply. Interactive filters on the *Filter* pick list include the *Date Range*, *Task Range*, and *Using Resource* filters. For example, when I select the *Task Range* interactive, the software displays the *Task Range* dialog shown in Figure 3 - 12.

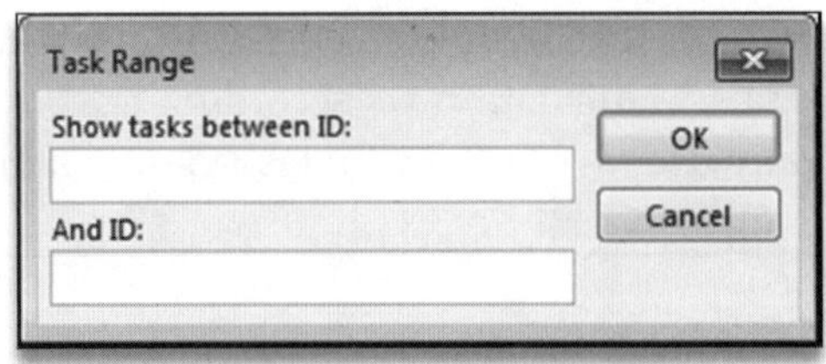

Figure 3 - 12: Task Range dialog

If you click the *More Filters* item near the bottom of the *Filter* pick list, the software displays the *More Filters* dialog shown in Figure 3 - 13. This dialog displays all available default and custom filters. After selecting any filter, click the *Apply* button to apply the filter as a standard filter, or click the *Highlight* button to apply the filter as a highlight filter. When you apply a filter as a highlight filter, Project 2013 displays all tasks (or resources) in the project, and highlights only the data that meet your filtering criteria using yellow cell background formatting. I discuss highlight filters in more detail in the following topical section.

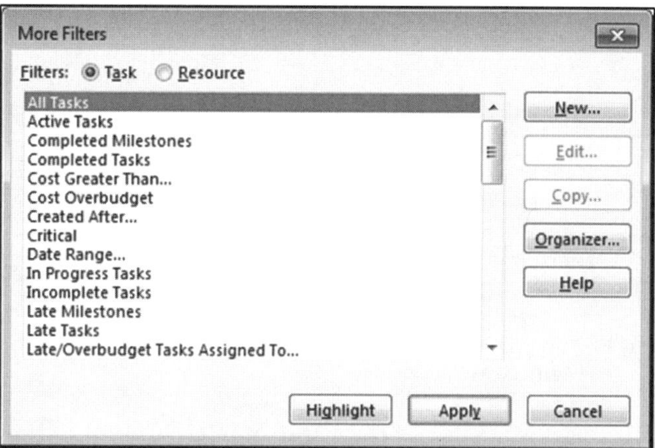

Figure 3 - 13: More Filters dialog

Best Practice: In the *More Filters* dialog, Project 2013 allows you to edit any filter by selecting it and then clicking the *Edit* button. Although the software allows you to do this, MSProjectExperts recommends that you do not modify any of the default filters included with the software. Instead, if no default filter meets your reporting needs, copy a filter that comes close and then modify that new filter to meet your reporting needs.

Information: Press the **F3** function key on your computer keyboard to apply the *[No Filter]* filter in any task view or the *All Resources* filter in any resource view.

Figure 3 - 14 shows the *Resource Group* filter applied as a standard filter to a project, filtering for members of the *Architect* group. Notice that the filter extracts five tasks in the *Pre-Renovation* phase and *Design* deliverable sections of the project. Jerry King is the only member of the *Architect* group, by the way, so notice that I assigned him to all five of these tasks.

	Task Mode	Task Name	Duration
0		SE Region Office Renovation	96.5 d
1		Pre-Renovation	25 d
2		Design	25 d
4		Create first draft plan	8 d
5		Review draft	2 d
6		Revise draft	4 d
7		Review and approve final plan	1 d
8		Design telecommunications plan	3 d

GANTT CHART — April 2014 / May 2014: Jerry King; Jerry King[50%],Steve Garcia[50%]; Jerry King[50%]; Jerry King[50%],Steve Ga; Travel Expense[$1,

Figure 3 - 14: Resource Group filter applied as a standard filter

To remove a filter and reapply the default *[No Filter]* filter, click the *Filter* pick list again and choose either the *[No Filter]* item or the *Clear Filter* item on the pick list.

Applying a Highlight Filter

When you apply any filter as a **highlight filter**, Project 2013 displays all rows in the project, but highlights the rows that meet the filter criteria using yellow cell background formatting. To apply any filter as a highlight filter, click the *View* tab. In the *Data* section of the *View* ribbon, click the *Highlight* pick list, and then select a highlight filter, as shown in Figure 3 - 15.

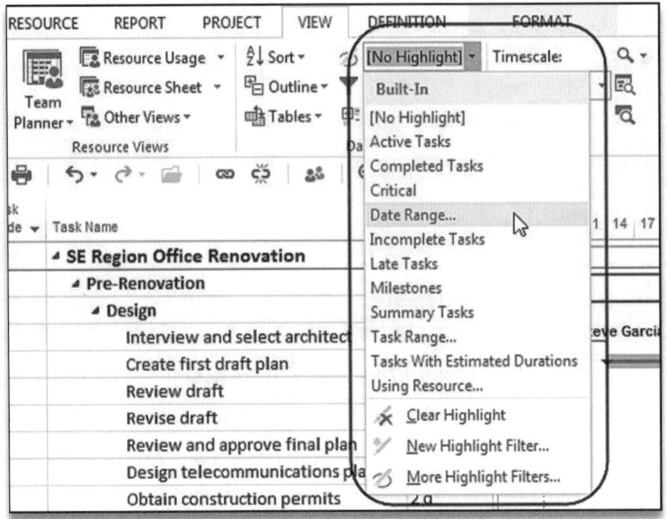

Figure 3 - 15: Apply a Highlight Filter

Notice in Figure 3 - 15 that the *Highlight* pick list allows you to choose from a list of the most commonly used filters, and provides other filtering options such as *Clear Highlight* to remove the highlight filter, *New Highlight Filter* to create a new highlight filter, and *More Highlight Filters* that opens the *More Filters* dialog. On the *Highlight* pick list, click the name of the filter you want to apply as a highlight filter.

If you click the *More Highlight Filters* item near the bottom of the *Highlight* pick list, the software displays the *More Filters* dialog shown previously in Figure 3 - 13. Remember that you can apply any filter as a highlight filter in the *More Filters* dialog by selecting the filter and then clicking the *Highlight* button.

Information: The list of filters shown on the *Highlight* pick list and the *Filter* pick list are **identical**. When you create a new filter and select the option to show it on the menu, Project 2013 displays the new filter on both the *Highlight* pick list and the *Filter* pick list automatically.

Information: You can also press the **F3** keyboard shortcut to remove the current highlight filter and reapply the *[No Filter]* or *All Resources* highlight filter.

Figure 3 - 16 shows the *Resource Group* filter applied as a highlight filter to a project, again filtering for members of the *Architect* group. Notice that the highlight filter displays all tasks in the project, but highlights the five tasks assigned to Jerry King (the architect).

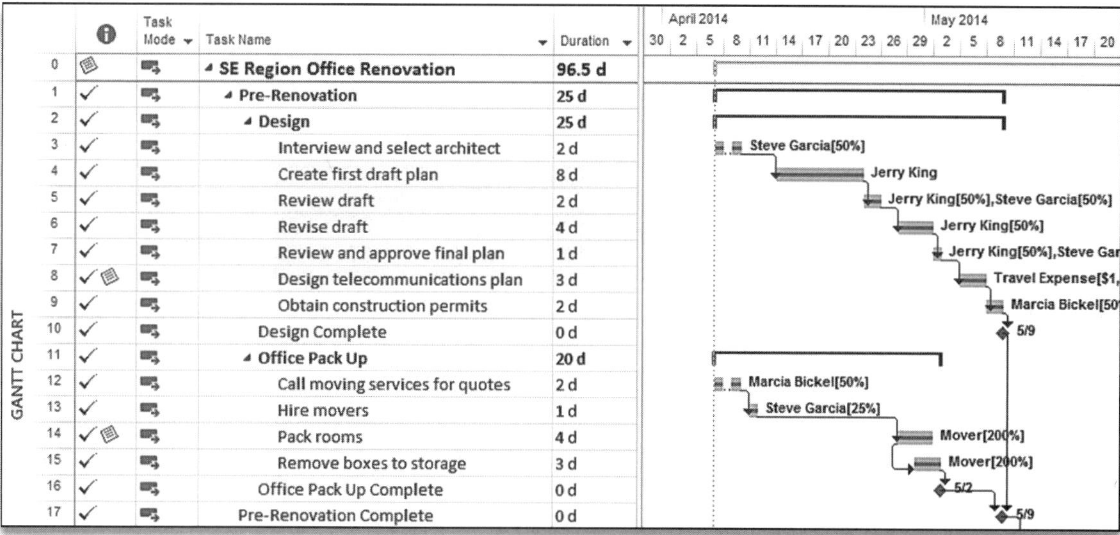

Figure 3 - 16: Resource Group filter applied as a highlight filter

To remove a *Highlight* filter and reapply the default *[No Filter]* filter, click the *Highlight* pick list again and choose either the *[No Highlight]* item or the *Clear Highlight* item on the pick list.

Using AutoFilter

AutoFilter is your third filtering option. Interestingly enough, Project 2013 actually offers you **two** ways to AutoFilter your project. To use either AutoFilter method, click the *AutoFilter* pick list arrow button in the column header of any column on which you want to filter, and the software displays the *AutoFilter* menu. Notice the *AutoFilter* menu for the *Duration* column shown in Figure 3 - 17. To apply an AutoFilter using the first method, deselect the *(Select All)* checkbox, select the checkboxes for one or more items on the menu, and then click the *OK* button. The software displays all rows that meet your AutoFilter criteria.

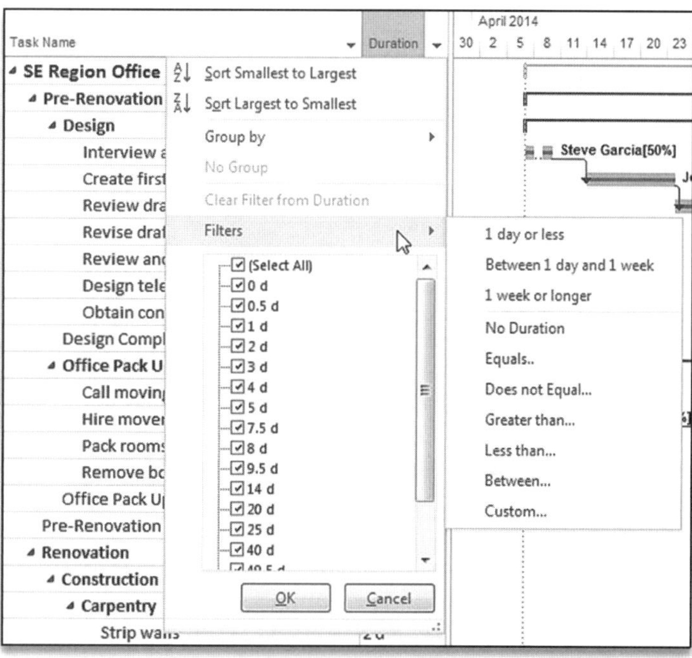

Figure 3 - 17: AutoFilter menu for the Duration column

Warning: When you apply an AutoFilter by selecting more than one checkbox on the *AutoFilter* menu, Project 2013 applies your filter criteria using a Boolean **Or** filter. This means that if you select the names of two resources, the software displays the tasks assigned to either of the selected resources.

To apply AutoFilter using the second method, click the *Filters* item on the *AutoFilter* menu and select one of the AutoFilters on the flyout menu. Notice in the *AutoFilter* menu shown previously in Figure 3 - 17 that the *Filters* flyout menu contains three default AutoFilters, including the *1 day or less*, the *Between 1 day and 1 week,* and the *1 week or longer* AutoFilters. Select one of the default AutoFilters and the software displays all rows that meet your AutoFilter criteria.

Notice that the *Filters* flyout menu also allows you to build your own custom AutoFilter by selecting an item like *Equals* on the flyout menu. If you select any of the flyout items other than the *No Duration* item, Project 2013 displays a *Custom AutoFilter* dialog similar to the one shown in Figure 3 - 18 when I selected the *Equals* item on the *Filters* flyout menu. Enter your own custom AutoFilter criteria in the *AutoFilter* dialog and then click the *OK* button. Again, the software displays all rows that meet your AutoFilter criteria.

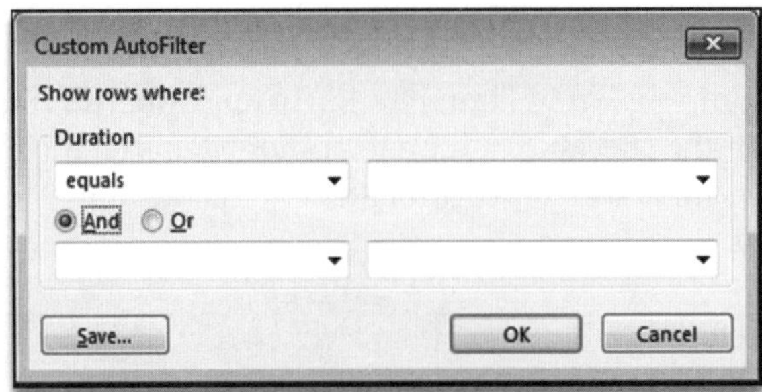

Figure 3 - 18: Custom AutoFilter dialog

Information: Notice that the *AutoFilter* menu shown previously in Figure 3 - 17 offers two options in addition to the AutoFiltering feature. You can click either the *Sort Smallest to Largest* or *Sort Largest to Smallest* item to apply sorting on the data in the column. You can also click the *Group by* item and apply grouping by selecting a relevant grouping item on the flyout menu.

Figure 3 - 19 shows my project after applying an AutoFilter to show all tasks with a *Duration* value of *0 days* so that I can see all of the milestones in my project. Notice that the software indicates that I applied AutoFilter to the *Duration* column by displaying a funnel symbol in place of the AutoFilter pick list arrow button.

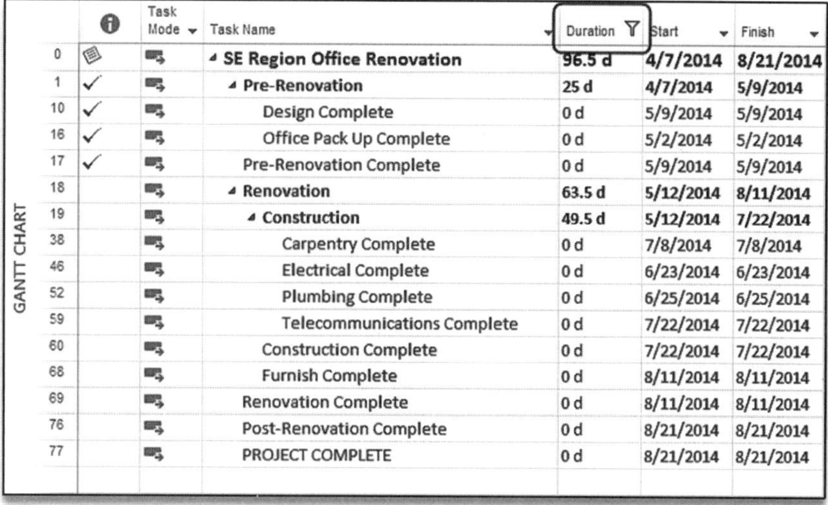

	Indicators	Task Mode	Task Name	Duration	Start	Finish
0			SE Region Office Renovation	96.5 d	4/7/2014	8/21/2014
1	✓		Pre-Renovation	25 d	4/7/2014	5/9/2014
10	✓		Design Complete	0 d	5/9/2014	5/9/2014
16	✓		Office Pack Up Complete	0 d	5/2/2014	5/2/2014
17	✓		Pre-Renovation Complete	0 d	5/9/2014	5/9/2014
18			Renovation	63.5 d	5/12/2014	8/11/2014
19			Construction	49.5 d	5/12/2014	7/22/2014
38			Carpentry Complete	0 d	7/8/2014	7/8/2014
46			Electrical Complete	0 d	6/23/2014	6/23/2014
52			Plumbing Complete	0 d	6/25/2014	6/25/2014
59			Telecommunications Complete	0 d	7/22/2014	7/22/2014
60			Construction Complete	0 d	7/22/2014	7/22/2014
68			Furnish Complete	0 d	8/11/2014	8/11/2014
69			Renovation Complete	0 d	8/11/2014	8/11/2014
76			Post-Renovation Complete	0 d	8/21/2014	8/21/2014
77			PROJECT COMPLETE	0 d	8/21/2014	8/21/2014

Figure 3 - 19: AutoFilter applied for tasks with 0 days Duration

To remove the current AutoFilter applied, click the funnel button in the column header in which you applied AutoFilter and then select the *Clear Filter from _____* item on the *AutoFilter* menu. Alternately, you can click the *Select All* item on the *AutoFilter* menu and then click the *OK* button.

Information: You can also press the **F3** keyboard shortcut to remove the current AutoFilter and reapply the *[No Filter]* or *All Resources* highlight filter.

Hands On Exercise

Exercise 3 - 3

Explore the new filters in Project 2013.

Information: To reduce the number of steps required to complete this Hands On Exercise, I modified the sample file so that you can see each of the new filters on both the *Filter* pick list and the *Highlight Filter* pick list.

1. Open the **Using New Filters 2013.mpp** sample file.
2. Click the *Project* tab to display the *Project* ribbon.
3. In the *Properties* section of the *Project* ribbon, click the *Project Information* button.
4. In the *Project Information* dialog, enter **02/02/15** in the *Current date* field (**not** in the *Start date* field) and then click the *OK* button.

I ask you to do the preceding step to temporarily "trick" Project 2013 into believing that today is actually Monday, February 2, 2015. After you save and close this sample project, the next time you open the project the *Current Date* value automatically reverts back to the date displayed on the system clock in your computer.

5. Click the *View* tab to display the *View* ribbon.
6. In the *Data* section of the *View* ribbon, click the *Filter* pick list and select the new *Completed Milestones* filter.

Using the *Completed Milestones* filter, notice how the software displays one completed milestone in the INSTALLATION phase of the project, and one completed milestone in the TRAINING phase of the project. You can determine that each milestone is completed by the blue check mark indicator shown in the *Indicators* column for each task.

7. Press the **F3** function key on your computer keyboard to clear the current filter.
8. Click the *Filter* pick list again and select the new *Late Milestones* filter.

Using the *Late Milestones* filter, notice how the software displays only the *Training Materials Created* milestone in the TRAINING phase of the project. Project 2013 determines that this milestone task is late because it is an incomplete milestone task that occurs earlier than the current date.

9. Press the **F3** function key on your computer keyboard to clear the current filter.
10. Click the *Filter* pick list again and select the new *Milestones Due This Month* filter.

When you use the *Milestones Due This Month* filter, Project 2013 uses the *Current Date* value to determine the current month. In this example, the software determines the current month is February 2015. Using this new filter, notice how the software displays two milestones due on February 1 (during the current month). Notice also that the software displays the late milestone task in the TRAINING phase. Remember that this filter displays milestones that occur during the current month, plus incomplete milestones in the past.

11. Press the **F3** function key on your computer keyboard to clear the current filter.
12. Click the *Filter* pick list again and select the new *No Actuals* filter.

Notice that the software displays the *Perform Server Stress Test* task in the INSTALLATION phase and the *Create Training Module 03* task in the TRAINING phase of the project. The *No Actuals* filter displays these two tasks because each of them is an unstarted task with a *Start* date earlier than the current date.

13. Press the **F3** function key on your computer keyboard to clear the current filter.
14. Click the *Filter* pick list again and select the new *No Resources Assigned* filter.

Notice that the software displays only the *Provide End User Training* task in the TRAINING phase of the project. The *No Resource Assigned* filter displays this task because the project manager forgot to assign team members to this task.

15. Press the **F3** function key on your computer keyboard to clear the current filter.

Before you apply the *Overallocated Tasks* filter, visually scan the *Indicators* column and look for any task on which an overallocated resource is assigned, shown using the "burning man" (red stick figure) indicator. You should see that there are four tasks with an overallocated resource assigned to them.

16. Click the *Filter* pick list again and select the new *Overallocated Tasks* filter.

Using the *Overallocated Tasks* filter, notice that the software displayed only **two** of the four tasks with overallocated resources assigned. Remember that this is due to an unfixed bug in the RTM version of Project 2013. The filter correctly shows Mike Andrews is overallocated on the *Perform Server Stress Test* task because this task occurs during nonworking time (on a weekend). The filter correctly shows Ruth Andrews is overallocated on the *Create Training Module 03* task because she is assigned at a *Units* value of *150%* on this task.

17. Press the **F3** function key on your computer keyboard to clear the current filter.
18. Click the *Filter* pick list again and select the new *Summary Task with Assigned Resources* filter.

Notice that the software displays the *Create Training Materials* summary task in the TRAINING phase. The *Summary Task with Assigned Resources* filter correctly displays the *Create Training Materials* summary task because the project manager accidently assigned a resource to this summary task.

19. Press the **F3** function key on your computer keyboard to clear the current filter.
20. Click the *Filter* pick list again and select the new *Tasks Due This Week* filter.

When you use the *Tasks Due This Week* filter, Project 2013 uses the *Current Date* value to determine the current week. In this example, the software determines the current week is February 1-7, 2015. Using this new filter, notice how the software displays two tasks due to finish during the current week. Notice that the *Perform Server Stress Test* task in the INSTALLATION phase is due to finish on February 1, while the *Conduct Skills Assessment* task in the TRAINING phase is due to finish on February 6.

21. Press the **F3** function key on your computer keyboard to clear the current filter.
22. Click the *Filter* pick list again and select the new *Tasks Starting Soon* filter.

When you use the *Tasks Starting Soon* filter, Project 2013 uses the *Current Date* value to determine the current week. In this example, the software determines the current week is February 1-7, 2015. Using this new filter, notice how the software displays two tasks scheduled to start during the current week. Notice also that the *Install Training Advisor Clients* task in the INSTALLATION phase and the *Conduct Skills Assessment* task in the TRAINING phase are both scheduled to start on February 2.

23. Press the **F3** function key on your computer keyboard to clear the current filter.
24. Click the *Filter* pick list again and select the new *Tasks with Duration < 8h* filter.

Using the *Tasks with Duration < 8h* filter, notice that the software displays only the milestone tasks in the project, along with their associated summary tasks.

25. Press the **F3** function key on your computer keyboard to clear the current filter.
26. Click the *Filter* pick list again and select the new *Upcoming Milestones* filter.

Using the *Upcoming Milestones* filter, notice that the software identifies three incomplete milestones earlier than the current date (in the past) and two milestone tasks later than the current date (in the future). Remember that this filter displays **all** incomplete milestones, regardless of whether they are scheduled in the past or in the future.

27. Press the **F3** function key on your computer keyboard to clear the current filter.
28. Save and close your **Using New Filters 2013.mpp** sample file.

Exercise 3 - 4

Apply a standard filter, a highlight filter, and AutoFilter in Project 2013.

1. Open the **Project Navigation 2013.mpp** sample file again.
2. Click the *View* tab to apply the *View* ribbon, if necessary.
3. In the *Data* section of the *View* ribbon, click the *Filter* pick list and select the *Using Resource…* filter.
4. In the *Using Resource* dialog, select the resource named *Russ Powell* and then click the *OK* button.

Notice how applying this filter as a standard filter displays only those tasks assigned to Russ Powell in the three phases of the project.

5. Press the **F3** function key on your computer keyboard to clear the current filter.
6. In the *Data* section of the *View* ribbon, click the *Highlight* pick list and select the *Using Resource…* filter.
7. In the *Using Resource* dialog, select *Russ Powell* again and click the *OK* button.

Notice how applying this filter as a highlight filter displays all tasks, but highlights all of Russ Powell's tasks using the yellow cell background color.

8. Press the **F3** function key on your computer keyboard to clear the current filter.
9. Drag the split bar to the right side so that you can see the *Resource Names* column.
10. Click the *AutoFilter* pick list button (arrow button) in the *Resource Names* column header.
11. In the *AutoFilter* menu, **deselect** the *(Select All)* checkbox.
12. In the *AutoFilter* menu, select the checkboxes for *Amy McKay* and *Russ Powell*, and then click the OK button.
13. Double-click the right edge of the *Resource Names* column header to widen the column.

Examine the names shown in the *Resource Names* column and notice how the *AutoFilter* displays all tasks assigned to either Amy McKay **or** Russ Powell. Keep in mind that *AutoFilter* uses the Boolean "or" logic rather than a Boolean "and" logic when filtering using multiple criteria.

14. Press the **F3** function key to clear the AutoFilter criteria.
15. Save but **do not** close the **Project Navigation 2013.mpp** sample file.

Understanding Groups

Project 2013 ships with 20 default groups, of which 13 are task groups and 7 are resource groups. You use groups to organize tasks or resources into groups with similar attributes or characteristics. Because the software applies groups within views, you must use task groups with task views and resource groups with resource views.

Applying a Group

To apply a group to your project data, click the *View* tab to display the *View* ribbon. In the *Data* section of the *View* ribbon, click the *Group By* pick list and select a group or select the *More Groups* item, as shown in Figure 3 - 20.

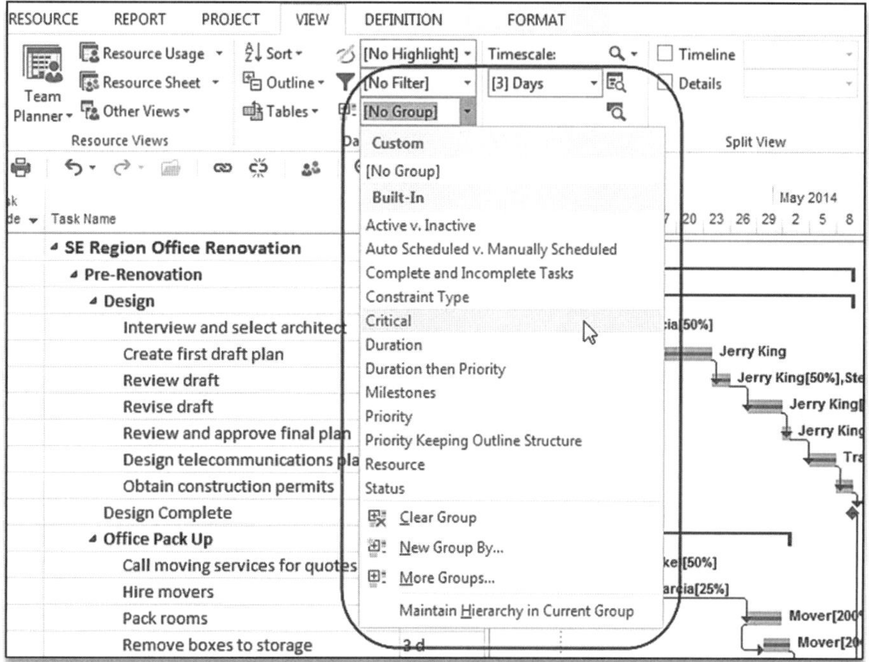

Figure 3 - 20: Apply a group

Notice that the *Group By* pick list allows you to choose from a list of most commonly used groups, plus you can choose additional grouping options. These additional options include *Clear Group* to remove the applied grouping, *New Group By* to create a new group from scratch, *More Groups* to display the *More Groups* dialog, and *Maintain Hierarchy in Current Group* to display the Work Breakdown Structure (WBS) of summary tasks for the grouped tasks.

If you select the *More Groups* item on the *Group By* pick list, the software displays the *More Groups* dialog shown in Figure 3 - 21. In the *More Groups* dialog, select any default or custom group and then click the *Apply* button.

Best Practice: In the *More Groups* dialog, Project 2013 allows you to edit any group by selecting the group and then clicking the *Edit* button. Although the software allows you to do this, MSProjectExperts recommends that you do not modify any of the default groups included with the software. Instead, if no default group meets your reporting needs copy a group that comes close and then modify that new group to meet your reporting needs.

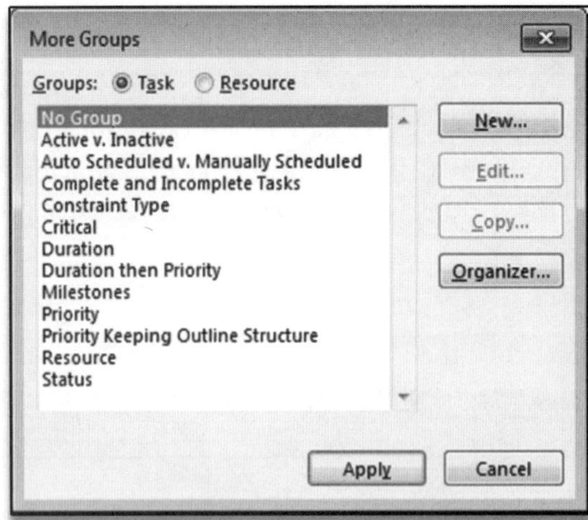

Figure 3 - 21: More Groups dialog

A very useful feature on the *Group By* pick list is the *Maintain Hierarchy in Current Group* item at the bottom of the list. When you apply a group in any task view, most of the default groups do not display the work breakdown structure (WBS) of summary tasks for the grouped tasks. This can create a confusing situation when you use same-named tasks in different summary task sections of your project. For example, Figure 3 - 22 shows a list of tasks in a project that includes summary tasks representing the phase and deliverable sections of the project. Notice that the Deliverable 1 and Deliverable 2 summary sections each contain four same-named tasks (Design, Build, Test, and Implement).

GANTT CHART

	Task Mode	Task Name	Duration	Start	Finish
1		**PHASE I**	**29 days**	**10/3/2016**	**11/10/2016**
2		**Deliverable 1**	**15 days**	**10/3/2016**	**10/21/2016**
3		Design	3 days	10/3/2016	10/5/2016
4		Build	5 days	10/6/2016	10/12/2016
5		Test	4 days	10/13/2016	10/18/2016
6		Implement	3 days	10/19/2016	10/21/2016
7		Deliverable 1 Complete	0 days	10/21/2016	10/21/2016
8		**Deliverable 2**	**14 days**	**10/24/2016**	**11/10/2016**
9		Design	4 days	10/24/2016	10/27/2016
10		Build	4 days	10/28/2016	11/2/2016
11		Test	3 days	11/3/2016	11/7/2016
12		Implement	3 days	11/8/2016	11/10/2016
13		Deliverable 2 Complete	0 days	11/10/2016	11/10/2016
14		PHASE I COMPLETE	0 days	11/10/2016	11/10/2016

Figure 3 - 22: Task list includes same-named tasks

In Figure 3 - 23, I applied the *Auto Scheduled v. Manually Scheduled* group to the task list shown previously in Figure 3 - 22. Notice how each grouping includes only regular tasks and milestone tasks, and does not include summary tasks. This means that I can see two tasks named *Design* in the *Auto Scheduled* group, but I cannot determine the WBS for either of these *Design* tasks.

	Task Mode	Task Name	Duration	Start	Finish
		Task Mode: Auto Scheduled	**29d**	**10/3/2016**	**11/10/2016**
3		Design	3 days	10/3/2016	10/5/2016
4		Build	5 days	10/6/2016	10/12/2016
7		Deliverable 1 Complete	0 days	10/21/2016	10/21/2016
9		Design	4 days	10/24/2016	10/27/2016
10		Build	4 days	10/28/2016	11/2/2016
13		Deliverable 2 Complete	0 days	11/10/2016	11/10/2016
14		PHASE I COMPLETE	0 days	11/10/2016	11/10/2016
		Task Mode: Manually Scheduled	***21d***	***10/13/2016***	***11/10/2016***
5		Test	4 days	10/13/2016	10/18/2016
6		Implement	3 days	10/19/2016	10/21/2016
11		Test	3 days	11/3/2016	11/7/2016
12		Implement	3 days	11/8/2016	11/10/2016

GANTT CHART

Figure 3 - 23: Auto Scheduled v. Manually Scheduled group does not include summary tasks

To eliminate the confusion about the WBS for each *Design* task, I click the *Group By* pick list again and select the *Maintain Hierarchy in Current Group* item. Figure 3 - 24 shows the result. Notice that the groupings now include the phase and deliverable summary sections for each regular task and milestone task. Because of this, I can now determine the WBS for each *Design* task in the *Auto Scheduled* group.

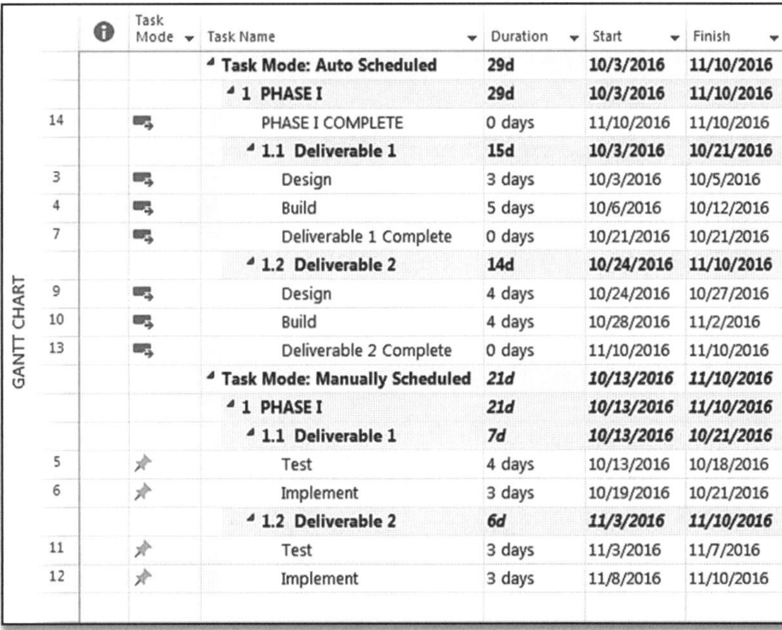

	Task Mode	Task Name	Duration	Start	Finish
		Task Mode: Auto Scheduled	**29d**	**10/3/2016**	**11/10/2016**
		1 PHASE I	**29d**	**10/3/2016**	**11/10/2016**
14		PHASE I COMPLETE	0 days	11/10/2016	11/10/2016
		1.1 Deliverable 1	**15d**	**10/3/2016**	**10/21/2016**
3		Design	3 days	10/3/2016	10/5/2016
4		Build	5 days	10/6/2016	10/12/2016
7		Deliverable 1 Complete	0 days	10/21/2016	10/21/2016
		1.2 Deliverable 2	**14d**	**10/24/2016**	**11/10/2016**
9		Design	4 days	10/24/2016	10/27/2016
10		Build	4 days	10/28/2016	11/2/2016
13		Deliverable 2 Complete	0 days	11/10/2016	11/10/2016
		Task Mode: Manually Scheduled	***21d***	***10/13/2016***	***11/10/2016***
		1 PHASE I	***21d***	***10/13/2016***	***11/10/2016***
		1.1 Deliverable 1	***7d***	***10/13/2016***	***10/21/2016***
5		Test	4 days	10/13/2016	10/18/2016
6		Implement	3 days	10/19/2016	10/21/2016
		1.2 Deliverable 2	***6d***	***11/3/2016***	***11/10/2016***
11		Test	3 days	11/3/2016	11/7/2016
12		Implement	3 days	11/8/2016	11/10/2016

GANTT CHART

Figure 3 - 24: Auto Scheduled v. Manually Scheduled group with "Maintain Hierarchy" applied

Information: The *Maintain hierarchy* option is available only when you apply a task group. You cannot display the hierarchy information for resource groups because resources do not have work breakdown structure information. This means that the software disables the *Maintain Hierarchy in Current Group* item on the *Group By* pick list in any resource view.

To remove a group and reapply the default *[No Group]* group, click the *Group By* pick list and select either the *[No Group]* item or the *Clear Group* item on the pick list.

Information: Press the **Shift + F3** key combination on your computer keyboard to remove the current group and reapply the *[No Group]* group.

Hands On Exercise

Exercise 3 - 5

Apply task and resource groups in Project 2013.

1. Return to the **Project Navigation 2013.mpp** sample file, if necessary.
2. Click the *View* tab to apply the *View* ribbon, if necessary
3. In the *Data* section of the *View* ribbon, click the *Group By* pick list and select the *Duration* group.

Notice that the *Duration* group organizes tasks into groups by their *Duration* value. To most project managers, this grouping is **not** very helpful.

4. In the *Resource Views* section of the *View* ribbon, click the *Resource Usage* button to apply the *Resource Usage* view.
5. Click the *Group By* pick list button and select the *Resource Group* item on the list.
6. Scroll down to the *Construction* grouping.

Notice that this group, when applied in the *Resource Usage* view, shows you the total amount of *Work* assigned to the resources in the *Construction* group (572 hours).

7. Click the *Group By* pick list button and select the *Assignments Keeping Outline Structure* item on the list.

Notice that this group, when applied in the *Resource Usage* view, shows you the Work Breakdown Structure (WBS) for every task assignment. To most project managers, this grouping is **very helpful**!

8. In the *Task Views* section of the *View* ribbon, click the *Gantt Chart* button to apply the *Gantt Chart* view.
9. Save and close your **Project Navigation 2013.mpp** sample file.

Module 04

Project Definition

Learning Objectives

After completing this module, you will be able to:

- Create a new project
- Define a new project using the six-step method recommended by MSProjectExperts
- Understand the date changes in Project 2013
- Set nonworking time and the working schedule on the Standard calendar
- Create new base calendars
- Specify the Task Mode setting for new tasks
- Specify options settings for a project
- Save your project using an alternate file type

Inside Module 04

Creating a New Project

To create a new project in Project 2013, click the *File* tab to display the *Backstage*. Click the *New* tab to display the *New* page shown in Figure 4 - 1.

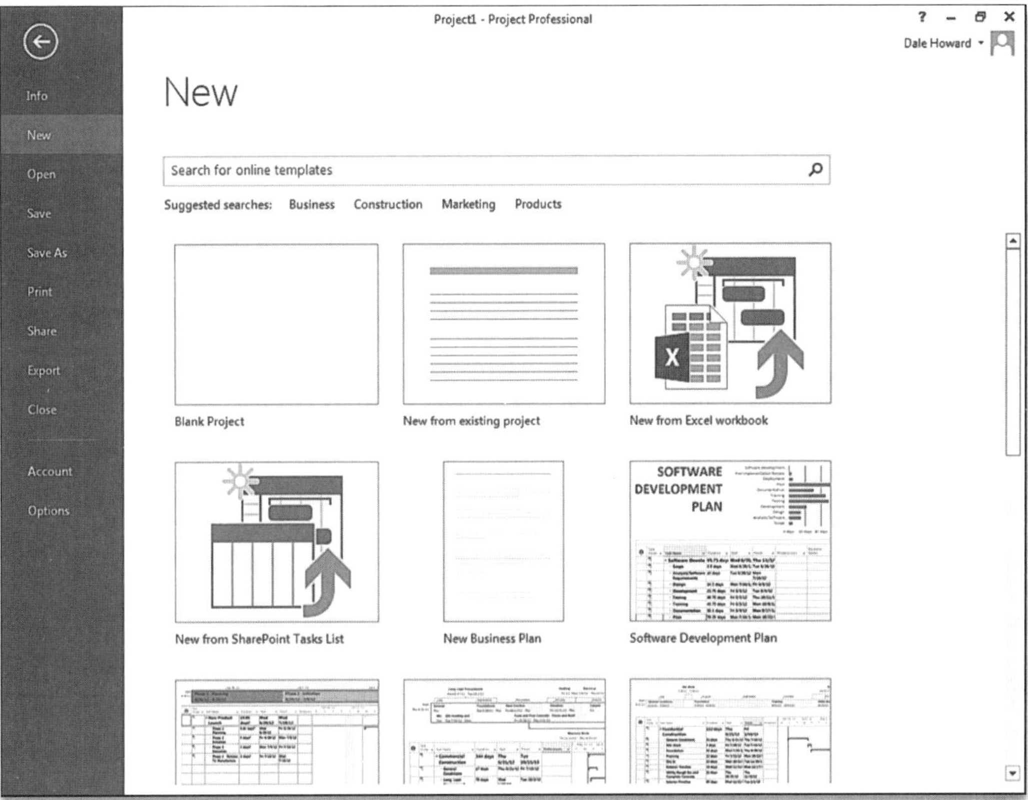

Figure 4 - 1: New page in the Backstage

The *New* page shows all of the types of templates available for you to use to create a new project. Notice that the *New* page includes the following types of templates:

- **Blank Project** – Use this template to create a new blank project that includes all of the options you specify in the *Project Options* dialog.
- **New from existing project** – Use this template to create a new project that is a copy of an existing project.
- **New from Excel workbook** – Use this template to create a new project from a Microsoft Excel workbook using the *Import/Export Wizard.*
- **New from SharePoint Tasks List** – Use this template to create a new project from a Tasks list in a SharePoint site. To use this feature, someone must first create the Tasks list in the SharePoint site.

In addition to the four types of templates listed previously, the *New* page also displays a selection of Project 2013 templates available in the *Office.com* website. Microsoft allows you to download and use any of these templates free of charge. Notice that each *Office.com* template button includes a preview picture of the file created from that template type.

Information: To pin one of the *Office.com* templates so that Project 2013 always displays the template at the top of the *Start* page and the *New* page in the *Backstage*, float your mouse pointer over the template icon and then click the "pushpin" symbol in the lower-right corner of the icon.

At the top of the *New* page, Project 2013 offers you a *Search for online templates* field in which you can search for other project templates in the *Office.com* website, along with four links on the *Suggested searches* line to allow you to search for commonly used templates such as business or construction templates. If the *New* page does not display the type of template you want to use to create a new project, you can use the search features on this page to locate an appropriate template in the *Office.com* website.

To search for a project template, enter your search term in the *Search for online templates* field and then click the *Start searching* button at the right end of the field. Alternately, you can click one of the links in the *Suggested searches* line, such as the *Marketing* link. During the search process, Project 2013 briefly displays a *SEARCHING THOUSANDS OF ONLINE TEMPLATES* message, and then reveals the search results on the *New* page as shown in Figure 4 - 2. Notice that using the search term *Products* yielded three project templates.

In addition, the *Category* sidepane on the right side of the page displays sub-categories of the templates available in the *Office.com* website. For example, notice that the *Office.com* website includes three *Analysis* templates. To further filter the list of templates, click one of the template categories shown in the *Category* list. Project 2013 shows you all of the templates that match the category you selected in the *Search for online templates* field or in the *Suggested searches* line, and the sub-category you selected in the *Category* list. After conducting a search for templates in the *Office.com* website, you can return to the unfiltered *New* page by clicking the *Home* button to the left of the *Search for online templates* field.

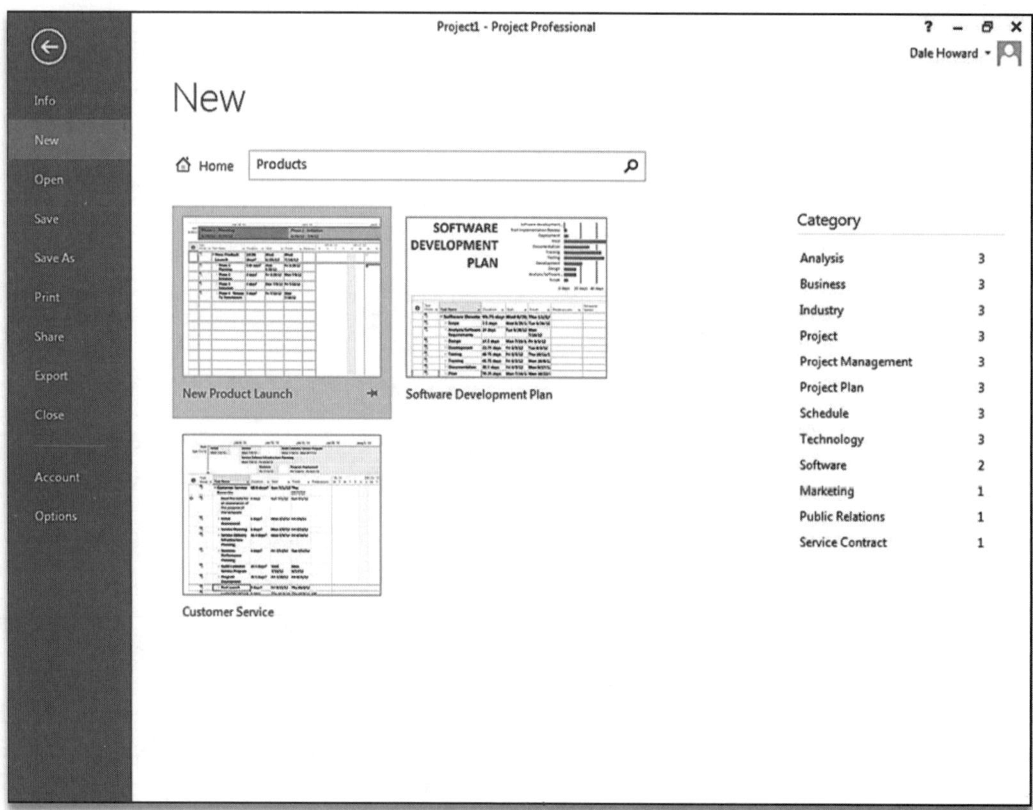

Figure 4 - 2: Search for a template in Office.com

Creating a New Project from a Template

Project 2013 offers several ways to create a new project from a template. To create a new blank project using the blank project template included with the software, click the *Blank Project* icon on the *New* page. The software creates a new blank project and applies the default *Gantt with Timeline* view.

To create a new project from one of the *Office.com* templates, click the icon for the template you want to use. Project 2013 displays a preview dialog for the selected template similar to the one shown in Figure 4 - 3.

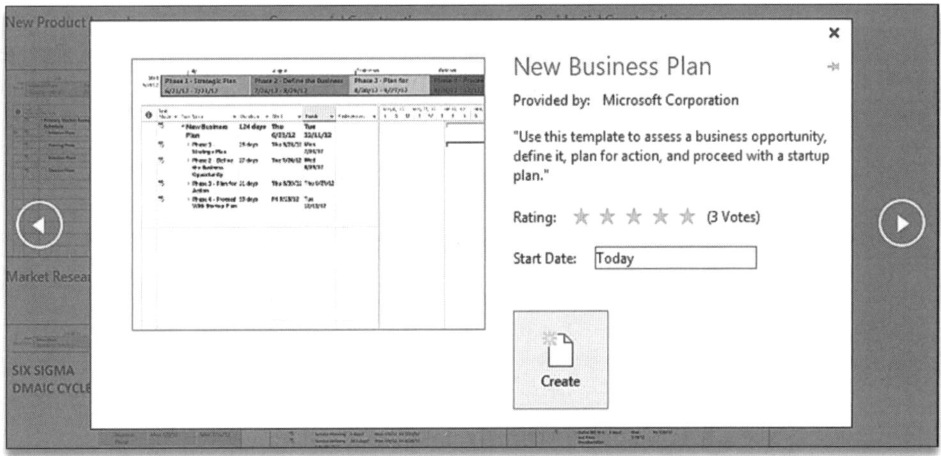

Figure 4 - 3: New Business Plan template preview dialog

Notice that the dialog shown in Figure 4 - 3 displays a preview of the *New Business Plan* template, which includes a pre-built *Timeline* report at the top of the template. The dialog also includes additional information about the template, including the name of the template creator (in this case, Microsoft Corporation), a description of when and how to use the template, and the rating of the template by members of the user community.

Information: To navigate in the preview dialog to the previous template or the next template on the *New* page, click the *Previous* or *Next* buttons (big white arrow buttons) on either side of the preview dialog.

To create a new project from the selected template, enter the *Start* date of the project in the *Start Date* field and then click the *Create* button. Project 2013 downloads a copy of the template, saves it in the default *Templates* folder on your computer's hard drive, and then creates a new project from the selected template, ready for you to use to plan your project.

Accessing Templates Stored in Your Templates Folder

Because of new functionality in Office 2013, the *New* page in the *Backstage* **does not** automatically allow you to create a new project from any template stored in your default *Templates* folder. This includes templates that you download from the *Office.com* website and templates that you create personally and save in your *Templates* folder. If you want to create a new project from any template stored in your *Templates* folder, you must complete the following steps first:

1. Click the *File* tab and then click the *Options* button in the *Backstage*.

2. Click the *Save* tab in the *Project Options* dialog. The software displays the *Save* page of the *Project Options* dialog shown in Figure 4 - 4.

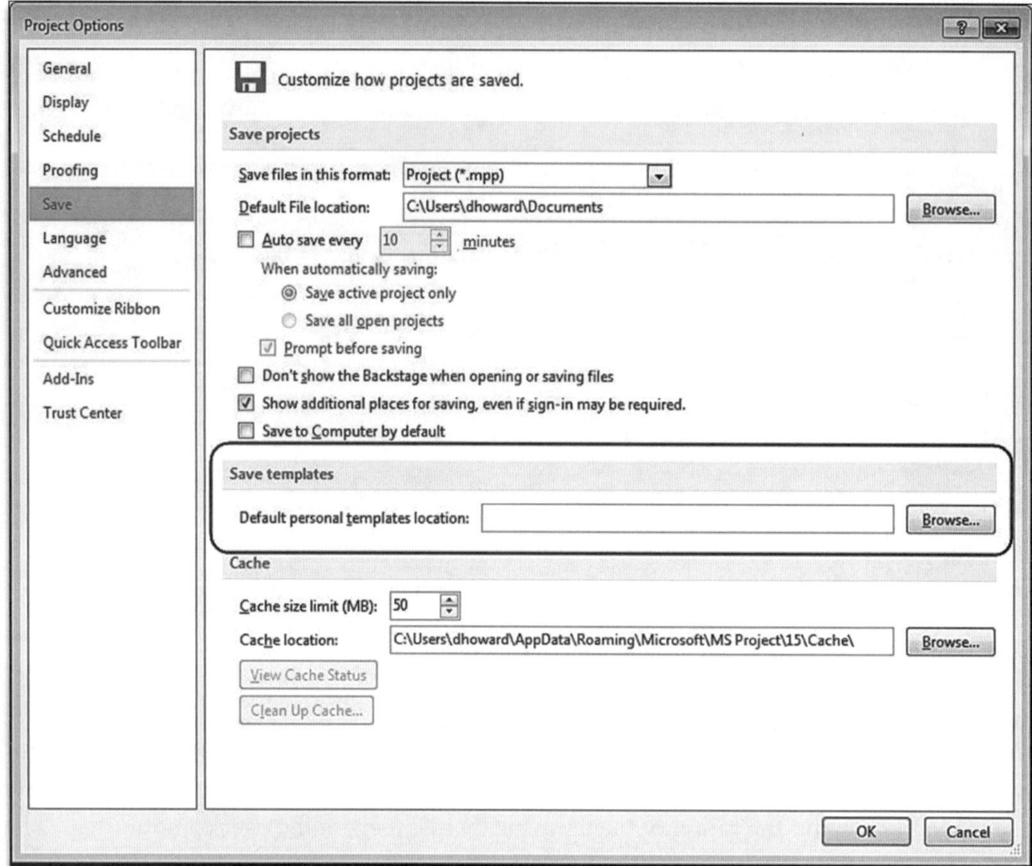

Figure 4 - 4: Project Options dialog, Save page

3. In the *Default personal templates location* field in the *Save templates* section of the dialog, manually enter the path for your default *Templates* folder based on the example below, or use the *Browse* button to navigate to your default *Templates* folder.

C:\Users\YourWindowsUserID\AppData\Roaming\Microsoft\Templates

4. Click the *OK* button.

The next time you navigate to the *Start* page or to the *New* page in the *Backstage*, Project 2013 displays two new links in the upper left corner of the page: the *FEATURED* link and the *PERSONAL* link. When selected, the *FEATURED* link displays *Office.com* templates plus the four default template types. Click the *PERSONAL* link to view project templates stored in your default *Templates* folder, as shown in Figure 4 - 5. Notice that I have four templates available for use in my default *Templates* folder, all downloaded from the *Office.com* website.

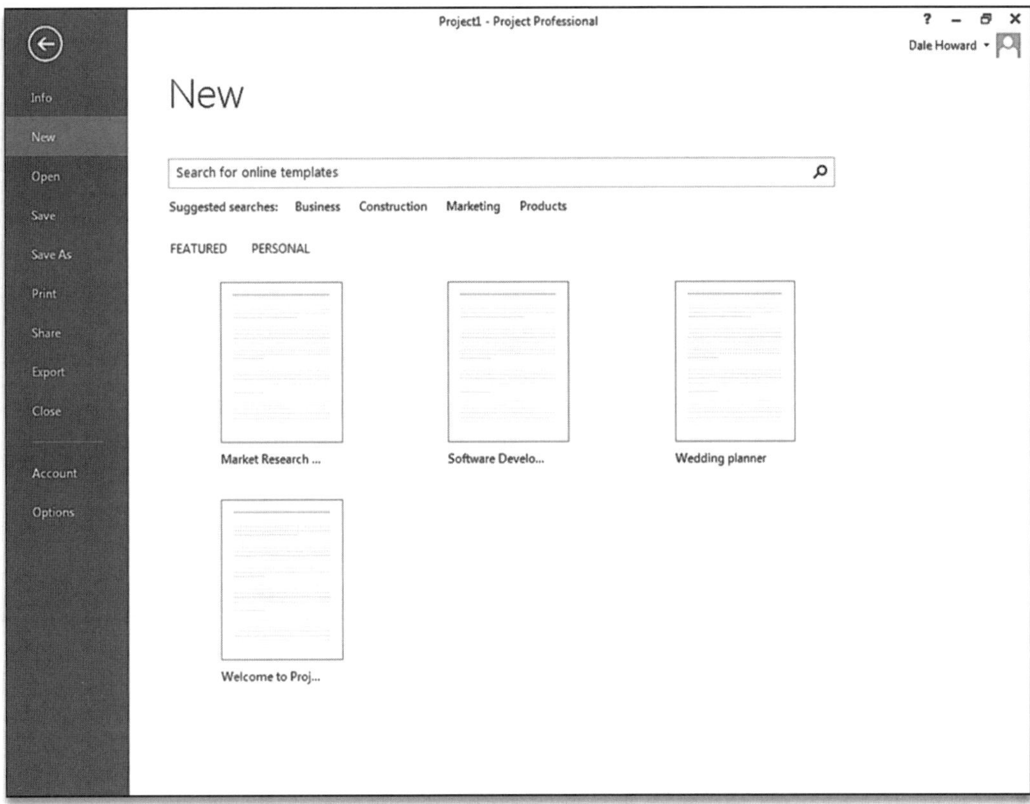

Figure 4 - 5: New page shows templates in the default Templates folder

Warning: If you want to use templates in the default *Templates* folder with any of your other Office 2013 applications, you must repeat the same process detailed above **in each of these applications individually**. There is currently no way to specify the default *Templates* folder for all of the Office 2013 applications simultaneously.

To create a new project from a template stored in your default *Templates* folder, click the *PERSONAL* link on the *New* page of the *Backstage* and then click the icon for the template you want to use. Project 2013 displays a preview dialog similar to the one shown in Figure 4 - 6. In this dialog, enter a date in the *Start Date* field and then click the *Create* button. The software creates the new project as a copy of the template you selected.

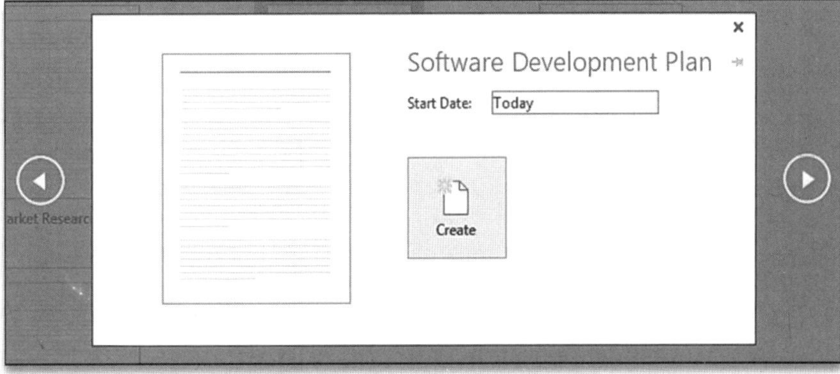

Figure 4 - 6: Create a new project

Information: To navigate in the dialog to the previous template or the next template on the *New* page, click the *Previous* or *Next* buttons (big white arrow buttons) on either side of the dialog.

Hands On Exercise

Exercise 4 - 1

Create a new project from an Office.com template.

Warning: Before you work this Hands On Exercise, confirm that you have Internet access. You must have Internet access to view and download available templates from the Office.com website.

1. Click the *File* tab and then click the *New* tab in the *Backstage*.
2. Examine the list of project templates available on the *New* page, including the templates available for download from the *Office.com* website.
3. In the *Search* section at the top of the page, click the *Marketing* link to search for marketing templates.
4. In the *Category* sidepane on the right side of the page, select the *Software* item to limit the search to software-related templates.
5. Click the icon for the *New Product Launch* template.

In the *New Product Launch* dialog, notice the preview image of the project template, along with the creator of the template (Microsoft), and the description of this template.

6. In the *Start Date* field in the *New Product Launch* dialog, enter a date **3 months in the future** and then click the *Create* button.
7. Click the *Task* tab to display the *Task* ribbon.
8. In the *View* section of the *Task* ribbon, click the *Gantt Chart* pick list button and select the *Gantt Chart* view.
9. Click the *File* tab and then click the *Save As* tab in the *Backstage*.
10. On the *Save As* page, click the *Computer* link and then click the *Browse* button.
11. In the *Save As* dialog, navigate to the folder where you unzipped your sample files for this class.
12. In the *Save As* dialog, enter **Launch New Mobile App 2013** in the *File name* field, and then click the *Save* button.
13. Click the *File* tab and then click the *Close* button to close your new project.

Exercise 4 - 2

Set up Project 2013 to access your *Templates* folder.

1. Click the *File* tab and then click the *Options* tab in the *Backstage*.

2. In the *Project Options* dialog, click the *Save* tab to display the *Save* page of the dialog.

3. In the *Default personal templates location* field in the *Save templates* section of the dialog, enter the path of your default *Templates* folder in the following form (or click the *Browse* button and browse to your default *Templates* folder):

   C:\Users\YourUserID\AppData\Roaming\Microsoft\Templates

4. Click the *OK* button to close the *Project Options* dialog.

5. Click the *File* tab and then click the *New* tab again in the *Backstage*.

At the top of the *New* page, notice the new *FEATURED* and *PERSONAL* links.

6. Click the *PERSONAL* link to see the *New Product Launch* template, which you just downloaded from the *Office.com* website.

7. Click the *New Product Launch* template on the *PERSONAL* page.

In the *New Product Launch* dialog, notice that you do not see a preview image of the project template, nor can you see the creator of the template or the description of this template. This is because the template is stored on your computer and not stored in the *Office.com* website.

8. In the upper right corner of the *New Product Launch* dialog, click the *Close* (**X**) button to return to the *New* page in the *Backstage*.

9. Press the **Escape** key on your computer keyboard to return to the main Project 2013 user interface.

Creating a New Project from an Existing Project

To create a new project from an existing project, click the *New from existing* button in the *New* page of the *Backstage*. Project 2013 displays the *New from Existing Project* dialog shown in Figure 4 - 7. In the dialog, navigate to a folder containing existing projects, select a project, and then click the *Open* button.

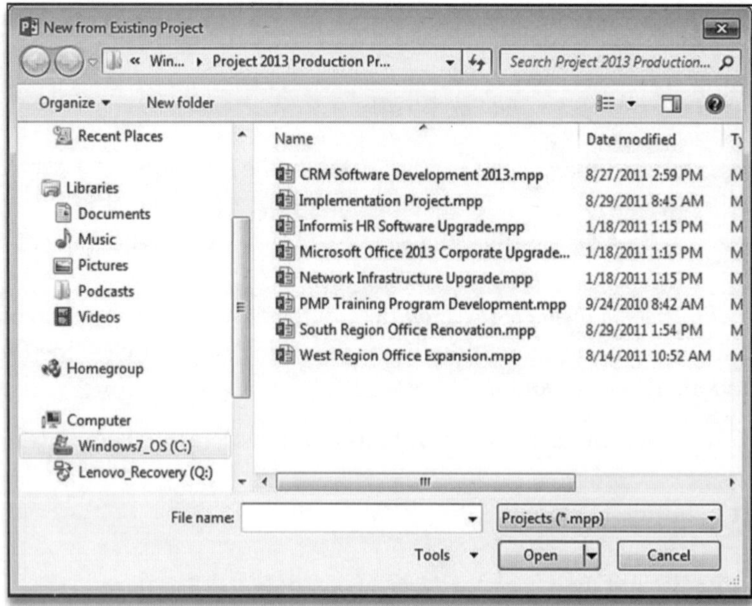

Figure 4 - 7: New from Existing Project dialog

When you use this method to create a new project, the software makes an **exact copy** of the existing project using the file name of the existing project. This means that the new project contains all of the data in the existing project, including task progress, constraints, deadline dates, resource names, resource assignments, baseline data, etc. At this point, you must clean up the project by performing actions such as removing task progress and removing/editing constraints and deadline dates.

When you are ready to save the new project created from an existing project, click the *File* tab and then click the *Save* button in the *Backstage*. Project 2013 displays the *Save As* page shown in Figure 4 - 8.

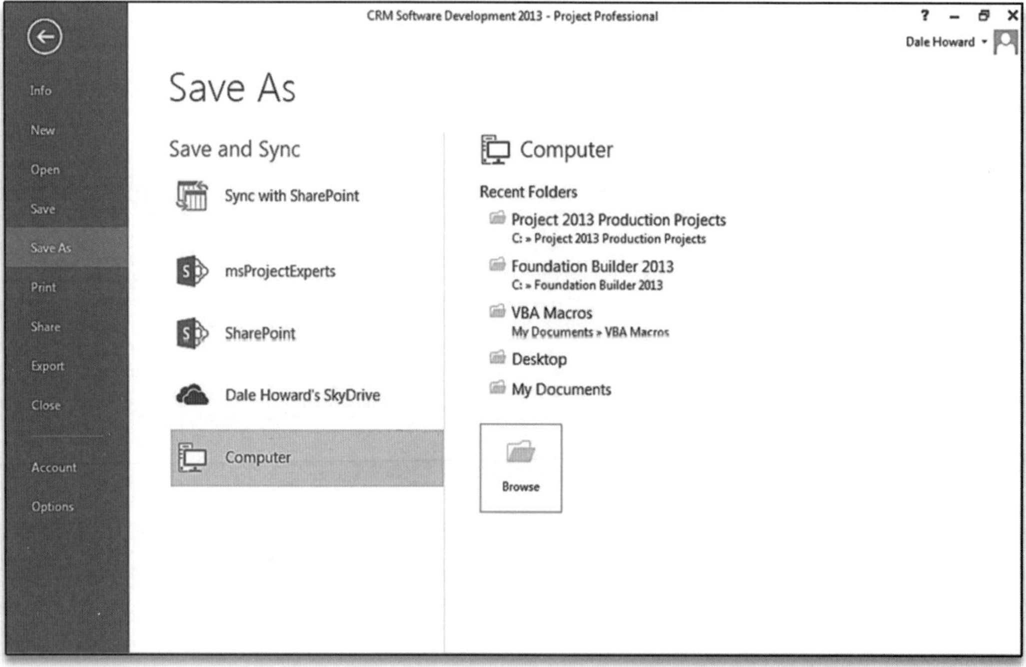

Figure 4 - 8: Save As page in the Backstage after creating a new project from an existing project

In the *Save As* page, click the *Browse* button. The software displays the *Save As* dialog shown in Figure 4 - 9. In the *Save As* dialog, navigate to the location where you want to save the new project, enter a new name for the project, and then click the *Save* button.

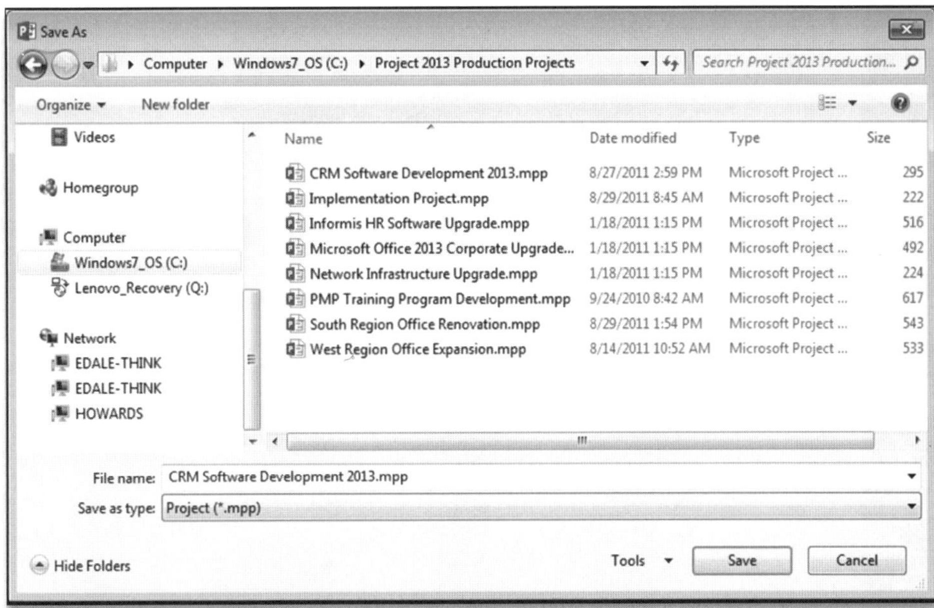

Figure 4 - 9: Save As dialog

Creating a New Project from an Excel Workbook

Project 2013 allows you to create a new project from the data stored in an Excel workbook. Before you use this feature, however, you must verify that the data in the Excel workbook conforms to the data required by Project 2013. At a minimum, the workbook should include the names of tasks, with items like *Duration* and *Work* specified for each task. The easiest way to see the Excel workbook data that Project 2013 requires is to export an existing project file as an Excel workbook and then to study the resulting Excel workbook.

Exporting a Project 2013 File as an Excel Workbook

To export an existing project as an Excel workbook, open the existing project and then complete the following steps:

1. Click the *File* tab and then click the *Export* tab to display the *Export* page in the *Backstage*.

2. On the *Export* page, select the *Save Project as File* option to view the file options for exporting a project, as shown in Figure 4 - 10.

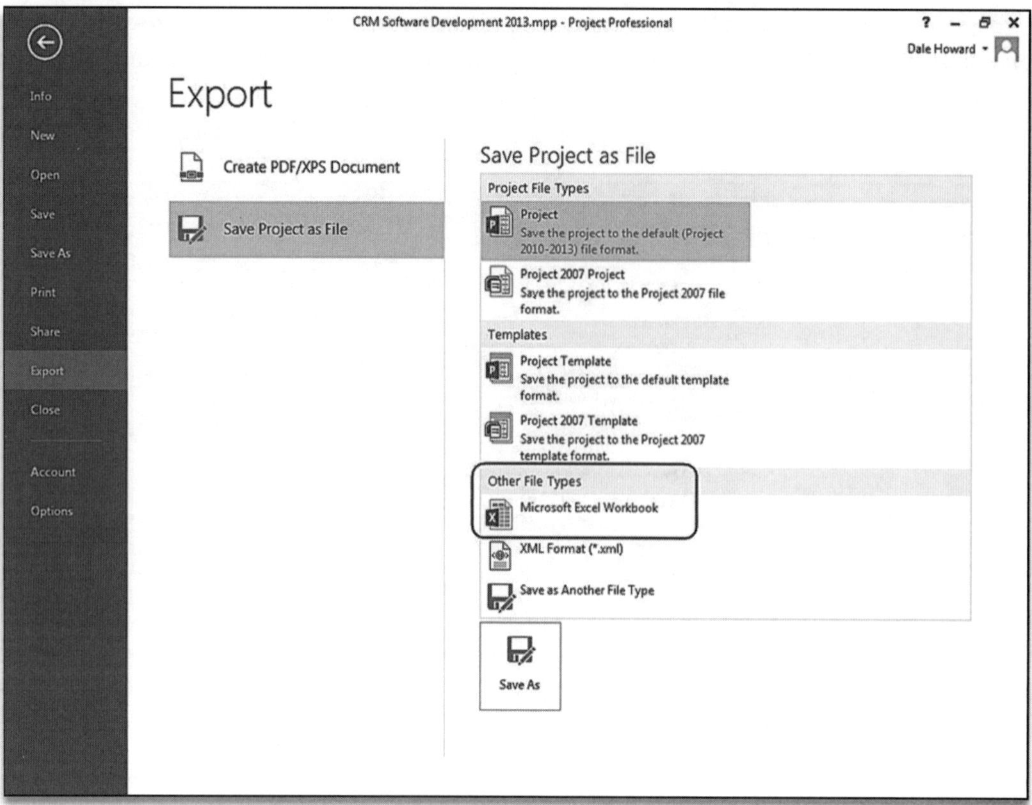

Figure 4 - 10: Export page in the Backstage

3. In the *Other File Types* section in the list of available file types, select the *Microsoft Excel Workbook* option, and then click the *Save As* button. The software displays the *Save As* dialog shown in Figure 4 - 11.

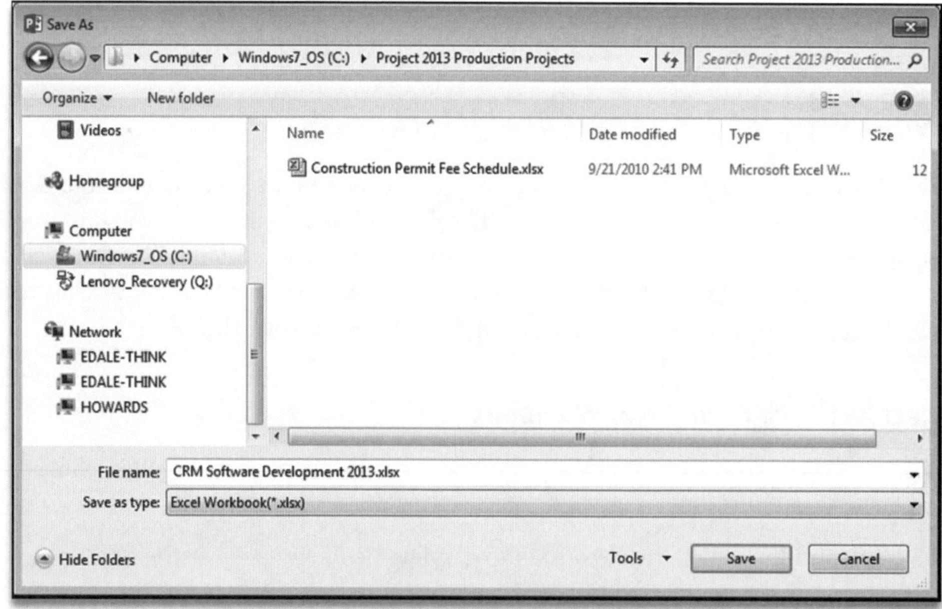

Figure 4 - 11: Save As dialog

4. In the *Save As* dialog, click the *Save* button. Project 2013 displays the *Welcome* page of the *Export Wizard* dialog shown in Figure 4 - 12.

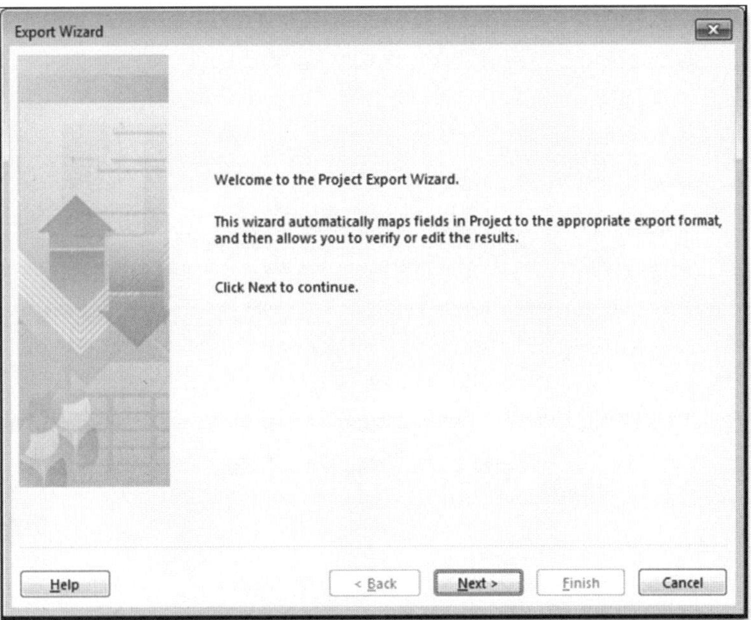

Figure 4 - 12: Export Wizard dialog, Welcome page

5. In the *Export Wizard* dialog, click the *Next* button. The software displays the *Data* page of the *Export Wizard* dialog shown in Figure 4 - 13.

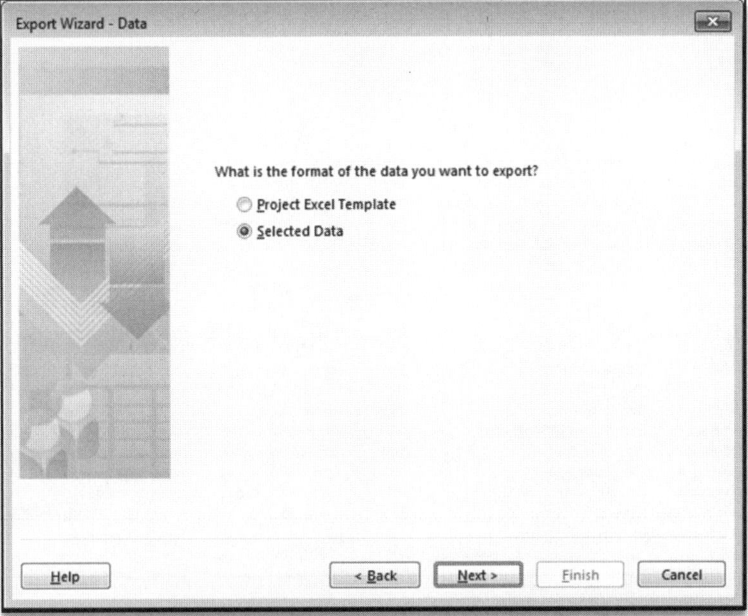

Figure 4 - 13: Export Wizard dialog, Data page

6. On the *Data* page of the *Export Wizard* dialog, select the *Project Excel Template* option, and then click the *Finish* button.

Warning: Because of an unfixed bug in the release (RTM) version of Project 2013, the software displays the false error dialog shown in Figure 4 - 14 after you click the *Finish* button in the *Export Wizard* dialog. To complete the export operation, click the *OK* button in the error dialog to allow the software to export the project file to an Excel workbook.

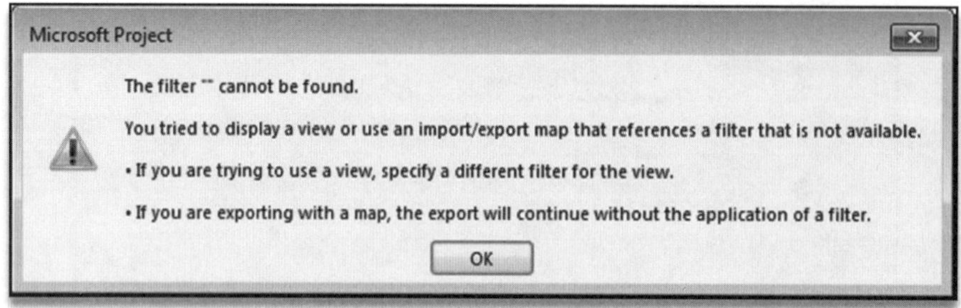

Figure 4 - 14: False error dialog

Using the *Project Excel* template, Project 2013 exports key data about project tasks, resources, and assignments into an Excel workbook. The resulting workbook contains three worksheets, labeled *Task_Table, Resource_Table,* and *Assignment_Table*. Each worksheet contains the type of data indicated in the name of the worksheet, meaning that you see the exported task data in the *Task_Table* worksheet. For example, Figure 4 - 15 shows the *Task_Table* worksheet for a Project 2013 file exported to an Excel workbook. Notice that this worksheet contains many of the relevant task columns required in Project 2013, including the *Name* (task name), *Duration, Start, Finish,* and *Predecessors* columns. After studying the exported project data in the Excel workbook, create your own new Excel workbook with the data you want to import into a Project 2013 project file.

	A	B	C	D	E	F	G	H	I
1	ID	Active	Task Mode	Name	Duration	Start	Finish	Predecessors	Outline L
2	0	Yes	Auto Scheduled	CRM Software Development	68 d	May 6, 2013 8:00 AM	August 12, 2013 8:00 AM		0
3	1	Yes	Auto Scheduled	Analysis/Software Requirements	11 d	May 6, 2013 8:00 AM	May 20, 2013 5:00 PM		1
4	2	Yes	Auto Scheduled	Conduct needs analysis	5 d	May 6, 2013 8:00 AM	May 10, 2013 5:00 PM		2
5	3	Yes	Auto Scheduled	Draft software specifications	3 d	May 13, 2013 8:00 AM	May 15, 2013 5:00 PM	2	2
6	4	Yes	Auto Scheduled	Develop budget	2 d	May 16, 2013 8:00 AM	May 17, 2013 5:00 PM	3	2
7	5	Yes	Auto Scheduled	Develop delivery timeline	1 d	May 20, 2013 8:00 AM	May 20, 2013 5:00 PM	4	2
8	6	Yes	Auto Scheduled	Analysis complete	0 d	May 20, 2013 5:00 PM	May 20, 2013 5:00 PM	5	2
9	7	Yes	Auto Scheduled	Design	9 d	May 21, 2013 8:00 AM	June 3, 2013 5:00 PM		1
10	8	Yes	Auto Scheduled	Develop functional specifications	5 d	May 21, 2013 8:00 AM	May 28, 2013 5:00 PM	6	2
11	9	Yes	Auto Scheduled	Develop prototype based on functiona	4 d	May 29, 2013 8:00 AM	June 3, 2013 5:00 PM	8	2
12	10	Yes	Auto Scheduled	Design complete	0 d	June 3, 2013 5:00 PM	June 3, 2013 5:00 PM	9	2
13	11	Yes	Auto Scheduled	Development	23 d	June 4, 2013 8:00 AM	July 5, 2013 5:00 PM		1
14	12	Yes	Auto Scheduled	Identify design parameters	2 d	June 4, 2013 8:00 AM	June 5, 2013 5:00 PM	10	2
15	13	Yes	Auto Scheduled	Develop code	20 d	June 6, 2013 8:00 AM	July 3, 2013 5:00 PM	12	2
16	14	Yes	Auto Scheduled	Developer testing	20 d	June 7, 2013 8:00 AM	July 5, 2013 5:00 PM	13SS+1d	2
17	15	Yes	Auto Scheduled	Development complete	0 d	July 5, 2013 5:00 PM	July 5, 2013 5:00 PM	14	2
18	16	Yes	Manually Scheduled	Testing	17 d	July 18, 2013 8:00 AM	August 12, 2013 8:00 AM		1
19	17	Yes	Manually Scheduled	Review modular code	5 d	July 18, 2013 8:00 AM	July 24, 2013 5:00 PM	15	2
20	18	Yes	Manually Scheduled	Test component modules to product s	2 d	July 25, 2013 8:00 AM	July 26, 2013 5:00 PM	17	2
21	19	Yes	Manually Scheduled	Identify anomalies to product specific	3 d	July 29, 2013 8:00 AM	July 31, 2013 5:00 PM	18	2
22	20	Yes	Manually Scheduled	Modify code	4 d				2
23	21	No	Manually Scheduled	Re-test modified code	2 d	August 8, 2013 8:00 AM	August 9, 2013 5:00 PM		2
24	22	Yes	Manually Scheduled	Testing Complete	0 d	August 12, 2013 8:00 AM	August 12, 2013 8:00 AM		2
25									
26									
27									

Task_Table / Resource_Table / Assignment_Table

Ready 100%

Figure 4 - 15: Task_Table worksheet in the Excel workbook

Best Practice: If you manually create an Excel workbook containing project data, MSProjectExperts recommends that you include the *Outline Level* column in the worksheet containing task data. Project 2013 needs the data in this column to display the Work Breakdown Structure (WBS) of summary tasks and subtasks when it imports the data from the Excel workbook. In addition, MSProjectExperts recommends that you name the columns in Excel using exactly the same names used in Project 2013, as doing so makes the import process much easier. This means that in your Excel workbook, you should use the *Name* column to refer to the *Task Name* column in Project 2013. The reason for this is because the real name of the *Task Name* column is actually *Name*. *Task Name* is simply the label or "nickname" for this column in Project 2013.

Creating a New Project from an Excel Workbook

After creating an Excel workbook containing project data, you are ready to create a new project from the Excel workbook by completing the following steps:

1. Using Project 2013, click the *File* tab and then click the *New* tab in the *Backstage*.

2. On the *New* page, click the *New from Excel Workbook* icon. The software displays the *Open* dialog shown in Figure 4 - 16.

Warning: Because of an unfixed bug in the release (RTM) version of Project 2013, the software sets the file type in the *Open* dialog to *XML Format (*.xml)* instead of the *Excel Workbook (*.xlsx)* file format. To work around this bug, click the *File Type* pick list in the lower right corner of the *Open* dialog and select the *Excel Workbook (*.xlsx)* file format.

3. In the *Open* dialog, navigate to the folder containing the Excel workbook you want to import as a new project file.

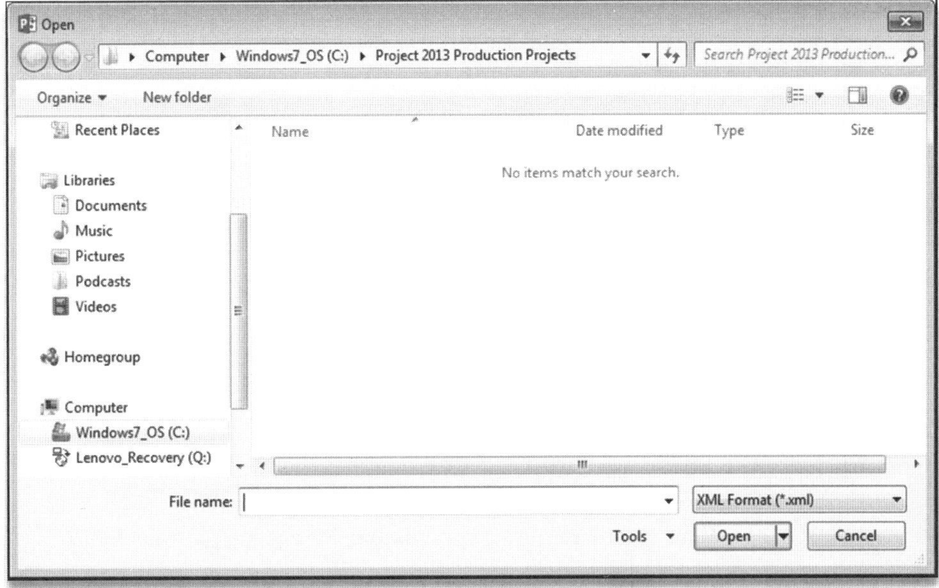

Figure 4 - 16: Open dialog

4. In the *Open* dialog, select the Excel workbook containing project data and then click the *Open* button. The software displays the *Welcome* page of the *Import Wizard* dialog shown in Figure 4 - 17.

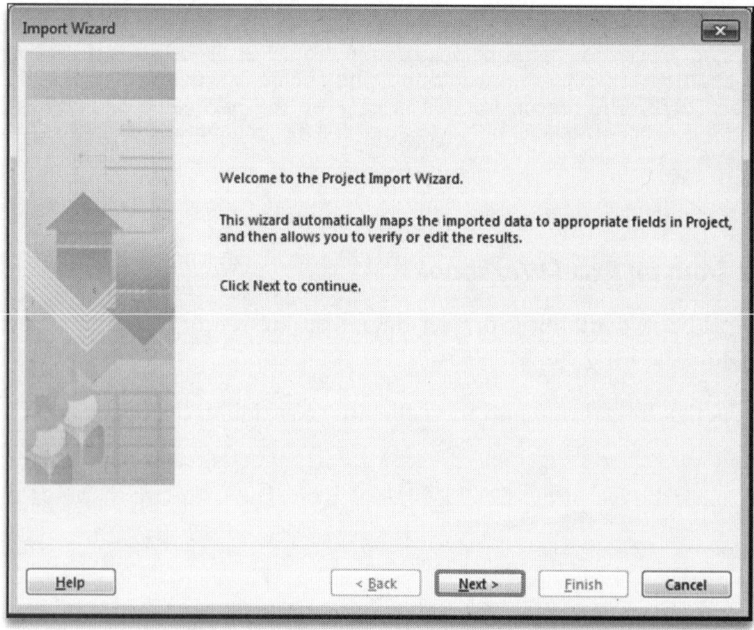

Figure 4 - 17: Import Wizard dialog, Welcome page

5. In the *Import Wizard* dialog, click the *Next* button. The software displays the *Map* page of the *Export Wizard* dialog shown in Figure 4 - 18.

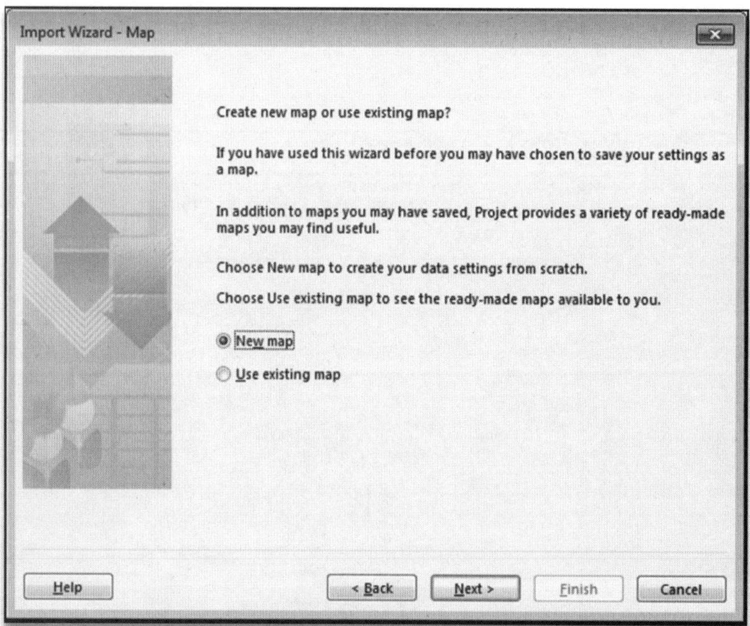

Figure 4 - 18: Import Wizard dialog, Map page

6. On the *Map* page of the dialog, leave the *New map* option selected, and then click the *Next* button. Project 2013 displays the *Import Mode* page of the *Import Wizard* dialog shown in Figure 4 - 19.

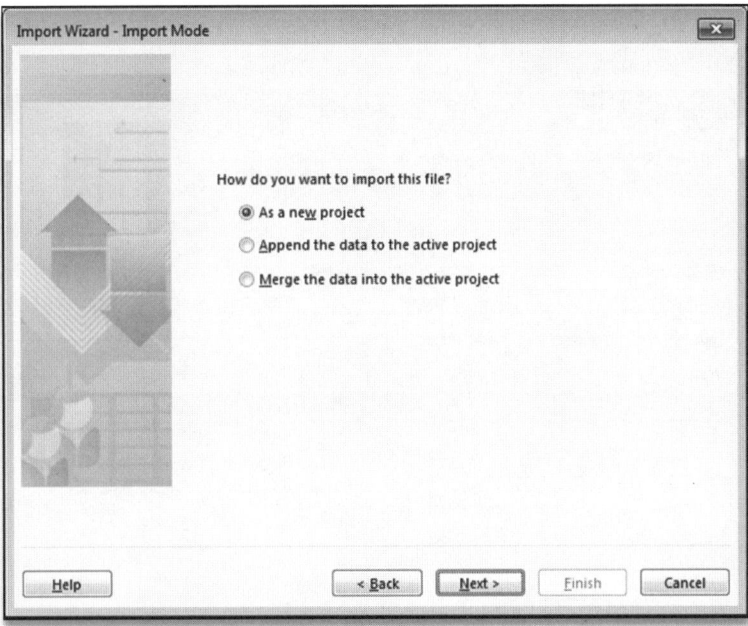

Figure 4 - 19: Import Wizard dialog, Import Mode page

7. On the *Import Mode* page of the dialog, leave the *As a new project* option selected, and then click the *Next* button. The software displays the *Map Options* page of the *Import Wizard* dialog shown in Figure 4 - 20.

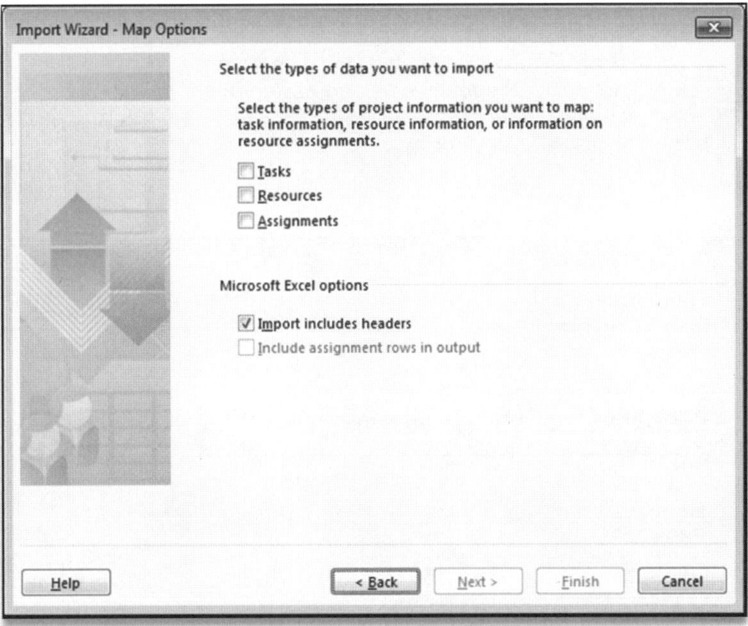

Figure 4 - 20: Import Wizard dialog, Map Options page

8. On the *Map Options* page of the dialog, select one or more of the checkbox options in the top half of the dialog to indicate how many worksheets the Excel workbook contains. For example, if your Excel workbook contains two worksheets, one with task data and the other with resource data, then select both the *Tasks* and *Resources* options. Click the *Next* button after selecting at least one checkbox option. Project 2013 displays the *Task Mapping* page of the *Import Wizard* dialog shown in Figure 4 - 21.

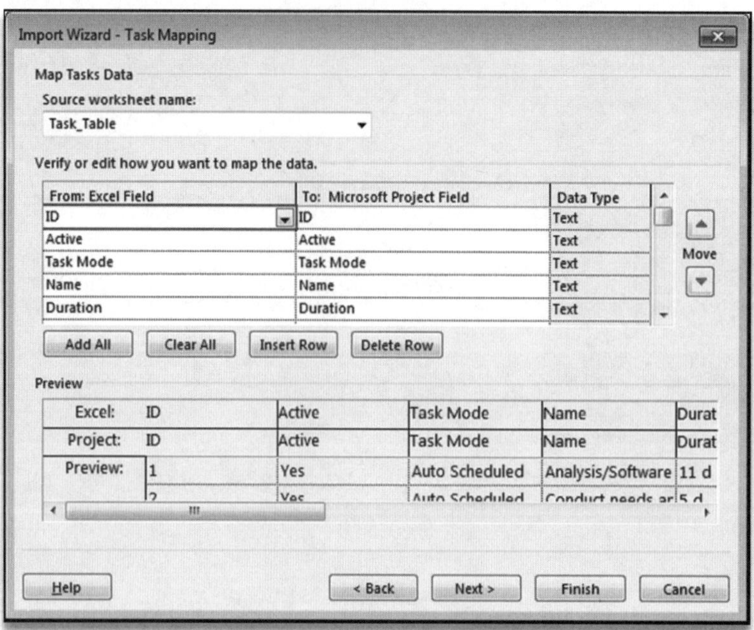

Figure 4 - 21: Import Wizard dialog, Task Mapping page

9. On the *Task Mapping* page of the dialog, map each field shown in the *From: Excel Field* column with a corresponding field in the *To: Microsoft Project Field* column, and then click the *Next* button. If you selected the *Resources* checkbox option on the *Map Options* page of the dialog, the software displays the *Resource Mapping* page of the *Import Wizard* dialog shown in Figure 4 - 22.

Information: If you did not select the *Resources* and *Assignments* checkbox options on the *Map Options* page of the *Import Wizard* dialog, click the *Finish* button instead of the *Next* button to complete the data import operation and create the new project from the Excel workbook.

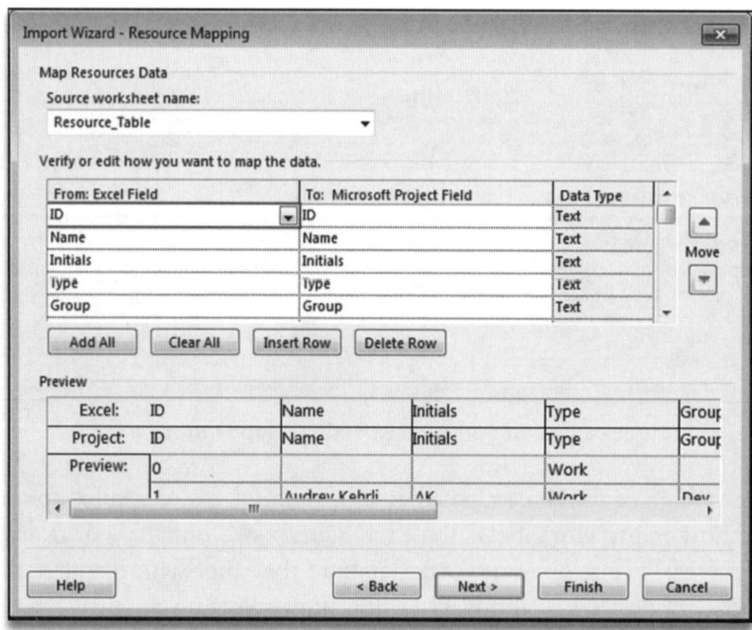

Figure 4 - 22: Import Wizard dialog, Resource Mapping page

10. On the *Resource Mapping* page of the dialog, map each field shown in the *From: Excel Field* column with a corresponding field in the *To: Microsoft Project Field* column, and then click the *Next* button. If you selected the *Assignments* checkbox option on the *Map Options* page of the dialog, the software displays the *Assignment Mapping* page of the *Import Wizard* dialog shown in Figure 4 - 23.

Information: If you did not select the *Assignments* checkbox option on the *Map Options* page of the *Import Wizard* dialog, click the *Finish* button instead of the *Next* button to complete the data import operation and create the new project from the Excel workbook.

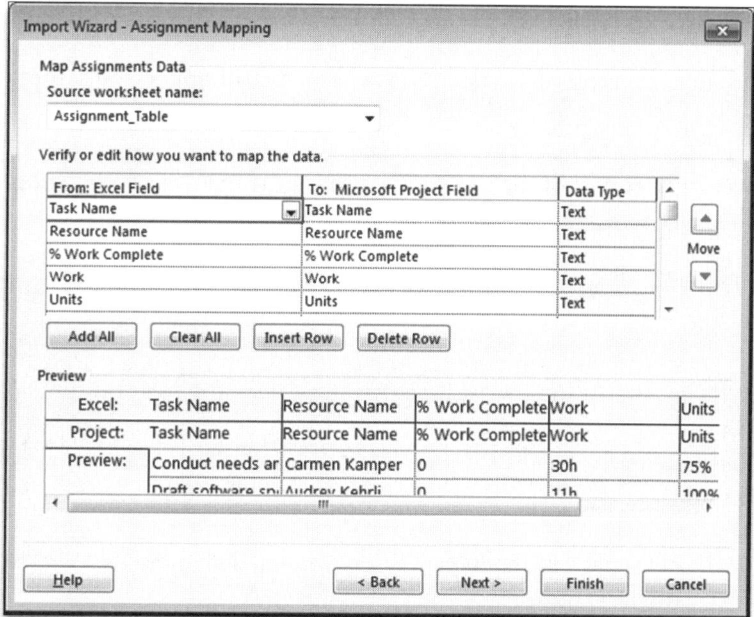

Figure 4 - 23: Import Wizard dialog, Assignment Mapping page

11. On the *Assignment Mapping* page of the dialog, map each field shown in the *From: Excel Field* column with a corresponding field in the *To: Microsoft Project Field* column, and then click the *Finish* button. Project 2013 completes the import process by creating a new project from the data in the Excel workbook.

Warning: One negative consequence of creating a new project from an Excel workbook is that Project 2013 places a Start No Earlier Than (SNET) constraint on **every** *Auto Scheduled* task in the project. To remove these unnecessary constraints, click the *Select All* button to select all tasks in the project, and then click the *Task* tab to display the *Task* ribbon. In the *Properties* section of the *Task* ribbon, click the *Information* button. In the *Multiple Task Information* dialog, click the *Advanced* tab to display the *Advanced* page of the dialog. On the *Advanced* page, click the *Constraint Type* pick list, select the *As Soon As Possible* constraint type, and then click the *OK* button.

Hands On Exercise

Exercise 4 - 3

Create a new project from an Excel workbook.

1. Click the *File* tab and then click the *New* tab in the *Backstage*.
2. On the *New* page in the *Backstage*, click the *New from Excel workbook* icon.
3. In the *Open* dialog, navigate to the folder where you unzipped the sample files that accompany this book.
4. In the lower right corner of the *Open* dialog, click the *File Type* pick list button and select the *Excel Workbook (*.xlsx)* item.
5. In the *Open* dialog, select the **Implement Training Advisor 2013.xlsx** sample file and then click the *Open* button.
6. On the *Welcome* page of the *Import Wizard* dialog, click the *Next* button.
7. On the *Map* page of the *Import Wizard* dialog, leave the *New map* option selected, and then click the *Next* button.
8. On the *Import Mode* page of the *Import Wizard* dialog, leave the *As a new project* option selected, and then click the *Next* button.
9. On the *Map Options* page of the *Import Wizard* dialog, select the *Tasks*, *Resources*, and *Assignments* checkboxes.
10. On the *Map Options* page of the *Import Wizard* dialog, leave the *Import includes headers* option selected, and then click the *Next* button.

On the *Task Mapping* page of the *Import Wizard* dialog, notice how Project 2013 cannot map the *Task Name* field in the *From: Excel Field* column with a corresponding field in the *To: Microsoft Project Field* column, as indicated by the *(not mapped)* text formatted in red.

11. Select the *(not mapped)* cell, click the pick list, and select the *Name* field.
12. On the *Task Mapping* page of the *Import Wizard* dialog, click the *Next* button.

On the *Resource Mapping* page of the *Import Wizard* dialog, notice how the software correctly maps every field in the Excel workbook with existing fields in Project 2013.

13. On the *Resource Mapping* page of the *Import Wizard* dialog, click the *Next* button.

On the *Assignment Mapping* page of the *Import Wizard* dialog, notice how the software correctly maps every field in the Excel workbook with existing fields in Project 2013.

14. On the *Assignment Mapping* page of the *Import Wizard* dialog, click the *Finish* button.
15. Examine the new project imported from the Excel workbook.
16. Click the *File* tab and then click the *Save As* tab in the *Backstage*.
17. On the *Save As* page, click the *Computer* link and then click the *Browse* button.
18. In the *Save As* dialog, navigate to the folder where you unzipped your sample files for this class.
19. In the *Save As* dialog, enter **Implement Training Advisor 2013** in the *File name* field, and then click the *Save* button.
20. Click the *File* tab and then click the *Close* button in the *Backstage*.

Creating a New Project from a SharePoint Tasks List

If your organization uses SharePoint 2013, but does not use the Project Server 2013 enterprise project management tool, you can leverage the power of SharePoint by creating a new project in Project 2013 from a *Tasks* list in a SharePoint site. This feature can be useful to your organization if you need to create a new project from a standard list of tasks defined by your organization. Before you can create a new project from a *Tasks* list in SharePoint, your organization must meet the following requirements:

- Your SharePoint administrator must create a SharePoint site for you.
- Your SharePoint administrator must share the SharePoint site with you and grant you *Full Control* permissions by adding you to the *Project Highlevel Owners* security group.
- Your SharePoint administrator must supply you with the URL of the site.
- In the SharePoint site, a knowledgeable person must create a new *Tasks* list containing the names of tasks for a standard project. Ideally, the *Tasks* list should include task dependencies, if possible.
- You must navigate to the *Tasks* list in the SharePoint site and then copy the URL to your Windows clipboard.

Figure 4 - 24 shows a short *Tasks* list in a SharePoint 2013 site. Notice that the *Tasks* list includes a summary task named *PHASE I*, with four subtasks named *Design*, *Build*, *Test*, and *Implement*. Notice also that I specified a predecessor for each task, along with a start date and a due date, and I assigned a resource to each task. In order to show all of this information to you, I modified the default *All Tasks* view to display all of the relevant columns to the right of the *Task Name* column.

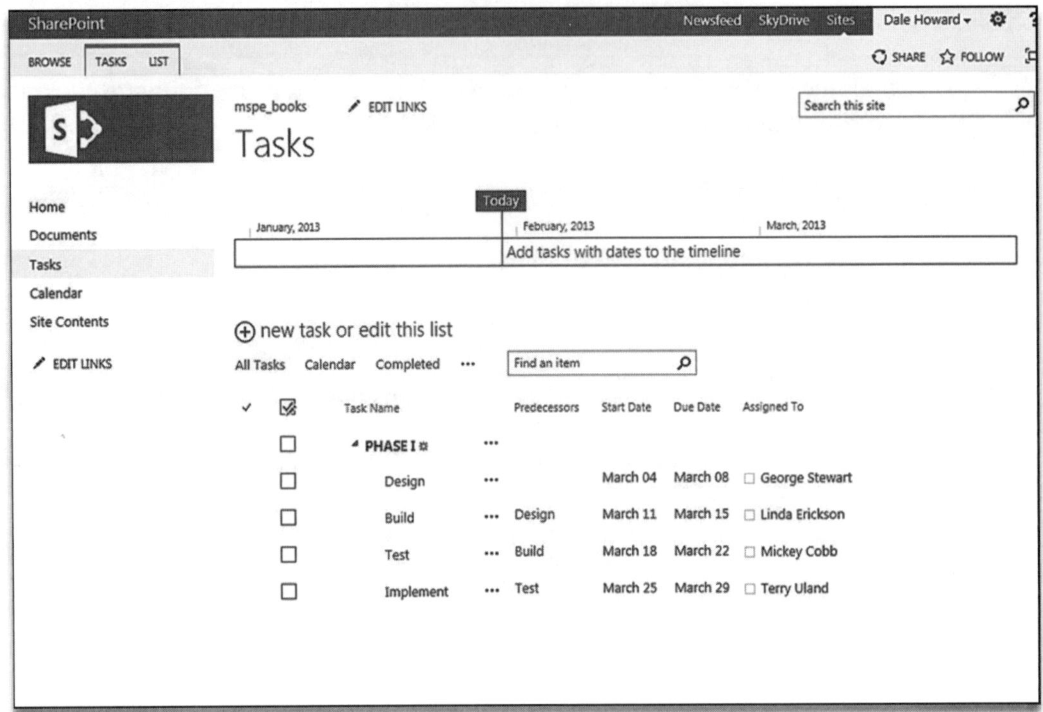

Figure 4 - 24: Tasks list in a SharePoint 2013 site

To create a new project from a *Tasks* list in a SharePoint site, complete the following steps in Project 2013:

1. Click the *File* tab and then click the *New* tab in the *Backstage*.
2. On the *New* page in the *Backstage*, click the *New from SharePoint Tasks List* icon. Project 2013 displays the *Import from SharePoint Site* dialog shown in Figure 4 - 25.

Figure 4 - 25: Import from SharePoint Site dialog

3. In the *Import from SharePoint Site* dialog, enter or paste the URL of the SharePoint site in the *Site URL* field.

Information: After you create at least one new project from a *Tasks* list in SharePoint, Project 2013 populates the *Site URL* field automatically by adding the URL of the SharePoint site to the pick list. When you create new projects from multiple SharePoint sites, the *Site URL* field displays a pick list containing the entire URL history.

4. Click the *Check Address* button in the *Import from SharePoint Site* dialog. If the URL is valid for the SharePoint site, the software activates the *Tasks List* pick list with a list of *Tasks* list items, as shown in Figure 4 - 26.

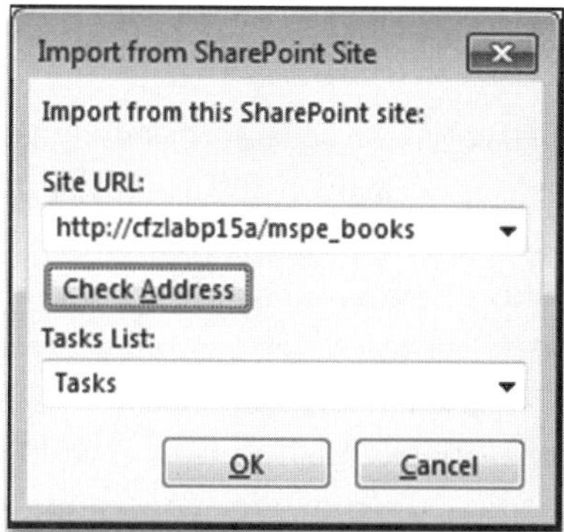

Figure 4 - 26: Tasks List populated with available Tasks List items

5. Click the *Tasks List* pick list and choose an available *Tasks* list, if needed, and then click the *OK* button. As Project 2013 collects the *Tasks* list information, the software displays the *Sync with Tasks List* dialog shown in Figure 4 - 27.

Figure 4 - 27: Sync with Tasks List dialog

After the software completes the process of creating a new project from a *Tasks* list in SharePoint, Project 2013 creates the new project using the *Tasks* list defined in the SharePoint site. How the software creates the tasks in your project depends on your default *Task Mode* setting for all new projects. If you specify *Manually Scheduled* as the default *Task Mode* setting for all new projects, Project 2013 creates each task as a *Manually Scheduled* task and sets dependencies on the tasks if the *Tasks* list in SharePoint contains dependency information in the *Predecessors* field. With the default *Task Mode* value set to *Manually Scheduled,* Figure 4 - 28 shows a new project created from the *Project Tasks* list shown previously in Figure 4 - 24. Notice that the software calculated a *Duration* value of *5 days* for each task, based on the dates I entered for the tasks in the *Start Date* and *Due Date* fields in the SharePoint site. Notice also that Project 2013 shows the resources assigned to each task.

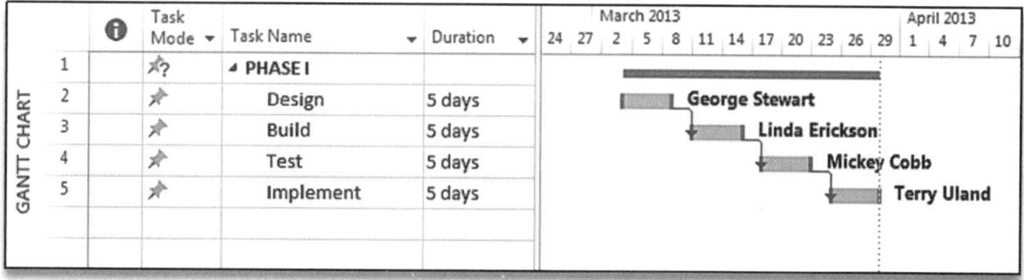

Figure 4 - 28: New project created from a Tasks list in SharePoint using Manually Scheduled tasks in all new projects

Information: If you do not enter dates in the *Start Date* and *Due Date* fields in the SharePoint site, Project 2013 leaves the *Duration*, *Start*, and *Finish* fields blank for each *Manually Scheduled* task. In addition, the software enters the *Current date* value in the *Scheduled Start* and *Scheduled Finish* column for each *Manually Scheduled* task.

If you specify *Auto Scheduled* as the default *Task Mode* setting for new projects, Project 2013 creates each task as an *Auto Scheduled* task and sets dependencies on the tasks if the *Tasks* list in SharePoint contains dependency information in the *Predecessors* field. With the default *Task Mode* value set to *Auto Scheduled*, Figure 4 - 29 shows a new project created from the *Project Tasks* list shown previously in Figure 4 - 24. Notice that the software calculated a *Duration* value of *5 days* for each task, based on the dates I entered for the tasks in the *Start Date* and *Due Date* fields in the SharePoint site. Notice also that the Project 2013 shows the resources assigned to each task. In addition, the software applied a *Finish No Earlier Than* constraint on each of the four subtasks. After creating a new project from a *Tasks* list in SharePoint, you should remove the constraint on each task.

	Task Mode	Task Name	Duration
1		PHASE I	20 days?
2		Design	5 days?
3		Build	5 days?
4		Test	5 days?
5		Implement	5 days?

Figure 4 - 29: New project created from a Tasks list in SharePoint using Auto Scheduled tasks in all new projects

Information: If you do not enter dates in the *Start Date* and *Due Date* fields in the SharePoint site, Project 2013 sets the *Current date* as the *Start date* for the project, and enters the default value of *1 day* in the *Duration* field for each *Auto Scheduled* task. Using the *Start date* for the project, along with dependencies and *Duration* values for each *Auto Scheduled* task, the software calculates the *Finish* date for each task.

Information: To specify the default *Task Mode* setting for all new projects, click the *File* tab and then click the *Options* button in the *Backstage*. In the *Project Options* dialog, click the *Schedule* tab. Click the *Scheduling options for this project* pick list and select the *All New Projects* item. Click the *New tasks created* pick list and select either *Manually Scheduled* or *Auto Scheduled*, and then click the *OK* button.

During the process of creating the new project from the *Tasks* list in SharePoint, Project 2013 applies a name to the project using the name of the SharePoint site, followed by a dash symbol, followed by the word *Tasks*. Because my SharePoint site is *mspe_books*, the name of my project is *mspe_books-Tasks.mpp*. When you create a new project from the *Tasks* list in SharePoint, Project 2013 assumes that you want to use the *Sync to SharePoint Tasks List* feature with the project. This means that if you click the *File* tab and then click the *Save* button, the software saves the project automatically in the *Site Assets* library in the SharePoint site. If you do not want to save your project in the SharePoint site, click the *File* tab and then click the *Save As* tab in the *Backstage*. Using the options on the *Save As* page, select an alternate location for the project, rename your project, if necessary, and then save the project in the alternate location.

Defining a New Project

After you determine your project requirements, you are ready to define the project in Project 2013 using the six-step method recommended by MSProjectExperts. You should use this six-step method when you open a new blank project or create a new project from a project template. The six-step method includes the following mandatory and optional steps:

1. Set the project start date.
2. Enter the project properties.
3. Display the Project Summary Task (aka Row 0 or Task 0).
4. Set the project working schedule using a calendar.
5. Set project options unique to this project.
6. Save the project according to your company's naming standards.

After completing the six-step initiating process, you are ready to begin the planning process. In this module, I discuss each of these steps as a major topical section.

Step #1 - Set the Project Start Date

Before I teach you how to set the *Start* date for a new project, I want you to understand the date changes made by Microsoft in the Project 2013 software. After I explain the significant date changes in the software, I will document how to specify the *Start* date for a new project.

Understanding Date Changes

In all previous versions of the software through Project 2010, the software would not support *Start* dates earlier than January 1, 1984 or *Finish* dates later than December 31, 2049. A major change in Project 2013 is that the software now allows dates up to **December 31, 2149**. With this simple change, Microsoft added 100 years to the life of any project!

Figure 4 - 30 shows a Project 2010 project in which I specified *December 30, 2049* as the *Start* date of the project. In this project, I added a task named *Design* and attempted to enter a *Duration* value of *5 days*. Notice that the software limits me to a *Duration* value of only *1 day* for the task, and notice that the *Timescale* shows no dates later than **December 31, 2049**.

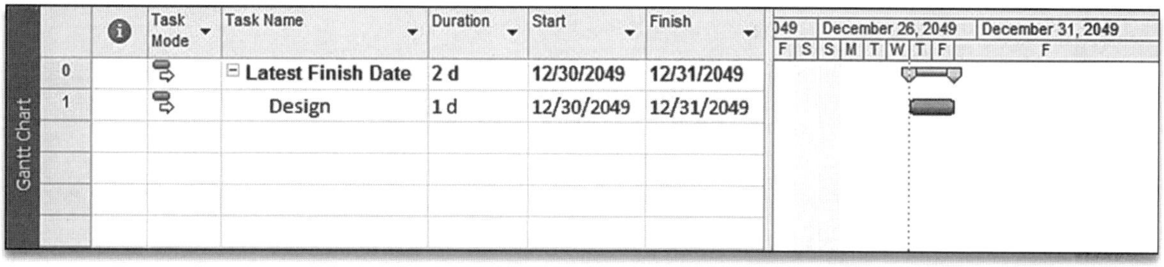

Figure 4 - 30: Latest possible Finish date in Project 2010

Figure 4 - 31 shows a similar project in Project 2013 in which I specified *December 30, 2149* as the *Start* date of the project. In this project, I added a task named *Design* and attempted to enter a *Duration* value of *5 days*. Notice that the software limits me to a *Duration* value of only *2 days*, and notice that the *Timescale* shows no dates later than **December 31, 2149**.

		Task Mode	Task Name	Duration	Start	Finish
0			Latest Finish Date	2 d	12/30/2149	12/31/2149
1			Design	2 d	12/30/2149	12/31/2149

Figure 4 - 31: Latest possible Finish date in Project 2013

If you use the *Project Information* dialog and attempt to enter either a *Start date* or *Finish date* value outside of the acceptable date range in Project 2013, the software displays the warning dialog shown in Figure 4 - 32. Notice that the warning dialog confirms the earliest and latest dates possible in the software.

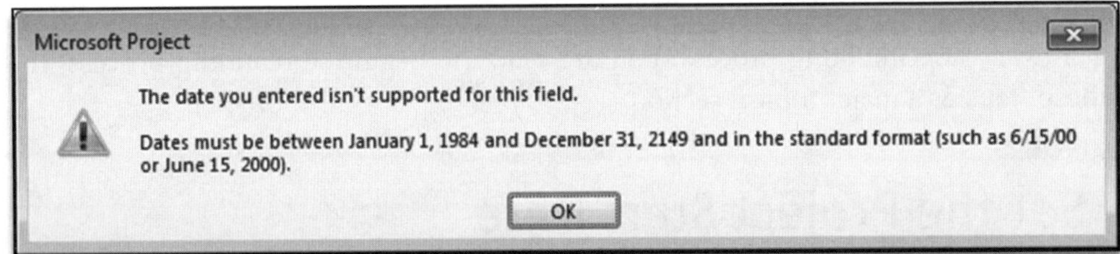

Figure 4 - 32: Date range warning dialog

Hands On Exercise

Exercise 4 - 4

Explore the new date changes in Project 2013.

1. Click the *File* tab and then click the *New* tab in the *Backstage*.
2. On the *New* page in the *Backstage*, click the *Blank Project* icon to create a new blank project.
3. Click the *Project* tab to display the *Project* ribbon.
4. In the *Properties* section of the *Project* ribbon, click the *Project Information* button.
5. In the *Start date* field, enter **3/18/2150** and then click the *OK* button.

Notice that the warning dialog reveals the acceptable range for dates in your project, spanning from January 1, 1984 to December 31, 2149.

6. Click the *OK* button to close the warning dialog.

7. In the *Start date* field, enter **12/29/2149** and then click the *OK* button.
8. In the lower left corner of the Project 2013 application window, click the *New Tasks* button and select the *Auto Scheduled* item on the menu.
9. Manually enter a new task named *Design*, enter a *Duration* value of *5 days* for this new task, and then press the **Enter** key on your computer keyboard.
10. Drag your split bar to the right so that you can see the *Finish* column, if necessary.

Notice that the software does not allow any date later than December 31, 2149. Because of this, Project 2013 shortens the *Duration* to only *3 days* to calculate a *Finish* date of *December 31, 2149* for the new task. Remember that this is the latest possible date in Project 2013.

11. Click the *File* tab and then click the *Close* tab in the *Backstage*.
12. When prompted in a dialog to save the changes to the new project, click the *No* button.

Setting the Project Start Date

When you define a new project in Project 2013, you must set the start date of the project. When you set a project's start date, you allow the software to calculate an estimated finish date based on the information you enter during the task, resource, and assignment planning process. To enter the start date for a new project, complete the following steps:

1. Click the *Project* tab to display the *Project* ribbon.
2. In the *Properties* section of the *Project* ribbon, click the *Project Information* button. The software displays the *Project Information* dialog shown in Figure 4 - 33.

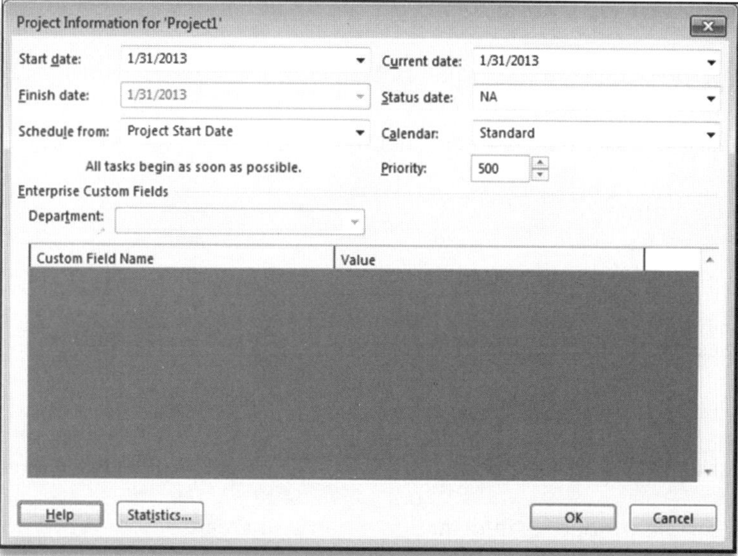

Figure 4 - 33: Project Information dialog, Set the Start date of the project

Information: You can also display the *Project Information* dialog by clicking the *Definition* tab to display your new custom *Definition* ribbon. In the *Start Date* section of the *Definition* ribbon, click the *Set Project Start Date* button to display the *Project Information* dialog.

3. Click the *Schedule from* pick list and select the *Project Start Date* item, if necessary.

4. Enter your desired project start date in the *Start date* field and then click the *OK* button.

Information: In the *Project Information* dialog, you do not see an *Enterprise Custom Fields* section in the bottom half of the dialog if you are using the **Standard** version of Project 2013. You only see an *Enterprise Custom Fields* section in the dialog if you are using the **Professional** version of the software.

Hands On Exercise

Exercise 4 - 5

You are the project manager of the Training Advisor Rollout project. The purpose of this project is to implement a new enterprise Learning Management System (LMS) that allows employees to create and manage their own professional development program by taking in-house and external training classes. You estimate the project start date at January 4, 2016. The target finish date for the project is June 24, 2016.

1. Open the **Training Advisor 04.mpp** sample file.

2. Click the *Project* tab to display the *Project* ribbon.

3. In the *Properties* section of the *Project* ribbon, click the *Project Information* button.

4. Enter *January 4, 2016* in the *Start date* field.

5. Click the *OK* button.

Notice how Project 2013 scrolls the Gantt chart to the start date of the project.

6. In the *Quick Access Toolbar*, click the *Save* button to save your project.

Step #2 - Enter the Project Properties

Although you may not enter file properties information when you create a new Word document or Excel spreadsheet, you should enter the properties information for each new project you create in Project 2013. When you enter properties information for a project, this action causes the software to populate the properties information **automatically** in various places throughout the project, such as in the headers and footers of printed views or in PDF files that you export. To enter the properties information for a new project, complete the following steps:

1. Click the *File* tab to display the *Backstage*.

2. Click the *Info* tab to display the *Information* page in the *Backstage*, as shown in Figure 4 - 34.

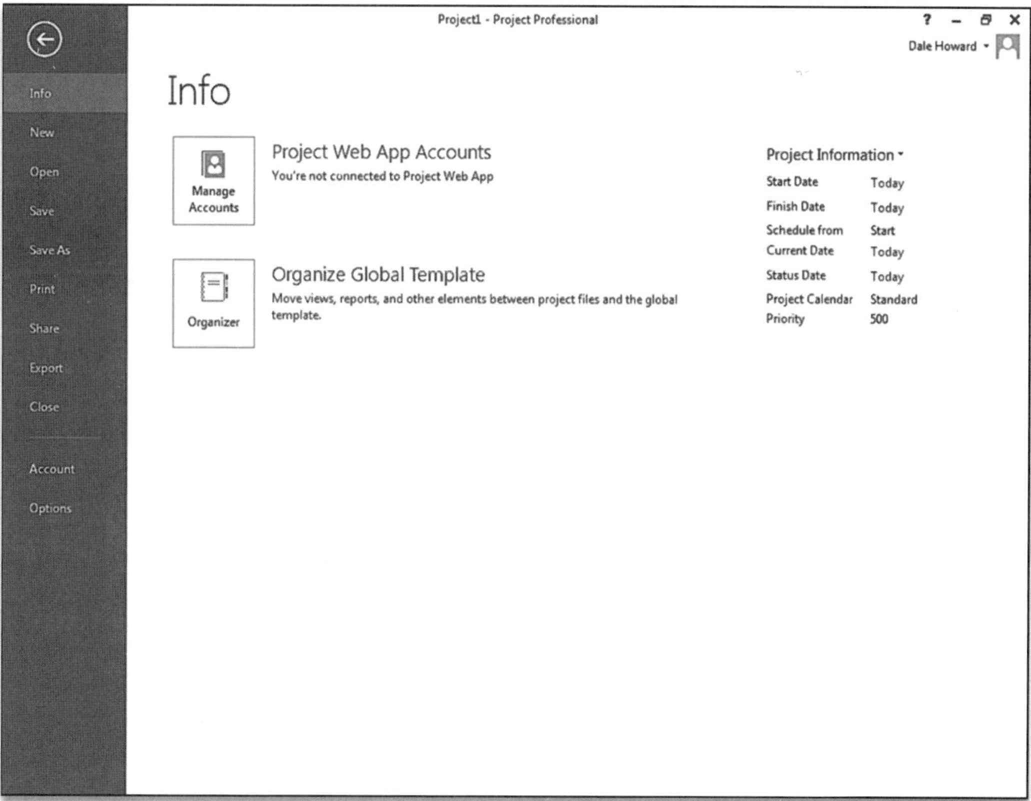

Figure 4 - 34: Info page in the Backstage

3. On the right side of the *Info* page, click the *Project Information* pick list and select the *Advanced Properties* item on the list, as shown in Figure 4 - 35.

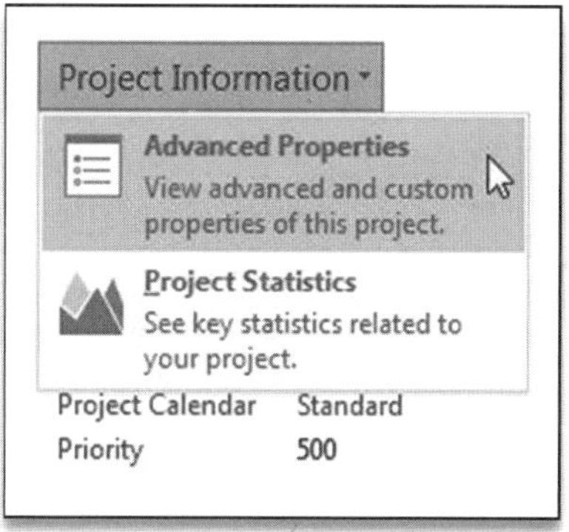

Figure 4 - 35: Project Information pick list

The software displays the *Properties* dialog for the new project shown in Figure 4 - 36.

Information: You can also display the *Properties* dialog by clicking the *Definition* tab to display your new custom *Definition* ribbon. In the *Properties* section of the *Definition* ribbon, click the *Set Project Properties* button to display the *Properties* dialog.

Figure 4 - 36: Properties dialog

4. Click the *Summary* tab, if necessary, and enter values in each of the fields.
5. Click the *OK* button when finished.

Table 4 - 1 provides descriptions and recommendations for using the fields in the *Properties* dialog.

Field Name	Description and Recommendations
Title	Displays as the task name for the Project Summary Task (Row 0), as the task name for subprojects inserted in a master project, and in the headers or footers of printed views and reports.
Subject	Used only for file searching.
Author	Enter your name. Optionally displayed in the headers or footers of printed views.

Field Name	Description and Recommendations
Manager	Enter your name. Displayed in the headers and footers of printed views.
Company	Enter the name of your company. Displayed in the headers and footers of printed views.
Category	Used only for file searching.
Keywords	Used only for file searching.
Comments	Displayed in the *Notes* field on the Project Summary Task.
Hyperlink base	Used as the base path address for all relative hyperlinks inserted within the project.
Template	Displays the name of the template you used to create the project plan. The software disables this field if you create the project as a new blank project.
Save preview picture	Displays a preview picture of your project file in the *Open* dialog.

Table 4 - 1: Project Properties fields

Hands On Exercise

Exercise 4 - 6

Enter the properties information for a project.

1. Return to your **Training Advisor 04.mpp** sample file.
2. Click the *File* tab and then click the *Info* tab in the *Backstage*.
3. On the right side of the *Info* page, click the *Project Information* pick list and select the *Advanced Properties* item.

4. In the *Properties* dialog, enter the information shown in Table 4 - 2.

Field Name	Description and Recommendations
Title	Training Advisor Rollout
Subject	enterprise software implementation
Author	Your name
Manager	Your name
Company	Name of your organization or company
Category	enterprise software implementation
Keywords	enterprise software implementation
Comments	Implement the Training Advisor software to allow employees to plan and direct their own continuing education program.
Hyperlink base	Leave blank
Template	Unused
Save preview picture	Leave deselected

Table 4 - 2: Properties information for the Training Advisor project

5. Click the *OK* button.

6. In the *Quick Access Toolbar*, click the *Save* button to save your project.

Step #3 - Display the Project Summary Task

The Project Summary Task, also known as Row 0 or Task 0, is the highest-level summary task in your project. The Project Summary Task summarizes or "rolls up" all task values in the entire project. For example, the value in the *Duration* column for the Project Summary Task represents the duration of the entire project, while the values in the *Work* and the *Cost* columns represent the total work and total cost for the entire project. By default, Project 2013 **does not** display the Project Summary Task automatically in any new blank project, so you must display it manually. To display the Project Summary Task, complete the following steps:

1. Apply the *Gantt Chart* view, if necessary.

2. Click the *Format* tab to display the *Format* ribbon with the *Gantt Chart Tools* applied.

3. In the *Show/Hide* section of the *Format* ribbon, select the *Project Summary Task* checkbox. The software displays the Project Summary Task (Row 0) in the current project, as shown in Figure 4 - 37.

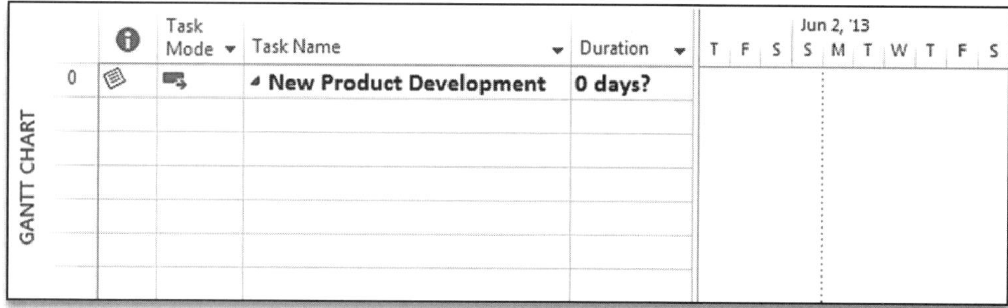

Figure 4 - 37: Project Summary Task (Row 0)

Information: You can also display the Project Summary Task by clicking the *Definition* tab to display your new custom *Definition* ribbon. In the *Project Summary Task* section of the *Definition* ribbon, select the *Display Project Summary Task* checkbox.

4. Widen the *Task Name* column, if necessary, to "best fit" the task name of the Project Summary Task.
5. If you widen the *Task Name* column, drag the split bar to the right side of the *Duration* column, as needed.

Notice the name of the Project Summary Task shown in Figure 4 - 37. Project 2013 uses the text you enter in the *Title* field of the *Properties* dialog as the task name of the Project Summary Task. Notice also the note indicator in the *Indicators* column to the left of the *Task Name* column. The software uses the text you enter in the *Comments* field of the *Properties* dialog as the body of the note for the Project Summary Task.

Hands On Exercise

Exercise 4 - 7

Display the Project Summary Task in a project.

1. Return to your **Training Advisor 04.mpp** sample file.
2. Click the *Format* tab to display the *Format* ribbon with the *Gantt Chart Tools* applied.
3. In the *Show/Hide* section of the *Format* ribbon, select the *Project Summary Task* checkbox.
4. Widen the *Task Name* column and then drag the split bar to the right edge of the *Duration* column.

Notice that the software uses the *Title* information from the *Properties* dialog as the task name of the Project Summary Task.

5. Float your mouse pointer over the note indicator in the *Indicators* column for the Project Summary Task.

Notice that the software uses the *Comments* information from the *Properties* dialog as the body of the note for the Project Summary Task.

6. In the *Quick Access Toolbar*, click the *Save* button to save your project.

Step #4 - Set the Project Working Schedule

To achieve a realistic working schedule for your project, you likely need to do one or more of the following:

- Add nonworking time to the *Standard* calendar to reflect your company holidays.
- Modify the *Standard* calendar in your project to reflect your company's working schedule, if different from the default working schedule.
- Create new base calendars to represent unique working schedules.
- Specify the *Project* calendar and the *Nonworking Time* calendar for your project.

I discuss each of these topics individually.

Adding Nonworking Time to the Standard Calendar

To add nonworking time representing company holidays to the *Standard* calendar in a project, complete the following steps:

1. Click the *Project* tab to display the *Project* ribbon.
2. In the *Properties* section of the *Project* ribbon, click the *Change Working Time* button. The software opens the *Change Working Time* dialog, as shown in Figure 4 - 38.

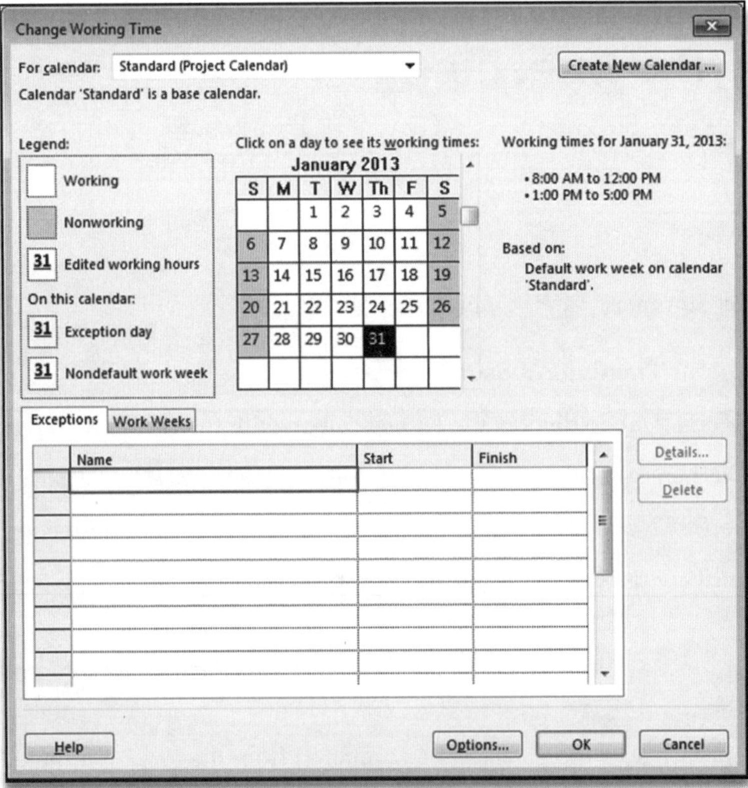

Figure 4 - 38: Change Working Time dialog

Information: You can also display the *Change Working Time* dialog by clicking the *Definition* tab to display your new custom *Definition* ribbon. In the *Set Working Schedule* section of the *Definition* ribbon, click the *Change Working Time* button to display the *Change Working Time* dialog.

3. Click the *For calendar* pick list at the top of the dialog and make sure you have the *Standard* calendar selected.

4. In the calendar grid at the top of the *Change Working Time* dialog, select the date of the next company holiday, such as Memorial Day.

Information: To set consecutive nonworking days, drag your mouse pointer over the dates in the calendar grid to select a block of days. For example, some companies mark as nonworking time the week between Christmas Day and New Year's Day. To select noncontiguous dates, select the first date, press and hold the **Control** key on your computer keyboard, and then select additional dates.

5. In the *Name* column of the *Exceptions* data grid at the bottom of the dialog, select the first blank row, and then type the name of the holiday.

6. Press either the **Right-Arrow** key or the **Tab** key on your computer keyboard to navigate to the *Start* column. Project 2013 sets the date as nonworking time, such as for the Memorial Day holiday shown in Figure 4 - 39.

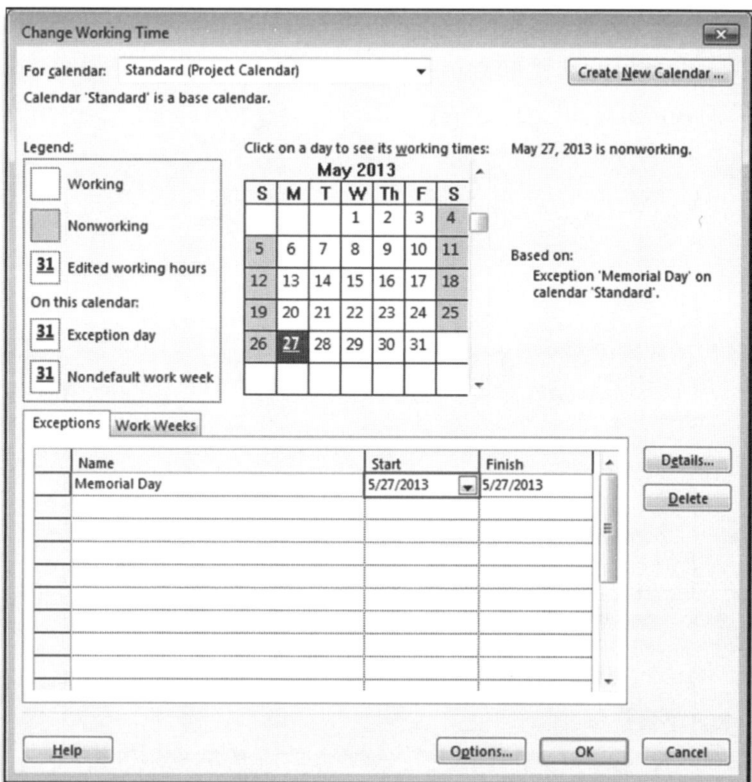

Figure 4 - 39: Memorial Day set as nonworking time

7. With the new holiday selected in the *Exceptions* data grid, click the *Details* button. The software displays the *Details* dialog for the selected holiday, as shown in Figure 4 - 40.

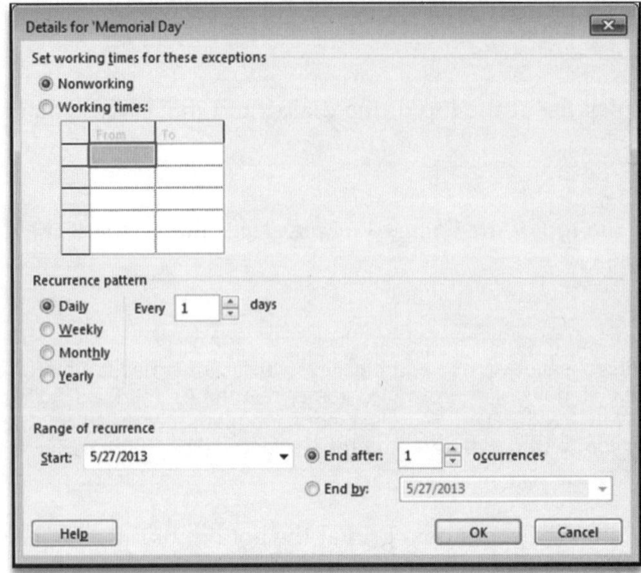

Figure 4 - 40: Details dialog for the Memorial Day holiday

8. In the *Set working times for these exceptions* section of the dialog, leave the *Nonworking* option selected.
9. In the *Recurrence Pattern* section, select the *Yearly* option, and then select the pattern of recurrence for the holiday. For example, Memorial Day always occurs on the last Monday of May every year.
10. In the *Range of Recurrence* section, select the *End after* option and then select the number of years for which you want to set the holiday (such as 5 years).

Figure 4 - 41 shows the *Details* dialog after setting the *Recurrence pattern* values to *Yearly* on the *Last Monday* of *May* and setting the *Range of recurrence* values to *End after* 5 occurrences.

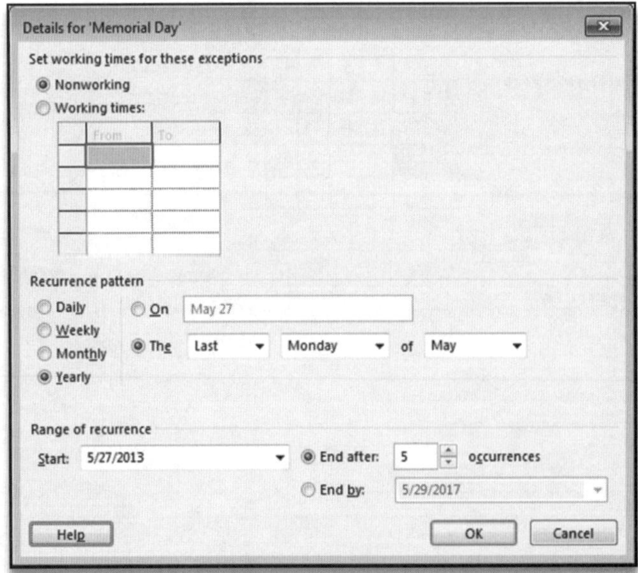

Figure 4 - 41: Details dialog after setting Memorial Day recurrence for 5 years

Information: You may need to set some holidays as partial working days. For example, some companies give their employees the afternoon off on Christmas Eve or New Year's Eve. To set a holiday as a partial working day, select the *Working times* option in the *Set working times for these exceptions* section of the dialog, and then enter the working schedule in the data grid. For example, to set the Christmas Eve holiday to show the afternoon as nonworking time, delete the *1:00 PM* and *5:00 PM* items on the second row of the data grid.

11. Click the *OK* button.
12. Repeat the preceding set of steps for each company holiday.

Warning: When you set a hard date as nonworking time, such as the New Year's day holiday on January 1, and then set the holiday to occur multiple times, some of the nonworking dates may fall on a weekend. Project 2013 **does not** automatically reset a Saturday holiday to the previous Friday, or reset a Sunday holiday to the following Monday. Instead, you must set these weekend occurrences as individual instances in the *Exceptions* grid. After you set a recurring company holiday on a hard date, scroll through the calendar grid looking for weekend occurrences, and then set individual exceptions according to your organization's policies.

Figure 4 - 42 shows the *Change Working Time* dialog after setting company holidays as nonworking days for the next 5 years through 2017. Notice that I created additional exceptions for the Christmas Day holiday in 2016 and the New Year's Day holiday in 2017 because these two holidays occur on a weekend during those two years.

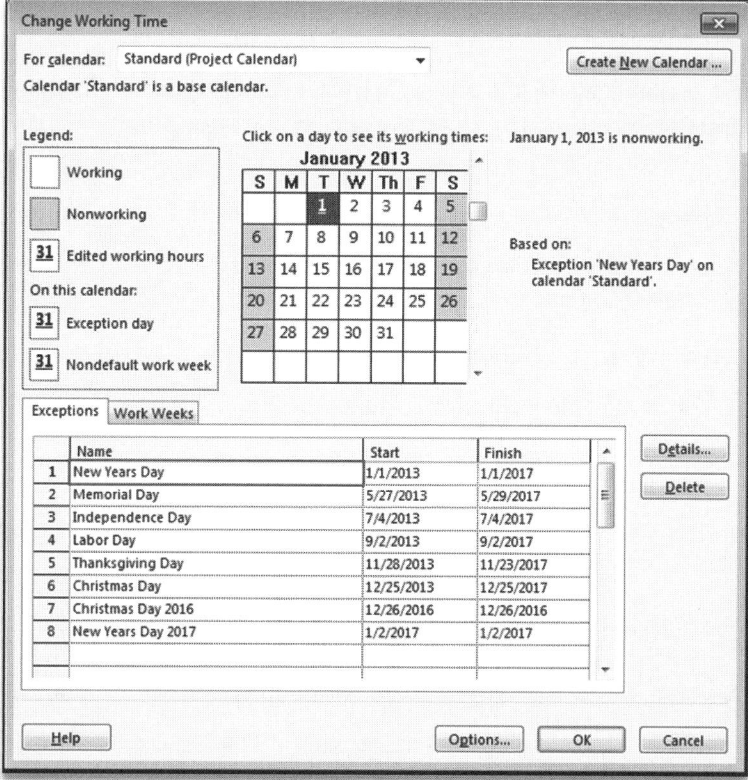

	Name	Start	Finish
1	New Years Day	1/1/2013	1/1/2017
2	Memorial Day	5/27/2013	5/29/2017
3	Independence Day	7/4/2013	7/4/2017
4	Labor Day	9/2/2013	9/2/2017
5	Thanksgiving Day	11/28/2013	11/23/2017
6	Christmas Day	12/25/2013	12/25/2017
7	Christmas Day 2016	12/26/2016	12/26/2016
8	New Years Day 2017	1/2/2017	1/2/2017

Figure 4 - 42: Change Working Time dialog with company holidays set as nonworking time

13. Click the *OK* button.

After you set your holidays as nonworking time on the *Standard* calendar, Project 2013 schedules no task work on any date specified as nonworking time.

Hands On Exercise

Exercise 4 - 8

Set a company holiday that occurs on a designated day of the week every year on the *Standard* calendar.

1. Return to the **Training Advisor 04.mpp** sample file.
2. Click the *Project* tab to display the *Project* ribbon.
3. In the *Properties* section of the *Project* ribbon, click the *Change Working Time* button.
4. Examine the list of company holidays already entered for the *Standard* calendar.

Notice that the holidays recur through 2018 with additional exceptions entered when a holiday occurs on a Saturday or Sunday (such as Christmas Day 2016).

5. In the *Calendar* grid at the top of the dialog, select *November 28, 2013* (the fourth Thursday of November is Thanksgiving Day).
6. On the first available blank line of the *Exceptions* data grid, enter *Thanksgiving Day* in the *Name* column, and then press the **Right-Arrow** key on your computer keyboard to navigate to the *Start* column.
7. With the *Thanksgiving Day* exception still selected, click the *Details* button.
8. In the *Recurrence pattern* section of the *Details* dialog, select the *Yearly* option, and then select the *Fourth Thursday of November* option.
9. Select the *End after* option and then select *6 occurrences.*
10. Click the *OK* button to close the *Details* dialog.
11. **Do not** close the *Change Working Time* dialog.

Exercise 4 - 9

Set a company holiday that occurs on a fixed date every year on the *Standard* calendar.

1. Make sure you have the *Change Working Time* dialog open for the **Training Advisor 04.mpp** sample file.
2. In the *Calendar* grid at the top of the dialog, select *July 4, 2013.*
3. On the first available blank line of the *Exceptions* data grid, enter *Independence Day* in the *Name* column, and then press the **Right-Arrow** key on your computer keyboard to navigate the *Start* column.
4. Click the *Details* button to display the *Details* dialog for the *Independence Day* exception.

5. In the *Recurrence pattern* section of the *Details* dialog, select the *Yearly* option, and then select the *On July 4* option.
6. Select the *End after* option and then select *6 occurrences.*
7. Click the *OK* button to close the *Details* dialog.
8. In the *Calendar* grid at the top of the dialog, scroll to and select *July 3, 2015.*

Notice that Independence Day (July 4) occurs on a Saturday in 2015.

9. Leave *July 3, 2015* selected in the *Calendar* grid.
10. On the first available blank line of the *Exceptions* data grid, enter *Independence Day 2015* in the *Name* column, and then press the **Right-Arrow** key on your computer keyboard to navigate the *Start* column.

Note: You just set an individual exception for the Independence Day holiday when it occurs on a weekend.

11. Click the *OK* button to close the *Change Working Time* dialog.
12. In the *Quick Access Toolbar,* click the *Save* button to save your project.

Exercise 4 - 10

Your organization holds its annual company picnic in the afternoon of the 2nd Friday of August, but the morning is working time. Set a company holiday that is a partial working day on the *Standard* calendar.

1. In the *Properties* section of the *Project* ribbon, click the *Change Working Time* button.
2. In the *Calendar* grid at the top of the dialog, select *August 9, 2013.*
3. On the first available blank line of the *Exceptions* data grid, enter *Annual Company Picnic* in the *Name* column, and then press the **Right-Arrow** key on your computer keyboard to navigate to the *Start* column.
4. With the *Annual Company Picnic* exception still selected, click the *Details* button.
5. In the *Set working times for these exceptions* section of the *Details* dialog, select the *Working times* option.
6. In the *Working times* data grid, select the line containing the *1:00 PM* to *5:00 PM* working schedule, and press the **Delete** key on your computer keyboard to delete the afternoon work.
7. Select the *Yearly* option in the *Recurrence pattern* section, and then select the *Second Friday of August* option.
8. Select the *End after* option and then select *6 occurrences.*
9. Click the *OK* button to close the *Details* dialog and then click the *OK* button to close the *Change Working Time* dialog.
10. In the *Quick Access Toolbar,* click the *Save* button to save your project.

Setting the Working Schedule

After entering your company holidays as nonworking time, you may also need to set your company's daily working schedule on the *Standard* calendar. By default, Project 2013 assumes a daily working schedule of 8:00 AM – 5:00 PM with one hour off for lunch, Monday through Friday, with Saturday and Sunday as nonworking times. To set any other type of daily working schedule, such as from 7:00 AM – 3:30 PM with a half-hour for lunch, complete the following steps:

1. In the *Properties* section of the *Project* ribbon, click the *Change Working Time* button.

2. At the top of the *Change Working Time* dialog, click the *For calendar* pick list and select the *Standard* calendar, if necessary.

3. Click the *Work Weeks* tab as shown in Figure 4 - 43.

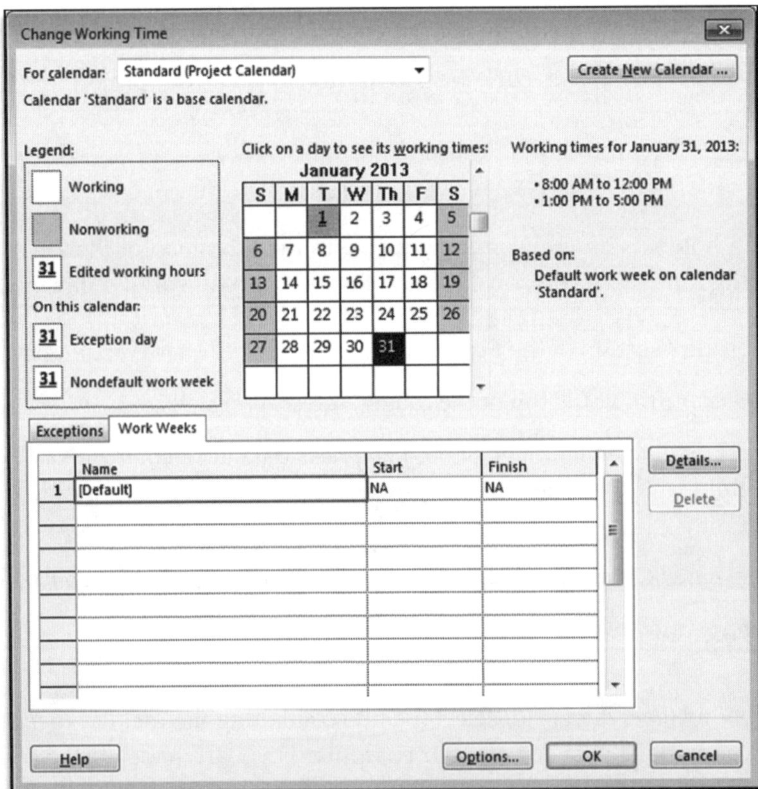

Figure 4 - 43: Change Working Time dialog, Work Weeks tab

4. In the *Work Weeks* data grid, leave the *[Default]* item selected and then click the *Details* button. The software displays the *Details* dialog for the default working schedule, as shown in Figure 4 - 44.

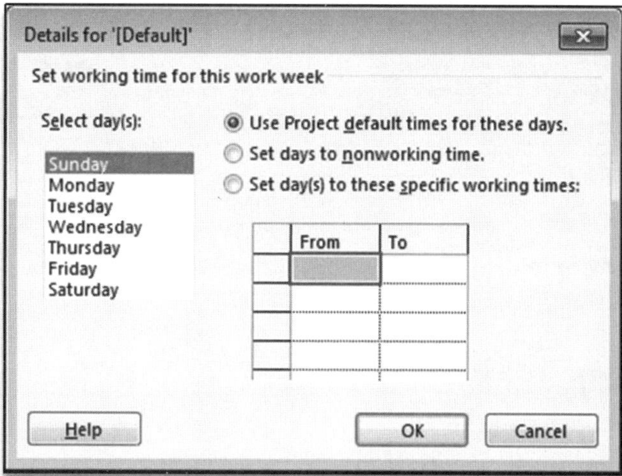

Figure 4 - 44: Details dialog

5. In the *Select day(s)* section of the *Details* dialog, select *Monday* through *Friday* in the list of days.
6. Select the *Set day(s) to these specific working times* option. The software displays the default 8:00 AM – 12:00 PM and 1:00 PM – 5:00 PM working time in the working times grid shown in Figure 4 - 45.

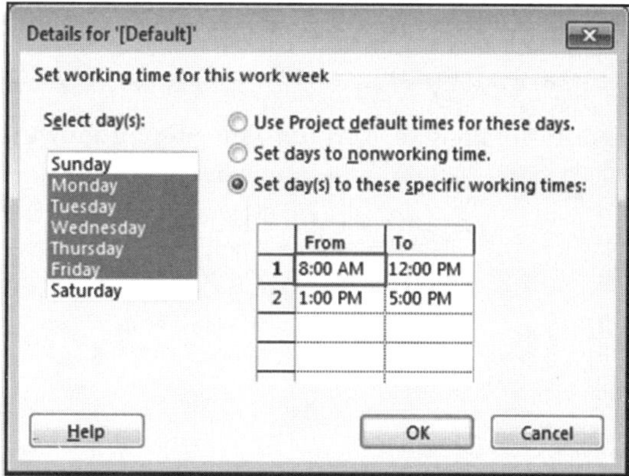

Figure 4 - 45: Default working schedule in the Details dialog

7. Change the first *From* value to *7:00 AM* and change the first *To* value set to *11:00 AM.*
8. Change the second *From* value to *11:30 AM* and change the second *To* value to *3:30 PM.*
9. Click the *OK* button to close the *Details* dialog.

To view the alternate working schedule, select any date in the *Calendar* grid and then examine the schedule shown in the upper right corner of the *Change Working Time* dialog. Notice that the dialog shown in Figure 4 - 46 reveals the alternate working schedule of 7:00 AM – 11:00 AM and 11:30 AM – 3:30 PM.

10. Click the *OK* button in the *Change Working Time* dialog.

Information: You can use the same preceding set of steps to modify the working schedule on any calendar by clicking the *For calendar* pick list and selecting the calendar whose working schedule you want to modify. For example, you might need to change a calendar to show shift work or weekend work.

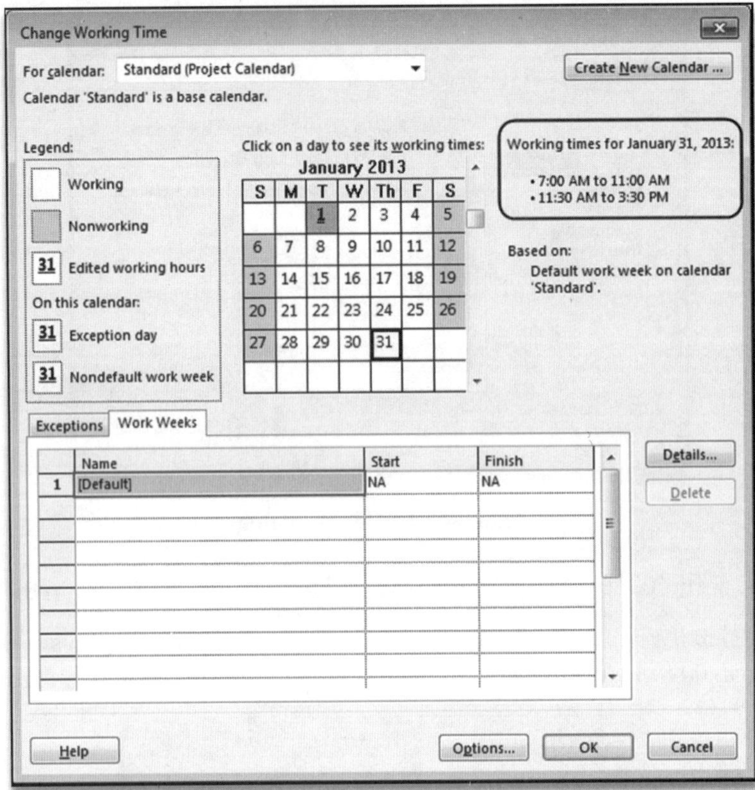

Figure 4 - 46: Change Working Time dialog shows the 7:00 AM – 3:30 PM alternate working schedule

Hands On Exercise

Exercise 4 - 11

Change the default working schedule on a calendar for staff members who work on the second shift from 3:00 PM – midnight each day.

1. Return to the **Training Advisor 04.mpp** sample file.
2. In the *Properties* section of the *Project* ribbon, click the *Change Working Time* button.
3. Click the *For calendar* pick list at the top of the *Change Working Time* dialog and select the *Second Shift* calendar.

Notice that the *Second Shift* base calendar already contains all company holidays, including the *Annual Company Picnic* partial working day every August.

4. In the *Change Working Time* dialog, click the *Work Weeks* tab.
5. In the *Work Weeks* data grid, select the *[Default]* item and then click the *Details* button.

6. In the *Select day(s)* section of the *Details* dialog, select *Monday* through *Friday* in the list of days.
7. Select the *Set day(s) to these specific working times* option.
8. Set the first *From* time to *3:00 PM* and set the first *To* time to *7:00 PM*.
9. Set the second *From* time to *8:00 PM* and set the second *To* time to *12:00 AM*.
10. Click the *OK* button to close the *Details* dialog.
11. Select any working day from Monday through Friday and examine the working schedule for that day shown in the upper right corner of the dialog.
12. Click the *OK* button to close the *Change Working Time* dialog.
13. In the *Quick Access Toolbar*, click the *Save* button to save your project.

Creating a New Base Calendar

A base calendar is a master calendar that represents a unique working schedule for your organization. Project 2013 uses base calendars to schedule all work for tasks in a project and to set the working schedule for each resource. The software offers three predefined base calendars: the *24 Hours* calendar, the *Night Shift* calendar, and the *Standard* calendar.

Because of unique scheduling needs in your project, you may need to create additional base calendars beyond the three default calendars that ship with the tool. For example, you may need to schedule work to occur on a 7-day work week schedule or to occur on a 4-day work week (10 hours/day and 4 days/week). You might even need to create international calendars, such as a calendar for your staff that live in other countries.

For each of these scheduling needs, you must create a new base calendar. For example, to create a new base calendar to schedule a 4-day work week with 10 hours of work each day, Monday through Thursday, complete the following steps:

1. In the *Properties* section of the *Project* ribbon, click the *Change Working Time* button.
2. In the *Change Working Time* dialog, click the *Create New Calendar* button in the upper right corner of the dialog. The software displays the *Create New Base Calendar* dialog as shown in Figure 4 - 47.

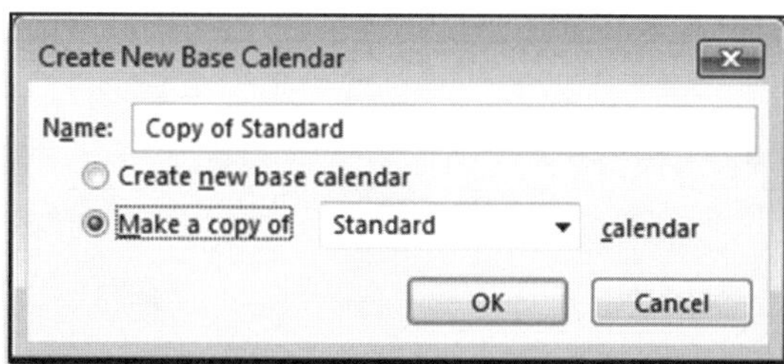

Figure 4 - 47: Create New Base Calendar dialog

3. In the *Name* field, enter a name for your new base calendar.
4. To copy the existing schedule of company holidays, select the *Make a copy of Standard calendar* option. To create an entirely new calendar without company holidays, select the *Create new base calendar* option.
5. Click the *OK* button.

6. Set the working and nonworking schedule for the new calendar using the steps detailed in the previous topical sections.
7. Click the *OK* button in the *Change Working Time* dialog.

For example, Figure 4 - 48 shows a custom *4x10 Work Week* base calendar I created. This calendar schedules work for 10 hours per day from 7:00 AM – 6:00 PM, Monday through Thursday, with every Friday marked as nonworking time.

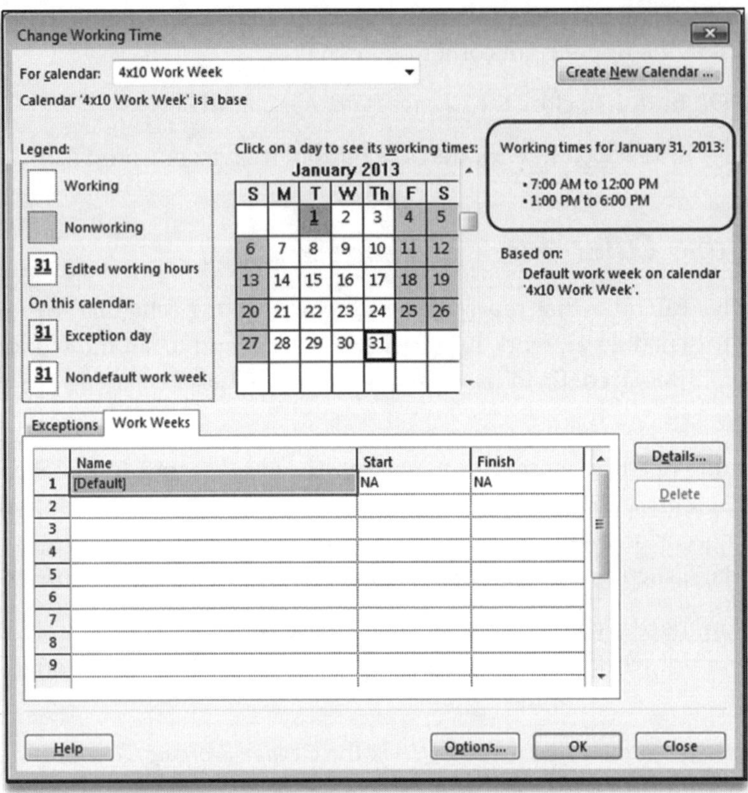

Figure 4 - 48: 4x10 Work Week base calendar

Hands On Exercise

Exercise 4 - 12

Create a new base calendar to schedule work to occur only on a Saturday or Sunday.

1. Return to the **Training Advisor 04.mpp** sample file.
2. In the *Properties* section of the *Project* ribbon, click the *Change Working Time* button.
3. In the *Change Working Time* dialog, click the *Create New Calendar* button.
4. In the *Create New Calendar* dialog, select the *Create new base calendar* option.

5. Enter the name *Weekend Work Only* in the *Name* field and click the *OK* button.
6. Click the *Work Weeks* tab, select the *[Default]* item in the data grid, and then click the *Details* button.
7. Using the **Control** key on your computer keyboard, select the *Sunday* and *Saturday* items in the *Select days* section of the *Details* dialog, and then release the **Control** key.
8. Select the *Set days to these specific working time* option.
9. In the *From* and *To* fields, enter the working schedule of *8:00 AM* to *12:00 PM* and *1:00 PM* to *5:00 PM*.
10. In the *Select days* section of the dialog, select *Monday* through *Friday* only.
11. Select the *Set days to nonworking time* option.
12. Click the *OK* button to close the *Details* dialog.
13. In the *Change Working Time* dialog, examine the working schedule for your new custom *Weekend Work Only* base calendar.
14. Click the *OK* button to close the *Change Working Time* dialog.
15. In the *Quick Access Toolbar,* click the *Save* button to save your project.

Setting the Project Calendar

Setting the *Project* calendar is an optional step, and is only required if your project schedule does not follow the schedule specified on the *Standard* calendar. For example, suppose that you work for an international company that has its headquarters in the United States. Although you work in the United States, you are the manager of a project in which most of the team members are from Canada. Because most team members are from Canada, the Canadian working schedule with Canadian holidays should drive the project schedule. In a situation like this, the project manager must change both the *Project* calendar and the *Non-Working Time* calendar to a calendar that contains Canadian holidays by completing the following steps:

1. Click the *Project* tab to display the *Project* ribbon.
2. In the *Properties* section of the *Project* ribbon, click the *Project Information* button.

Information: You can also display the *Project Information* dialog by clicking the *Definition* tab to display your new custom *Definition* ribbon. In the *Set Working Schedule* section of the *Definition* ribbon, click the *Set Project Calendar* button.

3. In the *Project Information* dialog, click the *Calendar* pick list and select the calendar with Canadian holidays, as shown in Figure 4 - 49.
4. Click the *OK* button.

Completing the preceding set of steps specifies the *Canadian Work Schedule* calendar as the *Project* calendar, which makes it the master calendar for scheduling all tasks in the project. This means that Project 2013 automatically schedules all tasks according to the working schedule shown on this calendar. If a task occurs on a Canadian national holiday, the software automatically reschedules the task to the next working day.

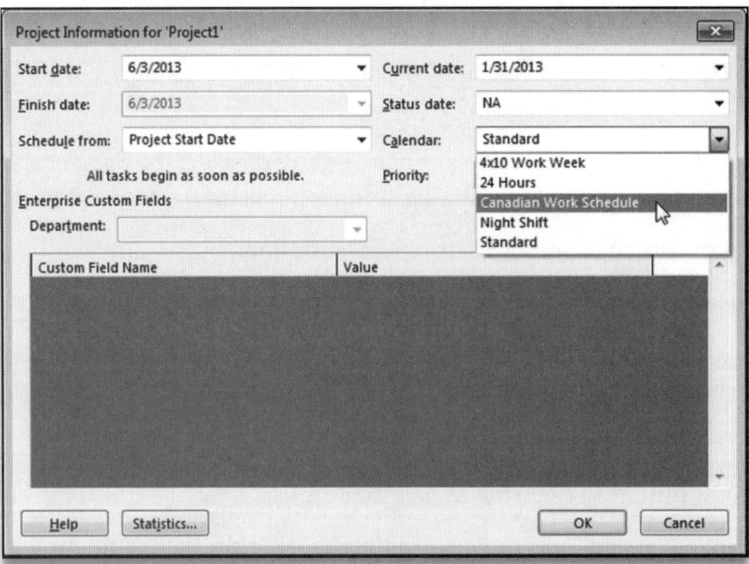

Figure 4 - 49: Project Information dialog
Set the Project calendar

After setting the *Project* calendar for the project, you must also set the *Non-Working Time* calendar. This calendar displays the nonworking time from the *Project* calendar as gray shaded bands in the Gantt chart. Setting the *Non-Working Time* calendar to the *Canadian Work Schedule* calendar allows you to see Canadian national holidays in the Gantt chart. To set the *Non-Working Time* calendar, complete the following steps:

1. Double-click anywhere in the *Timescale* bar. The software displays the *Timescale* dialog.
2. In the *Timescale* dialog, select the *Non-working time* tab.

Information: The fastest way to display the *Timescale* dialog with the *Non-working time* tab selected is to zoom to *Weeks Over Days* and then double-click anywhere in a gray shaded band in the Gantt chart. You can also right-click anywhere in the Gantt chart and select *Nonworking time* on the shortcut menu.

Information: You can also display the *Timescale* dialog with the *Non-working time* tab selected by clicking the *Definition* tab to display your new custom *Definition* ribbon. In the *Set Working Schedule* section of the *Definition* ribbon, click the *Set Nonworking Time Calendar* button.

3. On the *Non-working time* page of the dialog, click the *Calendar* pick list and select the alternate calendar with Canadian holidays, as shown in Figure 4 - 50.
4. Click the *OK* button.

Warning: You must complete **both sets of steps** to set an alternate working schedule for your project. If you set the *Project* calendar but fail to select the *Non-Working Time* calendar, Project 2013 schedules each task correctly, but you cannot confirm this schedule because you cannot see the holidays as gray shaded bands on the Gantt chart.

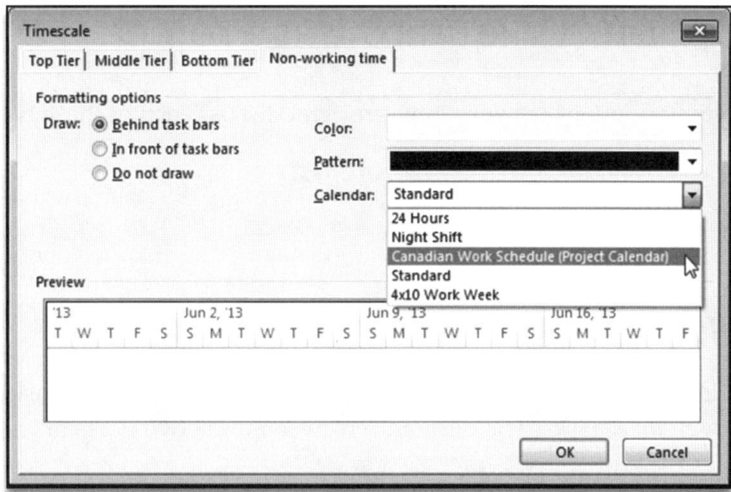

Figure 4 - 50: Timescale dialog, Non-working time tab

Information: Always keep in mind that the *Project* calendar sets the **initial schedule** for every task in the project. When you assign resources to tasks, Project 2013 schedules each task according to the calendars of the assigned resources. Therefore, even though the *Canadian Work Schedule* calendar governs the initial task schedule, if I assign an American worker to a task, the software reschedules the task according to the American working schedule.

Hands On Exercise

Exercise 4 - 13

Examine the *Project* calendar and *Non-Working Time* calendar for a project.

1. Return to the **Training Advisor 04.mpp** sample file.
2. In the *Properties* section of the *Project* ribbon, click the *Project Information* button.
3. In the *Project Information* dialog, click the *Calendar* pick list and examine the available calendars for use as the *Project* calendar.
4. Leave the *Standard* calendar selected on the *Calendar* pick list and click the *OK* button.
5. Double-click anywhere in the *Timescale* bar and then click the *Non-working time* tab.
6. On the *Non-working time* page of the *Timescale* dialog, click the *Calendar* pick list and examine the available calendars for use as the *Non-Working Time* calendar.
7. Leave the *Standard (Project Calendar)* item selected in the *Calendar* pick list and click the *OK* button.
8. In the *Quick Access Toolbar,* click the *Save* button to save your project.

Step #5 - Set Options Unique to this Project

You need to specify two types of options for your new project. I discuss each of these types of options individually:

- Set the default *Task Mode* option.
- Set options in the *Project Options* dialog.

Setting the Default Task Mode Option

The default *Task Mode* setting allows you to specify whether Project 2013 adds new tasks to your project as either *Auto Scheduled* or *Manually Scheduled* tasks. The difference between these two types of tasks is as follows:

- Project 2013 controls the schedule of each *Auto Scheduled* task by continuously updating the current *Start* date and *Finish* date for the task.
- **You** control the schedule of each *Manually Scheduled* task, which means that **you** must manually update the current *Start* date and *Finish* date for each task.

Microsoft added *Manually Scheduled* tasks as a new feature in Project 2010 and continues this feature in the 2013 version of the software. You can use the *Manually Scheduled* option for a task that you know you need to include in the project, but for which you do not have enough information to determine a *Duration* value, a *Start* date, or a *Finish* date. In other words, you want to leave the task as an unscheduled task.

The default *Task Mode* setting in Project 2013 is *Manually Scheduled,* which means that the software adds all new tasks as *Manually Scheduled* tasks. Every time you launch the software, you see the default *Task Mode* setting as a ScreenTip on the *Status* bar in the lower left corner of the application window, as shown in Figure 4 - 51.

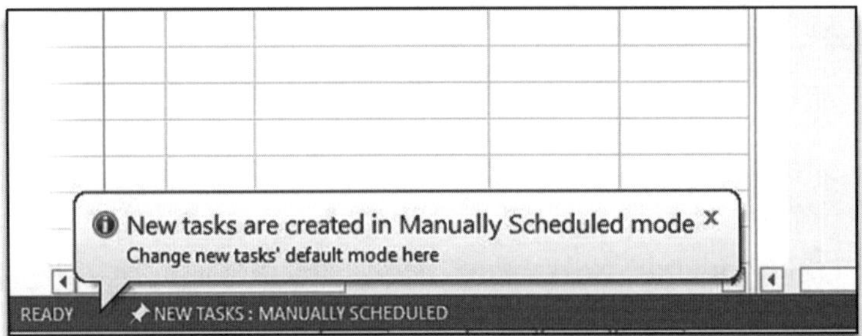

Figure 4 - 51: Task Mode option set to Manually Scheduled for all new tasks

To change the *Task Mode* setting and specify that all tasks must be *Auto Scheduled* in your new project, use either of the following methods:

- Click the *New Tasks* button on the *Status* bar and select the *Auto Scheduled* option.
- In the *Tasks* section of the *Task* ribbon, click the *Schedule Mode* pick list button and select the *Auto Schedule* item on the pick list.

When you create new tasks in your new project after selecting the default *Task Mode* option, Project 2013 creates them as *Auto Scheduled* tasks. If you want to specify the default *Task Mode* setting for all new blank projects, you must specify this setting in the *Project Options* dialog. I discuss this setting in the next section of this module.

Information: You can also specify the default *Task Mode* setting by clicking the *Definition* tab to display your new custom *Definition* ribbon. In the *Set Project Options* section of the *Definition* ribbon, click either the *New Tasks Auto Scheduled* button or the *New Tasks Manually Scheduled* button.

Setting Options in the Project Options Dialog

After you specify the default *Task Mode* setting for your new project, you are ready to specify options in the *Project Options* dialog. Project 2013 allows you to specify three types of options settings in the *Project Options* dialog:

- Application options that control how the software looks and works.
- Options specific to any project currently open.
- Options for all new projects created from a blank project.

To specify all three types of options settings, click the *File* tab and then click the *Options* button in the *Backstage*. The software displays the *General* page of the *Project Options* dialog shown in Figure 4 - 52.

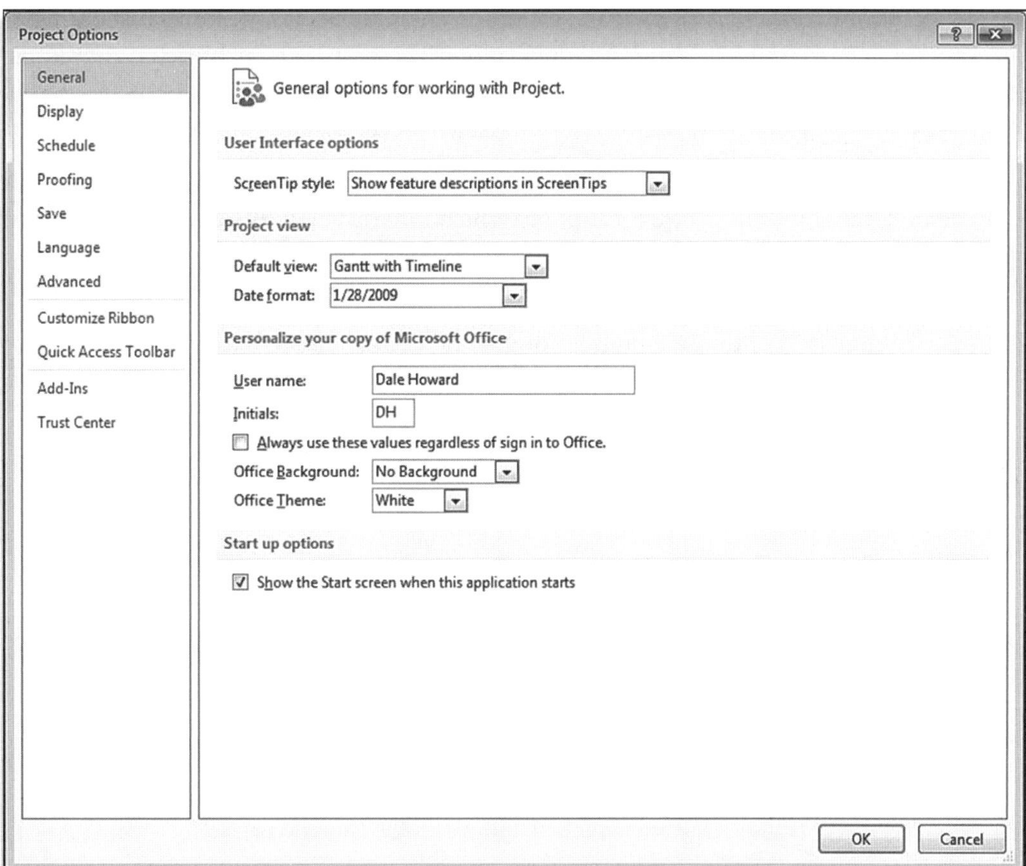

Figure 4 - 52: Project Options dialog, General page

Information: You can also specify the default *Task Mode* setting by clicking the *Definition* tab to display your new custom *Definition* ribbon. In the *Set Project Options* section of the *Definition* ribbon, click the *Set Project Options* button.

Notice in Figure 4 - 52 that the *Project Options* dialog includes tabs for eleven pages of options: *General, Display, Schedule, Proofing, Save, Language, Advanced, Customize Ribbon, Quick Access Toolbar, Add-Ins,* and *Trust Center*. With the exception of the *Customize Ribbon* and *Quick Access Toolbar* pages, which I discussed previously in Module 02, I discuss all of the other pages in detail below.

Information: Because Microsoft provides excellent *Help* articles for all of the options found in the *Project Options* dialog, I do not discuss each of these options individually. Instead, I focus on the new options found in Project 2013, and I document other important options of which you should be aware. To access *Help* for any option, press the **F1** function key or click the *Help* button (**?** button) in the upper right corner of the *Project Options* dialog.

Setting General Options

The *General* page of the *Project Options* dialog, shown previously in Figure 4 - 52, contains only application options. Remember that application options control how the software looks, works, and displays every project you open. The *General* page contains several sets of new options in Project 2013. These options include:

- The *Personalize your copy of Microsoft Office* section contains three new options that allow you to change the background pattern and background theme colors. These options include the *Always use these values regardless of sign in to Office* checkbox, the *Office Background* pick list, and the *Office Theme* pick list. I documented these options previously in this module while discussing the *Account* page in the *Backstage*.

- The new *Start up options* section contains a single option called *Show the Start screen when this application starts*. By default, the software selects this option, which forces Project 2013 to display the *Start* page every time to launch the software. If you disable this option, every time you launch Project 2013 the software opens a new blank project file and applies the *Gantt with Timeline* view to the project.

Table 4 - 3 shows the non-default options settings recommended by MSProjectExperts on the *General* page of the *Project Options* dialog.

Option	Setting
Date format	1/28/09
User name	Your name
Initials	Your initials
Show the Start screen when this application starts	Deselected

Table 4 - 3: Recommended options on the General page

Setting Display Options

Click the *Display* tab in the *Project Options* dialog to view the options on the *Display* page shown in Figure 4 - 53. As indicated at the top of the *Display* page, use the options on this page to control how Project 2013 displays project data on the screen. Project 2013 does not offer any new options on the *Display* page.

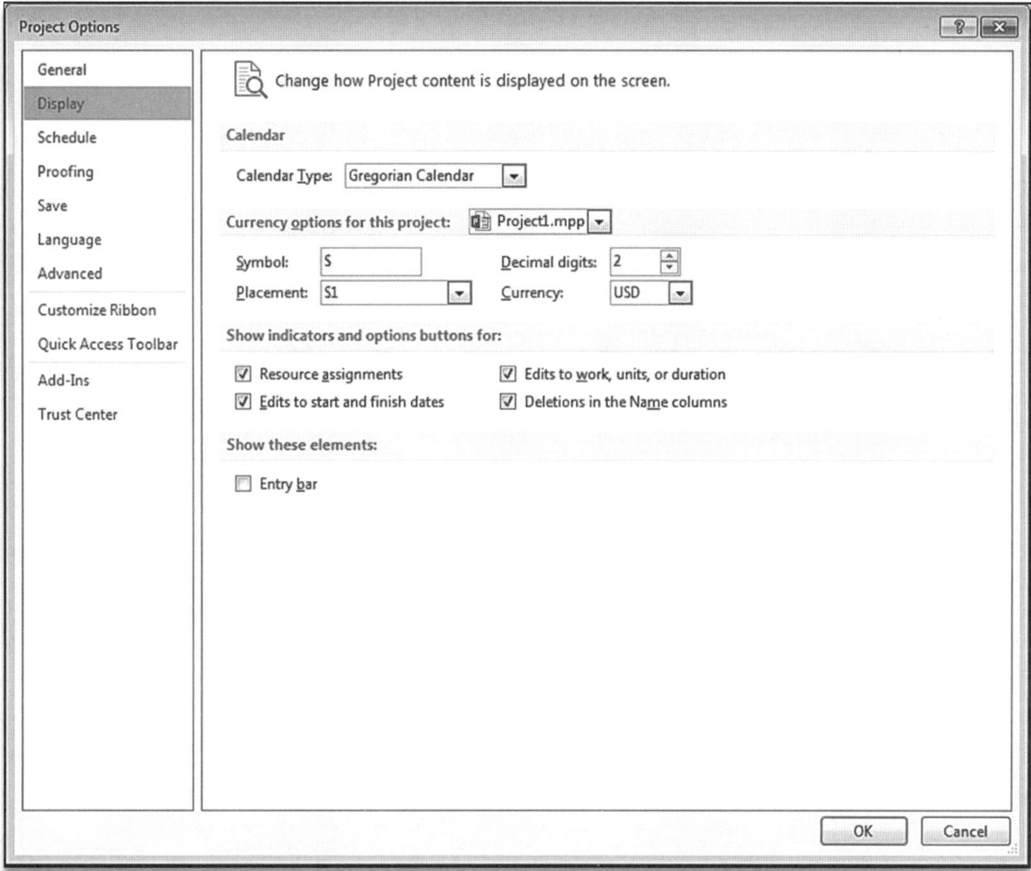

Figure 4 - 53: Project Options dialog, Display page

The *Display* page is the first page of many in the *Project Options* dialog in which Project 2013 allows you to specify option settings for any project currently open, regardless of whether that project is the active project,. You see this feature in the *Currency options for this project* section. Click the *Currency options for this project* pick list to view a list of projects currently open. By default, the pick list pre-selects the active project. Select any open project and specify your currency options for that project. Using this functionality means that you can specify a unique set of options settings for each open project. MSProjectExperts does not recommend any changes from the default settings on the *Display* page of the dialog.

Setting Schedule Options

Click the *Schedule* tab in the *Project Options* dialog to view the options on the *Schedule* page shown in Figure 4 - 54. As indicated at the top of the *Schedule* page, you use the options on this page to control scheduling, calendars, and calculations in Project 2013. The *Schedule* page includes sections in which you may specify the following types of options: *Calendar, Schedule, Scheduling,* and *Schedule Alerts,* along with two sections for *Calculation* options. Project 2013 does not offer any new options on the *Schedule* page.

Four of the six sections on the *Schedule* page allow you to specify options settings for any project currently open. The pick lists on the *Schedule* page, however, differ slightly from the pick list shown on the *Display* page. For example, if you click the *Calendar options for this project* pick list, the list includes all projects currently open, plus an *All New Projects* item. If you select the *All New Projects* item, the software allows you to specify options settings for all new blank projects you create from this point forward.

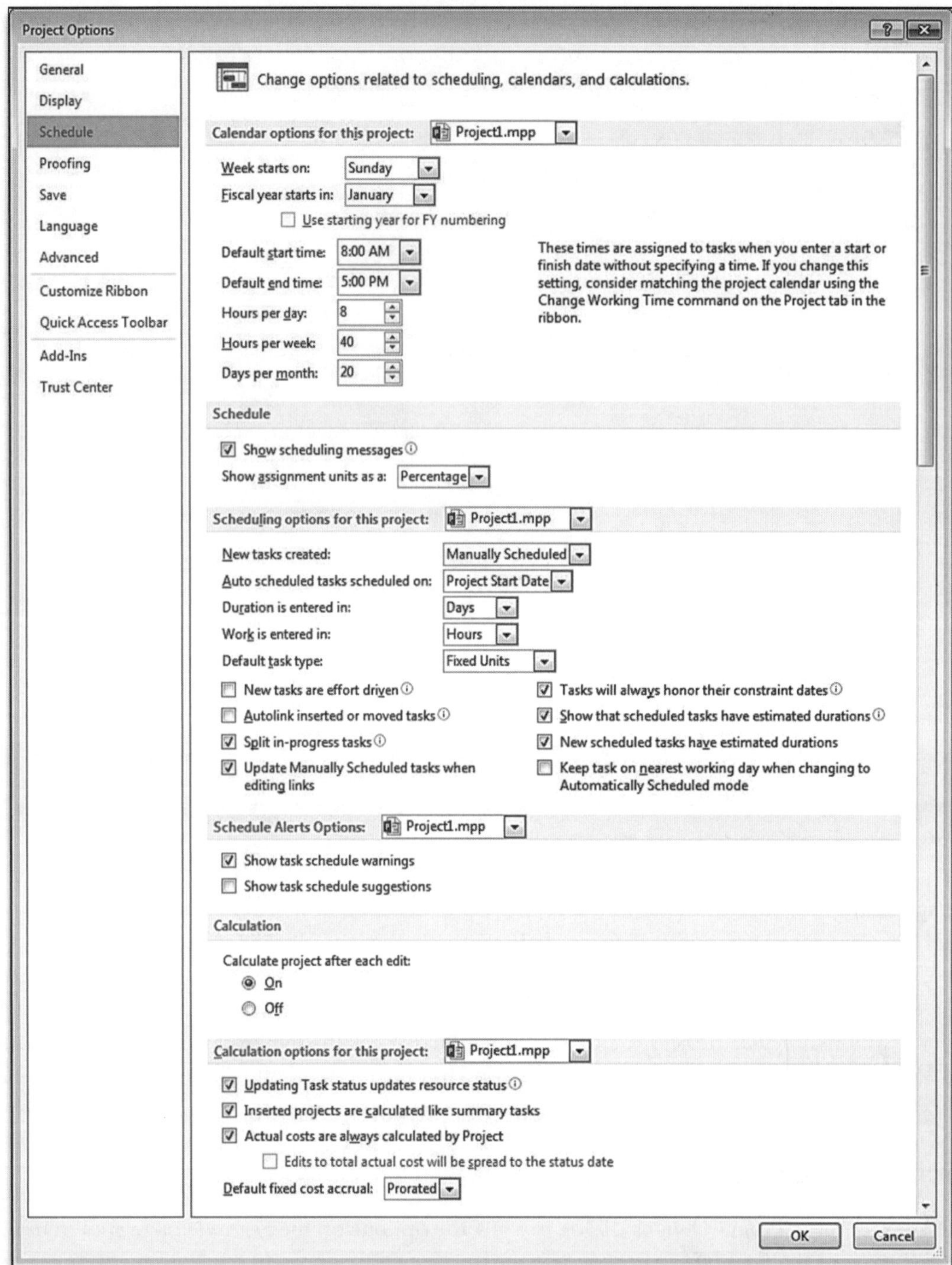

Figure 4 - 54: Project Options dialog, Schedule page

In the *Scheduling options for this project* section, you can use the *New tasks created* option to specify *Manually Scheduled* as the default *Task Mode* setting for all new projects. To do this, click the *Scheduling options for this project* pick list and select the *All New Projects* item. Then click the *New tasks created* pick list and select the *Auto Scheduled* item. When you click the *OK* button to close the *Project Options* dialog, Project 2013 sets the default *Task Mode* option to *Auto Scheduled* for every new blank project you create from this point forward.

Table 4 - 4 shows the non-default options settings recommended by MSProjectExperts on the *Schedule* page of the *Project Options* dialog. Furthermore, MSProjectExperts recommends you set these options for all open projects and for all new projects.

Option	Setting
New tasks created	Auto Scheduled
New tasks are effort driven	Selected
Show that scheduled tasks have estimated durations	Deselected
New scheduled tasks have estimated durations	Deselected
Show task schedule suggestions	Selected

Table 4 - 4: Recommended options on the Schedule page for all current and future project

Setting Proofing Options

Click the *Proofing* tab in the *Project Options* dialog to view the options on the *Proofing* page shown in Figure 4 - 55. As indicated at the top of the *Proofing* page, use the options on this page to control how Project 2013 corrects and formats text in your projects. There are no new options on the *Proofing* page and MSProjectExperts does not recommend any changes from the default settings.

Warning: Be careful about the default settings in the *AutoCorrect* dialog, accessed by clicking the *AutoCorrect Options* button at the top of the *Proofing* page. If you type the name of a task or resource in your project and you see the text suddenly changed without your permission, this means Project 2013 used an entry in the *AutoCorrect* dialog to change your text. To prevent the software from changing text without your permission, you may need to locate and delete those entries in the *AutoCorrect* dialog.

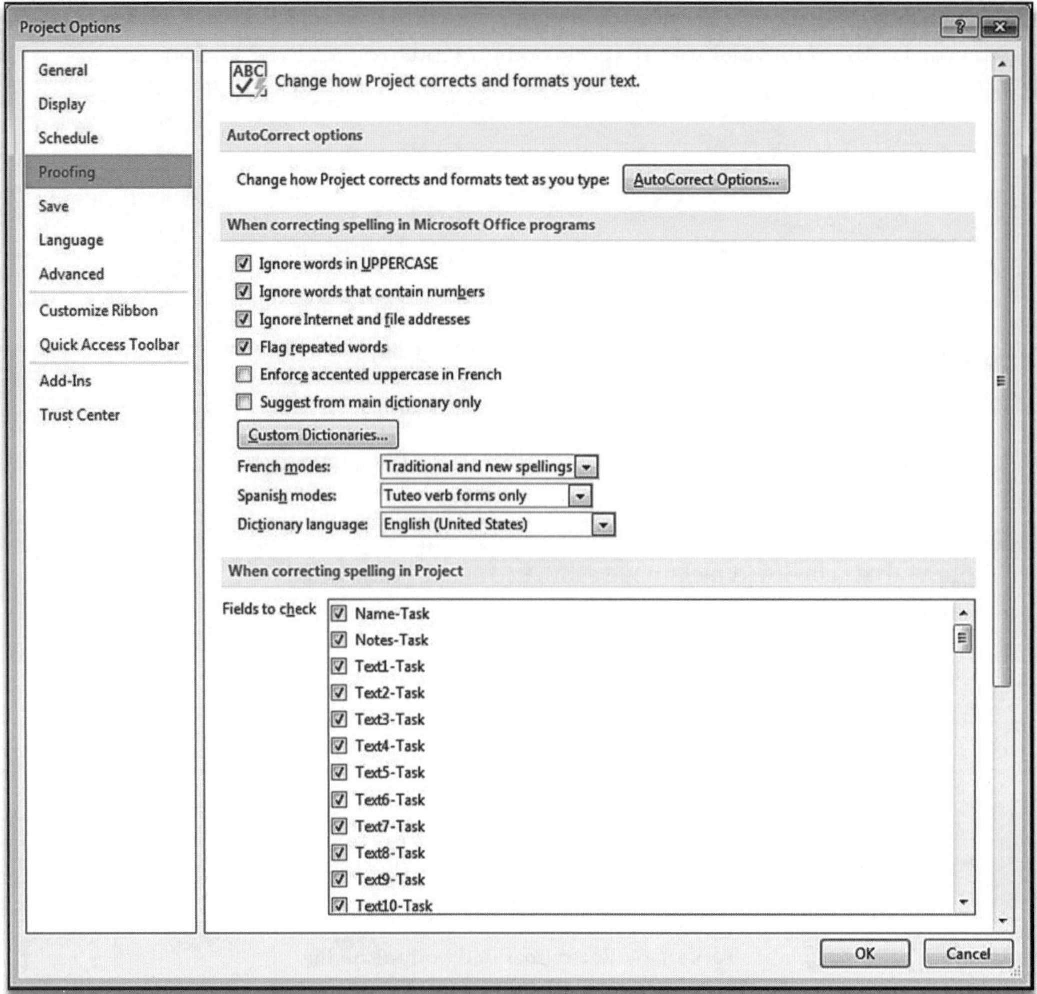

Figure 4 - 55: Project Options dialog, Proofing page

Setting Save Options

Click the *Save* tab in the *Project Options* dialog to view the options on the *Save* page shown in Figure 4 - 56. As indicated at the top of the *Save* page, use the options on this page to determine options for saving a project. The *Save* page contains only application options which control how the software saves your projects. Changes in Project 2013 on the *Save* page include three new options in the *Save projects* section:

- The *Don't show the Backstage when opening or saving files* option forces the software to hide the *Backstage* whenever you open or save a project file using the *Open* or *Save* buttons on your *Quick Access Toolbar.* With this option selected, when you click the *Open* button with no project currently open or you click the *Save* button, the software displays the *Open* or *Save As* dialog instead of displaying the *Backstage.* By default, the software deselects this option.

- The *Show additional places for saving, even if sign in may be required* option forces the software to display the *SkyDrive* link on the *Save As* page in the *Backstage.* By default, the software selects this option.

- The *Save to Computer by default* option forces the software to select the *Computer* link on the *Save As* page every time you save a new project file. By default, the software deselects this option.

The *Save Templates* section is entirely new in Project 2013 and contains only a single option, the *Default personal templates location* option. Remember that you must manually enter the path for your default *Templates* folder if you want to create new projects from templates you downloaded from the *Office.com* website or templates you created and saved.

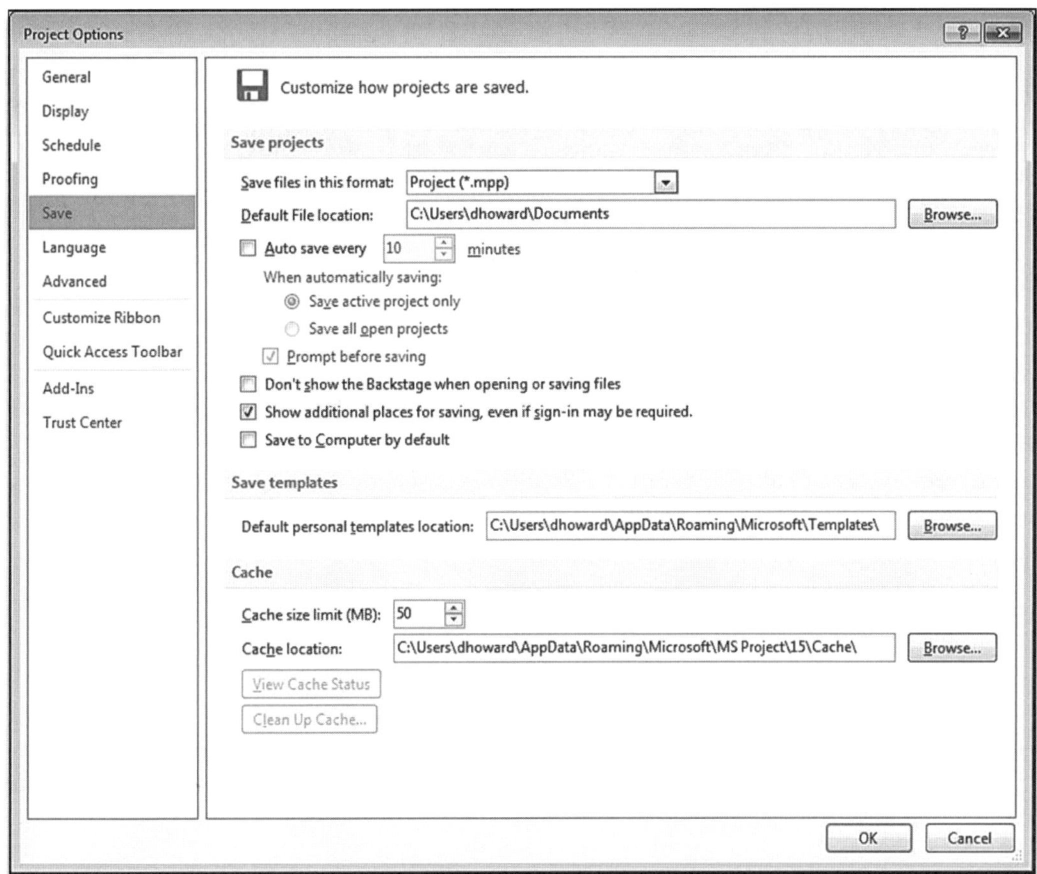

Figure 4 - 56: Project Options dialog, Save page

Table 4 - 5 shows the non-default options settings recommended by MSProjectExperts on the *Save* page of the *Project Options* dialog.

Option	Setting
Don't show the Backstage when opening or saving files	Selected
Show additional places for saving, even if sign in may be required	Deselected
Save to Computer by default	Selected

Table 4 - 5: Recommended options on the Save page

Warning: The *Save* page includes a *Cache* section at the bottom of the page only if you have the **Professional** version of Project 2013, as you use this feature with Project Server 2013. If you have the **Standard** version of the software, you do not see a *Cache* section on the *Save* page in the *Project Options* dialog.

Warning: If you like to perform a "what if" analysis in your project, and you select the *Auto save every ___ minutes* option, be sure to leave the *Prompt before saving* option selected. Otherwise, you risk the possibility of overwriting your production project with the "what if" changes, with no recourse to use the *Undo* button since the save action clears the *Undo* cache.

Backward Compatibility and Save Option Behavior

By default, Project 2013 is automatically backwards compatible with Project 2010. This means that you can create a project in the 2013 version of the software and a user with the 2010 version of the software can open and work with the project automatically. Microsoft designed Project 2013 to be backward compatible with three generations of the software. This means Project 2013 is also capable of saving projects in both the 2007 and 2000-2003 formats. Although the *Save files in this format* pick list in the *Save Projects* section is not a new option, it has a profoundly different effect on the behavior of your project client when you choose to save in an older project format as your default save option.

If you select either of the older project formats as the default on the *Save* page, the software creates all new blank projects in your selected format, and disables many version-specific features in Project 2013, such as being able to use *Manually Scheduled* tasks. When you create a new blank project the software presents the project in *Compatibility Mode,* which the software displays rather subtly in the *Title* bar at the top of the application window, as shown in Figure 4 - 57. Notice also how the software disables the *Manually Schedule* and *Auto Schedule* buttons in the *Task* ribbon.

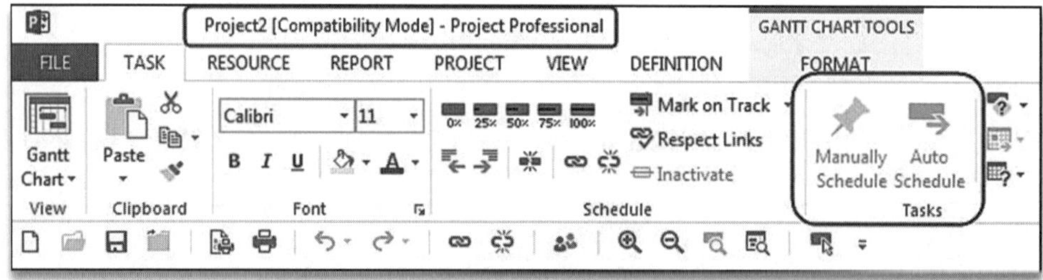

Figure 4 - 57: Compatibility Mode display

You cannot create *Manually Scheduled* tasks in new blank projects when you set your default to save in older formats. The same is true when you open projects saved in legacy formats. The software does not convert these for you automatically. Instead, it respects the limits of the legacy format and disables new scheduling features in Project 2013 for those projects. You can, however, continue to use these features when you open projects previously saved in the new Project 2013 file format and for new blank projects and existing projects saved in a legacy format after you deliberately save the project to the 2013 format. I discuss these limitations in more depth later in this module.

Best Practice: Because of the limitations with using older file formats, MSProjectExperts recommends as a best practice that you leave the default *Project (*.mpp)* option selected on the *Save files in this format* pick list on the *Save* page of the *Project Options* dialog.

Setting Language Options

Click the *Language* tab in the *Project Options* dialog to view and set options on the *Language* page shown in Figure 4 - 58. As indicated at the top of the *Language* page, use the options on this page to specify your language preference(s) for Project 2013. The *Choose Editing Languages* section includes a new option called *Let me know when I should download additional proofing tools.* By default, the software selects this option, which forces Project 2013 to warn you when you open a project file created in a language different from your selected editing languages.

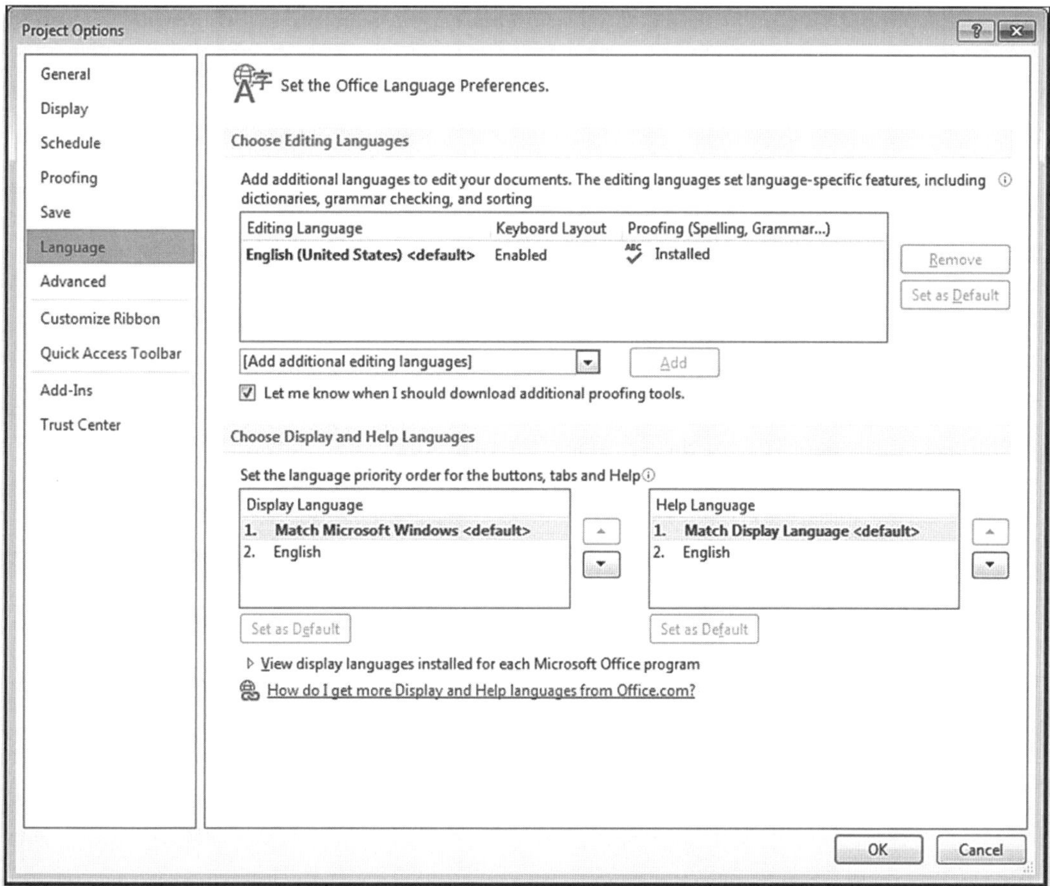

Figure 4 - 58: Project Options dialog, Language page

Before you can use the *Language* page, you must install one or more *Language Packs* for Office 2013 applications. After installing at least one *Language Pack*, you can specify the language you want to use for editing your projects, and choose the language the software uses to display your application and to display *Help* dialogs. If you do not install at least one *Language Pack*, the software limits you to the default options shown on the *Language* page.

Setting Advanced Options

Click the *Advanced* tab in the *Project Options* dialog to view the options on the *Advanced* page shown in Figure 4 - 59. As indicated at the top of the *Advanced* page, use the options on this page to specify advanced settings for Project 2013. The *Advanced* page includes sections where you specify the following types of options: *General, Project Web App, Planning Wizard, General options for this project, Edit, Display, Display options for this project, Cross project linking, Earned Value,* and *Calculation*. The *Display* section contains four new options:

- The *Show this number of Recent Projects* option determines the number of recent projects displayed in the *Recent Projects* section of the *Open* page in the *Backstage*. By default, the software specifies *25 projects* in this option.

- The *Quickly access this number of Recent Projects* option forces the software to display the names of the selected number of projects at the bottom of the sidepane on the left side of the *Backstage*. By default, the software does not select this option.

- The *Show this number of unpinned Recent Folders* option determines how many unpinned folders you see in the *Recent Folders* section of either the *Save As* page or the *Open* page in the *Backstage*. By default, the software specifies *5* folders in this option.

- The *Disable hardware graphics acceleration* does what the name implies. By default, the software does not select this option. Depending on the graphics hardware in your computer, you may see this option as disabled (grayed out) so that you cannot change the option.

Warning: The *Advanced* page includes a *Project Web App* section only in the **Professional** version of Project 2013 as you use this feature with Project Server 2013. If you have the **Standard** version of the software, you do not see the *Project Web App* section.

Best Practice: Although not a new option, the *Show Project Summary Task* option offers a new setting state. To display the Project Summary Task in all new blank projects, click the *Display options for this project* pick list and choose the *All New Projects* item, and then select the *Show Project Summary Task* option. In prior versions of Project, the software required you to select this option for each project individually.

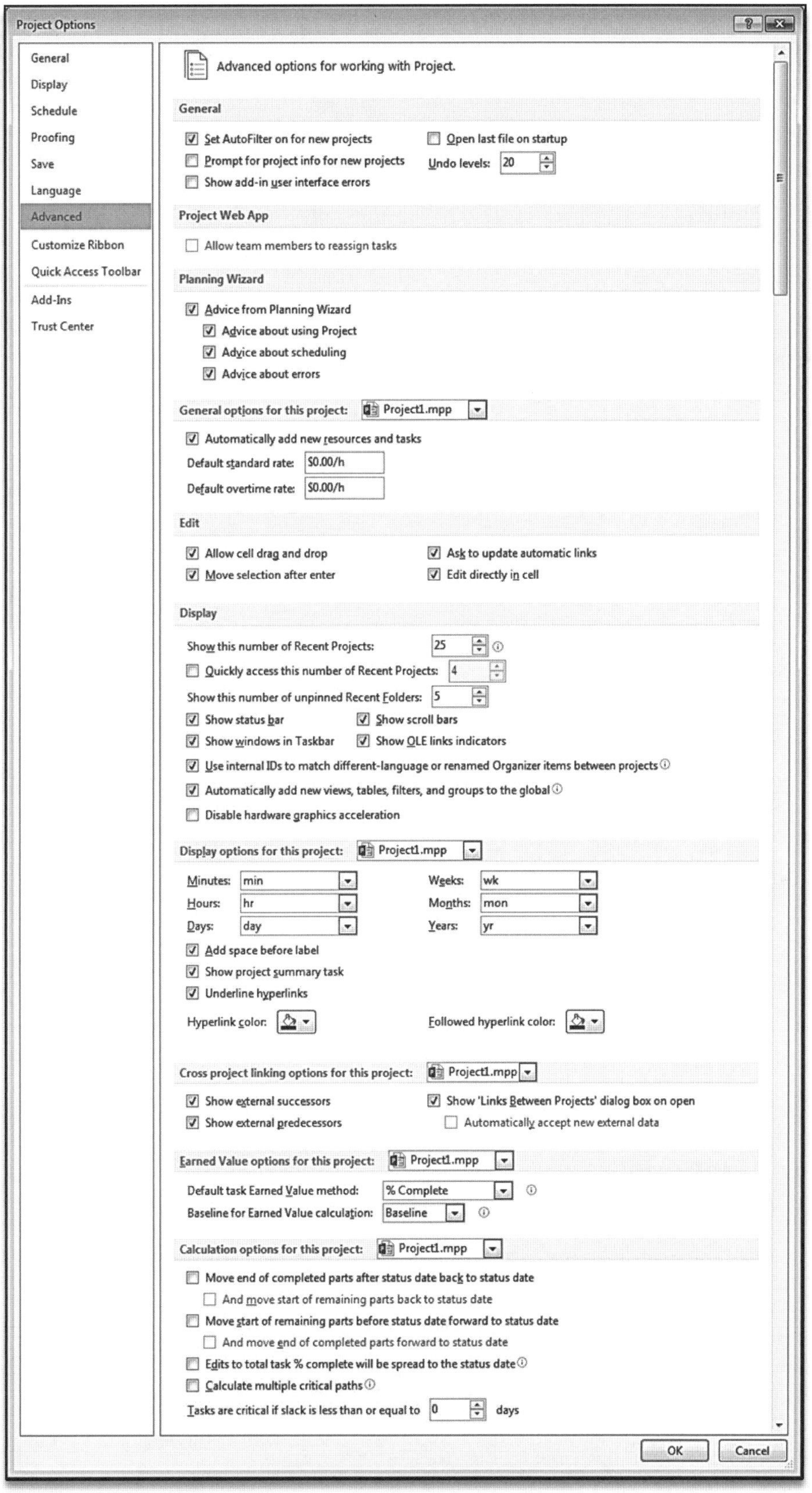

Figure 4 - 59: Project Options dialog, Advanced page

Table 4 - 6 shows the non-default options settings recommended by MSProjectExperts on the *Advanced* page of the *Project Options* dialog. Furthermore, MSProjectExperts recommends you set these options for all open projects and for all new projects.

Option	Setting
Automatically add new resources and tasks	Deselected
Minutes	m
Hours	h
Days	d
Weeks	w
Months	mo
Years	y
Show project summary task	Selected

Table 4 - 6: Recommended options on the Advanced page for all current and future projects

Setting Add-Ins Options

Click the *Add-Ins* tab in the *Project Options* dialog to view the options on the *Add-Ins* page shown in Figure 4 - 60. As indicated at the top of the *Add-Ins* page, use the options on this page to view and manage COM Add-Ins for the applications in the Office 2013 suite of tools.

Information: As with the 2010 version, Project 2013 **does not** include any of the pre-built macros found in the 2007 version and earlier. Note that the *Inactive Application Add-ins* section of the *Add-Ins* page shown in Figure 4 - 60 includes the familiar macros from Project 2007. This is because I also have Project 2007 installed on my computer. If you do not have Project 2007 installed on your computer, you do not see the 2007 macros displayed in the *Inactive Application Add-ins* section of the page.

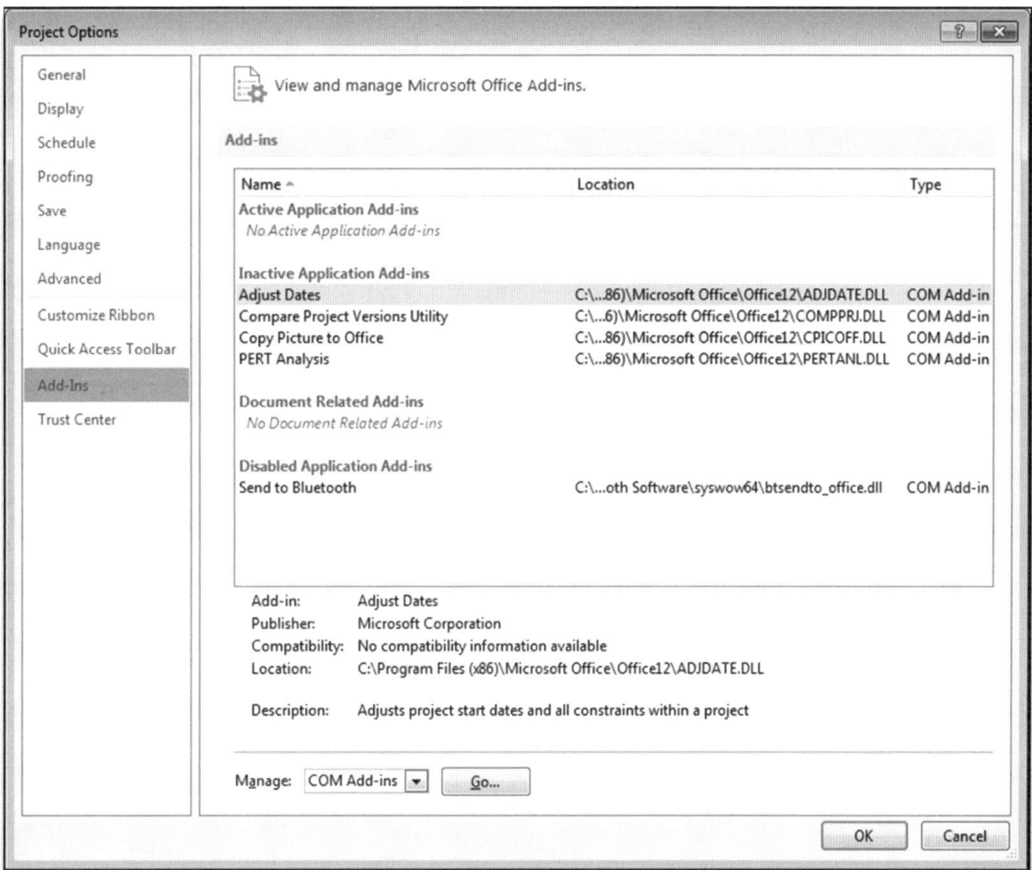

Figure 4 - 60: Project Options dialog, Add-Ins page

Setting Trust Center Options

Click the *Trust Center* tab in the *Project Options* dialog to view the options on the *Trust Center* page shown in Figure 4 - 61. As indicated at the top of the *Trust Center* page, use the options on this page to provide security for your project and for your computer. The *Trust Center* page in the *Project Options* dialog provides three sections of security-related information. The *Protecting your privacy* section includes four links, the *Show the Microsoft Project privacy statement*, the *Office.com privacy statement*, the *Customer Experience Improvement Program*, and the *Microsoft Office Feedback "Send a Smile" Privacy Statement* links. I do not discuss these options, as they are self-explanatory. The *Security & more* section includes the *Microsoft Trustworthy Computing* link that displays the *Microsoft Trustworthy Computing* website. Again, I do not discuss this option, as it self-explanatory.

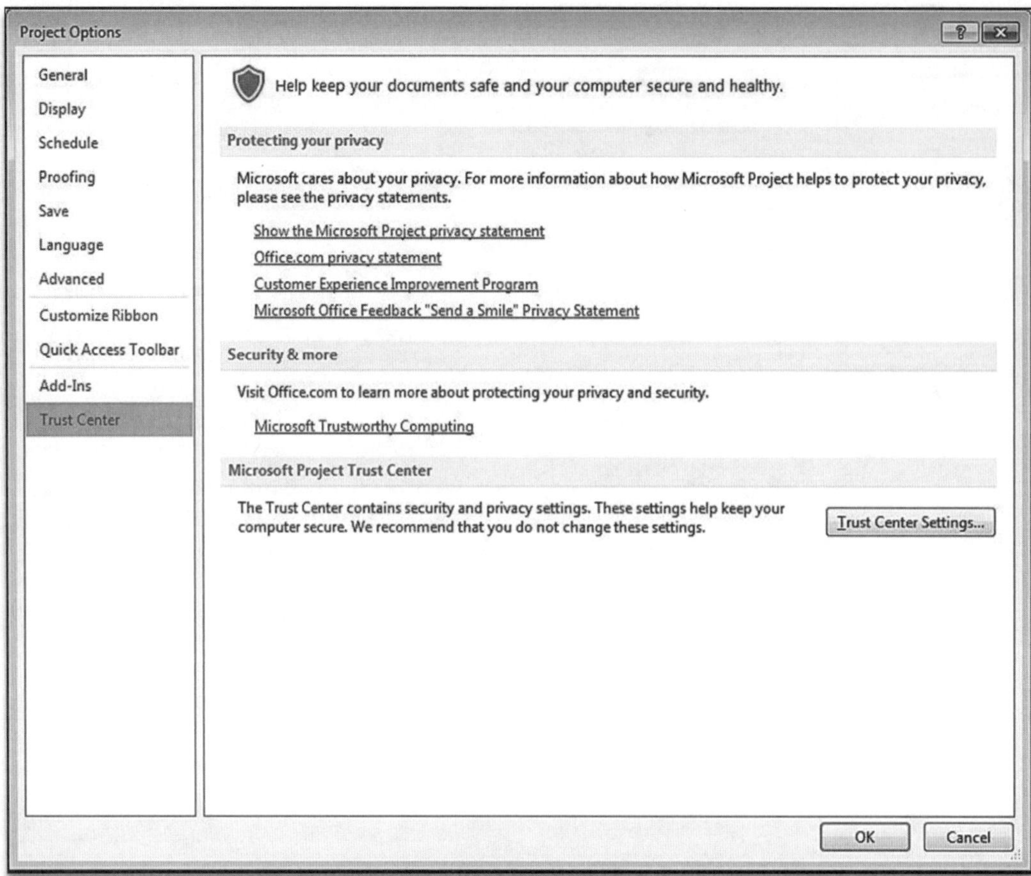

Figure 4 - 61: Project Options dialog, Trust Center page

In the *Microsoft Project Trust Center* section of the *Project Options* dialog, click the *Trust Center Settings* button to specify a range of security settings. The software displays the *Macro Settings* page of the *Trust Center* dialog shown in Figure 4 - 62 by default. Use the *Macro Settings* page to set your level of macro security.

By default, Project 2013 selects the *Disable all macros with notification* option, which prevents you from running macros in the application unless you authorize the macros to run. The software notifies you in a warning dialog about this limitation when you attempt to run a macro. If you do not intend to use macros ever, you can avoid the security warning by selecting the *Disable all macros without notification* option. To enable all macros and avoid the security warning entirely, you can select the *Disable all macros except digitally signed macros* option or select the *Enable all macros* option. Notice in the dialog shown in Figure 4 - 62 that Microsoft does not recommend selecting the *Enable all macros* option. This is because of the possibility that a macro might actually be a malicious virus instead.

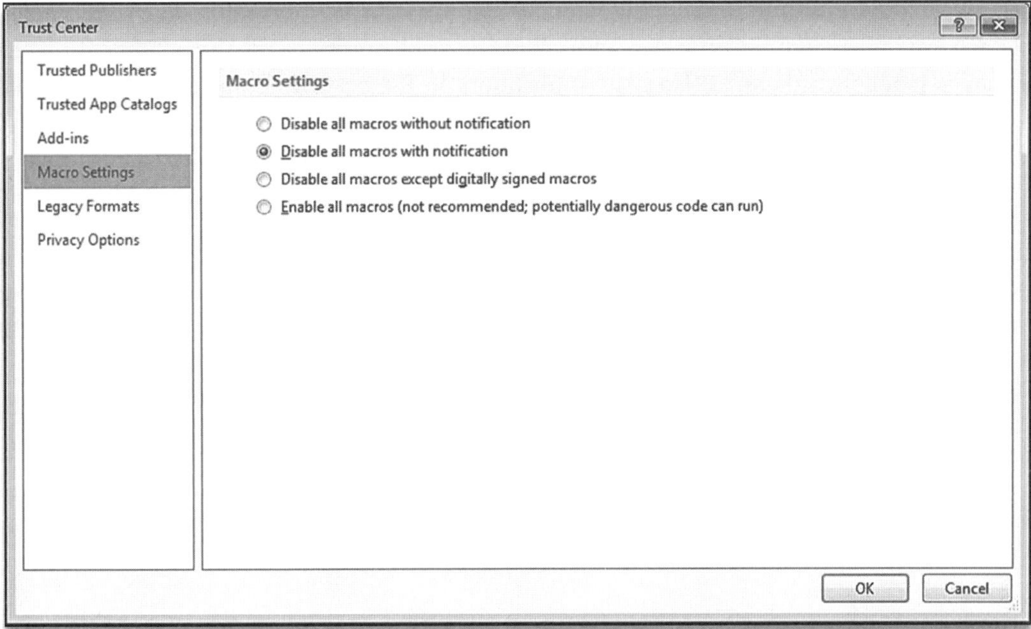

Figure 4 - 62: Trust Center dialog, Macro Settings page

Click the *Trusted Publishers* tab to display the *Trusted Publishers* page shown in Figure 4 - 63. The *Trusted Publishers* page shows macro authors whose VBA code you trust. Notice in the dialog shown in Figure 4 - 63 that I do not currently have a formal macro trust relationship with any macro authors.

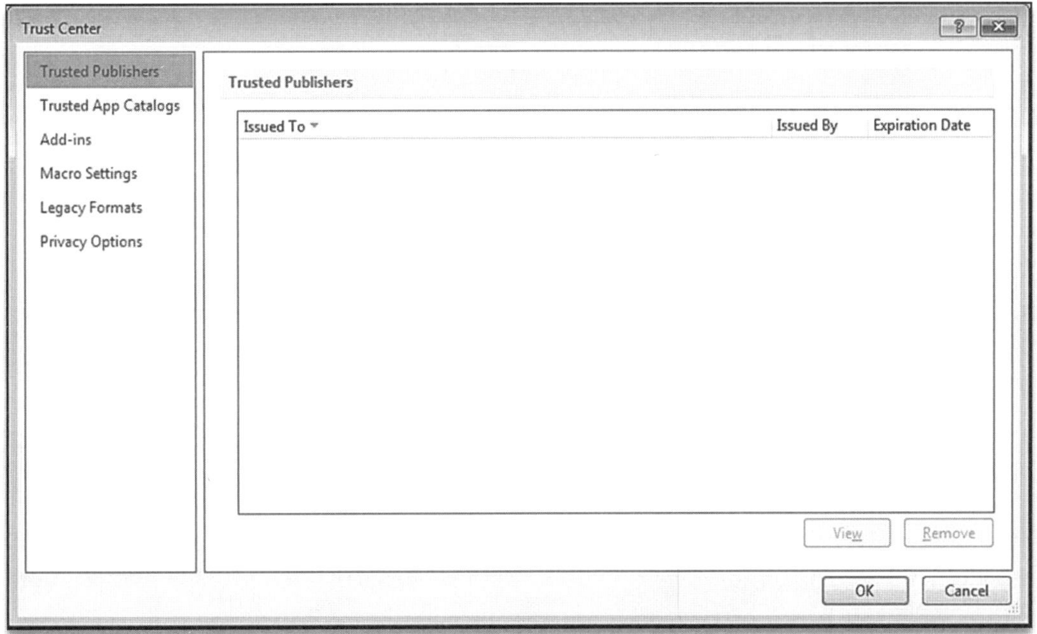

Figure 4 - 63: Trust Center dialog, Trusted Publishers page

Click the *Trusted App Catalogs* tab to display the new *Trusted App Catalogs* page shown in Figure 4 - 64. Use the options on this page to manage your Office Apps for all of the applications in the Office 2013 suite of tools. Office Apps are web pages loaded inside an Office 2013 application. In Project 2013, you can only use task pane Office Apps to help you work with a project file.

To trust an Office App catalog in Project 2013, enter the URL for the Office App catalog in the *Catalog URL* field, and then click the *Add Catalog* button to add the Office App to the list in the *Trusted Catalogs Table* section of the dialog. To remove any existing Office App catalog, select the catalog, and then click the *Remove* button. In addition, you can disable Office App catalogs by selecting either the *Don't allow any apps to start* option or the *Don't allow apps from the Office Store to start* option in the *Trusted App Catalogs* section at the top of the dialog.

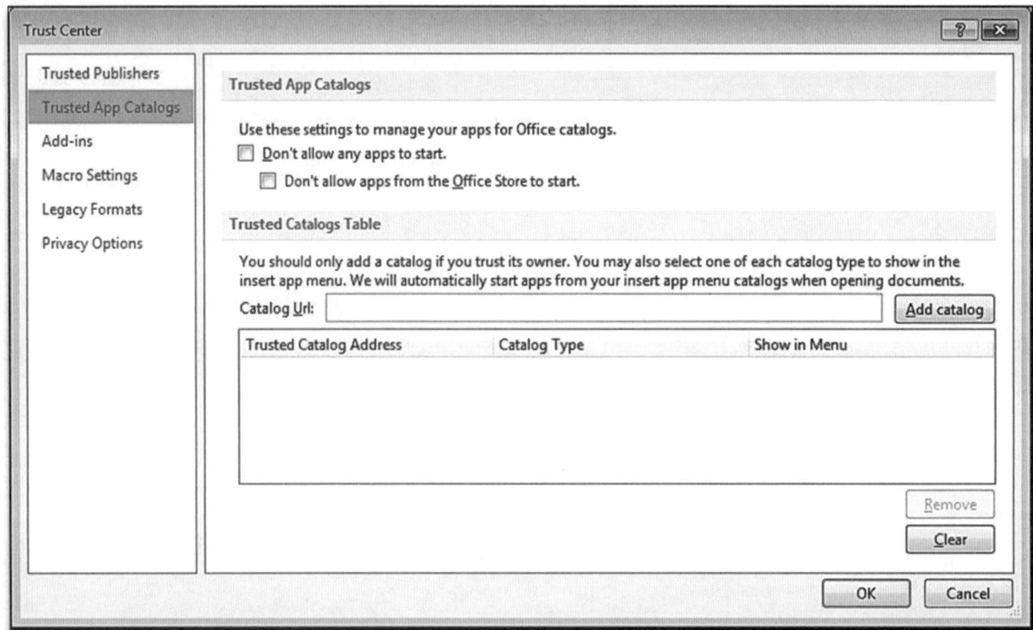

Figure 4 - 64: Trust Center dialog, Trusted App Catalogs page

Information: When you specify any of the preceding settings in the *Trust Center* dialog, the Office 2013 system saves these settings in the *Trust Center* dialog for every application in the Office 2013 suite of tools.

Click the *Add-Ins* tab to display the *Add-Ins* page shown in Figure 4 - 65. The *Add-Ins* page offers three options for working with COM Add-Ins, and none of these options are enabled by default. I do not discuss these options because they are self-explanatory.

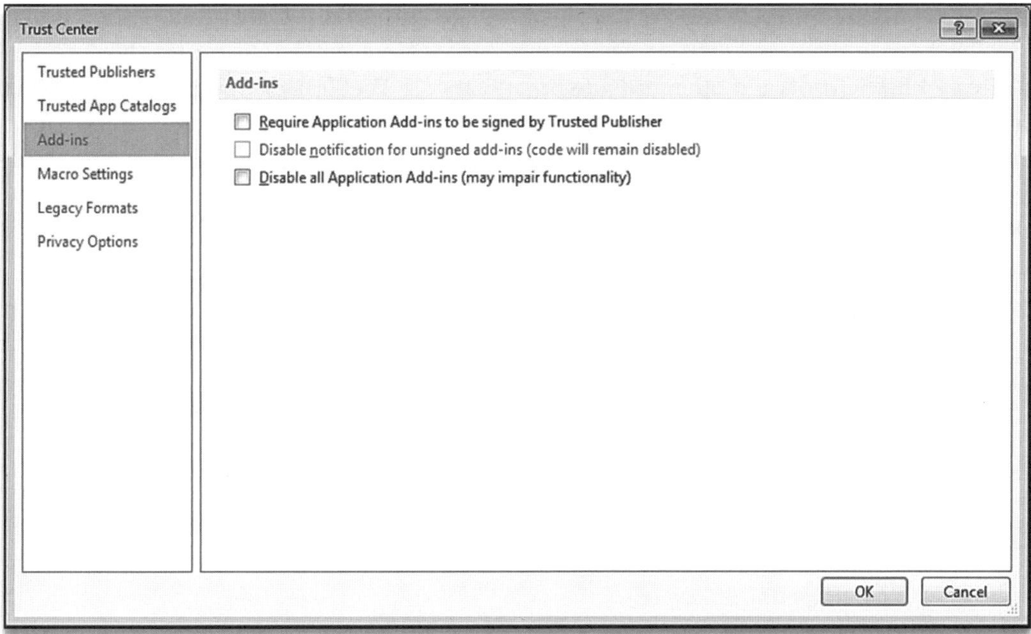

Figure 4 - 65: Trust Center dialog, Add-Ins page

Click the *Legacy Formats* tab to display the *Legacy Formats* page in the *Trust Center* dialog shown in Figure 4 - 66. The options on the *Legacy Formats* page control how Project 2013 works with non-default and legacy file formats. Legacy formats controlled by this setting include tab-delimited and comma-delimited text files. The default *Do not open/save file with legacy or non-default file formats in Project* option prevents you from opening or closing files that are non-default or legacy format. If you need to work with non-default or legacy files, select either the *Prompt when loading files with legacy or non-default file format* option or the *Allow loading files with legacy or non-default file formats* option in the dialog.

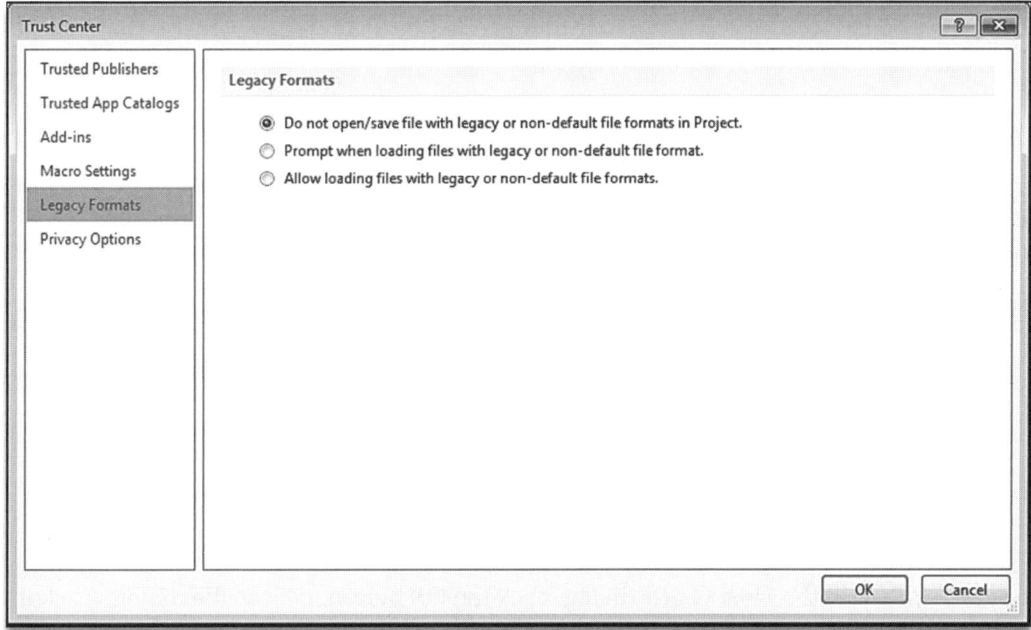

Figure 4 - 66: Trust Center dialog, Legacy Formats page

Click the *Privacy Options* tab to display the *Privacy Options* page in the *Trust Center* dialog shown in Figure 4 - 67. As the name of the page implies, use the settings on the *Privacy Options* page to control how much information Project 2013 shares with Microsoft and other outside organizations. The *Privacy Options* page contains six application options and one project-specific option. The names of the six application options reveal their function, so I do not discuss them individually. If you select the *Remove personal information from file properties on save* option, the single project-specific option, the software clears the *Author, Manager, Company* and *Last Saved By* fields in the *Properties* dialog each time you save the project.

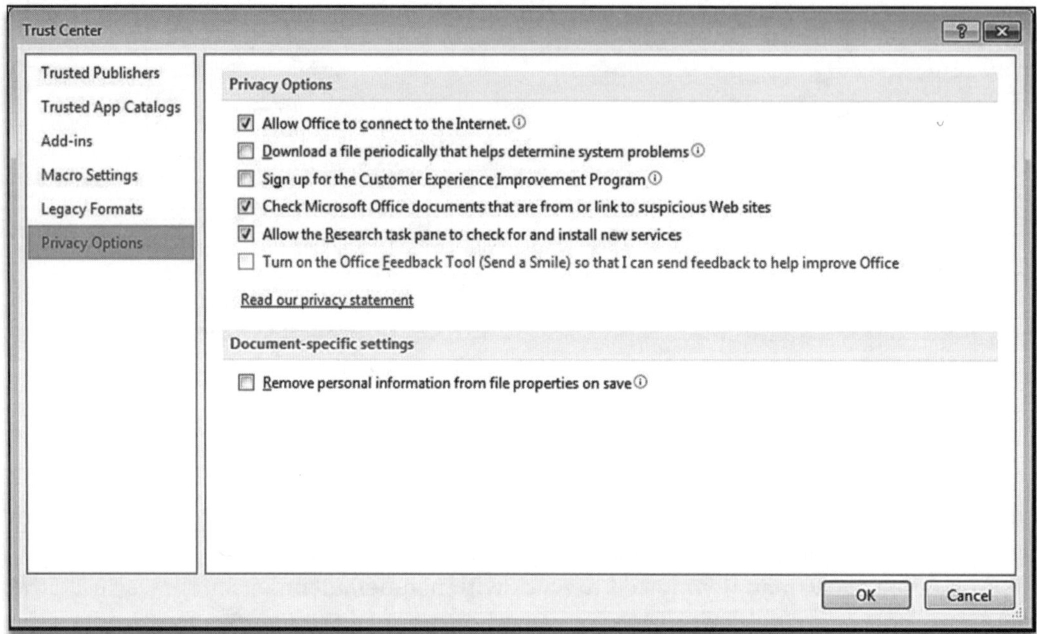

Figure 4 - 67: Trust Center dialog, Privacy Options page

Table 4 - 7 shows the non-default options settings recommended by MSProjectExperts on the *Trust Center* page of the *Project Options* dialog.

Option	Setting
Macro Settings	Enable all macros
Legacy Formats	Allow loading files with legacy or non-default file formats
Trusted App Catalogs	Add the URL for the Office Store catalog **https://office.microsoft.com**

Table 4 - 7: Recommended options for the Trust Center page

After selecting your options in the *Trust Center* dialog, click the *OK* button to close the dialog. Click the *OK* button to close the *Project Options* dialog.

Hands On Exercise

Exercise 4 - 14

In your new project, specify the settings recommended by MSProjectExperts in the *Project Options* dialog.

1. Return to the **Training Advisor 04.mpp** sample file.
2. Click the *File* tab and then click the *Options* tab in the *Backstage*.
3. On the *General* page of the *Project Options* dialog, set the following options:

Option	Setting
Date format	1/28/09
User name	Your name
Initials	Your initials
Show the Start screen when this application starts	Deselected

4. On the *Schedule* page, set the following options for the active project in the *Scheduling options for this project* section:

Option	Setting
New tasks are effort driven	Selected
Show that scheduled tasks have estimated durations	Deselected
New scheduled tasks have estimated durations	Deselected

5. On the *Schedule* page, click the *Scheduling options for this project* pick list, select the *All New Projects* item, and then set the following options for all new projects:

Option	Setting
New tasks created	Auto Scheduled
New tasks are effort driven	Selected
Show that scheduled tasks have estimated durations	Deselected
New scheduled tasks have estimated durations	Deselected

6. On the *Schedule* page, select the *Show task schedule suggestions* option for the active project in the *Schedule Alert Options* section.

7. On the *Schedule* page, click the *Schedule Alert Options* pick list, select the *All New Projects* item, and then select the *Show task schedule suggestions* option again for all new projects.

8. On the *Save* page, set the following options in the *Save projects* section:

Option	Setting
Don't show the Backstage when opening or saving files	Selected
Show additional places for saving, even if sign in may be required	Deselected
Save to Computer by default	Selected

9. On the *Advanced* page, deselect the *Automatically Add New Resources and Tasks* option for the active project in the *General Options for this Project* section.

10. On the *Advanced* page, click the *General options for this project* pick list, select the *All New Projects* item, and then deselect the *Automatically add new resources and tasks* option for all new projects.

11. On the *Advanced* page, set the following options for the active project in the *Display options for this project* section:

Option	Setting
Minutes	m
Hours	h
Days	d
Weeks	w
Months	mo
Years	y
Show project summary task	Selected

12. On the *Advanced* page, click the *Display options for this project* pick list, select the *All New Projects* item, and then specify **the same settings** that you set in the previous step.

13. On the *Trust Center* page, click the *Trust Center Settings* button.

14. On the *Legacy Formats* page of the *Trust Center* dialog, select the *Allow loading files with legacy or non-default file formats* option.

15. Click the *OK* button to close the *Trust Center* dialog.

16. Click the *OK* button to close the *Project Options* dialog.

17. In the *Quick Access Toolbar*, click the *Save* button to save your project.

Step #6 - Save the Project

The final step in the six-step project definition process is to save the project file according to your organization's naming conventions. To save your project, complete the following steps:

1. Click the *File* tab and then click the *Save* tab in the *Backstage*. If you set up Project 2013 with the *Project Options* dialog settings recommended by MSProjectExperts, the software displays the *Save As* dialog shown in Figure 4 - 68. By default, the software selects the *My Documents* folder in the *Save As* dialog.

Information: If you use the default settings in the *Project Options* dialog, Project 2013 displays the *Save As* page in the *Backstage*. On the *Save As* page, click the *Computer* link and then click the *Browse* button to display the *Save As* dialog.

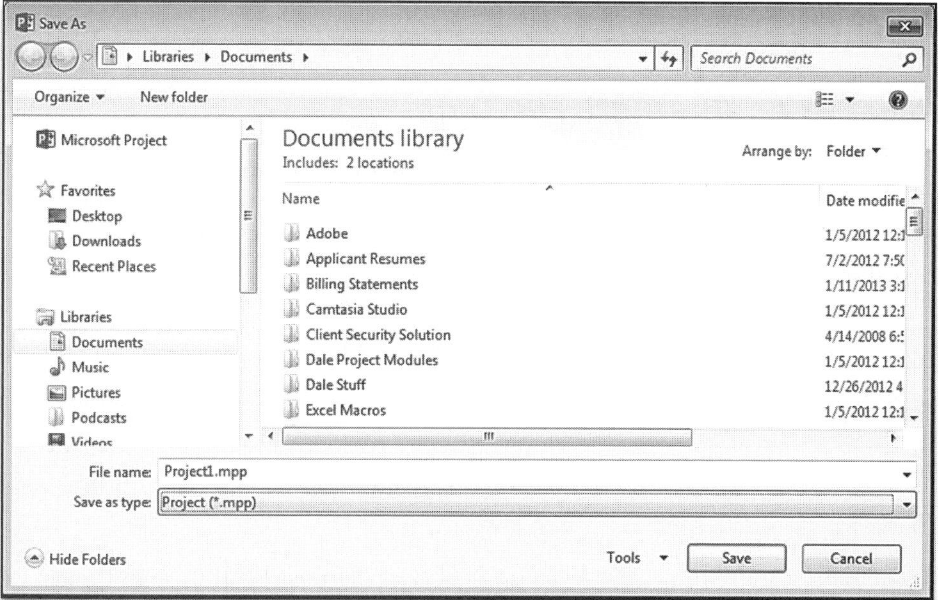

Figure 4 - 68: Save As dialog

2. In the *Save As* dialog, navigate to the location where you want to save your project.

3. In the *File name* field, enter a name for your project that conforms to your organization's naming convention.

4. Click the *Save* button.

Hands On Exercise

Exercise 4 - 15

Your organization's naming convention for project files includes the department name, the 3-letter initials of the project manager, and a brief description of the project in the file name. Save this project file using the company naming convention.

1. Return to the **Training Advisor 04.mpp** sample file.
2. Click the *File* tab and then click the *Save As* tab in the *Backstage*.
3. On the *Save As* page in the *Backstage*, click the *Computer* link and then click the *Browse* button.
4. In the *Save As* dialog, navigate to the folder where you unzipped your sample files for this class.
5. In the *Save As* dialog, edit the name of the file to include your department name, your own three-letter initials, and the words *Training Advisor*.
6. Click the *Save* button.
7. Click the *File* tab and then click the *Close* button in the *Backstage* to close the **Training Advisor 04.mpp** sample file.

Saving a Project as an Alternate File Type

Beyond saving a project using the default Project 2013 file type, the software allows you to save your project using alternate file types. When you save a new project file for the first time, the software selects the *Project (*.mpp)* option as the default file type, which saves the project file in the native Project 2013 file format.

Warning: In order to work with some of the following file types, you must change the settings on the *Legacy Formats* page of the *Trust Center* dialog, as discussed in the previous topic.

As I noted in the *Exporting a Project File to an Alternate File Type* topical section in Module 02, *Project 2013 Overview*, the file types available in Project 2013 include the following:

- **Project** – This is the default Project 2013 file type, which is also compatible with Project 2010.
- **Project 2007 Project** – This file type provides backwards compatibility with Project 2007.
- **Project 2000-2003 Project** – This file type provides backwards compatibility with the 2000, 2002, and 2003 versions of Project.
- **Project Template** – This file type allows you to save a project file as a Project 2013 project template, which is also compatible with Project 2010.
- **Project 2007 Template** – This file type allows you to save a project file as a Project 2007 project template.

- **Excel Workbook** – This file type allows you to save a project file as an Excel 2013 workbook, which is also compatible with Excel 2007 and 2010.
- **Excel Binary Workbook** – Select this file type to save the project file as a macro-enabled Excel workbook file stored in binary format rather than saving it in the XLSX format. Use this file format to save a very large Project file quickly and efficiently. This file type is compatible with Excel 2013, 2010, and 2007.
- **Excel 97-2003 Workbook** – Select this file type to save a project file as an Excel workbook using a format that allows Excel 97 through Excel 2003 to open the workbook directly without using a converter.
- **PDF File** – Select this file type to save a project file as a Portable Document Format (PDF) file. Using the PDF file type allows you to share project information with users who do not have any version of Project installed on their workstations.
- **XPS File** – Select this file type to save a project file as an XML Paper Specification file. Using the XPS file type allows you to share project information with users who do not have any version of Project installed on their workstations.
- **Text File** – Select this file type to save your project file as a *Tab Delimited* text file.
- **CSV File** – Select this file type to save your project file as a *Comma Delimited* text file.
- **XML Format** – Select this file type to save your project file as an Extensible Markup Language (XML) file.

Information: Many of the alternate file types require you to use the *Export Wizard* to save the file. Because the *Export Wizard* is a very complex tool with many options, I devote an entire module to the import/export process in this book's companion volume, *Ultimate Study Guide: Advanced, Microsoft Project 2013*. Therefore, in this module, I do not discuss how to save a project using most of the alternate file types, and focus instead on saving a project for use with earlier versions of the Project software.

Information: As I noted in the *Exporting a Project File to an Alternate File Type* topical section in Module 02, *Project 2013 Overview*, you can also save a project using an alternate file type from the *Export* page in the *Backstage*.

To save a Project 2013 file using an alternate file type, complete the following steps:

1. Click the *File* tab and then click the *Save As* tab in the *Backstage.*
2. On the *Save As* page in the *Backstage*, click the *Computer* link and then click the *Browse* button.
3. In the *Save As* dialog, navigate to the location where you want to save the project using an alternate file type.
4. In the *Save As* dialog, click the *Save as type* pick list and select an alternate file type, as shown in Figure 4 - 69.
5. In the *Save As* dialog, enter an alternate name for the file, if necessary.
6. Click the *Save* button.

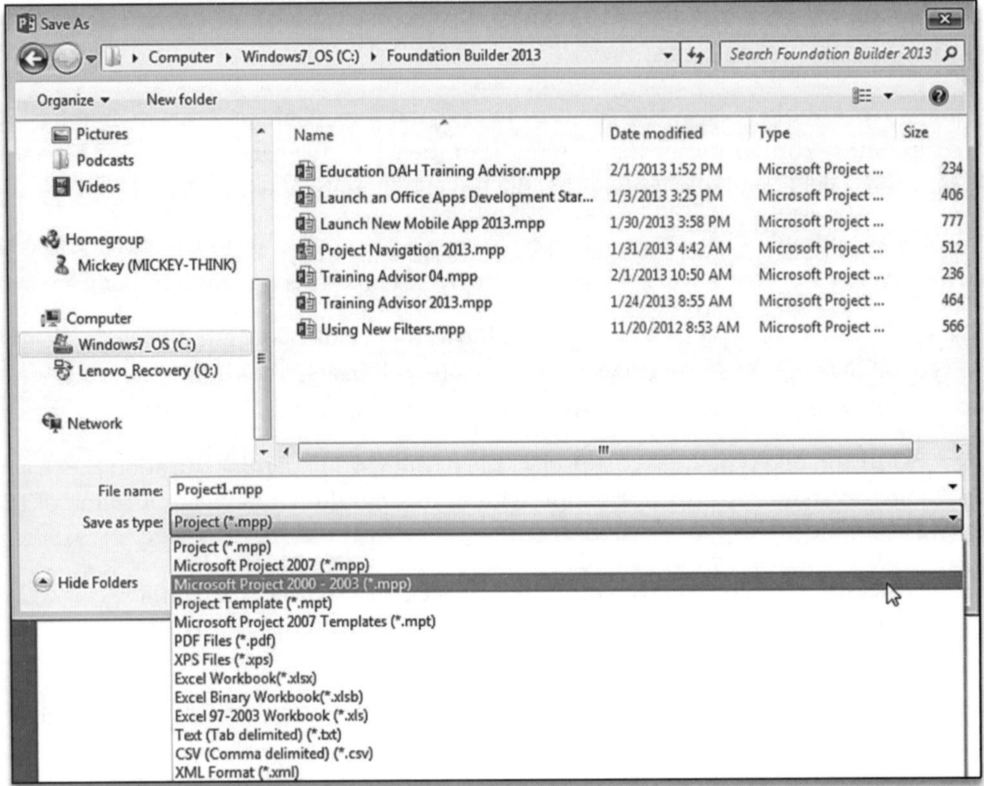

Figure 4 - 69: Select an alternate file type on the Save as type pick list

Saving a Project File as a PDF or XPS Document

Before you save a Project 2013 file as a PDF or XPS file, apply the view you want to display in the resulting file, such as the *Gantt Chart* view. Click the *File* tab and then click the *Save As* tab in the *Backstage*. In the *Save As* dialog, click the *Save as type* pick list, and then select either the *PDF Files (*.pdf)* item or the *XPS Files (*.xps)* item. Click the *Save* button and Project 2013 displays the *Document Export Options* dialog shown in Figure 4 - 70.

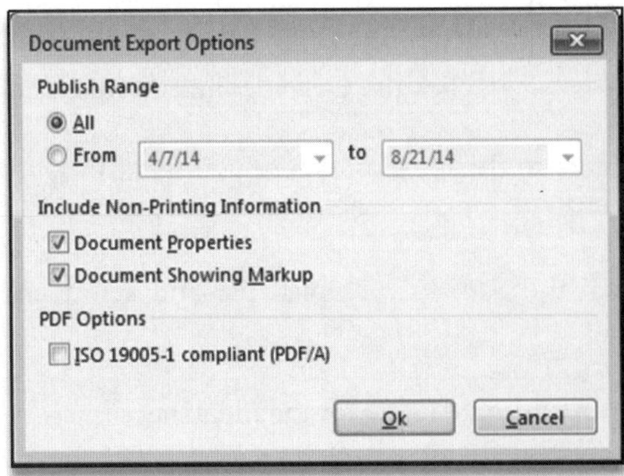

Figure 4 - 70: Document Export Options dialog

In the *Publish Range* section, select the *All* option to export all tasks in the project, along with the entire Gantt chart timeline if you applied the *Gantt Chart* view in the project. Select the *From* option and select a date range to print the task sheet on the left side with the date range specified for the Gantt chart.

In the *Include Non-Printing Information* section of the dialog, leave the *Document Properties* option and the *Document Showing Markup* option selected to include this information in the PDF or XPS file. Users can view this non-printing information in the PDF file by *Properties* item on the *File* menu in the Adobe Acrobat Reader software. Deselect one or both of these options to remove the non-printing information from the PDF or XPS file.

In the *PDF Options* section, select the *ISO 19500-1 Compliant (PDF/A)* option to save a PDF document in ISO compliant format. Do not select this option if you do not need an ISO compliant PDF file. Click the *OK* button to save the project file as a PDF file. Figure 4 - 71 shows a Project 2013 project file saved as a PDF document and displayed in the Adobe Acrobat Reader software.

Information: Companies use the PDF/A file format for the long-term archiving of electronic documents. This file format guarantees that users can reproduce the original document in exactly the same way years later.

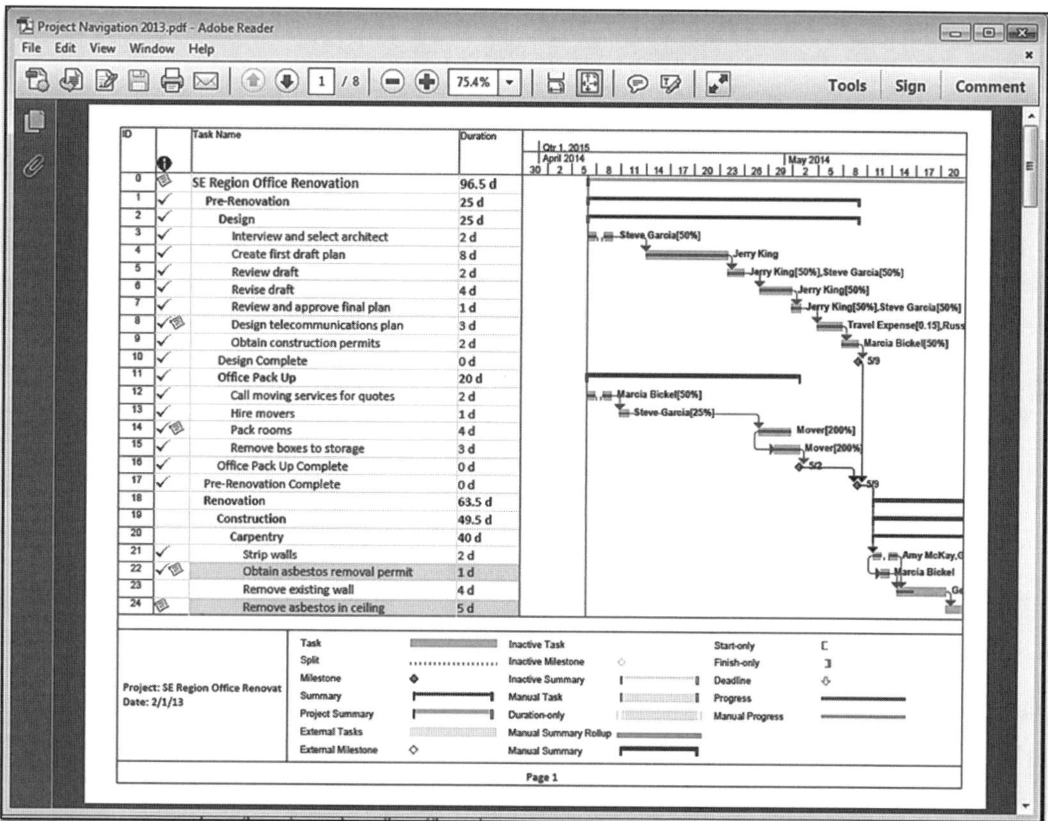

Figure 4 - 71: Project 2013 project file saved as a PDF document

Saving a Project Using an Older Project File Type

If you save a Project 2013 file using the Project 2007 file type, the software displays the *Saving to Previous Version – Compatibility Checker* warning dialog shown in Figure 4 - 72. The dialog warns you of Project 2013 features not supported in the 2007 version of the software, including *Inactive* tasks, *Manually Scheduled Tasks* and *Manually*

Scheduled Summary Tasks. Notice that the dialog also reveals how the software converts these features to work with the 2007 version of the software.

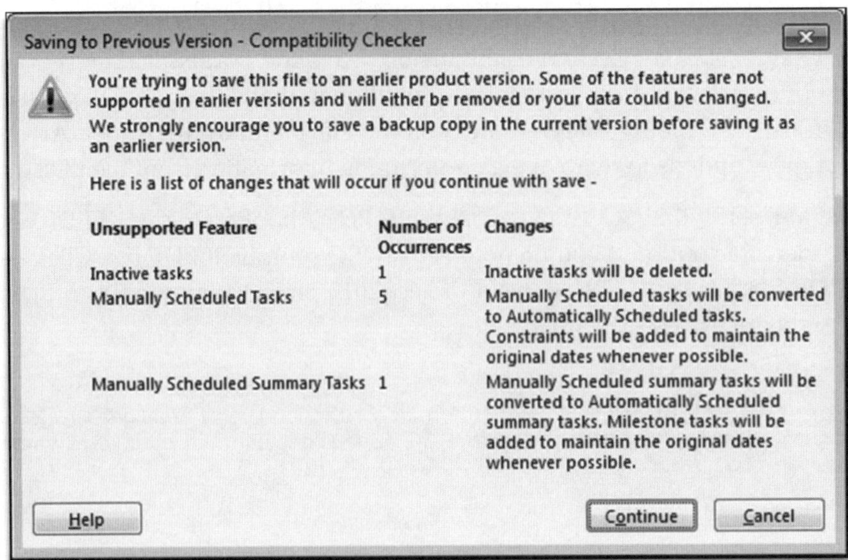

Figure 4 - 72: Saving to Previous Version – Compatibility Checker dialog

When you click the *Continue* button in the *Saving to Previous Version – Compatibility Checker* dialog, the software converts the data that relies on new features as follows:

- The software changes *Manually Scheduled* tasks to *Auto Scheduled* tasks, and adds Start No Earlier Than (SNET) constraints to the tasks to preserve current dates in the schedule. If a *Manually Scheduled* task is an unscheduled task with no *Start* date or *Finish* date, the software moves the task to the *Start* date of the project.
- The software changes *Manually Scheduled* summary tasks to *Auto Scheduled* summary tasks.
- After converting *Manually Scheduled* summary tasks to *Auto Scheduled* summary tasks, the software adds two milestone tasks immediately after the summary task to indicate the original start date and finish date for the summary task. The software adds a Must Start On (MSO) constraint to these milestone tasks.
- The software deletes *Inactive* tasks.
- The software removes *Strikethrough* font formatting on tasks.
- If you apply custom formatting to the *Team Planner* view, save the file as an earlier version, then close and re-open the file, you lose the custom formatting in the *Team Planner* view.
- When the user opens the project using Project 2007, the software converts 32-bit colors to the 16 colors used in all previous versions. These colors apply to font formatting, Gantt bar colors, and cell background formatting.
- When the user opens the project using Project 2007, the software hides the *Task Mode* column.
- When the user opens the project using Project 2007, the user cannot display the *Timeline* view.

If you save a Project 2013 file using the Project 2003 file type, the software displays the *Saving to Previous Version – Compatibility Checker* dialog shown previously in Figure 4 - 72. When you click the *Continue* button, the software displays the *Saving to Project 2013 2000-2003 format* dialog shown in Figure 4 - 73. The dialog warns you of Project 2013 features not supported in the earlier version of the software application.

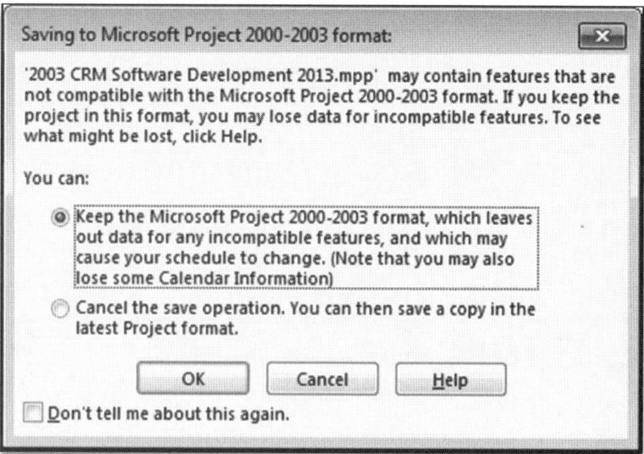

Figure 4 - 73: Saving to Microsoft Project 2000-2003 Format dialog

When you save a Project 2013 file in the Project 2000-2003 file format, the software converts the project in same manner as with saving the 2007 file format, and impacts your saved file in these additional ways:

- You lose any information contained in *Budget* fields, such as in the *Budget Cost* field.
- The software converts each *Cost* resource to a same-named *Material* resource, but you do not lose information contained in the *Cost* fields for the *Cost* resources.
- The software removes cell background formatting applied to tasks, but you do not lose font formatting.
- The software removes information contained in the *Assignment Owner* field and other fields added to Project since the 2003 version.
- The software converts recurring calendar exceptions to a series of multiple individual exceptions.
- The software removes all information related to enterprise custom fields.

Warning: MSProjectExperts strongly recommends that you **do not** exchange a project file with project managers who use Project 2007 and 2003, as doing so can lead to data loss in your project. For example, do not save a Project 2013 file as a 2007 version, ask a project manager using Project 2007 to update the project, and then reopen the 2007 version using Project 2013. In theory, you should not lose data "round tripping" the project between two different versions of the software. In reality, however, many users report the loss of project data due to "round tripping" the project between the two different versions of the software. If you must share a project with a project manager who uses Project 2007 or 2003, do so only for the purpose of allowing the project manager to view the data.

Opening a Project Created in an Older Version of Project

In Project 2013, when you open a project file created in an earlier version of the software, the software opens the file in *Compatibility Mode,* displaying this information in the *Title* bar of the application window as shown previously in Figure 4 - 57. While you have a project file open in *Compatibility Mode,* you cannot use any of the features specific to Project 2013, such as *Manually Scheduled* tasks or *Inactive* tasks. If you save the project file as a Project 2013 file, the software enables all of the new features in the software, but handles existing tasks and new tasks as follows:

- The software sets the default *Task Mode* option to *Auto Scheduled*, and sets all existing tasks to *Auto Scheduled*. You can then set the default *Task Mode* option to *Manually Scheduled* and set any existing tasks to *Manually Scheduled*, if necessary.
- The software does not display the *Task Mode* column automatically. To display this column, you must do so manually.
- The software does not display the *Gantt with Timeline* view automatically. To display this view, apply the *Gantt with Timeline* view manually.

Hands On Exercise

Exercise 4 - 16

Save your project using several alternate file types.

1. Open the **CRM Software Development 2013.mpp** sample file.
2. Click the *File* tab, click the *Save As* tab in the *Backstage*, select the *Computer* icon and then click the *Browse* button.
3. In the *Save As* dialog, click the *Save as type* pick list, select the *PDF Files (*.pdf)* item, and then click the *Save* button.
4. In the *Document Export Options* dialog, leave all of the default options selected and then click the *Ok* button.
5. Click the *File* tab, click the *Save As* tab in the *Backstage*, and then click the *Browse* button if necessary.
6. In the *Save As* dialog, change the file name to **CRM Software Development 2007**.
7. In the *Save As* dialog, click the *Save as type* pick list, select the *Project 2007 (*.mpp)* item, and then click the *Save* button.
8. In the *Saving to Previous Version - Compatibility Checker* dialog, click the *Continue* button.
9. Notice the *[Compatibility Mode]* label appended to the file name on the title bar at the top of the Project 2013 application window.
10. Notice how Project 2013 placed constraints on most of the tasks in the *Testing* phase of the project.
11. Click the *Task* tab to display the *Task* ribbon, and notice that the software disables the *Inactivate*, *Manually Schedule*, and *Auto Schedule* buttons.
12. Close the **CRM Software Development 2007.mpp** sample file, and when prompted in a warning dialog, click the *No* button to close it without saving further changes.

Module 05

Project Task Planning

Learning Objectives

After completing this module, you will be able to:

- Understand the task planning process
- Understand change highlighting
- Use Manually Scheduled tasks and Auto Scheduled tasks
- Use basic task planning skills to create a project schedule
- Set task dependencies, constraints, and deadline dates
- Document the task list with appropriate task notes
- Use cell background formatting to display tasks of interest
- Estimate task durations
- Determine task drivers
- Create recurring tasks
- Enter a fixed cost on a task

Inside Module 05

Understanding the Task Planning Process

After you define your project, you begin the planning process. The first step in the planning process is task planning. If you do not create your project from a template, then you must manually complete a series of steps in Project 2013 to complete the task planning process.

When you create a task list manually, you must thoughtfully analyze the activities required to complete the project. Depending on the size of your project, this may mean lots of typing! You can use either a "top down" or "bottom up" approach to create the initial task list. The "top down" approach begins by listing the major phases of the project, as well as the project deliverables under each phase. Under each deliverable you list the activities necessary to produce the deliverable. To help you with the process of "top down" planning, Project 2013 includes a feature that allows you to insert "top down" summary tasks. I discuss this new feature later in this module.

The "bottom up" approach works in the opposite direction. Using this approach, you list all of the activities in the project and then organize the activities into phase and deliverable summary sections. You can be effective in creating the task list for the project using either approach. Your organization may adhere to pre-defined project lifecycle standards, which obligate you to use a structured framework. Whenever you create a new project manually, it is a good idea to follow this methodology:

1. Create the task list.
2. Move the tasks into the proper sequence.
3. Create summary tasks to generate the project's Work Breakdown Structure (WBS).
4. Create project milestones.
5. Set task dependencies and document unusual task dependencies with a task note.
6. Set task constraints and deadline dates, and document all task constraints with a task note.
7. Set task calendars for any task with an alternate working schedule and document the task calendars with a task note.
8. Estimate task effort or durations according to your preferred or required methodologies.
9. Create recurring tasks (optional).
10. Enter known fixed costs.

In successive topical sections in this module, I discuss each of the steps in the preceding task planning methodology.

Auto-Wrapping Task Names

During the task planning process, you see the *Auto-Wrap Task Names* feature in Project 2013 when you enter a task name that exceeds the width of the *Task Name* column. This feature increases the row height automatically and wraps the text inside the cell. In all previous versions of the tool, the only way to auto-wrap task names was to manually increase the height of the task row until the task name wrapped completely within the cell. In Project 2013, the software auto-wraps task names in cells when one of several events occurs:

- You manually type a task name that exceeds the width of the *Task Name* column and then press the **Enter** key to complete the data entry. The software automatically increases the row height for that task to wrap the task name within the cell.

- You paste a task name that exceeds the width of the *Task Name* column. The software automatically increases the row height for that task to wrap the task name within the cell.

- You manually decrease the width of the *Task Name* column. The software automatically increases the row height for **every** task with a name exceeding the width of the *Task Name* column.

- You manually increase the width of the *Task Name* column. The software automatically decreases the row height for that task and un-wraps the text.

Warning: Project 2013 **does not** decrease the row height of wrapped tasks automatically when you double-click the right edge of the *Task Name* column header to "best fit" the contents of the column. To work around this limitation, click and hold the right edge of the *Task Name* column header and then drag the column edge to the right to manually make the column slightly wider. The software should decrease the row height of wrapped tasks automatically.

Understanding Change Highlighting

Whenever you make a change anywhere in a Project 2013 schedule, the software uses change highlighting to graphically show you all tasks impacted by the change. This behavior begins the moment you enter the first task in the project and continues until you complete the project. For example, if you change the schedule of any task with successors, the software applies the light blue cell background color in the *Duration, Start,* and/or *Finish* columns for every impacted task. Figure 5 - 1 shows a project before I make revisions to the schedule.

		Task Mode	Task Name	Duration	Start	Finish
0			**New Project**	**14 d**	**2/2/15**	**2/19/15**
1			**PHASE I**	**14 d**	**2/2/15**	**2/19/15**
2			Design	4 d	2/2/15	2/5/15
3			Build	3 d	2/6/15	2/10/15
4			Test	2 d	2/11/15	2/12/15
5			Implement	5 d	2/13/15	2/19/15
6			Phase I Completed	0 d	2/19/15	2/19/15

Figure 5 - 1: Project before schedule changes

Figure 5 - 2 shows the same project after I change the duration of the *Test* task from *2 days* to *4 days*. Notice how Project 2013 changes the cell formatting color for the *Duration* and *Finish* columns of the *Test* task, and changes the cell formatting color to the *Start* and/or *Finish* columns of each impacted task and summary task, including the Project Summary Task.

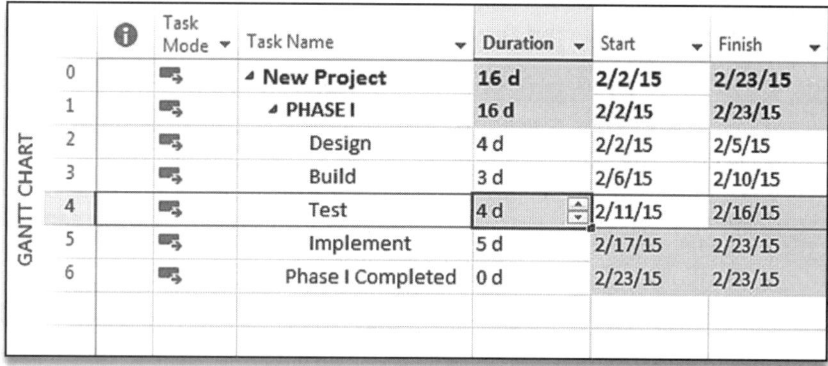

	Task Mode	Task Name	Duration	Start	Finish
0		New Project	16 d	2/2/15	2/23/15
1		PHASE I	16 d	2/2/15	2/23/15
2		Design	4 d	2/2/15	2/5/15
3		Build	3 d	2/6/15	2/10/15
4		Test	4 d	2/11/15	2/16/15
5		Implement	5 d	2/17/15	2/23/15
6		Phase I Completed	0 d	2/23/15	2/23/15

Figure 5 - 2: Project after making schedule changes

Information: To change the cell background color used to indicate changed tasks, click the *Format* tab to display the *Format* ribbon. In the *Format* section of the *Format* ribbon, click the *Text Styles* button. In the *Text Styles* dialog, click the *Item to Change* pick list and select the *Changed Tasks* item on the list. Click the *Background Color* pick list, select a different color, and then click the *OK* button.

Using the Selected Task Feature

In Project 2013, Microsoft improved the graphics used in Gantt-based views so that it is now easier to align each Gantt bar with its corresponding task name on the left side of the view. If you select any task in the task sheet portion of the *Gantt Chart* view, for example, the software displays a set of horizontal gridlines running across the entire screen to indicate the selected task. For example, notice in Figure 5 - 3 that I selected the *Develop budget* task, and that Project 2013 draws a pair of horizontal gridlines around the selected task's Gantt bar in the *Gantt Chart* portion of the view.

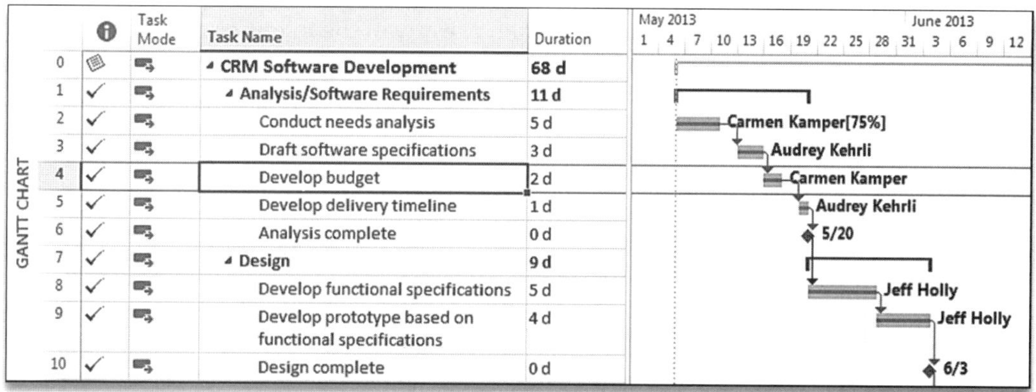

	Task Mode	Task Name	Duration
0		CRM Software Development	68 d
1		Analysis/Software Requirements	11 d
2		Conduct needs analysis	5 d
3		Draft software specifications	3 d
4		Develop budget	2 d
5		Develop delivery timeline	1 d
6		Analysis complete	0 d
7		Design	9 d
8		Develop functional specifications	5 d
9		Develop prototype based on functional specifications	4 d
10		Design complete	0 d

Figure 5 - 3: Horizontal gridlines show selected task

Using Basic Task Planning Skills

You should possess a variety of basic task skills to use Project 2013 effectively. I discuss each of these basic task planning skills in the following topical sections.

Understanding Task Mode

Described as task mode, Project 2013 offers two types of tasks for you to use in your projects: *Manually Scheduled* tasks and *Auto Scheduled* tasks. In versions prior to Project 2010, the software only offered *Auto Scheduled* tasks. An *Auto Scheduled* task is a task whose schedule is controlled by the Project 2013 software, and whose schedule is updated automatically every time you make a scheduling change in your project.

In the 2010 version of the software, Microsoft introduced a second type of task known as *Manually Scheduled* tasks, and continues to offer this feature in the 2013 version of the software. As the name implies, a *Manually Scheduled* task is a task whose schedule you control manually. Every time you make a scheduling change in your project, Project 2013 **does not update** the schedule of *Manually Scheduled* tasks. Instead, the software relies on you to manually reschedule the tasks as needed.

In your projects, you can use only *Auto Scheduled* tasks, *Manually Scheduled* tasks, or a mix of the two types of tasks. For the vast majority of the time, I recommend that you use *Auto Scheduled* tasks to allow the software to automatically calculate the schedule of tasks in your projects. Occasionally you may want to use a *Manually Scheduled* task as an unscheduled or "placeholder" task, such as when you know you may need the task eventually but are not ready to estimate a *Duration* value or to schedule the task with a *Start* and *Finish* date.

Entering New Tasks

To enter a new task in your project, complete the following steps:

1. In the lower left corner of the Project 2013 application window, click the *New Tasks* button and select either the *Auto Scheduled* or *Manually Scheduled* item on the menu.
2. Select a blank cell in the *Task Name* column of the task sheet.
3. Type the task name.
4. Press the **Enter** key, **Tab** key, or **Down-Arrow** key on your computer keyboard.

To edit the name of an existing task, select the task and then use any of the following methods:

- Double-click the task and edit the name in the *Task Information* dialog.
- Retype the task name.
- Press the **F2** function key on your computer keyboard and edit the task name.
- Select the name of the task and then click anywhere in the cell to enable in-cell editing.

When you enter a new *Auto Scheduled* task, the software sets a *Duration* value of *1 day* for the task, sets the *Start* date of the project as the *Start* date of the task, and then calculates the *Finish* date of the task. When you enter a new *Manually Scheduled* task, Project 2013 leaves the values blank in the *Duration, Start*, and *Finish* fields.

To change the *Task Mode* setting for any tasks from *Auto Scheduled* to *Manually Scheduled* or vice versa, complete the following steps:

1. Click the *Task* tab to display the *Task* ribbon.
2. Select the task(s) whose *Task Mode* setting you want to change.
3. In the *Tasks* section of the *Task* ribbon, click either the *Manually Schedule* button or the *Auto Schedule* button.

Information: To specify the *Task Mode* setting for an individual task, you can also select a cell in the *Task Mode* column for the task, click the pick list in the *Task Mode* cell, and choose either *Manually Scheduled* or *Auto Scheduled* from the list. You can also right-click on the task and select either *Manually Schedule* or *Auto Schedule* on the shortcut menu.

Working with Manually Scheduled Tasks

Figure 5 - 4 shows a project in which I included four *Auto Scheduled* tasks (*Design, Build, Test,* and *Implement*) and two *Manually Scheduled* tasks (*Rebuild* and *Retest*). Notice the following about this project:

- Project 2013 displays a unique indicator to the left of each task in the *Indicators* column to identify the *Task Mode* setting for each task.

- Every *Auto Scheduled* task includes a *1d* value in the *Duration* column, along with date values in the *Start* and *Finish* columns.

- The *Manually Scheduled* tasks have no values in the *Duration, Start,* or *Finish* columns. The software leaves the values blank in those three columns, allowing you to manually schedule the tasks as needed.

- The *Gantt Chart* view does not include Gantt bars for these two *Manually Scheduled* tasks.

GANTT CHART

	Task Name	Duration	Start	Finish
0	Develop MSP2013 Macros	1 d	2/2/15	2/2/15
1	Phase I	1 d	2/2/15	2/2/15
2	Design	1 d	2/2/15	2/2/15
3	Build	1 d	2/2/15	2/2/15
4	Test	1 d	2/2/15	2/2/15
5	Rebuild			
6	Retest			
7	Implement	1 d	2/2/15	2/2/15
8	Phase I Complete	0 d	2/2/15	2/2/15

Feb 1, '15 — F S S M T W T F — 2/2

Figure 5 - 4: New project includes both Manually Scheduled tasks and Auto Scheduled tasks

When you set a task to *Manually Scheduled,* Project 2013 allows you to specify values in the *Duration, Start,* and *Finish* columns in a number of ways, including:

- Specify **no values** in the *Duration, Start,* or *Finish* columns until you have an estimated duration, start, or finish date.

- Enter **text information** about an approximate duration (such as *TBD* or *About 1 Week*) in the *Duration* column, and enter text information about approximate dates (such as *Early June* or *Decision by 11/02/15*) in the *Start* and *Finish* columns.

- Enter **numerical values** to show an estimated duration (such as *5 days*) in the *Duration* column, and/or an estimated date (such as *3/18/2015*) in the *Start* and *Finish* columns.

In Figure 5 - 4 shown previously, you can see two *Manually Scheduled* tasks with no *Duration, Start,* or *Finish* values specified. I refer to these tasks as **unscheduled tasks**, meaning that you have not yet supplied the information necessary for Project 2013 to schedule the tasks. In Figure 5 - 5, you see an example of two *Manually Scheduled* tasks with text values entered in the *Duration* column (*About 1w* and *TBD*) and in the *Start* and *Finish* columns (*Late April* and *Early May*).

	Indicators	Task Mode	Task Name	Duration	Start	Finish
0			**Develop MSP2013 Macros**	**1 d**	**2/2/15**	**2/2/15**
1			**Phase I**	**1 d**	**2/2/15**	**2/2/15**
2			Design	1 d	2/2/15	2/2/15
3			Build	1 d	2/2/15	2/2/15
4			Test	1 d	2/2/15	2/2/15
5			Rebuild	*About 1w*	*Late April*	
6			Retest	*TBD*		*Early May*
7			Implement	1 d	2/2/15	2/2/15
8			Phase I Complete	0 d	2/2/15	2/2/15

Figure 5 - 5: Text-based Duration, Start, and Finish values for Manually Scheduled tasks

If you enter a numerical value (such as *5 days*) in only the *Duration* column for a *Manually Scheduled* task, Project 2013 displays a teal-colored Gantt bar with lightly-shaded ends for the task. If you also enter a numerical date value (such as *3/18/15*) in the *Start* or *Finish* columns, the software displays a solid teal-colored Gantt bar for the task. In Figure 5 - 6, notice that I entered numerical *Duration* values for the *Rebuild* and *Retest* tasks, and specified numerical date values in the *Start* and *Finish* columns for only the *Retest* task. Notice the two different types of Gantt bars for these tasks. Notice also the different indicators shown in the *Indicators* column for the *Rebuild* and *Retest* tasks. The pushpin with the question mark indicator on the *Rebuild* task shows that Project 2013 needs more information to schedule the task. The pushpin indicator for the *Retest* task shows that the software successfully scheduled the task.

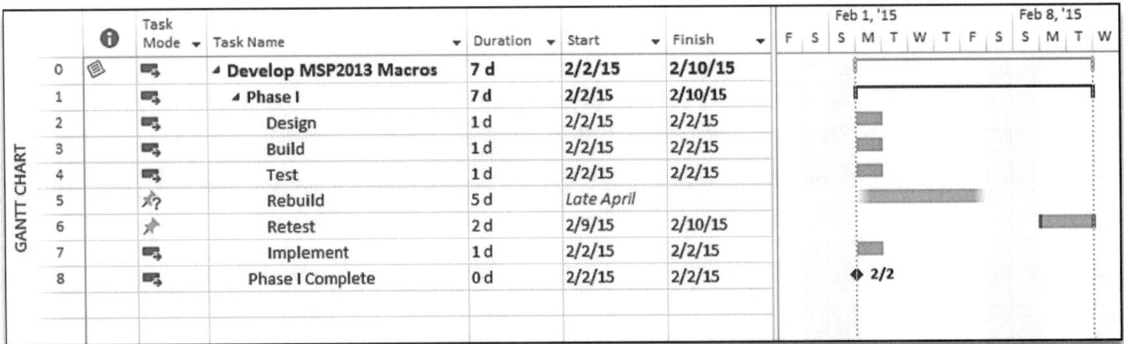

	Indicators	Task Mode	Task Name	Duration	Start	Finish
0			**Develop MSP2013 Macros**	**7 d**	**2/2/15**	**2/10/15**
1			**Phase I**	**7 d**	**2/2/15**	**2/10/15**
2			Design	1 d	2/2/15	2/2/15
3			Build	1 d	2/2/15	2/2/15
4			Test	1 d	2/2/15	2/2/15
5			Rebuild	5 d	*Late April*	
6			Retest	2 d	2/9/15	2/10/15
7			Implement	1 d	2/2/15	2/2/15
8			Phase I Complete	0 d	2/2/15	2/2/15

Figure 5 - 6: Manually Scheduled tasks with Duration and Start date values specified

Information: If you leave the *Duration* column blank, but enter a numerical date value in only the *Start* column, Project 2013 displays teal-colored left square bracket Gantt symbol. If you leave the *Duration* column blank, but enter a numerical date value in only the *Finish* column, the software displays teal-colored right square bracket Gantt symbol. If you leave the *Duration* column blank, but enter numerical date values in **both** the *Start* and *Finish* columns, the software calculates a numerical *Duration* value and then displays a solid teal-colored Gantt bar.

Hands On Exercise

Exercise 5 - 1

Use basic task planning skills to define the task list in a project.

1. Open the **Training Advisor 05a.mpp** sample file.
2. Scroll to the first blank row at the bottom of the existing task list and add the following new tasks:
    - Create Training Schedule
    - Provide End User Training

Notice that Project 2013 creates these two new tasks as *Manually Scheduled* tasks, controlled by the default *Task Mode* setting in the left end of the status bar at the bottom of the application window.

3. Drag your split bar to the right edge of the *Finish* column.
4. For the *Create Training Schedule* task, enter *5 days* in the *Duration* column and enter *Late March* in the *Start* column.
5. For the *Provide End User Training* task, enter *10 days* in the *Duration* column and enter *By May* in the *Finish* column.

Notice the unusual Gantt bar displayed by Project 2013 for these two *Manually Scheduled* tasks.

6. Select the *Conduct Skills Accessment* task, press the **F2** function key on your computer keyboard, and then change the spelling of *Accessment* to *Assessment*.
7. Drag the split bar to the right edge of the *Duration* column.
8. Save but **do not** close **Training Advisor 05a.mpp** sample file.

Moving Tasks

During the task planning process, you may create the task list with tasks in the wrong sequential order. To move a task, complete the following steps:

1. Click the task ID number (row header) on the far left end of the task and release the mouse button.
2. Click and hold the task ID number (row header) to "grab" the task.
3. Move the mouse pointer up or down on the screen to drag the task.

As you move the mouse pointer, you see a gray I-beam bar to indicate that you are moving the task, as shown in Figure 5 - 7.

		Task Mode	Task Name	Duration	Start	Finish
			New Project	**1 d**	**6/1/15**	**6/1/15**
1			Build	1 d	6/1/15	6/1/15
2			Test	1 d	6/1/15	6/1/15
3			Design	1 d	6/1/15	6/1/15
4			Implement	1 d	6/1/15	6/1/15

Figure 5 - 7: Moving a task

4. Drag the task until you position the gray I-beam indicator where you want to place the task.

5. Release the mouse button to complete the move and "drop" the task in its new location.

You can also move a group of tasks as a block by first selecting the ID numbers of all of the tasks you want to move. When you click and hold any one of the selected ID numbers, you can drag the entire block of tasks to a new location in the project. Additionally, when you move a summary task, all of its subtasks move with it.

Hands On Exercise

Exercise 5 - 2

Drag and drop tasks into the correct order in a project.

1. Return to the **Training Advisor 05a.mpp** sample file.

2. Click the row header for task ID #6, the *Load and Configure Software* task, and then release the mouse button.

3. Click and hold the row header for task ID #6 and then drag and drop the task immediately above task ID #5, the *Perform Server Stress Test* task.

4. Click and drag the row headers for task IDs #19 and #20 to select the tasks as a block, and then release the mouse button.

5. Click and hold the row header for either of the two selected tasks and then drag them as a block above task ID #18, the *Training Complete* task.

6. Save but **do not** close **Training Advisor 05a.mpp** sample file.

Inserting Tasks

While entering the task list, you may discover that you accidentally omitted one or more tasks. To insert new tasks in your project plan, select any cell in the row where you want to insert the new task and then use one of the following methods:

- Press the **Insert** key on your computer keyboard.
- Right-click in the row and then select the *Insert Task* item on the shortcut menu.
- In the *Insert* section of the *Task* ribbon, click the *Task* button.

Project 2013 adds a new blank task row automatically above the selected task. If you add the new task using the **Insert** key on your computer keyboard, the software simply adds a new blank task. If you use the *Task* button on the *Task* ribbon or the *Insert Task* item on the shortcut menu, the software adds a new task named <*New Task*>. After using any of these three methods to add the new task, you must still enter a name for the new task.

To add multiple new tasks simultaneously, select as many rows as the number of new tasks you would like to add, and use one of the preceding methods. For example, in Figure 5 - 8 I want to add two new tasks above the *Implement* task, so I select the *Implement* task and the row below it so that the software creates two blank rows above the *Implement* task.

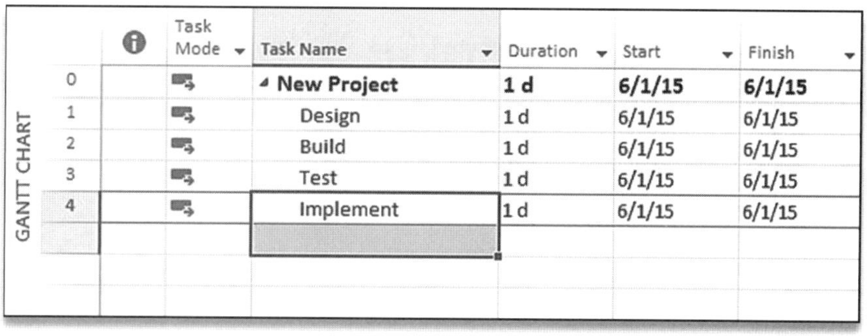

	Task Mode	Task Name	Duration	Start	Finish
0		**New Project**	**1 d**	**6/1/15**	**6/1/15**
1		Design	1 d	6/1/15	6/1/15
2		Build	1 d	6/1/15	6/1/15
3		Test	1 d	6/1/15	6/1/15
4		Implement	1 d	6/1/15	6/1/15

Figure 5 - 8: Preparing to insert two new tasks after the Test task

When I click the *Task* button on the *Task* ribbon, the software inserts two new tasks named <*New Task*> as shown in Figure 5 - 9.

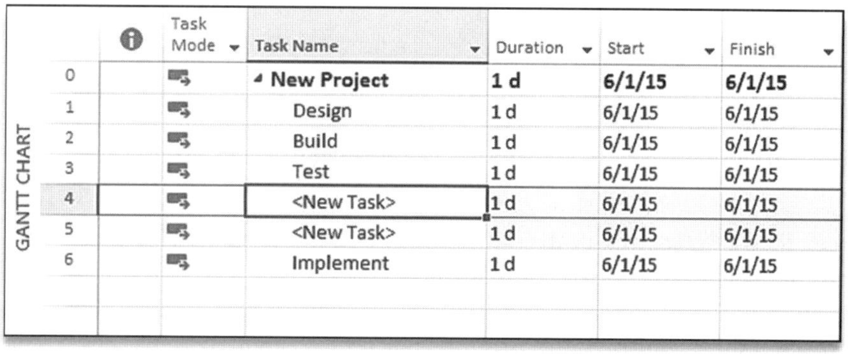

	Task Mode	Task Name	Duration	Start	Finish
0		**New Project**	**1 d**	**6/1/15**	**6/1/15**
1		Design	1 d	6/1/15	6/1/15
2		Build	1 d	6/1/15	6/1/15
3		Test	1 d	6/1/15	6/1/15
4		<New Task>	1 d	6/1/15	6/1/15
5		<New Task>	1 d	6/1/15	6/1/15
6		Implement	1 d	6/1/15	6/1/15

Figure 5 - 9: Two new tasks inserted above the Implement task

Hands On Exercise

Exercise 5 - 3

Members of the project team determined that your project is missing a necessary task in the *Testing* section of the project. Insert a new task called *Resolve Connectivity Errors* between the *Verify Connectivity* task and the *Testing Complete* task.

1. Return to the **Training Advisor 05a.mpp** sample file.

2. Select task ID #11, the *Testing Complete* task.

3. In the *Insert* section of the *Task* ribbon, click the *Task* button.

Because the default *Task Mode* setting for this project is *Manually Scheduled*, notice that Project 2013 created a new *Manually Scheduled* task named <*New Task*>.

4. With the new unnamed task still selected, click the *Auto Schedule* button in the *Tasks* section of the *Task* ribbon.

5. Change the name of the new task to *Resolve Connectivity Errors* and then press the **Enter** key on your computer keyboard.

6. Save but **do not** close **Training Advisor 05a.mpp** sample file.

Deleting Tasks

While entering a task list, you may find that you no longer need one or more tasks in the project plan. To delete a task, use one of the following methods:

- Right-click anywhere on the task row and select the *Delete Task* item on the shortcut menu.
- Click the task ID number and then press the **Delete** key on your computer keyboard.

If you select any cell in the *Task Name* column (rather than selecting the task ID number) and then press the **Delete** key on your computer keyboard, the software displays a *Smart Tag* (**X** button) to the left of the cell. When you float your mouse pointer over the *Smart Tag*, the software displays a pick list. Click the *Smart Tag* pick list and then select the *Delete the task* item. Figure 5 - 10 shows the *Smart Tag* while deleting a task.

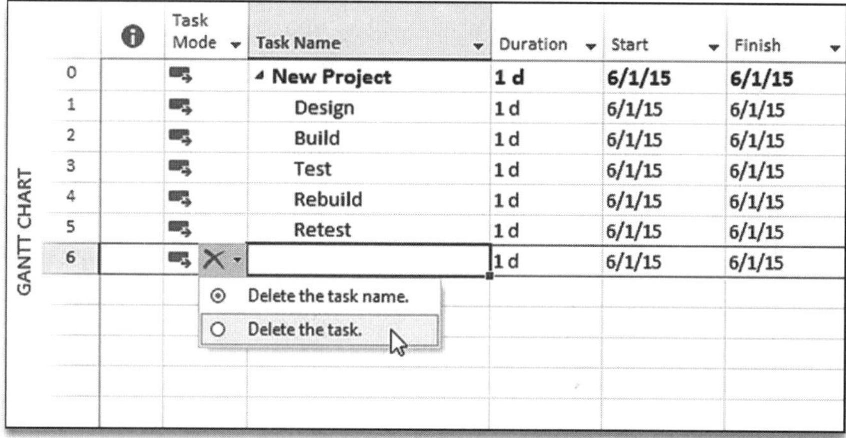

Figure 5 - 10: Smart Tag displayed after deleting a task

Information: When you select a cell in the *Resource Name* column in any resource view and press the **Delete** key on your computer keyboard, the software also displays a *Smart Tag* to the left of the cell. The choices are similar to those offered while deleting a cell in any task view.

Hands On Exercise

Exercise 5 - 4

Members of the project team concluded that they already know the server specifications for this project. Therefore, you do not need the *Determine Server Specifications* task and you need to delete it.

1. Return to the **Training Advisor 05a.mpp** sample file.
2. Select the row header for task ID #2, the *Determine Server Specifications* task.
3. Press the **Delete** key on your computer keyboard.
4. Save but **do not** close **Training Advisor 05a.mpp** sample file.

Creating the Work Breakdown Structure (WBS)

The Work Breakdown Structure (WBS) divides the project tasks into meaningful and logical components. The WBS consists of summary tasks representing major aspects of the project, such as phase and deliverable sections, along with subtasks in each summary section. Figure 5 - 11 shows a simple generic Work Breakdown Structure comprised of phase and deliverable sections, with four subtasks in each deliverable section.

		Task Mode	Task Name	Duration	Start	Finish
0			**Project Summary Task**	**1 d**	**3/2/15**	**3/2/15**
1			**PHASE I**	**1 d**	**3/2/15**	**3/2/15**
2			**Deliverable 1**	**1 d**	**3/2/15**	**3/2/15**
3			Design	1 d	3/2/15	3/2/15
4			Build	1 d	3/2/15	3/2/15
5			Test	1 d	3/2/15	3/2/15
6			Implement	1 d	3/2/15	3/2/15
7			**Deliverable 2**	**1 d**	**3/2/15**	**3/2/15**
8			Design	1 d	3/2/15	3/2/15
9			Build	1 d	3/2/15	3/2/15
10			Test	1 d	3/2/15	3/2/15
11			Implement	1 d	3/2/15	3/2/15

Figure 5 - 11: Work Breakdown Structure

To create a Work Breakdown Structure in a project, you must create a series of summary tasks and subtasks. The purpose of summary tasks is to summarize or "roll up" the data contained in the subtasks. Project 2013 offers you several ways to create summary tasks and subtasks. As with all previous versions of the software, you can create summary tasks and subtasks by completing the following steps:

1. Type the names of a summary task and its subtasks.
2. Select the tasks that you want to make subtasks of the summary task.
3. Click the *Indent task* button in the *Schedule* section of the *Task* ribbon.

In the project shown in Figure 5 - 12, I select the *Design* through *Implement* tasks to prepare to make them subtasks of the *PHASE I* task.

		Task Mode	Task Name	Duration	May 31, '15 F S S M T W T F
0			**New Project**	**1 d**	
1			PHASE I	1 d	
2			Design	1 d	
3			Build	1 d	
4			Test	1 d	
5			Implement	1 d	

Figure 5 - 12: Prepare to make PHASE I a summary task

After clicking the *Indent* button in the *Schedule* section of the *Task* ribbon, the software makes the four selected tasks subtasks of the *PHASE I* summary task. Figure 5 - 13 shows the result of this procedure.

		Task Mode	Task Name	Duration
0			◢ **New Project**	**1 d**
1			◢ **PHASE I**	**1 d**
2			Design	1 d
3			Build	1 d
4			Test	1 d
5			Implement	1 d

Figure 5 - 13: PHASE I summary task with four subtasks

Notice in Figure 5 - 13 how Project 2013 displays summary tasks and subtasks:

- It formats PHASE I in bold.
- It shows an outline indicator (***triangle symbol***) in front of the *PHASE I* task name.
- It changes the Gantt bar shape for *PHASE I.*
- It indents the *Design* through *Implement* tasks one level.

Best Practice: Converting an existing task to a summary task causes the software to roll up information from the subtasks to the summary task. This changes the behavior of the summary task, but it does not change any underlying data that you previously entered in the existing task before you converted it to a summary task. If you convert the summary task back to a regular task, any previously entered data reappears. Because this can cause surprising schedule changes, MsProjectExperts recommends that you create all of your summary tasks **from new tasks** rather than converting tasks in which you previously entered work or duration values.

Inserting Summary Tasks

The other method for creating summary tasks is to use the *Insert Summary Task* feature in Project 2013. Many project managers like to do "top down" task planning by creating summary tasks initially to represent phase and deliverable sections in the project, and then they add subtasks to each summary section. To do "top down" task planning in Project 2013, click the *Insert Summary Task* button in the *Insert* section of the *Task* ribbon. The software inserts a new unnamed summary task and subtask, as shown in Figure 5 - 14.

		Task Mode	Task Name	Duration
0			◢ **Project1**	**1 d**
1			◢ **<New Summary Task>**	**1 d**
2			<New Task>	1 d

Figure 5 - 14: Newly Inserted Summary Task during "top down" task planning process

After inserting the new summary task and subtask pair, you should edit the name of the summary task, replacing the default value with the name of the phase or deliverable section it represents. Similarly, you eventually edit the name of the subtask and add additional subtasks as needed. You can leave the name of the subtask with its original <New Task> name as a placeholder for a future subtask until you are ready to add detailed tasks to the summary section.

If you insert a summary task below another summary task and subtask pair, Project 2013 automatically indents the new summary task at the same level of indenture as the task immediately preceding it. This is the default behavior of the tool, and you cannot change it. For example, Figure 5 - 15 shows a new summary task and subtask pair inserted after the *Design* task. Notice that the software indented the new summary task at the same level as the *Design* task preceding it. To resolve the indenting situation shown in Figure 5 - 15, select the new summary task and then click the *Outdent Task* button in the *Schedule* section of the *Task* ribbon.

	Task Mode	Task Name	Duration
0		◢ Project1	1 d
1		◢ PHASE I	1 d
2		Design	1 d
3		◢ <New Summary Task>	1 d
4		<New Task>	1 d

Figure 5 - 15: New summary task indented at same level as the Design task preceding it

In addition to inserting summary tasks during "top down" task planning, Project 2013 also makes it easier to insert a summary task for a selected group of subtasks. For example, consider the set of four tasks shown in Figure 5 - 16. I want to show that each of these four tasks is a subtask in the *PHASE I* section of the project.

	Task Mode	Task Name	Duration
0		◢ New Project	1 d
1		Design	1 d
2		Build	1 d
3		Test	1 d
4		Implement	1 d

Figure 5 - 16: Four tasks ready for inclusion as subtasks of Phase I

To make these tasks a subtask in a new *PHASE I* summary task, select the four tasks, and then click the *Insert Summary Task* button on the *Task* ribbon. Project 2013 automatically inserts a new unnamed summary task and indents the four tasks as subtasks of the summary section, as shown in Figure 5 - 17. You can then rename the new summary task as desired.

	Task Mode	Task Name	Duration
0		New Project	1 d
1		<New Summary Task>	1 d
2		Design	1 d
3		Build	1 d
4		Test	1 d
5		Implement	1 d

Figure 5 - 17: Four tasks inserted as subtasks below the new unnamed summary task

Creating a Manually Scheduled Summary Task

In addition to creating *Manually Scheduled* tasks, Project 2013 also allows you to create *Manually Scheduled* summary tasks. For example, Figure 5 - 18 shows a project with a *Manually Scheduled* summary task with *Manually Scheduled* subtasks. Notice in Figure 5 - 18 that the software displays a different type of summary Gantt bar for *Manually Scheduled* summary tasks than it does for *Auto Scheduled* summary tasks.

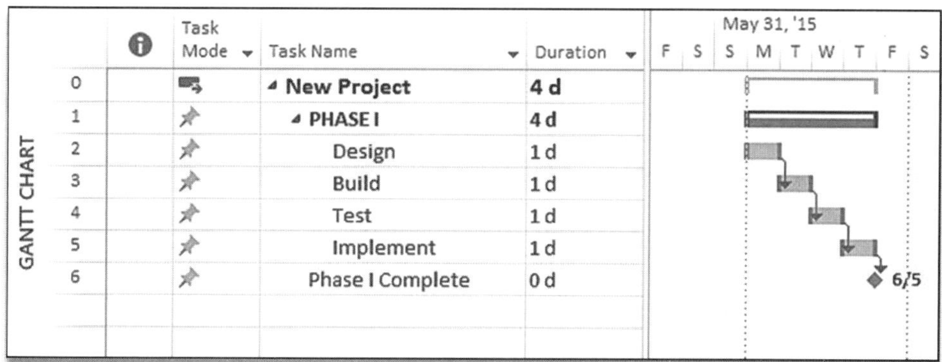

	Task Mode	Task Name	Duration
0		New Project	4 d
1		PHASE I	4 d
2		Design	1 d
3		Build	1 d
4		Test	1 d
5		Implement	1 d
6		Phase I Complete	0 d

Figure 5 - 18: Phase I as a Manually Scheduled summary task

The behavior of *Manually Scheduled* summary tasks is similar to the behavior of *Manually Scheduled* tasks, but with a few differences, including:

- Project 2013 formats the summary Gantt bar to show schedule warnings about schedule conflicts.
- Project 2013 shows a schedule warning in the *Finish* column of every task causing the schedule conflict with the *Manually Scheduled* summary task.

Notice in Figure 5 - 19 that the software formats the summary Gantt bar for the *PHASE I* summary task in red to show a schedule warning, indicating that the duration of the subtasks now exceeds the duration of the *Manually Scheduled* summary task. The software also shows schedule warnings in the *Finish* column for each subtask causing the schedule problem indicated by a red wavy line. To resolve the schedule problems, you can use the *Task Inspector* tool on the *PHASE I* summary task, which offers the option to extend the *Finish* date of the *Manually Scheduled* summary task. I discuss the *Task Inspector* feature later in this module.

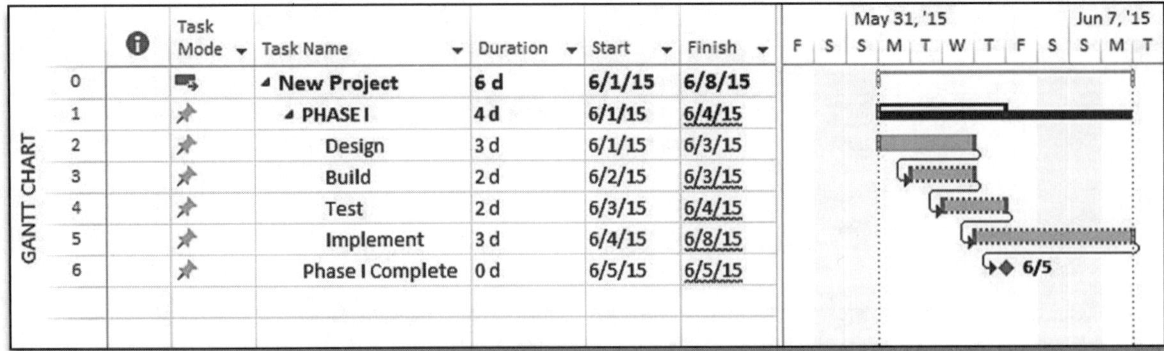

Figure 5 - 19: Schedule warnings on a Manually Scheduled summary task and subtasks

Hands On Exercise

Exercise 5 - 5

Create the Work Breakdown Structure by creating summary tasks that represent the phases of the project.

1. Return to the **Training Advisor 05a.mpp** sample file.
2. Select task IDs #8-10, from the *Install Training Advisor Clients* task to the *Resolve Connectivity Errors* task.
3. In the *Schedule* section of the *Task* ribbon, click the *Indent Task* button.
4. Leave the *Testing Complete* task at the same level as the *TESTING* summary task (**do not** indent this task).
5. Select task IDs #13-19, from the *Setup Test Training Server* task to the *Provide End User Training* task.
6. In the *Schedule* section of the *Task* ribbon, click the *Indent Task* button.
7. Leave the *Training Complete* task at the same level as the *TRAINING* summary task (**do not** indent this task).
8. Select task IDs #14-16, from the *Create Training Module 01* task to the *Create Training Module 03* task.
9. In the *Insert* section of the *Task* ribbon, click the *Insert Summary Task* button.

Notice how Project 2013 inserts the new summary task and indents the selected tasks as subtasks automatically.

10. Enter the name *Create Training Materials* for the new summary task you inserted.
11. Save but **do not** close **Training Advisor 05a.mpp** sample file.

Creating Milestones

In project management terms, we define a milestone as "a significant point in time" in a project, usually indicating the completion of something important. In Project 2013, you may use a milestone to indicate the beginning point of a project, the completion of a phase or a deliverable section, or the completion of the entire project. Most projects contain multiple milestones.

Best Practice: MSProjectExperts recommends that you include a milestone task for every phase and deliverable level summary task, plus one final milestone to show the completion of the entire project.

Project 2013 offers you several ways to create milestone tasks. As with all previous versions of the software, you can create milestones by inserting a new task and then changing the value in the *Duration* column to *0 days*. Notice in Figure 5 - 20 that the *Gantt Chart* symbol for a *Phase I Complete* milestone task is a black diamond that displays the finish date of the milestone to the right of the black diamond.

	Task Mode	Task Name	Duration
0		New Project	1 d
1		PHASE I	1 d
2		Design	1 d
3		Build	1 d
4		Test	1 d
5		Implement	1 d
6		Phase I Complete	0 d

Figure 5 - 20: Phase I Complete is a milestone task

Best Practice: In Figure 5 - 20, notice that indenture level for the *Phase I Complete* milestone task is the same as the *PHASE I* summary task. For ease of high-level reporting, MSProjectExperts recommends that you always outdent milestone tasks to the same level as the summary tasks they represent. With this structure in place, when you show and print *Outline Level 1* tasks (the phase sections of your project), you see each phase along with its corresponding milestone which shows the finish date of each phase.

Warning: When you outdent milestone tasks at the same level as summary tasks, as recommended in the previous Best Practice note, the milestone tasks no longer move with their summary tasks. Before you attempt to move the entire summary task section to another location in the project, you should temporarily indent the milestone to the task level.

Information: Project 2013 allows you to create a milestone for a task with a *Duration* value greater than *0 days* by completing the following steps:

1. Double-click the task to open the *Task Information* dialog.
2. Click the *Advanced* tab.
3. Select the *Mark task as milestone* option and then click the *OK* button.

Inserting a Milestone Task

The other method for creating milestone tasks is to use the *Insert Milestone* feature in Project 2013, which allows you to directly insert milestone tasks into your project. To create a milestone task by inserting it, select a row for the new milestone task and then click the *Milestone* button in the *Insert* section of the *Task* ribbon. The software automatically inserts a new task named *<New Milestone>* with a *Duration* value of *0 days*, as shown in Figure 5 - 21. After inserting a new milestone task, you should rename it.

		Task Mode	Task Name	Duration
0			New Project	1 d
1			PHASE I	1 d
2			Design	1 d
3			Build	1 d
4			Test	1 d
5			Implement	1 d
6			<New Milestone>	0 d

GANTT CHART — May 31, '15 — F S S M T W T F — 6/1

Figure 5 - 21: New inserted milestone task

Hands On Exercise

Exercise 5 - 6

Create milestone tasks to indicate the completion date for each phase and for project completion in a project.

1. Return to the **Training Advisor 05a.mpp** sample file.
2. Scroll down to the first blank line at the end of your project and add a new task named *Project Complete*.
3. Select the new *Project Complete* task and then click the *Auto Schedule* button in the *Tasks* section of the *Task* ribbon.
4. For the moment, leave the value in the *Duration* column as *1 day* for the *Project Complete* task.
5. For task ID #6, the *Installation Complete* task, change the value in the *Duration* column to *0 days*.

Notice that Project 2013 converted this task to a milestone task automatically.

6. Using the **Control** key on your computer keyboard, simultaneously select the following tasks:

   Task ID #11, the *Testing Complete* task

   Task ID #21, the *Training Complete* task

   Task ID #22, the *Project Complete* task

7. Click the *Information* button in the *Properties* section of the *Task* ribbon.

8. In the *Multiple Task Information* dialog, set the *Duration* value to *0 days*, and then click the *OK* button.

Notice that Project 2013 automatically converted all three selected tasks to milestones.

9. Select task ID #18, the *Conduct Skills Assessment* task.

10. In the *Insert* section of the *Task* ribbon, click the *Insert Milestone* button.

11. With the new milestone task still selected, click the *Auto Schedule* button in the *Tasks* section of the *Task* ribbon.

12. With the new milestone task still selected, click the *Outdent Task* button in the *Schedule* section of the *Task* ribbon.

Notice that this action outdents the new milestone task to the same level of indenture as the *Create Training Materials* summary task.

13. Change the name of the new milestone task to *Training Materials Created.*

14. Save but **do not** close **Training Advisor 05a.mpp** sample file.

Using Task Notes and Cell Background Formatting

Task notes are an important part of project documentation and are essential to understanding the historical information about any project. You can add notes to tasks at any time during the life of the project, from planning through closure. To add a note to a task, use any of the following methods:

- Select the task and then click the *Task Notes* button in the *Properties* section of the *Task* ribbon.

- Double-click the task and then click the *Notes* tab.

- Right-click the task and then select the *Notes* item on the shortcut menu.

Using any of the preceding methods, the software displays the *Notes* tab in the *Task Information* dialog. Type the text of the note and add formatting as needed, shown in Figure 5 - 22. Click the *OK* button when finished.

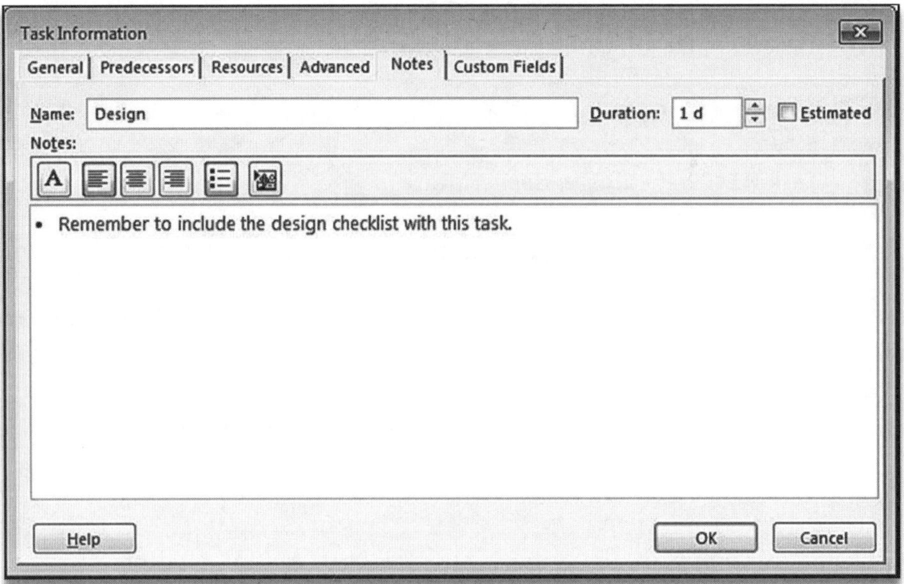

Figure 5 - 22: Task Information dialog, Notes page

Best Practice: MsProjectExperts recommends that you use "bulleted list" formatting for the text of your notes, as shown in Figure 5 - 22. When a task contains multiple notes, the bulleted list formatting makes the individual notes easier to read in the *Task Information* dialog, and when you print the project and include a *Notes* page at the end.

After you add a note to a task, Project 2013 displays a note indicator in the *Indicators* column to the left of the task, as shown in Figure 5 - 23. You can read the text of the note by floating your mouse pointer over the note indicator.

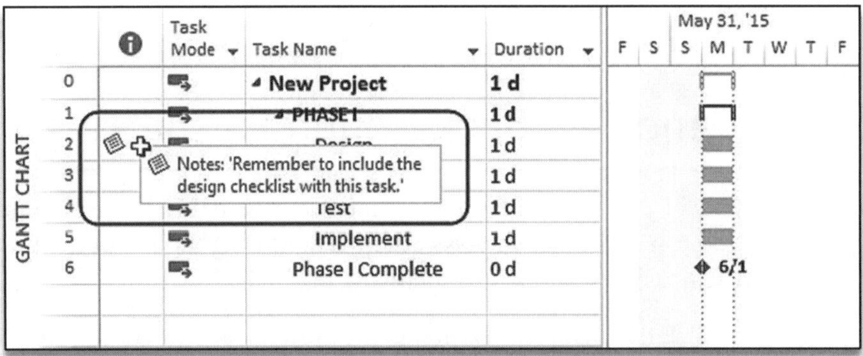

Figure 5 - 23: Notes indicator with screen tip text displayed

Using Cell Background Formatting

To easily identify tasks of interest, you can use cell background formatting in Project 2013. This feature is similar to the cell background formatting feature in Excel. You can manually apply cell background formatting for one or more tasks, or you can set it automatically using text styles. To manually set cell background formatting on any task, select the ID numbers of the tasks whose cell background color you want to format, and then use one of the following methods:

- In the *Font* section of the *Task* ribbon, click the *Background Color* button to format the cell background using the default *Yellow* color.
- In the *Font* section of the *Task* ribbon, click the *Background Color* pick list button and select a color in either the *Theme Colors* or *Standard Colors* sections of the pick list, as shown in Figure 5 - 24.

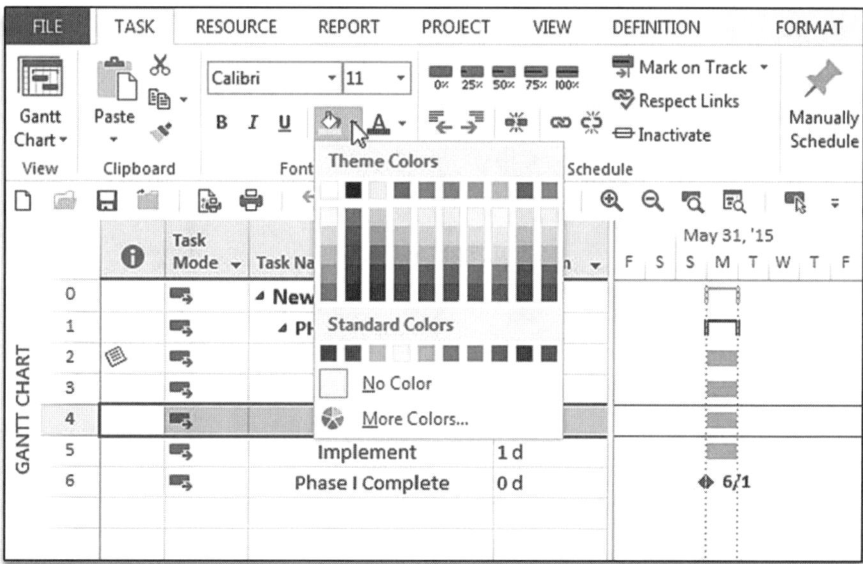

Figure 5 - 24: Background Color pick list

- In the *Font* section of *the Task* ribbon, click the *Background Color* pick list button and then click the *More Colors* item in the pick list. On the *Standard* page of the *Colors* dialog shown in Figure 5 - 25, select a color in the color palette, and then click the *OK* button.

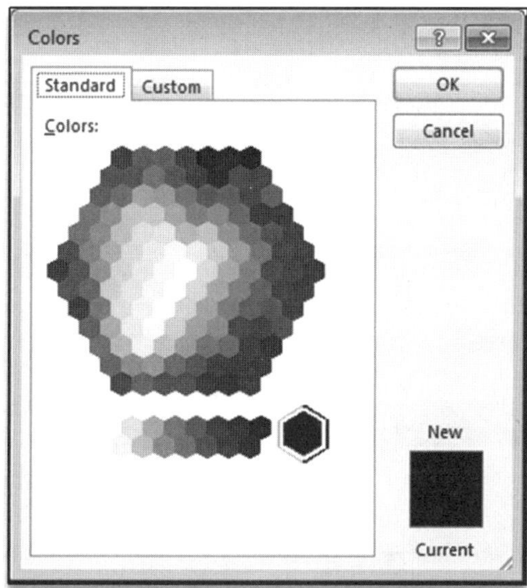

Figure 5 - 25: Colors dialog

- In the *Font* section of *the Task* ribbon, click the *Background Color* pick list button and then click the *More Colors* item at the bottom of the pick list. Click the *Custom* tab to display the *Custom* page of the *Colors* dialog shown in Figure 5 - 26. Click anywhere in the *Colors* palette to select an initial color and then drag the shading slider to the right of the *Colors* palette to "dial in" the exact *Red, Green,* and *Blue* values you want. Click the *OK* button when finished.

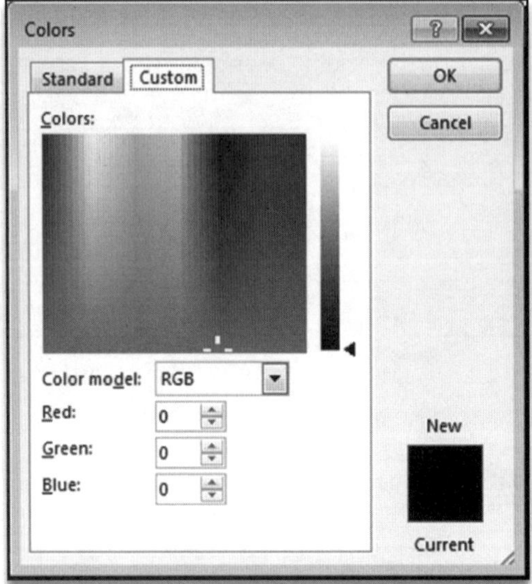

Figure 5 - 26: Colors dialog

- In the lower right corner of the *Font* section in the *Task* ribbon, click the *Font Dialog Launcher* icon. The software displays the *Font* dialog shown in Figure 5 - 27.

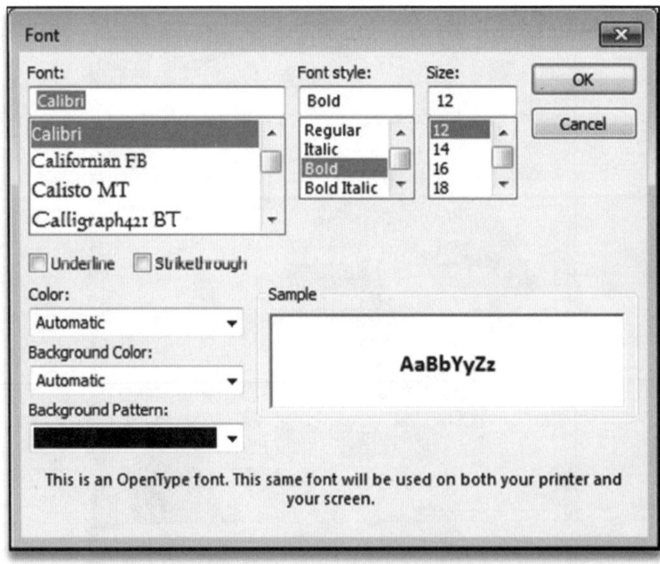

Figure 5 - 27: Font dialog

In the *Font* dialog, click the *Background Color* pick list and select the color of your background formatting. Click the *Background Pattern* pick list and select a pattern for the background color, if necessary. Click the *Color* pick list and select a different font color, if necessary. For example, if you select a dark color in the *Background Color* pick list, you should choose a lighter color in the *Color* pick list. Click the *OK* button when finished.

Warning: In the *Font* dialog, **do not** select the first pattern on the *Background Pattern* pick list (the white pattern). If you select this pattern, the software **does not** display any cell background formatting for the selected tasks.

Figure 5 - 28 shows background cell formatting for the *Test* task in a project.

		Task Mode	Task Name	Duration	May 31, '15
0			New Project	1 d	
1			PHASE I	1 d	
2			Design	1 d	
3			Build	1 d	
4			Test	1 d	
5			Implement	1 d	
6			Phase I Complete	0 d	6/1

Figure 5 - 28: Cell background formatting for the Test task

Using Automatic Cell Background Formatting

Project 2013 allows you to apply cell background formatting automatically to all tasks of a certain type, such as applying a particular color to all milestone tasks. To use automatic cell background formatting, click the *Format* tab to display the *Format* ribbon with the *Gantt Chart Tools* applied. In the *Format* section of the *Format* ribbon, click the *Text Styles* button. In the *Text Styles* dialog, click the *Item to Change* pick list as shown in Figure 5 - 29. On the *Item to Change* pick list, select the type of task you want to format automatically. For example, to apply cell background automatically to all milestone tasks, select the *Milestone Tasks* item. Click the *Background Color* pick list and select the color of your background formatting. Click the *Background Pattern* pick list and select a pattern for the background color, if necessary. Click the *Color* pick list and select a different font color, if necessary. For example, if you select a dark color in the *Background Color* pick list, you should choose a lighter color in the *Color* pick list. Click the *OK* button when finished. Project 2013 applies cell background formatting automatically to all tasks of the type you specify, including new tasks of that type you add to the project at a later time.

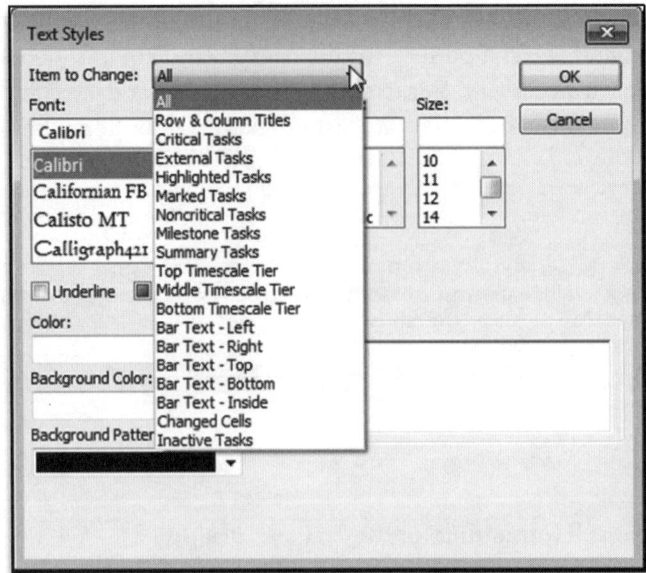

Figure 5 - 29: Text Styles dialog

Information: Cell background formatting, whether manual or automatic, is an attribute of the view in which you apply the formatting. When you apply cell background formatting to a task, Project 2013 applies formatting to the task for all tables in the current view only. For example, if you apply the standard *Yellow* color to a task displayed in the *Gantt Chart* view, the software applies the background formatting to the task in every task table you apply in the *Gantt Chart* view (such as the *Cost* and *Work* tables). However, if you display the *Tracking Gantt* view, the software does not apply any cell background formatting to the task in this view. This means that you can apply cell background formatting to different tasks in different views.

Hands On Exercise

Exercise 5 - 7

Add task notes and apply cell background formatting to tasks in a project.

1. Return to the **Training Advisor 05a.mpp** sample file.
2. Double-click task ID #8, the *Install Training Advisor Clients* task.
3. In the *Task Information* dialog, click the *Notes* tab.
4. On the *Notes* page of the *Task Information* dialog, click the *Bulleted List* button.
5. Enter the following text in the note field:

   Installation script location is \\corp\apps\training_advisor.

6. Click the *OK* button.

7. Float your cursor over the note indicator in the *Indicators* column to view the note on the *Install Training Advisor Clients* task.

8. Click the ID number (row header) for task ID #9, the *Verify Connectivity* task.

9. In the *Font* section of the *Task* ribbon, click the *Background Color* pick list button and select the *Gold, Lighter 60%* color (float your mouse pointer over the colors to find the correct color).

10. Click the *Format* tab to display the *Format* ribbon with the *Gantt Chart Tools* applied.

11. In the *Format* section of the *Format* ribbon, click the *Text Styles* button.

12. In the *Text Styles* dialog, click the *Item to Change* pick list and select the *Milestone Tasks* item on the list.

13. Click the *Background Color* pick list and choose the *Green, Lighter 60%* color in the *Theme Color* section of the pick list (float your mouse pointer over the colors to find the correct color).

14. Click the *OK* button.

Notice how the automatic cell background coloring calls attention to all of the milestone tasks and makes them easier to identify in the project.

15. Right-click the *Select All* button (upper left corner of the task sheet) and select the *Cost* table.

16. Save and close the **Training Advisor 05a.mpp** sample file.

Using Task Dependencies

After completing the initial steps in the task planning process, your next step is to determine the sequence in which tasks occur. This process requires you to determine and set task dependencies between tasks in the project.

Understanding Task Dependencies

When you set a dependency relationship between two tasks, Project 2013 designates the first task as the **predecessor task** and designates the second task as the **successor task** in the dependency relationship. The software offers you the following four default task dependency types:

- Finish-to-Start (abbreviated as FS)

- Start-to-Start (SS)

- Finish-to-Finish (FF)

- Start-to-Finish (SF)

Figure 5 - 30 shows an example for each of these four default dependency types.

	Task Mode	Task Name	Duration
1		Finish to Start (FS)	10 d
2		Task A	5 d
3		Task B	5 d
4			
5		Start to Start (SS)	5 d
6		Task C	5 d
7		Task D	5 d
8			
9		Finish to Finish (FF)	5 d
10		Task E	5 d
11		Task F	3 d
12			
13		Start to Finish (SF)	10 d
14		Task G	5 d
15		Task H	5 d

Figure 5 - 30: Four default task dependency types

A **Finish-to-Start (FS)** dependency means that the finish date of the predecessor task drives the start date of the successor task. Figure 5 - 30 shows an FS dependency between *Task A* and *Task B*. In this task pair, the finish date of *Task A* (the predecessor) drives the start date of *Task B* (the successor).

A **Start-to-Start (SS)** dependency means that the start date of the predecessor task drives the start date of the successor task. Figure 5 - 30 shows an SS dependency between *Task C* and *Task D*. In this task pair, the start date of *Task C* (the predecessor) drives the start date of *Task D* (the successor), which means that the two tasks start at the same time.

A **Finish-to-Finish (FF)** dependency means that the finish date of the predecessor task drives the finish date of the successor task. Figure 5 - 30 shows an FF dependency between *Task E* and *Task F*. In this task pair, the finish date of *Task E* (the predecessor) drives the finish date of *Task F* (the successor), which means the two tasks finish at the same time.

Best Practice: MsProjectExperts recommends that you be cautious with using the Finish-to-Finish (FF) dependency because it is extremely difficult to force two or more independent events to finish at precisely the same time. A best practice is to use an FF dependency as a predictive relationship to tell you when to start the successor task so that the linked tasks **might finish** at approximately the same time.

A **Start-to-Finish (SF)** dependency means that the start date of the predecessor task drives the finish date of the successor task. Figure 5 - 30 shows an SF dependency between *Task G* and *Task H*. In this task pair, the start date of *Task G* (the predecessor) drives the finish date of *Task H* (the successor).

Information: Many people confuse the meaning of the terms **predecessor** and **successor**, wrongly assuming that the predecessor is the task that occurs sequentially before the successor task. A better way to think of these two terms is as follows:

- The **predecessor** is the task that drives the schedule of the successor task.
- The **successor** is the task whose schedule is driven by the predecessor task.

In Project 2013, you can easily determine which task is the predecessor and which task is the successor because the software always draws the link line **from** the predecessor **to** the successor.

Setting Task Dependencies

To set a dependency in Project 2013, complete the following steps:

1. Select two or more tasks that are dependent on one another.
2. In the *Schedule* section of the *Task* ribbon, click the *Link the Selected Tasks* button.

When you complete these steps, Project 2013 sets a Finish-to-Start (FS) dependency on the selected tasks by default. To change the dependency type to any of the other three, continue with the following steps:

3. Double-click the link line between two dependent tasks. The software displays the *Task Dependency* dialog shown in Figure 5 - 31.

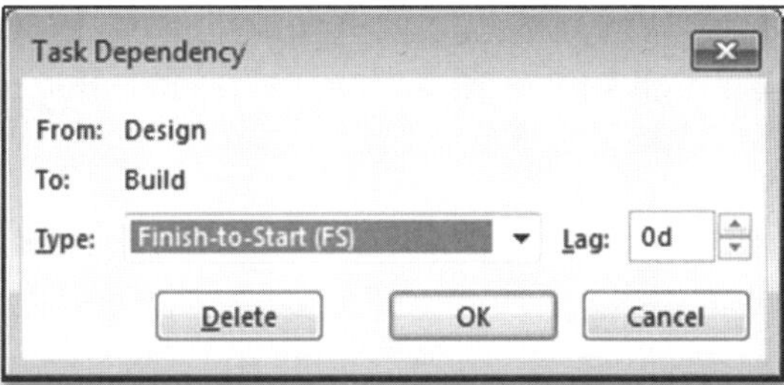

Figure 5 - 31: Task Dependency dialog

4. Click the *Type* pick list and select the desired dependency type.
5. Click the *OK* button.

Warning: Set task dependencies **only** on regular tasks and milestone tasks. **Do not** set dependencies on summary tasks, as doing this can lead to circular reference errors any time in the future. Circular reference errors are very difficult to troubleshoot and resolve, so it is better to avoid them by not setting task dependencies on summary tasks.

Warning: Be very careful when you use the **Control** key on your computer keyboard to select multiple tasks to link them. After selecting one task initially, when you press the **Control** key, Project 2013 assumes the first task you selected is the predecessor task and all other tasks you select are successor tasks. This means that when using the **Control** key to select multiple tasks, the order in which you select the tasks is very important in the dependency planning process!

Removing a Task Dependency

To remove a dependency relationship between two or more tasks, complete the following steps:

1. Select the tasks from which you want to remove the dependencies.
2. In the *Schedule* section of the *Task* ribbon, click the *Unlink Tasks* button.

Information: You can also remove a task dependency by double-clicking the link line between the dependent tasks. In the *Task Dependency* dialog, click the *Type* pick list and select the *(None)* item, or click the *Delete* button.

Hands On Exercise

Exercise 5 - 8

Set each of the four types of task dependencies for *Auto Scheduled* and *Manually Scheduled* tasks.

1. Open the **Dependency Planning 2013.mpp** sample file.

You determine that *Task A* through *Task D* are a "chain of events" that must occur sequentially. Link them with a Finish-to-Start (FS) dependency.

2. Select *Task A* through *Task D* and then click the *Link the Selected Tasks* button in the *Schedule* section of the *Task* ribbon.

You determine that *Task E* and *Task F* must start at the same time, and that *Task E* is the "driving event" between these two tasks. Set a Start-to-Start (SS) dependency on these two tasks.

3. Select *Task E* and *Task F* and then click the *Link the Selected Tasks* button in the *Schedule* section of the *Task* ribbon.
4. In the Gantt chart, double-click the link line between the Gantt bars for *Task E* and *Task F*.
5. In the *Task Dependency* dialog, click the *Type* pick list, select the *Start-to-Start (SS)* item on the list, and then click the *OK* button.

You determine that *Task G* and *Task H* must finish at the same time, and that *Task G* is the "driving event" between these two tasks. Set a Finish-to-Finish (FF) dependency on these two tasks.

6. Select *Task G* and *Task H* and then click the *Link the Selected Tasks* button in the *Schedule* section of the *Task* ribbon.
7. In the Gantt chart, double-click the link line between the Gantt bars for *Task G* and *Task H*.

8. In the *Task Dependency* dialog, click the *Type* pick list, select the *Finish-to-Finish (FF)* item on the list, and then click the *OK* button.

Your professor scheduled a World History final examination for 8:00 AM on Friday, March 6. You believe you need two days to study for the exam. The date and time of the exam determines when you need to finish studying. Set a Start-to-Finish (SF) dependency between the *World History Final Exam* task and the *Study for the Exam* task.

9. Select the *World History Final Exam* and *Study for the Exam* tasks and then click the *Link the Selected Tasks* button in the *Schedule* section of the *Task* ribbon.
10. In the Gantt chart, double-click the link line between the Gantt bars for these two tasks.
11. In the *Task Dependency* dialog, click the *Type* pick list, select the *Start-to-Finish (SF)* item on the list, and then click the *OK* button.
12. Save but **do not** close the **Dependency Planning 2013.mpp** sample file.

Using Lag Time with Dependencies

Lag time is a delay in the start or finish date of a successor task. You can use *Lag* time for a number of reasons, including situations such as the following:

- You need to plan for the delivery time delay between ordering equipment or supplies and receiving them in a FS dependency relationship.
- You require the completion of a portion (time or percentage) of the predecessor task before the successor task begins such as might be the case where you want to show that the painters can start painting after a portion of the dry wall work is complete in a SS dependency relationship.

You can enter *Lag* time as either a time value, such as *5 days*, or as a percentage of the duration of the predecessor task, such as *50%*. To enter *Lag* time on a task dependency, complete the following steps:

1. Double-click the link line between two dependent tasks.
2. In the *Task Dependency* dialog, enter a **positive** value in the *Lag* field (either as a time unit, such as *days*, or as a percentage).
3. Click the *OK* button.

In the *Task Dependency* dialog shown in Figure 5 - 32, notice that I added *2d* of *Lag* time to the FS dependency between the *Design* task and the *Build* task.

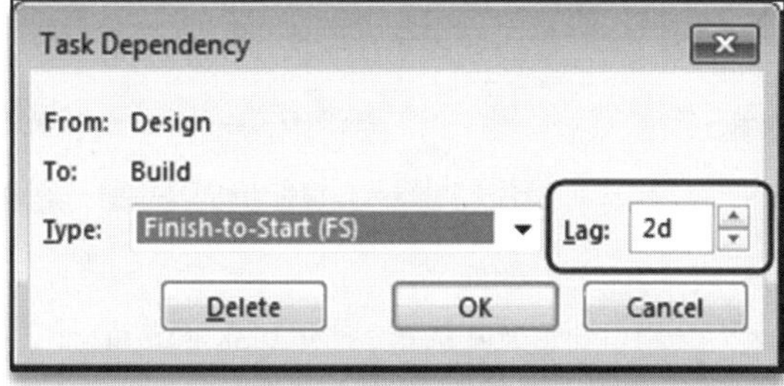

Figure 5 - 32: Task Dependency dialog with 3d Lag time entered

Figure 5 - 33 shows two different dependencies with *Lag* time. For the FS dependency between the *Pour Foundation* and *Frame Walls* tasks, I added *2 days* of *Lag* time. This dependency means that the *Frame Walls* task must start 2 days after the *Pour Foundation* task finishes. For the SS dependency between the *Test for Bugs* and *Fix Bugs* tasks, I added a *50% Lag* time. This means that the *Test for Bugs* task starts, and when it is 50% completed, the *Fix Bugs* task starts.

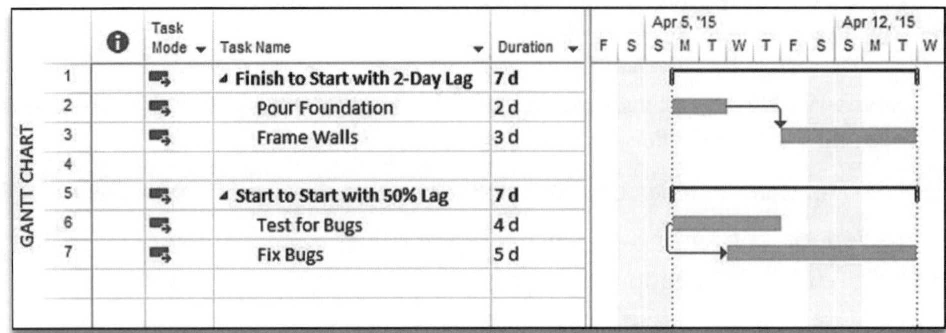

Figure 5 - 33: Lag time added to two different dependencies

Using Lead Time with Dependencies

Lead time is the opposite of *Lag* time, expressed by a negative *Lag* value. Most people use *Lead* time to create an overlap between two tasks linked with a Finish-to-Start (FS) dependency. To enter *Lead* time on a task dependency, complete the following steps:

1. Double-click the link line between two dependent tasks.
2. In the *Task Dependency* dialog, enter a **negative** value in the *Lag* field (either as a time unit, such as *days*, or as a percentage).
3. Click the *OK* button.

In the *Task Dependency* dialog shown in Figure 5 - 34, notice that I added *2d* of *Lag* time (-2d of *Lead* time) to the FS dependency between the *Design* task and the *Build* task.

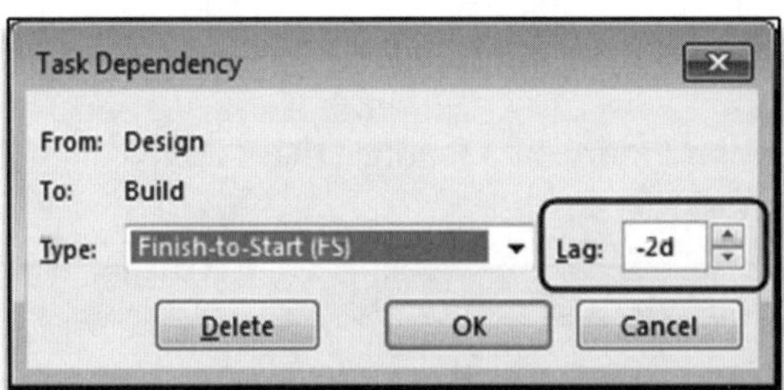

Figure 5 - 34: Task Dependency dialog with 2d Lead time added

In an FS dependency, *2 days* of *Lead* time means the successor task can start 2 days **before** the finish date of the predecessor task. Adding *2 days* of *Lead* time on an FS dependency creates an overlap between the dependent tasks as shown in Figure 5 - 35.

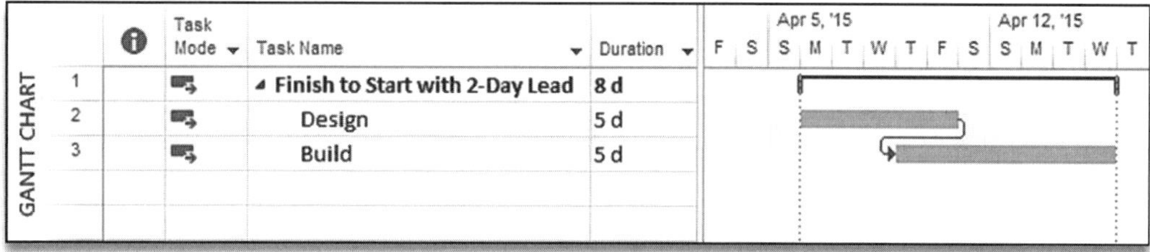

Figure 5 - 35: FS Dependency with 2 days of Lead time

Warning: Project managers often use *Lead* time to "fast track" a project by compressing the time it takes to complete a project schedule. Doing this is risky and can cause scheduling problems that result in an even later project finish date than originally scheduled. Because of this, MSProjectExperts recommends that you be very careful when using *Lead* time in your projects.

Hands On Exercise

Exercise 5 - 9

Add *Lag* time and *Lead* time on task dependencies.

1. Return to the **Dependency Planning 2013.mpp** sample file.

You determine that the *Setup Equipment* task cannot begin until 5 days after the *Order Equipment* task finishes. Set a Finish-to-Start (FS) dependency with *5 days* of *Lag* time for these two tasks.

2. Select the *Order Equipment* and *Setup Equipment* tasks and then click the *Link the Selected Tasks* button in the *Schedule* section of the *Task* ribbon.
3. In the Gantt chart, double-click the link line between the Gantt bars for these two tasks.
4. In the *Task Dependency* dialog, enter *5d* in the *Lag* field and then click the *OK* button.
5. Float your mouse pointer over the link line between these two tasks to see the screen tip indicating that the FS dependency includes 5 days of *Lag* time.

You determine that the *Decorate Rooms* task cannot start until the *Paint Rooms* task reaches 50% completion. Set a Start-to-Start (SS) dependency with *50% Lag* time for these two tasks.

6. Select the *Paint Rooms* and *Decorate Rooms* tasks and then click the *Link the Selected Tasks* button in the *Schedule* section of the *Task* ribbon.
7. In the Gantt chart, double-click the link line between the Gantt bars for these two tasks.
8. In the *Task Dependency* dialog, click the *Type* pick list and select the *Start-to-Start* (SS) dependency, manually type *50%* in the *Lag* field, and then click the *OK* button.

9. Float your mouse pointer over the link line between these two tasks to see the screen tip indicating that the SS dependency includes 50% *Lag* time.

You determine that Task J must start 2 days before Task I finishes. Set a Finish-to-Start (FS) dependency with *2 days* of *Lead* time between Task I and Task J.

10. Select *Task I* and *Task J* and then click the *Link the Selected Tasks* button in the *Schedule* section of the *Task* ribbon.
11. In the Gantt chart, double-click the link line between the Gantt bars for *Task I* and *Task J*.
12. In the *Task Dependency* dialog, enter *-2d* in the *Lag* field and then click the *OK* button.
13. Float your mouse pointer over the link line between these two tasks to see the screen tip indicating that the FS dependency includes 2 days of *Lead* time.

You determine that your team must complete the *Assemble Meeting Packets* task 5 days before the *Annual Shareholder Meeting* task begins. Because the start date of the *Annual Shareholder Meeting* task drives the finish date of the *Assemble Meeting Packets* task, set a Start-to-Finish (SF) dependency between these two tasks with *5 days* of *Lead* time.

14. Select the *Annual Shareholder Meeting* and *Assemble Meeting Packets* tasks, and then click the *Link the Selected Tasks* button in the *Schedule* section of the *Task* ribbon.
15. In the Gantt chart, double-click the link line between the Gantt bars for these two tasks.
16. In the *Task Dependency* dialog, click the *Type* pick list and select the *Start-to-Finish* (SF) dependency, enter *-5d* in the *Lag* field, and then click the *OK* button.
17. Float your mouse pointer over the link line between these two tasks to see the screen tip indicating that the SF dependency includes 5 days of *Lead* time.
18. Save but **do not** close the **Dependency Planning 2013.mpp** sample file.

Setting Task Dependencies on Manually Scheduled Tasks

If you specify task dependencies by linking *Manually Scheduled* tasks, Project 2013 **initially schedules** each *Manually Scheduled* task as follows:

- If you do not enter *Duration, Start,* or *Finish* values for a *Manually Scheduled* task, the software sets the *Duration* of the task to the default value of *1d* and then calculates the *Start* and *Finish* dates accordingly, based on its dependency relationship with its predecessor task.
- If you enter text in the *Duration* field for a *Manually Scheduled* task (such as *About 5 days*), the software leaves the text value in the *Duration* field, but treats the task as if it has a *Duration* value of *1 day,* and then calculates the *Start* and *Finish* dates accordingly.
- If you enter a numerical value in the *Duration* field for a *Manually Scheduled* task, the software maintains the numerical *Duration* value, and then calculates the *Start* and *Finish* dates accordingly.
- If you enter text in the *Start* and/or *Finish* fields for a *Manually Scheduled* task (such as *Early October*), the software replaces the textual date values with calculated dates in the *Start* and *Finish* fields.

- If you enter a numerical value in the *Start* field for a *Manually Scheduled* task, the software **ignores** the *Start* date and calculates the *Start* date based on its dependency relationship with its predecessor task.
- If you enter a numerical value in the *Finish* field for a *Manually Scheduled* task, the software honors the *Finish* date, calculates the *Duration* of the task based on the scheduled *Start* date and the current *Finish* date, and then schedules the task accordingly.

Information: When you link *Manually Scheduled* tasks using task dependencies, the software calculates the **initial schedule** of each task. If you later change the duration, start, or finish date of a *Manually Scheduled* task, Project 2013 **does not** recalculate the schedule of the *Manually Scheduled* task. I discuss this behavior in the next section of this module.

Hands On Exercise

Exercise 5 - 10

Set task dependencies on *Manually Scheduled* tasks.

1. Return to the **Dependency Planning 2013.mpp** sample file.
2. Scroll down to the group of *Manually Scheduled* tasks and then drag the split bar to the right edge of the *Finish* column.

Notice that these seven *Manually Scheduled* tasks include a mix of different types of information in the *Duration, Start,* and *Finish* fields. The one thing all of these tasks have in common is that they are all unscheduled tasks to some degree. Notice also the unusual Gantt bars for *Task M, Task O,* and *Task Q.*

3. Select *Task K* through *Task Q* and then click the *Link the Selected Tasks* button in the *Schedule* section of the *Task* ribbon.

Notice how Project 2013 calculates dates in the *Start* and *Finish* columns for every task, and calculates values in the *Duration* column for every task except *Task L.*

4. Save but **do not** close the **Dependency Planning 2013.mpp** sample file.

Understanding Schedule Warnings and Suggestions

When you link *Manually Scheduled* tasks and then later change the project schedule, Project 2013 recalculates the schedule for **only** *Auto Scheduled* tasks. It **does not** recalculate the schedule for *Manually Scheduled* tasks. Instead, the software calculates what the *Start* and *Finish* date **should be** for each *Manually Scheduled* task based on the task dependency relationships. The software stores these two dates in the *Scheduled Start* and *Scheduled Finish* fields. Then the software compares the current *Start* and *Finish* dates with the *Scheduled Start* and *Scheduled Finish* dates. If the dates in the *Scheduled Start* and *Scheduled Finish* fields are **later** than the dates in the *Start* and *Finish* fields, meaning that the schedule for the task is not correct, the software displays a schedule warning on the task by applying a red wavy underline to the date in the *Finish* column and by displaying a chopped up Gantt bar.

For example, in the schedule shown in Figure 5 - 36, I manually entered *Duration* values for the *Design*, *Build*, and *Test* tasks. This resulted in a schedule discrepancy for the *Manually Scheduled* task, *Rebuild*, creating the schedule warnings shown in both the task sheet (red wavy underline below the *Finish* date) and the Gantt chart (chopped up teal-colored Gantt bar).

	Task Mode	Task Name	Duration	Start	Finish
0		◢ New Project	7 d	6/1/15	6/9/15
1		◢ PHASE I	7 d	6/1/15	6/9/15
2		Design	2 d	6/1/15	6/2/15
3		Build	3 d	6/3/15	6/5/15
4		Test	2 d	6/8/15	6/9/15
5		Rebuild	1 d	6/4/15	6/4/15
6		Retest	1 d	6/5/15	6/5/15
7		Implement	1 d	6/8/15	6/8/15
8		Phase I Complete	0 d	6/8/15	6/8/15

Figure 5 - 36: Schedule discrepancy warning on a Manually Scheduled task

By default, Project 2013 only shows warnings about schedule discrepancies on *Manually Scheduled* tasks; however, you can configure the software to show optimization suggestions about how to optimize your schedule . As I noted in Module 04, *Project Definition*, you can enable optimization suggestions by selecting the *Show task schedule suggestions* option on the *Schedule* page of the *Project Options* dialog. Remember that you can choose to apply this option only to the current project or for all new projects. If you did not select this option in the *Project Options* dialog, you can select this option for the current project by clicking the *Inspect* pick list button in the *Tasks* section of the *Task* ribbon and then selecting the *Show Suggestions* item, as shown in Figure 5 - 37.

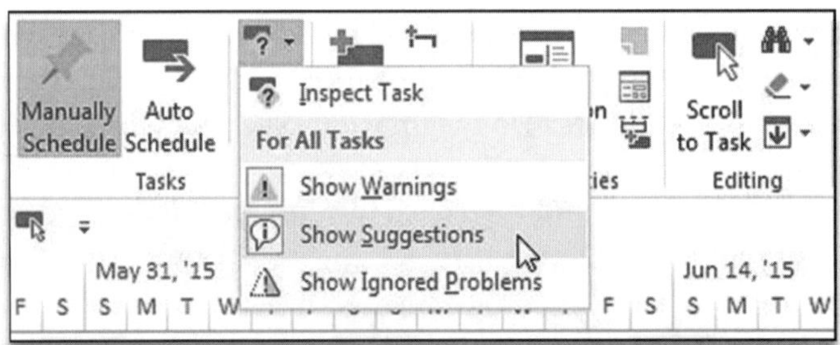

Figure 5 - 37: Enable optimization suggestions for Manually Scheduled tasks

When you enable optimization suggestions, Project 2013 examines the current *Start* and *Finish* date for each *Manually Scheduled* task and looks for opportunities to optimize. To do this, the software calculates the earliest that each *Manually Scheduled* task can start and finish based on the task dependency relationships. The software stores these two dates in the *Scheduled Start* and *Scheduled Finish* fields. Then the software compares the current *Start* and *Finish* dates with the *Scheduled Start* and *Scheduled Finish* dates. If the dates in the *Scheduled Start* and *Scheduled Finish* fields are **earlier** than the dates in the *Start* and Finish fields, meaning that the task could start earlier, the software displays an optimization suggestion on that task by applying a green wavy underline to the date in the *Finish* column.

For example, in the schedule shown in Figure 5 - 38, I manually entered a *Start* date of Friday, June 12 on the *Rebuild* task. This caused a gap between the *Finish* date of the *Test* task and the *Start* date of the *Rebuild* task, and resulted in an optimization suggestion from Project 2013.

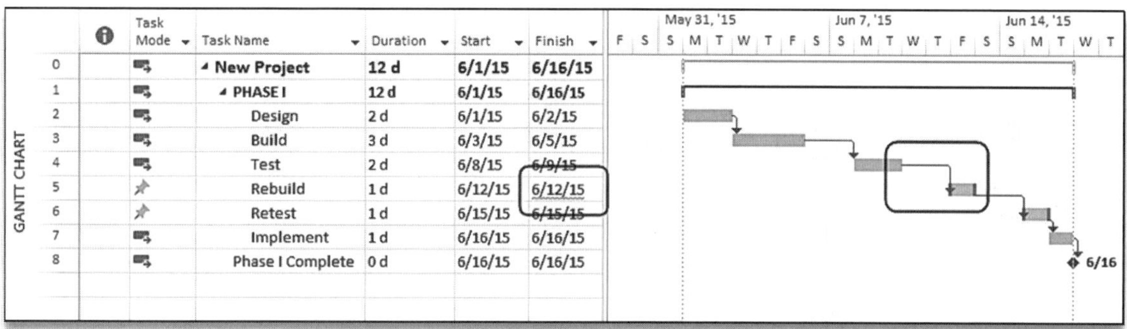

Figure 5 - 38: Optimization Suggestion on a Manually Scheduled task

If you float your mouse pointer over a schedule warning in the *Finish* column, the software displays a tool tip with the words, *Potential scheduling problem. Right-click to see options.* If you float your mouse pointer over an optimization suggestion in the *Finish* column, the software displays a tool tip with the words, *Potential scheduling optimization. Right-click to see options.* When you right-click in the *Finish* cell for the task as suggested in the tool tip, the shortcut menu provides three options for acting on the schedule warning or the optimization suggestion, including the *Fix in Task Inspector, Respect Links* and *Ignore Problems for this Task* items shown in Figure 5 - 39.

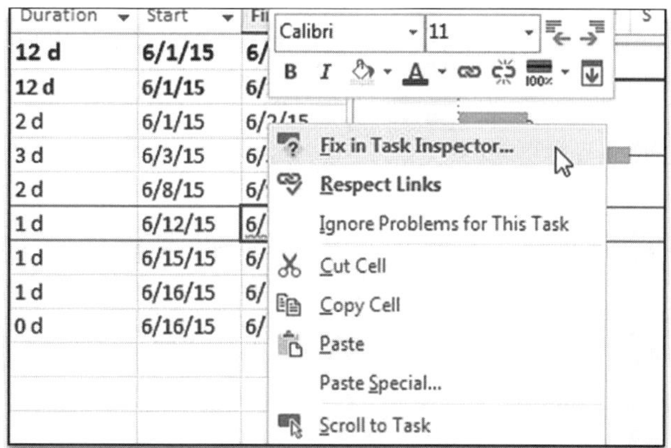

Figure 5 - 39: Shortcut menu for an optimization suggestion

Using the Respect Links Feature

Project 2013 allows you to respond to schedule warnings and optimization suggestions using the *Respect Links* feature. To use this feature, right-click any *Manually Scheduled* task with a schedule warning or optimization suggestion, and then select the *Respect Links* item on the shortcut menu. You can also access the *Respect Links* feature by clicking the *Respect Links* button in the *Schedule* section of the *Task* ribbon.

When you use the *Respect Links* feature, Project 2013 reschedules the task by changing the *Start* and *Finish* dates to the dates in the *Scheduled Start* and *Scheduled Finish* fields. When responding to a schedule warning, this means the software delays the *Manually Scheduled* task. When responding to an optimization suggestion, this means that the software reschedules the *Manually Scheduled* task to start earlier than currently scheduled. Keep in mind that this action might result in a new schedule warning or optimization suggestion on other *Manually Scheduled* tasks linked to the rescheduled task!

Using the Task Inspector

Project 2013 allows you to respond to schedule warnings and optimization suggestions on *Manually Scheduled* tasks using the *Task Inspector* tool. You can also use the *Task Inspector* to examine *Auto Scheduled* tasks to determine the reason for the current scheduled *Start* date of any task. To display the *Task Inspector*, click the *Inspect* button in the *Tasks* section of the *Task* ribbon. The software displays the *Task Inspector* on the left side of the application window. On a *Manually Scheduled* task with a schedule warning or optimization suggestion, you can also right-click the task and select the *Fix in Task Inspector* item on the shortcut menu.

Depending on the type of task you select, the *Task Inspector* includes either three sections or one section only. For example, Figure 5 - 40 shows the *Task Inspector* for a *Manually Scheduled* task with a schedule warning. Notice that the first section displays the reason for the schedule warning (the task needs to be delayed by 4 days). The *Actions* section offers the *Respect Links* button and the *Auto Schedule* button to resolve the schedule problem. The *Info* section reveals the reason for the scheduled start date of the selected task.

Figure 5 - 41 shows the *Task Inspector* for a task with an optimization suggestion. Notice that only the first section differs from the *Task Inspector* shown in Figure 5 - 40, and reveals the reason for the optimization suggestion (the task can start 2 days earlier than currently scheduled). Figure 5 - 42 shows the *Task Inspector* for an *Auto Scheduled* task and contains only a single section, the *Info* section. To close the *Task Inspector* sidepane, click the *Close* (**X**) button in the upper right corner of the pane.

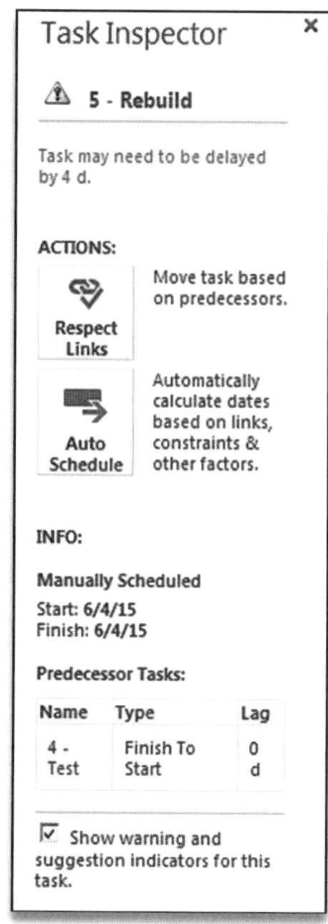

Figure 5 - 40: Task Inspector for a task with a warning

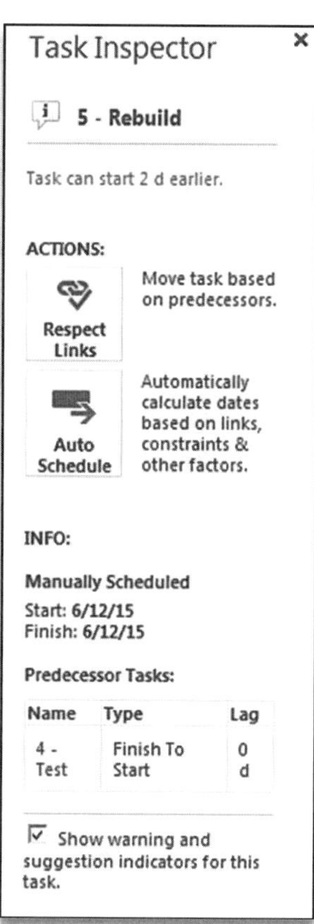

Figure 5 - 41: Task Inspector for a task with a suggestion

Figure 5 - 42: Task Inspector for an Auto Scheduled task

Hands On Exercise

Exercise 5 - 11

Respond to schedule warnings and optimization suggestions on *Manually Scheduled* tasks.

1. Return to the **Dependency Planning 2013.mpp** sample file.
2. For *Task L,* change the value in the *Duration* column to *3d* and then press the **Enter** key on your computer keyboard.

Notice that the software displays a schedule warning in the *Finish* column for *Task M* (the red wavy underline below the date) and changes the Gantt bar to the a chopped up Gantt bar.

3. Float your mouse pointer over the schedule warning for *Task M* and read the tool tip.
4. Right-click anywhere on *Task M* and then select the *Respect Links* item in the shortcut menu.

Notice that the software resolves the scheduling warning for *Task M,* but now shows a new schedule warning for *Task N.*

5. Select *Task K* through *Task Q,* and then click the *Respect Links* button in the *Schedule* section of the *Task* ribbon.

Notice that the software resolves the scheduling warning *Task N* and prevents schedule warnings for any of the remaining tasks .

6. For *Task Q,* change the date in the *Start* column to *March 19, 2015* and then press the **Enter** key on your computer keyboard.

Notice that the software displays an optimization suggestion for *Task Q* (the green wavy underline below the *Finish* date). Notice also the gap between the Gantt bars for *Task P* and *Task Q*. This gap indicates the reason for the optimization suggestion, since *Task Q* could start 2 days earlier based on the task dependency relationship with *Task P.*

7. Right-click anywhere on *Task Q* and then select the *Fix in Task Inspector* item on the shortcut menu.
8. In the *Actions* section of the *Task Inspector* sidepane, click the *Respect Links* button.

Notice that Project 2013 removes the gap between the Gantt bars for *Task P* and *Task Q* by scheduling *Task Q* to start immediately after *Task P* finishes.

9. Close the *Task Inspector* sidepane.
10. Save but **do not** close the **Dependency Planning 2013.mpp** sample file.

Using Alternate Methods to Set Dependencies

In addition to using the *Link the Selected Tasks* button, Project 2013 offers you several other ways for setting task dependencies. The first way is to manually enter the dependency information in the *Predecessors* column for each task. To use this method, apply the *Gantt Chart* view and then drag the split bar to the right until you see the *Predecessors* column, as shown in Figure 5 - 43. Notice the "shorthand" Project 2013 uses for dependencies in the *Predecessors* column:

- Since the predecessor for the *Build P1* task is the *Design P1* task (ID #2), the software displays the numeral 2 in the *Predecessors* column for the *Build P1* task, indicating a Finish-to-Start dependency with the *Design P1* task.
- The FS dependency between the *Design P1* and *Build P1* tasks includes 2 days of *Lag* time, indicated by the *+2d* text appended to the *2FS* text.
- The predecessor for the *Test P1* task is the *Build P1* task with a Start-to-Start dependency, indicated by the *3SS* text in the *Predecessors* column.
- The predecessor for the *Build P2* task is the *Design P2* task with a Finish-to-Finish dependency, indicated by the *8FF* text in the *Predecessors* column.

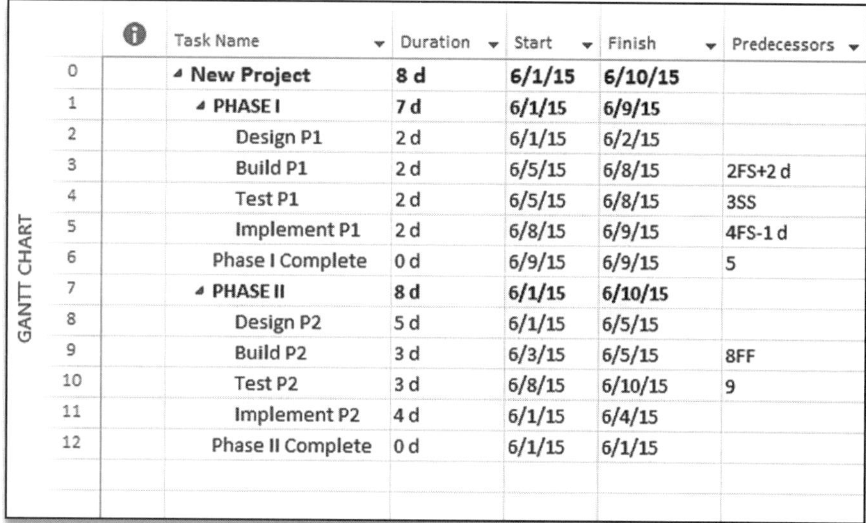

GANTT CHART

	Task Name	Duration	Start	Finish	Predecessors
0	**New Project**	**8 d**	**6/1/15**	**6/10/15**	
1	**PHASE I**	**7 d**	**6/1/15**	**6/9/15**	
2	Design P1	2 d	6/1/15	6/2/15	
3	Build P1	2 d	6/5/15	6/8/15	2FS+2 d
4	Test P1	2 d	6/5/15	6/8/15	3SS
5	Implement P1	2 d	6/8/15	6/9/15	4FS-1 d
6	Phase I Complete	0 d	6/9/15	6/9/15	5
7	**PHASE II**	**8 d**	**6/1/15**	**6/10/15**	
8	Design P2	5 d	6/1/15	6/5/15	
9	Build P2	3 d	6/3/15	6/5/15	8FF
10	Test P2	3 d	6/8/15	6/10/15	9
11	Implement P2	4 d	6/1/15	6/4/15	
12	Phase II Complete	0 d	6/1/15	6/1/15	

Figure 5 - 43: Predecessors column in the Gantt Chart view

If you want to manually enter dependency information for tasks in the *Predecessors* column, use the following approach:

- If the dependency is Finish-to-Start (FS) without any *Lag* time or *Lead* time, enter only the ID number of the predecessor task in the *Predecessors* column.
- If the dependency is Start-to-Start (SS), enter the ID number of the predecessor task plus the characters *SS* in the *Predecessors* column.
- If the dependency is Finish-to-Finish (FF), enter the ID number of the predecessor task plus the characters *FF* in the *Predecessors* column.
- If the dependency is Start-to-Finish (SF), enter the ID number of the predecessor task plus the characters *SF* in the *Predecessors* column.
- To add *Lag* time to any dependency relationship, append a plus sign character (+) along with the amount of *Lag* time to the dependency.
- To add *Lead* time to any dependency relationship, append a minus sign character (-) along with the amount of *Lead* time to the dependency.

The second way to set task dependencies is to use the *Task Entry* view following these steps:

1. Apply the *Gantt Chart* view.
2. Click the *View* tab to display the *View* ribbon.
3. In the *Split View* section of the *View* ribbon, select the *Details* option checkbox.

Remember that the *Task Entry* view is a combination view consisting of the *Gantt Chart* view in the top pane and the *Task Form* view in the bottom pane.

4. Right-click anywhere in the *Task Form* pane and select the *Predecessors & Successors* item on the shortcut menu.
5. Select any task in the *Gantt Chart* pane. Figure 5 - 44 shows the *Task Entry* view with the *Implement P2* task selected in the *Gantt Chart* pane and the *Predecessors & Successors* details applied in the *Task Form* pane.

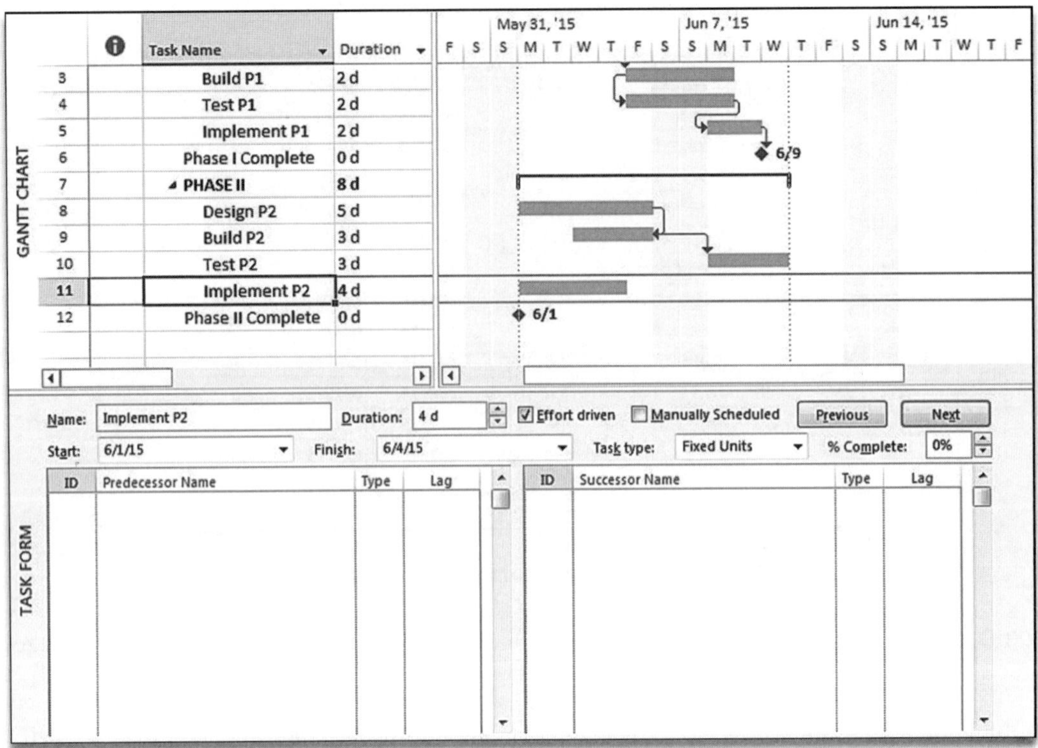

Figure 5 - 44: Task Entry view with Predecessors & Successors details

6. In the *Task Form*, click the first blank line in either the *Predecessor Name* column or the *Successor Name* column.
7. Click the pick list arrow button in the selected column and then select the name of the task from the list of tasks. Notice in Figure 5 - 45 that I am selecting the *Test P2* task in the *Predecessor Name* column for the *Implement P2* task.

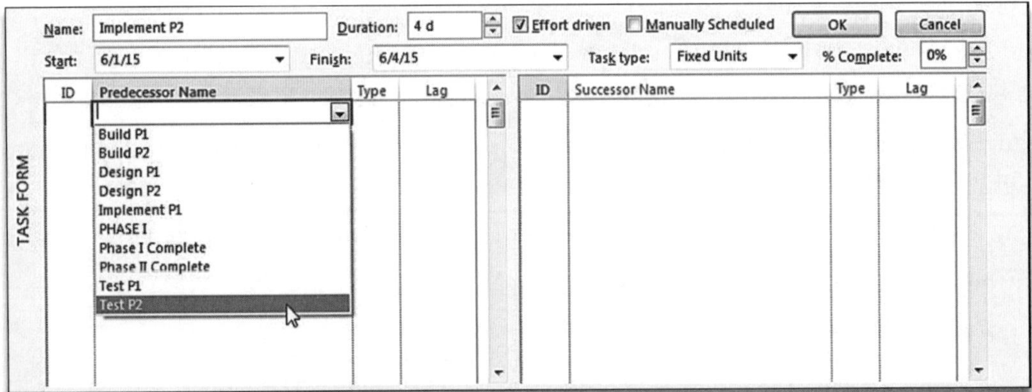

Figure 5 - 45: Select a task from the Predecessor Name column

8. Click the first blank line in the *Type* column, click the pick list arrow button, and then select a dependency type from the list of four possible dependencies.
9. Enter *Lag* time or *Lead* time in the *Lag* column as needed.
10. Click the *OK* button in the *Task Form* pane to apply the selected dependency.

Information: If you do not select a dependency type in the *Type* column of the *Task Form* pane, Project 2013 selects the *FS* item in the *Type* column and enters *0d* in the *Lag* column by default.

The third way to set task dependencies is to use the *Task Information* dialog by completing the following steps:

1. Double-click any successor task in the project.
2. In the *Task Information* dialog for the selected task, click the *Predecessors* tab.
3. Click the first blank line in the *Task Name* column on the *Predecessors* page, click the pick list arrow button, and then select a task from the list, as shown in Figure 5 - 46.

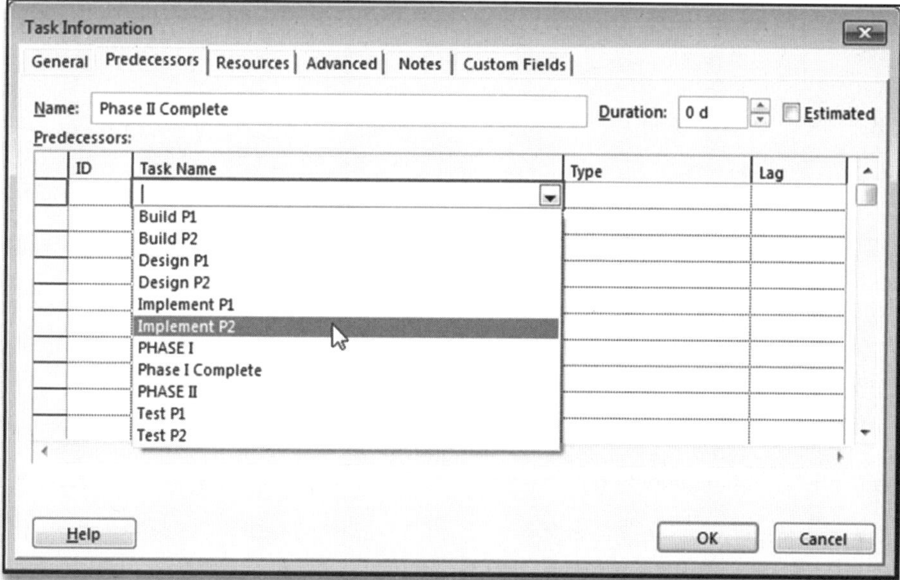

Figure 5 - 46: Task Information dialog, Predecessors page

When you select a task name in the *Task Name* column, the software automatically selects the *Finish-to-Start (FS)* item in the *Type* column and enters *0d* of *Lag* time in the *Lag* column.

4. Click the first cell of the *Type* column, click the pick list arrow button, and then select a different dependency type from the list, if needed.
5. Enter *Lag* time or *Lead* time in the *Lag* column as needed.
6. Click the *OK* button.

Information: Project 2013 actually offers one additional way to set task dependencies, although I do not recommend you use it. To set a task dependency using this final method, click and hold the Gantt bar of a predecessor task to "grab" the Gantt bar, and then drag the Gantt bar onto the Gantt bar of the successor task. As you drag the predecessor Gantt bar onto its successor, the software displays a link line between the tasks, a *Link Tasks* symbol on the link line, and a floating tooltip that shows you the impending dependency information. Release the mouse button to set the dependency. Using this method, Project 2013 always sets a Finish-to-Start dependency with *0 days* of *Lag* time on the two tasks.

Hands On Exercise

Exercise 5 - 12

Edit task dependencies using alternate methods.

1. Return to the **Dependency Planning 2013.mpp** sample file.

Using the *Predecessors* column, add *2 days* of *Lag* time to the to the Start-to-Start (SS) dependency between *Task E* and *Task F*.

2. Drag the vertical split bar to the right side of the *Predecessors* column.
3. Select the *Predecessors* cell for *Task F*, press the **F2** function key on your computer keyboard, and then add the *+2d* text to the end of the *6SS* text.
4. Press the **Enter** key on your computer keyboard to complete the editing.
5. Drag the vertical split bar back to the right side of the *Duration* column.

Using the *Task Entry* view, change the *Lag* time to *7 days* for the dependency between the *Order Equipment* task and the *Setup Equipment* task.

6. Select the *Order Equipment* task.
7. Right-click anywhere in the Gantt chart and select the *Show Split* item on the shortcut menu to display the *Task Entry* view.
8. Right-click anywhere in the *Task Form* pane and select the *Predecessors & Successors* item on the shortcut menu.
9. In the *Task Form* pane, change the value in the *Lag* column for the *Setup Equipment* successor task from *5d* to *7d* and then click the *OK* button.
10. Right-click anywhere in the Gantt chart and **deselect** the *Show Split* item on the shortcut menu to close the *Task Form*.

Using the *Task Information* dialog, designate *Task A* as a predecessor to *Task I* using the default Finish-to-Start (FS) dependency.

11. Double-click *Task I* to display the *Task Information* dialog, and then click the *Predecessors* tab.
12. On the *Predecessors* page of the dialog, click the *Task Name* cell on the first blank row, click the pick list button, and select *Task A* on the pick list.
13. Click the *OK* button.
14. Save and close the **Dependency Planning 2013.mpp** sample file.

Exercise 5 - 13

Set task dependencies in your Training Advisor Rollout project using any of the previous methods.

1. Open to the **Training Advisor 05b.mpp** sample file.
2. Individually select each of the following blocks of tasks and use the *Link the Selected Tasks* button to link each of the following task sequences with a Finish-to-Start (FS) dependency:

   Task IDs #2-6

   Task IDs #8-11

   Task IDs #13 and #15 (use the **Control** key to select only these two tasks)

   Task IDs #15-23

Historical records show that it normally takes the server vendor 8 days to deliver a server after we order it.

3. Double-click the link line between task IDs #2 and #3, the *Order Server* and *Setup Server* tasks.
4. In the *Task Dependency* dialog, enter *8 days* in the *Lag* field and then click the *OK* button.

Because of the time needed before training rooms become available, the *Provide End User Training* task cannot begin until 5 days after the *Create Training Schedule* task completes.

5. Double-click the link line between task IDs #20 and #21, the *Create Training Schedule* and the *Provide End User Training* tasks.
6. In the *Task Dependency* dialog, enter *5 days* in the *Lag* field and then click the *OK* button.
7. Using the **Control** key, select task IDs #6 and #8, the *Installation Complete* milestone and the *Install Training Advisor Clients* task.
8. In the *Schedule* section of the *Task* ribbon, click the *Link the Selected Tasks* button to link the selected tasks with a Finish-to-Start (FS) dependency.

Information: The previous step represents the best practice approach to linking phases or deliverables. Setting dependencies in this manner avoids the possibility of a circular reference error that could render you unable to open your project in the future!

9. Using the **Control** key, select task IDs #11 and #20, the *Testing Complete* milestone and the *Create Training Schedule* task.
10. In the *Schedule* section of the *Task* ribbon, click the *Link the Selected Tasks* button to link the selected tasks with a Finish-to-Start (FS) dependency.
11. Save but **do not** close the **Training Advisor 05b.mpp** sample file.

Exercise 5 - 14

Respond to schedule warnings in your Training Advisor Rollout project.

1. Return to the **Training Advisor 05b.mpp** sample file, if necessary.
2. Drag the split bar to the right side of the *Finish* column.
3. Notice the schedule warning in the *Finish* column for task ID #21, the *Provide End User Training* task, and in the Gantt bar for this task .
4. Right-click anywhere on the *Provide End User Training* task and then select the *Respect Links* item on the shortcut menu.
5. Select Task IDs #20 and #21, the *Create Training Schedule* and *Provide End User Training* tasks, both of which are *Manually Scheduled* tasks.
6. In the *Tasks* section of the *Task* ribbon, click the *Auto Schedule* button to convert these two tasks to *Auto Scheduled.*
7. On the status bar in the lower left corner of the Project 2013 application window, click the *New Tasks* button and select the *Auto Scheduled* option.

From this point forward, your Training Advisor Rollout project uses only *Auto Scheduled* tasks.

8. Drag the split bar back to the right side of the *Duration* column.
9. Save but **do not** close **Training Advisor 05b.mpp** sample file.

Setting Task Constraints and Deadline Dates

Project 2013 offers you two options to constrain tasks in the project schedule:

- Constraints
- Deadline dates

A constraint is a restriction that you set on the *Start* date or *Finish* date of a task. When you set a constraint on a task in Project 2013, you limit the software's ability to automatically reschedule the task when the schedule changes on predecessor tasks. Common reasons for using constraints include the following:

- **Contractual dates for task completion** when you have an obligation to complete a certain task in your project by a certain date.
- **Delivery dates for equipment and supplies** when a vendor guarantees delivery of equipment by a certain date.
- **Resource availability restrictions** when a resource cannot begin work on a task until after a certain date due to other project commitments.

Using a deadline date is a way to set a "soft target date" for the completion of a task. Unlike constraints, deadline dates **do not** limit the Project 2013 scheduling engine, but the software does show an indicator if the task's *Finish* date slips past the *Deadline* date.

Setting Constraints

To set a constraint on a task, complete the following steps:

1. Double-click the task whose schedule you need to constrain.
2. In the *Task Information* dialog, click the *Advanced* tab. Figure 5 - 47 shows the *Advanced* page of the *Task Information* dialog for the *Build* task.

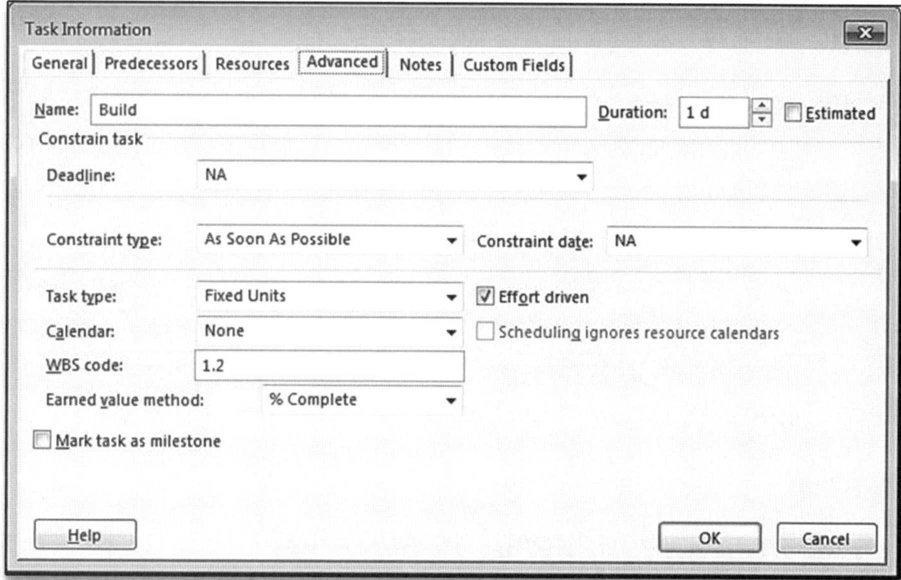

Figure 5 - 47: Task Information dialog, Advanced page

3. Click the *Constraint type* pick list and select a constraint.
4. Click the *Constraint date* pick list and select a date in the calendar date picker.

When setting a constraint on a task, it is wise to add a note to the task to document the reason for the constraint. Adding a note makes it easier for others to understand why you set the constraint originally, and you can use this information later to evaluate the historical data in your project. To add a constraint note to a task, continue with the following steps:

5. In the *Task Information* dialog, click the *Notes* tab.
6. Click the *Bulleted List* button.
7. Click in the *Notes* text field and enter the body of your note.

A good "shorthand" method for documenting a constraint is to include the following information in the body of the note:

- Abbreviation or acronym for the constraint type (such as *SNET*).
- The date of the constraint (such as *06/10/15*).
- The reason for setting the constraint (such as *Contractual delivery date for supplies*).

Figure 5 - 48 shows the *Notes* page of the *Task Information* dialog documenting the reason for a constraint.

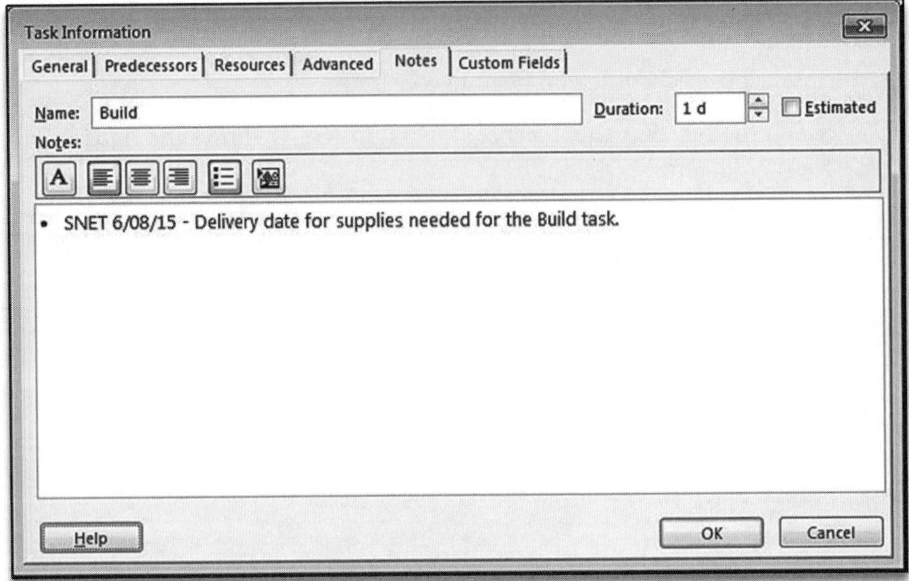

Figure 5 - 48: Task Information dialog, note documents a constraint

8. Click the *OK* button.

Understanding Flexible and Inflexible Constraints

In Project 2013, constraints are either **flexible** or **inflexible**. A flexible constraint allows the software to reschedule the task as required, while an inflexible constraint limits or even stops the tool from using its normal scheduling behavior. When you set a constraint, the software displays an indicator with a colored dot in the *Indicators* column to the left of the task, and the color of the dot reveals whether the task is flexible or inflexible. The information shown in Table 5 - 1 and Table 5 - 2 documents the behavior of Project 2013 when you set a constraint in a project scheduled from a start date.

Flexible Constraints		
Constraint Name	**Indicator Color**	**Constraint Description**
As Soon As Possible	None	Default constraint on new tasks when the project is scheduled from a *Start* date
As Late As Possible	None	Schedules the task as late as possible without any impact on project *Finish* date
Finish No Earlier Than	Blue	Task cannot finish earlier than the constraint date
Start No Earlier Than	Blue	Task cannot start earlier than the constraint date

Table 5 - 1: Flexible Constraints, project scheduled from a start date

Inflexible Constraints		
Constraint Name	**Indicator Color**	**Constraint Description**
Finish No Later Than	Red	Task cannot finish later than the constraint date
Must Finish On	Red	Task must finish on the constraint date
Must Start On	Red	Task must start on the constraint date
Start No Later Than	Red	Task cannot start later than the constraint date

Table 5 - 2: Inflexible Constraints, project scheduled from a start date

The *Project Information* dialog contains a special field known as the *Schedule from* field. To access the *Project Information* dialog, click the *Project Information* button in the *Properties* section of the *Project* ribbon. You use the *Schedule from* field to determine the scheduling direction for the Project 2013 scheduling engine. The default option in the *Schedule from* field is *Project Start Date,* which means that the software schedules from the *Start* date of your project **into the future** so that it can calculate the *Finish* date of your project. You can reverse the direction of the scheduling engine, however, by selecting *Project Finish Date* in the *Schedule from* field. With this option selected, the software schedules from the *Finish* date of your project **into the past** so that it can calculate the *Start* date of your project.

I mention the *Schedule from* option because this option also determines whether a constraint is flexible or inflexible. Shown previously, the information in Table 5 - 1 and Table 5 - 2 documents the behavior of the tool when you set a constraint in a project scheduled from a *Start* date. The information in Table 5 - 3 and Table 5 - 4 documents the behavior of the tool when you set a constraint in a project scheduled from a *Finish* date.

Flexible Constraints		
Constraint Name	**Indicator Color**	**Constraint Description**
As Soon As Possible	None	Schedules the task as soon as possible based on the project *Start* date and dependencies
As Late As Possible	None	Default constraint on new tasks when the project is scheduled from a *Finish* date
Finish No Later Than	Blue	Task cannot finish later than the constraint date
Start No Later Than	Blue	Task cannot start later than the constraint date

Table 5 - 3: Flexible Constraints, project scheduled from a finish date

Inflexible Constraints		
Constraint Name	**Indicator Color**	**Constraint Description**
Finish No Earlier Than	Red	Task cannot finish earlier than the constraint date
Must Finish On	Red	Task must finish on the constraint date
Must Start On	Red	Task must start on the constraint date
Start No Earlier Than	Red	Task cannot start earlier than the constraint date

Table 5 - 4: Inflexible Constraints, project scheduled from a finish date

Understanding Planning Wizard Messages about Constraints

When you set a task constraint in a project scheduled from a *Start* date, Project 2013 displays a *Planning Wizard* message when the resulting situation meets both of the following conditions:

- The constraint is *inflexible*, such as a *Finish No Later Than* constraint.
- The constrained task is a successor task, meaning that it has one or more predecessors.

Notice in the *Planning Wizard* message shown in Figure 5 - 49 that the software is warning how these two conditions can cause potential scheduling problems in your project, either now or any time in the future. The default response in this dialog is the first choice, which is to cancel setting the constraint. If you truly want to set an inflexible constraint and risk potential scheduling problems, select the third choice, *Continue*, and then click the *OK* button. The second option, by the way, makes no sense at all since selecting this option allows the software to change the constraint to a flexible constraint (Finish No Earlier Than), an outcome that defeats the purpose of setting the inflexible constraint in the first place!

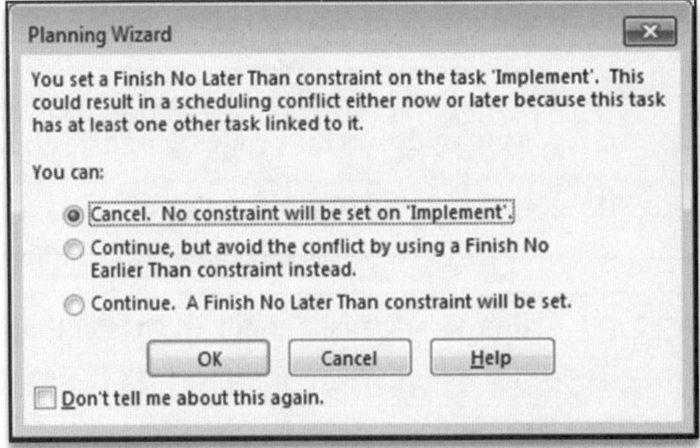

Figure 5 - 49: Planning Wizard message warns about setting a constraint

Best Practice: MSProjectExperts recommends that you **do not** select the *Don't tell me about this again* checkbox to disable *Planning Wizard* messages about scheduling issues. Seeing warning messages of this type is a good way to confirm you selected the constraint you desire, especially if it is an inflexible constraint on a task that has predecessor tasks.

Manually Entering a Start and Finish Date

Although I do not recommend doing so, Project 2013 allows you to manually enter *Start* dates and *Finish* dates on *Auto Scheduled* tasks. When you manually enter either a *Start* date or a *Finish* date, the software automatically adds a constraint to the task. If you manually enter a *Start* date for a task, the software adds a *Start No Earlier Than (SNET)* constraint on the task, using the date you entered as the constraint date. If you manually enter a *Finish* date on a task, the software adds a *Finish No Earlier Than (FNET)* constraint, using the date you entered as the constraint date. After you enter **both** dates, Project 2013 adds the constraint and then calculates the duration of the task.

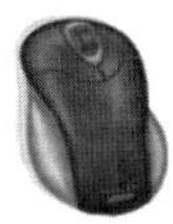

Hands On Exercise

Exercise 5 - 15

Two issues with the Training Advisor Rollout project necessitate the use of constraints:

- In the Statement of Work, the contractual finish date for the *Installation* phase is **February 5, 2016**.
- Because of commitments to other projects, there are no testers available to verify client connectivity until **February 8, 2016** or later.

In response to these issues, apply constraints to tasks in the Training Advisor Rollout project.

1. Return to the **Training Advisor 05b.mpp** sample file.
2. Double-click task ID #6, the *Installation Complete* milestone task.
3. In the *Task Information* dialog, click the *Advanced* tab.
4. On the *Advanced* page of the dialog, click the *Constraint type* pick list and select the *Finish No Later Than* constraint.
5. Click the *Constraint date* pick list and select the date *February 5, 2016* in the calendar date picker.
6. Click the *Notes* tab, click the *Bulleted List* button, and then enter the following comment in the notes field:

   FNLT 2/5/16 – Contractual finish date for Installation phase

7. Click the *OK* button.
8. If prompted by a *Planning Wizard* dialog, click the third choice, *Continue*, and then click the *OK* button.

9. Double-click task ID #9, the *Verify Connectivity* task.

10. In the *Task Information* dialog, click the *Advanced* tab.

11. Click the *Constraint type* pick list and select the *Start No Earlier Than* constraint.

12. Click the *Constraint date* pick list and select the date *February 8, 2016* in the calendar date picker.

13. Click the *Notes* tab, click the *Bulleted List* button, and then enter the following comment in the notes field:

    SNET 2/8/14 – Resource availability issue

14. Click the *OK* button to set the constraint.

15. Save but **do not** close the **Training Advisor 05b.mpp** sample file.

Using Deadline Dates

In addition to constraints, Project 2013 allows you to set deadline dates on tasks. Deadline dates are similar to constraints, but do not limit the scheduling engine. When you set a deadline date on a task, the software places a solid green arrow in the Gantt chart on the same line as the task's Gantt bar. To set a deadline date for any task, complete the following steps:

1. Double-click the task.
2. In the *Task Information* dialog, click the *Advanced* tab.
3. Click the *Deadline* pick list and select a date in the calendar date picker. Notice in Figure 5 - 50 that I set a deadline date of *6/17/15* on the *Phase I Complete* milestone task.

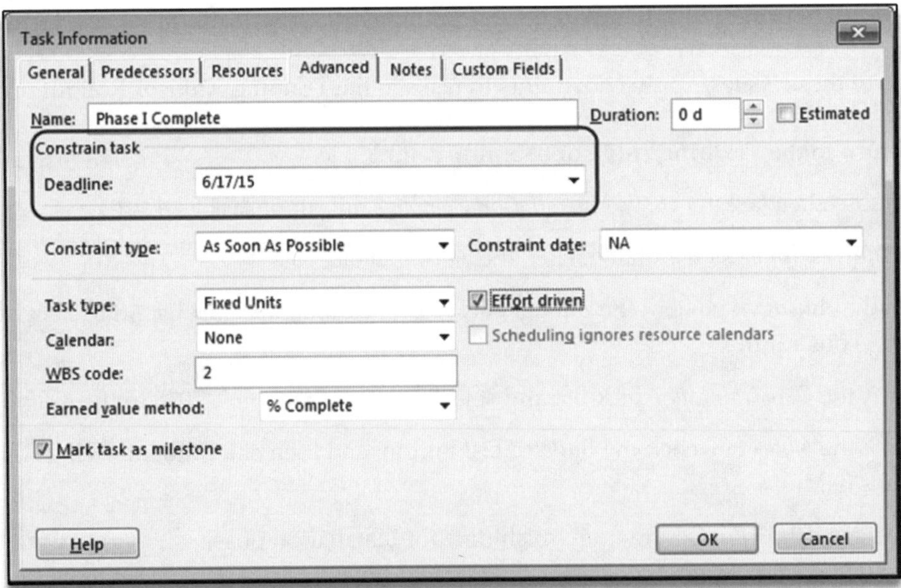

Figure 5 - 50: Set a deadline date in the Task Information dialog

4. Click the *OK* button.

Figure 5 - 51 shows how Project 2013 displays the deadline date in the *Gantt Chart* view. Notice that the software displays a solid green arrow to the right of the milestone symbol for the *Phase I Complete* task.

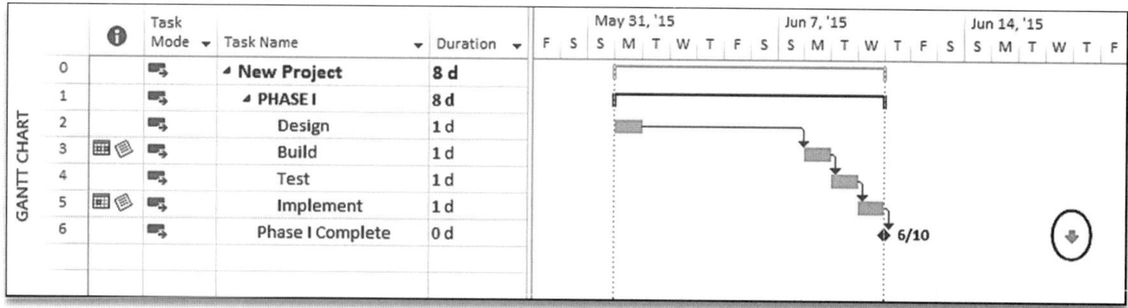

Figure 5 - 51: Deadline date indicator for the Phase I Complete milestone

Hands On Exercise

Exercise 5 - 16

The project manager set **Friday, April 29, 2016** as the target completion date for the Training Advisor Rollout project. Set this date as the deadline date for the entire project.

1. Return to the **Training Advisor 05b.mpp** sample file.
2. Click the *View* tab to display the *View* ribbon.
3. In the *Zoom* section of the *View* ribbon, click the *Timescale* pick list and select the *Weeks* item to apply the *Months Over Weeks* level of zoom.
4. Double-click task ID #23, the *Project Complete* milestone task.
5. In the *Task Information* dialog, click the *Advanced* tab.
6. Click the *Deadline* pick list and select *April 29, 2016* in the calendar date picker.
7. Click the *OK* button to set the deadline date on the task.
8. Scroll your Gantt chart to the right to the week of *April 24, 2016.*

Notice the solid green arrow for the deadline date in the Gantt chart for the *Project Complete* milestone task.

9. In the *Zoom* section of the *View* ribbon, click the *Timescale* pick list and select the *Days* item to apply the *Weeks Over Days* level of zoom.
10. On your computer keyboard, press **Control + Home** and then press **Alt + Home** to scroll back to the beginning of the project.
11. Save and close the **Training Advisor 05b.mpp** sample file.

Viewing Missed Constraints and Deadline Dates

Project 2013 gives you a limited warning when you miss a constraint date or a deadline date. When the *Start* or *Finish* date of a task slips past the constraint date for an **inflexible** constraint, such as when you miss a *Finish No Later Than (FNLT)* constraint, Project 2013 displays the *Planning Wizard* dialog shown in Figure 5 - 52. In this dialog, the software warns you of the schedule conflict, and gives you an opportunity to cancel the action or to allow the schedule conflict to occur.

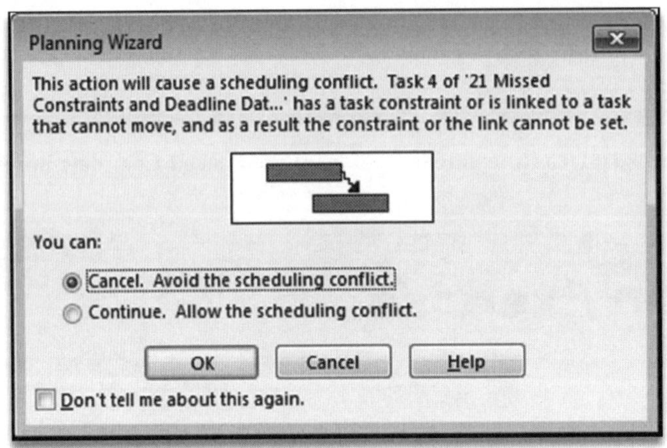

Figure 5 - 52: Planning Wizard message for a missed constraint date

The default setting in this *Planning Wizard* dialog is to cancel the action that caused the scheduling conflict. If you select the second choice, *Continue,* Project 2013 completes the scheduling change allowing the scheduling conflict; however, it does not remove the constraint causing the scheduling conflict. Figure 5 - 53 shows the missed constraint date on the *Test* task. Notice how the link line between the *Test* task and the *Implement* task "wraps back" in time, an indication of the missed constraint date.

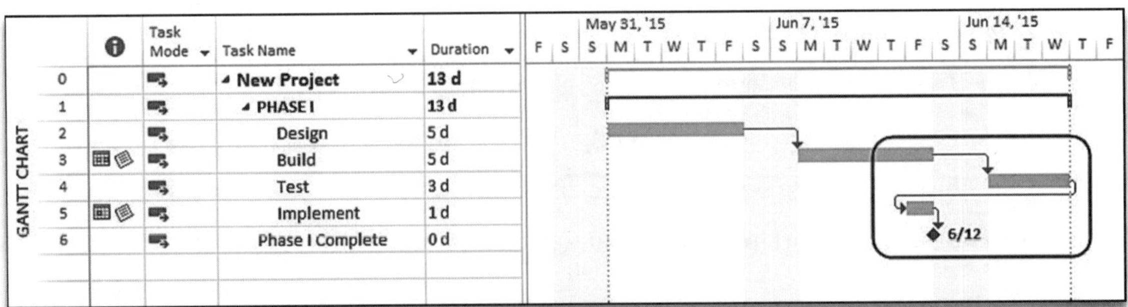

Figure 5 - 53: Missed constraint on the Phase I Complete milestone

When the finish date of a task slips past its deadline date, the software **does not** display a *Planning Wizard* warning dialog. Instead, it displays only a *Missed Deadline* indicator in the *Indicators* column. For example, Figure 5 - 54 shows the missed deadline date on the Phase I Complete milestone task with a *Missed Deadline* indicator in the *Indicators* column to the left of the task name.

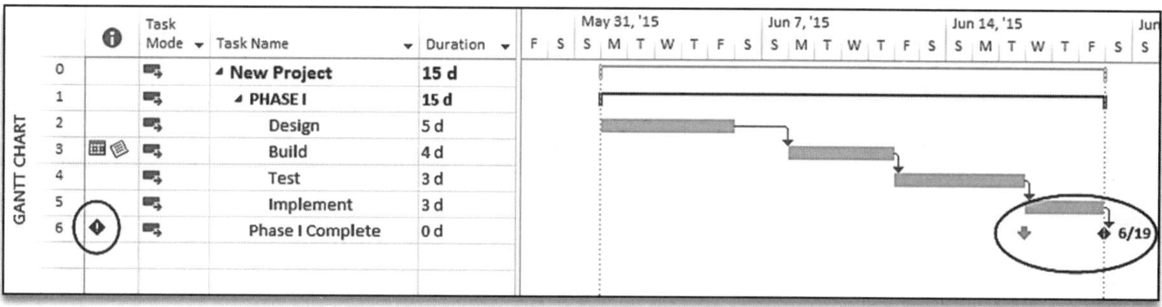

Figure 5 - 54: Missed deadline date on the Phase I Complete milestone

Assigning Task Calendars

Assign a **task calendar** when you want to manually override the current schedule for any task with a completely different schedule defined by a custom calendar. In Figure 5 - 55, Project 2013 schedules the *Design* task to finish on Wednesday, June 10, 2015. In order to "fast track" this task and make it finish earlier, I need to apply a task calendar that schedules work for 7 days per week.

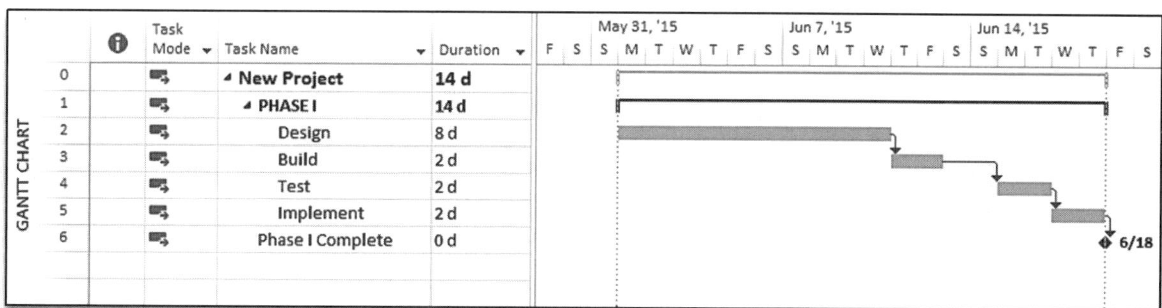

Figure 5 - 55: Build task scheduled for Monday and Tuesday

Information: Before you can assign a task calendar, you must create a new base calendar for this purpose. You learned how to create a new base calendar in Module 04, *Project Definition*.

After creating a base calendar that meets your scheduling needs, you can apply a task calendar to any task by completing the following steps:

1. Double-click the task whose schedule you want to override.

2. In the *Task Information* dialog, click the *Advanced* tab.

3. Click the *Calendar* pick list and select a base calendar from the list. For example, notice in Figure 5 - 56 that I am selecting the *7 Day Work Week* base calendar on the *Calendar* pick list. This special base calendar schedules work 7 days per week with 8 hours of work per day.

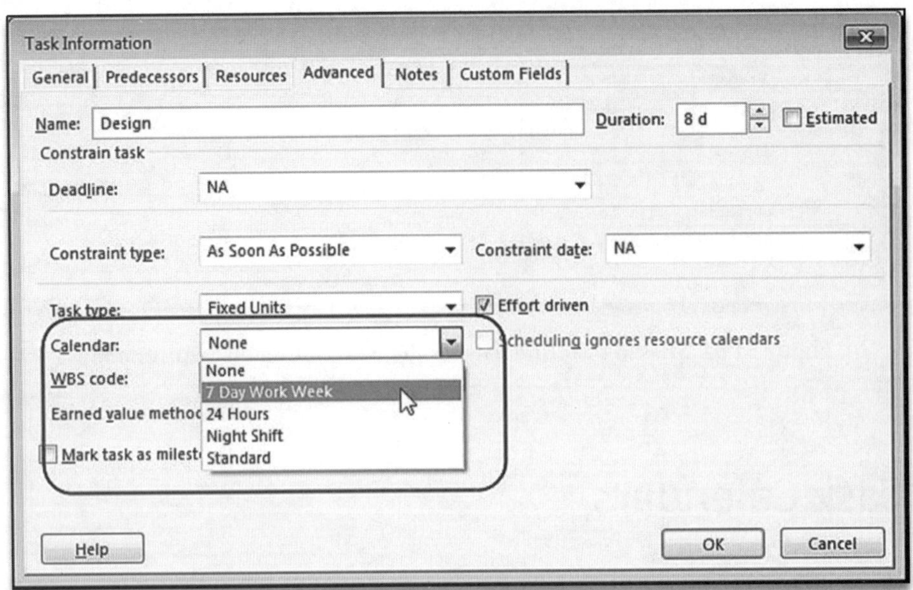

Figure 5 - 56: Select a task calendar in the Task Information dialog

4. Optionally, select the *Scheduling ignores resource calendars* option.
5. Click the *OK* button.

Information: The *Scheduling ignores resource calendars* option forces the software to ignore resource calendars in the task scheduling process. With this option selected, the software schedules assigned resources to work even when their base calendars indicate that they are not available for work. If you leave the *Scheduling ignores resource calendars* option **deselected**, then the software schedules the task using the **common working time** between the project calendar (set in the *Project Information* dialog) and the calendars of the resources assigned to the task. Selecting this option is useful when you need to schedule resources to work on days that are non-working time otherwise, such as on weekends and company holidays.

Figure 5 - 57 shows the same project after assigning the *7 Day Work Week* task calendar to the *Design* task. Notice how the software rescheduled the *Design* task to finish on Monday rather than Wednesday by scheduling two days of work on Saturday and Sunday. Notice also how Project 2013 displays a special task calendar indicator in the *Indicators* column for the task.

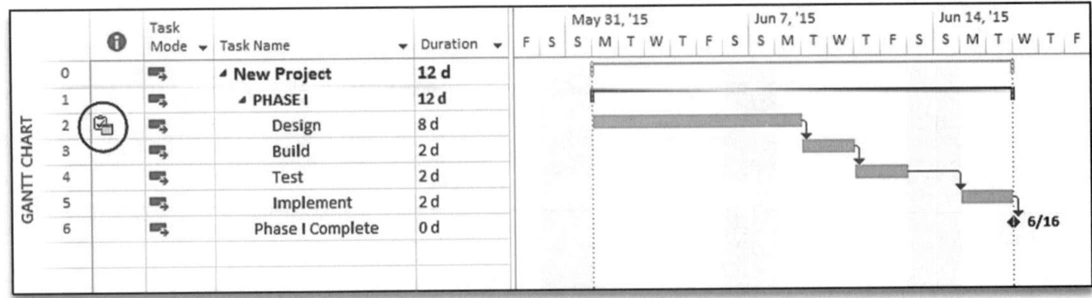

Figure 5 - 57: Build task rescheduled using a Task Calendar

Best Practice: When you assign a task calendar to override the schedule of a task, MSProjectExperts recommends that you always add a note to the task to document the reason for using the task calendar.

Hands On Exercise

Exercise 5 - 17

The *Perform Server Stress Test* task must occur only on a Saturday or a Sunday. Assign a task calendar to this task to schedule the work correctly in the Training Advisor Rollout project.

1. Open the **Training Advisor 05c.mpp** sample file.
2. Click the *Task* tab to display the *Task* ribbon, if necessary.
3. Double-click the *Perform Server Stress Test* task.
4. In the *Task Information* dialog, click the *Advanced* tab.
5. On the *Advanced* page of the dialog, click the *Calendar* pick list and select the *Weekend Work Only* calendar.
6. Select the *Scheduling ignores resource calendars* checkbox.
7. Click the *Notes* tab, click the *Bulleted List* button, and then enter the following comment in the notes field:

   Weekend Work Only task calendar - Task must occur on a Saturday and/or Sunday

8. Click the *OK* button.

Notice how Project 2013 schedules the task during the first available Saturday because of overriding the task schedule using the *Weekend Work Only* task calendar.

9. Save but **do not** close the **Training Advisor 05c.mpp** sample file.

Understanding Duration-Based and Effort-Based Planning

Project 2013 allows you to drive your schedule based on effort or duration. Generally speaking, duration-based planning is easier for most novice schedulers and more instinctive to the average user. It is somewhat easier to manage as it requires less work to estimate and less work to track. The tradeoff is that you lose a significant degree of accuracy and, in the final analysis, you gain much less insight into what went right or what went wrong in your project.

When using duration-based planning, you typically use the *Percent Complete* method to track your project. When using effort-based planning, you typically use the *Actual Work and Remaining Work* method to track your project. In the first scenario, you apply duration estimates to tasks. As you assign your resources, the software calculates the work values for you. Using the latter approach, you enter your work estimates and the software calculates the duration values for you.

Estimating duration is less accurate because when you ask a resource to estimate how long a task will take them to complete, they tend to factor in the non-project work they have on their plate. Typically, a resource will tell you that the task takes 5 days when the effort involved may only be 32 hours. This is only human nature! On the other hand, when you carefully ask a resource if they had nothing else on their plate, how many hours the task will consume, you are very likely to get a fairly accurate work estimate unless the type of work is unfamiliar to the resource. You may need to assure the resource that you will take their non-project workload into account when you produce the schedule.

Duration-based planning is a top-down approach and, as such, it does not indicate how you derived the duration estimate. Further, when you look at a slipping schedule, you must go back to your resources and ask questions like, "Are you working on it or not?" or "Is it more work than you expected?" When you estimate effort and collect *Actual Work and Remaining Work* tracking data, the answers to these questions become self-evident in the software. Furthermore, for many projects labor is the primary cost factor. Because Project 2013 calculates costs based on work, if you do not estimate and track work, you will not get very good cost data from the software.

By now you may be asking yourself if effort-based planning and tracking is much more accurate and insightful, and why anyone would use duration-based planning. The simple answer is that it is simple when compared to asking people to track their time for you. Unless your organization is already in the habit of collecting time from resources, effort-driven planning will meet with significant resistance from your resources.

Estimating Task Durations

After you create the task schedule, including setting task dependencies and constraints, you are ready to estimate task durations, wherever appropriate. According to Project 2013, duration is "the total span of active working time for a task." Another way to think of duration is the "window of opportunity" during which the team members work on the task.

Many novice users of Project 2013 wrongly assume that duration and work are interchangeable terms in a project. In some cases, this may be true, but in many cases, duration and work are two entirely different numbers. Consider the following examples:

- A resource must perform 40 hours of work during a 10-day time period. The duration of this task, therefore, is 10 days because it is the "window" during which the resource performs the work (40 hours).
- We allow an executive 5 days to approve a deliverable, but the executive will only perform 2 hours of actual work on the approval. The duration of this task, therefore, is 5 days because this is the "window" during which the executive performs the work (2 hours).

Notice in the two preceding examples that the duration or "window of opportunity" does not consider the amount of work performed on the task. The duration is simply the period of time during which team members perform the work, regardless of how much or how little work the task requires. There are several ways to determine a task duration estimate:

- Get the estimate from the team member who will actually perform the work on the task. This allows you to tap the skills, knowledge, and experience of the team member. This is a Project Management Institute best practice, by the way.

- If you cannot get the duration estimate from a team member, then get an estimate from a team leader who has experience in this type of work.
- If you cannot get a duration estimate from a team leader, study your organization's repository of completed projects and get an estimate based on historical data for similar tasks.
- If you cannot use any of the previous methods, then make a "guestimate" of the task, but validate your duration estimate later against the actual completion data for the task.

To enter duration values, simply type your estimate in the *Duration* column for each task. You may enter the duration value using any time unit, including hours, days, weeks, months, etc. By default, the software formats *Duration* values in *days*.

Hands On Exercise

Exercise 5 - 18

Enter estimated task durations for some of the tasks in the Training Advisor Rollout project.

1. Return to the **Training Advisor 05c.mpp** sample file.
2. Click the *View* tab to display the *View* ribbon.
3. In the *Zoom* section of the *View* ribbon, click the *Timescale* pick list and select the *Weeks* item to apply the *Months Over Weeks* level of zoom.
4. Enter estimated duration values in the *Duration* column for tasks as follows:

ID	Task Name	Duration
2	Order Server	2 days
3	Setup Server and Load O/S	4 days
4	Load and Configure Software	5 days
5	Perform Server Stress Test	2 days
13	Setup Test Training Server	3 days
15	Create Training Module 01	5 days
16	Create Training Module 02	5 days
17	Create Training Module 03	5 days

5. Do not change the previously-entered duration values for task ID #20-21, the *Create Training Schedule* and *Provide End User Training* tasks.

6. Leave the default *Duration* value of *1 day* for every other task in the project.
7. Save but **do not** close the **Training Advisor 05c.mpp** sample file.

Using the Task Inspector to Determine Task Drivers

A **task driver** is any factor that determines the *Start* date of an *Auto Scheduled* task. Task drivers can include any of the following factors:

- *Task Mode* setting, whether *Manually Scheduled* or *Auto Scheduled.*
- Constraints, such as *Start No Earlier Than (SNET)* constraint.
- Predecessor tasks (including *Lag* time or *Lead* time).
- Nonworking time on the project calendar and the resource calendars of the resources assigned to the task.
- Leveling delays caused by leveling resource overallocations.
- An *Actual Start* date on the task.

You can use the *Task Inspector* tool to determine the task drivers for any task by completing the following steps:

1. Click the *Task* tab to display the *Task* ribbon, if necessary.
2. In the *Tasks* section of the *Task* ribbon, click the *Inspect* button. Alternately, you can click the *Inspect* pick list and select the *Inspect Task* item.
3. Select the task whose drivers you want to determine.

The software displays the task drivers for the selected task in the *Factors Affecting Task* section of the *Task Inspector* sidepane, as shown in Figure 5 - 58. Notice that the *Task Inspector* sidepane shows that the task drivers on the selected task include a predecessor task, *Install new fuse box*, as well as the calendar for the assigned resource, *Bob Siclari*.

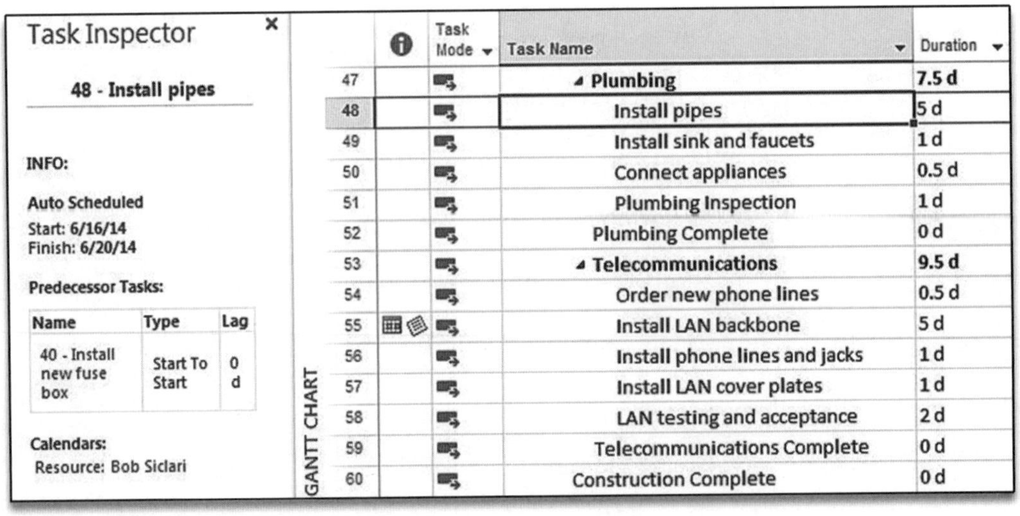

Task Inspector

48 - Install pipes

INFO:

Auto Scheduled

Start: 6/16/14

Finish: 6/20/14

Predecessor Tasks:

Name	Type	Lag
40 - Install new fuse box	Start To Start	0 d

Calendars:

Resource: Bob Siclari

	Task Mode	Task Name	Duration
47		Plumbing	7.5 d
48		Install pipes	5 d
49		Install sink and faucets	1 d
50		Connect appliances	0.5 d
51		Plumbing Inspection	1 d
52		Plumbing Complete	0 d
53		Telecommunications	9.5 d
54		Order new phone lines	0.5 d
55		Install LAN backbone	5 d
56		Install phone lines and jacks	1 d
57		Install LAN cover plates	1 d
58		LAN testing and acceptance	2 d
59		Telecommunications Complete	0 d
60		Construction Complete	0 d

GANTT CHART

Figure 5 - 58: Task drivers for the Install pipes task

4. To view the base calendar for any resource assigned to the selected task, click the name of the resource in the *Task Inspector* sidepane. Project 2013 displays the *Change Working Time* dialog for the selected resource, *Bob Siclari,* as shown in Figure 5 - 59.

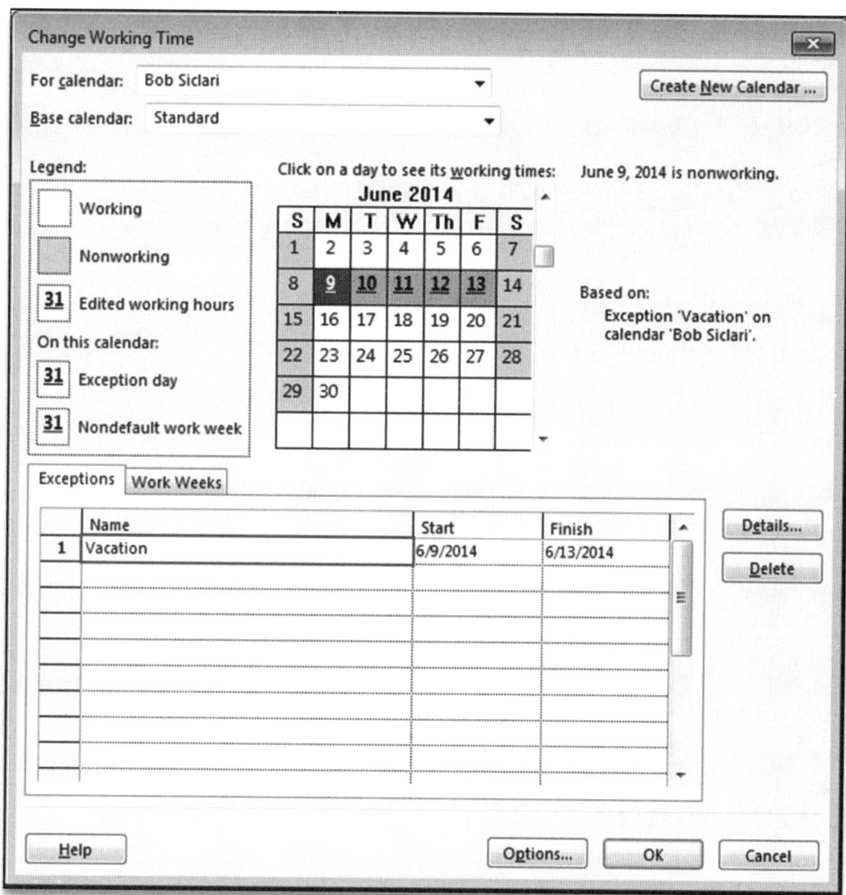

Figure 5 - 59: Change Working Time dialog for Bob Siclari

Notice in Figure 5 - 59 that I scheduled *Bob Siclari* for a week of vacation from June 9-13, 2014. This period of nonworking time affects the *Start* dates and/or *Finish* dates of any task to which I assign *Bob Siclari* during the week that is now nonworking time.

Information: I discuss how to enter nonworking time on resource calendars in Module 06, *Project Resource Planning*.

5. Close the *Task Inspector* sidepane when finished.

Hands On Exercise

Exercise 5 - 19

Determine task drivers for tasks in the Training Advisor Rollout project.

1. Return to the **Training Advisor 05c.mpp** sample file.
2. Click the *Task* tab to display the *Task* ribbon, if necessary.
3. In the *Tasks* section of the *Task* ribbon, click the *Inspect* button.
4. Select each of the following tasks individually and then use the *Task Inspector* to determine the task driver for the task:
    - Task ID #2, *Order Server*
    - Task ID #5, *Perform Server Stress Test*
    - Task ID #9, *Verify Connectivity*
    - Task ID #20, *Create Training Schedule*
5. Close the *Task Inspector* sidepane when finished.
6. Save but **do not** close the **Training Advisor 05c.mpp** sample file.

Viewing the Task Path for a Task

Over the years, several common questions asked by many project managers include the following:

- What is the task path of all predecessor tasks for a task in my project?
- Which task is the driving predecessor for a task in my project?
- What is the task path of all successors for a task in my project?
- Which task is the driven successor to a task in my project?

No version of the software earlier than Project 2013 offered a default feature to answer any of these questions. In fact, the only way to answer these questions was to use a custom macro written in the VBA programming language by a fellow Project MVP named Jack Dahlgren. With the release of Project 2013, however, you can use the new *Task Path* feature to determine the answer to all four common questions.

Before you can use the *Task Path* feature, your project must contain a list of tasks with dependencies set between all tasks. To use the feature, apply any Gantt-based view, such as the *Gantt Chart* view, and then select a task. Click the *Format* tab to display the *Format* ribbon with the *Gantt Chart Tools* applied. In the *Bar Styles* section of the *Format* ribbon, click the *Task Path* pick list button and select one of four options on the menu, as shown in Figure 5 - 60.

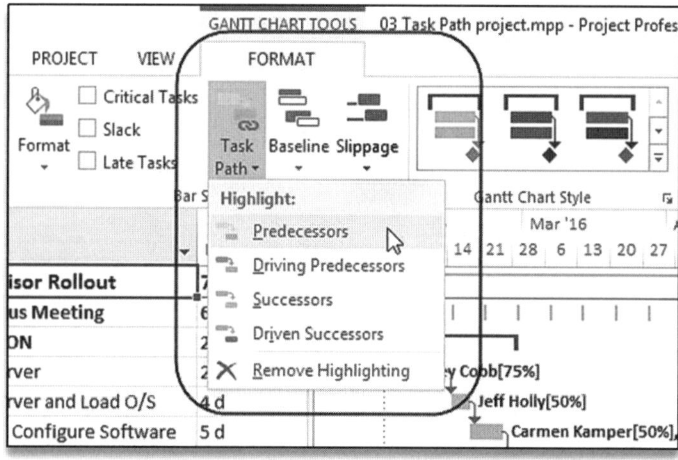

Figure 5 - 60: Task Path menu on the Format ribbon

Available options on the *Task Path* menu include:

- **Predecessors** – Select this option to display the complete task path of all predecessors for the selected task.

- **Driving Predecessors** – Select this option to display only those predecessors that directly affect the schedule of the selected task.

- **Successors** – Select this option to display the complete task path of all successors for the selected task.

- **Driven Successors** – Select this option to display only those successors whose schedule is directly affected by the selected task.

- **Remove Highlighting** – Select this option to remove all of the *Task Path* highlighting currently applied.

Information: When you select the *Predecessors* option on the *Task Path* menu, Project 2013 displays **all** predecessor tasks including completed tasks, which are predecessors for the selected task. When you select the *Driving Predecessors* option, however, the software may include the last completed task in the chain of completed tasks, plus all other incomplete tasks that are driving predecessors for the selected task. When you select the *Successors* option, Project 2013 displays all successor tasks including completed tasks, which are successors of the selected task. When you select the *Driven Successors* option, however, the software **does not** display any completed tasks and only displays incomplete tasks, which are driven successors of the selected task.

If you select the *Predecessors* option on the *Task Path* menu, Project 2013 formats the Gantt bars of all predecessor tasks using a light orange color. Figure 5 - 61 shows all predecessor tasks for task ID #8, the *Design P2* task. Notice the software reveals that the predecessors include all five tasks in the *PHASE I* section of the project.

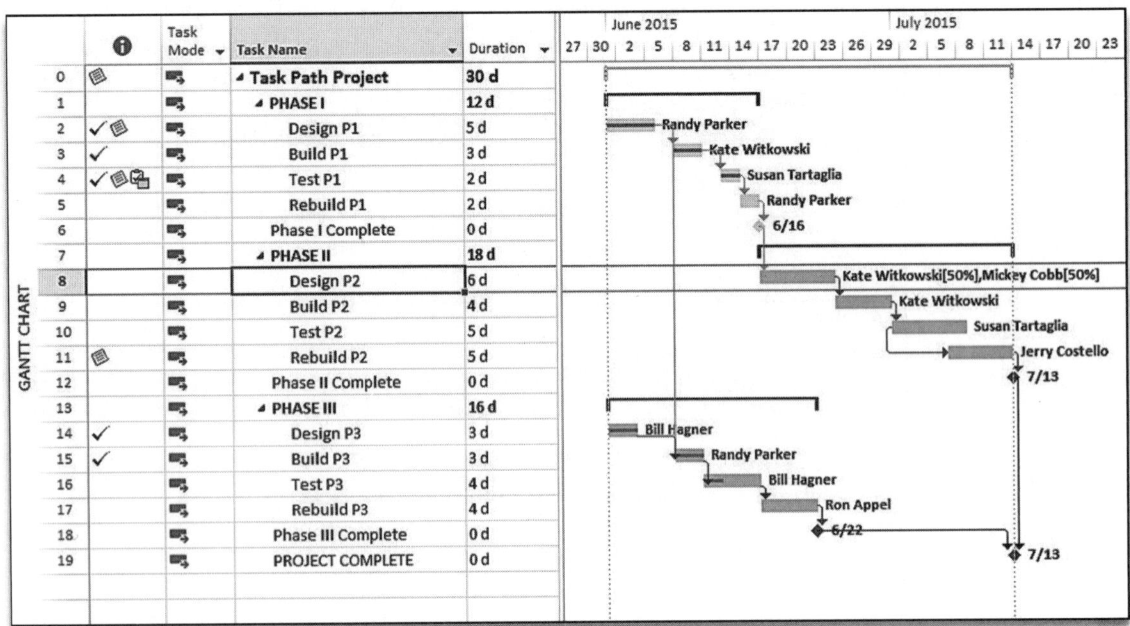

Figure 5 - 61: Task Path – Predecessors option applied

If you select the *Driving Predecessors* option on the *Task Path* menu, Project 2013 formats the Gantt bars of all driving predecessor tasks using a dark orange color. Remember that driving predecessors are only those predecessor tasks that directly affect the schedule of the selected task. Figure 5 - 62 shows all of the driving predecessor tasks for task ID #8, the *Design P2* task. Notice the software reveals that the driving predecessors include only the last three tasks in the *PHASE I* section of the project, but do not include the *Design P1* and *Build P1* tasks because they are completed tasks.

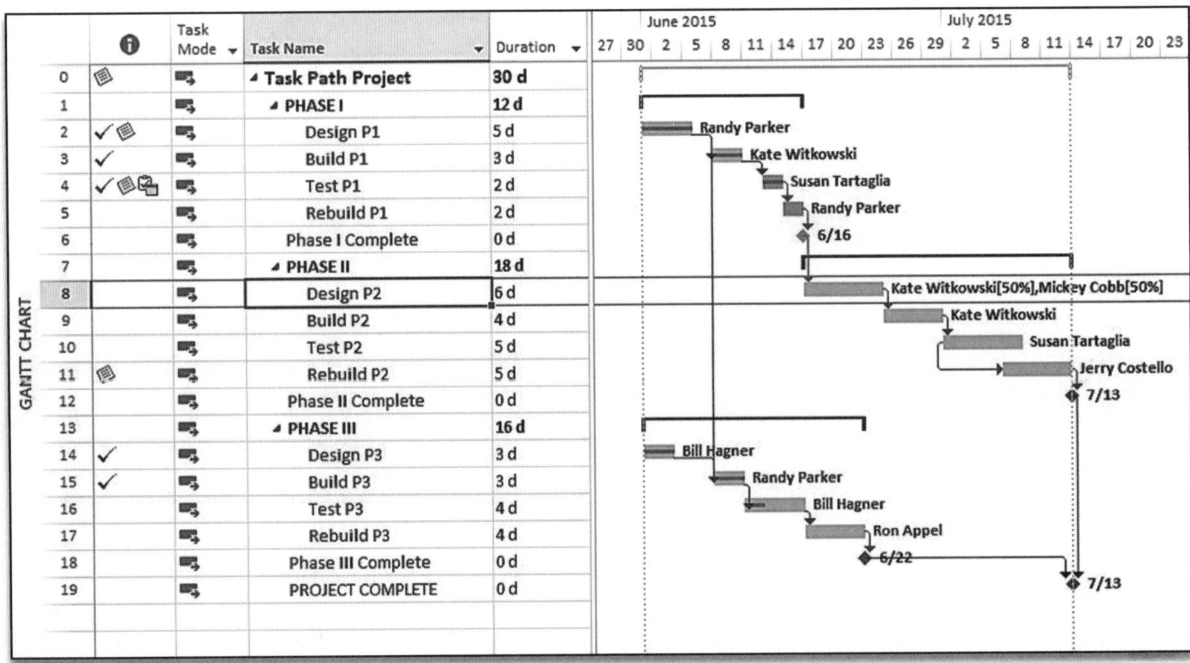

Figure 5 - 62: Task Path – Driving Predecessors option applied

If you select the *Successors* option on the *Task Path* menu, Project 2013 formats the Gantt bars of all successor tasks using a light purple color. Figure 5 - 63 shows all successor tasks for task ID #8, the *Design P2* task. Notice the software reveals that the successors include all of the other tasks in the *PHASE* II section of the project, along with the *PROJECT COMPLETE* milestone task.

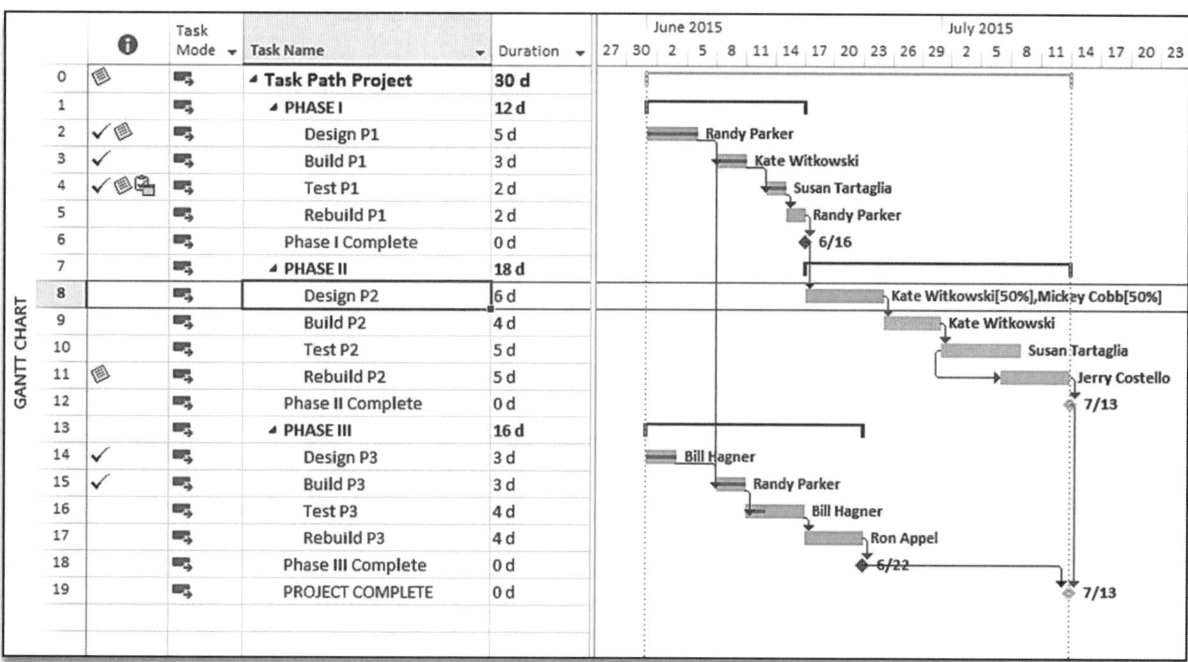

Figure 5 - 63: Task Path – Successors option applied

If you select the *Driven Successors* option on the *Task Path* menu, Project 2013 formats the Gantt bars of all driven successor tasks using a dark purple color. Remember that driven successors are only those successor tasks whose schedule is directly affected by the selected task. Figure 5 - 64 shows all driven successor tasks for task ID #8, the *Design P2* task. Notice the software reveals that the driven successor tasks include all of the other tasks in the *PHASE* II section of the project, along with the *PROJECT COMPLETE* milestone task.

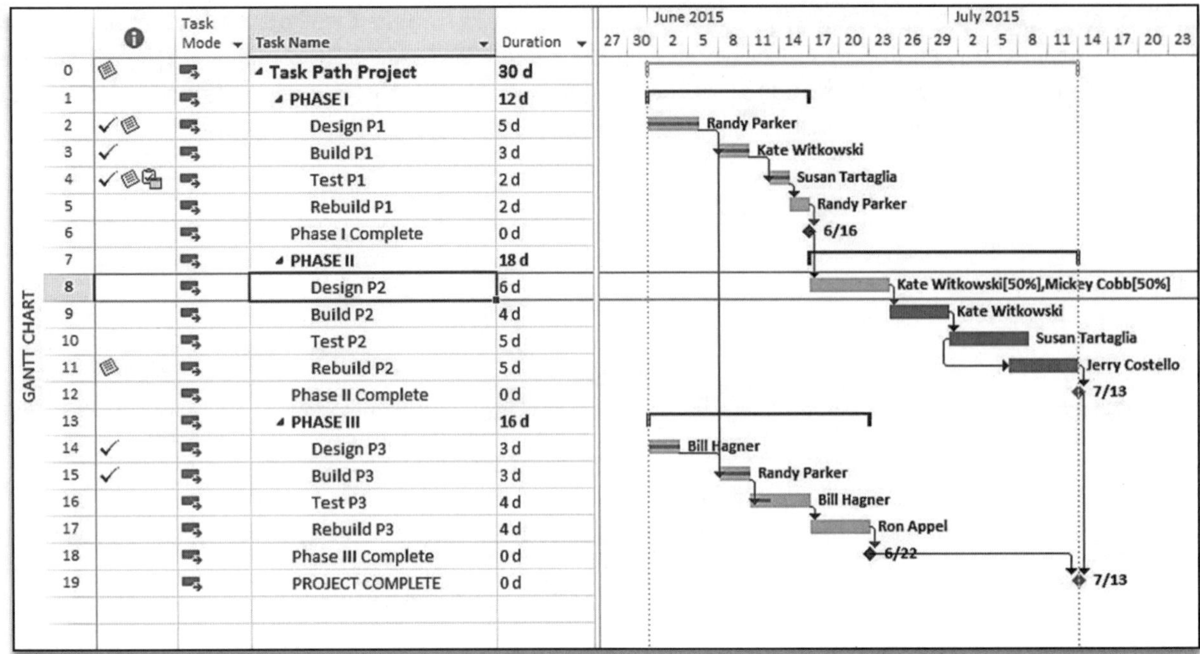

Figure 5 - 64: Task Path – Driven Successors option applied

Information: When you select one of the four options on the *Task Path* menu, Project 2013 leaves the option selected until you remove it. This allows you to select a series of tasks individually to see the *Predecessors* or *Successors* for each of the tasks you select. Beyond this, the software also allows you to select multiple items on the *Task Path* menu. For example, if you select both the *Predecessors* and *Driving Predecessors* options, the software allows you to determine which tasks are *Predecessors* and which tasks are *Driving Predecessors* based on the colors of the Gantt bars.

To clear a selected option on the *Task Path* menu, click the *Task Path* pick list button and deselect the selected item. To clear one or more items on the *Task Path* menu simultaneously, click the *Task Path* pick list button and then click the *Remove Highlighting* item on the menu.

Hands On Exercise

Exercise 5 - 20

Experiment with the new Task Path feature in Project 2013.

1. Open the **Project Navigation 2013.mpp** sample file.
2. Click the *Task* tab to display the *Task* ribbon.
3. In the *Views* section of the *Task* ribbon, click the *Gantt Chart* pick list button and select the *Gantt Chart* view, if necessary.
4. Click the *Format* tab to display the *Format* ribbon.

5. Select task ID #28, the *Plaster* task.
6. In the *Bar Styles* section of the *Format* ribbon, click the *Task Path* pick list button and select the *Predecessors* item on the menu.

Notice that Project 2013 uses a light orange color to highlight the Gantt bars of all of the tasks in the *Pre-Renovation* phase and the first seven tasks in the *Carpentry* sub-deliverable section of the project.

7. Click the *Task Path* pick list button and select the *Remove Highlighting* item.
8. Click the *Task Path* pick list button and select the *Driving Predecessors* item.

Notice that the software uses a dark orange color to highlight the Gantt bars of five driving predecessor tasks, from the *Remove existing wall* task to the *Put up dry wall* tasks. Remember that driving predecessors are only those predecessor tasks that directly affect the schedule of the selected task.

9. Click the *Task Path* pick list button and select the *Remove Highlighting* item.
10. Select task ID #23, the *Remove existing wall* task.
11. Click the *Task Path* pick list button and select the *Successors* item.

Notice that Project 2013 uses a light purple color to highlight the Gantt bars of every remaining task in the project from task ID #24, the *Remove asbestos in ceiling* task, through task ID #77, the *PROJECT COMPLETE* milestone task.

12. Click the *Task Path* pick list button and select the *Remove Highlighting* item.
13. Click the *Task Path* pick list button and select the *Driven Successors* item.

Notice that the software uses a dark purple color to highlight the Gantt bar of only task ID #24, the *Remove asbestos in ceiling* task. This is the only task whose schedule is directly driven by the selected task. Task ID #25, the *Asbestos removal inspection* task, is not a driven successor because it has a Must Start On constraint, which is the driving factor that controls the *Start* date of the task.

14. Click the *Task Path* pick list button and select the *Remove Highlighting* item.
15. Save and close the **Project Navigation 2013.mpp** sample file.

Creating Recurring Tasks

In Project 2013, a recurring task is any task that repeats on a regular cycle. Many project managers use a recurring task for project-related meetings, such as a project team meeting or a project status meeting. You can insert a recurring task anywhere in a project plan, although most people prefer to insert a recurring task at the beginning or the end of the project.

Warning: Using a recurring task almost always creates resource overallocations at the hourly level in your project for every resource you assign to both the recurring task and regular tasks. Therefore, use recurring tasks cautiously, and prepare for the presence of hourly resource overallocations as a result.

To insert a recurring task into a project plan, complete the following steps:

1. Select the task row where you want to insert the recurring task.
2. Click the *Task* tab to display the *Task* ribbon, if necessary.
3. In the *Insert* section of the *Task* ribbon, click the *Task* pick list button and select the *Recurring Task* item. Project 2013 displays the *Recurring Task Information* dialog shown in Figure 5 - 65.

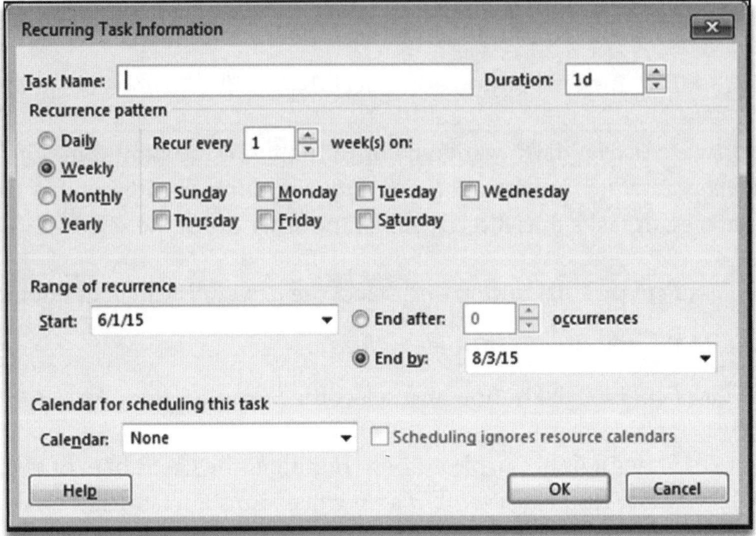

Figure 5 - 65: Recurring Task Information dialog

4. In the *Recurring Task Information* dialog, enter a name for the recurring task in the *Task Name* field.
5. In the *Duration* field, enter the duration of the recurring task (normally entered in hours).
6. In the *Recurrence pattern* section, select how often the task occurs and when it occurs.

Figure 5 - 66 through Figure 5 - 69 show the options available in the *Recurrence pattern* section with the *Daily, Weekly, Monthly,* and *Yearly* recurrence options selected. Notice in Figure 5 - 68, for example, that you can set a monthly recurring task to occur on a specific date each month, such as the 15th or the 30th, or you can set it to occur on a certain time of the month, such as on the last Friday of each month.

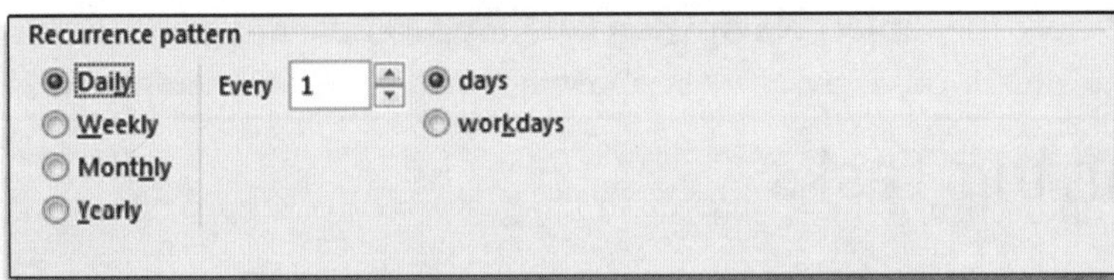

Figure 5 - 66: Daily recurrence pattern options

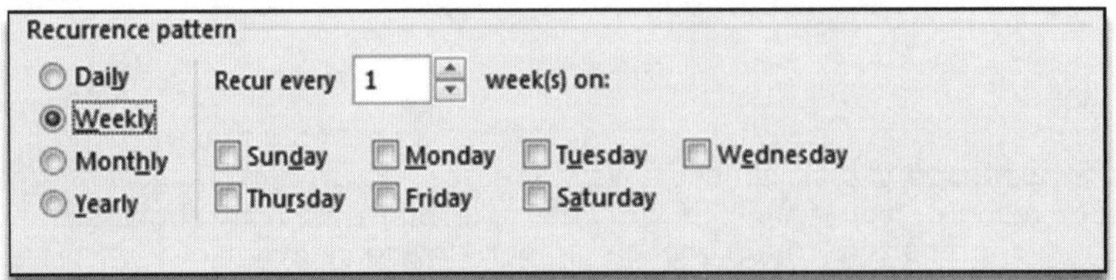

Figure 5 - 67: Weekly recurrence pattern options

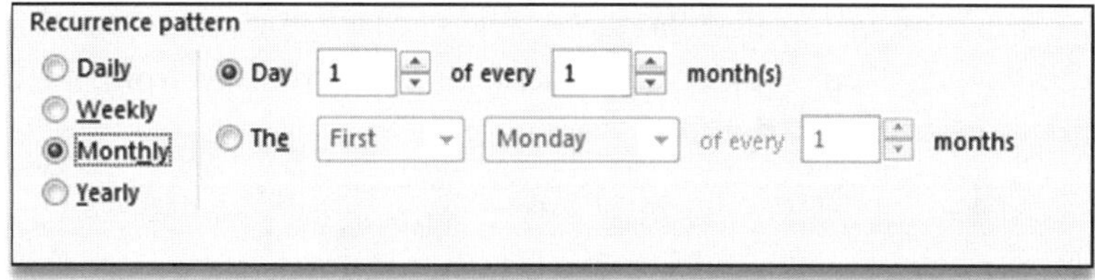

Figure 5 - 68: Monthly recurrence pattern options

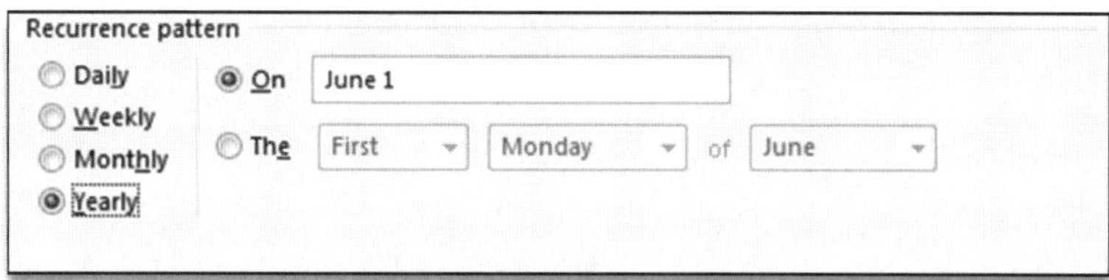

Figure 5 - 69: Yearly recurrence pattern options

Information: To create a recurring task that occurs on a quarterly basis (every third month), select the *Monthly* option in the *Recurrence pattern* section of the dialog, and then set the task to occur every 3 months.

7. In the *Range of Recurrence* section, select the date of the first occurrence in the *Start* field if you do not want the first instance of the recurring task to occur during the first week of the project. If you do not select an alternate date in the *Start* field, the software enters the *Start* date of the project in this field, and then calculates the date of the first occurrence of the recurring task from the *Start* date of the project.

8. In the *Range of Recurrence* section, select the *End by* option, or select the *End after* option and then specify the number of occurrences in the *occurrences* field. If you select the *End by* option in the *Recurring Task Information* dialog, Project 2013 calculates the number of occurrences needed in the project based on the *Start* date and *Finish* date of the project.

Information: If you select the *End by* option in the *Recurring Task Information* dialog, Project 2013 calculates the number of occurrences needed in the project based on the *Start* date and *Finish* date of the project.

9. Leave the *Calendar* field value set to *None*. You should only select a value in the *Calendar* field if you need to override the schedule of the recurring task with a custom task calendar.

10. Click the *OK* button.

In Figure 5 - 70, I created a recurring task called *Bi-Weekly Project Meeting*. Notice that this 4-hour meeting occurs every two weeks on Wednesday, and that Project 2013 calculates 5 occurrences from 6/1/15 (the project start date) through 8/3/15 (the scheduled project finish date).

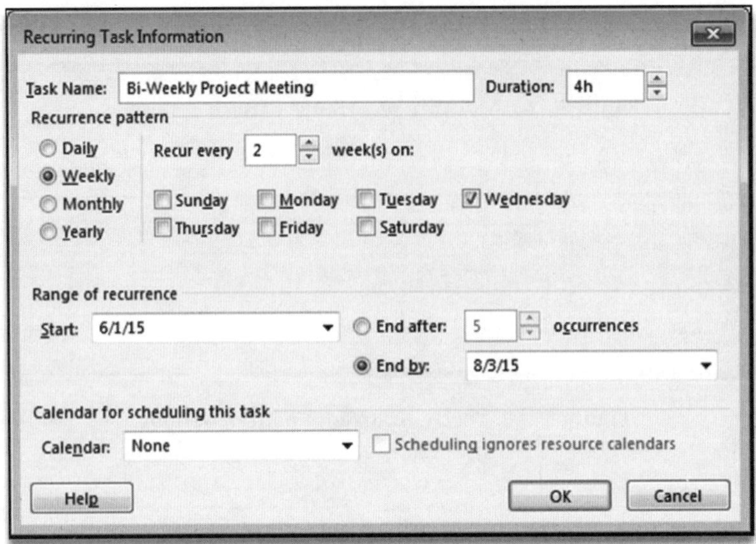

Figure 5 - 70: Recurring Task Information dialog, set up to create the Bi-Weekly Meeting

When you click the *OK* button, Project 2013 creates the recurring task in your project. Figure 5 - 71 shows the *Bi-Weekly Project Meeting* recurring task with the five individual instances of the meeting. In the Gantt chart, you can see the Gantt bars for the first two meeting instances. Notice that the values in the *Duration* column reveal that each meeting is 4 hours. Notice that the software names each meeting instance using the name of the recurring task and appending successive numerals to each task name. If desirable, Project 2013 allows you to edit the name of each instance of a recurring task, if needed. For example, some companies refer to the first project status meeting as the *Project Kick-Off* meeting, and refer to the last meeting as the *Project Closure* meeting.

	Task Mode	Task Name	Duration
0		New Project	45 d
1		Bi-Weekly Project Meeting	39.5 d
2		Bi-Weekly Project Meeting 1	4 h
3		Bi-Weekly Project Meeting 2	4 h
4		Bi-Weekly Project Meeting 3	4 h
5		Bi-Weekly Project Meeting 4	4 h
6		Bi-Weekly Project Meeting 5	4 h
7		PHASE I	25 d
8		Design	7 d
9		Build	2 d
10		Test	3 d
11		Rebuild	4 d
12		Retest	3 d
13		Implement	6 d
14		Phase I Complete	0 d
15		PHASE II Complete	20 d
16		Design	5 d
17		Build	2 d
18		Test	5 d
19		Implement	8 d
20		Phase II Complete	0 d

GANTT CHART — May 31, '15 · Jun 7, '15 · Jun 14, '15 — F S S M T W T F S S M T W T F S S M T W T F S

Figure 5 - 71: Bi-Weekly Project Meeting recurring task

Notice in Figure 5 - 71 that the software displays a *recurring task* indicator (circular arrows) in the *Indicators* column, and shows an *Expand/Collapse* indicator (black triangle symbol) to the left of the name of the recurring task. Click *Expand/Collapse* indicator to expand or collapse the instances of the recurring task. Figure 5 - 72 shows the collapsed *Bi-Weekly Project Meeting* recurring task.

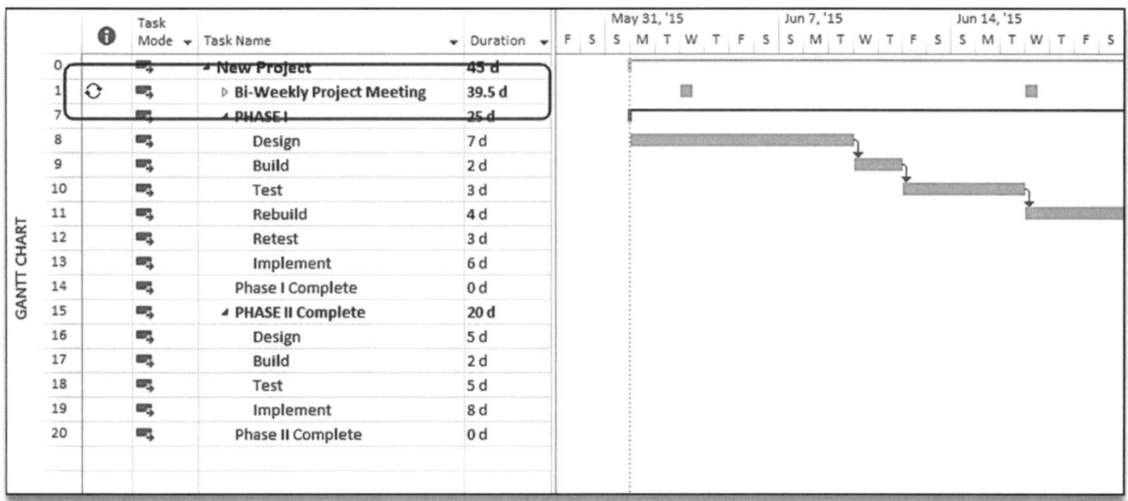

Figure 5 - 72: Bi-Weekly Project Meeting recurring task, meeting instances collapsed

Information: Notice in the two previous figures that the *Duration* value of the *Bi-Weekly Project Meeting* recurring task is *39.5 days*. Project 2013 calculates the *Duration* of a recurring task as the number of working days from the *Start* date of the first recurring task instance and the *Finish* date of the last instance. In the example of the *Bi-Weekly Project Meeting* recurring task, there are **39** working days from the *Start* date of the first instance to the *Start* date of the fifth instance. Because the *Duration* of the fifth instance is **.5** days, the software calculates the *Duration* as *39 days + .5 days = 39.5 days*.

Hands On Exercise

Exercise 5 - 21

The team leaders from the project team must attend a 2-hour project status meeting every Monday, beginning the second week of the project. The project manager estimates approximately 14 meetings. Therefore, create a recurring task in the Training Advisor Rollout project to account for these project status meetings.

1. Return to the **Training Advisor 05c.mpp** sample file.
2. Select task ID #1, the *INSTALLATION* summary task.
3. In the *Insert* section of the *Task* ribbon, click the *Task* pick list button and select the *Recurring Task* item.

4. In the *Recurring Task Information* dialog, create the recurring task using the following information:
    - **Name** – Project Status Meeting
    - **Duration** – 2h
    - **Recurrence Pattern** – Weekly, Every 1 week on Monday
    - **Start** – 1/11/16
    - **End after** – 14 occurrences
    - **Calendar** – None
5. Click the *OK* button to create the recurring task.
6. Examine the occurrences of the new *Project Status Meeting* recurring task.
7. Click the *Collapse* indicator (black triangle symbol) to collapse the occurrences of the *Project Status Meeting* recurring task.
8. Save but do not close the **Training Advisor 05c.mpp** sample file.

Planning for Known Fixed Costs

The final step in the task planning process is to plan for known fixed costs on tasks. Examples of fixed costs include the cost of a building permit, the cost of a piece of equipment or hardware, or the cost of room rental. Most tasks do not have a fixed cost associated with them, but if a task does have a known fixed cost associated with it, you can enter the fixed cost amount by completing the following steps:

1. Apply any task view, such as the *Gantt Chart* view.
2. Right-click the *Select All* button and select the *Cost* table on the shortcut menu.
3. Drag the split bar to the right side of the *Fixed Cost Accrual* column.
4. Enter the known fixed cost for the task in the *Fixed Cost* column.
5. Click the *Fixed Cost Accrual* pick list for the task and select the accrual method you want to use to allocate the fixed cost amount on the task.
6. Double-click the task and then select the *Notes* tab in the *Task Information* dialog.
7. Enter a note documenting the reason for the fixed cost and then click the *OK* button.

Step #4 above mentions that you need to select a *Fixed Cost Accrual* method for the task. The method you select determines how the software assesses the amount of the fixed cost on the task. The *Fixed Cost Accrual* column offers you three methods for accruing a fixed cost on a task in Project 2013:

- The *Start* method causes the software to assess the entire fixed cost amount at the beginning of the task.
- The *End* method causes the software to assess the entire fixed cost amount at the end of the task.
- The *Prorated* method causes the software to distribute the fixed cost amount evenly over the duration of the task.

Figure 5 - 73 shows the *Cost* table for a construction project that contains a task called *Obtain construction permits*. This task has a known fixed cost associated with it, which is the cost of all the required construction permits. To plan for this known fixed cost, I entered *$4,350* in the *Fixed Cost* column, and selected the *End* option in the *Fixed Cost Accrual* column.

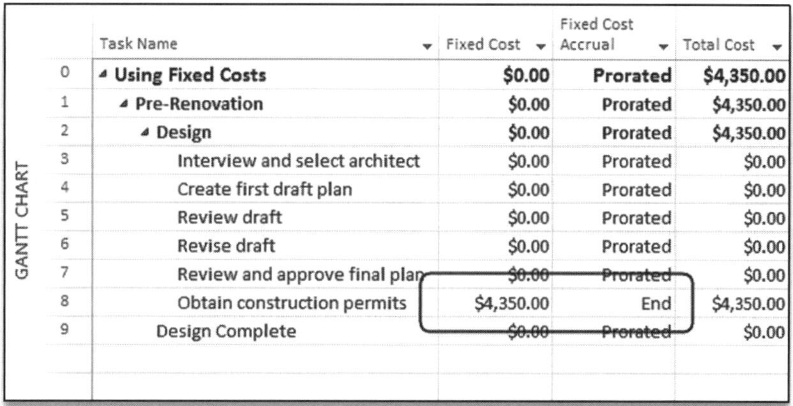

	Task Name	Fixed Cost	Fixed Cost Accrual	Total Cost
0	**Using Fixed Costs**	**$0.00**	**Prorated**	**$4,350.00**
1	**Pre-Renovation**	**$0.00**	**Prorated**	**$4,350.00**
2	**Design**	**$0.00**	**Prorated**	**$4,350.00**
3	Interview and select architect	$0.00	Prorated	$0.00
4	Create first draft plan	$0.00	Prorated	$0.00
5	Review draft	$0.00	Prorated	$0.00
6	Revise draft	$0.00	Prorated	$0.00
7	Review and approve final plan	$0.00	Prorated	$0.00
8	Obtain construction permits	$4,350.00	End	$4,350.00
9	Design Complete	$0.00	Prorated	$0.00

Figure 5 - 73: Enter Fixed Cost information in the Cost table

Information: Notice in Figure 5 - 73 shown previously that the fixed cost amount of $4,350 does not roll up to its summary tasks or to the Project Summary Task (Row 0). This column is one of only a few whose values **do not** roll up to their respective summary tasks. This allows you to enter a value in the *Fixed Cost* column for the Project Summary Task to show a fixed cost associated with the entire project or on a summary task to show a fixed cost associated with a Phase or Deliverable section of the project. Notice, however, that Project 2013 **does** include the fixed cost amount in the *Total Cost* column.

Hands On Exercise

Exercise 5 - 22

Plan for a known fixed cost, the cost of a new server, in the Training Advisor Rollout project.

1. Return to the **Training Advisor 05c.mpp** sample file.
2. Right-click the *Select All* button and select the *Cost* table on the shortcut menu.
3. Drag the split bar to the right side of the *Total Cost* column.
4. For task ID #17, the *Order Server* task, enter *$6,509* in the *Fixed Cost* column.
5. For the *Order Server* task, select the *End* option in the *Fixed Cost Accrual* column.
6. Double-click the *Order Server* task and then select the *Notes* tab in the *Task Information* dialog.
7. On the *Notes* page, click the *Bulleted List* button and then enter the following note:

   Fixed Cost of $6,509 for a Dell PowerEdge T620 server.

8. Click the *OK* button to close the *Task Information* dialog.
9. Right-click the *Select All* button and select the *Entry* table on the shortcut menu.
10. Save and close the **Training Advisor 05c.mpp** sample file.

Module 06

Project Resource Planning

Learning Objectives

After completing this module, you will be able to:

- Understand project resources
- Create a Work resource
- Create a Generic resource
- Create a Material resource
- Create Cost resources
- Enter basic and custom information for each type of resource
- Sort resources
- Insert a new resource
- Use Lync integration with Project 2013

Inside Module 06

Defining Project Resources

Project 2013 defines resources in a variety of ways and organizes them conceptually in the resource organization chart shown in Figure 6 - 1.

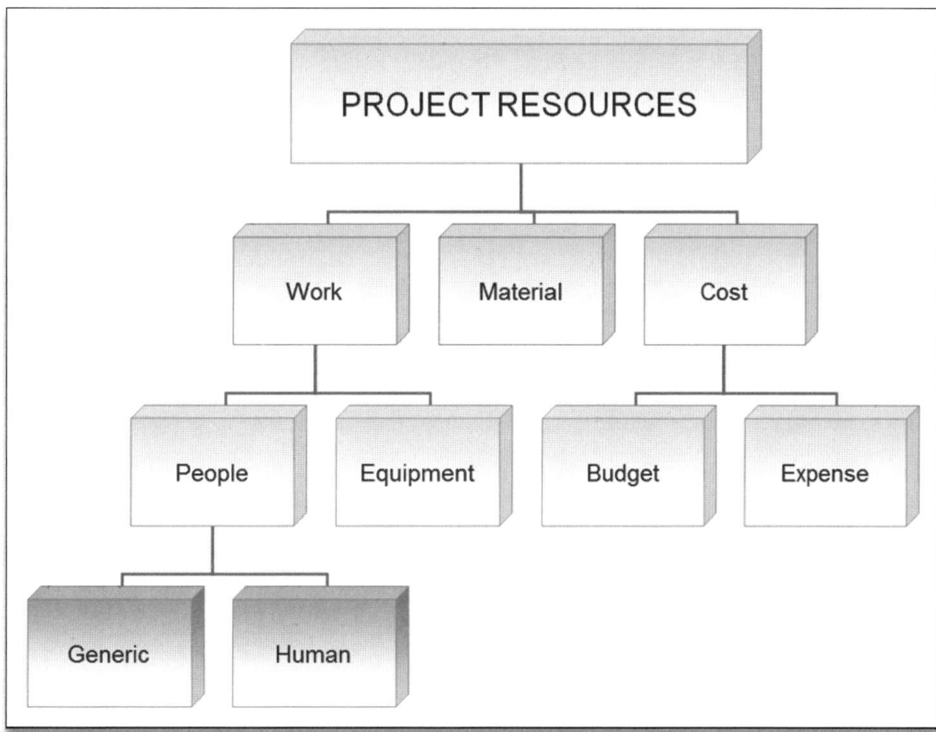

Figure 6 - 1: Resource organization chart

Project 2013 allows you to define three basic resource types: *Work, Material,* and *Cost*. You use *Work* resources to model people and equipment, while you use *Material* resources to represent the supplies consumed during the project lifecycle. You use *Cost* resources to track budget costs and project expenses unrelated to the *Work* resources assigned to tasks. *Work* resources affect both the schedule and the cost of the project, while *Material* and *Cost* resources affect only the project cost.

Information: Unfortunately, Project 2013 does not recognize a formal type of resource called *Equipment*. Therefore, if you want to use equipment resources in your projects, understand in advance that the software treats equipment resources the same as human resources in determining the project schedule.

Project 2013 organizes people resources into two groups: generic and human resources. A human resource is a specific individual whom you can identify by name, such as Mickey Cobb. A generic resource is a skill-based placeholder resource, such as a SQL Server DBA. Generic resources allow you to specify the skills required for a task assignment before you know which human resources are available to work on the task. You can later replace generic resources with human resources who possess the same skills.

You should identify all resources that you may eventually assign to tasks, and then enter the appropriate *Max. Units* availability for each resource into the *Resource Sheet* view to show their availability for project work. The software measures the *Max. Units* availability of *Work* resources as a percentage, where 100% represents a full-time worker and 50% represents a part-time worker such as a college intern. For a human resource, you should not enter a *Max. Units* value greater than 100%.

Information: You cannot realistically expect that any of your *Work* resources are available at 100%, and even equipment has service downtime. People attend meetings, answer phone calls, make trips to the bathroom, and stop to chat with coworkers as a matter of course. To drive an accurate schedule, you should consider reducing resource availability based on your organization's reality. In some organizations, for example, resource availability for project work is as little as 25%.

The software also measures the *Max. Units* availability of generic resources as a percentage; however, this percentage may exceed 100%. For example, to show that I have four full-time SQL Server DBAs available for project work, I enter the *Max. Units* availability as 400% for a generic resource called SQL Server DBA.

Information: In Project 2013, you cannot enter a *Max. Units* value for *Material* or *Cost* resources. This is because *Material* and *Cost* resources affect only project costs and do not affect the project schedule.

Prior to assigning resources to tasks, you should enter a variety of basic and custom resource information for each resource in your project. You enter basic information in the columns of the *Resource Sheet* view. You enter custom information, such as vacation time and alternate cost rates, in the *Resource Information* dialog for each resource.

Creating Work Resources

The first step in the resource planning process is to enter the basic resource information in the *Resource Sheet* view for the *Work* resources in your project team. To apply the *Resource Sheet* view, click the *Resource* tab to display the *Resource* ribbon. In the *View* section of the *Resource* ribbon, click the *Team Planner* pick list button and select the *Resource Sheet* view. Figure 6 - 2 shows the *Resource Sheet* view with the resource *Entry* table applied.

Figure 6 - 2: Resource Sheet view with the Entry table applied

In the *Resource Sheet* view, enter information in the following columns for each project team member:

- In the *Resource Name* column, enter the first and last name of each human resource.

Information: You may optionally enter the name of each human resource in "last name, first name" format; however, you **cannot** use the comma character to separate the last name from the first name because the comma character is reserved by Windows as the list separator character. Instead, use the semi-colon character or a space character to separate the last name and first name of each resource.

- In the *Type* column, select the *Material* value if the resource is a *Material* resource or the *Cost* value if the resource is a *Cost* resource. Otherwise, leave the value set as the default *Work* value for a human resource or a generic resource.
- In the *Material Label* column, enter text to describe how you measure the consumption of the *Material* resource. For example, I measure the consumption of concrete in cubic yards. The software does not allow you to enter a *Material Label* value for *Work* or *Cost* resources.
- In the *Initials* column, enter the initials of each resource. By default, Project 2013 auto-populates in the *Initials* column only the first letter of the first word from the *Resource Name* column.
- In the *Group* column, enter the skill, team, department, or some other name to use for grouping and filtering the resources in your project team.
- In the *Max. Units* column, enter a percentage representing the maximum amount of an average working day the resource is available for project work on this project. Enter 100% or your discounted availability only for resources that are available for full-time project work, and enter a value less than 100% for resources who are available to work less than full-time.
- In the *Std. Rate* column, enter the rate at which you cost the resource's work. The default measure is hourly cost, such as $50.00/hour, but you may also enter a cost using any other time units, such as $1,200/week.
- In the *Ovt. Rate* column, enter the rate at which you cost overtime work. In Project 2013, overtime work is any work you enter explicitly in the *Overtime Work* or *Actual Overtime Work* fields.

Warning: MSProjectExperts recommends that you **never** enter a resource's actual salary in any of the resource cost fields. Doing so may result in privacy issues with your company's HR department and could even cause dissension and morale problems with project staff. In fact, some European Union countries have laws prohibiting this practice. Instead, use "blended" or averaged rates for resources across a team, a department, a business unit, or even your entire organization.

- In the *Cost/Use* column, enter the "flat rate" that accrues each time you use the resource in the project. The *Cost/Use* column is similar to the "trip charge" billed by a plumber to get the plumber to show up at your home.

Information: Most project managers do not use the *Cost/Use* column because the software accrues this rate **every time** you assign the resource to a task in your project. This means that if you assign a resource ten times, you accrue ten *Cost/Use* instances. Most people believe the column would work better if Project 2013 accrued the *Cost/Use* rate only once per project.

- In the *Accrue At* column, select a value that determines how Project 2013 applies the timephased costs when you assign the selected resource to a task. You can apply the cost at the beginning of the task by selecting the *Start* value or at the end of the task by selecting the *End* value. The default value, *Prorated*, applies the cost evenly across the duration of the task.

- In the *Base Calendar* column, select the base calendar that Project 2013 uses to set up the resource's personal calendar. If you entered your company holidays on the *Standard* calendar, and then specified this calendar as the resource's base calendar, then the resource's personal calendar automatically inherits all company holidays from the *Standard* calendar.
- The *Code* column is a free text field in which you may enter any type of additional information about the resource, such as the cost center code or work phone number for the resource.

Information: Similar to Excel, you can speed up the entry of resources by using the Fill Handle tool to fill data from one cell to consecutive cells above or below it. To do so, select the cell whose content you want to fill into other cells, click and hold the Fill Handle tool in the lower right corner of the selected cell, then drag up or down to fill as many cells as you want.

Figure 6 - 3 shows the *Resource Sheet* view with a new resource named *George Stewart*. Notice that I filled in every available column for this resource except for the *Cost/Use* column.

RESOURCE SHEET

	ℹ	Resource Name	Type	Material Label	Initials	Group	Max. Units	Std. Rate	Ovt. Rate	Cost/Use	Accrue At	Base Calendar	Code
1		George Stewart	Work		GS	Engineering	100%	$50.00/h	$75.00/h	$0.00	Prorated	Standard	80222

Figure 6 - 3: Resource Sheet view shows a new Work resource

Hands On Exercise

Exercise 6 - 1

Enter *Work* resources in the project team for the Training Advisor Rollout project.

1. Open the **Training Advisor 06.mpp** sample file.
2. Click the *Resource* tab to display the *Resource* ribbon.
3. In the *View* section of the *Resource* ribbon, click the *Team Planner* pick list button, and select the *Resource Sheet* view.

Information: Remember that you only see the *Team Planner* pick list button if you use the **Professional** version of Project 2013. If you use the **Standard** version of the software, click the *Resource Sheet* pick list button, and then select the *Resource Sheet* view.

4. In the *Name Column*, select the first blank cell at the bottom of the list of resources already entered in the *Resource Sheet* view of the project.
5. Add a new *Work* resource using the basic resource information shown in Table 6 - 1.

Column	Value to Enter/Select
Resource Name	Audrey Kehrli
Type	Work
Material Label	
Initials	AK
Group	Test
Max. Units	100%
Std. Rate	$50.00/h
Ovt. Rate	$75.00/h
Cost/Use	$0.00
Accrue At	Prorated
Base Calendar	Standard
Code	500

Table 6 - 1: Create a Work resource

6. Save but **do not** close the **Training Advisor 06.mpp** sample file.

Entering Custom Resource Information

The second step in the resource planning process is to enter custom resource information for each *Work* resource on your project team. Custom resource data includes information such as vacation time, alternate cost rates, or notes about the resource. To enter this information, display the *Resource Information* dialog using one of the following methods:

- Select the resource and then click the *Information* button in the *Properties* section of the *Resource* ribbon.
- Right-click the resource and then select the *Information* item on the shortcut menu.

Information: In previous versions of the software prior to Project 2013, the software allowed you to double-click a resource to display the *Resource Information* dialog. Because of the new Lync integration feature, when you double-click a resource, the software displays the *Lync contact card* dialog for any Lync-enabled resource. To enable a resource for Lync integration, by the way, you must enter an e-mail address for the resource. If you double-click a resource that is not Lync-enabled, the software does nothing.

Figure 6 - 4 shows the *Resource Information* dialog for a resource named George Stewart. Notice a number of fields on the *General* page of the dialog show information I entered previously in the *Resource Sheet* view of the project.

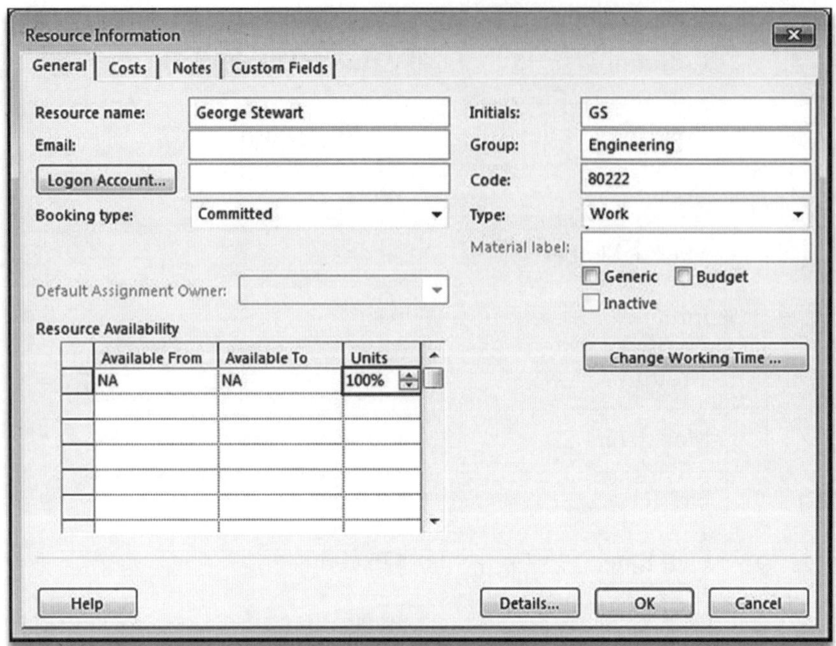

Figure 6 - 4: Resource Information dialog, General page

The *Resource Information* dialog includes four pages of information for each resource, including the *General, Costs, Notes,* and *Custom Fields* pages. I discuss each of these pages separately.

Entering General Information

The *General* page includes some of the information you already entered in the *Resource Sheet* view of the project in the *Resource Name, Type, Initials, Group,* and *Code* columns. This page in the dialog allows you to enter additional information, including the resource's e-mail address, Windows user account, and availability information. From this page, you can also designate a *Work* resource as a generic resource by selecting the *Generic* option.

Use the data grid in the *Resource Availability* section to enter changes in the availability of a resource, such as when a part-time employee becomes a full-time employee on a specific date. You can also use this section to indicate changes in the number of generic resources available, for example, to show that your organization will add two new network engineers on August 1 of the current year.

Figure 6 - 5 shows the changes in availability for the resource, George Stewart, who changes from full-time to part-time to attend graduate school during the 2015-2106 school year. Notice how his *Units* availability changes from *100%* (full-time) to *50%* (half-time) and then returns to *100%* (full-time) again. The software automatically updates these availability changes in the *Max. Units* field for the resource.

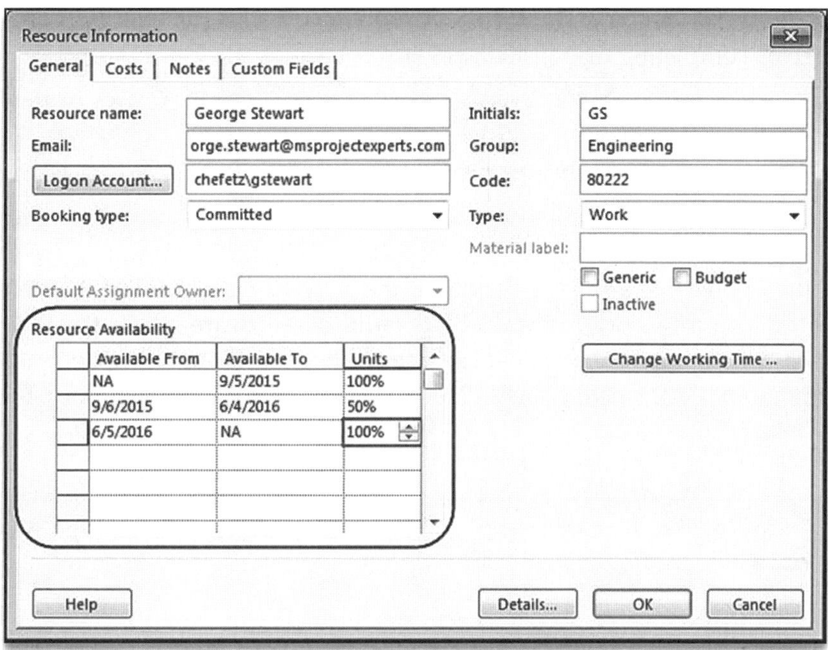

Figure 6 - 5: Resource Information dialog, changes to Resource Availability

Best Practice: MSProjectExperts recommends that you always document changes in the *Resource Availability* section of the *Resource Information* dialog by adding a note for the resource.

Changing Working Time

There are several situations that require you to change the working schedule for a resource, which are:

- The resource works a schedule different from the schedule specified on the *Standard* calendar.
- You need to add nonworking time for the resource, such as vacation or planned sick leave.
- You need to make minor modifications to the resource's working schedule, such as adding Saturday work for a specific period of time.

I discuss how to configure each of these schedule needs separately.

Setting an Alternate Working Schedule

If you want to create an alternate working schedule for a resource, and the schedule differs from the *Standard* calendar, there are two ways to accomplish this. To use the first method, you must create a custom base calendar in the project. Refer back to Module 04, if necessary, for the steps needed to create a custom base calendar. After you create the custom base calendar, simply select that new calendar as the *Base Calendar* column for the selected resource in the *Resource Sheet* view of the project.

If a base calendar with the schedule you want does not exist already, you can specify the non-standard working schedule for the resource by completing the following steps:

1. On the *General* page of the *Resource Information* dialog, click the *Change Working Time* button.

The software displays the *Change Working Time* dialog for the selected resource. For example, Figure 6 - 6 shows the *Change Working Time* dialog for George Stewart. By default, the software selects the *Exceptions* tab at the bottom of the dialog. Notice that because the *Standard* calendar is the *Base Calendar* for George Stewart, his calendar inherits nonworking time from the *Standard* calendar, such as the Memorial Day exception I selected in the dialog.

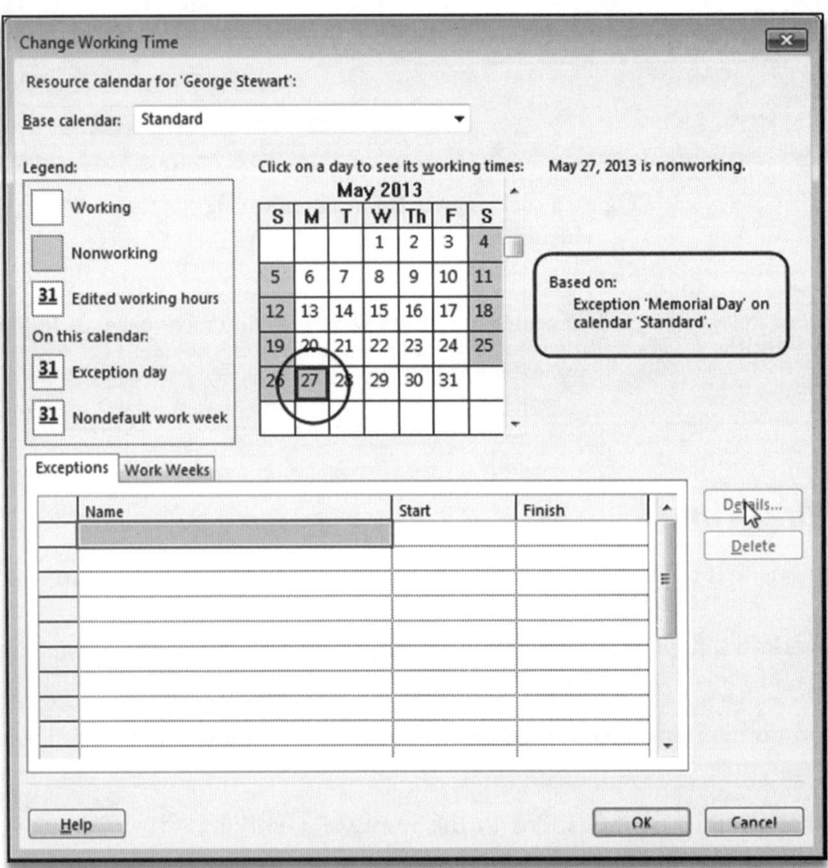

Figure 6 - 6: Change Working Time dialog, Exceptions tab

2. In the bottom half of the dialog, click the *Work Weeks* tab. Figure 6 - 7 shows the *Work Weeks* tab in the *Change Working Time* dialog for George Stewart.

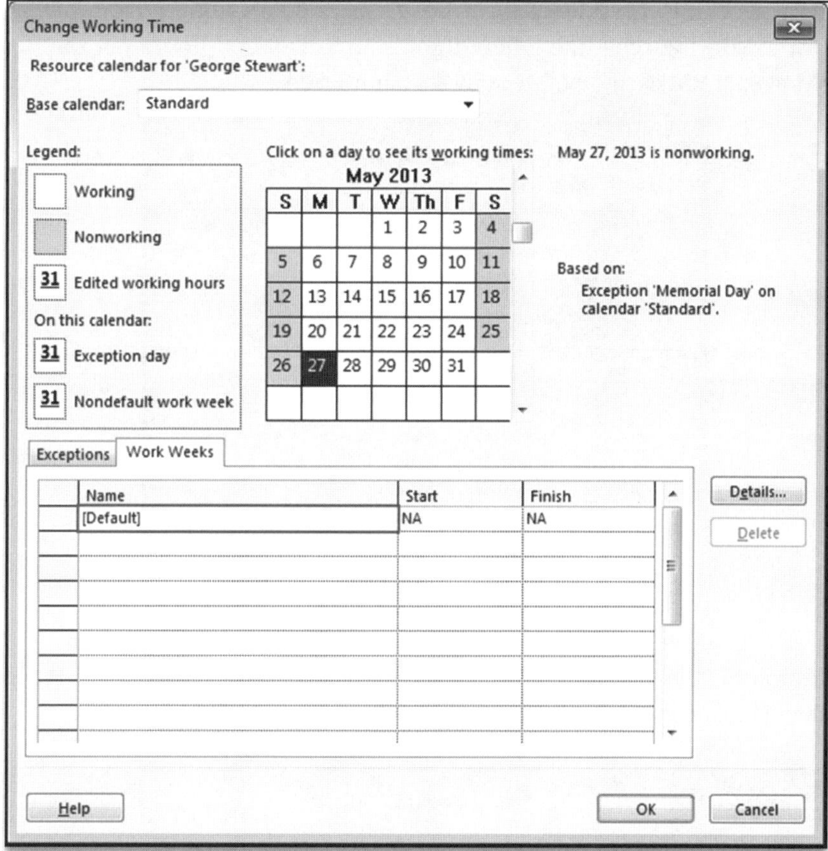

Figure 6 - 7: Change Working Time dialog, Work Weeks tab

3. Select the *[Default]* item in the *Work Weeks* data grid and then click the *Details* button. The software displays the *Details* dialog for the default working schedule shown in Figure 6 - 8.

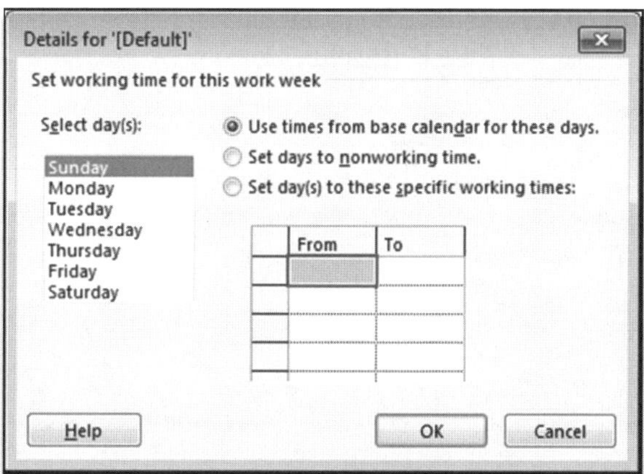

Figure 6 - 8: Details dialog for the default working schedule

4. In the *Select day(s)* list, select the days whose schedule you want to change, such the Monday through Friday.

5. In the upper right corner of the dialog, select the *Set day(s) to these specific working times* option.

6. Enter the alternate working schedule in the *Working times* data grid. For example, Figure 6 - 9 shows the *Details* dialog for a working schedule where the resource works 9 hours per day from 8:00 AM to 12:30 PM and 1:30 PM to 6:00 PM each day, Monday through Friday.

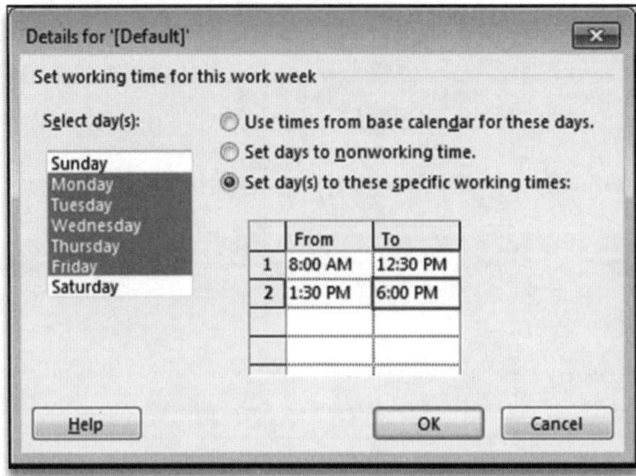

Figure 6 - 9: Details dialog shows alternate working schedule

7. Click the *OK* button to close the *Details* dialog. Figure 6 - 10 shows the *Change Working Time* dialog with the new alternate working schedule for George Stewart.

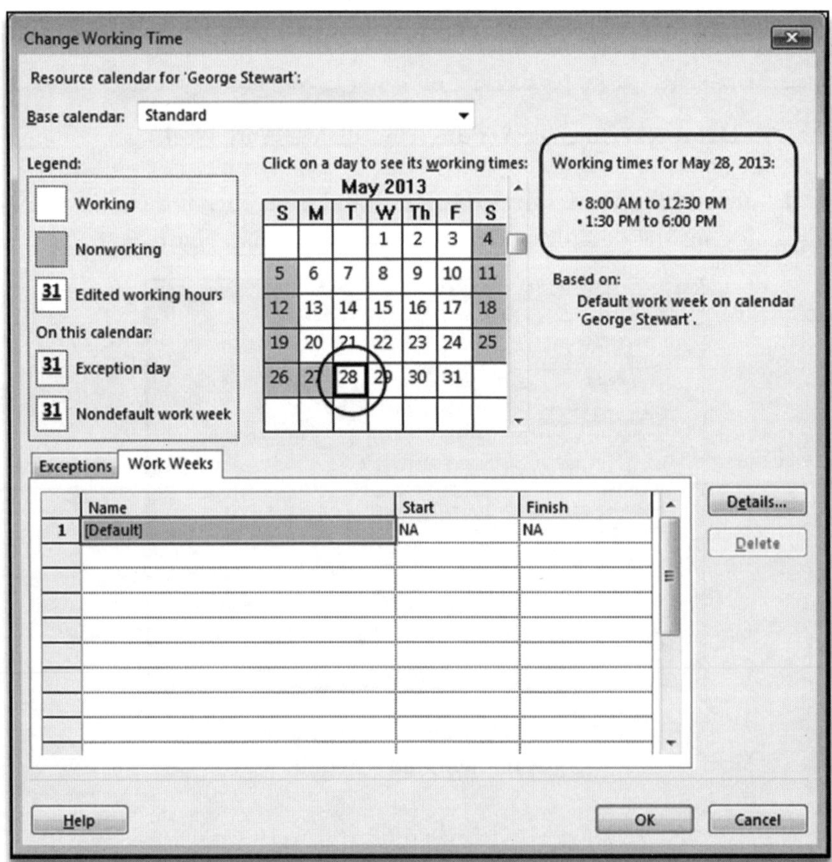

Figure 6 - 10: Change Working Time dialog with alternate working schedule

Entering Nonworking Time

Project 2013 allows you to enter nonworking time, such as vacations and planned medical leave, for each individual resource. To enter nonworking time for a resource, complete the following steps in the *Resource Information* dialog:

1. On the *General* page of the *Resource Information* dialog, click the *Change Working Time* button.

2. Click the *Exceptions* tab. The software displays the *Exceptions* tab of the *Change Working Time* dialog, shown previously in Figure 6 - 6.

3. In the calendar grid at the top of the page, select the days you want to set as nonworking time.

4. In the *Exceptions* data grid in the bottom half of the dialog, select the *Name* cell in the first blank line.

5. In the *Name* cell of the *Exceptions* data grid, enter a name for the nonworking time instance, such as *Vacation*.

6. Press the **Enter** key on your computer keyboard. The software automatically sets the selected time period as nonworking time, such as the vacation time for George Stewart in August 2015 as shown in Figure 6 - 11.

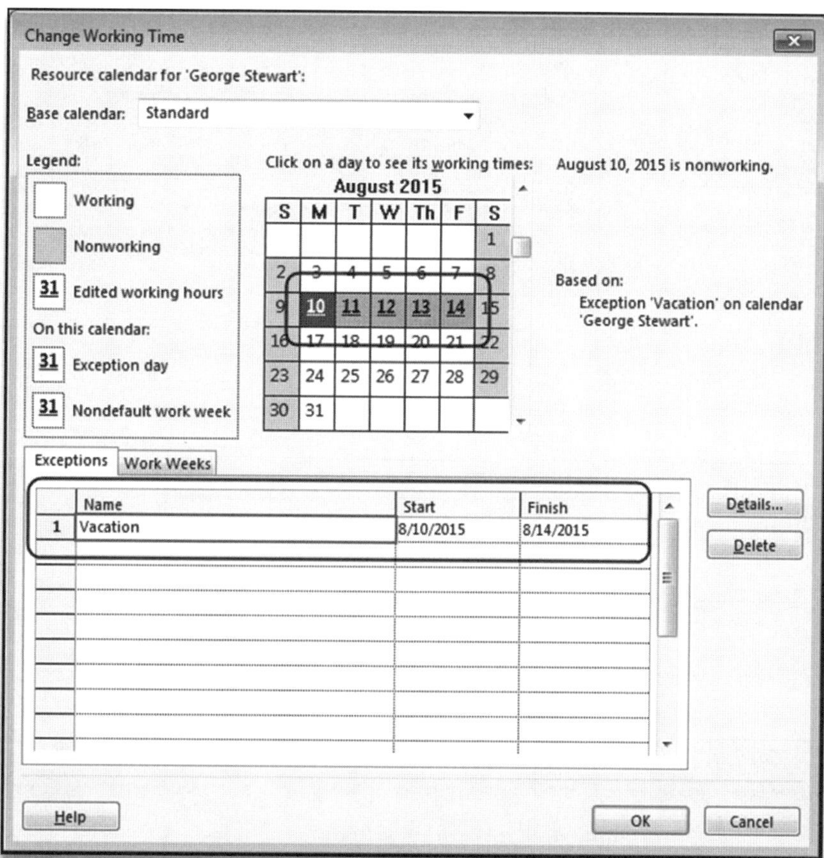

Figure 6 - 11: Planned vacation for George Stewart in August 2015

Setting Working Schedule Changes

At some point, you may need to set an alternate working schedule for a limited period of time, such as when a resource might work an extended work week during summer months. To set an alternate working schedule for a resource for a specific period of time, complete the following steps in the *Resource Information* dialog:

1. On the *General* page of the *Resource Information* dialog, click the *Change Working Time* button.

2. Click the *Work Weeks* tab.

3. In the *Work Weeks* data grid, select the first blank row below the *[Default]* line.

4. In the *Name* cell of the blank row, enter a name for the alternate working schedule and then press the **Right-Arrow** key on your computer keyboard. Make sure you leave selected the name of the alternate working schedule.

5. Enter the starting date of the schedule change in the *Start* field and enter the ending date in the *Finish* field for the alternate working schedule. For example, Figure 6 - 12 shows the June 2015 working schedule I want to change for George Stewart.

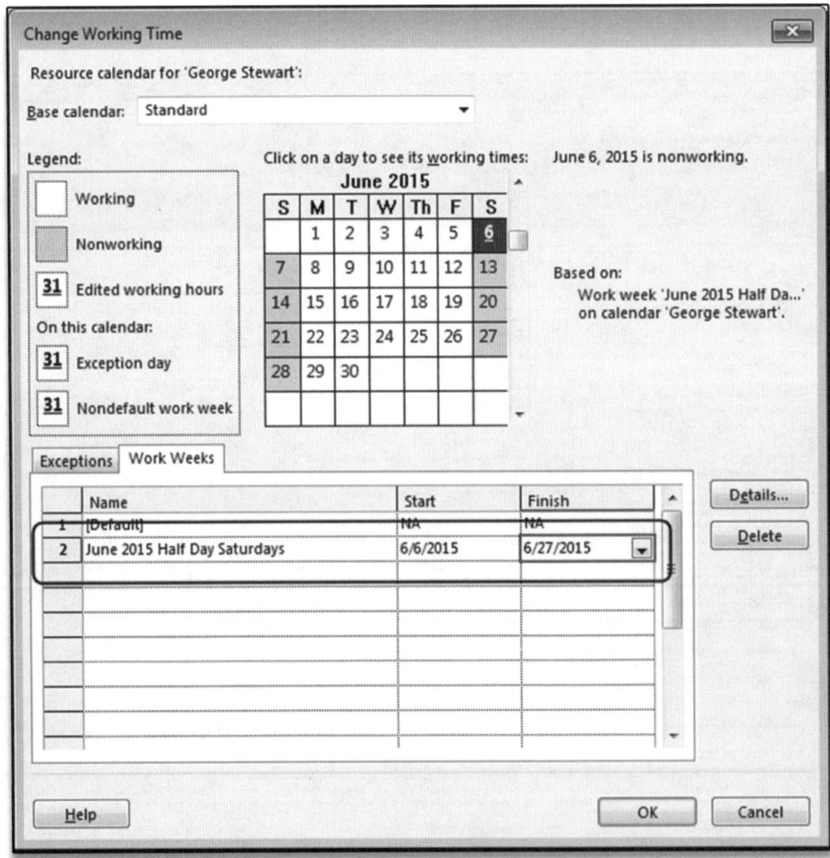

Figure 6 - 12: Working schedule includes Saturdays for June 2015 only

6. With the alternate work schedule still selected, click the *Details* button. The software displays the *Details* dialog shown previously in Figure 6 - 9.

7. In the *Details* dialog for the alternate working schedule, set the working schedule for each day of the week, as needed. The *Details* dialog shown in Figure 6 - 13 displays the Saturday work schedule for George Stewart during June 2015 only.

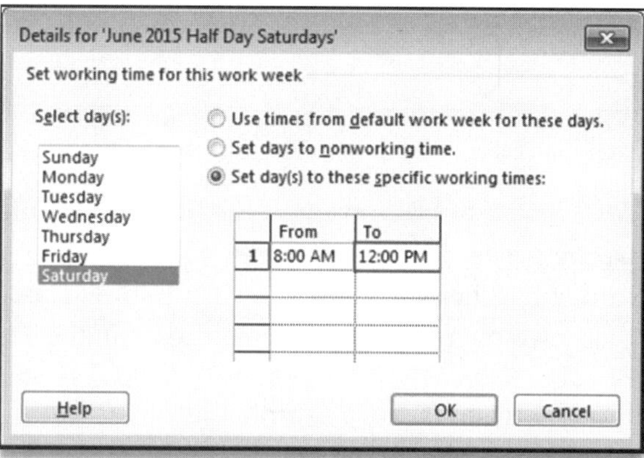

Figure 6 - 13: Details dialog shows Saturdays as work days in June 2015 only

8. Click the *OK* button to close the *Details* dialog. Figure 6 - 14 shows the *Change Working Time* dialog for George Stewart with the June 2015 schedule change to show half-day working days on Saturday.

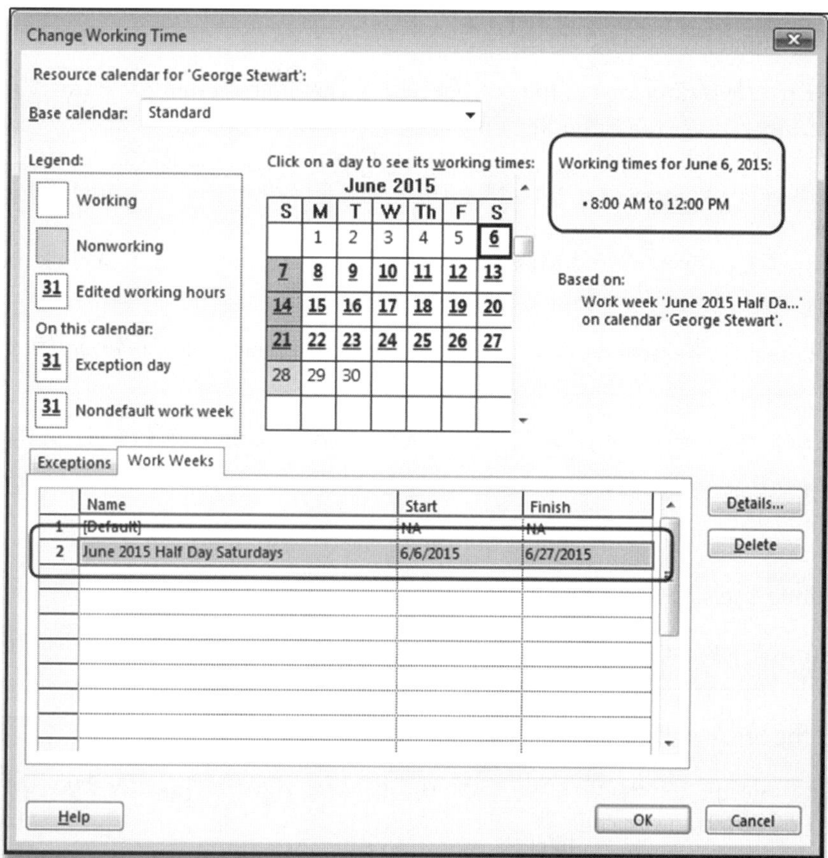

Figure 6 - 14 Change Working Time dialog shows Saturdays as work days in June 2015 only

Hands On Exercise

Exercise 6 - 2

The functional manager for Mickey Cobb approved her vacation request for a week of vacation from March 14-18, 2016. The working schedule for Audrey Kehrli is four days each week from Monday through Thursday only, working 10 hours/day, with every Friday as nonworking time. Specify working schedule information for these two members of the project team in the Training Advisor Rollout project.

1. Return to the **Training Advisor 06.mpp** sample file.
2. Right-click the resource named *Mickey Cobb* and then select the *Information* item on the shortcut menu.
3. On the *General* page of the *Resource Information* dialog, click the *Change Working Time* button.
4. Click the *Exceptions* tab, if necessary.
5. In the top half of the *Change Working Time* dialog, scroll the calendar grid to *March 2016*.
6. In the calendar grid, select the dates *March 14-18, 2016*.
7. In the *Exceptions* data grid in the bottom half of the dialog, enter the name *Vacation* for the exception and then press the **Enter** key on your computer keyboard.

Notice how Project 2013 marks March 14-18, 2016 as nonworking time in the calendar grid.

8. Click the *OK* button to close the *Change Working Time* dialog and then click the *OK* button again to close the *Resource Information* dialog.
9. Right-click the resource named *Audrey Kehrli* and then select the *Information* item on the shortcut menu.
10. In the *Resource Information* dialog, click the *Change Working Time* button on the *General* page.
11. Click the *Work Weeks* tab.
12. In the *Work Weeks* data grid at the bottom of the dialog, select the *[Default]* item, if necessary.
13. Click the *Details* button.
14. In the *Select days* list on the left side of the *Details* dialog, select the *Monday* through *Thursday* items.
15. Select the *Set day(s) to these specific working times* option.
16. On the first row of the data grid on the right side of the dialog, enter *8:00 AM* in the *From* cell and enter *1:00 PM* in the *To* cell.
17. On the second row of the data grid on the right side of the dialog, enter *2:00 PM* in the *From* cell and enter *7:00 PM* in the *To* cell.
18. In the *Select days* list on the left side of the *Details* dialog, select only the *Friday* item.

19. Select the *Set days to nonworking time* option.
20. Click the *OK* button to close the *Details* dialog.
21. In the calendar grid at the top of the *Change Working Time* dialog, select any Monday through Thursday date and examine the working schedule shown in the upper right corner of the *Change Working Time* dialog.
22. In the calendar grid at the top of the dialog, select any Friday and notice that Friday is a non-working day.
23. Click the *OK* button to close the *Change Working Time* dialog and then click the *OK* button again to close the *Resource Information* dialog.
24. Save but **do not** close the **Training Advisor 06.mpp** sample file.

Entering Cost Information

To enter custom cost information for any resource, display the *Resource Information* dialog for the resource and then click the *Costs* tab. The *Resource Information* dialog *Costs* page, shown in Figure 6 - 15, displays the *Standard Rate, Overtime Rate,* and *Per Use Cost* fields for the selected resource. In addition, the *Cost rate tables* section of the page also contains five cost rate tables labeled *A (Default)* through *E*. Cost rate table *A* contains the rates you entered in the *Resource Sheet* view in the *Std. Rate, Ovt. Rate,* and *Cost/Use* columns. You can use cost rate tables *B* through *E* to specify alternate cost rates. You can set the cost rates on any of the cost rate tables so that the rate changes on a given day automatically, such as when a resource receives a salary increase or when your organization increases the billing rate to clients.

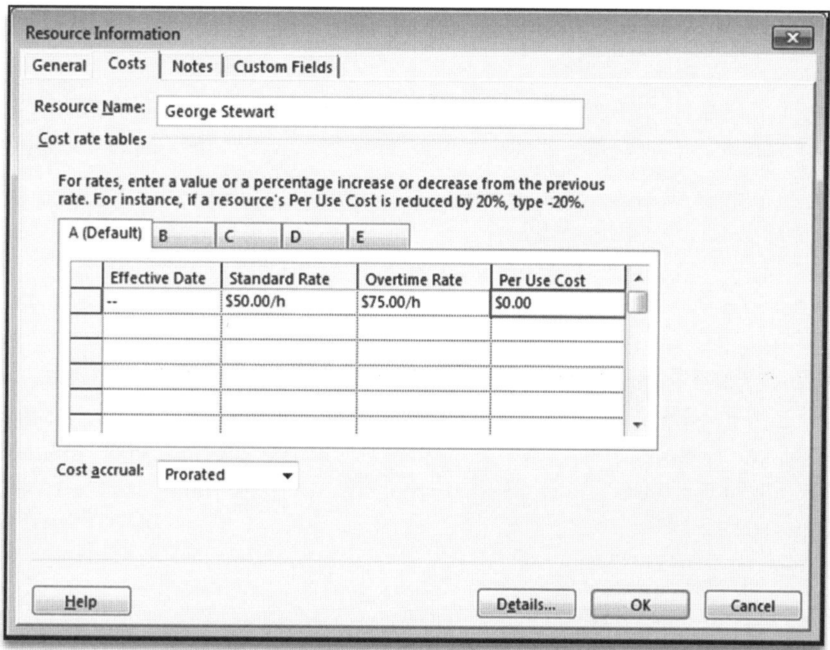

Figure 6 - 15: Resource Information dialog, Costs page

As a part of the cost model for your project, you may need to change cost rates on a specific date for a resource on the project team. For example, on January 1 of next year, George Stewart's *Standard Rate* increases by $10/hour and the resource's *Overtime Rate* increases by $15/hour.

To define a new cost rate that begins on a specific date, select the *A (Default)* cost rate table tab and then enter the date in the *Effective Date* field on the **first blank line** of the data grid. Enter the new rates in the *Standard Rate* cell and *Overtime Rate* cell on that line, such as shown in Figure 6 - 16.

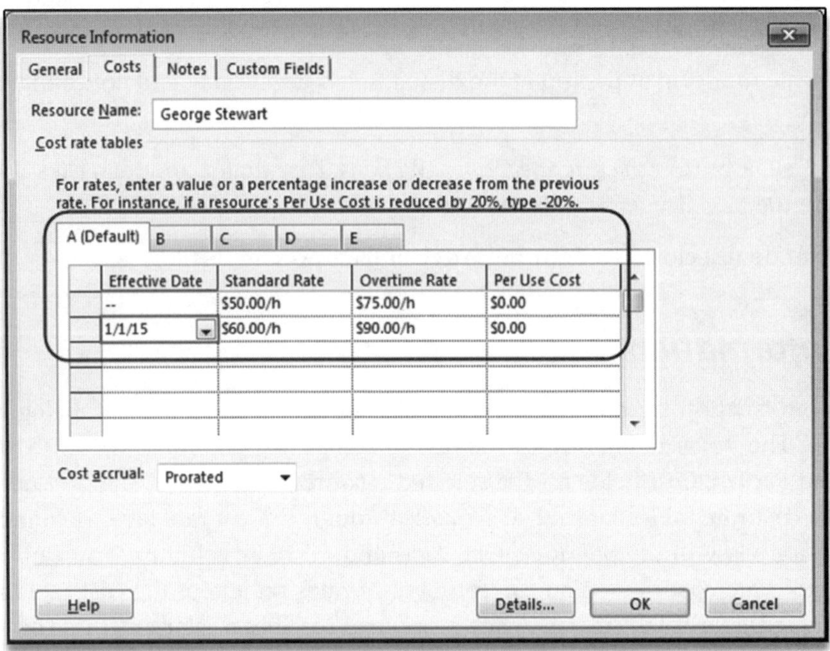

Figure 6 - 16: Resource Information dialog
Cost rate increase on 1/1/15

Information: When you enter a cost rate change for a resource, Project 2013 automatically costs all work for the resource at the new cost rate beginning on the date you enter in the *Effective Date* field. Using the example shown previously in Figure 6 - 16, the software costs all of George Stewart's task work at $50/hour before 1/1/15 and at $60/hour beginning 1/1/15 and thereafter.

You might have a team member who plays multiple roles in a project, and whose cost depends on the team member's role in the project. For example, we cost George Stewart's work at $50/hour for engineering tasks but cost his work at $150/hour for tasks in which he must provide expert witness testimony before any governmental entity. To specify an alternate cost rate for a resource, select one of the alternate cost rate table tabs (*B* through *E*) in the *Cost rate tables* section of the *Costs* page and then enter the alternate rate(s) on the **first blank line** of the data grid, as shown in Figure 6 - 17.

Best Practice: MSProjectExperts recommends that you always document your use of alternate cost rates with a resource note. The note should explain how to use the alternate rates shown on cost rate tables *B* through *E*. You do not need to use a note to document the rate shown on cost rate table *A (Default)* since this is the default cost rate for all tasks until you choose an alternate cost rate.

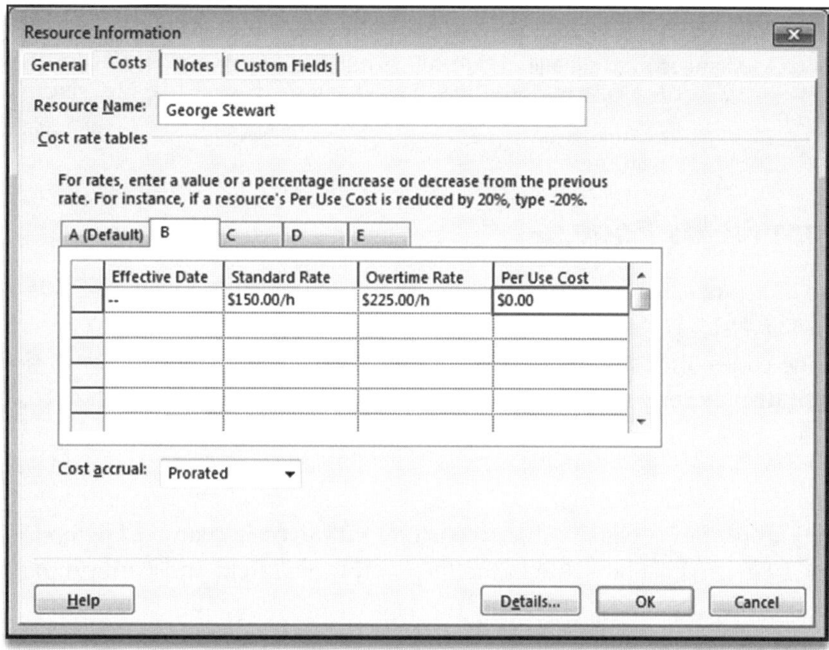

Figure 6 - 17: Resource Information dialog, alternate cost rate for expert witness testimony work on cost rate table B

Entering Resource Notes

Use the *Notes* page in the *Resource Information* dialog to record additional information about the selected resource, such as changes in availability and notes about how to use alternate cost rates. Figure 6 - 18 shows the *Notes* page in the *Resource Information* dialog with a note added about the alternate cost rate for George Stewart.

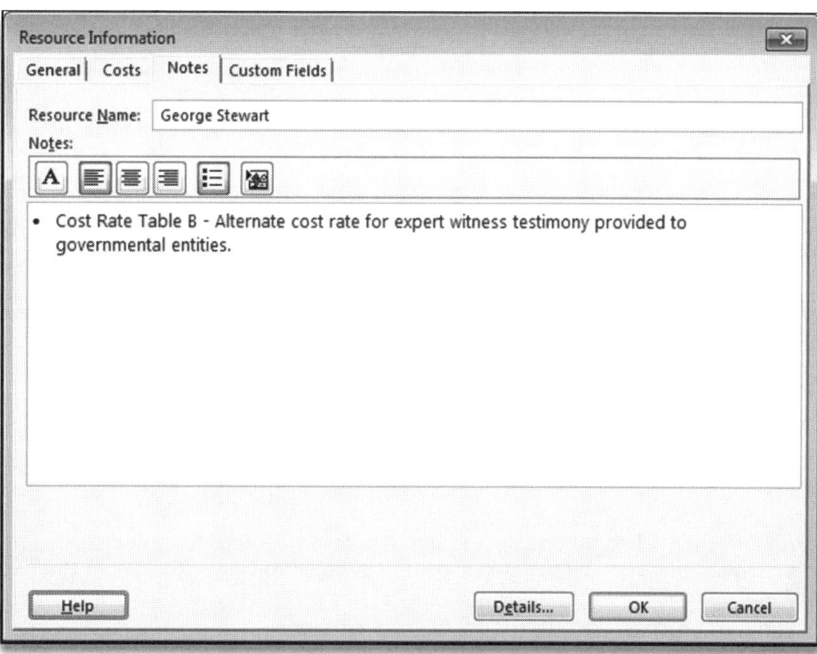

Figure 6 - 18: Resource Information dialog, Notes page

Best Practice: MSProjectExperts recommends the use of resource notes to document important resource information such as changes in availability and use of alternate cost rates. This makes it easier for others to understand how Project 2013 calculates both the schedule and the cost of tasks to which you assign the resource.

Using the Custom Fields Page

The *Custom Fields* page in *the Resource Information* dialog shows any custom resource fields available in your project. By default, the *Custom Fields* page is blank in the *Resource Information* dialog. If you create any local custom resource fields or outline codes, they appear on the *Custom Fields* page. If your organization uses Project Server 2013, then this page also displays any custom enterprise resource fields created by the Project Server administrator.

Figure 6 - 19 shows the *Custom Fields* page with two custom outline codes named *Engineering Skill* and *Region Office*. Notice that I selected *Electrical* as the value in the *Engineering Skill* field and I am preparing to select *Denver* as the value in the *Region Office* field.

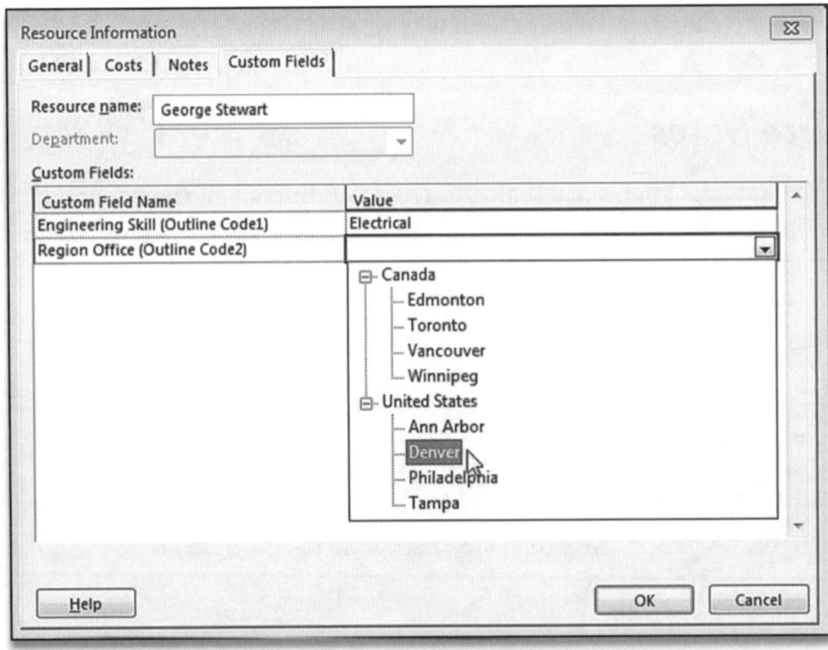

Figure 6 - 19: Resource Information dialog, Custom Fields page

When you finish setting up the *Work* resource, click the *OK* button to close the *Resource Information* dialog.

Information: In Module 13 of this book, I teach you how to create different types of custom fields, including custom *Outline Code* fields such as the two shown previously in Figure 6 - 19 on the *Custom Fields* page of the *Resource Information* dialog.

Hands On Exercise

Exercise 6 - 3

The cost rates for Ruth Andrews increase by 25% on April 1, 2016. Mike Andrews works on the Help Desk primarily, but does occasional testing work that you cost at the same rate as members of Test team. Enter custom cost information and notes for these two members of the project team in the Training Advisor Rollout project.

1. Return to the **Training Advisor 06.mpp** sample file.
2. Right-click the resource named *Ruth Andrews* and then select the *Information* item on the shortcut menu.
3. Click the *Costs* tab to display the *Costs* page in the *Resource Information* dialog.
4. Select the cost rate table *A (Default)* page in the *Cost rate tables* section of the *Costs* page, if necessary.
5. On the **first blank line** of the data grid, enter *April 1, 2016* in the *Effective Date* column, enter *25%* in the *Standard Rate* column and enter *25%* in the *Overtime Rate* column.

Information: From the previous step, you now know that you can specify a rate increase by entering the new cost amount, or by entering a percentage value and let Project 2013 calculate the new cost rate for you.

6. Click the *OK* button to close the *Resource Information* dialog.
7. Right-click the resource named *Mike Andrews* and then select the *Information* item on the shortcut menu.
8. Click the *Costs* tab to display the *Costs* page in the *Resource Information* dialog.
9. Click the *B* tab in the *Cost rate tables* section of the *Costs* page.
10. On the first line of the data grid on the cost rate table *B* page, enter *$50/hour* in the *Standard Rate* column and *$75/hour* in the *Overtime Rate* column.
11. Click the *Notes* tab to display the *Notes* page of the *Resource Information* dialog.
12. On the *Notes* page, click the *Bulleted List* button and then enter the following text in the *Notes* field:

    Cost Rate Table B – Alternate cost rate for testing tasks.

13. Click the *OK* button to close the *Resource Information* dialog.
14. Save but do close the **Training Advisor 06.mpp** sample file.

Creating Generic Resources

Generic resources are skill-based or placeholder resources that you can assign to tasks before you know the actual human resources to assign. You can also use generic resources to model project costs in the early stages of the project before you begin assigning any human resources. To create a generic resource, complete the following steps in the *Resource Sheet* view of your project:

1. Enter the name of the generic resource in the *Resource Name* column.

2. Enter all other basic information in the columns of the *Resource Sheet* view as you would for a non-generic resource.

3. Right-click the generic resource and then select the *Information* item on the shortcut menu.

4. On the *General* page of the *Resource Information* dialog, select the *Generic* checkbox on the right side of the dialog.

Information: You only see a *Generic* checkbox if you use the **Professional** version of Project 2013. If you use the **Standard** version of the software, you cannot create a true generic resource, but you can create a generic-like resource instead, based on the resource's name. For example, using the **Standard** version of Project 2013, you know that a resource named *Mickey Cobb* is a human resource and a resource named *SQL Server DBA* is a generic-like resource.

5. In the *Resource Availability* data grid, enter a *Units* value representing the number of full-time generic resources available in the current project.

6. Specify cost information on the *Costs* page.

7. Specify custom field values on the *Custom Fields* page, if needed.

8. Click the *OK* button.

Figure 6 - 20 shows the *Resource Information* dialog for a generic resource named Electrical Engineer. Notice that I set the *Units* value in the *Resource Availability* section to *400%* indicating that our organization has four full-time electrical engineers to perform project work.

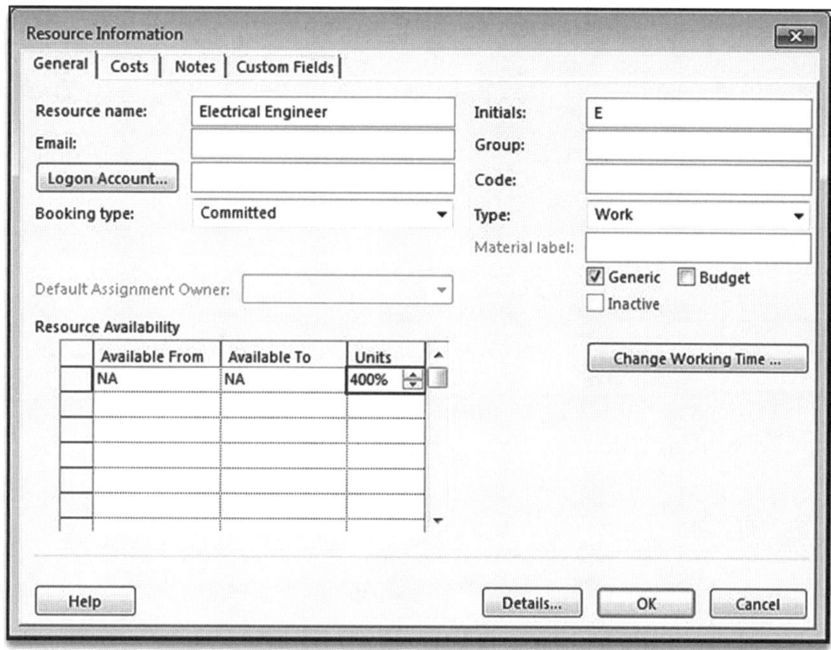

Figure 6 - 20: Resource Information dialog for a Generic resource

Hands On Exercise

Exercise 6 - 4

Create a generic resource in the Training Advisor Rollout project.

1. Return to the **Training Advisor 06.mpp** sample file.
2. At the bottom of the resource list in the *Resource Sheet* view of the project, add a new generic resource using the basic resource information shown in Table 6 - 2.

Column	Value to Enter/Select
Resource Name	Training Developer
Type	Work
Material Label	
Initials	TD
Group	TechEd

Column	Value to Enter/Select
Max. Units	500%
Std. Rate	$40.00/h
Ovt. Rate	$60.00/h
Cost/Use	$0.00
Accrue At	Prorated
Base Calendar	Standard
Code	401

Table 6 - 2: Create a generic resource

3. Widen the *Resource Name* column, if necessary.
4. Right-click the *Training Developer* resource and select the *Information* item on the shortcut menu.
5. On the *General* page of the *Resource Information* dialog, select the *Generic* checkbox, and then click the *OK* button.

Information: If you use the **Standard** version of Project 2013, you do not have a *Generic* checkbox in the *Resource Information* dialog; therefore, simply omit the preceding step.

6. Save but **do not** close the **Training Advisor 06.mpp** sample file.

Creating Material Resources

You use *Material* resources to represent the supplies consumed during the life of the project. To create a *Material* resource, complete the following steps in the *Resource Sheet* view of your project:

1. Enter the name of the *Material* resource in the *Resource Name* column.
2. In the *Type* column for the *Material* resource, click the pick list button and select the *Material* item.
3. Enter a value in the *Material Label* column to indicate how you measure the consumption of the *Material* resource.
4. In the *Initials* column, enter the initials of the *Material* resource, if appropriate.
5. In the *Group* column, enter the group to which the *Material* resource belongs, if appropriate.
6. In the *Std. Rate* column, enter the cost for each unit consumed, as specified in the *Material Label* column.

The *Material Label* column allows you to define your own consumption units corresponding with the costs that you set. For instance, in a construction project I measure the consumption of concrete in **cubic yards**, so I should enter *Cubic Yards* in the *Material Label* column for this *Material* resource. In an IT project, I measure the consumption of servers as **each**, so I should enter *Each* in the *Material Label* column for this *Material* resource.

The point is that you should make the label in the *Material Label* column correspond to how you measure the consumption of the *Material* resource. In Figure 6 - 21, notice that I entered a *Material* resource called *120V UPS Unit* whose consumption is *Each* and which we cost at *$549/each.*

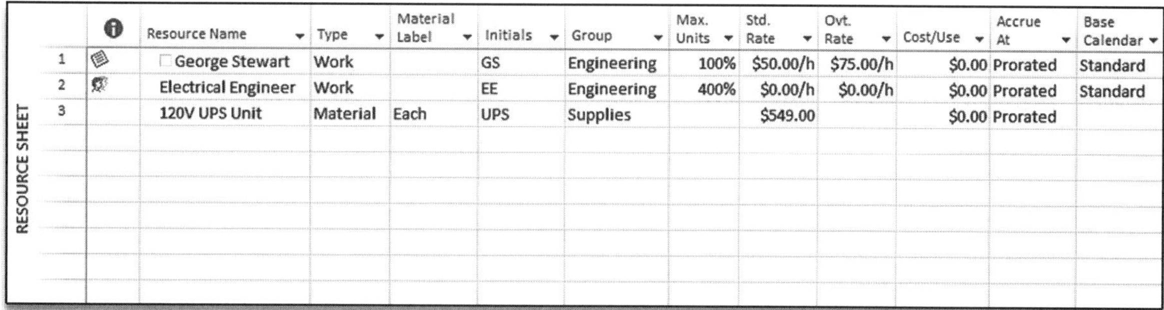

		Resource Name	Type	Material Label	Initials	Group	Max. Units	Std. Rate	Ovt. Rate	Cost/Use	Accrue At	Base Calendar
1		George Stewart	Work		GS	Engineering	100%	$50.00/h	$75.00/h	$0.00	Prorated	Standard
2		Electrical Engineer	Work		EE	Engineering	400%	$0.00/h	$0.00/h	$0.00	Prorated	Standard
3		120V UPS Unit	Material	Each	UPS	Supplies		$549.00		$0.00	Prorated	

Figure 6 - 21: 120V UPS Unit resource is a Material resource

Information: When you create a *Material* resource, you cannot enter information in the *Max. Units, Ovt. Rate,* and *Base Calendar* columns. You can optionally enter information in the *Cost/Use* and *Code* columns, if necessary.

Hands On Exercise

Exercise 6 - 5

Create a *Material* resource in the Training Advisor Rollout project.

1. Return to the **Training Advisor 06.mpp** sample file.
2. At the bottom of the resource list in the *Resource Sheet* view of the project, add a new *Material* resource using the basic resource information shown in Table 6 - 3.

Column	Value to Enter/Select
Resource Name	Student Materials
Type	Material
Material Label	Sets
Initials	SM

Column	Value to Enter/Select
Group	Supplies
Max. Units	
Std. Rate	$50.00
Ovt. Rate	
Cost/Use	$0.00
Accrue At	Prorated
Base Calendar	
Code	900

Table 6 - 3: Create a Material resource

3. Save but do not close the **Training Advisor 06.mpp** sample file.

Creating Cost Resources

Cost resources, added originally in Project 2007, allow you to specify a project budget and to track additional project costs in a more robust manner than using the *Fixed Cost* column. For example, you might use *Cost* resources in the following situations:

- You need to specify an overall monetary budget to your project. For example, your organization allocates $1,500,000 as the budget for your project and you need to enter this information in your project.
- You need to track additional project costs and show the total extra expenditure as a line item in a resource view in your project. For example, you need to track travel expenses for the resources assigned to tasks in your project, and need to report on travel expenses as line item expenditures in your project.

Project 2013 provides you with two types of *Cost* resources: *Budget Cost* resources and *Expense Cost* resources. To use *Cost* resources effectively you may need to create at least one *Budget Cost* resource and at least one *Expense Cost* resource in your project.

Creating a Budget Cost Resource

To create a *Budget Cost* resource, complete the following steps in the *Resource Sheet* view of your project:

1. Enter the name of the *Budget Cost* resource in the *Resource Name* column.
2. In the *Type* column for the *Cost* resource, click the pick list button and select the *Cost* item.
3. Enter additional information for the *Budget Cost* resource in the *Initials, Group, Accrue At,* and *Code* columns, as needed.
4. Right-click the *Budget Cost* resource and then select the *Information* item on the shortcut menu.

5. On the *General* page of the *Resource Information* dialog, select the *Budget* checkbox on the right side of the dialog, as shown in Figure 6 - 22.

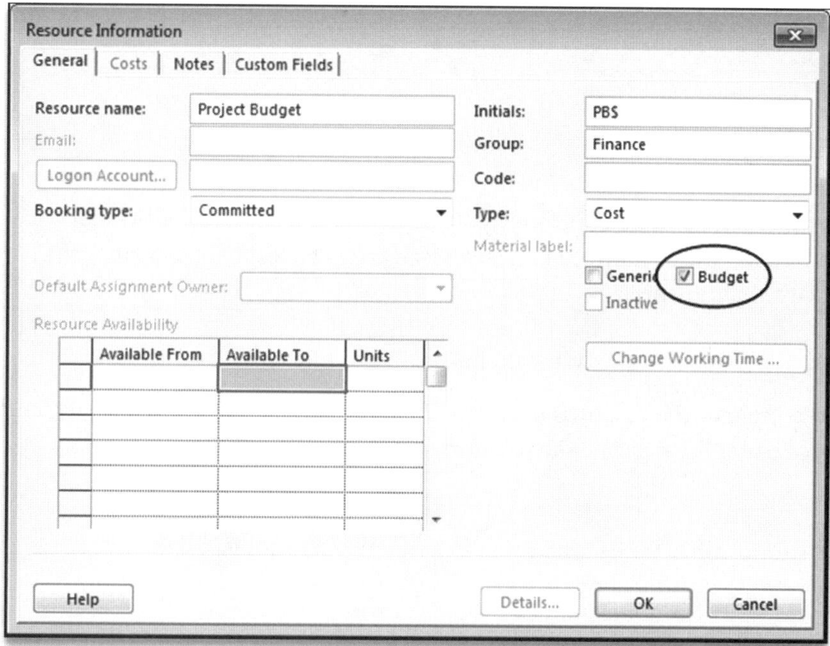

Figure 6 - 22: Create a Budget Cost resource

6. Click the *OK* button.

Creating an Expense Cost Resource

The steps needed to create an *Expense Cost* resource are nearly identical to those needed to create a *Budget Cost* resource. To create an *Expense Cost* resource, complete the following steps in the *Resource Sheet* view of your project:

1. Enter the name of the *Expense Cost* resource in the *Resource Name* column.
2. In the *Type* column for the *Cost* resource, click the pick list button and select the *Cost* item.
3. Enter additional information for the *Expense Cost* resource in the *Initials, Group, Accrue At,* and *Code* columns, as needed.

Figure 6 - 23 shows two *Cost* resources in my project. I created a *Budget Cost* resource named *Project Budget* and an *Expense Cost* resource named *Travel Expense.*

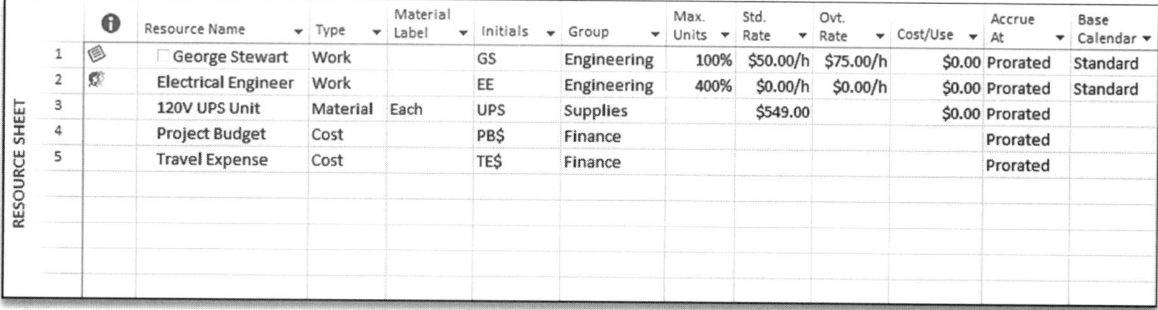

	Resource Name	Type	Material Label	Initials	Group	Max. Units	Std. Rate	Ovt. Rate	Cost/Use	Accrue At	Base Calendar
1	George Stewart	Work		GS	Engineering	100%	$50.00/h	$75.00/h	$0.00	Prorated	Standard
2	Electrical Engineer	Work		EE	Engineering	400%	$0.00/h	$0.00/h	$0.00	Prorated	Standard
3	120V UPS Unit	Material	Each	UPS	Supplies		$549.00		$0.00	Prorated	
4	Project Budget	Cost		PB$	Finance					Prorated	
5	Travel Expense	Cost		TE$	Finance					Prorated	

Figure 6 - 23: Two new Cost resources added to the project

Hands On Exercise

Exercise 6 - 6

In your Training Advisor Rollout project, you need to enter an overall budget for your project, and you need to track the amount of money spent on software licenses. Create a *Budget Cost* resource and an *Expense Cost* resource in your project.

1. Return to the **Training Advisor 06.mpp** sample file.
2. At the bottom of the resource list in the *Resource Sheet* view of the project, add a new *Budget Cost* resource using the basic resource information shown in Table 6 - 4.

Column	Value to Enter/Select
Resource Name	Project Budget
Type	Cost
Material Label	
Initials	PB$
Group	Finance
Max. Units	
Std. Rate	
Ovt. Rate	
Cost/Use	
Accrue At	Prorated
Base Calendar	
Code	999

Table 6 - 4: Create a Budget Cost resource

3. Right-click the *Project Budget* resource and then select the *Information* item on the shortcut menu.
4. On the *General* page of the *Resource Information* dialog, select the *Budget* checkbox on the right side of the dialog.
5. Click the *OK* button.

6. At the bottom of the resource list in the *Resource Sheet* view of the project, add a second *Cost* resource using the basic resource information shown in Table 6 - 5.

Column	Value to Enter/Select
Resource Name	Software Licenses
Type	Cost
Material Label	
Initials	SL$
Group	Finance
Max. Units	
Std. Rate	
Ovt. Rate	
Cost/Use	
Accrue At	Prorated
Base Calendar	
Code	999

Table 6 - 5: Create an Expense Cost resource

7. Save but do not close the **Training Advisor 06.mpp** sample file.

Sorting Resources in the Resource Sheet View

After you create the resources needed for your project team, you may want to sort the resources in either a default or custom order. To sort the resources in the *Resource Sheet* view, complete the following steps:

1. Click the *View* tab to display the *View* ribbon.

2. In the *Data* section of the *View* ribbon, click the *Sort* pick list.

3. To apply a default sort, select the *by Cost, by Name,* or *by ID* item on the *Sort* pick list. To apply a custom sort, select the *Sort By* item. Project 2013 displays the *Sort* dialog shown in Figure 6 - 24.

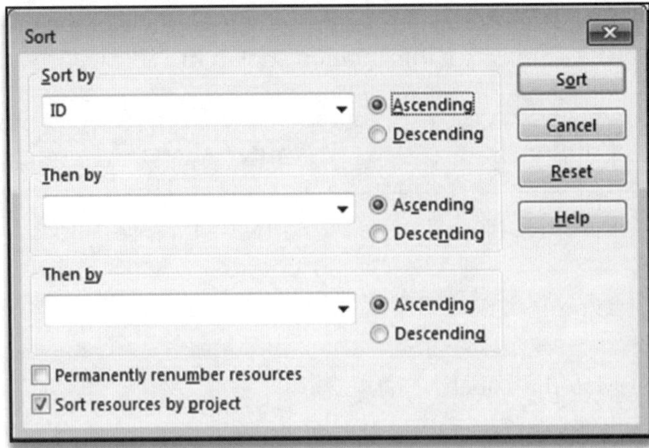

Figure 6 - 24: Sort dialog

4. Select the fields upon which you want to sort using the *Sort by* pick list and the two *Then by* pick lists.
5. Select either the *Ascending* or *Descending* option for the *Sort by* pick list and the two *Then by* pick lists.
6. Select the *Permanently renumber resources* option.
7. Leave the *Sort resources by project* option selected .
8. Click the *Sort* button to sort the resources according to the sorting criteria you specify in the *Sort* dialog.

Hands On Exercise

Exercise 6 - 7

Sort the resources in your project team for the Training Advisor Rollout project. Apply a three-level sorting by the resource *Type* value, then by the *Group* value, and finally by the *Resource Name* value.

1. Return to the **Training Advisor 06.mpp** sample file.
2. Click the *View* tab to display the *View* ribbon.
3. In the *Data* section of the *View* ribbon, click the *Sort* pick list and select the *Sort By* item.
4. In the *Sort* dialog, click the *Sort by* pick list and select the *Type* field.
5. Select the *Descending* option for the *Sort by* pick list.
6. Click the top *Then by* pick list and select the *Group* field.
7. Leave the *Ascending* option selected for the top *Then by* pick list.
8. Click the bottom *Then by* pick list and select the *Name* field.

Notice that the real name of the *Resource Name* column is actually the *Name* column. Microsoft applies the title *Resource Name* to the column for ease of use.

9. Leave the *Ascending* option selected for the bottom *Then by* pick list.
10. Select the *Permanently renumber resources* and *Sort resources by project* options, if not already selected.
11. Click the *Sort* button to sort the resources using this custom sorting order.
12. Study the unusual sorting order for the resources shown in the *Resource Sheet* view of your project.
13. Click the *Task* tab to display the *Task* ribbon.
14. In the *View* section of the *Task* ribbon, click the *Gantt Chart* pick list button, and select the *Gantt Chart* view.
15. Save and close the **Training Advisor 06.mpp** sample file.

Inserting New Resources in the Resource Sheet View

Project 2013 allows you to insert new resources in any resource view using the *Add Resources* pick list button in the *Resource* ribbon. To insert a new resource in your project using this feature, complete the following steps in the *Resource Sheet* view:

1. Click the *Resource* tab to display the *Resource* ribbon.
2. In the *View* section of the *Resource* ribbon, click the *View* pick list button and select the *Resource Sheet* view.
3. In the *Insert* section of the *Resource* ribbon, click the *Add Resources* pick list button shown in Figure 6 - 25.

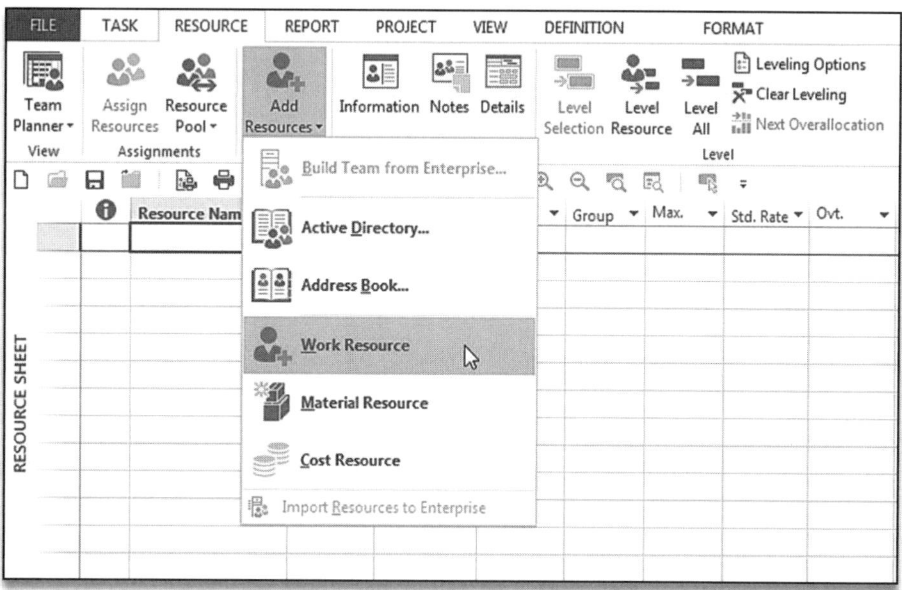

Figure 6 - 25: Add Resources pick list

4. On the *Add Resources* pick list, select the *Work Resource, Material Resource,* or *Cost Resource* item. Project 2013 inserts a new resource based on the type you selected. Notice in Figure 6 - 26 that I created one new resource of each type (*Work, Material,* and *Cost*).

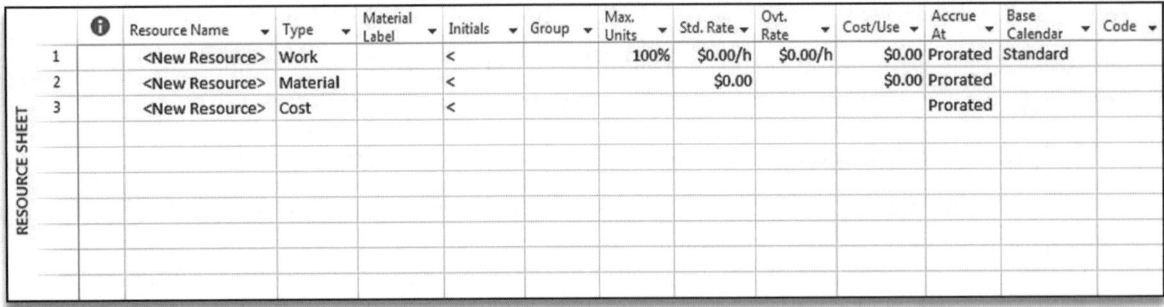

		Resource Name	Type	Material Label	Initials	Group	Max. Units	Std. Rate	Ovt. Rate	Cost/Use	Accrue At	Base Calendar	Code
1		<New Resource>	Work		<		100%	$0.00/h	$0.00/h	$0.00	Prorated	Standard	
2		<New Resource>	Material		<			$0.00		$0.00	Prorated		
3		<New Resource>	Cost		<						Prorated		

Figure 6 - 26: Work, Cost, and Material resources inserted in a project

When you insert a new resource using the *Add Resources* pick list, Project 2013 creates the new resource by inserting *<New Resource>* in the *Resource Name* column, inserting the < symbol in the *Initials* column, and selecting the *Prorated* value in the *Accrue At* column for all three types of resources. For a *Work* resource, the software also selects the *Work* value in the *Type* column, defaults the *Max. Units* value to *100%*, enters *$0.00/hr* in the *Std. Rate* and *Ovt. Rate* columns, enters *$0.00* in the *Cost/Use* column, and selects the *Standard* calendar in the *Base Calendar* column. For a *Material* resource, the software selects the *Material* value in the *Type* column and enters *$0.00* in the *Std. Rate* and *Cost/Use* columns. For a *Cost* resource, the software selects the *Cost* value in the *Type* column. After you insert any of the three types of resources, you must rename the resource and provide any other basic and custom resource information you want to use for the selected resource.

Information: When you insert a new *Cost* resource, the software creates an *Expense Cost* resource automatically. If you need to create a new *Cost* resource as a *Budget Cost* resource, right-click the *Cost* resource and select the *Information* item on the shortcut menu. On the *General* page of the *Resource Information* dialog, select the *Budget* option, and then click the *OK* button.

Setting Up and Using Lync Integration

In order to use the new Lync integration feature with Project 2013, your organization must use the Lync software. In addition, you must meet the following requirements:

- You must enter the name of each team member in the *Resource Name* column in the *Resource Sheet* view of your project.
- You must enter the e-mail address of each team member in the *Email* field found on the *General* page of the *Resource Information* dialog for the resource.
- You must install the Lync client software on the computer running Project 2013 and you must have the Lync client software application running.

You use the new Lync integration to foster communication between you and your team members. Lync integration is available in most resource views in Project 2013, in any task view that displays resources, such as the *Gantt Chart* view with the *Entry* table applied, and even in the *Assign Resources* dialog. You can also use Lync integration in any SharePoint page that displays the names of team members.

To use the new Lync integration feature, float your mouse pointer over the name of any team member in either Project 2013 or in SharePoint. The software displays a Lync floating dialog that allows you to use the software to communicate with the team member. For example, Figure 6 - 27 shows the Lync floating dialog for a resource named Marlene Roth, accessed by floating my mouse pointer over her name in the *Resource Sheet* view.

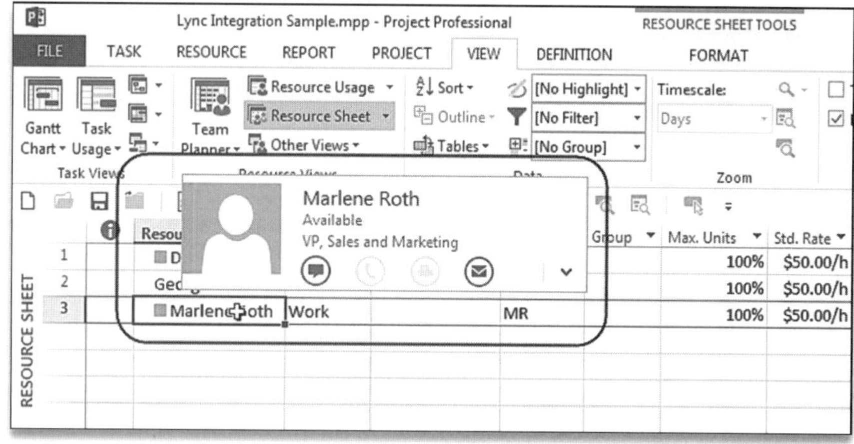

Figure 6 - 27: Lync floating dialog in the Resource Sheet view

When you double-click the name of any Lync-enabled resource in the *Resource Sheet* view of your project, Project 2013 displays the Lync contact card dialog shown in Figure 6 - 28. The Lync contact card dialog displays the name of the resource, their current status according to their Outlook calendar, and their job title. Use the hyperlinks in the contact card dialog to contact the resource by sending an instant message through Lync or by sending an e-mail message through Outlook. By the way, Project 2013 displays the Lync contact card dialog when you double-click the name of a Lync-enabled resource in any view or dialog, including task views such as the *Gantt Chart* view.

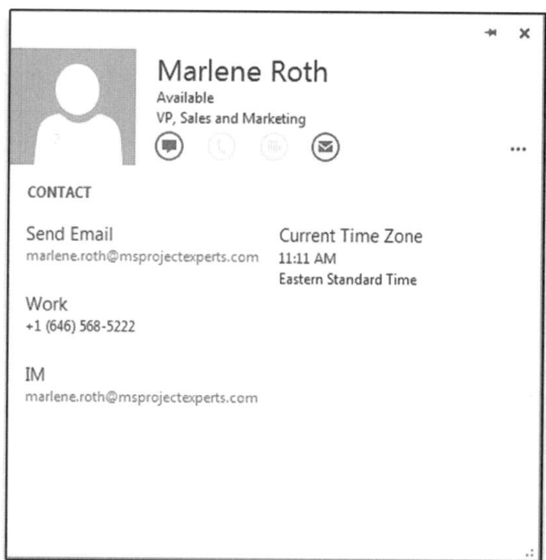

Figure 6 - 28: Lync contact card for a resource

Figure 6 - 29 shows the Lync floating dialog for Marlene Roth, accessed by floating my mouse pointer over her name in the *Resource Names* column of the *Gantt Chart* view. At the bottom of this floating dialog, click one of the four buttons to use the Lync application to send the user an instant message, to call the user, to start a video call with the user, or send an e-mail message to the user. You can also open the Lync contact card for the user, shown previously in Figure 6 - 28, by clicking the down arrow button (**v**) in the lower right corner of the floating dialog.

Figure 6 - 29: Lync floating dialog in the Gantt Chart view

If you click the first button to send an instant message, for example, Project 2013 displays the Lync instant message dialog. Use the dialog to hold an instant message conversation with the user, such as the conversation with Marlene Roth shown in Figure 6 - 30.

Figure 6 - 30: Lync instant message dialog

Module 07

Project Assignment Planning

Learning Objectives

After completing this module, you will be able to:

- Understand work estimation techniques
- Assign resources to tasks using the Task Entry view and the Assign Resources dialog
- Understand and use Task Types
- Change the Cost Rate Table for an assignment
- Use Effort-Driven scheduling to shorten task duration
- Assign a Material resource to tasks
- Assign Budget Cost and Expense Cost resources to tasks
- Use filtering and graphing in the Assign Resources dialog
- Use the Team Planner view to analyze resource allocation
- Locate and level resource overallocations in Resource views and in Task views
- Understand how Manually Scheduled tasks interact with resource assignments

Inside Module 07

Understanding Assignments

After you complete task planning and resource planning, you are ready to do assignment planning. When you assign a resource to a task, Project 2013 creates an assignment in the Project 2013 data model, as shown in Figure 7 - 1. A good way to think of an assignment is "who does what, when, and how much on a task." When thinking about assignments, keep in mind that there may be many assignments related to one task. Each resource you assign to a task creates a new assignment.

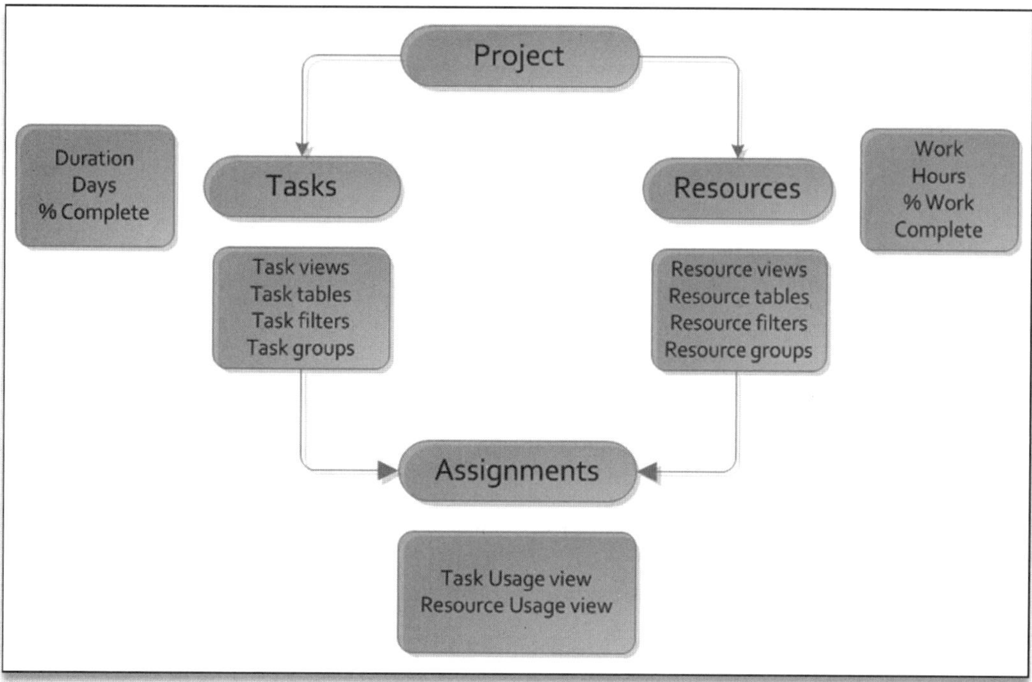

Figure 7 - 1: Complete Project 2013 Data Model

Using a Work Estimation Methodology

In addition to the duration-based planning you performed in Module 05, *Project Task Planning,* you may also need to estimate work or effort prior to assigning resources to tasks. Determining a reasonable work estimate for a task assignment can be challenging, especially if the task is a new type never performed by any resource in your organization.

Some companies use specific rules or methodologies for work estimating. I describe these methodologies as the "4 and 40" rule or the "8 and 80" rule. In the "4 and 40" rule, for example, no resource may perform less than 4 hours of work on any task, nor perform more than 40 hours of work. If a task requires less than 4 hours of work, you should merge the task with another task. If a task requires more than 40 hours of work, then you should split the task into one or more tasks that require 40 hours of work or less. The "8 and 80" rule follows the same type of restrictions: no less than 8 hours of work for a resource on a task, and no more than 80 hours of work.

Assigning Resources Using a Best Practice

The Project Management Institute (PMI) recommends that you involve resources in the estimating process by asking them to provide work estimates on their task assignments. This is a best practice for the following reasons:

- Based on their skills, knowledge, and experience, your resources' work estimates are more accurate than "pulling a number out of thin air."
- Getting work estimates from your resources gives you their "buy in" and gives them a sense of ownership in the project.
- It is easier to hold a resource to a work estimate if the resource actually provided the estimate.
- Resources are more likely to give you accurate progress reports on tasks for which they provided the work estimates.
- If it is not possible to involve the resources in the estimating process, get the work estimates from Subject Matter Experts (SME), such as team leaders, and then allow the resources to approve the estimates.

Assigning Resources to Tasks

After you enter project team members in the *Resource Sheet* view of your project, you are ready to assign team members to tasks. Like all previous versions of the tool, Project 2013 offers two powerful tools for assigning resources to tasks, which are:

- *Task Entry* view
- *Assign Resources* dialog

In addition to the *Task Entry* view and the *Assign Resources* dialog for assigning resources, Project 2013 also includes a *Team Planner* view that you can use to analyze resource assignments. In the remainder of this module, I present an in-depth treatment of how to use each of these tools for assignment planning and analysis, along with additional information on how to level resource overallocations.

Warning: During the resource assignment process, **do not** assign resources to summary tasks, as this greatly increases the work hours and costs for your project. Instead, if you need to show a resource as the responsible person for a summary section of the project, use the built-in *Contact* field, create a custom field and name it *Responsible Person*, or assign the resource to the milestone for the summary section of that project.

Using the Task Entry View

The *Task Entry* view is the most powerful way to assign resources to tasks because it gives you total control over all of the elements in the Project 2013 scheduling engine. Using the *Task Entry* view, you can do all of the following in a single location:

- Assign multiple resources simultaneously, and specify different *Units* and *Work* values for each resource.
- Enter the *Duration* value of the task.
- Set the *Task Type* for the task to determine whether the software fixes or "locks" the *Units, Work,* or *Duration* value for the task.
- Specify the *Effort Driven* status of the task to determine what happens when you add or remove resources on the task.
- Set the *Task Mode* for the task as either *Manually Scheduled* or *Auto Scheduled.*

Information: The only disadvantage of using the *Task Entry* view is that you cannot assign resources to multiple tasks simultaneously. This means that you cannot use the *Task Entry* view to assign resources to a recurring task, for example.

To apply the *Task Entry* view, complete the following steps:

1. In the *View* section of the *Task* ribbon, click the *Gantt Chart* pick list button and select the *Gantt Chart* view (if you do not have the *Gantt Chart* view displayed already).

2. Click the *View* tab to display the *View* ribbon.

3. In the *Split View* section of the *View* ribbon, select the *Details* checkbox. Project 2013 displays the *Task Entry* view, shown in Figure 7 - 2.

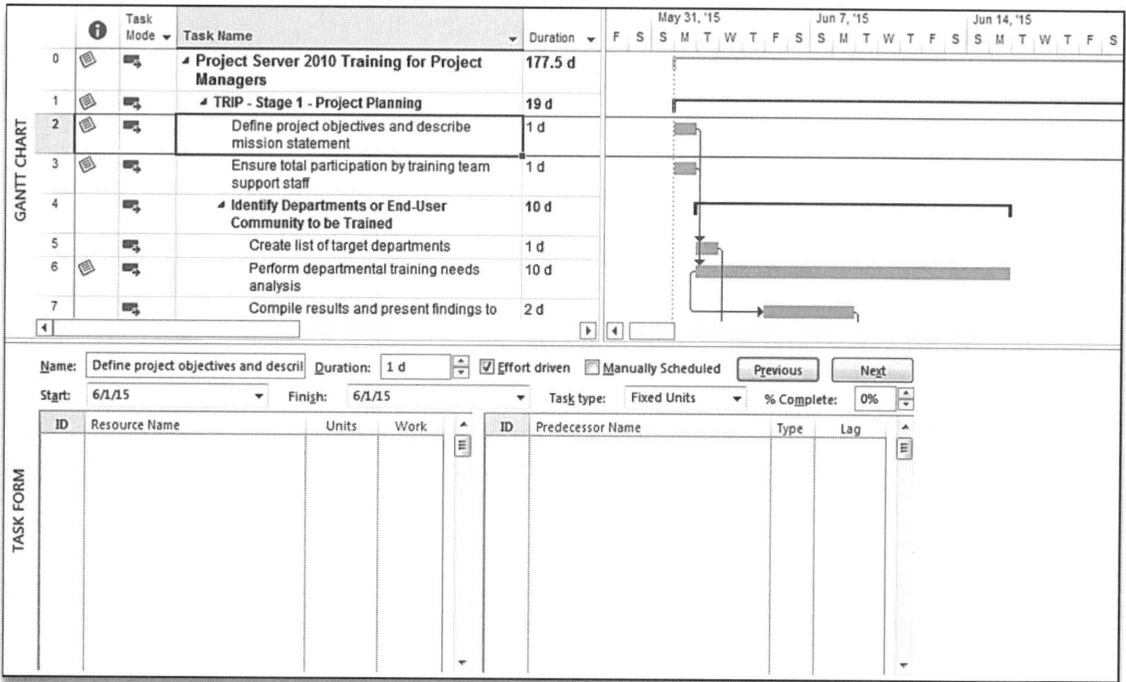

Figure 7 - 2: Task Entry view

Information: Another way to display the *Task Entry* view is to right-click anywhere in the Gantt chart and to select the *Show Split* item on the shortcut menu. To close the *Task Form* pane and return to the *Gantt Chart* view, right-click anywhere in the Gantt chart and deselect the *Show Split* item on the shortcut menu.

The *Task Entry* view is a combination view consisting of two other views, each displayed in a separate pane. The *Task Entry* view includes the *Gantt Chart* view in the top pane and the *Task Form* view in the bottom pane. To assign a resource to a task using the *Task Entry* view, take the following steps:

1. Select a single task in the *Gantt Chart* pane.

2. In the *Task Form* pane, select the first blank cell in the *Resource Name* column and then click the pick list button in that cell. The software displays the list of resources you added to the *Resource Sheet* view, displayed alphabetically, as shown in Figure 7 - 3.

3. In the pick list of team members shown in the *Resource Name* column, select a resource.

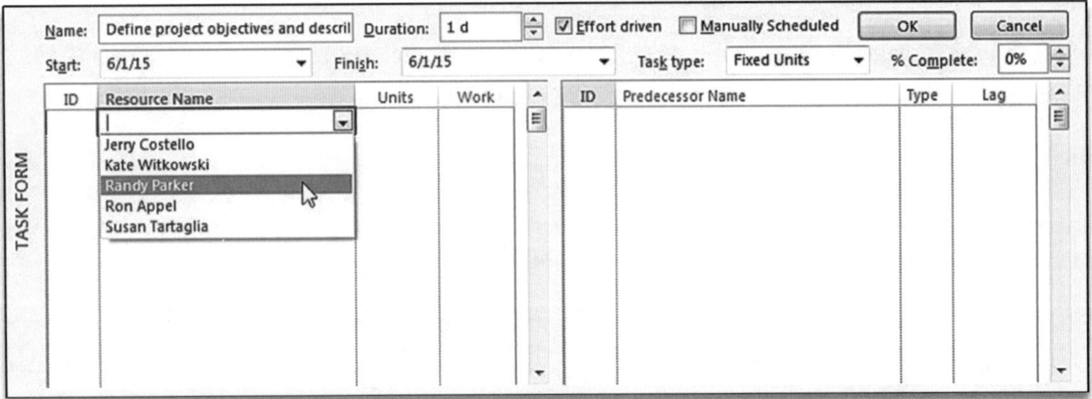

Figure 7 - 3: Task Entry view, select a resource

4. Click the first blank cell in the *Units* column and then select or enter a *Units* value for the selected resource.

Information: In the *Units* column, you can use the spin control feature to select a value, but Project 2013 displays only *Units* values in 50% increments (0%, 50%, 100%, etc.). You cannot use the spin control to select *Units* values such as 25% or 75%; instead, you must manually type the *Units* value you need.

5. Click in the first blank cell in the *Work* column and enter the estimated work hours for the resource.

6. Repeat steps #2-4 for each additional resource you want to assign to the task.

7. Click the *OK* button.

Warning: Do not click the *OK* button in the *Task Form* pane until you finish selecting all of the resources you want to assign, and you finish setting both the *Units* and *Work* values for each resource.

Project 2013 assigns the resource to the task and then calculates the *Duration* value based on the *Units* and *Work* values you enter. Notice in Figure 7 - 4 that I assigned a resource named *Randy Parker* to the task at a *Units* value of *50%* and *16* hours of work. Based on these two numbers, the software calculated a *Duration* value of *4 days* for the task.

Notice also in Figure 7 - 4 that the software changed the *OK* and *Cancel* buttons to the *Previous* and *Next* buttons. Using the *Previous* and *Next* buttons, you can navigate easily from task to task during the assignment process.

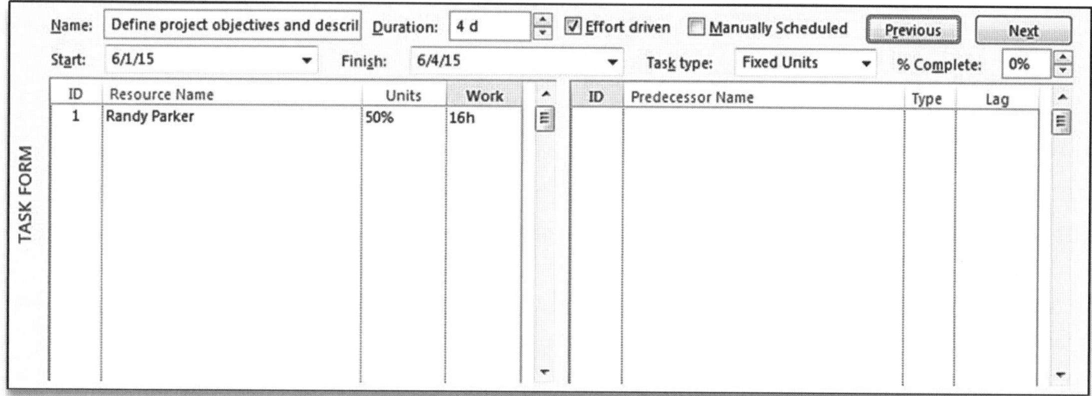

Figure 7 - 4: Task Entry view, Duration calculated after assigning a resource with Units and Work

8. Click the *Next* button to select the next task in the project and to continue assigning resources to tasks.

To assign resources to a task for which you already entered an estimated *Duration* value previously, complete the following steps:

1. In the *Gantt Chart* pane, select the task with the estimated *Duration* value.
2. In the *Task Form* pane, select the name of a resource from the list in the *Resource Name* column.
3. Enter a *Units* value for the resource in the *Units* column.
4. **Do not** enter a *Work* value.
5. Repeat steps #2-4 for each additional resource you want to assign to the task.
6. Click the *OK* button.

Project 2013 calculates the *Work* value for each resource assigned to the task. Notice in Figure 7 - 5 that I assigned three resources to work full-time on the task with a *Duration* value of *10 days,* so the software calculated *80 hours* in the *Work* column for each resource.

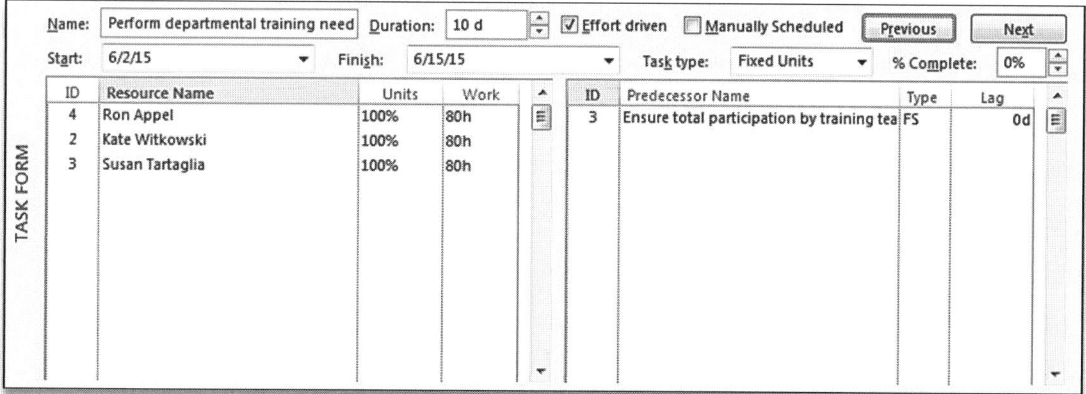

Figure 7 - 5: Task Entry view, Work calculated after assigning resources with Units and Duration

Hands On Exercise

Exercise 7 - 1

The assignment process is already under way in the Training Advisor Rollout project, with resources assigned to all tasks in the *Installation* phase of the project. Apply the *Task Entry* view and then assign resources to the remaining tasks in the project.

1. Open the **Training Advisor 07.mpp** sample file.
2. Click the *View* tab to display the *View* ribbon.
3. In the *Split View* section of the *View* ribbon, select the *Details* checkbox to apply the *Task Entry* view.

Testing phase: Several members of the *NetOps* team have very limited availability to work in the Training Advisor Rollout project, but provided work estimates for the tasks they must perform in this project. Assign resources to tasks in the *Testing* phase of the project.

4. In the *Gantt Chart* pane, select task ID #23, the *Install Training Advisor Clients* task.
5. Right-click anywhere in the *Task Form* pane and select the *Resources & Predecessors* item on the shortcut menu, if necessary.
6. In the *Task Form* pane, click the pick list on the first blank line of the *Resource Name* column and select *Dave Harbaugh* from the list of project team members.
7. Set the *Units* value to *50%*, enter a *Work* value of *48 hours*, and then click the *OK* button to complete the assignment.
8. In the *Task Form*, click the *Next* button to select task ID #24, the *Verify Connectivity* task.
9. Assign *Mike Andrews* to the *Verify Connectivity* task at *50%* units and *40 hours* of work, and then click the *OK* button.
10. Click the *Next* button to select task ID #25, the *Resolve Connectivity Errors* task.
11. Assign *Bob Jared* to the *Resolve Connectivity Errors* task at *25%* units and *40 hours* of work, and then click the *OK* button.

For the last three tasks, notice how Project 2013 calculated a *Duration* value for the task based on the values you entered in the *Units* and *Work* columns for the assignment.

12. In the *Gantt Chart* pane, select task ID #34, the *Conduct Skills Assessment* task.
13. Assign *Chuck Kirkpatrick* and *Kent Bergstrand* to the *Conduct Skills Assessment* task at *50%* units each and *40 hours* of work each, and then click the *OK* button.
14. Click the *Next* button to task ID #35, the *Create Training Schedule* task.

15. Assign *Kent Bergstrand* to the *Create Training Schedule* task at *25%* units and then click the *OK* button (**do not** enter a value in the *Work* column).

Since you previously estimated the *Duration* value of *5 days* for this task during the task planning process, notice how Project 2013 calculates a *10 hour* value in the *Work* field automatically.

16. In the *Split View* section of the *View* ribbon, **deselect** the *Details* checkbox to close the *Task Form* pane.
17. Press **Control + Home** on your computer keyboard to scroll back to the top of the task list.
18. Save but **do not** close the **Training Advisor 07.mpp** sample file.

Using the Assign Resources Dialog

The *Assign Resources* dialog is a second tool you can use in the assignment process. The *Assign Resources* dialog is ideal for assigning resources to recurring tasks, such as meetings, because it allows you to select and assign multiple resources to the recurring task. The *Assign Resources* dialog is also ideal for assigning one or more resources to multiple tasks simultaneously, and for replacing one resource with another on multiple tasks simultaneously. Although the *Assign Resources* dialog offers you a simple interface to assign resources to tasks quickly, keep in mind that it does not have all of the options available in the *Task Entry* view.

Using the *Assign Resources* dialog, you have no control over most of the attributes of the scheduling engine. This means you cannot specify the *Duration*, the *Work*, the *Task Type*, the *Effort Driven* status, or the *Task Mode* for a task. Furthermore, you cannot assign multiple resources to a task and individually select different *Units* values for each resource. To display the *Assign Resources* dialog, use one of the following methods:

- In the *Assignments* section of the *Resource* ribbon, click the *Assign Resources* button.
- Right-click any task and then select the *Assign Resources* item on the shortcut menu.

Project 2013 displays the *Assign Resources* dialog with your project team members sorted alphabetically, as shown in Figure 7 - 6.

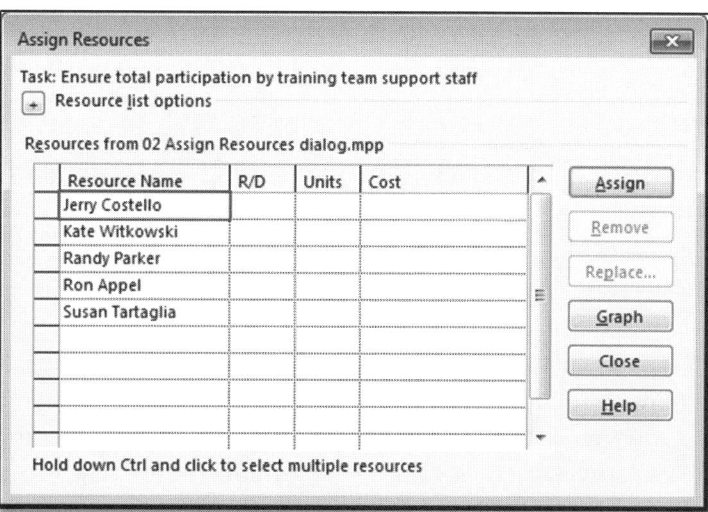

Figure 7 - 6: Assign Resources dialog

To assign a resource to tasks using the *Assign Resources* dialog, complete the following steps:

1. Select one or more tasks.
2. Select a single resource in the list of resources shown in the dialog.
3. Select or enter a *Units* value.
4. Click the *Assign* button.

The *Assign Resources* dialog indicates that you assigned the resource to the selected tasks by moving the assigned resource to the beginning of the list, and by adding a checkmark indicator to the left of the resource's name. Notice in Figure 7 - 7 that I assigned *Jerry Costello* to work full time (*100%* units) on the selected task. If you previously entered cost rates for your resources in the *Std. Rate* column of the *Resource Sheet* view, Project 2013 also calculates a cost value in the *Cost* column of the *Assign Resources* dialog for each assigned resource. Notice in Figure 7 - 7 that Jerry Costello's assignment on the selected task costs the project *$400,* as indicated in the *Cost* column.

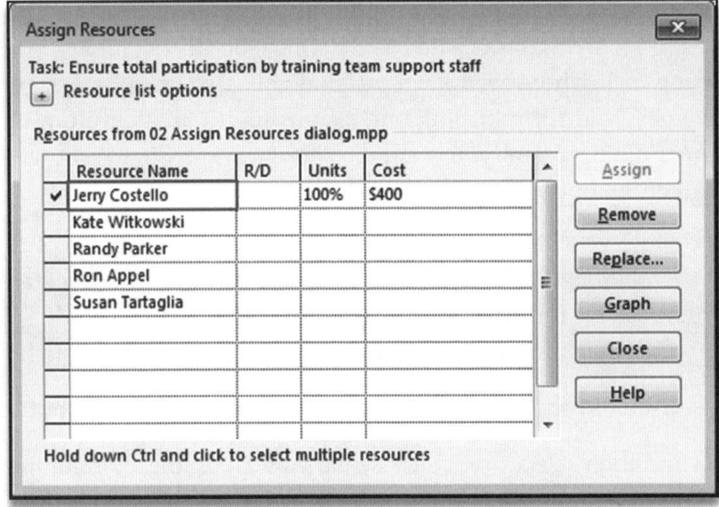

Figure 7 - 7: Assign Resources dialog with one resource assigned to a task

To assign multiple resources to tasks using the *Assign Resources* dialog, complete the following steps:

1. Select one or more tasks.
2. In the *Assign Resources* dialog, select multiple resources using either the **Control** key or the **Shift** key on your computer keyboard.
3. **Do not** set a *Units* value for any resource.
4. Click the *Assign* button.

If you do not enter a *Units* value when assigning a resource in the *Assign Resources* dialog, Project 2013 enters the *Max. Units* value for the resource from the *Resource Sheet* view of your project. This means that if the *Max. Units* value for a resource is *50%*, and you do not supply a *Units* value when assigning this resource, the *Assign Resources* dialog assigns the resource with a *Units* value of *50%* automatically. The exception to this rule is for resources that have a *Max. Units* value greater than 100%, such as generic resources. In this case, if you do not supply a *Units* value for the generic resource, the *Assign Resources* dialog assigns this generic resource with a *Units* value of only *100%* automatically.

Warning: **Do not** use the *Assign Resources* dialog to assign multiple resources to a task that requires using a different *Units* value for each resource. The software assigns the first resource at the *Units* value you select and then adds each of the other resources as **helpers** on the task using *Effort Driven* scheduling, decreasing the duration of the task accordingly. This behavior is one of the major reasons that new users find Project 2013 so frustrating! Instead, use the *Task Entry* view when you need to assign multiple resources with different *Units* values.

Hands On Exercise

Exercise 7 - 2

Assign resources to tasks in the Training Advisor Rollout project using the *Assign Resources* dialog.

1. Return to the **Training Advisor 07.mpp** sample file.
2. Click the *Resource* tab to display the *Resource* ribbon.
3. In the *Assignments* section of the *Resource* ribbon, click the *Assign Resources* button.
4. Select task ID #1, the *Project Status Meeting* recurring task.
5. In the *Assign Resources* dialog, use the **Control** key on your computer keyboard to select the following resources as a group:

   Audrey Kehrli – Test team leader

   Carolyn Fross – administrative assistant

   Helen Howard – NetOps team leader

   Melena Keeth – TechEd team leader

   Richard Sanders – project manager

6. Click the *Assign* button to assign these five resources to the *Project Status Meeting* recurring task.

Notice how Project 2013 assigned these five resources at a *Units* value of *100%* since you did not supply a *Units* value for any of them in the *Assign Resources* dialog.

7. Click the *expand* symbol (the white arrowhead sign) to the left of the *Project Status Meeting* recurring task to expand the occurrences of this recurring task.

Notice in the Gantt chart that although you **do not** see the resources assigned to the *Project Status Meeting* recurring task itself, you **do see** the resources assigned to each of the individual occurrences of the recurring task.

8. Click the *collapse* symbol (the triangle symbol) to the left of the *Project Status Meeting* recurring task to collapse the occurrences of this recurring task.

9. Select task IDs #30-32, from the *Create Training Module 01* task to the *Create Training Module 03* task.

10. In the *Assign Resources* dialog, select the *Training Developer* resource, enter a *Units* value of *100%*, and click the *Assign* button.

After completing the training materials and setting the training schedule, the company plans to offer three sets of concurrent training classes at three different locations on the corporate campus.

11. Select task ID #36, the *Provide End User Training* task.

12. In the *Assign Resources* dialog, use the **Control** key on your computer keyboard to select the following resources as a group:

    Chuck Kirkpatrick

    Kent Bergstrand

    Ruth Andrews

13. Click the *Assign* button to assign these three resources to the *Provide End User Training* task.

14. Click the *Close* button to close the *Assign Resources* dialog.

15. Save but **do not** close the **Training Advisor 07.mpp** sample file.

Understanding the Duration Equation

When you assign a resource to a task using the *Task Entry* view, and you enter a *Units* value and a *Work* value for the resource, Project 2013 calculates the *Duration* value for the task automatically. How does the software calculate duration? The software uses a simple formula known as the **Duration Equation**, written as follows:

Duration = **W**ork ÷ (**H**ours **P**er **D**ay × **U**nits)

or

D = W ÷ (HPD × U)

The default *Hours Per Day* value is 8 hours per day. You can locate this value by clicking the *File* tab and then clicking the *Options* item in the *Backstage*. In the *Project Options* dialog, click the *Schedule* tab. You find the *Hours per day* option in the *Calendar options for this project* section, as shown in Figure 7 - 8.

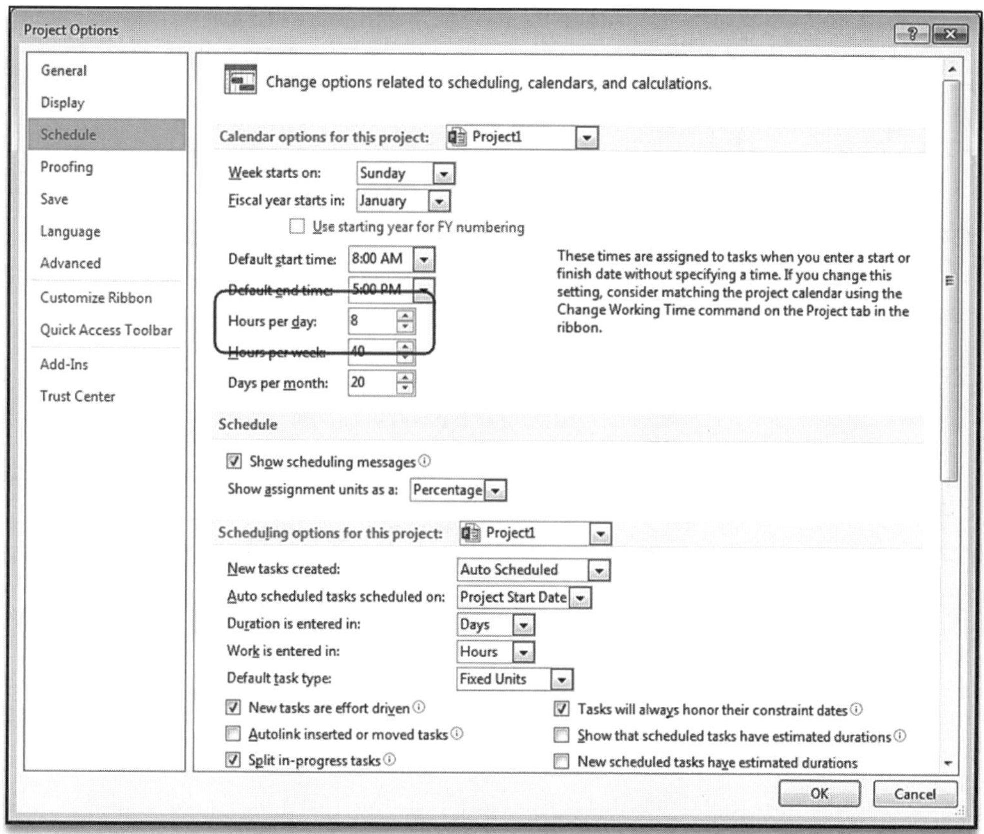

Figure 7 - 8: Project Options dialog, Schedule tab shows the Hours per day setting

To demonstrate how the Duration Equation works, I assign a resource to a task at *50% Units* and *40 hours* of work. Using the Duration Equation, Project 2013 calculates the *Duration* value at *10 days* as follows:

$$D = W \div (HPD \times U)$$

$$D = 40 \div (8 \times 50\%)$$

$$D = 40 \div 4 = 10 \text{ days}$$

When you assign a resource to a task and enter *Duration* and *Units* values (rather than *Units* and *Work* values), Project 2013 calculates the *Work* value. How does the software calculate work? The software uses a modified version of the Duration Equation, rewritten to solve for the *Work* variable as follows:

Work = **D**uration × **H**ours **P**er **D**ay × **U**nits

or

$$W = D \times HPD \times U$$

For example, I assign a resource to work *50% Units* on a task with a *Duration* value of *10 days*, Project 2013 calculates *40 hours* of work as follows:

$$W = D \times HPD \times U$$

$$W = 10 \times 8 \times 50\%$$

$$W = 10 \times 4 = 40 \text{ hours}$$

You can also rewrite the Duration Equation to solve for the *Units* variable as follows:

Units = **Work** ÷ (**Duration** × **Hours Per Day**)

or

$$U = W \div (D \times HPD)$$

For example, I assign a resource *40 hours* of work on a task with a *Duration* value of *10 days*, Project 2013 calculates a *Units* value of 50% as follows:

$$U = W \div (D \times HPD)$$

$$U = 40 \div (10 \times 8)$$

$$U = 40 \div 80 = .5 \text{ or } 50\%$$

Understanding Task Types

You can specify the *Task Type* setting for any task to one of three types: *Fixed Units, Fixed Work,* or *Fixed Duration.* You can select **only one** *Task Type* setting for each task. The default *Task Type* setting for every task is *Fixed Units,* unless you specify otherwise in the *Project Options* dialog. To specify the *Task Type* setting for any task, select the task and then use one of the following methods:

- Apply the *Task Entry* view. In the *Task Form,* click the *Task Type* pick list and select the desired *Task Type* setting.
- Double-click the task and then click the *Advanced* tab in the *Task Information* dialog. Click the *Task Type* pick list and select the desired *Task Type* setting.
- In the *Properties* section of the *Task* ribbon, click the *Information* button, and then click the *Advanced* tab in the *Task Information* dialog. Click the *Task Type* pick list and select the desired *Task Type* setting.
- Right-click the task and then select the *Information* item on the shortcut menu. In the *Task Information* dialog, click the *Advanced* tab. Click the *Task Type* pick list and select the desired *Task Type* setting.

Information: You can also specify the *Task Type* setting for multiple tasks simultaneously by selecting a group of tasks first. In the *Properties* section of the *Task* ribbon, click the *Information* button and then click the *Advanced* tab in the *Multiple Task Information* dialog. Click the *Task Type* pick list and select the desired *Task Type* setting for the selected tasks.

Specify the *Task Type* setting for tasks using the following information as your guide:

- **Fixed Units** – Project 2013 locks the *Units* value for all resources assigned to a *Fixed Units* task. Use the *Fixed Units* setting when a resource has a known availability to perform work on tasks in your project. For example, you assign a resource to work on a task at a *Units* value of *50%* because the resource also works half time on the Help Desk. Use the *Fixed Units* task type on this task to guarantee that the software does not recalculate the *Units* value if you change either the *Work* or *Duration* values on the task.
- **Fixed Work** – the software locks the *Work* value for all resources assigned to a *Fixed Work* task. Use the *Fixed Work* setting when you are certain about the number of hours to complete a task. For example, you hire a consultant to work on a project task, and the work is set at 40 hours by contract. Use the *Fixed Work* task type on this task to guarantee that Project 2013 does not recalculate the *Work* value if you change either the *Units* or *Duration* values on the task.

- **Fixed Duration** – the software locks the *Duration* value on a *Fixed Duration* task. Use the *Fixed Duration* setting when you are certain of the *Duration* value for a task, such as when you have a known "window of opportunity" to complete the task. For example, you have a task called Shareholder Conference and the conference lasts 3 days. Use the *Fixed Duration* task type on this task to guarantee that the software does not recalculate the *Duration* value of *3 days* if you change either the *Units* or *Work* values on the task.

The *Task Type* setting you select fixes or "locks" one of the three variables in the Duration Equation for the selected task. When you change one of the two non-fixed variables, Project 2013 calculates the other non-fixed variable automatically. Table 7 - 1 shows the behavior of all three *Task Types* when you change the non-fixed variable, and when you change the fixed variable

Task Type	Fixed Variable	You Change	Recalculated Variable
Fixed Units	Units	Work	Duration
Fixed Units	Units	Duration	Work
Fixed Units	Units	Units	Duration
Fixed Work	Work	Units	Duration
Fixed Work	Work	Duration	Units
Fixed Work	Work	Work	Duration
Fixed Duration	Duration	Units	Work
Fixed Duration	Duration	Work	Units
Fixed Duration	Duration	Duration	Work

Table 7 - 1: Task Type behavior

The only exception to the *Task Type* behavior documented in Table 7 - 1 occurs when you initially assign a resource to a *Fixed Duration* task and enter a value in the *Work* field. In this situation, Project 2013 does the following:

- In the *Units* field in the *Task Form* pane, the software enters the *Max. Units* value for the resource from the *Resource Sheet* view of your project.
- In the background, the software calculates the correct *Units* value, but does not display it in the *Units* field in the *Task Form* pane. Instead, the software stores this value in the *Peak* field, which you cannot see in the *Task Form* pane.
- The software assigns the resource using the correctly calculated *Units* value stored in the *Peak* field.

If you want to see the values in the *Units* and *Peak* fields, you can add the *Assignment Units* field and the *Peak* field to the *Task Usage* view of your project. At this point, however, do not despair. I provide an in-depth discussion of the behavior of the *Assignment Units* and *Peak* fields in the next section of this module.

When you change a non-fixed variable for any task type Project 2013 automatically recalculates the other non-fixed variable. When you change the **fixed** variable, however, the software invokes one of the programming decisions implemented by the software development team many years ago. For example, which variable should the software recalculate when you change the *Units* value on a *Fixed Units* task, or you change the *Work* value on a *Fixed Work* task, or you change the *Duration* value on a *Fixed Duration* task? We refer to the decisions made by the software development team as the programming biases. These programming biases are as follows:

- If you change the *Units* variable on a *Fixed Units* task, Project 2013 **always** recalculates the *Duration* variable.
- If you change the *Work* variable on a *Fixed Work* task, Project 2013 **always** recalculates the *Duration* variable.
- If you change the *Duration* variable on a *Fixed Duration* task, Project 2013 **always** recalculates the *Work* variable.

As you can see, Project 2013 has a bias to calculate changes in *Duration* rather than to *Work* or *Units*. If the software cannot change *Duration*, it has a bias to calculate changes in *Work* rather than *Units*.

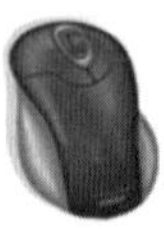

Hands On Exercise

Exercise 7 - 3

Learn more about *Task Types* by changing the variables in the Duration Equation for tasks with different *Task Types*.

1. Open the **Understanding Task Types 2013.mpp** sample file.
2. In the *Task Usage* pane, select the *Fixed Units 1* task.
3. Click the *Task* tab to display the *Task* ribbon, if necessary.
4. In the *Editing* section of the *Task* ribbon, click the *Scroll to Task* button to show the timephased *Work* hours in the timephased grid (right side of the view).
5. In the *Task Form* pane, change the *Work* value to *48h* and then click the *OK* button.
6. Click the *Next* button in the *Task Form* pane to select the *Fixed Units 2* task.
7. In the *Task Form* pane, change the *Duration* value to *8d* and then click the *OK* button.

For these *Fixed Units* tasks, notice that when you change the *Work* variable, Project 2013 recalculates the *Duration* variable, and when you change the *Duration* variable, the software recalculates the *Work* variable.

8. Click the *Next* button in the *Task Form* pane to select the *Fixed Units 3* task.
9. In the *Task Form* pane, change the *Units* value to *100%* and then click the *OK* button.

For this *Fixed Units* task, notice that when you change the *Units* variable, Project 2013 recalculates the *Duration* variable. This behavior is the first of three programming biases I discussed in the previous topical subsection.

10. Click the *Next* button in the *Task Form* pane to select the *Fixed Work 1* task.
11. In the *Task Form* pane, change the *Units* value to *100%* and then click the *OK* button.

For this *Fixed Work* task, notice that when you change the *Units* variable, Project 2013 recalculates the *Duration* variable.

12. Click the *Next* button in the *Task Form* pane to select the *Fixed Work 2* task.
13. In the *Task Form* pane, change the *Duration* value to *5d* and then click the *OK* button.

For this *Fixed Work* task, notice that when you change the *Duration* variable, Project 2013 **did not** recalculate the *Units* variable as expected. Or **did it** change the *Units* variable, but the software does not display the recalculated *Units* variable in the *Task Form* pane?

14. Drag the split bar to the right side of the *Peak* column.
15. Scroll down to view the assignment information for *Debbie Kirkpatrick* on the *Fixed Work 2* task, if necessary.

In the custom *_Assignment Units and Peak* table displayed in the *Task Usage* pane, notice that Project 2013 includes **two fields** related to the assignment units: the *Assignment Units* and *Peak* fields. The *Units* field you see in the *Task Form* pane is actually the *Assignment Units* field, which shows the **original** *Units* value on the task (*50%*). The *Peak* field contains the **new** *Units* value after you changed the *Duration* value on the *Fixed Work* task. Notice that the *Peak* field shows the **correct** *Units* value of *100%*. Notice also in the timephased grid on the right side of the view that the software schedules the *Work* hours correctly at 8 hours per day based on the *Units* value of *100%* in the *Peak* field. Therefore, even though the *Units* value does not seem to be correct in the *Task Form* pane (*50%*), the software **does schedule the task correctly** using the value shown in the *Peak* field (*100%*).

Warning: If you are a previous user of any prior version of Project 2013, you undoubtedly find the behavior of the *Units* field in the *Task Form* pane **confusing**, along with the interaction between the *Assignment Units* field and the *Peak* field. Because of this, I provide an in-depth treatment of the *Peak* field and the *Assignment Units* field in the next topical subsection of this module.

16. Click the *Next* button in the *Task Form* pane to select the *Fixed Work 3* task.
17. In the *Task Form* pane, change the *Work* value to *32h* and then click the *OK* button.

For this *Fixed Work* task, notice that when you change the *Work* variable, Project 2013 recalculates the *Duration* variable. This behavior is the second of three programming biases I discussed in the previous topical subsection.

18. Click the *Next* button in the *Task Form* pane to select the *Fixed Duration 1* task.
19. In the *Task Form* pane, change the *Units* value to *100%* and then click the *OK* button.

For this *Fixed Duration* task, notice that when you change the *Units* variable, Project 2013 recalculates the *Work* variable.

20. Click the *Next* button in the *Task Form* pane to select the *Fixed Duration 2* task.
21. In the *Task Form* pane, change the *Work* value to *60h* and then click the *OK* button.

For this *Fixed Duration* task, notice that when you change the *Work* variable, Project 2013 **did not** recalculate the *Units* variable. Once again, examine the *Task Usage* pane and notice that the *Peak* field contains the expected value of *75%*. Notice also in the timephased grid that the software schedules the *Work* hours correctly at 6 hours per day based on the *75%* value in the *Peak* field.

22. Click the *Next* button in the *Task Form* pane to select the *Fixed Duration 3* task.
23. In the *Task Form* pane, change the *Duration* value to *6d* and then click the *OK* button.

For this *Fixed Duration* task, notice that when you change the *Duration* variable, Project 2013 recalculates the *Work* variable. This behavior is the final of three programming biases I discussed in the previous topical subsection.

24. Click the *View* tab and then **deselect** the *Details* checkbox in the *Split View* section of the *View* ribbon.
25. Save but **do not** close the **Understanding Task Types 2013.mpp** sample file.

Understanding the Peak and Assignment Units Fields

To gain a thorough understanding of the behavior of the *Assignment Units* and *Peak* fields, it helps to understand how the software works when you initially assign a resource to a task. Suppose that I assign a resource named *Henry Baum* to the *Design* task at a *Units* value of *100%* and *40 hours* of *Work,* as shown in Figure 7 - 9. Notice that Project 2013 calculates a *Duration* value of *5 days* for this *Fixed Work* task.

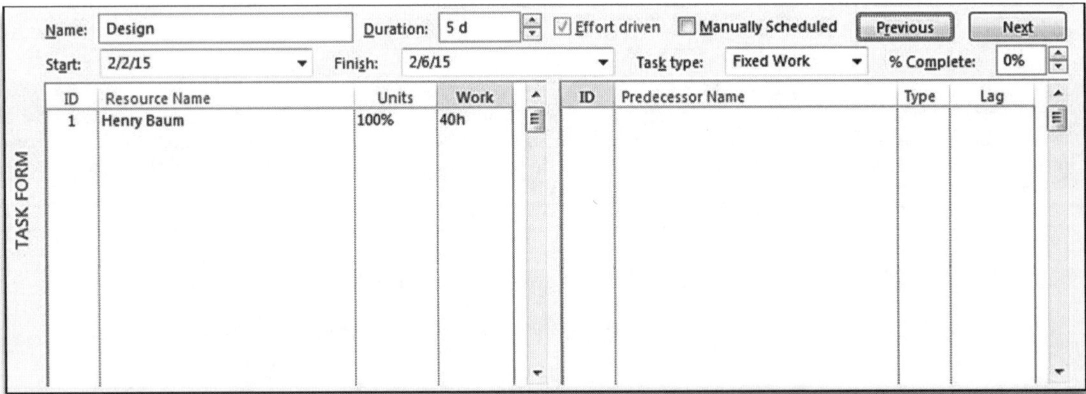

Figure 7 - 9: Resource assigned at 100% Units to the Design task

When I assign *Henry Baum* to the *Design* task, the software creates a resource assignment on the task and captures the original *Units* value of *100%*. You can see the resource assignment information in either the *Task Usage* view or *Resource Usage* view of a project. Figure 7 - 10 shows the initial assignment information in the *Task Usage* view for *Henry Baum's* resource assignment on the *Design* task. Notice that the software assigns the *40 hours* of *Work* using a flat pattern of 8 hours per day over the *Duration* of *5 days* for the task.

		Task Mode	Task Name	Work	Details	Feb 1, '15 S	M	T	W	T	F	S
TASK USAGE	0		**Understanding Units**	**40 h**	Work		8h	8h	8h	8h	8h	
	1		Design	40 h	Work		8h	8h	8h	8h	8h	
			Henry Baum	*40 h*	Work		8h	8h	8h	8h	8h	
					Work							
					Work							

Figure 7 - 10: Task Usage view shows the resource assignment information

Although not displayed by default in either the *Task Usage* view or *Resource Usage* view, Project 2013 offers several additional assignment fields you can use to understand how the software handles the original *Units* value on the resource assignment. These additional fields include:

- *Assignment Units* (an assignment field)
- *Peak* (an assignment field)
- *Percent Allocation* (a timephased assignment field)
- *Peak Units* (a timephased assignment field)

To add the *Assignment Units* field to either the *Task Usage* view or the *Resource Usage* view, right-click the *Work* column header. The software displays the shortcut menu shown in Figure 7 - 11.

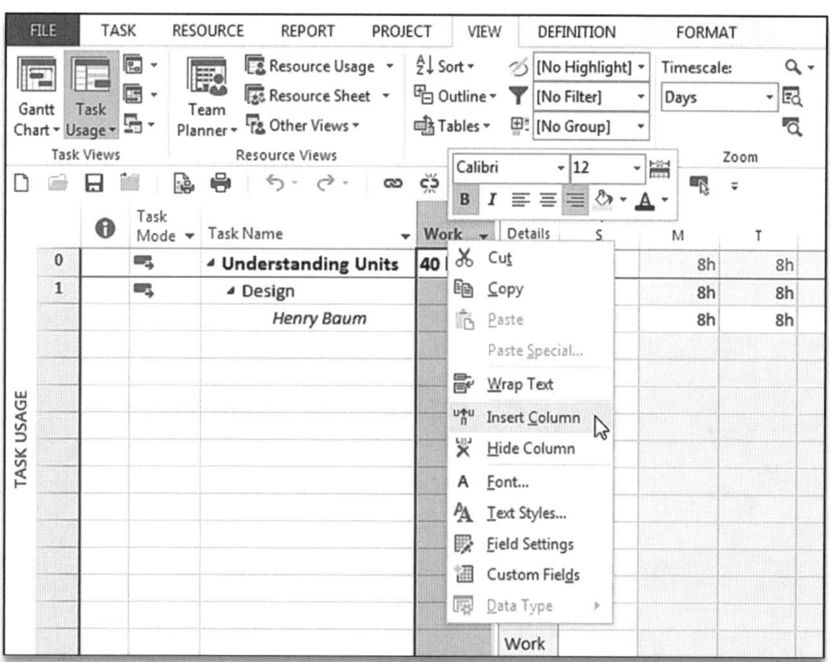

Figure 7 - 11: Shortcut menu to add a new field

Select the *Insert Column* item in the menu and then select the *Assignment Units* field from the lengthy pick list of available fields. Project 2013 inserts the *Assignment Units* field to the left of the *Work* field, as shown in Figure 7 - 12.

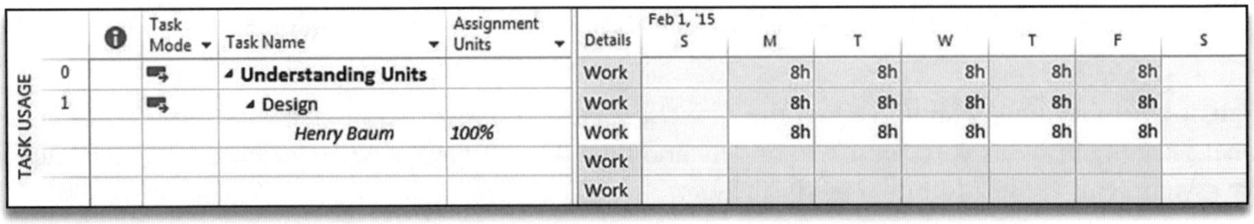

TASK USAGE		Task Mode	Task Name	Assignment Units	Details	Feb 1, '15 S	M	T	W	T	F	S
0			Understanding Units		Work		8h	8h	8h	8h	8h	
1			Design		Work		8h	8h	8h	8h	8h	
			Henry Baum	100%	Work		8h	8h	8h	8h	8h	
					Work							
					Work							

Figure 7 - 12: Assignment Units column added to the Task Usage view

After adding the *Assignment Units* field to the *Task Usage* view or *Resource Usage* view, you can also add the *Percent Allocation* timephased assignment field to the timephased grid on the right side of the view. To add the *Percent Allocation* field, right-click anywhere in the timephased grid and select the *Detail Styles* item on the shortcut menu, as shown in Figure 7 - 13.

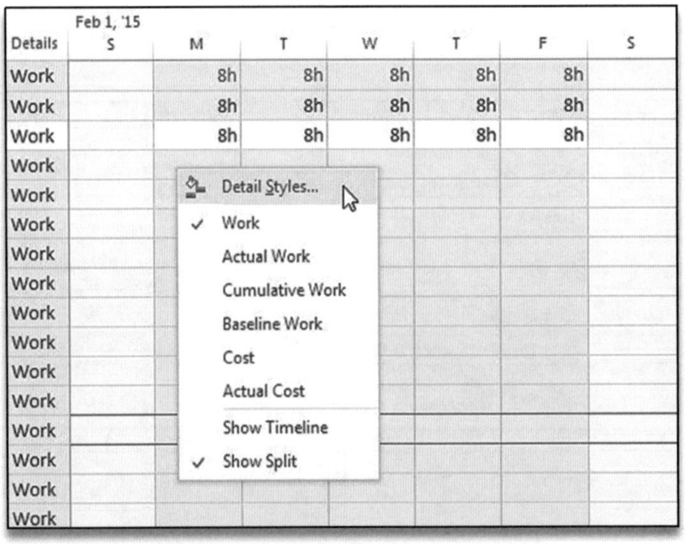

Details	Feb 1, '15 S	M	T	W	T	F	S
Work		8h	8h	8h	8h	8h	
Work		8h	8h	8h	8h	8h	
Work		8h	8h	8h	8h	8h	
Work							
Work							
Work							
Work							
Work							
Work							
Work							
Work							
Work							
Work							
Work							
Work							
Work							

Detail Styles...
✓ Work
Actual Work
Cumulative Work
Baseline Work
Cost
Actual Cost
Show Timeline
✓ Show Split

Figure 7 - 13: Shortcut menu to add a new timephased field to the timephased grid

The software displays the *Detail Styles* dialog shown in Figure 7 - 14. The *Detail Styles* dialog shows you the list of all available timephased fields in the *Available Fields* list on the left side of the dialog.

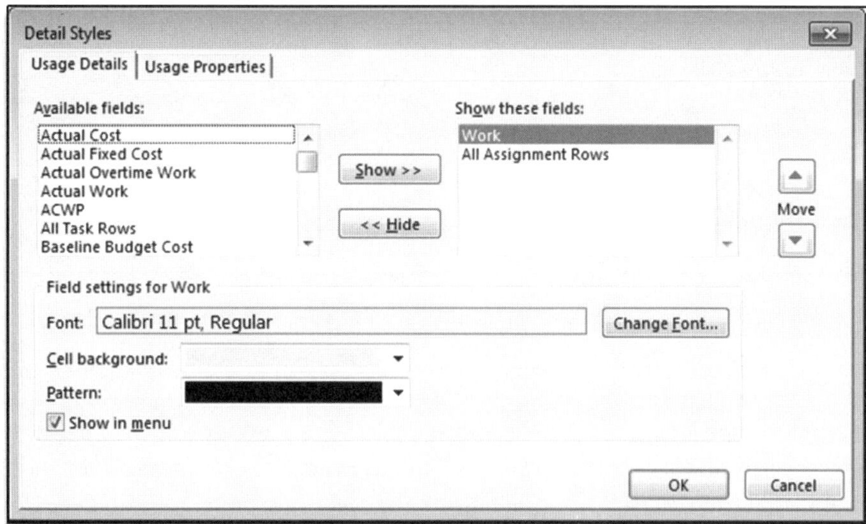

Figure 7 - 14: Detail Styles dialog

In the *Detail Styles* dialog, scroll to the bottom of the *Available Fields* list and select the *Percent Allocation* field. Click the *Show* button to add the *Percent Allocation* field to the *Show these fields* list. Click the *OK* button to add the *Percent Allocation* timephased assignment field to the timephased grid, as shown in Figure 7 - 15.

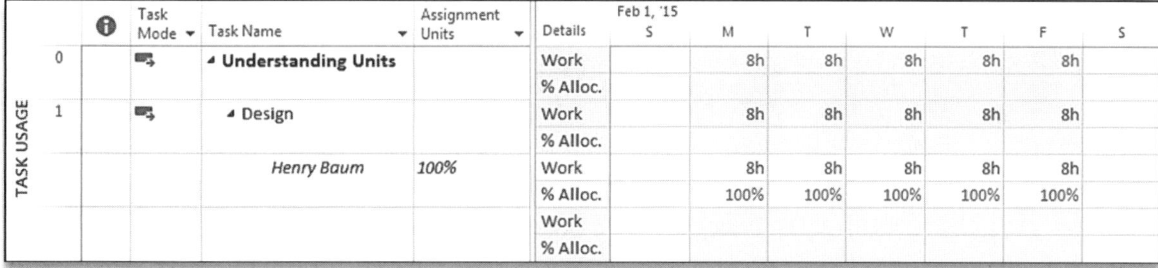

Figure 7 - 15: Percent Allocation field added to the timephased grid

When I assigned *Henry Baum* to the *Design* task, I assigned him at a *Units* value of *100%*, which represents the **original** *Units* value for his task assignment. Notice in Figure 7 - 15 shown previously that the *Percent Allocation* timephased field shows the **original** *Units* value of *100%* for Henry Baum's assignment on the *Design* task.

To add the *Peak* field to the *Task Usage* view or *Resource Usage* view, drag the split bar to the right of the *Work* column and then right-click the *Work* column header. Click the *Insert Column* item in the menu and then select the *Peak* field from the pick list of available fields. The software displays the *Peak* field to the right of the *Assignment Units* field, as shown in Figure 7 - 16. Notice that both the *Peak* field and the *Assignment Units* field show the same *Units* value of 100%.

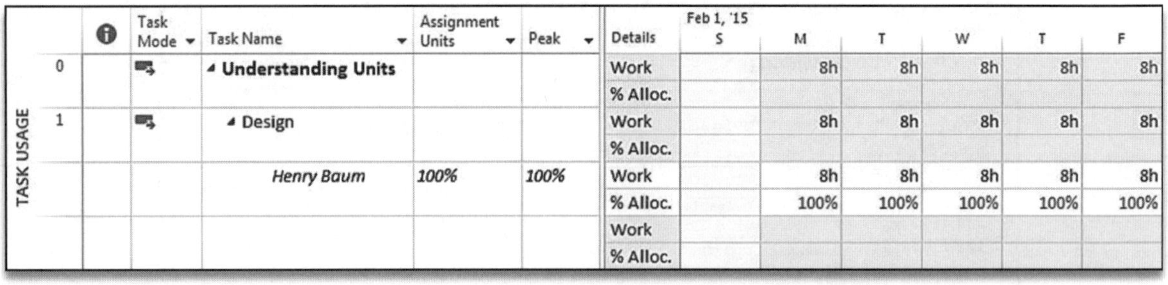

	Task Mode	Task Name	Assignment Units	Peak	Details	Feb 1, '15 S	M	T	W	T	F
0		**Understanding Units**			Work		8h	8h	8h	8h	8h
					% Alloc.						
1		Design			Work		8h	8h	8h	8h	8h
					% Alloc.						
		Henry Baum	*100%*	*100%*	Work		8h	8h	8h	8h	8h
					% Alloc.		100%	100%	100%	100%	100%
					Work						
					% Alloc.						

Figure 7 - 16: Peak field added to the Task Usage view

To add the *Peak Units* timephased assignment field to the *Task Usage* view or *Resource Usage* view, right-click anywhere in the timephased grid and select the *Detail Styles* item on the shortcut menu. In the *Detail Styles* dialog, select the *Peak Units* field from the *Available Fields* list. Click the *Show* button to add the *Peak Units* field to the *Show These Fields* list and then click the *OK* button to add the *Peak Units* timephased field to the timephased grid, as shown in Figure 7 - 17.

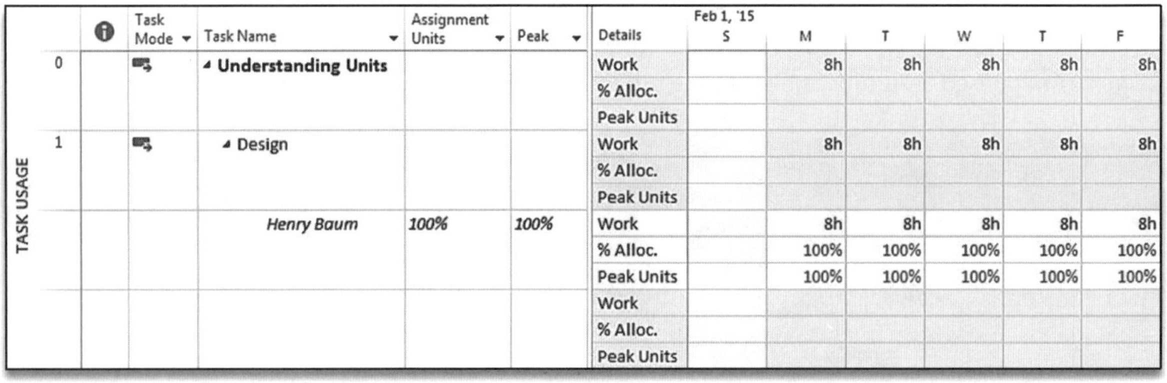

	Task Mode	Task Name	Assignment Units	Peak	Details	Feb 1, '15 S	M	T	W	T	F
0		**Understanding Units**			Work		8h	8h	8h	8h	8h
					% Alloc.						
					Peak Units						
1		Design			Work		8h	8h	8h	8h	8h
					% Alloc.						
					Peak Units						
		Henry Baum	*100%*	*100%*	Work		8h	8h	8h	8h	8h
					% Alloc.		100%	100%	100%	100%	100%
					Peak Units		100%	100%	100%	100%	100%
					Work						
					% Alloc.						
					Peak Units						

Figure 7 - 17: Peak Units field added to the timephased grid

When you make any change to the project that causes the Project 2013 scheduling engine to recalculate the *Units* value on the assignment, such as when you change the *Duration* value on a *Fixed Work* task, or you change the *Work* value on a *Fixed Duration* task, the software responds as follows:

- The software displays the **original** *Units* value in the *Assignment Units* field.
- The software captures the **recalculated** *Units* value in the *Peak* field.
- Using the **recalculated** *Units* value in the *Peak* field, the software reschedules the timephased work accordingly in the timephased grid.

For example, I change the value in the *Duration* field to *10 days,* as shown in Figure 7 - 18. Notice that Project 2013 **does not** show the recalculated *Units* value in the *Task Form* pane.

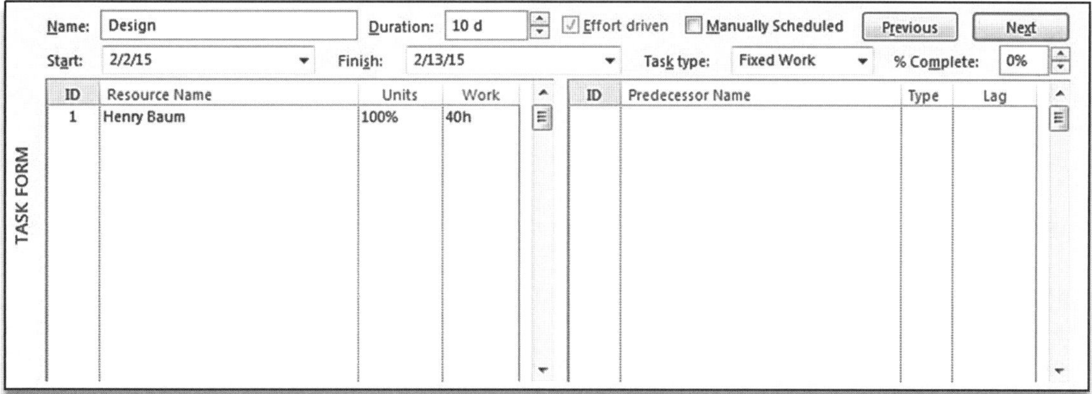

Figure 7 - 18: Change the Duration value to 10 days

Instead, Project 2013 does the following in the *Task Usage* view shown in Figure 7 - 19:

- The software displays the **original** *Units* value of **100%** in the *Assignment Units* field.
- The software captures the **recalculated** *Units* value of **50%** in the *Peak* field.
- Using the new **50%** value in the *Peak* field, the software reschedules the timephased work at 4 hours per day in the timephased grid.

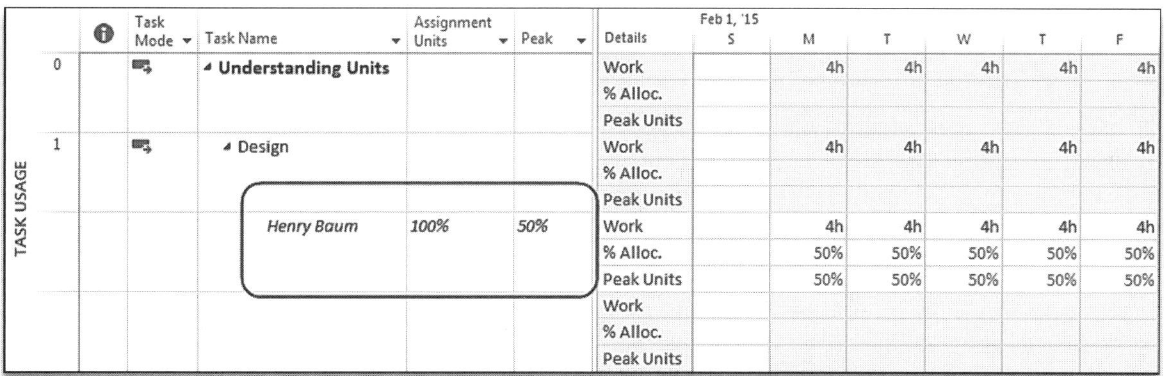

Figure 7 - 19: Peak field captures the recalculated Units value

Notice in Figure 7 - 19 shown previously that the timephased *Percent Allocation* field shows the correct assignment *Units* value on Henry Baum's assignment in the timephased grid. Notice also that the software correctly schedules the timephased *Work* value for this task at 4 hours per day using the *50%* value.

Information: Beyond the challenging behavior of the *Assignment Units* and *Peak* fields, as documented in this section of the module, you may see additional challenging behavior in Project 2013 when you begin entering progress in your project. I provide thorough documentation about this additional new behavior in *Module 08: Project Execution*.

Hands On Exercise

Exercise 7 - 4

Study the *Assignment Units* and *Peak* fields in Project 2013.

1. Return to the **Understanding Task Types 2013.mpp** sample file.
2. Right-click anywhere in the timephased grid and select the *Detail Styles* item on the shortcut menu.
3. In the *Detail Styles* dialog, select the *Percent Allocation* field in the *Available fields* list and then click the *Show* button to add the field to the *Show these fields* list.
4. In the *Available fields* list, select the *Peak Units* field and then click the *Show* button.
5. Click the *OK* button.
6. In the timephased grid, double-click the right edge of the *Details* column header to "best fit" the column width.
7. Click the *Task* tab to display the *Task* ribbon.
8. Select the name of the assigned resource, *Debbie Kirkpatrick*, on the *Fixed Work 2* task and then click the *Scroll to Task* button in the *Editing* section of the *Task* ribbon.
9. Examine the values in the *Assignment Units* field (the **original** *Units* value) and the *Peak field* (**re-calculated** *Units* value) for *Debbie Kirkpatrick's* assignment on the *Fixed Work 2* task.
10. Examine the timephased *Work* and *Percent Allocation* fields in the timephased grid for *Debbie Kirk-patrick's* assignment .
11. Examine the values in the *Assignment Units* field and the *Peak* field for *Greg Owens'* assignment on the *Fixed Duration 2* task.
12. Examine the timephased *Work* and *Percent Allocation* fields in the timephased grid for *Greg Ow-ens'* assignment .
13. Save and close the **Understanding Task Types 2013.mpp** sample file.

Setting the Cost Rate Table

Project 2013 offers you two special assignment views, the *Task Usage* and *Resource Usage* views, in which you can select the *Cost Rate Table* used to calculate the cost of an assignment. To apply the *Task Usage* view, use one of the following methods:

- In the *View* section of the *Task* ribbon, click the *Gantt Chart* pick list button, and then select the *Task Usage* view from the list.
- In the *Task Views* section of the *View* ribbon, click the *Task Usage* button.

Figure 7 - 20 shows the *Task Usage* view for a project. By default, the *Task Usage* view consists of the task *Usage* table on the left side and the timephased grid on the right side. The *Task Name* column shows a list of all project tasks, along with the resource assignments for each task. Below each task, the software indents the resource assignments one level, and formats them in italics to distinguish them from the tasks. The timephased grid displays the timephased *Work* field for each task and resource assignment, with the assigned work phased over time. Project 2013 formats the timephased *Work* cells of each task using the gray cell background color and of each resource assignment using a white cell background color.

TASK USAGE

	Task Mode	Task Name	Work	Details	May 31, '15 S	M	T	W	T	F	S
0		**Cost Rate Tables**	**480 h**	Work		8h	8h	8h	16h	16h	
1		**Phase I**	**240 h**	Work		8h	8h	8h	16h	16h	
2		Design P1	24 h	Work		8h	8h	8h			
		Cindy McNair	*24 h*	Work		8h	8h	8h			
3		Build P1	64 h	Work					16h	16h	
		Jerry King	*32 h*	Work					8h	8h	
		Marcia Bickel	*32 h*	Work					8h	8h	
4		Test P1	80 h	Work							
		Cindy McNair	*40 h*	Work							
		George Stewart	*40 h*	Work							
5		Implement P1	72 h	Work							
		George Stewart	*24 h*	Work							
		Leanne Owens	*24 h*	Work							
		Steve Garcia	*24 h*	Work							
6		Phase I Complete	0 h	Work							
7		**Phase II**	**240 h**	Work							
8		Design P2	24 h	Work							
		Cindy McNair	*24 h*	Work							
9		Build P2	64 h	Work							
		Jerry King	*32 h*	Work							
		Marcia Bickel	*32 h*	Work							
10		Test P2	80 h	Work							
		Cindy McNair	*40 h*	Work							
		George Stewart	*40 h*	Work							
11		Implement P2	72 h	Work							
		George Stewart	*24 h*	Work							
		Leanne Owens	*24 h*	Work							
		Steve Garcia	*24 h*	Work							

Figure 7 - 20: Task Usage view

To apply the *Resource Usage* view, use one of the following methods:

- In the *View* section of the *Resource* ribbon, click the *Team Planner* pick list button (or *Resource Sheet* pick list button), and then select the *Resource Usage* view from the list.

- In the *Resource Views* section of the *View* ribbon, click the *Resource Usage* button.

Figure 7 - 21 shows the *Resource Usage* view. By default, the *Resource Usage* view consists of the resource *Usage* table on the left and the timephased grid on the right. The *Resource Name* column displays a list of all project resources, along with the task assignments for each resource. Below each resource, the software indents the task assignments one level, and formats them in italics to distinguish them from the resources. The timephased grid displays the timephased *Work* field for each resource and task assignment, with the assigned work phased over time. Project 2013 formats the timephased *Work* cells of each resource using the gray cell background color and of each task assignment using a white cell background color.

Information: In addition to the names of all resources on the project team, the *Resource Name* column includes an additional item named *Unassigned Resources*. This item displays tasks not yet assigned to any resource, such as milestone tasks. At the conclusion of the assignment planning process, the *Unassigned Resources* item should not include any regular tasks in your project, and should include only milestone tasks.

RESOURCE USAGE

		Resource Name	Work	Details	May 31, '15 S	M	T	W	T	F	S
		▷ Unassigned	0 h	Work							
1		◢ Cindy McNair	128 h	Work		8h	8h	8h			
		Design P1	*24 h*	Work		8h	8h	8h			
		Test P1	*40 h*	Work							
		Design P2	*24 h*	Work							
		Test P2	*40 h*	Work							
2		◢ George Stewart	128 h	Work							
		Test P1	*40 h*	Work							
		Implement P1	*24 h*	Work							
		Test P2	*40 h*	Work							
		Implement P2	*24 h*	Work							
3		◢ Jerry King	64 h	Work					8h	8h	
		Build P1	*32 h*	Work					8h	8h	
		Build P2	*32 h*	Work							
4		◢ Leanne Owens	48 h	Work							
		Implement P1	*24 h*	Work							
		Implement P2	*24 h*	Work							
5		◢ Marcia Bickel	64 h	Work					8h	8h	
		Build P1	*32 h*	Work					8h	8h	
		Build P2	*32 h*	Work							
6		◢ Steve Garcia	48 h	Work							
		Implement P1	*24 h*	Work							
		Implement P2	*24 h*	Work							
				Work							
				Work							

Figure 7 - 21: Resource Usage view

To see the cost of any assignment, complete the following steps:

1. Apply either the *Task Usage* or *Resource Usage* view.

2. Right-click the *Select All* button and select the *Cost* table from the shortcut menu.

3. Right-click anywhere in the timephased grid and then select the *Cost* item from the shortcut menu.

4. Right-click anywhere in the timephased grid again and then **deselect** the *Work* item from the shortcut menu.

Figure 7 - 22 shows you the *Resource Usage* view with the *Cost* table applied, and with the timephased *Cost* field shown in the timephased grid. With the *Cost* table applied in the *Resource Usage* view, the *Cost* column shows you the total cost of each task assignment for every resource.

RESOURCE USAGE

	Resource Name	Cost	Details	May 31, '15 S	M	T	W	T	F	S
	~~Unassigned~~	~~$0.00~~	~~Cost~~							
1	◢ Cindy McNair	$6,400.00	Cost		$400.00	$400.00	$400.00			
	Design P1	*$1,200.00*	Cost		$400.00	$400.00	$400.00			
	~~*Test P1*~~	~~*$2,000.00*~~	~~Cost~~							
	Design P2	*$1,200.00*	Cost							
	Test P2	*$2,000.00*	Cost							
2	◢ George Stewart	$6,400.00	Cost							
	Test P1	*$2,000.00*	Cost							
	Implement P1	*$1,200.00*	Cost							
	Test P2	*$2,000.00*	Cost							
	Implement P2	*$1,200.00*	Cost							
3	◢ Jerry King	$3,200.00	Cost					$400.00	$400.00	
	Build P1	*$1,600.00*	Cost					$400.00	$400.00	
	Build P2	*$1,600.00*	Cost							
4	◢ Leanne Owens	$2,400.00	Cost							
	Implement P1	*$1,200.00*	Cost							
	Implement P2	*$1,200.00*	Cost							
5	◢ Marcia Bickel	$3,200.00	Cost					$400.00	$400.00	
	Build P1	*$1,600.00*	Cost					$400.00	$400.00	
	Build P2	*$1,600.00*	Cost							
6	◢ Steve Garcia	$2,400.00	Cost							
	Implement P1	*$1,200.00*	Cost							
	Implement P2	*$1,200.00*	Cost							
			Cost							
			Cost							

Figure 7 - 22: Resource Usage view with Cost table and Cost details applied

By default, Project 2013 **always** applies the *Standard Rate* value from *Cost Rate Table A* at the time you initially assign a resource to a task. After assigning the resource to a task, you can then modify the *Cost Rate Table* used to calculate the cost for that assignment. Notice in Figure 7 - 22 shown previously that total cost for the *Design P1* task assigned to *Cindy McNair* is $1,200, phased over time at $400.00 per day. The software calculated these costs using her *Standard Rate* value of *$50/hour* on *Cost Rate Table A*. To change the *Cost Rate Table* for an assignment, complete the following steps:

1. Apply either the *Task Usage* or *Resource Usage* view.

2. Double-click the assignment for which you want to change the *Cost Rate Table*. The software displays the *Assignment Information* dialog shown in Figure 7 - 23.

3. Click the *Cost rate table* pick list button and then select an alternate value (*B* through *E*).

4. Click the *OK* button.

Information: You can also display the *Assignment Information* dialog using several other methods. To use the first method, right-click an assignment and then select the *Information* item on the shortcut menu. To use the second method, select the assignment and then click the *Information* button in the *Assignment* section of the *Format* ribbon. To use the third method, select multiple assignments using either the **Control** key or the **Shift** key on your computer keyboard. With multiple assignments selected, you can right-click any of the selected assignments and select the *Information* item on the shortcut menu or you can click the *Information* button in the *Assignment* section of the *Format* ribbon. When you use the third method with multiple assignments selected, Project 2013 displays the *Multiple Assignment Information* dialog in which you can edit all of the selected assignments simultaneously.

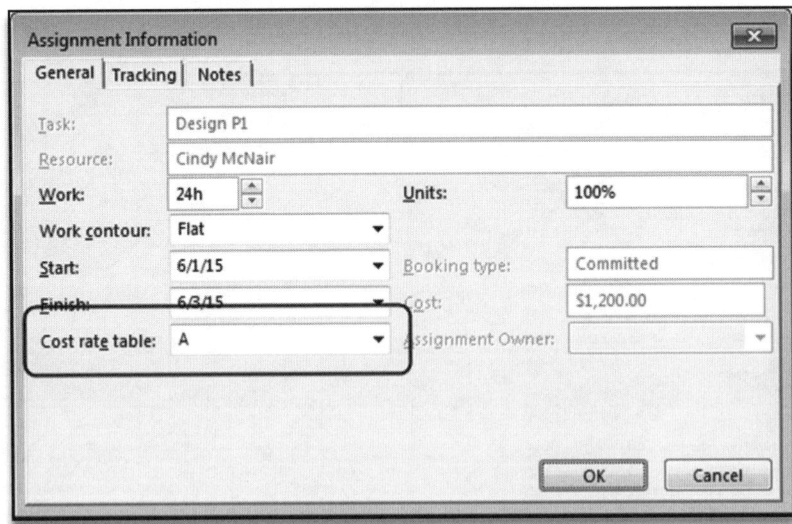

Figure 7 - 23: Assignment Information dialog

When you select an alternate rate on the *Cost rate table* pick list, Project 2013 automatically recalculates the cost for that assignment using the *Standard Rate* from the alternate *Cost Rate Table* you select. Figure 7 - 24 shows the *Resource Usage* view after selecting the *B* table in the *Cost rate table* field for Cindy McNair. Notice that the cost for the *Design P1* task assigned to *Cindy McNair* is now $2,400, phased over time at $800.00 per day using her alternate rate of *$100/hour* on *Cost Rate Table B.*

RESOURCE USAGE

	Resource Name	Cost	Details	May 31, '15 S	M	T	W	T	F	S
	Unassigned	$0.00	Cost							
1	Cindy McNair	$7,600.00	Cost		$800.00	$800.00	$800.00			
	Design P1	*$2,400.00*	Cost		$800.00	$800.00	$800.00			
	Test P1	*$2,000.00*	Cost							
	Design P2	*$1,200.00*	Cost							
	Test P2	*$2,000.00*	Cost							
2	George Stewart	$6,400.00	Cost							
	Test P1	*$2,000.00*	Cost							
	Implement P1	*$1,200.00*	Cost							
	Test P2	*$2,000.00*	Cost							
	Implement P2	*$1,200.00*	Cost							
3	Jerry King	$3,200.00	Cost					$400.00	$400.00	
	Build P1	*$1,600.00*	Cost					$400.00	$400.00	
	Build P2	*$1,600.00*	Cost							
4	Leanne Owens	$2,400.00	Cost							
	Implement P1	*$1,200.00*	Cost							
	Implement P2	*$1,200.00*	Cost							
5	Marcia Bickel	$3,200.00	Cost					$400.00	$400.00	
	Build P1	*$1,600.00*	Cost					$400.00	$400.00	
	Build P2	*$1,600.00*	Cost							
6	Steve Garcia	$2,400.00	Cost							
	Implement P1	*$1,200.00*	Cost							
	Implement P2	*$1,200.00*	Cost							
			Cost							
			Cost							

Figure 7 - 24: Resource Usage view after selecting Cost Rate Table B rate

To change the *Cost Rate Table* for multiple assignments, the fastest method is to temporarily insert the *Cost Rate Table* column in either the *Task Usage* or *Resource Usage* view with the *Cost* table applied. To insert the *Cost Rate*

Table column, right-click the *Cost* column header, select the *Insert Column* item in the shortcut menu, and then select the *Cost Rate Table* field in the list of available fields. Figure 7 - 25 shows the *Resource Usage* view with the *Cost Rate Table* column inserted in the *Cost* table. Notice that the *Cost Rate Table* column shows that I selected the *B* rate for the *Design P1* task assigned to *Cindy McNair*. After inserting the *Cost Rate Table* column, you can use copy and paste or use the *Fill Handle* to copy the alternate *Cost Rate Table* selection to additional assignments as needed.

	Resource Name	Cost Rate Table	Cost	Details	May 31, '15 S	M	T	W	T	F	S
	Unassigned		$0.00	Cost							
1	Cindy McNair		$7,600.00	Cost		$800.00	$800.00	$800.00			
	Design P1	*B*	*$2,400.00*	Cost		$800.00	$800.00	$800.00			
	Test P1	*A*	*$2,000.00*	Cost							
	Design P2	*A*	*$1,200.00*	Cost							
	Test P2	*A*	*$2,000.00*	Cost							
2	George Stewart		$6,400.00	Cost							
	Test P1	*A*	*$2,000.00*	Cost							
	Implement P1	*A*	*$1,200.00*	Cost							
	Test P2	*A*	*$2,000.00*	Cost							
	Implement P2	*A*	*$1,200.00*	Cost							
3	Jerry King		$3,200.00	Cost					$400.00	$400.00	
	Build P1	*A*	*$1,600.00*	Cost					$400.00	$400.00	
	Build P2	*A*	*$1,600.00*	Cost							
4	Leanne Owens		$2,400.00	Cost							
	Implement P1	*A*	*$1,200.00*	Cost							
	Implement P2	*A*	*$1,200.00*	Cost							
5	Marcia Bickel		$3,200.00	Cost					$400.00	$400.00	
	Build P1	*A*	*$1,600.00*	Cost					$400.00	$400.00	
	Build P2	*A*	*$1,600.00*	Cost							
6	Steve Garcia		$2,400.00	Cost							
	Implement P1	*A*	*$1,200.00*	Cost							
	Implement P2	*A*	*$1,200.00*	Cost							
				Cost							
				Cost							

RESOURCE USAGE

Figure 7 - 25: Resource Usage view with Cost Rate Table column inserted

Hands On Exercise

Exercise 7 - 5

Although Mike Andrews works primarily on the Help Desk, in the Training Advisor Rollout project he works on two tasks that involve testing work. For all testing tasks, you must cost his assignments using the higher *Standard Rate* value for testing that you specified previously on *Cost Rate Table B*.

1. Return to the **Training Advisor 07.mpp** sample file.
2. Click the *View* tab to display the *View* ribbon.
3. In the *Resource Views* section of the *View* ribbon, click the *Resource Usage* button.
4. Collapse the assignments for the *Unassigned* resource by clicking the *Collapse* symbol (black triangle symbol) to the left of the resource name.
5. Click the *Task* tab to display the *Task* ribbon.

6. Select resource ID #2, *Mike Andrews*, and then click the *Scroll to Task* button in the *Editing* section of the *Task* ribbon.

Notice that Project 2013 scrolls the timephased grid to the weekend *Work* hours for the *Perform Server Stress Test* task.

7. Right-click the *Select All* button and select the *Cost* item on the shortcut menu.
8. Widen the *Resource Name* column as needed and then drag the split bar to the right edge of the *Cost* column.
9. Right-click anywhere in the timephased grid and select the *Cost* item on the shortcut menu.
10. Right-click again in the timephased grid and **deselect** the *Work* item on the shortcut menu.

Notice the current cost information for *Mike Andrews* and for his task assignments in the *Cost* column of the *Cost* table and in the timephased *Cost* field shown in the timephased grid. The software calculates the cost of his task assignments using the *Standard Rate* value of *$30/hour* specified on *Cost Rate Table A*.

Information: Project 2013 formats the name *Mike Andrews* in red because the software thinks that he is overallocated. This is because you assigned him to work on a task that occurs only on a Saturday and Sunday. Because these days are nonworking time, the software assumes he must be overallocated, which is not the case at all! I discuss how to address this false overallocation warning in the last topical section of this module.

11. Double-click the *Perform Server Stress Test* task assignment for *Mike Andrews*.

12. In the *Assignment Information* dialog, click the *Cost rate table* pick list, select the *B* value, and then click the *OK* button.

Notice how Project 2013 recalculates the cost of this task assignment using the *Standard Rate* value of *$50/hour* specified on *Cost Rate Table B*.

13. Select the *Verify Connectivity* task for *Mike Andrews* and then click the *Scroll to Task* button in the *Editing* section of the *Task* ribbon.

14. Right-click the *Verify Connectivity* task for *Mike Andrews* and select the *Information* item on the shortcut menu.

15. In the *Assignment Information* dialog, click the *Cost rate table* pick list, select the *B* value, and then click the *OK* button.

16. Right-click anywhere in the timephased grid and select the *Work* item in the shortcut menu.

17. Right-click again in the timephased grid and **deselect** the *Cost* item in the shortcut menu.

18. Right-click the *Select All* button and select the *Usage* table on the shortcut menu.

19. In the *View* section of the *Task* ribbon, click the *Gantt Chart* pick list button and select the *Gantt Chart* view.

20. Save but **do not** close the **Training Advisor 07.mpp** sample file.

Assigning Material Resources

You use *Material* resources in a project to track project consumables. You can assign *Material* resources using either of two methods:

- Fixed consumption rate
- Variable consumption rate

You should assign a *Material* resource at a **fixed consumption rate** when the amount of the resource consumed does not depend upon the duration of the task. For example, when you assign the *Material* resource named *Paper* at *25 Reams* to a *Project Administration* task, this action consumes 25 reams of paper regardless of whether the task takes 30 days or 12 months to complete.

You should assign a *Material* resource at a **variable consumption rate** when the amount of the resource consumed depends directly on the duration of the task. For example, you assign the *Material* resource named *Gasoline* to the task *Excavate Site* at *100 gallons/day*. Using this method, you know that the excavation consumes 500 gallons of gasoline in 5 days or 2,000 gallons in 20 days. When you assign a *Material* resource to a task, make sure that you use the correct assignment method.

To assign a *Material* resource to a task, complete the following steps:

1. Apply the *Gantt Chart* view.
2. Click the *View* tab to display the *View* ribbon.
3. In the *Split View* section of the *View* ribbon, select the *Details* checkbox to apply the *Task Entry* view.
4. Select a task in the *Gantt Chart* pane.
5. In the *Resource Name* column of the *Task Form* pane, click the pick list and select a *Material* resource from the list of resources.
6. Enter the consumption for the *Material* resource in the *Units* column.

Information: To assign the *Material* resource using a fixed consumption rate, enter only a number in the *Units* field, such as **25** to the consumption of the resource at 25 units. To assign the *Material* resource using a variable consumption rate, enter a number plus a slash symbol plus a time period in the *Units* field, such as **100/d** to show the consumption of the resource at 100 units per day.

7. Click the *OK* button.

Project 2013 shows the total consumption of the *Material* resource in the *Work* column of the *Task Form* pane. For example, Figure 7 - 26 shows the fixed consumption assignment of 25 reams for the *Paper* resource assigned to the *Project Administration* task over the 30-day duration of the task.

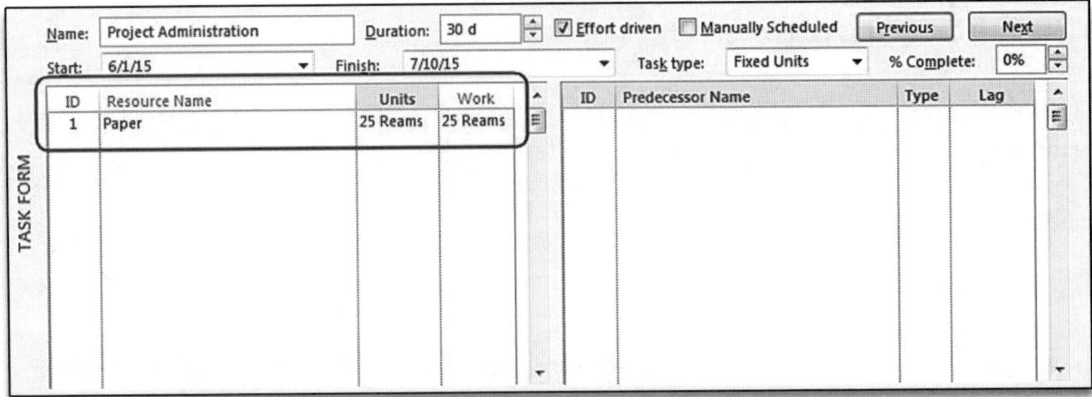

Figure 7 - 26: Material resource Paper assigned at a fixed consumption rate

Figure 7 - 27 shows the assignment after I change the *Duration* value of the task from *30 days* to *12 months*. Notice the number of reams of the *Paper* resource consumed does not change on this task because I assigned this *Material* resource using the **fixed consumption rate** method.

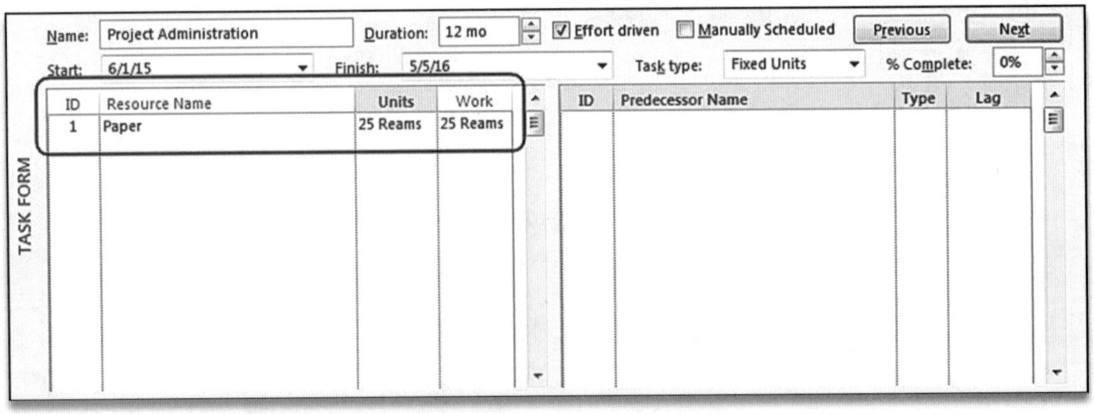

Figure 7 - 27: No change in Paper consumption at a fixed consumption rate assignment when the Duration increases

Figure 7 - 28 shows the variable consumption rate applied to the assignment of the *Gasoline* resource on the *Excavate Site* task. Figure 7 - 29 demonstrates how the consumption amount changes after I increase the *Duration* value of the task from *5 days* to *20 days*. Notice that the amount of the *Gasoline* resource consumed **changes in proportion** to the *Duration* of the task, from *500 gallons* used in *5 days to 2,000 gallons* used in *20 days*.

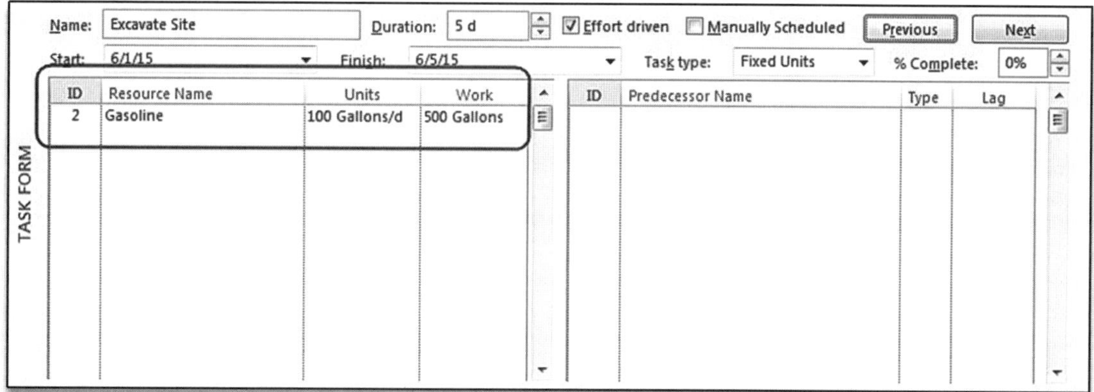

Figure 7 - 28: Material resource Gasoline assigned at a variable consumption rate

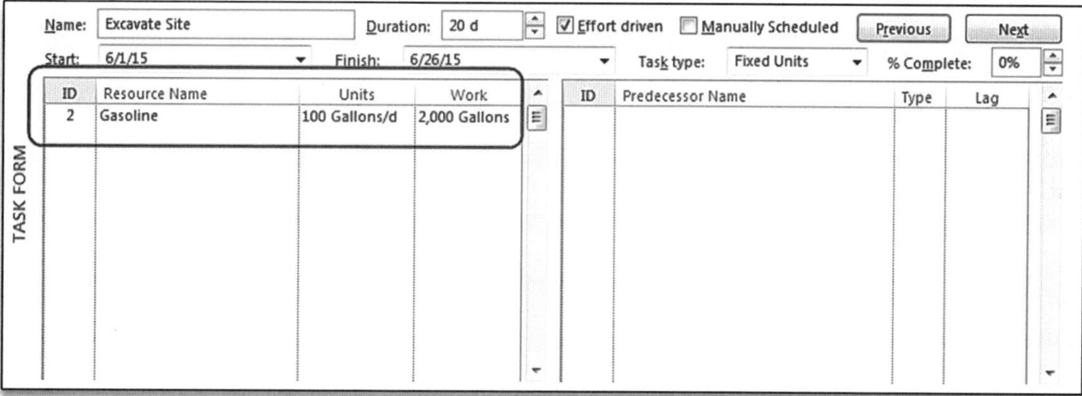

Figure 7 - 29: Consumption of the Gasoline resource changes as Duration changes

Hands On Exercise

Exercise 7 - 6

Assign a *Material* resource to a task in the Training Advisor Rollout project.

1. Return to the **Training Advisor 07.mpp** sample file.
2. Click the *View* tab to display the *View* ribbon.
3. In the *Split View* section of the *View* ribbon, select the *Details* checkbox to apply the *Task Entry* view.
4. In the *Gantt Chart* pane, select task ID #36, the *Provide End User Training* task.
5. In the *Task Form* pane, select the first blank cell below the name of the last resource in the *Resource Name* column.
6. Click the *Resource Name* pick list and select the *Student Materials* resource.

7. In the *Units* column for the *Student Materials* resource, manually type ***36/d*** in the *Units* cell to set a variable consumption rate of 36 sets per day.

Information: I estimated the variable consumption rate for the student materials as 12 students per class multiplied by 3 concurrent classes each day, which means we consume a maximum of 36 sets of student materials for each day of training. This value ensures that I order enough sets of student materials to supply all of the students in all of the sessions of the training classes.

8. Click the *OK* button.

Notice that Project 2013 calculated 360 sets of student materials needed during the 10-day duration for this task.

9. In the *Split View* section of the *View* ribbon, **deselect** the *Details* checkbox to close the *Task Form* pane.
10. Save but **do not** close the **Training Advisor 07.mpp** sample file.

Assigning Cost Resources

As I noted in Module 06, *Project Resource Planning*, Project 2013 offers you two types of *Cost* resources: *Budget Cost* and *Expense Cost* resources. The process of assigning each type of *Cost* resource requires a unique set of steps; therefore, I describe each process individually.

Assigning a Budget Cost Resource

Project 2013 allows you to assign a *Budget Cost* resource to **only** the Project Summary Task (Row 0 or Task 0), allowing you to specify an overall budget for the entire project. On the other hand, the software **does not** allow you assign a *Budget Cost* resource to individual tasks or to summary tasks, thus preventing you from setting a budget on phases, deliverables, or individual tasks. To specify an overall budget for your entire project, complete the following steps:

1. Click the *View* tab to display the *View* ribbon.
2. In the *Task Views* section of the *View* ribbon, click the *Task Usage* button to display the *Task Usage* view.
3. In the *Task Usage* view of your project, select the Project Summary Task (Row 0).

Information: If you do not see the Project Summary Task in your project, click the *Format* tab to display the *Format* ribbon. In the *Show/Hide* section of the *Format* ribbon, select the *Project Summary Task* option to display the Project Summary Task.

4. Click the *Resource* tab to display the *Resource* ribbon.
5. In the *Assignments* section of the *Resource* ribbon, click the *Assign Resources* button.
6. In the *Assign Resources* dialog, select your *Budget Cost* resource and then click the *Assign* button.
7. Click the *Close* button to close the *Assign Resources* dialog.

Figure 7 - 30 shows that I assigned my *Project Budget* resource, which is a *Budget Cost* resource, to the Project Summary Task in my SE Region Office Renovation project.

TASK USAGE

	Task Name	Work	Details	S	M	T	W	T	F	S
0	SE Region Office Renovation	974 h	Work		8h	8h	6h		6h	
	Project Budget		Work							
1	Pre-Renovation	282 h	Work		8h	8h	6h		6h	
2	Design	156 h	Work		4h	4h	2h		4h	
3	Interview and select architect	10 h	Work		4h	4h	2h			
	Steve Garcia	*10 h*	Work		4h	4h	2h			
4	Create first draft plan	52 h	Work						4h	
	Jerry King	*52 h*	Work						4h	
5	Review draft	10 h	Work							
	Jerry King	*4 h*	Work							
	Steve Garcia	*6 h*	Work							
6	Revise draft	20 h	Work							
	Jerry King	*20 h*	Work							
7	Review and approve final plan	8 h	Work							
	Jerry King	*4 h*	Work							
	Steve Garcia	*4 h*	Work							
8	Design telecommunications plan	48 h	Work							
	Jerry King	*12 h*	Work							
	Russ Powell	*24 h*	Work							
	Steve Garcia	*12 h*	Work							
9	Obtain construction permits	8 h	Work							
	Marcia Bickel	*8 h*	Work							
10	Design Complete	0 h	Work							

Figure 7 - 30: Budget Cost resource assigned to the Project Summary Task

8. Right-click the *Select All* button and select the *Cost* item on the shortcut menu to apply the *Cost* table.
9. Right-click the *Fixed Cost* column header, select the *Insert Column* item on the shortcut menu, and then select the *Budget Cost* item from the list of available fields.
10. Right-click anywhere in the timephased grid and then select the *Detail Styles* item in the shortcut menu.
11. In the *Available fields* list on the left side of the *Detail Styles* dialog, select the *Budget Cost* field, and click the *Show* button to add the field to the *Show these fields* list on the right side of the dialog. Figure 7 - 31 shows the *Detail Styles* dialog with the *Budget Cost* field added to the *Show these fields* list.

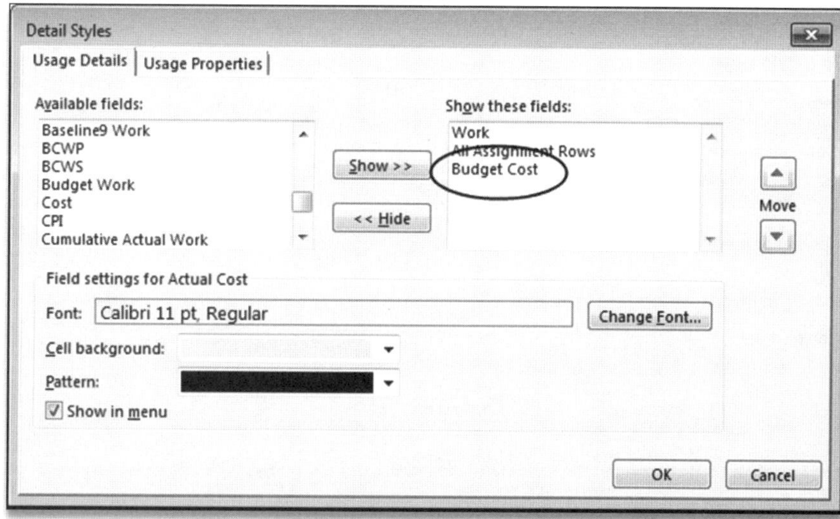

Figure 7 - 31: Detail Styles dialog with Budget Cost field added

12. Click the *OK* button to close the *Details Styles* dialog.

13. In the timephased grid, double-click the right edge of the *Details* column header to "best fit" the column width. Figure 7 - 32 shows the *Task Usage* view with the *Budget Cost* column displayed in the *Cost* table on the left side of the view and with the timephased *Budget Cost* field displayed in the timephased grid on the right side of the view.

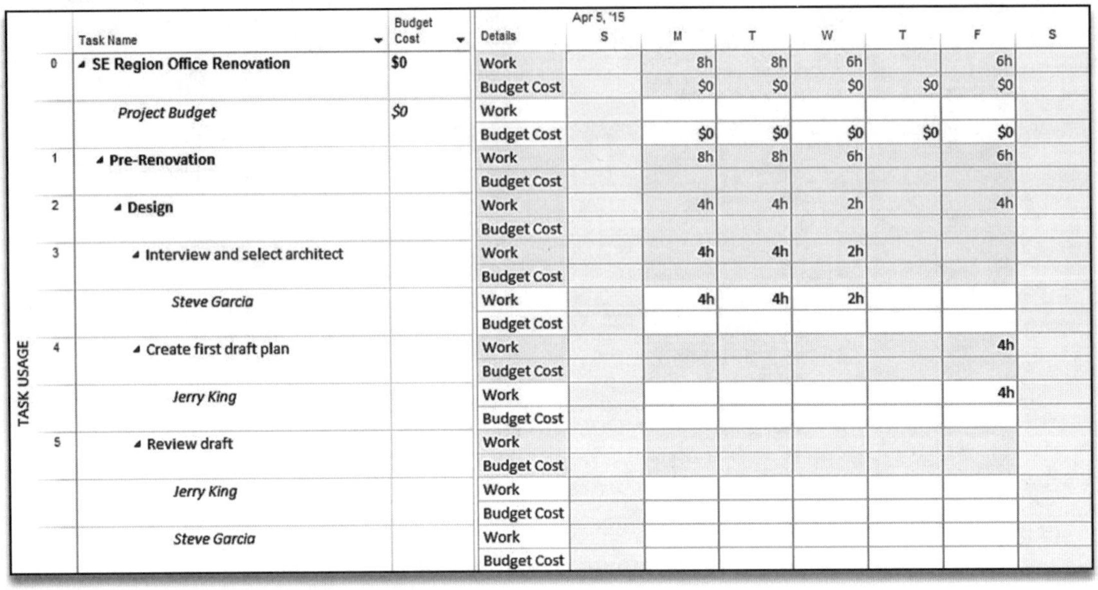

TASK USAGE

	Task Name	Budget Cost	Details	Apr 5, '15 S	M	T	W	T	F	S
0	◢ SE Region Office Renovation	$0	Work		8h	8h	6h		6h	
			Budget Cost		$0	$0	$0	$0	$0	
	Project Budget	*$0*	Work							
			Budget Cost		$0	$0	$0	$0	$0	
1	◢ Pre-Renovation		Work		8h	8h	6h		6h	
			Budget Cost							
2	◢ Design		Work		4h	4h	2h		4h	
			Budget Cost							
3	◢ Interview and select architect		Work		4h	4h	2h			
			Budget Cost							
	Steve Garcia		Work		4h	4h	2h			
			Budget Cost							
4	◢ Create first draft plan		Work						4h	
			Budget Cost							
	Jerry King		Work						4h	
			Budget Cost							
5	◢ Review draft		Work							
			Budget Cost							
	Jerry King		Work							
			Budget Cost							
	Steve Garcia		Work							
			Budget Cost							

Figure 7 - 32: Task Usage view prepared to enter project budget

14. In the *Budget Cost* column for the *Budget Cost* resource assignment on the Project Summary Task, enter your planned budget for the entire project and then press the **Enter** key on your computer keyboard. Figure 7 - 33 shows the *Budget Cost* amount of *$320,000* for the *Project Budget* resource I assigned to the Project Summary Task.

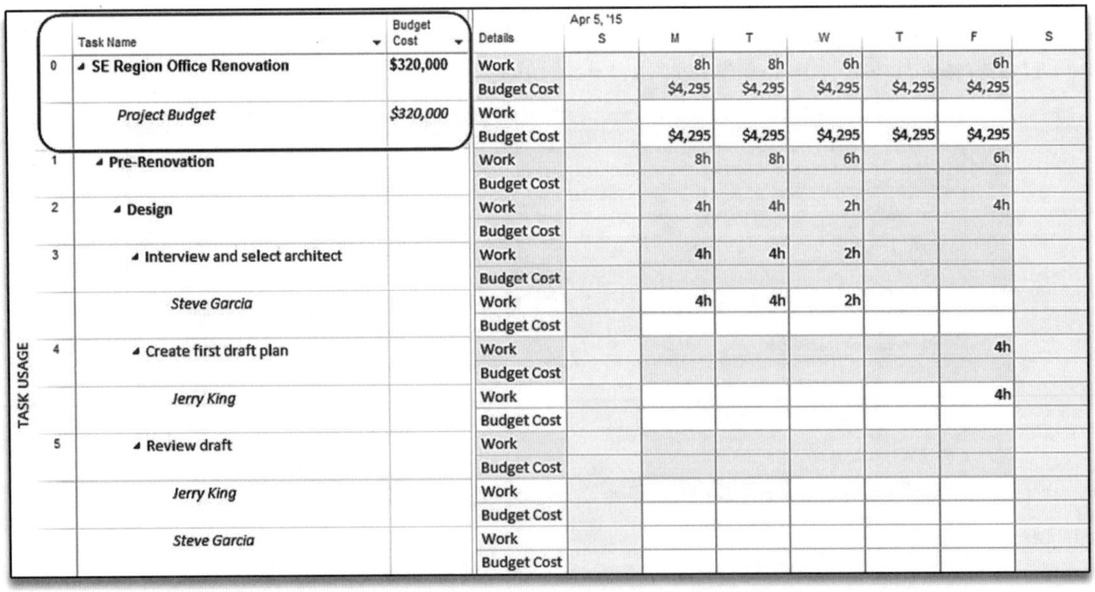

TASK USAGE

	Task Name	Budget Cost	Details	Apr 5, '15 S	M	T	W	T	F	S
0	◢ SE Region Office Renovation	$320,000	Work		8h	8h	6h		6h	
			Budget Cost		$4,295	$4,295	$4,295	$4,295	$4,295	
	Project Budget	*$320,000*	Work							
			Budget Cost		$4,295	$4,295	$4,295	$4,295	$4,295	
1	◢ Pre-Renovation		Work		8h	8h	6h		6h	
			Budget Cost							
2	◢ Design		Work		4h	4h	2h		4h	
			Budget Cost							
3	◢ Interview and select architect		Work		4h	4h	2h			
			Budget Cost							
	Steve Garcia		Work		4h	4h	2h			
			Budget Cost							
4	◢ Create first draft plan		Work						4h	
			Budget Cost							
	Jerry King		Work						4h	
			Budget Cost							
5	◢ Review draft		Work							
			Budget Cost							
	Jerry King		Work							
			Budget Cost							
	Steve Garcia		Work							
			Budget Cost							

Figure 7 - 33: Budget Cost amount for entire project

If you set the *Accrue At* value to *Prorated* for the *Budget Cost* resource in the *Resource Sheet* view of your project, then Project 2013 apportions the *Budget Cost* amount evenly across the time span of the entire project. You see the timephased *Budget Cost* amounts in each day ($4,295 each day) of the timephased grid shown previously in Figure 7 - 33. If you want to reapportion the *Budget Cost* information in another manner, such as on a monthly basis, then complete the following additional steps:

15. Click the *View* tab to display the *View* ribbon.
16. In the *Zoom* section of the *View* ribbon click the *Timescale* pick list button and select the level of zoom you want to apply to the *Timescale*, such as *Months*.
17. In the timephased grid, enter your anticipated *Budget Cost* values in the *Budget Cost* cells for your *Budget Cost* resource assignment. In Figure 7 - 34, notice that I entered my *Project Budget* values on a monthly basis, roughly timephased in proportion to the planned *Work* hours for each month.

TASK USAGE

	Task Name	Budget Cost	Details		2nd Quarter			3rd Quarter	
				Mar	Apr	May	Jun	Jul	Aug
0	SE Region Office Renovation	$320,000	Work		226h	412h	188h	148h	
			Budget Cost		$80,000	$80,000	$100,000	$60,000	
	Project Budget	*$320,000*	Work						
			Budget Cost		$80,000	$80,000	$100,000	$60,000	
1	Pre-Renovation		Work		226h	56h			
			Budget Cost						
2	Design		Work		100h	56h			
			Budget Cost						
3	Interview and select architect		Work		10h				
			Budget Cost						
	Steve Garcia		Work		10h				
			Budget Cost						
4	Create first draft plan		Work		52h				
			Budget Cost						
	Jerry King		Work		52h				
			Budget Cost						
5	Review draft		Work		10h				
			Budget Cost						
	Jerry King		Work		4h				
			Budget Cost						
	Steve Garcia		Work		6h				
			Budget Cost						

Figure 7 - 34: Project Budget information entered in timephased grid

Information: In addition to the *Budget Cost* field, Project 2013 includes an additional budget field called *Budget Work*. This field allows you to specify an overall budget for working hours for your project in addition to specifying a monetary budget. Before you can use the *Budget Work* field, however, you must first create a *Budget Work* resource by creating a new *Work* resource and then selecting the *Budget* checkbox in the *Resource Information* dialog for the new resource. After creating the new *Budget Work* resource, assign this resource to your Project Summary Task in the *Task Usage* view. Insert the *Budget Work* field and then enter your overall budget of working hours for the entire project in this field.

Assigning an Expense Cost Resource

After you enter your project budget using a *Budget Cost* resource, you can assign *Expense Cost* resources to your project so that you can track additional project expenses. Project 2013 allows you to assign *Expense Cost* resources to any type of task in the project, including summary tasks, subtasks, and milestone tasks. The software **does not** allow you to assign an *Expense Cost* resource to the Project Summary Task, however. To assign an *Expense Cost* resource to tasks in your project, complete the following steps:

1. Using the customized *Task Usage* view documented in the previous topical section, select any task in the project, including a regular task, a summary task, or a milestone task.

2. Click the *Resource* tab to display the *Resource* ribbon, if necessary.

3. In the *Assignments* section of the *Resource* ribbon, click the *Assign Resources* button.

4. In the *Assign Resources* dialog, select your *Expense Cost* resource and then click the *Assign* button.

Figure 7 - 35 shows the *Assign Resources* dialog after assigning an *Expense Cost* resource named *Travel Expense*. I intend to use this *Expense Cost* resource to capture the total amount of the travel expenses for my project so that I can report this amount as a line item expenditure.

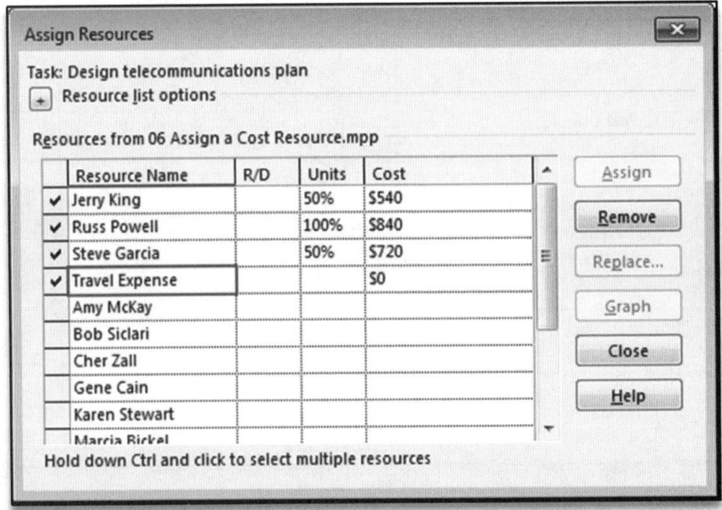

Figure 7 - 35: Assign Resources dialog after assigning an Expense Cost resource

5. In the *Cost* column of the *Assign Resources* dialog, enter the amount of **anticipated expenditure** for the *Expense Cost* resource and then press the **Enter** key on your computer keyboard.

Figure 7 - 36 shows the *Assign Resources* dialog after entering my estimated expenditure for travel expenses on the selected task. Notice that I anticipate the travel expenses at *$1,525* for this task.

6. Continue selecting tasks, using the *Assign Resources* dialog to assign the *Expense Cost* resource, and entering anticipated expenditures in the *Cost* column of the dialog.

7. Click the *Close* button to close the *Assign Resources* dialog.

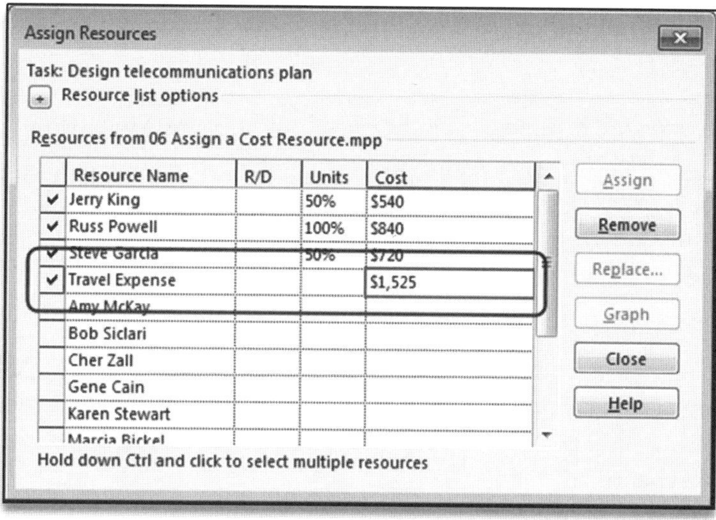

Figure 7 - 36: Assign Resources dialog after assigning an Expense Cost resource

Hands On Exercise

Exercise 7 - 7

Your organization assigns a $225,000 overall budget for your Training Advisor Rollout project. Assign a *Budget Cost* resource to your project so that you can enter the overall monetary budget for your project.

Information: To limit the amount of time required to complete this Hands On Exercise, the **Training Advisor 07.mpp** sample file contains a custom view called *_Cost Resources* that you can use to assign *Cost* resources in a project. If you want to use this custom view for your own projects, the final steps of Exercise 7 - 8 show you how to copy the custom view to your own Global.mpt file, which makes the custom view available for all of the current and future projects you manage.

1. Return to the **Training Advisor 07.mpp** sample file.
2. Click the *Task* tab to display the *Task* ribbon.
3. In the *View* section of the *Task* ribbon, click the *Gantt Chart* pick list button, and select the *_Cost Resources* item in the *Custom* section of the list.
4. Select the Project Summary Task (Row 0).
5. In the *Editing* section of the *Task* ribbon, click the *Scroll to Task* button to bring the cost information into view in the timephased grid.
6. Click the *Resource* tab to display the *Resource* ribbon.
7. In the *Assignments* section of the *Resource* ribbon, click the *Assign Resources* button.
8. In the *Assign Resources* dialog, select the *Project Budget* resource and then click the *Assign* button.

Notice how Project 2013 allows you to assign this *Budget Cost* resource to the Project Summary Task (Row 0).

9. In the *Assign Resources* dialog, click the *Close* button to close the dialog.
10. In the left side of the view, enter *$225,000* in the *Budget Cost* column for the *Project Budget* assignment and then press the **Enter** key on your computer keyboard.
11. Click the *View* tab to display the *View* ribbon.
12. In the *Zoom* section of the *View* ribbon, click the *Timescale* pick list and then select the *Quarters* item.
13. In the timephased grid on the right side of the view, select the *Qtr 1* cell for the *Budget Cost* row for the *Project Budget* assignment, enter *$175,000* in the cell, and then press the **Enter** key on your computer keyboard.
14. Select the *Qtr 2* cell for the *Budget Cost* row for the *Project Budget* assignment, enter *$50,000* in the cell, and then press the **Enter** key on your computer keyboard.
15. Save but **do not** close the **Training Advisor 07.mpp** sample file.

Exercise 7 - 8

The Training Advisor software vendor charges $75,000 for the license for the server software, plus $50,000 for the number of client software licenses needed by your organization. Assign an *Expense Cost* resource to your project so that you can track the total cost of software licenses.

1. Return to the **Training Advisor 07.mpp** sample file, if necessary.
2. Select task ID #19, the *Load and Configure Software* task.
3. Click the *Resource* tab to display the *Resource* ribbon.
4. In the *Assignments* section of the *Resource* ribbon, click the *Assign Resources* button.
5. In the *Assign Resources* dialog, select the *Software Licenses* resource and then click the *Assign* button.
6. In the *Cost* column of the *Assign Resources* dialog, enter *$75,000* for the *Software Licenses* resource and then press the **Enter** key on your computer keyboard.
7. Scroll down and select task ID #23, the *Install Training Advisor Clients* task.
8. In the *Assign Resources* dialog, select the *Software Licenses* resource and then click the *Assign* button.
9. In the *Cost* column of the *Assign Resources* dialog, enter *$50,000* for the *Software Licenses* resource and then press the **Enter** key on your computer keyboard.
10. In the *Assign Resources* dialog, click the *Close* button to close the dialog.

Notice how Project 2013 applied your planned costs for software licenses in the *Cost* column on the left side of the view for each assignment of the software *Licenses* resource.

11. Click the *Task* tab to display the *Task* ribbon.

12. In the *View* section of the *Task* ribbon, click the *Gantt Chart* pick list button and select the *Gantt Chart* view.

Information: Steps #13-18 document the process for copying the *_Cost Resources* custom view from the **Training Advisor 07.mpp** sample file to your Global.mpt file. If you complete these steps, you make the *_Cost Resources* custom view available for use in every current and future project you open. If you do not want to use the *_Cost Resources* custom view, then skip steps #13-18 and complete step #19 only.

13. Click the *File* tab and then click the *Info* tab in the *Backstage*.

14. On the *Info* page in the *Backstage*, click the *Organizer* button.

15. In the list of views on the right side of the *Organizer* dialog, select the *_Cost Resources* custom view in the project and click the *Copy* button to copy the view to your Global.mpt file.

16. Click the *Tables* tab to display the *Tables* page of the dialog.

17. In the list of tables on the right side of the *Organizer* dialog, select the *_Cost Resources* custom table in the project and click the *Copy* button to copy the table to your Global.mpt file.

18. Click the *Close* button to close the *Organizer* dialog.

19. Save but **do not** close the **Training Advisor 07.mpp** sample file.

Using Effort Driven Scheduling

In Project 2013, you can designate each task individually as either an *Effort Driven* task or a *non-Effort Driven* task. The *Effort Driven* status of any task determines how the software responds when you add or remove resources on a task to which you previously assigned one or more resources. The default setting for every task in Project 2013 is *Effort Driven*. To assign additional resources as helpers to a task using *Effort Driven* scheduling, complete the following steps:

1. Select a task to which you previously assigned at least one resource.
2. Click the *View* tab to display the *View* ribbon.
3. In the *Split View* section of the *View* ribbon, select the *Details* checkbox to apply the *Task Entry* view.
4. In *Task Form* pane, select the *Effort driven* option, if not already selected.
5. Select one or more additional resources in the *Resource Name* column, and set a *Units* value for each additional resource.
6. **Do not** enter a *Work* value for any of the additional resources.
7. Click the *OK* button.

When you add a resource to an *Effort Driven* task, Project 2013 keeps the *Remaining Work* value constant and allocates the *Remaining Work* value proportionately to each resource based on the *Units* value of each resource. Consider the following examples of how the software allocates the *Remaining Work* value based on the *Units* values of each resource:

- I assign *Ann Dyer* to the *Design* task at a *Units* value of *100%* and *80 hours* of *Work*, and the software calculates a *Duration* value of *10 days* for the task. Using *Effort Driven* scheduling, I add *Kevin Holthaus* to the task at a *Units* value of *100%*. Project 2013 shortens the *Duration* value to *5 days* and allocates the *80 hours* of *Remaining Work* evenly between the two resources (*40 hours* each to *Ann Dyer* and to *Kevin Holthaus*), as shown in Figure 7 - 37.

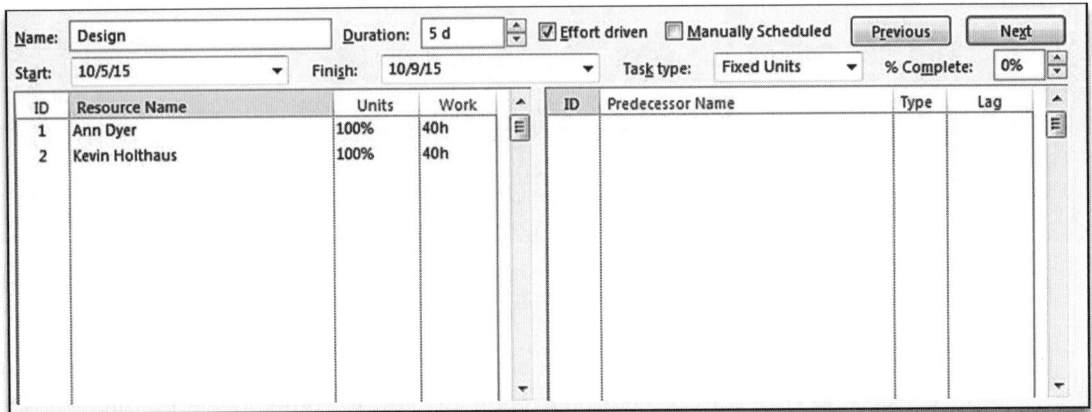

Figure 7 - 37: Using Effort Driven scheduling with identical Units values

- I assign *Ann Dyer* to the *Design* task at a *Units* value of *100%* and *80 hours* of *Work*, and the software calculates a *Duration* value of *10 days* for the task. Using *Effort Driven* scheduling, I add *Kevin Holthaus* to the task at a *Units* value of *50%*. In this situation, Project 2013 shortens the *Duration* to *6.67 days* and allocates the *80 hours* of *Remaining Work* **proportionately** between the two resources (*53.33 hours* to *Ann Dyer* and *26.67 hours* to *Kevin Holthaus*), as shown in Figure 7 - 38.

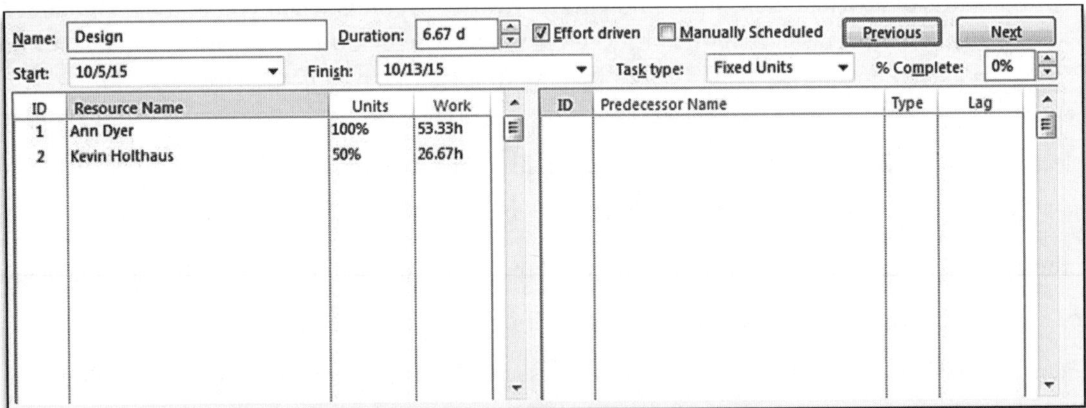

Figure 7 - 38: Effort Driven scheduling with different Units values

How does Project 2013 actually determine the proportionate split of the *80 hours* of *Remaining Work*? The *Units* value of *100%* for *Ann Dyer* is two-thirds of the total *Units* of *150%* for both resources (100/150 = 2/3), so the software allocates *Ann Dyer* two-thirds of the total *Remaining Work*, which is *53.33 hours* (80 x 2/3 = 53.33). The *Units* value of *50%* for *Kevin Holthaus* is one-third of the total *Units* value (50/150 = 1/3), so the software allocates *Kevin Holthaus* one-third of the total *Remaining Work*, which is *26.67 hours* (80 x 1/3 = 26.67).

Best Practice: When you assign additional resources to an *Effort Driven* task, MSProjectExperts recommends that you also increase the *Work* hours for each resource in the range of **10% to 20%** to account for the increased communications overhead between the resources.

Information: When you remove a resource from an *Effort Driven* task with multiple resources already assigned, Project 2013 **increases** the *Duration* value of the task and allocates the *Remaining Work* value proportionately for each remaining resource. This behavior is also known as *Effort Driven* scheduling, although most people do not realize this.

Remember that when you assign additional resources to an *Effort Driven* task, Project 2013 allocates the *Remaining Work* value proportionately between all of the assigned resources. So how does the software respond when you add a helper to a task that already contains some completed work? Consider the following example:

- I assign *Michelle Leitinger* to the *Build* task at a *Units* value of *100%* and *80 hours* of *Work*, and the software calculates a *Duration* value of *10 days* for the task. After she completes *40 hours* of *Actual Work*, this leaves *40 hours* of *Remaining Work* on the task. Using *Effort Driven* scheduling, I add *Susan Risser* to the task at a *Units* value of *100%*. Project 2013 shortens the *Duration* value to *7.5 days* and allocates the *40 hours* of *Remaining Work* evenly between the two resources (*20 hours* each to *Michelle Leitinger* and *Susan Risser*), as shown in Figure 7 - 39.

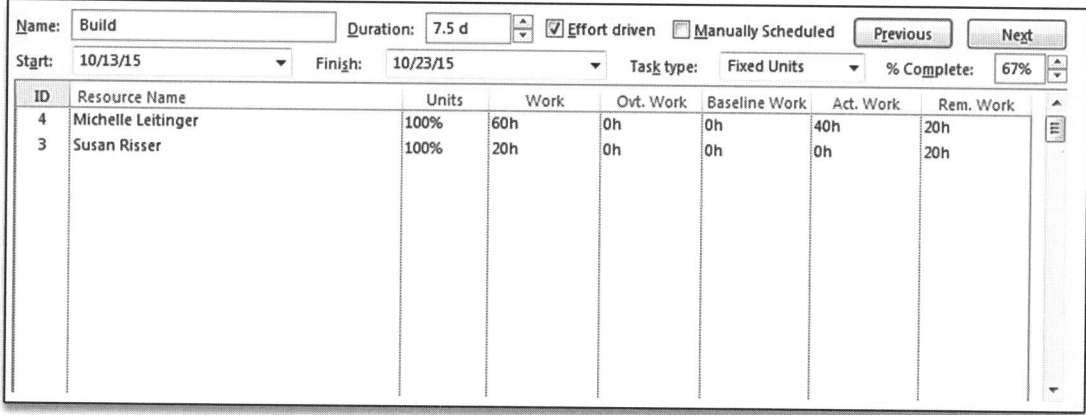

Figure 7 - 39: Using Effort Driven scheduling on a task with completed work

In Figure 7 - 39 shown previously, you see the *Task Form* pane with the *Work* details applied. To view the *Work* details, right-click anywhere in the *Task Form* pane and then select the *Work* item on the shortcut menu. Notice in Figure 7 - 39 that the software allocates only the *40 hours* of *Remaining Work* between the two resources. This gives *60 hours* of total *Work* to *Michelle Leitinger* (*40 hours* of *Actual Work* + *20 hours* of *Remaining Work*) and gives *20 hours* of total *Work* to *Susan Risser* (*0 hours* of *Actual Work* + *20 hours* of *Remaining Work*).

Information: On *Fixed Units* or *Fixed Work* tasks, assigning additional resources using *Effort Driven* scheduling shortens the *Duration* value of the task. On a *Fixed Duration* task, however, assigning additional resources using *Effort Driven* scheduling **does not** shorten the *Duration* value, but does allocate the *Remaining Work* proportionately between the resources.

Using Non-Effort Driven Scheduling

In the real world, not all tasks are *Effort Driven* in nature, meaning that no matter how many helpers you add to the task, the *Duration* value remains unchanged. The classic example is adding additional drivers to drive the school bus along its route; this task takes 2 hours to complete regardless of how many helpers you give to the driver. When you add additional resources to a *non-Effort Driven* task, Project 2013 increases the total *Work* value on the task, and does not decrease the *Duration* value of the task. Conversely, when you remove a resource from a *non-Effort Driven* task, the software decreases the total *Work* value on the task, and does not increase the *Duration* value.

To specify a task as *non-Effort Driven* and then assign additional resources to the task, complete the following steps:

1. Select the task you want to make *non-Effort Driven.*
2. Click the *View* tab to display the *View* ribbon.
3. In the *Split View* section of the *View* ribbon, select the *Details* checkbox to apply the *Task Entry* view.
4. In the *Task Form* pane, **deselect** the *Effort driven* checkbox.
5. Click the *OK* button.
6. Select one or more additional resources in the *Resource Name* column, and set a *Units* value for each additional resource.
7. **Do not** enter a *Work* value for any of the additional resources.
8. Click the *OK* button.

Figure 7 - 40 shows the same example I used previously in Figure 7 - 37, except that I changed the task to *non-Effort Driven*. Notice how the *Duration* value remained the same while Project 2013 increased the total amount of *Work* by assigning *80 hours* of *Work* to *Kevin Holthaus* in addition to the *80 hours* of *Work* previously assigned to *Ann Dyer*.

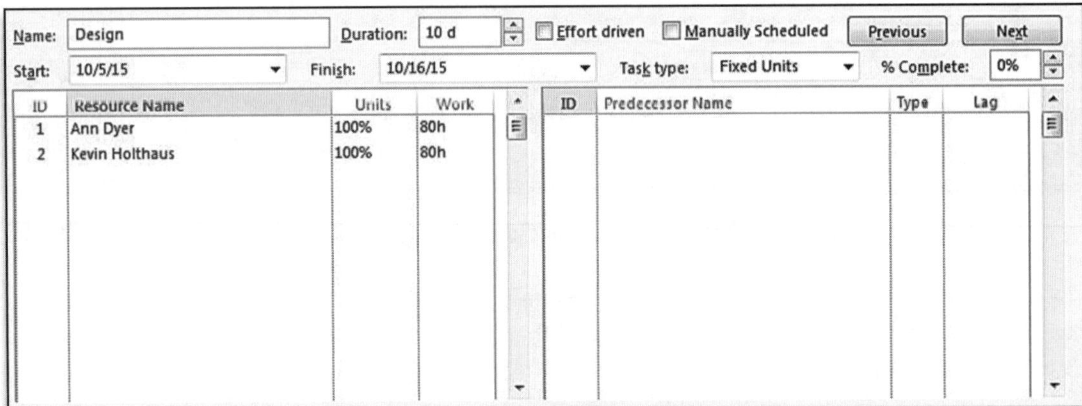

Figure 7 - 40: Using non-Effort Driven scheduling Project 2013 increases total work

Hands On Exercise

Exercise 7 - 9

After reviewing the project schedule, senior management in your organization made a decision to shorten the duration of the *Resolve Connectivity Errors* task by assigning an additional resource to assist with the work. Use *Effort Driven* scheduling to shorten the *Duration* value of this task.

1. Return to the **Training Advisor 07.mpp** sample file.
2. Click the *View* tab to display the *View* ribbon.
3. In the *Split View* section of the *View* ribbon, select the *Details* checkbox to apply the *Task Entry* view.
4. In the *Gantt Chart* pane, select task ID # 25, the *Resolve Connectivity Errors* task.
5. In the *Task Form* pane, make sure the *Effort driven* checkbox is selected (if not, select it and then click the *OK* button).
6. In the *Task Form* pane, add *Terry Uland* to the task at a *Units* value of *25%* (**do not** enter a *Work* value) and then click the *OK* button.

Notice how Project 2013 decreased the *Duration* value of the task to only *10 days*.

7. To account for the increased communication needs between the assigned resources, increase the *Work* value for each resource to *24 hours* and then click the *OK* button.

Notice now how the software increased the *Duration* value to *12 days*, which probably represents a more realistic *Duration* value for this task.

8. In the *Split View* section of the *View* ribbon, **deselect** the *Details* checkbox to close the *Task Form* pane and reapply the *Gantt Chart* view.
9. Save but **do not** close the **Training Advisor 07.mpp** sample file.

Exercise 7 - 10

Learn more about *Effort Driven* scheduling by adding a resource to a task where the existing resource has completed some actual work on the task.

1. Open the **Using Effort Driven Scheduling 2013.mpp** sample file.
2. Click the *View* tab to display the *View* ribbon.
3. In the *Split View* section of the *View* ribbon, select the *Details* checkbox to apply the *Task Entry* view.
4. In the *Gantt Chart* pane, select the *Implement* task.

5. Right-click anywhere in the *Task Form* pane and then select the *Work* details on the shortcut menu.

Notice in the *Task Form* pane that *Greg Owens* previously completed *24 hours* of *Actual Work* on this task. Notice also that he has *40 hours* of *Remaining Work* left to complete this task.

6. In the *Task Form* pane, add *Cindy McNair* at a *Units* value of *100%* and then click the *OK* button.

Notice that Project 2013 allocated the *40 hours* of *Remaining Work* proportionately between the two resources. This means that *Greg Owens* now has *24 hours* of *Actual Work* plus *20 hours* of *Remaining Work* (*44 hours* of total *Work*), while *Cindy McNair* has *20 hours* of *Remaining Work.*

7. Save and close the **Using Effort Driven Scheduling 2013.mpp** sample file.

Replacing Resources Assigned to Tasks

After assigning generic or skill-based resources to tasks, on a future date you may eventually need to replace these generic resources with human resources. The *Assign Resources* dialog allows you to locate human resources with the necessary availability and then to perform the resource replacement. This dialog contains a number of filtering options that you access by clicking the *Resource list options* button (+ button) at the top of the dialog. Figure 7 - 41 shows the *Assign Resources* dialog with the *Resource list options* section expanded.

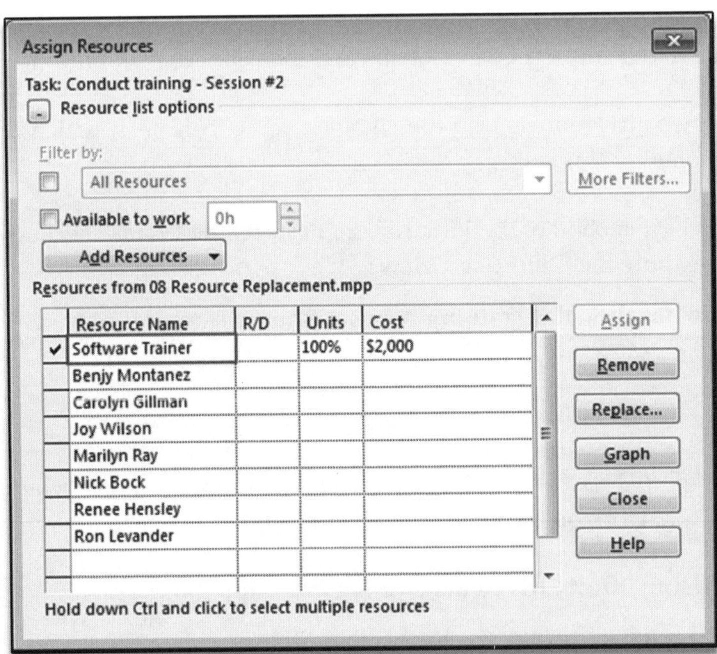

Figure 7 - 41: Assign Resources dialog with Resource list options expanded

The options in the *Resource list options* section of the dialog allow you to apply a filter to locate the right type of human resource to replace an assigned resource. Before you can apply any filter, however, you must make sure you populated the *Resource Sheet* view with some type of data upon which you can filter. For example, you might populate the *Group* column with data used to identify the skills or role for each resource in your project. After meeting this requirement, you can filter for a value in this column using the default *Group...* filter.

To apply a filter to the resources shown in the *Assign Resources* dialog, select the *Filter by* checkbox option, click the *Filter by* pick list, and select any default or custom filter, such as the *Group...* filter. The *Assign Resources* dialog displays only those resources that meet your filtering criteria. For example, in Figure 7 - 42, I selected the *Group...* filter and used this filter to locate members of the *Training* group. Notice that three human resources are members of the *Training* group.

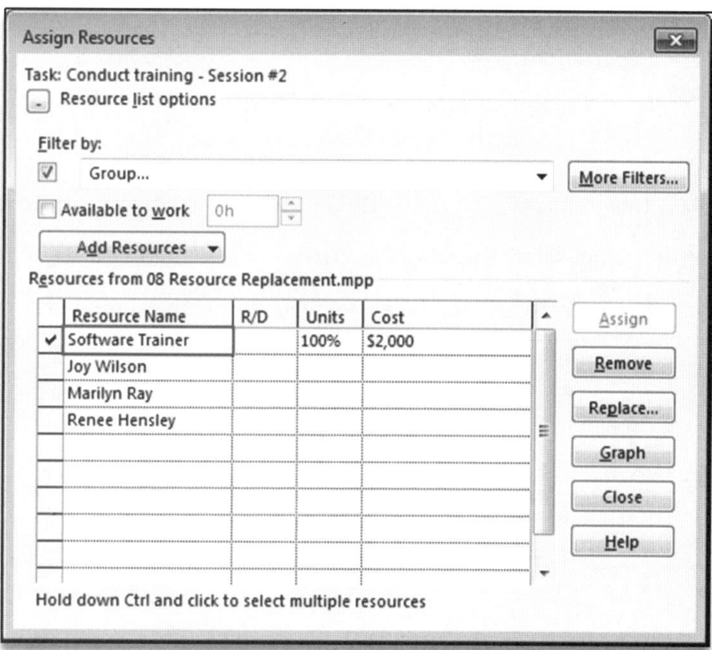

Figure 7 - 42: Apply a filter in the Assign Resources dialog

After you apply a filter, you can also filter further to identify resources with the necessary availability during the scheduled time frame for the selected task. Select the *Available to work* checkbox option and enter the number of hours of work required for the selected task in the *Available to work* field. Notice in Figure 7 - 43 that I refined the filter to locate trainers who have at least *40 hours* of availability to work on the *Conduct training – Session #2* selected task. The *Assign Resources* dialog reveals there are only two trainers who have at least *40 hours* of availability to work on this task, *Joy Wilson* and *Renee Hensley*.

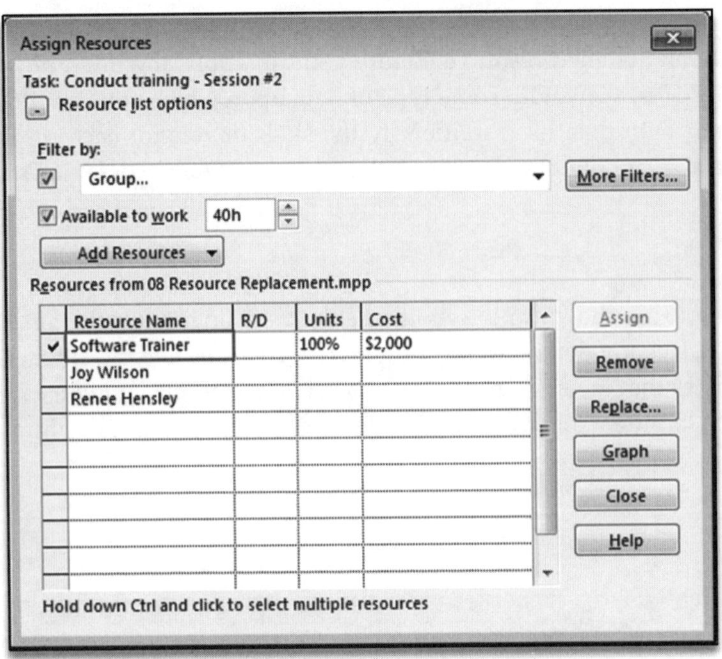

Figure 7 - 43: Use the Available to work filter in the Assign Resources dialog

After filtering, you can replace the assigned resource with another resource by completing the following steps:

1. In the *Assign Resources* dialog, select the resource currently assigned to the task.
2. Click the *Replace* button. The software displays the *Replace Resource* dialog shown in Figure 7 - 44.

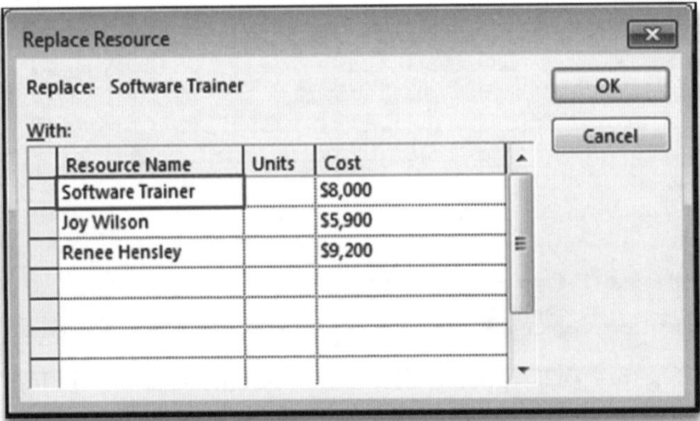

Figure 7 - 44: Replace Resource dialog

3. In the *Replace Resource* dialog, select the new resource and then click the *OK* button.

Information: When a team member leaves your project team before you complete the project, you can use the *Assign Resources* dialog to reassign all of the *Remaining Work* for the departing resource. Project 2013 leaves the *Actual Work* assigned to the departing resource, and transfers only the *Remaining Work* to the new resource. This preserves the historical record of the *Actual Work* performed by the departing resource.

Using the Resource Graph

Beyond the filtering capabilities in the *Resource list options* section of the *Assign Resources* dialog, Project 2013 also allows you to display a resource graph for your project team members. To use this feature, select one or more tasks and then click the *Graph* button in the *Assign Resources* dialog. The software displays a combination view with the *Gantt Chart* view in the top pane and the *Resource Graph* view in the bottom pane, as shown in Figure 7 - 45. The software leaves the *Assign Resources* dialog open, so before you study this custom combination view, you should click the *Close* button to close the *Assign Resources* dialog.

The *Resource Graph* pane shows you a graph with allocation and overallocation information for each of the resources assigned to the selected tasks. By default, the *Resource Graph* pane initially displays the first resource assigned to the first selected task in the left side of the pane. Notice In Figure 7 - 45 that I assigned three resources to the selected task, but the *Resource Graph* pane shows the first resource assigned, *Joy Wilson.*

The default information displayed in *Resource Graph* pane is a graph with *Peak Units* information for each resource assigned to the selected tasks. *Peak Units*, by the way, represents the maximum *Units* value assigned to each resource in all time periods. The graph shows allocation information with blue columns, and shows overallocation information with red columns, for all tasks to which I assigned the current resource in the project.

If you see the resource's name formatted in red, and see red columns anywhere in the graph for a selected resource, then this resource is overallocated. Notice in the graph shown in the *Resource Graph* pane in Figure 7 - 45 that I accidentally overallocated Joy Wilson at a *Peak Units* value of *150%* during the week of June 7, indicated by the red bar extending above the *Max. Units* line of *100%* (thick black horizontal line in the graph). When a resource's *Peak Units* value exceeds the resource's *Max. Units* value in any time period, Project 2013 considers the resource overallocated.

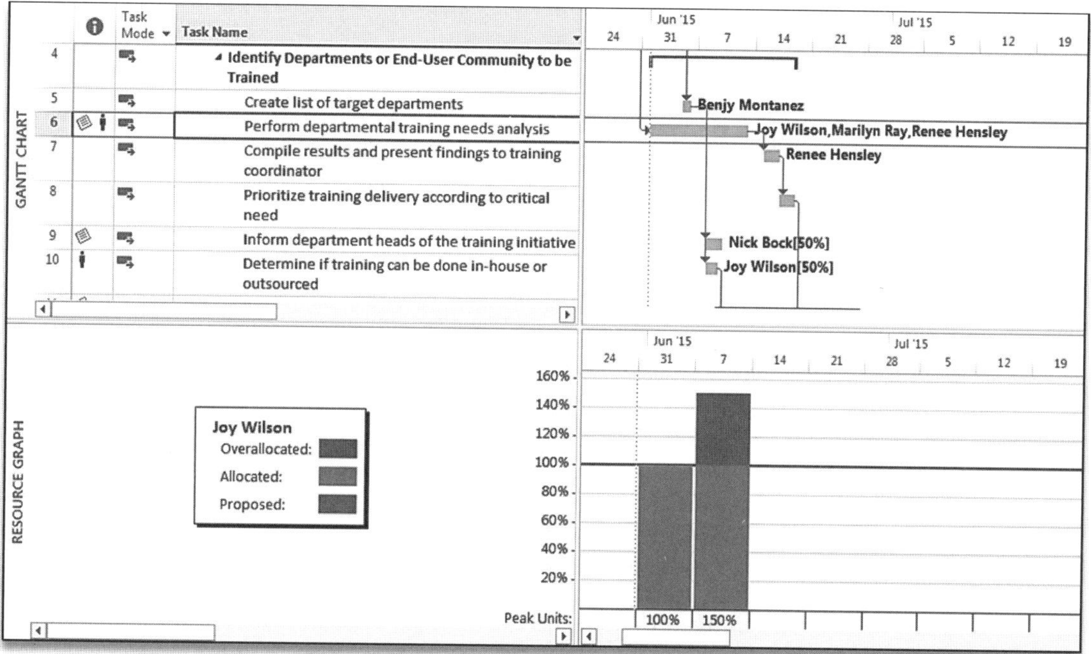

Figure 7 - 45: Combination view with Gantt Chart pane and Resource Graph pane

Information: If you use the **Professional** version of Project 2013, you may also see a third type of information about *Proposed* resource assignments, indicated by purple columns. You can only use this feature, however, if you use Project Server 2013. If your organization does not use Project Server 2013, you do not see any purple columns in the *Resource Graph* pane.

On the left side of the *Resource Graph* pane, use the horizontal scroll bar at the bottom to individually scroll to each of the resources assigned to the selected tasks. On the right side of the *Resource Graph* pane, you can scroll using the horizontal scroll bar to display allocation information in past or in future time periods for all tasks to which you assigned the resource.

The timescale at the top of the *Resource Graph* pane displays the same level of zoom displayed in the timescale at the top of the *Gantt Chart* pane. Using the options in the *Zoom* section of the *View* ribbon, you can zoom the timescales to show more or less detailed allocation information in both the *Gantt Chart* pane and the *Resource Graph* pane. Before you can change the zoom level, however, you first need to click in the *Gantt Chart* pane to activate it.

The *Resource Graph* pane allows you to display other assignment information beyond the *Peak Units* data. Right-click anywhere in the graph side of the *Resource Graph* pane and Project 2013 displays a shortcut menu with other sets of assignments details shown below the *Peak Units* item, as shown in Figure 7 - 46.

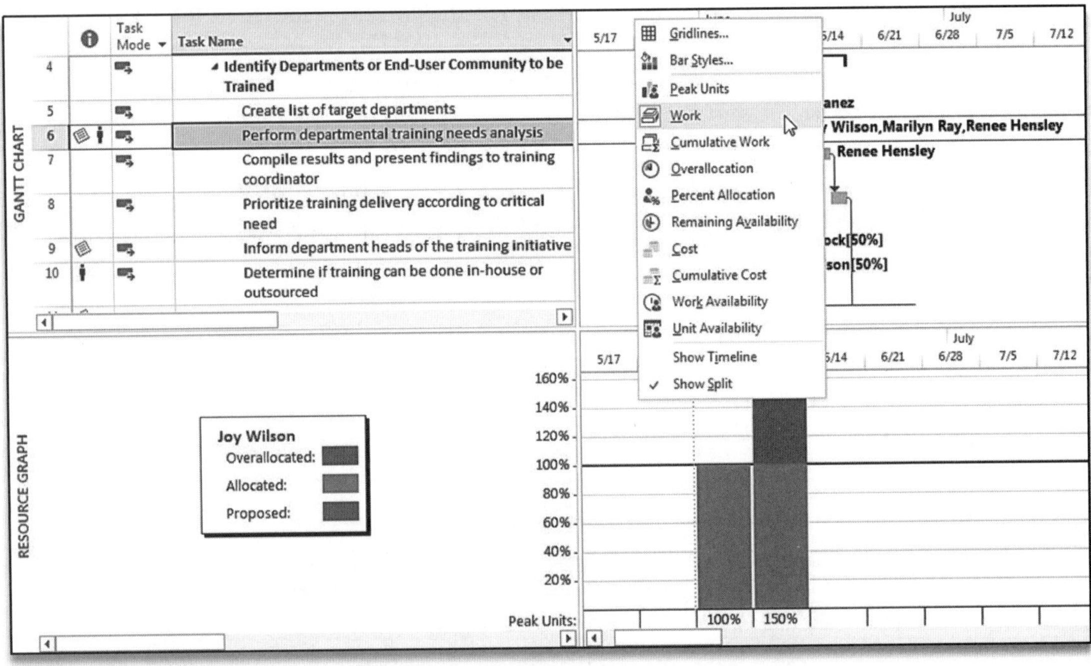

Figure 7 - 46: Right-click in the Resource Graph to view other allocation details

The *Resource Graph* pane allows you to display the following sets of assignment details in the graph:

- **Peak Units** – The graph displays *Peak Units* information as a percentage, and shows allocation data with blue columns and overallocation data with red columns. The combined stacked columns value represents the total *Peak Units* field value in any time period.
- **Work** – The graph displays *Work* information in hours, and shows allocation data with blue columns and overallocation data with red columns. The combined stacked columns value represents the total number of hours of assigned work in any time period

- **Cumulative Work** – The graph displays blue columns representing the resource's *Cumulative Work* in hours during each time period.
- **Overallocation** – The graph displays *Overallocation* information in hours using red columns.
- **Allocation** – The graph shows the percentage of work allocated (the *Percent Allocation* field) for each time period. Project 2013 uses the formula *Percent Allocation* = *Work* / *Capacity* x 100 to calculate the *Percent Allocation* value for each time period. For example, if you assign a resource to work full-time on a task with a *Duration* value of *1 day*, the software calculates the *Percent Allocation* value as *100%* **for that one day**. However, if you do not assign any other tasks to the resource during that week, then the software calculates the *Percent Allocation* value **for that entire week** as only *20%* (8/40 x 100%).
- **Remaining Availability** – The graph displays only *Remaining Availability* information in hours using blue columns. The software uses the formula *Remaining Availability* = *Capacity* – *Work* to calculate the *Remaining Availability* value for each time period. For example, if a resource is available to work 8 hours/day, where the *Max. Units* value is *100%*, and you assign a resource to work at a *Units* value of *50%* on a task with a *Duration* value of *5 days*, the software calculates the *Remaining Availability* for the resource as *4 hours* per day and *20 hours* for the entire week.
- **Cost** – The graph displays blue columns representing the resource cost over time using the currency you specify on the *Display* page of the *Project Options* dialog. The software uses the formula *Cost* = *Standard Rate* x *Work* to calculate the *Cost* value in each time period.
- **Cumulative Cost** – The graph displays blue columns representing the *Cumulative Cost* for the resource in each time period using your selected currency option.
- **Work Availability** – The graph displays *Work Availability* information in hours using blue columns. The software uses the value in the *Max. Units* field plus the working schedule of the resource to calculate the *Work Availability* value in each time period.
- **Unit Availability** –The graph displays *Unit Availability* information as a percentage using blue columns. The software uses the value in the *Max. Units* field plus the working schedule of the resource to calculate the *Unit Availability* value in each time period.

To close the *Resource Graph* pane, use one of the following methods:

- Double-click the split bar between the *Gantt Chart* pane and the *Resource Graph* pane.
- Click the *View* tab and then **deselect** the *Details* checkbox in the *Split View* section of the *View* ribbon.

Hands On Exercise

Exercise 7 - 11

Locate an available human resource with the right skills to replace the generic resource assigned to the Training Advisor Rollout project and then substitute an available human resource for a generic resource.

1. Return to the **Training Advisor 07.mpp** sample file.

2. Select task IDs #30-32, the *Create Training Module 01*, *Create Training Module 02*, and *Create Training Module 03* tasks.
3. Click the *Resource* tab to display the *Resource* ribbon.
4. In the *Assignments* section of the *Resource* ribbon, click the *Assign Resources* button.
5. In the *Assign Resources* dialog, click the *Resource list options* button (the + button) to expand the filtering options, if necessary.
6. Select the *Filter by* checkbox, click the *Filter by* pick list button, and then select the *Group…* filter.
7. In the *Group* dialog, type **TechEd** in the *Group name* field, and then click the *OK* button.

Notice how Project 2013 shows you only the resources who are members of the *TechEd* team, specified previously in the *Group* column in the *Resource Sheet* view.

8. In the *Assign Resources* dialog, select the *Available to work* checkbox and then enter *120 hours* in the *Available to work* field.

When you set the *Available to work* option to *120 hours*, it guarantees that the filtered resource list contains only those resources that are available to work full-time on the three selected tasks. Notice that four human resources have the right skills **and** have 120 hours of availability to work on the selected tasks.

9. In the *Assign Resources* dialog, select the *Training Developer* resource and then click the *Replace* button.
10. In the *Replace Resource* dialog, select *Ruth Andrews* and then click the *OK* button.
11. Click the *Close* button to close the *Assign Resources* dialog.
12. Save but **do not** close the **Training Advisor 07.mpp** sample file.

Understanding Resource Overallocation

During the resource assignment process, you may accidentally overallocate one or more resources in the project. A **resource overallocation** occurs when you assign more work to a resource than the resource can do during the working time available, resulting in a *Units* value that exceeds the *Max. Units* value for the resource. Each of the following situations results in an overallocated resource:

- You assign a resource to work 32 hours in a single day.
- You assign a resource to work 160 hours in a single week.
- You assign a resource to work 30 minutes in a 15-minute time period.

Leveling is the process you use to resolve resource overallocations so that your project resources are no longer overallocated. The third bullet point reveals an important truth about leveling overallocated resources:

Not all overallocations are worth leveling.

You should definitely level the overallocations I describe in the first two bulleted items above, because either situation would likely cause your project finish date to slip. The third situation is not worth leveling, however, as the amount of time spent leveling this overallocation is not worth the effort.

Information: In addition to the three previous examples, you can also overallocate a resource by assigning the resource to a task at a *Units* value of *200%* when the *Max. Units* value for the resource is *100%*. You cannot resolve this type of overallocation using the built-in leveling tool in Project 2013. Instead, you must manually resolve this type of overallocation by reducing the *Units* value for the resource's assignment on the task.

Locating Resource Overallocations

Project 2013 offers you two views in which you can locate overallocated resources: the *Resource Usage* view and the *Team Planner* view. Keep in mind that the *Team Planner* view is only available in the **Professional** version of the software. If you are using the **Standard** version of Project 2013, you cannot use the *Team Planner* view.

To apply the *Resource Usage* view, click the *Resource* tab to display the *Resource* ribbon. In the *View* section of the *Resource* ribbon, click the *Team Planner* pick list button, and then select the *Resource Usage* view. Because Project 2013 formats overallocated resources with red text, look for any resource names formatted in red. To determine the time periods during which your resources are overallocated, click the *Next Overallocation* button in the *Level* section of the *Resource* ribbon. When you click the *Next Overallocation* button, Project 2013 scrolls the timephased grid and selects the start of the first resource overallocation, as shown in Figure 7 - 47.

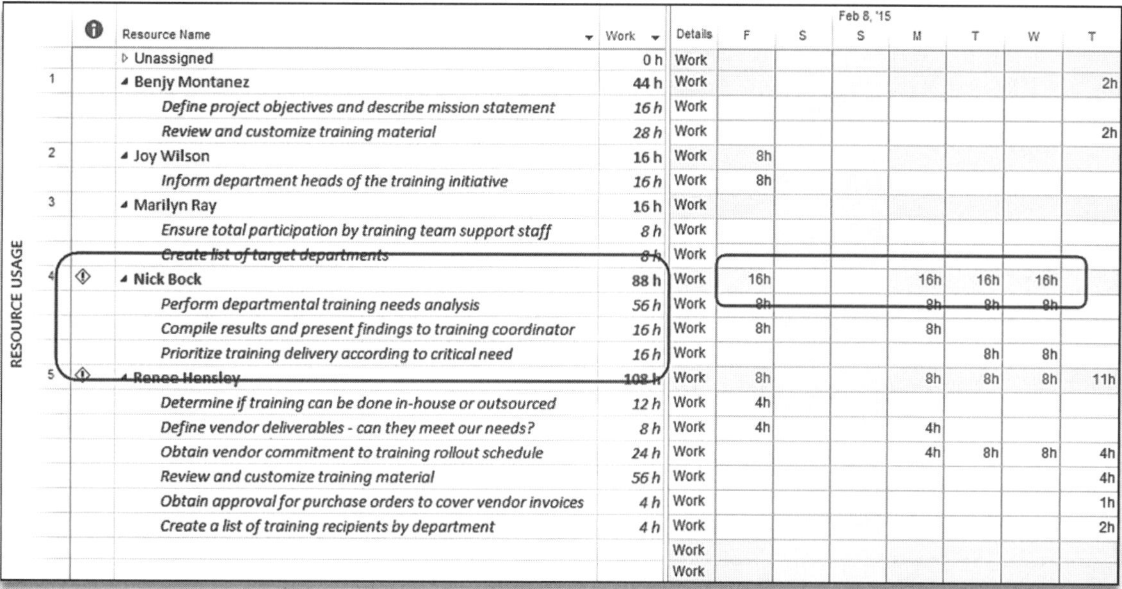

		Resource Name	Work	Details	F	S	Feb 8, '15 S	M	T	W	T
		▷ Unassigned	0 h	Work							
1		◢ Benjy Montanez	44 h	Work							2h
		Define project objectives and describe mission statement	*16 h*	Work							
		Review and customize training material	*28 h*	Work							2h
2		◢ Joy Wilson	16 h	Work	8h						
		Inform department heads of the training initiative	*16 h*	Work	8h						
3		◢ Marilyn Ray	16 h	Work							
		Ensure total participation by training team support staff	*8 h*	Work							
		Create list of target departments	*8 h*	Work							
4	◈	◢ Nick Bock	88 h	Work	16h			16h	16h	16h	
		Perform departmental training needs analysis	*56 h*	Work	8h			8h	8h	8h	
		Compile results and present findings to training coordinator	*16 h*	Work	8h			8h			
		Prioritize training delivery according to critical need	*16 h*	Work					8h	8h	
5	◈	◢ Renee Hensley	108 h	Work	8h			8h	8h	8h	11h
		Determine if training can be done in-house or outsourced	*12 h*	Work	4h						
		Define vendor deliverables - can they meet our needs?	*8 h*	Work	4h			4h			
		Obtain vendor commitment to training rollout schedule	*24 h*	Work				4h	8h	8h	4h
		Review and customize training material	*56 h*	Work							4h
		Obtain approval for purchase orders to cover vendor invoices	*4 h*	Work							1h
		Create a list of training recipients by department	*4 h*	Work							2h
				Work							
				Work							

Figure 7 - 47: Resource Usage view shows first overallocation

Warning: Because of an unfixed bug in the release (RTM) version of Project 2013, clicking the *Next Overallocation* button may not scroll to any times periods during which a resource is overallocated. Instead, the software only displays the dialog shown in Figure 7 - 48.

Notice in Figure 7 - 47 shown previously that I assigned *Nick Bock* to work 16 hours each day in a four-day period during the weeks of February 1 and February 8. I accidentally caused this overallocation when I assigned him to work on three overlapping tasks, each of which requires full-time work. As you continue to click the *Next Overal-*

location button, Project 2013 selects the start of each successive overallocation. When the software cannot locate any more resource overallocations, it displays the dialog shown in Figure 7 - 48.

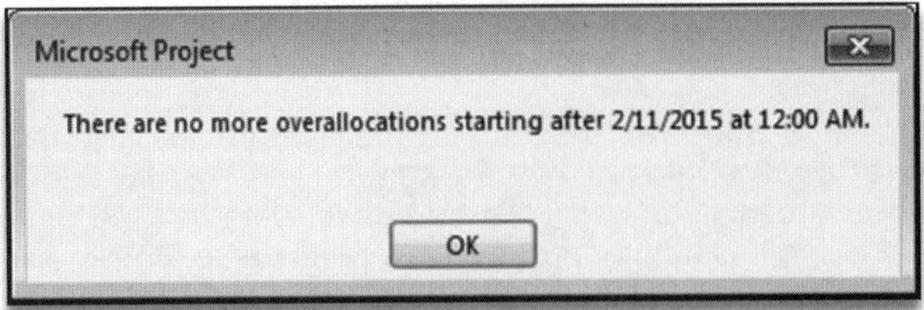

Figure 7 - 48: No more resource overallocations

To apply the *Team Planner* view, click the *Resource* tab to display the *Resource* ribbon. In the *View* section of the *Resource* ribbon, click the *Team Planner* button. Because Project 2013 formats overallocated resources with red text, look for any resource names formatted in red. The software also applies red borders on Gantt bars of the tasks assigned to an overallocated resource, indicating the time period during which the resource is overallocated.

Figure 7 - 49 shows the *Team Planner* view. Notice the red borders around the Gantt bars for some of the tasks assigned to *Nick Bock* and to *Renee Hensley*, the two overallocated resources in this project. Because the *Team Planner* view presents assignment information graphically using Gantt bars, it is very easy to see why any resource is overallocated. In the case of *Nick Bock*, he is overallocated because I accidentally assigned him to work full-time on three parallel tasks.

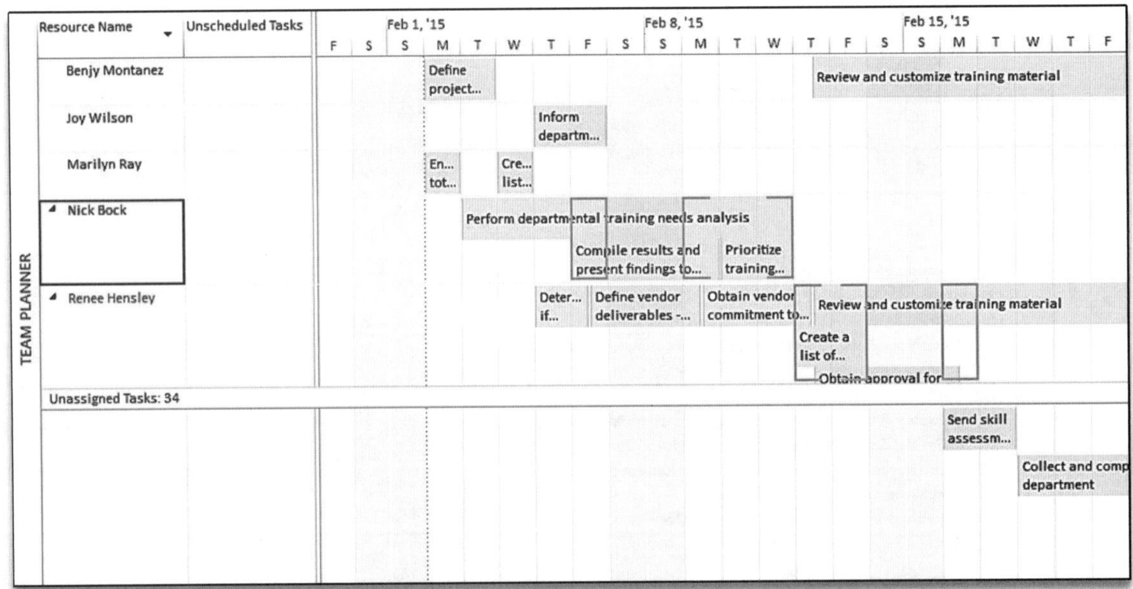

Figure 7 - 49: Team Planner view shows resource overallocations

Leveling Overallocated Resources

As I previously stated, leveling is the process you use to resolve resource overallocations. There are many ways to level overallocated resources, including each of the following:

- Substitute an available resource for the overallocated resource.
- Increase the availability of overallocated resources.

- Schedule overtime for the overallocated resource.
- Manually delay tasks with overallocated resources.
- Delay the start of a resource assignment on a task.
- Adjust the project schedule using task constraints to eliminate resource assignment conflicts.
- Split tasks by interrupting the work on a task to make resources available for other assignments.
- Adjust dependencies and add *Lag* time.
- Add resources to an *Effort Driven* task to shorten the duration of the task.
- Look for potential overlapping work opportunities, such as Finish-to-Start dependencies that do not have a true "finish to start" relationship.
- Negotiate with your project sponsor or customer to delay the finish date of the project.
- Negotiate with your project sponsor or customer to reduce the feature set (scope) of the project.
- Use the built-in leveling tool in Project 2013 with either the *Resource Usage* view or *Team Planner* view.

Notice that using the built-in leveling tool in Project 2013 appears last on the preceding list! Each of the preceding leveling methods is powerful and useful for leveling overallocated resources; however, most users assume the only way to level is to use the built-in leveling tool found in Project 2013. Given the complexity of using the software's leveling capabilities, the average user of Project 2013 is far better off using any of the other manual leveling methods. The key to using any method for resource leveling is to remember that you must take **complete control** of all leveling decisions.

Leveling Overallocations Using the Resource Usage View

Many Project 2013 users attempt to level all of their overallocated resources simultaneously in the *Gantt Chart* view using the built-in leveling tool. Although this approach can work in some situations, most often it leads to frustration. This approach does not give you insight into how the software leveled the overallocations, and can lead to failure because you did not take control over the leveling process. A much better approach is to level overallocated resources using the following methodology:

1. Level each overallocated resource individually in the *Resource Usage* view.
2. Study the results of the leveling process in the *Leveling Gantt* view.
3. Clear unacceptable leveling results and then level the overallocated resource using any other method.
4. Repeat steps #1-3 for each overallocated resource.

Setting Leveling Options

Before you begin the process of leveling overallocated resources in the *Resource Usage* view, you should specify your leveling options by clicking the *Leveling Options* button in the *Level* section of the *Resource* ribbon. The software displays the *Resource Leveling* dialog shown in Figure 7 - 50.

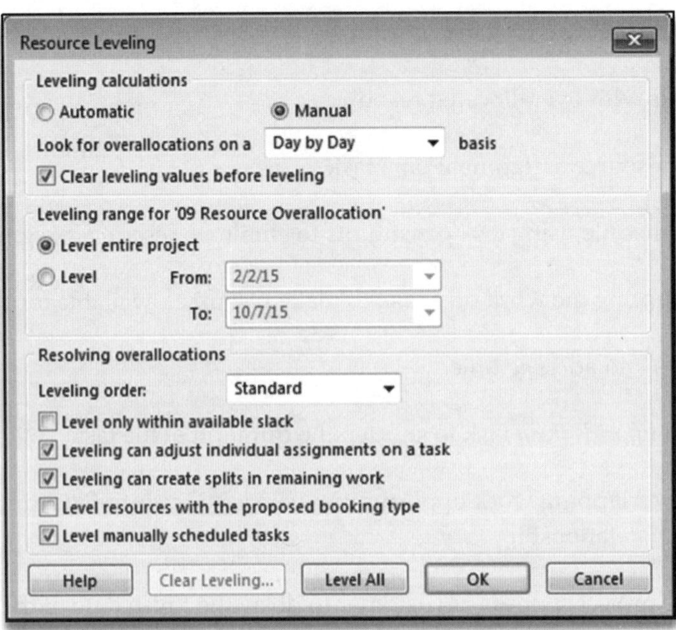

Figure 7 - 50: Resource Leveling dialog

In the *Leveling calculations* section of the *Resource Leveling* dialog, you find the *Look for overallocations on a _____ basis* option. This option controls the granularity used by Project 2013 to determine whether resources are overallocated. The default setting is *Day by Day*, which means that the software only shows you overallocations during which resources are overallocated in full day time periods. Click the *Look for overallocations on a _____ basis* pick list and select any other option, as needed. The finest level of granularity is the *Minute by Minute* setting and the coarsest level of granularity is the *Month by Month* setting. When Project 2013 locates a resource overallocation at the granularity level you specify, the software formats the name of the resource in red, and displays a yellow indicator in the *Indicators* column to the left of the resource name. If you float your mouse pointer over the yellow indicator, the software simply displays a *This resource is overallocated* message in the tooltip.

Warning: Be very cautious in using either the *Minute by Minute* or *Hour by Hour* settings on the *Look for overallocations on a _____ basis* pick list. Using either setting forces the software to show many overallocations that are not worth the time and effort to level, including overallocations in 15-minute time periods.

In the *Resource Leveling* dialog, there are several options in the *Resource overallocations* section of the dialog that you may want to change from their default setting. These options include:

- Set the *Leveling order* option to the *Priority, Standard* value. By selecting this option, you force the software to consider first the *Priority* number of each task in the software's algorithm of five leveling factors. The other factors include predecessor task relationships, the *Start* date of each task, the *Total Slack* value for each task, and whether the task has an inflexible constraint.

- Select the *Level only within available slack* option to guarantee that the leveling operation does not change the *Finish* date of your project. With this option selected, Project 2013 levels overallocations until it reaches the point where it must delay the *Finish* date of your project. At this point, the software discontinues the leveling process and displays a warning dialog. At this point, you must stop using the built-in leveling tool and use an alternate method for leveling the remaining overallocations.

- If your project contains *Manually Scheduled* tasks with overallocated resources, and you want to manually reschedule the tasks to resolve these overallocations, then you should **deselect** the *Level manually scheduled tasks* option. If you leave this option selected, Project 2013 delays or splits any *Manually Scheduled* tasks with overallocated resources assigned to them.

Warning: MSProjectExperts recommends that you **never** select the *Automatic* option in the *Leveling calculations* section of the *Resource Leveling* dialog. When applied, the *Automatic* leveling option causes Project 2013 to level all overallocated resources automatically in all open projects without asking your permission. This means that you lose control over the leveling process.

After you select your leveling options in the *Resource Leveling* dialog, click the *OK* button. Project 2013 saves your option selections in this dialog so that you do not need to reselect them every time you want to level resource overallocations.

Warning: Do not click the *Level All* button in the *Resource Leveling* dialog. If you click the *Level All* button, the software levels **all** of the overallocated resources in your project in a single operation. Again, this means that you lose control over the leveling process.

Leveling an Overallocated Resource

To start the process of leveling overallocated resources, select the most critical resource in the project. You must decide the criteria used to determine which resource is most critical. Your criteria might include which resource is the most in demand for project work, which resource is the most highly skilled, which resource is assigned to the most *Critical* tasks in the project, etc. After selecting this resource, click the *Level Resource* button in the *Level* section of the *Resource* ribbon. Project 2013 displays the *Level Resources* dialog shown in Figure 7 - 51.

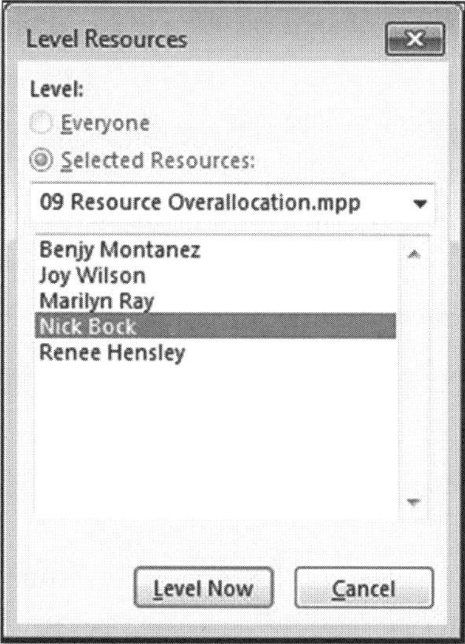

Figure 7 - 51: Level Resources dialog

The *Level Resources* dialog selects the same resource you selected in the *Resource Usage* view. Click the *Level Now* button in the dialog to level the overallocations for the first selected resource using the leveling options you set in the *Resource Leveling* dialog. When you use the built-in leveling tool to level an overallocated resource, Project 2013 resolves the overallocation using one or both of the following methods:

- The software delays tasks or assignments.

- The software splits tasks or assignments.

If Project 2013 cannot level overallocations for the selected resource, such as when you select the *Level only within available slack* option in the *Resource Leveling* dialog, the software displays the warning dialog shown in Figure 7 - 52. If you previously selected multiple resources to level in a single operation, you can click the *Skip* button to continue the leveling process with the next overallocated resource, or you can click the *Skip All* button to skip all overallocations that the software cannot resolve. If you selected only your critical resource, as guided in this module, then you must click the *Stop* button to stop the leveling process entirely. At this point, you must level the overallocated resource using one of the manual methods presented earlier in the *Leveling Overallocated Resources* topical section of this module.

Information: The warning dialog shown in Figure 7 - 52 is what you see if you attempt to level a resource that you accidentally overallocated by assigning the resource to a task at a *Units* value that is greater than its *Max. Units* value, such as when you assign the resource with a *Units* value of *200%* when the *Max. Units* value for the resource is *100%*.

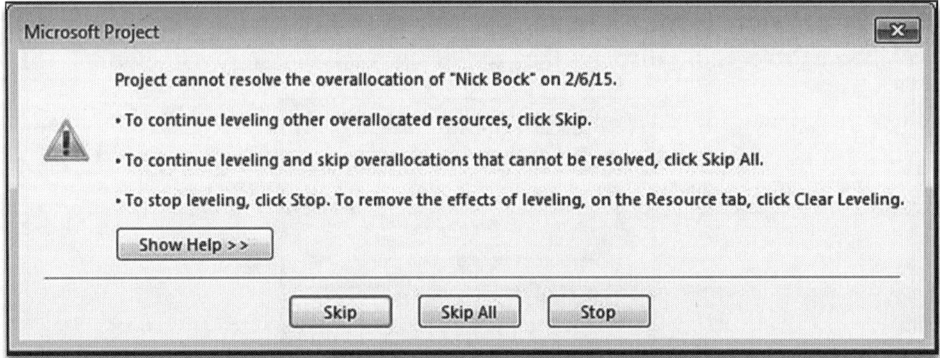

Figure 7 - 52: Warning dialog during leveling

Viewing Leveling Results

To see the results of leveling the first overallocated resource, you must apply the *Leveling Gantt* view. The best way to apply the *Leveling Gantt* view is to open a new window containing this view by completing the following steps:

1. Click the *View* tab to display the *View* ribbon.
2. In the *Window* section of the *View* ribbon, click the *New Window* button. Project 2013 displays the *New Window* dialog shown in Figure 7 - 53.

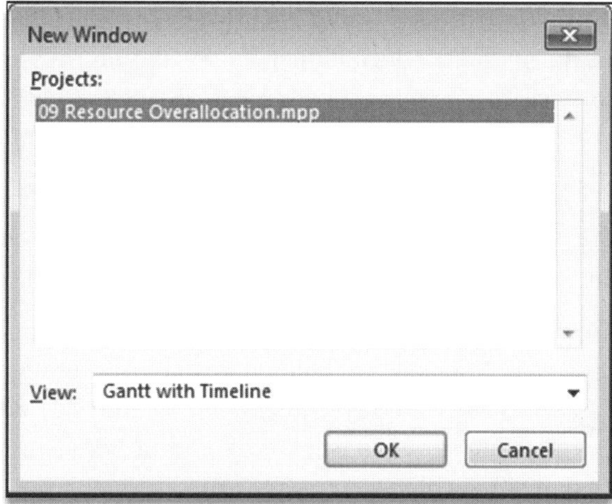

Figure 7 - 53: New Window dialog

3. At the bottom of the *New Window* dialog, click the *View* pick list button and select the *Leveling Gantt* item.
4. Click the *OK* button. The software displays the *Leveling Gantt* view shown in Figure 7 - 54.

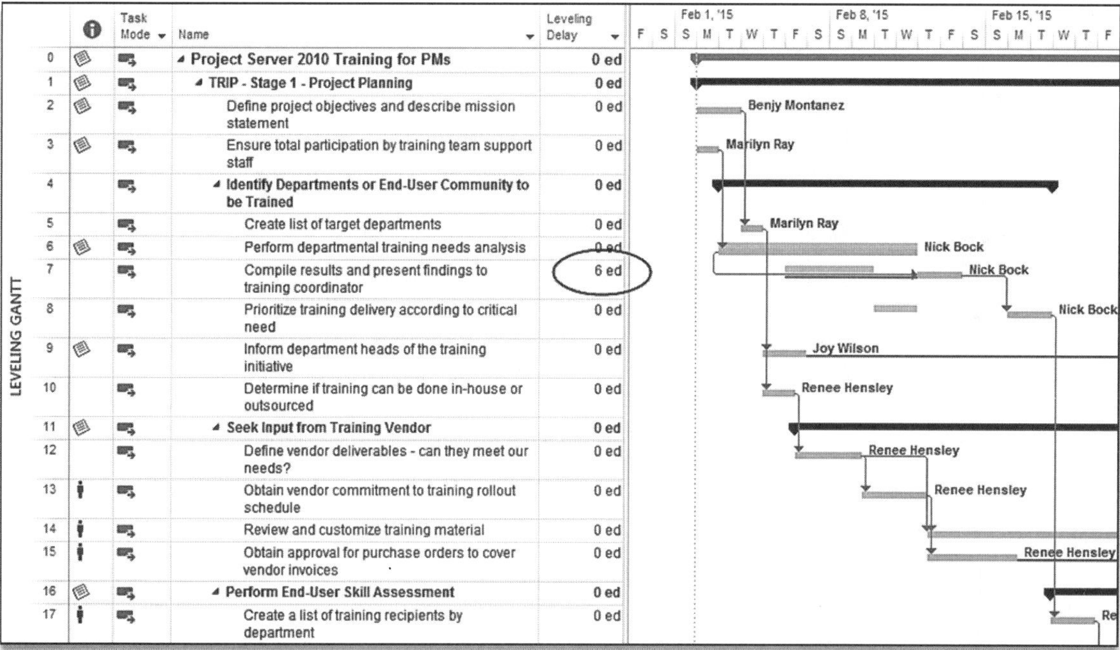

	Name	Leveling Delay
0	Project Server 2010 Training for PMs	0 ed
1	TRIP - Stage 1 - Project Planning	0 ed
2	Define project objectives and describe mission statement	0 ed
3	Ensure total participation by training team support staff	0 ed
4	Identify Departments or End-User Community to be Trained	0 ed
5	Create list of target departments	0 ed
6	Perform departmental training needs analysis	0 ed
7	Compile results and present findings to training coordinator	6 ed
8	Prioritize training delivery according to critical need	0 ed
9	Inform department heads of the training initiative	0 ed
10	Determine if training can be done in-house or outsourced	0 ed
11	Seek Input from Training Vendor	0 ed
12	Define vendor deliverables - can they meet our needs?	0 ed
13	Obtain vendor commitment to training rollout schedule	0 ed
14	Review and customize training material	0 ed
15	Obtain approval for purchase orders to cover vendor invoices	0 ed
16	Perform End-User Skill Assessment	0 ed
17	Create a list of training recipients by department	0 ed

Figure 7 - 54: Leveling Gantt view

The *Leveling Gantt* view includes the *Delay* table on the left and the *Leveling Gantt* chart on the right. The symbols used in the *Leveling Gantt* view are as follows:

- The **tan Gantt bars** represent the pre-leveled schedule for each task you assigned to the overallocated resource that you just leveled. Figure 7 - 54 shown previously reveals that I created the resource overallocation for Nick Bock accidentally by assigning him to work full-time on three parallel tasks (task ID numbers #6, 7, and 8).
- The **light blue Gantt bars** represent the schedule of all tasks after the software levels the resource overallocation.

- The **brown underscore** to the left of any Gantt bar represents the amount of delay applied to the task schedule to level the resource overallocation. Figure 7 - 54 shown previously reveals the delay symbol to the left of the Gantt bar for task ID #7. In the leveling process, Project 2013 delayed task ID #7, which then delayed task ID #8 due to a Finish-to-Start dependency relationship, which resolved Nick Bock's resource overallocation.

- The **teal underscore** to the right of any Gantt bar represents the *Total Slack* for that task, which signifies the amount of time you can delay the task without delaying the finish date of the entire project.

The *Delay* table includes the *Leveling Delay* column to the right of the *Task Name* column. This column shows the amount of delay the software applies to a task to level a resource overallocation. By default, Project 2013 measures the amount of *Leveling Delay* in **elapsed days** (displayed as **edays** or **ed**). Each elapsed day is a 24-hour calendar day that ignores nonworking time, such as weekends and holidays. In Figure 7 - 54 shown previously, notice that the software delayed task ID #7 six elapsed days (6 ed).

Clearing Leveling Results

As you study the results of leveling an overallocated resource, you may find that Project 2013 did not level an overallocation as you expected. In these situations, you must clear the unacceptable leveling result and then level using another method. To clear an unacceptable leveling result, complete the following steps:

1. Click the *Resource* tab to display the *Resource* ribbon.
2. Select only the tasks leveled in an unacceptable manner.
3. In the *Level* section of the *Resource* ribbon, click the *Clear Leveling* button. Project 2013 displays the *Clear Leveling* dialog shown in Figure 7 - 55.

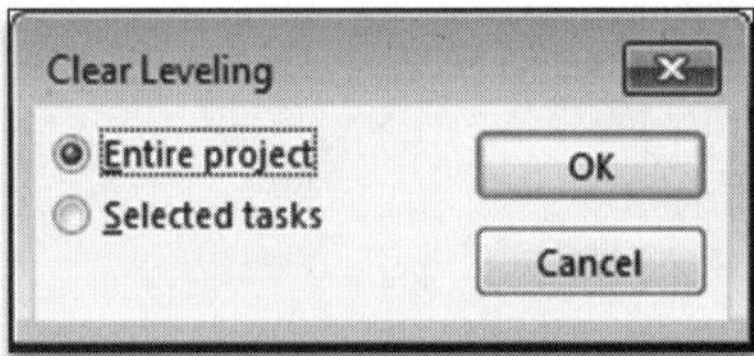

Figure 7 - 55: Clear Leveling dialog

4. In the *Clear Leveling* dialog, choose the *Selected tasks* option and then click the *OK* button.

The software sets the *Leveling Delay* value back to the default value to *0d* for each selected task. At this point, you must level the resource overallocation using another method. You have many options available to you, including using one of the manual leveling methods I previously discussed. Another option is to set a *Priority* number on tasks showing the relative importance of each task, and then re-level the overallocations in the *Resource Usage* view.

Setting Task Priority Numbers

When you set task *Priority* numbers on tasks assigned to an overallocated resource, Project 2013 levels the resource overallocation by factoring in the task *Priority* numbers you assign. The software delays tasks with lower *Priority* numbers while maintaining the original schedule of the task with the highest *Priority* number. To set a *Priority* number on tasks with overallocated resources, complete the following steps:

1. Double-click a task assigned to an overallocated resource. Project 2013 displays the *Task Information* dialog shown in Figure 7 - 56.
2. Click the *General* tab, if necessary.
3. Set a value between *0* and *1000* in the *Priority* field.

Remember that *0* signifies the lowest priority and *1000* signifies the highest priority for any task.

4. Click the *OK* button.
5. Repeat steps #1-4 for each task to which you assigned the overallocated resource.

When setting *Priority* numbers on multiple tasks, be sure to specify a unique priority number for each task. After setting task *Priority* numbers, return to the *Resource Usage* window and then level the overallocated resource again.

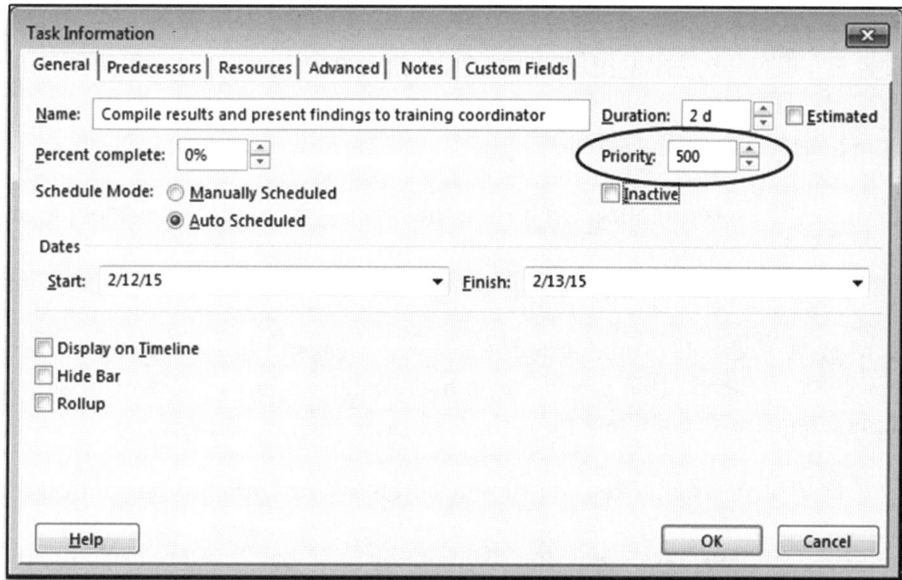

Figure 7 - 56: Task Information dialog – Set a Priority number

Information: An alternate method for setting *Priority* numbers to tasks is to insert the *Priority* field temporarily in the *Leveling Gantt* view by completing the following steps:

1. Right-click the *Leveling Delay* column header and select the *Insert Column* item on the shortcut menu.
2. In the pick list of available fields, select the *Priority* field.
3. Enter values in the *Priority* column for each task with an overallocated resource assigned.

Information: For the sake of simplicity, I offer only a brief presentation on resource leveling in this book. For an in-depth treatment of all aspects of resource leveling, refer to the *Advanced Resource Leveling* module of the companion volume to this book, *Ultimate Study Guide: Advanced, Microsoft Project 2013*.

Hands On Exercise

Exercise 7 - 12

Locate resource overallocations and then level overallocated resources.

1. Return to the **Training Advisor 07.mpp** sample file.
2. Click the *Resource* tab to display the *Resource* ribbon.
3. In the *View* section of the *Resource* ribbon, click the *Team Planner* pick list button and select the *Resource Usage* view.
4. Scroll the timephased grid to the week of **January 3, 2016** and select *Monday, January 3* in the timephased grid.
5. In the *Level* section of the *Resource* ribbon, click the *Next Overallocation* button.

Notice that Mickey Cobb is overallocated during the first two days of the week of January 3.

6. In the *Level* section of the *Resource* ribbon, click the *Next Overallocation* button again.

Notice that Mike Andrews is overallocated during the weekend of January 23-24 because you assigned him to work on a weekend. This is not a true overallocation, however, and in situations like this you should simply ignore the overallocation.

7. In the *Level* section of the *Resource* ribbon, click the *Next Overallocation* button one final time.

Notice that Project 2013 displays a warning dialog indicating that it cannot find any more overallocations in the project.

8. Click the *OK* button to close the warning dialog.
9. In the *Level* section of the *Resource* ribbon, click the *Leveling Options* button.
10. In the *Resource Leveling* dialog, click the *Leveling order* pick list and select the *Priority, Standard* order.
11. Click the *OK* button to close the *Resource Leveling* dialog.
12. Scroll the timephased grid back to the week of *January 3, 2016*.
13. Scroll down the list of resources and select *Mickey Cobb*.
14. In the *Level* section of the *Resource* ribbon, click the *Level Resource* button.
15. Click the *Level Now* button in the *Level Resources* dialog.

Notice that Project 2013 no longer formats Mickey Cobb's name in red, indicating that the software leveled her overallocation successfully.

16. Click the *View* tab to display the *View* ribbon.
17. In the *Window* section of the *View* ribbon, click the *New Window* button.
18. In the *New Window* dialog, click the *View* pick list and select the *Leveling Gantt* item, and then click the *OK* button.
19. Widen the *Task Name* column, as needed, and then drag the split bar to the right edge of the *Leveling Delay* column.
20. Press **Control + Home** and then press **Alt + Home** on your computer keyboard to scroll your project back to the beginning.

Notice that Project 2013 leveled Mickey Cobb's resource overallocation by setting a *Leveling Delay* value of *2 elapsed days* on task ID #28, the *Setup Test Training Server* task.

21. Click the *Close Window* button (**X** button) in the upper right corner of the *Leveling Gantt* window to close the window.
22. Save but **do not** close the **Training Advisor 07.mpp** sample file.

Leveling Resource Overallocations in the Team Planner View

For novice users of Project 2013, the *Team Planner* view is an excellent location in which to hone valuable leveling skills. This view allows you to analyze the current state of resource assignments in your project using a friendly graphical display. To apply the *Team Planner* view, click the *Resource* tab to display the *Resource* ribbon. In the *View* section of the *Resource* ribbon, click the *Team Planner* button. The software displays the *Team Planner* view for your project, as shown in Figure 7 - 57.

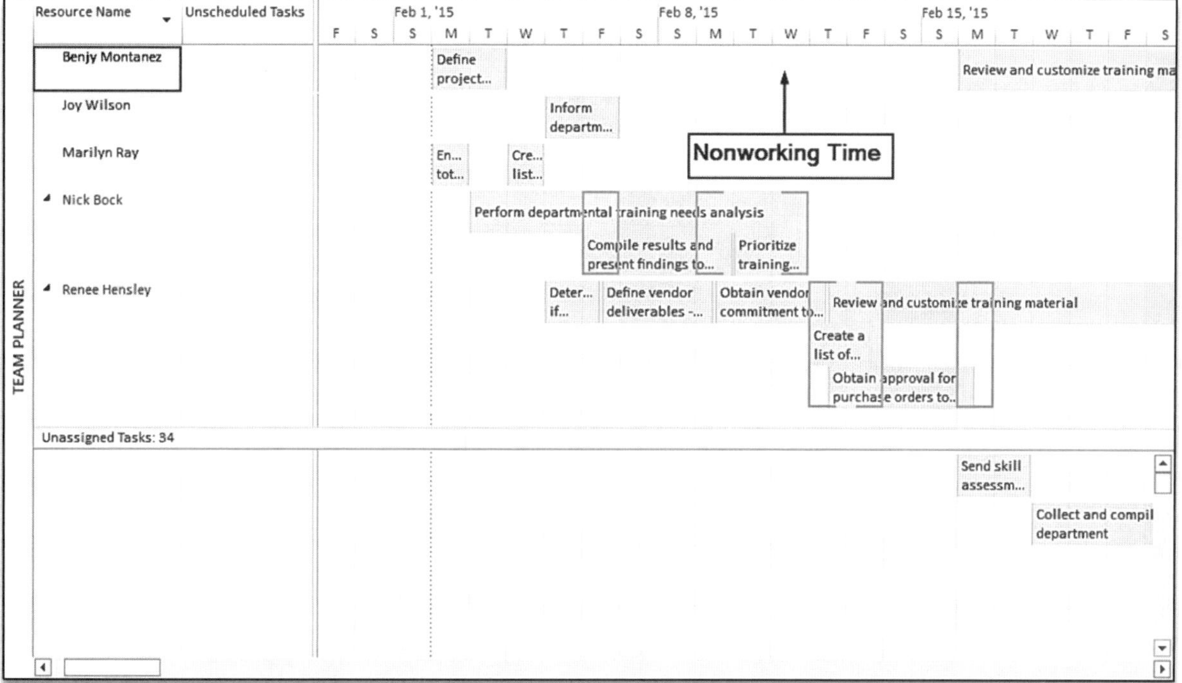

Figure 7 - 57: Team Planner view

Warning: Remember that only the **Professional** version of Project 2013 includes the *Team Planner* view. If you use the **Standard** version of the software, the *Team Planner* view is not an available view.

The *Team Planner* view displays resource and assignment information in two panes. The top pane is the *Resource* pane and shows resources from the *Resource Sheet* view of your project, sorted alphabetically by ID number. Assigned tasks for each resource appear as light blue Gantt bars on the right side of the pane. Unlike the *Gantt Chart* view, however, the *Team Planner* view displays the Gantt bars arranged horizontally on a single line for each resource. *Unscheduled Tasks* (*Manually Scheduled* tasks with no *Duration, Start,* or *Finish* date) that are already assigned to a resource appear in the *Unscheduled Tasks* column to the right of the resource name in the top pane.

The right half of the *Resource* pane also shows nonworking time for each resource, displayed as a gray shaded band for each time period. Nonworking time includes weekends and company holidays for all resources, plus vacation and planned sick leave for each resource individually. On the right side of the *Resource* pane shown previously in Figure 7 - 57, you can also see that *Benjy Montanez* has a week of nonworking time scheduled during the week of February 8, indicated by the gray shaded band in the *Gantt Chart* area for this resource. To learn more about any resource's nonworking time for any time period, double-click the gray shaded band for that time period of interest. Project 2013 displays the *Change Working Time* dialog shown in Figure 7 - 58. Notice that *Benjy Montanez* is scheduled to take a SQL Server training class during that week. Click the *Cancel* button to close the *Change Working Time* dialog for the selected resource.

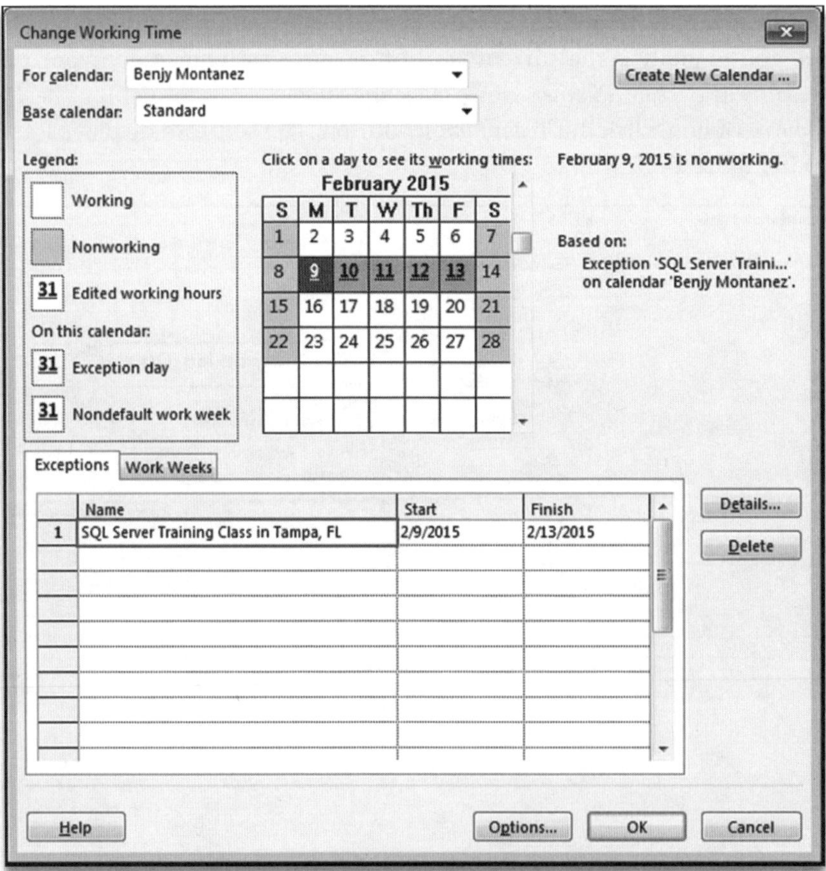

Figure 7 - 58: Change Working Time dialog, Week of training for Benjy Montanez

The bottom pane of the *Team Planner* view is the *Unassigned Tasks* pane and shows the list of tasks not yet assigned to any resource, sorted by task ID number. The right side of the *Unassigned Tasks* pane shows Gantt bars with the current schedule for each unassigned task, based on the schedule specified in the *Gantt Chart* view of the project.

To view additional information about any task, float your mouse pointer over the Gantt bar of the task. Project 2013 displays a screen tip for the selected Gantt bar, as shown in Figure 7 - 59. The screen tip displays summary information about the task, including items like the *Task Mode* setting, *Start* date, *Finish* date, *Duration*, etc.

Information: Because you cannot see summary tasks in the *Team Planner* view, you can use the screen tip to determine the summary tasks for any selected task. Float your mouse pointer over the Gantt bar for any task and examine the *Path* information shown in the screen tip. The *Path* information shows you the complete path of all summary tasks for the selected task, including the Project Summary Task.

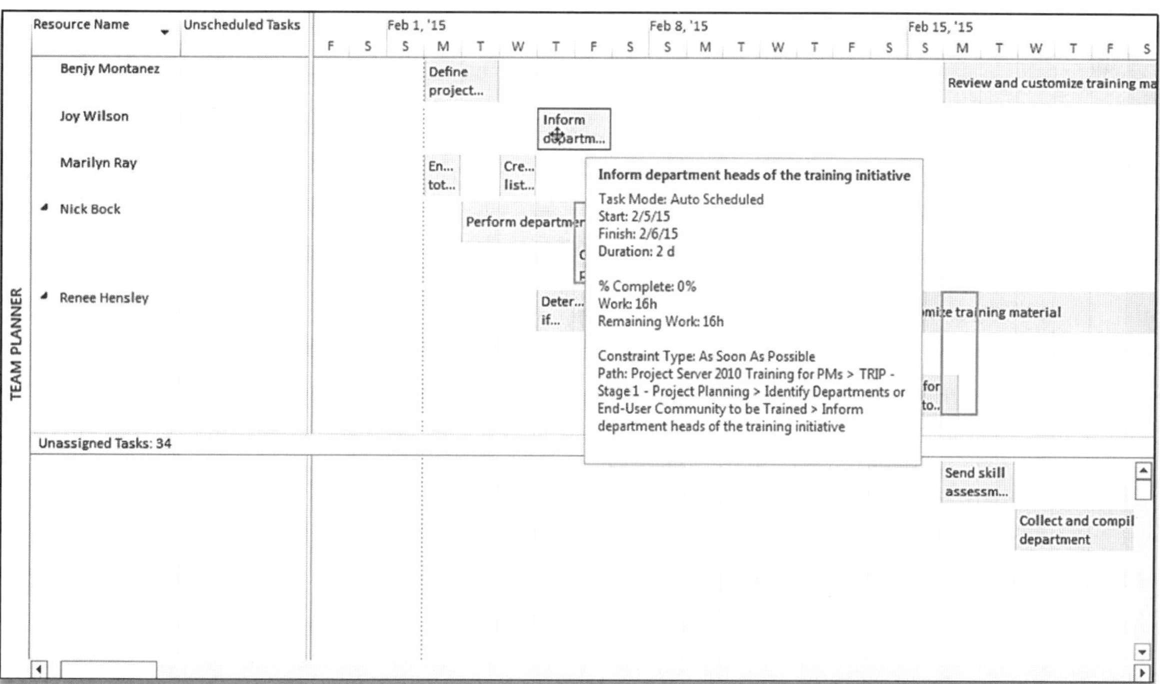

Figure 7 - 59: Schedule information for the selected task

The *Team Planner* view uses special colors and formatting to display task information for each assigned and unassigned task. The key to understanding the color formatting is as follows:

- Light blue Gantt bars represent unstarted *Auto Scheduled* tasks.
- Light teal (turquoise) Gantt bars represent *Manually Scheduled* tasks.
- Dark blue in a Gantt bar represents task progress for both *Auto Scheduled* tasks and *Manually Scheduled* tasks.
- Light gray Gantt bars represent external tasks in another project.
- Dark gray Gantt bars with white text represent late tasks (tasks where the current *% Complete* progress does not extend to the *Status Date* of the project).
- Resource names formatted in red represent overallocated resources.
- Red borders on a Gantt bar represent time periods of overallocation for a resource.

Leveling a Resource Overallocation

Using the *Team Planner* view, Project 2013 allows you to level resource overallocations using three different methods:

- Level the resource overallocation using the built-in leveling tool in the software.
- Reassign a task that is causing an overallocation by dragging the task to a different resource.
- Reschedule a task that is causing an overallocation by dragging it to a different time period.

Before you level resource overallocations using the built-in leveling tool with the *Team Planner* view, you should specify your leveling options. In the *Level* section of the *Resource* ribbon, click the *Leveling Options* button. The software displays the *Resource Leveling* dialog shown previously in Figure 7 - 50. Refer back to the *Setting Leveling Options* topical section of this module and review the recommended settings, if necessary.

To level an overallocated resource using the *Team Planner* view, select the resource and then click the *Level Resource* button in the *Level* section of the *Resource* ribbon. Remember that when you use the built-in leveling tool to level an overallocated resource, Project 2013 resolves the overallocation using one or both of the following methods:

- The software delays tasks or assignments.
- The software splits tasks or assignments.

Figure 7 - 60 shows the *Team Planner* view after leveling the resource overallocations for *Nick Bock* using the built-in leveling tool in Project 2013. Notice that the software delayed several of the tasks assigned to Nick Bock to resolve the overallocation.

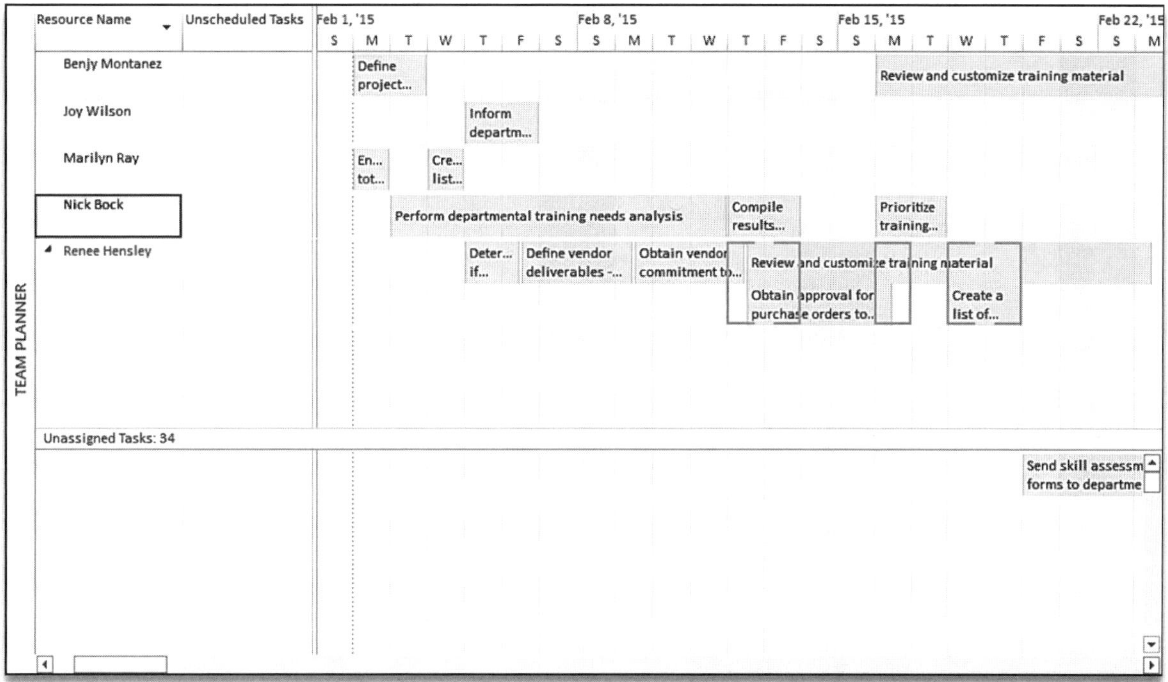

Figure 7 - 60: Team Planner view after leveling Nick Bock's overallocations

If you prefer to use a manual approach to level a resource overallocation, Project 2013 allows you to use the *Team Planner* view to do either of the following:

- Drag an assigned task to a different time period to reschedule the task.
- Drag an assigned task to a different resource.

To reschedule a task to a different time period, click and hold the task's Gantt bar to "grab" the task, and then drag it to the new time period. Keep in mind, however, that when you reschedule a task by dragging it to a new time period, Project 2013 sets a *Start No Earlier Than* (SNET) constraint on the task automatically. If you drag a task beyond the right edge of the *Team Planner* view, the software scrolls the view automatically so that you do not need to release the mouse button and scroll manually.

Warning: Project 2013's use of SNET constraints in the *Team Planner* view may be contrary to the best interests of your scheduling model if you want to maintain a fully dynamic model. SNET constraints prevent a task from moving to an earlier *Start* date even if an earlier *Start* becomes available. You can easily clear leveling delays added by the built-in leveling tool with a press of a button, but you must manually remove constraints added by dragging tasks in the *Team Planner* view.

To reassign a task to another resource, click and hold the task's Gantt bar to "grab" the task, and then drag it to the new resource and drop it on the desired time period. For example, Figure 7 - 61 shows the *Team Planner* view after I dragged two tasks assigned to *Nick Bock* and reassigned them to *Marilyn Ray*. These two tasks were the tasks causing the resource overallocation for Nick Bock.

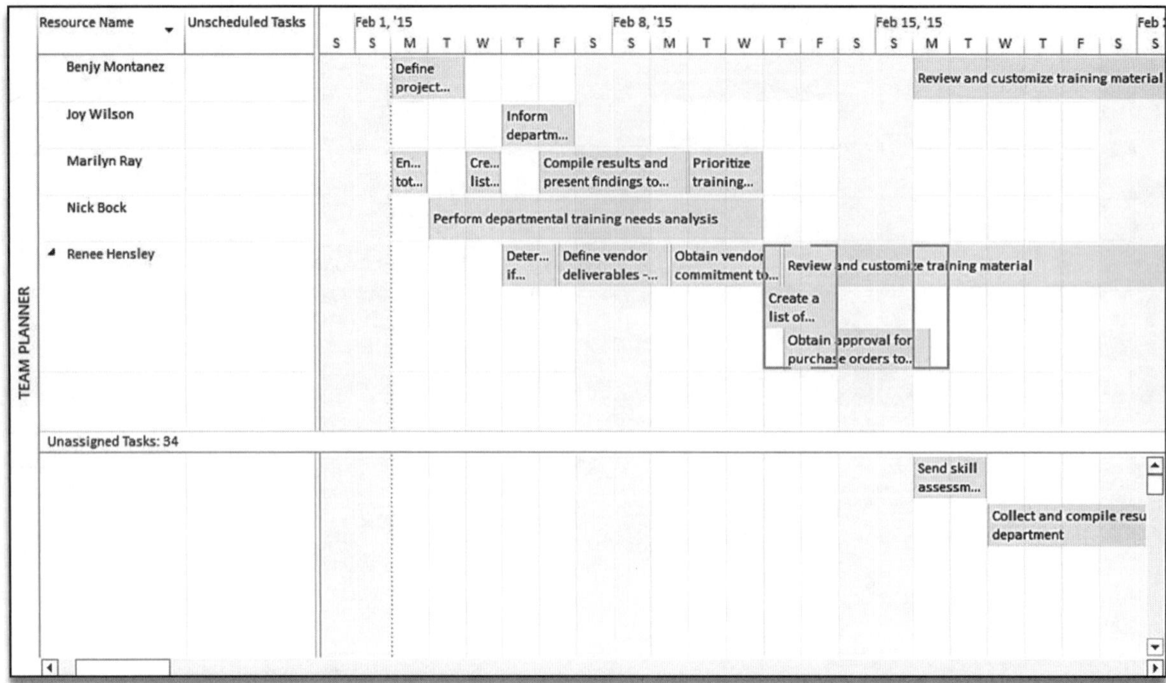

Figure 7 - 61: Resolve a resource overallocation by dragging tasks to another resource

Information: You can also reassign a task to another resource by right-clicking the Gantt bar for the task, choosing the *Reassign To* item on the shortcut menu, and then selecting the name of the new resource.

In addition to dragging tasks to manually level resource overallocations, you can also use the *Team Planner* view to assign resources to tasks. To assign an *Unassigned Task* to any resource using the *Team Planner* view, click and hold the task's Gantt bar to "grab" the task, and then drag the task's Gantt bar from the bottom pane to the top pane and drop it in the time period during which you want to schedule the task for the selected resource. Keep in mind that when you assign a task to a resource using this method, Project 2013 assigns the task to the resource at a *Units* value of *100%* automatically, indicating full-time work on the task.

Information: To reassign or reschedule multiple tasks simultaneously, press and hold the **Control** key to select multiple tasks, and then drag and drop the block of selected tasks. Project 2013 does not allow you to drag and drop multiple unassigned tasks simultaneously in the *Team Planner* view, however.

Changing Schedule Information in the Team Planner View

As you analyze assignment information in the *Team Planner* view, at some point you may need to revise schedule information. Project 2013 allows you to revise your project as follows in the *Team Planner* view:

- You can change the *Task Mode* option for a task by right-clicking the Gantt bar for the task and selecting either the *Auto Schedule* or *Manually Schedule* item on the shortcut menu.

- You can set a task to *Inactive* status by right-clicking the Gantt bar for the task and choosing the *Inactivate Task* item on the shortcut menu. When you set a task to *Inactive* status, Project 2013 hides the task in the *Team Planner* view.

- You can change information for any task (such as setting a constraint or applying a task calendar) by double-clicking the Gantt bar for the task and entering the information in the *Task Information* dialog. You can also right-click the Gantt bar for the task and choose the *Information* item on the shortcut menu.

- You can apply the *Task Details Form* in a split view arrangement with the *Team Planner* view by clicking the *Task* tab to display the *Task* ribbon. In the *Properties* section of the *Task* ribbon, click the *Display Task Details* button. When you select the Gantt bar for any assigned or unassigned task in the top pane, the *Task Details Form* in the bottom pane displays relevant information about the task and its assigned resources. Notice in Figure 7 - 62 that the *Task Details Form* displays information about the *Perform departmental training needs analysis* task whose Gantt bar I selected in the top pane. To close the *Task Details Form,* double-click the split bar between the *Team Planner* pane and the *Task Details Form* pane.

Information: To display any other view in the bottom pane, click the *View* tab to display the *View* ribbon. In the *Split View* section of the *View* ribbon, click the *Details* pick list and select any view that does not include a timescale. On the default *Details* pick list, eligible views include the *Resource Form*, *Resource Sheet*, *Task Form*, *Task Details Form*, and *Network Diagram* views. If you select the *More Views* item on the *Details* pick list, you can select and display any of the following additional views in the bottom pane: *Descriptive Network Diagram*, *Relationship Diagram*, *Resource Name Form*, *Task Name Form*, *Task Sheet*, and *Timeline* views. If you attempt to display any view with a timescale in the bottom pane, Project 2013 displays an error message.

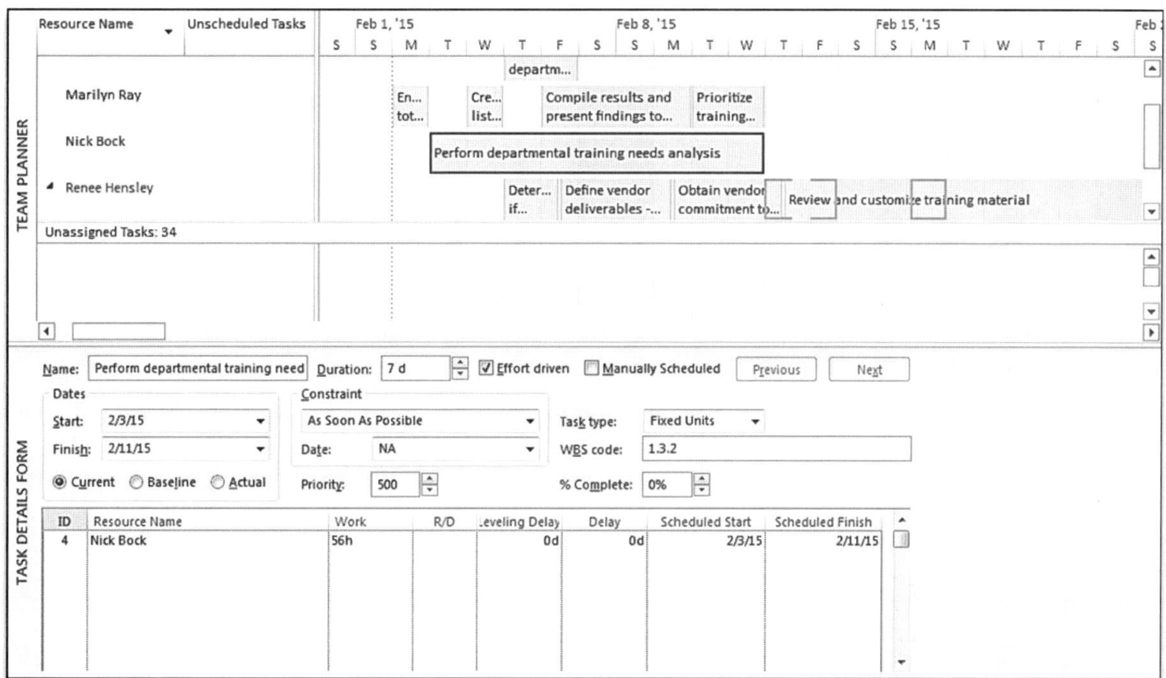

Figure 7 - 62: Task Details Form applied in a split-screen arrangement with the Team Planner view

- You can prevent resource overallocations in your project by clicking the *Format* tab to display the *Format* ribbon. In the *Schedule* section of the *Format* ribbon, click the *Prevent Overallocations* button. With this option enabled, the software levels all existing overallocations in the project immediately, and levels any future resource overallocation when it occurs, such as when you drag a task or assign a task that causes a resource overallocation. Project 2013 indicates in the *Team Planner* view that you enabled this option by highlighting the *Prevent Overallocations* button and by displaying a *Prevent Overallocations: On* indicator at the left end of the status bar at the bottom of the application window, as shown in Figure 7 - 63.

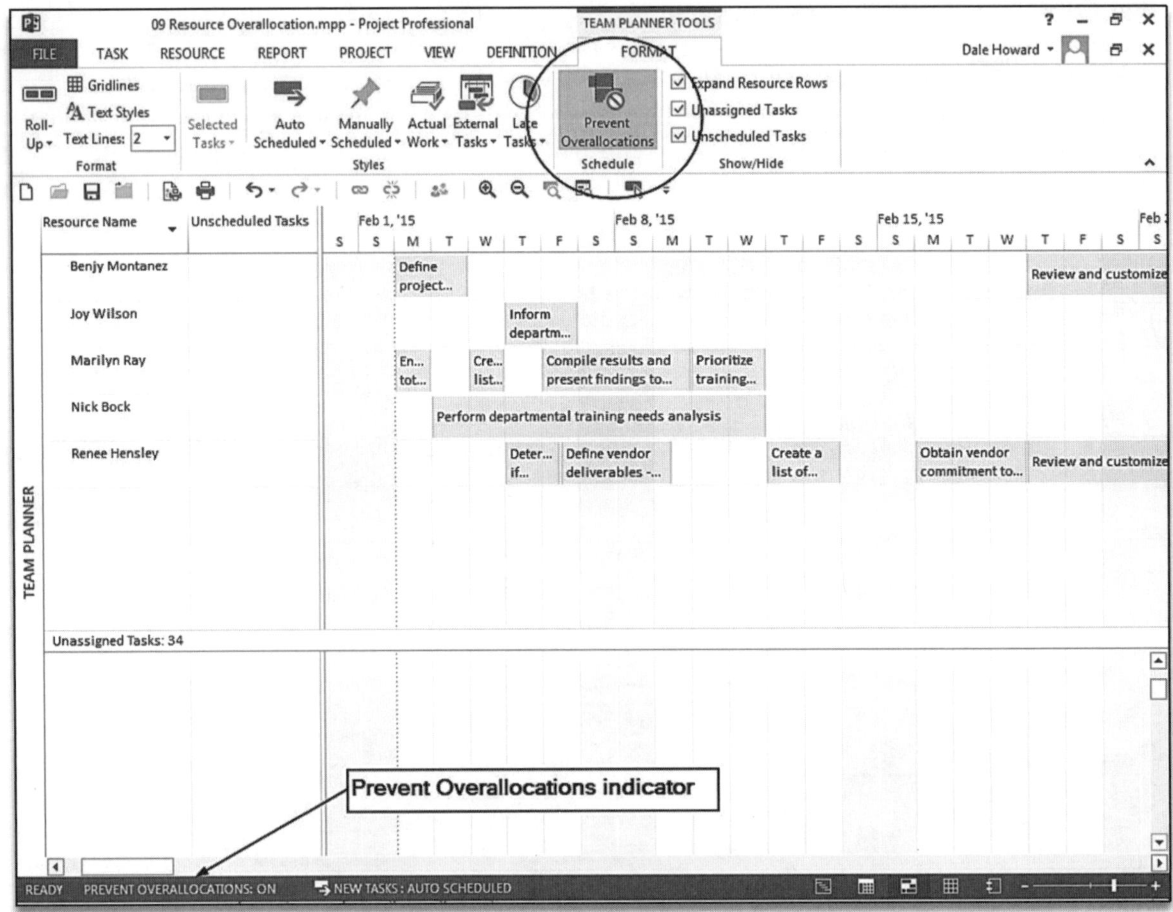

Figure 7 - 63: Prevent Overallocations option selected

Information: During the execution stage of your project, you can also enter progress against a task by right-clicking the task's Gantt bar and selecting a *% Complete* value in the *Mini Toolbar* section of the shortcut menu. The *Mini Toolbar* offers you the *0%, 25%, 50%, 75%,* and *100%* buttons with which to enter progress on a task quickly.

Hands On Exercise

Exercise 7 - 13

Warning: You can only work this exercise if you are using the **Professional** version of Project 2013. If you are using the **Standard** version of the software, then you must skip this exercise because your version of Project 2013 does not include the *Team Planner* view.

Use the *Team Planner* view to analyze resource assignments and to level resource overallocations.

1. Open the **Using the Team Planner View 2013.mpp** sample file.

2. Click the *Resource* tab to display the *Resource* ribbon.

3. In *View* section of the *Resource* ribbon, click the *Team Planner* button.

4. In the *Team Planner* view, examine the tasks currently assigned to each resource. You may need to scroll to the right, as needed, to view task assignments for each resource and unassigned tasks .

5. Scroll to the week of **August 28, 2016** for *Dan Morton* and notice the week of nonworking time (gray shaded cells).

6. Double-click anywhere in the gray shaded cells during the week of nonworking time for *Dan Morton* to display the *Change Working Time* dialog and reveal the reason for the nonworking time.

Notice that Dan Morton has a week of planned vacation during the week of August 28, 2016.

7. Click the *Cancel* button to close the *Change Working Time* dialog.

8. In the *Level* section of the *Resource* ribbon, click the *Leveling Options* button.

9. In the *Resource Leveling* dialog, click the *Leveling Order* pick list and select the *Priority, Standard* order, if necessary.

10. Click the *OK* button to close the *Resource Leveling* dialog.

11. In the *Resource* pane, scroll to the weeks of **July 31** and **August 7, 2016** and notice the red borders on the Gantt bars for the three tasks assigned to *Dan Morton*, indicating he is an overallocated resource on these three tasks.

12. Select *Dan Morton* and then click the *Level Resource* button in the *Resource* ribbon

Notice that Project 2013 delayed two of the three tasks assigned to *Dan Morton* to resolve the overallocation.

13. Select the overallocated resource, *Marilyn Ray*, and then scroll to the right to locate her resource overallocation beginning the week of **August 21, 2016**.

14. Drag the Gantt bar for the *Initiate End-User Placement Matrix* task from *Marilyn Ray* to *Cassie Endicott*. **Note:** Be sure to keep the **same time schedule** for the task when you drag the Gantt bar to *Cassie Endicott*.

Notice that this action leveled the resource overallocation for *Marilyn Ray*.

15. Select the overallocated resource, *Renee Hensley*, and then scroll to the week of **August 7, 2016** to locate her resource overallocation.

16. Drag the Gantt bar for the *Obtain approval for purchase orders to cover vendor invoices* task until it starts **immediately after** the *Review and customize training material* task.

Notice that this action manually delayed the task to resolve the overallocation.

17. Click the *Task* tab to display the *Task* ribbon.

18. In the *View* section of the *Task* ribbon, click the *Gantt Chart* pick list button, and then select the *Gantt Chart* view.

19. Locate task ID #15, the *Obtain approval for purchase orders to cover vendor invoices* task that you manually delayed to a later date for *Renee Hensley*.

In the *Indicators* column, notice that the indicator for this task reveals Project 2013 applied a *Start No Earlier Than (SNET)* constraint on this task. This is the consequence of dragging and dropping task Gantt bars in the *Team Planner* view.

20. Save and close the **Using the Team Planner View 2013.mpp** sample file.

Leveling Resource Overallocations in a Task View

Another powerful feature in Project 2013 helps you to locate and level resource overallocations on a task-by-task basis in any task view, such as the *Gantt Chart* view. To locate a resource overallocation in a task view, apply any task view. Look in the *Indicators* column for any task with a "red stick figure" or "burning man" indicator, which identifies the task as assigned to an overallocated resource. For example, Figure 7 - 64 shows the *Gantt Chart* view of a project with an overallocated resource. Notice the special "burning man" indicator in the *Indicators* column for task IDs #13, #14, #15, and #17, indicating that I have an overallocated resource assigned to these four tasks. In this situation, the overallocated resource is *Larry Barnes*. The overallocation is a consequence of assigning *Larry Barnes* to work on four parallel tasks.

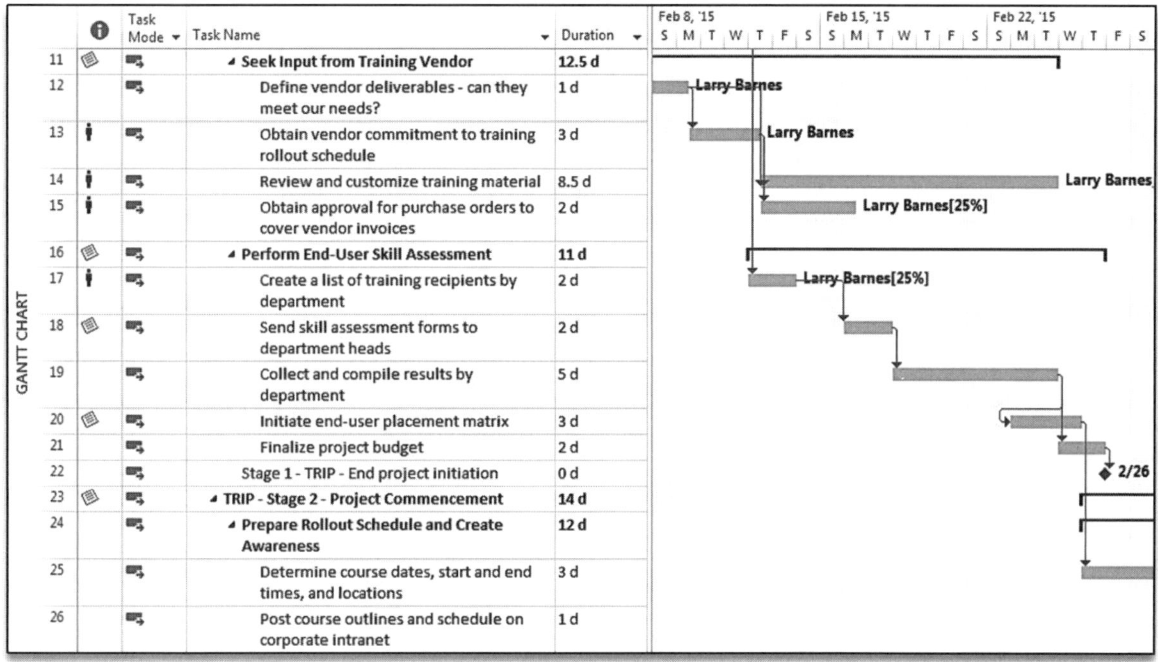

	Task Mode	Task Name	Duration
11		Seek Input from Training Vendor	12.5 d
12		Define vendor deliverables - can they meet our needs?	1 d
13		Obtain vendor commitment to training rollout schedule	3 d
14		Review and customize training material	8.5 d
15		Obtain approval for purchase orders to cover vendor invoices	2 d
16		Perform End-User Skill Assessment	11 d
17		Create a list of training recipients by department	2 d
18		Send skill assessment forms to department heads	2 d
19		Collect and compile results by department	5 d
20		Initiate end-user placement matrix	3 d
21		Finalize project budget	2 d
22		Stage 1 - TRIP - End project initiation	0 d
23		TRIP - Stage 2 - Project Commencement	14 d
24		Prepare Rollout Schedule and Create Awareness	12 d
25		Determine course dates, start and end times, and locations	3 d
26		Post course outlines and schedule on corporate intranet	1 d

Figure 7 - 64: Four tasks with an overallocated resource assigned

Project 2013 allows you to level the resource overallocation on these four tasks by delaying the tasks individually, on a task-by-task basis in the *Gantt Chart* view. Before you use this method, you must decide which tasks you want to delay and which tasks you want to leave alone. After you make this important decision, right-click the first task you want to delay. The software displays the shortcut menu shown in Figure 7 - 65. Notice that the shortcut menu offers three methods for dealing with the overallocation.

Figure 7 - 65: Shortcut menu for a task assigned to an overallocated resource

The first option on the shortcut menu is *Fix in Task Inspector*. If you select this option, the software opens the *Task Inspector* sidepane on the left side of the *Gantt Chart* view, as shown in Figure 7 - 66. The *Task Inspector* sidepane offers two options in the *Actions* section for resolving the resource overallocation. Click the *Reschedule Task* button to delay the task to the first available time period that resolves the overallocation. Click the *Team Planner* button to display the *Team Planner* view, in which you can level the resource using any of the methods I discussed earlier this module.

Task Inspector

15 - Obtain approval for purchase orders to cover vendor invoices

Resources overallocated due to work on other tasks
Larry Barnes

ACTIONS:

Reschedule Task — Move task to resources' next available time.

Team Planner — View overallocated resources in Team Planner.

INFO:

Auto Scheduled
Start: 2/12/15
Finish: 2/16/15

Predecessor Tasks:

Name	Type	Lag
13 - Obtain vendor commitment to training rollout schedule	Finish To Start	0 d

GANTT CHART

	Task Mode	Task Name	Duration
11		Seek Input from Training Vendor	12.5 d
12		Define vendor deliverables - can they meet our needs?	1 d
13		Obtain vendor commitment to training rollout schedule	3 d
14		Review and customize training material	8.5 d
15		Obtain approval for purchase orders to cover vendor invoices	2 d
16		Perform End-User Skill Assessment	11 d
17		Create a list of training recipients by department	2 d
18		Send skill assessment forms to department heads	2 d
19		Collect and compile results by department	5 d
20		Initiate end-user placement matrix	3 d
21		Finalize project budget	2 d
22		Stage 1 - TRIP - End project initiation	0 d
23		TRIP - Stage 2 - Project Commencement	14 d
24		Prepare Rollout Schedule and Create Awareness	12 d
25		Determine course dates, start and end times, and locations	3 d
26		Post course outlines and schedule on corporate intranet	1 d
27		Establish support through help desk for post-training questions	1 d
28		Reserve training rooms	1 d
29		Coordinate equipment needs with IT support staff	1 d

Figure 7 - 66: Task Inspector for a task assigned to an overallocated resource

The second option on the shortcut menu is the *Reschedule to Available Date* option. If you select this option, Project 2013 delays the task to the first available time period that resolves the overallocation. Selecting this option is the same as clicking the *Reschedule Task* button in the *Task Inspector* sidepane.

The third option on the shortcut menu is the *Ignore Problems for This Task* option. If you select this option, the software hides the "burning man" indicator for that task in the *Indicators* column, but does nothing to resolve the resource overallocation. This is the method you can use to hide false overallocation warnings.

Warning: Do not use the *Ignore Problems for This Task* option as your standard method for dealing with resource overallocation issues, since using this option serves only to hide your resource overallocation problems in task views. Instead, use this option specifically to hide false overallocation warnings, such as when you assign a resource to work on a task which takes place during a weekend.

Information: If you use the *Ignore Problems for This Task* option to hide false overallocation warnings, at some point you may want to see the warnings again. To resolve this issue, click the *Task* tab to display the *Task* ribbon. Select the task in which you applied the *Ignore Problems for This Task* option. In the *Tasks* section of the *Task* ribbon, click the *Inspect* pick list button and select the *Show Ignored Problems* item on the pick list.

Hands On Exercise

Exercise 7 - 14

Locate and resolve resource overallocations in the *Gantt Chart* view.

1. Open the **Leveling in a Task View 2013.mpp** sample file.
2. Scroll down through the list of tasks and look for any task that shows the "burning man" indicator in the *Indicators* column, indicating the task has an overallocated resource assigned to it.

Note: You should see that task IDs #6, 7, 8, 13, 14, 15, 19, and 20 have an overallocated resource assigned to them.

3. Float your mouse pointer over the overallocation indicator for task ID #7, the *Compile results and present findings to training coordinator* task, and read the text in the screen tip.
4. Right-click anywhere on task ID #7 and then select the *Fix in Task Inspector* item on the shortcut menu.
5. In the *Task Inspector* sidepane, read the available information about the resource overallocation on this task.
6. In the *Actions* section of the *Task Inspector* sidepane, click the *Reschedule Task* button to level the resource overallocation on this task.

Notice that this action resolved the resource overallocation on task IDs #6 and #8 .

7. Close the *Task Inspector* sidepane.
8. Right-click anywhere on task ID #14, the *Review and customize training material* task, and then select the *Reschedule To Available Date* item on the shortcut menu.
9. Right-click anywhere on task ID #20, the *Initiate end-user placement matrix* task, and then select the *Reschedule To Available Date* item on the shortcut menu.

Using the *Reschedule To Available Date* feature, notice that you easily resolved the remaining resource overallocations.

10. Save and close the **Leveling in a Task View 2013.mpp** sample file.

Exercise 7 - 15

Hide overallocation warnings for a task assigned to an overallocated resource.

1. Return to the **Training Advisor 07.mpp** sample file.
2. Click the *Task* tab to display the *Task* ribbon.
3. In the *View* section of the *Task* ribbon, click the *Gantt Chart* pick list button, and then select the *Gantt Chart* view.

Notice that task ID #20, the *Perform Server Stress Test* task, displays the "burning man" indicator in the *Indicators* column. As I stated earlier in this module, the "burning man" indicator reveals that Project 2013 believes the assigned resource is overallocated because the task occurs during nonworking time on a Saturday and Sunday. In reality, the assigned resource is **not overallocated** because you intentionally scheduled this task to occur on a weekend due to unique scheduling requirements for this type of work.

4. Right-click anywhere on task ID #20 and select the *Ignore Problems for This Task* item on the shortcut menu.

Notice that Project 2013 no longer displays a "burning man" indicator for this task.

5. Save and close the **Training Advisor 07.mpp** sample file.

Module 08

Project Execution

Learning Objectives

After completing this module, you will be able to:

- Reschedule an unstarted project to a new start date
- View the Critical Path for a project
- Save an original baseline for a project
- Understand the proper use of the multiple Baseline fields in Project 2013
- Understand the three primary methods for entering project progress
- Enter progress for a Cost resource
- Reschedule uncompleted work from past reporting periods into the current reporting period
- Reschedule a task to a future time period
- Set a task to Inactive status
- Understand how to synchronize your project with a new or existing SharePoint site
- Include additional fields in the synchronization process
- Add users to your SharePoint site
- Collaborate on a project in a SharePoint Site

Inside Module 08

Understanding the Execution Process

Project execution is the process of doing the actual work described in the project plan. During the executing stage of each project, you typically perform each of the following actions:

- Display the Critical Path
- Save an original project baseline
- Enter project progress
- Analyze project variance
- Revise the project
- Manage project changes
- Report on project progress

In this module, I discuss the topics shown in the first three bulleted list items, plus I discuss additional topics relevant to the executing stage of a project. In succeeding modules, I discuss the other actions you need to perform in Project 2013 during the executing stage of your project.

Rescheduling an Unstarted Project

Project managers may occasionally face the problem of rescheduling the *Start* date of an unstarted project. Common reasons for rescheduling an unstarted project include budget shortfalls, a lack of resources, and executive uncertainties. For example, consider the unstarted project shown in Figure 8 - 1. When I originally planned the project, I did the following:

- I set the *Start* date of the project to *May 4*.
- I set a *Finish No Later Than* constraint of *May 22* on the *Phase I Complete* milestone task.
- I set a *Start No Earlier Than* constraint of *July 6* on the *Test Beta Classes* task.
- I set a *Deadline* date of *July 1* on the *Phase II Complete* milestone to signify the target finish date of Phase II.
- I set a *Deadline* date of *August 7* on the *Project Complete* milestone to signify the target finish date of the entire project.

Information: To make it easier for you to see the *Deadline* date symbols in the Gantt chart shown in Figure 8 - 1, I removed the dates that Project 2013 usually displays to the right of each milestone symbol. This way you can easily see both the *Milestone* symbols and the *Deadline* date symbols on the *Phase II Complete* and *Project Complete* milestone tasks.

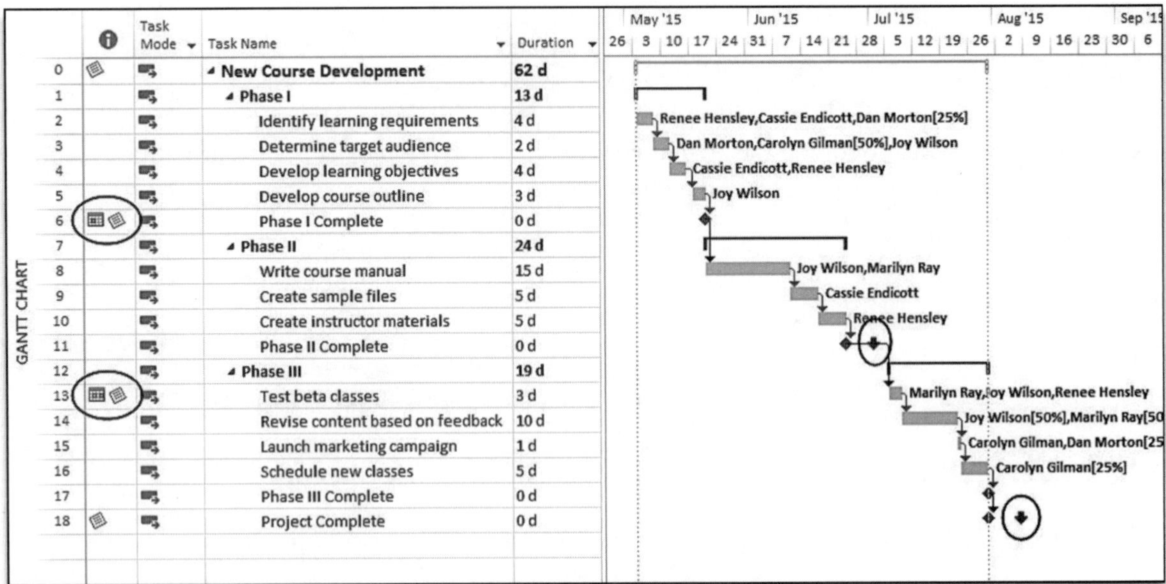

Figure 8 - 1: Unstarted project

Shortly before team members begin work on this project, company management announces a 4-week delay to allow the project team members to work on a higher priority project. To reschedule the *Start* date of an unstarted project, click the *Project* tab to display the *Project* ribbon. In the *Schedule* section of the *Project* ribbon, click the *Move Project* button. Project 2013 displays the *Move Project* dialog shown in Figure 8 - 2.

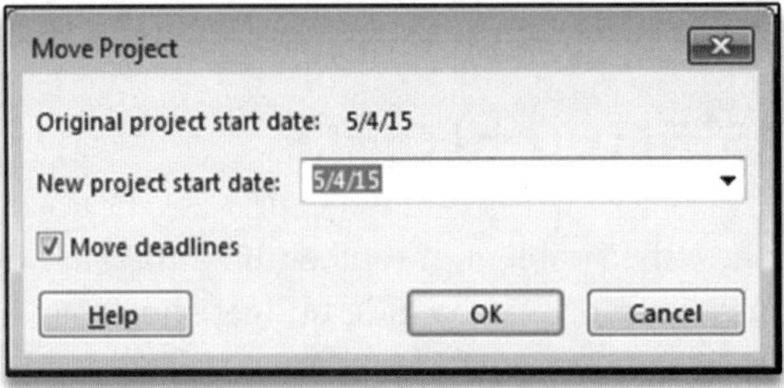

Figure 8 - 2: Move Project dialog

In the *Move Project* dialog, the software displays the current *Start* date of the project in the *Original project start date* field. To reschedule the project, enter or select a new date in the *New project start date* field. If you want the software to reschedule *Deadline* dates, leave the *Move deadlines* option selected. When you click the *OK* button, Project 2013 reschedules your project using the following actions:

- The software enters your new project *Start* date in the *Start date* field of the *Project Information* dialog.
- The software reschedules the dates of constraints and *Deadline* dates, based on the duration difference measured in working days between the original *Start* date and the new *Start* date of the project.

Figure 8 - 3 shows the unstarted project rescheduled to start 4 weeks (20 working days) later than originally planned. After entering the new project *Start* date of *June 1* in the *Move Project* dialog, Project 2013 did the following:

- The software entered *June 1* in the *Start date* field of the *Project Information* dialog.
- The software changed the *Finish No Later Than* constraint date on the *Phase I Complete* milestone task to *June 20* (20 working days later than the original constraint date).

- The software changed the *Start No Earlier Than* constraint date on the *Test Beta Classes* task to *August 3* (20 working days later than the original constraint date).
- The software changed the *Deadline* date on the *Phase II Complete* milestone task to *July 30* (20 working days later than the original *Deadline* date).
- The software changed the *Deadline* date on the *Project Complete* milestone task to *September 5* (20 working days later than the original *Deadline* date).

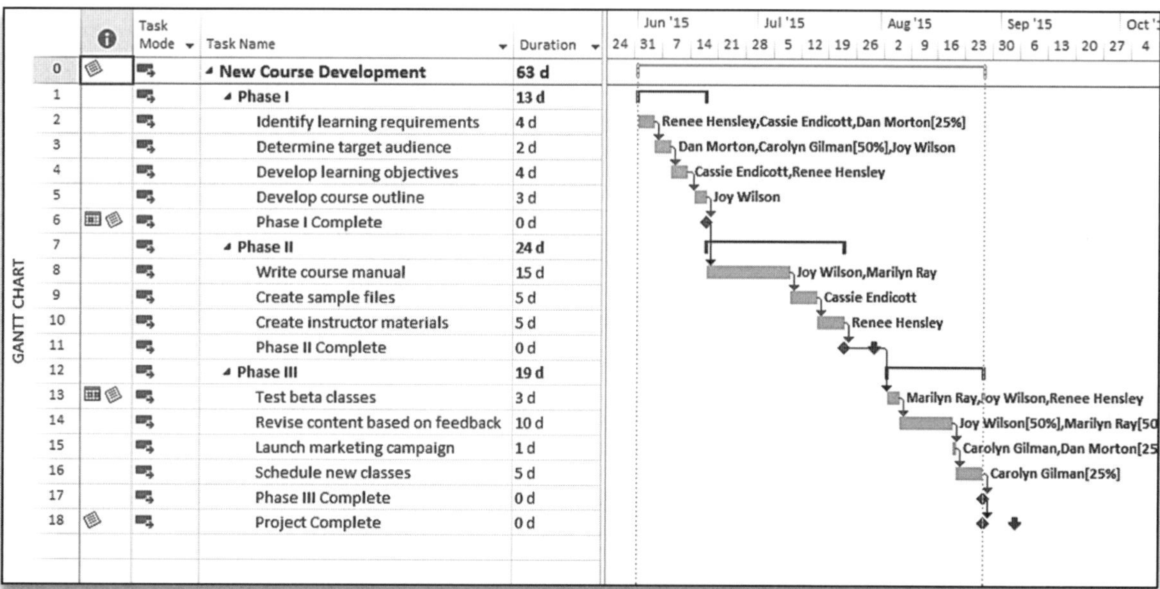

Figure 8 - 3: Unstarted project rescheduled 20 days later

Keep in mind that when you use the *Move Project* dialog to reschedule your project, Project 2013 assumes that you want to move *Constraint* dates and *Deadline* dates **exactly** the same number of days that you moved the project *Start* date. In reality, this may not be true, and you may need to change the *Constraint* dates and *Deadline* dates manually. In addition, if you set a baseline for the unstarted project before rescheduling it, you may want to set a new baseline for the project to capture the new schedule information.

Hands On Exercise

Exercise 8 - 1

Reschedule the *Start* date of an unstarted project to a date four months in the future due to a shortage of resources to work on the project.

1. Open the **Reschedule an Unstarted Project 2013.mpp** sample file.
2. Examine the *Indicators* column and notice that three tasks include constraints and the *Project Complete* milestone tasks includes a *Deadline* date.

3. Float your mouse pointer over the constraint indicators in the *Indicators* column and examine the *Constraint* dates for the three tasks with constraints.
4. Float your mouse pointer over the *Deadline* date symbol (red diamond) in the Gantt chart for the *Project Complete* milestone task and examine the current *Deadline* date.
5. Click the *Project* tab to display the *Project* ribbon.
6. In the *Schedule* section of the *Project* ribbon, click the *Move Project* button.
7. In the *Move Project* dialog, enter **June 6, 2016** in the *New project start date* field.
8. In the *Move Project* dialog, leave the *Move deadlines* option **selected**, and then click the *OK* button to reschedule the project.

Notice that Project 2013 displays *Change Highlighting* on the *Duration* values of the Project Summary Task (Row 0) and on the *TRAINING* summary task. This indicates a change in duration due to the Independence Day company holiday after rescheduling the project *Start* date.

9. Float your mouse pointer over the constraint indicators in the *Indicators* column and examine the **new** *Constraint* dates for the three tasks with constraints.
10. Float your mouse pointer over the *Deadline* date symbol (red diamond) in the Gantt chart for the *Project Complete* milestone task and examine the **new** *Deadline* date.
11. Save and close the **Reschedule an Unstarted Project 2013.mpp** sample file.

Viewing the Critical Path

Project 2013 defines the **Critical Path** as "The series of tasks that must be completed on schedule for a project to finish on schedule." Every task on the Critical Path is a **Critical task**. By default, all tasks on the Critical Path have a *Total Slack* value of *0 days,* which means they cannot slip without delaying the project *Finish* date. If the *Finish* date of any *Critical* task slips by even 1 day, the project's *Finish* date slips .

Project 2013 defines a **non-Critical task** as any task that is 100% complete or any task with a *Total Slack* value greater than *0 days*. A non-Critical task can slip by its amount of *Total Slack* before it impacts the *Finish* date of the project. For example, if a task has *5 days* of *Total Slack*, the task must finish more than 5 days late before the resulting slippage changes the *Finish* date of the project. To manage your project well, you should be aware of the non-Critical tasks in your project, but you should focus your energies on managing the tasks on the Critical Path.

Information: Project 2013 automatically calculates the *Total Slack* value for each task to determine the Critical Path of the project. To view the *Total Slack* for any task, click the *View* tab to display the *View* ribbon. In the *Data* section of the *View* ribbon, click the *Tables* button, and then select the *Schedule* table. The *Total Slack* column is the last column on the right side of the *Schedule* table.

In Project 2013, the Critical Path may run from the *Start* date to the *Finish* date of the project, or it may begin anywhere in the project and run to the *Finish* date of the project. This behavior is a key difference from the traditional Critical Path Method (CPM) definition of Critical Path.

Information: If you make changes to your project, either by entering actual progress or by making plan revisions, keep in mind that the Critical Path may change.

There are a number of ways to determine the Critical Path in any project in Project 2013. The simplest method is to format the *Gantt Chart* view to display red Gantt bars for *Critical* tasks. To format the *Gantt Chart* view to display the Critical Path, complete the following steps:

1. Apply the *Gantt Chart* view.
2. Click the *Format* tab to display the *Format* ribbon.
3. In the *Bar Styles* section of the *Format* ribbon, select the *Critical Tasks* checkbox.
4. Optionally select the *Slack* checkbox .

In the formatted *Gantt Chart* view shown in Figure 8 - 4, notice that Project 2013 displays the following:

- **Red bars** represent *Critical* tasks on the Critical Path. These tasks have a *Total Slack* value of *0 days*.
- **Blue bars** represent non-Critical tasks. These tasks have a *Total Slack* value greater than *0 days*.
- A **black stripe** to the right of any Gantt bar represents the amount of *Total Slack* for the task.

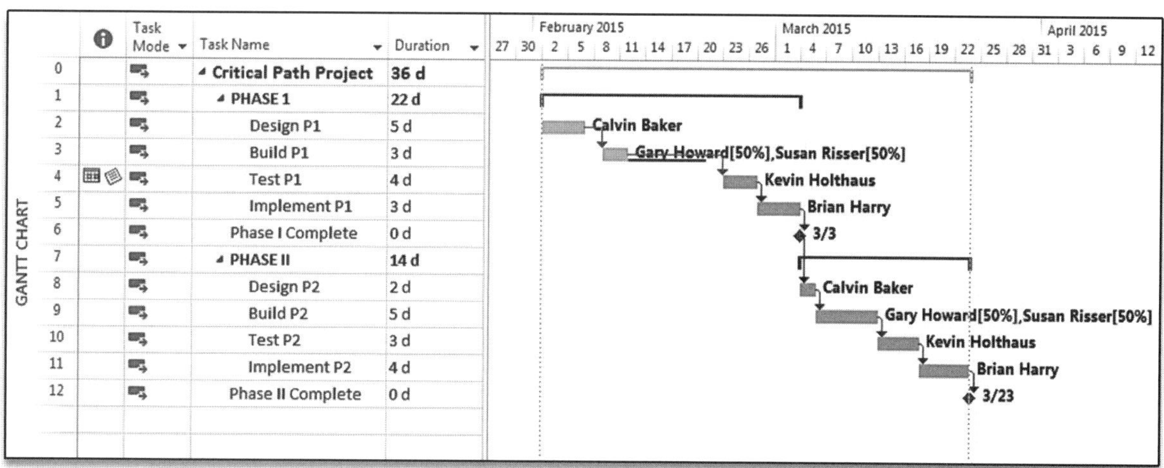

Figure 8 - 4: Gantt Chart formatted to show the Critical Path and Total Slack

Information: You can also view the Critical Path in any project by applying the *Tracking Gantt* view. Take note, however, that the *Tracking Gantt* view displays Gantt bars for both the Critical Path and for the baseline schedule of the project. Remember that red Gantt bars show Critical tasks, blue Gantt bars show non-Critical tasks, and gray Gantt bars show the original baseline schedule of each task.

Viewing the "Nearly Critical" Path

In Project 2013, you can change the software's definition of a Critical task by clicking the *File* tab and then clicking the *Options* tab in the *Backstage*. In the *Project Options* dialog, select the *Advanced* tab and then scroll down to the *Calculation options for this project* section of the dialog. To change the software's definition of a *Critical* task, change the *Tasks are critical if slack is less than or equal to* option to a value **greater than** *0 days*, and then click the *OK* button.

Using this technique is a helpful way to see the "nearly Critical tasks" in your project. "Nearly Critical tasks" are those tasks that are not on the true Critical Path, but are close enough to impact the *Finish* date of the project if they slip by an amount greater than their *Total Slack* value. For example, I have a task with only *1 day* of *Total Slack,* so this task is not a true Critical task since it has a *Total Slack* value greater than 0 days. However, if this task slips by only 2 days, the *Finish* date of the project slips . Therefore, it is not a bad idea to identify the "nearly Critical tasks" in any project.

Hands On Exercise

Exercise 8 - 2

Display the Critical Path in your Training Advisor Rollout project.

1. Open the **Training Advisor 08.mpp** sample file.
2. Click the *Format* tab to display the *Format* ribbon.
3. In the *Bar Styles* section of the *Format* ribbon, select the *Critical Tasks* checkbox.

Notice that Project 2013 displays *Critical* tasks with red Gantt bars and non-Critical tasks with blue Gantt bars.

4. Right-click the *Select All* button (upper left corner of the task sheet) and select the *Schedule* table on the shortcut menu.
5. In the *Schedule* table, drag the split bar to the right so that you can view the *Total Slack* column on the far right side of the *Schedule* table.

Notice that the *Total Slack* value for every Critical task is *0 days,* indicating that these tasks cannot slip without delaying the project *Finish* date. Notice also that the first three tasks in the *INSTALLATION* phase have *1 day* of *Total Slack,* indicating that they can slip no more than one day without impacting the *Finish* date of the project.

6. Right-click the *Select All* button and select the *Entry* table on the shortcut menu.
7. Drag the split bar to the right edge of the *Duration* column.
8. Click the *File* tab and then click the *Options* tab in the *Backstage.*
9. In the *Project Options* dialog, select the *Advanced* tab, and then scroll down to the *Calculation options for this project* section of the dialog.
10. Change the *Tasks are critical if slack is less than or equal to* option value to *1 day,* and then click the *OK* button.

Notice that Project 2013 displays red Gantt bars for the first three tasks in the *INSTALLATION* phase. The software now shows the true Critical Path, along with "nearly Critical tasks." You can use this technique at any time to see "nearly Critical tasks" in any project.

11. Click the *Undo* button in your *Quick Access Toolbar* to redisplay only the true Critical Path in the project.
12. Save but **do not** close the **Training Advisor 08.mpp** sample file.

Working with Project Baselines

Prior to executing a project, you should save a baseline for your project. A baseline represents a snapshot of the work, cost, and schedule estimates as represented in your initial project plan. Your baseline should represent the schedule your stakeholders approved before you begin tracking progress. All of the variance measurements that Project 2013 calculates for you are dependent on the existence of a baseline. Saving a project baseline provides you with a way to analyze project variance by comparing the current state of the project against the original planned state of the project (the baseline).

When you save a baseline in Project 2013, the software captures the current values for five important task fields and two important resource fields, and then saves these values in a corresponding set of *Baseline* fields. Table 8 - 1 shows the original fields and their corresponding *Baseline* fields.

Data Type	Field	Baseline Field
Task	Duration	Baseline Duration
Task	Start	Baseline Start
Task	Finish	Baseline Finish
Task	Work	Baseline Work
Task	Cost	Baseline Cost
Resource	Work	Baseline Work
Resource	Cost	Baseline Cost

Table 8 - 1: Baseline information

In addition to the five important task fields captured in the baseline, Project 2013 also captures the information in several other task fields. The software captures the extra cost information in the *Fixed Cost* and *Fixed Cost Accrual* fields, saving this information in the *Baseline Fixed Cost* and *Baseline Fixed Cost Accrual* fields, respectively. The software also captures the estimated task schedule information in the *Scheduled Duration, Scheduled Start*, and *Scheduled Finish* fields, saving this information in the *Baseline Estimated Duration, Baseline Estimated Start*, and *Baseline Estimated Finish* fields respectively. Project 2013 uses these estimated schedule fields primarily with the *Manually Scheduled* tasks feature. If you use *Budget Cost* resources in your project, Project 2013 also captures budget information in the *Budget Cost* and *Budget Work* fields, saving this information in the *Baseline Budget Cost* and *Baseline Budget Work* fields, respectively.

Information: Project 2013 also saves the timephased values for both tasks and resources in the timephased *Baseline Work* and *Baseline Cost* fields. You can view these timephased values in the timephased grid portion of either the *Task Usage* or *Resource Usage* views.

Saving a Project Baseline

To save a baseline for the entire project in Project 2013, complete the following steps:

1. Click the *Project* tab to display the *Project* ribbon.
2. In the *Schedule* section of the *Project* ribbon, click the *Set Baseline* pick list button, and then select the *Set Baseline* item on the list. The software displays the *Set Baseline* dialog shown in Figure 8 - 5.

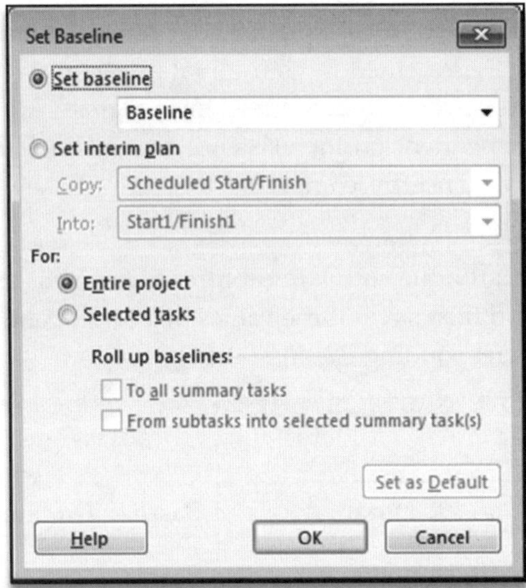

Figure 8 - 5: Set Baseline dialog

3. Leave the *Set baseline* option selected at the top of the dialog.
4. Leave the *Baseline* item selected in the *Set baseline* pick list.
5. In the *For:* section of the dialog, leave the *Entire project* option selected.
6. Click the *OK* button.

Best Practice: MsProjectExperts recommends that you save an original baseline for the entire project only once during the life of the project. After a change control procedure that adds new tasks to your project, you should update the baseline with information for only the new tasks. This maintains the integrity of your original project baseline.

Saving a "Rolling Baseline"

Some project managers must begin the executing stage for a project that is not completely planned, but they still need to save a baseline for the portion that is completely planned. To understand this unique baseline need, consider the following example:

- Your project consists of three consecutive phases, named Phase I, Phase II, and Phase III.
- You must completely plan the tasks in Phase I, but do only "skeleton planning" for the tasks in Phase II and Phase III.
- You must baseline the Phase I tasks and then begin the execution of the Phase I tasks.

- As the work progresses in Phase I, you do the detailed planning for the tasks in Phase II and then you must baseline only the Phase II tasks.
- As the work begins in Phase II, you do the detailed planning for tasks in Phase III and then you must baseline only the Phase III tasks.

The preceding description characterizes the need for saving a "rolling baseline" to capture the baseline information in a series of rolling waves. The "rolling baseline" process captures the original values in Phase I, then later appends the baseline information from Phase II, and finally appends the baseline information from Phase III . To save a "rolling baseline" for each set of selected tasks in a project, complete the following steps:

1. Select the tasks you are ready to baseline.
2. In the *Schedule* section of the *Project* ribbon, click the *Set Baseline* pick list button, and then select the *Set Baseline* item on the list.
3. Leave the *Set baseline* option selected at the top of the dialog.
4. Leave the *Baseline* item selected in the *Set baseline* pick list.
5. In the *For:* section of the dialog, choose the *Selected tasks* option.
6. In the *Roll up baselines:* section, select the *To all summary tasks* option, as shown in Figure 8 - 6.

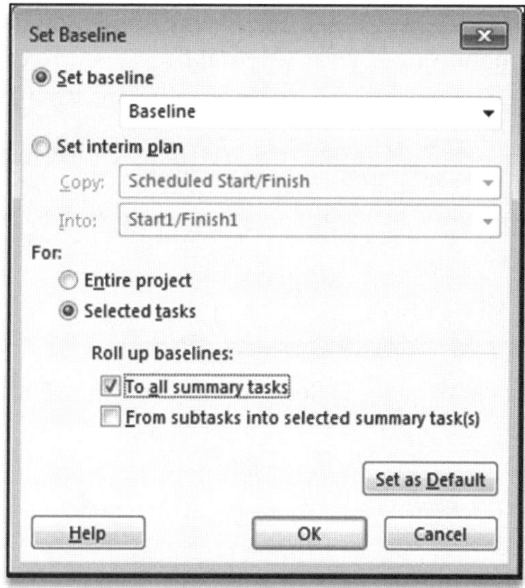

Figure 8 - 6: Set Baseline dialog, ready to baseline selected tasks

7. Click the *Set as Default* button.
8. Click the *OK* button.
9. When you baseline the Phase II and Phase III tasks, click the *Yes* button in the warning dialog about overwriting the baseline.

Saving Over a Previous Baseline

To determine whether you previously saved an original baseline in a project, click the *Set Baseline* pick list button and select the *Set Baseline* item on the list. The *Set Baseline* dialog indicates whether you previously saved a baseline by displaying the *last saved on* date in the *Set baseline* field, as displayed in Figure 8 - 7. If you do not see a *last saved on* date in the *Set baseline* field, this means you have not baselined your project yet.

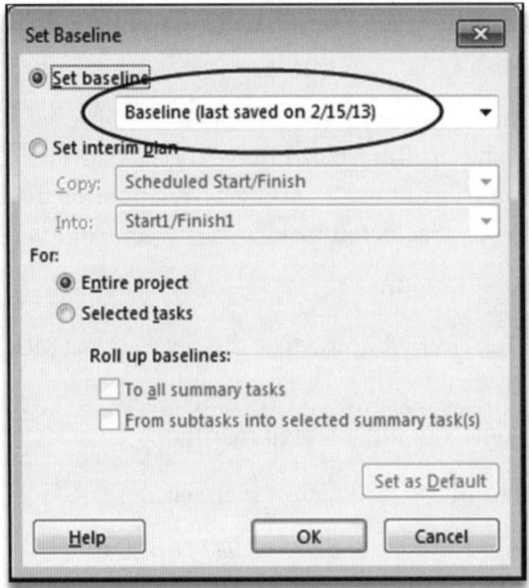

Figure 8 - 7: Last saved on date in the Set Baseline dialog

If you attempt to save baseline information over your original baseline, Project 2013 displays the warning dialog shown in Figure 8 - 8. Click the *Yes* button to save your new baseline information.

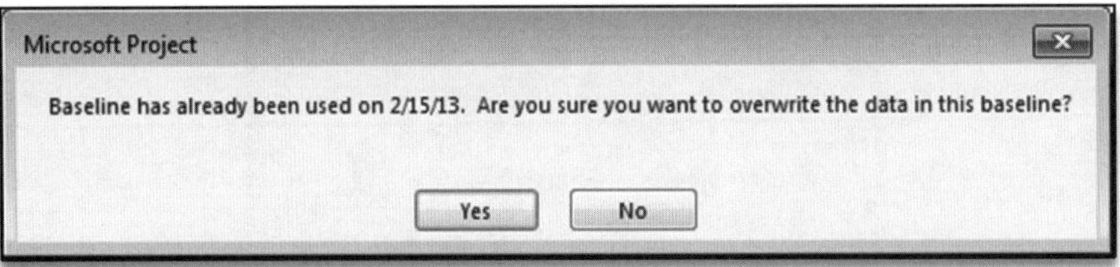

Figure 8 - 8: Warning dialog to overwrite original baseline

Information: If you are saving additional baseline information in the "rolling baseline" process, then click the *Yes* button in the warning dialog shown in Figure 8 - 8. When doing this in a "rolling baseline" process, the software **does not** overwrite your original baseline information as indicated in the dialog, but simply appends the new information to the original baseline.

Viewing the Project Baseline

When you save a project baseline, Project 2013 copies the current values from one set of fields into the corresponding set of baseline fields. You can view the baseline data for your project tasks by completing the following steps:

1. Display any task view, such as the *Gantt Chart* view.
2. Right-click the *Select All* button and then select the *More Tables* item on the shortcut menu.
3. In the *More Tables* dialog, select the *Baseline* table, and then click the *Apply* button. Figure 8 - 9 shows the task *Baseline* table applied to the *Gantt Chart* view.

	Task Name	Baseline Dur.	Baseline Start	Baseline Finish	Baseline Work	Baseline Cost
0	**Critical Path Project**	**36 d**	**2/2/15**	**3/23/15**	**232 h**	**$23,200.00**
1	**PHASE 1**	**22 d**	**2/2/15**	**3/3/15**	**120 h**	**$12,000.00**
2	Design P1	5 d	2/2/15	2/6/15	40 h	$4,000.00
3	Build P1	3 d	2/9/15	2/11/15	24 h	$2,400.00
4	Test P1	4 d	2/23/15	2/26/15	32 h	$3,200.00
5	Implement P1	3 d	2/27/15	3/3/15	24 h	$2,400.00
6	Phase I Complete	0 d	3/3/15	3/3/15	0 h	$0.00
7	**PHASE II**	**14 d**	**3/4/15**	**3/23/15**	**112 h**	**$11,200.00**
8	Design P2	2 d	3/4/15	3/5/15	16 h	$1,600.00
9	Build P2	5 d	3/6/15	3/12/15	40 h	$4,000.00
10	Test P2	3 d	3/13/15	3/17/15	24 h	$2,400.00
11	Implement P2	4 d	3/18/15	3/23/15	32 h	$3,200.00
12	Phase II Complete	0 d	3/23/15	3/23/15	0 h	$0.00

Figure 8 - 9: Gantt Chart view, Baseline table applied

Information: If you float your mouse pointer over the *Baseline Dur.* column header, you quickly discover that this column is **not** the *Baseline Duration* column. Instead, this column is actually the *Baseline Estimated Duration* column, included in this table to make it easier to work with baselines on *Manually Scheduled* tasks. Microsoft applied a *Title* to this column so that the *Baseline* table in Project 2013 looks like the *Baseline* table found in Project 2007 and earlier versions of the software.

Unlike the default task *Baseline* table, Project 2013 **does not** contain a default **resource** *Baseline* table that shows only the baseline values for each resource. To display the *Baseline Work* and *Baseline Cost* values for each resource, complete the following steps:

1. Apply the *Resource Sheet* view.
2. Right-click the *Type* column header and then select the *Insert Column* item on the shortcut menu.
3. In the pick list of available fields, select the *Baseline Work* field.
4. Right-click the *Type* column header again and then select *Insert Column* on the shortcut menu.
5. In the pick list of available fields, select the *Baseline Cost* field. Figure 8 - 10 shows the *Resource Sheet* view with the *Baseline Work* and *Baseline Cost* inserted temporarily in the resource *Entry* table.

		Resource Name	Baseline Work	Baseline Cost	Type	Material Label	Initials
1		Gary Howard	32 h	$3,200.00	Work		GH
2		Brian Harry	56 h	$5,600.00	Work		BH
3		Susan Risser	32 h	$3,200.00	Work		SR
4		Calvin Baker	56 h	$5,600.00	Work		CB
5		Kevin Holthaus	56 h	$5,600.00	Work		KH

Figure 8 - 10: Resource Sheet view with baseline fields

Information: To remove the *Baseline Work* and *Baseline Cost* fields from the *Resource Sheet* view, select the column headers of both *Baseline* fields. Right-click the selected column headers and then choose the *Hide Column* item on the shortcut menu.

Clearing the Project Baseline

You may need to clear the baseline information for a project, such as when management decides to delay the start of your project indefinitely. In a situation like this, your baseline information is invalid when your executives finally determine a new project *Start* date. To clear the baseline values for your project complete the following steps:

1. In the *Schedule* section of the *Project* ribbon, click the *Set Baseline* pick list button and select the *Clear Baseline* item. Project 2013 displays the *Clear Baseline* dialog shown in Figure 8 - 11.

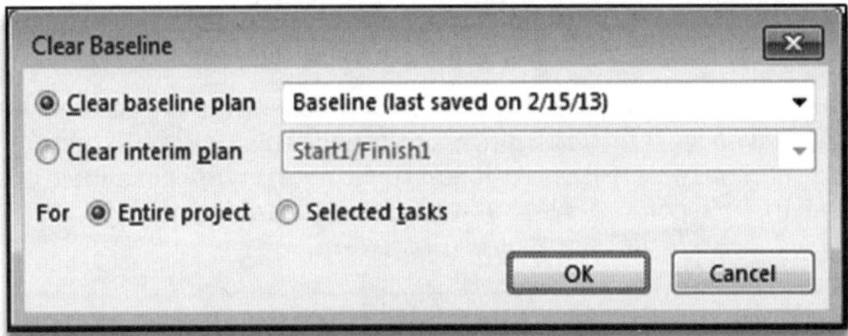

Figure 8 - 11: Clear Baseline dialog

2. Leave the *Clear baseline plan* option selected.

3. On the *Clear baseline plan* pick list, leave the *Baseline* item selected.

4. Leave the *Entire project* option selected.

5. Click the *OK* button.

Information: You can clear the baseline for only selected tasks only by choosing the *Selected tasks* option in the *Clear Baseline* dialog.

Using Additional Baselines

Beyond the original project baseline that you save in the *Baseline* set of fields, Project 2013 allows you to save baseline information in up to ten additional sets of baseline fields, numbered *Baseline 1* through *Baseline 10*. You can select one by clicking the *Set baseline* pick list in the *Set Baseline* dialog shown in Figure 8 - 12.

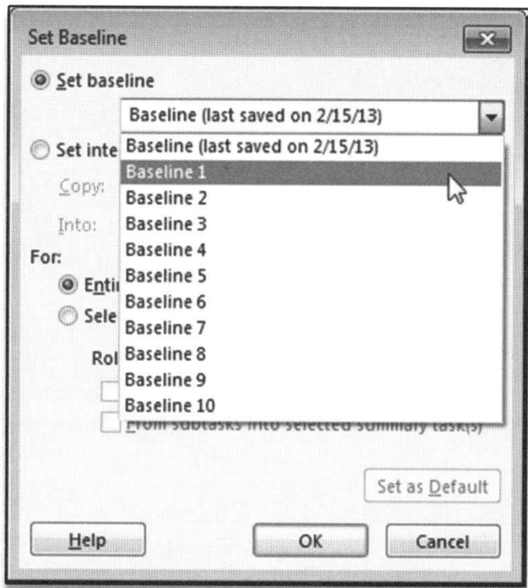

Figure 8 - 12: Set Baseline dialog with additional baseline fields

There are three serious limitations to saving baseline information in one of the additional sets of baseline fields. The first limitation is that none of the additional baseline fields (such as the *Baseline 5 Duration* field) appears in any default tables in Project 2013. This means that you must create one or more custom tables to view the additional baseline information. The second limitation is that Project 2013 calculates all task variance using the default *Baseline* set of fields. This means that if you want the software to calculate variance using any other set of baseline fields (such as the *Baseline 5* set of fields) you must change the *Baseline for Earned Value calculation* setting on *Advanced* page of the *Project Options* dialog to force the software to calculate variance using another set of baseline fields. The third limitation is that the *Tracking Gantt* view displays gray Gantt bars (the baseline schedule) using the default *Baseline* set of fields. This means that if you want to display gray Gantt bars using any other set of baseline fields, you must select the new baseline field on the *Baseline* pick list button in the *Bar Styles* section of the *Format* ribbon.

Best Practice: MSProjectExperts recommends that you use the ten additional sets of *Baseline* fields to back up historic baseline data from the *Baseline* set of fields. After you save your original baseline initially in the *Baseline* set of fields, save the baseline information a second time to *Baseline 1* set of fields. When you need to rebaseline your project, such as after a major change control procedure, save the new baseline information in the *Baseline* set of fields, and then save it a second time in the *Baseline 2* set of fields. By doing this each time you make a significant baseline change, you capture the historical data about the baseline before you rebaselined the project.

Beyond the primary baseline fields and additional sets of baseline fields, Project 2013 allows you to save a partial set of baseline information as an *Interim Plan*. When you save an *Interim Plan*, the software saves the *Scheduled Start* date in the *Start1* field and the *Scheduled Finish* date in the *Finish1* field for each task in the project, but saves no information about the *Duration*, *Cost*, or *Work* values for each task. Because of this, *Interim Plan* information is limited in its usefulness. To save an *Interim Plan*, select the *Set interim plan* option in the *Set Baseline* dialog, as shown in Figure 8 - 13. Click the *Into* pick list and select the set of *Start* and *Finish* fields you want to use, such as *Start5* and *Finish5*, and then click the OK button.

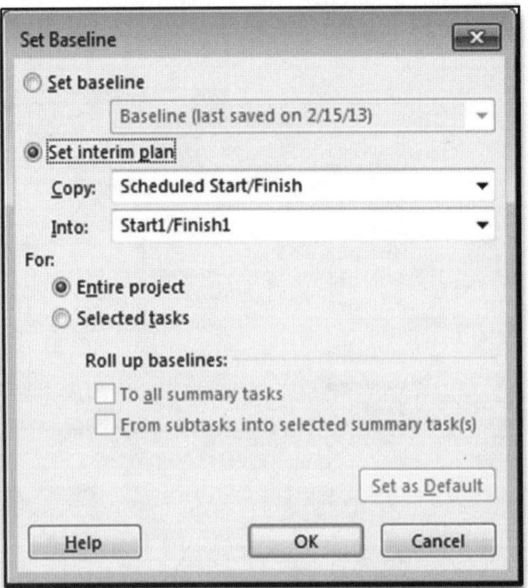

Figure 8 - 13: Save Interim Plan

Information: Project 2013 uses the *Scheduled Start* and *Scheduled Finish* fields primarily with *Manually Scheduled* tasks. For *Auto Scheduled* tasks, the *Scheduled Start* field always contains the same date as the *Start* field, and the *Scheduled Finish* field always contains the same date in the *Finish* field.

Hands On Exercise

Exercise 8 - 3

Now that you have completed your project planning, you are ready to save a baseline for the Training Advisor Rollout project.

1. Return to the **Training Advisor 08.mpp** sample file.
2. Right-click the *Select All* button and select the *More Tables* item on the shortcut menu.
3. In the *More Tables* dialog, select the *Baseline* table and click the *Apply* button.
4. Widen the *Task Name* column, as needed, and then drag the vertical split bar all the way to the right so that you can see all of the columns in the *Baseline* table.

Notice that none of the columns in the *Baseline* table display any baseline information yet, showing either *0* or *NA* values in each column.

5. Click the *Project* tab to display the *Project* ribbon.

6. In the *Schedule* section of the *Project* ribbon, click the *Set Baseline* pick list button, and then select the *Set Baseline* item.
7. In the *Set Baseline* dialog, leave the *Set Baseline* option selected, and leave the *Baseline* item selected in the *Set Baseline* pick list.
8. In the *For:* section of the *Set Baseline* dialog, leave the *Entire project* option selected.
9. Click the *OK* button.

Notice the software saved baseline values for every task in the project in all five baseline columns shown in the *Baseline* table.

10. Right-click the *Select All* button again and select the *Entry* table on the shortcut menu to reapply the *Entry* table.
11. Drag the vertical split bar back to the right edge of the *Duration* column.
12. In the *Schedule* section of the *Project* ribbon, click the *Set Baseline* pick list button, and select the *Set Baseline* item again.

Notice that the *Set baseline* pick list displays a *last saved on* date for the current baseline.

13. Click the *Cancel* button to exit the *Set Baseline* dialog.
14. Save and close the **Training Advisor 08.mpp** sample file.

Tracking Project Progress

After your project team members begin working on tasks in your project, your next step is to begin collecting actual progress from them so that you can enter project progress. You must stress the importance of tracking actual data to your team members and confirm that they are delivering accurate information to you in a timely manner. Collecting actual project data is the first step toward a clear understanding of the current state of the project.

Project 2013 includes many fields in which you can enter task progress, all of which you find in the task *Tracking* table. In my opinion, a better way to enter task progress is using one of three methods, which I describe as follows:

- Percent Complete
- Actual Work + Remaining Work
- Daily Timesheet + Remaining Work

Each of these methods for tracking project progress offers advantages and disadvantages. No matter which method you use, you must manually enter actual progress reported to you by your team members. To help them report their progress to you, you might print paper timesheets or create Excel spreadsheets in which your team members can record their actual progress and then report it to you so that you can enter it in your project.

Entering Progress Using Percent Complete

The simplest method of tracking progress is to ask your team members to estimate the cumulative percentage of the work that they have completed to date on each task during the reporting period. This method works better for construction projects, where it is more common to estimate the amount of work completed. This method is much less reliable in other environments, such as with software development projects.

The chief limitation of the Percent Complete tracking method is that it is not date-sensitive. In fact, when you enter a *Percent Complete* value for a task in Project 2013, the software assumes that the task **started and finished as scheduled**. If you want to use the Percent Complete method for tracking project progress, you can address this date limitation by gathering the following progress information from each team member for each task assignment:

- Actual Start date
- Percent Complete
- Actual Finish date

During each reporting period, your team members should report the actual date they began work on a task, along with their estimate of the percentage of work completed to date on the task. When the task is complete, your team members should report the actual date that they completed work on the task. Based on the information your team members provide for you, you can manually enter actual progress using the Percent Complete method by completing the following steps:

1. Apply the *Gantt Chart* view.
2. Right-click the *Select All* button and select the *Tracking* table on the shortcut menu.
3. Widen the *Task Name* column, if necessary.
4. Drag the vertical split bar to the right of the *% Complete* column.
5. "Drag and drop" the *% Complete* column between the *Actual Start* and *Actual Finish* columns.
6. Enter the actual start date of each task in the *Actual Start* column.
7. Enter an estimated percent complete in the *% Complete* column.
8. When the assigned resources complete a task, enter the actual completion date in the *Actual Finish* column.

Information: The preceding steps work well when you enter progress on tasks with only a single resource assigned. If you want use the *Percent Complete* method to enter progress on tasks with multiple resources assigned, and want to enter progress for each assigned resource individually, you can use a variation of the preceding set of steps. Display the *Task Usage* view instead of the *Gantt Chart* view, and then apply the *Tracking* table. Right-click the *Actual Finish* column header, select the *Insert Column* item on the shortcut menu, and then select the *% Work Complete* column. You can now enter progress using a modified version of the Percent Complete method of tracking progress on tasks with multiple resources assigned.

Figure 8 - 14 shows the *Tracking* table set up for the Percent Complete method of tracking progress, and with progress entered on the first two tasks. Notice that the *Design P1* task is 100% complete with both an *Actual Start* date and an *Actual Finish* date entered for the task. Notice that the *Build P1* task is only 50% complete with an *Actual Start* date and a *% Complete* value entered, but with no *Actual Finish* date entered.

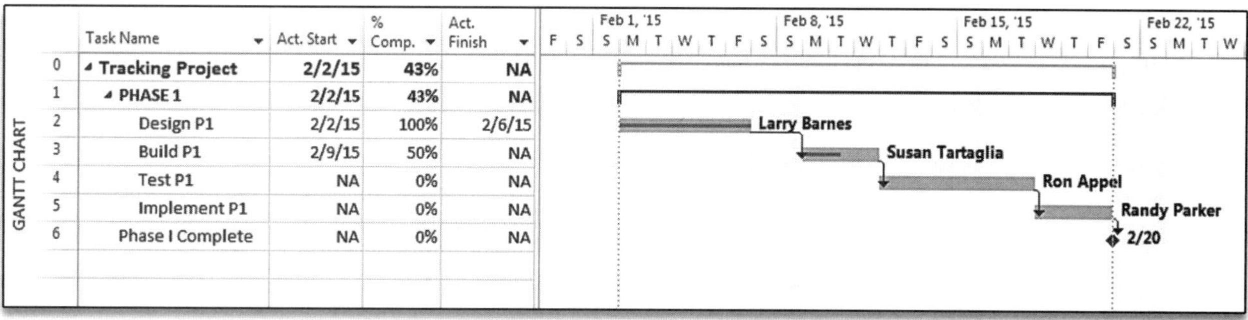

	Task Name	Act. Start	% Comp.	Act. Finish
0	Tracking Project	2/2/15	43%	NA
1	PHASE 1	2/2/15	43%	NA
2	Design P1	2/2/15	100%	2/6/15
3	Build P1	2/9/15	50%	NA
4	Test P1	NA	0%	NA
5	Implement P1	NA	0%	NA
6	Phase I Complete	NA	0%	NA

Figure 8 - 14: Progress entered in the Tracking table using the Percent Complete method

Hands On Exercise

Exercise 8 - 4

Enter task progress for the first two weeks of the Training Advisor Rollout project using the Percent Complete method.

1. Open the **Training Advisor 08 – Percent Complete.mpp** sample file.
2. Right-click the *Select All* button and select the *Tracking* table on the shortcut menu.
3. Click the *% Complete* column header to select the column, and then release the mouse button.
4. Click and hold the column header of the *% Complete* column to "grab" the column, and then drag and drop the column between the *Actual Start* and *Actual Finish* columns.
5. For task ID #17, the *Order Server* task, enter *01/04/16* in the *Actual Start* column and enter *01/05/16* in the *Actual Finish* column, and press the **Enter** key on your computer keyboard after you enter each date.

Notice that Project 2013 automatically marks the task as complete by entering *100%* in *the % Complete* column and by displaying a dark blue progress line in the Gantt bar for the task.

6. For task ID #28, the *Setup Test Training Server* task, enter *100%* in the *% Complete* column, and then press the **Enter** key on your computer keyboard.

Notice that Project 2013 enters the current *Start* date of the task in the *Actual Start* column and enters the current *Finish* date of the task in the *Actual Finish* column.

7. For task ID #30, the *Create Training Module 01* task, enter *01/13/16* in the *Actual Start* field, and then press the **Enter** key on your computer keyboard.

Notice that Project 2013 delays the Gantt bar for this task to a date two days later than the original *Start* date. The reason for the late start date is because *Ruth Andrews*, the assigned resource, called in sick on Monday and Tuesday of that week.

8. For task ID #30, the *Create Training Module 01* task, enter *60%* in the *% Complete* column, and then press the **Enter** key on your computer keyboard.
9. Add a task note to the *Creating Training Module 01* task to document the reason for the schedule slippage (2 days of sick leave for the resource *Ruth Andrews*).
10. Expand the occurrences of the *Project Status Meeting* recurring task.
11. Enter *100%* in the *% Complete* column for the *Project Status Meeting 1* task and then press the **Enter** key on your computer keyboard.
12. Collapse the occurrences of the *Project Status Meeting* recurring task.
13. Save and close the **Training Advisor 08 – Percent Complete.mpp** sample file.

Entering Progress Using Actual Work and Remaining Work

Another tracking method requires your team members to report the total number of actual work hours they performed to date for each task, and to provide their estimate on the number of remaining work hours for each task. For example, a team member reports 20 hours of actual work to date on a 40-hour task, but estimates 30 hours of remaining work (rather than 20 hours) because the original 40-hour estimate of work was too low.

This tracking method allows you to see date slippage, based on any increased remaining work estimates submitted by your team members. However, this method may not present a true picture of task progress, especially if a task started late. When using this method for tracking project progress, Project 2013 once again assumes that each task **started and finished as currently scheduled**.

If you want to use the Actual Work and Remaining Work method of tracking project progress, you can address the date limitation issue by obtaining the following progress information from each team member for each task assignment:

- Actual Start date
- Actual Work
- Remaining Work estimate
- Actual Finish date

During each reporting period, team members report the actual date they began work on a task, the number of hours of actual work completed to date, and their estimate on the number of remaining work hours. When a task is complete, team members report the actual date that they completed the work. Based on the information your team members provide, you can manually enter actual progress using the Actual Work and Remaining Work method by completing the following steps:

1. Apply the *Gantt Chart* view.
2. Right-click the *Select All* button and select the *Tracking* table on the shortcut menu.
3. Widen the *Task Name* column, if necessary.
4. "Drag and drop" the *Actual Work* column between the *Actual Start* and *Actual Finish* columns.

5. Right-click the *Actual Finish* column header and select the *Insert Column* item on the shortcut menu.

6. In the list of available columns, select the *Remaining Work* column.

7. Drag the vertical split bar to the right edge of the *Actual Finish* column.

8. Enter the actual start date of the task in the *Actual Start* column.

9. Enter the number of hours of actual work completed to date in the *Actual Work* column.

10. Enter a revised remaining work estimate in the *Remaining Work* column, if necessary.

11. When the assigned resource completes a task, enter the actual completion date in the *Actual Finish* column.

Information: The preceding steps work well when you enter progress on tasks with only a single resource assigned. If you want to use the Actual Work and Remaining Work method to enter progress on tasks with multiple resources assigned, and want to enter progress for each assigned resource individually, you can use a variation of the preceding set of steps. Display the *Task Usage* view instead of the *Gantt Chart* view, and then apply the *Tracking* table. Drag and drop the *Actual Work* field between the *Actual Start* and *Actual Finish* fields, and then insert the *Remaining Work* field to the right of the *Actual Work* field. You can now enter progress using a modified Actual Work and Remaining Work method of tracking progress on tasks with multiple resources assigned.

Figure 8 - 15 shows the *Tracking* table set up for the Actual Work and Remaining Work method of tracking progress and with progress entered for the first task. The project manager originally scheduled *24 hours* of *Work* on the *Build P1* task. The resource assigned to the task, *Larry Barnes,* reported that he performed *24 hours* of *Actual Work* on the task, and increased the *Remaining Work* estimate to *16 hours*. This means the task will finish late, based on the increased *Remaining Work* estimate.

	Task Name	Act. Start	Act. Work	Remaining Work	Act. Finish
0	**Tracking Project**	**2/2/15**	**24 h**	**96 h**	**NA**
1	**PHASE 1**	**2/2/15**	**24 h**	**96 h**	**NA**
2	Design P1	2/2/15	24 h	16 h	NA
3	Build P1	NA	0 h	24 h	NA
4	Test P1	NA	0 h	32 h	NA
5	Implement P1	NA	0 h	24 h	NA
6	Phase I Complete	NA	0 h	0 h	NA

Figure 8 - 15: Progress entered in the Tracking table using the Actual Work and Remaining Work method

Best Practice: When a team member increases their *Remaining Work* estimate, MSProjectExperts recommends that you add a task note to document the reason for changes in the *Remaining Work* value. Doing so may assist in the estimating process in future projects.

Hands On Exercise

Exercise 8 - 5

Enter task progress for the first two weeks of the Training Advisor Rollout project using the Actual Work and Remaining Work method.

1. Open the **Training Advisor 08 – Actual and Remaining Work.mpp** sample file.
2. Right-click the *Select All* button and select the *Tracking* table on the shortcut menu.
3. Drag the split bar to the right side of the *Actual Work* column.
4. Click the *Actual Work* column header to select the column, and then release the mouse button.
5. Click and hold the column header of the *Actual Work* column to "grab" the column, and then drag and drop the column between the *Actual Start* and *Actual Finish* columns.
6. Right-click the *Actual Finish* column header and select the *Insert Column* item on the shortcut menu.
7. In the list of available columns, select the *Remaining Work* column.
8. Drag the vertical split bar to the right edge of the *% Complete* column.
9. For task ID #17, the *Order Server* task, enter *1/4/16* in the *Actual Start* column and enter *01/05/16* in the *Actual Finish* column.

Notice in the *% Complete* column that Project 2013 marks the task as 100% complete. Notice also that the software calculates *12 hours* of *Actual Work* and sets the *Remaining Work* value to *0 hours*.

10. For task ID #28, the *Setup Test Training Server* task, enter *24h* in the *Actual Work* column.

Notice that Project 2013 marks the task as 100% complete by setting the *Remaining Work* value to *0 hours*, by entering the current *Start* date of the task in the *Actual Start* column, and by entering the current *Finish* date of the task in the *Actual Finish* column.

11. For task ID #30, the *Create Training Module 01* task, enter *01/13/16* in the *Actual Start* field.

Notice that Project 2013 delays the Gantt bar for this task to a date two days later than the original *Start* date. The reason for the late *Start* date is because Ruth Andrews, the assigned resource, was sick on Monday and Tuesday of that week.

12. For the *Create Training Module 01* task, enter *24h* in the *Actual Work* column and then enter *32h* in the *Remaining Work* column.

After Ruth Andrews began work on the *Create Training Module 01* task, she discovered her original work estimate of 40 hours was too low, which is why she increased the remaining work estimate by 16 hours.

Because of the late start and the increased remaining work estimate, this task is seriously behind schedule.

13. Add a task note to the *Creating Training Module 01* task to document the reason for the schedule slippage (2 days of sick leave for the resource *Ruth Andrews*).
14. Expand the occurrences of the *Project Status Meeting* recurring task.
15. Enter *10h* in the *Actual Work* column for the *Project Status Meeting 1* task.
16. Collapse the occurrences of the *Project Status Meeting* recurring task.
17. Save and close the **Training Advisor 08 – Actual and Remaining Work.mpp** sample file.

Entering Progress Using a Daily Timesheet

The most challenging method of tracking project progress is the Daily Timesheet method, which requires your team members to record their actual work hours in some type of daily timesheet. In addition, your team members must also record their estimate of the remaining work hours on each task at the end of the week. To use this method of tracking progress, you must manually create some type of form in which your team members can record progress, such as a paper timesheet you print for them or an electronic timesheet in Microsoft Excel you create for them.

This Daily Timesheet method of tracking progress is date sensitive because your team members report their *Actual Work* on a daily basis. When you enter progress for your team members using the Daily Timesheet method, Project 2013 infers the *Actual Start* date based on the first day on which you enter actual progress on the task. Likewise, the software infers the *Actual Finish* date of the task as the date that completes the total work on the task.

Best Practice: MSProjectExperts recommends that project team members record actual project progress on a daily basis, and submit their progress to the project manager on a weekly basis. Even though team members may protest, studies show that it takes an average of only 5 minutes per day to collect and record project progress, even if you use a paper timesheet.

Based on the information your team members provide for you in their paper or electronic timesheets, you can manually enter actual progress using the Daily Timesheet method by completing the following steps:

1. Click the *View* tab to display the *View* ribbon.
2. In the *Resource Views* section of the *View* ribbon, click the *Resource Usage* button to display the *Resource Usage* view.
3. Widen the *Resource Name* column, if necessary.
4. Scroll the timephased grid (gray/white timesheet) to the current week, if necessary.
5. In the *Zoom* section of the *View* ribbon, click the *Timescale* pick list and select the *Days* item on the list.
6. Right-click anywhere in the timephased grid and then select the *Actual Work* item on the shortcut menu.
7. Widen the *Details* column in the timephased grid, if necessary.
8. In the *Split View* section of the *View* ribbon, select the *Details* option checkbox to display the *Resource Form* view in the lower pane.

9. Right-click anywhere in the *Resource Form* pane and select the *Work* details on the shortcut menu.

10. In the *Resource Usage* pane, click the *Select All* button to select all of the resources and their assignments.

11. In the *Data* section of the *View* ribbon, click the *Outline* pick list button, and then select the *Hide Subtasks* item to collapse all of the task assignments for every resource.

12. Click the *Expand* symbol (white arrow symbol) for a resource to expand the task assignments for that resource.

Figure 8 - 16 shows the *Resource Usage* view, set up to enter progress for the tasks assigned to *Larry Barnes* using the Daily Timesheet method.

Information: After you expand the task assignments for a resource, click the *Task* tab to display the *Task* ribbon. Select any task assignment and then click the *Scroll to Task* button in the *Editing* section of the *Task* ribbon to scroll to the planned work hours in the timephased grid.

Information: In the timephased grid, gray cells show the timephased values for resources, while the white cells show the timephased values for task assignments. When you enter progress in the timephased grid, be sure to enter your *Actual Work* hours in the white cells and not the gray cells.

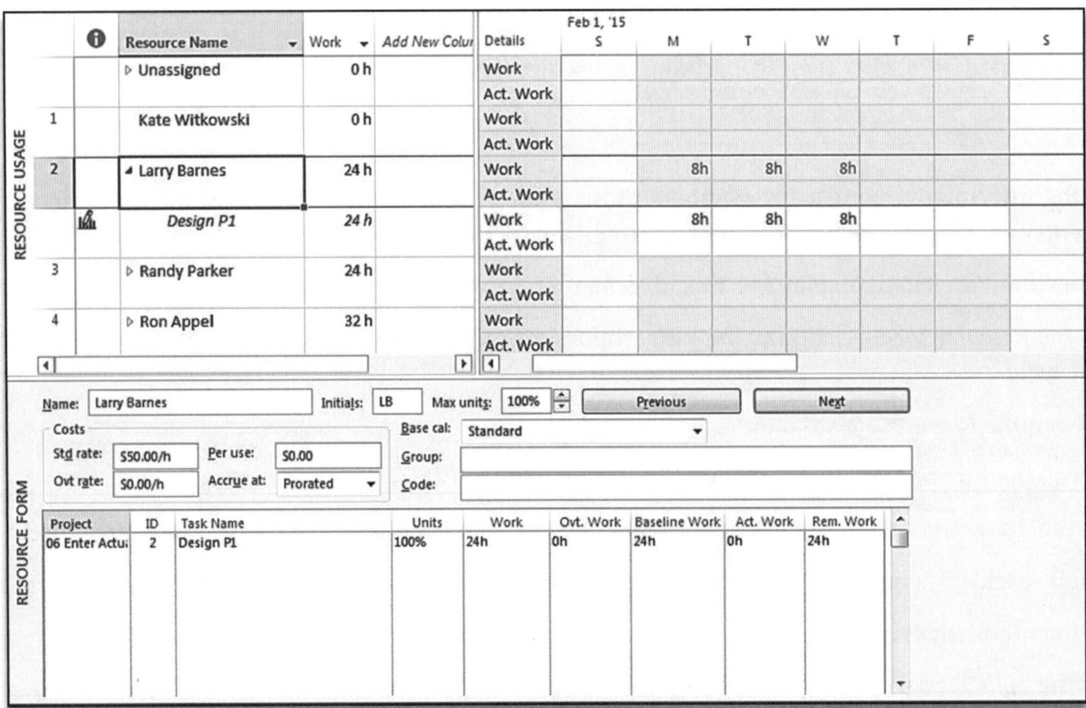

Figure 8 - 16: Ready to enter progress using the Daily Timesheet method

To enter *Actual Work* values and adjust the *Remaining Work* value for any resource's task assignment, complete the following steps:

1. For the selected resource, select the *Actual Work* task assignment cell (white cell) in the timephased grid.
2. Type the actual work values in the *Actual Work* assignment cell for each day of the week, as reported by the resource.
3. In the *Resource Form* pane, select the *Remaining Work* value for the correct task assignment.
4. Increase or decrease the selected *Remaining Work* value, as needed.
5. Click the *OK* button in the *Resource Form* pane when finished.

Figure 8 - 17 shows that I entered actual progress for *Larry Barnes* on the *Design P1* task assignment during the week of February 1. Notice that I entered *0 hours* of *Actual Work* on Wednesday, indicating the resource performed no work that day. In the *Resource Form* pane, notice that I also increased the *Remaining Work* estimate from *0 hours* to *8 hours* for the *Design P1* task assignment.

Information: When you use the Daily Timesheet method of tracking progress, one of the oddities you notice about Project 2013 is that planned *Work* hours change to the hours you entered in the *Actual Work* cells. This is not a bug in the software; it is default behavior. The theory behind how the software works is this: "Actuals always replace estimates." Suppose you have 8 hours of planned work for a resource to do on Monday. The resource reports back that he only did 4 hours of actual work on Monday. So, how much work is there on Monday? There are now only 4 hours of work on Monday, and Project 2013 reschedules the remaining 4 hours of uncompleted work to the next day. If you want to see the original number of hours of planned work for a task, you must add the *Baseline Work* details to the timephased grid.

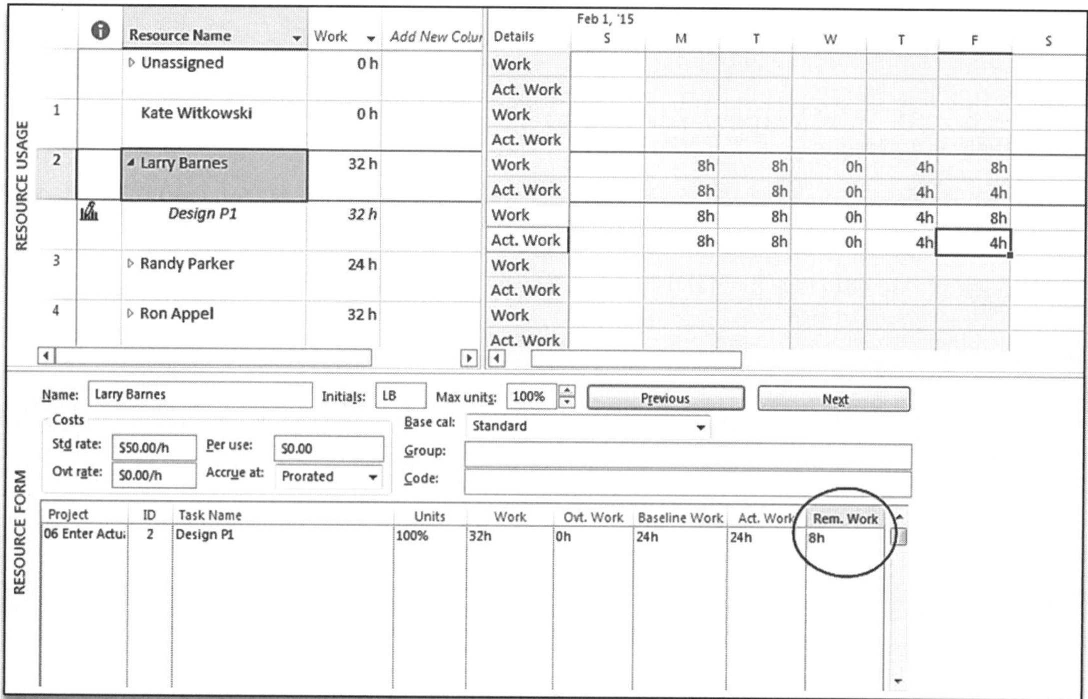

Figure 8 - 17: Actual Work entered and Remaining Work revised

Hands On Exercise

Exercise 8 - 6

Set up the Training Advisor Rollout project to use the Daily Timesheet method.

1. Open the **Training Advisor 08 – Daily Timesheet.mpp** sample file.
2. Click the *View* tab to display the *View* ribbon.
3. In the *Resource Views* section of the *View* ribbon, click the *Resource Usage* button to display the *Resource Usage* view.
4. Widen the *Resource Name* column, if necessary.
5. Scroll the timephased grid (gray/white timesheet) to the week of *January 3, 2016*.
6. In the *Zoom* section of the *View* ribbon, click the *Timescale* pick list and select the *Days* item on the list, if necessary.
7. Right-click anywhere in the timephased grid and then select the *Actual Work* item on the shortcut menu.
8. Widen the *Details* column in the timephased grid.
9. In the *Split View* section of the *View* ribbon, select the *Details* option checkbox to display the *Resource Form* view in the lower pane.
10. Right-click anywhere in the *Resource Form* pane and select the *Work* details on the shortcut menu.
11. In the *Resource Usage* pane (top pane), click the *Select All* button to select all of the resources and their assignments.
12. In the *Data* section of the *View* ribbon, click the *Outline* pick list button, and then select the *Hide Subtasks* item to collapse all of the task assignments for every resource.
13. Save but **do not** close the **Training Advisor 08 – Daily Timesheet.mpp** sample file.

Exercise 8 - 7

Enter task progress for the first three weeks of the Training Advisor Rollout project using the Daily Timesheet method.

1. Return to the **Training Advisor 08 – Daily Timesheet.mpp** sample file, if necessary.
2. In the *Resource Usage* pane, click the *Expand* symbol (white arrow symbol) for *Mickey Cobb* to expand her task assignments.
3. Using the following paper timesheet data for *Mickey Cobb*, enter *Actual Work* values in the white row of the timephased grid and then adjust the *Remaining Work* value in the *Resource Form* pane:

Name: **Mickey Cobb**	Week Of: **1/3/16**					
Task Name	**M**	**T**	**W**	**Th**	**F**	**Remaining Work**
Order Server	8	2				0
Setup Test Training Server			8	8	8	0

4. In the *Resource Usage* pane, click the *Collapse* symbol (black triangle symbol) for *Mickey Cobb* to collapse her task assignments.
5. In the *Resource Usage* pane, click the *Expand* symbol (white arrow symbol) for *Ruth Andrews* to expand her task assignments.
6. Scroll the timephased grid to the week of *January 10, 2016*.
7. Using the following paper timesheet data for *Ruth Andrews*, enter *Actual Work* values in the white row of the timephased grid, adjust the *Remaining Work* value in the *Resource Form* pane if needed, and add a task *Note* for her:

Name: **Ruth Andrews**	Week Of: **1/10/16**					
Task Name	**M**	**T**	**W**	**Th**	**F**	**Remaining Work**
Create Training Module 01	8	8				24
Task Notes	Resource worked Monday and Tuesday but called in sick the rest of the week.					

Important Information: To add a task note while entering actual progress in this special combination view, double-click the name of the task assignment in the *Resource Form* pane to open the *Task Information* dialog. Click the *Notes* tab and then enter the text of the note.

8. In the *Resource Usage* pane, click the *Collapse* symbol (black triangle symbol) for *Ruth Andrews* to collapse her task assignments.
9. In the *Resource Usage* pane, click the *Expand* symbol (white arrow symbol) for *Jeff Holly* to expand his task assignments.
10. Scroll the timephased grid to the week of *January 17, 2016*.
11. Using the following paper timesheet data for *Jeff Holly*, enter *Actual Work* values in the white row of the timephased grid and then adjust the *Remaining Work* value in the *Resource Form* pane:

Name: **Jeff Holly**	Week Of: **01/17/16**					
Task Name	**M**	**T**	**W**	**Th**	**F**	**Remaining Work**
Setup Server and Load O/S			4	4	8	24

12. In the *Split View* section of the *View* ribbon, **deselect** the *Details* option checkbox to close the *Resource Form* pane.
13. In the *Task Views* section of the *View* ribbon, click the *Gantt Chart* button to reapply the *Gantt Chart* view.
14. Click the *Task* tab to display the *Task* ribbon.
15. Select task ID #21, the *Installation Complete* milestone task, and then click the *Scroll to Task* button in the *Editing* section of the *Task* ribbon to bring the Gantt bar into view for this milestone task.

Notice that Project 2013 **does not** reschedule the *Installation Complete* milestone task to 2/8/16 as you might expect, based on the FS dependency with its predecessor task. This is because the milestone task has a *Finish No Later Than* constraint set for 2/5/16. Due to the schedule slippage on *Setup Server and Load O/S* task, you cannot meet the contractual obligation on this milestone task, so you re-negotiated with the project sponsor for a *Finish* date of 2/12/16 for the *Installation Complete* phase.

16. Double-click task ID #21, the *Installation Complete* milestone task, and then click the *Advanced* tab in the *Task Information* dialog.
17. Click the *Constraint date* pick list and select the *2/12/16* constraint date.
18. Click the *Notes* tab, click the *Bulleted List* button, and then add the following note:

    FNLT 2/12/16 - Unable to meet original contractual finish date for the Installation phase.

19. Click the *OK* button to close the *Task Information* dialog.
20. Save but **do not** close the **Training Advisor 08 – Daily Timesheet.mpp** sample file.

Exercise 8 - 8

You receive an e-mail message from *Jeff Holly* stating, "The server was delivered two days later than scheduled. After starting the server setup, I encountered an unanticipated database software upgrade that cost $995. Because of this, I must redo 4 hours of work that I did previously." Add this additional status information to the Training Advisor Rollout project.

1. Return to the **Training Advisor 08 – Daily Timesheet.mpp** sample file, if necessary.
2. Right-click the *Select All* button and select the *Cost* table on the shortcut menu.

Notice the planned *Fixed Cost* value of *$6,509* you entered during task planning on the *Order Server* task.

3. In the *Fixed Cost* column for task ID #18, the *Setup Server and Load O/S* task, enter *$995* for the price of the unanticipated database software upgrade.
4. Double-click the *Setup Server and Load O/S* task and then click the *Notes* tab in the *Task Information* dialog.
5. On the *Notes* page of the dialog, click the *Bulleted List* button, and then add the following note:

   Server delivered two days late. $995 extra cost for unanticipated DB software upgrade. Resource must redo 4 hours of work done previously.

6. Click the *OK* button when finished.
7. Right-click the *Select All* button and select the *Entry* table on the shortcut menu.
8. Save but **do not** close the **Training Advisor 08 – Daily Timesheet.mpp** sample file.

Exercise 8 - 9

Enter project progress for the first two *Project Status Meeting* occurrences.

1. Click the *Expand* symbol (white arrow symbol) for the *Project Status Meeting* recurring task to expand all of the occurrences.
2. Select the *Project Status Meeting 1* task and then click the *Scroll to Task* button in the *Editing* section of the *Task* ribbon to bring the Gantt bar into view for the meeting.
3. In the *Schedule* section of the *Task* ribbon, click the *100%* button.

The fastest and most reliable way to mark a meeting completed is to select it and then click the *100%* button on the *Task* ribbon.

4. Select the *Project Status Meeting 2* task and then click the *100%* button in the *Schedule* section of the *Task* ribbon.
5. Click the *Collapse* symbol (black triangle symbol) for the *Project Status Meeting* recurring task to collapse all of the occurrences
6. Save and close the **Training Advisor 08 – Daily Timesheet.mpp** sample file.

Entering Progress for an Expense Cost Resource

To enter actual cost information for an *Expense Cost* resource, click the *View* tab to display the *View* ribbon. In the *Task Views* section of the *View* ribbon, click the *Task Usage* button to display the *Task Usage* view. In the *Data* section of the *View* ribbon, click the *Tables* pick list button and select the *Cost* table. In the *Cost* table, drag and drop the *Actual* and *Total Cost* columns to the left of the *Fixed Cost* column.

Right-click in the timephased grid and select the *Cost* details. Right-click again in the timephased grid and select the *Actual Cost* details on the shortcut menu. Right-click one final time in the timephased grid and **deselect** the *Work* details on the shortcut menu.

Select the task to which you assigned the *Expense Cost* resource and then enter the actual expenditure in the *Actual* column for the *Expense Cost* resource assignment. Project 2013 evenly distributes the *Actual Cost* amount across the duration of the task in the timephased grid. If you want to time phase the *Actual Cost* expenditure to show how you actually spent the money, re-type the *Actual Cost* values in the timephased grid. Figure 8 - 18 shows a slightly-modified *Task Usage* view after I entered *$16,599* of actual expense in the *Actual Cost* column for the *Testing Equipment* cost resource assigned to the *Test P1* task.

Information: If you enter an *Actual Cost* amount that is **less than** the original estimated *Cost* amount for an *Expense Cost* resource, you should reduce the *Remaining Cost* value to *$0.00* for the *Expense Cost* resource assignment. To do this, drag the split bar to the right to expose the *Remaining Cost* column in the *Cost* table. In the *Remaining Cost* column, set the value to *$0.00* for the *Expense Cost* resource assignment. When you do variance analysis, Project 2013 shows you that the expenditure came in "under budget" for the assignment.

TASK USAGE

	Task Name	Actual Cost	Total Cost	Details	Feb 15, '15 S	M	T	W	T	F
0	**Tracking Project**	**$22,199.00**	**$23,399.00**	Cost		$4,549.75	$4,549.75	$4,549.75	$4,549.75	$400.00
				Act. Cost		$4,549.75	$4,549.75	$4,549.75	$4,549.75	
1	**PHASE 1**	$22,199.00	$23,399.00	Cost		$4,549.75	$4,549.75	$4,549.75	$4,549.75	$400.00
				Act. Cost		$4,549.75	$4,549.75	$4,549.75	$4,549.75	
2	Design P1	$2,000.00	$2,000.00	Cost						
				Act. Cost						
	Larry Barnes	*$2,000.00*	*$2,000.00*	Cost						
				Act. Cost						
3	Build P1	$2,000.00	$2,000.00	Cost						
				Act. Cost						
	Susan Tartaglia	*$2,000.00*	*$2,000.00*	Cost						
				Act. Cost						
4	Test P1	$18,199.00	$18,199.00	Cost		$4,549.75	$4,549.75	$4,549.75	$4,549.75	
				Act. Cost		$4,549.75	$4,549.75	$4,549.75	$4,549.75	
	Ron Appel	*$1,600.00*	*$1,600.00*	Cost		$400.00	$400.00	$400.00	$400.00	
				Act. Cost		$400.00	$400.00	$400.00	$400.00	
	Test Equipment	*$16,599.00*	*$16,599.00*	Cost		~~$4,149.75~~	~~$4,149.75~~	~~$4,149.75~~	~~$4,149.75~~	
				Act. Cost		$4,149.75	$4,149.75	$4,149.75	$4,149.75	
5	Implement P1	$0.00	$1,200.00	Cost						$400.00
				Act. Cost						
	Randy Parker	*$0.00*	*$1,200.00*	Cost						$400.00
				Act. Cost						

Figure 8 - 18: Task Usage view after entering Actual Cost expenditure for an Expense Cost resource

To modify the *Task Usage* view shown previously in Figure 8 - 18, I dragged and dropped the *Actual Cost* and *Total Cost* columns to the left of the *Fixed Cost* column in the *Cost* table. I then modified the title shown in the column header of the *Actual* column to show the real name of the column, *Actual Cost*. To modify the title of the *Actual* column, right-click in the *Actual* column header and then select the *Field Settings* item on the shortcut menu. In the *Field Settings* dialog shown in Figure 8 - 19, delete the word *Actual* in the *Title* field and then click the *OK* button.

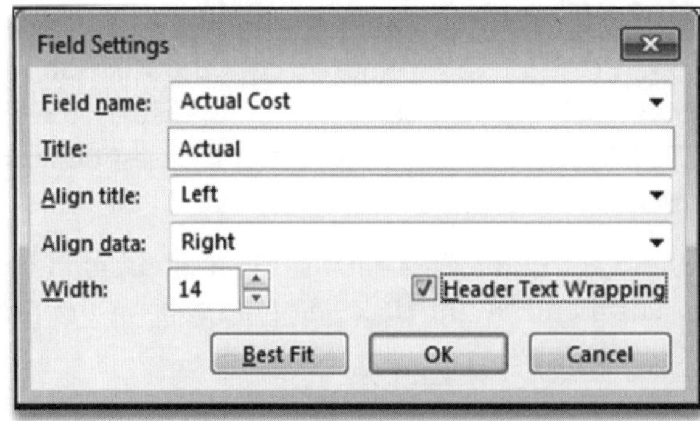

Figure 8 - 19: Field Settings dialog

Information: When you leave the *Title* field blank in the *Field Settings* dialog, Project 2013 displays the real name of the field in the column header. You can enter any type of information in the *Title* field to make it easier to shorten the name of the column or to identify the purpose of the column.

Hands On Exercise

Exercise 8 - 10

Today is Monday, February 1, 2016 and task progress has been entered through the week of January 24, 2016. To prepare for loading and configuring the Training Advisor server software, *Carmen Kamper* purchased the necessary software licenses from the software vendor. Enter actual expense information for an *Expense Cost* resource in your Training Advisor Rollout project.

1. Open the **Training Advisor Rollout 08 – Expense Cost Resource.mpp** sample file.
2. Click the *Task* tab to display the *Task* ribbon, if necessary.
3. In the *View* section of the *Task* ribbon, click the *Gantt Chart* pick list button and select the *_Cost Resources* view in the *Custom* section at the top of the pick list.
4. Scroll down and then select task ID #19, the *Load and Configure Software* task assigned to *Carmen Kamper*.
5. In the *Editing* section of the *Task* ribbon, click the *Scroll to Task* button to bring the timephased *Cost* hours into view for the task.
6. Drag the split bar to the right to expose the *Actual Cost* column.
7. Enter *$84,000* in the *Actual Cost* column for the *Software Licenses* resource assignment.

The extra cost of $9,000 for server software licenses is for the Training Advisor server software installed on the test training server.

8. Double-click the *Load and Configure Software* task and then select the *Notes* tab in the *Task Information* dialog.
9. On the *Notes* page of the dialog, click the *Bulleted List* button, and then add the following note:

    $9,000 of additional cost for the software license for the test training server.

10. Click the *OK* button when finished.
11. In the *View* section of the *Task* ribbon, click the *Gantt Chart* button to reapply the *Gantt Chart* view.
12. Save and close the **Training Advisor Rollout 08 – Expense Cost Resource.mpp** sample file.

Rescheduling Uncompleted Work

Regardless of which method of tracking progress you use, after entering actual progress in your project plan in Project 2013 you must also locate and reschedule uncompleted work that remains in a past reporting period. Uncompleted tasks usually fall into one of the following situations:

- The resource(s) assigned to the task reported no actual progress on the task during the last reporting period (no progress).
- The resource(s) assigned to the task reported progress on the task, but reported no progress on one or more of the final days of the last reporting period (interrupted partial progress).

Figure 8 - 20 shows a project that contains both completed and uncompleted work during the first reporting period of the project. In the sample project, today is Monday, April 13, represented by the green vertical line in the Gantt chart in the right side of the project. Notice in the *PHASE I* section that *Myrta Hansen* completed all of her scheduled work during the April 5 reporting period. Notice in the *PHASE II* section that *Nick Bock* completed only part of his scheduled work during the April 5 reporting period. Notice in the *PHASE III* section that *Lisa Glaus* did not complete any of her scheduled work during the April 5 reporting period. Because both *Nick Bock* and *Lisa Glaus* failed to complete their scheduled work during the April 5 reporting period, the current project schedule is **no longer accurate** because of uncompleted work scheduled in the past prior to Monday, April 13.

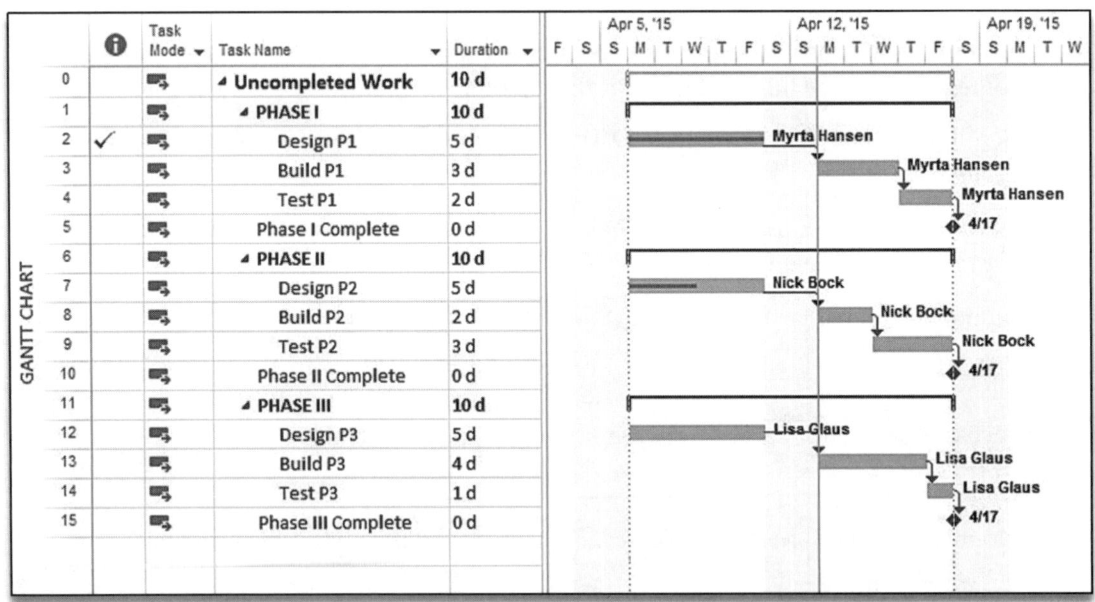

Figure 8 - 20: Uncompleted work in a past reporting period for two tasks

To address situations such as the one shown in Figure 8 - 20, you must reschedule uncompleted work from the past reporting period into the current reporting period by completing a two-step process:

1. Set the *Status* date.
2. Reschedule all uncompleted work in the past to the current reporting period.

I discuss these two steps individually.

Setting the Status Date

To enter the *Status* date for your project, click the *Project* tab to display the *Project* ribbon. In the *Properties* section of the *Project* ribbon, click the *Project Information* button. Project 2013 displays the *Project Information* dialog shown in Figure 8 - 21. This dialog offers three important date options in the *Start date, Current date,* and *Status date* fields. As part of the six-step process to define a new project, you enter the *Start* date of your project in the *Start date* field. The software automatically fills in the date in the *Current date* field with the date from the system clock in your computer. Optionally, such as for simulation purposes, you can change the date in the *Current date* field.

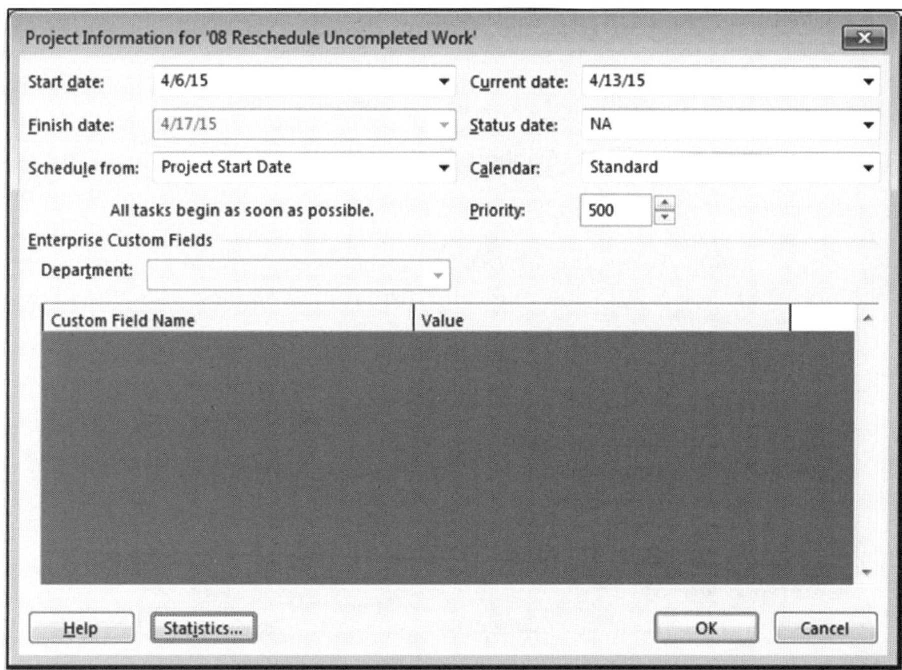

Figure 8 - 21: Project Information dialog
Set the Current date or the Status date

By default, the software sets the *Status* date value to *NA* unless you manually enter a *Status* date. The *Status* date should represent the last day of the previous reporting period during which team members should report progress. The date you enter in the *Status date* field can be the date of a Friday, Saturday, or Sunday as needed. For example, today is Monday, April 13. You see this date in the *Current date* field in the *Project Information* dialog shown previously in Figure 8 - 21. The *Status* date for this project can be April 10 (Friday), April 11 (Saturday), or April 12 (Sunday). For the sake of consistency, I recommend you always select the date for Sunday in case team members worked over the weekend. To enter a *Status* date for your project, click the *Status date* pick list and select a date. Click the *OK* button when finished.

Project 2013 also allows you to specify a *Status* date by clicking the *Status Date* button in In the *Status* section of the *Project* ribbon. The software displays the *Status Date* dialog shown in Figure 8 - 22. In the *Status Date* dialog, click the *Status Date* pick list and select a date. Click the *OK* button when finished.

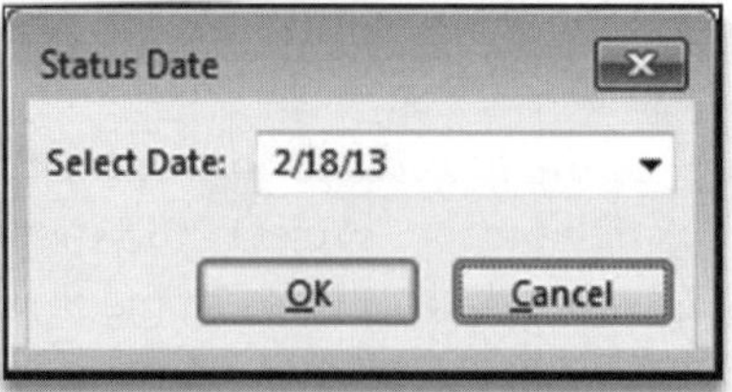

Figure 8 - 22: Status Date dialog

Rescheduling Uncompleted Work

After you specify the *Status* date, you are ready to reschedule uncompleted work from the past into the current reporting period by completing the following steps:

1. Optionally select tasks with uncompleted work in past reporting periods.
2. Click the *Project* tab to display the *Project* ribbon.
3. In the *Status* section of the *Project* ribbon, click the *Update Project* button.
4. In the *Update Project* dialog, select the *Reschedule uncompleted work to start after* option, as shown in Figure 8 - 23. Notice that Project 2013 automatically displays the *Status* date value in this field.

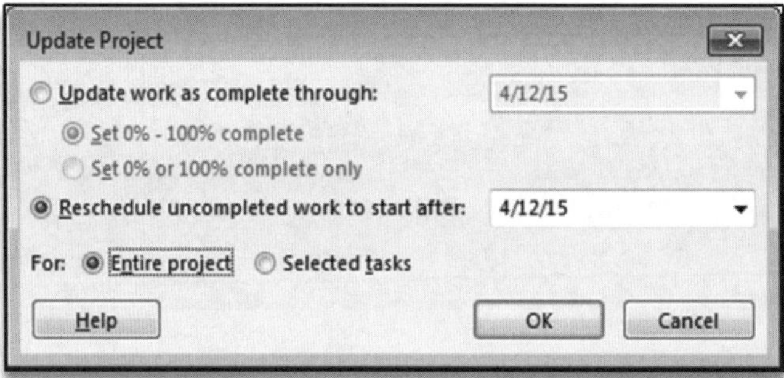

Figure 8 - 23: Update Project dialog

Warning: If you do not enter a *Status* date value in either the *Project Information* dialog or in the *Status Date* dialog, then you must enter your *Status* date in the *Reschedule uncompleted work to start after* field in the *Update Project* dialog. If you fail to enter the *Status* date, then the *Reschedule uncompleted work to start after* field always displays the *Current* date, which may give unacceptable results when you reschedule the uncompleted work.

In the *Update Project* dialog, Project 2013 allows you to select either the *Entire project* option or the *Selected tasks* option. Selecting the *Entire project* option offers you the more aggressive approach because the software finds every instance of uncompleted work in the past, and reschedules the work for you automatically. If you prefer to take a more conservation approach, you must first select tasks with uncompleted work in the past, and then you can choose the *Selected tasks* option in the *Update Project* dialog. Click the *OK* button when finished.

If your project contains constraints of any type, Project 2013 displays the *Planning Wizard* dialog shown in Figure 8 - 24. The dialog warns you about potentially unscheduled tasks due to constraint dates, and encourages you to locate these tasks using a filter, and then to manually reschedule the tasks. In reality, the software can reschedule tasks with *flexible* constraints (such as *Start No Earlier Than*), but it cannot reschedule tasks with *inflexible* constraints (such as *Finish No Later Than*). If your project does contain inflexible constraints, follow the guidance shown in the dialog to locate these tasks and then reschedule them manually. Click the *OK* button to close the dialog.

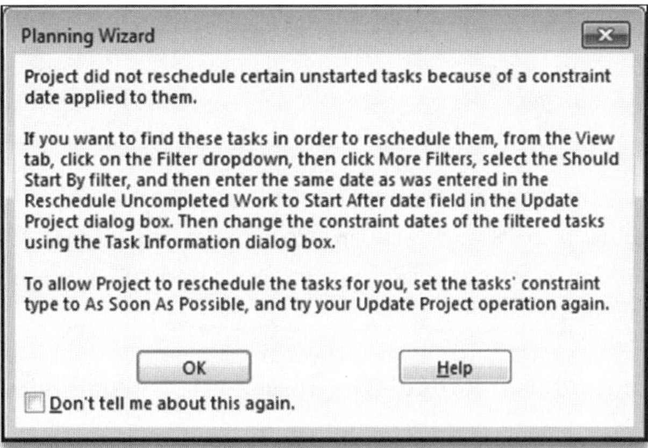

Figure 8 - 24: Planning Wizard dialog warns about constraints

Project 2013 reschedules uncompleted work from past reporting periods by splitting in-progress tasks and by setting a *Start No Earlier Than (SNET)* constraint on unstarted tasks. Figure 8 - 25 shows the new project schedule after rescheduling uncompleted work. Notice that the software split the in-progress *Design P2* task assigned to *Nick Bock,* as indicated by the split indicator (…) in the middle of the Gantt bar. The software also rescheduled the entire unstarted *Design P3* task assigned to *Lisa Glaus* by applying a *Start No Earlier Than (SNET)* constraint to the task.

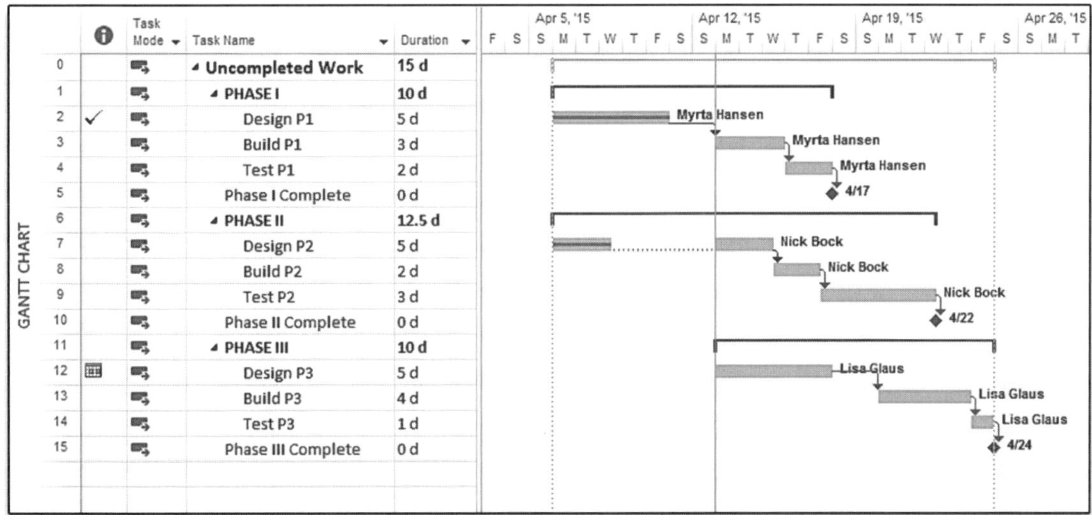

Figure 8 - 25: Uncompleted work rescheduled to the current reporting period

Information: Do not fear selecting the *Entire project* option in the *Update Project* dialog to take a more aggressive approach to the process of rescheduling uncompleted work. If you select this option and then reschedule the uncompleted work from the past, you can easily determine which tasks the software rescheduled by looking for tasks with the light blue change highlighting. Generally speaking, the first task in a block of tasks with light blue change highlighting is the task that the software rescheduled.

Hands On Exercise

Exercise 8 - 11

Today is Monday, February 1, 2016 and task progress has been entered through the week of January 24, 2016. Enter the *Status* date and then reschedule uncompleted work from the past reporting period into the current reporting period.

1. Open the **Training Advisor Rollout 08 – Reschedule Uncompleted Work.mpp** sample file.
2. Scroll the Gantt chart so that you can see the weeks of **January 24 and 31, 2016.**

Notice that *Carmen Kamper* only completed 1 day of work on task ID #19, the *Load and Configure Software* task. Due to her continuing illness, notice also that *Ruth Andrews* did no work on task ID #31, the *Create Training Module 02* task.

3. Click the *Project* tab to display the *Project* ribbon.
4. In the *Properties* section of the *Project* ribbon, click the *Project Information* button.
5. In the *Project Information* dialog, manually enter the date **1/31/16** in the *Status date* field, and then click the *OK* button.
6. In the *Schedule* section of the *Project* ribbon, click the *Update Project* button.
7. In the *Update Project* dialog, select the *Reschedule uncompleted work to start after* option.
8. Leave the *Status* date value shown in the *Reschedule uncompleted work to start after* field.
9. Leave the *Entire project* option selected and then click the *OK* button.
10. In the *Planning Wizard* dialog, click the *OK* button.

Notice how Project 2013 split task ID #19, the *Load and Configure Software* task, which is an in-progress task. Notice also, how the software moved task ID #31, the *Create Training Module 02* task, by applying a *Start No Earlier Than* constraint to the task.

11. Save and close the **Training Advisor Rollout 08 – Reschedule Uncompleted Work.mpp** sample file.

Rescheduling a Task

Project managers occasionally need to reschedule one or more tasks in a project to show a delay in a project that is already under way. A common reason for this is when management pulls the resources off one project to go and help on a failing project. For example, consider the project shown in Figure 8 - 26. After team members completed all of the tasks in the *Phase I* section of the project, I learned that I must put the remainder of the project "on hold" for a month (4 weeks or 20 working days). Therefore, I must reschedule the tasks in the project beginning with the *Write Course Manual* task.

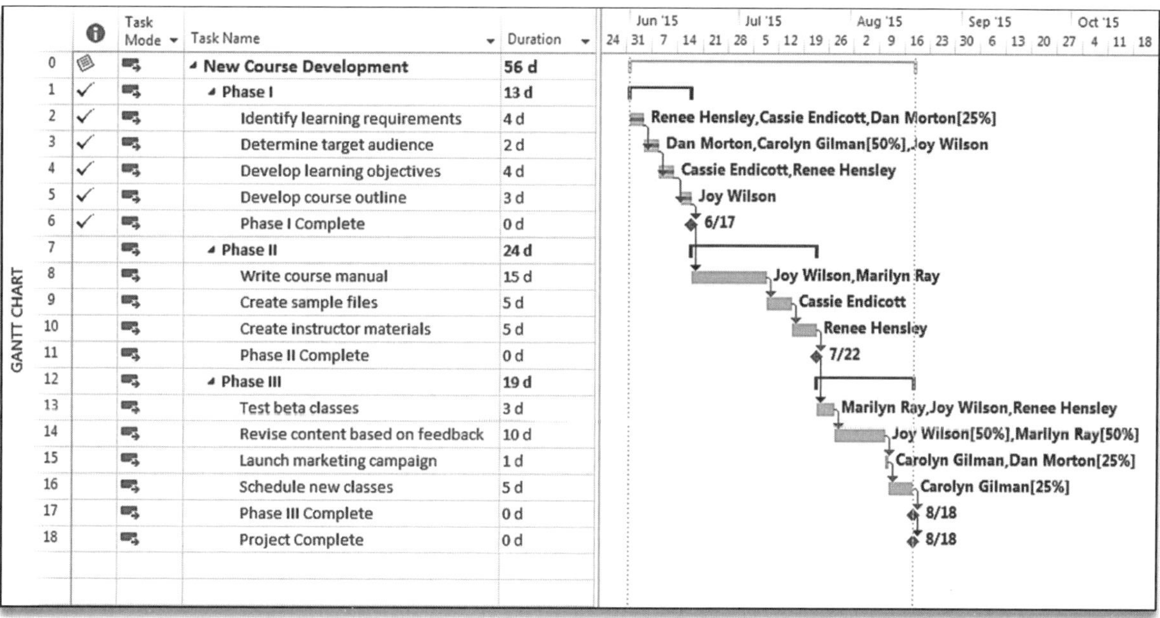

Figure 8 - 26: In-progress project

To move tasks, click the *Task* tab to display the *Task* ribbon. Select the tasks you want to move and then click the *Move* pick list button in the *Tasks* section of the *Task* ribbon, as shown in Figure 8 - 27. The *Move* pick list includes three sections that allow you to reschedule the selected tasks.

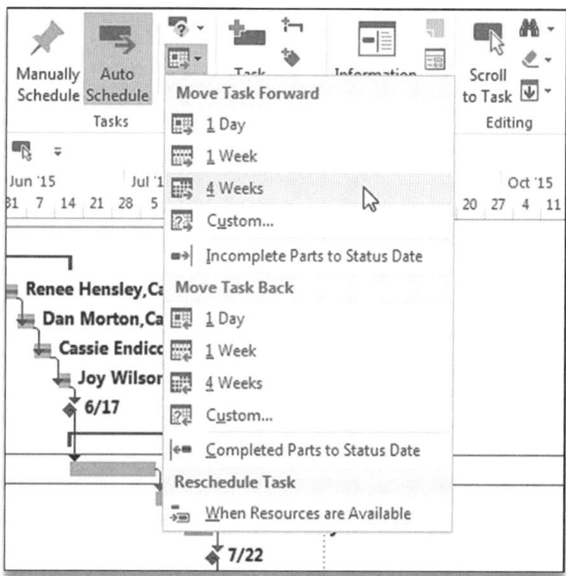

Figure 8 - 27: Move pick list

The *Move Task Forward* section offers options that allow you to reschedule the selected tasks into the future by 1 day, by 1 week, by 4 weeks, by a specific amount of time you specify, or by rescheduling uncompleted work forward to the *Status* date of the project. The *Move Task Back* section offers you options that allow you to reschedule the selected tasks into the past by 1 day, by 1 week, by 4 weeks, by a specific amount of time you specify, or by rescheduling completed work back to the *Status* date of the project. The *Reschedule Task* section includes a single option that allows you to delay the task until the assigned resource is available. This final option allows you to manually level an overallocated resource assigned to the selected task.

If you select the *Custom* item in the *Move Task Forward* section of the *Move* pick list, Project 2013 displays the *Move tasks forward* dialog shown in Figure 8 - 28. Enter a number of working days in the *Move selected tasks forward by ____ working days* field and then click the *OK* button. If you select the *Custom* item in the *Move Task Backward* section of the *Move* pick list, by the way, the software displays a *Move tasks backward* dialog that is identical to the *Move tasks forward* dialog in every way except for the name of the dialog.

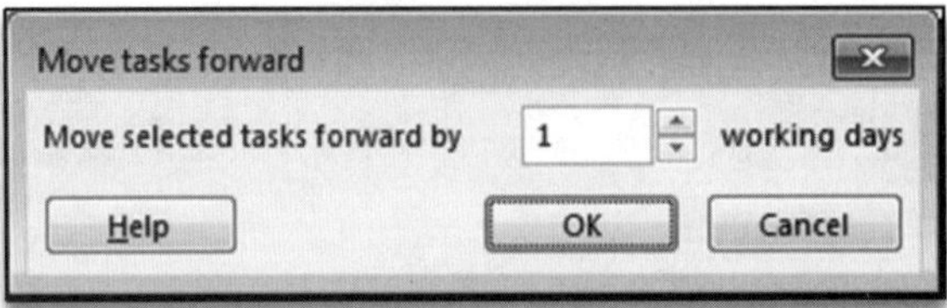

Figure 8 - 28

To delay my project by four weeks, I select the *Write course manual* task (the first task in the *Phase II* section of the project), and then I select the *4 Weeks* item on the *Move* pick list. Project 2013 reschedules this task and all successor tasks 4 weeks into the future by setting a *Start No Earlier Than* (SNET) constraint on the task, as shown in Figure 8 - 29. The new *Finish* date for the project is now September 15, exactly 20 working days later than the original *Finish* date of August 18.

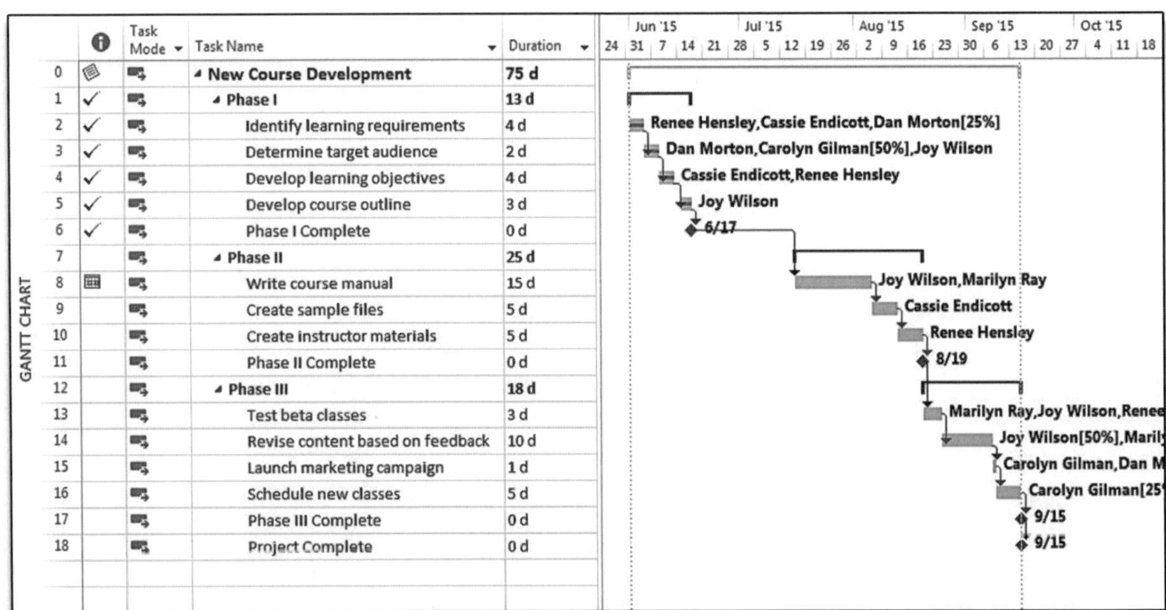

Figure 8 - 29: New project scheduling after delaying the Write Course Manual task four weeks

Information: If you use the *Move* feature on an in-progress task, Project 2013 moves only the incomplete part of the task forward, but does not move any part of the task backwards. If you attempt to use the *Move* feature on a completed task, the software does not move the task forward or backward since the task is completed and cannot move.

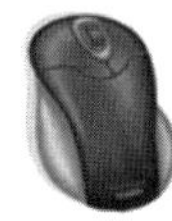

Hands On Exercise

Exercise 8 - 12

Due to a lack of resources, management put a project "on hold" for two weeks. Delay all incomplete tasks by two weeks (10 working days).

1. Open the **Reschedule a Task 2013.mpp** sample file.

Notice that all tasks are completed in the *Analysis/Software Requirements* and *Design* sections of the project. Notice that the current *Finish* date of the project is **July 25**, as shown to the right of the *Testing Complete* milestone.

2. Select task ID #12, the *Identify design parameters* task.
3. Click the *Task* tab to display the *Task* ribbon, if necessary.
4. In the *Tasks* section of the *Task* ribbon, click the *Move* pick list button and then select the *Custom* item in the *Move Task Forward* section of the pick list.
5. In the *Move tasks forward* dialog, enter *10 days* in the *Move selected tasks forward by ____ working days* field and then click the *OK* button.

Notice that the new *Finish* date of the project is **August 8**, exactly 10 working days later than the previous Finish date of **July 25**, as shown to the right of the *Testing Complete* milestone.

6. Save and close the **Reschedule a Task 2013.mpp** sample file.

Setting Tasks to Inactive

After you baseline a project and begin tracking progress, you may discover that you no longer need some tasks in the project. Best practices with Project 2013 dictate that you should **never** delete a task with a baseline. This is because when you delete the task, you lose the baseline data on the task, thereby losing the ability to track variance on the deleted task. Furthermore, when you delete a baselined task, this causes negative variance in your project without any way to determine why you have negative variance! Instead, best practice dictates that you **cancel** the unneeded task, rather than delete it.

To cancel an unneeded task using the **Standard** version of Project 2013, I recommend you use the following approach:

1. In the task *Work* table, set the *Remaining Work* value to *0h* on the task. When you complete this step, Project 2013 changes the Gantt bar to the *Milestone* symbol (a black diamond).
2. Double-click the *Milestone* symbol for the cancelled task and choose another symbol that you want to use to represent a cancelled task.
3. Change the *Cell Background Color* of the task to a color representing a cancelled task.

4. Add a note to the task to document the reason for cancelling it.

Cancelling an unneeded task in the **Professional** version of Project 2013 is much simpler than cancelling the task in the **Standard** version. To cancel a task you simply need to set the task to *Inactive* status. Consider the project shown in Figure 8 - 30. After the project team completed all tasks in the *Phase I* and *Phase II* sections of the project, management decided to cancel the first two tasks in the *Phase III* section to "fast track" project completion.

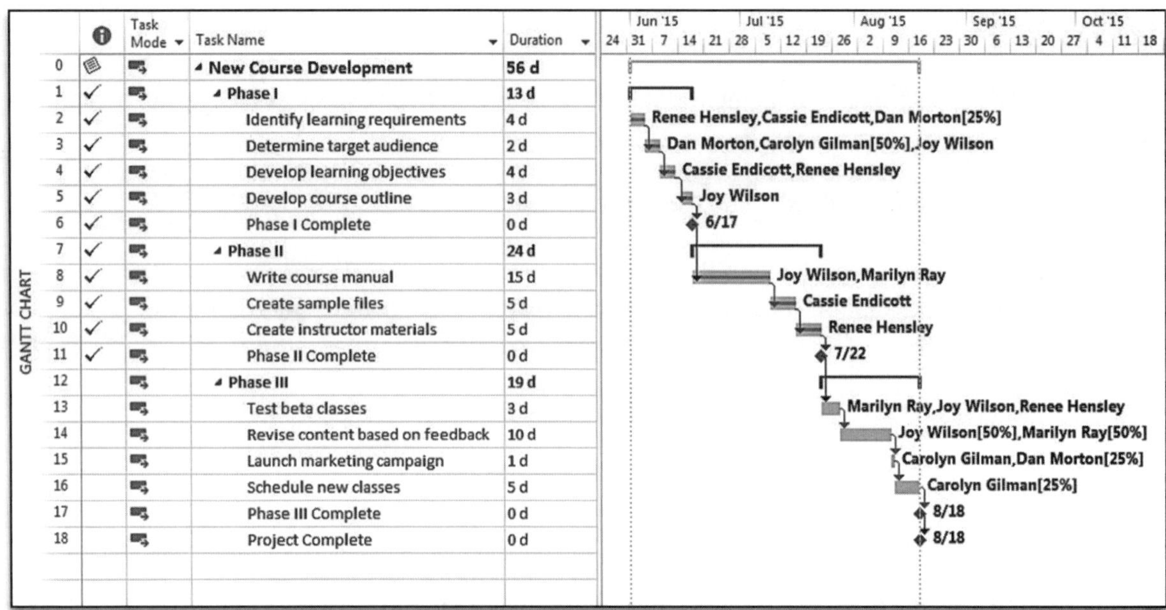

Figure 8 - 30: Project cancelled before cancelling tasks in Phase III

Warning: Remember that the *Inactivate Task* feature is available **only** in the **Professional** version of Project 2013. You cannot use this feature if you have the **Standard** version of the software. If you have the **Standard** version of the software, use the four-step method documented previously.

To cancel tasks by setting them to *Inactive* status in Project 2013, select one or more tasks, and then click the *Inactivate* button in the *Schedule* section of the *Task* ribbon. Figure 8 - 31 shows the *Inactivate* button on the *Task* ribbon, along with its floating tool tip.

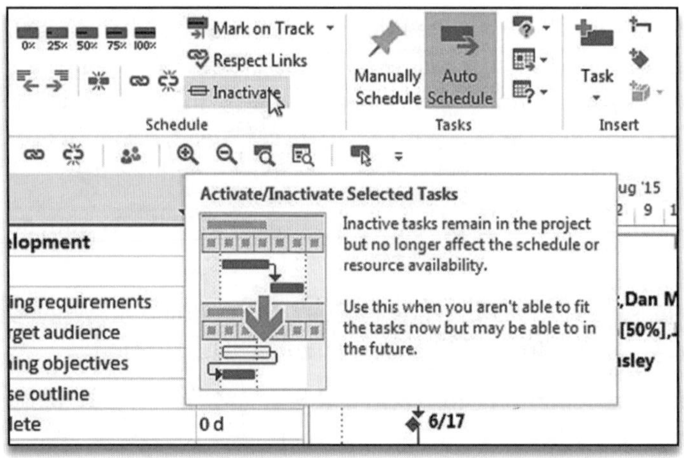

Figure 8 - 31: Inactivate button and Tooltip

Figure 8 - 32 shows the project after setting the first two tasks in the *Phase III* section to *Inactive* status. When you cancel a task using the *Inactivate* button, Project 2013 does the following:

- The software formats the text of the *Inactive* task using the strikethrough font effect and the gray font color.

- The software formats the Gantt bar of the *Inactive* task using a hollow (unfilled) pattern.

- The software treats the *Inactive* task as if it has *0h* of *Remaining Work*. This means the *Inactive* task no longer affects resource availability for resources assigned to it, as indicated in the tool tip shown previously in Figure 8 - 31.

- The software **cancels** the dependency relationship between the *Inactive* task and its successor task, and schedules the successor task as if it is linked to the last predecessor task **before** the *Inactive* task.

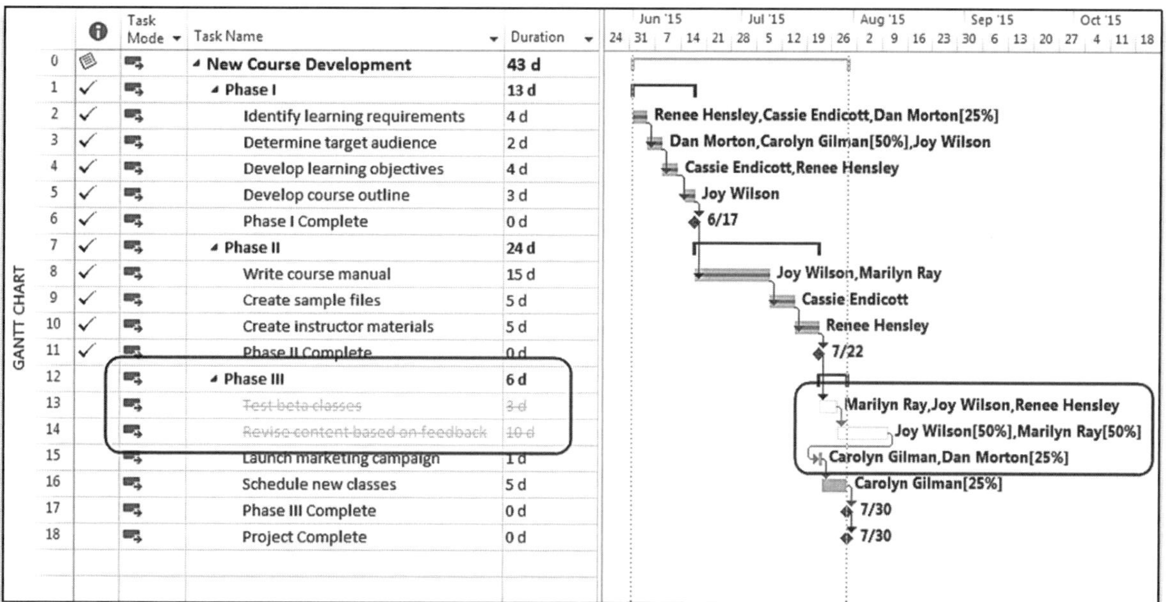

Figure 8 - 32: Last four tasks cancelled in Phase III

Figure 8 - 33 shows the two *Inactive* tasks in the task *Work* table. Notice that the Project 2013 shows *-152h* of *Work Variance* (in the *Variance* column) on the *Phase III* summary task and on the *Project Summary Task*, caused by inactivating two tasks with 152 hour of work assigned to each task.

	Task Name	Work	Baseline	Variance	Actual	Remaining	% W. Comp.
0	New Course Development	540 h	692 h	-152 h	520 h	20 h	96%
1	Phase I	200 h	200 h	0 h	200 h	0 h	100%
2	Identify learning requirements	72 h	72 h	0 h	72 h	0 h	100%
3	Determine target audience	40 h	40 h	0 h	40 h	0 h	100%
4	Develop learning objectives	64 h	64 h	0 h	64 h	0 h	100%
5	Develop course outline	24 h	24 h	0 h	24 h	0 h	100%
6	Phase I Complete	0 h	0 h	0 h	0 h	0 h	100%
7	Phase II	320 h	320 h	0 h	320 h	0 h	100%
8	Write course manual	240 h	240 h	0 h	240 h	0 h	100%
9	Create sample files	40 h	40 h	0 h	40 h	0 h	100%
10	Create instructor materials	40 h	40 h	0 h	40 h	0 h	100%
11	Phase II Complete	0 h	0 h	0 h	0 h	0 h	100%
12	Phase III	20 h	172 h	-152 h	0 h	20 h	0%
13	~~Test beta classes~~	~~72 h~~	~~72 h~~	~~0 h~~	~~0 h~~	~~72 h~~	~~0%~~
14	~~Revise content based on feedback~~	~~80 h~~	~~80 h~~	~~0 h~~	~~0 h~~	~~80 h~~	~~0%~~
15	Launch marketing campaign	10 h	10 h	0 h	0 h	10 h	0%
16	Schedule new classes	10 h	10 h	0 h	0 h	10 h	0%
17	Phase III Complete	0 h	0 h	0 h	0 h	0 h	0%
18	Project Complete	0 h	0 h	0 h	0 h	0 h	0%

Figure 8 - 33: Work table shows cancelled tasks

Remember that when you set a task to *Inactive* status, Project 2013 schedules successor tasks as if they are no longer linked to the *Inactive* task. For example, Figure 8 - 34 shows the *Gantt Chart* view of the two *Inactive* tasks, zoomed to the *Weeks Over Days* level of zoom. Notice that the software schedules task ID #19, the *Launch marketing campaign* task, as if it is no longer linked to task ID #18, the cancelled *Revise content based on feedback* task. Instead, notice that the software schedules the *Launch marketing campaign* task as if it was linked to task ID #11, the *Phase II Complete* milestone task.

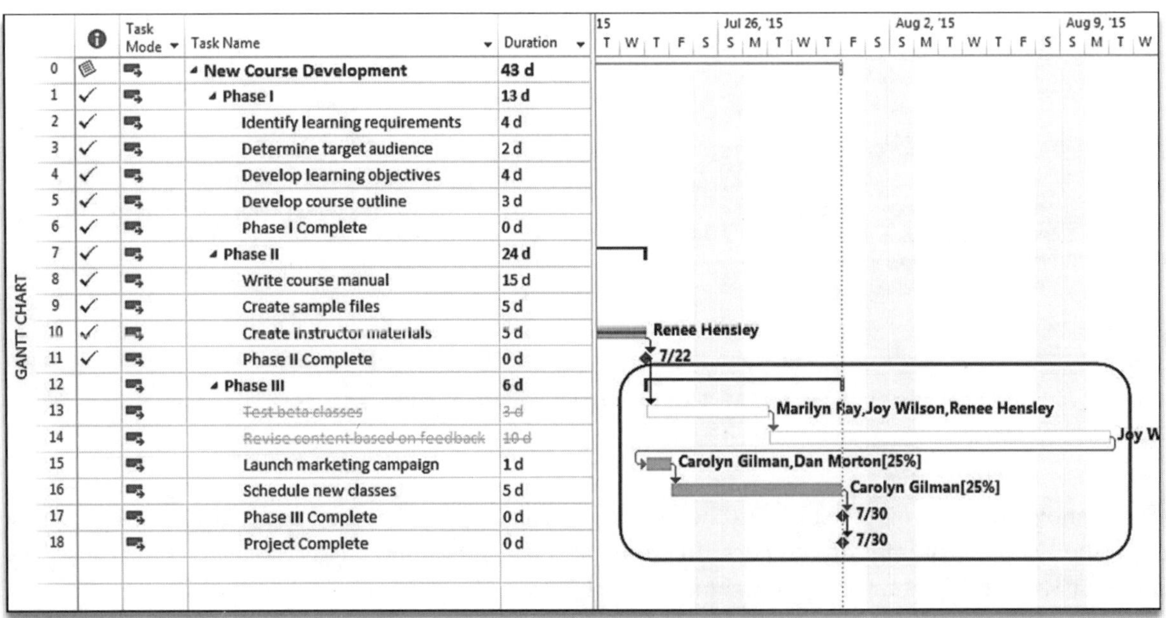

	Task Mode	Task Name	Duration
0		New Course Development	43 d
1		Phase I	13 d
2		Identify learning requirements	4 d
3		Determine target audience	2 d
4		Develop learning objectives	4 d
5		Develop course outline	3 d
6		Phase I Complete	0 d
7		Phase II	24 d
8		Write course manual	15 d
9		Create sample files	5 d
10		Create instructor materials	5 d
11		Phase II Complete	0 d
12		Phase III	6 d
13		~~Test beta classes~~	~~3 d~~
14		~~Revise content based on feedback~~	~~10 d~~
15		Launch marketing campaign	1 d
16		Schedule new classes	5 d
17		Phase III Complete	0 d
18		Project Complete	0 d

Figure 8 - 34: Inactive tasks do not control the schedule of successor tasks

Warning: Project 2013 does not allow you to cancel a completed task or an in-progress task by setting it to *Inactive* status. To cancel the uncompleted work on an in-progress task, apply the task *Work* table and then set the *Remaining Work* value to *0h* for the task.

Information: If you set a task to *Inactive* status using the *Inactivate* button, and later find you need the task after all, you can reset the task to *Active* status by selecting the task and then clicking the *Inactivate* button again.

Hands On Exercise

Exercise 8 - 13

Team members report that a task is no longer needed in the project; therefore, cancel the unneeded task by setting its status to *Inactive*.

Warning: You can only work this Hands On Exercise if you use the **Professional** version of Project 2013. If you use the **Standard** version, you must skip this exercise.

1. Open the **Inactivate a Task 2013.mpp** sample file.
2. Right-click the *Select All* button and select the *Work* table on the shortcut menu.
3. Drag the split bar to the right of the *Variance* column.

Notice that the *Work Variance* (shown in the *Variance* column) is currently *0h* for the *Project Summary Task* and for the *Testing* summary task.

4. Click the *Task* tab to display the *Task* ribbon.
5. Select task ID #21, the *Re-test modified code* task.
6. In the *Schedule* section of the *Task* ribbon, the *Inactivate* button.

Notice that the *Work Variance* is now *-16h* for the *Project Summary Task* and for the *Testing* summary task, caused by setting the *Re-test modified code* task to *Inactive* status.

7. Right-click the *Select All* button and select the *Entry* table on the shortcut menu.
8. Drag the split bar to the right of the *Duration* column.

9. Double-click task ID #21, the *Re-test modified code* task, and then select the *Notes* tab in the *Task Information* dialog.
10. On the *Notes* page of the dialog, click the *Bulleted List* button and add the following note:

    July 5, 2016 – Task cancelled as unneeded by team members.

11. Click the *OK* button to close the *Task Information* dialog.
12. Save and close the **Inactivate a Task 2013.mpp** sample file.

Using the Sync with SharePoint Tasks List Feature

Project 2013 offers an improved version of the *Sync with SharePoint Tasks List* feature introduced previously in Project 2010. This feature leverages the power of SharePoint by publishing your project file to a SharePoint site as a *Tasks* list, and then synchronizing your project tasks with the *Tasks* list. This feature enables two-way communication between you and your project team members, as it allows you to display the current task schedule to all team members, and allows your team members to submit task updates for their assigned tasks.

Information: If you want to use the *Sync with SharePoint Tasks List* feature with SharePoint Online (Office 365 SharePoint), you can use the default Team Site included as a part of SharePoint Online. If you want to sync with a completely new SharePoint site in SharePoint Online, however, your SharePoint administrator must either give you permission in SharePoint Online to create a new SharePoint site or must create a new SharePoint site for you.

To use this improved *Sync with SharePoint Tasks List* feature, open a project that you want to synchronize with a *Tasks* list in SharePoint. Click the *File* tab and then click the *Save As* tab to display the *Save As* page in the *Backstage*. On the *Save As* page of the *Backstage*, click the *Sync with SharePoint* icon in the *Save and Sync* section of the page. The software refreshes the *Save As* page as shown in Figure 8 - 35.

Notice that the *Sync with a SharePoint Tasks List* pane in the right half of the page includes three fields in which you must select an option or enter information. Using the improved *Sync with SharePoint Tasks List* feature, you can do one of the following:

- Create a new SharePoint site, save the project to the site, and then use the site to collaborate with your team members.
- Save your project to an existing SharePoint site and then use the existing site to collaborate with your team members.

Warning: Before you can perform either of the above actions, your SharePoint administrator must provide you with access to SharePoint, and must provide you with either the URL of the SharePoint server (to create a new site) or the URL of the existing SharePoint site.

By default, Project 2013 selects the *New SharePoint Site* item on the *Sync with* pick list and displays the name of the project in the *Project name* field. If you previously logged in to an Office 365 SharePoint location in Project 2013, the software also displays the URL of the Office 365 SharePoint site in the *Site address* field.

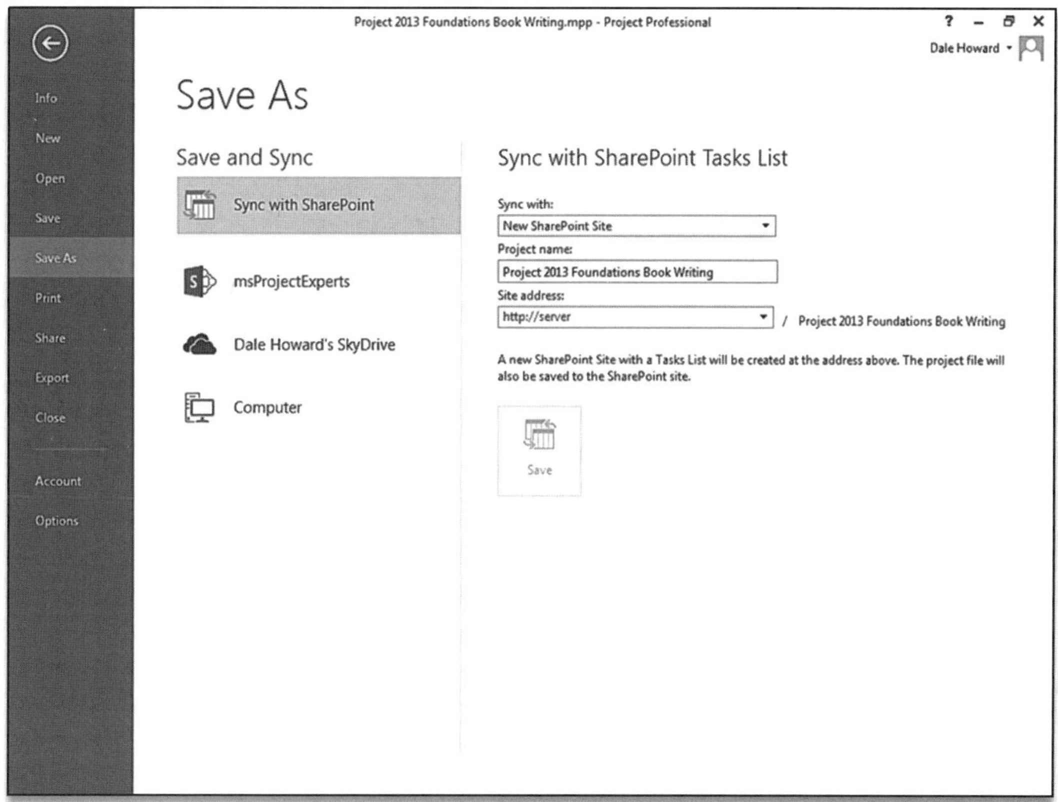

Figure 8 - 35: Save As page in the Backstage

Creating a New SharePoint Site

To create a new SharePoint site in which you and your team can collaborate on the project, complete the following steps:

1. Click the *Sync with* pick list and select the *New SharePoint Site* item on the list, if necessary.
2. Edit the name of the project in the *Project name* field, if necessary.

Warning: If you use spaces in the name of your project in the *Project name* field, the software substitutes the *%20* text string for each space when creating the URL for the new SharePoint site. If you do not want to see the *%20* text string in the URL, replace the space characters with the underscore (_) character instead.

3. Enter or edit the URL of the SharePoint server in the *Site Address* field.
4. Click the *Save* button.

Project 2013 creates the URL of the new SharePoint site using the URL of the SharePoint server, along with the name of the project, in the following form:

http://SharePointServerName/ProjectName

As the software creates the new SharePoint site, it displays a series of *Sync with Tasks List* dialogs, such as the one shown in Figure 8 - 36. The dialogs allow you to monitor the progress as the software creates the site, verifies that the list exists, reads the list properties, reads the list items, and then updates the SharePoint site and the active project.

Figure 8 - 36: Sync with Tasks List dialog

During the synchronization process, the software may display a resource error dialog similar to the one shown in Figure 8 - 37. The message in this dialog indicates that a resource assigned to tasks in the project, Myrta Hansen, does not have access to the SharePoint site. To resolve this problem, I must manually share the site with this resource. I discuss how to add resources to the SharePoint site in the *Adding Users to the SharePoint Site* section of this module.

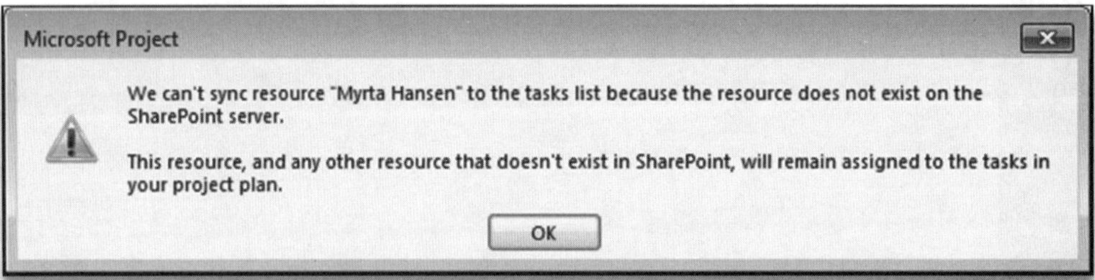

Figure 8 - 37: Sync resource error dialog

When the software completes the process of creating the new SharePoint site, it launches Internet Explorer and navigates to the *Home* page of the new SharePoint site. Figure 8 - 38 shows the *Home* page of the new SharePoint site for my project.

Information: When Project 2013 creates the new SharePoint site, the software creates the site using the *Project Site* template.

Notice that the *Home* page includes each of the following elements:

- The *Quick Launch* menu on the left side of the page offers links for *Home, Documents, Tasks, Calendar,* and *Site Contents.*
- The *Project Summary* section at the top of the page displays late tasks that are overdue, along with upcoming tasks in the project that are due in the current week or during the next week. Notice that the *Project Summary* section shows 1 late task and two upcoming tasks. The *Design* task is late, the *Build* task is due in 2 days, and the *Test* task is not due until next week.
- The *Getting started with your site* section in the middle of the page displays a carousel of commands helpful to a new SharePoint user. If your team members are experienced SharePoint users, you can hide the carousel by clicking the *REMOVE THIS* link immediately above the carousel.

- The *Newsfeed* section at the bottom of the page allows you and your team members to hold a conversation about any subject related to the project.
- The *Documents* section in the lower right corner of the page allows you to upload documents related to the project.

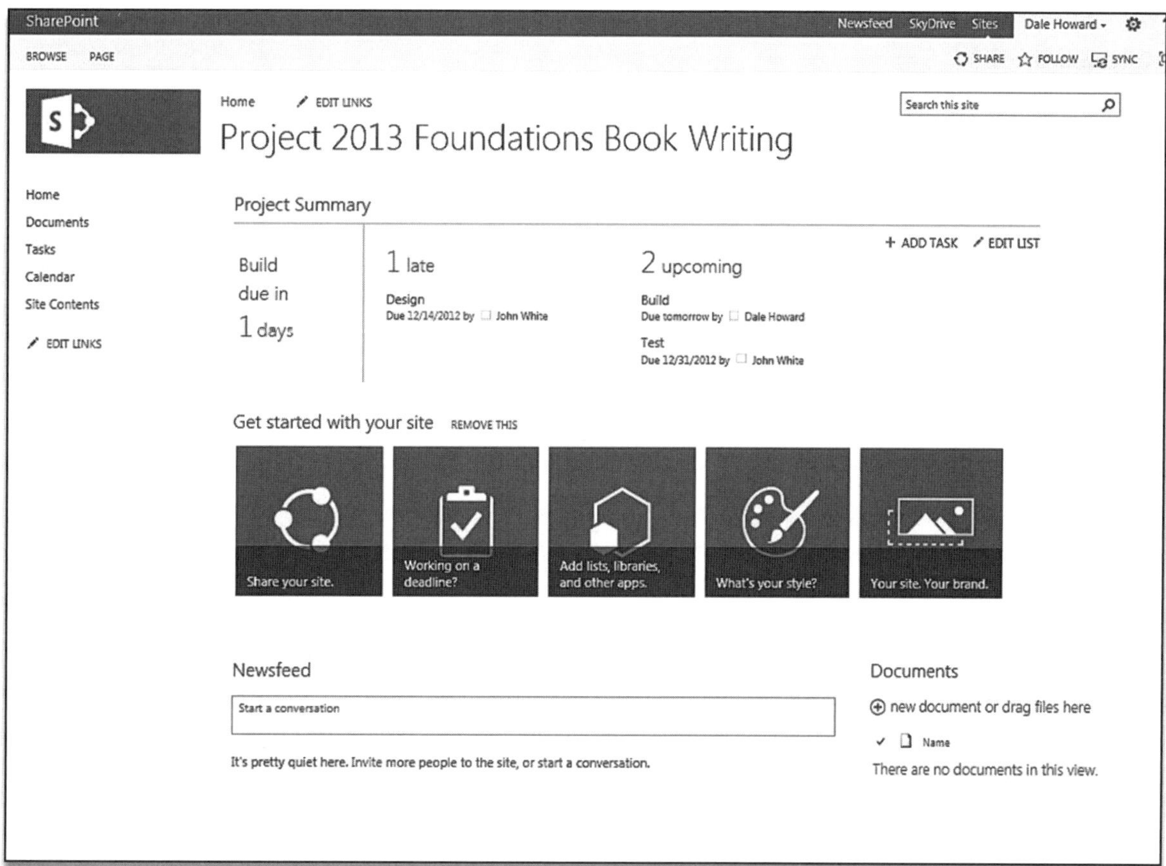

Figure 8 - 38: New SharePoint site Home page

When Project 2013 saves the project in the new SharePoint site, the software appends *-Tasks* to the end of the file name, and saves the file in the *Site Assets* library of the new SharePoint site. For example, the name of the project I saved in the new SharePoint site is **Project_2013_Foundations_Book_Writing-Tasks.mpp**. You can locate your project file in the new SharePoint site by entering a URL similar to the following:

http://ServerName/ProjectName/SiteAssets

Warning: By default, the new SharePoint site does not display a link for the *Site Assets* library in the *Quick Launch* menu on the left side of the *Home* page. To display the *Site Assets* library as a link in the *Quick Launch* menu, click the *Site Contents* link to display the *Site Contents* page, and then click the *Site Assets* icon. On the *Site Assets* page, click the *Library* tab to display the *Library* ribbon. In the *Settings* section of the *Library* ribbon, click the *Library Settings* button. In the *General Settings* section of the *Settings* page, click the *List name, description, and navigation* link. On the *General Settings* page, select the *Yes* option in the *Navigation* section of the page, and then click the *Save* button.

Hands On Exercise

Exercise 8 - 14

Prepare a project to synchronize with a new SharePoint site.

Warning: Before you can work the following Hands On Exercises, your organization must use SharePoint 2013, and you must have access to an existing SharePoint site. If you do not have access to an existing SharePoint site, ask your SharePoint administrator to create a new site for you and to supply you with the URL for the site. As you work through this exercise, Project 2013 will create a new SharePoint site that is a sub-site of the existing SharePoint site.

1. Open the **Implement Budget Pro 2013.mpp** sample file.
2. In the *Resource Sheet* view of the project, replace the *Resource 1* resource with yourself.
3. Replace the *Resource 2*, *Resource 3*, and *Resource 4* resources with the names of real people who work with you in your organization.
4. In the *User Logon Account* column, enter the Windows network user ID for each of the four resources in the form of **DomainName/UserName**.
5. In the *Initials* column, enter the 2-letter initials for each of your four resources.
6. In the *View* section of the *Task* ribbon, click the *Gantt Chart* pick list button and select the *Gantt Chart* view.
7. Click the *Project* tab to display the *Project* ribbon.
8. In the *Properties* section of the *Project* ribbon, click the *Project Information* button.
9. In the *Project Information* dialog, click the *Start* date pick list and select the date of *Monday* of the **previous week** (not Monday of the current week), and then click the *OK* button.
10. In the *Schedule* section of the *Project* ribbon, click the *Set Baseline* pick list button and then select the *Set Baseline* item on the pick list.
11. In the *Set Baseline* dialog, leave all of the default settings in place and then click the *OK* button.
12. Click the *File* tab and then click the *Save* button in the *Backstage*.

Exercise 8 - 15

Synchronize a project with a new SharePoint site.

1. Click the *File* tab and then click the *Save As* tab in the *Backstage*.
2. On the *Save As* page in the *Backstage*, click the *Sync with SharePoint* icon.
3. In the *Sync with SharePoint Tasks List* section of the *Save As* page, do the following:

- Click the *Sync with* pick list and select the *New SharePoint Site* item, if necessary.
- In the *Project name* field, replace the spaces in the project name with the underscore character (_).
- In the *Site address* field, enter the URL of the existing SharePoint site.

4. In the *Sync with SharePoint Tasks List* section of the *Save As* page, click the *Save* button.
5. In the *Sync with Tasks List* dialog, monitor the progress as Project 2013 works with SharePoint to create a new SharePoint site and to synchronize your project with the site.
6. If you see a warning dialog about resources that do not exist in the SharePoint server, click the *OK* button.
7. Maximize the new Internet Explorer window, if necessary, to see the new SharePoint site for your project.

Exercise 8 - 16

Create a link for the *Site Assets* library in the *Quick Launch* menu on the *Home* page SharePoint site.

1. Click the *Site Contents* link in the *Quick Launch* menu.
2. On the *Site Contents* page, click the *Site Assets* icon.
3. At the top of the *Site Assets* page, click the *Library* tab to display the *Library* ribbon.
4. In the *Settings* section of the *Library* ribbon, click the *Library Settings* button.
5. In the *General Settings* section of the *Settings* page, click the *List name, description, and navigation* link.
6. On the *General Settings* page, select the *Yes* option in the *Navigation* section of the page, and then click the *Save* button.
7. In the *Quick Launch* menu, click the new *Site Assets* link.

Notice that Project 2013 saved your project in the *Site Assets* library in the SharePoint site using the file name **Implement Budget Pro 2013-Tasks.mpp**.

8. Click the *Home* link at the top of the *Quick Launch* menu to return to the *Home* page of your SharePoint site.
9. Examine the *Project Summary* section at the top of the *Home* page, looking for any late tasks and upcoming tasks. Ideally, you should see at least one late task and several upcoming tasks.

Using an Existing SharePoint Site

Project 2013 also allows you to use an existing SharePoint site where you and your team can collaborate on the project. Ideally, you should use a SharePoint site created using the *Project Site* template, but you can use any existing SharePoint site and then customize it as needed. To collaborate using an existing SharePoint site, complete the following steps:

1. Click the *Sync with* pick list and select the *Existing SharePoint Site* item on the list. The software updates the *Sync with a SharePoint Tasks List* section of the *Save As* page in the *Backstage.*

Information: By default, the *Site Address* pick list contains the URL of every SharePoint site accessed by Project 2013. Click the pick list and select the URL of a previously used SharePoint site, or manually enter the URL of a new SharePoint site.

2. Enter the URL of the existing SharePoint site in the *Site address* field similar to the one shown in Figure 8 - 39.

Information: If you previously logged into an Office 365 SharePoint location in Project 2013, the software displays the URL of the Office 365 SharePoint site in the *Site address* field by default. In addition, the software displays a list of all recently used SharePoint sites in the *Site Address* field. You have the option, therefore, to manually enter a URL in the *Site Address* field or to click the *Site Address* pick list and select a URL in the list.

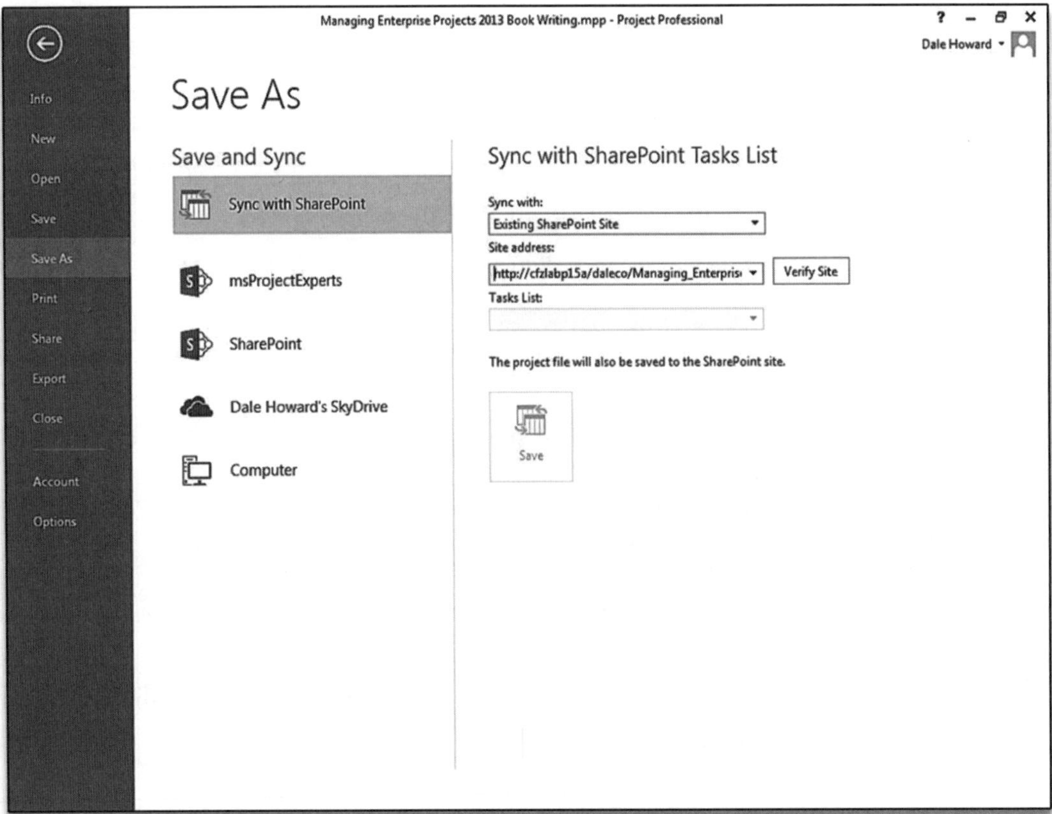

Figure 8 - 39: Updated Sync with SharePoint Tasks List section of the Save As page in the Backstage

3. Click the *Verify Site* button to confirm that the existing SharePoint site contains at least one *Tasks* list. If successful, the *Sync with SharePoint Tasks List* section of the *Save As* page appears similar to the one shown in Figure 8 - 40.

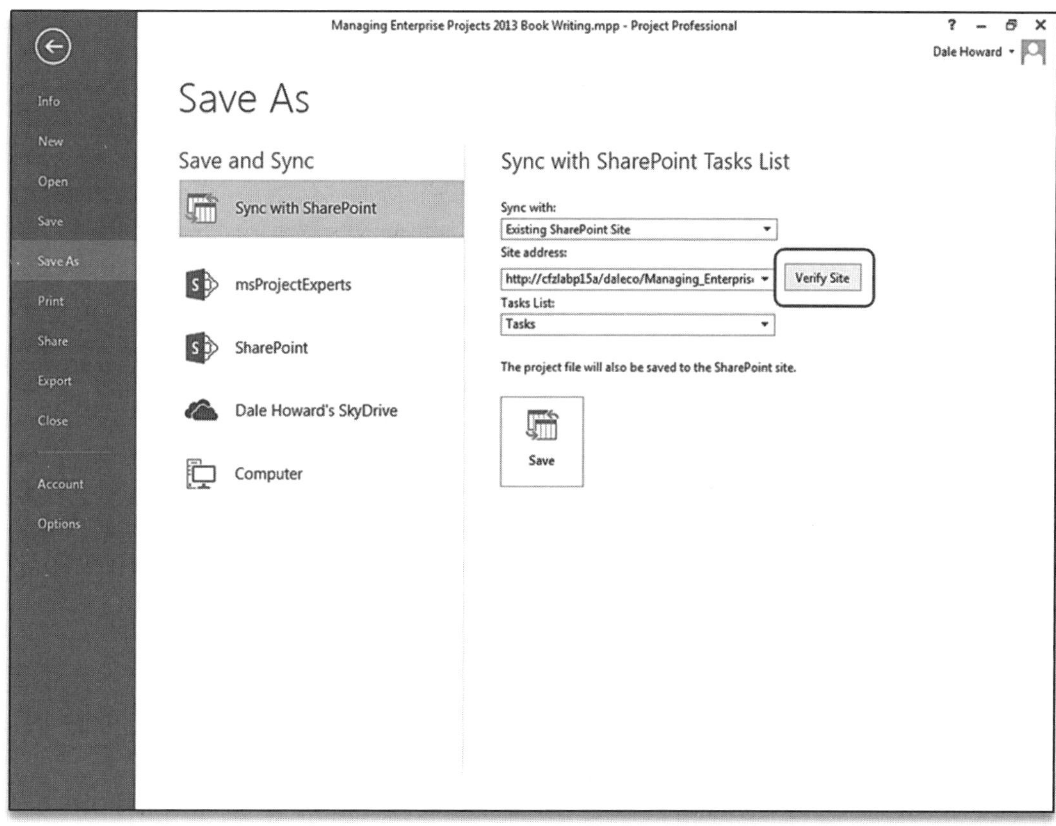

Figure 8 - 40: Tasks list confirmed in the Save As page in the Backstage

Warning: If your existing SharePoint site does not already contain an existing *Tasks* list, such as with the Team Site in SharePoint Online, the software **does not** allow you to continue to the synchronization process unless you create a *Tasks* list. The easiest way to create a *Tasks* list is to type the word *Tasks* (or any other name) in the *Tasks List* field and then click the *Save* button to begin the synchronization process. To manually create a *Tasks* list in the SharePoint site, navigate to the *Home* page of the SharePoint site and click the *Add lists, libraries, and other apps* button in the *Get started with your site* carousel. On the *Add an App* page, click the *Tasks* button, enter a name for the new *Tasks* list in the *Adding Tasks* dialog, and then click the *Create* button.

Warning: If you want to synchronize more than one project in an existing SharePoint site, you must create a *Tasks* list for each project. Remember to give each *Tasks* list a unique name so that you can easily select it in the next step listed below.

If you incorrectly enter the URL of an existing SharePoint site, Project 2013 displays the error dialog shown in Figure 8 - 41. Notice that the dialog lists three possible reasons why it cannot verify the site, including the possibility that the URL for the site is not correct.

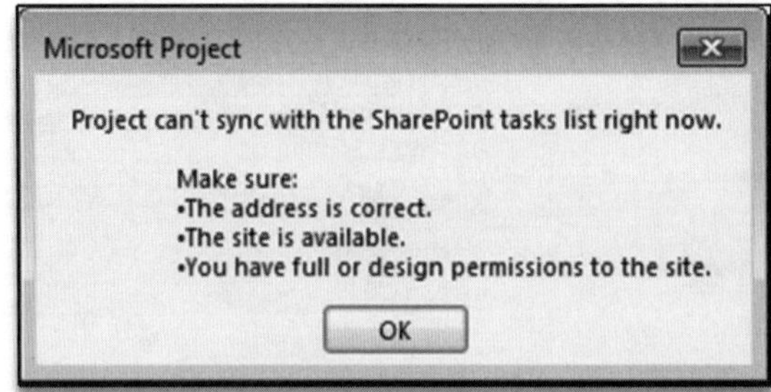

Figure 8 - 41: SharePoint Tasks list error dialog

4. Click the *Tasks List* pick list and select the desired *Tasks* list, if necessary.

5. Click the *Save* button.

As the software saves the project in the existing SharePoint site, it displays a series of *Sync with Tasks List* dialogs, such as the one shown previously in Figure 8 - 36. The dialogs allow you to monitor the progress as the software creates the site, verifies that the list exists, reads the list properties, reads the list items, and then updates the SharePoint site and the active project.

During the synchronization process, the software may display a resource error dialog similar to the one shown previously in Figure 8 - 37. This message in the dialog indicates that a resource assigned to tasks in the project does not have access to the SharePoint site. To resolve this problem, you must manually share the site with this resource. I discuss how to add resources to the SharePoint site in the *Adding Users to the SharePoint Site* section of this module.

After the process completes, you must navigate manually to the *Home* page of the existing SharePoint site and then click the *Tasks* link in the *Quick Launch* menu to see the updated *Tasks* list, such as the list shown in Figure 8 - 42. Notice that the *Tasks* page contains a list of tasks from the active project, along with a timeline at the top of the page.

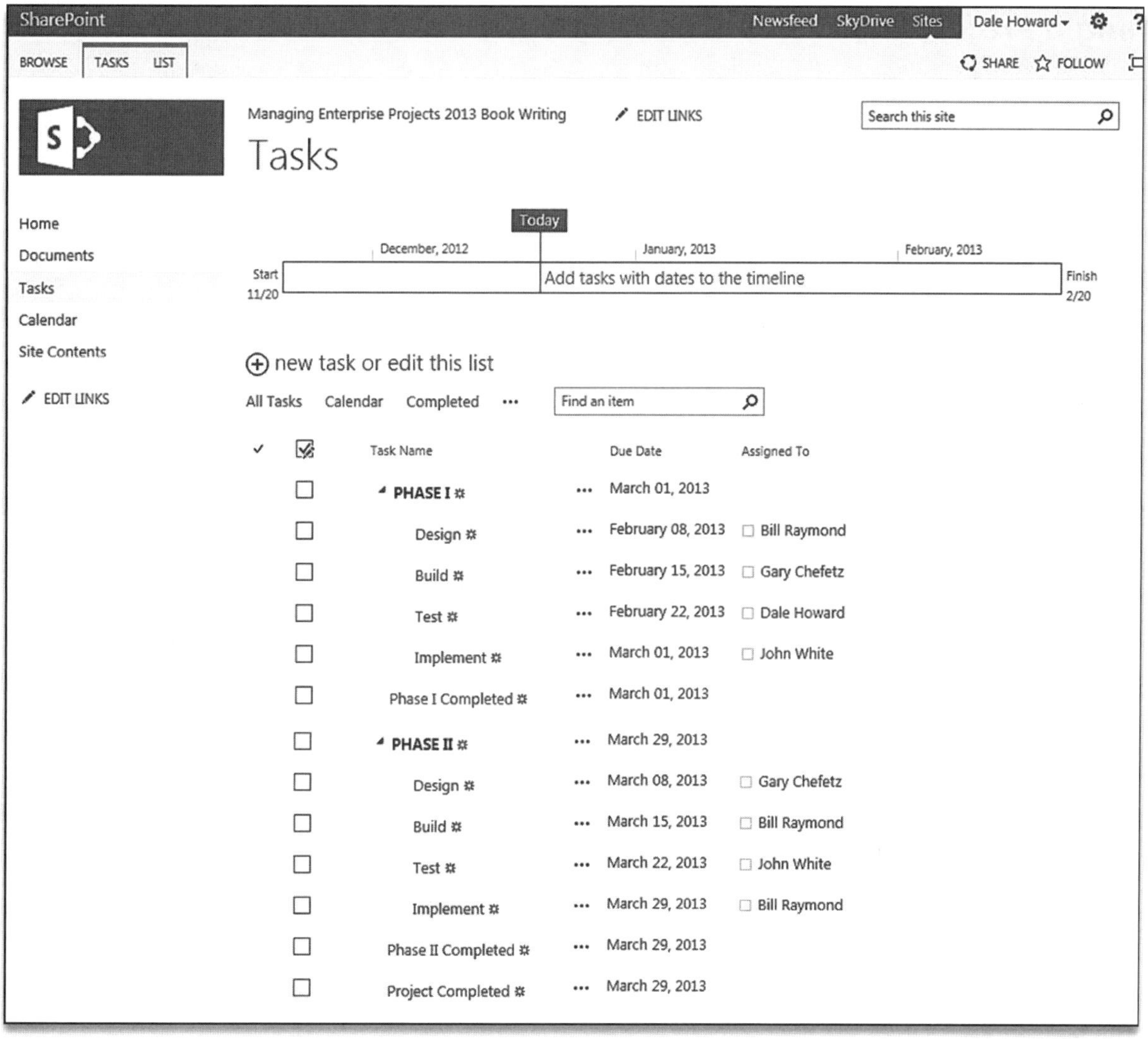

Task Name	Due Date	Assigned To
PHASE I	March 01, 2013	
Design	February 08, 2013	Bill Raymond
Build	February 15, 2013	Gary Chefetz
Test	February 22, 2013	Dale Howard
Implement	March 01, 2013	John White
Phase I Completed	March 01, 2013	
PHASE II	March 29, 2013	
Design	March 08, 2013	Gary Chefetz
Build	March 15, 2013	Bill Raymond
Test	March 22, 2013	John White
Implement	March 29, 2013	Bill Raymond
Phase II Completed	March 29, 2013	
Project Completed	March 29, 2013	

Figure 8 - 42: SharePoint Tasks list contains tasks from the project

Notice in steps #1-5 listed previously in this topical section that Project 2013 **does not** allow you to enter a name for your project. When the software saves your project in the existing SharePoint site, the software applies a generic name for the project based on the title of existing SharePoint site, and then appends "*-Tasks*" to the end of the file name. For example, the software names the project I synchronized with the existing site shown in Figure 8 - 42 as **Managing Enterprise Projects 2013 Book Writing-Tasks.mpp**, and saves the file in the *Site Assets* library of the SharePoint site. You can locate your project file in the SharePoint site by entering a URL similar to the following:

http://ServerName/SiteName/SiteAssets

Warning: By default, an existing SharePoint site does not show the *Site Assets* library in the *Quick Launch* menu on the left side of the *Home* page. To display the *Site Assets* library as a link in the *Quick Launch* menu, click the *Site Contents* link to display the *Site Contents* page, and then click the *Site Assets* icon. On the *Site Assets* page, click the *Library* tab to display the *Library* ribbon. In the *Settings* section of the *Library* ribbon, click the *Library Settings* button. In the *General Settings* section of the *Settings* page, click the *List name, description, and navigation* link. On the *General Settings* page, select the *Yes* option in the *Navigation* section of the page, and then click the *Save* button.

Opening a Project Saved in a SharePoint Site

After you close a project saved in a new or existing SharePoint site, you can reopen the project in Project 2013 by clicking the *File* tab and then clicking the *Open* tab in the *Backstage*. In the *Recent Projects* section of the *Open* page, the software displays all recently opened projects, including projects saved in a SharePoint site, as shown in Figure 8 - 43. Notice the two projects saved in SharePoint sites, each indicated with *–Tasks* appended at the end of the file name.

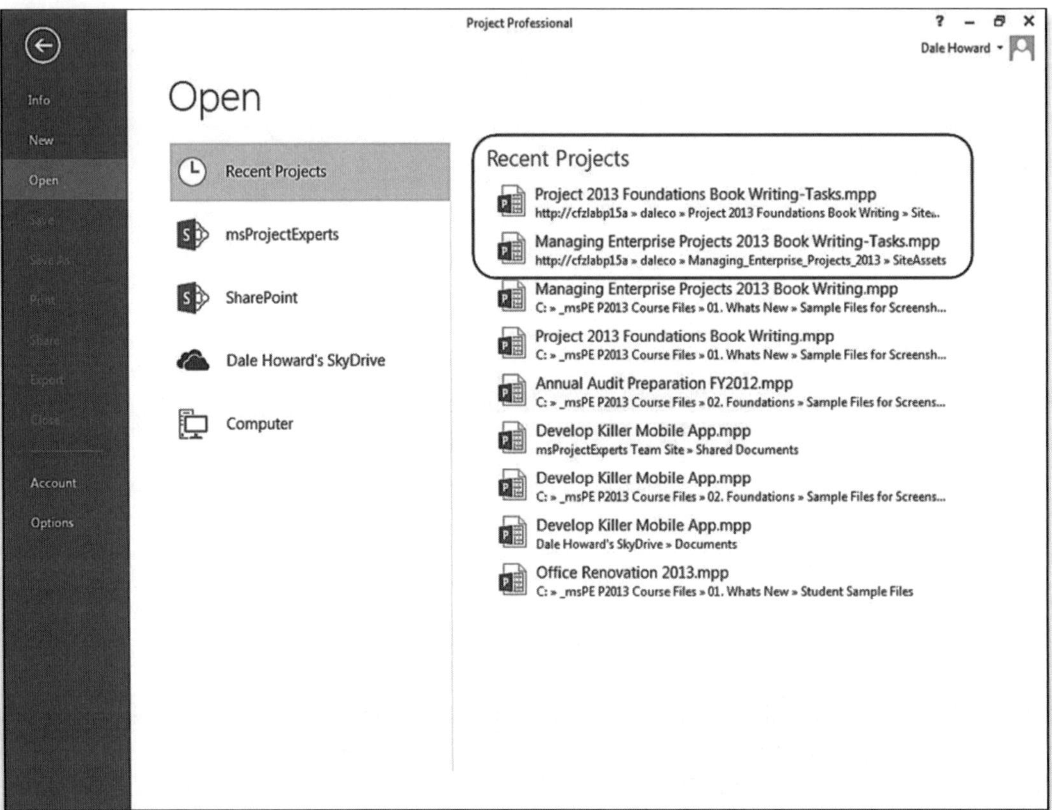

Figure 8 - 43: Recent Projects section shows projects saved in SharePoint

Notice also that the *Open* page displays a new link named *SharePoint*. Click the *SharePoint* link and the software refreshes the *Open* page as shown in Figure 8 - 44. Notice that the *SharePoint* section displays two recent folders named *SiteAssets*, each representing a SharePoint library in which I saved a project.

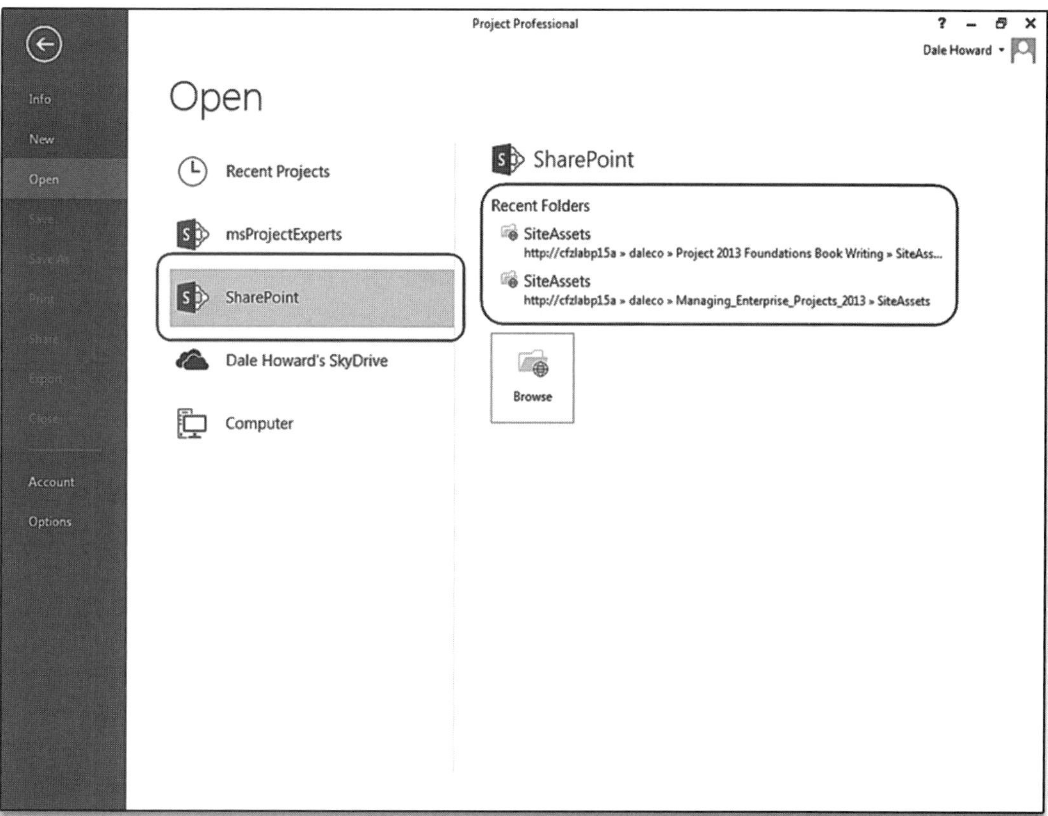

Figure 8 - 44: Open page shows recent SharePoint folders

To open a project saved in a SharePoint site, click the name of the project in the *Recent Projects* section of the *Open* page in the *Backstage*. Alternately, you can click one of the folders in the *SharePoint* section of the *Open* page and then open the project using the *Open* dialog. As the software opens the project, it displays a *Downloading* dialog similar to the one shown in Figure 8 - 45, and then displays a series of *Sync with Tasks List* dialogs such as the one shown previously in Figure 8 - 36.

Figure 8 - 45: Downloading dialog

Information: You can also open the project file directly from the SharePoint site by navigating to the *Site Assets* library in the SharePoint site. Click the *Open Menu* button (the **...** symbol) to the right of the project file name and select the *EDIT* item in the shortcut menu.

Warning: If you attempt to open the project file by clicking the name of the project in the *Site Assets* library, the SharePoint software system opens the project in *Read-Only* mode in Project 2013. To open the project in *Read/Write* mode, you must follow the steps listed in the previous informational note.

Updating the Fields Synchronized with SharePoint

When you initially synchronize your project with a *Tasks* list in SharePoint, Project 2013 uses the information in the project file to create a series of fields in the *Tasks* list. Most of the SharePoint fields map to a corresponding field in the project file, but several of the SharePoint fields do not map to any field in Project 2013. Table 8 - 2 shows the list of SharePoint fields and the corresponding fields in Project 2013. Notice that the *Priority* and *Task Status* fields in SharePoint do not have any corresponding fields in Project 2013.

SharePoint Tasks Field	Project 2013 Field
Title	Name (Task Name)
Start Date	Start
Due Date	Finish
% Complete	% Complete
Assigned To	Resource Names
Predecessors	Predecessors
Priority	No corresponding Project field
Task Status	No corresponding Project field

Table 8 - 2: Corresponding fields in a SharePoint tasks list and a Project 2013 file

In addition to the standard fields included in the synchronization process, Project 2013 allows you to add other fields, including both standard fields and custom fields. You can add these additional fields for reporting purposes or give team members additional information about their task assignments. To add other fields to the task synchronization process, complete the following steps:

1. Click the *File* tab and then click the *Info* tab to display the *Info* page in the *Backstage*. Notice that the *Info* page shown in Figure 8 - 46 includes a *Save and Sync Your Project* section at the top of the page.

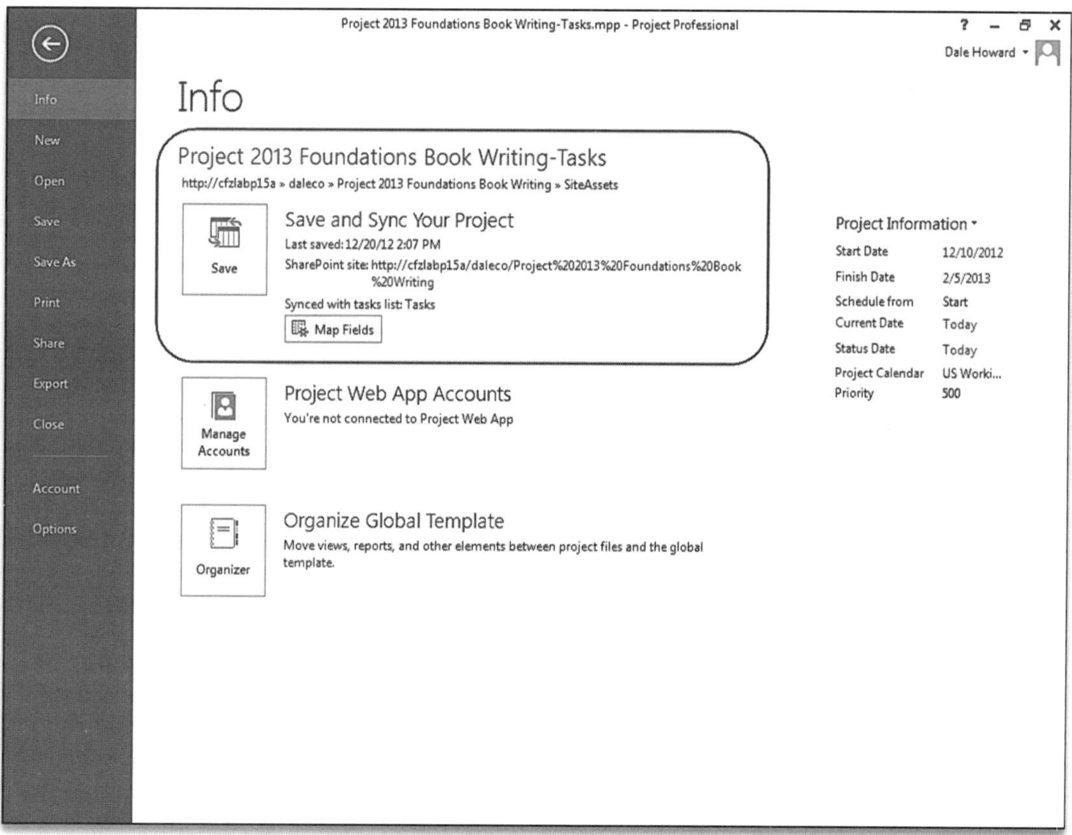

Figure 8 - 46: Save and Sync Your Project section in the Info page

2. In the *Save and Sync Your Project* section of the *Info* page, click the *Map Fields* button.

The software displays the *Map Fields* dialog shown in Figure 8 - 47. Notice the list of fields used for the synchronization process, including the *Priority* and *Task Status* fields created in a *Tasks* list in SharePoint. Project 2013 **does not** allow you to select the *Sync* checkbox for the *Priority* and *Task Status* fields in the *Map Fields* dialog. This is because there are no Project 2013 fields that correspond to these two SharePoint fields.

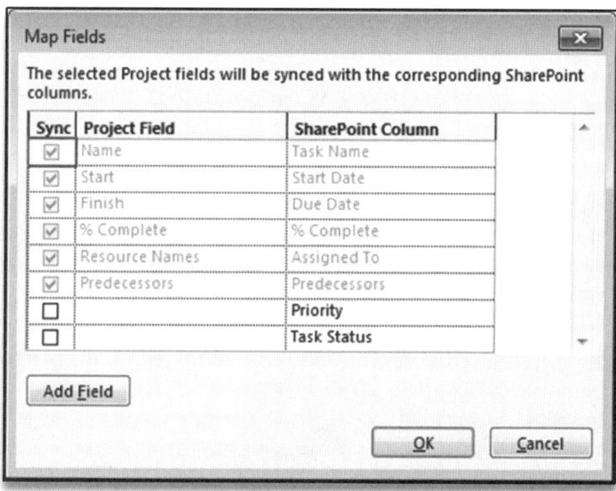

Figure 8 - 47: Map Fields dialog

3. In the *Map Fields* dialog, click the *Add Field* button. The software displays the *Add Field* dialog shown in Figure 8 - 48.

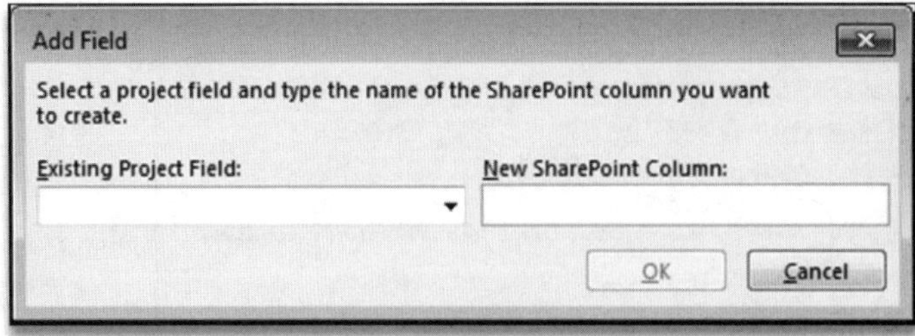

Figure 8 - 48: Add Field dialog

4. In the *Add Field* dialog, click the *Existing Project Field* pick list and select a default or custom field in Project 2013. The system enters the name of the field in the *New SharePoint Column* field automatically.
5. In the *Add Field* dialog, optionally edit the field name in the *New SharePoint Column* field and then click the *OK* button.
6. Repeat steps #3-5 for every field you want to add to the synchronization process.
7. Click the *OK* button to close the *Map Fields* dialog.

If you add certain fields in the *Map Fields* dialog, such as the *Actual Start* or *Actual Finish* fields, the software may display a warning dialog like the one shown in Figure 8 - 49. This warning indicates that Project 2013 will ignore the dates my team members enter in the *Actual Start* field in the SharePoint site, and will override the *Actual Start* date with the current *Start* date instead during each synchronization cycle. In essence, this dialog reveals it is **totally useless** to add fields like *Actual Start, Actual Finish,* or *Actual Work* to the SharePoint synchronization process!

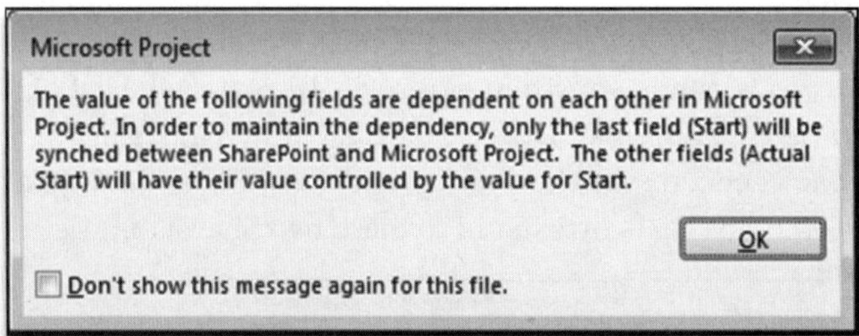

Figure 8 - 49: Warning dialog

Information: The default method of tracking progress in the SharePoint site is very simple. Your team members can update their progress by entering dates in the *Start* and *Finish* fields, and can update their progress by entering a number in the *% Complete* field. The system ignores information they add to fields that are more accurate for tracking progress, such as the *Actual Start* and *Actual Finish* fields.

8. In the *Save and Sync Your Project* section of the *Info* page, click the *Save* button.

Information: You can also synchronize your project with SharePoint by clicking the *Save* button on your *Quick Access Toolbar*.

When Project 2013 completes the synchronization process with SharePoint, the software automatically adds the new fields you select in the *Map Fields* dialog to the SharePoint site. This behavior alone is a major improvement over Project 2010, which required the project manager to manually edit the Project site so that users could see and use the new fields.

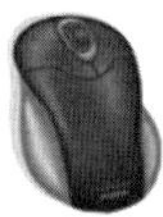

Hands On Exercise

Exercise 8 - 17

Open the project from the SharePoint site and add new fields to the synchronization process.

1. Leave your Internet Explorer application window open and return to your Project 2013 application.

Notice that the name of your project is **Implement Budget Pro 2013-Tasks.mpp**, as shown in the title bar at the top of your Project 2013 application window.

2. Click the *File* tab and then click the *Close* button in the *Backstage*.
3. Leave your Project 2013 application window open and return to your Internet Explorer application window.
4. Click the *Site Assets* link in the *Quick Launch* menu.
5. On the *Site Assets* page, click the *Open Menu* button (the **...** symbol) to the right of the **Implement Budget Pro 2013-Tasks.mpp** file name and select the *EDIT* item in the shortcut menu.
6. In the *Downloading* dialog, monitor the progress of the file download, and in the *Sync with Tasks List* dialog in Project 2013, monitor the progress of the synchronization process.
7. If you see a warning dialog about resources that do not exist in the SharePoint server, click the *OK* button.
8. Click the *File* tab and then click the *Info* tab in the *Backstage*, if necessary.
9. In the *Save and Sync Your Project* section of the *Info* page, click the *Map Fields* button.
10. In the *Map Fields* dialog, click the *Add Field* button.
11. In the *Add Field* dialog, click the *Existing Project Field* pick list and select the *Notes* field, and then click the *OK* button.
12. In the *Map Fields* dialog, click the *OK* button.
13. In the *Save and Sync Your Project* section of the *Info* page, click the *Save* button.
14. In the *Sync with Tasks List* dialog in Project 2013, monitor the progress of the synchronization process.
15. If you see a warning dialog about resources that do not exist in the SharePoint server, click the *OK* button.

Adding Users to the SharePoint Site

Before your team members can collaborate with you on your project using the SharePoint site, they must have permission to access the site. If your team members do not already have access, you can grant them access to the site by completing the following steps:

1. Launch your Internet Explorer application and navigate to the *Home* page of your SharePoint site.

2. In the *Get started with your site* section of the *Home* page, click the *Share your site* button in the carousel. SharePoint displays the *Share* dialog shown in Figure 8 - 50.

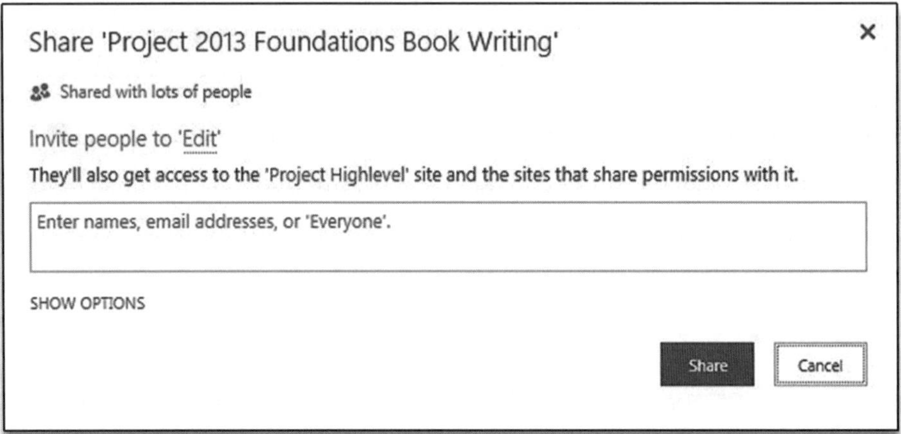

Figure 8 - 50: Share dialog

3. To see the list of users who currently have access to the SharePoint site, click the *lots of people* link in the upper left corner of the *Share* dialog. SharePoint displays the *Shared With* dialog shown in Figure 8 - 51. Notice that Dale Howard, Gary Chefetz, and John White currently have access to the SharePoint site, along with the domain users group.

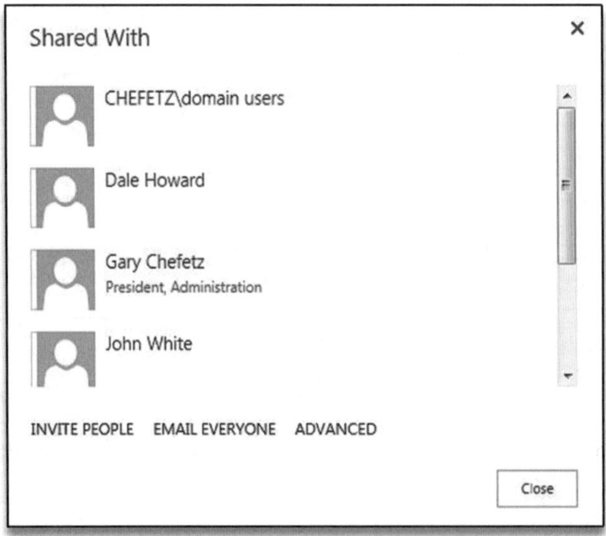

Figure 8 - 51: Shared With dialog

Information: If you click the *INVITE PEOPLE* link in the *Shared With* dialog shown previously in Figure 8 - 51, SharePoint displays the *Share* dialog shown previously in Figure 8 - 50. If you click the *EMAIL EVERYONE* link, the software creates a new e-mail message, adds the name of the site in the *Subject* line, and adds each current user in the *To* line of the message. If you click the *ADVANCED* link, the software displays the *Permissions* page for your SharePoint site. Because setting custom SharePoint permissions is beyond the scope of this book, I do not show this page, nor do I discuss it.

4. Click the *Close* button to close the *Shared With* dialog after you determine which users currently have access to the SharePoint site.
5. In the *Invite people to 'Edit'* section of the *Share* dialog, enter the Windows network user ID, the e-mail address, or the name of the user.
6. As you enter the information for a user, the *Share* dialog displays a pick list of user names corresponding to each user you enter, as shown in Figure 8 - 52. Select a user name from the pick list to add the user.

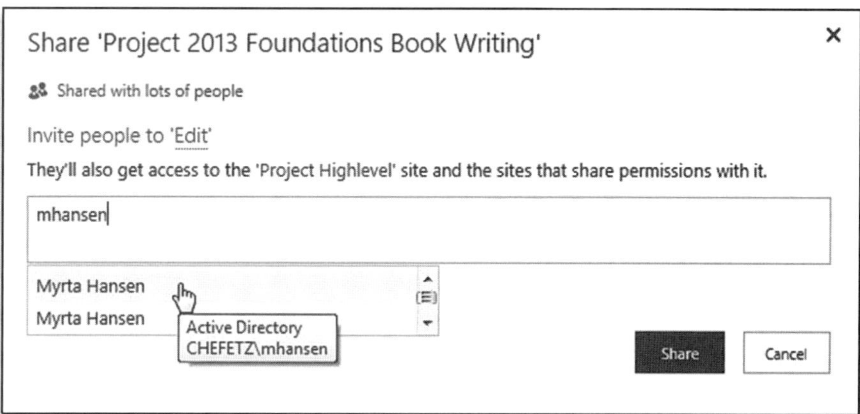

Figure 8 - 52: Share dialog shows available users

7. After adding the names of additional users in the *Share* dialog, click the *SHOW OPTIONS* link in the lower left corner of the dialog. SharePoint expands the dialog to display the *Select a group or permission level* section, as shown in Figure 8 - 53. Notice in the dialog that I want to grant access to the SharePoint site to three additional users: Myrta Hansen, Terry Uland, and Linda Erickson.

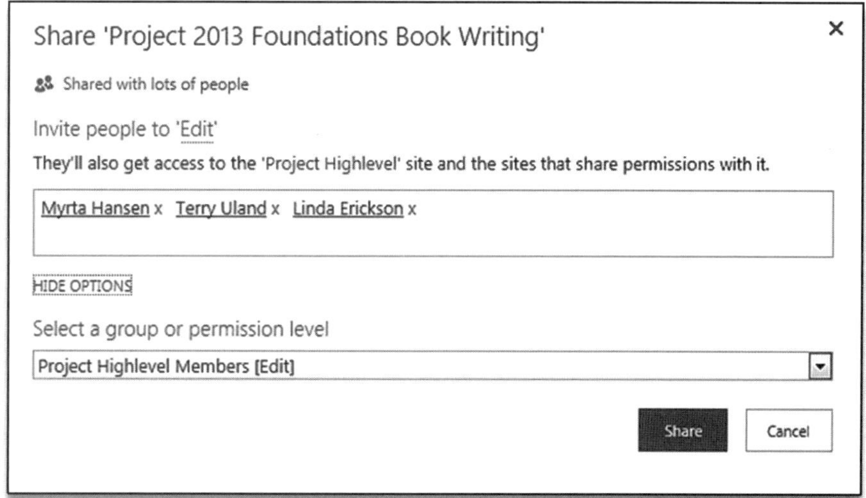

Figure 8 - 53: Share dialog, refreshed to show options

8. Click the *Select a group or permission level* pick list and select a SharePoint group or permission level you want to grant to the additional users. Permission levels include *Excel Services Viewers [View Only]*, *Project Highlevel Members [Edit]*, *Project Highlevel Owners [Full Control]*, and *Project Highlevel Visitors [Read]*. SharePoint selects the *Project Highlevel Members [Edit]* by default.

Information: To see exactly what the *Edit* permission means, float your mouse pointer over the *'Edit'* link in the upper left corner of the dialog. With the *Edit* permission, your new users can add, edit, and delete lists. Your new users can also add, edit, and delete list items and documents. The *Edit* permission, by the way, is the ideal permission for team members.

9. Click the *Share* button.

The software adds the new users to the SharePoint site using the permissions you grant them. After adding users to your site, be sure to open your project in Project 2013 and click the *Save* button on the *Quick Access Toolbar* to synchronize the information in the project with the new users you added to the site.

Hands On Exercise

Exercise 8 - 18

Add your team members to the SharePoint site.

1. Leave the **Implement Budget Pro 2013-Tasks.mpp** project file open in your Project 2013 application window, but return to your Internet Explorer application window.
2. At the top of the *Quick Launch* menu, click the *Home* link to return to the *Home* page of the SharePoint site.
3. In the *Getting started with your site* section of the *Home* page, click the *Share your site* button in the carousel.
4. In the *Share* dialog, type the name of your first team member.
5. In the list of users shown at the bottom of the *Share* dialog, select the name of your team member.
6. In the *Share* dialog, repeat the preceding two steps for your second and third team members.
7. Click the *Share* button.
8. In the *Getting started with your site* section of the *Home* page, click the *Share your site* button again in the carousel.
9. In the *Share* dialog, click the *lots of people* link in the upper left corner of the dialog.
10. In the *Shared With* dialog, scroll through the list of users who have access to the SharePoint site.
11. Click the *Close* button to close the *Shared With* dialog and then click the *Cancel* button to close the *Share* dialog.

12. Leave your Internet Explorer application window open and return to your Project 2013 application window.

13. In Project 2013, click the *File* tab and then click the *Save* button in the *Backstage* to save the **Implement Budget Pro 2013-Tasks.mpp** project file.

Warning: At the end of the synchronization process, you should no longer see a warning dialog about resources that do not exist in the SharePoint server. If you see this dialog again, note the name of the resource shown in the dialog, and then add the resource as a user in the SharePoint site using the preceding steps in this exercise.

Collaborating Using the SharePoint Site

You and the team members in your project can collaborate together about the project using the SharePoint site. Remember that you must add your team members to the SharePoint site before they can access the site. To collaborate with you by reporting task progress, a team member must complete the following steps:

1. Navigate to the *Home* page of the SharePoint site and then click the *Tasks* link in the *Quick Launch* menu. The software displays the *Tasks* list for the project, as shown previously in Figure 8 - 42.

2. Click the name of the task on which you want to report progress. SharePoint displays the *Tasks* page for the selected task with the *View* ribbon applied. For example, Figure 8 - 54 shows the *Tasks* page for the *Design* task, assigned to a team member named John White. Notice that by default, the software displays only the *Task Name, Start Date, Due Date, Assigned To,* and *% Complete* fields.

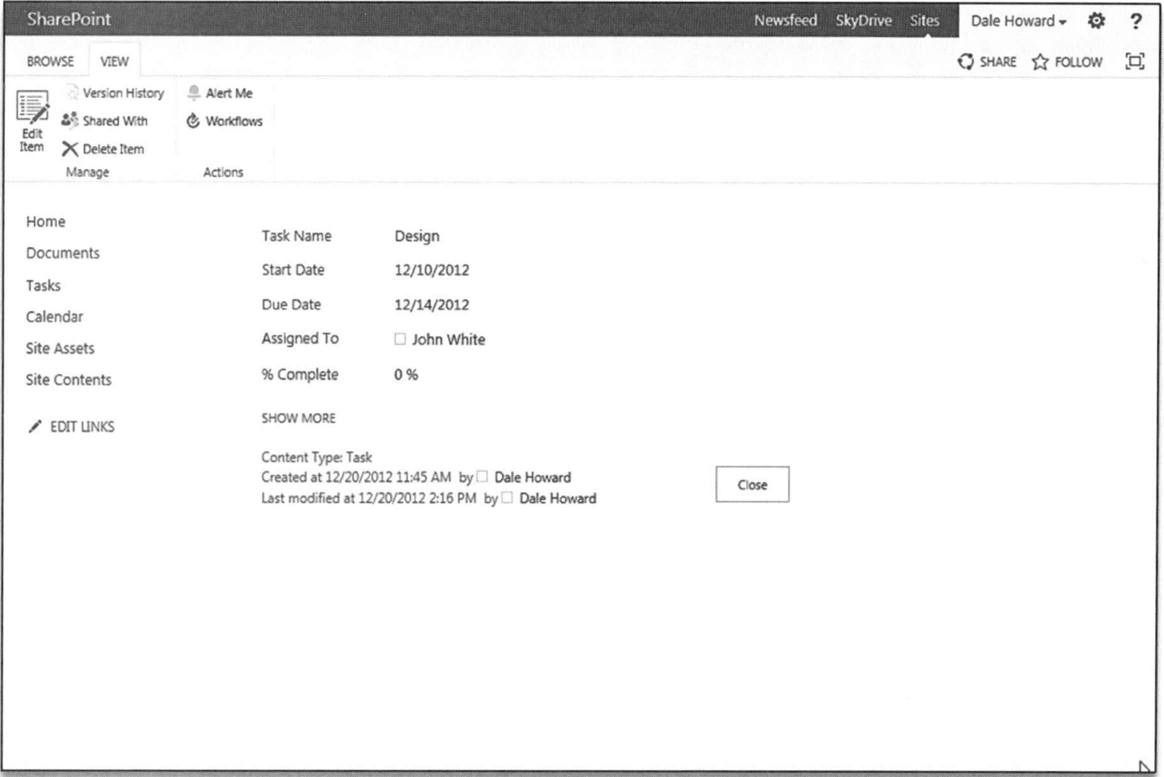

Figure 8 - 54: Tasks page for a selected task

3. In the *Manage* section of the *View* ribbon, click the *Edit Item* button. SharePoint redisplays the *Tasks* page in editing mode with the *Edit* ribbon applied. To see all available fields, click the *SHOW MORE* link near the bottom of the page. The software refreshes the page as shown in Figure 8 - 55. Notice that the *Tasks* page now includes all of the default fields, plus the two custom fields I added, which are the *Actual Start* and *Actual Finish* fields.

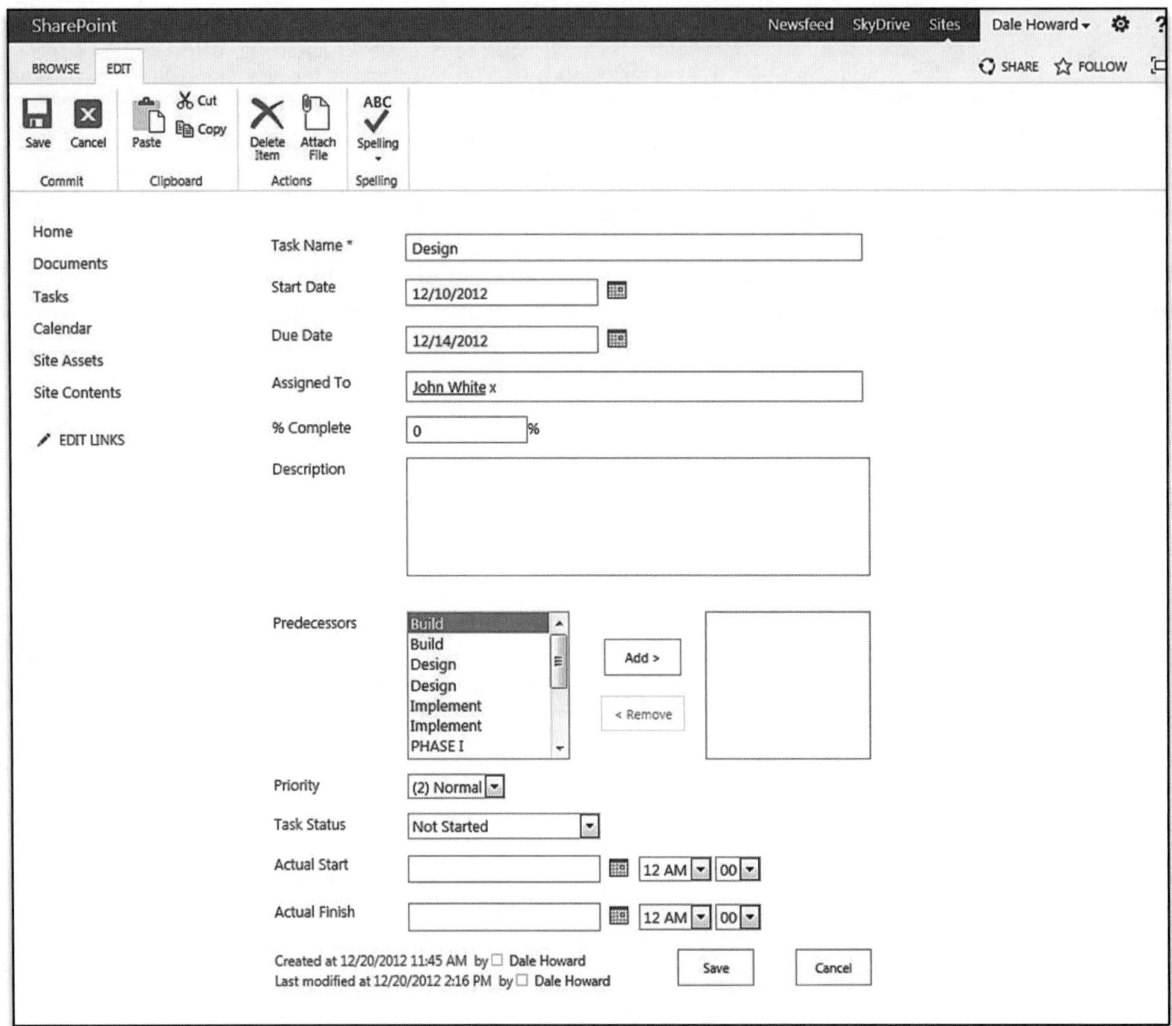

Figure 8 - 55: Tasks page in editing mode

4. Using the fields available on the *Tasks* page, enter progress according to your company's methodology for tracking progress. At a minimum, this means you should enter a *% Complete* value to show your current estimated progress on the task.

5. When finished, click either the *Save* button at the bottom of the page or the *Save* button in the *Commit* section of the *Edit* ribbon. If the team member enters a *100%* value in the *% Complete* field, the software updates the *Tasks* page to show task completion for the selected task. Notice in Figure 8 - 56 that the *Tasks* page shows completion for the *Design* task, indicated by the strikethrough formatting applied to the task name, and with the checkbox selected to the left of the task.

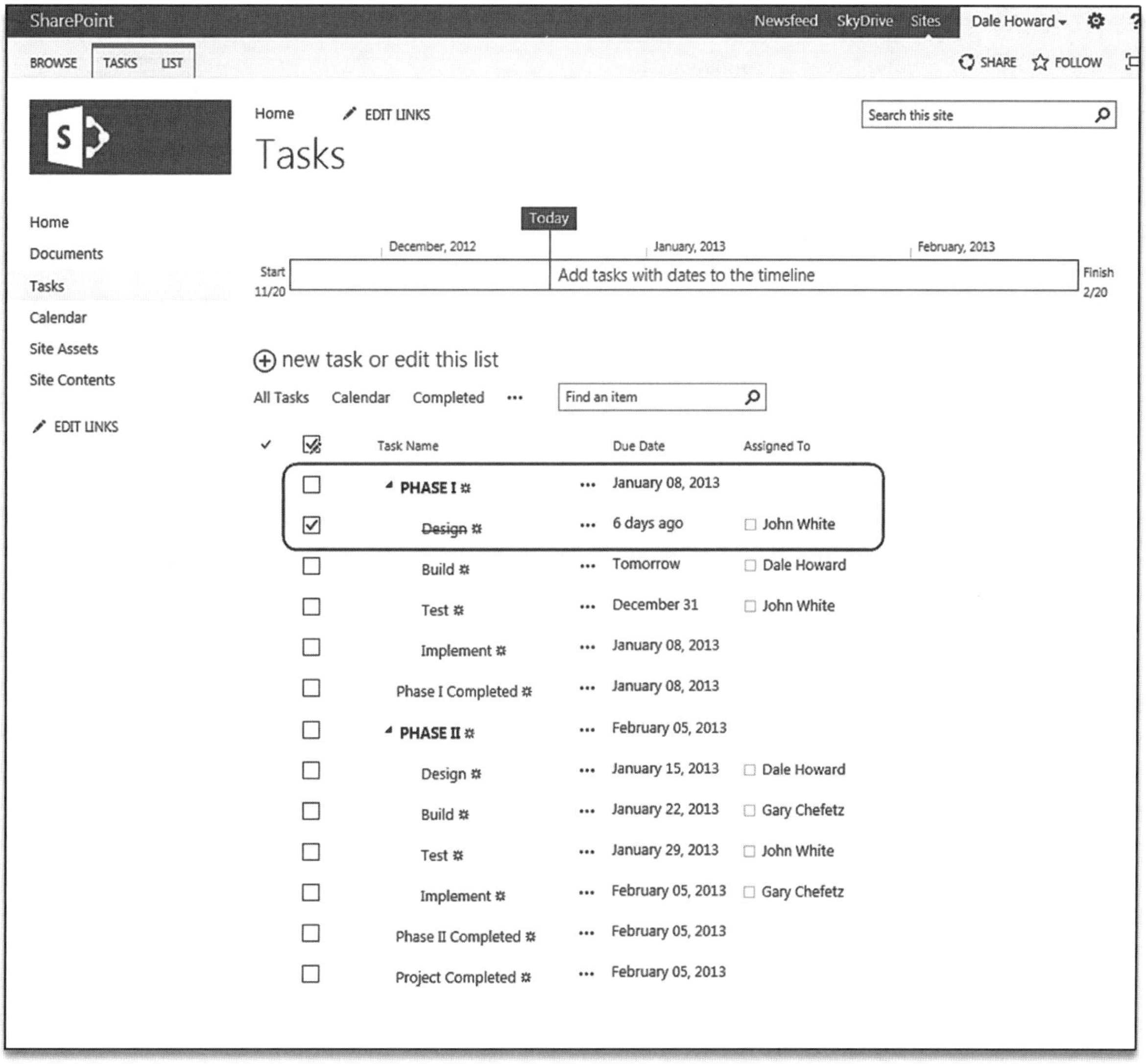

SharePoint | Newsfeed | SkyDrive | Sites | Dale Howard

BROWSE | TASKS | LIST | SHARE | FOLLOW

Home | EDIT LINKS | Search this site

Tasks

Home
Documents
Tasks
Calendar
Site Assets
Site Contents
EDIT LINKS

Today
December, 2012 | January, 2013 | February, 2013
Start 11/20 | Add tasks with dates to the timeline | Finish 2/20

new task or edit this list

All Tasks | Calendar | Completed | ... | Find an item

Task Name	Due Date	Assigned To
PHASE I	January 08, 2013	
~~Design~~	6 days ago	John White
Build	Tomorrow	Dale Howard
Test	December 31	John White
Implement	January 08, 2013	
Phase I Completed	January 08, 2013	
PHASE II	February 05, 2013	
Design	January 15, 2013	Dale Howard
Build	January 22, 2013	Gary Chefetz
Test	January 29, 2013	John White
Implement	February 05, 2013	Gary Chefetz
Phase II Completed	February 05, 2013	
Project Completed	February 05, 2013	

Figure 8 - 56: Design task completed by team member

After team members enter progress in the *Tasks* list in SharePoint, the project manager can open the project in Project 2013 and resynchronize the project to import the updates into the project. Figure 8 - 57 shows the project after synchronizing it with the progress entered by John White in the SharePoint site. Notice that the synchronization progress marked the *Design* task as *100% complete* in the *Phase I* section of the project.

Warning: If a team member changes the *Start Date* value for the task, SharePoint **does not** update the *Due Date* value correspondingly. For example, if a team member changes the *Start Date* value to a date two days later, the software does not change the *Due Date* value to a date that is two days later. This means that when you accept the task update from your team member into your Project 2013 plan, the software **shortens** the duration of the task by 2 days! Therefore, stress to your team members that they should report progress by only updating the *% Complete* value, and they **should not** change the *Start Date* or *Due Date* values unless absolutely necessary.

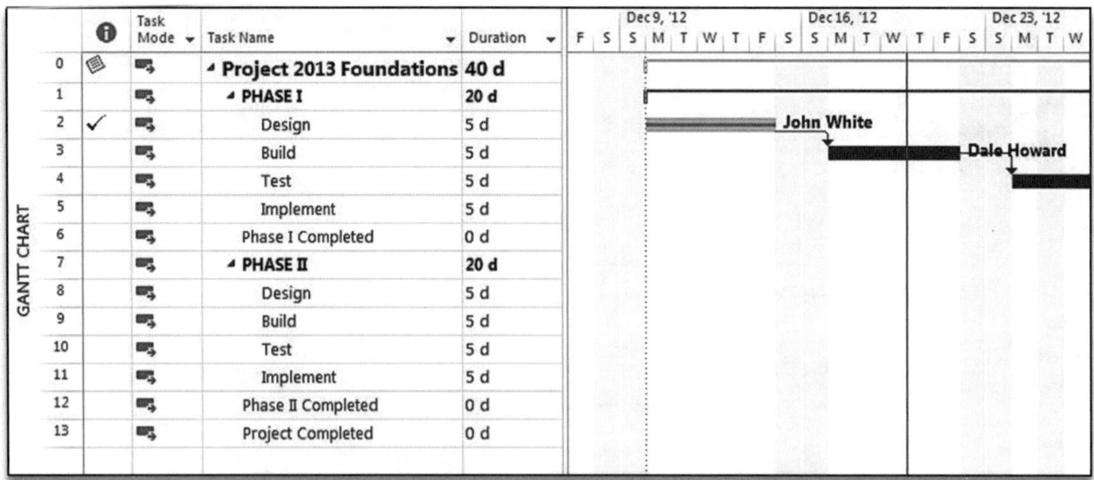

Figure 8 - 57: Project 2013 file updated with progress entered on the Design task by the team member in the SharePoint site

Hands On Exercise

Exercise 8 - 19

Enter progress on a task in the SharePoint site and then synchronize the project.

1. Leave the **Implement Budget Pro 2013-Tasks.mpp** project file open in your Project 2013 application window open, and return to your Internet Explorer application window.
2. In the *Quick Launch* menu, click the *Tasks* link.
3. On the *Tasks* page of the SharePoint site, examine the list of tasks and the resource assigned to each task.
4. Click the *Order Server* task to display additional details about the task.
5. In the *Manage* section of the *View* ribbon, click the *Edit Item* button.
6. Near the bottom of the pagc, click the *SIIOW MORE* link to display all of the details about the *Order Server* task.
7. Examine the information shown in the *Notes* field at the bottom of the page.
8. In the *% Complete* field, enter the value *100,* and then click the *Save* button in either the *Edit* ribbon or at the bottom of the page.
9. Note that SharePoint indicates that the *Order Server* task is completed using the strikethrough font formatting and by selecting the checkbox to the left of the task.
10. Close your Internet Explorer application window and return to your Project 2013 application window.

11. Click the *File* tab and then click the *Save* button in the *Backstage* to save the **Implement Budget Pro 2013-Tasks.mpp** project file.

At the conclusion of the synchronization process, notice that Project 2013 shows the *Order Server* task is completed, indicated by the progress line drawn through the middle of the task's Gantt bar, and by the check mark in the *Indicators* column.

12. Close the **Implement Budget Pro 2013-Tasks.mpp** project file and then exit Project 2013.

Module 09

Variance Analysis, Plan Revision, and Change Control

Learning Objectives

After completing this module, you will be able to:

- Understand the different types of project variance
- Understand the difference between "estimated" variance and "actual" variance
- Create a custom view to analyze Duration variance
- Create custom views, tables, filters, and groups
- Use the Organizer to manage default and custom views, tables, filters, and groups
- Define plan revision and change control
- Revise a project plan to bring it back on schedule
- Understand how the Autolink feature works when you insert a new task between two other tasks with dependencies
- Use change control procedures to add a new task to a project
- Baseline a project after adding new tasks
- View the schedule of multiple baselines in a project

Inside Module 09

Understanding Variance

At the end of every reporting period, you should analyze project variance by comparing actual progress and remaining estimates against the original project baseline. This is the way you determine schedule slippage and overruns, as well as identifying existing and/or potential problems with your project schedule. Analyzing variance is the first step in revising the project plan to bring it back on track with its original goals and objectives.

Understanding Variance Types

In Module 08, I documented that when you save a baseline in Project 2013, the software baselines the current values for five important task fields. These fields include the *Duration, Start, Finish, Work,* and *Cost*. Because the software saves five task values in a project baseline, the software calculates five types of task variance:

- Duration variance
- Start variance
- Finish variance
- Work variance
- Cost variance

About Those Extra Task Baseline Fields

In Module 08, I noted that in addition to the five important task fields captured in the baseline, Project 2013 also captures extra baseline information in several other task fields . The software captures the extra baseline information in the following fields: the *Baseline Fixed Cost* and *Baseline Fixed Cost Accrual* fields; the *Baseline Estimated Duration, Baseline Estimated Start,* and *Baseline Estimated Finish* fields; and the *Baseline Budget Cost* and *Baseline Budget Work* fields.

Even though Project 2013 captures the extra task baseline information in these seven fields, the software **does not** include any corresponding variance fields for these fields. This means that if you want to analyze Fixed Cost variance, for example, there is no default field called *Fixed Cost Variance*. So, if you want to analyze Fixed Cost variance, you must create a custom task field containing a formula to calculate this variance. The same is true for the other six extra baseline fields. I discuss how to create a custom field containing a formula in Module 13, *Digging Deeper into Project 2013*.

Calculating Variance

To calculate variance, Project 2013 uses the following formula:

Variance = (Actual Progress + Remaining Estimates) - Baseline

In Project 2013, a positive variance is unfavorable to the project, and means that the project schedule is late, or that work and/or cost are over budget. Negative variance is favorable to the project, and means that the project is ahead of schedule, or that work and/or cost are under budget.

For example, suppose that the actual work for a task is 60 hours, the remaining work estimate is 40 hours, and the baseline work for the task is 80 hours. Using the formula above, Project 2013 calculates the work variance as:

Work Variance = (Actual Work + Remaining Work) – Baseline Work

Work Variance = (60 hours + 40 hours) – 80 hours

Work Variance = 100 hours - 80 hours

Work Variance = 20 hours

The resulting 20-hour work variance is unfavorable to the project because the total work hours exceed the original baseline work budget. Using another example, suppose that the actual work for a task is 32 hours, the remaining work estimate is 0 hours, and the baseline work for the task is 40 hours. Using the formula above, Project 2013 calculates the work variance as:

Work Variance = (Actual Work + Remaining Work) – Baseline Work

Work Variance = (32 hours + 0 hours) – 40 hours

Work Variance = 32 hours - 40 hours

Work Variance = -8 hours

The resulting -8 hours of work variance is favorable to the project because the total work hours for the project are now less than the original baseline work budget.

Understanding Actual vs. Estimated Variance

Project 2013 measures two types of variance in any project: **Actual Variance** and **Estimated Variance**. It is important that you understand the distinction between the two. Actual variance occurs when an actual value, such as *Actual Work*, exceeds its original baseline. For example, suppose that a task has a baseline work of 40 hours, but the task is complete and the actual work on the task is 50 hours. Using the formula for variance, Project 2013 calculates the variance as follows:

Work Variance = (Actual Work + Remaining Work) – Baseline Work

Work Variance = (50 hours + 0 hours) – 40 hours

Work Variance = 10 hours

Because the task is complete and the actual work exceeds the baseline work by 10 hours, this type of variance is actual variance. In other words, the task went over its baseline budget on work and it is now too late for the project manager to do anything about it.

On the other hand, estimated variance is variance that "might" occur, based on the estimates submitted by the project team members. Estimated variance occurs when actual progress plus remaining estimates (such as actual work + remaining work) exceeds the baseline. For example, a task has a baseline work of 40 hours. At the end of the first week of work on the task, the resource reports 25 hours of actual work, plus a remaining work estimate of 30 hours. Using the formula for variance, Project 2013 calculates the variance as follows:

Work Variance = (Actual Work + Remaining Work) – Baseline Work

Work Variance = (25 hours + 30 hours) – 40 hours

Work Variance = 55 hours – 40 hours

Work Variance = 15 hours

The 15 hours of work variance is only an "estimate" at this point, which is caused by the resource "estimating" 15 hours more work than originally scheduled. Estimated variance is very important to you because it is variance that "might" occur and which gives you time to mitigate the possible slippage or overrun.

Analyzing Project Variance

Project 2013 offers you the following locations from which to analyze project variance:

- *Tracking Gantt* view
- *Variance* table
- *Work* table
- *Cost* table

The *Tracking Gantt* view and the *Variance* table allow you to analyze start and finish variance for tasks. The *Work* and *Cost* tables allow you to analyze work and cost variance, respectively.

Information: Project 2013 does not offer a default table in which to analyze *Duration* variance. If you want to see *Duration* variance, you must create your own custom table for this purpose. Later in this module, I teach you how to create a custom view that you can use to analyze *Duration* variance.

Analyzing Date Variance

Date variance is a major concern for every project manager because many projects have an inflexible project finish date. You can analyze date variance graphically by applying the *Tracking Gantt* view. To apply the *Tracking Gantt* view, use one of the following methods:

- In the *View* section of the *Task* ribbon, click the *Gantt Chart* pick list button, and then select the *Tracking Gantt* view.
- In the *View* section of the *Resource* ribbon, click the *Team Planner* pick list button, and then select the *Tracking Gantt* view.
- In the *Tasks Views* section of the *View* ribbon, click the *Gantt Chart* pick list button, and then select the *Tracking Gantt* view.
- Right-click in the *View Bar* on the far left side of any view and select the *Tracking Gantt* view on the shortcut menu.

Project 2013 applies the *Tracking Gantt* view shown in Figure 9 - 1.

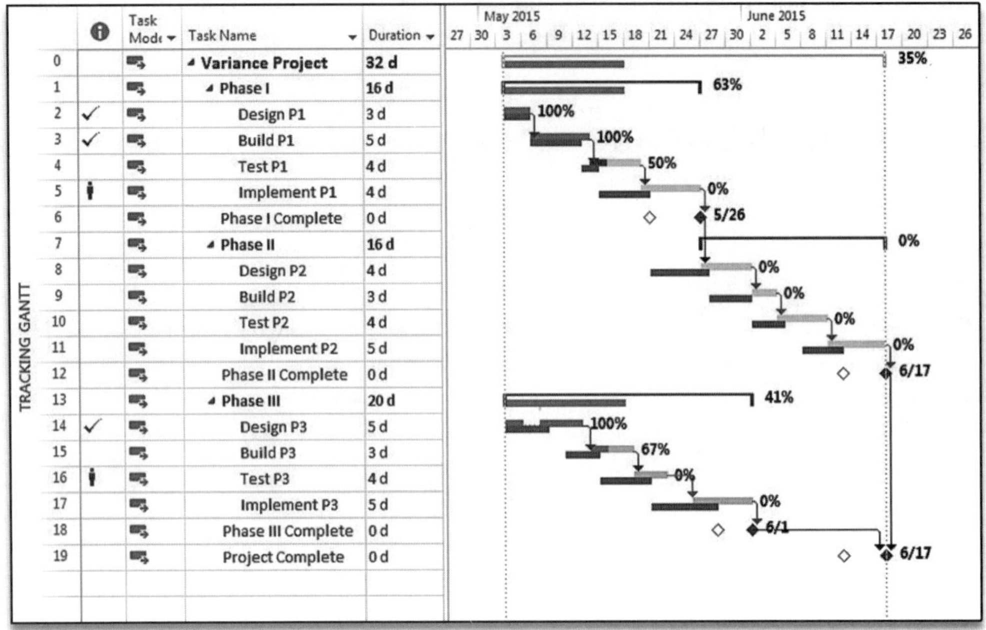

	Task Name	Duration
0	Variance Project	32 d
1	Phase I	16 d
2	Design P1	3 d
3	Build P1	5 d
4	Test P1	4 d
5	Implement P1	4 d
6	Phase I Complete	0 d
7	Phase II	16 d
8	Design P2	4 d
9	Build P2	3 d
10	Test P2	4 d
11	Implement P2	5 d
12	Phase II Complete	0 d
13	Phase III	20 d
14	Design P3	5 d
15	Build P3	3 d
16	Test P3	4 d
17	Implement P3	5 d
18	Phase III Complete	0 d
19	Project Complete	0 d

Figure 9 - 1: Tracking Gantt view

Following is a description of the symbols shown in the *Tracking Gantt* view:

- Light red Gantt bars represent planned work for tasks on the Critical Path.
- Light blue Gantt bars represent planned work for tasks not on the Critical Path.
- Light teal Gantt bars represent planned work for *Manually Scheduled* tasks not on the Critical Path.
- Dark red Gantt bars represent completed work for tasks on the Critical Path.
- Dark blue Gantt bars represent completed work for tasks not on the Critical Path.
- Dark teal Gantt bars represent completed work for *Manually Scheduled* tasks not on the Critical Path.
- Dark gray Gantt bars represent the baseline schedule for each task.
- Black solid diamonds represent the current schedule for each milestone task.
- Teal solid diamonds represent the current schedule for *Manually Scheduled* milestone tasks.
- Hollow diamonds represent the baseline schedule for each milestone task.
- The percentage value at the right end of each Gantt bar represents the % *Complete* field value for each task.
- The gray bar on the bottom half of each summary task Gantt bar represents the cumulative % *Complete* field value for all of the subtasks for the summary task.

Information: To see every possible symbol that Project 2013 can display in the *Tracking Gantt* view, double-click anywhere in the white part of the Gantt chart. The software displays the *Bar Styles* dialog, which shows you the definition for every symbol used in the *Tracking Gantt* view.

The *Tracking Gantt* view allows you to see schedule slippage presented graphically. Using this view, you can compare red, blue, or teal Gantt bars (the current schedule of each task) with their accompanying gray Gantt bars (the baseline schedule for each task). If a red, blue, or teal Gantt bar slips to the right of its gray Gantt bar, then the task is slipping. Additionally, if a black or teal diamond slips to the right of its hollow diamond, then the milestone task is slipping. Using the *Tracking Gantt* view to analyze schedule variance is the easiest way to see the slippage in all phases of the project, as well as the overall slippage for the total project.

While in the *Tracking Gantt* view, use the *Variance* table to view the date variance in a numerical format, such as in days. To apply the *Variance* table, use either of the following methods:

- Right-click the *Select All* button and select the *Variance* table in the shortcut menu.
- In the *Tables* section of the *View* ribbon, click the *Tables* pick list, and then select the *Variance* table.

Project 2013 displays the *Variance* table shown in Figure 9 - 2.

TRACKING GANTT

	Task Mode	Task Name	Start	Finish	Baseline Start	Baseline Finish	Start Var.	Finish Var.
0		**Variance Project**	**5/4/15**	**6/17/15**	**5/4/15**	**6/12/15**	**0 d**	**3 d**
1		**Phase I**	**5/4/15**	**5/26/15**	**5/4/15**	**5/20/15**	**0 d**	**3 d**
2		Design P1	5/4/15	5/6/15	5/4/15	5/6/15	0 d	0 d
3		Build P1	5/7/15	5/13/15	5/7/15	5/12/15	0 d	1 d
4		Test P1	5/14/15	5/19/15	5/13/15	5/14/15	1 d	3 d
5		Implement P1	5/20/15	5/26/15	5/15/15	5/20/15	3 d	3 d
6		Phase I Complete	5/26/15	5/26/15	5/20/15	5/20/15	3 d	3 d
7		**Phase II**	**5/27/15**	**6/17/15**	**5/21/15**	**6/12/15**	**3 d**	**3 d**
8		Design P2	5/27/15	6/1/15	5/21/15	5/27/15	3 d	3 d
9		Build P2	6/2/15	6/4/15	5/28/15	6/1/15	3 d	3 d
10		Test P2	6/5/15	6/10/15	6/2/15	6/5/15	3 d	3 d
11		Implement P2	6/11/15	6/17/15	6/8/15	6/12/15	3 d	3 d
12		Phase II Complete	6/17/15	6/17/15	6/12/15	6/12/15	3 d	3 d
13		**Phase III**	**5/4/15**	**6/1/15**	**5/4/15**	**5/28/15**	**0 d**	**2 d**
14		Design P3	5/4/15	5/12/15	5/4/15	5/8/15	0 d	2 d
15		Build P3	5/14/15	5/18/15	5/11/15	5/14/15	3 d	2 d
16		Test P3	5/19/15	5/22/15	5/15/15	5/20/15	2 d	2 d
17		Implement P3	5/26/15	6/1/15	5/21/15	5/28/15	2 d	2 d
18		Phase III Complete	6/1/15	6/1/15	5/28/15	5/28/15	2 d	2 d
19		Project Complete	6/17/15	6/17/15	6/12/15	6/12/15	3 d	3 d

Figure 9 - 2: Variance table applied in the Tracking Gantt view

To analyze date variance, examine each value in the *Start Variance* and *Finish Variance* columns. Figure 9 - 2 shows that the *Finish Variance* value for the Project Summary Task (Row 0) is *3 days*, revealing that this project is 3 days late on its finish date, caused by the late finish for the tasks in the *Phase I* section. Because of the *3 days* of *Finish Variance* in the *Phase I* section, all of the tasks in the *Phase II* section are 3 days late . Notice also that the tasks in the *Phase III* section are each 2 days late on their finish date due to the late finish of the *Design P3* task.

Analyzing Work Variance

Use the *Work* table to analyze work variance and to determine when project work exceeds its original planned work budget. To apply the *Work* table, use either of the following methods:

- Right-click the *Select All* button and select the *Work* table in the shortcut menu.

- In the *Tables* section of the *View* ribbon, click the *Tables* pick list, and then select the *Work* table.

Project 2013 displays the *Work* table shown in Figure 9 - 3.

TRACKING GANTT

	Task Name	Work	Baseline	Variance	Actual	Remaining	% W. Comp.
0	**Variance Project**	**488 h**	**464 h**	**24 h**	**176 h**	**312 h**	**36%**
1	**Phase I**	**168 h**	**136 h**	**32 h**	**120 h**	**48 h**	**71%**
2	Design P1	24 h	24 h	0 h	24 h	0 h	100%
3	Build P1	80 h	64 h	16 h	80 h	0 h	100%
4	Test P1	32 h	16 h	16 h	16 h	16 h	50%
5	Implement P1	32 h	32 h	0 h	0 h	32 h	0%
6	Phase I Complete	0 h	0 h	0 h	0 h	0 h	0%
7	**Phase II**	**152 h**	**152 h**	**0 h**	**0 h**	**152 h**	**0%**
8	Design P2	32 h	32 h	0 h	0 h	32 h	0%
9	Build P2	48 h	48 h	0 h	0 h	48 h	0%
10	Test P2	32 h	32 h	0 h	0 h	32 h	0%
11	Implement P2	40 h	40 h	0 h	0 h	40 h	0%
12	Phase II Complete	0 h	0 h	0 h	0 h	0 h	0%
13	**Phase III**	**168 h**	**176 h**	**-8 h**	**56 h**	**112 h**	**33%**
14	Design P3	40 h	40 h	0 h	40 h	0 h	100%
15	Build P3	24 h	32 h	-8 h	16 h	8 h	67%
16	Test P3	64 h	64 h	0 h	0 h	64 h	0%
17	Implement P3	40 h	40 h	0 h	0 h	40 h	0%
18	Phase III Complete	0 h	0 h	0 h	0 h	0 h	0%
19	Project Complete	0 h	0 h	0 h	0 h	0 h	0%

Figure 9 - 3: Work table applied in the Tracking Gantt view

To analyze work variance, examine each value in the *Variance* column. In Figure 9 - 3 shown previously, the *Variance* value for the Project Summary Task (Row 0) reveals that this project is currently 24 hours over budget. The *Phase I* section is currently 32 hours over its work budget. The *Build P1* task is 16 hours over budget, and the task is completed; therefore, the *Build P1* task shows actual variance. The *Test P1* task is also 16 hours over budget, but the task is only 50% complete; therefore, the *Test P1* task shows estimated variance. Notice also in Figure 9 - 3 that the *Build P3* task shows *-8 hours* in the *Variance* column, indicating that this task is currently 8 hours under budget on work.

Information: In the *Work* table, the real name of the *Variance* column is *Work Variance*. Microsoft uses the shorter name as the title of this column for display purposes only. Remember that you can see the real name of the column by floating your mouse pointer over the *Variance* column header. The software displays a tool tip that shows the title of the column, followed by the real name of the column in parentheses.

Analyzing Cost Variance

Use the *Cost* table to analyze cost variance and to determine when project costs exceed its original planned cost budget. To apply the *Cost* table, display any task view (such as the *Tracking Gantt* view) and then use either of the following methods:

- Right-click the *Select All* button and select the *Cost* table in the shortcut menu.

- In the *Tables* section of the *View* ribbon, click the *Tables* pick list, and then select the *Cost* table.

Project 2013 displays the *Cost* table shown in Figure 9 - 4.

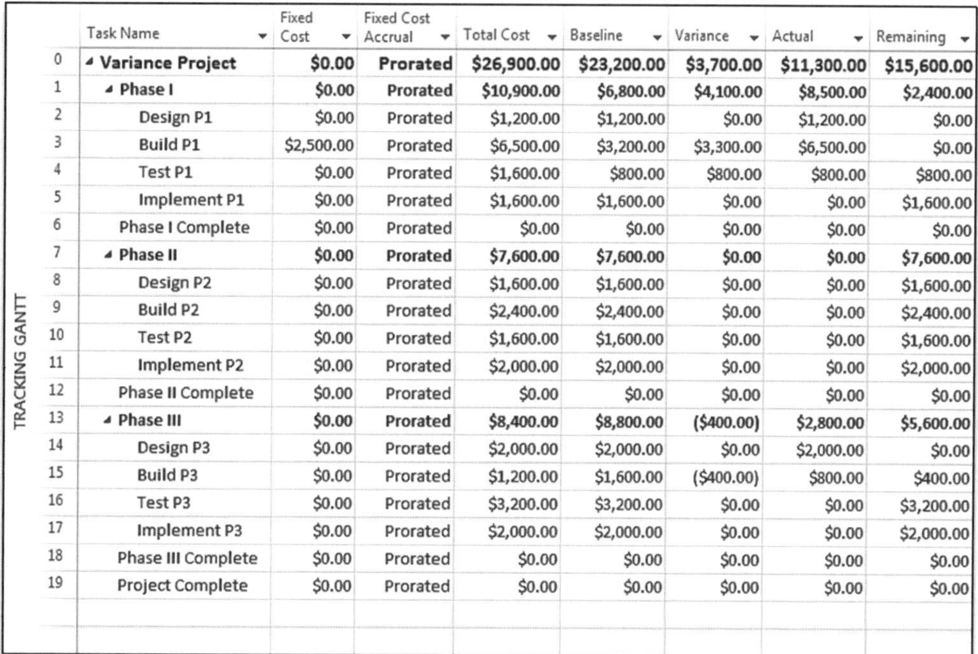

	Task Name	Fixed Cost	Fixed Cost Accrual	Total Cost	Baseline	Variance	Actual	Remaining
0	**Variance Project**	**$0.00**	**Prorated**	**$26,900.00**	**$23,200.00**	**$3,700.00**	**$11,300.00**	**$15,600.00**
1	**Phase I**	**$0.00**	**Prorated**	**$10,900.00**	**$6,800.00**	**$4,100.00**	**$8,500.00**	**$2,400.00**
2	Design P1	$0.00	Prorated	$1,200.00	$1,200.00	$0.00	$1,200.00	$0.00
3	Build P1	$2,500.00	Prorated	$6,500.00	$3,200.00	$3,300.00	$6,500.00	$0.00
4	Test P1	$0.00	Prorated	$1,600.00	$800.00	$800.00	$800.00	$800.00
5	Implement P1	$0.00	Prorated	$1,600.00	$1,600.00	$0.00	$0.00	$1,600.00
6	Phase I Complete	$0.00	Prorated	$0.00	$0.00	$0.00	$0.00	$0.00
7	**Phase II**	**$0.00**	**Prorated**	**$7,600.00**	**$7,600.00**	**$0.00**	**$0.00**	**$7,600.00**
8	Design P2	$0.00	Prorated	$1,600.00	$1,600.00	$0.00	$0.00	$1,600.00
9	Build P2	$0.00	Prorated	$2,400.00	$2,400.00	$0.00	$0.00	$2,400.00
10	Test P2	$0.00	Prorated	$1,600.00	$1,600.00	$0.00	$0.00	$1,600.00
11	Implement P2	$0.00	Prorated	$2,000.00	$2,000.00	$0.00	$0.00	$2,000.00
12	Phase II Complete	$0.00	Prorated	$0.00	$0.00	$0.00	$0.00	$0.00
13	**Phase III**	**$0.00**	**Prorated**	**$8,400.00**	**$8,800.00**	**($400.00)**	**$2,800.00**	**$5,600.00**
14	Design P3	$0.00	Prorated	$2,000.00	$2,000.00	$0.00	$2,000.00	$0.00
15	Build P3	$0.00	Prorated	$1,200.00	$1,600.00	($400.00)	$800.00	$400.00
16	Test P3	$0.00	Prorated	$3,200.00	$3,200.00	$0.00	$0.00	$3,200.00
17	Implement P3	$0.00	Prorated	$2,000.00	$2,000.00	$0.00	$0.00	$2,000.00
18	Phase III Complete	$0.00	Prorated	$0.00	$0.00	$0.00	$0.00	$0.00
19	Project Complete	$0.00	Prorated	$0.00	$0.00	$0.00	$0.00	$0.00

Figure 9 - 4: Cost table applied in the Tracking Gantt view

To analyze cost variance, examine each value in the *Variance* column. In Figure 9 - 4, the *Variance* value for the Project Summary Task (Row 0) reveals that the project is currently $3,700 over budget. This variance is because the *Phase I* section is currently $4,100 over budget while the *Phase III* section is currently $400 **under** budget (indicated by the -$400 value in the *Variance* column). Notice that a significant part of the cost variance in the *Phase I* section arises from the *$2,500* of extra cost in the *Fixed Cost* column for the *Build P1* task. Remember that you can use the *Fixed Cost* column to track unanticipated task costs.

Information: In the *Cost* table, the real name of the *Variance* column is *Cost Variance*. Microsoft uses the shorter name as the title of this column for display purposes only. Remember that you can see the real name of the column by floating your mouse pointer over the *Variance* column header. The software displays a tool tip that shows the title of the column, followed by the real name of the column in parentheses.

Hands On Exercise

Exercise 9 - 1

Actual progress is current through Friday, February 12, 2016 in your Training Advisor Rollout project. The red dashed line in the *Gantt Chart* view indicates that the "current" date is Monday, February 15, 2016. Analyze schedule, date, work, and cost variance in your project.

1. Open the **Training Advisor 09.mpp** sample file.

2. Click the *Task* tab to display the *Task* ribbon.

3. In the *View* section of the *Task* ribbon, click the *Gantt Chart* pick list button, and then select the *Tracking Gantt* view.

4. If necessary, select the Project Summary Task (Row 0) and then click the *Scroll to Task* button in the *Editing* section of the *Task* ribbon to scroll the Gantt bars into view.

5. Scroll to the right through the *Tracking Gantt* chart to analyze schedule slippage for each task in the project.

6. Right-click the *Select All* button and select the *Variance* table in the shortcut menu.

7. Drag the split bar to the right edge of the *Finish Variance* column.

8. In the *Start Variance* and *Finish Variance* columns, analyze the schedule slippage data for every task in the project.

For the Project Summary Task (Row 0), notice in the *Finish Variance* column that the project is currently 5 days late. Notice also that the *INSTALLATION, TESTING,* and *TRAINING* phases are also 5 days late. Notice finally that the *Create Training Materials* deliverable section is 13 days late.

9. Right-click the *Select All* button and select the *Work* table in the shortcut menu.
10. Examine the data in the *Variance* column and analyze work variance for every task in the project.

For the Project Summary Task (Row 0), notice in the *Variance* column that the project is currently 46 hours over budget on work. Notice that the *INSTALLATION* phase is 6 hours over budget and that the *TRAINING* phase is 40 hours over budget. Notice finally that task ID #17, the *Order Server* task, finished 2 hours **under** budget, as evidenced by the *-2h* value in the *Variance* column.

11. Right-click the *Select All* button and select the *Cost* table in the shortcut menu.
12. Examine the data in the *Variance* column and analyze cost variance for every task in the project.

For the Project Summary Task (Row 0), notice in the *Variance* column that the project is currently $26,895 over budget on cost. Notice that the *INSTALLATION* phase is $10,295.00 over budget, the *TESTING* phase is $15,000 over budget, and the *TRAINING* phase is $1,600 over budget.

13. Double-click task ID #23, the *Install Training Advisor Clients* task, and then click the *Notes* tab in the *Task Information* dialog.

Notice that the task note explains why this task is $15,000 over budget, due to a need for more desktop software licenses for the new regional office in Irvine, CA.

14. Click the *Cancel* button to close the *Task Information* dialog.
15. Right-click the *Select All* button and select the *Entry* table in the shortcut menu.
16. Drag the split bar back to the right edge of the *Duration* column.
17. Press **Control + Home** and **Alt + Home** on your computer keyboard to go to the beginning of the project.
18. Save but **do not** close the **Training Advisor 09.mpp** sample file.

Understanding Custom Views

An experienced project manager once said to me, "Project 2013 is like a black hole. It takes, but it won't give back." He was describing his frustration with gathering meaningful information about his projects. He knew the information was "in there somewhere" but he just could not find it! Using custom views, you can quickly locate pertinent project information, including project variance.

Earlier in this module, I explained that Project 2013 does not include a default table that allows you to analyze *Duration* variance. Using a custom view that includes a custom table, you can analyze *Duration* variance. Before I teach you how to create this custom view and table, it helps to understand what constitutes a view in Project 2013.

What Is A View?

Most of us think of a view as a "way of looking at our data." However, Project 2013 formally defines a view as follows:

View = Table + Filter + Group + Screen

In order to extract meaningful information from your projects, such as *Duration* variance information, you may need to create your own custom views so that you can see:

- Columns of data you want to see (the table)
- Only the rows of data you want to see (the filter)
- Rows grouped the way you want to see them (the group)
- Your data displayed on the screen using your desired layout (the screen)

Creating a New Custom View Using a Four-Step Method

A "best practice" approach for creating custom views is to apply a four-step method. These four steps are:

1. Select an existing table or create a new custom table.

2. Select an existing filter or create a new custom filter.

3. Select an existing group or create a new custom group.

4. Create the new view using the desired table, filter, group, and screen.

Creating a Custom Table

The first step requires you to select an existing table or to create a new custom table if no existing table meets your reporting needs. Because a table is a collection of columns, a key question to ask during this step is, "What columns do I want to see in my new view?" The answer to this question determines whether you select an existing table or create a new custom table. If no existing table contains the columns you want to see, then you must create a custom table.

The easiest way to create a new table is to copy an existing table and then modify the copy. To create a new table using this method, complete the following steps:

1. Click the *View* tab to display the *View* ribbon.

2. In the *Data* section of the *View* ribbon, click the *Tables* pick list and select the *More Tables* item. Project 2013 displays the *More Tables* dialog shown in Figure 9 - 5.

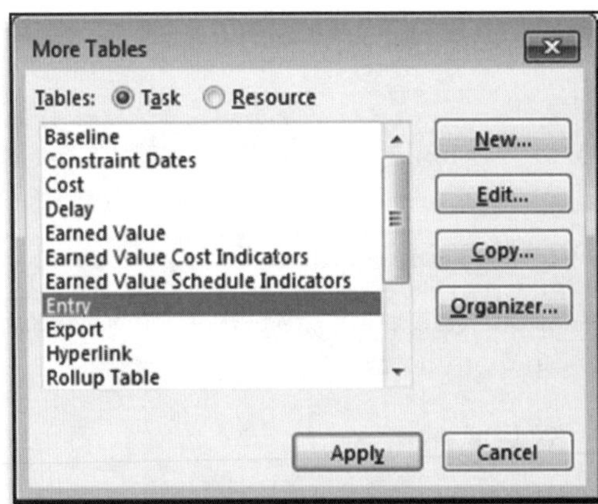

Figure 9 - 5: More Tables dialog

3. From the list of default and custom tables, select an existing table and then click the *Copy* button. Project 2013 displays the *Table Definition* dialog shown in Figure 9 - 6.

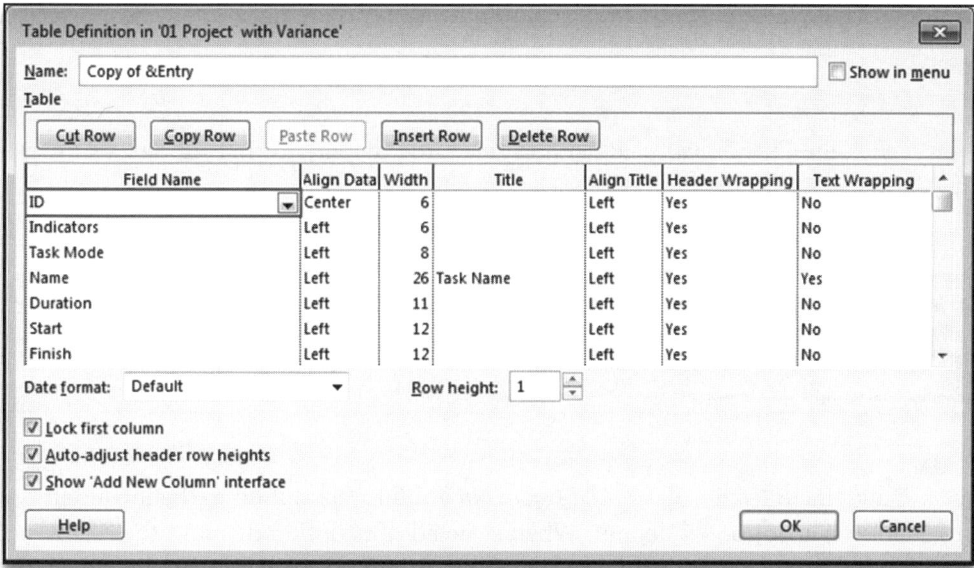
Table Definition in '01 Project with Variance'

Name: Copy of &Entry   Show in menu

Table

Cut Row | Copy Row | Paste Row | Insert Row | Delete Row

Field Name	Align Data	Width	Title	Align Title	Header Wrapping	Text Wrapping
ID	Center	6		Left	Yes	No
Indicators	Left	6		Left	Yes	No
Task Mode	Left	8		Left	Yes	No
Name	Left	26	Task Name	Left	Yes	Yes
Duration	Left	11		Left	Yes	No
Start	Left	12		Left	Yes	No
Finish	Left	12		Left	Yes	No

Date format: Default   Row height: 1

Lock first column

Auto-adjust header row heights

Show 'Add New Column' interface

Help   OK   Cancel

Figure 9 - 6: Table Definition dialog

4. In the *Name* field, enter an original name for the new custom table such as *_Duration vs. Work.*

Information: In Figure 9 - 6 shown previously, the ampersand character **(&)** in the name of the table precedes the hotkey character associated with the table. To access the *Entry* table using hotkeys, press the **Alt** key to activate *KeyTips*, press the **W** key to display the *View* ribbon, press **TA** key combination to select the *Tables* pick list, and then press the **E** key to select the *Entry* table.

5. Select the *Show in menu* option if you want to see the table displayed on the *Tables* pick list.

6. To delete any field you do not want to see in your new custom table, select the field and then click the *Delete Row* button in the dialog or press the **Delete** key on your computer keyboard.

7. To add a new field at the bottom of the list of fields, click the blank row below the last field in the *Field Name* column, click the pick list button in the blank row, and then select the name of your field from the list.

8. To insert a new field between two other fields in the list, select the row where you want to insert the new field, and then click the *Insert Row* button. Click in the *Field Name* column in the blank row, click the pick list button, and then select the name of your field from the list.

9. For each field you add to the *Table Definition* dialog, enter or select a value in the *Align Data, Width, Align Title, Header Wrapping,* and *Text Wrapping* columns.

Information: The *Text Wrapping* column allows you to specify whether Project 2013 wraps text in the field automatically when the length of the text string exceeds the width of the column. The software wraps text in the *Name* field (*Task Name* column) by default. When you add new fields to the table, the software sets the *Text Wrapping* value to *Yes* for each new field, but you can change the value to *No* as needed.

10. If you want to display alternate text in the column header for any field, enter the alternate text in the *Title* field.

11. If necessary, click the *Date format* pick list and select the display format for dates shown in your custom table.

Information: The *Date* format pick list is a little-known feature of Project 2013 that allows you to select a unique date format for dates shown only in your custom table. The software applies the selected date format to **only** the custom table, while applying the default date format to every other default table.

The *Table Definition* dialog includes the *Show 'Add New Column' Interface* option in the lower left corner of the dialog. The software enables this option by default. When selected, this option displays the *Add New Column* virtual column as the last column on the right side of the table. If you do not want to see the *Add New Column* virtual column in your new table, **deselect** this option.

Figure 9 - 7 shows the *Table Definition* dialog for a new custom table I created to show the differences between the *% Complete* field values and the *% Work Complete* field values for every task. Notice in the dialog that I included a title for the *% Complete* field to show that this field actually represents the *% Duration Complete* value for each task. Notice that I also deselected the new *Show 'Add New Column' Interface* option to hide the *Add New Column* virtual column in my new custom table.

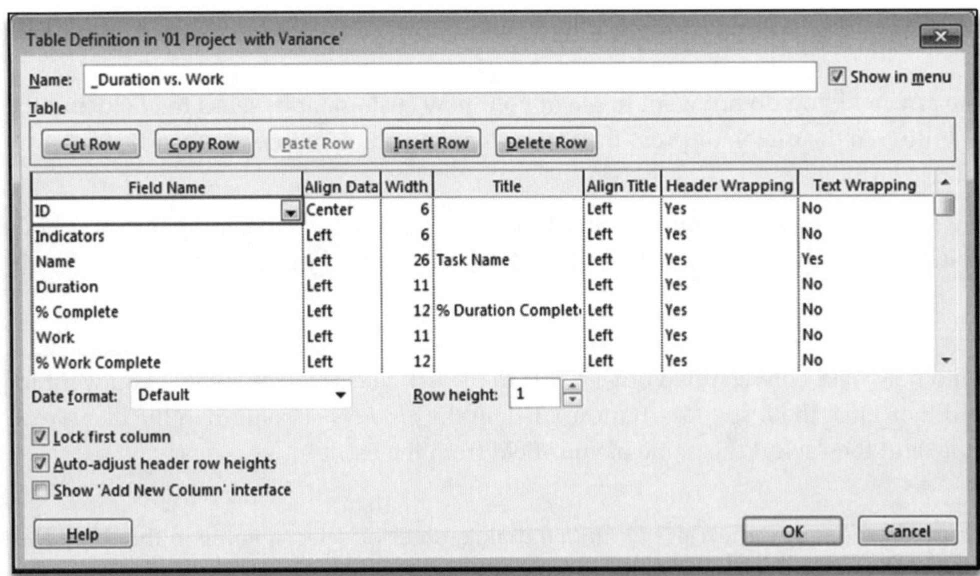

Figure 9 - 7: Completed custom table definition

12. Click the *OK* button to close the *Table Definition* dialog.

13. Click the *Apply* button to display your new table. Figure 9 - 8 shows the new custom *_Duration vs. Work* table I created using the previous steps, applied in the *Gantt Chart* view.

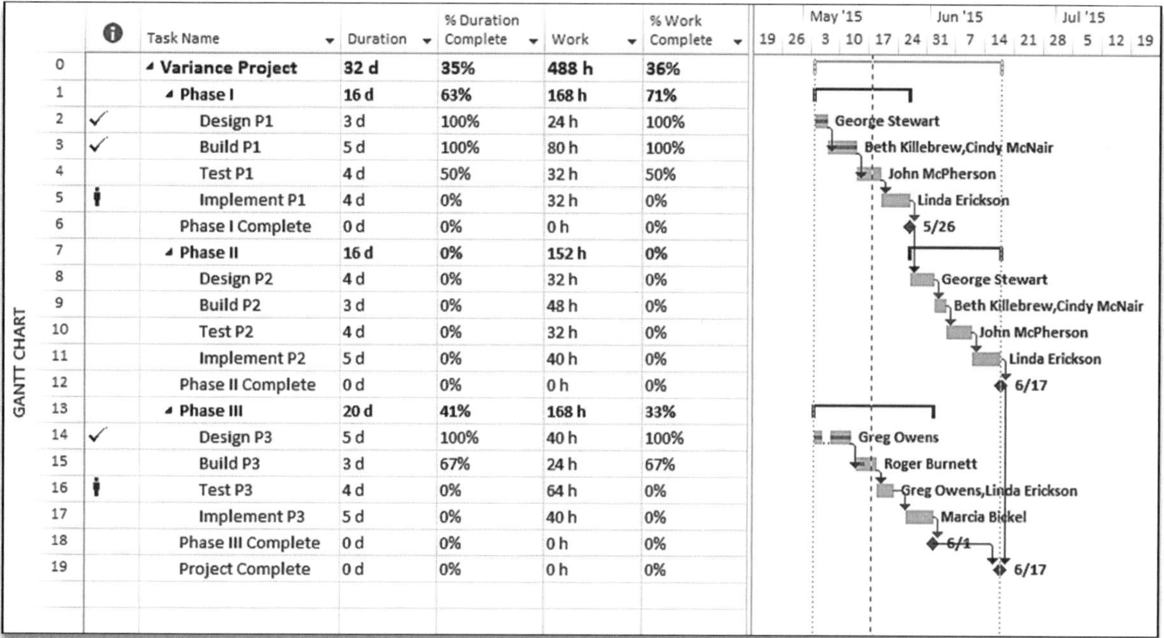

		Task Name	Duration	% Duration Complete	Work	% Work Complete
0		Variance Project	32 d	35%	488 h	36%
1		Phase I	16 d	63%	168 h	71%
2	✓	Design P1	3 d	100%	24 h	100%
3	✓	Build P1	5 d	100%	80 h	100%
4		Test P1	4 d	50%	32 h	50%
5		Implement P1	4 d	0%	32 h	0%
6		Phase I Complete	0 d	0%	0 h	0%
7		Phase II	16 d	0%	152 h	0%
8		Design P2	4 d	0%	32 h	0%
9		Build P2	3 d	0%	48 h	0%
10		Test P2	4 d	0%	32 h	0%
11		Implement P2	5 d	0%	40 h	0%
12		Phase II Complete	0 d	0%	0 h	0%
13		Phase III	20 d	41%	168 h	33%
14	✓	Design P3	5 d	100%	40 h	100%
15		Build P3	3 d	67%	24 h	67%
16		Test P3	4 d	0%	64 h	0%
17		Implement P3	5 d	0%	40 h	0%
18		Phase III Complete	0 d	0%	0 h	0%
19		Project Complete	0 d	0%	0 h	0%

Figure 9 - 8: New custom _Duration vs. Work table

Information: When you use the *More Tables* dialog to create a new table, Project 2013 copies the new table automatically to your Global.mpt file. This makes the new custom table available for all of your current and future projects.

Hands On Exercise

Exercise 9 - 2

Create a new custom table to show *Duration* variance data.

1. Return the **Training Advisor 09.mpp** sample file.
2. Click the *View* tab to display the *View* ribbon.
3. In the *Data* section of the *View* ribbon, click the *Tables* pick list, and then select the *More Tables* item.
4. In the *More Tables* dialog, select the *Work* table, and then click the *Copy* button.
5. In the *Table Definition* dialog, enter *_Duration* in the *Name* field and then select the *Show in menu* option.

Information: The underscore character preceding the table name allows users to easily identify that this table is a custom table rather than a default table.

Best Practice: MSProjectExperts recommends that you use a unique naming convention, such as preceding the name with an underscore character, when creating custom objects such as views, tables, filters, or groups. Using a naming convention separates your customization objects from the default objects included in Project 2013.

6. In the data grid, select the *Name* field and then click the *Insert Row* button.
7. In the *Field Name* column, click the pick list for the new blank row, and then select the *Indicators* field on the list of available fields.
8. For the *Indictors* field, specify each of the following values:

Align Data	Width	Title	Align Title	Header Wrapping	Text Wrapping
Left	9		Left	Yes	No

9. Using the information shown in Table 9 - 1, replace the existing fields shown in the *Original Field* column with different fields shown in the *New Field* column. For example, replace the *Work* field with the *Duration* field in the *Table Definition* dialog. Please note that you do not need to replace the *ID*, *Indicators*, and *Name* fields.

Original Field	New Field
ID	ID
Indicators	Indicators
Name	Name
Work	Duration
Baseline Work	Baseline Duration
Work Variance	Duration Variance
Actual Work	Actual Duration
Remaining Work	Remaining Duration
% Work Complete	% Complete

Table 9 - 1: Field list for the _Duration table

10. Press the **Backspace** key on your keyboard to remove the value in the *Title* column for every field **except** for the *Task Name* field.

Warning: To delete the text for any field in the *Title* column, you must select the text and then press the **Backspace** key on your computer keyboard. If you press the **Delete** key, Project 2013 removes the entire field rather than deleting the text.

11. Select the *Duration Variance* field and then click the *Cut Row* button.

12. Select the *Duration* field and then click the *Paste Row* button.

By completing the two preceding steps, you moved the most important column in the table (the *Duration Variance* column) to the immediate right of the *Task Name* column. Arranging the columns in this order makes it easier to spot tasks with duration slippage.

13. In the lower left corner of the *Table Definition* dialog, **deselect** the *Show 'Add New Column' Interface* option.

14. Click the *OK* button.

15. Select your new custom table, if necessary, and then click the *Apply* button to display the new custom table.

16. Widen the *Task Name* column, if needed.

17. Drag the split bar to the far right side of the new custom table and study the information shown in every column.

18. Save but do not close the **Training Advisor 09.mpp** sample file.

Creating a Custom Filter

The second step for creating a new view is to select an existing filter, or to create a new filter if no existing filter meets your reporting requirements. You use a filter to extract the exact rows of data you want to see in your view. A key question to ask before completing this step is, "What rows of data do I want to see in my new view?" The answer to this question determines whether you select an existing filter or create a new custom filter. If no existing filter meets your filtering criteria, then you must create a custom filter by completing the following steps:

1. Click the *View* tab to display the *View* ribbon.
2. In the *Data* section of the *View* ribbon, click the *Filter* pick list and select the *More Filters* item. Alternately, you can click the *Highlight Filter* pick list and select the *More Highlight Filters* item. Project 2013 displays the *More Filters* dialog shown in Figure 9 - 9.

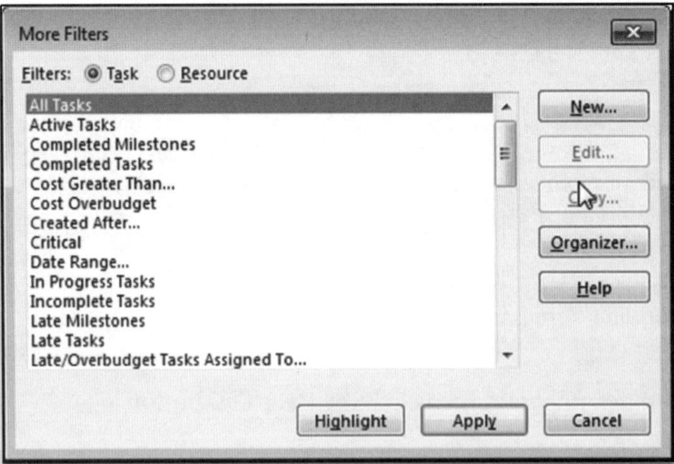

Figure 9 - 9: More Filters dialog

3. Click the *New* button in the *More Filters* dialog. Project 2013 displays the *Filter Definition* dialog shown in Figure 9 - 10.

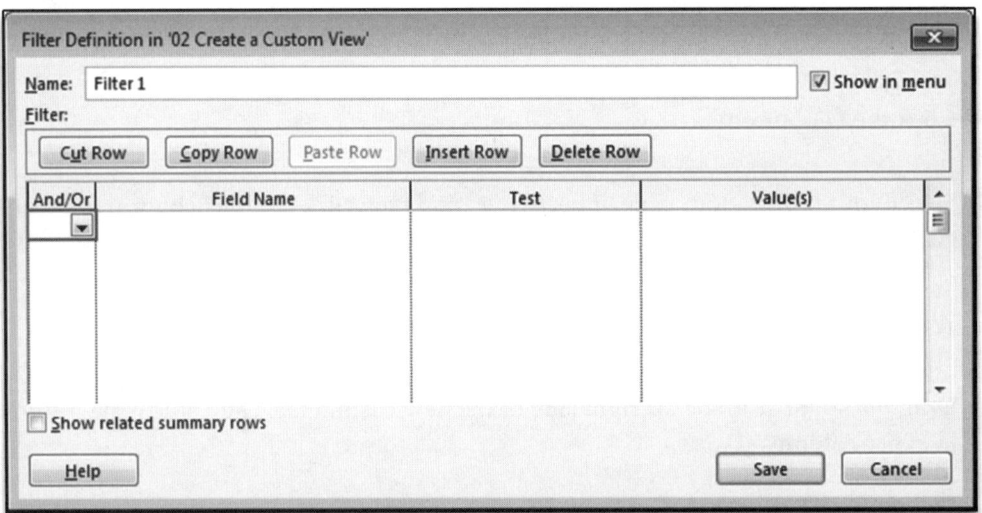

Figure 9 - 10: Filter Definition dialog for a new custom filter

Information: Two alternate methods you can use to display the *Filter Definition* dialog from the *View* ribbon are to click the *Filter* pick list and select the *New Filter* item, or to click the *Highlight Filter* pick list and select the *New Highlight Filter* item. If you use either of these two methods, you bypass the *More Filters* dialog completely, and the resulting *Filter Definition* dialog contains an *Apply* button in addition to the *Save* and *Cancel* buttons.

4. Enter a name for the new filter in the *Name* field.
5. Select the *Show in menu* option if you want your new filter to display in *Filter* and *Highlight Filter* pick lists in the *View* ribbon.
6. In the data grid, enter your desired filter criteria in the *Field Name, Test, Value(s),* and *And/Or* columns.

Information: To create a compound filter with multiple lines of filtering criteria, you must select an *And* value or an *Or* value for each line after the first line.

7. Select the *Show related summary rows* option if you want to see all summary tasks for every task that meets your filter criteria, regardless of whether the summary task meets the filter criteria.

Information: Selecting the *Show related summary rows* option guarantees that the filter shows you the Work Breakdown Structure (WBS) for each task displayed by the filter. This helps you to identify the phase and/or deliverable section of the project for each task the filter displays.

Figure 9 - 11 shows the *Filter Definition* dialog with criteria for a new custom filter. Using Boolean AND logic, this filter first determines whether the *Work Variance* value is greater than *0 hours,* indicating the task is over budget on work. Then the filter determines whether the *Baseline Work* value does not equal *0 hours* to eliminate milestone tasks. Using these criteria, the new custom filter displays all tasks that exceed their original budget of work hours specified in the *Baseline Work* field.

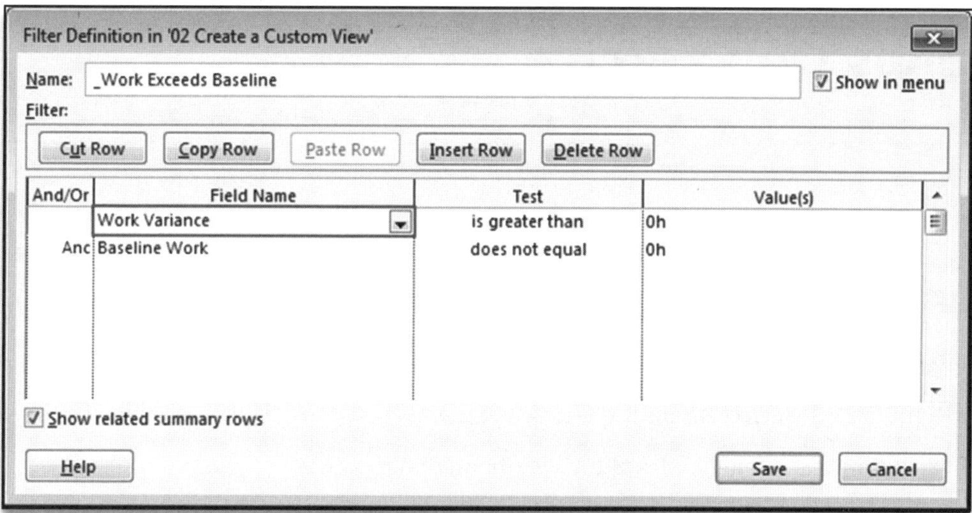

Figure 9 - 11: Filter criteria in the Filter Definition dialog

Information: The *_Work Exceeds Baseline* filter shown in Figure 9 - 11 displays every task where the current *Work* value exceeds the original budget of work hours specified in the *Baseline Work* field. The filter displays completed, in-progress, and unstarted tasks that are over budget on work. This differs from the behavior of the default *Work Overbudget* filter that displays only completed and in-progress tasks in which the *Actual Work* value exceeds the *Baseline Work* value.

8. Click the *Save* button to close the *Filter Definition* dialog.

9. In the *More Filters* dialog, select your new custom filter, if necessary, and then click the *Apply* button to test the filter.

Figure 9 - 12 shows the *_Work Exceeds Baseline* filter applied in the *Gantt Chart* view with the *Work* table displayed. Notice that this custom filter displays two tasks where the *Work Variance* value is greater than *0 hours,* including a completed task (*Build P1*), and an in-progress task (*Test P1*).

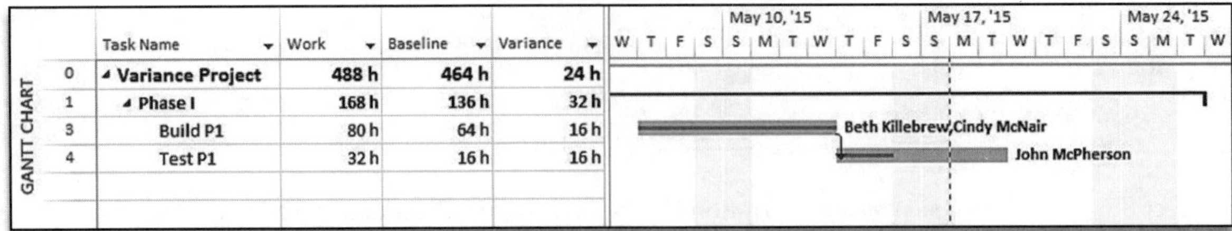

Figure 9 - 12: _Work Exceeds Baseline filter applied in the Gantt Chart view

10. After you confirm the filter works correctly as designed, press the **F3** function key to reapply the *[No Filter]* filter.

Information: When you create a new filter, Project 2013 copies the new filter automatically into your Global.mpt file. This makes the new custom filter available for all of your current and future projects.

Hands On Exercise

Exercise 9 - 3

Create a custom filter to locate tasks whose *Duration* value exceeds their *Baseline Duration* value.

1. Return the **Training Advisor 09.mpp** sample file.
2. Right-click the *Select All* button and select the new custom *_Duration* table, if necessary.
3. Click the *View* tab to display the *View* ribbon, if necessary.
4. In the *Data* section of the *View* ribbon, click the *Filter* pick list, and then select the *More Filters* item.
5. In the *More Filters* dialog, click the *New* button.
6. In the *Filter Definition* dialog, enter the filter criteria shown in Table 9 - 2.

Name	_Duration Variance > 0d		
Show in menu	Selected		
And/Or	**Field Name**	**Test**	**Value(s)s**
	Duration Variance	is greater than	0d
Show related summary rows		Selected	

Table 9 - 2: Filter criteria

7. Click the *Save* button to save the new filter.

8. Select your new filter in the *More Filters* dialog, if necessary, and then click the *Apply* button to test the filter.

Notice that the filter displays one task in the *INSTALLATION* phase of the project (the *Setup Server and Load O/S* task) and two tasks in the *TRAINING* phase of the project (the *Create Training Module 01* and *Create Training Module 03* tasks).

9. After you confirm the filter works correctly as designed, press the **F3** function key on your computer keyboard to clear the current filter.

10. Right-click the *Select All* button and select the *Entry* table.

11. Drag the split bar to the right edge of the *Duration* column.

12. Save but do not close the **Training Advisor 09.mpp** sample file.

Creating a Custom Group

The third step in creating a new view is to select an existing group or to create a new group if no existing group meets your reporting needs. In Project 2013, groups allow you to categorize, sort, and summarize your project data. Because very few default groups exist in Project 2013, it is likely that you need to create a new group as a part of any new custom view to which you want to apply grouping. To create a new custom group, complete the following steps:

1. Click the *View* tab to display the *View* ribbon.

2. In the *Data* section of the *View* ribbon, click the *Group By* pick list and select the *More Groups* item. Project 2013 displays the *More Groups* dialog shown in Figure 9 - 13.

Figure 9 - 13: More Groups dialog

3. In the *More Groups* dialog, click the *New* button. Project 2013 displays the *Group Definition* dialog shown in Figure 9 - 14.

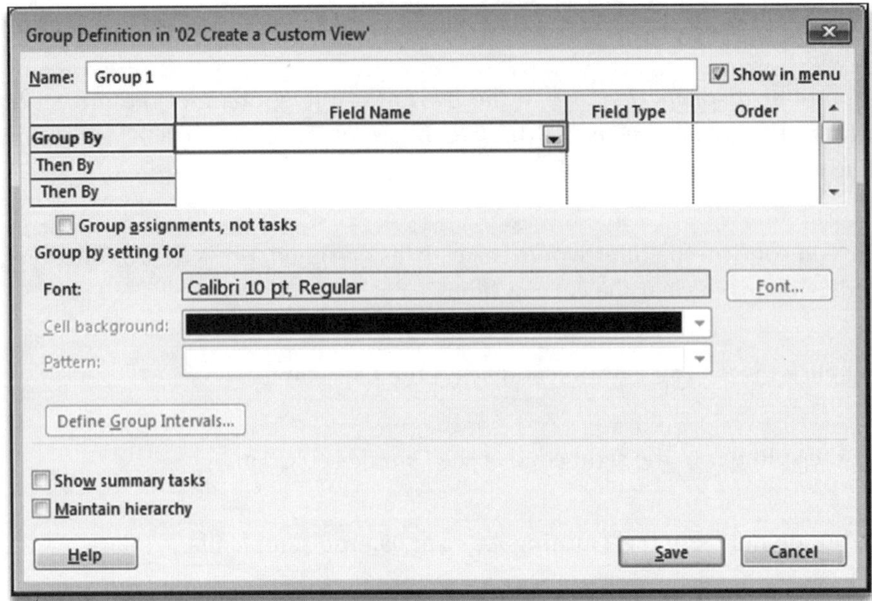

Figure 9 - 14: Group Definition dialog

Information: An alternate method to display the *Group Definition* dialog from the *View* ribbon is to click the *Group By* pick list and select the *New Group By* item. Using this method, you bypass the *More Groups* dialog completely, and the resulting *Group Definition* dialog contains an *Apply* button in addition to the *Save* and *Cancel* buttons.

4. Enter a name for the new custom group in the *Name* field and then select the *Show in menu* option if you want the new custom group to display in the *Group By* pick list in the *View* ribbon.

5. In the data grid, enter the desired grouping information on the *Group By* line in the *Field Name, Field Type,* and *Order* columns.

6. To create multi-level grouping, enter additional grouping information in one or more of the *Then By* lines in the data grid.

Information: You can create a custom group that applies grouping on assignments in any assignment view. This means that you can create a task group that applies grouping to resource assignments in the *Task Usage* view, and you can create a resource group that applies grouping to the task assignments in the *Resource Usage* view. To create a group that applies grouping on assignments, first select the *Group assignments, not tasks* option, click the *Field Type* pick list for the assignment field upon which you want to group, and then select the *Assignments* value on the list.

7. If you want to specify grouping intervals, click the *Define Group Intervals* button. Project 2013 displays the *Define Group Interval* dialog shown in Figure 9 - 15.

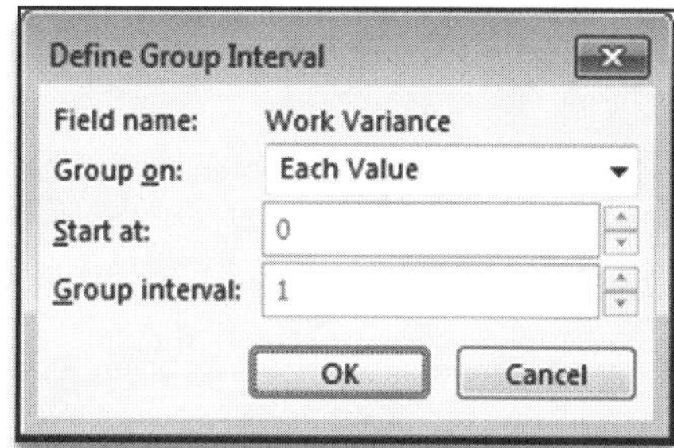

Figure 9 - 15: Define Group Interval dialog

You use the options in the *Define Group Interval* dialog to set up grouping with specific interval ranges. Based on the type of field you select, Project 2013 offers the appropriate interval options in the *Group on* pick list. For example, notice in Figure 9 - 15 shown previously that I selected the *Work Variance* field. Because the *Work Variance* field contains time data, the *Group on* pick list contains group interval options for *Minutes, Hours, Days, Weeks,* and *Months.* For my reporting criteria, I want to group tasks by their *Work Variance* value, grouped in 8-hour intervals, generating groups from 0-8h, 8-16h, 16-24h, etc.

In addition, the *Define Group Interval* dialog also includes a *Start at* field. You can use this field to specify the starting value of your first group interval. For example, if you set the *Group on* value to *Hours,* set the *Group interval* value to *8,* and leave the *Start at* value to *0,* the software creates the first group interval as **0h - < 8h**. If you change the *Start at* value to *2,* the software creates the first group interval as **2h - < 10h**. If you want to specify a value in the *Start at* field, the value you select **must be less than** the value you specify in the *Group interval* field; otherwise, the *Start at* value you specify has no effect on the group intervals created when you apply the group.

Information: When you specify a value in the *Start at* field, the software **may not** create the group intervals you expect. This is because Project 2013 must create a group interval for every task in the project. Using the preceding example, I have a number of tasks in the project that have a 0h value in the *Work Variance* field. If I set the *Start at* value to 2, the software **does not** create the first group interval as **2h - < 10h**. Instead, the software creates the first group interval as **-6h - < 2h** so that there is a group interval for tasks with *0h* value in the *Work Variance* column.

8. In the *Define Group Interval* dialog, select your desired interval values in the *Group on, Start at,* and *Group interval* fields. Figure 9 - 16 shows the completed *Define Group Interval* dialog with grouping set in 8-hour intervals.

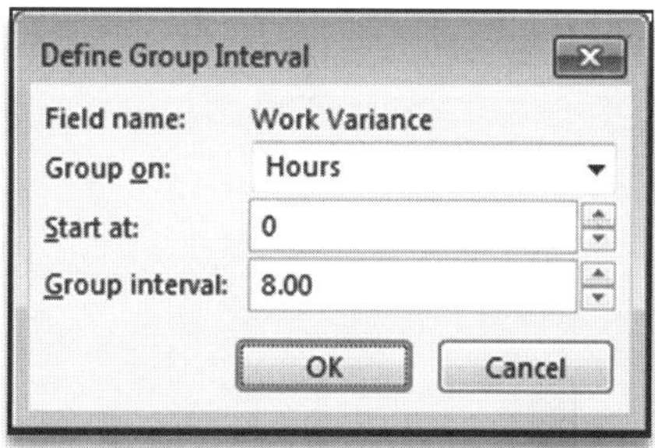

Figure 9 - 16: Define Group Interval dialog with 8-hour intervals

Information: If you do not specify grouping intervals, Project 2013 creates a separate group interval for each set of values in the field on which you apply grouping.

9. Click the *OK* button to close the *Define Group Interval* dialog.
10. Click the *Cell background* pick list and select an alternate color other than the default tan color, if necessary.
11. Click the *Pattern* pick list and select an alternate pattern other than the default solid pattern, if necessary.
12. Click the *Font* button and select alternate font settings, if necessary.

Information: By changing the values in the *Cell Background* and *Pattern* fields, you can create your own color scheme for each grouping level in your custom group.

13. Select the *Show summary tasks* option if you want to see summary tasks included in the grouping intervals.

Warning: If you select the *Show summary tasks* option, Project 2013 **does not** maintain the Work Breakdown Structure (WBS) for your project when you apply the group. This means that the software might list a summary task in one grouping interval and one of its subtasks in a different grouping interval. If you want to see the WBS for each task, **do not** select the *Show summary tasks* option and select the *Maintain hierarchy* option instead.

14. If you want to show the WBS of summary tasks for each task with the group applied, select the *Maintain hierarchy* option.

Figure 9 - 17 shows the completed *Group Definition* dialog for the custom *_Work Variance* group. Notice that I selected the *Maintain hierarchy* option since I want to see the WBS for every task.

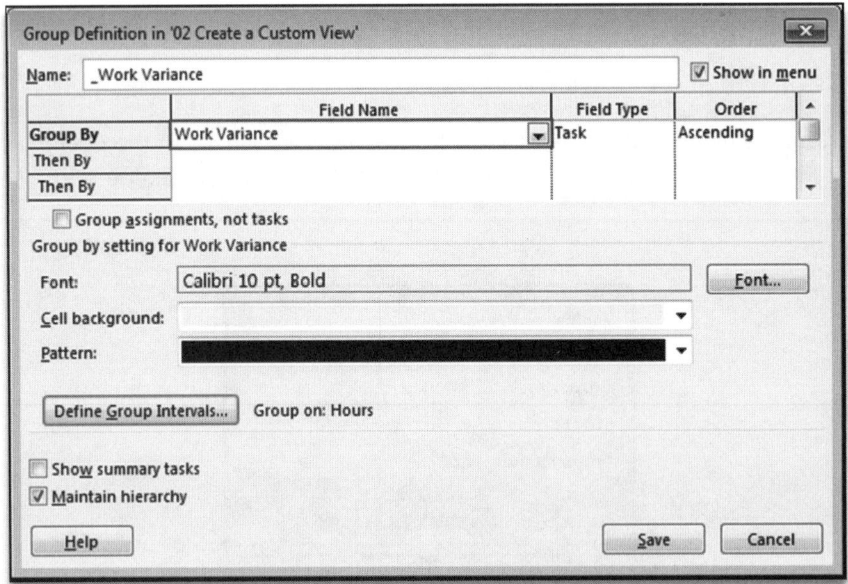

Figure 9 - 17: Completed _Work Variance group definition in the Group Definition

15. Click the *Save* button to close the *Group Definition* dialog.

16. In the *More Groups* dialog, select your new custom group, if necessary, and then click the *Apply* button to test it.

Warning: When applying a task group, do not apply the group in any view containing a *Gantt Chart* screen, as this action generates a "tangled spaghetti" pattern with the link lines between Gantt bars. Instead, for better results, always apply a task group while displaying the *Task Sheet* view.

Figure 9 - 18 shows the custom *_Work Variance* group applied to the *Task Sheet* view with the *Work* table displayed. Because I set the *Group interval* value to *8* in the *Define Group Interval* dialog, the software creates groups in intervals of 8 hours each, as expected. Because I also selected the *Maintain hierarchy* option in the *Group Definition* dialog, notice that Project 2013 displays the WBS for each task in each group interval.

	Task Name	Work	Baseline	Variance	Actual	Remaining	% W. Comp.
	Work Variance: -16 h - <-8 h	**24 h**	**32 h**	**-8 h**	**16 h**	**8 h**	**66%**
	5 Phase III	**24 h**	**32 h**	**-8 h**	**16 h**	**8 h**	**66%**
15	Build P3	24 h	32 h	-8 h	16 h	8 h	67%
	Work Variance: 0 h - <8 h	**352 h**	**352 h**	**0 h**	**64 h**	**288 h**	**18%**
	1 Phase I	**56 h**	**56 h**	**0 h**	**24 h**	**32 h**	**42%**
2	Design P1	24 h	24 h	0 h	24 h	0 h	100%
5	Implement P1	32 h	32 h	0 h	0 h	32 h	0%
	2 Phase I Complete	**0 h**	**0 h**	**0 h**	**0 h**	**0 h**	**0%**
6	Phase I Complete	0 h	0 h	0 h	0 h	0 h	0%
	3 Phase II	**152 h**	**152 h**	**0 h**	**0 h**	**152 h**	**0%**
8	Design P2	32 h	32 h	0 h	0 h	32 h	0%
9	Build P2	48 h	48 h	0 h	0 h	48 h	0%
10	Test P2	32 h	32 h	0 h	0 h	32 h	0%
11	Implement P2	40 h	40 h	0 h	0 h	40 h	0%
	4 Phase II Complete	**0 h**	**0 h**	**0 h**	**0 h**	**0 h**	**0%**
12	Phase II Complete	0 h	0 h	0 h	0 h	0 h	0%
	5 Phase III	**144 h**	**144 h**	**0 h**	**40 h**	**104 h**	**27%**
14	Design P3	40 h	40 h	0 h	40 h	0 h	100%
16	Test P3	64 h	64 h	0 h	0 h	64 h	0%
17	Implement P3	40 h	40 h	0 h	0 h	40 h	0%
	6 Phase III Complete	**0 h**	**0 h**	**0 h**	**0 h**	**0 h**	**0%**
18	Phase III Complete	0 h	0 h	0 h	0 h	0 h	0%
	7 Project Complete	**0 h**	**0 h**	**0 h**	**0 h**	**0 h**	**0%**
19	Project Complete	0 h	0 h	0 h	0 h	0 h	0%
	Work Variance: 16 h - <24 h	**112 h**	**80 h**	**32 h**	**96 h**	**16 h**	**85%**
	1 Phase I	**112 h**	**80 h**	**32 h**	**96 h**	**16 h**	**85%**
3	Build P1	80 h	64 h	16 h	80 h	0 h	100%
4	Test P1	32 h	16 h	16 h	16 h	16 h	50%

Figure 9 - 18: _Work Variance group applied in the Task Sheet view

Information: When you create a new group, Project 2013 copies the new group automatically into your Global.mpt file. This makes the new custom group available for all of your current and future projects.

Hands On Exercise

Exercise 9 - 4

Create a new custom group to apply grouping tasks by *Duration Variance* in descending order in 1-day intervals.

1. Return to the **Training Advisor 09.mpp** sample file.
2. Click the *View* tab to display the *View* ribbon, if necessary.
3. In the *Task Views* section of the *View* ribbon, click the *Gantt Chart* pick list button, and then select the *More Views* item.
4. In the *More Views* dialog, select the *Task Sheet* view, and then click the *Apply* button.
5. Right-click the *Select All* button and select the new custom *_Duration* table.
6. In the *Data* section of the *View* ribbon, click the *Group By* pick list, and then select the *More Groups* item.
7. In the *More Groups* dialog, click the *New* button.
8. In the *Group Definition* dialog, set up the group criteria using the information shown in Table 9 - 3.

Name	_Duration Variance
Show in menu	Selected
Field Name	Duration Variance
Field Type	Task
Order	Descending
Group assignments not tasks	Not selected
Show summary tasks	Not selected
Maintain hierarchy	Selected

Table 9 - 3: Group Definition information

9. Click the *Define Group Intervals* button and set up group intervals in the *Define Group Interval* dialog using the information shown in Table 9 - 4.

Group on	Days
Start at	0.00
Group interval	1.00

Table 9 - 4: Group interval information

10. Click the *OK* button to close the *Define Group Interval* dialog.

11. Click the *Save* button to close the *Group Definition* dialog.

12. Select your new custom group, if necessary, and then click the *Apply* button to test the group.

13. Click the *Collapse* symbol (black triangle symbol) to collapse the *Duration Variance: 0d - <1d* section to hide tasks with a *Duration Variance* value less than 1 day.

14. Press **Shift + F3** as the shortcut key to clear the current group.

15. Right-click the *Select All* button and select the *Entry* table.

16. In the *Task Views* section of the *View* ribbon, click the *Gantt Chart* pick list button, and then select the *Gantt Chart* view.

17. Drag the split bar to the right edge of the *Duration* column, if necessary.

18. Save but do not close the **Training Advisor 09.mpp** sample file.

Creating a New Custom View

The final step in the view creation process is to combine your desired screen, table, filter, and group into a new custom view. The screen selection is a very important component of any custom view, as it controls what appears on the right side of the new custom view. For example, when choosing a screen, you determine whether the right side of the view displays a *Gantt Chart* screen of some type (such as in the *Tracking Gantt* view), a timephased grid screen (such as in the *Resource Usage* view), or no screen at all (such as in the *Task Sheet* view).

Warning: Carefully select your *Screen* option because you **cannot** change the screen selection after you complete the process of creating your new custom view. If you accidentally select the wrong screen, you must delete the new view using the *Organizer* dialog and then create the new view again from scratch.

To create your new custom view, complete the following steps:

1. Click the *View* tab to display the *View* ribbon.

2. In the *Task Views* section of the *View* ribbon, click the *Gantt Chart* pick list and select the *More Views* item. Project 2013 displays the *More Views* dialog shown in Figure 9 - 19.

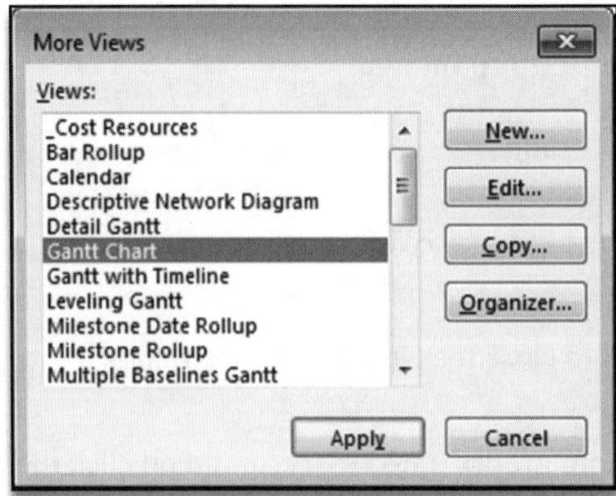

Figure 9 - 19: More Views dialog

3. In the *More Views* dialog, click the *New* button. Project 2013 displays the *Define New View* dialog shown in Figure 9 - 20.

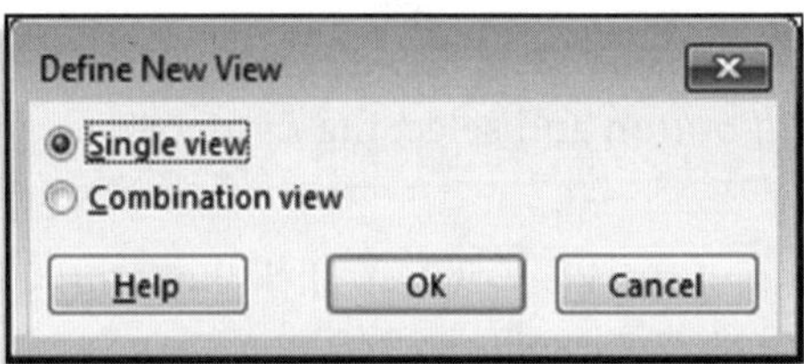

Figure 9 - 20: Define New View dialog

4. To create a custom single pane view, leave the default *Single view* option selected and click the *OK* button. Project 2013 displays the *View Definition* dialog shown in Figure 9 - 21.

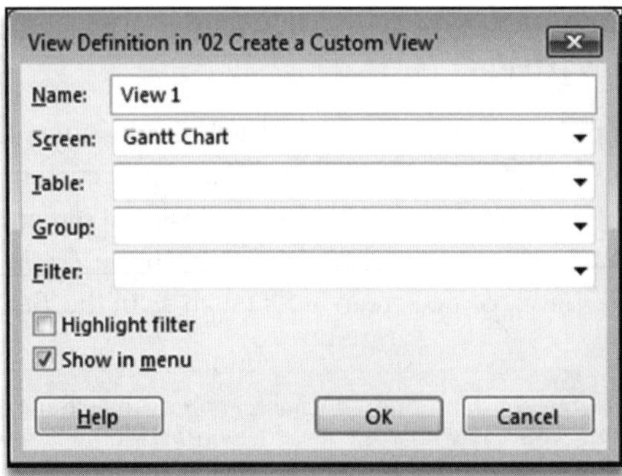

Figure 9 - 21: View Definition dialog

Information: You can also start the process of creating a new custom view by selecting any existing view in the *More Views* dialog and then clicking the *Copy* button. The limitation of using this method is that Project 2013 **does not** allow you to change the *Screen* value when creating a single pane view.

5. In the *View Definition* dialog, enter a name for the new custom view in the *Name* field.

6. Click the *Screen* pick list and select the screen you want to appear on the right side of the view. Project 2013 offers you a list of sixteen screen choices, each of which matches up with one of the default views you see in the software.

7. Click the *Table* pick list and select the table you want to use in your custom view. You can select any default table or any custom table you created previously.

8. Click the *Group* pick list and select the group you want to use in your custom view. You can select any default group or any custom group you created previously.

Information: When creating a new custom view, you **must** select a *Group* value in the *View Definition* dialog, even if you **do not** want to use a group in your view. If you fail to select a group when creating your new view, Project 2013 displays an error message when you click the *OK* button to complete the view. If you do not want to use a group in your view, select the *No Group* value in the *Group* field.

9. Click the *Filter* pick list and select the filter you want to use in your custom view. You can select any default filter or any custom filter you created previously.

10. Select the *Highlight filter* option if you want to apply the selected filter as a highlight filter.

Information: Remember that a highlight filter displays all tasks in your project, but highlights only those tasks that meet your filter criteria. By default, Project 2013 highlights the tasks using the yellow cell background color.

11. Select the *Show in menu* option if you want to see the new custom view on any view menu.

When you select the *Show in menu* option, Project 2013 adds the new custom view in the *Custom Views* section at the top of the *Gantt Chart* pick list in the *View* section of the *Task* ribbon, or at the top of the *Team Planner* pick list in the *View* section of the *Resource* ribbon. The software also displays the new custom view in the *Custom Views* section at the top of any pick list in either the *Task Views* or *Resource Views* section of the *View* ribbon.

The software chooses the appropriate pick list based on the *Screen* option you select in the *View Definition* dialog. For example, if you select the *Gantt Chart* item on the *Screen* pick list, the software adds the custom view to the *Gantt Chart* pick list in the *Task Views* section of the ribbon. If you select the *Resource Usage* item on the *Screen* pick list, the software adds the custom view to the *Resource Usage* pick list in the *Resource Views* section of the ribbon.

Figure 9 - 22 shows the completed *View Definition* dialog. I intend to use this new custom view to display tasks that are over budget on work, compared against the original work budget specified in the *Baseline Work* field.

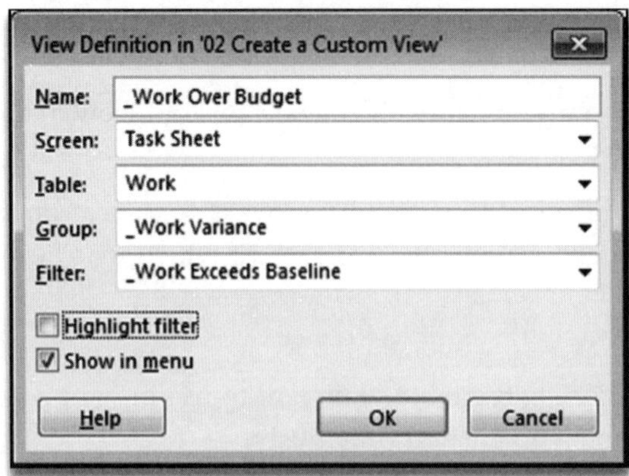

Figure 9 - 22: Completed custom view criteria in the View Definition dialog

12. Click the *OK* button to close the *View Definition* dialog.

13. In the *More Views* dialog, select your new custom view, if necessary, and then click the *Apply* button to test your new view.

Figure 9 - 23 shows the new custom *_Work Over Budget* view, as defined in the *View Definition* dialog shown previously in Figure 9 - 22. Notice that the view displays only those tasks with a value greater than 0 hours in the *Work Variance* column. Notice also that I can see the WBS for each task because I selected the *Maintain hierarchy* option when I created the custom group included in this view.

_WORK OVER BUDGET

	Task Name	Work	Baseline	Variance	Actual	Remaining	% W. Comp.
	Work Variance: 0 h - <8 h	**44 h**	**40 h**	**4 h**	**0 h**	**44 h**	**0%**
	5 Phase III	**44 h**	**40 h**	**4 h**	**0 h**	**44 h**	**0%**
17	Implement P3	44 h	40 h	4 h	0 h	44 h	0%
	Work Variance: 8 h - <16 h	**40 h**	**32 h**	**8 h**	**0 h**	**40 h**	**0%**
	3 Phase II	**40 h**	**32 h**	**8 h**	**0 h**	**40 h**	**0%**
10	Test P2	40 h	32 h	8 h	0 h	40 h	0%
	Work Variance: 16 h - <24 h	**112 h**	**80 h**	**32 h**	**96 h**	**16 h**	**85%**
	1 Phase I	**112 h**	**80 h**	**32 h**	**96 h**	**16 h**	**85%**
3	Build P1	80 h	64 h	16 h	80 h	0 h	100%
4	Test P1	32 h	16 h	16 h	16 h	16 h	50%

Figure 9 - 23: New custom _Work Over Budget view

Information: When you create a new view, Project 2013 copies the new view automatically into your Global.mpt file. This makes the new custom view available for all of your current and future projects.

Hands On Exercise

Exercise 9 - 5

Make a copy of the *Tracking Gantt* view and then modify the copy to create a custom view that shows all tasks with a *Duration Variance* value greater than *0 days*. Apply the filter as a highlight filter.

1. Return to the **Training Advisor 09.mpp** sample file.
2. Click the *View* tab to display the *View* ribbon, if necessary.
3. In the *Task Views* section of the *View* ribbon, click the *Gantt Chart* pick list, and then select the *More Views* item.
4. In the *More Views* dialog, select the *Tracking Gantt* view, and then click the *Copy* button.
5. In the *View Definition* dialog, enter or select the information shown in Table 9 - 5.

Name	_Duration Slippage
Table	_Duration
Group	No Group
Filter	_Duration Variance > 0d
Highlight filter	Selected
Show in menu	Selected

Table 9 - 5: View Definition information

6. Click the *OK* button to close the *View Definition* dialog.
7. Select your new custom view, if necessary, and then click the *Apply* button.
8. Drag the split bar to the right side of the *Duration Variance* column.
9. In the *Zoom* section of the *View* ribbon, click the *Timescale* pick list and select the *Weeks* level of zoom.
10. Study the *Duration Variance* information shown in this new custom view.

Notice that this new custom view uses the yellow cell background color to highlight every task with a *Duration Variance* value greater than *0 days*. This new custom view allows you to easily spot any task whose *Duration* is greater than the original *Baseline Duration*, meaning that the task is slipping.

11. Save but **do not** close to the **Training Advisor 09.mpp** sample file.

Creating a Combination View

Remember that a combination view consists of two views, each tiled in its own pane. Because of this, the steps needed to create a combination view are much different than the steps needed to create a single-screen view. As documented in the previous topical section, you use the four-step method to create a single-screen view. To create a combination view, however, complete the following steps:

1. Click the *View* tab to display the *View* ribbon.

2. In the *Task Views* section of the *View* ribbon, click the *Gantt Chart* pick list, and then select the *More Views* item. Project 2013 displays the *More Views* dialog shown previously in Figure 9 - 19.

3. In the *More Views* dialog, click the *New* button. Project 2013 displays the *Define New View* dialog shown previously in Figure 9 - 20.

4. Select the *Combination view* option and click the *OK* button. Project 2013 displays the *View Definition* dialog shown in Figure 9 - 24.

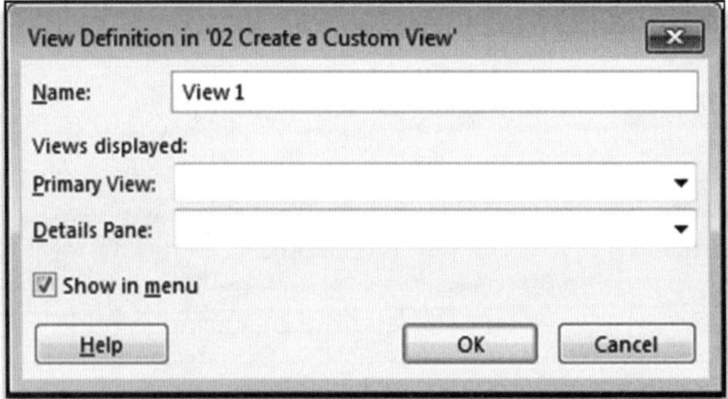

Figure 9 - 24: View Definition dialog, ready to create for a new combination view

5. Enter a name for your new combination view in the *Name* field.

6. Select your desired views in the *Primary View* and *Details Pane* pick lists.

Information: The view you select in the *Primary View* field appears in the top pane of the combination view. The view you select in the *Details Pane* pick list appears in the bottom pane of the combination view.

7. Select the *Show in menu* option if you want to see the new custom view in the appropriate view menu.

Figure 9 - 25 shows the *View Definition* dialog with the definition of a new combination view I intend to use to analyze resource overallocation data. When I apply this new view, I can select any overallocated resource in the *Resource Usage* pane (top pane) and see immediately the severity of overallocation in the *Resource Graph* pane (bottom pane).

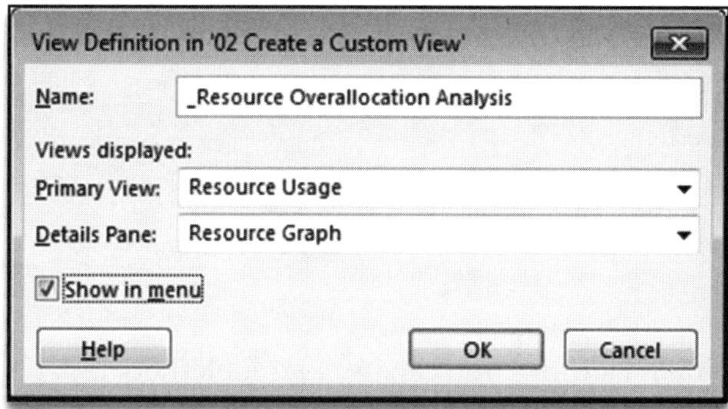

Figure 9 - 25: View Definition dialog with a new combination view

8. Click the *OK* button to close the *View Definition* dialog.

9. Select your new custom view, if necessary, and then click the *Apply* button.

Figure 9 - 26 shows my new custom *_Resource Overallocation Analysis* combination view. Notice the view reveals that I assigned *Linda Erickson* accidentally to two parallel tasks. Because of this, I now assign her at a total *Units* value of *200%* from Thursday through Tuesday, which means she is overallocated. Facing an overallocation of this nature, I can level this resource overallocation using one of the techniques I discussed previously in Module 07, *Project Assignment Planning*.

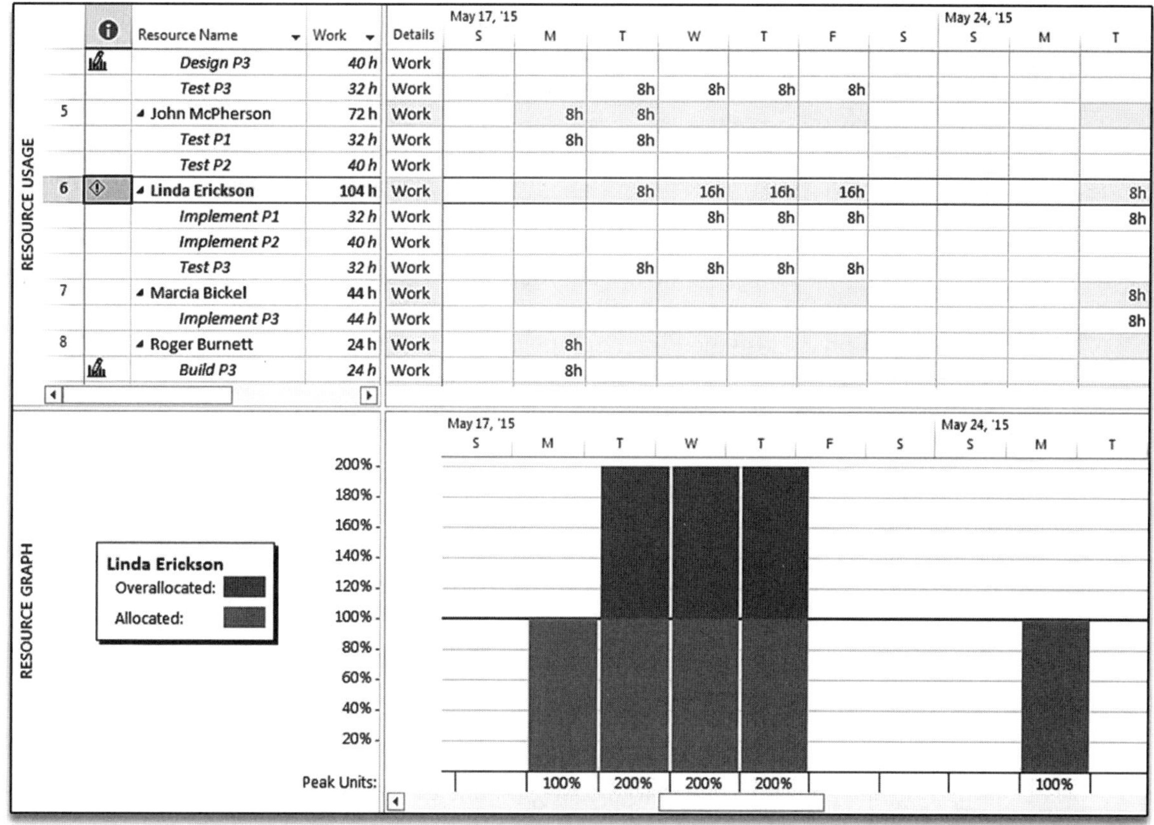

Figure 9 - 26: _Resource Overallocation Analysis combination view

Hands On Exercise

Exercise 9 - 6

Create a custom combination view that you can use to troubleshoot task dependency problems.

1. Return to the **Training Advisor 09.mpp** sample file.
2. Click the *View* tab to display the *View* ribbon.
3. In the *Task Views* section of the *View* ribbon, click the *Gantt Chart* pick list, and then select the *More Views* item.
4. In the *More Views* dialog, click the *New* button.
5. In the *Define New View* dialog, select the *Combination view* option and then click the *OK* button.
6. In the *View Definition* dialog, enter or select the information in Table 9 - 6:

Name	_Dependency Analysis
Primary View	Gantt Chart
Details Pane	Relationship Diagram
Show in menu	Selected

Table 9 - 6: View Definition information

7. Click the *OK* button to close the *View Definition* dialog.
8. Select your new custom view, if necessary, and then click the *Apply* button.
9. In the *Gantt Chart* pane, select task ID #35, the *Create Training Schedule* task.

In the *Relationship Diagram* pane, notice that the *Create Training Schedule* task has two predecessors and only one successor.

10. Select several other tasks in the *Gantt Chart* pane and experiment with using this new custom combination view.
11. Double-click anywhere in the split bar between the top pane and the bottom pane to close the *Relationship Diagram* pane and return to the single-pane *Gantt Chart* view.
12. Save but **do not** close the **Training Advisor 09.mpp** sample file.

Using the Organizer

Every time you launch Project 2013, the software opens the Global.mpt file in the background. The Global.mpt file is your "library" of default objects that ship with the software, including default views, tables, filters, groups, reports, etc. The Global.mpt file also serves as the "library" of the personal objects you create.

As I stated previously, when you create a custom view, table, filter, and/or group in Project 2013, the software creates these objects in the project file and then adds them to the Global.mpt file automatically. By adding these objects to the Global.mpt file automatically, the software makes the view, table, filter, and/or group available to every current and future project you manage.

Information: If you do not want Project 2013 to add custom views, tables, filters, and/or groups to the Global.mpt file automatically, you can disable this option. With this option disabled, you must manually add new custom views, tables, filters, and/or groups to the Global.mpt file using the *Organizer* dialog. To disable the automatic functionality, click the *File* tab and then click the *Options* tab in the *Backstage*. In the *Project Options* dialog, click the *Advanced* tab. In the *Display* section of the *Advanced* page of the dialog, **deselect** the *Automatically add new views, tables, filters, and groups to the global* option. Click the *OK* button when finished.

If you edit an existing view, table, filter, or group, keep in mind that Project 2013 changes the object in the project only, but **does not** change the object in the Global.mpt file. This means you must copy the edited object from the project to the Global.mpt file to make the new version of the object available to every current and future project.

To manage the objects in the Global.mpt file, you must use the *Organizer* dialog. To access this dialog, click the *File* tab, click the *Info* tab in the *Backstage*, and then click the *Organizer* button on the *Info* page of the *Backstage*. The software displays the *Organizer* dialog shown in Figure 9 - 27.

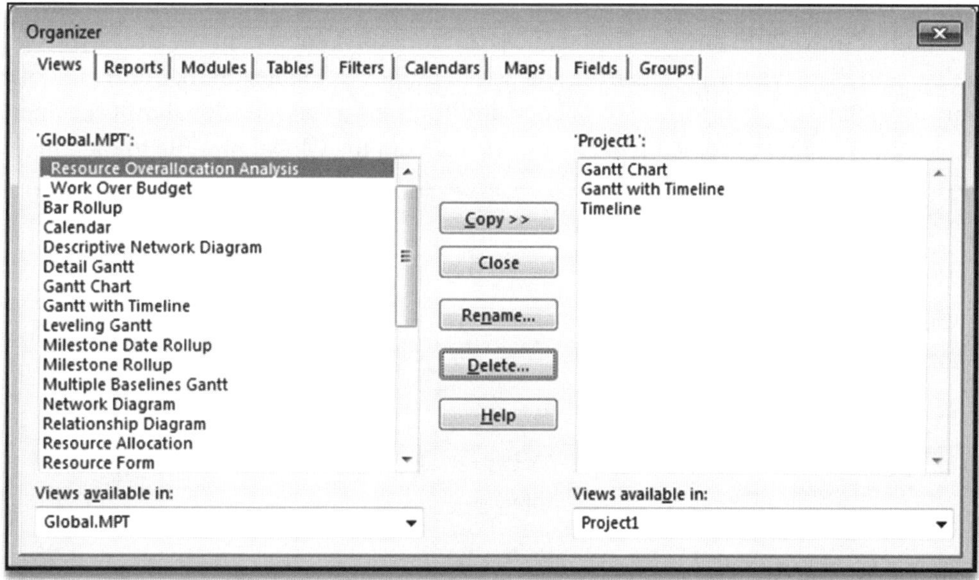

Figure 9 - 27: Organizer dialog

You can use the *Organizer* dialog to manage any of the custom objects you create in a project and/or in the Global.mpt file. Notice also in Figure 9 - 27 that the *Organizer* dialog shows two custom views in the list on the left side of the dialog (in the Global.mpt file), but shows only three default views in the list on the right side of the dialog (in the project file).

The *Organizer* dialog includes nine tabs that allow you to manage all of the default and custom objects available in Project 2013. These objects include views, tables, filters, groups, reports, fields, calendars, maps, and modules.

When you create a new custom object in a project file and/or in the Global.mpt file, you can use the *Organizer* dialog to do any of the following:

- Copy custom objects from one file to another.
- Rename a custom object.
- Delete a custom object.

Copying Custom Objects

To copy a custom object to or from the Global.mpt file, complete the following steps in the *Organizer* dialog:

1. Select the appropriate tab in the *Organizer* dialog for the type of object you want to manage (such as a filter or a view).
2. On the *Tables, Filters,* and *Groups* pages of the dialog, select either the *Task* or *Resource* option, depending on which type of object you want to copy.
3. Select one or more objects on one side of the dialog.
4. Click the *Copy* button to copy the selected object(s) to the other side of the dialog.
5. Click the *Close* button when finished.

Using this technique, you can copy custom objects between the Global.mpt file and a project file, or between two project files. By default, Project 2013 always displays objects from the Global.mpt file in the list on the left side of the *Organizer* dialog, and displays the objects from the active project in the list on the right side of the dialog. Using this default arrangement, you can copy objects back and forth between the Global.mpt file and the active project file. Notice in Figure 9 - 28 that I copied two custom views from the Global.mpt file to the *Project1* project.

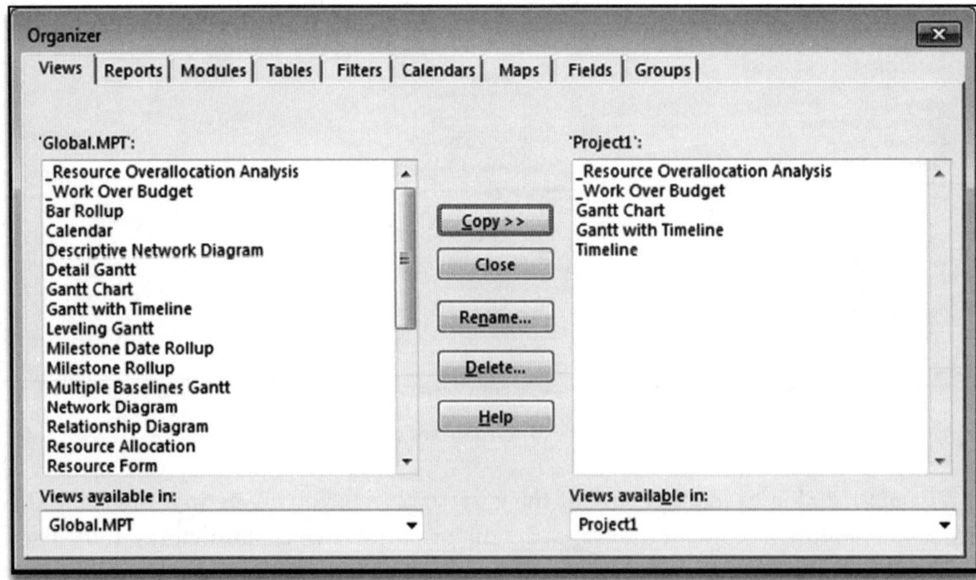

Figure 9 - 28: Copy a custom view from the Global.mpt file to a project file

Warning: When you use the *Organizer* dialog to manually copy a new custom view to the Global.mpt file, do not forget to copy any new tables, filters, and/or groups you created that are part of the custom view. If you neglect to copy all objects included in the new custom view, Project 2013 displays an error message when you attempt to apply the new view in any project.

Information: When you use the *Organizer* dialog to copy an object to the Global.mpt file, Project 2013 copies the object to the Global.mpt **currently loaded in memory**. When you exit Project 2013, the software saves the changes to the Global.mpt file on your hard drive.

You can also use the *Organizer* dialog to copy objects from one project file to another. To perform this copy operation, complete the following steps:

1. Open each project.
2. Click the *File* tab, click the *Info* tab in the *Backstage*, and then click the *Organizer* button.
3. Select the appropriate tab in the *Organizer* dialog for the type of object you want to manage.
4. On the *Tables, Filters,* and *Groups* pages of the dialog, select either the *Task* or *Resource* option, depending on which type of object you want to copy.
5. Click the pick list in the **lower left corner** of the dialog and select one of the open projects.
6. Click the pick list in the **lower right corner** of the dialog and select the other project.
7. Select one or more objects in the list on one side of the dialog and then click the *Copy* button to copy the selected objects to the list on the other side of the dialog.
8. Click the *Close* button when finished.

Renaming and Deleting Custom Objects

You can also use the *Organizer* dialog to rename existing objects or to delete unneeded objects in either the Global.mpt file or in a project. To rename an object using the *Organizer* dialog, complete the following steps:

1. Select the appropriate tab in the *Organizer* dialog for the type of object you want to manage.
2. On the *Tables, Filters,* and *Groups* pages of the dialog, select either the *Task* or *Resource* option, depending on which type of object you want to rename.
3. Select the object on either the right side or the left side of the dialog and then click the *Rename* button. Project 2013 displays the *Rename* dialog shown in Figure 9 - 29.

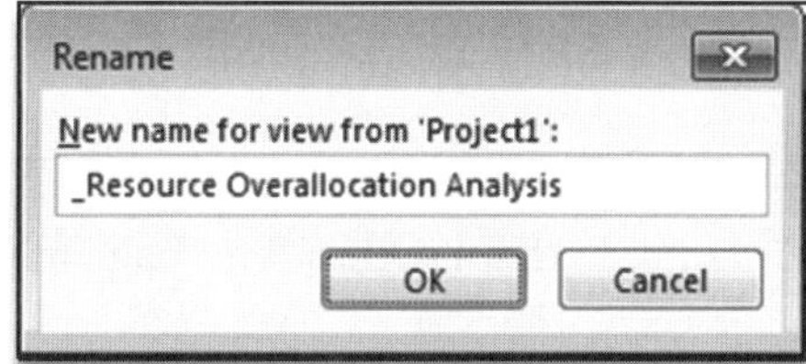

Figure 9 - 29: Rename dialog

4. Enter the new name for the object.

5. Click the *OK* button.
6. Click the *Close* button when finished.

To delete a custom object that you no longer need, complete the following steps in the *Organizer* dialog:

1. Select the appropriate tab in the *Organizer* dialog for the type of object you want to delete.
2. On the *Tables, Filters,* and *Groups* pages of the dialog, select either the *Task* or *Resource* option, depending on which type of object you want to delete.
3. Select the object on either the right side or the left side of the dialog and then click the *Delete* button. Project 2013 displays the confirmation dialog shown in Figure 9 - 30.

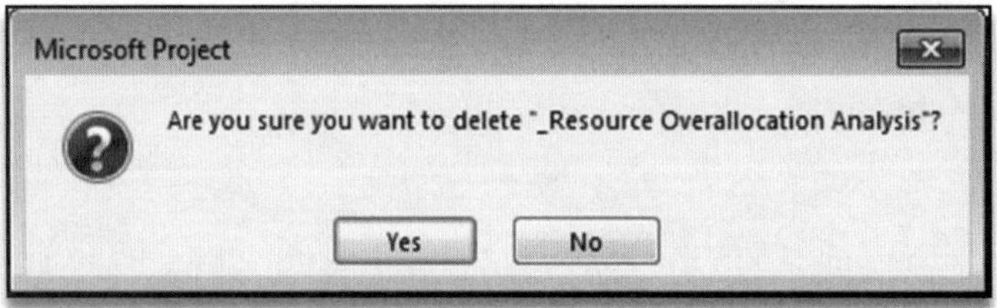

Figure 9 - 30: Deletion confirmation dialog

4. Click the *Yes* button to delete the object.
5. Click the *Close* button when finished.

Warning: When you delete or rename a custom object, there is no *Undo* command to reverse your action. If you accidentally delete or rename a custom object, the only way to recover the original is to open a project containing the original object (if such a project even exists), and use the *Organizer* dialog to copy the object back to the Global.mpt file.

Hands On Exercise

Exercise 9 - 7

Use the *Organizer* dialog to view the new custom objects created in Exercises 9-2 through 9-6.

1. Return to the **Training Advisor 09.mpp** sample file.
2. Click the *File* tab, click the *Info* tab in the *Backstage,* and then click the *Organizer* button.
3. If necessary, click the *Views* tab to display the *Views* page in the *Organizer* dialog.

Notice the new *_Dependency Analysis* and *_Duration Slippage* views in the list on the **left side** of the *Organizer* dialog (in the Global.mpt file) and in the list on the **right side** of the dialog (in the **Training Advisor 09.mpp** sample file).

4. Click the *Tables* tab in the *Organizer* dialog.

Notice the new *_Duration* table in the lists on both sides of the dialog.

5. Click the *Filters* tab in the *Organizer* dialog.

Notice the new *_Duration Variance > 0d* filter in the lists on both sides of the dialog.

6. Click the *Groups* tab in the *Organizer* dialog.

Notice the new *_Duration Variance* group in the lists on both sides of the dialog.

7. Click the *View* tab again in the *Organizer* dialog.
8. In the list of views on the **right side** of the dialog (in the **Training Advisor 09.mpp** sample file), select the *_Dependency Analysis* view, and then click the *Rename* button.
9. In the *Rename* dialog, enter the new name *_Dependency Relationships* and click the *OK* button.
10. In the list of views on the **right side** of the dialog (in the **Training Advisor 09.mpp** file), select the *Copy of Gantt Chart* view, and then click the *Delete* button.
11. In the confirmation dialog, click the *Yes* button to confirm the deletion.
12. Click the *Close* button to close the *Organizer* dialog.
13. Click the *Back* button (large left-arrow button) again to exit the *Backstage*.
14. Save but **do not** close the **Training Advisor 09.mpp** sample file.

Revising a Project Plan

After completing variance analysis, you may need to revise your project plan to bring it "back on track" against its original goals, objectives, and schedule. There are a number of strategies for revising a project plan, but each one requires careful consideration before you make the revision. You should perform a "what-if" analysis before making plan revisions, especially if you need formal approval to make the revisions.

Project 2013 offers a number of methods for revising a project plan. These methods include:

- Add resources to *Effort Driven* tasks to shorten the duration of the task.
- Ask project team members to work overtime or on weekends.
- Increase project team availability for your project.
- Modify dependencies, including reducing or removing *Lag* time, or adding *Lead* time.
- Reduce the scope of the project.
- Renegotiate the project finish date.

Potential Problems with Revising a Plan

Prior to employing any of the preceding techniques, you should be aware of potential problems that may arise when you implement the revisions. Some of the potential problems include:

- Adding resources to an *Effort Driven* task can increase the total work on the task due to increased communication needs between the team members.
- Asking team members to work overtime on a regular basis can increase your employee turnover rate.
- Increasing team member availability for your project reduces their availability for other projects, potentially causing those projects to slip.
- Reducing *Lag* time on task dependencies can create an overly optimistic project schedule.
- Adding *Lead* time on task dependencies can create a scheduling crisis when the predecessor task must finish completely, thus negating the intent of adding the *Lead* time.
- The scope of your project may be non-negotiable.
- The finish date of your project may be non-negotiable.

Hands On Exercise

Exercise 9 - 8

Revise the Training Advisor Rollout project by adding resources and adjusting resource availability to bring it "back on track" against its original baseline schedule.

1. Return to the **Training Advisor 09.mpp** sample file.
2. Click the *View* tab to display the *View* ribbon, if necessary.
3. In the *Task Views* section of the *View* ribbon, click the *Gantt Chart* pick list button, and then select the *Tracking Gantt* view.
4. In the *Split View* section of the *View* ribbon, select the *Details* checkbox.

Information: The temporary combination view you just created (*Tracking Gantt* view in the top pane and *Task Form* view in the bottom pane) is an excellent view to use when revising your project. This view shows you the immediate result of each revision compared against the original project baseline schedule.

5. In the *Zoom* section of the *View* ribbon, click the *Timescale* pick list, and select the *Weeks* item to zoom to the *Months Over Weeks* level of zoom.

Due to commitments to his Help Desk work, *Mike Andrews* is only able to work half-time on the *Verify Connectivity* task. You negotiate with his functional manager to "borrow" *Mike Andrews* to work three-quarter time on this task to complete it sooner. You now owe *Mike Andrew's* functional manager a **big favor** in return!

6. Select task ID #24, the *Verify Connectivity* task.

7. Scroll your *Tracking Gantt* chart to the right so that you can see the Gantt bar for the selected task.
8. In the *Task Form* pane, increase the *Units* value for *Mike Andrews* to *75%*, and then click the *OK* button.

Notice that Project 2013 shortens the *Duration* value of this task to *6.67 days*. Remember that on a *Fixed Units* task, when you change the *Units* value, the software always recalculates the *Duration* value of the task.

9. In the *Task Form* pane, click the *Next* button to select task ID #25, the *Resolve Connectivity Errors* task.
10. Scroll your *Tracking Gantt* chart to the right so that you can see the Gantt bar for the selected task.
11. In the *Task Form* pane, click the first blank row below *Terry Uland*.
12. In the *Task Form* pane, add *Jeff Holly* with a *Units* value of *25%* (**do not** enter a value in the *Work* field) and click the *OK* button.
13. To account for the increased communication needs, add *4h* of extra work in the *Work* field for each *Work* resource and then click the *OK* button. You should now see *20 hours* of *Work* assigned to each resource.
14. In the *Split View* section of the *View* ribbon, **deselect** the *Details* checkbox to close the *Task Form* pane and return to a single-pane *Tracking Gantt* view.

If you compare the project's current schedule (red Gantt bar) to its original baseline schedule (dark gray Gantt bar) for the *Resolve Connectivity Errors* task, your project should appear slightly **ahead** of schedule.

15. In the *Task Views* section of the *View* ribbon, click the *Gantt Chart* pick list button, and then select the *Gantt Chart* view.
16. Save but **do not** close the **Training Advisor 09.mpp** sample file.

Using a Change Control Process

Change control is the process of managing requested changes in your project. Change requests can arise from a variety of sources, including your customer, your project sponsor, your project stakeholders, your company's executives, your fellow project managers, and even from your project team members. Because each change can result in schedule slippage and cost overruns, it is important that you manage all changes in your project. Remember the old project management saying, "Either you manage change, or change manages you!"

Your change control process should identify and maximize the benefits of change, and should avoid all changes that offer no benefit to the project or that impact the project negatively. Document your change management process in both the Statement of Work document and in the "rules of engagement" with your project sponsor and/or client. Following is an example of a change management process:

- Use a paper or electronic change request form to initiate the change request.
- Perform an impact analysis to assess the impact of the change on the project. Determine who does the impact analysis and how they report the results.

- Calculate the cost of the impact analysis and determine who pays for it. Remember that an impact analysis is never free!
- Enlist the support of an executive in your organization with the authority to accept or reject the change request.
- Apply a procedure for implementing an approved change request.
- In your project plan, indicate the tasks you changed or added because of the change request.

Inserting New Tasks in a Project

The most common change request is to add new tasks to a project. When you insert a new task between two dependent tasks, the *Autolink* feature of Project 2013 determines whether the software automatically adds dependency links to the new task. If you **disabled** the *Autolink* feature in the *Project Options* dialog, per my directions in Module 04, *Project Definition,* the software does not automatically link the new task to the existing tasks in the project. However, if you **enabled** the *Autolink* feature, then Project 2013 handles the task linking operation as follows when you insert a new task between two dependent tasks:

- If the dependent tasks have a Finish-to-Start (FS) dependency, the software automatically links the new task to the existing tasks using the Finish-to-Start FS dependency.
- If the dependent tasks have any other type of dependency (SS, FF, or SF), then Project 2013 **does not** automatically link the new task to the existing tasks. Instead, the software leaves the new task unlinked.

Figure 9 - 31 shows a sample project containing four task pairs, with each task pair linked using a different dependency type. After inserting a new task in each task pair (by right-clicking and selecting the *Insert Task* item on the shortcut menu), you can see how Project 2013 uses the *Autolink* feature as described above. Notice that the software automatically links the new task inserted between *Task A* and *Task C* because these two tasks have an FS dependency, but does not link the new task in the other three task pairs.

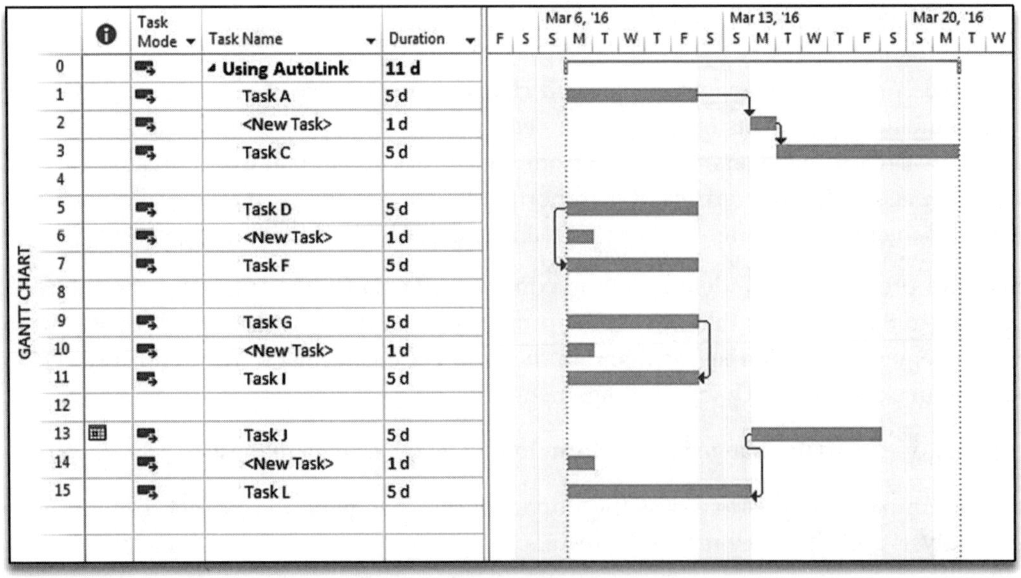

		Task Mode	Task Name	Duration
0			Using AutoLink	11 d
1			Task A	5 d
2			<New Task>	1 d
3			Task C	5 d
4				
5			Task D	5 d
6			<New Task>	1 d
7			Task F	5 d
8				
9			Task G	5 d
10			<New Task>	1 d
11			Task I	5 d
12				
13			Task J	5 d
14			<New Task>	1 d
15			Task L	5 d

Figure 9 - 31: Autolink behavior

Best Practice: Because you should always make task dependency decisions, and not the software, MsProjectExperts recommends that you **disable** the *Autolink* feature. If this is not possible due to corporate policy, then break the task dependency links on the tasks in the section where you intend to insert a new task. After inserting the new task, establish appropriate task dependencies for the tasks in that section of your project.

If you already enabled the *Autolink* feature, you can disable this feature of Project 2013 by clicking the *File* tab and then clicking the *Options* tab in the *Backstage*. In the *Project Options* dialog, select the *Schedule* tab. In the *Scheduling options for this project* section, **deselect** the *Autolink inserted or moved tasks* option. To disable the *Autolink* feature for all new projects as well, click the *Scheduling options for this project* pick list and select the *All New Projects* item. **Deselect** the *Autolink inserted or moved tasks* option again, and then click the *OK* button.

Best Practice: When you add new tasks to a project through a change control process, MsProjectExperts recommends that you format the new tasks with a unique color. You can format the font, the cell background color, and/or the Gantt bar color, as needed. Keep in mind that these formatting changes are visible only in the view in which you apply the formatting.

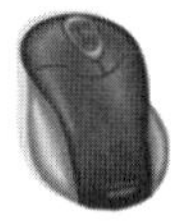

Hands On Exercise

Exercise 9 - 9

While working on the *Create Training Module 03* task, *Ruth Andrews* believes the course training materials need one additional module. She requests that you add a new task named *Create Training Module 04* in the *Create Training Materials* section of the project. After reviewing the change request and its impact to the project, you approve the change request.

1. Return to the **Training Advisor 09.mpp** sample file.
2. Click the *Task* tab to display the *Task* ribbon.
3. Select task ID #33, the *Training Materials Created* milestone task, and then press the **Insert** key on your computer keyboard.
4. In the new blank row, enter the name *Create Training Module 04* and enter a *Duration* value of *5 days* for the new task.

Because you disabled the *Autolink* feature in this project, notice that Project 2013 **does not** automatically link the new task with the other tasks in the *Create Training Materials* section. This means that you have full control over the task linking process.

5. Select task IDs #32-34, from the *Create Training Module 03* task to the *Training Materials Created* milestone task, and then click the *Unlink Tasks* button in the *Schedule* section of the *Task* ribbon.
6. With task IDs #32-24 still selected, click the *Link Tasks* button to link the three selected tasks with a default Finish-to-Start (FS) dependency.

7. Click the *View* tab to display the *View* ribbon.
8. In the *Split View* section of the *View* ribbon, select the *Details* checkbox.
9. In the *Gantt Chart* pane, select task ID #33, the new *Create Training Module 04* task.
10. In the *Task Form* pane, select *Ruth Andrews*, enter a *Units* value of *100%*, and then click the *OK* button to assign her to the new task.
11. In the *Split View* section of the *View* ribbon, **deselect** the *Details* checkbox to return to the single-pane *Gantt Chart* view.
12. Double-click task ID #33, the new *Create Training Module 04* task, and then click the *Notes* tab in the *Task Information* dialog.
13. Click the *Bulleted List* button and then enter the following note:

    2/10/16 – New task added through change control at request of Ruth Andrews.

14. Click the *OK* button to close the *Task Information* dialog.
15. Click the gray row header for task ID #33 to select the entire task row for the new task, and then click the *Task* tab to display the *Task* ribbon.
16. In the *Font* section of the *Task* ribbon, click the *Background Color* pick list and select the *Orange, Lighter 60%* item in the *Theme Colors* section of the pick list.
17. Select any other task to see the cell background color applied to the new task.
18. Save but **do not** close the **Training Advisor 09.mpp** sample file.

Updating the Project Baseline

After you add new tasks to your project through change control, you must update the baseline for your project. There are a number of methodologies you can use for updating a baseline, including the following:

- Rebaseline all tasks in the project using the default *Baseline* set of fields. This method destroys all variance that existed in the project before you added the new tasks, and makes the project appear perfectly on schedule.
- Back up your current baseline into one of the ten additional sets of baseline fields (the *Baseline 1* through *Baseline 10* sets of fields), and then rebaseline your entire project using the default *Baseline* set of fields. This approach maintains the historical record shown in the original baseline for the project, but destroys all variance that existed in the project before you added the new tasks.
- Back up your current baseline into one of the ten additional sets of baseline fields, and then baseline only the new tasks in the project using the default *Baseline* set of fields. Project 2013 offers you the option to baseline only the new tasks without rolling up the baseline data to summary tasks, or to baseline the new tasks and roll up the baseline values to each summary task to which the new tasks are subtasks, including the Project Summary Task (Row 0).
- Back up your original baseline into one of the ten additional sets of baseline fields, and then baseline only unstarted tasks using the default *Baseline* set of fields. This approach maintains the historical record

shown in the original baseline for the project, maintains the variance recorded on all completed and in-progress tasks, but sets a new baseline for all unstarted tasks.

- Baseline all tasks in the project using one of the ten additional sets of baseline fields (the *Baseline 1* through *Baseline 10* sets of fields). If you want to use this technique, you must change the baseline Project 2013 uses to calculate variance. You must also change how the software displays the baseline schedule, shown by the dark gray Gantt bars in the *Tracking Gantt* view of your project.

Information: The default *Baseline* set of fields includes the following fields: *Baseline Start, Baseline Finish, Baseline Duration, Baseline Work, and Baseline Cost*. The ten additional sets of baselines, named *Baseline 1* through *Baseline 10*, include a corresponding set of fields. For example, the *Baseline1* set of fields includes the following fields: *Baseline 1 Start, Baseline 1 Finish, Baseline 1 Duration, Baseline 1 Work*, and *Baseline 1 Cost*.

Backing Up an Original Baseline

Before you update your baseline after a change control procedure, it is wise to back up the current baseline data stored in the default *Baseline* set of fields. This is true, regardless of whether you rebaseline the entire project, or only baseline selected tasks or unstarted tasks. As you know by now, Project 2013 offers you 11 sets of fields in which to save baseline data. These sets of fields include the default *Baseline* set of fields, plus the *Baseline 1* through *Baseline 10* sets. You can use any of these ten sets of alternate baseline fields to back up the current baseline before you rebaseline your project.

To back up your current baseline values, complete the following steps:

1. Click the *Project* tab to display the *Project* ribbon.
2. In the *Schedule* section of the *Project* ribbon, click the *Set Baseline* pick list button, and then select the *Set Baseline* item. Project 2013 displays the *Set Baseline* dialog shown in Figure 9 - 32.

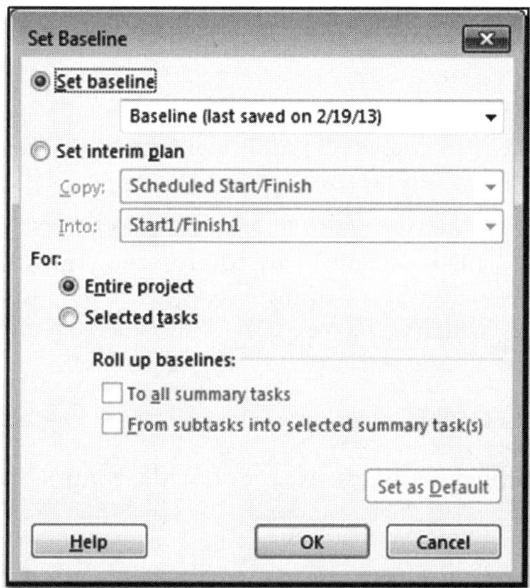

Figure 9 - 32: Set Baseline dialog

3. In the *Set Baseline* dialog, select the *Set interim plan* option.
4. Click the *Copy* pick list and select the *Baseline* item.

5. Click the *Into* pick list and select the next available set of baseline fields into which you want to back up the current baseline of the project, as shown in Figure 9 - 33.

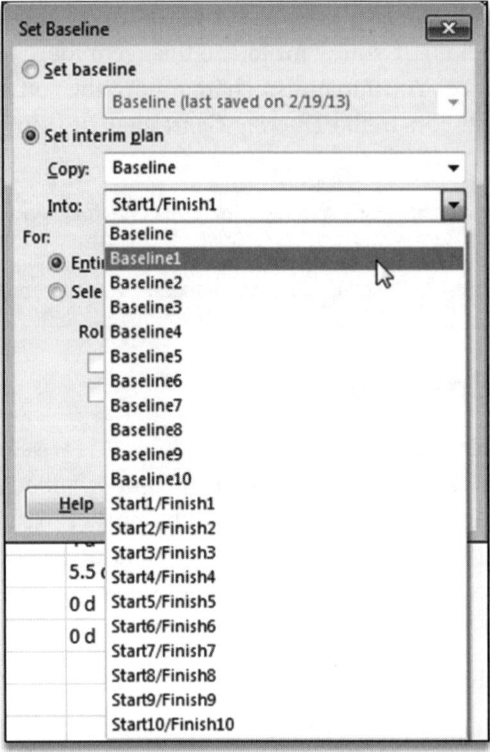

Figure 9 - 33: Backup the current baseline into the Baseline 1 set of fields

6. In the *For:* section of the dialog, leave the *Entire project* option selected.
7. Click the *OK* button.

When you use this procedure, Project 2013 copies all baseline information from the *Baseline* set of fields to the set of fields for the alternate baseline. For example, if you select the *Baseline 1* set of fields in the *Into* pick list, the software copies the values for every task in the *Baseline Start* field to the *Baseline 1 Start* field, the *Baseline Finish* field to the *Baseline 1 Finish* field, etc. This is a useful way to preserve your original project baseline for historical purposes before you rebaseline your project. You can use this process for up to ten change control procedures, at which point you run out of alternate sets of baseline fields.

Rebaselining the Entire Project

To rebaseline an entire project using the default *Baseline* set of fields, complete the following steps:

1. Click the *Project* tab to display the *Project* ribbon.
2. In the *Schedule* section of the *Project* ribbon, click the *Set Baseline* pick list button, and then select the *Set Baseline* item. Project 2013 displays the *Set Baseline* dialog shown previously in Figure 9 - 32.
3. Leave the *Set baseline* option selected and the *Baseline* value selected in the *Set baseline* pick list.
4. In the *For:* section of the dialog, leave the *Entire project* option selected.
5. Click the *OK* button. Project 2013 displays the confirmation dialog shown in Figure 9 - 34.

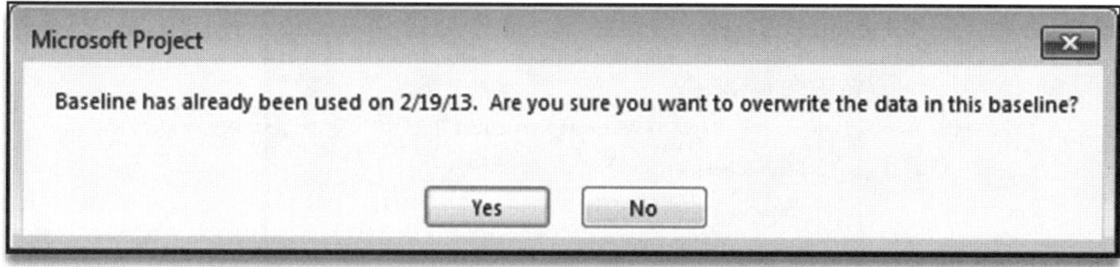

Figure 9 - 34: Overwrite baseline confirmation dialog

6. In the confirmation dialog, click the *Yes* button.

Warning: Using this process, you lose all of the historical variance information in your project, because the process sets the variance values back to *0* in the *Start Variance, Finish Variance, Duration Variance, Work Variance,* and *Cost Variance* fields. Because of this, MSProjectExperts strongly recommends that you **do not** use this methodology for updating the baseline in your project, unless this is the mandatory methodology of your organization.

Baselining Only Selected Tasks

After adding new tasks to the project through a change control procedure, an ideal method for updating the baseline is to baseline **only** the new tasks. Project 2013 offers you two methods for baselining only selected tasks, which are:

- Baseline only the selected tasks, but do not roll up the baseline values to any summary tasks in the project. Using this technique, the data for the new tasks shows as variance against the original project baseline.

- Baseline only the selected tasks, but roll up the baseline values to all summary tasks in the project. When you choose this option, the baseline data rolls up to all summary tasks for which the selected tasks are subtasks, including the Project Summary Task (Row 0). Using this technique, the data for the new tasks does not show as variance against the original project baseline.

To baseline only selected tasks using either of these options, complete the following steps:

1. Select only the new tasks added to the project through the change control procedure.

2. Click the *Project* tab to display the *Project* ribbon.

3. In the *Schedule* section of the *Project* ribbon, click the *Set Baseline* pick list button, and then click the *Set Baseline* item. Project 2013 displays the *Set Baseline* dialog.

4. Leave the *Set baseline* option selected and leave the *Baseline* value selected in the *Set baseline* pick list.

5. In the *For:* section of the dialog, choose the *Selected tasks* option, as shown in Figure 9 - 35.

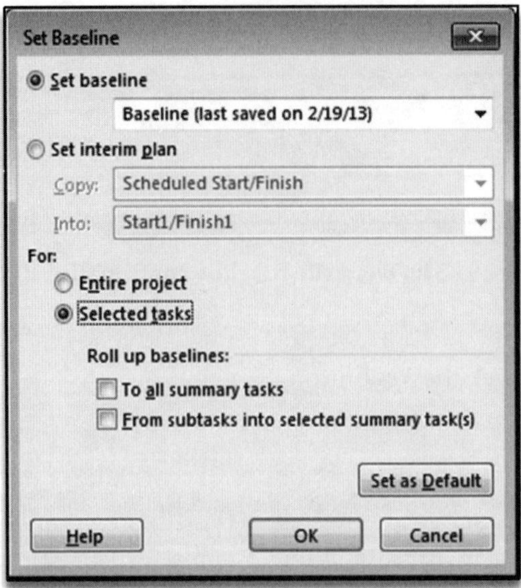

Figure 9 - 35: Set Baseline dialog to baseline selected tasks

6. If you want to roll up the baseline values to summary tasks, choose one of the following options in the *Roll up baselines* section:

    - Select the *To all summary tasks* option if you want the software to roll up the baseline values to all summary tasks for which the selected tasks are subtasks and to the Project Summary Task.

    - Select the *From subtasks into selected summary tasks* option if you want the software to roll up the baseline values to only the summary tasks currently selected (you must select these summary tasks **before** you begin the process of updating the baseline).

Warning: Because of an unfixed bug in the release (RTM) version of Project 2013, selecting the *To all summary tasks* option does not work correctly for tasks whose current *Finish* date is **earlier** than the *Baseline Finish* date. When you choose the *Selected tasks* option along with the *To all summary tasks* option, the summary tasks ignore the original baseline data beyond the new *Finish* date for all subtasks. This means that the new baseline data is **less than expected**. You see this especially for work-related columns, such as *Work*, *Baseline Work*, and *Work Variance* columns. Until Microsoft released a fix for this bug, there is no easy way to work around the bug, short of manually rebaselining tasks which the software did not calculate the baseline data correctly.

Information: If you do not want to roll up the baseline values to any summary tasks, do not select either of the checkboxes in the *Roll up baselines* section of the dialog. This means that data from the selected tasks continues to show as variance against the current project baseline.

7. To save the current options in the *Roll up baselines* section of the dialog, click the *Set as Default* button.

8. Click the *OK* button. Project 2013 warns you about overwriting the baseline data in the confirmation dialog shown previously in Figure 9 - 34.

9. Click the *Yes* button in the confirmation dialog.

Information: In spite of the warning in the dialog, using this procedure does not actually "overwrite" the data in your original baseline. Instead, this procedure "appends" the baseline data from the new tasks to the current project baseline.

Rebaselining Only Unstarted Tasks

After adding new tasks to the project through a change control procedure, the final method for updating a baseline is to rebaseline only unstarted tasks. Using this method yields the following results:

- Your project continues to use the original baseline values on all completed and in-progress tasks, preserving current project variance on these tasks.
- The software updates the baseline on all unstarted tasks and resets their variance values to 0.

To rebaseline only unstarted tasks, complete the following steps:

1. Click the *View* tab to display the *View* ribbon.
2. In the *Data* section of the *View* ribbon, click the *Filter* pick list button, and then select the *More Filters* item. Project 2013 displays the *More Filters* dialog shown in Figure 9 - 36.

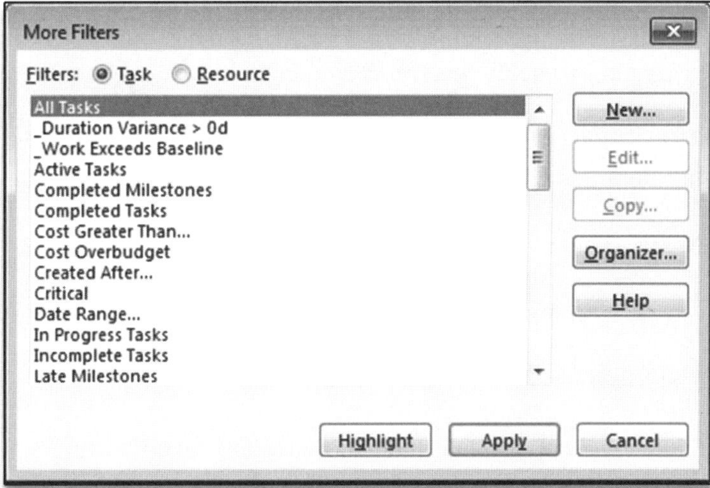

Figure 9 - 36: More Filters dialog

3. In the *More Filters* dialog, select the *Unstarted Tasks* item, and then click the *Apply* button. Project 2013 hides both completed tasks and in-progress tasks, displaying only unstarted tasks.
4. Click the *Select All* button to select all tasks in the project, including summary tasks and the Project Summary Task (Row 0).
5. Click the *Project* tab to display the *Project* ribbon.
6. In the *Schedule* section of the *Project* ribbon, click the *Set Baseline* pick list button, and then select the *Set Baseline* item. Project 2013 displays the *Set Baseline* dialog.
7. Leave the *Set baseline* option selected and leave the *Baseline* value selected in the *Set baseline* pick list.
8. In the *For:* section of the dialog, choose the *Selected tasks* option.
9. **Do not** select either checkbox in the *Roll up baselines* section of the dialog.

10. Click the *OK* button.

11. When the software warns you about overwriting the original baseline, click the *Yes* button in the confirmation dialog.

12. Press the **F3** function key on your computer keyboard to reapply the *[No Filter]* filter and redisplay all tasks in the project.

Hands On Exercise

Exercise 9 - 10

Back up the original project baseline information in the *Baseline 1* set of fields for the Training Advisor Rollout project.

1. Return to the **Training Advisor 09.mpp** sample file.
2. Click the *Project* tab to display the *Project* ribbon.
3. In the *Schedule* section of the *Project* ribbon, click the *Set Baseline* pick list button, and then select the *Set Baseline* item.
4. In the *Set Baseline* dialog, select the *Set interim plan* option.
5. Click the *Copy* pick list and select the *Baseline* item.
6. Click the *Into* pick list and select the *Baseline 1* item.
7. Leave the *Entire project* option selected and then click the *OK* button.
8. Save but **do not** close the **Training Advisor 09.mpp** sample file.

Exercise 9 - 11

Baseline only selected tasks in the Training Advisor Rollout project.

1. Return to the **Training Advisor 09.mpp** sample file.
2. Click the *Task* tab to display the *Task* ribbon.
3. In the *View* section of the *Task* ribbon, click the *Gantt Chart* pick list button, and then select the *Tracking Gantt* view.
4. Select task ID #33, the new *Create Training Module 04* task.

5. In the *Editing* section of the *Task* ribbon, click the *Scroll to Task* button to bring the Gantt bar into view for the new *Create Training Module 04* task.

Notice that Project 2013 displays no baseline schedule (no dark gray Gantt bar) for the new *Create Training Module 04* task. This is because the new task lacks baseline information.

6. Click the *Project* tab to display the *Project* ribbon.

7. In the *Schedule* section of the *Project* ribbon, click the *Set Baseline* pick list button, and then select the *Set Baseline* item.

8. In the *Set Baseline* dialog, leave the *Set baseline* option selected and leave the *Baseline* value selected in the *Set baseline* pick list.

9. In the *For:* section of the dialog, choose the *Selected tasks* option.

10. In the *Roll up baselines* section of the dialog, select the *To all summary tasks* option.

11. Click the *OK* button.

12. When the software warns you about overwriting the current baseline, click the *Yes* button in the confirmation dialog.

Notice in the *Tracking Gantt* chart that Project 2013 now displays the baseline schedule (dark gray Gantt bar) for the new *Create Training Module 04* task.

13. Click the *Task* tab to display the *Task* ribbon.

14. In the *View* section of the *Task* ribbon, click the *Gantt Chart* pick list button, and then select the *Gantt Chart* view.

15. Save but **do not** close the **Training Advisor 09.mpp** sample file.

Rebaselining the Entire Project Using an Alternate Baseline

To rebaseline an entire project using one of the ten alternate sets of baseline fields, such as the *Baseline 1* set of fields, complete the following steps:

1. Click the *Project* tab to display the *Project* ribbon.

2. In the *Schedule* section of the *Project* ribbon, click the *Set Baseline* pick list button, and then select the *Set Baseline* item. Project 2013 displays the *Set Baseline* dialog.

3. In the *Set Baseline* dialog, click the *Set baseline* pick list and choose one of the ten alternate sets of baseline fields, such as the *Baseline 1* item shown in Figure 9 - 37.

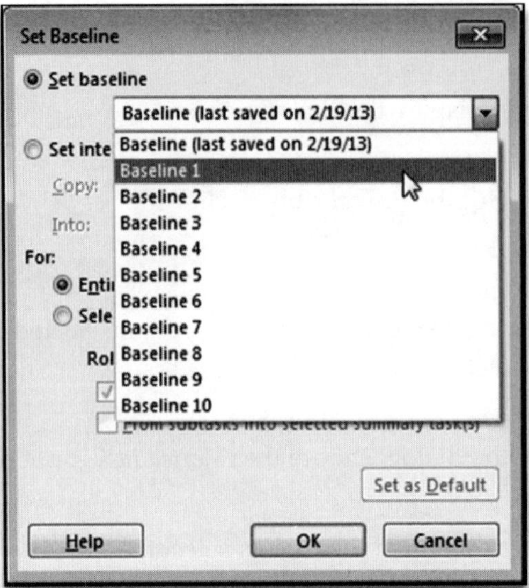

Figure 9 - 37: Set Baseline dialog, select the Baseline 1 set of fields

4. In the *For:* section of the dialog, select the *Entire project* option.

5. Click the *OK* button.

After you rebaseline your project using one of alternate sets of baseline fields, you must change the baseline used by Project 2013 to calculate variance, and you must make this change in two locations in the software. To the baseline used to calculate variance, complete the following steps:

1. Click the *File* tab and then click the *Options* tab in the *Backstage*.

2. In the *Project Options* dialog, click the *Advanced* tab.

3. In the *Earned Value options for this project* section of the dialog, click the *Baseline for Earned Value calculation* pick list, and select the alternate baseline used during the rebaselining process, as shown in Figure 9 - 38.

4. Click the *OK* button.

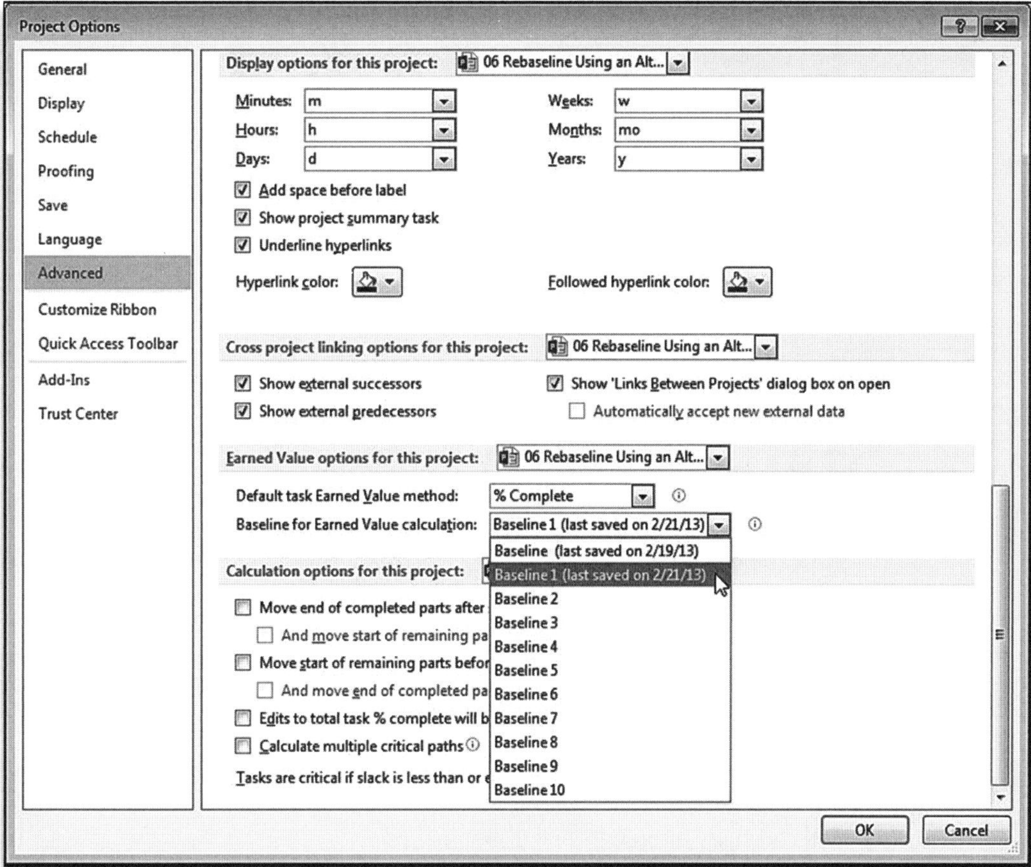

Figure 9 - 38: Select an alternate set of baseline fields

When you change the *Baseline for Earned Value calculation* option in the *Project Options* dialog, you change how Project 2013 calculates variance in your project. After changing this option, the software uses the alternate set of baseline fields to calculate all variance in the project. This affects the *Start Variance, Finish Variance, Duration Variance, Work Variance,* and *Cost Variance* fields, and you see the results in the task *Work, Cost,* and *Variance* tables. For example, if you selected the *Baseline 1* set of fields in step #3 above, the software calculates the values in the *Work Variance* field for every task using the following formula: **Work Variance = Work – Baseline 1 Work.**

In addition to changing the set of baseline fields used to calculate variance in Project 2013, you must also change the baseline schedule shown in the *Tracking Gantt* view. To change this view, complete the following additional set of steps:

1. Click the *Task* tab to display the *Task* ribbon.

2. In the *View* section of the *Task* ribbon, click the *Gantt Chart* pick list button, and then select the *Tracking Gantt* view.

3. Click the *Format* tab to display the *Format* ribbon.

4. In the *Bar Styles* section of the *Format* ribbon, click the *Baseline* pick list button, and then select the alternate baseline used during the rebaselining process, as shown in Figure 9 - 39.

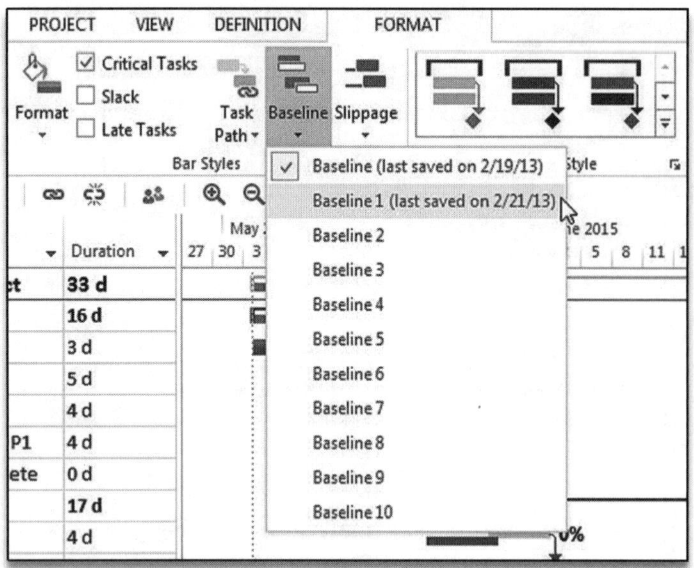

Figure 9 - 39: Select the alternate set of baseline fields for the Tracking Gantt view

Warning: If you want to use this methodology for rebaselining a project using an alternate set of baseline fields, you **must always** complete the steps used to change the baseline used to calculate variance **and** the steps used to show the correct baseline schedule in the *Tracking Gantt* view. If you fail to complete these two extra sets of steps, you cannot analyze project variance accurately, and you do not see the accurate baseline schedule in the *Tracking Gantt* view.

For example, Figure 9 - 40 shows the default *Tracking Gantt* view of a project after the project manager rebaselined the entire project using the *Baseline 1* set of fields. Because the *Tracking Gantt* view still uses the default *Baseline* set of fields to create the gray Gantt bars, the baseline schedule shown with the gray Gantt bars is not correct.

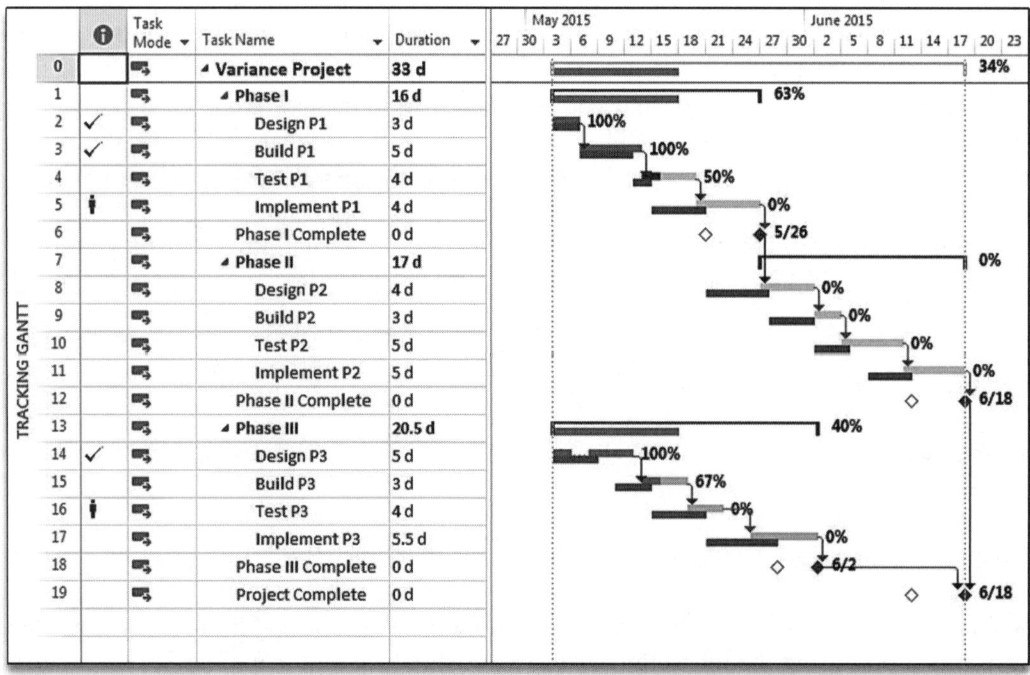

Figure 9 - 40: Tracking Gantt view using the Baseline schedule

Figure 9 - 41 shows the *Tracking Gantt* view after the project manager selected the *Baseline 1* set of fields in the *Baseline* pick list on the *Formatting* ribbon. The *Tracking Gantt* view now uses the *Baseline 1* set of fields to show the baseline schedule, which results in an accurate baseline schedule.

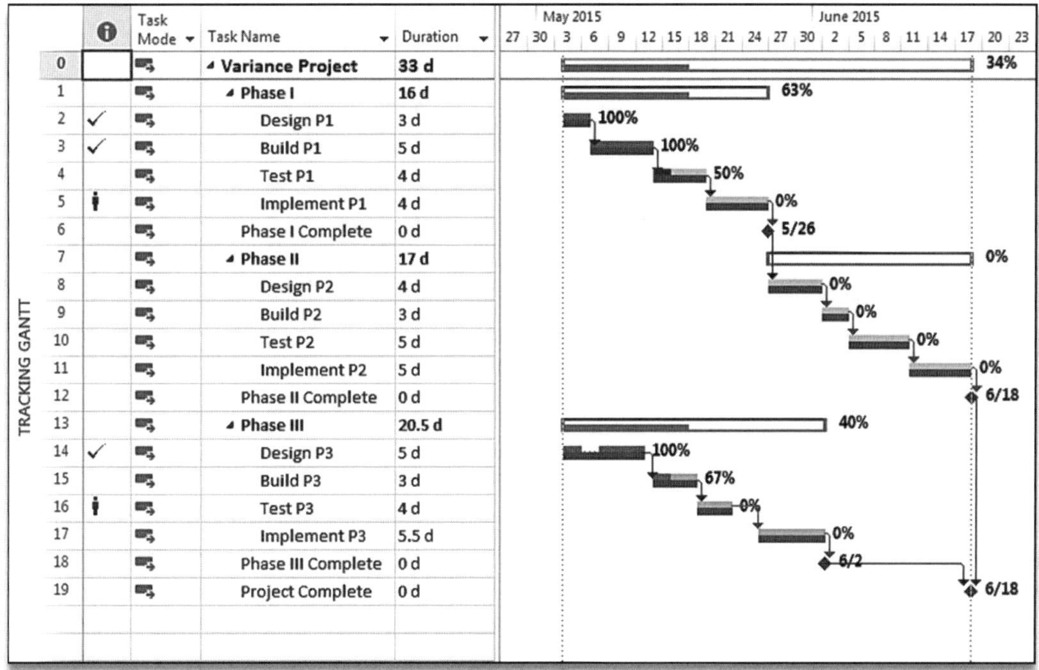

Figure 9 - 41: Tracking Gantt view using the Baseline 1 schedule

Hands On Exercise

Exercise 9 - 12

Rebaseline the entire Training Advisor Rollout project using the *Baseline 2* set of fields.

1. Return to the **Training Advisor 09.mpp** sample file.

2. Click the *Project* tab to display the *Project* ribbon.

3. In the *Schedule* section of the *Project* ribbon, click the *Set Baseline* pick list button, and then select the *Set Baseline* item.

4. In the *Set Baseline* dialog, select the *Set baseline* pick list and select the *Baseline 2* item.

5. In the *For:* section of the dialog, leave the *Entire project* option selected.

6. Click the *OK* button.

7. Save but **do not** close the **Training Advisor 09.mpp** sample file.

Exercise 9 - 13

Configure Project 2013 to use the *Baseline 2* set of fields to calculate variance and to display the *Baseline 2* schedule in the *Tracking Gantt* view.

1. Return to the **Training Advisor 09.mpp** sample file.
2. Click the *File* tab and then click the *Options* item in the *Backstage.*
3. In the *Project Options* dialog, click the *Advanced* tab.
4. In the *Earned Value options for this project* section of the dialog, click the *Baseline for Earned Value calculation* pick list and select the *Baseline* 2 item.
5. Click the *OK* button.
6. Click the *Task* tab to display the *Task* ribbon.
7. In the *View* section of the *Task* ribbon, click the *Gantt Chart* pick list button, and then select the *Tracking Gantt* view.

Notice that the *Tracking Gantt* view shows the incorrect baseline schedule (gray Gantt bars) using the original *Baseline* set of fields.

8. Click the *Format* tab to display the *Format* ribbon.
9. In the *Bar Styles* section of the *Format* ribbon, click the *Baseline* pick list button, and then select the *Baseline* 2 item.

Notice that the *Tracking Gantt* view now shows the correct baseline schedule (gray Gantt bars) using the new *Baseline* 2 set of fields.

10. Save but **do not** close the **Training Advisor 09.mpp** sample file.

Viewing Multiple Baselines

When you use multiple baselines in a project, you can use the *Multiple Baselines Gantt* view to display up to three baselines simultaneously. To apply this special view, complete the following steps:

1. Click the *Task* tab to display the *Task* ribbon.
2. In the *View* section of the *Task* ribbon, click the *Gantt Chart* pick list button, and then select the *More Views* item.
3. In the *More Views* dialog, select the *Multiple Baselines Gantt* view, and then click the *Apply* button.

In the *Multiple Baselines Gantt* view, Project 2013 displays the baseline schedule for only the *Baseline, Baseline 1,* and *Baseline* 2 sets of fields. For each task, the software displays a blue Gantt symbol for the *Baseline* schedule, a red Gantt symbol for the *Baseline 1* schedule, and green Gantt symbol for the *Baseline* 2 schedule.

Hands On Exercise

Exercise 9 - 14

View alternate baseline schedule information in a project.

1. Return to the **Training Advisor 09.mpp** sample file.
2. Click the *Task* tab to display the *Task* ribbon.
3. In the *View* section of the *Task* ribbon, click the *Gantt Chart* pick list button, and then select the *More Views* item.
4. In the *More Views* dialog, select the *Multiple Baselines Gantt* view, and then click the *Apply* button.
5. Select the Project Summary Task (Row 0) and then click the *Scroll to Task* button in the *Editing* section of the *Task* ribbon to scroll the Gantt bars into view.
6. Click the *View* tab to display the *View* ribbon.
7. In the *Zoom* section of the *View* ribbon, click the *Timescale* pick list and select the *Weeks* item.
8. Study the three baseline schedules shown by the three sets of Gantt bars for each task in the project.
9. Save but **do not** close the **Training Advisor 09.mpp** sample file.

Exercise 9 - 15

Configure Project 2013 to use the original *Baseline* set of fields to calculate variance and to display the *Baseline* schedule in the *Tracking Gantt* view.

1. Return to the **Training Advisor 09.mpp** sample file.
2. Click the *File* tab and then click the *Options* item in the *Backstage*.
3. In the *Project Options* dialog, click the *Advanced* tab.
4. In the *Earned Value options for this project* section of the dialog, click the *Baseline for Earned Value calculation* pick list, and select the *Baseline* item.
5. Click the *OK* button.
6. Click the *Task* tab to display the *Task* ribbon.
7. In the *View* section of the *Task* ribbon, click the *Gantt Chart* pick list button, and then select the *Tracking Gantt* view.
8. Click the *Format* tab to display the *Format* ribbon.
9. In the *Bar Styles* section of the *Format* ribbon, click the *Baseline* pick list button, and then select the *Baseline* item.

10. Click the *Task* tab to display the *Task* ribbon.
11. In the *View* section of the *Task* ribbon, click the *Gantt Chart* pick list button, and then select the *Gantt Chart* view.
12. Save and close the **Training Advisor 09.mpp** sample file.

Module 10

Basic Project Reporting

Learning Objectives

After completing this module, you will be able to:

- Understand reporting features in Project 2013
- Use enhanced copy and paste between Office applications
- Use and format the Timeline view
- Create a custom view and table by modifying and saving an existing view and table
- Reset a customized view to its default settings
- Print views
- Format the Gantt Chart view using multiple methods
- Format the Team Planner view and the Task Usage view
- Attach documentation to the project
- Export a Project 2013 image to another application

Inside Module 10

Reporting in Project 2013

During project execution, you must report project progress to one or more stakeholder groups. These typically include your project sponsor, your customer, your company executives, and even your project team. Project 2013 offers you a number of ways to report basic information about your project:

- Copy and paste Project 2013 data to another Office application.
- Use the *Timeline* view in combination with the *Gantt Chart* view.
- Create custom views.
- Modify default views.
- Print default and custom views.
- Attach documents to the project file.
- Export a project image to another application.

I discuss each of these reporting options separately.

Using Enhanced Copy and Paste

As part of your reporting process during the execution stage of a project, you may need to copy and paste project data to another application. When you copy data from Project 2013 and paste the data into another application in the Office family, the paste operation works as follows:

- The Office application pastes the Project 2013 data in a table format that you can modify as needed.
- The Office application indents tasks to reflect their hierarchy in the project.
- The Office application retains field names as column headers for each column of data.
- The Office application maintains complete text formatting and cell background color formatting. The text formatting includes the fonts, font sizes, font styles, and font colors, as well as other formatting such as bold, italic, underline, strikethrough, etc.

For example, Figure 10 - 1 shows a task list in a project. Notice the work breakdown structure in my project, along with the tasks highlighted using cell background formatting. I select the task information from the *Task Name* column through the *Finish* column, and from the *Project Summary Task* (Row 0) to the *Project Complete* milestone task, and then copy the information to the Windows clipboard.

		Task Mode	Task Name	Duration	Start	Finish
0			**New Course Development**	**63 d**	**6/1/15**	**8/27/15**
1			**Phase I**	**13 d**	**6/1/15**	**6/17/15**
2			Identify learning requirements	4 d	6/1/15	6/4/15
3			Determine target audience	2 d	6/5/15	6/8/15
4			Develop learning objectives	4 d	6/9/15	6/12/15
5			Develop course outline	3 d	6/15/15	6/17/15
6			Phase I Complete	0 d	6/17/15	6/17/15
7			**Phase II**	**31 d**	**6/18/15**	**7/31/15**
8			Write course manual	15 d	6/18/15	7/8/15
9			Edit course manuals	5 d	7/9/15	7/15/15
10			Create sample files	5 d	7/16/15	7/22/15
11			Test sample files and exercises	2 d	7/23/15	7/24/15
12			Create instructor materials	5 d	7/27/15	7/31/15
13			Phase II Complete	0 d	7/31/15	7/31/15
14			**Phase III**	**19 d**	**8/3/15**	**8/27/15**
15			Test beta classes	3 d	8/3/15	8/5/15
16			Revise content based on feedback	10 d	8/6/15	8/19/15
17			Launch marketing campaign	1 d	8/20/15	8/20/15
18			Schedule new classes	5 d	8/21/15	8/27/15
19			Phase III Complete	0 d	8/27/15	8/27/15
20			Project Complete	0 d	8/27/15	8/27/15

GANTT CHART

Figure 10 - 1: Task list in Project 2013

After opening a new blank document in Word, I paste the contents of the Windows clipboard directly into the document shown in Figure 10 - 2. Notice how Word pastes the project data into a table with the correct column headers at the top of each column. Notice also how Word maintains the level of indenture for each task, along with the cell background formatting.

Task Name	Duration	Start	Finish
New Course Development	**63 d**	**6/1/15**	**8/27/15**
Phase I	**13 d**	**6/1/15**	**6/17/15**
Identify learning requirements	4 d	6/1/15	6/4/15
Determine target audience	2 d	6/5/15	6/8/15
Develop learning objectives	4 d	6/9/15	6/12/15
Develop course outline	3 d	6/15/15	6/17/15
Phase I Complete	0 d	6/17/15	6/17/15
Phase II	**31 d**	**6/18/15**	**7/31/15**
Write course manual	15 d	6/18/15	7/8/15
Edit course manuals	5 d	7/9/15	7/15/15
Create sample files	5 d	7/16/15	7/22/15
Test sample files and exercises	2 d	7/23/15	7/24/15
Create instructor materials	5 d	7/27/15	7/31/15
Phase II Complete	0 d	7/31/15	7/31/15
Phase III	**19 d**	**8/3/15**	**8/27/15**
Test beta classes	3 d	8/3/15	8/5/15
Revise content based on feedback	10 d	8/6/15	8/19/15
Launch marketing campaign	1 d	8/20/15	8/20/15
Schedule new classes	5 d	8/21/15	8/27/15
Phase III Complete	0 d	8/27/15	8/27/15
Project Complete	0 d	8/27/15	8/27/15

Figure 10 - 2: Project 2013 task data pasted into Word

When you copy data from an application in the Office family, and paste the data into Project 2013, the paste operation retains custom text formatting and cell background color formatting. Depending on the Office application, the paste operation may also retain other information. For example, if you paste a bulleted list from Word into the *Task Name* field in Project 2013, the paste operation converts the bulleted tasks into subtasks of the first task, making it a summary task.

Warning: Be very wary about pasting data from PowerPoint into your Project 2013 files. Keep in mind that the paste operation retains complete text formatting information, including bullets and the very large font sizes used in PowerPoint.

Figure 10 - 3 shows a project task list created in Word. Notice that I use several levels of bulleted text to indicate phase and deliverable summary tasks. Notice that I also use the text highlight feature in the application to highlight the *Deliverable 1 Complete, Deliverable 2 Complete,* and *Phase I Complete* tasks. I select and copy the entire task list to the Windows clipboard.

- PHASE I
  - Deliverable 1
    - Design
    - Build
    - Test
    - Implement
  - Deliverable 1 Complete
  - Deliverable 2
    - Design
    - Build
    - Test
    - Implement
  - Deliverable 2 Complete
- Phase I Complete

Figure 10 - 3: Task list created in Word

After creating a new blank project in Project 2013, I paste the contents of the Windows clipboard directly into the first blank line of the project, as shown in Figure 10 - 4. Notice how Project 2013 uses the various levels of the bulleted text to create summary tasks and subtasks, and that the software applies cell background formatting to the three milestone tasks. Notice also that Project 2013 uses the same font and font size settings from Word. After pasting text from another Office application, you may need to change the font and font size settings on the tasks in your Project 2013 plan.

Information: In Project 2013, the default font for tasks is the *Calibri* font, and the default font size for tasks is *11 point*. The default font for the Project Summary Task (Row 0) is the *Calibri* font, and the default font size is *12 point*. The software also applies the *Bold* font style to summary tasks and to the Project Summary Task.

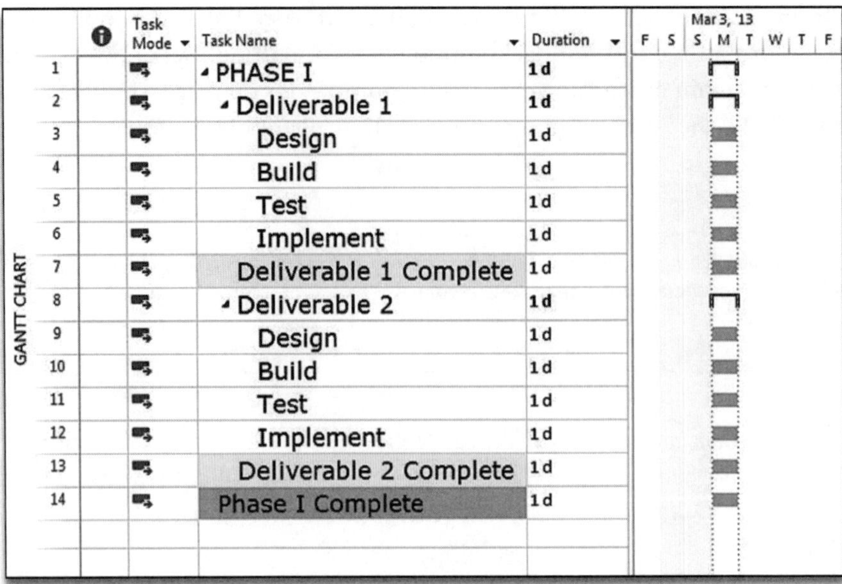

Figure 10 - 4: Task list from Word pasted into Project 2013

Information: The fastest way to set the default *Font, Font Style*, and *Font Size* settings for tasks in your Project 2013 file is to click the *Gantt Chart* pick list button on the *Task* ribbon and to select the *Reset to Default* item on the pick list. In the confirmation dialog, click the *Yes* button to reset all default settings for task fonts, including the *Font, Font Style*, and *Font Size* settings. After completing these two steps, you lose the cell background formatting applied to any tasks, and you must reapply it if you want to retain the formatting.

Hands On Exercise

Exercise 10 - 1

Copy and paste task data from Project 2013 to another Office application.

1. Open the **Project Navigation 2013.mpp** sample file.
2. Click the *Task* tab to display the *Task* ribbon.
3. Drag the split bar to the right of the *Finish* column so that you can see the *Start* and *Finish* columns completely.
4. Select all of the tasks in the *Pre-Renovation* phase of the project (task IDs #1-17), including the information in the *Task Name, Duration, Start,* and *Finish* columns.
5. In the *Clipboard* section of the *Task* ribbon, click the *Copy* button.
6. Launch your Word application, preferably either the 2010 or 2013 version of Word.
7. In a new blank Word document, click the *Paste* button.

Notice how the Word application pastes the Project 2013 data into a table, correctly labels each column, and maintains the levels of indenture for every task.

8. Close the Word document without saving it and leave the Word application open.
9. Return to your Project 2013 application window.
10. Click the *File* tab and then click the *Close* tab in the *Backstage* to close the **Project Navigation 2013.mpp** sample file without saving it.
11. Press the **Escape** key on your computer keyboard to exit the *Backstage* and return to the main Project 2013 user interface.

Exercise 10 - 2

Copy and paste task data from an Office application to Project 2013.

1. Return to your Word application window.
2. Open the **Three Phase Task List.docx**sample file.
3. Select all of the tasks shown in the sample document.
4. In the *Clipboard* section of the *Home* ribbon, click the *Copy* button.
5. Return to your Project 2013 application window.
6. Click the *File* tab and then click the *New* tab in the *Backstage*.
7. On the *New* page, click the *Blank Project* template to create a new blank project.
8. In the first blank row, select the cell in the *Task Name* column.
9. In the *Clipboard* section of the *Task* ribbon, click the *Paste* button.

Notice how Project 2013 pastes the Word data into the project, creating summary tasks and subtasks, while maintaining the font formatting for each task.

10. In the *View* section of the *Task* ribbon, click the *Gantt Chart* pick list button, and select the *Reset to Default* item.
11. When prompted in a warning dialog, click the *Yes* button to reset the task list to the default settings for the *Gantt Chart* view.
12. Widen the *Task Name* column, as needed, and then drag the split bar to the right edge of the *Duration* column.
13. Click the *File* tab and then click the *Save As* tab in the *Backstage*.
14. On the *Save As* page in the *Backstage*, select the *Computer* icon, and then select the name of your student files folder in the *Recent Folders* list.
15. In the *Save As* dialog, enter *Three Phase Project* in the *File name* field, and then click the *Save* button.
16. Click the *File* tab and then click the *Close* tab in the *Backstage*.

17. Press the **Escape** key on your computer keyboard to exit the *Backstage* and return to the main Project 2013 user interface.

18. Return to your Word application window.

19. Click the *File* tab and then click the *Close* tab to close the **Three Phase Task List.docx** sample file without saving it.

20. Exit your Word application and return to your Project 2013 application window.

Using the Timeline View

Project 2013 includes one default *Timeline* view that displays the current project schedule using a timeline presentation similar to what you see in Microsoft Visio or in any other timeline software application. You can modify the default *Timeline* view to show your current project schedule according to your reporting requirements and you can create new *Timeline* views as needed. You can also export any *Timeline* view to other Office applications, such as PowerPoint.

The *Gantt with Timeline* view is the default view for every new project you create in Project 2013. In fact, you see this view every time you launch the software, because the software always creates a new blank project on application launch. The *Gantt with Timeline* view is a combination view that shows the *Timeline* view in the top pane and the *Gantt Chart* view in the bottom pane. Figure 10 - 5 shows the *Gantt with Timeline* view applied to an in-progress project.

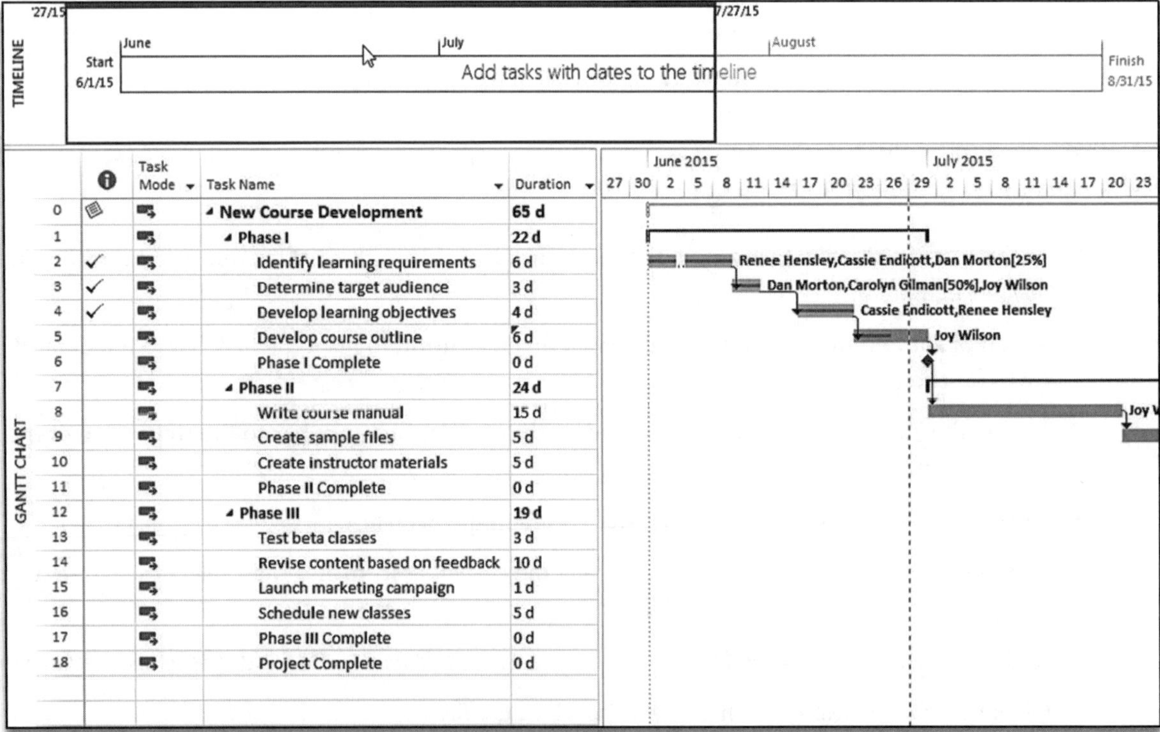

Figure 10 - 5: Gantt with Timeline view for an in-progress project

Information: If you do not see the *Gantt with Timeline* view when you open a project, apply the *Gantt Chart* view and then click the *View* tab. In the *Split View* section of the *View* ribbon, select the *Timeline* checkbox.

Depending on your level of zoom applied in your project, the *Timeline* view shows the following information by default:

- The white *Timeline* bar represents the time span of the entire project, with the project *Start* date displayed on the left end of the bar and the project *Finish* date displayed at the right end of the bar. Notice in Figure 10 - 5 shown previously that the project runs from 6/01/15 to 8/31/15, indicated by the dates on the left and right of the white *Timeline* bar.

- The software divides the *Timeline* bar into date segments consistent with the level of zoom you have currently applied in the *Gantt Chart* pane. Notice in Figure 10 - 5 shown previously that Project 2013 displays tick marks for months across the top of the *Timeline* bar.

- The software indicates the current date with the word *Today* displayed in a green text above the *Timeline* bar and with an green line in the *Timeline* bar.

- The software uses two green vertical lines to show the time span of the project currently visible in the *Gantt Chart* view. These green vertical lines show the beginning and ending dates of this time span. If you float your mouse pointer anywhere between the two green vertical lines, Project 2013 displays a green border around the entire time span, such as you see in Figure 10 - 5 shown previously. The software refers to the thick green border at the top of the *Timeline* view as the *Pan & Zoom* bar.

- The software uses faint shading for the portion of the *Timeline* bar not visible in the *Gantt Chart* view. Figure 10 - 5 shown previously indicates that project information is not visible past 7/27/15 in the *Gantt Chart* view, indicated by the faint shading in the *Timeline* bar after that date.

Information: As you scroll right or left in the *Gantt Chart* view, the *Pan & Zoom* bar scrolls with you to indicate the portion of the timeline currently visible in the *Gantt Chart* pane. Conversely, if you drag the *Pan & Zoom* bar to the left or right, the software scrolls the Gantt chart with you. If you drag the left or right gridline of the *Pan & Zoom* bar to either the right or left, the software zooms the *Timescale* in the *Gantt Chart* view in response.

Adding a Task to the Timeline

To add any task to the *Timeline* view, right-click the name of the task in the task list on the left side of the *Gantt Chart* view and then select the *Add to Timeline* item on the shortcut menu. To add multiple tasks to the *Timeline* view, select a block of tasks, right-click anywhere in the selected block of tasks, and then select the *Add to Timeline* item on the shortcut menu. Project 2013 adds the selected tasks to the *Timeline* view as shown in Figure 10 - 6. Notice that I added the *Phase I, Phase II,* and *Phase III* summary tasks to the *Timeline* view, along with the first three subtasks in the *Phase II* section of the project. By default, the software formats each bar you add to the *Timeline* view using a light blue cell background color.

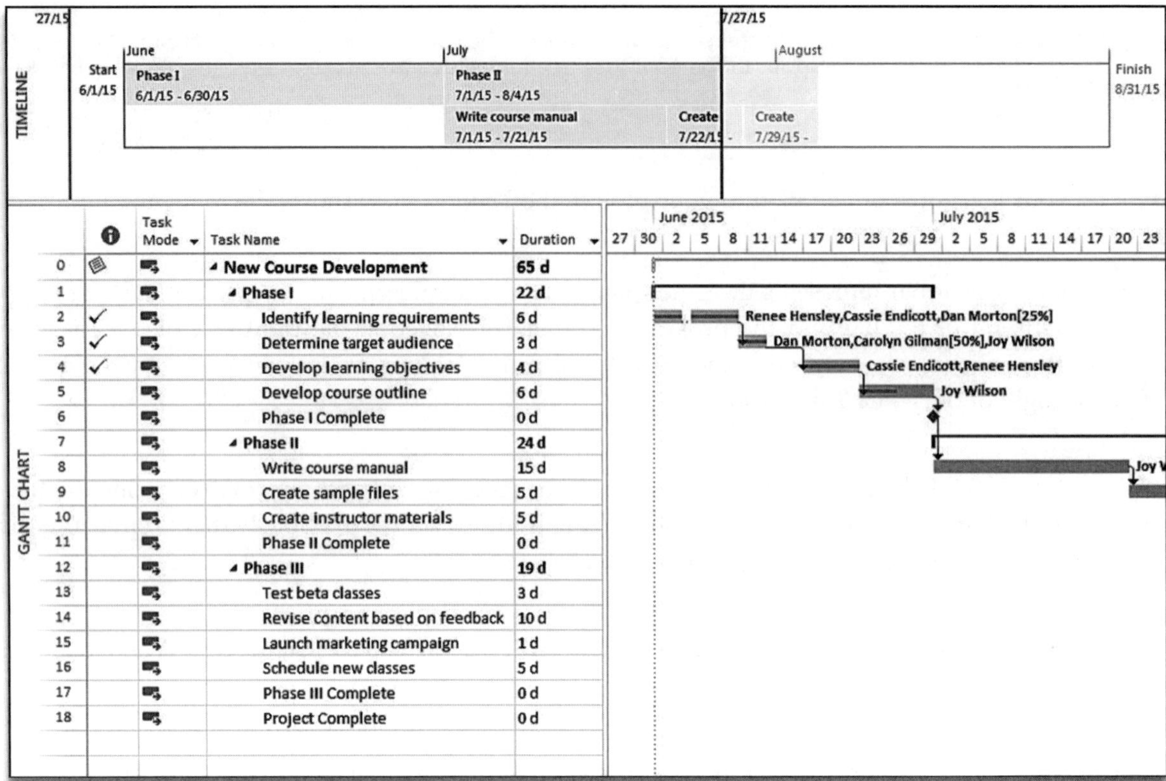

Figure 10 - 6: Tasks added to the Timeline view

Information: You can also add a task in the *Timeline* view by double-clicking the task and then selecting the *Display on Timeline* option on the *General* page of the *Task Information* dialog. If you select multiple tasks, you can add a task in the *Timeline* view by displaying the *Task* ribbon and then clicking the *Information* button in the *Properties* section of the *Task* ribbon. In the *Multiple Task Information* dialog, select the *Display on Timeline* option on the *General* page and click the *OK* button.

After you add tasks to the *Timeline* view, you can rearrange the tasks on the *Timeline* bar using any of the following techniques:

- Drag a task to a new row above or below its current position in the *Timeline* bar.
- Drag a task above or below the *Timeline* bar to display the task as a callout.
- Drag a block of tasks by selecting them while pressing and holding the **Control** key on your keyboard, and then dragging the block of the selected tasks to a new position.
- Right-click any task in the *Timeline* bar and select the *Display as Callout* item on the shortcut menu.
- Drag a new callout from the top of the *Timeline* bar to a position below the *Timeline* bar.
- Convert a callout to a task bar by right-clicking the callout and then selecting the *Display as Bar* item on the shortcut menu.

When you drag tasks into a new position in the *Timeline* bar, or create callouts above or below the *Timeline* bar, Project 2013 adjusts the height of the *Timeline* view automatically to accommodate the new information. For example, Figure 10 - 7 shows my *Timeline* view after I created two callouts, one above the *Timeline* bar and the other below it, and dragged the *Phase II* task and one of its subtasks to a new row in the *Timeline* bar.

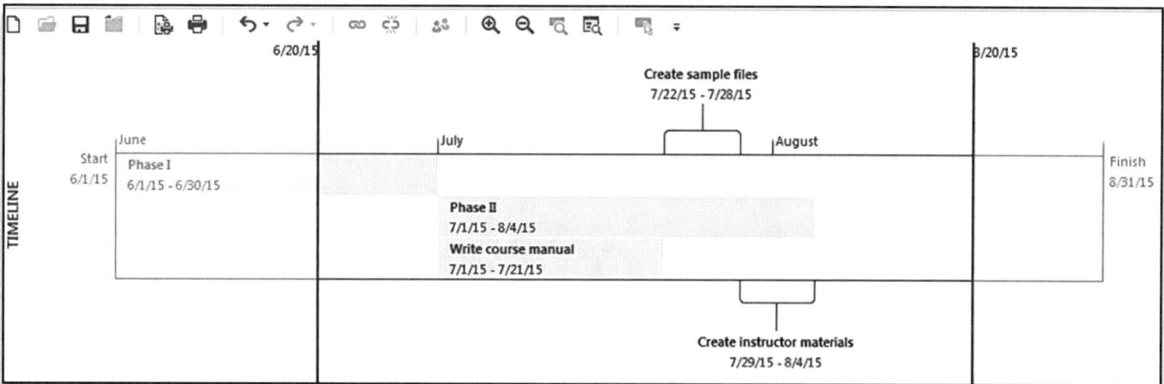

Figure 10 - 7: Tasks shown as callouts in the Timeline view

To remove a task or a callout from the *Timeline* view, right-click the task bar or the callout and then select the *Remove from Timeline* item on the shortcut menu. Project 2013 also allows you to scroll to any task in the *Gantt Chart* pane by right-clicking the task bar or task callout in the *Timeline* pane, and selecting the *Scroll to Selected Task* item on the shortcut menu. The software selects the task in the *Gantt Chart* pane and then scrolls the Gantt chart to the beginning of the selected task, in a manner similar to the functionality of the *Scroll to Task* button in the *Task* ribbon.

Hands On Exercise

Exercise 10 - 3

Add tasks to the *Timeline* view.

1. Open the **Project Navigation 2013.mpp** sample file.
2. Click the *View* tab to display the View ribbon.
3. In the *Split View* section of the *View* ribbon, select the *Timeline* option.
4. Click and hold the split bar along the bottom edge of the *Timeline* pane and drag it down to approximately **triple** the height of the current *Timeline* pane.
5. Right-click the *Pre-Renovation* summary task and then select the *Add to Timeline* item on the shortcut menu.

Notice how Project 2013 adds a bar to the *Timeline* bar representing the *Pre-Renovation* summary task.

6. Using the **Control** key on your computer keyboard, select the following summary tasks as a group:
    - Renovation
    - Construction
    - Furnish

7. Release the **Control** key, right-click one of the selected tasks, and then select the *Add to Timeline* item on the shortcut menu.

8. Using the **Control** key on your keyboard, select the three tasks highlighted with the green cell background color (task IDs #22, 24, and 25).

9. Release the **Control** key, right-click one of the selected tasks, and then select the *Add to Timeline* item on the shortcut menu.

10. In the *Timeline* view, right-click the *Obtain asbestos removal permit* task bar (the left-most item in the third row) and select the *Display as Callout* item on the shortcut menu.

Notice how Project 2013 displays this task as a callout **above** the *Timeline* bar.

11. In the *Timeline* pane, click and hold the text box for the *Obtain asbestos removal permit* callout to "grab" it, and then drag the text box up and away from the *Timeline* bar approximately *1/2 inch.*

12. In the *Timeline* pane, right-click the task bar for the *Asbestos removal inspection* task (the right-most item in the third row), and select the *Display as Callout* item on the shortcut menu.

13. In the *Timeline* pane, click and hold the *Asbestos removal inspection* text box to "grab" it, and then drag the text box up and away from the *Timeline* bar approximately *1/2 inch.*

14. Click and hold the split bar along the bottom edge of the *Timeline* pane and drag it down to add approximately one additional inch to the height of the *Timeline* pane.

15. In the *Timeline* pane, click and hold the *Remove asbestos in ceiling* task bar to "grab it" and then drag it **below** the *Timeline* bar until you see an outline of a callout, and then release the mouse button.

Notice how Project 2013 displays this task as a callout **below** the *Timeline* bar.

16. In the *Timeline* pane, press and hold the **Control** key on your computer keyboard and select the *Renovation* and *Construction* task bars in the *Timeline* view.

17. Release the **Control** key, and then drag the two selected task bars **one row below** their current position in the *Timeline* bar.

18. Save but do not close the **Project Navigation 2013.mpp** sample file.

Formatting the Timeline View

To format the *Timeline* view, click anywhere in the *Timeline* pane to activate the pane, and then click the *Format* tab. Project 2013 displays the contextual *Format* ribbon with the *Timeline Tools* applied, shown in Figure 10 - 8. Using the features on the *Format* ribbon, the software offers you many ways to format the *Timeline* view.

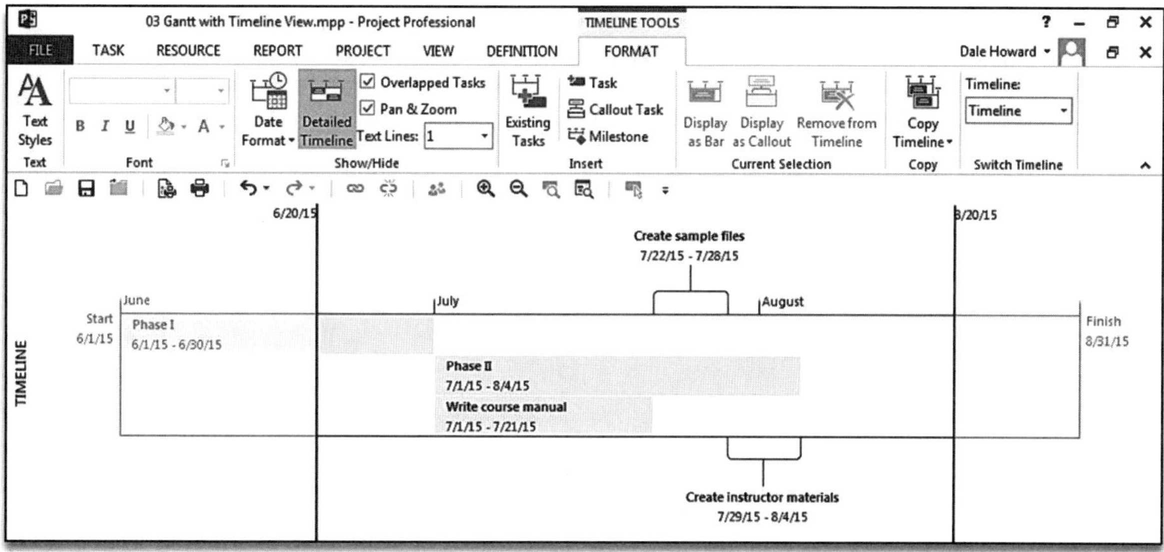

Figure 10 - 8: Format ribbon with the Timeline Tools applied

Using the Text Tools

To format the text for specific set of objects shown in the *Timeline* view, such as all milestone dates, click the *Text Styles* button in the *Text* section of the contextual *Format* ribbon. Project 2013 displays the *Text Styles* dialog shown in Figure 10 - 9. Select any type of object on the *Item to Change* pick list, such as the *Milestone Date* item. Change the formatting options in the *Font, Font styles, Size,* and *Color* fields. Optionally select the *Underline* or *Strikethrough* options as needed, and then click the *OK* button. Project 2013 applies the specified text formatting to all objects of the type you selected.

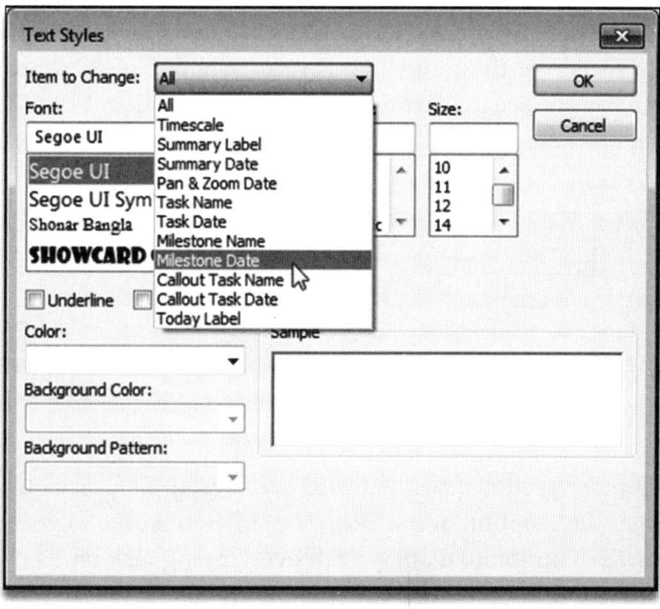

Figure 10 - 9: Text Styles dialog, Item to Change pick list

Information: Notice in Figure 10 - 9 shown previously that Project 2013 **does not** allow you to change the *Background Color* or *Background Pattern* options in the *Text Styles* dialog for the *Timeline* view. The software limits you to changing only text formatting options such as the *Font* and *Color* items.

Information: You can also display the *Text Styles* dialog by right-clicking anywhere in the white part of the *Timeline* view and then selecting the *Text Styles* item on the shortcut menu.

Using Font Tools

To change the font or the cell background color of an individual object in the *Timeline* view, select the object and then change the formatting using the options in the *Font* section of the contextual *Format* ribbon. To display the *Font* dialog, click the *Font* dialog launcher icon in the lower right corner of the *Font* section of the ribbon. To change the background color of a task bar, for example, select the bar and choose a new color on the *Background Color* pick list.

Using Show/Hide Tools

To change the date format of the dates shown in the *Timeline* view, click the *Date Format* pick list button in the *Show/Hide* section and select a new date format. By default, the *Timeline* view uses the date format specified in the *Date Format* field on the *General* page of the *Project Options* dialog. On the *Date Format* pick list, Project 2013 also allows you to hide some of the dates shown by default on the *Timeline* view. To hide the dates shown for each task, click the *Date Format* pick list and **deselect** the *Task Dates* option. To hide the current date, **deselect** the *Current Date* option on the *Date Format* pick list. To hide the dates shown above the *Timeline* bar, **deselect** the *Timescale* option on the *Date Format* pick list.

To remove the details from the *Timeline* view, such as the names of tasks and task dates, click the *Detailed Timeline* toggle button in the *Show/Hide* section of the contextual *Format* ribbon. The software completely removes all details from the *Timeline* view. As you can see in Figure 10 - 10, without the details, the *Timeline* view is probably not very useful to you. To redisplay the details in the *Timeline* view, click the *Detailed Timeline* toggle button again.

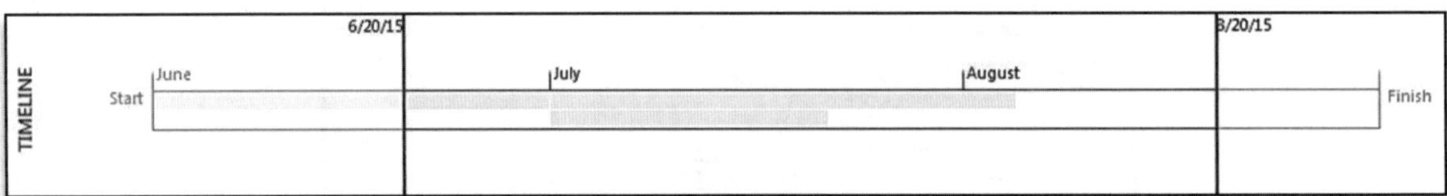

Figure 10 - 10: Timeline view with details removed

If your project contains parallel task sections, and you display overlapping tasks from these parallel sections in the *Timeline* view, the *Overlapped Tasks* option in the *Show/Hide* section works to your advantage. By default, Project 2013 selects the *Overlapped Tasks* option to display each overlapping task on its own row in the *Timeline* view. For example, Figure 10 - 11 shows a different project with multiple parallel task sections and with each summary task section displayed on the *Timeline* view. Notice how Project 2013 displays each overlapping section on its own task row in the *Timeline* view.

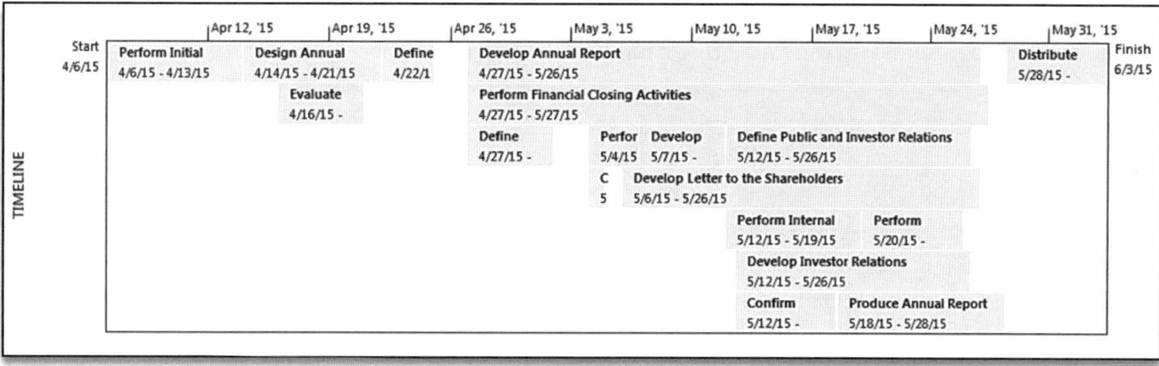

Figure 10 - 11: Timeline with Overlapped Tasks option selected

Figure 10 - 12 shows the same *Timeline* view with the *Overlapped Tasks* option deselected. Notice how the software displays all tasks on a single task row in the *Timeline* view, rendering the information all but impossible to read. For this reason, I recommend you leave the *Overlapped Tasks* option selected for the *Timeline* view.

Figure 10 - 12: Timeline with Overlapped Tasks option deselected

In the *Show/Hide* section of the contextual *Format* ribbon, the *Pan & Zoom* option allows you to display or hide the two green vertical lines in the *Timeline* that show the time span of the project currently visible in the *Gantt Chart* view. If you select the *Pan & Zoom* option, the software displays the *Pan & Zoom* bar (the two green vertical lines); if you deselect this option, the software hides the *Pan & Zoom* bar.

The final option in the *Show/Hide* section is the *Text Lines* option, which allows you to determine how many lines of text to display for every task shown in the *Timeline* view. By default, the software sets the *Text Lines* value to *1 line*. Because of this, the software truncates long task names when displayed in the *Timeline* view. For example, in the *Timeline* view shown in Figure 10 - 13 notice how the software truncates the names of two of the three sub-tasks shown in the *Phase II* section with the *Text Lines* value set to the default *1 line* value.

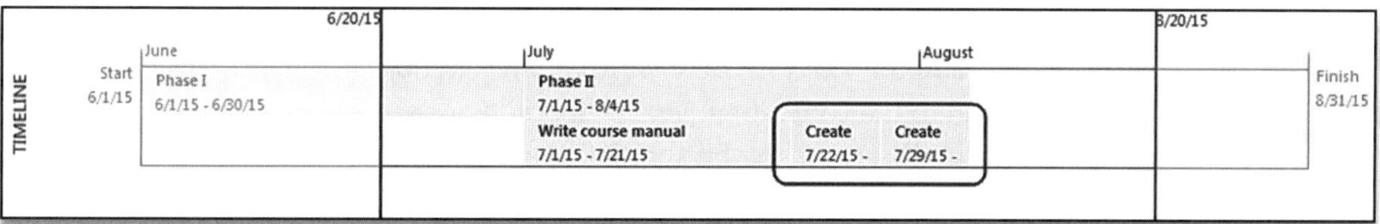

Figure 10 - 13: Timeline view with the Text Lines option set to 1 line

Figure 10 - 14 shows the same *Timeline* view with the *Text Lines* value set to *3 lines*. Notice that you can now read the full name of all three subtask in the *Phase II* section.

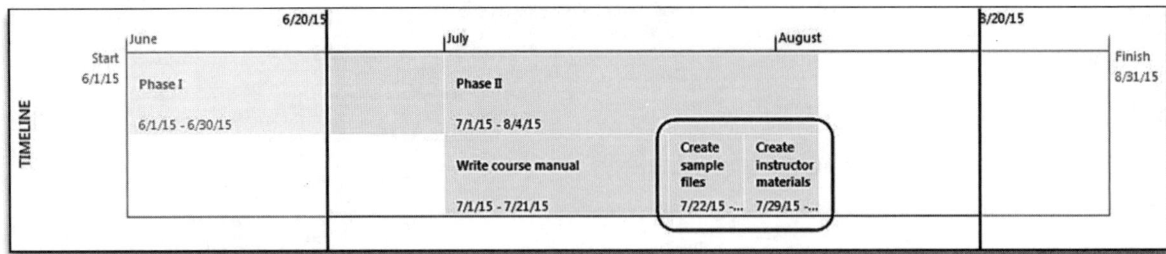

Figure 10 - 14: Timeline view with the Text Lines option set to 3 lines

Figure 10 - 15 shows a completed *Timeline* view after I formatted it using methods I documented in this section of the module. To format the *Timeline* view, I did the following:

- I added the *Phase III* summary task and the *Project Complete* milestone task to the *Timeline* view.
- I changed the two tasks to callouts in the *Phase II* section.
- I dragged the *Create instructor materials* callout to a position below the *Timeline* bar.
- I changed the *Date Format* option to the *Jan 28* format.
- I changed the *Background Color* setting for each task individually.
- I changed the *Font Color* setting to *White* for the *Phase III* bar and the *Write course manual* bar.
- Using the *Text Styles* dialog, I changed the *Font Color* setting to *Red* for the dates of every callout.
- I changed the *Text Lines* value to 2 to display two lines of text in each bar.
- I deselected the *Pan & Zoom* option to hide the *Pan & Zoom* bar.

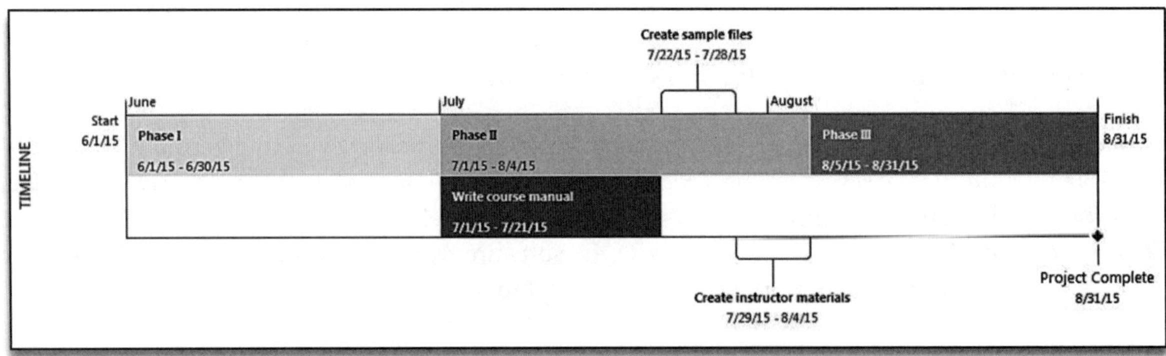

Figure 10 - 15: Timeline view after applying custom formatting

To change the type of object displayed in the *Timeline* view, or to remove an object from the *Timeline* view, use the buttons in the *Current Selection* section of the contextual *Format* ribbon. For example, to change a callout to a task bar, select the callout and then click the *Display as Bar* button. To change a task bar to a callout, select the task bar and then click the *Display as Callout* button. To remove a task or a callout from the *Timeline* view, select the task or callout and then click the *Remote from Timeline* button.

Warning: While you have the *Timeline* pane activated, be careful not to click the *Zoom* button in the *Zoom* section of the *View* ribbon and then to select either the *Zoom In* or *Zoom Out* option. If you zoom in or zoom out with the *Timeline* pane activated, you cannot use the *Zoom In* or *Zoom Out* options to return to the default level of zoom applied to the *Timeline* view. To return to the default level of zoom, you must click the *Zoom Entire Project* button in the *Zoom* section of the *View* ribbon. You can also right-click anywhere in the *Timeline* pane and select the *Zoom to Screen* item on the shortcut menu.

Adding Tasks Using the Contextual Format Ribbon

In addition to the formatting options available on the contextual *Format* ribbon with the *Timeline Tools* applied, this ribbon also offers options for adding or removing tasks in the *Timeline* view. In the *Insert* section of the *Format* ribbon, Project 2013 includes four buttons that allow you to add new tasks to the *Timeline* view. To add a new existing task to the *Timeline* view, click the *Existing Tasks* button. The software displays the *Add Tasks to Timeline* dialog shown in Figure 10 - 16. To add a task to the *Timeline* view, select the checkbox to the left of the task name, and then click the *OK* button.

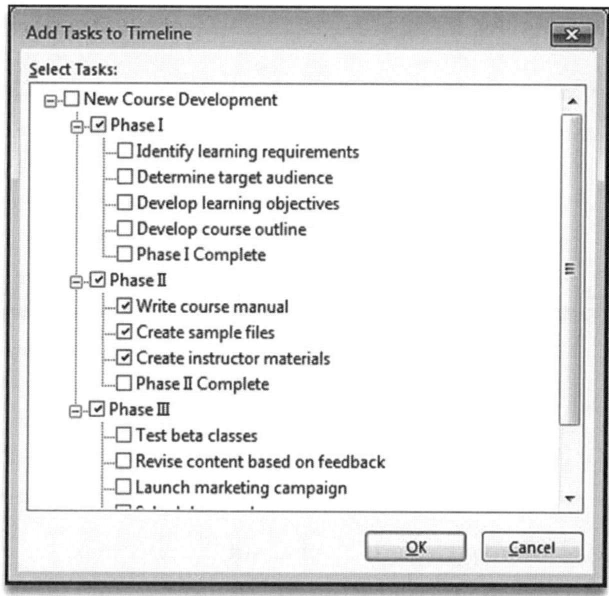

Figure 10 - 16: Add Tasks to Timeline dialog

The software adds the selected task(s) to the *Timeline* view. For example, notice in Figure 10 - 17 that I added the *Phase I Complete* milestone task to the *Timeline* view.

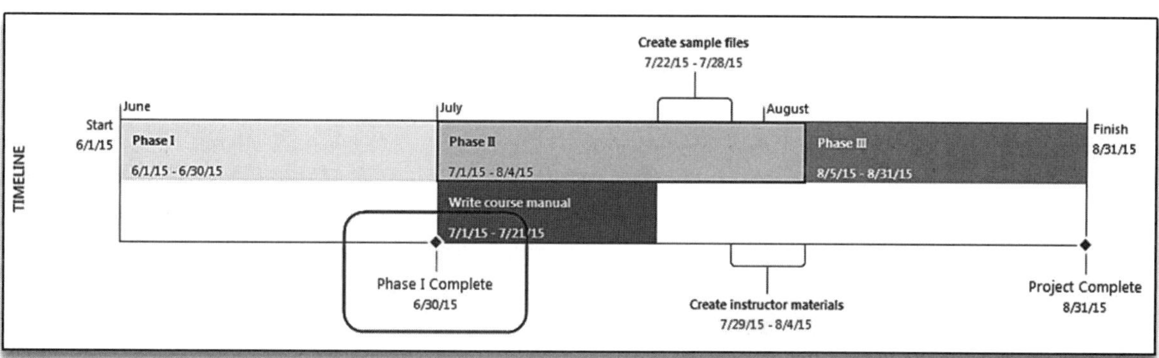

Figure 10 - 17: Milestone task added to the Timeline view

To add a completely new task to your project and simultaneously add the new task to the *Timeline* view, click the *Task* button, the *Callout Task* button, or the *Milestone* button in the *Insert* section of the contextual *Format* ribbon. Project 2013 displays the *Task Information* dialog shown in Figure 10 - 18.

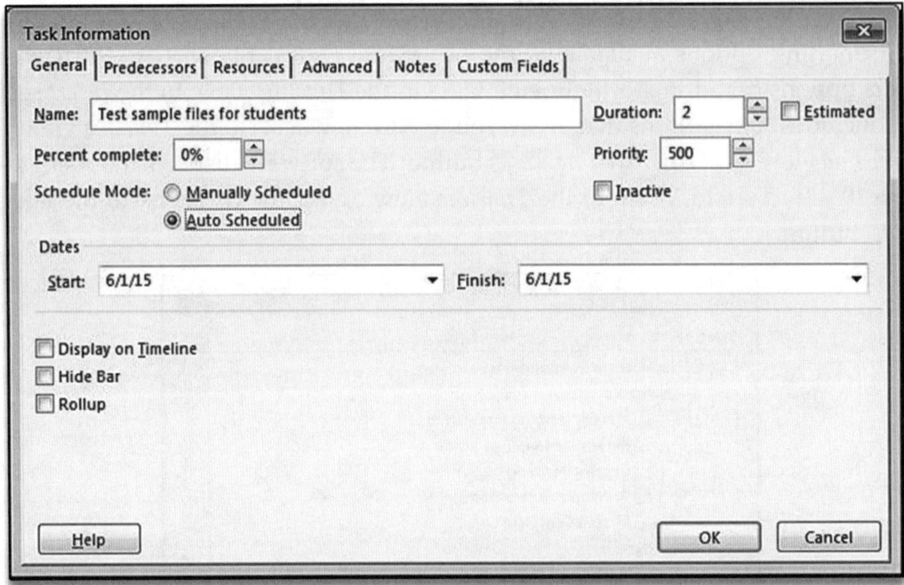

Figure 10 - 18: Task Information dialog

In the *Task Information* dialog, enter complete information about the new task, including information in the *Name* and *Duration* fields, and select the desired *Schedule Mode* option. Assuming you want to display the new task in the *Timeline* view, be sure to select the *Display on Timeline* option. If necessary, select predecessor tasks on the *Predecessors* page and assign resources to the new task on the *Resources* page. Click the *OK* button to add the new task to the project and to the *Timeline* view. Project 2013 creates the new task as the last task in the task list, and adds the new task to the *Timeline* view. Figure 10 - 19 shows the new *Test student sample files* task. After creating the new task, you must drag the task to the correct place in the project and set additional dependencies as needed.

Information: You can also insert a new task in the project and add it to the *Timeline* view by right-clicking anywhere in the white part of the *Timeline* view, selecting the *Insert Task* menu item, and then selecting the *Callout Task*, *Task*, or *Milestone* item on the flyout menu.

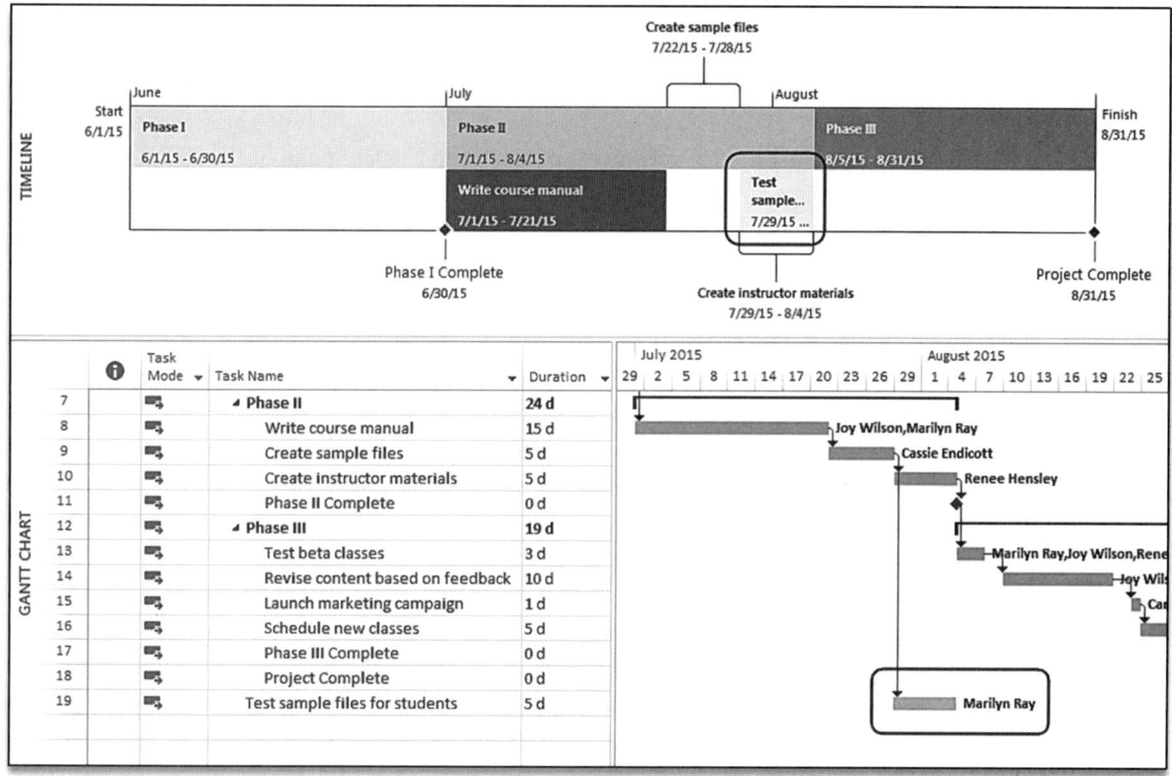

Figure 10 - 19: New task added to the project and to the Timeline view

Hands On Exercise

Exercise 10 - 4

Customize the *Timeline* view.

1. Return to the **Project Navigation 2013.mpp** sample file.
2. Click anywhere in the *Timeline* pane to activate the pane.
3. Click the *Format* tab to display the contextual *Format* ribbon with the *Timeline Tools* applied.
4. In the *Text* section of the *Format* ribbon, click the *Text Styles* button.
5. In the *Text Styles* dialog, click the *Item to Change* pick list and select the *Callout Task Name* item.
6. Click the *Color* pick list and select the *Orange, Darker 25%* color in the *Theme Colors* section of the dialog.
7. Click the *OK* button.

Notice how Project 2013 automatically formatted the text color for all three of the callouts simultaneously.

8. In the *Timeline* view, click the task bar for the *Construction* summary task.
9. In the *Font* section of the *Format* ribbon, click the *Background Color* pick list button, and then select the *More Colors* item.
10. In the *Colors* dialog, select the *Custom* tab to display the *Custom* page of the dialog.
11. On the *Custom* page of the dialog, enter the following values in the *Red, Green,* and *Blue* fields as shown in Table 10 - 1:

Color Field	Value
Red	184
Green	28
Blue	24

Table 10 - 1: Color values

Notice that Project 2013 displays a deep "cherry red" background color to the selected task bar in the *Timeline* bar.

12. In the *Font* section of the *Format* ribbon, click the *Color* pick list button, and select the *Yellow* color in the *Standard Colors* section.

Notice how the yellow text color accents nicely with the cherry red background color of the task bar for the *Construction* summary task.

13. In the *Show/Hide* section of the *Format* ribbon, click the *Date Format* pick list button, and then **deselect** the *Timescale* item at the bottom of the pick list.
14. In the *Show/Hide* section of the *Format* ribbon, **deselect** the *Pan & Zoom* option.
15. In the *Insert* section of the *Format* ribbon, click the *Existing Tasks* button.
16. In the *Add Tasks to Timeline* dialog, select the checkbox for the *PROJECT COMPLETE* milestone task and then click the *OK* button.
17. Save but do not close the **Project Navigation 2013.mpp** sample file.

Creating a New Timeline View

In addition to the one default *Timeline* view included with Project 2013, the software allows you to create additional custom *Timeline* views. To create a custom *Timeline* view, complete the following steps:

1. In the *Split View* section of the *View* ribbon, **deselect** the *Timeline* checkbox to close the *Timeline* pane and display only the single-pane *Gantt Chart* view.
2. In the *Task Views* section of the *View* ribbon, click the *Gantt Chart* pick list button, and then select the *More Views* item. Project 2013 displays the *More Views* dialog shown in Figure 10 - 20.

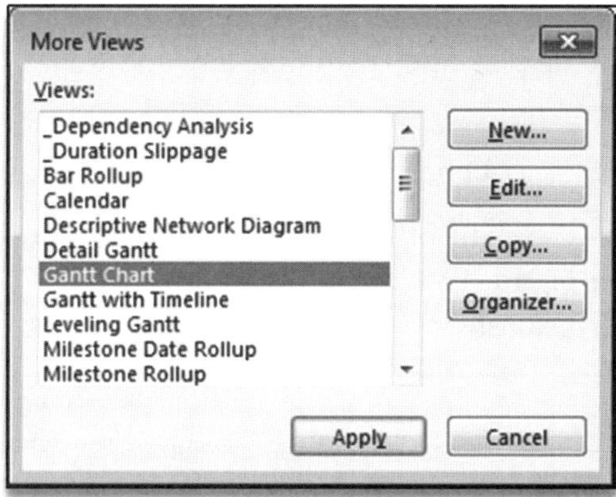

Figure 10 - 20: More Views dialog

3. In the *More Views* dialog, click the *New* button. Project 2013 displays the *Define New View* dialog shown in Figure 10 - 21.

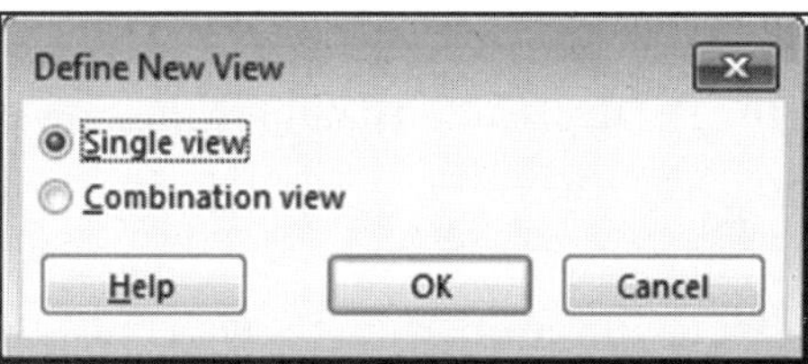

Figure 10 - 21: Define New View dialog

4. In the *Define New View* dialog, select the *Single view* option, and then click the *OK* button. Project 2013 displays the *View Definition* dialog for a new view, as shown in Figure 10 - 22.

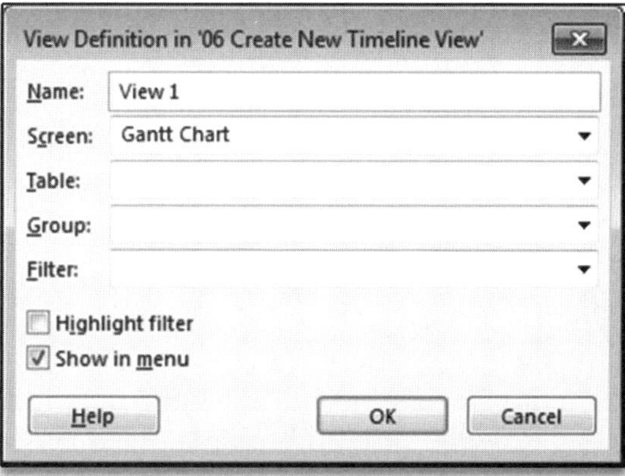

Figure 10 - 22: View Definition dialog

5. In the *View Definition* dialog, enter a descriptive name in the *Name* field. For example, I want to create a new *Timeline* view that shows major milestones in the project, so I enter the name *Timeline Milestones* in the *Name* field.
6. In the *View Definition* dialog, click the *Screen* pick list and select the *Timeline* screen.
7. Click the *OK* button to close the *View Definition* dialog and then click the *OK* button to close the *More Views* dialog.

After creating the new *Timeline* view, how do you actually display it so that you can customize the new *Timeline* view? Complete the following steps to display and customize any additional *Timeline* views you create in Project 2013:

1. In the *Split View* section of the *View* ribbon, select the *Timeline* checkbox.
2. Click the *Timeline* pick list to the right of the *Timeline* checkbox to see the list of all available *Timeline* views. For example, notice in Figure 10 - 23 that I can now see my new *Timeline Milestones* view in the *Custom* section of the *Timeline* pick list.

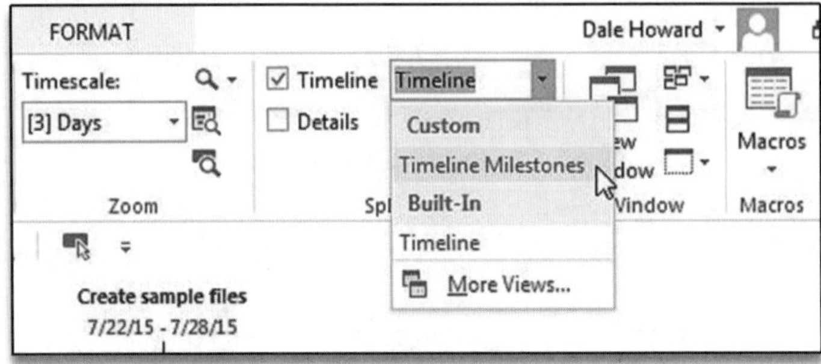

Figure 10 - 23: Display the Timeline Milestones view

3. In the *Custom* section of the *Timeline* pick list, select your new *Timeline* view.
4. Add tasks to the new *Timeline* view and format the view, as needed, using the formatting features presented in the previous topical section of this book.

Figure 10 - 24 shows my new custom *Timeline Milestones* view, created by adding each milestone to the view and then formatting some of the milestones. Notice that I dragged two of the milestones above the *Timeline* bar.

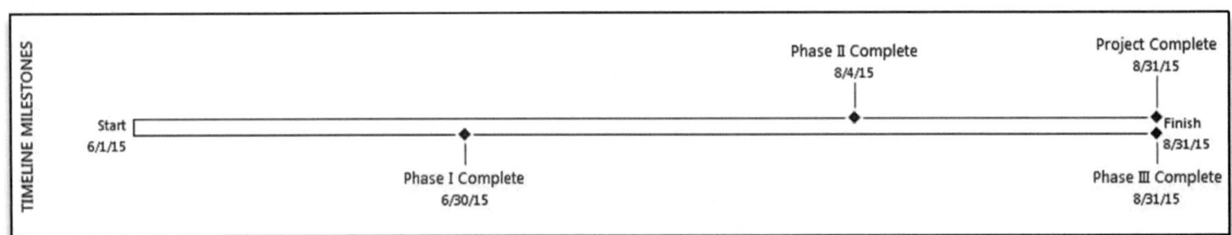

Figure 10 - 24: New Timeline Milestones view

Exporting the Timeline View

Project 2013 allows you to export the entire *Timeline* view to any Office application, such as PowerPoint or Word. To copy the *Timeline* view, click the *Copy Timeline* pick list button in the *Copy* section of the contextual *Format* ribbon. The *Copy Timeline* pick list contains three choices, including *For E-Mail, For Presentation,* and *Full Size.*

If you select the *Full Size* item on the *Copy Timeline* pick list, Project 2013 copies the full-size image of the current *Timeline* view to your Windows clipboard. If you select the *For Presentation* item, the software optimizes the image for use in PowerPoint by reducing the image size to approximately 90% of full size. If you select the *For E-Mail* item, the software optimizes the image for use in Microsoft Outlook by reducing the image size to approximately 60% of full size.

After copying the *Timeline* view to your clipboard, paste the image in one of the Office applications. If you use an application that has image editing capabilities, such as Word or PowerPoint, you can continue to refine your

Timeline view presentation. For example, Figure 10 - 25 shows the *Timeline* view after I pasted the image into a PowerPoint presentation and applied additional formatting. Notice that I used the *Bevel* feature to give the tasks a 3-D appearance, and I used the *Glow* feature to alter the appearance of the *Project Complete* milestone task.

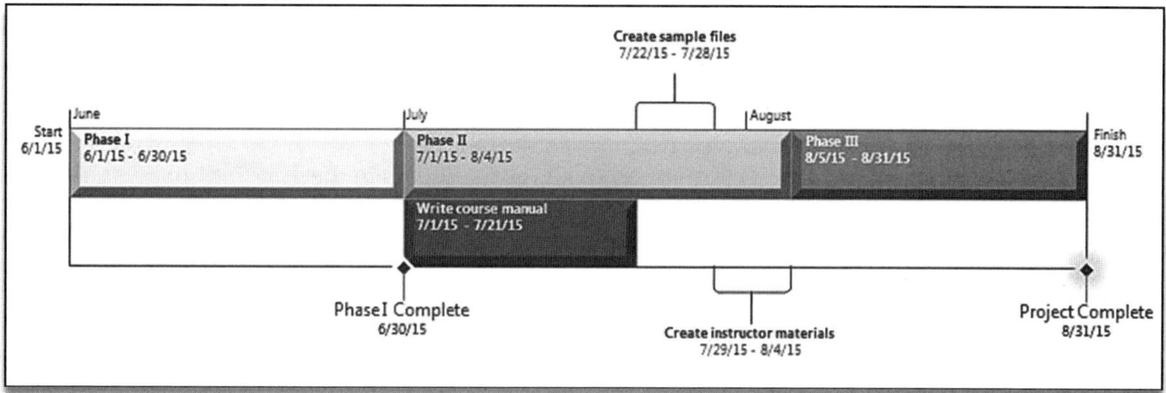

Figure 10 - 25: Timeline view formatted in PowerPoint

Information: You can also copy the *Timeline* view by right-clicking anywhere in the white part of the *Timeline* view, selecting the *Copy Timeline* item from the shortcut menu, and then selecting the *For E-Mail, For Presentation*, or *Full Size* item on the flyout menu.

Hands On Exercise

Exercise 10 - 5

Export the *Timeline* view to another Office application.

1. Return to the **Project Navigation 2013.mpp** sample file.
2. Click anywhere in the *Timeline* pane to select it.
3. In the *Copy* section of the *Format* ribbon, click the *Copy Timeline* pick list button and then select the *For Presentation* item.
4. Launch your PowerPoint application and create a slide using the *Title Only* layout.
5. In the new blank PowerPoint slide, click in the *Click to add title* text box and then manually type *Office Renovation Project* in the text box.
6. Click anywhere in the white part of the slide and then click the *Paste* button in the *Clipboard* section of the *Home* ribbon in PowerPoint.
7. Click anywhere in the pasted *Timeline* image and then use the **Down-Arrow** and **Right-Arrow** keys on your computer keyboard to manually center the image on the slide.

8. Using the **Control** key on your computer keyboard, select each of the task bars in the *Timeline* image to select all four task bars as a group, and then release the **Control** key.
9. Click the *Format* tab to display the contextual *Format* ribbon with the *Drawing Tools* applied in PowerPoint.
10. In the *Shape Styles* section of the *Format* ribbon, click the *Shape Effects* pick list, select the *Bevel* item, and then select the *Angle* item on the flyout menu.

Notice how PowerPoint applies 3-D formatting to all four task bars in the *Timeline* image.

11. Exit your PowerPoint application without saving the new presentation, and then return to your Project 2013 application window.
12. Click the *File* tab and then click the *Save* tab in the *Backstage*.
13. Click the *File* tab and then click the *Close* tab to close the **Project Navigation 2013.mpp** sample file.

Creating a New Table by Customizing an Existing Table

In the preceding module, I taught you two methods for creating a custom table. These methods included creating a new table from scratch and creating a new table by copying an existing table. Project 2013 offers you several additional ways to work with tables, which include the following:

- Customize any default table and save it as a new table.
- Use the *Add New Column* virtual column to customize the existing table.
- Reset a customized table back to its original default settings.

Saving a Customized Table as a New Table

The first of these three additional methods for working with tables is to customize any default table and then to save it as a new table. After you save the new custom table, the software then allows you to reset the original table back to its default settings. To customize any existing table, complete the following steps:

1. Right-click the *Select All* button and select any default table for temporary customization.
2. Drag the split bar to the right to expose all of the columns in the selected table.
3. Right click the column header of any column you want to remove and then select the *Hide Column* item on the shortcut menu.
4. To add a new column to the table, right-click the column header where you want to insert the column, and then select the *Insert Column* item in the shortcut menu. From the list of available columns, select the new column you want to add.

Information: You can also insert a new column in the table by clicking the pick list button in the *Add New Column* virtual column and selecting the column from the list of available columns.

5. To change the settings for any column, such as the title displayed in the column header, right-click the column you want to change and select the *Field Settings* item on the shortcut menu. Project 2013 displays the *Field Settings* dialog shown in Figure 10 - 26.

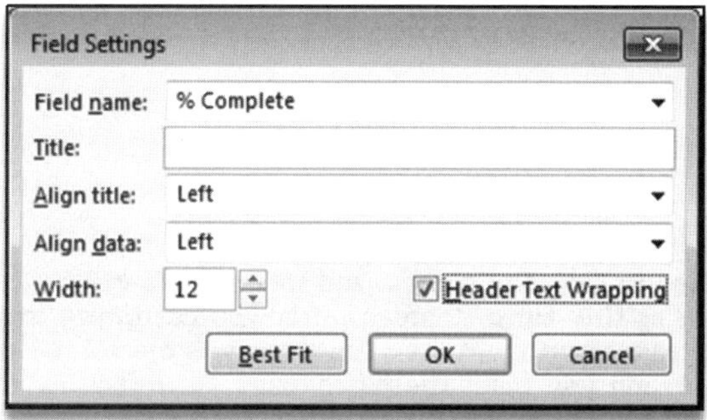

Figure 10 - 26: Field Settings dialog

The *Field Settings* dialog allows you to enter text in the *Title* field to specify an alternate name for the column. In addition, you can specify values in the *Align title* and *Align data* fields to specify whether to align the column and its data on the left, on the right, or centered. Finally, you can set the width of the column in the *Width* field and you can specify whether to use the *Header Text Wrapping* feature by selecting this option.

6. In the *Field Settings* dialog, specify the column options you want and click the *OK* button.

Information: If you click the *Best Fit* button in the *Field Settings* dialog, Project 2013 sets the column width automatically to the width of the longest entry in the column.

After customizing the default table, you are ready to save the customized table as a new table, and then to reset the customized table back to its original default settings. To save the customized table as a new table and then reset the customized table back to its original default settings, complete the following steps:

1. Click the *View* tab to display the *View* ribbon.
2. In the *Data* section of the *View* ribbon, click the *Tables* pick list, and select the *Save Fields as a New Table* item on the list. Project 2013 displays the *Save Table* dialog shown in Figure 10 - 27.

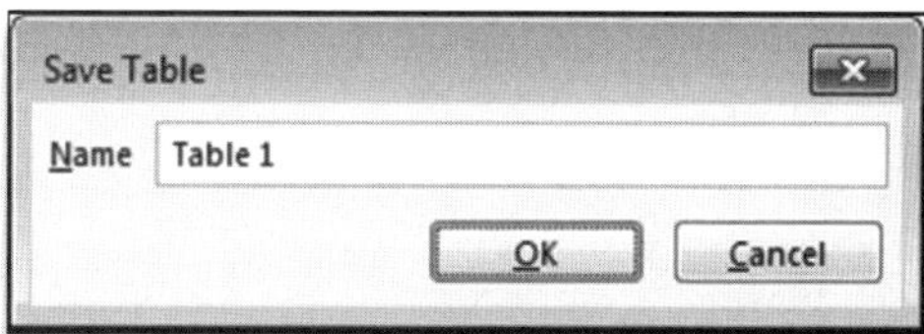

Figure 10 - 27: Save Table dialog

3. In the *Save Table* dialog, enter a name for the new custom table in the *Name* field, and then click the *OK* button.
4. Right-click the *Select All* button and select the **original table** you temporarily customized to create the new table.
5. In the *Data* section of the *View* ribbon, click the *Tables* pick list and select the *Reset to Default* item.

Project 2013 resets the customized table back to its original default settings. This action includes resetting the original list of columns, plus all formatting for the data in each column, and adding the *Add New Column* virtual column.

Information: If you intend to save the customized table as a part of a customized view, you **do not** need to save the customized table **at this time**. Instead, after you customize the table, then customize the view and save the customized view as a new view. When you do this, Project 2013 **also saves** the customized table as a new table automatically. When you reset the customized view back to its default settings, the software also resets the customized table back to its default settings.

Customizing a Table Using the Add New Column Feature

I noted previously in this book that every default table in Project 2013 includes the *Add New Column* virtual column on the far right side of the table. You can use this feature as an alternate method of adding columns in a new custom table. The software offers you several ways to insert a new column using the *Add New Column* virtual column, including the following:

- Click the column header at the top of the *Add New Column* virtual column and select a default or custom field from the list of available fields.
- Click the column header at the top of the *Add New Column* virtual column and then manually type the name of any default field in the blank column header.
- Click the column header at the top of the *Add New Column* virtual column and then manually type the name of a new custom field in the blank column header.
- Type data in any cell in the *Add New Column* virtual column.

When you type the name of a new custom field in the *Add New Column* virtual column header, the software creates a new custom *Text* field automatically, using the next available unused *Text* field. The software then redisplays the *Add New Column* virtual column to the right of the new custom column. For example, Figure 10 - 28 shows the new *Schedule Risk* column I added to a custom table using the *Add New Column* virtual column.

GANTT CHART

		Task Mode	Task Name	Duration	Schedule Risk	Add New Column
0			◢ **Killer iPhone App Development**	**67 d**		
1			◢ **Analysis/Software Requirements**	**13 d**		
2			Conduct needs analysis	5 d		
3			Draft software specifications	5 d		
4			Develop budget	2 d		
5			Develop delivery timeline	1 d		
6			Analysis complete	0 d		
7			◢ **Design**	**11 d**		
8			Develop functional specifications	5 d		
9			Develop prototype based on functional specifications	6 d		
10			Design complete	0 d		
11			◢ **Development**	**26 d**		
12			Identify design parameters	5 d		
13			Develop code	20 d		
14			Developer testing (primary debugging)	20 d		
15			Development complete	0 d		
16			◢ **Testing**	**17 d**		
17			Review modular code	5 d		
18			Test component modules to product specifications	2 d		
19			Identify anomalies to product specifications	3 d		
20			Modify code	5 d		
21			Re-test modified code	2 d		
22			Testing Complete	0 d		
23			Projct Complete	0 d		

Figure 10 - 28: New custom Schedule Risk column added

When you create a new custom column using this method, keep in mind that Project 2013 offers **only 30** custom *Text* fields. If you attempt to exceed this number by creating the thirty-first custom column, the software displays the *Delete Custom Fields* dialog shown in Figure 10 - 29. Because of the limit of 30 custom *Text* fields, you must delete an existing custom *Text* field by selecting the option checkbox for one or more fields and then clicking the *Delete Custom Fields* button in the dialog. When prompted in a confirmation dialog, click the *Yes* button to delete the selected fields.

Figure 10 - 29: Delete Custom Fields dialog

When you type data in the *Add New Column* virtual column without typing a name in the column header, Project 2013 automatically selects the next available custom field using the data type you entered. For example, if you type *$500* in the *Add New Column* field, the software selects and inserts the next unused custom *Cost* field. If you enter *5d* in the *Add New Column* field, the software selects and inserts the next unused custom *Duration* field. For example, Figure 10 - 30 shows the new *Number3* column that the software added automatically after I typed the number *12357* in the *Add New Column* virtual column.

		Task Mode	Task Name	Duration	Schedule Risk	Number3	Add New Column
0			**Killer iPhone App Development**	**67 d**		**0**	
1			**Analysis/Software Requirements**	**13 d**		**0**	
2			Conduct needs analysis	5 d		12357	
3			Draft software specifications	5 d		0	
4			Develop budget	2 d		0	
5			Develop delivery timeline	1 d		0	
6			Analysis complete	0 d		0	
7			**Design**	**11 d**		**0**	
8			Develop functional specifications	5 d		0	
9			Develop prototype based on functional specifications	6 d		0	
10			Design complete	0 d		0	
11			**Development**	**26 d**		**0**	
12			Identify design parameters	5 d		0	
13			Develop code	20 d		0	
14			Developer testing (primary debugging)	20 d		0	
15			Development complete	0 d		0	
16			**Testing**	**17 d**		**0**	
17			Review modular code	5 d		0	
18			Test component modules to product specifications	2 d		0	
19			Identify anomalies to product specifications	3 d		0	
20			Modify code	5 d		0	
21			Re-test modified code	2 d		0	
22			Testing Complete	0 d		0	
23			Projct Complete	0 d		0	

Figure 10 - 30: New custom Number column

If you create a new custom column by typing a value in the *Add New Column* virtual column, I strongly recommend that you either change the *Title* of the column or rename the field to display relevant information that identifies the column. To change the *Title* of a column, right-click the column header and select the *Field Settings* item on the shortcut menu. Project 2013 displays the *Field Settings* dialog shown previously in Figure 10 - 26. Enter a name for the column in the *Title* field and then click the *OK* button. When you enter a *Title* for a column, the column continues to retain its original name, such as *Number3*, but the column header displays the *Title* information instead of the column name. I like to think of the column *Title* as the "nickname" of the column.

To rename a column and give it a completely new name, right-click its column header and select the *Custom Fields* item on the shortcut menu. The software displays the *Custom Fields* dialog with the new field selected, as shown in Figure 10 - 31. Click the *Rename* button, enter a new name for the field in the *Rename Field* dialog, and then click the *OK* button. Click the *OK* button to close the *Custom Fields* dialog.

Information: You can also rename the new field in the *Custom Fields* dialog by clicking the selected field and then typing a name for the field. This means you can bypass using the *Rename* button if you prefer.

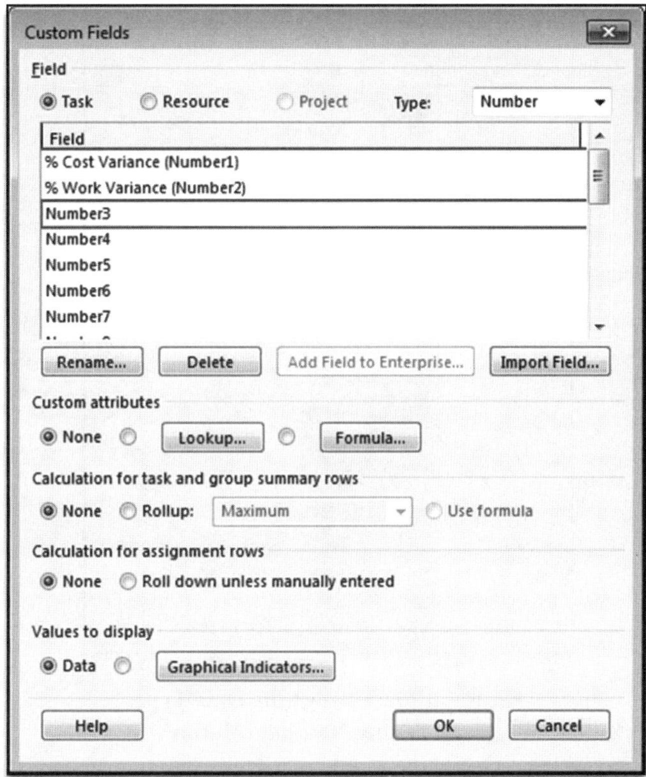

Figure 10 - 31: Custom Fields dialog

After creating a new custom column using either of the two previous methods, Project 2013 also allows you to change the *Data Type* used for the column. For example, after I typed a number in the *Add New Column* virtual column, the software added the *Number1* field automatically. However, if I need to be able to enter alphanumeric data in this column, I must convert the *Data Type* from *Number* to *Text*. To change the *Data Type* for any custom column, right-click the column header, select the *Data Type* item on the shortcut menu, and then select the desired *Data Type* item on the fly out menu as shown in Figure 10 - 32. Notice that I renamed the custom *Number3*column to *SAP Number* using the *Custom Fields* dialog. Notice also that the fly out menu shows the original *Data Type* value for this column, the *Number* type.

When you change the *Data Type* for a custom column, Project 2013 selects the next available unused column with that *Data Type*. In my project, after converting the *SAP Number* column from a *Number* field to a *Text* field, the software selected the *Text7* field (the next available unused *Text* field), applied the *SAP Number* name to the *Text7* field, and then removed the *SAP Number* name from the *Number3* field.

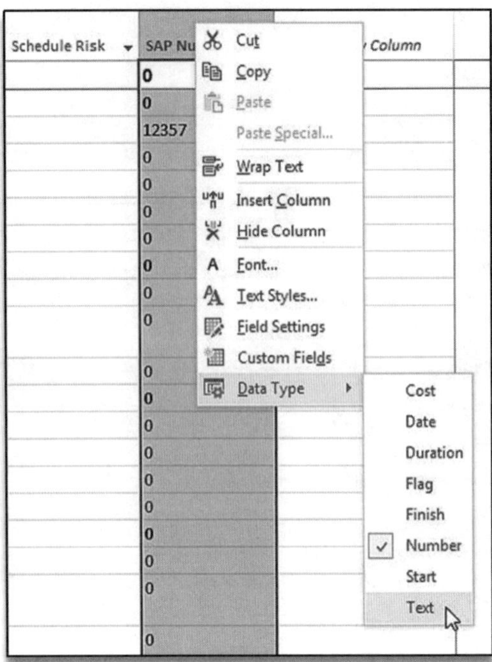

Figure 10 - 32: Change the Data Type for a custom Number column

If you attempt to convert the *Data Type* for a column to an invalid type based on the data already in the column, Project 2013 displays a warning dialog such as the one shown in Figure 10 - 33. For example, the software displays this dialog when I attempt to change the *SAP Number* column to the *Flag* data type. Notice in the dialog that if I click the *Yes* button to continue with the conversion operation, the software deletes all of the non-conforming data in this column. In my situation, I must click the *No* button because I do not want to delete the data in this column.

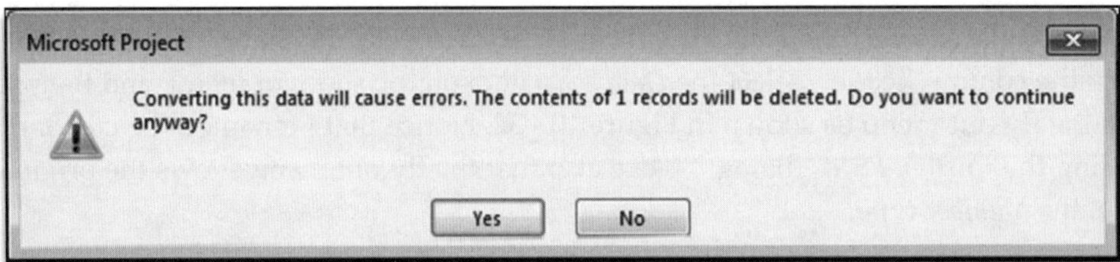

Figure 10 - 33: Warning dialog after changing to an invalid Data Type

Warning: When you add columns to any default table, remember that this action changes the definition of the default table from this point forward. Because a number of views share common tables between them, adding columns to the table in one view causes the columns to appear in other views. For example, if you add columns to the *Entry* table in the *Gantt Chart* view, you see these additional columns in the *Tracking Gantt* view and the *Task Sheet* view because all three views use the *Entry* table by default.

Hands On Exercise

Exercise 10 - 6

Add several new custom columns using the *Add New Column* virtual column.

1. Open the **Customize an Existing Table 2013.mpp** sample file.
2. Drag the split bar to the far right side of the *Gantt Chart* view to expose all of the columns in the *Entry* table.
3. Click and drag across the column headers of the *Duration, Start, Finish, Predecessors,* and *Resource Names* columns to select these five columns.
4. Right-click anywhere in the column headers of the five selected columns, and then select the *Hide Column* item on the shortcut menu to hide the five selected columns.
5. Click the column header of the *Add New Column* virtual column and select the *Responsible Person (Text1)* column from the list of available columns.
6. Click the column header of the *Add New Column* virtual column and select the *Cost Center ID (Text2)* column from the list of available columns.

Note: The *Responsible Person* and *Cost Center ID* columns are **custom columns** I created specifically for this Hands On Exercise. These two columns **are not** default columns included in Project 2013.

7. In the *Add New Column* virtual column, select the cell for task ID #8, the *Initial Planning Complete* milestone task.
8. Type a *Yes* value in the selected cell in the *Add New Column* virtual column.

Notice how Project 2013 adds the new *Flag1* column to the left of the *Add New Column* virtual column.

9. In the *Flag1* column, select a *Yes* value for the following tasks:
    - Task ID #18, the *Annual Report Design Complete* milestone task
    - Task ID #23, the *SEC 10-K and Proxy Documentation Production Schedules Complete* milestone task
    - Task ID #58, the *Annual Report Creation Complete* milestone task
    - Task ID #103, the *Production of Annual Report Complete* milestone task
10. Right-click the *Flag1* column header and select the *Custom Fields* item on the shortcut menu.
11. In the *Custom Fields* dialog, select the *Flag1* field, and then click the *Rename* button.

12. In the *Rename Field* dialog, enter the name *Major Milestone* in the *New name for Flag1* field and then click the *OK* button.

13. Click the *OK* button to close the *Custom Fields* dialog.

14. Right-click the *Major Milestone* column header and select the *Field Settings* item on the shortcut menu.

15. In the *Field Settings* dialog, select the *Center* value in the *Align title* and *Align data* fields.

16. Set the *Width* field value to *14* and then click the *OK* button.

17. Save and close the **Customize an Existing Table 2013.mpp** sample file.

Creating a New View by Customizing an Existing View

In Module 08, *Project Execution,* I showed you how to format the *Gantt Chart* view using the *Format* ribbon to display the *Critical Path* in your project, and to optionally show the *Total Slack* for each task. In the previous topical section of this module, I showed you how to customize an existing table using several methods. After you customize any default view and table, Project 2013 allows you to save in a single action **both** the customized view and the customized table as an entirely new custom view and table. After you save the customized view and table, you can also reset the original view and table back to their default settings in a single action. For example, Figure 10 - 34 shows a customized *Gantt Chart* view with a customized *Entry* table applied.

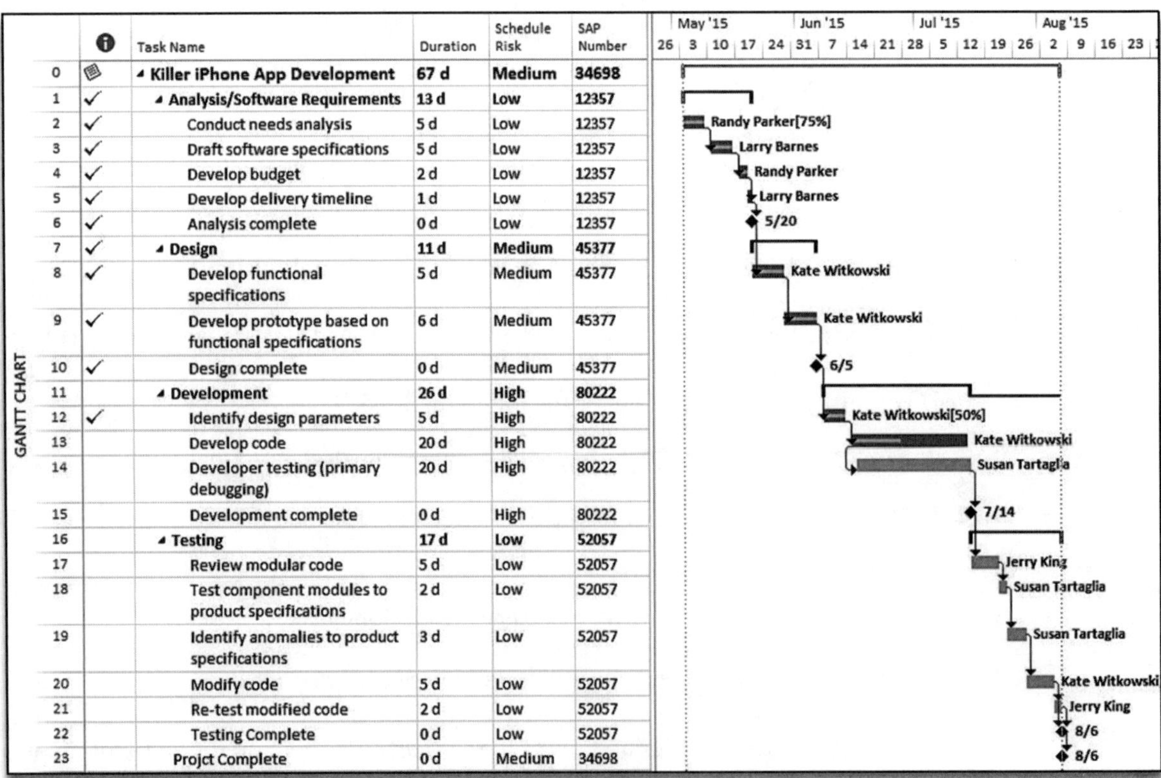

		Task Name	Duration	Schedule Risk	SAP Number
0		Killer iPhone App Development	67 d	Medium	34698
1	✓	Analysis/Software Requirements	13 d	Low	12357
2	✓	Conduct needs analysis	5 d	Low	12357
3	✓	Draft software specifications	5 d	Low	12357
4	✓	Develop budget	2 d	Low	12357
5	✓	Develop delivery timeline	1 d	Low	12357
6	✓	Analysis complete	0 d	Low	12357
7	✓	Design	11 d	Medium	45377
8	✓	Develop functional specifications	5 d	Medium	45377
9	✓	Develop prototype based on functional specifications	6 d	Medium	45377
10	✓	Design complete	0 d	Medium	45377
11		Development	26 d	High	80222
12	✓	Identify design parameters	5 d	High	80222
13		Develop code	20 d	High	80222
14		Developer testing (primary debugging)	20 d	High	80222
15		Development complete	0 d	High	80222
16		Testing	17 d	Low	52057
17		Review modular code	5 d	Low	52057
18		Test component modules to product specifications	2 d	Low	52057
19		Identify anomalies to product specifications	3 d	Low	52057
20		Modify code	5 d	Low	52057
21		Re-test modified code	2 d	Low	52057
22		Testing Complete	0 d	Low	52057
23		Projct Complete	0 d	Medium	34698

Figure 10 - 34: Customized Gantt Chart view

To customize the default *Gantt Chart* view and *Entry* table shown previously in Figure 10 - 34, I completed the following steps:

- I removed the *Task Mode* column.
- I created two new columns called *Schedule Risk* and *SAP Number*, and then populated a value in each of these fields for every task in the project.
- I formatted the *Gantt Chart* view by selecting the *Critical Path* and *Slack* options in the *Bar Styles* section of the *Format* ribbon.
- I changed the color scheme of the *Gantt Chart* view using one of the color schemes in the *Gantt Chart Style* section of the *Format* ribbon.

After customizing a default view and table, you can save them as a new custom view and table by completing the following steps:

1. Display the customized view and table.
2. Click the *Task* tab to display the *Task* ribbon.
3. In the *View* section of the *Task* ribbon, click the *Gantt Chart* pick list button, and then select the *Save View* item on the pick list menu. Project 2013 displays the *Save View* dialog shown in Figure 10 - 35.

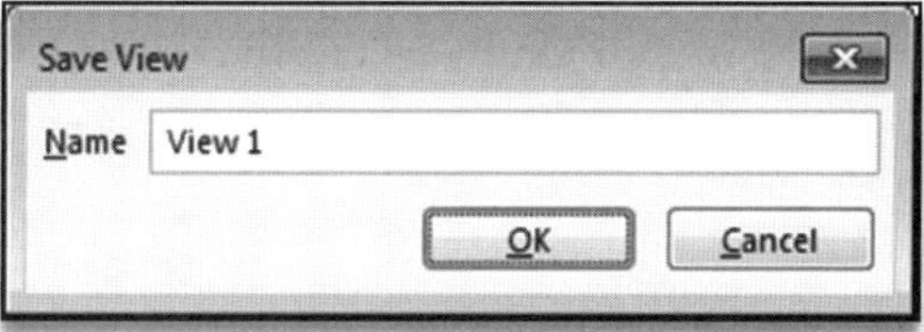

Figure 10 - 35: Save View dialog

4. In the *Save View* dialog, enter an original name for the custom view in the *Name* field, and then click the *OK* button.

Information: You can also save a customized view as a new view using several other ribbons. For example, on the *Resource* ribbon, click the *Team Planner* pick list button, and then select the *Save View* item on the menu. On the *View* ribbon, click **any** pick list button in either the *Task Views* or *Resource Views* section of the ribbon, and then select the *Save View* item on the menu.

After completing the previous set of steps, Project 2013 adds your new view and table to your current project **and** to your Global.mpt file automatically. By adding the view and table to the Global.mpt file, the software makes them available to all current and future projects. To see your new view and table in the Global.mpt file, click the *File* tab and then click the *Organizer* button on the *Info* page of the *Backstage*. The software displays the *Views* page of the *Organizer* dialog shown in Figure 10 - 36. Notice that the software added the new custom view named *_Company Tracking* to the list on the left side of the dialog (in the Global.mpt file) and to the list on the right side of the dialog (in the active project).

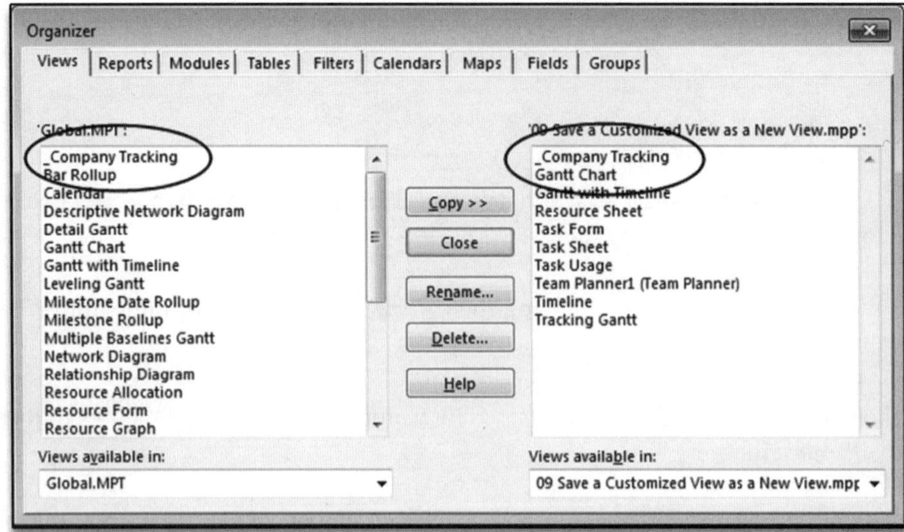

Figure 10 - 36: Organizer dialog, Views page

If you click the *Tables* tab, you can see your new custom table on the left side of the dialog (in the Global.mpt file) and in the right side of the dialog (in the active project). Notice in Figure 10 - 37 that the software named my new custom table using the name of the view, and appending *Table 1* to the table name. In this case, the software named my new custom table *_Company Tracking Table 1*.

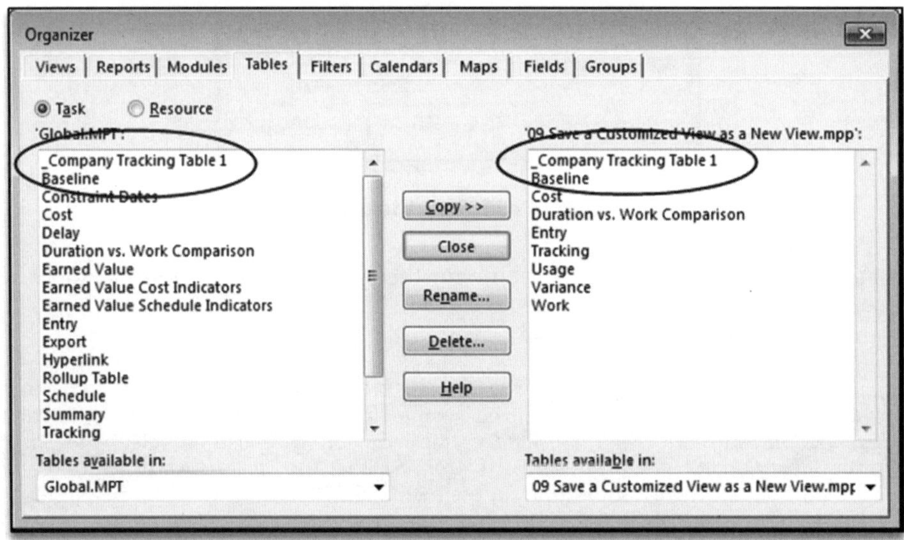

Figure 10 - 37: Organizer dialog, Tables page

At this point, you have the option to edit the name of the table, if necessary. To edit the table name, select the table on the left side of the dialog and then click the *Rename* button. In the *Rename* dialog, enter a new name for the table (such as removing the *Table 1* text from the table name) and then click the *OK* button. Repeat this process for the name of the table on the right side of the dialog. Click the *Close* button to close the *Organizer* dialog and then press the **Escape** key on your computer keyboard to exit the *Backstage*.

Resetting a Default View and Table after Customization

After you create a new custom view and table by customizing a default view and table, I strongly recommend that you reset the customized default view and table to their original default settings. To do this, complete the following steps:

1. Click the *Task* tab to display the *Task* ribbon.
2. In the *View* section of the *Task* ribbon, click the *Gantt Chart* pick list button, and then select the name of the **original** view that you customized and saved as a new view (such as the *Gantt Chart* view).
3. Click the *Gantt Chart* pick list button again and then select the *Reset to Default* item. Project 2013 displays the confirmation dialog shown in Figure 10 - 38.

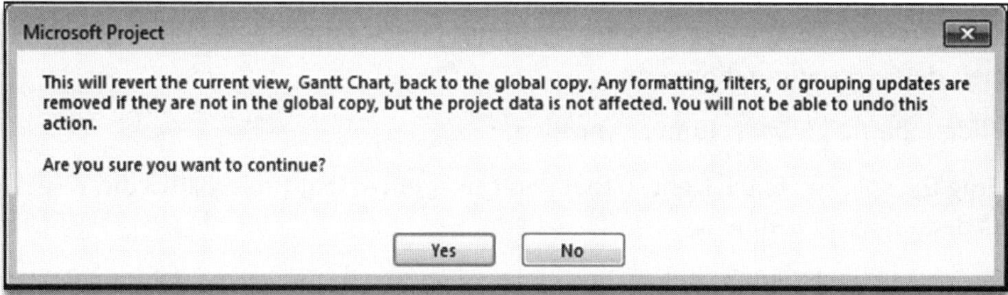

Figure 10 - 38: Confirmation dialog to reset a view to its default settings

4. In the confirmation dialog, click the *Yes* button.

Information: As noted in the previous topical section, you can also reset a view to its default settings by clicking any view pick list button on either the *Resource* ribbon or the *View* ribbon.

The software resets both the view and table to their original default settings prior to customization. This means if you added or removed columns in the table, the software resets the table to the original default list of columns and resets the column width for every column.

Hands On Exercise

Exercise 10 - 7

Create a new custom view by saving a customized default view.

1. Open the **Customize an Existing View 2013.mpp** sample file.
2. Drag the split bar to the right edge of the *Responsible Person* column.
3. Click the *Format* tab to display the contextual *Format* ribbon with the *Gantt Chart Tools* applied.

4. In the *Bar Styles* section of the *Format* ribbon, select the *Critical Tasks* option and the *Slack* option.
5. In the *Gantt Chart Style* gallery in the *Format* ribbon, select any *Gantt Chart* style in the *Scheduling Styles* section of the carousel.
6. Click the *Task* tab to display the *Task* ribbon.
7. Click the *Gantt Chart* pick list button and then select the *Save View* item on the list.
8. In the *Save View* dialog, enter the name *_PMO Information* in the *Name* field, and then click the *OK* button.
9. Click the *Gantt Chart* pick list button again and select the *Gantt Chart* view.
10. Click the *Gantt Chart* pick list button again and select the *Reset to Default* item on the list.
11. In the confirmation dialog, click the *Yes* button to reset the *Gantt Chart* view and the *Entry* table to their default configuration settings.
12. Widen the *Task Name* column, as needed.
13. Drag the split bar to the right so that you can confirm that Project 2013 did reset the *Entry* table to its default list of columns.
14. Click the *File* tab and then click the *Organizer* button on the *Info* page in the *Backstage*.

Notice the new *_PMO Information* view on both the left and right sides of the *Organizer* dialog.

Exercise 10 - 8

Rename and delete objects using the *Organizer* dialog.

1. Click the *Tables* tab in the *Organizer* dialog.
2. Select the *_PMO Information Table 1* item on the **left side** of the *Organizer* dialog (in the Global.mpt file) and then click the *Rename* button.
3. Enter the new name *_PMO Tracking Info* in the *Rename* dialog and click the *OK* button.
4. Select the *_PMO Information Table 1* item on the **right side** of the *Organizer* dialog (in the sample project file) and then click the *Delete* button.
5. Click the *Yes* button in the confirmation dialog to confirm the deletion.
6. Click the *Fields* tab.
7. Select the three custom fields (*Cost Center ID, Major Milestone,* and *Responsible Person*) on the right side of the dialog and then click the *Copy* button to copy them to your Global.mpt file.
8. Click the *Close* button to close the *Organizer* dialog.
9. Press the **Escape** key on your computer keyboard to exit the *Backstage*.
10. Save and close the **Customize an Existing View 2013.mpp** sample file.

Information: With the completion of this exercise, you now have a new custom view, a new custom table, and three custom fields for tracking project information. If you want to use the *Responsible Person* and *Cost Center ID* fields in your own organization, you **must** edit the items in the lookup table for each of these fields. To edit these two fields, use the *Custom Fields* dialog (in the *Properties* section of the *Project* ribbon, click the *Custom Fields* button). If you do not want to use the custom view, tables, and fields, use the *Organizer* dialog to delete all of these custom objects from your Global.mpt file.

Formatting the Gantt Chart

As part of your project communication process, you may need to format the Gantt chart portion of the *Gantt Chart* view for printing or display purposes. In Module 08, *Project Execution,* I taught you how to format the Gantt chart to display *Critical* tasks and to display the *Slack* for each task. I repeated this information again earlier in this module to teach you how to create a new view by customizing a default view. In these two situations, I only "scratched the surface" of the view formatting capabilities available in Project 2013. Now I want to show you the complete view formatting capabilities of the tool, which allow you to format the *Gantt Chart* view or any other default or custom view.

To format the Gantt chart, apply the *Gantt Chart* view and then click the *Format* tab. The software displays the contextual *Format* ribbon with the *Gantt Chart Tools* applied, indicated by the purple area above the *Format* tab shown in Figure 10 - 39.

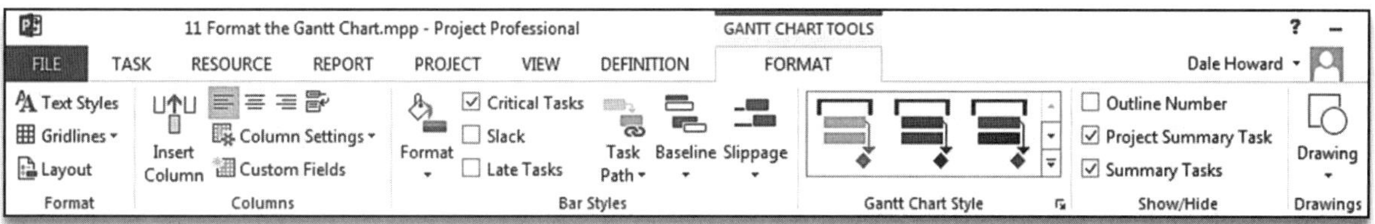

Figure 10 - 39: Format ribbon with the Gantt Chart Tools applied

Using the Format Tools

The *Format* section of the contextual *Format* ribbon contains three buttons, which allow you to format a number of items that appear in Project 2013. Use these buttons to format text styles, gridlines, and progress lines, and to control the layout of Gantt bars in any *Gantt Chart* view. I discuss each of these items separately.

Formatting Text Styles

When you click the *Text Styles* button in the *Format* section of the contextual *Format* ribbon, the software displays the *Text Styles* dialog. This dialog offers you the automatic formatting capabilities for both text and cell background formatting. For example, you can use this dialog to apply a cell background color to every milestone task and to apply a different cell background color to every summary task. When you click the *Item to Change* pick list, as shown in Figure 10 - 40, you see the list of every text object to which you can apply the automatic formatting.

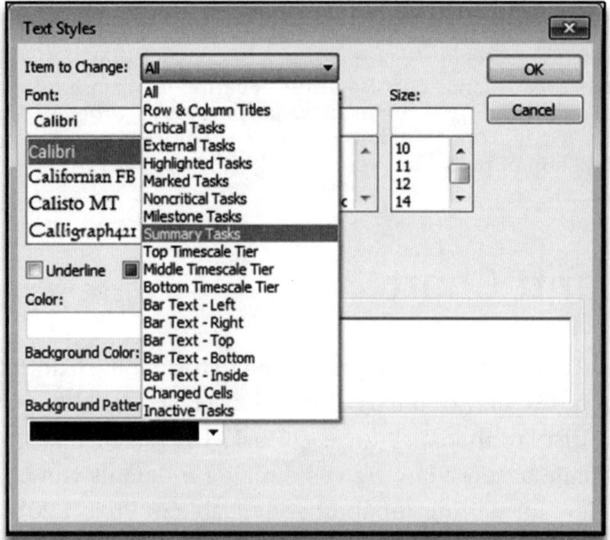

Figure 10 - 40: Text Styles dialog
Item to Change pick list

To apply automatic formatting to any object in a project, complete the following steps in the *Text Styles* dialog:

1. Click the *Item to Change* pick list and select an object, such as the *Summary Tasks* object.
2. Select the desired font formatting options in the *Font*, *Font Style*, and *Size* fields.
3. Select the *Underline* or *Strikethrough* checkboxes, as needed.
4. Select color formatting in the *Color*, *Background Color*, and *Background Pattern* pick lists, as needed.
5. Repeat steps #1-4 for each object you want to format automatically.
6. Click the *OK* button when finished.

Formatting Gridlines

When you click the *Gridlines* pick list button in the *Format* section of the *Format* ribbon, the software displays two options on the list: the *Gridlines* item and the *Progress Lines* item. If you select the *Gridlines* item, Project 2013 displays the *Gridlines* dialog. Figure 10 - 41 shows the formatting for the *Current Date* gridline in the *Gridlines* dialog.

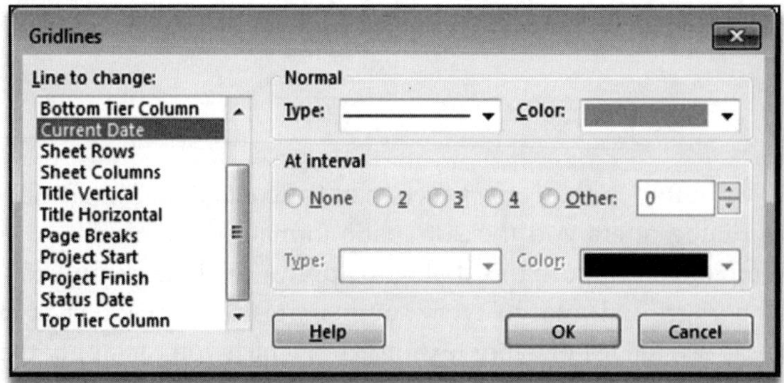

Figure 10 - 41: Gridlines dialog, Current Date formatting

To change any gridline, select a gridline item in the *Line to change* list. In the *Gridlines* dialog, select the relevant values in the *Type* and *Color* fields, and in the *At interval* section of the dialog. Click the *OK* button to apply the formatting to the selected gridline.

Best Practice: As a part of your project reporting process, if you select a date in the *Status date* field in the *Project Information* dialog, MSProjectExperts recommends that you also apply formatting to the *Status Date* gridline. This makes the *Status Date* gridline visible in the *Gantt Chart* view. For example, in the *Gridlines* dialog, select the *Status Date* item in the *Line to change* list, select the last item on the *Type* pick list (the -- - -- - -- item), and then select the *Red* color on the *Color* pick list. This creates a very visible reminder of the date currently entered in the *Status Date* field for your project.

Figure 10 - 42 shows a project in which I formatted the *Status Date* gridline using the preceding best practice recommendation. In this project, June 26th (Friday) is the *Status Date* of the project, representing the last day of the previous reporting period. The red dashed line is the *Status Date* gridline, which represents the date for which all task progress must be current or else the task is behind schedule. The solid green gridline on June 29th is the *Current Date* for the project, by the way.

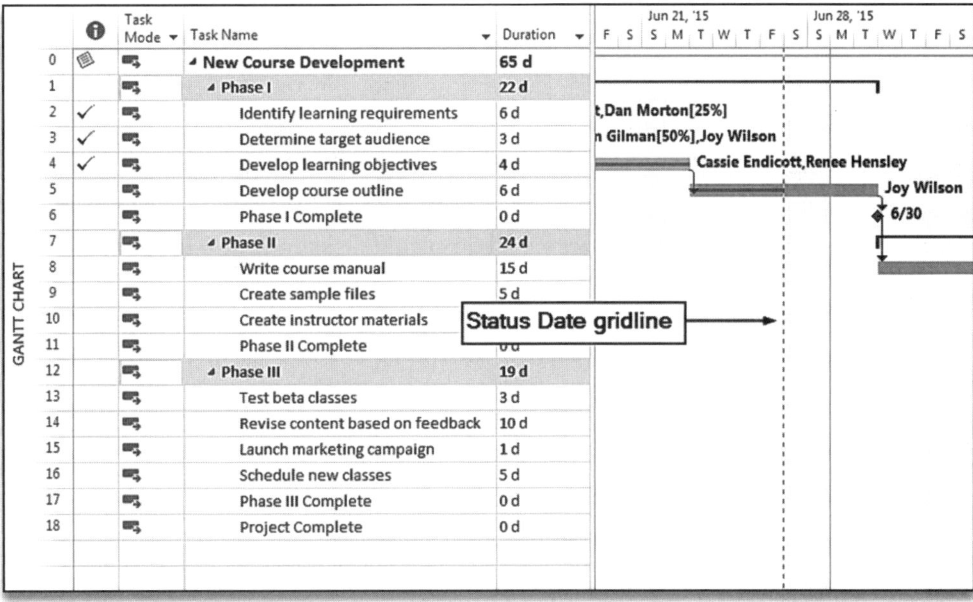

Figure 10 - 42: Status Date gridline displayed in the Gantt Chart view

Displaying and Formatting Progress Lines

You can use the *Progress Lines* feature in Project 2013 to quickly locate tasks whose progress is behind schedule. A task that is behind schedule is any task whose cumulative *% Complete* value is less than the expected *% Complete* value, as of the *Status Date* value you specify in the project. For example, by the *Status Date* of my project, a task is only 25% complete when it should be 50% complete; therefore, this task is behind schedule.

In the *Format* section of the *Format* ribbon, click the *Gridlines* pick list button, and then select the *Progress Lines* item. The software displays the *Progress Lines* dialog with the *Dates and Intervals* tab selected, shown in Figure 10 - 43. On the *Dates and Intervals* page of the dialog, Project 2013 allows you to select the type of progress line(s) you want to display.

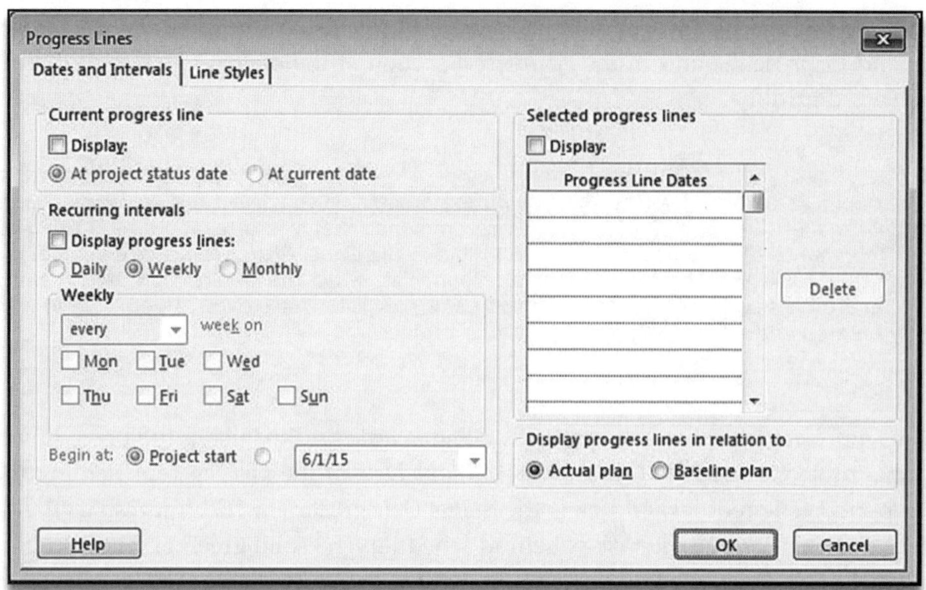

Figure 10 - 43: Progress Lines dialog, Dates and Intervals page

To display the most commonly used progress line, select the *Display* checkbox in the *Current progress line* section of the dialog, and then select the *At project status date* option. Selecting this option assumes you entered a date value in the *Status Date* field in the *Project Information* dialog, of course. You have the option to select the *At current date* option if you want to do so. Click the *OK* button to display the progress line in your project.

Figure 10 - 44 shows a project with a progress line displayed. The progress line connects with the current progress point on any in-progress task, but does not connect with completed tasks or future unstarted tasks. If the progress line "spikes" to the left, the task is behind schedule, as of the *Status Date* value you specified for the project. Most of the time, you should focus your attention on any task whose progress line spikes to the left. Notice in Figure 10 - 44 that the progress line "spikes" to the left for the *Write course manual* task and the *PHASE II* summary task, indicating that these this task is behind schedule.

		Task Mode	Task Name	Duration
0			New Course Development	63 d
1	✓		Phase I	20 d
2	✓		Identify learning requirements	6 d
3	✓		Determine target audience	3 d
4	✓		Develop learning objectives	4 d
5	✓		Develop course outline	4 d
6	✓		Phase I Complete	0 d
7			Phase II	24 d
8			Write course manual	15 d
9			Create sample files	5 d
10			Create instructor materials	5 d
11			Phase II Complete	0 d
12			Phase III	19 d
13			Test beta classes	3 d
14			Revise content based on feedback	10 d
15			Launch marketing campaign	1 d
16			Schedule new classes	5 d
17			Phase III Complete	0 d
18			Project Complete	0 d

Figure 10 - 44: Progress Line displayed in the Gantt Chart view

In the *Progress Lines* dialog, the software offers you several other progress line options. For example, if you select the *Display progress lines* option in the *Recurring intervals* section of the dialog, Project 2013 allows you to set up recurring progress lines on a daily, weekly, or monthly basis, as shown in Figure 10 - 45. If you select this option, you must also select other relevant information in this section of the dialog. For example, if you select the *Weekly* option, you must select an item in the *Weekly* pick list, and then select the checkbox for at least one day of the week. Beyond this, you must select a *Begin at* option to determine whether the recurring progress line begins on the project start date or on a day you specify manually.

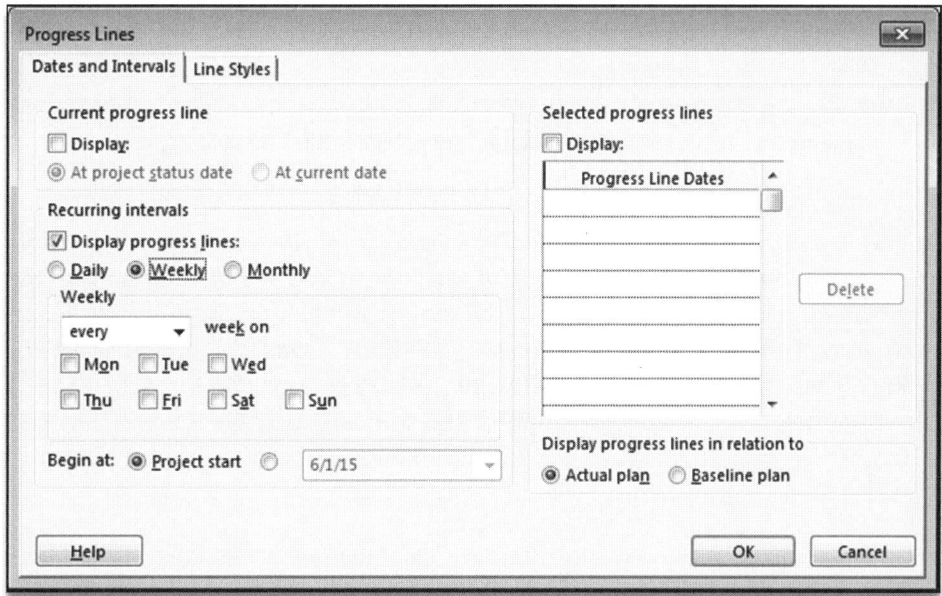

Figure 10 - 45: Progress Lines dialog, select a recurring progress line

Another progress line option in the *Progress Lines* dialog allows you to specify progress lines on **specific dates** in your project, such as on the dates of key milestones. To use this feature, select the *Display* checkbox in the *Selected progress lines* section of the dialog. For each line in the *Progress Line Dates* data grid, select or enter a date for a progress line you want to display in the project. For example, in Figure 10 - 46 notice that I am currently selecting another progress line on 7/3/15. Because of the visual confusion you may create by displaying multiple progress lines, you may want to delete progress lines that you no longer need. To delete a progress line, select the date in the *Progress Line Dates* data grid and then click the *Delete* button.

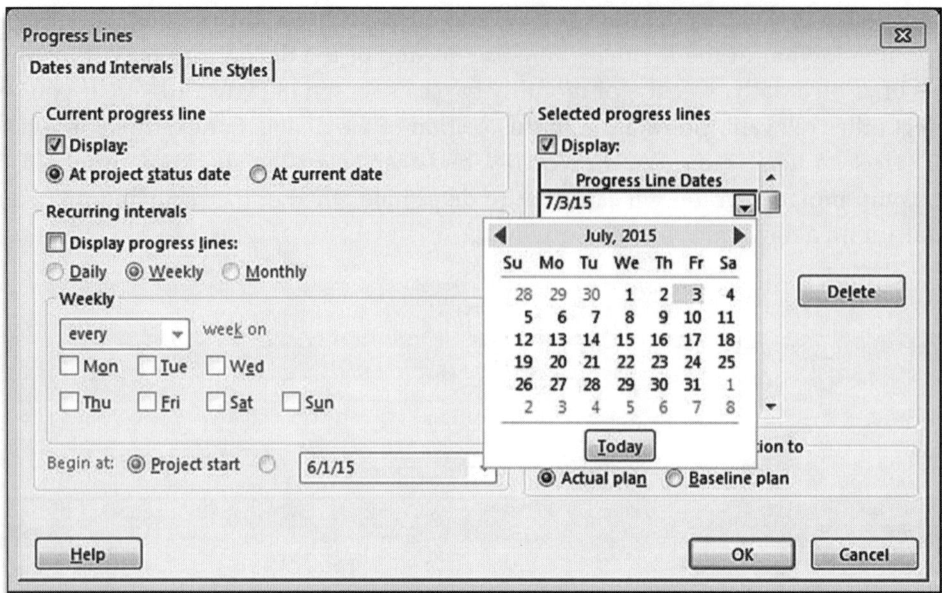

Figure 10 - 46: Progress Lines dialog, set progress lines on specific dates

The final progress lines option you can select on the *Dates and Intervals* page is whether to display progress lines based on current progress or on the baseline schedule of the project. You see these options in the *Display progress lines in relation to* section in the lower right corner of the dialog. By default, the software selects the *Actual plan* option, but you may select the *Baseline plan* option instead. With the *Actual plan* option selected, Project 2013 displays the progress line(s) based on the current schedule of the project, based on the *Actual Start* and *Actual Finish* dates for each task. If you select the *Baseline plan* option, the software displays the progress line(s) based on the baseline schedule of the project, based on the *Baseline Start* and *Baseline Finish* dates for each task.

After you specify the type of progress line you want to see, click the *Line Styles* tab in the *Progress Lines* dialog to format the display of the progress line. The software displays the *Line Styles* page of the dialog shown in Figure 10 - 47. Using the options on the *Line Styles* page, the software allows you to control the types, shapes, colors, and date display for the progress line as follows:

- In the *Progress line type* section of the dialog, select one of four display types. By default, the software selects the item in the upper left corner of the section.

- In the *Line style* section of the dialog, select values in the *Line type, Line color, Progress point shape,* and *Progress point color* pick lists. The software allows you to format the shape and color for the current progress line and for all other progress lines.

- In the *Date display* section of the dialog, select the *Show date for each progress line* option to show the date for the progress line at the top of the progress line, directly below the *Timescale* bar. In the *Date display* section, you can also click the *Format* pick list and choose the formatting for the date. Additionally, you can click the *Change Font* button and select the font used for the date displayed on the progress line.

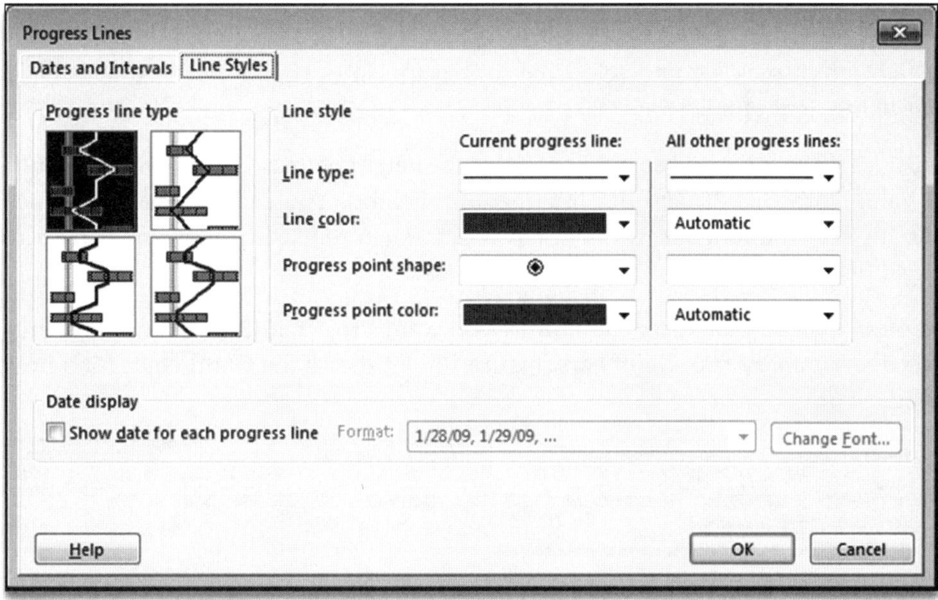

Figure 10 - 47: Progress Lines dialog, Line Styles page

Formatting the Display of Gantt Bars

In the *Format* section of the *Format* ribbon, click the *Layout* button, and the software displays the *Layout* dialog shown in Figure 10 - 48. You use the options in this dialog to control how Project 2013 lays out Gantt bars in any task view, such as in the *Gantt Chart* view.

Figure 10 - 48: Layout dialog

The *Layout* dialog contains three sections in which you control how the software displays Gantt bars. In the *Links* section, select one of three options that control how the software displays the link lines between dependent tasks. By default, Project 2013 selects the third option (straight link lines), but you can select the second option to display curving link lines, or the first option to display no link lines at all.

The *Bars* section contains a number of available options, including:

- Click the *Date format* pick list and select the format for dates shown with Gantt bars. The software displays dates to the right of milestone tasks by default.

- Click the *Bar height* pick list and select a value for the height of each Gantt bar. By default, the software selects a *12* value in the *Bar Height* pick list (medium height). You can increase the value in the *Bar height* field if you increase the font size for the names of tasks in the task list, or you can decrease the value in the *Bar height* field if you decrease the font size for tasks.

- Select the *Always roll up Gantt bars* checkbox if you want Project 2013 to roll up the Gantt bar symbols on their respective summary task Gantt bars. Figure 10 - 49 shows the Gantt chart for a project with this option selected.

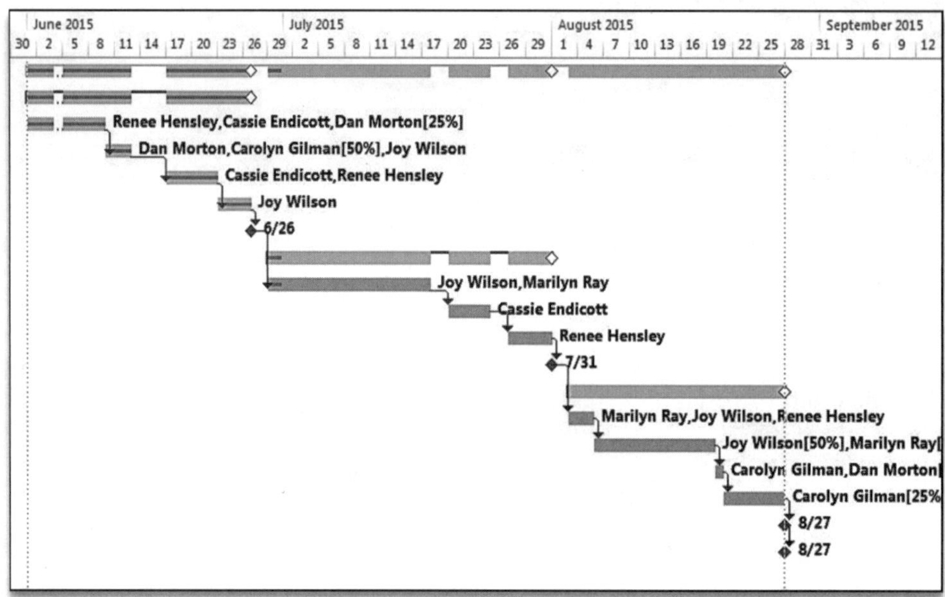

Figure 10 - 49: Gantt bars rolled up to their summary tasks

- If you select the *Always roll up Gantt bars* checkbox, the software activates a second checkbox. If you select the *Hide rollup bars when summary expanded* checkbox, the software hides summary Gantt bars when you collapse a summary task, and displays only the rolled up Gantt bars from its subtasks. If you expand a summary task, the software displays only the summary Gantt bar for the summary task. Keep in mind that this behavior is the **opposite** of how you might expect it to work!

- Use the *Round bars to whole days* option to determine how Project 2013 displays the length of the Gantt bar for any task whose *Duration* value is not a whole number, such as when a task has a duration of *3.25 days*. If you select this option, the software sets the length of the Gantt bar to a rounded *Duration* of *3 days*. If you deselect this option, the software sets the length of the Gantt bar to the exact *Duration* value. Keep in mind that this option **does not** affect values in the *Duration*, *Start*, and *Finish* fields for any task; this option only affects how the software displays Gantt bars.

- Select the *Show bar splits* checkbox if you want the software to display the split symbol (**...**) in the Gantt bars of tasks containing a task split. Task splits usually occur when you enter an *Actual Work* value of *0h* in the timephased grid of either the *Task Usage* or *Resource Usage* view. Entering 0 hours of actual work indicates that the resource performed no work during the specified time period, such as on a day when the resource called in sick. If you deselect the *Show bar splits* checkbox, Project 2013 displays every Gantt bar as a solid bar, even if the task contains a task split.

Warning: Because of an unfixed bug in the release (RTM) version of Project 2013, the software **does not** allow you to **deselect** the *Show bar splits* checkbox in the *Layout* dialog. Instead, the software displays an error dialog and does not allow you to proceed any further.

- Select *Show drawings* checkbox if you want to add drawing objects to your Gantt chart using the *Drawing* button in the *Drawings* section of the *Format* ribbon. If you deselect this option, Project 2013 disables the *Drawing* button so that you cannot add drawings to the Gantt chart.

When finished, click the *OK* button to close the *Layout* dialog and apply the selected layout options to the *Gantt Chart* view of your project.

Hands On Exercise

Exercise 10 - 9

Format the text styles, gridlines, and the layout of Gantt bars in the *Gantt Chart* view of a project.

1. Open the **Formatting Views 2013.mpp** sample file.
2. Click the *Format* tab to display the contextual *Format* ribbon with the *Gantt Chart Tools* applied.
3. Click the *Text Styles* button in the *Format* section of the *Format* ribbon.
4. In the *Text Styles* dialog, click the *Item to Change* pick list and select the *Milestone Tasks* item.
5. Click the *Background Color* pick list and select the *Gold, Lighter 60%* color in the *Theme Colors* section of the dialog.
6. Click the *OK* button.

Notice how Project 2013 formats the cell background color of every milestone task with the gold color.

7. Click the *Gridlines* pick list button and then select the *Gridlines* item on the list.
8. In the *Gridlines* dialog, select the *Status Date* item at the bottom of the *Line to change* list.
9. Click the *Type* pick list and select the last item on the list (the -- - -- - -- - item).
10. Click the *Color* pick list and select the *Red* color in the *Standard Colors* section of the pick list.
11. Click the *OK* button.

Notice how Project 2013 displays the *Status Date* of the project using a red dashed vertical line in the Gantt chart.

12. Click the *Layout* pick list button.
13. In the *Layout* dialog, select the second item in the *Links* section, and then click the *OK* button.

Notice how Project 2013 changes the straight link lines to the curving link lines for all tasks with dependencies.

14. Save but **do not** close the **Formatting Views 2013.mpp** sample file.

Using the Columns Tools

Earlier in this module, I taught you several ways to insert columns in a default table and view in Project 2013. The *Columns* section of the contextual *Format* ribbon provides one more way to insert columns in a table and view. To insert a new column in the *Gantt Chart* view, for example, click anywhere in the column where you want to insert the new column, and then click the *Insert Column* button in the *Columns* section of the *Format* ribbon. Project 2013 inserts a new column to the left of the selected column and displays the list of available task fields, as shown in Figure 10 - 50. To complete the insertion process, select the column you want to insert from the list of available columns.

Alternately, with the list of available columns displayed, you can also type the name of the column you want to insert. When you type the name of a column, remember that the software creates a new custom *Text* field using the name you enter. Because I discussed creating fields previously in this module, I do not discuss this topic again. If necessary, refer back to the *Customizing a Table Using the Add New Column Feature* topical section of this module and review the process for creating custom fields.

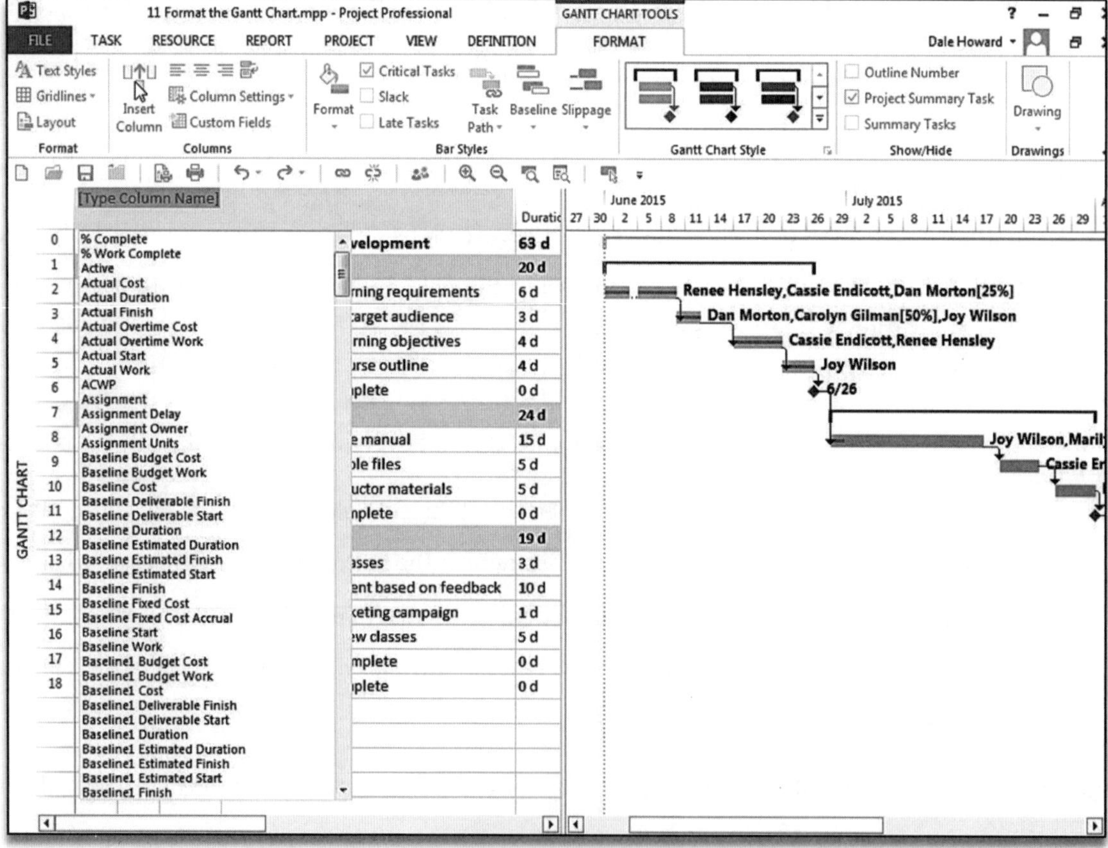

Figure 10 - 50: Insert a new column to the left of the Task Name column

To align the data in any column, click anywhere in a column and then click the *Align Left*, the *Center*, or the *Align Right* button in the *Columns* section of the *Format* ribbon. The software changes the alignment of the data in the column, but does not change the alignment of the text in the column header.

To control text wrapping for any column, click anywhere in the column you want to change and then select or deselect the *Wrap Text* toggle button in the *Columns* section of the *Format* ribbon. By default, Project 2013 enables the *Wrap Text* feature for only the *Task Names* column in task views and the *Resource Names* column in resource views. With the *Text Wrapping* feature enabled, the software increases the row height of tasks automatically for task names longer than the new width of the *Task Name* column.

Before you attempt to use the *Column Settings* pick list button in the *Columns* section of the *Format* ribbon, be certain to select a column in your Project 2013 project file. When you click the *Column Settings* pick list button, the software displays the pick list menu shown in Figure 10 - 51.

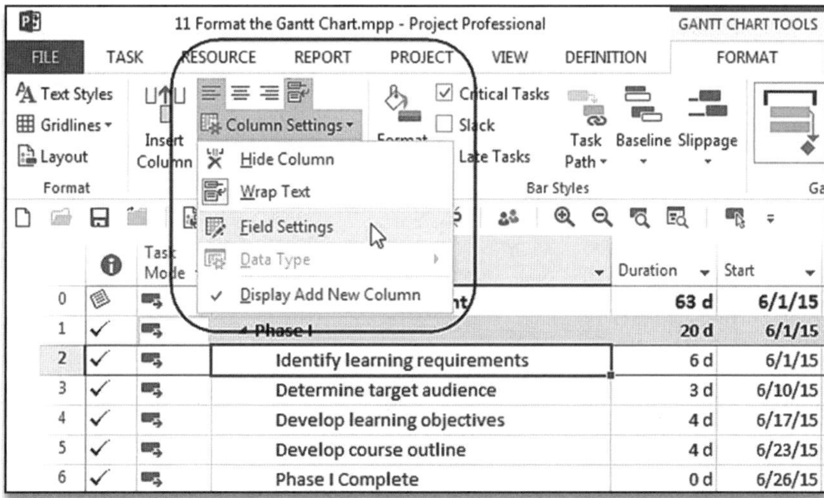

Figure 10 - 51: Column Settings pick list menu

In the *Column Settings* pick list menu, click the *Hide Column* item to hide the selected column. Select or deselect the *Wrap Text* item to enable or disable automatic text wrapping in the selected column. Select the *Field Settings* item to display the *Field Settings* dialog shown in Figure 10 - 52. Because I discussed the *Field Settings* dialog previously in this module, I do not discuss this topic again. If necessary, refer back to the *Customizing a Table Using the Add New Column Feature* topical section of this module and review the information about the *Field Settings* dialog.

Figure 10 - 52: Field Settings dialog

In the *Column Settings* pick list menu, deselect the *Display Add New Column* item if you do not want to display the *Add New Column* virtual column on the far right side of the current table. You can display or hide the *Add New*

Column virtual column for each table individually. Keep in mind that the software automatically displays the *Add New Column* virtual column in every default table included in Project 2013, but you can disable this feature on a table by table basis, as needed.

If you click the *Custom Fields* button in the *Columns* section of the *Format* ribbon, Project 2013 displays the *Custom Fields* dialog shown in Figure 10 - 53. Because I discussed the *Custom Fields* dialog previously in this module, I do not discuss this topic again. If necessary, refer back to the *Customizing a Table Using the Add New Column Feature* topical section of this module and review the information about the *Custom Fields* dialog.

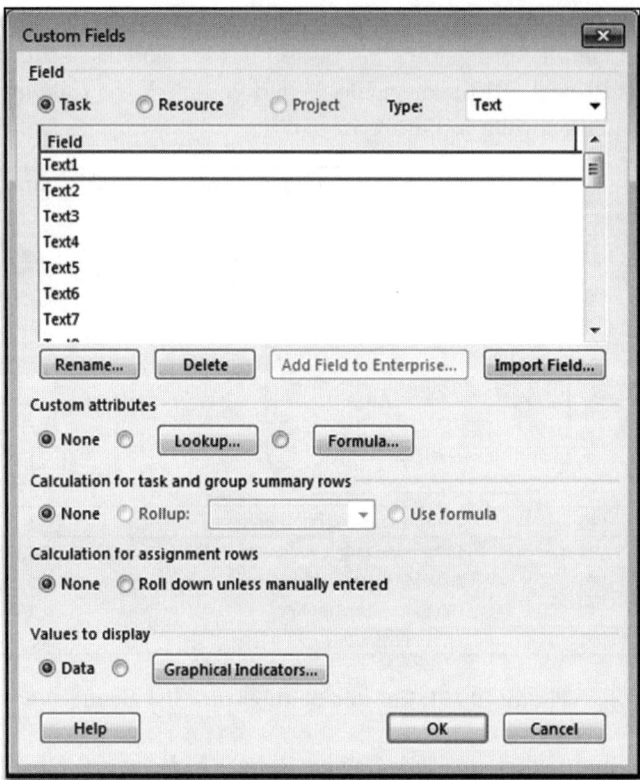

Figure 10 - 53: Custom Fields dialog

Hands On Exercise

Exercise 10 - 10

Format the columns in the *Gantt Chart* view of a project.

1. Return to the **Formatting Views 2013.mpp** sample file.
2. Click the *Task Mode* column header to select the entire column.
3. In the *Columns* section of the *Format* ribbon, click the *Insert Column* button, and then select the *% Complete* field from the list of available fields.

4. Double-click the right edge of the *% Complete* column header to "best fit" the column automatically.
5. With the *% Complete* column still selected, click the *Center* button to center the data in the *% Complete* column.
6. With the *% Complete* column still selected, click the *Column Settings* pick list button, and then select the *Field Settings* item.
7. In the *Field Settings* dialog, click the *Align Title* pick list, and select the *Center* item.
8. Click the *OK* button.
9. Click the *Task Mode* column header to select the entire column.
10. In the *Columns* section of the *Format* ribbon, click the *Column Settings* pick list button, and select the *Hide Column* item on the pick list.
11. Save but **do not** close the **Formatting Views 2013.mpp** sample file.

Using the Bar Styles Tools

The *Bar Styles* section of the contextual *Format* ribbon contains a number of powerful tools that allow you to customize the *Gantt Chart* view to display project information exactly the way you want to see it. When you click the *Format* pick list button, the software displays two options on the pick list menu: the *Bar* item and the *Bar Styles* item. If you want to format the appearance of individual Gantt bars in the *Gantt Chart* view, select the tasks whose Gantt bars you want to format, then click the *Format* pick list button and select the *Bar* item. Project 2013 displays the *Format Bar* dialog shown in Figure 10 - 54.

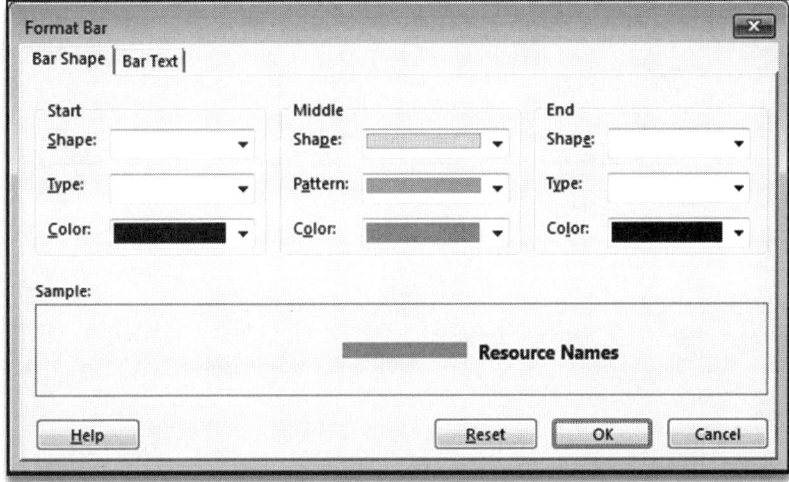

Figure 10 - 54: Format Bar dialog, Bar Shape tab

On the *Bar Shape* tab of the *Format Bar* dialog, the software offers three sections of fields that you use to format the shape and color of the selected Gantt bars. Use the *Shape, Type,* and *Color* pick lists in the *Start* and *End* sections to control the shapes used to draw the start and end of each selected Gantt bar. Use the *Shape, Pattern,* and *Color* pick lists in the *Middle* section to format the middle of the selected Gantt bars. Notice in Figure 10 - 54 shown previously that the Gantt bars for the selected tasks do not contain any start or end shape information. Figure 10 - 55 shows the *Bar Styles* dialog with custom information in the *Start, Middle,* and *End* sections of the dialog.

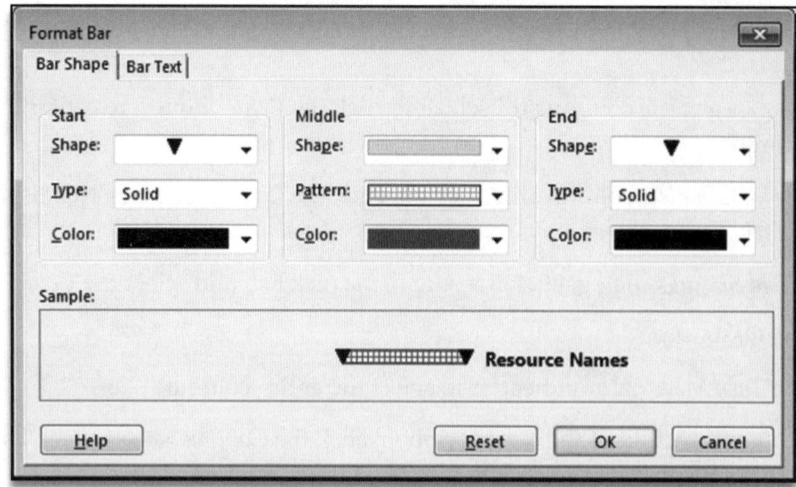

Figure 10 - 55: Format Bar dialog, Bar Shape tab with custom information in the Start, Middle, and End sections

In the *Format Bar* dialog, select the *Bar Text* tab to display the *Bar Text* page shown in Figure 10 - 56. Beyond formatting the shape and color of selected Gantt bars, you can use the *Bar Text* page of the dialog to display text information with the selected Gantt bars. By default, Project 2013 selects the *Resource Names* field in the *Right* pick list. This causes the software to display the names of assigned resources to the right of Gantt bars for the selected tasks. You have the option to remove the *Resource Names* field from the *Right* pick list, if you like, and to select any field in the *Left, Right, Top, Bottom,* and *Inside* fields. For example, to display the *% Complete* field to the left of the selected Gantt bars, click the *Left* pick list and select the *% Complete* field. When finished, click the *OK* button to apply the new formatting to the Gantt bars for the selected tasks.

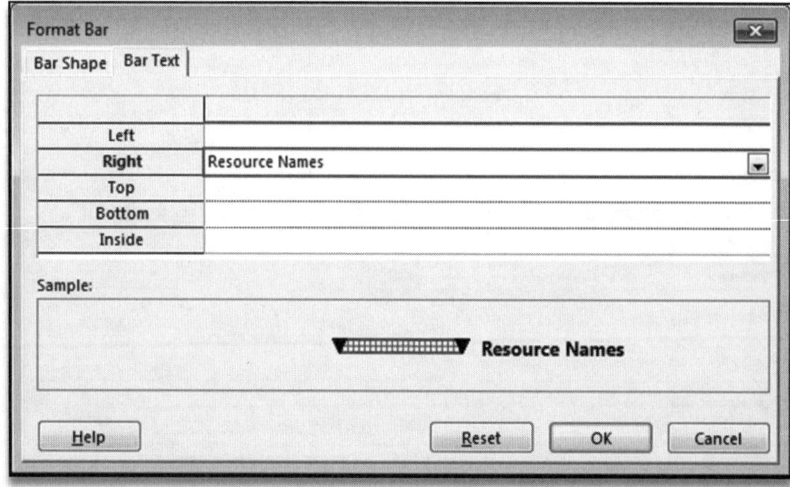

Figure 10 - 56: Format Bar dialog, Bar Text tab

If you want to format all of the Gantt bars in a project in a single action, click the *Format* pick list, and then select the *Bar Styles* item. The software displays the *Bar Styles* dialog shown in Figure 10 - 57 with the *Task* item selected. The *Bar Styles* dialog contains the definition of every object shown in the *Gantt Chart* view, including items like the Gantt bars for regular tasks and the symbols for milestone tasks and summary tasks. You can change the appearance of any *Gantt Chart* item by selecting its definition row in the *Bar Styles* dialog and then editing the information in the *Start, Middle,* and *End* sections of the *Bars* tab at the bottom of the dialog. If you click the *Text* tab in the bottom of the dialog, you see a data grid identical to the one shown on the *Bar Text* tab of the *Format Bar* dialog shown previously in Figure 10 - 56. To change the text displayed with any object, first select the object in the top part of the dialog, and then select the *Text* tab to configure the text information you want to show with the selected object. Click the *OK* button when finished.

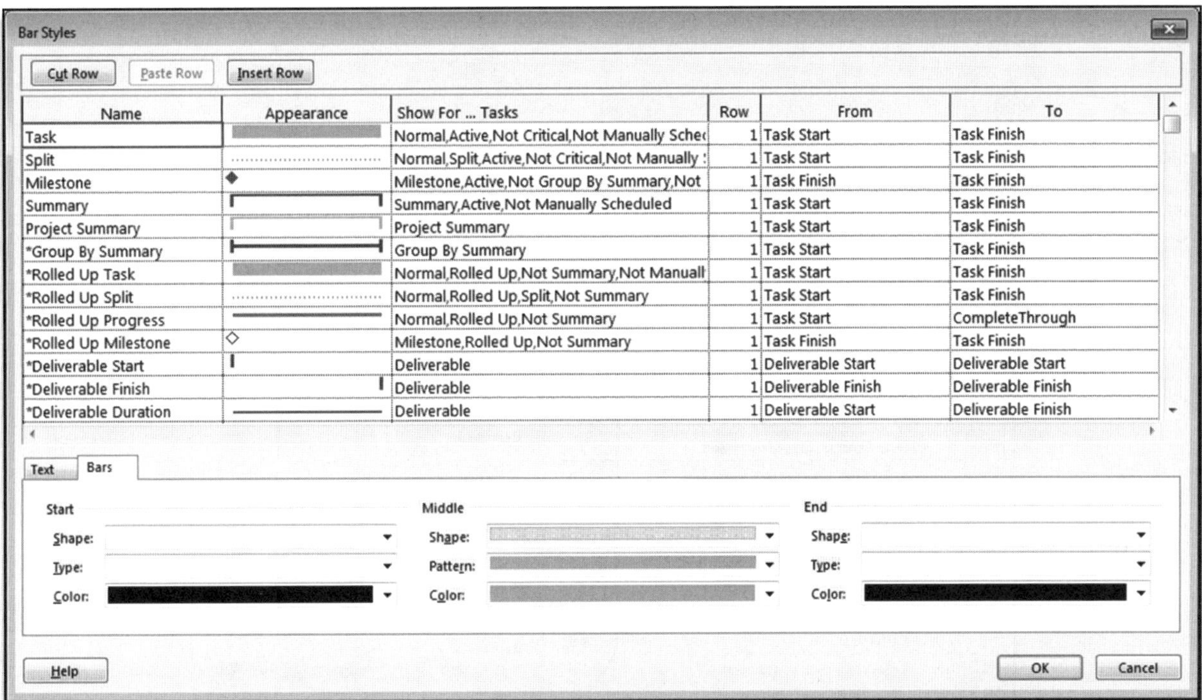

Figure 10 - 57: Bar Styles dialog with Task item selected

Warning: When you use the *Bar Styles* dialog to change the bar style for a particular *Gantt Chart* item, such as the *Critical* item, Project 2013 does not apply the new bar style for any individual Gantt bars whose bar style you applied manually using the *Format Bar* dialog.

As noted previously in Module 08, *Project Execution*, you can use the checkbox options in the *Bar Styles* section of the contextual *Format* ribbon to display the *Critical Path* in your project. To display the *Critical Path* in your project, select the *Critical Tasks* checkbox in the *Bar Styles* section of the contextual *Format* ribbon. Project 2013 formats the *Gantt Chart* view with red bars representing critical tasks, and with blue bars representing non-critical tasks. Remember that critical tasks have a *Total Slack* value of *0 days* and cannot slip without changing the finish date of the project. Non-critical tasks have a *Total Slack* value **greater than** *0 days* and can slip by the amount of the *Total Slack* before they impact the finish date of the project.

To display the *Total Slack* in your project, select the *Slack* checkbox in the *Bar Styles* section of the contextual *Format* ribbon. Project 2013 displays a dark blue underscore to the right of the Gantt bar of every task with a *Total Slack* value *greater than 0 days*.

In Project 2013, a *Late* task is any task whose current *% Complete* value is less than the expected *% Complete* value, as of the *Status Date* value you specify in the project. To display the *Late* tasks in your project, select the *Late Tasks* checkbox in the *Bar Styles* section of the contextual *Format* ribbon. Project 2013 displays *Late* tasks using dark gray Gantt bars.

As noted previously in Module 08, *Project Execution*, you can display your operating baseline in the *Gantt Chart* view by clicking the *Baseline* pick list button in the *Bar Styles* section of the contextual *Format* ribbon. The *Baseline* pick list displays a list of eleven available sets of *Baseline* fields, and indicates the save date for each set of *Baseline* fields, as shown in Figure 10 - 58. On the *Baseline* pick list, select the baseline you want to show in the *Gantt Chart* view. Project 2013 displays the selected baseline information using a gray bar for each task to represent the original baseline schedule for the task.

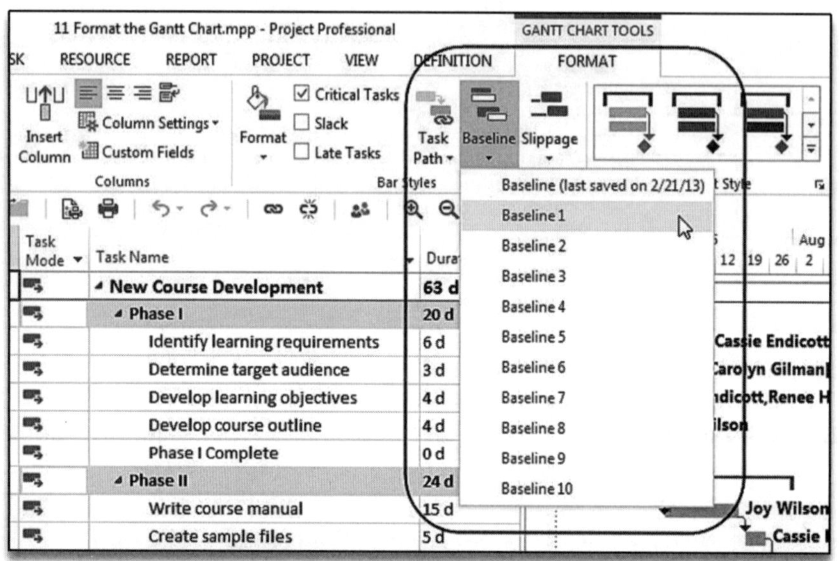

Figure 10 - 58: List of available Baselines on the Baseline pick list

To view the current amount of schedule slippage in your *Gantt Chart* view, click the *Slippage* pick list button in the *Bar Styles* section of the contextual *Format* ribbon. The *Slippage* pick list includes the same list of *Baseline* fields as on the *Baseline* pick list shown previously in Figure 10 - 58. Select one of the available sets of *Baseline* fields on the *Slippage* pick list. Project 2013 displays a dark blue underscore stripe to the left of the Gantt bar for every slipping task. The length of the *Slippage* indicator represents the amount of slippage for each task.

Using the Gantt Chart Style Tools

The only option in the *Gantt Chart Style* section of the contextual *Format* ribbon is the *Gantt Chart Style* carousel. Using this tool, you can customize the color scheme and appearance of all the symbols shown in the Gantt chart, including the symbols for regular tasks, summary tasks, milestone tasks, *Deadline* date indicators, and more. To change the color scheme used for every symbol in the Gantt chart, click either the *up-arrow* or *down-arrow* buttons in the *Gantt Chart Style* carousel to view the list of available color schemes, and then select a color scheme. Alternately, you can click the *More* button directly below the *down-arrow* button in the *Gantt Chart Style* carousel to display a list of all available color schemes, as shown in Figure 10 - 59.

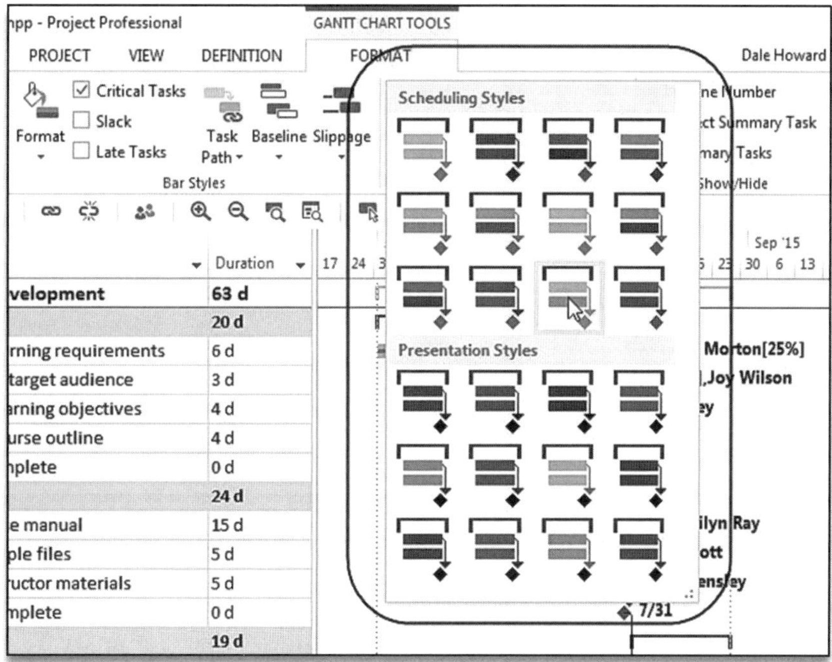

Figure 10 - 59: Available color styles in the Gantt Chart Styles pick list

Notice that the *Gantt Chart Styles* carousel organizes the available color schemes into two sections. Select a color scheme in the *Scheduling Styles* section to format your *Gantt Chart* view for day-to-day project management work. Select a color scheme in the *Presentation Styles* section to format your *Gantt Chart* view for a presentation.

After you select a color scheme on the *Gantt Chart Styles* carousel, you can also click the *Format Bar Styles Dialog Launcher* button (little arrow button) in the lower right corner of the *Gantt Chart Styles* section of the contextual *Format* ribbon. The software launches the *Bar Styles* dialog shown previously in Figure 10 - 57, with the selected color scheme applied to every object in the dialog.

Using the Show/Hide Tools

The *Show/Hide* section of the contextual *Format* ribbon contains three option checkboxes that allow you to show extra detail in the *Task Sheet* on the left side of your *Gantt Chart* view. Remember that the *Task Sheet* displays the list of tasks on the left side of any task view, such as the *Gantt Chart* view or the *Tracking Gantt* view. Unless you specify otherwise in the *Project Options* dialog, the software selects only the *Summary Tasks* option by default in each new project you create. Deselect the *Summary Tasks* option to hide summary tasks in your project temporarily to show only regular tasks and milestone tasks in your project, as shown in Figure 10 - 60.

	Task Mode	Task Name	Duration	
2	✓	Identify learning requirements	6 d	Renee Hensley,Cassie Endicott,Dan Morton[25%]
3	✓	Determine target audience	3 d	Dan Morton,Carolyn Gilman[50%],Joy Wilson
4	✓	Develop learning objectives	4 d	Cassie Endicott,Renee Hensley
5	✓	Develop course outline	4 d	Joy Wilson
6	✓	Phase I Complete	0 d	6/26
8		Write course manual	15 d	Joy Wilson,Marilyn Ray
9		Create sample files	5 d	Cassie Endicott
10		Create instructor materials	5 d	Renee Hensley
11		Phase II Complete	0 d	7/31
13		Test beta classes	3 d	Marilyn Ray,Joy Wilson,Renee Hensley
14		Revise content based on feedback	10 d	Joy Wilson[50%],Marilyn Ray[50%]
15		Launch marketing campaign	1 d	Carolyn Gilman,Dan Morton[25%]
16		Schedule new classes	5 d	Carolyn Gilman[25%]
17		Phase III Complete	0 d	8/27
18		Project Complete	0 d	8/27

Figure 10 - 60: Summary Tasks option deselected in the Show/Hide section

With the *Summary Tasks* option selected, you can also select the *Project Summary Task* option to display the Project Summary Task (Row 0 or Task 0) in your project. Remember that the Project Summary Task is the highest level summary task in your project, and summarizes all of the information in the project. It shows you the current *Start* date and the current calculated *Finish* date of the project, the current *Duration* of the project, the current amount of *Work* and *Cost* for the project, and shows you all variance for the project. Because of this, I strongly recommend you include the Project Summary Task in the *Gantt Chart* view of every project you manage! Figure 10 - 61 shows a project with summary tasks and the Project Summary Task displayed in the project.

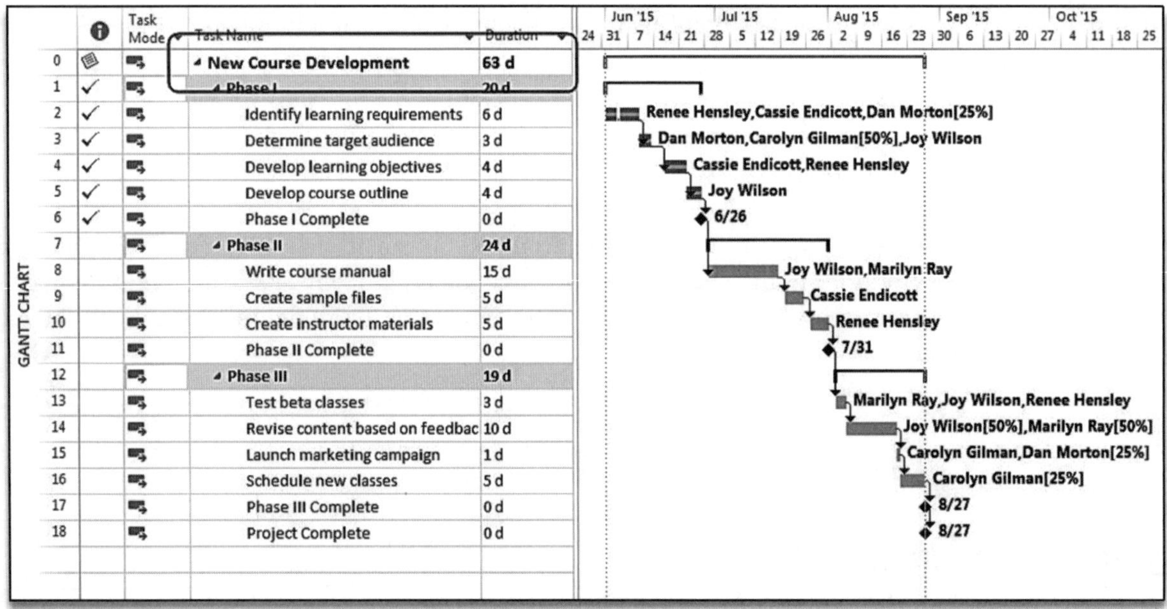

Figure 10 - 61: Project Summary Task option selected in the Show/Hide section

The final option you can select in the *Show/Hide* section of the contextual *Format* ribbon is the *Outline Number* option. When you select this option, Project 2013 displays an outline number to the left of every task in the *Task Sheet* part of the *Gantt Chart* view, as shown in Figure 10 - 62. Notice the numbering system for the outline numbers to the left of each task. The *Phase I* summary task is the first task at the first level of indent, so Project 2013 assigns the number **1** to this task. The *Phase II* summary task is the second task at the first level of indent, so the software assigns the number **2** to this task. The *Phase III* complete is the third task at the first level of indent, so the software assigns the number **3** to this task. The *Identify learning requirements* is the first task in the *Phase I* summary task section, so Project 2013 assigns the number **1.1** to this task. Notice that the *Develop course outline* task is the fourth task in the *Phase I* summary task section, so the software assigns the number **1.4** to this task.

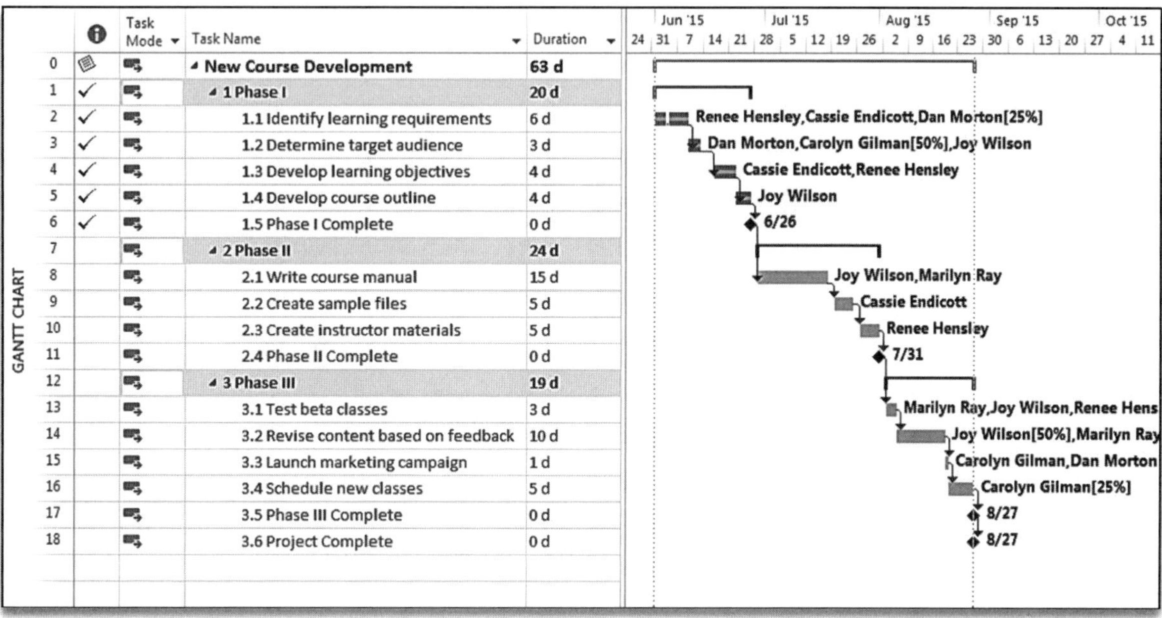

Figure 10 - 62: Outline Number option selected in the Show/Hide section

Using the Drawing Tools

The *Drawing* section of the contextual *Format* ribbon contains a single option. When you click the *Drawing* pick list button, the software displays the pick list shown in Figure 10 - 63. Use the items on this pick list to draw shapes such as ovals, rectangles, or text boxes in your *Gantt Chart* view.

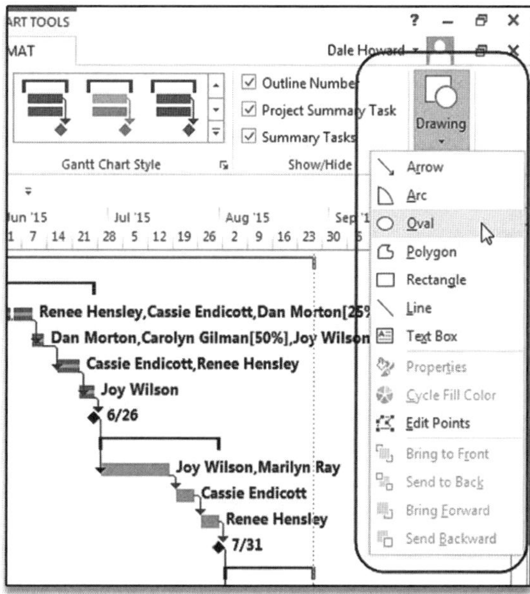

Figure 10 - 63: Drawing pick list

To add a text box shape to your *Gantt Chart* view, complete the following steps:

1. In the *Drawing* section of the *Format* ribbon, click the *Drawing* pick list button and select the *Text Box* item.

Project 2013 changes your mouse pointer arrow to a thin crosshair pointer with which to draw the object.

2. Click and hold your mouse button anywhere in the Gantt chart and then drag the crosshair away from the starting location, such as dragging down and to the right.
3. Release the mouse button.

The software displays the new *Text Box* shape in the Gantt chart. The shape includes "grab handles" around the outer edges. You can use these "grab handles" to resize the shape, if necessary.

4. Click in the center of the *Text Box* shape and type the text you want to display.
5. Use the "grab handles" to resize the *Text Box* shape, if necessary.
6. To move the *Text Box* shape, click and hold on the outer edge of the shape to "grab" it and then drag and drop it in a new location.
7. With the *Text Box* shape still selected, click the *Drawing* pick list button, and select the *Properties* item.

Project 2013 displays the *Format Drawing* dialog with the *Line & Fill* tab selected, as shown in Figure 10 - 64. Use the options in the *Line* and *Fill* sections of the *Line & Fill* page to change the appearance of the text box shape. For example, you might click the *Line* pick list in the *Line* section and select a thicker line. You might click the *Color* pick list in the *Fill* section and select a background color such as yellow.

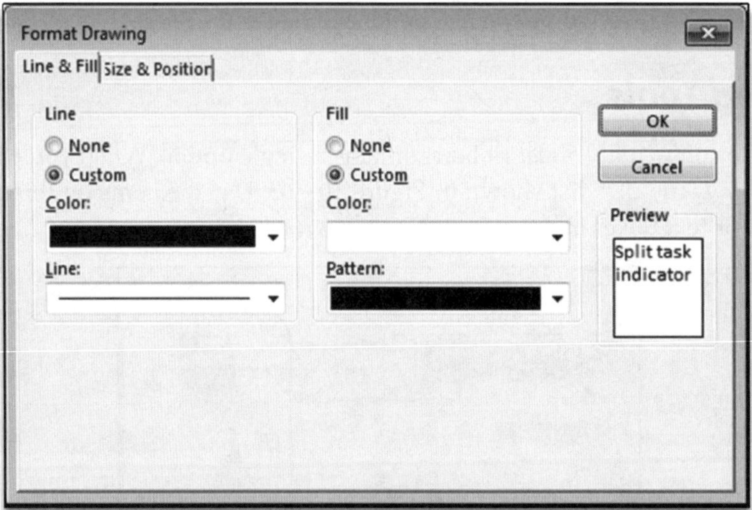

Figure 10 - 64: Format Drawing dialog, Line & Fill tab

Information: Unlike the thousands of colors available when you specify font colors or cell background colors, the *Color* pick lists in the *Format Drawing* dialog only offer you a small palette of **16 colors**.

If you click the *Size & Position* tab in the *Format Drawing* dialog, the software displays the *Size & Position* page shown in Figure 10 - 65. The options on the *Size & Position* page allow you to "anchor" the text box drawing in the Gantt chart by attaching the drawing to a date on the timescale, or by attaching the drawing to a specific task. If you attach the drawing to the timescale, the software allows you to specify the distance of the drawing from the timescale by entering a value in the *Vertical* field. If you select the *Attach to task* option, you must manually enter the ID number of the task in the *ID* field, and specify an *Attachment point* option to determine whether to attach the drawing at the left or right end of the Gantt bar. The software also allows you to enter values in the *Horizontal* and *Vertical* fields to determine the distance of the drawing from the selected Gantt bar. Additionally, you can also enter values in the *Height* and *Width* fields in the *Size* section of the dialog to manually control the size of the drawing. Click the *OK* button when finished to format the new *Text Box* shape according to your specifications.

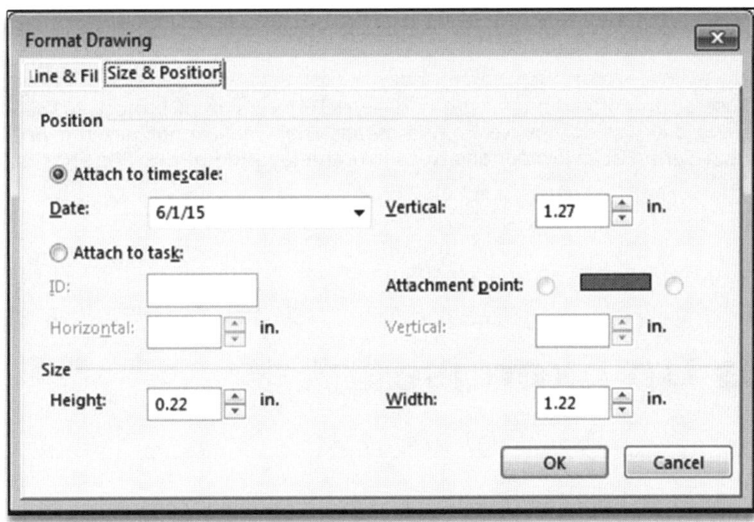

Figure 10 - 65: Format Drawing dialog, Size & Position tab

Figure 10 - 66 shows the *Gantt Chart* view of a project after I created a *Text Box* shape and an *Arrow* shape. Together, these two shapes point to a task split in the middle of a Gantt bar.

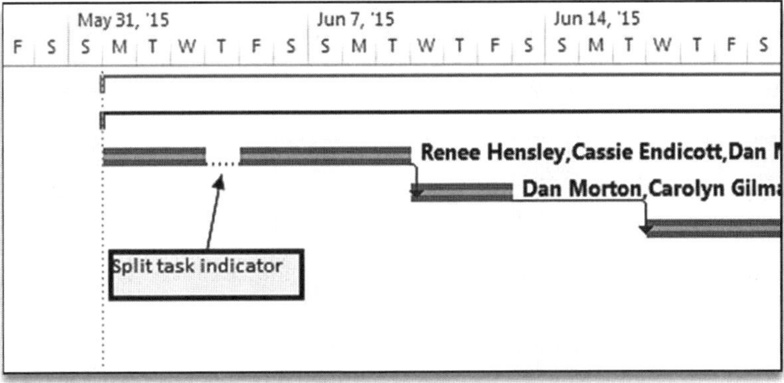

Figure 10 - 66: Text box and arrow drawings point to a task split

Beyond a selection of shapes and the *Properties* item, the *Drawing* pick list includes several additional options. With any shape selected, such as a *Text Box* shape, click the *Cycle Fill Color* item repeatedly to cycle through the 16 available colors on the *Color* pick list in the *Fill* section of the *Line & Fill* page of the *Format Drawing* dialog. The color cycle begins with the dark red color in the middle of the *Color* pick list.

If you create a *Polygon* shape, Project 2013 requires you to draw an outline of the exact type of polygon you want to see. When you connect the last line of the polygon with the starting point to close the *Polygon* shape, the software displays edit points around the border of the polygon. You can click and hold an edit point to "grab" the edit point, and then change the shape of the polygon. To remove the edit points, click the *Drawing* pick list button and deselect the *Edit Points* item. The software removes the edit points and replaces them with "grab handles" around the outside of the entire *Polygon* shape. You can use the "grab handles" to resize the *Polygon* shape.

If you layer your drawing shapes, you can use the final four choices on the *Drawing* pick list to control the order of the layers. For example, suppose that you overlay four drawing shapes on top of one another. Select any one of the four shapes and then select either the *Bring to Font* or *Send to Back* item on the *Drawing* pick list to move the selected shape in front of or behind all of the other shapes. Click the *Bring Forward* or *Send Backward* item on the *Drawing* pick list to move the selected shape one layer forward or one layer backward.

Warning: Because of an unfixed bug in the release (RTM) version of Project 2013, the four options at the bottom of the *Drawing* pick list do not work. This means that you cannot use the *Bring to Front*, *Send to Back*, *Bring Forward*, and *Send Backward* options to control the layering of drawing shapes.

Hands On Exercise

Exercise 10 - 11

Format the objects displayed in the *Gantt Chart* view of a project.

1. Return to the **Formatting Views 2013.mpp** sample file.
2. In the *Bar Styles* section of the *Format* ribbon, select the *Critical Tasks* option.
3. Scroll through the Gantt chart and look for *Critical* tasks (tasks with red Gantt bars).
4. Leave the *Critical Tasks* option selected and then select the *Slack* option.
5. Scroll through the Gantt chart and look for tasks with slack (tasks with a dark blue underscore to the right of the Gantt bar).
6. In the *Bar Styles* section of the *Format* ribbon, click the *Baseline* pick list button, and then select the *Baseline* item (the first baseline item listed).
7. Scroll through the Gantt chart and look for the baseline schedule of each task (gray Gantt bars).
8. Click the *Slippage* pick list button and select the *Baseline* item (the first baseline listed).
9. Scroll through the Gantt chart and look for slipping tasks (tasks with a dark blue underscore to the left of the Gantt bar).
10. In the *Gantt Chart Style* section of the *Format* ribbon, click the *More* button to see the complete list of styles available.
11. In the *Scheduling Styles* section of the *Gantt Chart Style* carousel, select the second style in the first row (light and dark purple Gantt bars).
12. In the *Bar Styles* section of the *Format* ribbon, click the *Format* pick list button, and then select the *Bar Styles* item to open the *Bar Styles* dialog.

13. In the *Bar Styles* dialog, scroll through the list of items, noting the color and shape of each item.

14. Click the *Cancel* button when finished.

15. In the *Show/Hide* section of the *Format* ribbon, select the *Outline Number* option.

16. Widen the *Task Name* column, as needed, and then drag the split bar to the right edge of the *Duration* column.

Notice how Project 2013 displays the *Outline Number* value to the left of each task in the *Task Name* field.

17. Save but **do not** close the **Formatting Views 2013.mpp** sample file.

Formatting the Team Planner View

In Module 07, *Project Assignment Planning*, I taught you how to use the *Team Planner* view in Project 2013. To customize this view, apply the *Team Planner* view and then click the *Format* tab. The software displays the contextual *Format* ribbon with the *Team Planner Tools* applied, as shown in Figure 10 - 67.

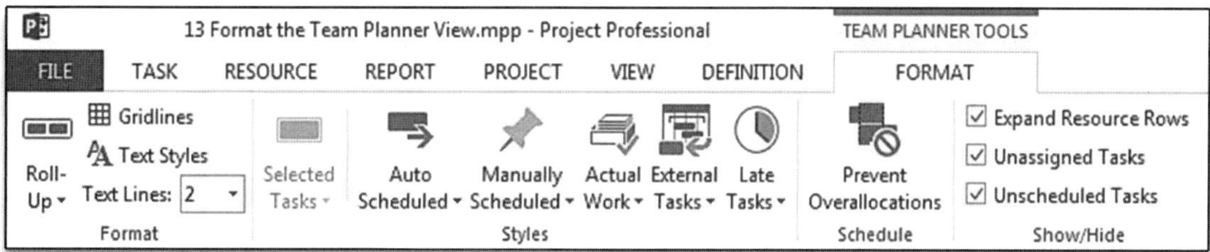

Figure 10 - 67: Format ribbon with the Team Planner Tools applied

Warning: Remember that only the **Professional** version of Project 2013 includes the *Team Planner* view. If you use the **Standard** version of the software, the *Team Planner* view is not an available view.

In the *Format* section of the *Format* ribbon, click the *Roll-Up* pick list button and select the level of WBS information to display for each Gantt bar shown on the right side of the *Team Planner* view. By default, the software selects the *All Subtasks* item on the *Roll-Up* pick list. When I created my project, I set it up so that summary tasks at *Outline Level 1* represent the phases of the project and summary tasks at *Outline Level 2* represent the deliverable sections in the project. Figure 10 - 68 shows the *Team Planner* view after selecting the *Outline Level 2* item on the *Roll-Up* pick list. Project 2013 displays the name of each *Outline Level 2* summary task (the deliverables) as Gantt bars in the *Team Planner* view. Notice also that the software displays the selected outline level for the *Team Planner* view with an indicator at the left end of the status bar at the bottom of the application window.

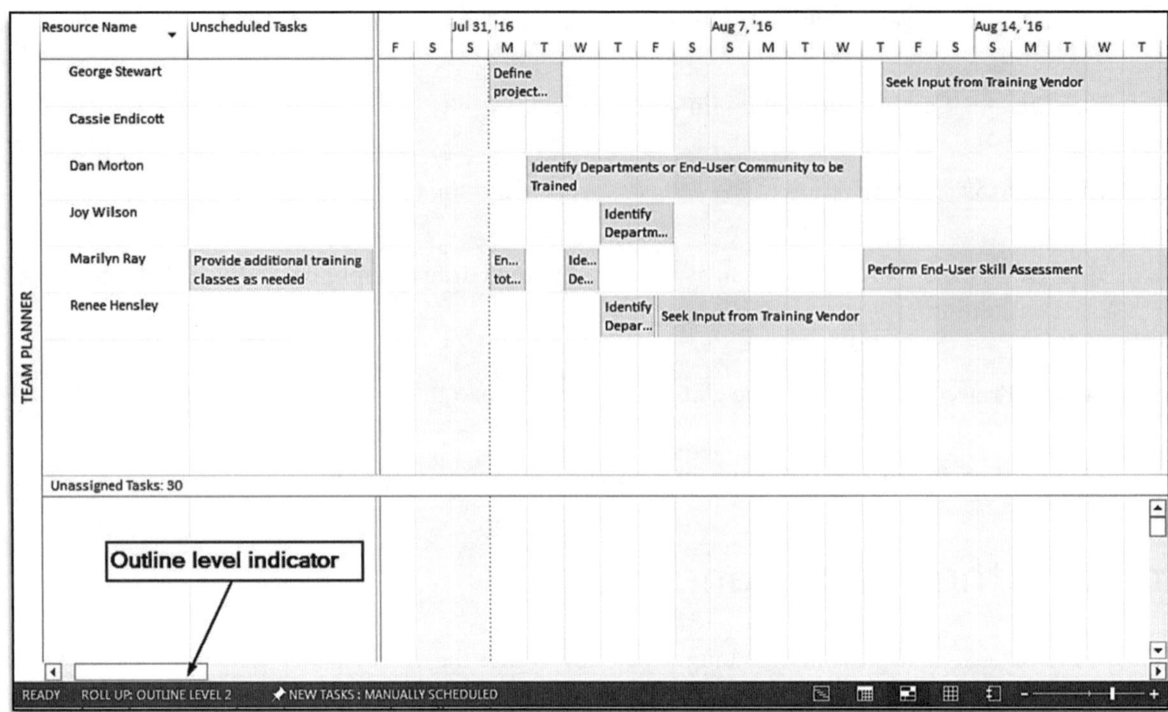

Figure 10 - 68: Team Planner view showing Outline Level 1 task information

Project 2013 allows you to customize the display of gridlines and text in the *Team Planner* view. In the *Format* section of the *Format* ribbon, click the *Gridlines* button to change the gridline display. The software displays the *Gridlines* dialog shown in Figure 10 - 69. In the *Gridlines* dialog, select an item in the *Line to change* list and select the formatting on the *Type* and *Color* pick lists. Click the *OK* button when finished to apply the gridline formatting.

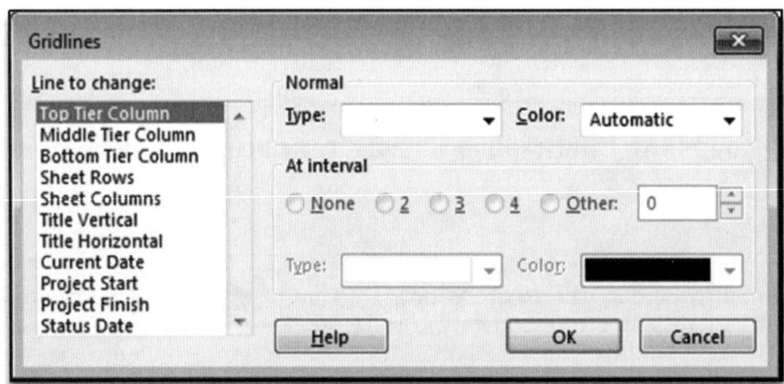

Figure 10 - 69: Gridlines dialog

Information: To display the *Status* date as a red dashed line in the *Team Planner* view, select the *Status Date* item in the *Line to Change* list, select the last item on the *Type* pick list, and choose the *Red* color on the *Color* pick list.

In the *Format* section of the *Format* ribbon, click the *Text Styles* button to customize how the software displays text in the *Team Planner* view. The software displays the *Text Styles* dialog. In the *Text Styles* dialog, click the *Item to Change* pick list as shown in Figure 10 - 70 and select the item you want to format. Choose your desired text formatting for the selected item and then click the *OK* button when finished.

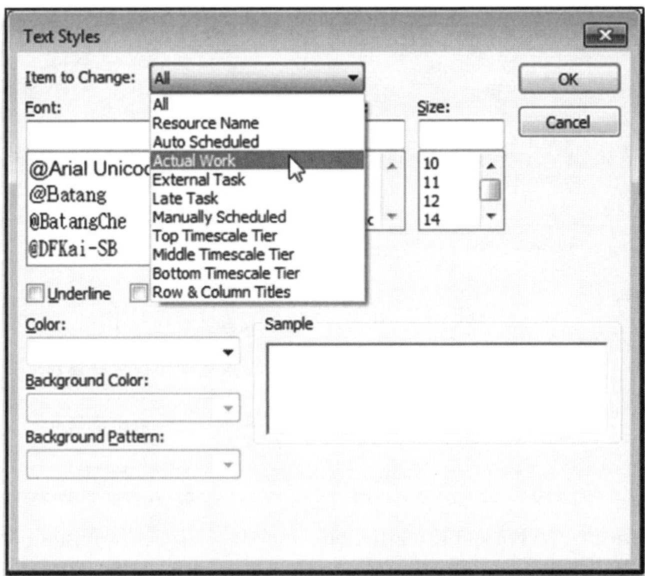

Figure 10 - 70: Text Styles dialog

In the *Format* section of the *Format* ribbon, specify a value in the *Text Lines* field. By default, Project 2013 sets the *Text Lines* value to 2 so that it displays the text in each Gantt bar in only two rows. If you use long task names in your project, the software may truncate the names of the tasks in each Gantt bar. In this case, select a value greater than 2 in the *Text Lines* field.

Project 2013 also allows you to format the colors of the Gantt bars shown in the *Team Planner* view. Notice in the *Format* ribbon shown previously in Figure 10 - 67 that the *Styles* section includes the *Selected Tasks, Auto Scheduled, Manually Scheduled, Actual Work, External Tasks,* and *Late Tasks* pick list buttons. To change the formatting of an individual Gantt bar or group of Gantt bars, select the Gantt bars you want to format, click the *Selected Tasks* pick list button. To change the Gantt bars for a particular type of tasks, such as *Manually Scheduled* tasks, click the pick list button for the type of task whose Gantt bar you want to format. When you click the pick list button, the software displays a pick list of available formatting items. Notice in Figure 10 - 71, for example, that I want to change the *Fill Color* value for all *Manually Scheduled* tasks.

To change the formatting for Gantt bars, the software allows you to specify both a *Border Color* value and a *Fill Color* value from a palette of values. With the exception of the *Selected Tasks* pick list, all of the other pick lists in the *Styles* section of the *Format* ribbon contain a *Reset to Default* item. If you change the color of any type of Gantt bar, and want to restore the original default value, simply select the *Reset to Default* item on the appropriate pick list.

Information: Project 2013 does not format the Gantt bars for *Manually Scheduled* tasks using the dark teal color the way it did in the 2010 version of the software. If you want to format *Manually Scheduled* tasks to match their counterpart in Project 2010, click the *Manually Scheduled* pick list button in the *Styles* section of the *Format* ribbon, select the *Fill Color* item, and then select the *More Colors* item on the flyout menu. In the *Colors* dialog, click the *Custom* tab. On the *Custom* page of the *Colors* dialog, set the *Red* value to *24*, set the *Green* value to *197*, set the *Blue* value to *206*, and then click the *OK* button.

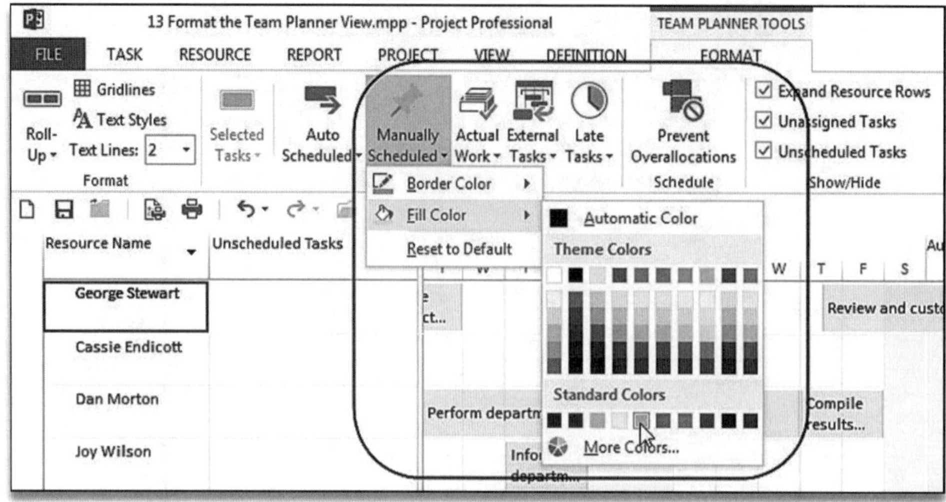

Figure 10 - 71: Format the Fill Color for Manually Scheduled tasks

As you format the *Team Planner* view for your project, Project 2013 also allows you to determine which items to display in this view. The *Show/Hide* section of the *Format* ribbon offers three option checkboxes that control the items you see in the *Team Planner* view. By default, the software selects the *Expand Resource Rows* option so that you see the Gantt bars for parallel tasks on separate rows for each resource. If you **deselect** the *Expand Resource Rows* option, the software displays all tasks on a single row for each resource, and "stacks" Gantt bars in front of each other. Although deselecting this option may save vertical screen space, you may find it difficult to read the text contained in Gantt bars stacked on top of each other. Figure 10 - 72 shows the top half of the *Team Planner* view with the *Expand Resource Rows* option deselected. Notice that you cannot read the names of overlapping tasks when the software displays all of them on a single row.

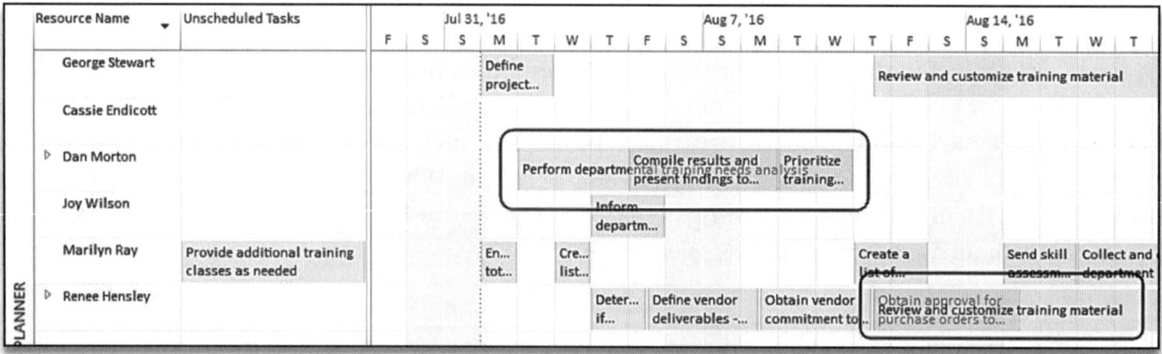

Figure 10 - 72: Expand Resource Rows option deselected

Information: You can also collapse parallel tasks onto one row for any resource individually by clicking the *Expand/Collapse* indicator to the left of the resource's name.

In the *Schedule* section of the *Format* ribbon, you can click the *Prevent Overallocations* toggle button to prevent resource overallocations in your project. With this option enabled, the software levels all existing overallocations in the project immediately, and levels any future resource overallocation when it occurs, such as when you drag a task or assign a task that causes a resource overallocation. Project 2013 indicates in the *Team Planner* view that you enabled this option by highlighting the *Prevent Overallocations* button with a light green cell background color, and by displaying a *Prevent Overallocations: On* indicator at the left end of the status bar at the bottom of the application window.

Project 2013 also allows you to determine which type of tasks to display. By default, the software selects the *Unassigned Tasks* and *Unscheduled Tasks* options in the *Show/Hide* section of the *Format* ribbon. If you do not want to see the *Unassigned Tasks* pane in the bottom half of the *Team Planner* view, deselect the *Unassigned Tasks* option. If you do not want to see the *Unscheduled Tasks* column on the left side of the *Team Planner* view, deselect the *Unscheduled Tasks* option. Figure 10 - 73 shows the *Team Planner* view with the *Unassigned Tasks* and *Unscheduled Tasks* options deselected in the *Show/Hide* section of the *Format* ribbon.

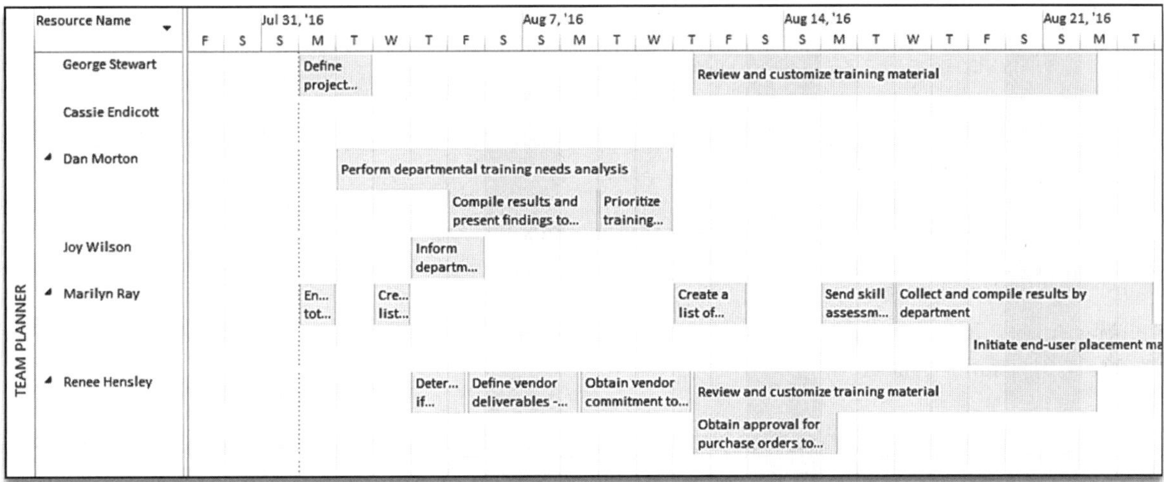

Figure 10 - 73: Team Planner view with Unassigned Tasks and Unscheduled Tasks hidden

A final formatting option in the *Team Planner* view is not obvious: zooming the *Timescale* in the Gantt chart portion of the view. As I stated earlier in this section, Project 2013 zooms the *Timescale* to the *Weeks Over Days* level of zoom. You can display any level of zoom you want. Click the *View* tab and then click the *Zoom* pick list button in the *Zoom* section of the *View* ribbon to zoom in or zoom out, as needed.

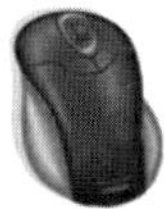

Hands On Exercise

Exercise 10 - 12

Customize the *Team Planner* view.

1. Return to the **Formatting Views 2013.mpp** sample file.
2. Click the *Resource* tab to display the *Resource* ribbon.
3. In the *View* section of the ribbon, click the *Team Planner* button.
4. Click the *Format* tab to display the contextual *Format* ribbon with the *Team Planner Tools* applied.
5. In the *Show/Hide* section of the *Format* ribbon, deselect the *Unassigned Tasks* checkbox.

Notice that Project 2013 hides the *Unassigned Tasks* section at the bottom of the *Team Planner* view.

6. In the right side of the *Team Planner* view, scroll to the week of *June 5, 2016*.
7. In the *Format* section of the *Format* ribbon, click the *Roll Up* pick list, and select the *Outline Level 1* item on the list.

Notice how Project 2013 displays the first-level summary tasks (the phases) for each resource in the *Team Planner* view.

8. In the *Format* section of the *Format* ribbon, click the *Roll Up* pick list, and select the *Outline Level 2* item on the list.

Notice how Project 2013 displays the second-level summary tasks (the deliverables) for each resource in the *Team Planner* view.

9. In the *Format* section of the *Format* ribbon, click the *Roll Up* pick list, and select the *Outline Level 3* item on the list.

Notice how Project 2013 displays the third-level summary tasks (the sub-deliverables) for each resource in the *Team Planner* view.

10. In the *Format* section of the *Format* ribbon, click the *Roll Up* pick list one final time, and select the *All Subtasks* item on the list.
11. In the *Styles* section of the *Format* ribbon, click the *Manually Scheduled* pick list, select the *Fill Color* item, and then select the *Light Green* color in the *Standard Colors* section of the color palette.

Notice how Project 2013 changed the fill color for the *Manually Scheduled* task assigned to both *Marcia Bickel* and *Steve Garcia*.

12. Click the *Manually Scheduled* pick list again and select the *Reset to Default* item on the list.
13. Save but **do not** close the **Formatting Views 2013.mpp** sample file.

Formatting Other Views

As I noted in Module 02, *Project 2013 Overview*, the software offers a contextual *Format* ribbon for every default view in the software. When you select any view and display the contextual *Format* ribbon, the ribbon contains a set of options unique to the selected view. For example, if you select the *Task Usage* view, the software displays the contextual *Format* ribbon with the *Task Usage Tools* applied, as shown in Figure 10 - 74. With the *Task Usage* view displayed, the contextual *Format* ribbon contains several of the same sections shown for the *Gantt Chart* view, and contains two additional sections.

The *Details* section contains six option checkboxes that control the details (rows) displayed in the timephased grid on the right side of the view (gray and white timesheet-like grid). By default, Project 2013 selects only the *Work* option, which displays only the *Work* details in the timephased grid. Select additional checkboxes in the *Details* section as you require. To choose from a complete list of details available for the timephased grid, click the *Add Details* button in the *Details* section. The software displays the *Detail Styles* dialog, in which you can select from a complete list of rows for the timephased grid.

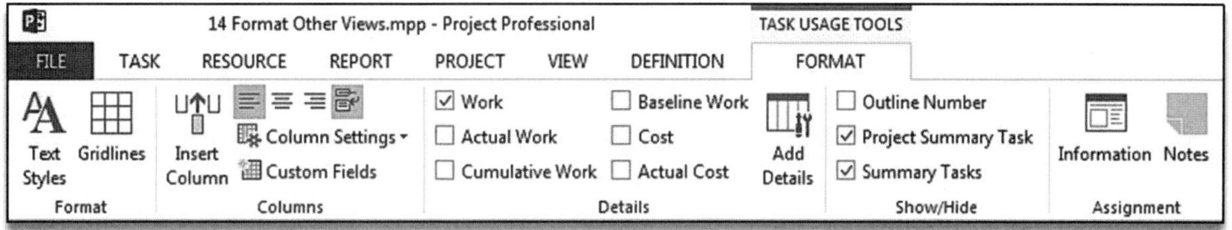

Figure 10 - 74: Format ribbon with the Task Usage Tools applied

When you select a resource assignment (italicized resource name below a task) in the *Task Usage* view, the software activates the two buttons in the *Assignment* section of the contextual *Format* ribbon. Click the *Information* button to display the *Assignment Information* dialog for the selected resource assignment. To add a note to a resource assignment, click the *Notes* button to display the *Assignment Information* dialog with the *Notes* tab selected.

Information: The contextual *Format* ribbon for the *Resource Usage* view is nearly identical to the ribbon shown for the *Task Usage* view. This is because both of these views are assignment views that display assignment information, along with a timephased grid on the right side of the view.

I do not discuss the contextual *Format* ribbon for every view in Project 2013. However, the information in this module can serve as an effective guide for you to format any view in the software.

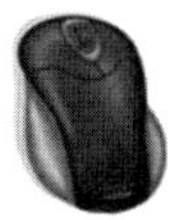

Hands On Exercise

Exercise 10 - 13

Format the *Task Usage* view of a project.

1. Return to the **Formatting Views 2013.mpp** sample file.

2. Click the *View* tab to display the *View* ribbon.

3. In the *Task Views* section of the *View* ribbon, click the *Task Usage* button.

4. Click the *Format* tab to display the contextual *Format* ribbon with the *Task Usage Tools* applied.

5. In the *Details* section of the *Format* ribbon, select the *Actual Work* and *Baseline Work* details.

Notice how Project 2013 displays these two additional detail rows in the timephased grid on the right side of the *Task Usage* view.

6. Double-click the right edge of the *Details* column header in the timephased grid to "best fit" the column automatically.

7. In the *Details* section of the *Format* ribbon, click the *Add Details* button.

8. In the *Detail Styles* dialog, select the *Actual Work* item in the *Show these fields* list, and then click the *Hide* button.

9. In the *Available fields* list, select the *Cost* field, and then click the *Show* button.

10. Click the *OK* button to close the *Detail Styles* dialog.

11. Below task ID #3, the *Interview and select architect* task, select the resource name *Steve Garcia.*

12. In the *Assignment* section of the *Format* ribbon, click the *Information* button.

Notice that Project 2013 displays the *Assignment Information* dialog for Steve Garcia's assignment on the *Interview and select architect* task.

13. Click the *OK* button to close the *Assignment Information* dialog.

14. Save and close the **Formatting Views 2013.mpp** sample file.

Printing Views

In Project 2013, you can print any default or custom view by clicking the *File* tab and then clicking the *Print* tab in the *Backstage.* The software displays the *Print* page of the *Backstage* as shown in Figure 10 - 75. The software divides the *Print* page into two panes. In the left pane, you can set printing options; in the right pane you see a print preview of the project. On the *Print* page, you can control any of the following printing options:

- Specify the number of copies to print in the *Copies* field.
- Select an available printer in the *Printer* pick list.
- Set printer options by clicking the *Printer Properties* link.
- Specify the date range for printing project information by clicking the *Settings* pick list and choosing a pre-defined date range.
- Manually enter a date range in the *Dates* and *To* fields.
- Specify the number of pages to print by selecting a value in the *Pages* and *To* fields.
- Specify the orientation of the printout on the *Print Orientation* pick list.
- Specify the paper size on the *Paper Size* pick list.
- Display the *Page Setup* dialog by clicking the *Page Setup* link.
- View the print preview of the project on the right side of the page.
- Navigate through the pages of the print preview using the buttons in the lower right corner of the page.

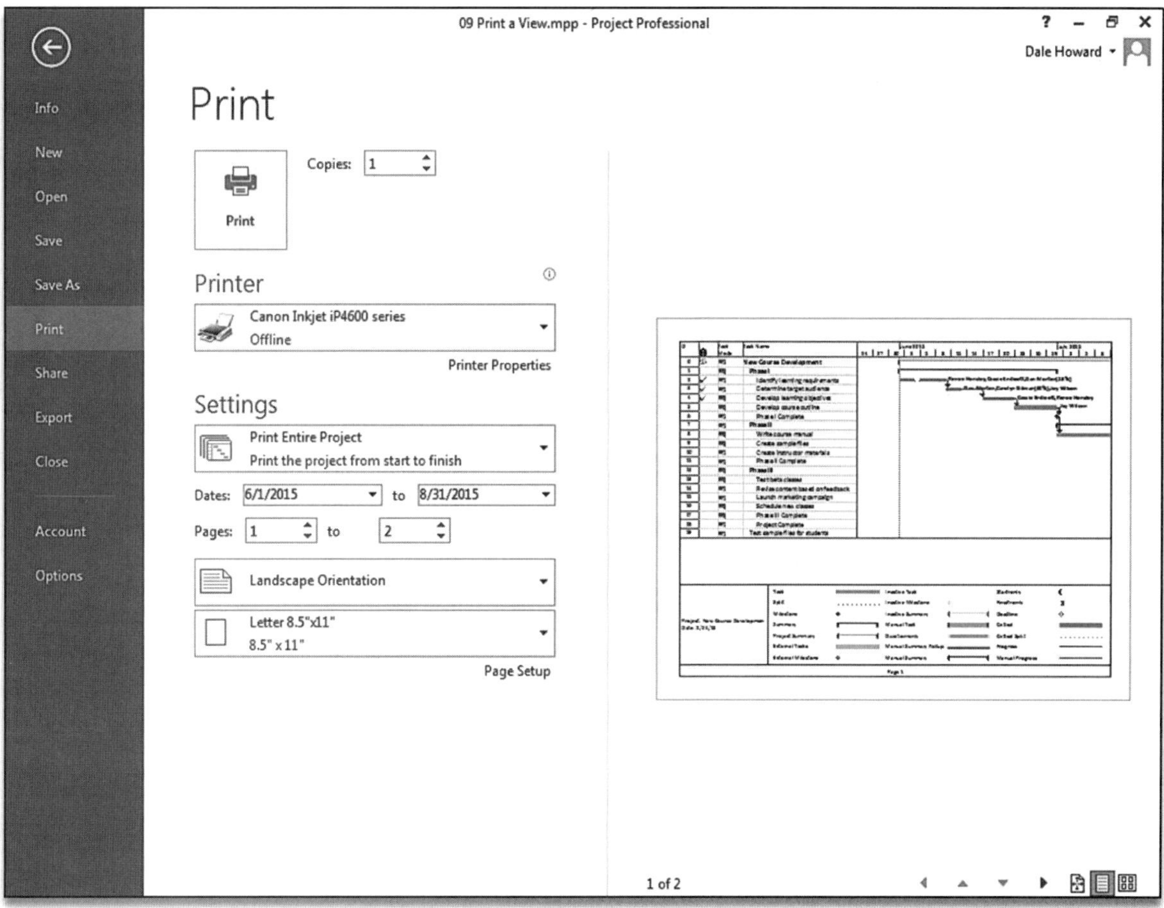

Figure 10 - 75: Print page of the Backstage

Warning: In the print preview pane, you may notice that you do not see all of the columns that you expect the software to print. One of the issues you may face when printing a view is that Project 2013 prints only those columns that are **completely visible** in the *Task Sheet* portion of the view. Therefore, before printing any view, confirm that all of the columns you want to print are completely visible. This means you may need to drag the split bar to the right to expose a column completely for printing.

Using Page Setup

To customize the printout of your view, you may want to specify additional settings in the *Page Setup* dialog. To access the *Page Setup* dialog, click the *Page Setup* link on the *Print* page of the *Backstage*. Project 2013 displays the *Page Setup* dialog with the *Page* tab selected shown in Figure 10 - 76.

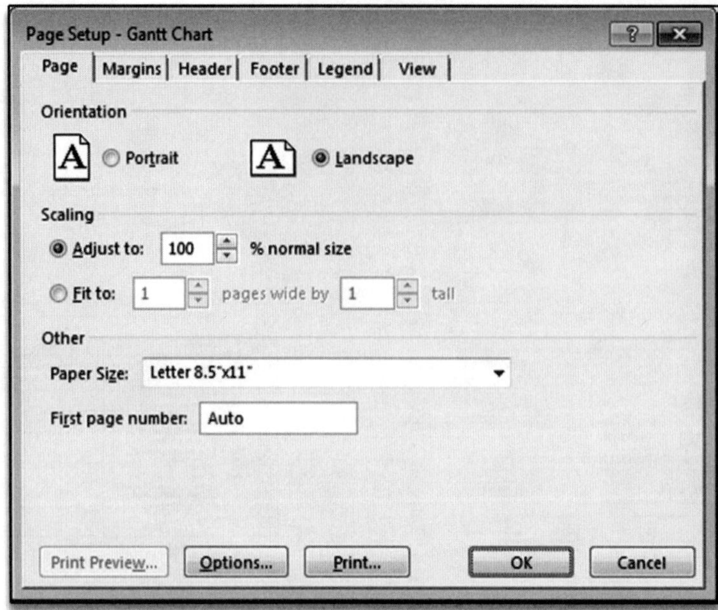

Figure 10 - 76: Page Setup dialog, Page tab selected

Table 10 - 2 through Table 10 - 7 describe the options available on each page of the *Page Setup* dialog. Figure 10 - 76 through Figure 10 - 83 show each page of the *Page Setup* dialog.

Page options	
Orientation	Select the *Portrait* or *Landscape* option.
Scaling	Use the *Adjust to* option to reduce or enlarge the printed image by a percentage of the original size. Use the *Fit to* option to scale the printed view to a specific number of pages.
Other	Set the *Paper Size* option. Set the *First page number* option.

Table 10 - 2: Page options

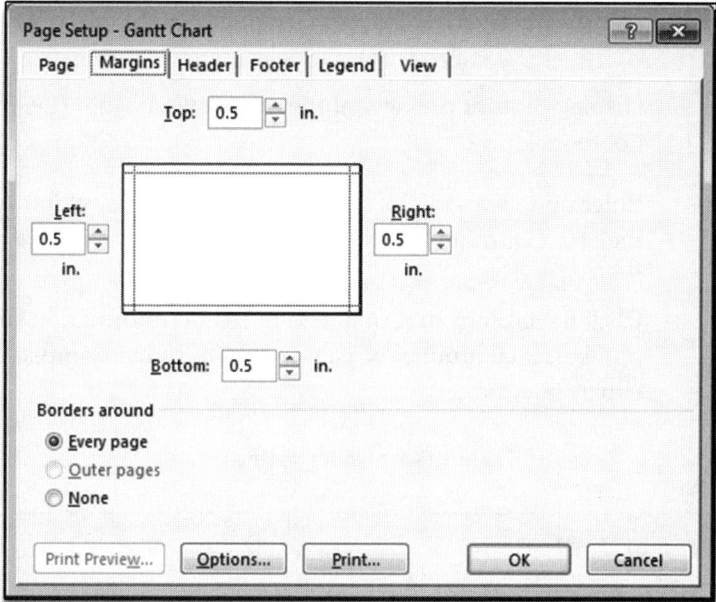

Figure 10 - 77: Page Setup dialog, Margins tab selected

Margins options	
Margins	Set the top, bottom, left, and right margins.
Borders around	Place borders around every page, outer pages only, or no pages.

Table 10 - 3: Margins options

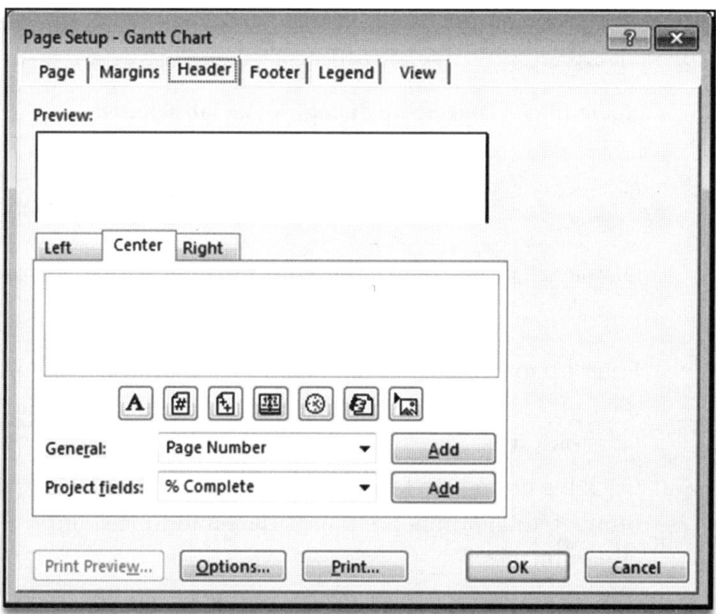

Figure 10 - 78: Page Setup dialog, Header tab selected

Header options	
Preview	Displays a print preview of the completed header (the preview is not to scale).
Alignment	Enter up to five lines of text, field codes, or project information in the *Left*, *Center*, and *Right* tab sections using the *General* and *Project fields* pick lists. Click the buttons to format text or to add information such as page number, total number of pages, date and time stamps, file name, or clipart images.

Table 10 - 4: Header options

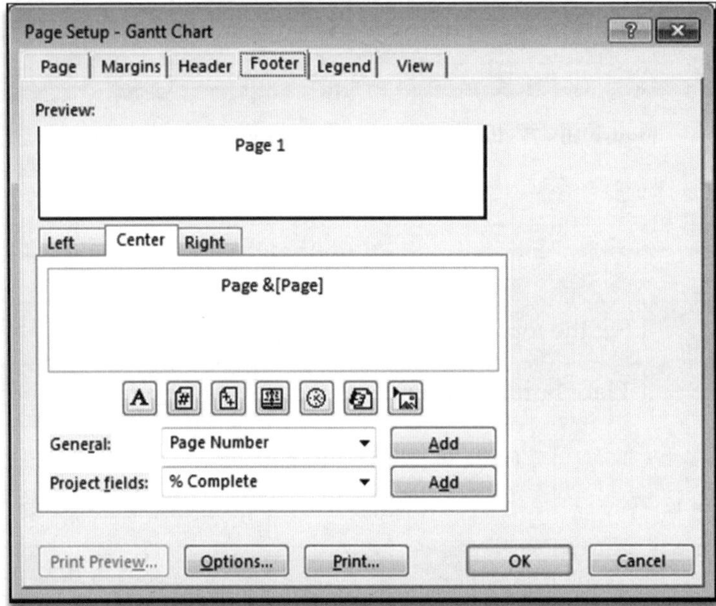

Figure 10 - 79: Page Setup dialog, Footer tab selected

Footer options	
Preview	Displays a print preview of the completed footer (the preview is not to scale).
Alignment	Enter up to five lines of text, field codes, or project information in the *Left*, *Center*, and *Right* tab sections using the *General* and *Project fields* pick lists. Click the buttons to format text or to add information such as page number, total number of pages, date and time stamps, file name, or clipart images.

Table 10 - 5: Footer options

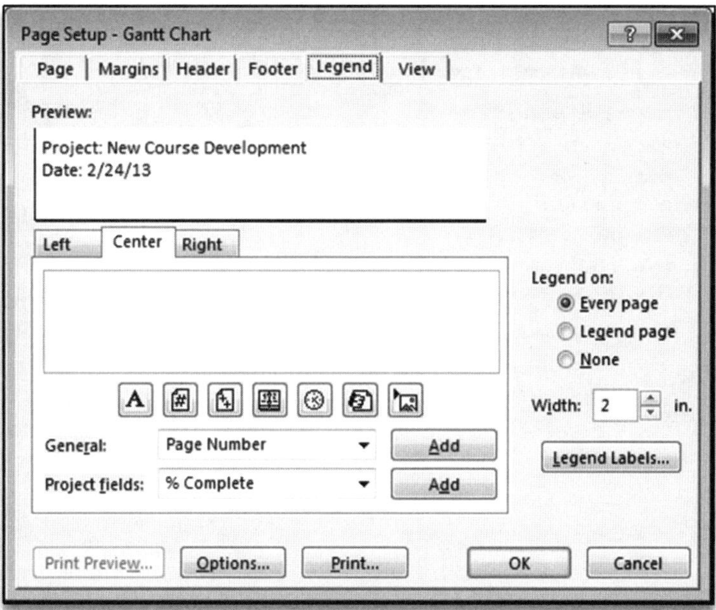

Figure 10 - 80: Page Setup dialog, Legend tab selected

Legend options	
Preview	Displays a print preview of the completed legend text (the preview is not to scale).
Alignment	Enter up to five lines of text, field codes, or project information in the *Left*, *Center*, and *Right* tab sections using the *General* and *Project fields* pick lists. Click the buttons to format text or to add information such as page number, total number of pages, date and time stamps, file name, or clipart images.
Legend on	Print the legend on every page, on a separate legend page, or select the *None* option to prevent the legend from printing. Specify a value up to *5 inches* in the *Width* field to control the width of the text section on the left side of the legend.
Legend Labels	Click the *Legend Labels* button to change the font for the legend text.

Table 10 - 6: Legend options

Information: You see the legend at the bottom of the printed page **only** when printing the *Network Diagram* view or any view that includes a Gantt chart, such as the *Tracking Gantt* view. For all other views, Project 2013 disables the *Legend* page. The legend includes a text section on the left side where you can include custom information.

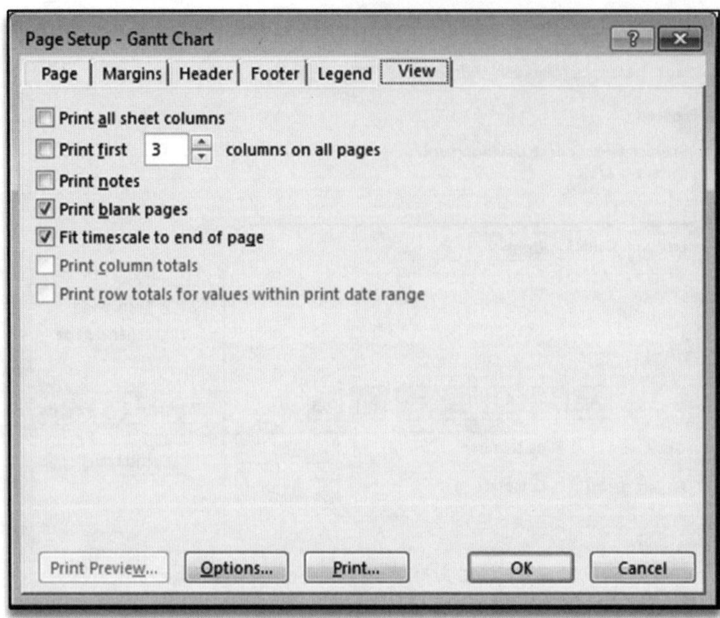

Figure 10 - 81: Page Setup dialog, View tab selected

Information: Project 2013 enables the last two options on the *View* page when printing either the *Task Usage* view or the *Resource Usage* view. For all other views, the software disables these two options.

View options	
Print all sheet columns	Print all columns in the table regardless of how many columns are currently visible in the view.
Print first ___ columns on all pages	Print a specific number of columns to print on every page.
Print notes	Print all task notes on one or more additional pages at the end of the printout.
Print blank pages	Print the blank pages in large *Network Diagram* view.
Fit timescale to end of page	Fit the timescale in the available space on each page.
Print row total for values within print date range	Print a total value at the right end of each row for only the selected date range (used only with the *Task Usage* or *Resource Usage* view).
Print column totals	Print a total at the bottom of each column (used only with the *Task Usage* or *Resource Usage* view).

Table 10 - 7: View options

Information: Use the *Print first ___ columns on all pages* option to solve the problem of Project 2013 not printing partially-hidden columns. This option guarantees that the software prints the selected number of columns on every page, regardless of the number of columns presently visible in the view. If additional columns are entirely visible in the view, the software prints all of them, but only on the first page.

Hands On Exercise

Exercise 10 - 14

Use the *Page Setup* dialog to print a specific number of columns in a view in the Training Advisor Rollout project.

1. Open the **Training Advisor 10.mpp** sample file.
2. Drag the vertical split bar to the left to cover up approximately half of the *Duration* column.
3. Click the *File* tab and then click the *Print* tab in the *Backstage.*
4. Click anywhere in the print preview pane to zoom into the print preview.

Notice that Project 2013 does not display the *Duration* column in the print preview pane. Remember that this is because the *Duration* column does not display completely.

5. In the *Print* page of the *Backstage,* click the *Page Setup* link to display the *Page Setup* dialog.
6. Click the *View* tab in the *Page Setup* dialog.
7. Select the *Print first __ columns on all pages* option and then set this option to *5 columns.*
8. Click the *OK* button to return to the *Print* page of the *Backstage.*

Notice in the print preview pane that the software displays the *Duration* column. This is because you selected the *Print first 5 columns* option on the *View* tab of the *Page Setup* dialog.

9. Leave the **Training Advisor 10.mpp** sample file open for the next exercise.

Exercise 10 - 15

Use the *Page Setup* dialog to add one or more notes pages when you print the *Gantt Chart* view.

1. Return to the **Training Advisor 10.mpp** sample file, if necessary.
2. In the *Print* page of the *Backstage,* click the *Page Setup* link to display the *Page Setup* dialog.
3. Click the *View* tab in the *Page Setup* dialog.
4. Select the *Print notes* option.

5. Click the *OK* button to return to the *Print* page of the *Backstage.*

6. In the print preview pane, click the *Page Right* button ▶ until you see the notes page.

7. Click anywhere in the notes page to zoom in and see larger text in the print preview pane.

Notice that the notes page displays every task containing a note, and displays the full text of each note, including bullets.

8. Scroll left and right in the print preview pane, as needed, to read the text of the notes.

9. Press the **Escape** key on your computer keyboard to exit the *Backstage.*

10. Save but **do not** close the **Training Advisor 10.mpp** sample file.

Creating a Header or Footer

Creating a header or footer in a printed view is similar to the process for creating a header or footer in Excel. To create a header or footer, complete the following steps:

1. Click the *File* tab and then click the *Print* tab in the *Backstage.*

2. In the *Print* page of the *Backstage,* click the *Page Setup* link to display the *Page Setup* dialog.

3. In the *Page Setup* dialog, select either the *Header* or the *Footer* tab.

4. Click the *Left, Center,* or *Right* tab in the page.

5. Click the *General* pick list, select a field, and then click the *Add* button.

6. Click the *Project fields* pick list, select a field, and then click the *Add* button.

7. Click one of the buttons at the bottom of the *Alignment* section to insert additional information, such as page numbers or the current date.

8. Manually enter text, as needed.

Figure 10 - 82 and Figure 10 - 83 show a custom header I set up for the *Gantt Chart* view. Figure 10 - 82 shows the left-aligned header information, while Figure 10 - 83 shows the right-aligned header information. Notice that the left-aligned header includes the project title (the *&[Title]* field) and the current view (the *&[View]* field), while the right-aligned header contains the name of the project manager (the *&[Author]* field) and the project sponsor (indicated by the *&[Manager]* field). Notice also that I manually added the *Project Manager* text after the *&[Author]* field and added the *Project Sponsor* text after the *&[Manager]* field.

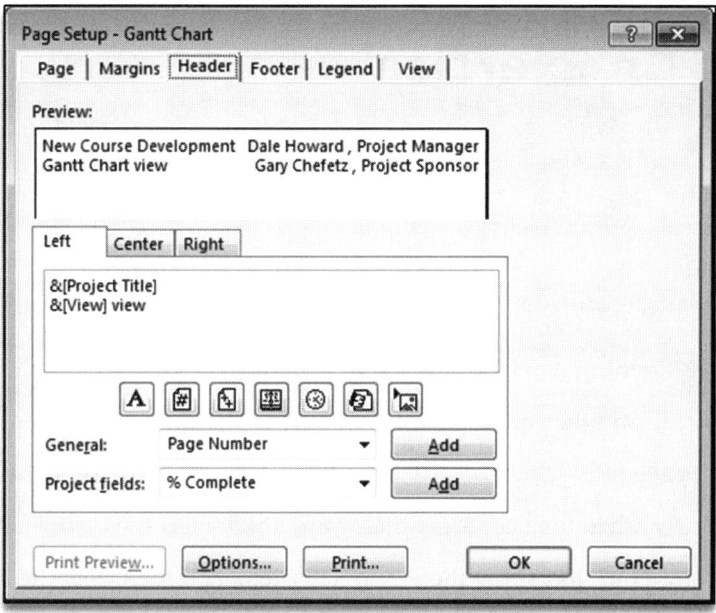

Figure 10 - 82: Page Setup dialog
Left section of Header page

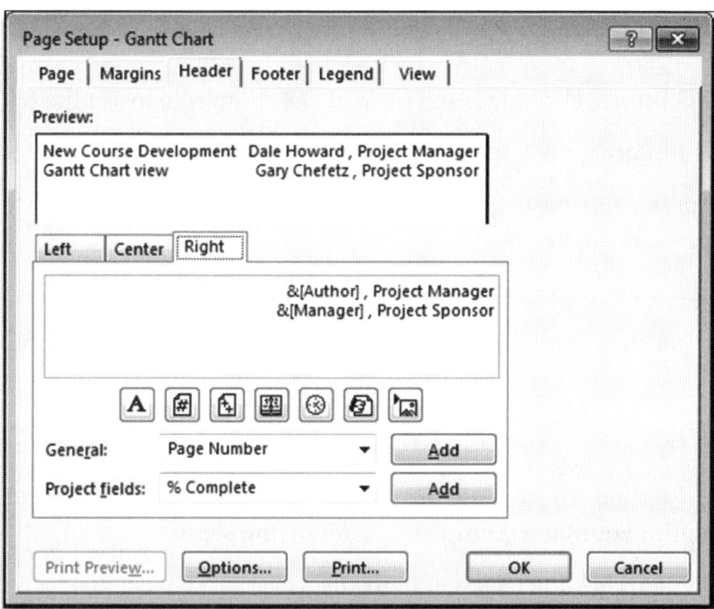

Figure 10 - 83: Page Setup dialog
Right section of Header page

Information: Use exactly the same process to enter custom legend information on the *Legend* page of the *Page Setup* dialog.

Hands On Exercise

Exercise 10 - 16

Use the *Page Setup* dialog to create a custom header for printing the *Gantt Chart* view.

1. Return to the **Training Advisor 10.mpp** sample file.
2. Click the *File* tab and then click the *Print* tab in the *Backstage*.
3. On the *Print* page of the *Backstage*, click the *Page Setup* link to display the *Page Setup* dialog.
4. Click the *Header* tab in the *Page Setup* dialog and then select the *Center* tab, if necessary.
5. Click the *General* pick list, select the *Project Title* item, and then click the *Add* button.
6. Click in the text area to the right of the *&[Project Title]* field and then press the **Enter** key on your computer keyboard.
7. In the new blank link on the *Center* page, manually type your own name, followed by the words *Project Manager* (such as *Dale Howard, Project Manager*).
8. Press the **Enter** key on your computer keyboard.
9. In the row of buttons, click the *Insert Current Date* button to insert the &[*Date]* field.
10. Click the *OK* button to view the new header in the print preview pane.
11. In the print preview pane, click in the header area of the print preview to zoom in and read the text of the new custom header.
12. Press the **Escape** key on your computer keyboard to exit the *Backstage*.
13. Save but **do not** close the **Training Advisor 10.mpp** sample file.

Setting Print Options

After you select your desired options in the *Page Setup* dialog, you are ready to set up print options. To set up your print options and then print your view, complete the following steps:

1. Click the *File* tab and then click the *Print* tab in the *Backstage*.
2. On the left side of the *Print* page, select your desired printing options as follows:
    - Click the *Printer* pick list and select the printer.
    - Click the *Printer Properties* link and set up the printer to print your view.
    - Click the *Date Range* pick list button and select a pre-defined date range. The pre-defined date range options include *Print Entire Project, Print Specific Dates, Print Specific Pages*, and *Print Custom Dates and Pages*. The *Settings* pick list includes additional options to include a notes page, to print all columns in the current table, and to print the left columns of each page.

- If you do not select a pre-defined date range, you can manually enter a date range in the *Dates* and *to* fields.
- Specify the number of pages to print by entering values in the *Pages* and *to* fields.
- Specify the orientation of the printout on the *Print Orientation* pick list.
- Specify the paper size on the *Paper Size* pick list.

3. Click the *Print* button.

Hands On Exercise

Exercise 10 - 17

Remove the *Legend* section from the bottom of the page and then print a selected date range for the *Gantt Chart* view.

1. Return to the **Training Advisor 10.mpp** sample file.
2. Click the *File* tab and then click the *Print* tab in the *Backstage*.
3. Click the *Page Setup* link to display the *Page Setup* dialog.
4. In the *Page Setup* dialog, click the *Legend* tab.
5. On the *Legend* page of the dialog, select the *None* option in the *Legend on* section on the right side of the dialog, and then click the *OK* button.
6. Click the *Dates* pick list and select the *1/4/2016* date.
7. Click the *To* pick list and select the *1/29/16* date.

Notice that the print preview pane displays only that portion of the *Gantt Chart* view between your two selected dates.

8. If you have a printer available, click the *Print* button to print the customized *Gantt Chart* view of your project.
9. Save and close the **Training Advisor 10**.mpp sample file.

Information: The changes you make in the *Page Setup* dialog and the *Print* page become part of the view currently applied. If you want these changes to apply to every current and future project, click the *Organizer* button on the *Info* page of the *Backstage* and then copy the current view from the active project (on the right side of the dialog) to your Global.mpt file (on the left side of the dialog).

Attaching Documentation to a Project

In addition to adding notes to tasks, Project 2013 also offers you two other methods for attaching documentation to a project. These methods include:

- Link a document to a task in the project.
- Add a hyperlink to a task in the project.

Linking a Document to a Task in a Project

To include additional documentation in a project, you can insert a link or "shortcut" to a document for any task in a Project 2013 file. The advantage of this approach is that the software allows you to link multiple documents to a single task in a project. To link a document to a task, complete the following steps:

1. Double-click the task to which you want to link a document.
2. In the *Task Information* dialog, select the *Notes* tab.
3. On the *Notes* page of the *Task Information* dialog, click the *Insert Object* button. Project 2013 displays the *Insert Object* dialog shown in Figure 10 - 84.

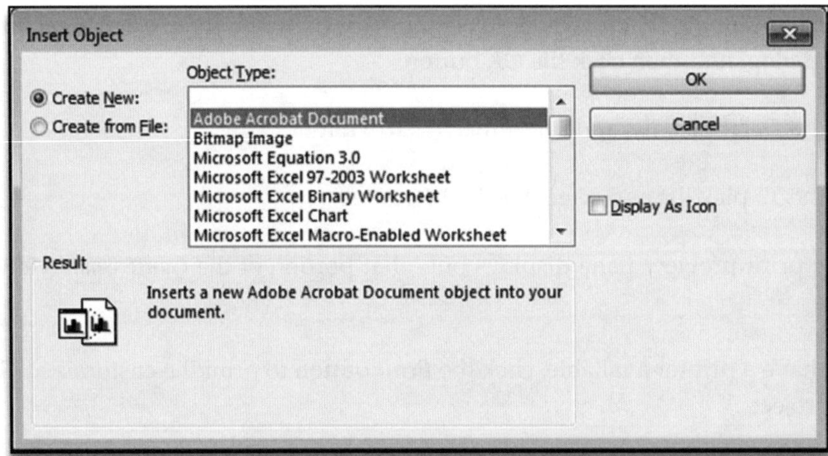

Figure 10 - 84: Insert Object dialog

4. In the *Insert Object* dialog, select the *Create from File* option. The software refreshes the dialog as shown in Figure 10 - 85.

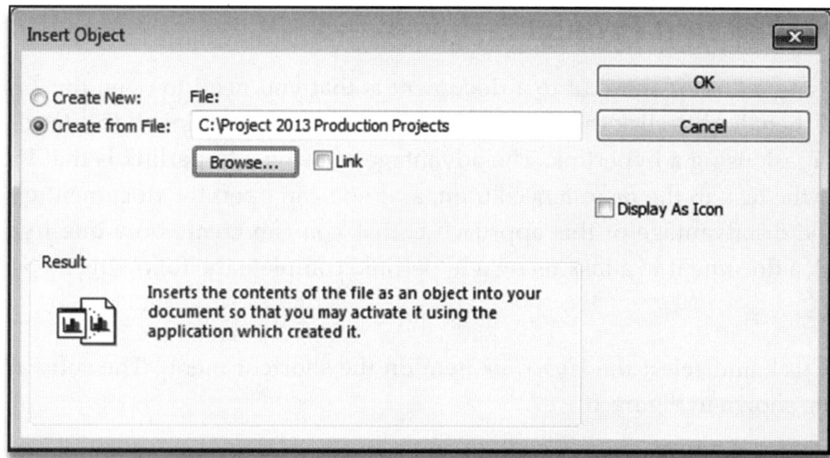

Figure 10 - 85: Insert Object dialog, Create from File options

5. Click the *Browse* button to display the *Browse* dialog.
6. In the *Browse* dialog, navigate to the location of the document you want to link.
7. In the *Browse* dialog, select a document, and then click the *Insert* button. Project 2013 displays the path to the document in the *File* field.
8. Select the *Link* checkbox.
9. Select the *Display as Icon* checkbox.
10. Click the *OK* button. Project 2013 displays the link to the document in the *Notes* page of the *Task Information* dialog, as shown Figure 10 - 86.

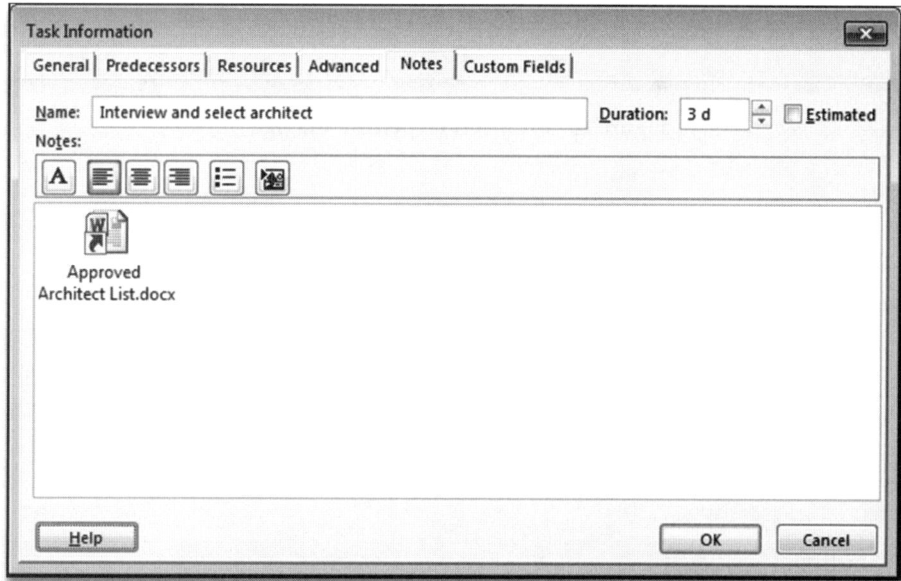

Figure 10 - 86: Task Information dialog shows the link to a document

11. Click the *OK* button to close the *Task Information* dialog.

Inserting a Hyperlink in a Project

The disadvantage of using a link or shortcut to a document is that you need to open the *Task Information* dialog, click the *Notes* tab, and then double-click the shortcut to open the document linked to a task. Another approach is to link a document to a task using a hyperlink. The advantage of using a hyperlink is that Project 2013 displays a hyperlink indicator for the task in the *Indicators* column, and you can open the document quickly by clicking the hyperlink indicator. The disadvantage of this approach is that you can create only **one hyperlink per task** in a Project 2013 file. To link a document to a task using a hyperlink, complete the following steps:

1. Right-click the task and select the *Hyperlink* item on the shortcut menu. The software displays the *Insert Hyperlink* dialog shown in Figure 10 - 87.

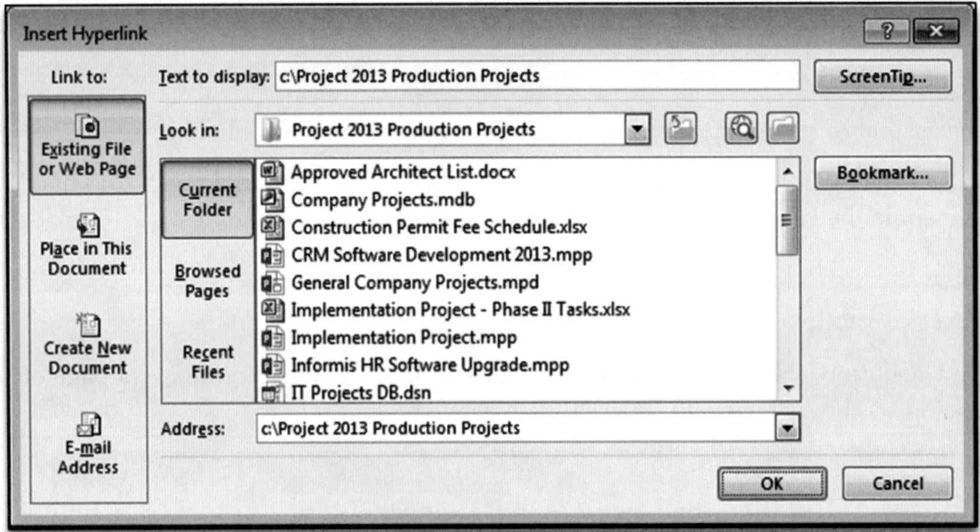

Figure 10 - 87: Insert Hyperlink dialog

2. In the *Insert Hyperlink* dialog, use the *Look in* pick list to navigate to the folder containing the document for which you want to create the hyperlink.

3. In the *Insert Hyperlink* dialog, select a document.

4. Edit the text in the *Text to display* field to give a friendly name to the hyperlink.

5. Click the *OK* button.

Project 2013 displays a hyperlink indicator in the *Indicators* column to the left of the task name. If you float your mouse pointer over the hyperlink indicator, you can read the text you entered in the *Text to display* field, as shown in Figure 10 - 88.

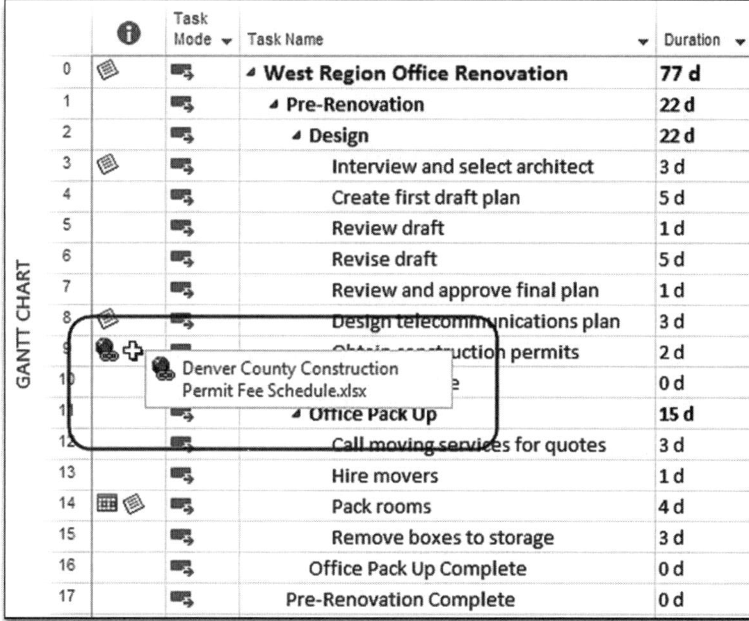

Figure 10 - 88: ScreenTip for hyperlink indicator

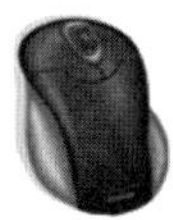

Hands On Exercise

Exercise 10 - 18

Attach a document to a project using a link (shortcut) and a hyperlink.

1. Open the **Linking Documents 2013.mpp** sample file.
2. Double-click task ID #2, the *Design P1* task.
3. In the *Task Information* dialog, select the *Notes* tab.
4. On the *Notes* page of the *Task Information* dialog, click the *Insert Object* button.
5. In the *Insert Object* dialog, select the *Create from File* option, and then click the *Browse* button.
6. In the *Browse* dialog, navigate to the folder containing your student sample files, if necessary.
7. In the *Browse* dialog, select the **Design Specifications 2013.docx** document, and then click the *Insert* button.
8. In the *Insert Object* dialog, select the *Link* checkbox and select the *Display as Icon* checkbox.
9. Click the *OK* button to close the *Insert Object* dialog.
10. Double-click the *Design Specifications.docx* shortcut to open the document in your Word application.
11. Close and do not save the *Design Specifications.docx* document and then exit the Word application.

12. Click the *OK* button to close the *Task Information* dialog.
13. Right-click task ID #3, the *Build P1* task, and then select the *Hyperlink* item on the shortcut menu.
14. In the *Insert Hyperlink* dialog, use the *Look in* pick list to navigate to the folder containing your student sample files, if necessary.
15. In the *Insert Hyperlink* dialog, select the **Expense Report 2013.xlsx** workbook file.
16. In the *Text to display* field, enter the text *Build Expenses*.
17. Click the *OK* button.
18. Float your mouse pointer over the hyperlink indicator for the *Build P1* task.
19. Click the hyperlink indicator for the *Build P1* task to open the workbook in your Excel application.
20. If prompted in a *Microsoft Project Security Notice* dialog, click the *Yes* button.
21. Close and do not save the workbook and then exit your Excel application.
22. Save and close the **Linking Documents 2013.mpp** sample file.

Exporting a Project Image to another Application

As a part of the communication and reporting process, project managers may occasionally need to export an image of a project view to another application. For example, you might need to export a picture of the *Gantt Chart* view to Word for inclusion in a project status report. The *Copy Picture* tool provides you this functionality by allowing you to copy a screenshot of your project so that you can paste the picture in other applications, such as Word, PowerPoint, or Visio. To use the *Copy Picture* tool, complete the following steps:

1. Apply the view you want to export to another application, such as the *Tracking Gantt* view.

Information: After applying the view you want to capture in the image, if possible, set up the view so that it fits on one screen. Although you can capture larger areas than a single screen, it is more difficult to get the results you want as the image gets larger. You may also need to adjust the position of the vertical split bar to show the columns you want to capture in the table portion of the view.

2. Click the *Task* tab to display the *Task* ribbon.
3. In the *Clipboard* section of the *Task* ribbon, click the *Copy* pick list button, and then select the *Copy Picture* item on the list, as shown in Figure 10 - 89.

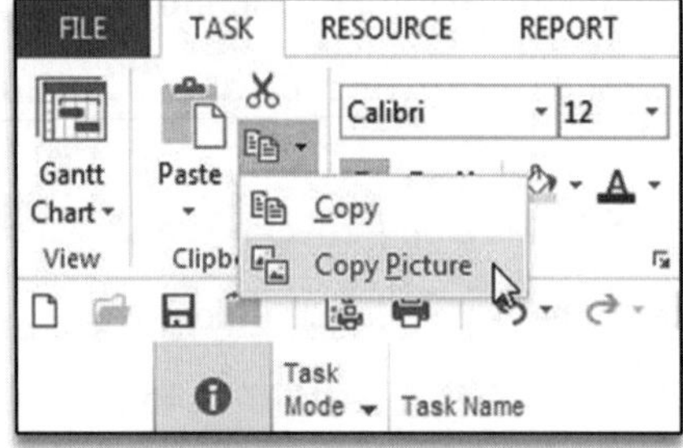

Figure 10 - 89: Copy Picture tool

The software displays the *Copy Picture* dialog shown in Figure 10 - 90. The *Copy Picture* dialog contains three sections in which you must configure options for the exported picture. Use the options in the *Render image* section as follows:

- Select the *For screen* option if you intend to paste the picture into an application to be viewed onscreen, such as in a PowerPoint presentation.

- Select the *For printer* option if you intend to paste the picture into an application to be printed, such as in a Word document.

- Select the *To GIF image file* option if you want to save the picture as a GIF image file for use in another application or in a web page, for example. If you choose this option, click the *Browse* button and browse to a folder in which to save the GIF image file and then give the image file a name. By default, the system names the GIF image file using the name of the Project 2013 file.

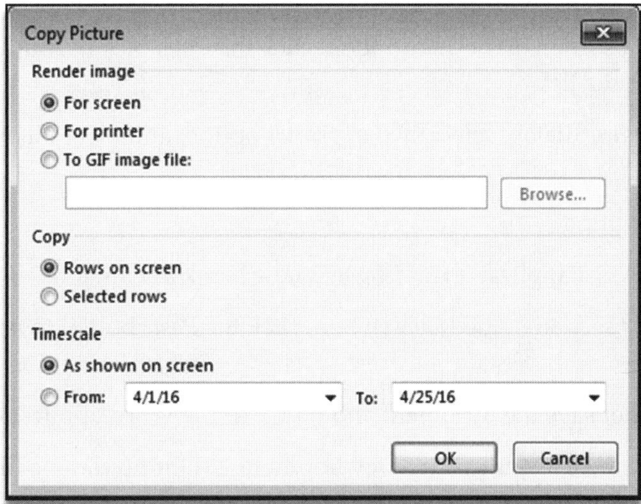

Figure 10 - 90: Copy Picture dialog

In the *Copy* section of the *Copy Picture* dialog, use the options as follows:

- Select the *Rows on screen* option to capture only the rows currently visible in the view.

- Select the *Selected rows* option to capture only the rows you selected in the view. Prior to using this option, you must actually select the rows you want to capture.

If the applied view contains a *Timescale* bar, such as in the *Gantt Chart, Tracking Gantt, Task Usage,* and *Resource Usage* views, use the options in the *Timescale* section as follows:

- Select the *As shown on screen* option to capture the date range shown in the timescaled part of the view. Prior to using this option, you should zoom the *Timescale* to show the date range you want to capture.

- Select a date in the *From* and *To* fields to capture a specific date range.

When you finish selecting your desired options in the *Copy Picture* dialog, click the *OK* button to capture the picture of your project. If you selected either the *For screen* or *For printer* option, the system copies a picture of your project to the Windows clipboard, from which you can paste the picture into another application. Switch to the other application, select the paste location, and then paste the picture into the document.

Hands On Exercise

Exercise 10 - 19

Export an image file to another Microsoft Office application.

1. Open the **CRM Software Development 2013.mpp** sample file.
2. Click the *Task* tab to display the *Task* ribbon, if necessary.
3. In the *View* section of the *Task* ribbon, click the *Gantt Chart* pick list button and then select the *Tracking Gantt* view.
4. In the *Clipboard* section of the *Task* ribbon, click the *Copy* pick list button, and then select the *Copy Picture* item on the list.
5. In the *Copy Picture* dialog, select the *For printer* option, and leave all of the other default options selected.
6. Click the *OK* button.
7. Launch your Word application and open a new blank document.
8. In the *Clipboard* section of the *Home* ribbon, click the *Paste* button to paste the image into the Word document.
9. Close and do not save the document and then exit the Word application.
10. Save and close the **CRM Software Development 2013.mpp** sample file.

Module 11

Advanced Project Reporting

Learning Objectives

After completing this module, you will be able to:

- Understand the new reports added to Project 2013
- Customize an existing report
- Customize a chart and a table
- Add a new chart or table in an existing report
- Create a new report
- Print a report
- Delete an existing report
- Share a report with another Office application
- View and modify Visual Reports
- Create custom Visual Reports

Inside Module 06

Understanding the New Reports

Prior to Project 2013, all previous versions of the software offered six categories of built-in reports. Although the previous versions allowed users to preview and print reports, the reports feature had two significant limitations:

- Users cannot export the report data to other Office applications, such as to Excel or PowerPoint.
- The reports contain textual data only, such as the type of data you might find in an Excel workbook, but the reports do not include any type of graphical data, such as charts.

For example, Figure 11 - 1 shows the *Project Summary* report in *Print Preview* mode in Project 2010. Notice how the report contains only textual data. My only choice is to print this report to paper since the software does not allow me to export it to Excel.

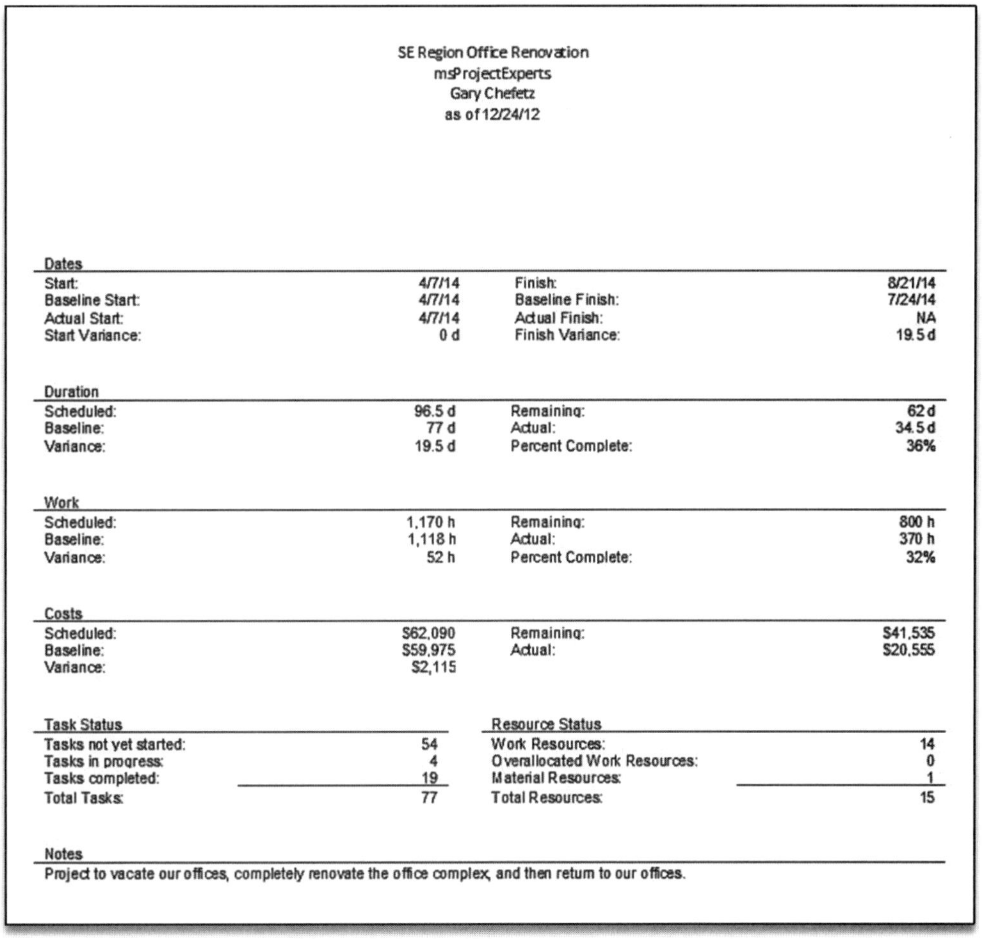

SE Region Office Renovation
msProjectExperts
Gary Chefetz
as of 12/24/12

Dates			
Start:	4/7/14	Finish:	8/21/14
Baseline Start:	4/7/14	Baseline Finish:	7/24/14
Actual Start:	4/7/14	Actual Finish:	NA
Start Variance:	0 d	Finish Variance:	19.5 d

Duration			
Scheduled:	96.5 d	Remaining:	62 d
Baseline:	77 d	Actual:	34.5 d
Variance:	19.5 d	Percent Complete:	36%

Work			
Scheduled:	1,170 h	Remaining:	800 h
Baseline:	1,118 h	Actual:	370 h
Variance:	52 h	Percent Complete:	32%

Costs			
Scheduled:	$62,090	Remaining:	$41,535
Baseline:	$59,975	Actual:	$20,555
Variance:	$2,115		

Task Status		Resource Status	
Tasks not yet started:	54	Work Resources:	14
Tasks in progress:	4	Overallocated Work Resources:	0
Tasks completed:	19	Material Resources:	1
Total Tasks:	77	Total Resources:	15

Notes

Project to vacate our offices, completely renovate the office complex, and then return to our offices.

Figure 11 - 1: Print preview in Project 2010 of the Project Summary report

With the introduction of Project 2013, the software now offers a powerful new reporting engine that generates graphical dashboard reports, which you can view, print, or export to another Office application. To use any of these new reports, click the *Report* tab to display the *Report* ribbon shown in Figure 11 - 2. Notice that the *View Reports* section of the *Report* ribbon contains eight pick list buttons that allow you to work with the new reporting feature.

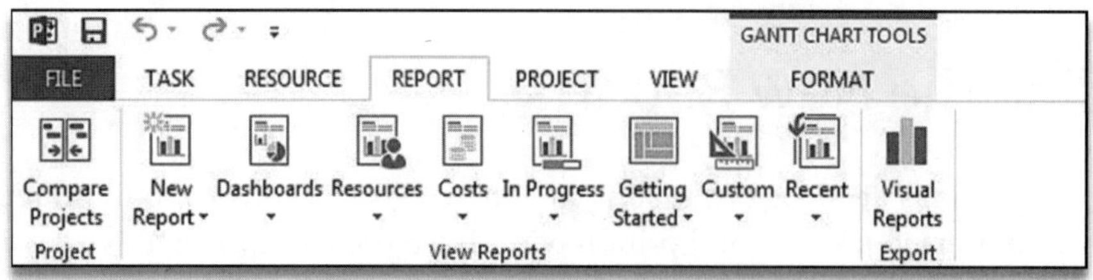

Figure 11 - 2: Report ribbon

Viewing a Report

Project 2013 organizes the default reports into five categories: *Dashboards, Resources, Costs, In Progress,* and *Getting Started.* To view a report, click one of these five pick list buttons and select a report, or click the *Recent* pick list button and select a recently used report. For example, to view an overview report about key data in your project, click the *Dashboards* pick list button and select the *Project Overview* report.

Figure 11 - 3 shows the new *Project Overview* report in Project 2013. Notice that the software displays the name of the report vertically along the left side of the report. Notice also that the report shows you a graphical table with a summary of the current *% Complete* for the project (*36%*), with a chart that shows the *% Complete* by first level tasks, along with two tables that show milestones due (not yet completed) and late tasks. If you compare the two *Project Overview* reports shown in Figure 11 - 1 and Figure 11 - 3, the difference between the two is absolutely striking!

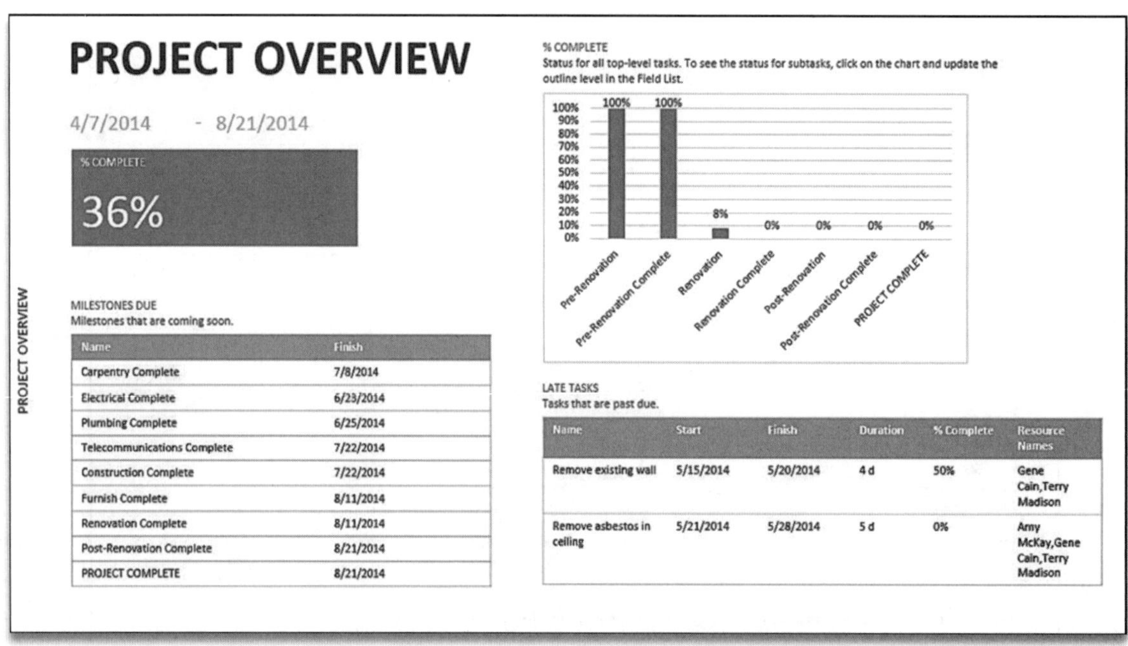

Name	Finish
Carpentry Complete	7/8/2014
Electrical Complete	6/23/2014
Plumbing Complete	6/25/2014
Telecommunications Complete	7/22/2014
Construction Complete	7/22/2014
Furnish Complete	8/11/2014
Renovation Complete	8/11/2014
Post-Renovation Complete	8/21/2014
PROJECT COMPLETE	8/21/2014

Name	Start	Finish	Duration	% Complete	Resource Names
Remove existing wall	5/15/2014	5/20/2014	4 d	50%	Gene Cain,Terry Madison
Remove asbestos in ceiling	5/21/2014	5/28/2014	5 d	0%	Amy McKay,Gene Cain,Terry Madison

Figure 11 - 3: Project Overview report in Project 2013

Another way to view a report is to click the *Custom* pick list button and select the *More Reports* item on the pick list. You can also select the *More Reports* item at the bottom of the *Dashboards, Resources, Costs, In Progress, Getting Started,* or *Recent* pick lists. Project 2013 displays the *Reports* dialog with the *Custom* tab selected. Click one of the tabs along the left side of the dialog to see reports in that section. For example, Figure 11 - 4 shows the *Reports* dialog with the *Costs* tab selected. To view any report using the *Reports* dialog, select the report and then click the *Select* button.

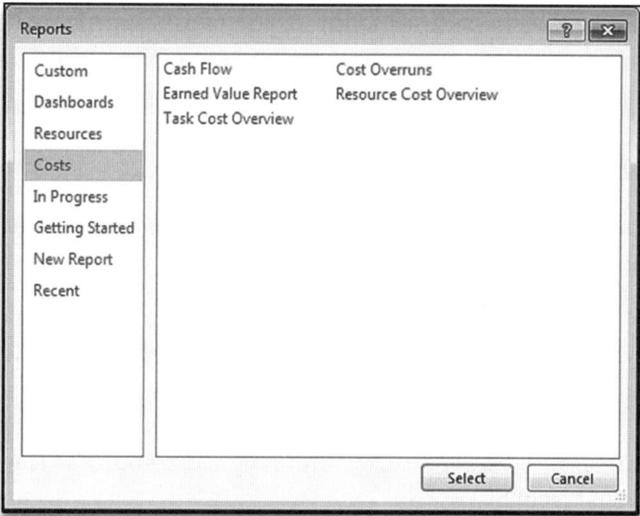

Figure 11 - 4: Reports dialog

When you view one of the new reports in Project 2013, the software displays a new *Design* ribbon with the *Report Tools* applied as shown in Figure 11 - 5. The software organizes the *Design* ribbon into five sections. Use the buttons in the *View* section to apply a view or a different report. Use the buttons in the *Themes* section to apply a set of theme colors, fonts, and effects to your report. Use the buttons in the *Insert* section to insert a graphical image, a graphical shape, a new chart, a new table, or a text box. Use the buttons in the *Report* section to manage your reports or to copy the current report to the Windows clipboard so that you can export the report data to another Office application. Use the buttons in the *Page Setup* section to prepare your report for printing.

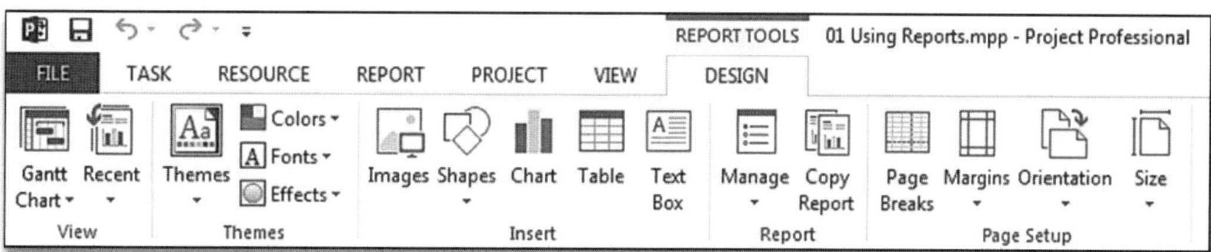

Figure 11 - 5: Design ribbon with the Report Tools applied

Every report in Project 2013 can contain any of the following types of objects:

- **Text boxes** – The software uses text boxes to show the title of the report, plus additional information about other objects in the report. For example, the *Project Overview* title shown previously in Figure 11 - 3 is a text box, as are the *Milestones Due* and *Late Tasks* labels, along with their descriptions.

- **Fields** – The software uses fields to display project data in a format similar to text boxes. You find two fields immediately below the title of the *Project Overview* report, which are the *Start* and *Finish* dates fields.

- **Tables** – The software uses tables to display data from project fields. For example, the *% Complete* value you see in the upper left corner of the *Project Overview* report is actually a table. In addition, you also see tables containing project data in the *Milestones Due* and *Late Tasks* sections of the *Project Overview* report.

- **Charts** – The software uses charts to graphically display data about your project. You see a *% Complete* chart about first level tasks in the upper right corner of the *Project Overview* report.

- **Hyperlinks** – The software uses hyperlinks to direct you to a *Help* article in Office.com that is relevant to the type of report currently displayed. For example, the *Burndown* report contains a *Try setting a baseline* hyperlink in an information text section at the bottom of the report.

Understanding Dashboard Reports

Click the *Dashboards* pick list button to see the five default dashboard reports that display project data in a dashboard format. These new dashboard reports include the following:

- *Project Overview* report shown previously in Figure 11 - 3 includes three tables and one chart that display high-level summary information about your project. The table in the upper left corner of the report shows the current *Percent Complete* for the project. The *Milestones Due* table displays a list of upcoming milestone tasks along with their *Finish* dates. The *Late Tasks* table displays a list of late tasks, along with their *Start* date, *Finish* date, *Duration*, *% Complete* values, and assigned resources. The *% Complete* chart shows the *Percent Complete* for all first level tasks.

Information: In Project 2013, a **late task** is any task with a *Late* value in the *Status* field. By default, the software sets a *Late* value in the *Status* field when the time-phased cumulative percent complete (represented by the black progress line in a Gantt bar) does not reach the *Status Date* you specify for the project. If you do not specify a *Status Date*, then the software uses the *Current Date* to determine late tasks.

- The *Burndown* report shown in Figure 11 - 6 contains two charts arranged horizontally. The *Work Burndown* chart is a line chart that compares the completed work with remaining work, timephased at the two-week level. This chart displays the information using the new *Remaining Cumulative Actual Work, Remaining Cumulative Work,* and *Baseline Remaining Cumulative Work* fields. The *Task Burndown* chart is a line chart that compares the number of completed tasks with the remaining tasks, timephased at the two-week level. This chart uses the new *Baseline Remaining Tasks, Remaining Tasks,* and *Remaining Actual Tasks* fields. Below the *Work Burndown* chart, the report displays a *Try setting a baseline* hyperlink that points to the *Set and save a baseline* page in the Office.com website. Below the *Task Burndown* chart, the report displays a *Learn more* hyperlink that points to the *Create a burndown report* page in the Office.com website.

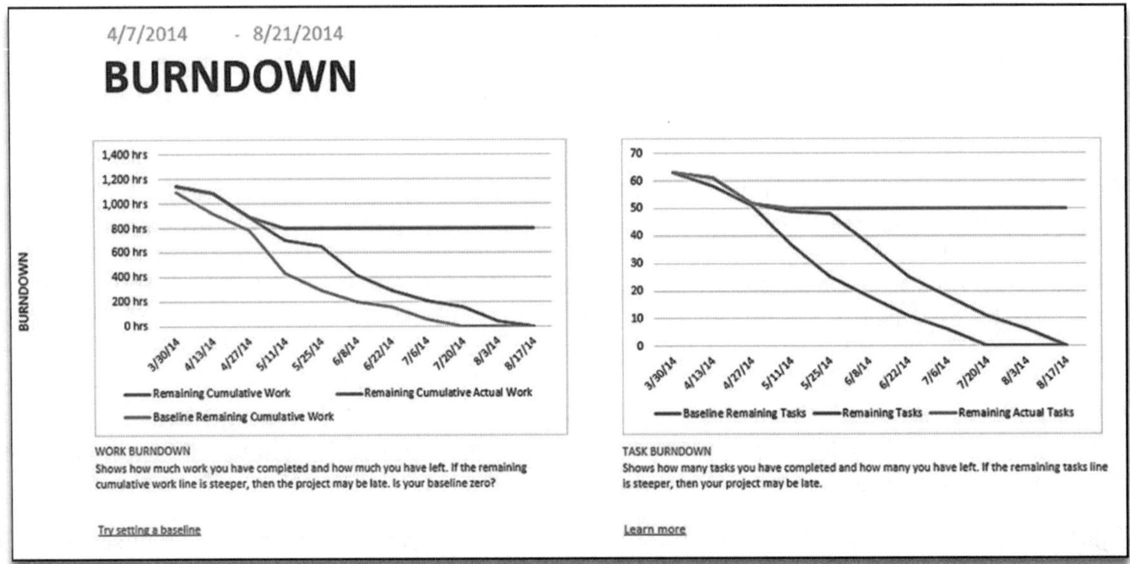

Figure 11 - 6: Burndown report

Warning: Due to the small size of the *Work Burndown* and *Task Burndown* charts, Project 2013 does not display the dates properly on the X-axis of each chart. To display the dates properly, you must edit each chart by changing the date format. I discuss how to customize a chart in the *Customizing a Chart* topical section later in this module.

- The *Cost Overview* report shown in Figure 11 - 7 contains four tables and two charts that display cost-related information about your project. The upper left corner of the report includes three tables, which display the current values in the *Cost, Remaining Cost,* and *% Complete* fields for the entire project. The *Cost Status* table shows you the current cost-related fields for every first level task. These fields include the *Actual Cost, Remaining Cost, Baseline Cost, Cost,* and *Cost Variance* fields. The *Progress Versus Cost* chart is a line chart that compares the *Cumulative Percent Complete* field with the *Cumulative Cost* field, timephased at the two-week level. The *Cost Status* chart is a combination chart that shows stacked columns for *Remaining Cost* and *Actual Cost,* with a line for *Baseline Cost.* This chart shows the data for all first level tasks. In the description section of the *Cost Status* chart, the report displays a *Try setting a baseline* hyperlink pointing to the *Set and save a baseline* page in the Office.com website.

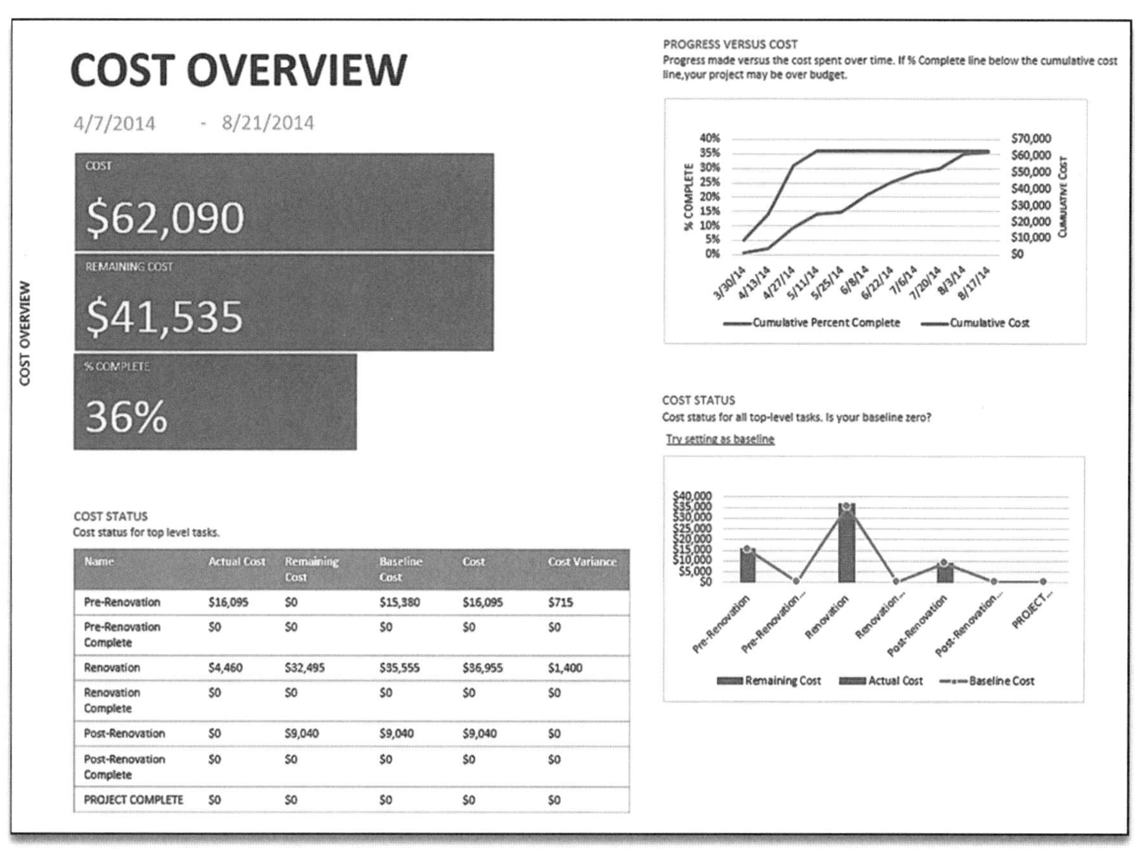

Name	Actual Cost	Remaining Cost	Baseline Cost	Cost	Cost Variance
Pre-Renovation	$16,095	$0	$15,380	$16,095	$715
Pre-Renovation Complete	$0	$0	$0	$0	$0
Renovation	$4,460	$32,495	$35,555	$36,955	$1,400
Renovation Complete	$0	$0	$0	$0	$0
Post-Renovation	$0	$9,040	$9,040	$9,040	$0
Post-Renovation Complete	$0	$0	$0	$0	$0
PROJECT COMPLETE	$0	$0	$0	$0	$0

Figure 11 - 7: Cost Overview report

- The *Upcoming Tasks* report shown in Figure 11 - 8 contains two tables and one chart that display task-related information about your project. The table in the upper left corner of the dialog shows the total *% Work Complete* value for the entire project. The *Tasks Starting Soon* table shows any task scheduled to start during the current week, based on the date in the *Current Date* field, and includes the *Resource Names, Start, Finish,* and *Work* fields. The *Remaining Tasks* chart is a column chart, which displays the *% Complete* value for any task scheduled to finish this week, based on the date in the *Current Date* field.

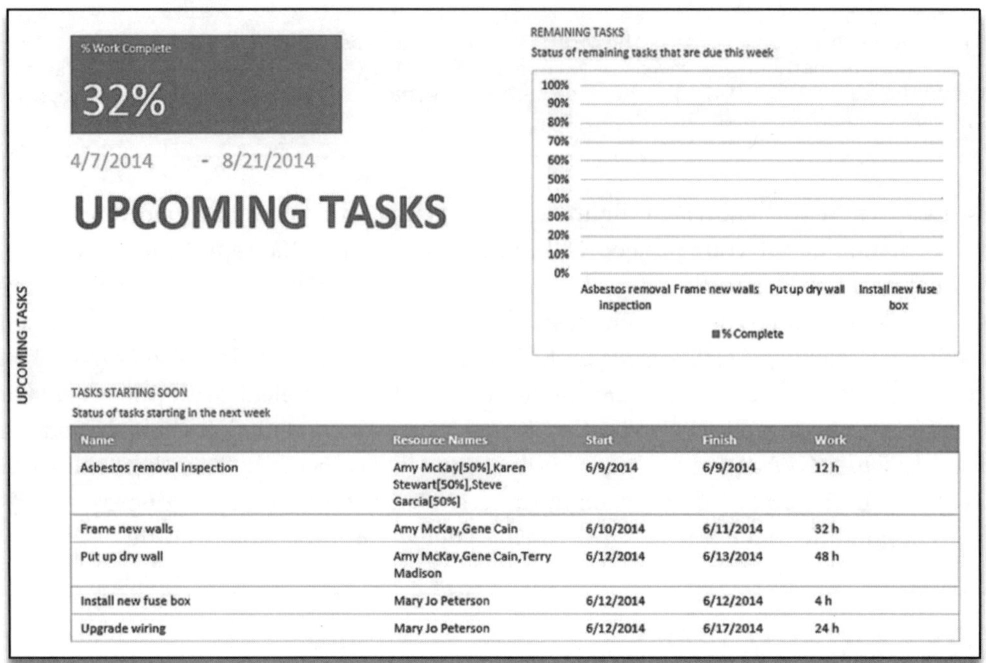

Name	Resource Names	Start	Finish	Work
Asbestos removal inspection	Amy McKay[50%],Karen Stewart[50%],Steve Garcia[50%]	6/9/2014	6/9/2014	12 h
Frame new walls	Amy McKay,Gene Cain	6/10/2014	6/11/2014	32 h
Put up dry wall	Amy McKay,Gene Cain,Terry Madison	6/12/2014	6/13/2014	48 h
Install new fuse box	Mary Jo Peterson	6/12/2014	6/12/2014	4 h
Upgrade wiring	Mary Jo Peterson	6/12/2014	6/17/2014	24 h

Figure 11 - 8: Upcoming Tasks report

- The *Work Overview* report shown in Figure 11 - 9 includes four charts and three tables that display information about task and resource work in your project. The right side of the report contains three tables, which display the current values in the *% Work Complete, Remaining Work,* and *Actual Work* fields for the entire project. The *Work Burndown* chart is a line chart that compares the completed work with the remaining work, timephased at the two-week level. This chart displays the information using the new *Remaining Cumulative Work, Remaining Cumulative Actual Work,* and *Baseline Remaining Cumulative Work* fields. The *Work Stats* chart is a combination chart that shows stacked columns for *Actual Work* and *Remaining Work,* with a line for *Baseline Work.* This chart shows the data for all first level tasks. The *Resource Stats* chart is a stacked bar chart that shows stacked bars with *Actual Work* and *Remaining Work* for each *Work* resource in your project. The *Remaining Availability* chart is a line chart that displays the *Remaining Availability,* timephased at the two-week level for each *Work* resource in your project.

Warning: Due to the small size of the *Remaining Availability* chart, Project 2013 can only show a small number of resources in the chart. To limit the number of resources shown in the *Remaining Availability* chart, you must customize the chart to filter for only the resources you want to see displayed in the chart. I discuss how to customize a chart in the *Customizing a Chart* topical section later in this module.

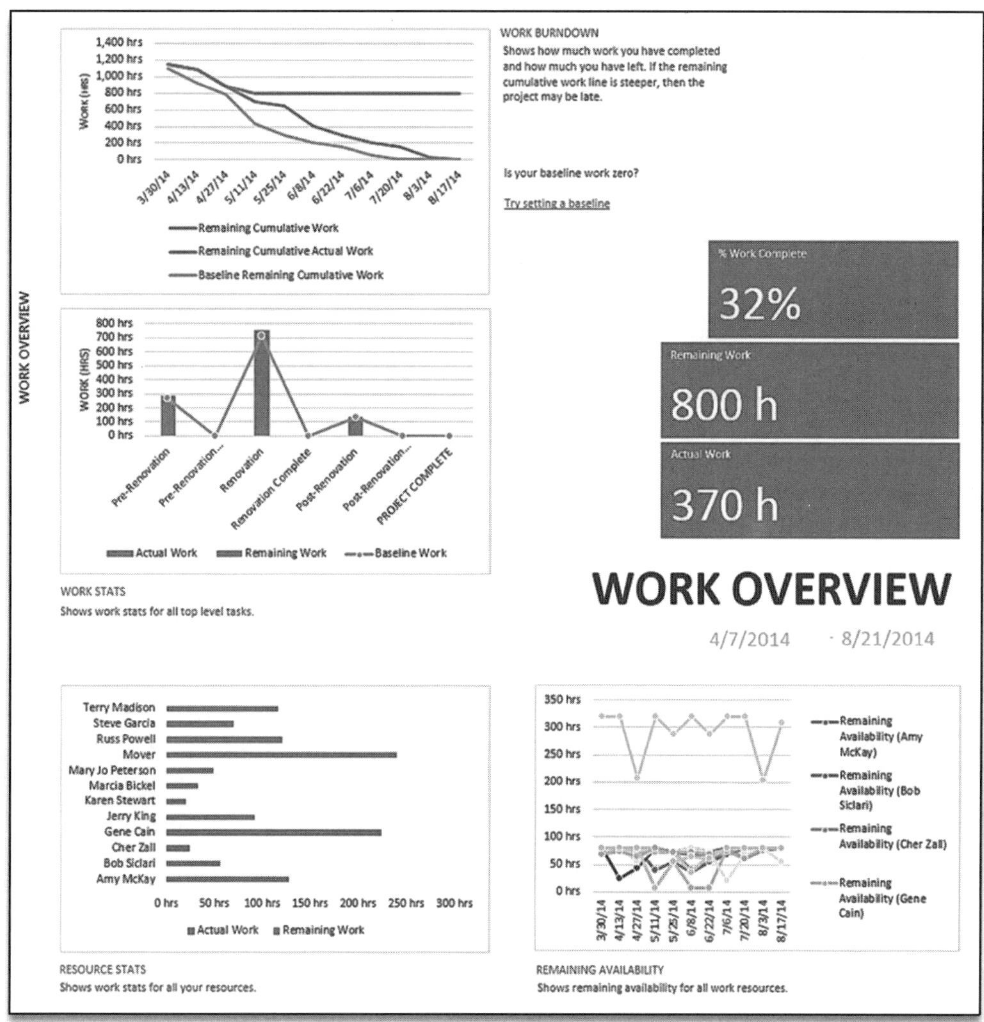

Figure 11 - 9: Work Overview report

Understanding Resource Reports

Click the *Resources* pick list button to see the two default resource reports that display information about the resources in your project team. These new resource reports include the following:

- The *Overallocated Resources* report shown in Figure 11 - 10 contains two charts that display information about overallocated resources in your project team. The *Work Status* chart is a stacked column chart that shows the *Actual Work* and *Remaining Work* for each overallocated resource. The *Overallocation* chart is a line chart that shows the total *Overallocation* for each overallocated resource, timephased at the daily level, from the *Start* date to the *Finish* date of the project.

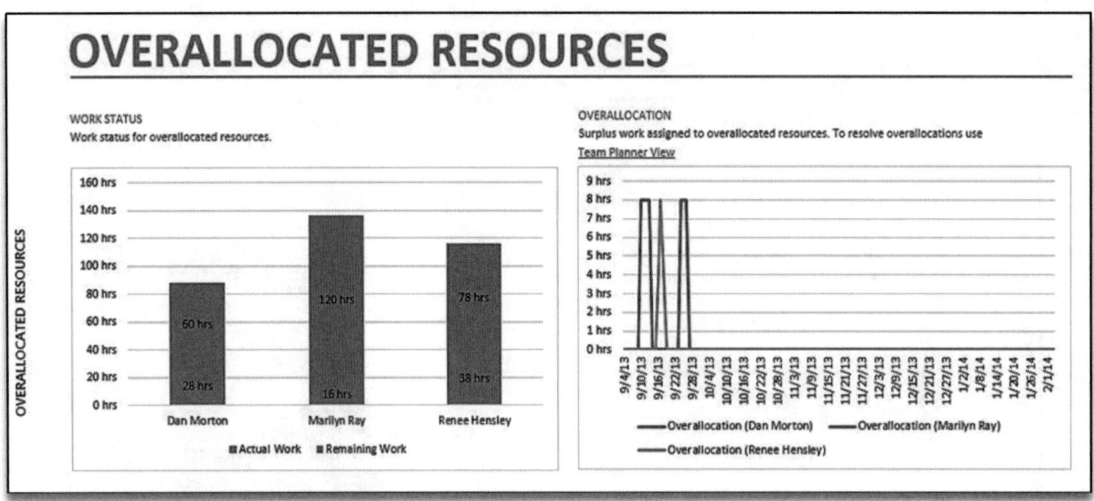

Figure 11 - 10: Overallocated Resources report

Warning: Due to the small size of the *Overallocation* chart, Project 2013 compresses the time periods shown along the X-axis of the chart. If you want to limit the number of time periods shown in the *Overallocation* chart, you must edit the *Time* category to format the timescale with the time periods you want to see. I discuss how to customize a chart in the *Customizing a Chart* topical section later in this module.

- The *Resource Overview* report shown in Figure 11 - 11 contains two charts and one table that display work-related information about each of the *Work* resources in your project team. The *Resource Stats* chart is a combination chart that shows stacked columns for *Actual Work* and *Remaining Work,* with a line for *Baseline Work* for each of the *Work* resources in your project team. The *Work Status* chart is a column chart that shows the *% Work Complete* for each of the *Work* resources in your project team. The *Resource Status* table shows the status of *Remaining Work* for each resource and includes the *Start, Finish,* and *Remaining Work* fields.

Information: In the *Resource Status* table, the *Start* field contains the earliest *Start* date of any task assigned to each resource, while the *Finish* field contains the latest *Finish* date of any task assigned to each resource. The *Remaining Work* field shows the total *Remaining Work* for all tasks assigned to each resource.

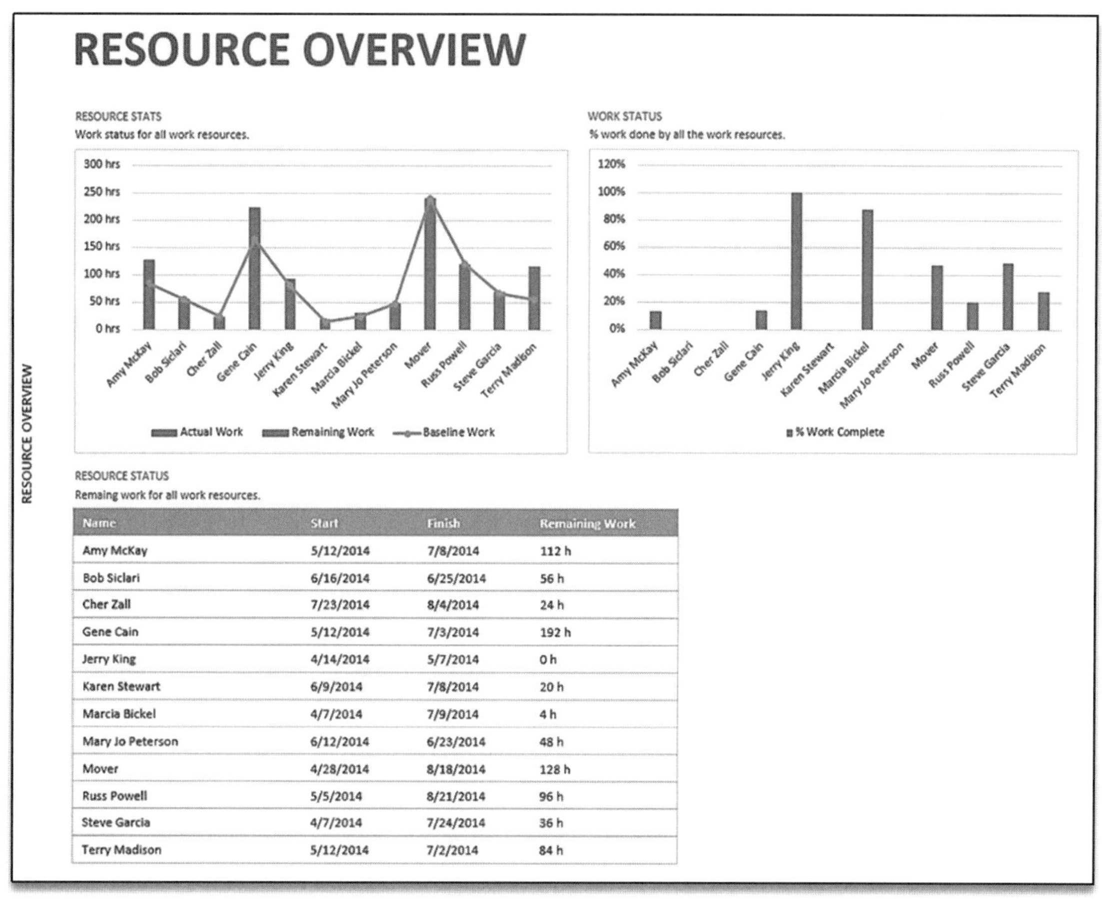

Name	Start	Finish	Remaining Work
Amy McKay	5/12/2014	7/8/2014	112 h
Bob Siclari	6/16/2014	6/25/2014	56 h
Cher Zall	7/23/2014	8/4/2014	24 h
Gene Cain	5/12/2014	7/3/2014	192 h
Jerry King	4/14/2014	5/7/2014	0 h
Karen Stewart	6/9/2014	7/8/2014	20 h
Marcia Bickel	4/7/2014	7/9/2014	4 h
Mary Jo Peterson	6/12/2014	6/23/2014	48 h
Mover	4/28/2014	8/18/2014	128 h
Russ Powell	5/5/2014	8/21/2014	96 h
Steve Garcia	4/7/2014	7/24/2014	36 h
Terry Madison	5/12/2014	7/2/2014	84 h

Figure 11 - 11: Resource Overview report

Understanding Cost Reports

Click the *Costs* pick list button to see the five default cost reports that display project cost information. These new cost reports include the following:

- The *Cash Flow* report shown in Figure 11 - 12 contains a chart, two tables, and an informational text box. The table at the top of the report, shown as a gray-shaded box, displays the *Actual Cost, Baseline Cost, Remaining Cost,* and *Cost Variance* fields for the entire project. The chart is a combination chart that shows a column for *Cost* and a line for *Cumulative Cost,* timephased by quarters for the entire project. The table at the bottom of the report shows you the current cost and earned value data for every first level task. The fields in the table include the *Remaining Cost, Actual Cost, Cost, ACWP (Actual Cost of Work Performed), BCWP (Budgeted Cost of Work Performed),* and *BCWS (Budgeted Cost of Work Scheduled)* fields. The informational text box to the right of the chart explains the meaning of the data in the chart and the table at the bottom of the report.

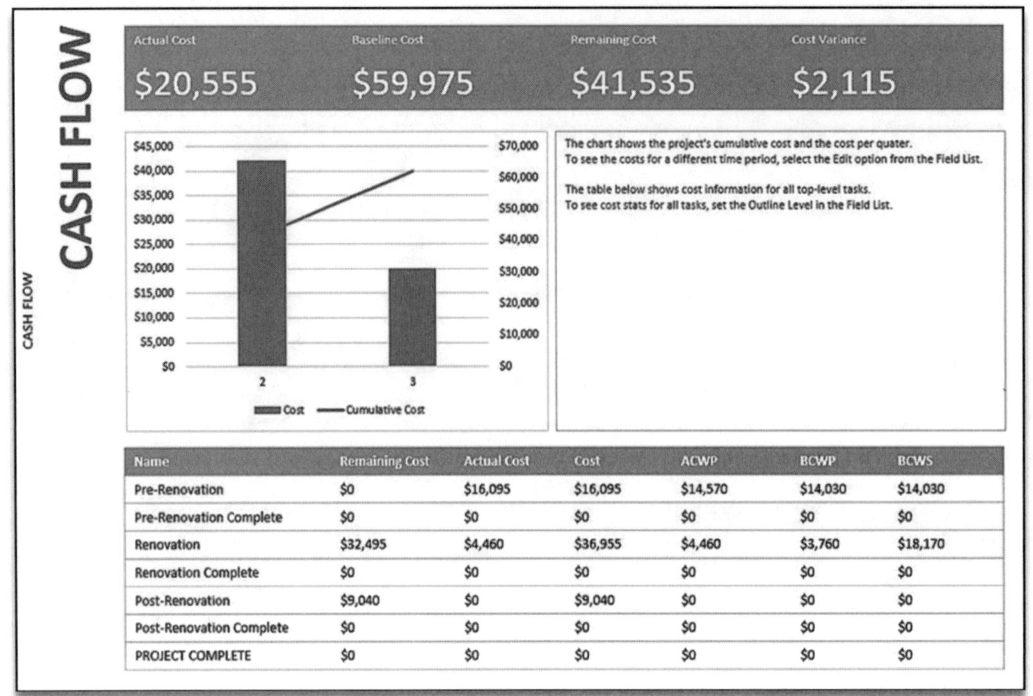

Name	Remaining Cost	Actual Cost	Cost	ACWP	BCWP	BCWS
Pre-Renovation	$0	$16,095	$16,095	$14,570	$14,030	$14,030
Pre-Renovation Complete	$0	$0	$0	$0	$0	$0
Renovation	$32,495	$4,460	$36,955	$4,460	$3,760	$18,170
Renovation Complete	$0	$0	$0	$0	$0	$0
Post-Renovation	$9,040	$0	$9,040	$0	$0	$0
Post-Renovation Complete	$0	$0	$0	$0	$0	$0
PROJECT COMPLETE	$0	$0	$0	$0	$0	$0

Figure 11 - 12: Cash Flow report

- The *Cost Overruns* report shown in Figure 11 - 13 contains two charts and two tables. The *Task Cost Variance* chart is a line chart that shows the *Cost Variance* data for every first level task in the project. The table immediately below this chart shows you the status and current cost data for every first level task. The fields in the table include the *% Work Complete, Cost, Baseline Cost,* and *Cost Variance* fields. The *Resource Cost Variance* chart is a column chart that shows the *Cost Variance* for every *Work* and *Cost* resource in your project team. The table immediately below this chart shows you the cost information for every *Work* resource in your project team. The fields in this table include the *Cost, Baseline Cost,* and *Cost Variance* fields.

Information: The table immediately below the *Resource Cost Variance* chart displays only the *Work* resources in your project team. If you use *Cost* and *Material* resources in your project, in addition to *Work* resources, you may want to customize this table to filter for all resources. I discuss how to customize a table in the *Customizing a Table* topical section later in this module.

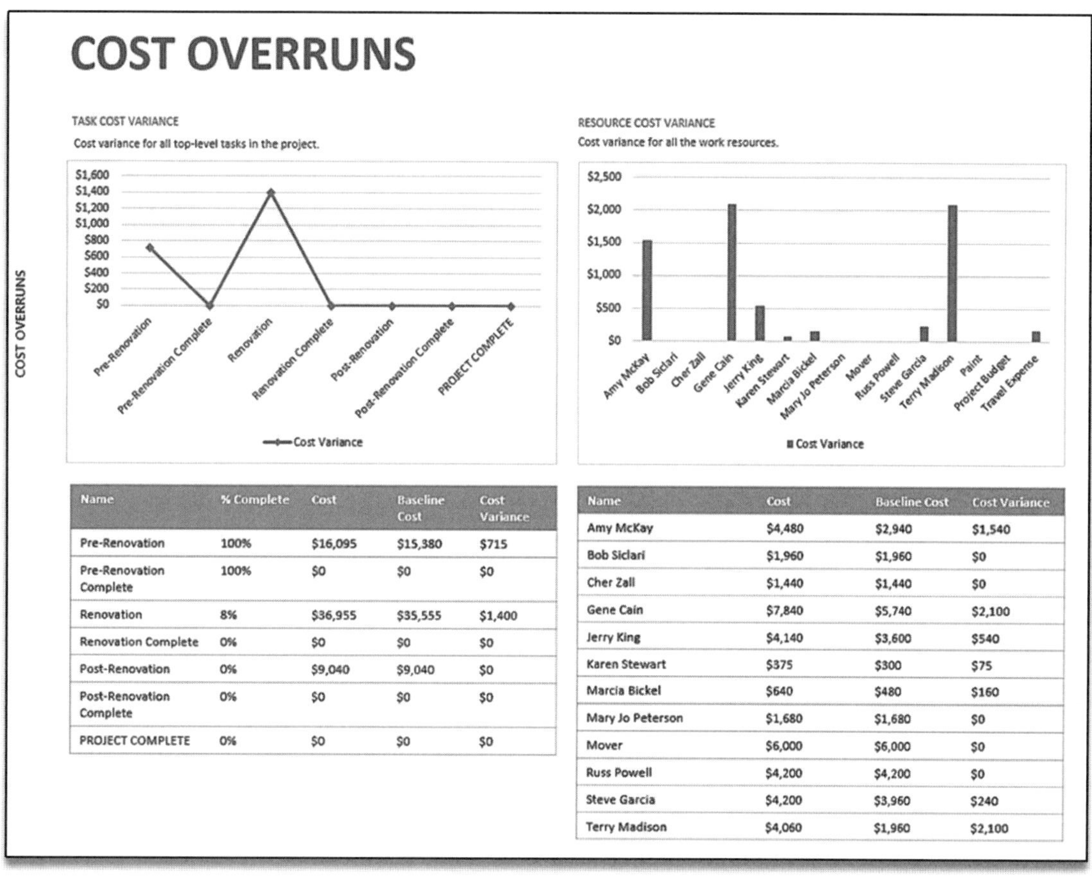

Name	% Complete	Cost	Baseline Cost	Cost Variance
Pre-Renovation	100%	$16,095	$15,380	$715
Pre-Renovation Complete	100%	$0	$0	$0
Renovation	8%	$36,955	$35,555	$1,400
Renovation Complete	0%	$0	$0	$0
Post-Renovation	0%	$9,040	$9,040	$0
Post-Renovation Complete	0%	$0	$0	$0
PROJECT COMPLETE	0%	$0	$0	$0

Name	Cost	Baseline Cost	Cost Variance
Amy McKay	$4,480	$2,940	$1,540
Bob Siclari	$1,960	$1,960	$0
Cher Zall	$1,440	$1,440	$0
Gene Cain	$7,840	$5,740	$2,100
Jerry King	$4,140	$3,600	$540
Karen Stewart	$375	$300	$75
Marcia Bickel	$640	$480	$160
Mary Jo Peterson	$1,680	$1,680	$0
Mover	$6,000	$6,000	$0
Russ Powell	$4,200	$4,200	$0
Steve Garcia	$4,200	$3,960	$240
Terry Madison	$4,060	$1,960	$2,100

Figure 11 - 13: Cost Overruns report

- The *Earned Value* report shown in Figure 11 - 14 contains one table, three charts, and one informational text box. The table at the top of the report, shown as a blue-shaded box, displays the *EAC (Estimate at Completion), ACWP (Actual Cost of Work Performed),* and *BCWP (Budgeted Cost of Work Performed)* fields for the entire project. The *Earned Value Over Time* chart is a line chart that shows the *ACWP (Actual Cost of Work Performed), BCWP (Budgeted Cost of Work Performed),* and *BCWS (Budgeted Cost of Work Scheduled)* fields, timephased at the weekly level. In the description section of the *Earned Value Over Time* chart, the report contains a *Learn more about earned value* hyperlink that points to the *Earned value analysis, for the rest of us* page in the Office.com website. The *Variance Over Time* chart is a line chart that shows the *CV (Cost Variance)* and *SV (Schedule Variance)* fields, timephased at the weekly level. The *Indices Over Time* chart is a line chart that shows the *SPI (Schedule Performance Index)* and *CPI (Cost Performance Index)* fields, timephased at the weekly level. The informational text box to the left of the charts briefly explains the concept of earned value management.

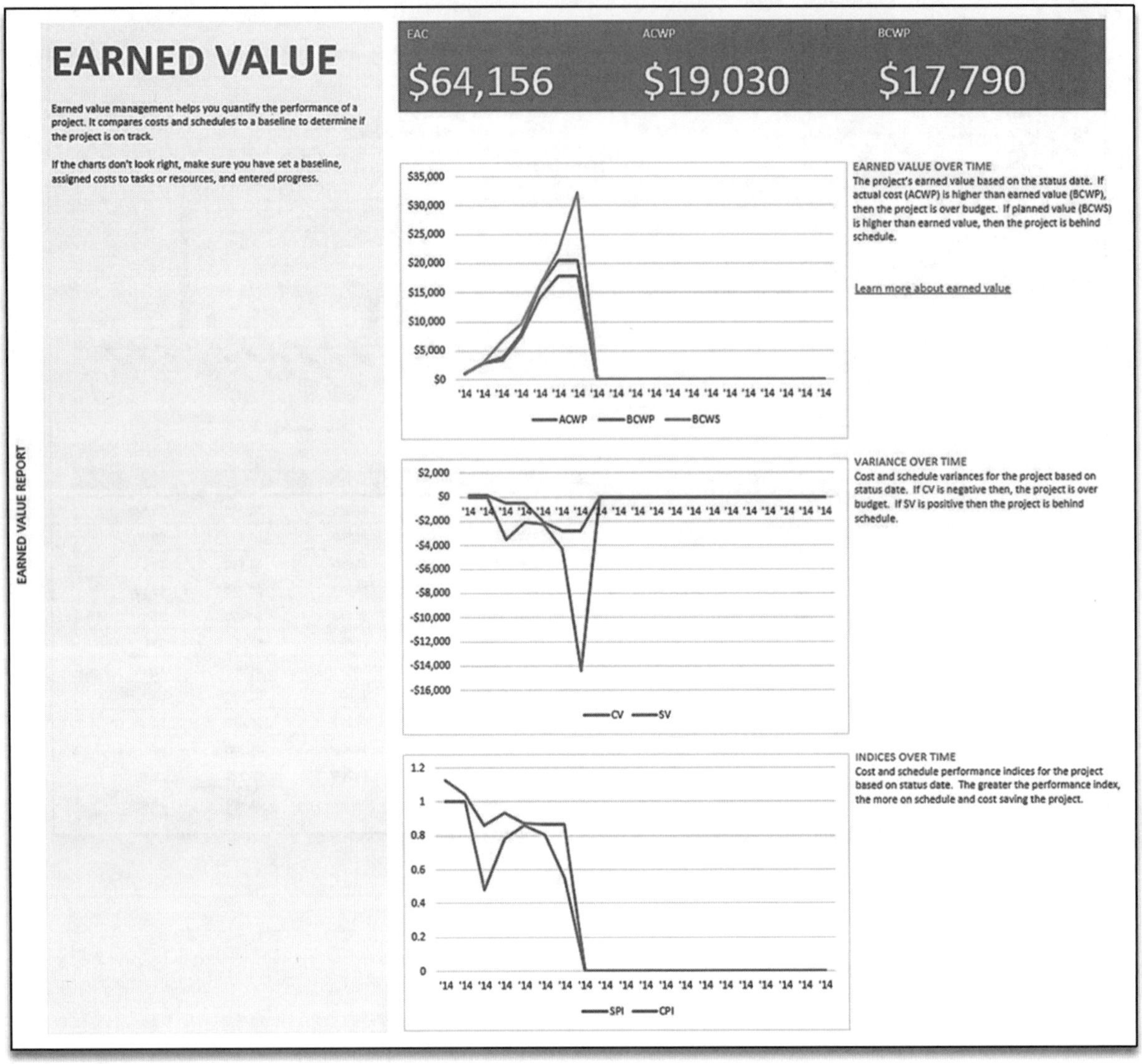

EARNED VALUE

Earned value management helps you quantify the performance of a project. It compares costs and schedules to a baseline to determine if the project is on track.

If the charts don't look right, make sure you have set a baseline, assigned costs to tasks or resources, and entered progress.

EAC $64,156 | ACWP $19,030 | BCWP $17,790

EARNED VALUE OVER TIME
The project's earned value based on the status date. If actual cost (ACWP) is higher than earned value (BCWP), then the project is over budget. If planned value (BCWS) is higher than earned value, then the project is behind schedule.

Learn more about earned value

VARIANCE OVER TIME
Cost and schedule variances for the project based on status date. If CV is negative then, the project is over budget. If SV is positive then the project is behind schedule.

INDICES OVER TIME
Cost and schedule performance indices for the project based on status date. The greater the performance index, the more on schedule and cost saving the project.

EARNED VALUE REPORT

Figure 11 - 14: Earned Value report

- The *Resource Cost Overview* report shown in Figure 11 - 15 contains two charts and one table. The *Cost Status* chart is a combination chart that displays stacked columns for *Actual Cost* and *Remaining Cost,* with a line for *Baseline Cost*. The *Cost Distribution* chart is a pie chart that displays *Cost* information distributed by resource type for *Work, Material,* and *Cost* resources. The *Cost Details* table shows work and cost information for each *Work* resource in your project team, and includes the *Actual Work, Actual Cost,* and *Standard Rate* columns.

Warning: Because of the small size of the *Cost Status* chart, Project 2013 overlaps the resource names on the X-axis over the *Legend* element at the bottom of the chart. To resolve this situation, you must edit the chart to display the *Legend* element at the top of the chart. I discuss how to customize a chart in the *Customizing a Chart* topical section later in this module.

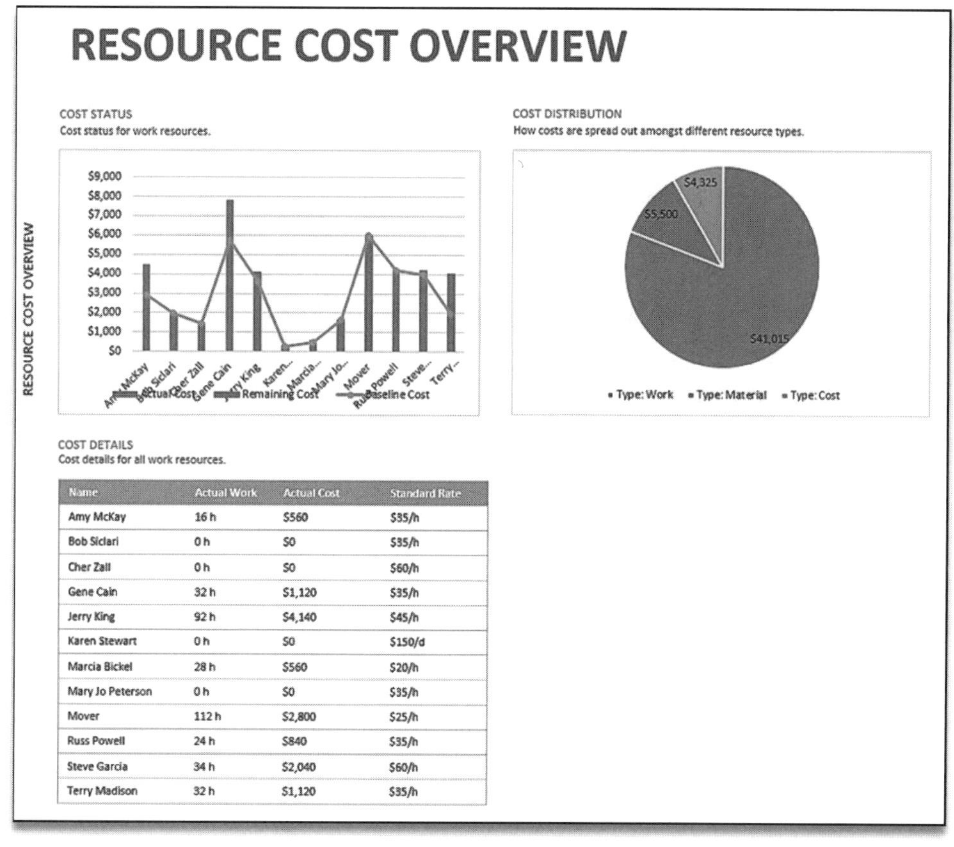

Name	Actual Work	Actual Cost	Standard Rate
Amy McKay	16 h	$560	$35/h
Bob Siclari	0 h	$0	$35/h
Cher Zall	0 h	$0	$60/h
Gene Cain	32 h	$1,120	$35/h
Jerry King	92 h	$4,140	$45/h
Karen Stewart	0 h	$0	$150/d
Marcia Bickel	28 h	$560	$20/h
Mary Jo Peterson	0 h	$0	$35/h
Mover	112 h	$2,800	$25/h
Russ Powell	24 h	$840	$35/h
Steve Garcia	34 h	$2,040	$60/h
Terry Madison	32 h	$1,120	$35/h

Figure 11 - 15: Resource Cost Overview report

Information: The *Cost Details* table displays only the *Work* resources in your project team. If you use *Cost* and *Material* resources in your project, in addition to *Work* resources, you may want to customize this table to filter for all resources. I discuss how to customize a table in the *Customizing a Table* topical section later in this module.

- The *Task Cost Overview* report shown in Figure 11 - 16 contains two charts and a table that display information about the cost of tasks in your project. The *Cost Status* chart is a combination chart that shows stacked columns for *Actual Cost* and *Remaining Cost*, with a line for *Baseline Cost*. This chart shows the data for all first level tasks. The *Cost Distribution* chart is a pie chart that displays *Cost* distribution based on the *Status* value for every task in the project. The *Status* field determines whether a task is completed, on schedule, a future task, or a late task. The *Cost Status* table shows you the current cost-related fields for every first level task. These fields include the *Fixed Cost, Actual Cost, Remaining Cost, Cost, Baseline Cost,* and *Cost Variance* fields.

Information: Remember that a **late task** is any task with a *Late* value in the *Status* field. By default, the software sets a *Late* value in the *Status* field when the time-phased cumulative percent complete (represented by the black progress line in a Gantt bar) does not reach the *Status Date* you specify for the project. If you do not specify a *Status Date*, then the software uses the *Current Date* to determine late tasks.

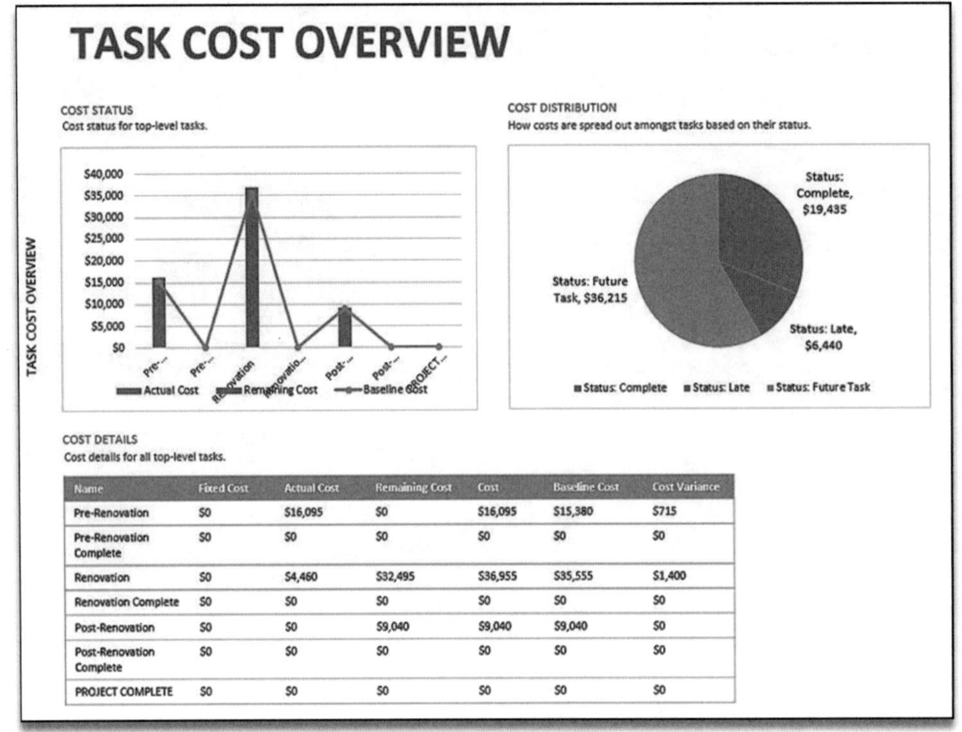
TASK COST OVERVIEW

TASK COST OVERVIEW

COST STATUS
Cost status for top-level tasks.

COST DISTRIBUTION
How costs are spread out amongst tasks based on their status.

COST DETAILS
Cost details for all top-level tasks.

Name	Fixed Cost	Actual Cost	Remaining Cost	Cost	Baseline Cost	Cost Variance
Pre-Renovation	$0	$16,095	$0	$16,095	$15,380	$715
Pre-Renovation Complete	$0	$0	$0	$0	$0	$0
Renovation	$0	$4,460	$32,495	$36,955	$35,555	$1,400
Renovation Complete	$0	$0	$0	$0	$0	$0
Post-Renovation	$0	$0	$9,040	$9,040	$9,040	$0
Post-Renovation Complete	$0	$0	$0	$0	$0	$0
PROJECT COMPLETE	$0	$0	$0	$0	$0	$0

Figure 11 - 16: Task Cost Overview report

Warning: Because of the small size of the *Cost Status* chart, Project 2013 overlaps the task names on the X-axis over the *Legend* element at the bottom of the chart. To resolve this situation, you must edit the chart to display the *Legend* element at the top of the chart. I discuss how to customize a chart in the *Customizing a Chart* topical section later in this module.

Understanding In Progress Reports

Click the *In Progress* pick list button to see the four default reports that display progress information about tasks in your project. These new *In Progress* reports include the following:

- The *Critical Tasks* report shown in Figure 11 - 17 contains a chart and a table. The chart in the upper left corner of the report is a pie chart that displays *Cost* distribution based on the *Status* value for every task in the project. The *Status* field determines whether a task is completed, on schedule, a future task, or a late task. The table displays schedule-related information about every *Critical* task in the project, and includes the *Start, Finish, % Complete, Remaining Work,* and *Resource Names* columns. In the description section of table, the report contains a *Learn more about managing your project's critical path* hyperlink that points to the *Show the critical path of your project* page in the Office.com website.

Information: The table in the *Critical Tasks* report does not display any completed tasks. Remember that Project 2013 does not consider completed tasks to be *Critical* tasks. By definition, a *Critical* task is any uncompleted task with a *Total Slack* value of 0 days.

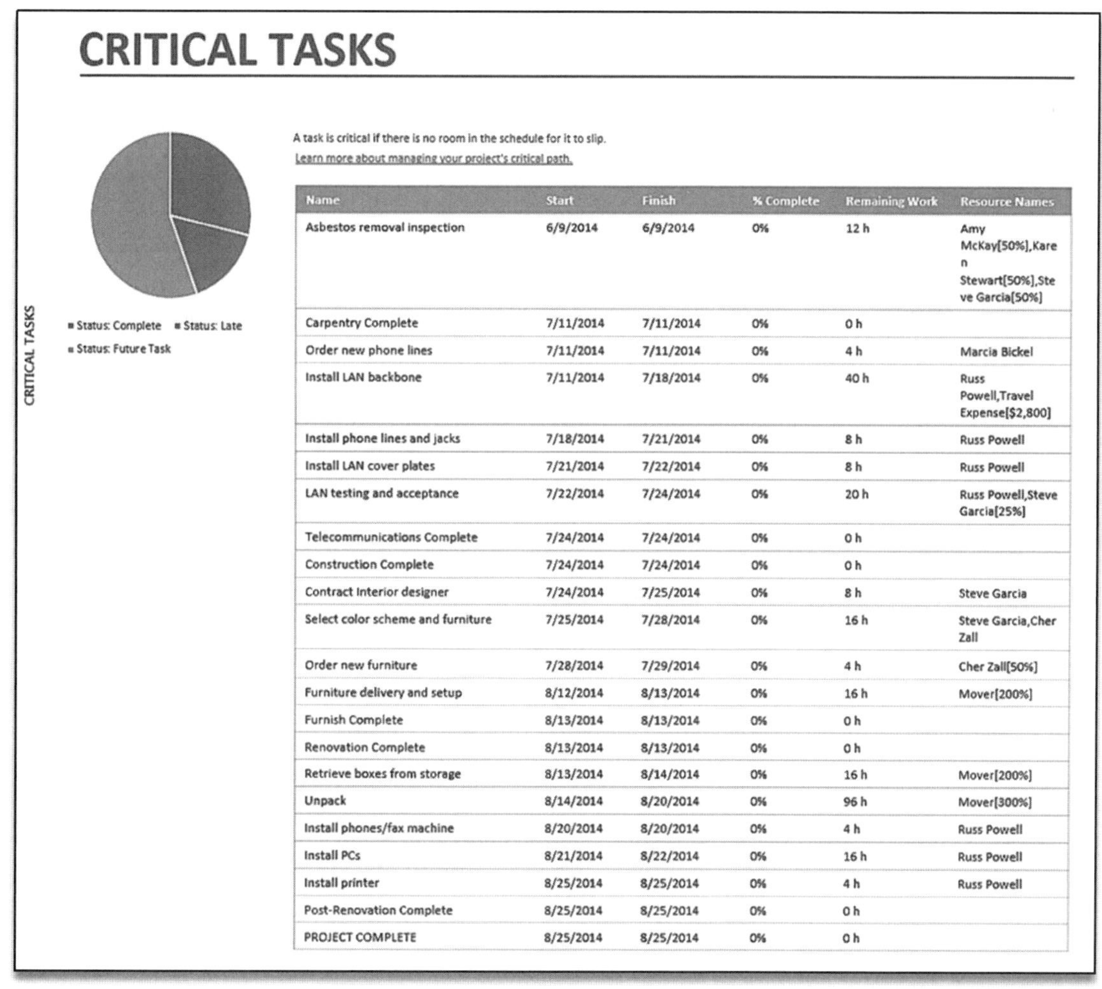

CRITICAL TASKS

A task is critical if there is no room in the schedule for it to slip.
Learn more about managing your project's critical path.

Name	Start	Finish	% Complete	Remaining Work	Resource Names
Asbestos removal inspection	6/9/2014	6/9/2014	0%	12 h	Amy McKay[50%],Karen Stewart[50%],Steve Garcia[50%]
Carpentry Complete	7/11/2014	7/11/2014	0%	0 h	
Order new phone lines	7/11/2014	7/11/2014	0%	4 h	Marcia Bickel
Install LAN backbone	7/11/2014	7/18/2014	0%	40 h	Russ Powell,Travel Expense[$2,800]
Install phone lines and jacks	7/18/2014	7/21/2014	0%	8 h	Russ Powell
Install LAN cover plates	7/21/2014	7/22/2014	0%	8 h	Russ Powell
LAN testing and acceptance	7/22/2014	7/24/2014	0%	20 h	Russ Powell,Steve Garcia[25%]
Telecommunications Complete	7/24/2014	7/24/2014	0%	0 h	
Construction Complete	7/24/2014	7/24/2014	0%	0 h	
Contract interior designer	7/24/2014	7/25/2014	0%	8 h	Steve Garcia
Select color scheme and furniture	7/25/2014	7/28/2014	0%	16 h	Steve Garcia,Cher Zall
Order new furniture	7/28/2014	7/29/2014	0%	4 h	Cher Zall[50%]
Furniture delivery and setup	8/12/2014	8/13/2014	0%	16 h	Mover[200%]
Furnish Complete	8/13/2014	8/13/2014	0%	0 h	
Renovation Complete	8/13/2014	8/13/2014	0%	0 h	
Retrieve boxes from storage	8/13/2014	8/14/2014	0%	16 h	Mover[200%]
Unpack	8/14/2014	8/20/2014	0%	96 h	Mover[300%]
Install phones/fax machine	8/20/2014	8/20/2014	0%	4 h	Russ Powell
Install PCs	8/21/2014	8/22/2014	0%	16 h	Russ Powell
Install printer	8/25/2014	8/25/2014	0%	4 h	Russ Powell
Post-Renovation Complete	8/25/2014	8/25/2014	0%	0 h	
PROJECT COMPLETE	8/25/2014	8/25/2014	0%	0 h	

Figure 11 - 17: Critical Tasks report

- The *Late Tasks* report shown in Figure 11 - 18 contains a chart and a table. The chart in the upper left corner of the report is a pie chart that displays *Cost* distribution based on the *Status* value for every task in the project. The *Status* field determines whether a task is completed, on schedule, a future task, or a late task. The table displays schedule-related information about every *Late* task in the project, and includes the *Start, Finish, % Complete, Remaining Work,* and *Resource Names* columns.

Information: Remember that in Project 2013, a **late task** is any task with a *Late* value in the *Status* field. By default, the software sets a *Late* value in the *Status* field when the time-phased cumulative percent complete (represented by the black progress line in a Gantt bar) does not reach the *Status Date* you specify for the project. If you do not specify a *Status Date*, then the software uses the *Current Date* to determine late tasks.

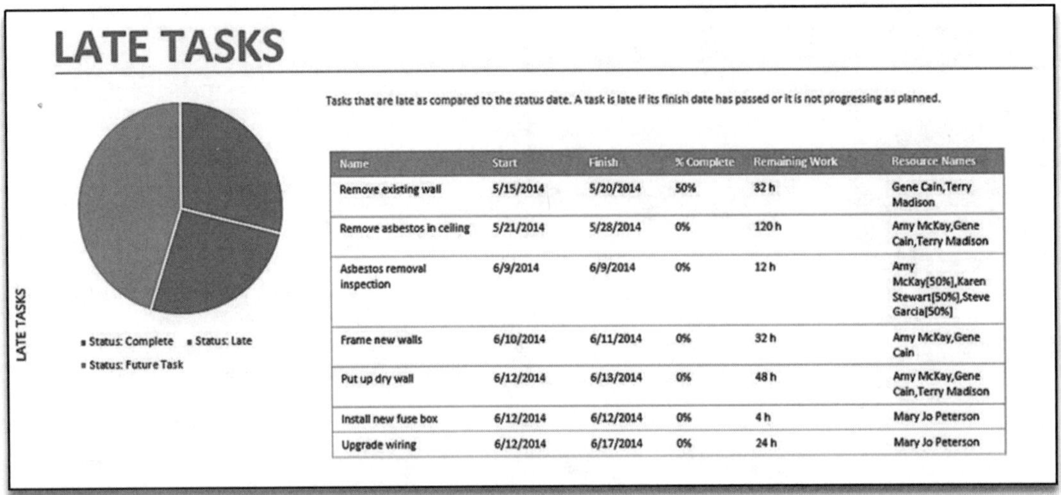

Name	Start	Finish	% Complete	Remaining Work	Resource Names
Remove existing wall	5/15/2014	5/20/2014	50%	32 h	Gene Cain,Terry Madison
Remove asbestos in ceiling	5/21/2014	5/28/2014	0%	120 h	Amy McKay,Gene Cain,Terry Madison
Asbestos removal inspection	6/9/2014	6/9/2014	0%	12 h	Amy McKay[50%],Karen Stewart[50%],Steve Garcia[50%]
Frame new walls	6/10/2014	6/11/2014	0%	32 h	Amy McKay,Gene Cain
Put up dry wall	6/12/2014	6/13/2014	0%	48 h	Amy McKay,Gene Cain,Terry Madison
Install new fuse box	6/12/2014	6/12/2014	0%	4 h	Mary Jo Peterson
Upgrade wiring	6/12/2014	6/17/2014	0%	24 h	Mary Jo Peterson

Figure 11 - 18: Late Tasks report

- The *Milestone Report* shown in Figure 11 - 19 contains three tables and one chart. The *Late Milestones* table displays any milestone task whose *Status* value is *Late,* and includes the *Finish* date of the milestone task. The *Milestones Up Next* table displays uncompleted milestones in the past or milestones that are due during the current month, and includes the *Finish* date of the milestone task. The *Completed Milestones* table displays all milestones with a *% Complete* value of *100%,* and includes the *Finish* date of the milestone task. The chart on the right side of the report is a line chart that shows data from the new *Remaining Tasks* and *Remaining Actual Tasks* fields.

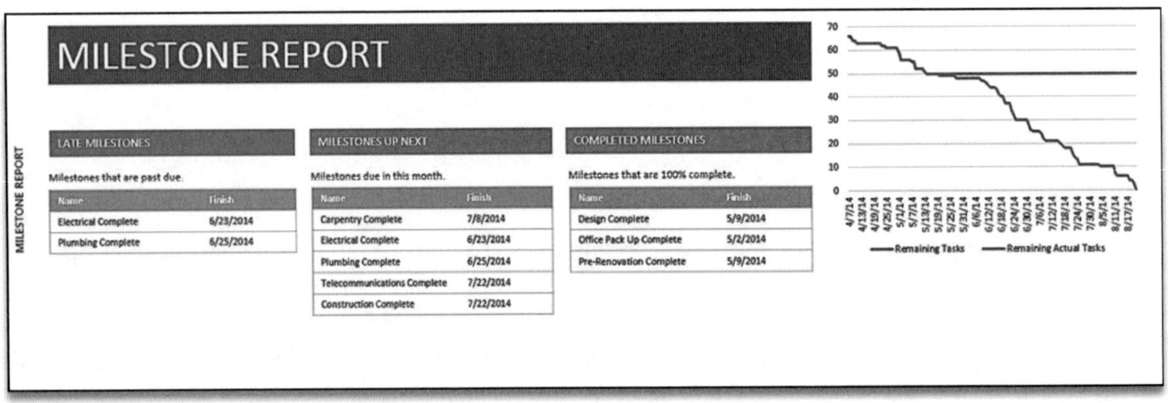

Name	Finish
Electrical Complete	6/23/2014
Plumbing Complete	6/25/2014

Name	Finish
Carpentry Complete	7/8/2014
Electrical Complete	6/23/2014
Plumbing Complete	6/25/2014
Telecommunications Complete	7/22/2014
Construction Complete	7/22/2014

Name	Finish
Design Complete	5/9/2014
Office Pack Up Complete	5/2/2014
Pre-Renovation Complete	5/9/2014

Figure 11 - 19: Milestone Report

- The *Slipping Tasks* report shown in Figure 11 - 20 contains a chart and a table. The chart in the upper left corner of the report is a line chart that shows data from the new *Remaining Cumulative Work* and *Remaining Cumulative Actual Work* fields. The table displays all slipping tasks, and includes the *Start, Finish, % Complete, Remaining Work,* and *Resource Names* columns. Remember that by definition in Project 2013, a slipping task is any uncompleted task whose *Finish* date is later than its *Baseline Finish* date. This means that a completed task cannot be a slipping task.

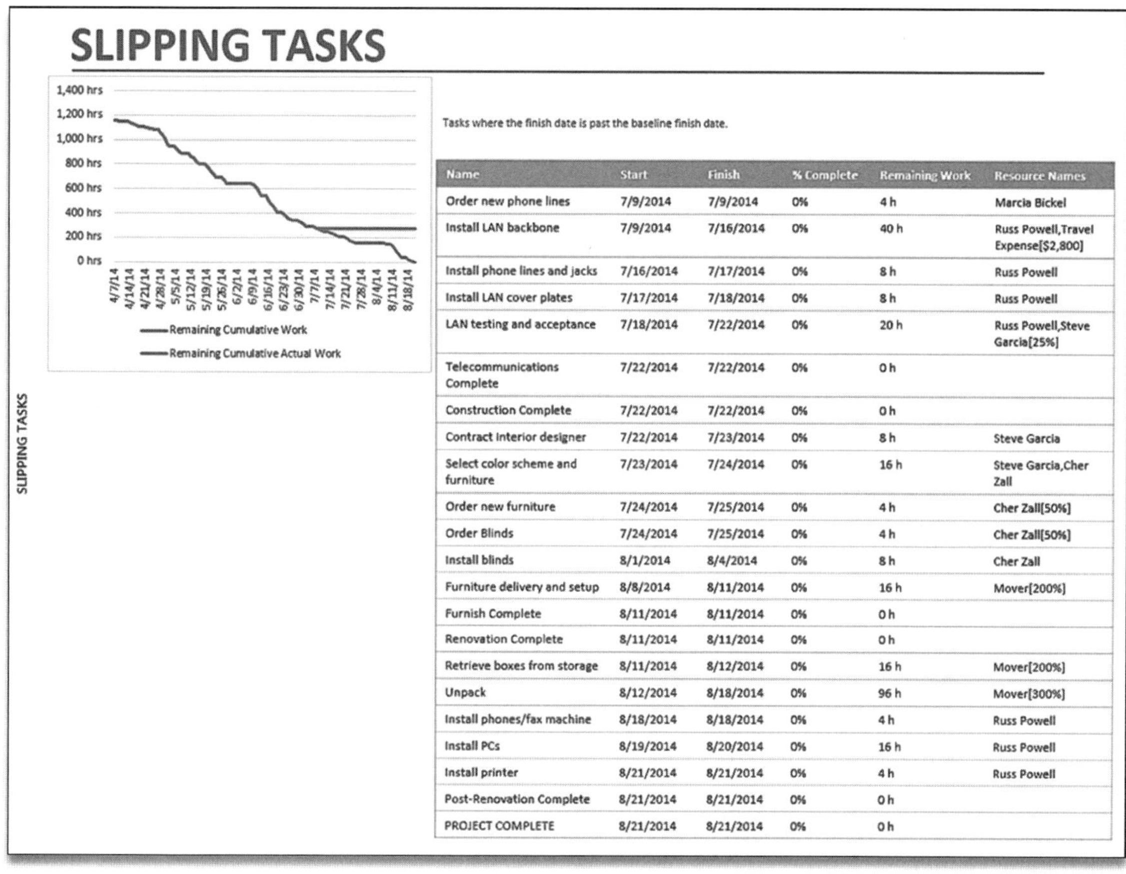

Name	Start	Finish	% Complete	Remaining Work	Resource Names
Order new phone lines	7/9/2014	7/9/2014	0%	4 h	Marcia Bickel
Install LAN backbone	7/9/2014	7/16/2014	0%	40 h	Russ Powell,Travel Expense[$2,800]
Install phone lines and jacks	7/16/2014	7/17/2014	0%	8 h	Russ Powell
Install LAN cover plates	7/17/2014	7/18/2014	0%	8 h	Russ Powell
LAN testing and acceptance	7/18/2014	7/22/2014	0%	20 h	Russ Powell,Steve Garcia[25%]
Telecommunications Complete	7/22/2014	7/22/2014	0%	0 h	
Construction Complete	7/22/2014	7/22/2014	0%	0 h	
Contract interior designer	7/22/2014	7/23/2014	0%	8 h	Steve Garcia
Select color scheme and furniture	7/23/2014	7/24/2014	0%	16 h	Steve Garcia,Cher Zall
Order new furniture	7/24/2014	7/25/2014	0%	4 h	Cher Zall[50%]
Order Blinds	7/24/2014	7/25/2014	0%	4 h	Cher Zall[50%]
Install blinds	8/1/2014	8/4/2014	0%	8 h	Cher Zall
Furniture delivery and setup	8/8/2014	8/11/2014	0%	16 h	Mover[200%]
Furnish Complete	8/11/2014	8/11/2014	0%	0 h	
Renovation Complete	8/11/2014	8/11/2014	0%	0 h	
Retrieve boxes from storage	8/11/2014	8/12/2014	0%	16 h	Mover[200%]
Unpack	8/12/2014	8/18/2014	0%	96 h	Mover[300%]
Install phones/fax machine	8/18/2014	8/18/2014	0%	4 h	Russ Powell
Install PCs	8/19/2014	8/20/2014	0%	16 h	Russ Powell
Install printer	8/21/2014	8/21/2014	0%	4 h	Russ Powell
Post-Renovation Complete	8/21/2014	8/21/2014	0%	0 h	
PROJECT COMPLETE	8/21/2014	8/21/2014	0%	0 h	

Figure 11 - 20: Slipping Tasks report

Understanding Getting Started Reports

Click the *Getting Started* pick list button to see the five default reports that help you to get started using Project 2013 as your project scheduling tool. These new *Getting Started* reports include the following:

- The *Best Practices Analyzer* report shown in Figure 11 - 21 contains two charts and two tables. Use this report to make sure that your project follows four best practices for task and assignment planning. The *Remaining Work* chart is a column chart that shows the *Remaining Work* for every unstarted task that has a *Start Date* earlier than the *Current Date*. The *Unassigned Work* chart is a column chart that shows the *Work* value for every task that has no resources assigned to it. The *Tasks with Durations Less Than 8 Hours* table shows every task with a *Duration* value less than *8 hours*, even if the task is completed, and includes the *Scheduled Duration* and *Work* columns. The *Summary Tasks with Assigned Resources* table displays every summary task with at least one resource assigned to it. In a project that you plan and manage well, you should not see data in the charts or the tables in this report.

Warning: Because of an unfixed bug in the release (RTM) version of Project 2013, the *Summary Tasks with Assigned Resources* table **does not** show any data, even if you assigned resources to summary tasks in the project. To work around this bug, click one of the column headers in the *Summary Tasks with Assigned Resources* table to display the *Field List* sidepane on the right side of the report. In the *Field List* sidepane, select the *Show Hierarchy* checkbox option at the bottom of the sidepane. Click anywhere outside the table to hide the *Field List* sidepane.

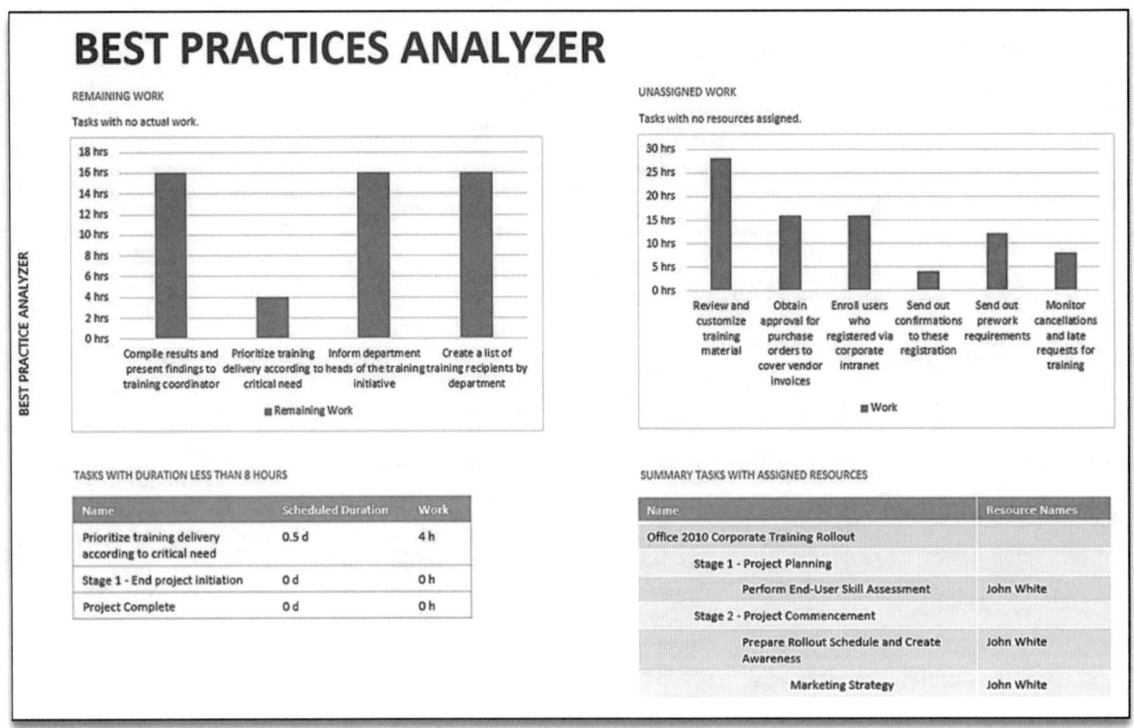

Name	Scheduled Duration	Work
Prioritize training delivery according to critical need	0.5 d	4 h
Stage 1 - End project initiation	0 d	0 h
Project Complete	0 d	0 h

Name	Resource Names
Office 2010 Corporate Training Rollout	
Stage 1 - Project Planning	
Perform End-User Skill Assessment	John White
Stage 2 - Project Commencement	
Prepare Rollout Schedule and Create Awareness	John White
Marketing Strategy	John White

Figure 11 - 21: Best Practices Analyzer report

- On the *Getting Started* pick list, select the *Getting Started with Project* item to display the *Welcome to Project 2013* report shown in Figure 11 - 22. This report is actually a wizard you can use to advance your knowledge about how to organize tasks, create reports, and share project data with your project team. If you click the *Start* button or click the *Organize tasks* button in this report, Project 2013 displays the *Organize Tasks* report shown in Figure 11 - 23. If you click the *Create reports* button, the software displays the *Create Reports* report shown in Figure 11 - 24. If you click the *Share with your team* button, the software displays the *Share with your Team* report shown in Figure 11 - 25. If you click the *Skip Intro* button, the software exits the report and displays a *Gantt with Timeline* view of your project.

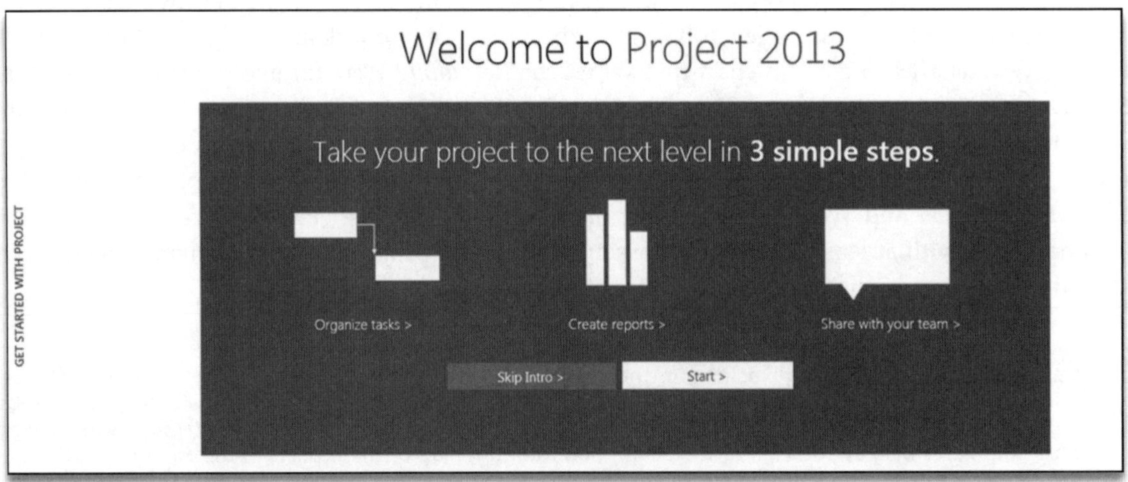

Figure 11 - 22: Welcome to Project 2013 report

- On the *Getting Started* pick list, select the *Organize Tasks* item to display the *Organize Tasks* report shown in Figure 11 - 23. The *Organize Tasks* report provides a brief tutorial on how to add task details, measure progress in your project, and manage task dependencies. At the bottom of each topical section, click the *Learn more* hyperlink to see more information about that topic. For example, if you click the *Learn more* hyperlink at the bottom of the *Add task details* section of the report, the software displays the *Change a task duration* page in the Office.com website. If you click the *Skip & go to your tasks* hyperlink in the upper right corner of the report, the software exits the *Organize Tasks* report and displays the *Gantt with Timeline* view in your project. Otherwise, you can click the *Next* button to display the *Create Reports* report shown in Figure 11 - 24.

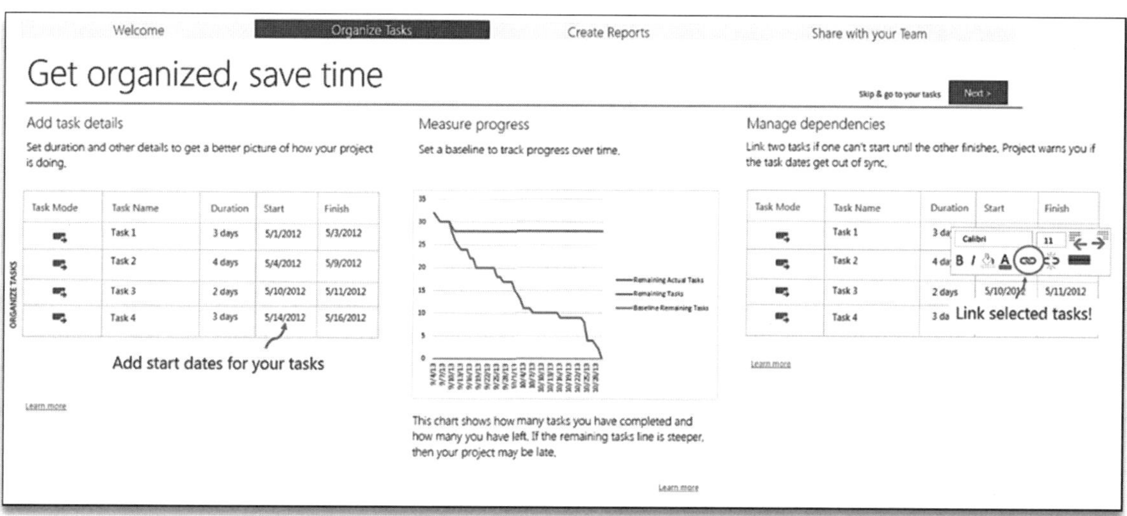

Figure 11 - 23: Organize Tasks report

- On the *Getting Started* pick list, select the *Create reports* item to display the *Create Reports* report shown in Figure 11 - 24. This report continues the brief tutorial by explaining the new reporting feature in Project 2013. The *Create Reports* report contains one table and two charts. The table in the upper left corner of the report displays the *% Complete* value for the entire project. The *Task Burndown* chart is a line chart that compares the number of completed tasks with the remaining tasks, timephased at the weekly level. Remember that this chart uses the new *Baseline Remaining Tasks, Remaining Tasks,* and *Remaining Actual Tasks* fields. The *Work Status* chart is a stacked column chart that shows the *Actual Work* and *Remaining Work* for each *Work* resource in your project team. Click the *Learn how to create a burndown* hyperlink to navigate to the *Create a burndown report* page in the Office.com website. If you click the *Skip & go to your tasks* hyperlink in the upper right corner of the report, the software exits the *Create Reports* report and displays the *Gantt with Timeline* view in your project. Otherwise, you can click the *Next* button to display the *Share with your Team* report shown in Figure 11 - 25.

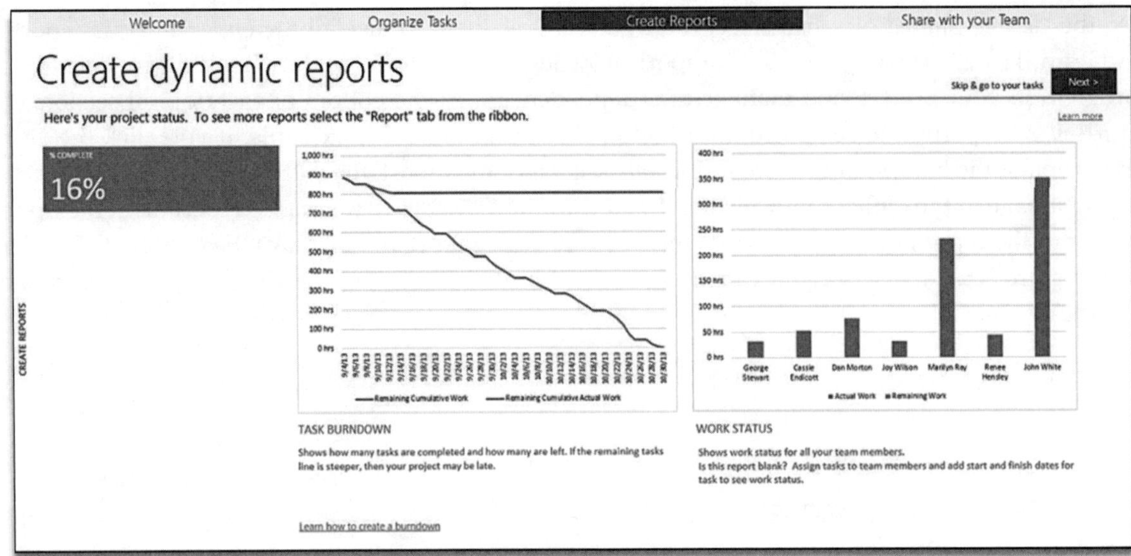

Figure 11 - 24: Create Reports report

- On the *Getting Started* pick list, select the *Share with your team* item to display the *Share with your Team* report shown in Figure 11 - 25. This report continues the brief tutorial by explaining how to synchronize a project with a SharePoint tasks list. Click the *Learn more hyperlink* to view a video on the *Collaborating with your Team* page in the Office.com website. Click the *Done* button in the upper right corner of the report to exit the report and navigate to the *Gantt with Timeline* view in your project.

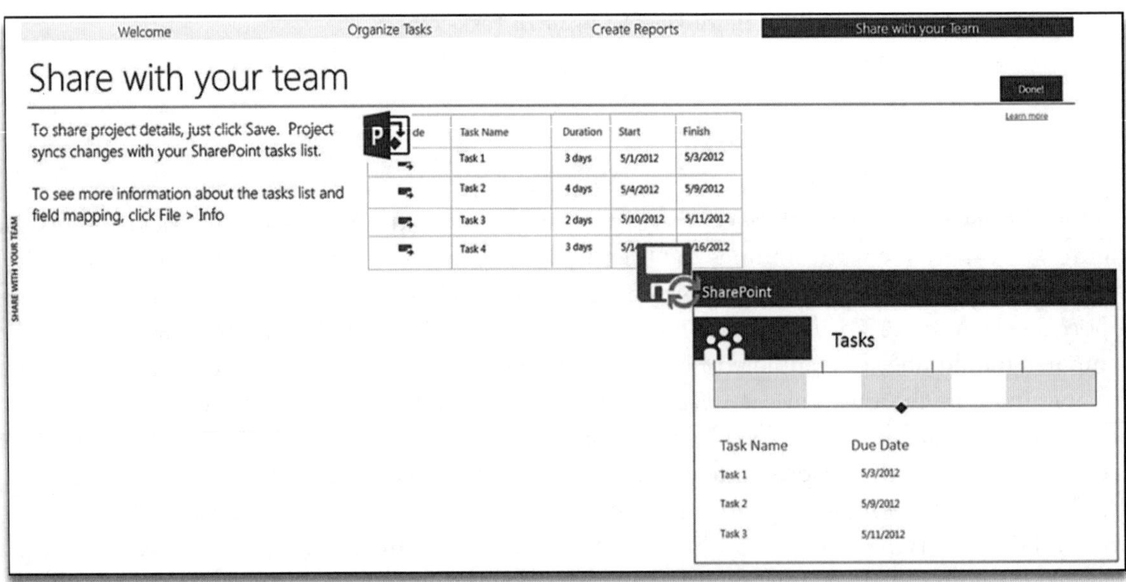

Figure 11 - 25: Share with your Team report

Hands On Exercise

Exercise 11 - 1

Explore the new reports in Project 2013.

1. Open the **Using Reports 2013.mpp** sample file from your sample files folder.

2. Click the *Report* tab to display the *Report* ribbon.

3. In the *View Reports* section of the *Report* ribbon, click the *Dashboards* pick list button and select the *Project Overview* item in the pick list.

Notice how Project 2013 displays the *Design* ribbon with the *Report Tools* applied.

4. Click anywhere in the *Milestones Due* table and notice how the software displays the *Field List* sidepane on the right side of the page.

Information: If you do not see the *Field List* sidepane when you click in the *Milestones Due* table, click the second *Design* tab to display the *Design* ribbon with the *Table Tools* applied. In the *Show/Hide* section of the *Design* ribbon, click the *Table Data* button to display the *Field List* sidepane on the right side of the report.

5. Examine the selected options in the *Field List* sidepane on the right side of the report, including the fields selected in the *Select Fields* section of the sidepane, along with the items selected on the *Filter, Group By, Outline Level,* and *Sort By* pick lists.

6. Click anywhere in the *% Complete* chart and then examine the selected options in the *Field List* sidepane.

7. Click the *Report* tab to display the *Report* ribbon again.

8. In the *View Reports* section of the *Report* ribbon, click the *Resources* pick list button and select the *Resource Overview* item in the pick list.

9. Study the data shown in the *Resource Stats* and the *Work Status* charts, along with the data shown in the *Resource Status* table.

10. Click anywhere in the *Resource Stats* chart and examine the fields selected in the *Select Fields* section of the *Field List* sidepane.

11. Click the *Report* tab to display the *Report* ribbon again.

12. In the *View Reports* section of the *Report* ribbon, click the *Costs* pick list button and select the *Task Cost Overview* item in the pick list.

13. Examine the data shown in the *Cost Status* and the *Cost Distribution* charts, along with the data shown in the *Cost Details* table.

14. Click the *Report* tab to display the *Report* ribbon again.

15. In the *View Report* section of the *Report* ribbon, click the *In Progress* pick list button and select the *Critical Tasks* item in the pick list.

16. Examine the data shown in the pie chart, along with the tasks shown in the table.

17. Click the *Learn more about managing your project's critical path* hyperlink at the top of the table.

18. Study the information shown on the *Show the critical path of your project* page in the Office.com website and then close the Internet Explorer when finished.

19. Save but **do not** close the **Using Reports 2013.mpp** sample file.

Customizing an Existing Report

Project 2013 offers you multiple ways to customize an existing report. These methods include: customizing a chart, customizing a table, customizing a text box, adding a new chart, adding a new table, and adding a new text box. In addition, you can also add new images and new shapes to the report, and you can move and resize all report objects.

Customizing a Chart

To customize a chart in your report, click one time in the chart you want to customize. The software refreshes the user interface as shown in Figure 11 - 26. Notice that when I select the *% Complete* chart in the *Project Overview* report, the user interface includes the following elements:

- On the far right side of the report, the software displays the *Field List* sidepane.

- To the right of the selected chart, the software displays three formatting buttons: the *Chart Elements, Chart Styles,* and *Chart Filters* buttons.

- At the top of the user interface, the software displays the *Design* and *Format* ribbon tabs with the *Chart Tools* applied.

You can use any of these three options to customize a chart, plus you can double-click any chart element to edit that individual element. I discuss each of these chart customization options individually.

Information: Customizing a chart in Project 2013 is nearly identical to customizing a chart in Excel 2013. The more experience you have with formatting an Excel chart, the better you will be at formatting a Project chart.

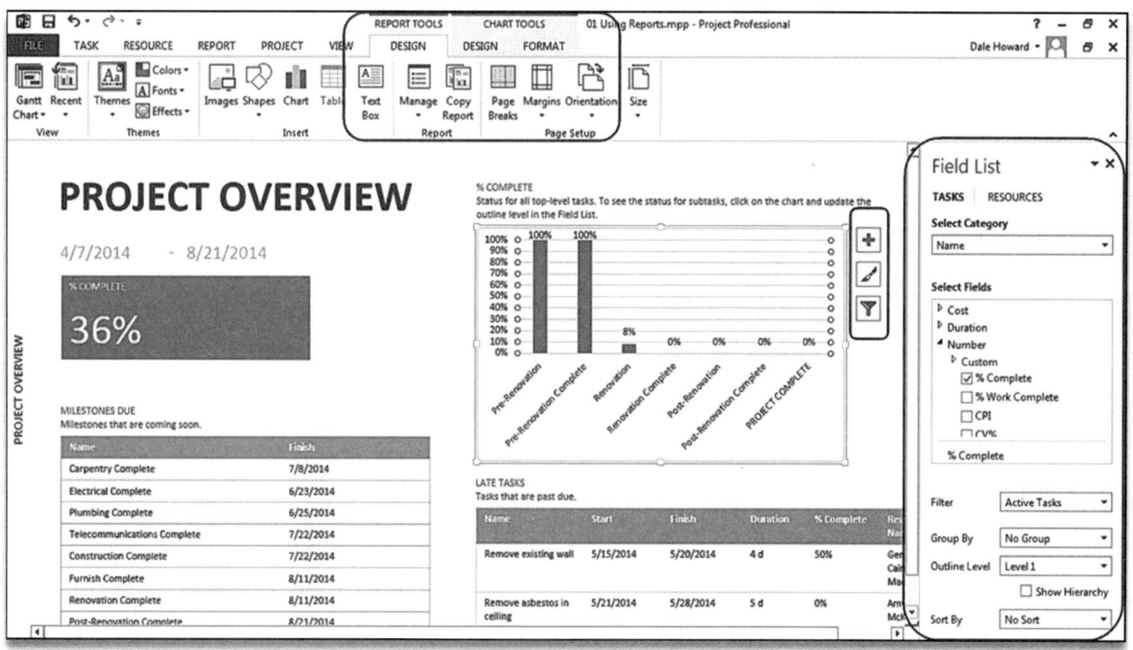

Figure 11 - 26: Select a chart for customization

Using the Field List sidepane

In the upper left corner of the *Field List* sidepane on the right side of the report, Project 2013 displays two tabs: the *Tasks* and *Resources* tab. The software selects the correct tab for the type of data shown in the chart. For example, notice in Figure 11 - 26 shown previously that the software selects the *Tasks* tab since the *% Complete* chart displays task data.

Warning: If you click the *Resources* tab while you have a task chart selected, or if click the *Tasks* tab while you have a resource chart selected, the software automatically removes all of the chart data and forces you to create a totally new chart from scratch for the type of data selected.

Click the *Select Category* pick list to select the type of fields you want displayed at the bottom of the selected chart. For the *% Complete* chart, the available categories include the *Time, ID, Name, Resource Names,* and *Unique ID* fields. By default, the software selects the *Name* field in the *Select Category* pick list, which displays the name of each task shown in the chart.

The *Select Fields* section of the sidepane displays the types of fields available for display in the selected chart, which include *Cost, Duration, Number,* and *Work* fields for a task chart. By default, the software expands the types of fields used in the selected chart. In the *% Complete* chart, the software expands the *Number* type, which shows the list of available *Number* fields for inclusion in the report. To expand any other type of field to see the available fields of that type, click the *Expand* symbol (white arrow button) to the left of the field type. In the bottom half of the *Select Fields* section, the software displays the fields currently included in the chart. By default, the *% Complete* chart includes only the *% Complete* field. To include any other fields in the chart, expand the field type and select the checkboxes for the fields you want to add. For example, I need to add the *% Work Complete* field in the *Number* section. To remove any current fields from the chart, deselect the checkbox for any field you want to omit.

Information: If you add additional fields to your chart, you can change the display order of the fields by manually dragging the fields up and down in the list of selected fields shown at the bottom of the *Select Fields* section of the *Field List* sidepane. If you right-click the name of any displayed field in the bottom half of the *Select Fields* section, the software displays a shortcut menu. On this shortcut menu, select the *Move Up* or *Move Down* item on the shortcut menu to move the field in the selected chart. Select the *Remove Field* item on the shortcut menu to remove the field from the selected chart. Select the *Field Settings* item on the shortcut menu to display the *Field Settings* dialog, in which you can apply a label or display name for the field in the selected chart.

The bottom of the *Field List* sidepane offers you options to filter, group, sort, and display the outline level of task data shown in the selected chart. By default, the *% Complete* chart includes the *Active Tasks* filter, the *No Group* item selected in the *Group By* pick list, the *Outline Level* option set to *Level 1*, with the *Show Hierarchy* checkbox option deselected, and the *Sort By* option set to *No Sort*.

Because the default filtering shows all *Active* tasks at outline level 1, and because I prefer to outdent milestones at the same outline level as the summary tasks they represent, the *% Complete* chart shows both summary tasks and milestone tasks. My reporting requirement, however, is to show **only** summary tasks at both outline level 1 and outline level 2. To meet this reporting requirement, I must complete the following steps:

1. Click the *Filter* pick list and select the *Summary Tasks* filter. Project 2013 displays only summary tasks at outline level 1.

2. Click the *Outline Level* pick list and select the *Level 2* item. The software displays only summary tasks at outline level 2; but at this point, I cannot see the outline level 1 summary tasks.

3. Select the *Show Hierarchy* checkbox.

The software displays Level 1 and Level 2 summary tasks in the chart. In the *% Complete* chart shown in Figure 11 - 27, the Level 1 summary tasks are the *Pre-Renovation* and *Renovation* tasks on the bottom row, while the Level 2 summary tasks are the *Design, Office Pack Up, Construction,* and *Furnish* tasks in the top row.

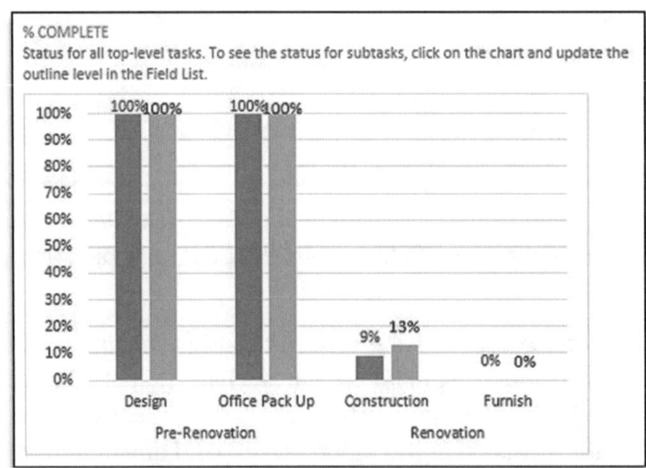

Figure 11 - 27: Updated % Complete chart

Edit the selected chart using the *Filter, Group By, Outline Level,* and *Sort By* pick lists, along with selecting the *Show Hierarchy* checkbox option as needed. When you finish editing the selected chart, click anywhere outside of the chart to close the *Field List* sidepane.

Information: If you close the *Field List* sidepane by clicking the *Close* button (**X**) in the upper right corner of the sidepane, Project 2013 offers you two methods to redisplay the sidepane. To use the first method, click the *Design* tab with the *Chart Tools* applied and then click the *Chart Data* button in the *Show/Hide* section of the *Design* ribbon. To use the second method, right-click anywhere in the selected chart and then click the *Show Field List* item at the bottom of the shortcut menu.

Using the Formatting Buttons

If you click the *Chart Elements* button on the right side of the chart, Project 2013 displays the *Chart Elements* menu shown in Figure 11 - 28. In the *Chart Elements* menu, select the checkboxes of any additional elements you want to add to the chart, and deselect the checkboxes for any elements you do not want to show. For example, notice in Figure 11 - 28 that the software selects the *Axes, Data Labels,* and *Gridlines* chart elements by default.

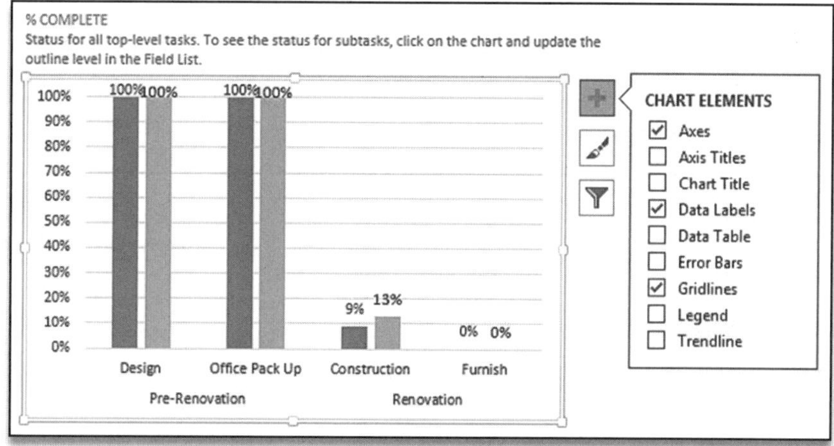

Figure 11 - 28: Chart Elements menu

When you select the checkbox to show an additional element in the chart or float your mouse pointer over the element, the software displays a right-arrow button at the end of the line. When you click this right-arrow button for any chart element, the software displays a flyout menu with additional options that control how to display the element. For example, if I click the right-arrow button to the right of the *Chart Title* element, Project 2013 displays the flyout menu shown in Figure 11 - 29. Notice that the flyout menu includes the *Above Chart, Centered Overlay,* and *More Options* items, which I can use to control where to display the *Chart Title* element in the chart.

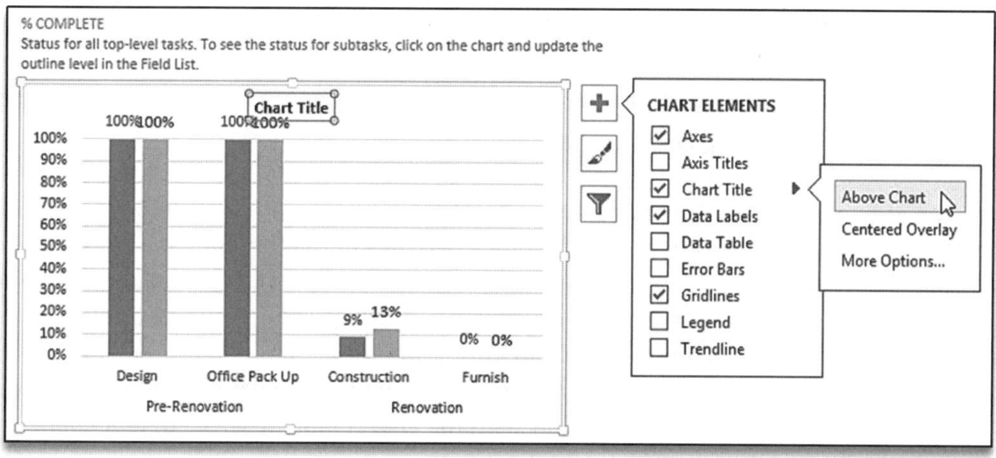

Figure 11 - 29: Flyout menu for the Chart Title element

Warning: If you select the *More Options* item on the *Chart Title* flyout menu and you still have the *Field List* sidepane open, the software displays an additional *Format Chart Title* sidepane to the right of the *Field List* sidepane. With two sidepanes open at the same time, you may want to close the *Field List* sidepane by clicking the *Close* button (**X**) in the upper right corner of the sidepane.

If I select the *More Options* item on the *Chart Title* flyout menu, the software adds the *Chart Title* element at the top of the chart, and then displays the *Format Chart Title* sidepane on the right side of the report. Figure 11 - 30 shows the *Format Chart Title* sidepane for the *Chart Title* chart element in the *% Complete* chart.

Information: If you add the *Chart Title* element to a chart, you must rename it, and you may also need to move it to a new location in the chart so that it does not cover up other chart data. To rename the *Chart Title* element, right-click anywhere in the element and select the *Edit Text* item on the shortcut menu. In the *Chart Title* element, delete the old name and enter a new title, and then click anywhere outside of the element. For example, I need to rename the *Chart Title* element to its new name, *Percent Complete Comparison*. To move the *Chart Title* element, click and hold anywhere on the edge of the element, and then drag and drop the element in its new location. For example, I need to move the *Chart Title* element to the upper right corner of the chart.

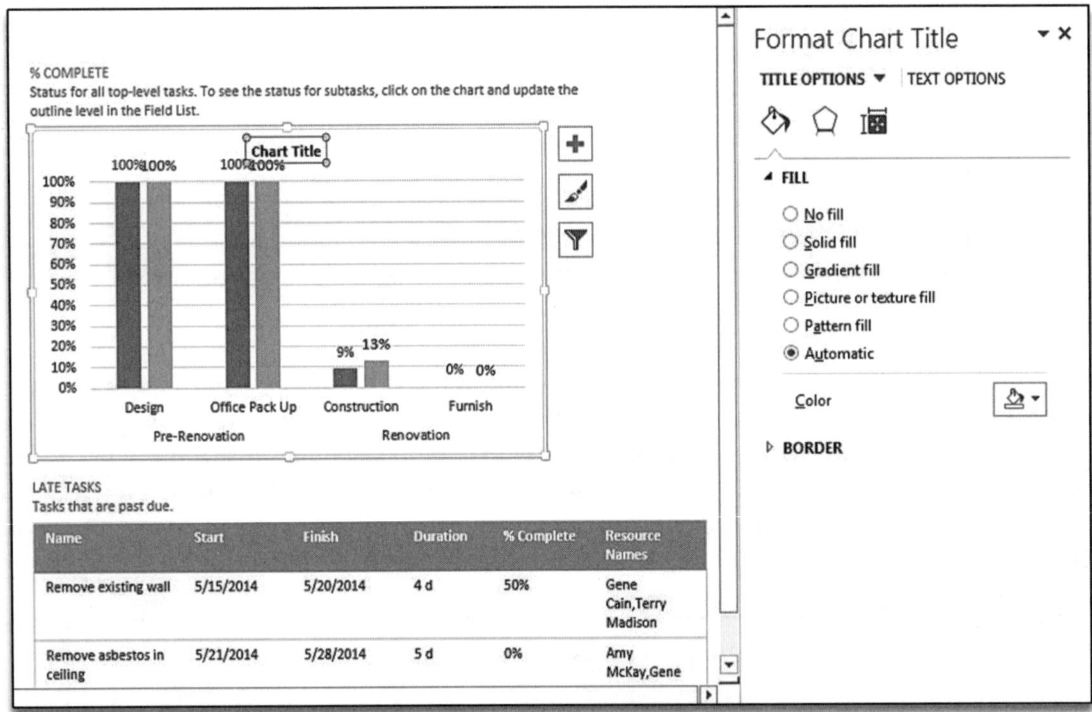

Figure 11 - 30: Format Chart Title sidepane

The *Format Chart Title* sidepane allows you to format the chart element currently selected, which in this case is the *Chart Title* element. The *Format Chart Title* sidepane includes two tabs at the top: the *Title Options* tab and the *Text Options* tab. Notice in the *Format Chart Title* sidepane shown previously in Figure 11 - 30 that the *Title Options* tab is actually a pick list. If you click the *Title Options* pick list, Project 2013 displays a list of additional items you can format in the sidepane, including items such as the *Chart Area*, the *Horizontal (Category) Axis*, and the *Vertical (Value) Axis*. If you select any other item on the *Title Options* pick list, the software selects the new chart element in the chart, changes the name of the sidepane to correspond with the chart element selected, and changes the name of the pick list. For example, if you select the *Chart Area* item on the pick list, the software selects the *Chart Area* element in the chart, changes the name of the sidepane to *Format Chart Area,* and changes the name of the pick list to *Chart Options.*

Click either of the two tabs at the top of the sidepane to see a set of buttons that indicate the available options for formatting the selected chart element. With the *Chart Title* element selected, when you click the *Title Options* tab, the software offers you the following buttons, which you can use to format the title:

- Click the *Fill & Line* button to display options for formatting the fill color and background, as well as formatting the borders of the *Chart Title* element. With the *Fill & Line* button selected, the sidepane displays two formatting sections: the *Fill* and *Border* sections. You may need to click the *Expand* indicator to the left of a section to see the settings in that section. Using the options available in the *Fill* and *Border* sections, specify your formatting options for the *Chart Title* element.

- Click the *Effects* button to see all available effects options. With the *Effects* button selected, the sidepane displays four sections of effects options: the *Shadow, Glow, Soft Edges,* and *3-D Format* sections. To view the available options in any of these four sections, you must first click the *Expand* indicator to the left of the section. Use the options in any of these four sections to apply various effects to the *Chart Title* element.

- Click the *Size & Properties* button to see the available options for size and alignment of the selected chart element. With the *Size & Properties* button selected, the sidepane displays only one section, the *Alignment* section. Use the options in the *Alignment* section of the sidepane to format the size and alignment of the *Chart Title* element.

Information: If you click the *Title Options* pick list and select either the *Horizontal (Category) Axis* item or the *Vertical (Value) Axis* item, Project 2013 displays an additional button called *Axis Options*. With the *Axis Options* button selected, the sidepane displays four sections of axis options: the *Axis Options, Tick Marks, Labels,* and *Numbers* sections. If you select one of the *Series* items on the *Title Options* pick list, such as the *Series % Complete* item, the software displays an additional button called *Series Options*. With the *Series Options* button selected, the sidepane displays only one section, the *Series Options* section.

When you click the *Text Options* tab at the top of the *Format Chart Title* sidepane, Project 2013 offers you the following buttons, which you can use to format the title text:

- Click the *Text Fill & Outline* button to display the options for formatting the fill color and outline of the text in the selected element. With the *Text Fill & Outline* button selected, the sidepane displays two formatting sections: the *Text Fill* and *Text Outline* sections. Using the options available in the *Text Fill* and *Text Outline* sections, specify your formatting options for the text in the *Chart Title* element.

- Click the *Text Effects* button to see all available effects options for formatting text. With the *Text Effects* button selected, the sidepane displays six sections of effects options: the *Shadow, Reflection, Glow, Soft Edges, 3-D Format,* and *3-D Rotation* sections. To view the available options in any of these six sections, you must first click the *Expand* indicator to the left of the section. Use the options in any of these six sections to apply various effects to the text in the *Chart Title* element.

- Click the *Text Box* button to see the available options for the alignment and direction of the text box used for the selected chart element. With the *Text Box* button selected, the sidepane displays only one section, the *Text Box* section. Use the options in the *Text Box* section of the sidepane to format the alignment and text direction of the *Chart Title* element.

If you click the *Chart Styles* button on the right side of the selected chart, Project 2013 displays the *Chart Styles* menu shown in Figure 11 - 31. This menu includes two tabs at the top, the *Style* tab and the *Color* tab with the *Style* tab selected by default. The *Style* page of the menu displays 16 pre-formatted styles, labeled *Style 1* through

Style 16, which you can apply to your chart. You see the label, by the way, when you float your mouse pointer over the style preview. Select any style in the list, as needed. When you initially apply a style, the software applies a gray color theme by default to all of the elements in the selected chart.

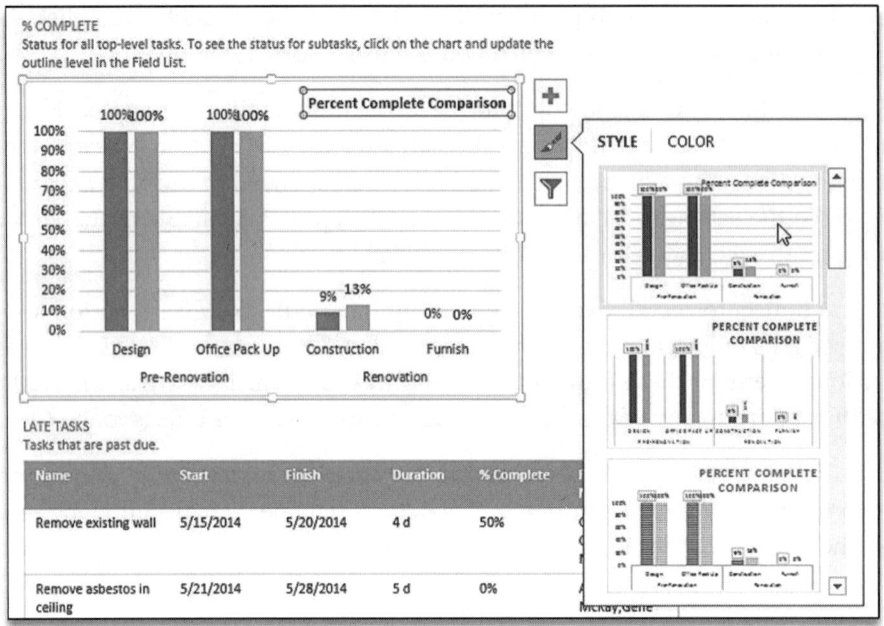

Figure 11 - 31: Chart Styles menu, Style tab selected

If you select a pre-formatted style on the *Style* page of the menu, you may want to change the color theme from the default gray colors. To do so, click the *Color* tab to display the *Color* page of the menu. Figure 11 - 32 shows the *Color* page of the menu after I applied the *Style 5* style to my chart. The *Color* page offers you two sections of theme colors, which you can apply to the selected chart. Select one of the theme colors in either the *Colorful* section or the *Monochromatic* section to apply the theme colors to the elements in the selected chart.

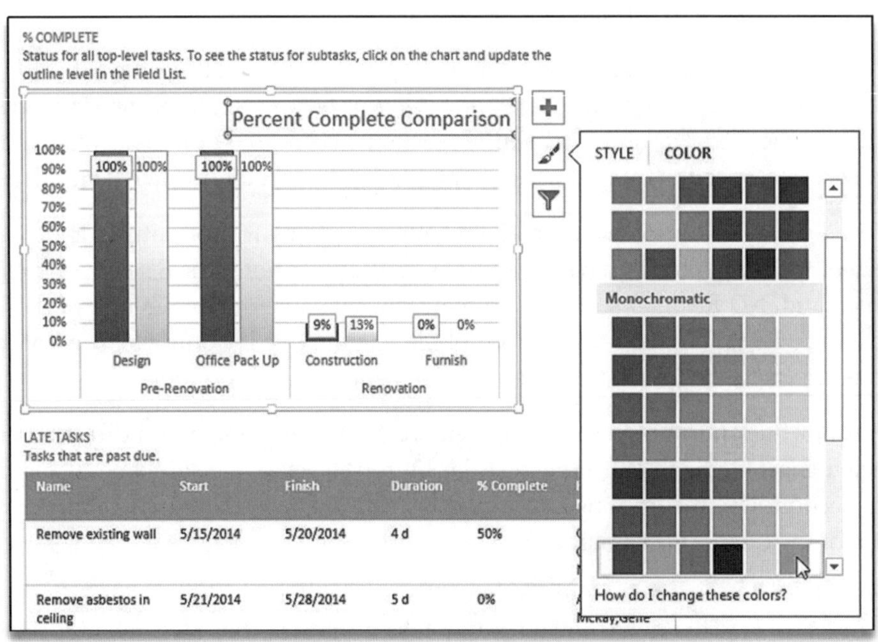

Figure 11 - 32: Chart Styles menu, Color tab selected

Information: If you float your mouse pointer over the *How do I change these colors* hyperlink at the bottom of the *Color* page in the *Chart Styles* menu, Project 2013 displays the *Change Theme Colors* tooltip that explains how to change the colors used in the report.

If you click the *Chart Filters* button on the right side of the chart, Project 2013 displays the *Values* menu. Figure 11 - 33 shows the *Values* menu after I applied the *Color 4* theme colors to my chart. The *Values* menu offers you a number of checkboxes organized into a *Series* section and a *Categories* section. The checkboxes in the *Series* section generally represent numerical fields, such as the *% Complete* and *% Work Complete* fields used in the *% Complete* chart, and show the data on the Y-axis of the chart. The checkboxes in the *Categories* section generally represent task or resource data, such as the first level tasks used in the *% Complete* chart, and show this data on the X-axis of the chart. You can select or deselect any of the checkboxes, as needed, to apply filtering to the data shown in the selected chart. Select the checkboxes for only the data you want to display in your chart and then click the *Apply* button. Click anywhere outside the *Values* menu to hide the menu.

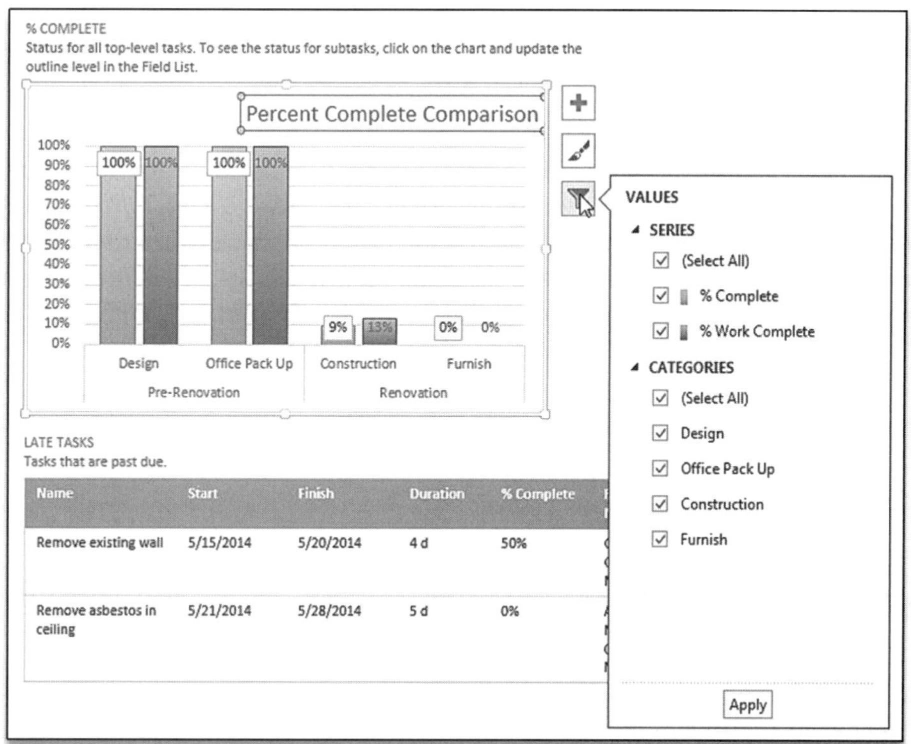

Figure 11 - 33: Chart Filter menu, Values page

Using Other Format Sidepanes

If you double-click any element in a chart, Project 2013 displays a *Format* sidepane for the selected chart element. For example, if I double-click one of the columns in the *% Complete* chart, the software displays the *Format Data Point* sidepane with the *Series Options* button selected, as shown in Figure 11 - 34.

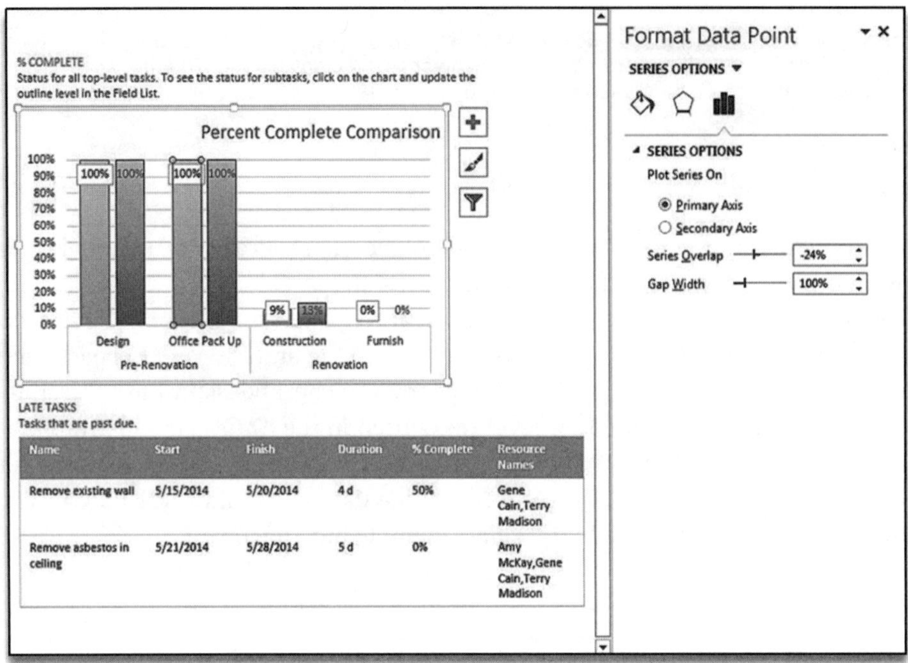

Figure 11 - 34: Format Data Point sidepane

Notice that the *Format Data Point* sidepane contains a *Series Options* pick list at the top, with three options buttons immediately below the pick list. Click these three buttons to display the *Fill & Line, Effects,* and *Series Options* pages in the sidepane. Click the *Series Options* pick list at the top of the sidepane to see the chart elements available for formatting. For example, in the *% Complete* chart, the *Series Options* pick list offers the following chart elements for formatting: *Chart Area, Chart Title, Horizontal (Category) Axis, Plot Area, Vertical (Value) Axis, Vertical (Value) Axis Major Gridlines, Series "% Complete", Series "% Complete" Data Labels, Series "% Work Complete"*, and *Series "% Work Complete" Data Labels.*

Information: The *Series Options* pick list contains the list of all chart elements available for formatting in the selected chart. This means that you may see different pick list items depending on the type of chart you format. For example, when formatting the *Cost Distribution* chart in the *Task Cost Overview* report, the *Series Options* pick list contains only the following elements for formatting: *Chart Area*, *Legend*, *Plot Area*, *Series "Cost"*, and *Series "Cost" Data Labels.*

If you select any other chart element on the *Series Options* pick list, Project 2013 redisplays the *Format* sidepane to show the options available for formatting the selected chart element. For example, when I select the *Plot Area* element on the pick list, the software displays the *Format Plot Area* sidepane with the *Effects* option selected. Use any of these available options to format the elements in the cart.

Using the Design Ribbon with the Chart Tools Applied

If you click the rightmost of the two *Design* tabs at the top of your Project 2013 application window, the software displays the *Design* ribbon with the *Chart Tools* applied, as shown in Figure 11 - 35. The software divides the *Design* ribbon into four sections: the *Chart Layouts, Chart Styles, Show/Hide,* and *Type* sections.

Figure 11 - 35: Design ribbon with the Chart Tools applied

When you click the *Add Chart Element* pick list button in the *Chart Layouts* section of the *Design* ribbon, the software shows you a pick list of available chart elements, including elements such as the *Axes, Axis Titles, Chart Title,* and *Legend* elements. The elements available on the *Chart Elements* pick list are identical to the elements on the *Chart Elements* menu shown previously in Figure 11 - 28. Use the *Add Chart Element* pick list button to add and position any additional elements to the selected chart.

If you click the *Quick Layout* pick list button in the *Chart Layouts* section of the *Design* ribbon, the software offers you 11 pre-defined layouts labeled *Layout 1* through *Layout 11.* Use these quick layouts to quickly lay out all of the elements in the selected chart. For example, the *Layout 2* quick layout centers the *Chart Title* and *Legend* elements across the top of the chart, and resizes the *Plot Area* element, as needed. Figure 11 - 36 shows the *% Complete* chart formatted using the *Layout 2* item on the *Quick Layout* pick list.

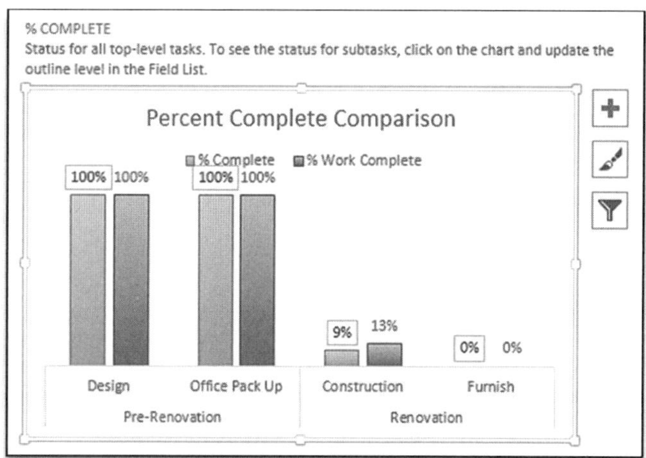

Figure 11 - 36: Layout 2 quick format applied

Information: If your chart does not already include the elements used in the selected *Quick Layout* item, Project 2013 automatically adds the missing elements. For example, if you did not include the *Legend* element in your chart, and then you select the *Layout 2* item on the *Quick Layout* pick list, the software adds this element for you automatically.

Information: After you apply an option on the *Quick Layout* pick list, Project 2013 allows you to use "drag and drop" to manually place the chart elements in a new location, if necessary.

The *Chart Styles* section of the *Design* ribbon contains a gallery of 16 pre-formatted chart styles, labeled *Style 1* through *Style 16*, which you can apply to your chart. The list of styles available in the *Chart Styles* gallery are identical to the list of styles on the *Style and Color* menu shown previously in Figure 11 - 31. Select any style in the gallery, as needed.

Click the *Chart Data* button in the *Show/Hide* section of the *Design* ribbon to display or hide the *Field List* sidepane shown previously in Figure 11 - 26. Click the *Change Chart Type* button in the *Type* section of the *Design* ribbon to change the type of chart displayed in your report. Project 2013 displays the *Change Chart Type* dialog shown in Figure 11 - 37.

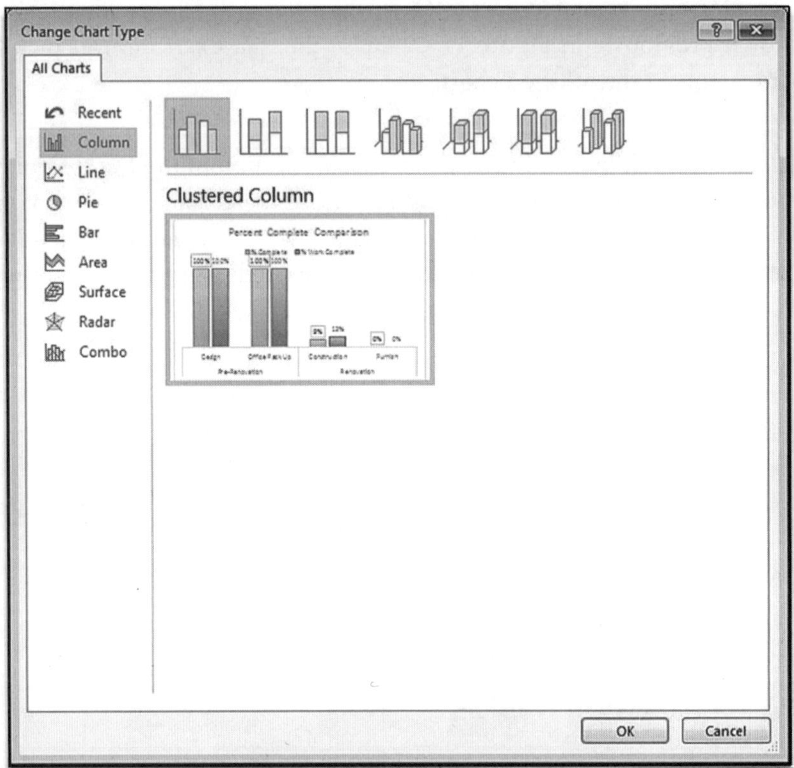

Figure 11 - 37: Change Chart Type dialog

The *Change Chart Type* dialog allows you to select any type of chart available in the software. In the list of chart types on the left side of the dialog, the software allows you to choose from among the *Column, Line, Pie, Bar, Area, Surface, Radar,* and *Combo* chart types. The dialog also includes the *Recent* item in the list to allow you to choose a recently applied chart type. Select a chart type in the list on the left side of the *Change Chart Type* dialog and the software displays a list of sub-types across the top of the dialog. For example, if you select the *Bar* chart type, Project 2013 offers you 6 sub-types, including the *Clustered Bar, Stacked Bar, 100% Stacked Bar, 3-D Clustered Bar, 3-D Stacked Bar,* and the *3-D 100% Stacked Bar* sub-types.

To change the chart type, select a chart type in the list on the left side of the dialog, and then select a sub-type in the list across the top of the *Change Chart Type* dialog. The software shows you a preview of the selected chart type in the middle of the dialog. To see a magnified preview of the chart type you select, float your mouse pointer over the preview image. Click the *OK* button to apply the new chart type to the selected chart. For example, Figure 11 - 38 shows the *% Complete* chart with the *3-D Clustered Bar* chart type applied.

Information: Because of the extremely small size of the *% Complete* chart, notice in Figure 11 - 38 how the data labels (percentages at the right of each bar) overlap each other and how the words in the axis labels (summary tasks on the left side of the chart) do not wrap correctly. To resolve this problem, you must increase the size of the *% Complete* chart. I discuss how to increase the size of a chart later in this module.

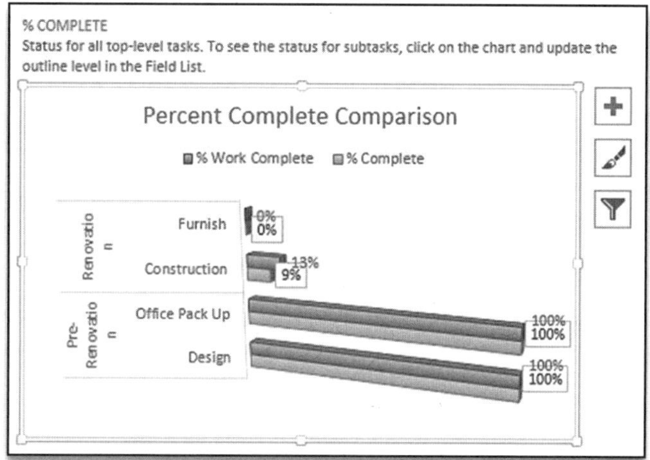

Figure 11 - 38: % Complete chart with 3-D Clustered Bar chart type applied

Using the Format Ribbon with the Chart Tools Applied

If you click the *Format* tab, Project 2013 displays the *Format* ribbon with the *Chart Tools* applied, as shown in Figure 11 - 39. The software divides the *Format* ribbon into six sections: the *Current Selection, Insert Shapes, Shape Styles, WordArt Styles, Arrange,* and *Size* sections.

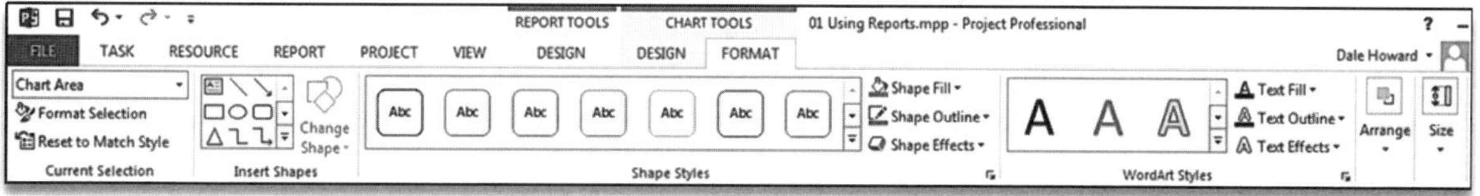

Figure 11 - 39: Format ribbon with the Chart Tools applied

To use the features in the *Current Selection* section of the *Format* ribbon, first click the *Chart Elements* pick list and select the chart element you want to format. For example, you might select the *Chart Title* element for formatting. To format the selected chart element, click the *Format Selection* button. The software displays the *Format* sidepane for the selected element. This means that if you select the *Chart Title* element and then click the *Format Selection* button, Project 2013 displays the *Format Chart Title* sidepane, such as the one shown previously in Figure 11 - 30. Apply the formatting you want in the sidepane and then close the sidepane when finished. If you do not like the current formatting of any element in the selected chart, select the element and then click the *Reset to Match Style* button. The software clears the current formatting on the selected element and then resets the element back to the current visual style applied to the chart.

The *Insert Shapes* section of the *Format* ribbon offers a gallery of available shapes. Click the *More* button in the lower right corner of the *Insert Shapes* gallery to see all of the available shapes that you can insert into the selected chart. The software organizes the shapes in the gallery into the *Recently Used Shapes, Lines, Rectangles, Basic Shapes, Block Arrows, Equation Shapes, Flowchart, Stars and Banners,* and *Callouts* sections. When you select a shape in the gallery, Project 2013 changes your mouse pointer into an *Insert Shape* crosshair pointer. Using this crosshair pointer, click and hold the mouse button and trace an outline of the size of the shape you want in the location where you want the shape. When you release the mouse button, the software creates the new shape and displays the *Format* ribbon with the *Drawing Tools* applied, as shown in Figure 11 - 40.

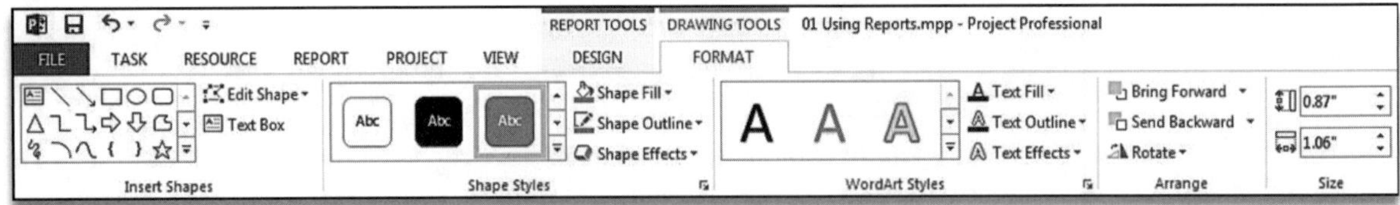

Figure 11 - 40: Format ribbon with the Drawing Tools applied

After inserting the new shape, you can resize and move the shape as needed. You can also type explanatory text into the shape by clicking in the shape and then typing the text. Beyond this, the software offers you all of the features in the *Format* ribbon with the *Drawing Tools* applied to further format the shape to your reporting specifications.

Information: Because I do not intend this book to be a reference book on Excel charting, I do not provide an in-depth discussion of the features in the *Format* ribbon with the *Drawing Tools* applied. On the other hand, keep in mind that this ribbon contains many of the same features as the *Format* ribbon with the *Chart Tools* applied.

Click anywhere in the chart and then return to the *Format* ribbon with the *Chart Tools* applied. The *Shape Styles* section offers a gallery of available shape styles, with additional buttons for formatting the fill, outline, and effects used with a shape. Before you can use any of these shape styles options, you must first select an element in your chart, such as the *Chart Title* element. After selecting the element, click the *More* button in the lower right corner of the *Shape Styles* gallery to see all 42 of the available shape styles. Select one of the shape styles in the gallery, as needed. Click the *Shape Fill* button to add a fill color, a picture, a gradient, or a texture to the selected chart element. Click the *Shape Outline* button to apply a color to the outline around the selected element, as well as to control the thickness of the outline and the type of outline, such as solid or dashed. Click the *Shape Effects* button to apply an effect to the selected element such as adding a shadow or applying beveling.

Information: To add a shadow to your chart, select the chart, and then click the *Shape Effects* pick list button and select one of the effects in the *Shadow* section of the flyout menu.

The *WordArt Styles* section of the *Format* ribbon offers a gallery of available WordArt styles, with additional buttons for formatting the fill, outline, and text effects used with a WordArt shape. Before you can use any of these WordArt options, you must first select any element containing text in your chart, such as the chart title or the chart legend. After selecting the element, click the *More* button in the lower right corner of the *WordArt Styles* gallery to see all 20 of the available WordArt styles, or to remove the current WordArt style. Select one of the WordArt styles in the gallery, as needed. Click the *Text Fill* button to add a fill color, a picture, a gradient, or a texture to the selected text element. Click the *Text Outline* button to apply a color to the outline around the selected text element, as well as to control the thickness of the outline and the type of outline, such as solid or dashed. Click the *Text Effects* button to apply an effect to the selected text element such as adding a shadow or applying beveling.

If you add two or more shapes to the selected chart, you can use the features in the *Arrange* section of the *Format* ribbon to layer the shapes. Before you can use these features, however, you must first select one of the shapes. When you click the *Bring Forward* pick list button, you can choose whether to bring the shape forward or to bring the shape to the front of all of the other shapes. When you click the *Send Backward* pick list button, you can choose whether to send the shape backward or to send the shape to the back of all of the other shapes.

The *Size* section of the *Format* ribbon allows you to control the precise size of the selected chart. Use the spin controls (up and down arrows) in the *Height* and *Width* fields to specify the exact dimensions of the selected chart. For example, you might want to increase the size of the chart to increase the readability of the chart data.

Moving and Resizing a Chart

The final step in modifying an existing chart is to move or resize the chart, as needed. To move a chart to a new location in the report, click anywhere the chart, then click and hold the mouse button to "grab" the chart. Drag the chart to a new location in the report and then release the mouse button to "drop" the chart into its new location. To resize the chart, you can use the *Height* and *Width* fields in the *Size* section of the *Format* ribbon, as I discussed in the previous topical section. Alternately, you can also click the chart to select it and then resize the chart using the "grab handles" in the corners and the sides of the chart. For example, to make a chart wider, click and hold the "grab handle" on the right side of the chart and then drag the chart edge to the right to widen the chart. When you finish formatting the chart, click anywhere outside of the selected chart.

Using Additional Chart Formatting Options

In addition to the chart formatting options presented in the *Customizing a Chart* topical section of this module, Project 2013 also allows you to edit a chart by right-clicking any element in the chart. The software displays a shortcut menu appropriate for the selected element, which offers you even more ways to customize your chart. For example, Figure 11 - 41 shows the shortcut menu when I right-click the Y-axis in the *% Complete* chart. You may need to use this advanced chart editing capability when you mix the types of data displayed in the chart, such as when you include both *Work* and *Cost* data in the same chart.

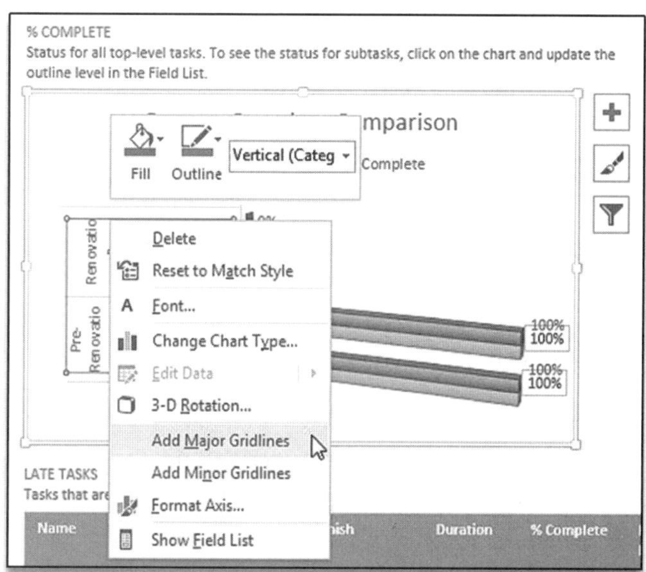

Figure 11 - 41: Shortcut menu to format the Y-axis

Hands On Exercise

Exercise 11 - 2

Customize a chart in a report in Project 2013.

1. Return to the **Using Reports 2013.mpp** sample file, if necessary.
2. Click the *Report* tab to display the *Report* ribbon.
3. In the *View Reports* section of the *Report* ribbon, click the *Dashboards* pick list button and select the *Work Overview* report.
4. Click anywhere in the *Work Stats* chart to select the chart for editing and to display the *Field List* sidepane.
5. Click the *Chart Elements* button (+ button) on the right side of the chart and select the checkbox for the *Chart Title* element in the flyout menu.
6. Click anywhere in the new *Chart Title* element in the chart, delete the default text, and enter *Work Comparison by Phase* as the title of the chart.
7. With the *Work Stats* chart still selected, click the *Filter* pick list in the *Field List* sidepane and select the *Summary Tasks* filter.
8. Click the *Chart Styles* button on the right side of the chart and select the *Style 8* item on the flyout menu.
9. Click the *Chart Styles* button again, click the *Color* tab at the top of the flyout menu, and select the *Color 4* color scheme in the *Colorful* section of the flyout menu.
10. Click anywhere in the *Resource Stats* chart to select the chart.
11. Click the second *Design* tab to display the *Design* ribbon with the *Chart Tools* applied.
12. In the *Type* section of the *Design* ribbon, click the *Change Chart Type* button.
13. In the *Change Chart Type* dialog, select the *3-D Stacked Bar* chart type, and then click the *OK* button.
14. With the *Resource Stats* chart still selected, click the *Filter* pick list in the *Field List* sidepane and select the *Group...* filter.
15. In the *Group* dialog, type the name *Construction* and then click the *OK* button.
16. Click the *Format* tab to display the *Format* ribbon with the *Chart Tools* applied.
17. In the *Shape Styles* section of the *Format* ribbon, click the *Shape Effects* pick list button, select the *Shadow* item on the menu, and then select the *Offset Right* item in the *Outer* section of the flyout menu.
18. Save but **do not** close the **Using Reports 2013.mpp** sample file.

Customizing a Table

To customize a table in your report, click anywhere in the table you want to customize. Project 2013 refreshes the user interface as shown in Figure 11 - 42. Notice that when I click the *Milestones Due* table in the *Project Overview* report, the user interface includes the following elements:

- On the far right side of the report, the software displays the *Field List* sidepane.

- At the top of the user interface, the software adds the *Design* and *Layout* ribbon tabs with the *Table Tools* applied, but leaves selected the *Design* ribbon with the *Report Tools* applied.

You can use either of these two options to customize a table. I discuss these two methods of table customization individually.

Information: Customizing a table in Project 2013 is very similar to customizing a table in Word 2013. The more experience you have with formatting Word tables, the better you will be at formatting a table in Project 2013.

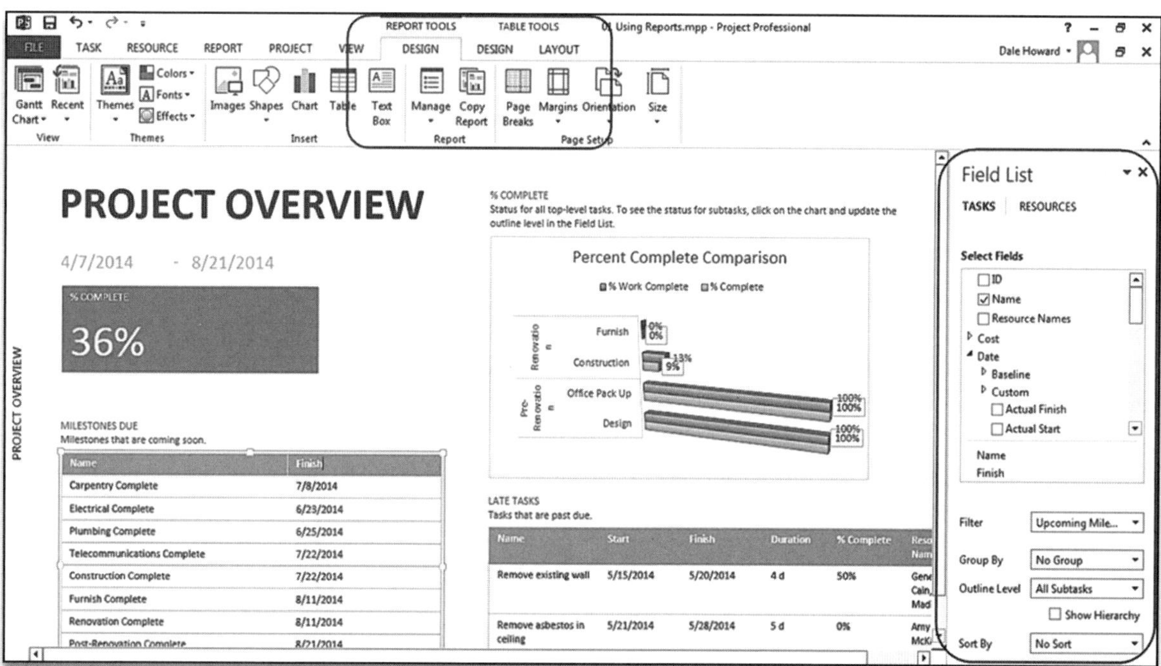

Figure 11 - 42: Select a table for customization

Using the Field List Sidepane

At the top of the *Field List* sidepane on the right side of the report, Project 2013 displays two tabs: the *Tasks* and *Resources* tab. The software selects the correct tab for the type of data shown in the table. For example, notice in Figure 11 - 42 shown previously that the software selects the *Tasks* tab since *Milestones Due* table displays task data.

Warning: If you click the *Resources* tab while you have a task table selected, the software replaces the list of tasks with the names of every resource, but includes all of the columns currently displayed in the table. In addition, the software displays a list of resource fields in the *Select Fields* section of the *Field List* sidepane.

The *Select Fields* section of the sidepane displays the types of fields available for display in the selected table, which include the *ID, Name,* and *Resource Names* fields, plus sections for *Cost, Date, Duration, Flag, Number, Work,* and *Other Fields*. By default, the software expands the types of fields used in the selected table. With the *Milestones Due* table selected, the software expands the *Date* section, which shows the list of available *Date* fields for inclusion in the table. To expand any other type of field to see the available fields of that type, click the *Expand* symbol to the left of the field type.

In the bottom half of the *Select Fields* section, the software displays the fields currently included in the table. By default, the *Milestones Due* table includes only the *Name* and *Finish* fields. To include any other fields in the table, expand the field type and select the checkboxes for the fields you want to add. To remove any current fields from the table, deselect the checkbox for any field you want to omit.

Information: If you add additional fields to your table, you can decrease the width of each column in the table by double-clicking anywhere on the right edge of the column header for the column whose width you want to decrease. You can also change the display order of the fields by moving the fields up and down in the list of selected fields shown at the bottom of the *Select Fields* section of the *Field List* sidepane.

Information: If you right-click on the name of any displayed field in the bottom half of the *Select Fields* section, the software displays a shortcut menu. Select the *Move Up* or *Move Down* item on the shortcut menu to move the field in the selected table. Select the *Remove Field* item on the shortcut menu to remove the field from the selected table. Select the *Field Settings* item on the shortcut menu to display the *Field Settings* dialog, in which you can apply a label or display name for the field in the selected table.

The bottom of the *Field List* sidepane offers you options to filter, group, sort, and display the outline level of task data shown in the selected table. By default, the *Milestones Due* table includes the *Upcoming Milestones* filter, the *No Group* item selected in the *Group By* pick list, the *Outline Level* option set to *All Subtasks,* with the *Show Hierarchy* checkbox option deselected, and with the *Sort By* option set to *No Sort*. To customize my report, I want the *Milestones Due* table to show only those milestones at outline levels 1 and 2, which represent the phase and deliverable milestones in my project. To meet this reporting requirement, I must click the *Outline Level* pick list and select the *Level 2* item on the pick list. Figure 11 - 43 shows the updated *Milestones Due* table.

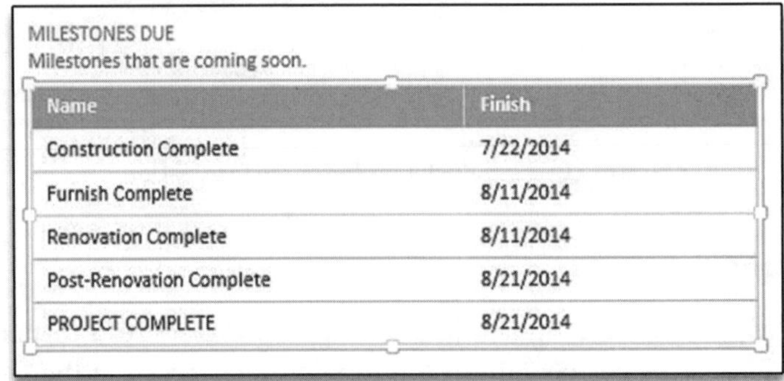
MILESTONES DUE
Milestones that are coming soon.

Name	Finish
Construction Complete	7/22/2014
Furnish Complete	8/11/2014
Renovation Complete	8/11/2014
Post-Renovation Complete	8/21/2014
PROJECT COMPLETE	8/21/2014

Figure 11 - 43: Updated Milestones Due table

Information: If you select the *Show Hierarchy* checkbox at the bottom of the *Field List* sidepane, Project 2013 displays the summary task for each milestone in the table.

Edit the selected table using the *Filter, Group By, Outline Level,* and *Sort By* pick lists, along with selecting the *Show Hierarchy* checkbox option, as needed. If you are finished editing the selected table, click anywhere outside the table to close the *Field List* sidepane.

Information: If you close the *Field List* sidepane by clicking the *Close* button (**X**) in the upper right corner of the sidepane, Project 2013 offers you two methods to redisplay it. To use the first method, click the *Design* tab with the *Table Tools* applied and then click the *Table Data* button in the *Show/Hide* section of the *Design* ribbon. To use the second method, right-click anywhere in the selected table and then click the *Show Field List* item at the bottom of the shortcut menu.

Using the Design Ribbon with the Table Tools Applied

If you click the rightmost of the two *Design* tabs, Project 2013 displays the *Design* ribbon with the *Table Tools* applied, as shown in Figure 11 - 44. The software divides the *Design* ribbon into four sections: the *Table Style Options, Table Styles, WordArt Styles,* and *Show/Hide* sections.

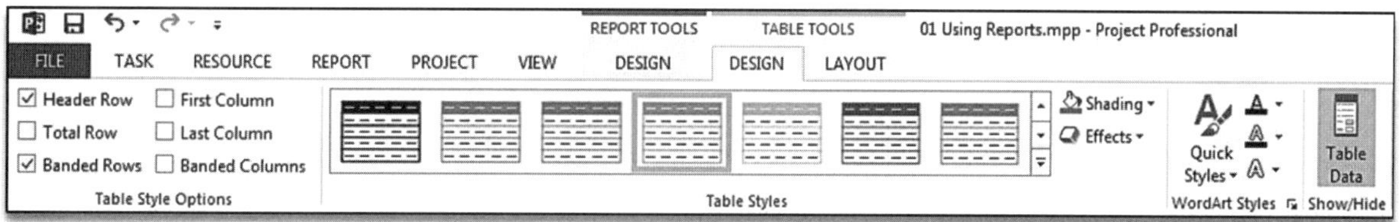

Figure 11 - 44: Design ribbon with the Table Tools applied

In the *Table Style Options* section of the *Design* ribbon, the software selects the *Header Row* and *Banded Rows* options by default. When selected, the *Header Row* option displays the field names as column headers in the first row of the table. I recommend you leave this option selected. When selected, the *Banded Rows* option formats the rows in the table with a gray gridline along the bottom of each row. If desirable, I recommend you leave this option selected. If the table contains work or cost information, you can select the *Total Row* to add an additional total row at the bottom of the table. If you select the *First Column* option, the software formats all cells in the first column with *Bold* font formatting. If you select the *Last Column* option, the software formats all cells in the last column with *Bold* font formatting. If you select the *Banded Columns* option, the software formats the columns in the table with a gray gridline along the right edge of each column

Information: The behavior of the options in the *Table Styles Options* section of the *Design* ribbon depends on the table style you choose in the *Table Styles* gallery. For example, if you choose a style in the *Medium* section of the *Table Styles* gallery, selecting the *Banded Rows* option displays alternating light and dark row colors in the selected table. Because of this, you may need to experiment with the settings in these two sections of the *Design* ribbon with the *Table Tools* applied.

The *Table Styles* section of the *Design* ribbon contains a gallery of 74 pre-formatted table styles, which you can apply to the selected table. Project 2013 divides these table styles into sections labeled *Best Match for Document, Light, Medium,* and *Dark*. The default style applied to the *Milestones Due* table is the *Light Style 2 – Accent 3* style. Select any style in the gallery, as needed, to change the style of your table. Select one or more cells in the table and then click the *Shading* pick list button to add a fill color, a picture, a gradient, or a texture to the selected cells. Click the *Effects* button to apply an effect to the selected table, such as adding a shadow or a reflection around the table. On the *Effects* menu, if you click the *Shadow Options* item at the bottom of the *Shadow* flyout menu, or you click the *Reflection Options* item at the bottom of the *Reflection* menu, Project 2013 displays the *Format Shape* sidepane, which gives you access to every option for formatting the shadow and reflection for the selected table.

The *WordArt Styles* section of the *Format* ribbon offers a gallery of available WordArt styles, with additional buttons for formatting the fill, outline, and WordArt effects used with the text in a table. Before you can use any of these WordArt options, you must first select one or more cells in the table. Click the *Quick Styles* pick list button to see all 20 of the available WordArt styles, or to remove the current WordArt style. Select one of the WordArt styles in the gallery, as needed. Click the *Text Fill* pick list button to add a fill color, a picture, a gradient, or a texture to the selected text. Click the *Text Outline* pick list button to apply a color to the outline around the selected text, as well as to control the thickness of the outline and the type of outline, such as solid or dashed. Click the *Text Effects* pick list button to apply an effect to the selected text, such as adding a shadow or applying beveling.

Click the *Table Data* button in the *Show/Hide* section of the *Design* ribbon to display or hide the *Field List* sidepane shown previously in Figure 11 - 42.

Using the Layout Ribbon with the Table Tools Applied

If you click the *Layout* tab, Project 2013 displays the *Layout* ribbon with the *Table Tools* applied, as shown in Figure 11 - 45. The software divides the *Layout* ribbon into five sections: the *Table, Cell Size, Alignment, Table Size,* and *Arrange* sections.

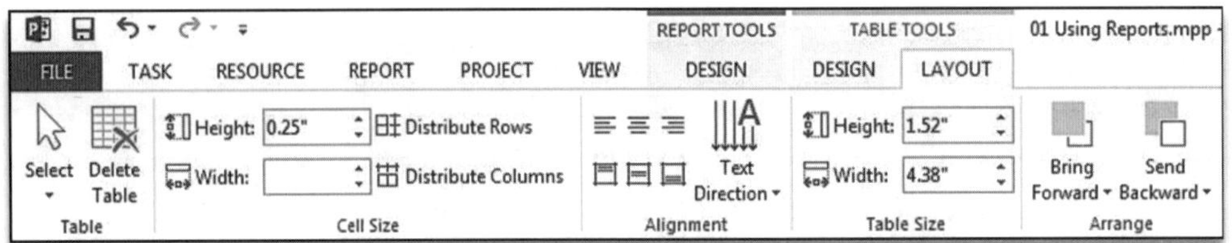

Figure 11 - 45: Layout ribbon with the Chart Tools applied

In the *Table* section of the *Layout* ribbon, click the *Select* pick list button. With any cell selected in the table, you can click the *Select Column* item on the pick list to select all cells in the current column, or click the *Select Row* item to select all cells in the current row. You can also choose the *Select Table* item on the pick list to select the entire table. To delete the selected table, click the *Delete Table* button or press the **Delete** key on your computer keyboard. The software does not warn you about deleting the selected table, but you can undo the deletion by clicking the *Undo* button in the *Quick Access Toolbar*.

Use the commands in the *Cell Size* section of the *Layout* ribbon to change the height and width of any cells in the selected table. Before you use these commands, be sure to select at least one cell in the table. Adjust the number in the *Height* field to adjust the height of the selected row. Adjust the number in the *Width* field to change the width of the selected column. Click the *Distribute Rows* button to set the row height for all rows the same as the tallest row in the selected table. Click the *Distribute Columns* button to set the column width for all columns the same as the widest column in the selected table.

Use the commands in the *Alignment* section of the *Layout* ribbon to control the alignment and text direction of the any cells in the selected table. Before you use these commands, be sure to select at least one cell in the table. Use the *Align Left, Center,* and *Align Right* buttons to align the text horizontally in the selected cells. Use the *Align Top, Center Vertically,* and *Align Bottom* buttons to align the text vertically in the selected cells. Click the *Text Direction* pick list button to set the text direction as horizontal, to rotate the text 90 degrees or 270 degrees, or to stack the text in the selected cells. If you select the *More Options* item at the bottom of the *Text Direction* pick list, Project 2013 displays the *Format Shape* sidepane with the *Text Options* tab selected, which gives you access to every option for formatting the text direction and setting margins in the selected cells.

The *Table Size* section of the *Format* ribbon allows you to control the precise size of the selected table. Use the spin controls (up and down arrows) in the *Height* and *Width* fields to control the height and width of the selected table.

If the selected table overlaps images, shapes, or charts that you added to your report, use the commands in the *Arrange* section of the *Layout* ribbon to layer the selected table with other objects. When you click the *Bring Forward* pick list button, you can choose whether to bring the table forward or to bring the table to the front of all of the other objects. When you click the *Send Backward* pick list button, you can choose whether to send the table backward or to send the table to the back of all of the other objects.

Hands On Exercise

Exercise 11 - 3

Customize a table in a report in Project 2013.

1. Return to the **Using Reports 2013.mpp** sample file, if necessary.
2. Click the *Report* tab to display the *Report* ribbon.
3. In the *View Reports* section of the *Report* ribbon, click the *Dashboards* pick list button and select the *Project Overview* report.
4. Click anywhere in the *Milestones Due* table to select the table for editing and to display the *Field List* sidepane.
5. In the *Field List* sidepane, do each of the following:
   - Click the *Filter* pick list and select the *Summary Tasks* filter.
   - Click the *Outline Level* pick list and select the *Level 2* item.
   - Select the *Show Hierarchy* checkbox.
6. Click anywhere in the *% Complete* table (orange box in the upper left corner of the report) to select the table for editing and to display the *Field List* sidepane.
7. In the *Select Fields* section of the *Field List* sidepane, select the checkbox for the *% Work Complete* field.
8. Click the second *Design* tab to display the *Design* ribbon with the *Table Tools* applied.
9. In the *Table Styles* section of the *Design* ribbon, select the *Themed Style 1 – Accent 1* color theme in the *Theme Styles* gallery.
10. Click the *Layout* tab to display the *Layout* ribbon with the *Table Tools* applied.
11. Click and drag to select all four cells in the newly-formatted *% Complete* table.

12. In the *Cell Size* section of the *Layout* ribbon, set the *Width* value to *2.2 inches.*

13. Click anywhere in the white part of the *Project Overview* report to deselect the selected table.

14. Save but **do not** close the **Using Reports 2013.mpp** sample file.

Adding a New Chart

To add a new chart to a report, click anywhere in the white area of the report and then click the *Design* tab to display the *Design* ribbon with the *Report Tools* applied. In the *Insert* section of the *Design* ribbon, click the *Chart* button. The software displays the *Insert Chart* dialog shown in Figure 11 - 46.

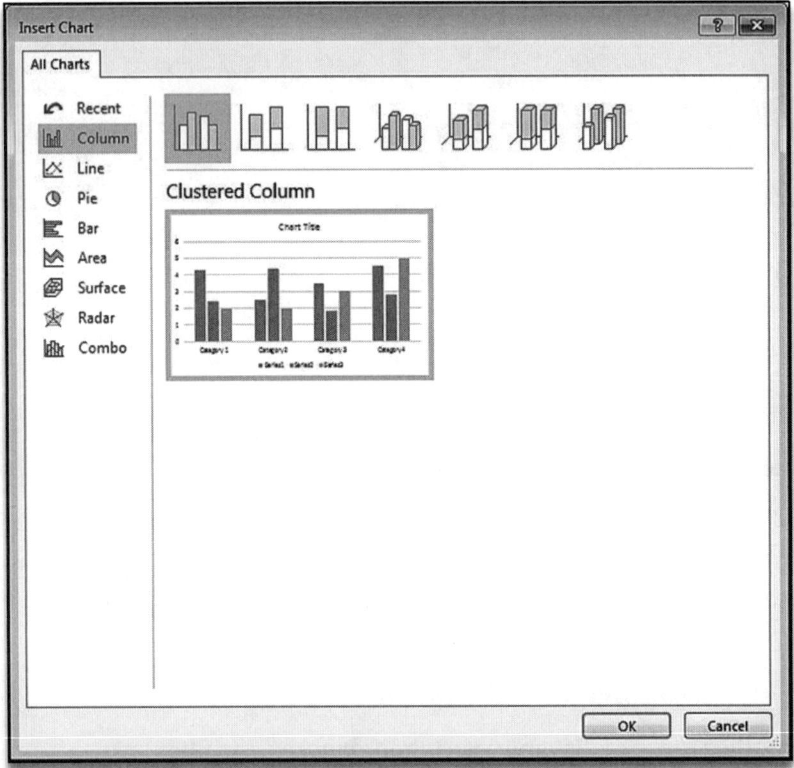

Figure 11 - 46: Insert Chart dialog

Warning: Make sure that you **do not** have an existing chart selected when you click the *Chart* button. If you do have an existing chart selected, the software displays the *Change Chart Type* dialog instead of the *Insert Chart* dialog, and then the software reformats your existing chart with the new chart type you select in the dialog.

The *Insert Chart* dialog allows you to select any type of chart available in the software. In the list of chart types on the left side of the dialog, the software allows you to choose from among the *Column, Line, Pie, Bar, Area, Surface, Radar,* and *Combo* chart types. The dialog also includes the *Recent* item in the list to allow you to choose from among recently used chart types. When you select a chart type in the list on the left side of the *Change Chart Type* dialog, the software displays a list of sub-types across the top of the dialog. For example, if you select the *Pie* chart type, Project 2013 offers you 5 sub-types, including the *Pie, 3-D Pie, Pie of Pie, Bar of Pie,* and the *Doughnut* sub-types.

Information: To make any chart type the default type for all new charts you add to reports, right-click on any of the sub-types at the top of the dialog and select the *Set as Default Chart* item on the shortcut menu.

To insert a new chart, select a chart type in the list on the left side of the dialog and then select a sub-type in the list across the top of the dialog. The software shows you a preview of the selected chart type in the middle of the dialog. To see a magnified preview of the chart type you select, float your mouse pointer over the preview image. Click the *OK* button to create the new chart. Project 2013 displays the new chart in the middle of the report. For example, Figure 11 - 47 shows the new 3-D Pie chart I added to the report. The software also displays the *Design* ribbon with the *Chart Tools* applied and displays the *Field List* sidepane on the right side of the report.

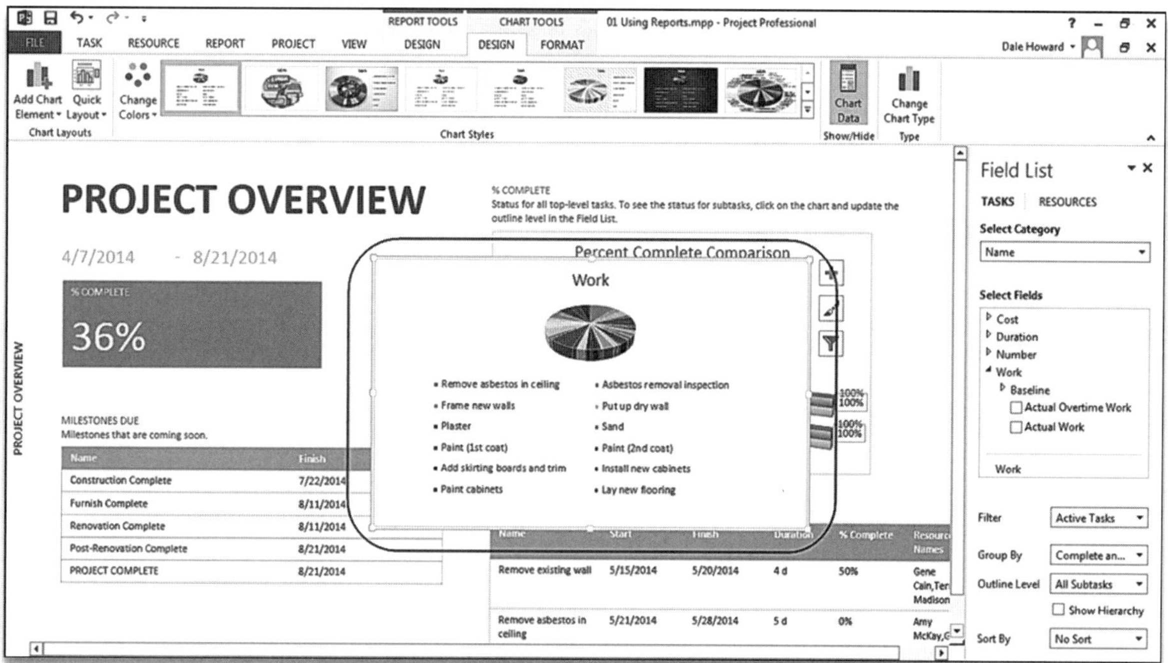

Figure 11 - 47: New 3-D Pie chart inserted in the Project Overview report

To properly format the new chart, you may need to use some or all of the techniques I previously presented in the *Customizing a Chart* topical section in this module. For example, I want to format the new 3-D pie chart to show the total *Work* value by project phase. To show this information in the chart, I must complete the following steps:

1. In the *Field List* sidepane, click the *Filter* pick list and select the *Summary Tasks* filter.

2. In the *Field List* sidepane, click the *Group By* pick list and select the *No Group* item.

3. In the *Field List* sidepane, click the *Outline Level* pick list and select the *Level 1* item. In my projects, summary tasks at the first level of indent represent the phases of the project.

4. Click the *Chart Elements* button on the right of the chart, select the *Data Labels* checkbox, and then select the *More Options* item on the flyout menu.

5. In the *Format Data Labels* sidepane, **select** the *Category Name, Value, Percentage,* and *Legend Key* checkboxes, and then **deselect** the *Show Leader Lines* checkbox.

6. In the *Format Data Labels* sidepane, select the *Outside End* option in the *Label Position* section of the sidepane. When finished, close the *Format Data Labels* sidepane.

7. Reselect the chart, if necessary, then click the *Chart Styles* button on the right side of the chart, and select the *Style 7* item in the *Style* menu.

8. Click the *Chart Elements* button on the right of the chart and then **deselect** the *Legend* checkbox.

9. Click in the *Chart Title* element, delete the existing text, and then change the name of the chart to *Total Work by Phase.*

10. In the *Size* section of the *Format* ribbon, reduce the *Height* value to *2.7″* and reduce the *Width* value to *4.3″*.

11. Double-click anywhere in the pie portion of the chart to display the *Format Data Series* sidepane.

12. In the *Format Data Series* sidepane, change the *Angle of the first slice* value to *90 degrees.*

13. In the *Format Data Series* sidepane, change the *Pie Explosion* value to *5%* and then close the *Format Data series* sidepane.

14. Click the border (outer edge) of the chart to select only the chart.

15. In the *Shape Styles* section of the *Format* ribbon, click the *Shape Effects* pick list button, select the *Shadow* item, and then click the *Offset Diagonal Bottom Left* item on the flyout menu.

16. Close the *Field List* sidepane.

17. Drag and drop the new chart to the right of the *% Complete* chart.

Figure 11 - 48 shows the new 3-D pie chart after completing all of the preceding steps.

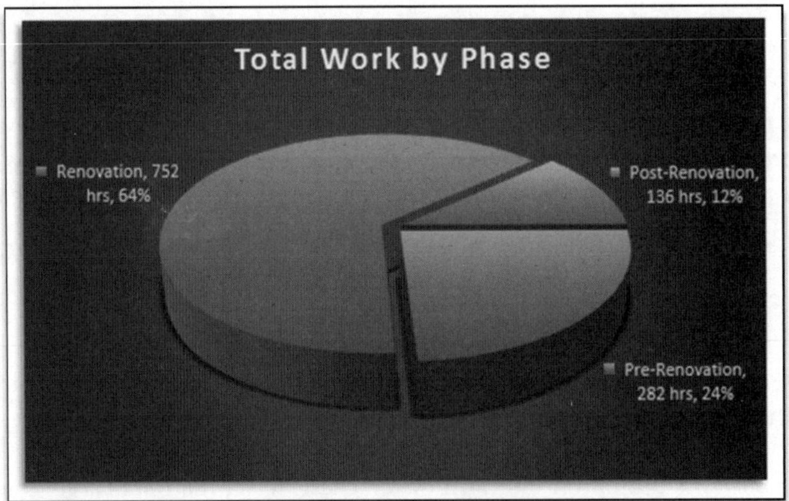

Figure 11 - 48: Completed 3-D pie chart added to the Project Overview report

Hands On Exercise

Exercise 11 - 4

Add a new chart to a report in Project 2013.

1. Return to the **Using Reports 2013.mpp** sample file, if necessary.
2. Click the *Report* tab to display the *Report* ribbon.
3. In the *View Reports* section of the *Report* ribbon, click the *Dashboards* pick list button and select the *Cost Overview* report.
4. In the *Insert* section of the *Design* ribbon, click the *Chart* button.
5. In the *Insert Chart* dialog, select the *Pie* item on the left side of the dialog, select the *3-D Pie* item at the top of the dialog, and then click the *OK* button.
6. Close the *Field List* sidepane on the right side.
7. Click and hold the new chart and drag it to the right of the *Progress Versus Cost* chart (align the top edges of the new chart with the *Progress Versus Cost* chart).
8. Use your horizontal screen bar to scroll past the right side of the new chart so that you can see the new chart completely when you display the *Field List* sidepane again in step #10.
9. With the new chart still selected, click the second *Design* tab to display the *Design* ribbon with the *Chart Tools* applied.
10. In the *Show/Hide* section of the *Design* ribbon, click the *Chart Data* button to display the *Field List* sidepane again.
11. In the *Field List* sidepane, do each of the following:
    - **Deselect** the *Work* checkbox in the *Select Fields* section of the sidepane.
    - Expand the *Cost* section (click the little white arrow to the left of the *Cost* item) and then **select** the checkbox for the *Cost* field.
    - Click the *Filter* pick list and select the *Summary Tasks* filter.
    - Click the *Group By* pick list and select the *No Group* item.
    - Click the *Outline Level* pick list and select *Level 1*.
12. In the *Chart Styles* section of the *Design* ribbon, click the *Style 3* button in the *Chart Styles* gallery.
13. Close the *Field List* sidepane again.
14. Click anywhere in the *Cost* title in the new chart and change the title to *Cost by Phase*.
15. Right-click anywhere in the pie chart itself and select the *Format Data Labels* item in the shortcut menu.

16. In the *Format Data Labels* sidepane, **select** the *Value* checkbox and then **deselect** the *Percentage* checkbox.

17. Click two separate times (not a double-click) in the *Pre-Renovation* slice (blue slice) of the pie chart to display the *Format Data Point* sidepane.

18. In the *Format Data Point* sidepane, set the *Point Explosion* value to 25%.

19. Right-click anywhere in the *Legend* chart element and then select the *Format Legend* item in the shortcut menu.

20. In the *Format Legend* sidepane, select the *Top* option in the *Legend Options* section of the sidepane.

21. Close the *Format Legend* sidepane.

22. Save but **do not** close the **Using Reports 2013.mpp** sample file.

Adding a New Table

To add a new table to a report, click anywhere in the white area of the report and then click the *Design* tab to display the *Design* ribbon with the *Report Tools* applied. In the *Insert* section of the *Design* ribbon, click the *Table* button. Project 2013 displays the new table in the middle of the report, as shown in Figure 11 - 49. Notice that the software displays the *Field List* sidepane on the right, and displays the *Design* and *Layout* ribbon tabs with the *Table Tools* applied. To properly format the new table, you may need to use some or all of the techniques I previously presented in the *Customizing a Table* topical section in this module.

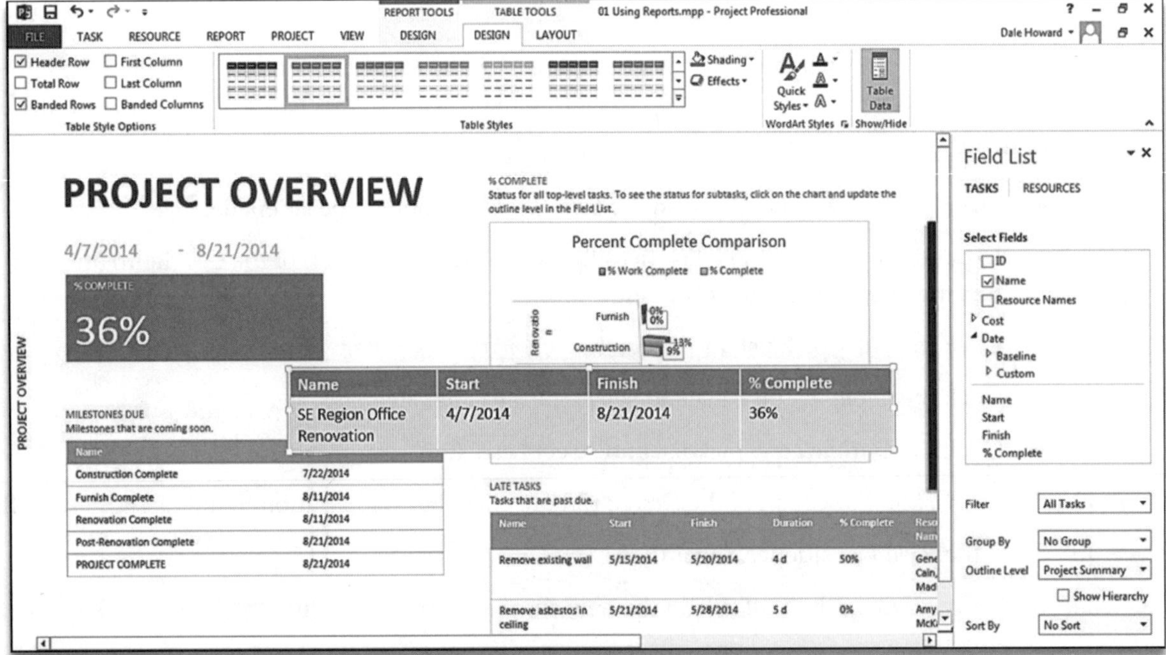

Figure 11 - 49: New table inserted in the Project Overview report

In my new table, I want to show *Work* and *Cost* by level 1 and 2 summary tasks (phase and deliverable sections of the project). To meet this reporting requirement, I must do the following:

1. In the *Field List* sidepane, **deselect** the *Finish, Start,* and *% Complete* checkboxes, and then select the *Work* and *Cost* checkboxes.
2. In the *Field List* sidepane, click the *Filter* pick list and select the *Summary Tasks* filter.
3. In the *Field List* sidepane, click the *Group By* pick list and leave the *No Group* item selected.
4. In the *Field List* sidepane, click the *Outline Level* pick list and select the *Level 2* item, and then select the *Show Hierarchy* checkbox. By selecting the *Show Hierarchy* checkbox, this allows me to show level 2 summary tasks, which represent the deliverables in my project, plus their level 1 summary tasks, which represent the phases of my project.
5. Click the rightmost of the two *Design* tabs to display the *Design* ribbon with the *Table Tools* applied, if necessary.
6. In the gallery in the *Table Styles* section of the *Design* ribbon, select the *Medium Style 2 - Accent 3* style to match the table style applied to the default tables in the *Project Overview* report.
7. Select all of the cells in the table and then click the *Task* tab to display the *Task* ribbon.
8. In the *Font* section of the *Task* ribbon, leave the *Calibri (Body)* font selected in the *Font* pick list, and then select the *9 point* size in the *Font Size* pick list. This allows me to match the font and font size used in the default tables in the *Project Overview* report.
9. Click the *Layout* tab to display the *Layout* ribbon with the *Table Tools* applied.
10. Click anywhere in the *Name* column of the table and then set the *Width* value to *2"* in the *Cell Size* section of the *Layout* ribbon.
11. Using the same technique, set the *Width* value of the *Work* and *Cost* columns to *1.2"* each.
12. In the *Table Styles* section of the *Design* ribbon, click the *Effects* pick list button, select the *Shadow* item, and then click the *Offset Diagonal Bottom Left* item on the flyout menu.
13. Drag and drop the new table below the *Milestones Due* table.
14. Close the *Field List* sidepane.

Figure 11 - 50 shows the new table after completing all of the preceding steps.

Name	Work	Cost
Pre-Renovation	282 h	$16,095
Design	156 h	$12,935
Office Pack Up	126 h	$3,160
Renovation	752 h	$36,955
Construction	696 h	$34,155
Furnish	56 h	$2,800
Post-Renovation	136 h	$9,040

Figure 11 - 50: Completed table added to the Project Overview report

Hands On Exercise

Exercise 11 - 5

Add a new table in a report in Project 2013.

1. Return to the **Using Reports 2013.mpp** sample file, if necessary.
2. Click the *Report* tab to display the *Report* ribbon.
3. In the *View Reports* section of the *Report* ribbon, click the *In Progress* pick list button and select the *Late Tasks* report.
4. In the *Insert* section of the *Design* ribbon, click the *Table* button.
5. In the *Field List* sidepane, do each of the following:
    - **Deselect** the *Finish, Start,* and *% Complete* fields in the *Select Fields* section of the sidepane.
    - Expand the *Duration* section along with its *Baseline* subsection, and then **select** the *Baseline Duration, Duration,* and *Duration Variance* fields.
    - Click the *Filter* pick list and select the *Summary Tasks* filter.
    - Click the *Outline Level* pick list and select *Level 1.*
    - Select the *Show Hierarchy* checkbox.
6. Click and hold anywhere on the edge of the new table and drag it below the table at the top of the report, aligning the left edges of the two tables.
7. Click the second *Design* tab to display the *Design* ribbon with the *Table Tools* applied, if necessary.
8. In the *Table Styles* section of the *Design* ribbon, select the *Light Style 3 – Accent 3* style in the *Light* section of the *Table Styles* gallery.
9. Click the *Task* tab to display the *Task* ribbon.

Warning: Before you complete the next step in this Hands On Exercise, confirm that you have the entire table section and not just one cell in the table. Click anywhere on the edge of the table to select the entire table.

10. In the *Font* section of the *Task* ribbon, click the *Font Size* pick list and select the *9 point* font size.
11. Click and drag all of the cells in the *Baseline Duration, Duration,* and *Duration Variance* columns to select those three columns.
12. Click the *Layout* tab to display the *Layout* ribbon with the *Table Tools* applied.
13. In the *Cell Size* section of the *Format* ribbon, set the *Width* value to *1.5 inches* for the three selected columns.
14. Save but **do not** close the **Using Reports 2013.mpp** sample file.

Adding a Text Box Shape

When you add a new table or a new chart to your report, you may want to include a title and description for the chart or table. For example, in the *Project Overview* report, Project 2013 includes a title and description for each chart and table in the report. To include a title and description, you must insert a new *Text Box* shape, add the title and description, and then format the shape. The fastest and easiest way to add a *Text Box* shape, however, is to copy any existing *Text Box* shape and then to change the text displayed in the shape. This allows you to duplicate the formatting of the default *Text Box* shapes included in each report.

For example, I want to include a title and description for the new 3-D pie chart and for the new table I added to the *Project Overview* report, shown previously in Figure 11 - 48 and Figure 11 - 50. If I want to go to the bother of manually adding a new title and description, I must complete the following steps:

1. Click the *Design* tab to display the *Design* ribbon with the *Report Tools* applied.
2. In the *Insert* section of the *Design* ribbon, click the *Text Box* button. Project 2013 changes the default mouse pointer into a special *Insert Shape* crosshair pointer.
3. Using this crosshair pointer, click and hold the mouse button and trace an outline of the size of the shape and in the location where I want the *Text Box* shape. When I release the mouse button, the software creates the new shape and displays the *Format* ribbon with the *Drawing Tools* applied, as shown previously in Figure 11 - 40.
4. Enter the required title and description text in the *Text Box* shape and then select the text.
5. Click the *Task* tab to display the *Task* ribbon.
6. Use the features in the *Font* section of the *Task* ribbon to format the text.

Information: To match the formatting of the title text displayed in each default report, format the text in your new *Text Box* shape as follows:

- Font Effect - All Caps
- Font - Calibri (Body)
- Font Size - 9 point
- Font Color - Blue, Accent 1

Information: To match the formatting of the description text displayed in each default report, format the text in your new *Text Box* shape as follows:

- Font - Calibri (Body)
- Font Size - 9 point
- Font Color - White, Background 1, Darker 50%

7. Click and hold anywhere on the edge of the new *Text Box* shape and then drag and drop the shape to its final location, as needed.
8. Narrow the width of the new title to match the width of the table or chart
9. Optionally, I can also use the formatting features in the *Format* ribbon with the *Drawing Tools* applied to apply additional formatting to the *Text Box* shape.

To quickly create a title and description for a new chart or table by copying an existing title and description, I must complete the following steps:

1. Click the *Task* tab to display the *Task* ribbon.

2. Click anywhere in the title and description label to select it.

3. In the *Clipboard* section of the *Task* ribbon, click the *Copy* button.

4. Click anywhere outside of the selected title and description to **deselect** the object.

5. In the *Clipboard* section of the *Task* ribbon, click the *Paste* button. Project 2013 pastes a copy of the selected object slightly below and to the right of the selected object.

6. With the new title and description label still selected, press the **Up-Arrow**, **Down-Arrow**, **Left-Arrow**, and **Right-Arrow** keys on your computer keyboard to move the label to its new location.

Information: You can also move the new label by clicking and holding on the outer edge of the selected object and then dragging and dropping it to a new location in the report.

7. Click anywhere in the new label, delete the old text, and then enter the new title and description text.

8. Format the title and description text to match the formatting used in the default labels in the report.

9. Narrow the width of the new label to match the width of the table or chart.

Figure 11 - 51 shows the new title and description for the table I added to the *Project Overview* report.

WORK AND COST
Shows total work and cost by phase and deliverable sections.

Name	Work	Cost
Pre-Renovation	282 h	$16,095
Design	156 h	$12,935
Office Pack Up	126 h	$3,160
Renovation	752 h	$36,955
Construction	696 h	$34,155
Furnish	56 h	$2,800
Post-Renovation	136 h	$9,040

Figure 11 - 51: Title and description added to the new table

If you select any shape, including a title and description label, the *Arrange* section of the *Format* ribbon now contains an additional *Rotate* button not seen when you selected a chart or a table. If you want to rotate a *Text Box* shape or any other type of shape, you can use the *Rotate* pick list button for this purpose. When you click the *Rotate* pick list button, you can choose whether to rotate the shape 90 degrees left or right, or to flip the shape horizontally or vertically. If you click the *More Rotation Options* at the bottom of the *Rotate* pick list, Project 2013 displays the *Format Shape* sidepane, which gives you access to every option for formatting the shape.

Hands On Exercise

Exercise 11 - 6

Use copy and paste to add a title and description text box label in a report in Project 2013.

1. Return to the **Using Reports 2013.mpp** sample file, if necessary.
2. Click the *Report* tab to display the *Report* ribbon.
3. In the *View Reports* section of the *Report* ribbon, click the *Dashboard* pick list button and select the *Cost Overview* report.
4. Click anywhere in the *Progress Versus Cost* text label and then click anywhere on the edge of the label to select it.
5. Click the *Task* tab to display the *Task* ribbon.
6. In the *Clipboard* section of the *Task* ribbon, click the *Copy* button and then click the *Paste* button.
7. Click and hold anywhere on the edge of the newly-pasted label and then drag the new label immediately above the *Cost By Phase* chart.
8. Edit the text in the new label to display the following:

   COST BY PHASE
   Total cost by first-level summary tasks.
9. Click the *Report* tab to display the *Report* ribbon.
10. In the *View Reports* section of the *Report* ribbon, click the *In Progress* pick list button and select the *Late Tasks* report.
11. Right-click anywhere in the blank part of the *Late Tasks* report and then select the *Keep Source Formatting* item in the *Paste Options* section of the shortcut menu.
12. Click and hold anywhere on the edge of the newly-pasted label and then drag the new label immediately above the new table you added to the *Late Tasks* report.

Warning: Before you can do the preceding step, you may need to drag the new table down in the *Late Tasks* report to make room for the new label text box.

13. Edit the text in the new label to display the following:

    DURATION VARIANCE
    Baseline Duration, Duration, and Duration Variance information for every first-level and second-level summary task in the project.
14. Save but **do not** close the **Using Reports 2013.mpp** sample file.

Adding Images and Shapes

After adding a new chart and table, as well as adding a title and description label for each, you may also want to add an image or other shapes to your report. To add an image, click the *Design* tab to display the *Design* ribbon with the *Report Tools* applied. In the *Insert* section of the *Design* ribbon, click the *Images* button. Project 2013 displays the *Insert Picture* dialog shown in Figure 11 - 52.

Figure 11 - 52: Insert Picture dialog

In the *Insert Picture* dialog, navigate to the location where you store image files, select an image file, and then click the *Open* button. The software inserts the new image in the middle of the report and then displays the *Format* ribbon with the *Picture Tools* applied, as shown in Figure 11 - 53.

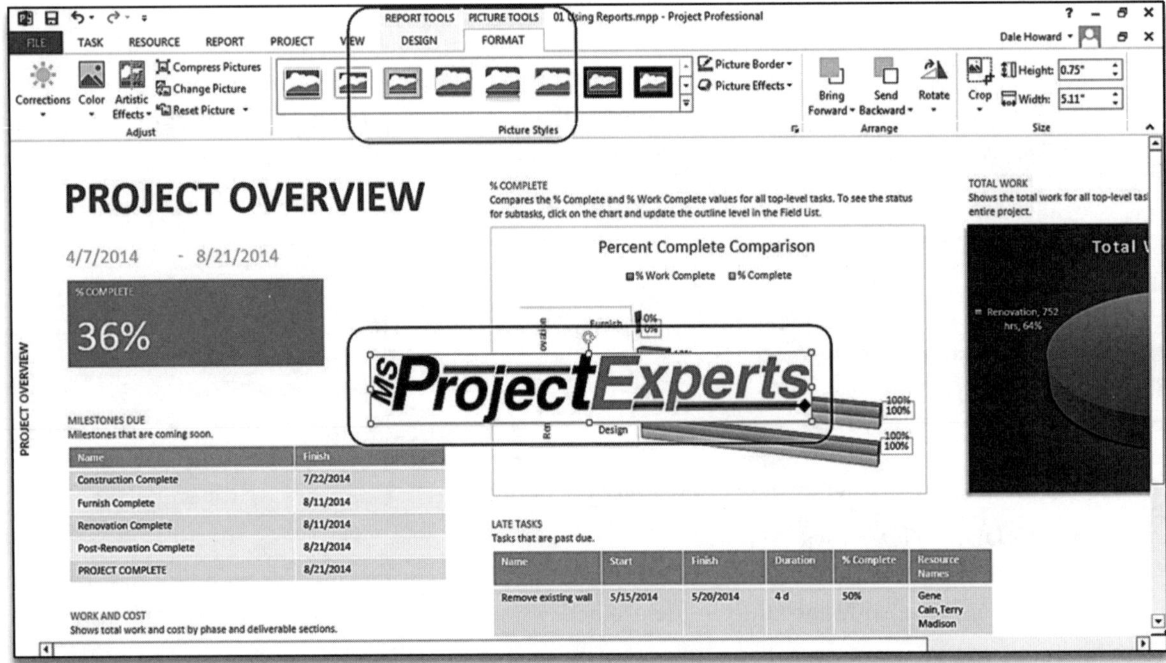

Figure 11 - 53: Insert a new image in the Project Overview report

After inserting the new image, click and hold the image and then drag and drop the image to the desired location in your report. If you want to resize the new image, you can click and hold one of the "grab handles" around the outside edge of the image and then drag the edge to resize the image. If you want to resize the new image proportionately, right-click the image and then select the *Size and Position* item on the shortcut menu. Project 2013 displays the *Format Picture* sidepane, in which you can resize the image proportionately by changing the *Scale Height* and *Scale Width* fields by the same amount, such as changing the value in each field to *75%*.

Information: Keep in mind that you may need to reorganize the layout of current charts and tables to make room for the new image in your report. To quickly "lasso" a block of charts and tables, click and hold anywhere in the white part of the report and then draw an outline of the area you want to select. As you do so, Project 2013 draws a gray shaded box to indicate the block you want to select. When you release the mouse button, the software selects every object in the block. Once selected, you can easily move all of the selected objects as a single block.

To insert a new shape in your report, click the *Design* tab to display the *Design* ribbon with the *Report Tools* applied. In the *Insert* section of the *Design* ribbon, click the *Shapes* pick list button to see the gallery of available shapes. The software organizes the shapes in the gallery into the *Recently Used Shapes, Lines, Rectangles, Basic Shapes, Block Arrows, Equation Shapes, Flowchart, Stars and Banners,* and *Callouts* sections. When you select a shape in the gallery, Project 2013 changes the default mouse pointer into a special *Insert Shape* mouse pointer. Using this special mouse pointer, click and hold the mouse button and trace an outline of the size of the shape you want in the location where you want the shape. When you release the mouse button, the software creates the new shape and displays the *Format* ribbon with the *Drawing Tools* applied, as shown previously in Figure 11 - 40.

After you insert the new shape in your report, click anywhere in the shape and then type the text you want to display in the shape. Select the text and then click the *Task* tab to display the *Task* ribbon. Use the features in the *Font* section of the *Task* ribbon to format the text. Click and hold anywhere on the edge of the new shape and then drag and drop the shape to its final location, as needed. Optionally, you may also want to use the formatting features in the *Format* ribbon with the *Drawing Tools* applied to apply additional formatting to the shape.

Information: Because I do not intend this book to be a reference book on how to edit graphical objects such as shapes, I do not provide an in-depth discussion of the features in the *Format* ribbon with the *Drawing Tools* applied.

If you want to resize the new shape, you can click and hold one of the "grab handles" around the outside edge of the shape and then drag the edge to resize the image. If you want to resize the new image proportionately, right-click the shape and then select the *Format Shape* item on the shortcut menu. In the *Format Shape* sidepane, click the *Size & Properties* button at the top of the sidepane. Project 2013 redisplays the *Format Shape* sidepane. You can resize the image proportionately by changing the *Scale Height* and *Scale Width* fields by the same amount, such as changing the value in each field to *75%*.

Figure 11 - 54 shows the final version of the *Project Overview* report. By the way, I edited this report using all of the features documented in this module.

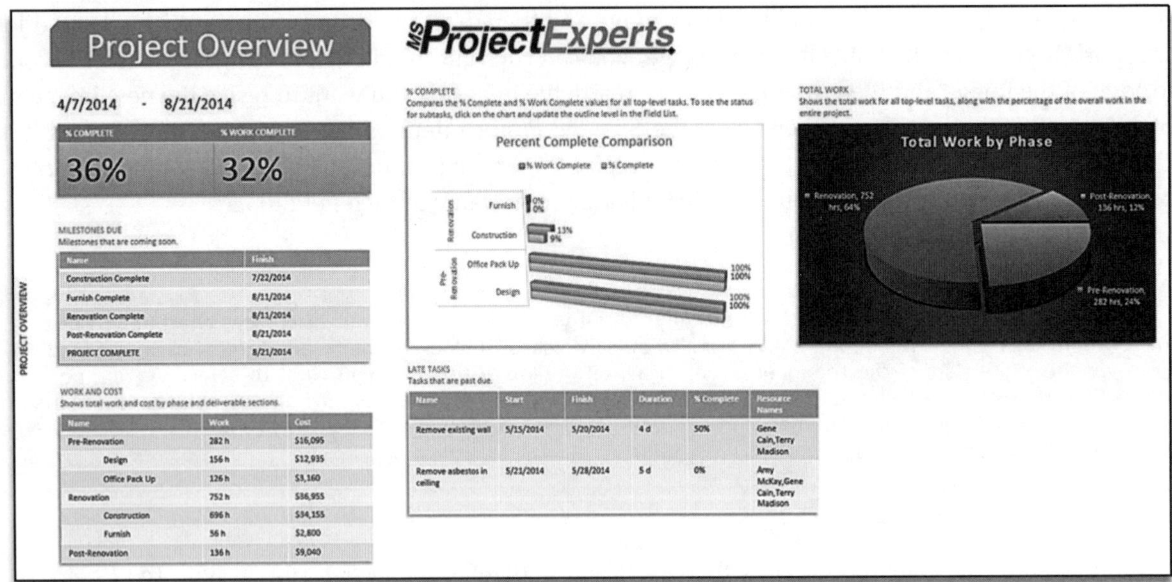

Figure 11 - 54: Final version of the Project Overview report

Notice in Figure 11 - 54 that this new version of the *Project Overview* report includes the following changes:

- At the top of the report, I removed the original *Text Box* title of the report, replaced it with a *Snip Same Side Corner Rectangle* shape, and added the *Project Overview* text as the title.
- I inserted and resized an image file of our company logo at the top of the report.
- I changed the *Font* color to *Black* for the *Start Date* and *Finish Date* fields below the title of the report.
- I added the *% Work Complete* field to the table in the upper left corner of the report and applied the *Themed Style 1 – Accent 1* formatting to the table. In addition, I resized the *Width* value for each column to *2.2 inches.*
- I resized the *% Complete* chart to match the size of the *Total Work* chart.
- I formatted the *Milestones Due* table to display level 2 milestone tasks.
- I added a new *Work and Cost* table in the lower left corner of the report. This table shows the total *Work* and *Cost* by level 1 and level 2 summary tasks (the phases and deliverables in the project).
- I added a title and description to the new *Work and Cost* table, using the same text formatting as in the default tables in the report.
- I added the *% Work Complete* field to the *% Complete* chart, changed the title and layout of the chart, and then formatted the chart to show level 1 and level 2 summary tasks (the phases and deliverables in the project).
- I added a new *Total Work* 3-D pie chart to the report, which shows the total *Work* by only level 1 summary tasks (the phases in the project).
- I added a title and description to the new *Total Work* pie chart, using the same text formatting as in the default tables in the report.
- I applied the same formatting to *Milestones Due, Work and Cost,* and *Late Tasks* tables.
- I rearranged the objects to create a visually pleasing report.

Creating a New Report

In addition to the default reports included in Project 2013, you may want to create new reports to meet your organization's reporting needs. To create a new report, complete the following steps:

1. Click the *Report* tab to display the *Report* ribbon.
2. In the *View Reports* section of the *Report* ribbon, click the *New Report* pick list button to display the *New Report* pick list shown in Figure 11 - 55. Notice that the software offers you four types of reports: a blank report, a report containing a chart, a report containing a table, and a comparison report containing two charts.

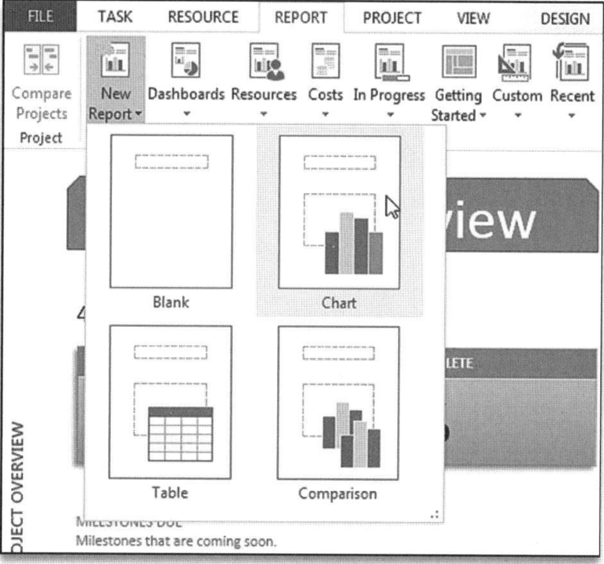

Figure 11 - 55: New Report pick list

Information: To create a new report, you can also click any other pick list button in the *View Reports* section of the *Report* ribbon and then select the *More Reports* item at the bottom of the pick list. The software displays the *Reports* dialog shown previously in Figure 11 - 4. In the *Reports* dialog, click the *New Report* tab to display the same four reports offered on the *New Report* pick list shown previously in Figure 11 - 55.

3. Select one of the available report types on the *New Report* pick list. The software displays the *Report Name* dialog shown in Figure 11 - 56.

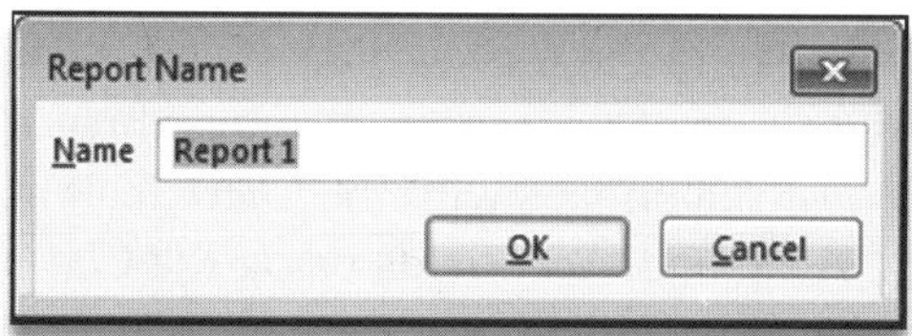

Figure 11 - 56: Report Name dialog

4. Enter a name for your report in the *Report Name* dialog and then click the *OK* button. Project 2013 creates a new report, ready for editing.

When you create a blank report, the software creates the new report similar to the one shown in Figure 11 - 57. Notice that the new report contains only a single *Text Box* shape that displays the name of the report. To set up the new *Blank* report, you must manually add and format all of the required reporting elements, such as charts, tables, shapes, and text boxes. You can manually add each of these elements using the buttons in the *Insert* section of the *Design* ribbon with the *Report Tools* applied, or you can copy and paste these elements from existing reports.

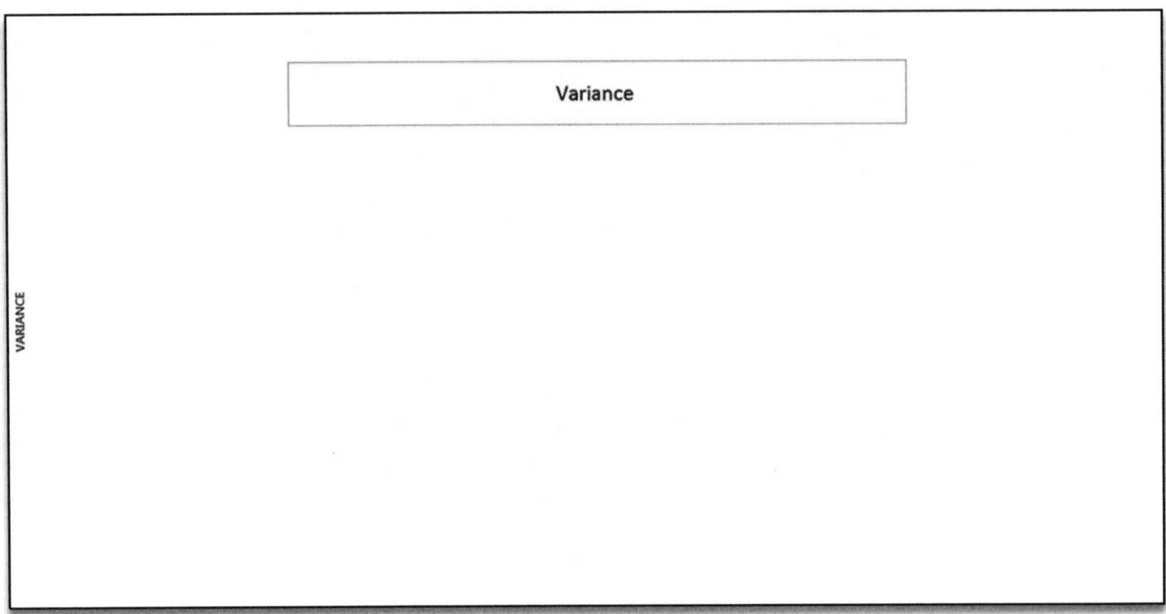

Figure 11 - 57: New blank report

When you create a new *Chart* report, Project 2013 creates the new report similar to the one shown in Figure 11 - 58. As I documented previously in the *Customizing a Chart* section of this module, the software displays the *Field List* sidepane on the right side of the report, displays three formatting buttons to the right of the chart, and displays the *Design* and *Format* ribbon tabs with the *Chart Tools* applied. By default, the chart displays data from the *Actual Work, Remaining Work,* and *Work* fields using the *Clustered Column* chart type. The software also applies the *Active Tasks* filter and sets the *Outline Level* field to *Level 1* in the *Field List* sidepane. To set up the new *Chart* report, you may need to edit the chart, and then you must manually add and format all of the required reporting elements, such as charts, tables, shapes, and text boxes.

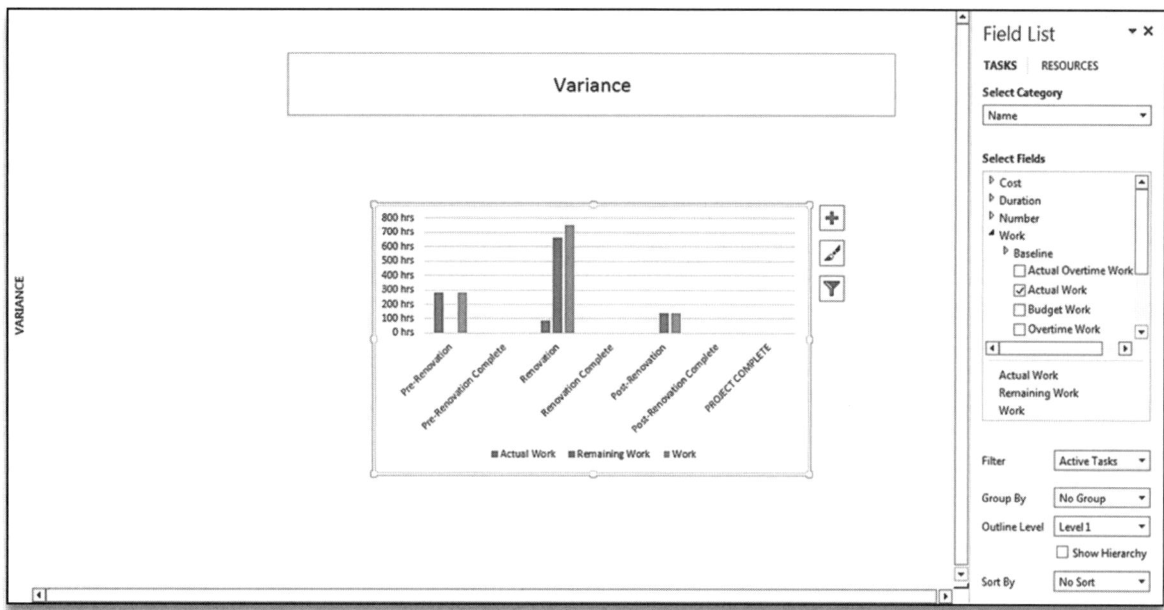

Figure 11 - 58: New Chart report

When you create a new *Table* report, Project 2013 creates a new report similar to the one shown in Figure 11 - 59. As I documented previously in the *Customizing a Table* section of this module, the software displays the *Field List* sidepane on the right side of the report and displays the *Design* and *Layout* ribbon tabs with the *Table Tools* applied. By default, the table displays a single row of data from the *Name, Start, Finish,* and *% Complete* fields with the *Medium Style 2 – Accent 1* style applied to the table. The software also applies the *All Tasks* filter and sets the *Outline Level* field to *Project Summary* in the *Field List* sidepane. To set up the new *Table* report, you may need to edit the table, and then you must manually add and format all of the required reporting elements, such as charts, tables, shapes, and text boxes.

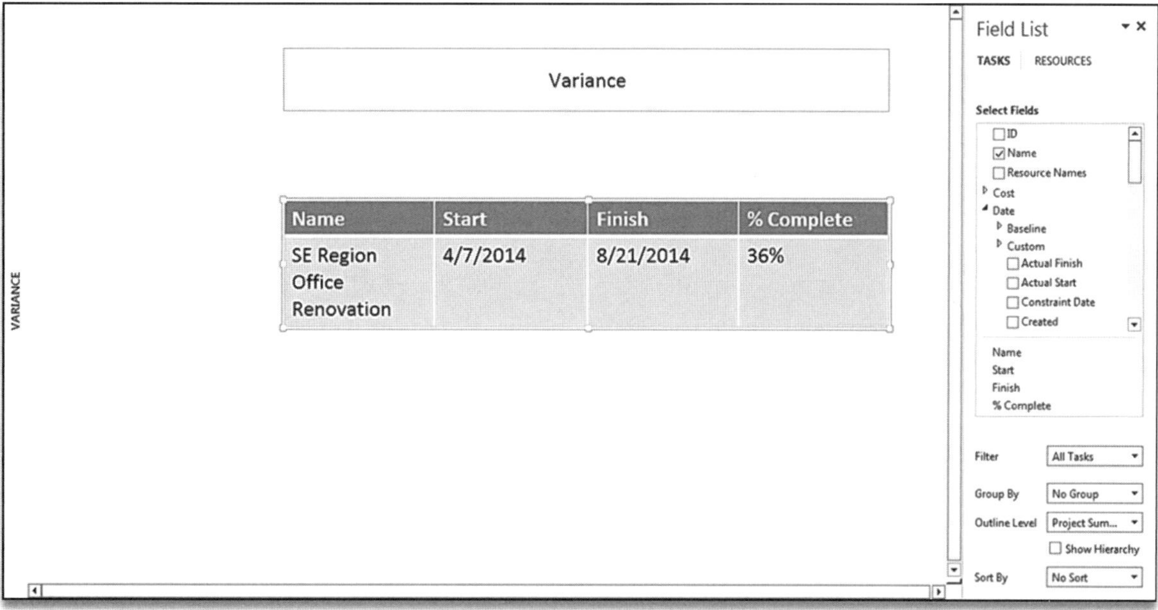

Figure 11 - 59: New Table report

When you create a new *Comparison* report, Project 2013 creates a new report containing two charts, similar to the one shown in Figure 11 - 60. As I documented previously in the *Customizing a Chart* section of this module, the software displays the *Field List* sidepane on the right side of the report, displays three formatting buttons to the right of the first chart, and displays the *Design* and *Format* ribbon tabs with the *Chart Tools* applied. By default, each chart displays data from the *Actual Work, Remaining Work,* and *Work* fields using the *Clustered Column* chart type. For each chart, the software also applies the *Active Tasks* filter and sets the *Outline Level* field to *Level 1* in the *Field List* sidepane. To set up the new *Comparison* report, you may need to edit the chart, and then you may need to manually add and format additional reporting elements, such as charts, tables, shapes, and text boxes.

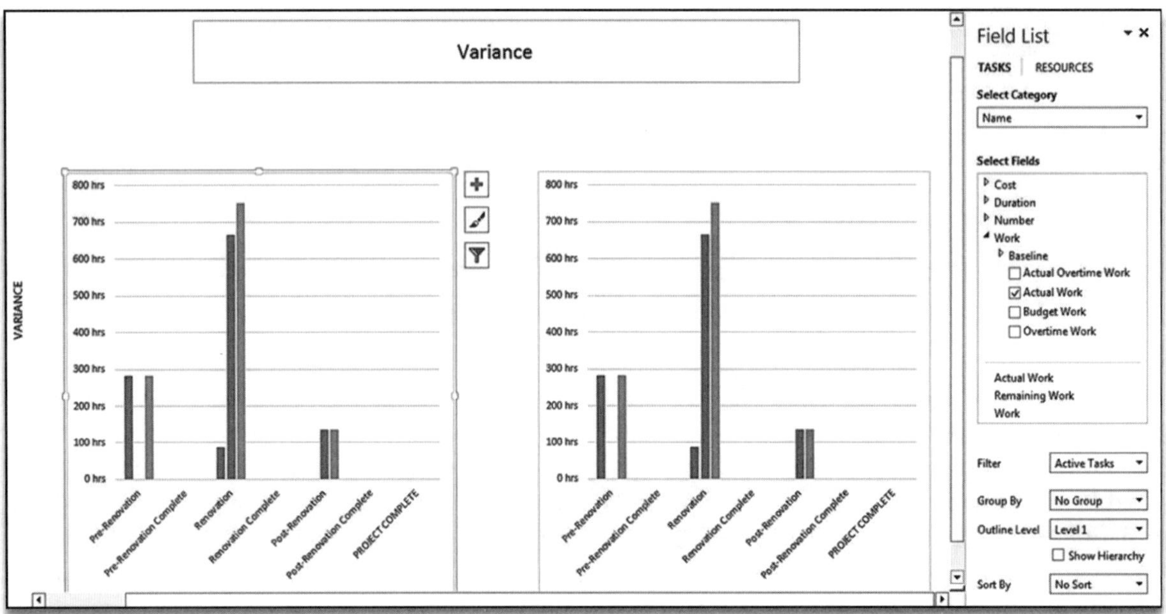

Figure 11 - 60: New Comparison report

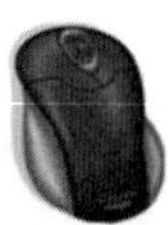

Hands On Exercise

Exercise 11 - 7

Create a new comparison report in Project 2013.

1. Return to the **Using Reports 2013.mpp** sample file, if necessary.
2. Click the *Report* tab to display the *Report* ribbon.
3. In the *View Reports* section of the *Report* ribbon, click the *New Report* pick list button and select the *Comparison* report.
4. In the *Report Name* dialog, enter *Overall Project Variance* in the *Name* field, and then click the *OK* button.

5. With the left-most chart selected, do each of the following in the *Field List* sidepane:
   - **Deselect** the *Actual Work, Remaining Work,* and *Work* fields and then **select** the *Work Variance* field in the *Select Fields* section of the sidepane.
   - Click the *Filter* pick list and select the *Summary Tasks* filter.
6. Click the second *Design* tab to display the *Design* ribbon with the *Chart Tools* applied.
7. In the *Type* section of the *Design* ribbon, click the *Change Chart Type* button.
8. Select the *3-D Clustered Column* item at the top of the dialog and then click the *OK* button.
9. Select the second chart and then do each of the following in the *Field List* sidepane:
   - **Deselect** the *Actual Work, Remaining Work,* and *Work* fields.
   - Expand the *Cost* section and then **select** the *Cost Variance* field.
   - Click the *Filter* pick list and select the *Summary Tasks* filter.
10. In the *Type* section of the *Design* ribbon, click the *Change Chart Type* button.
11. Select the *3-D Clustered Column* item at the top of the dialog and then click the *OK* button.
12. Click anywhere outside of the selected chart in the white part of the new report.
13. In the *Insert* section of the *Design* ribbon, click the *Chart* button.
14. In the *Insert Chart* dialog, select the *3-D Clustered Column* item at the top of the dialog and then click the *OK* button.
15. Do the following in the *Field List* sidepane:
   - **Deselect** the *Actual Work, Remaining Work,* and *Work* fields.
   - Expand the *Duration* section and then **select** the *Duration Variance* field.
   - Click the *Filter* pick list and select the *Summary Tasks* filter.
16. Click the *Format* tab to display the *Format* ribbon with the *Chart Tools* applied.
17. In the *Size* section of the *Format* ribbon, set the *Height* value to *5 inches* and set the *Width* value to *4.5 inches*.
18. Close the *Field List* sidepane.
19. Manually drag and drop the three charts so that they display in one row across the report, with the *Work Variance* chart on the left, the *Cost Variance* chart in the middle, and then *Duration Variance* Chart on the right.
20. Save but **do not** close the **Using Reports 2013.mpp** sample file.

Exercise 11 - 8

Add a table to the comparison report in Project 2013.

1. Click the *Design* tab to display the *Design* ribbon with the *Report Tools* applied.
2. In the *Insert* section of the *Design* ribbon, click the *Table* button.

3. In the *Field List* sidepane, do each of the following:
    - **Deselect** the *Finish, Start,* and *% Complete* checkboxes.
    - Collapse the *Date* section and then expand the *Cost, Duration,* and *Work* sections.
    - In the relevant sections, **select** the *Start Variance, Finish Variance, Duration Variance, Work Variance,* and *Cost Variance* fields.
    - Click the *Filter* pick list and select the *Summary Tasks* filter.
    - Click the *Outline Level* pick list and select the *Level 2* item.
    - Select the *Show Hierarchy* checkbox.

Information: You find the *Start Variance* and *Finish Variance* fields in the *Duration* section of the *Field List* sidepane. The software includes these two fields in the *Duration* section, rather than the *Date* section, because they display variance as a time span (duration) measured by default in days.

4. Close the *Field List* sidepane, but leave the entire table selected.
5. Click the *Task* tab to display the *Task* ribbon.
6. In the *Font* section of the *Task* ribbon, click the *Font Size* pick list and select the *10 point* size.
7. Click and drag the column headers of the *Start Variance, Finish Variance, Duration Variance, Work Variance,* and *Cost Variance* columns to select those five columns.
8. Click the *Layout* tab to display the *Layout* ribbon with the *Table Tools* applied.
9. In the *Cell Size* section of the *Layout* ribbon, set the *Width* value to *1.6 inches.*
10. Scroll down far enough so that you can see the blank area below the three charts in your *Overall Project Variance* report.
11. Click and hold anywhere on the edge of the table and then drag the table into the blank area immediately below the three charts.
12. If you want, you may optionally add title and description text fields above or below each of the three charts and the table in the new *Overall Project Variance* report.
13. Save but **do not** close the **Using Reports 2013.mpp** sample file.

Formatting a New Report

In addition to the capabilities of formatting charts, tables, and shapes, Project 2013 also allows you to format the report itself using the tools in the *Themes* section of the *Design* ribbon with the *Report Tools* applied. Click the *Themes* pick list button to see a gallery of *Custom* and *Office* themes for your report, along with options to browse for additional themes or to save the current theme as a new custom theme. By default, the software applies the *Office* theme to all new reports. Figure 11 - 61 shows the *Themes* gallery with the *Office* theme selected. When you select an alternate theme for your report, the software applies the new theme colors and text styles to all of the elements in your report, including charts, tables, and shapes.

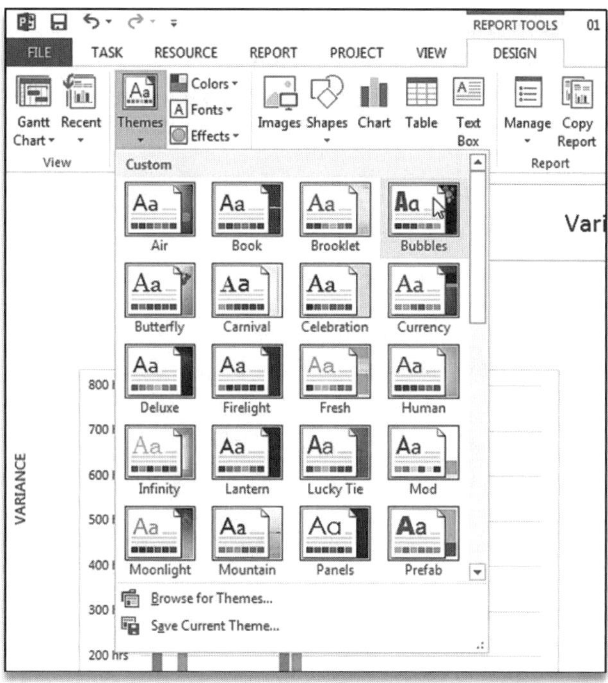

Figure 11 - 61: Themes gallery

Click the *Colors* pick list button to see a gallery of *Custom* and *Office* theme colors for your report, along with the option to create your own set of theme colors. By default, the software applies the *Office* theme to all new reports. Figure 11 - 62 show the *Colors* gallery with the *Bubbles* theme colors selected. When you select an alternate set of theme colors on the *Colors* pick list, Project 2013 changes the colors used in the current theme, but the software does not change the fonts or the effects used in the theme.

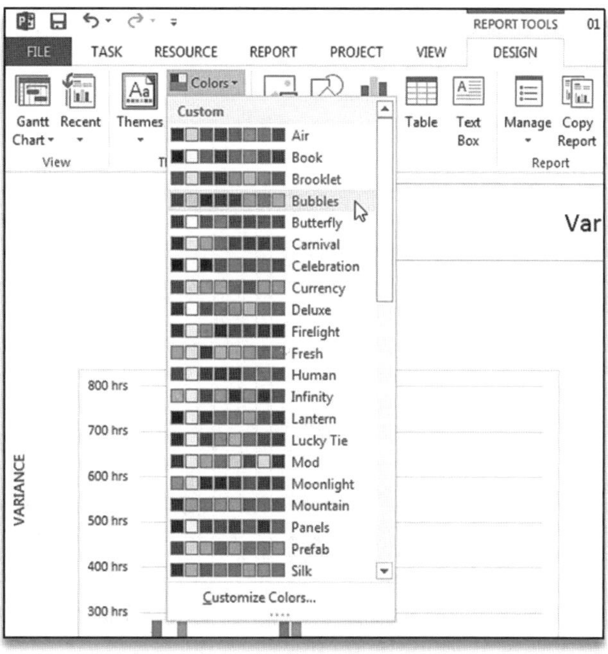

Figure 11 - 62: Colors gallery

If you select the *Customize Colors* item at the bottom of the *Colors* pick list, the software displays the *Create New Theme Colors* dialog shown in Figure 11 - 63. Create your new set of theme colors using the options in the *Theme colors* section of the dialog and view the results in the *Sample* section. To reset the theme colors to their original setting, click the *Reset* button. When finished, enter a name for your new set of theme colors in the *Name* field and then click the *Save* button.

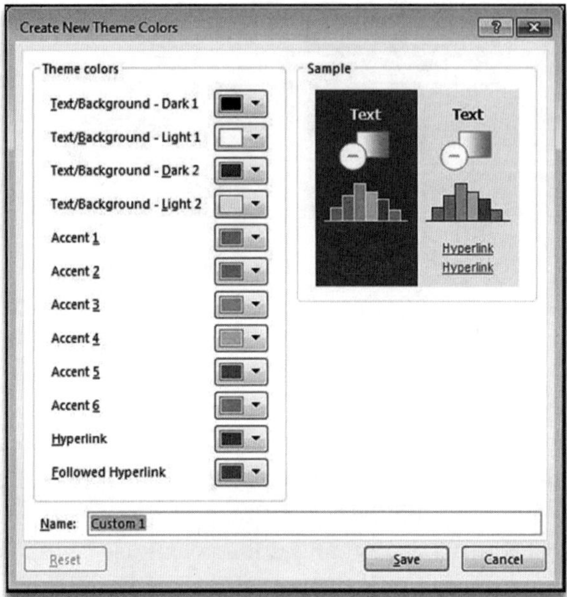

Figure 11 - 63: Create New Theme Colors dialog

Information: When you create a new set of theme colors in Project 2013, the software makes the color theme available to all of the other software applications in the Office 2013 suite of tools.

Click the *Fonts* pick list button to see a gallery of *Custom* and *Office* theme fonts for your report, along with the option to create your own font theme. By default, the software applies the *Office* font to all new reports. Figure 11 - 64 shows the *Font* gallery with the *Bubbles* theme fonts selected. When you select an alternate set of theme fonts on the *Fonts* pick list, Project 2013 changes only the fonts used in the current theme, but the software does not change the colors or the effects used in the theme.

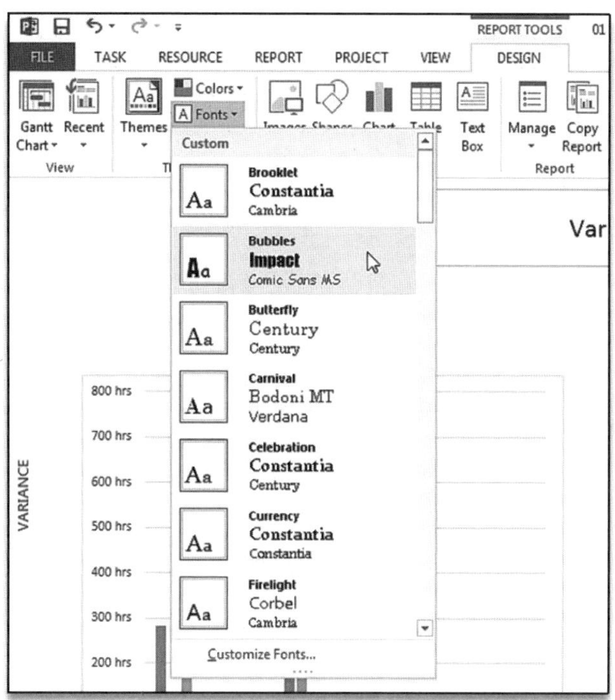

Figure 11 - 64: Font gallery

If you select the *Customize Fonts* item at the bottom of the *Fonts* pick list, the software displays the *Create New Theme Fonts* dialog shown in Figure 11 - 65. Create your new set of theme fonts by selecting the fonts you want to use in the *Heading font* and *Body font* fields. When finished, enter a name for your new set of theme fonts in the *Name* field and then click the *Save* button.

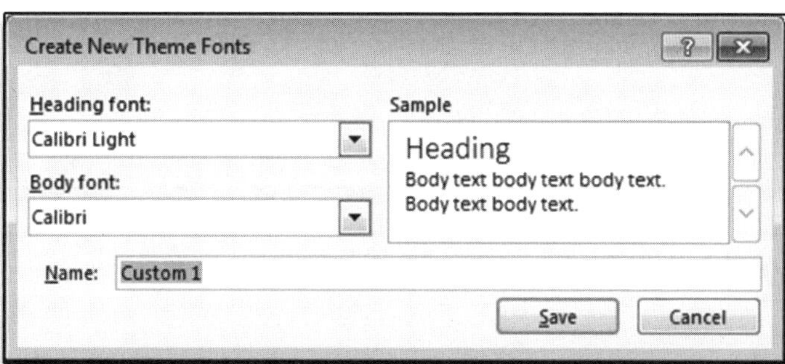

Figure 11 - 65: Create New Theme Fonts dialog

Information: When you create a new set of theme fonts in Project 2013, the software makes the font theme available to all of the other software applications in the Office 2013 suite of tools.

Click the *Effects* pick list to see a gallery of *Custom* and *Office* theme effects for your report. Keep in mind that an **effect** is a set of visual attributes that you can apply to the chart elements in your report. By default, the software applies the *Office* font to all new reports. Figure 11 - 66 shows the *Effects* gallery with the *Bubbles* effects selected. When you select an alternate set of theme effects on the *Effects* pick list, Project 2013 changes only the effects used in the current theme, but the software does not change the colors or the fonts used in the theme.

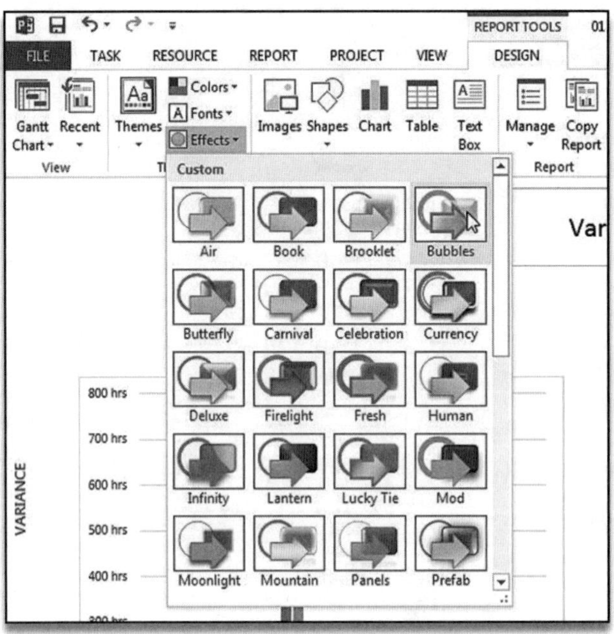

Figure 11 - 66: Effects gallery

If you select a set of theme colors or create a new custom set of theme colors, you select a set of theme fonts or create a new set of theme fonts, and/or you apply an effect, the software allows you to save these custom settings as a new custom theme. When you click the *Themes* pick list and select the *Save Current Theme* item at the bottom of the pick list, the software displays the *Save Current Theme* dialog shown in Figure 11 - 67. Enter a name for the new theme in the *File name* field and then click the *Save* button.

Information: When you create a new theme in Project 2013, the software makes the theme available to all of the other software applications in the Office 2013 suite of tools.

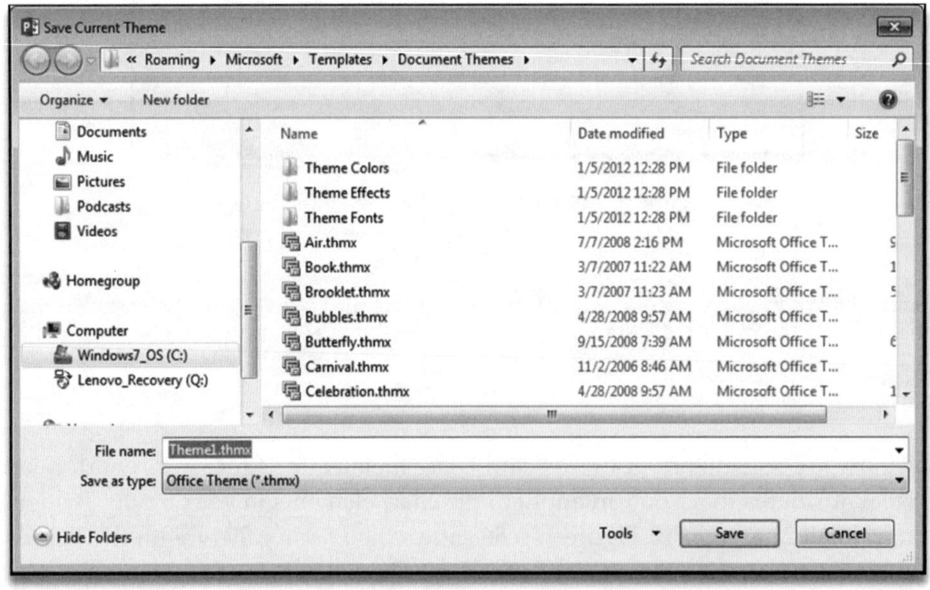

Figure 11 - 67: Save Current Theme dialog

Figure 11 - 68 shows my completed *Variance* report, created as a new *Comparison* report. In the *Work Variance* chart, I selected the *Baseline Work, Work,* and *Work Variance* fields, applied the *3-D Clustered Column* chart type, and then added the *Data Labels* chart element to the *Work Variance* bars. In the *Cost Variance* chart, I selected the *Baseline Cost, Cost,* and *Cost Variance* fields, applied the *3-D Clustered Column* chart type, and then added the *Data Labels* chart element to the *Cost Variance* bars. I added the *Date and Duration Variance* table, selected the *Start Variance, Finish Variance,* and *Duration Variance* fields, and displayed level 1 and level 2 summary tasks (the phases and deliverables in the project.) Notice that I also added a title and a description to both charts and to the table. After creating this new report, I applied the *Metropolitan* theme to the report.

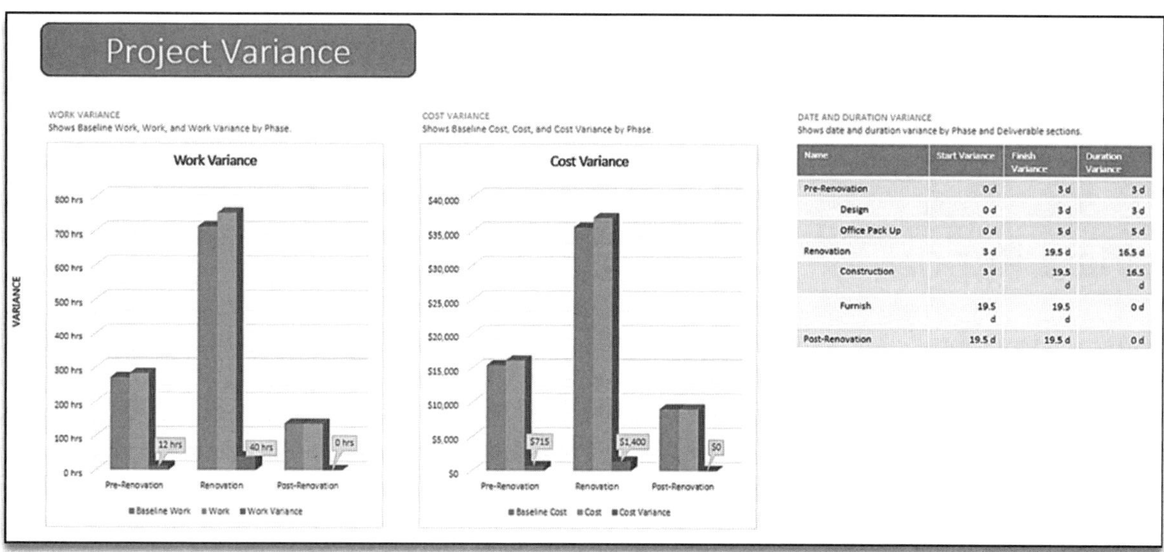

Name	Start Variance	Finish Variance	Duration Variance
Pre-Renovation	0 d	3 d	3 d
Design	0 d	3 d	3 d
Office Pack Up	0 d	5 d	5 d
Renovation	3 d	19.5 d	16.5 d
Construction	3 d	19.5 d	16.5 d
Furnish	19.5 d	19.5 d	0 d
Post-Renovation	19.5 d	19.5 d	0 d

Figure 11 - 68: Variance report

Hands On Exercise

Exercise 11 - 9

Add a custom title and then format the new report in Project 2013.

1. Return to the **Using Reports 2013.mpp** sample file, if necessary.
2. Click anywhere on the edge of the *Overall Project Variance* title field at the top of the report to select the entire field, and then press the **Delete** key on your computer keyboard.
3. Click the *Design* tab to display the *Design* ribbon with the *Report Tools* applied, if necessary.
4. In the *Insert* section of the *Design* ribbon, click the *Shape* pick list button and select the *Rounded Rectangle* shape in the *Rectangles* section of the pick list.
5. Click and hold your mouse button, and then trace the outline of a new shape in the blank area above the three charts.

6. Double-click anywhere in the new shape to display the *Format* ribbon with the *Drawing Tools* applied.
7. In the *Size* section of the *Format* ribbon, set the *Height* value to *1 inch* and set the *Width* value to *5 inches*.
8. With the new shape still selected, type the words *Overall Project Variance* in the shape.
9. Click the *Design* tab to display the *Design* ribbon with the *Report Tools* applied.
10. In the *Themes* section of the *Design* ribbon, click the *Themes* pick list button and select the *Celebration* theme in the *Custom* section of the pick list.
11. Select the *Overall Project Variance* text in the new shape, right-click in the selected text, and then select the Bold formatting button on the shortcut menu.
12. Save but **do not** close the **Using Reports 2013.mpp** sample file.

Printing a Report

To prepare a report for printing, click the *Design* tab to display the *Design* ribbon with the *Report Tools* applied. In the *Page* Setup section of the *Design* ribbon, click the *Margins* pick list button. The *Margins* pick list displays three default margins settings: *Normal, Wide,* and *Narrow,* along with a *Custom Margins* option to apply custom margins you specified previously. Select one of the three default margins settings. To specify your own custom margins settings, click the *Custom Margins* item at the bottom of the *Margins* pick list. The software displays the *Page Setup* dialog for the selected report, with the *Margins* tab selected, as shown in Figure 11 - 69. On the *Margins* page of the *Page Setup* dialog, specify your custom margins settings in the *Top, Left, Right,* and *Bottom* fields, and then click the *OK* button when finished.

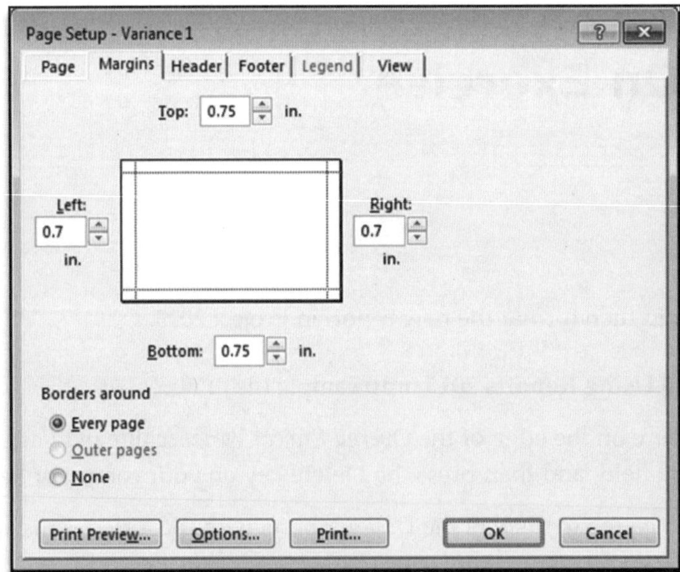

Figure 11 - 69: Page Setup dialog for a report

Click the *Orientation* pick list button to specify the print orientation. The *Orientation* pick list offers two standard orientation options: *Portrait* and *Landscape*. Select your orientation setting on this pick list. Click the *Size* pick list button and then select one of the available options for paper size.

When you finish setting up the report for printing, click the *Page Breaks* button. Project 2013 displays dashed lines in the report to show the current printable area of the report.

To print your report, click the *File* tab and then click the *Print* tab in the *Backstage*. The software displays a print preview of your report, and allows you to further customize the printing of your report. For example, if your report is slightly too large to fit on one page, click the *Page Setup* link at the bottom of the *Print* page. In the *Page Setup* dialog, click the *Page* tab, select the *Fit to 1 pages wide by 1 tall* option, and then click the *OK* button. Click the *Print* button to print the report.

Sharing a Report with another Office Application

Another powerful reporting feature in Project 2013 allows you to easily share your reports with another application in the Office family of tools, such as with PowerPoint 2013. To share your report with another application, display the report you want to share, and then click the *Design* tab to display the *Design* ribbon with the *Report Tools* applied. In the *Report* section of the *Design* ribbon, click the *Copy Report* button. The software copies the entire report to the Windows Clipboard, ready for you to paste into another Office application.

After you launch a Office application, set up the document into which you want to paste the report data. For example, in PowerPoint 2013, you might want to insert a new *Blank* slide in your presentation. When ready, click the *Paste* button in the *Clipboard* section of the *Home* ribbon to paste the report data into your selected Office application. When you paste the report, the software leaves every object selected in the report, allowing you to see every individual element of the report. For example, Figure 11 - 70 shows the *Burndown* report pasted into a slide in PowerPoint 2013. Notice that you can clearly see every element selected in the report, as evidenced by the outline and "grab handles" around each of the report elements.

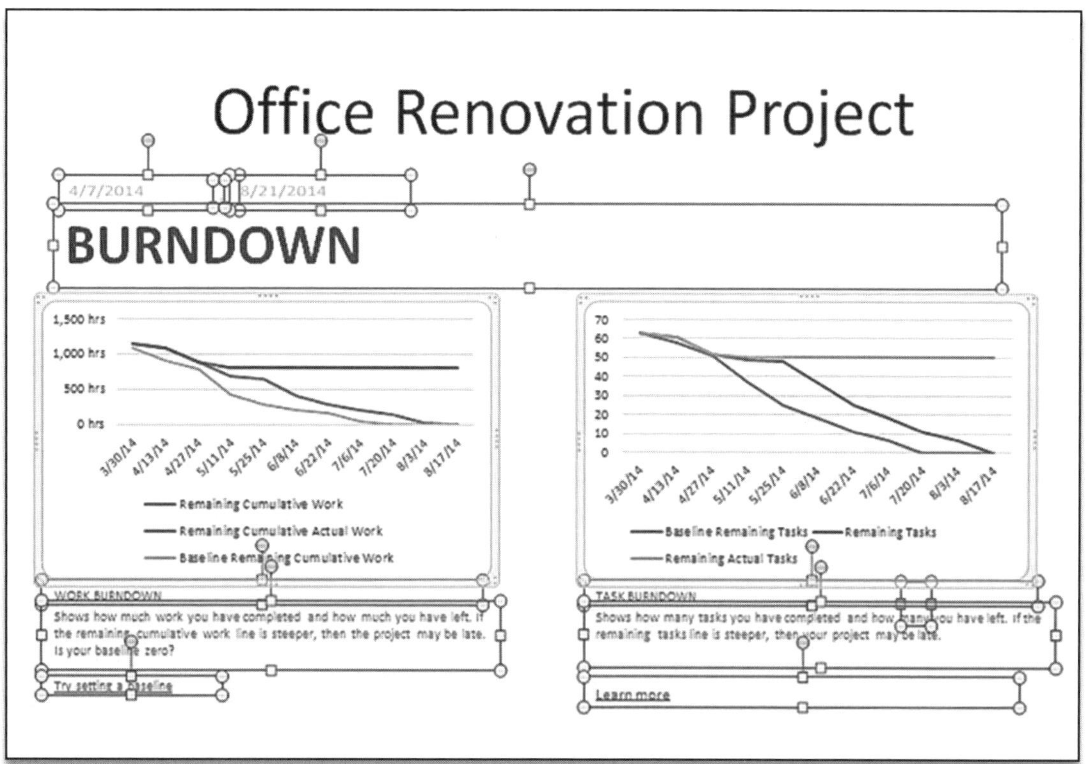

Figure 11 - 70: Burndown report pasted into a PowerPoint slide

Warning: When you paste a report containing multiple tables and/or charts into PowerPoint, the pasted report elements may extend beyond the edges of the slide. In this situation, leave every element selected and then shrink the report elements by completing the following steps:

1. Click the *Format* tab to display the *Format* ribbon with the *Picture Tools* applied.
2. In the lower right corner of the *Size* section of the *Format* ribbon, click the *Size and Position* task pane launcher button (the little arrow button).
3. In the *Format Picture* sidepane on the right side of the PowerPoint 2013 window, select the *Lock aspect ratio* checkbox.
4. In the *Format Picture* sidepane, change the percentage values shown in the *Scale Height* and *Scale Width* fields until the report data fits properly in the slide.
5. Select and move the report elements around in the slide to arrange the elements as needed.

Warning: When you paste a large report containing multiple tables and charts into a Word document, the software stacks the report elements on top of each other even if you set the page orientation to *Landscape* and set the margins to *Narrow* in the document. In response, you must use the same set of steps shown in the preceding *Warning* note to shrink the report elements as a group, and then manually move each report element individually in the document to rearrange the report. Because of the sheer amount of work you must do to rearrange the report elements manually, I do not recommend you paste Project 2013 report data into a Word document.

After pasting the report data into the Office application, you can now use the full graphical image editing capabilities of the tool. For example, in the *Burndown* report, use the **Control** key on your computer keyboard to select the *Work Burndown* chart, along with its title and description. With all three elements selected, click the *Format* tab to display the *Format* ribbon with the *Drawing Tools* applied. In the *Arrange* section of the *Format* ribbon, click the *Group* pick list button and then select the *Group* item on the pick list to group all three elements together to form a single element.

Information: To rapidly select a number of report elements simultaneously, "lasso" the elements by clicking and holding your mouse button to trace an imaginary rectangle around all of the elements you want to select.

Hands On Exercise

Exercise 11 - 10

Share a report from Project 2013 with another Office application.

1. Return to the **Using Reports 2013.mpp** sample file, if necessary.
2. Click the *Report* tab to display the *Report* ribbon.

3. In the *View Reports* section of the *Report* ribbon, click the *Dashboards* pick list button and select the *Burndown* item in the pick list.
4. In the *Report* section of the *Report* ribbon, click the *Copy Report* button.
5. Launch PowerPoint 2013 (or any earlier version of the software if you do not have the 2013 version of the software).
6. In the *Slides* section of the *Home* ribbon in PowerPoint, click the *New Slide* pick list and select the *Title Only* layout for the new slide.
7. Click anywhere in the title of the new slide and enter *Using Reports 2013* as the title.
8. Click anywhere in the blank part of the slide outside of the title field.
9. In the *Clipboard* section of the *Home* ribbon, click the *Paste* button.

Warning: Remember that when you paste a large report containing multiple tables and charts into PowerPoint, the pasted report elements may extend beyond the edges of the slide. To resolve this problem, you must reduce the size of the pasted image.

10. In PowerPoint, click the *Format* tab to display the *Format* ribbon with the *Picture Tools* applied.
11. In the *Size* section of the *Format* ribbon, click the *Size and Position Task Pane Launcher* button (the little arrow in the lower right corner of the section).
12. In the *Format Picture* sidepane on the right side of the PowerPoint 2013 window, select the *Lock aspect ratio* checkbox.
13. In the *Format Picture* sidepane, set the values in the *Scale Height* and *Scale Width* fields to *75%*.
14. Close the *Format Picture* sidepane.

Information: If you have PowerPoint 2010, click the *Size and Position Dialog Launcher* button (little arrow in the lower right corner) in the *Size* section of the *Format* ribbon. In the *Format Picture* dialog, select the *Lock aspect ratio* checkbox, set the values in the *Height* and *Width* fields to *75%*, and then click the *OK* button.

15. With the pasted objects still selected, use the **Down-Arrow** and **Right-Arrow** keys on your computer keyboard to center the pasted image horizontally and vertically as needed.
16. Save the PowerPoint presentation as **Office Renovation Project 2013.pptx** and then close the presentation.
17. Exit your PowerPoint application and return to your Project 2013 application window.

Managing Reports

Project 2013 allows you to manage your default and custom reports several ways, including renaming, copying, and deleting reports. To rename a report, display the report you want to rename and then click the *Design* tab to display the *Design* ribbon with the *Report Tools* applied. In the *Report* section of the *Design* ribbon, click the *Manage* pick list button and select the *Rename* item in the pick list. The software displays the *Rename* dialog shown in Figure 11 - 71. Enter the new name of the report in the dialog and then click the *OK* button to rename the report. The software displays the new name of the report vertically along the left side of the report pane.

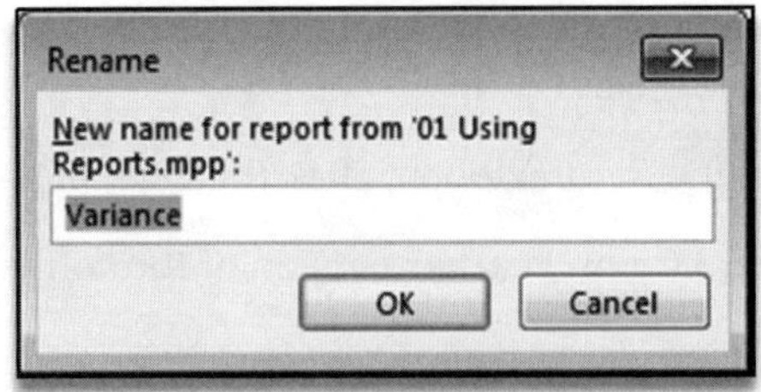

Figure 11 - 71: Rename dialog

To copy or delete a report, click the *Manage* pick list button and then select the *Organizer* item on the pick list. The software displays the *Organizer* dialog with the *Reports* tab selected, as shown in Figure 11 - 72. The *Organizer* dialog shows you the list of all default and custom reports in both the Global.mpt file and in the current project.

Warning: Before you can delete a report using the *Organizer* dialog, you must display a view such as the *Gantt Chart* view, or display any report other than the report you want to delete. This is because Project 2013 prevents you from deleting the report currently displayed.

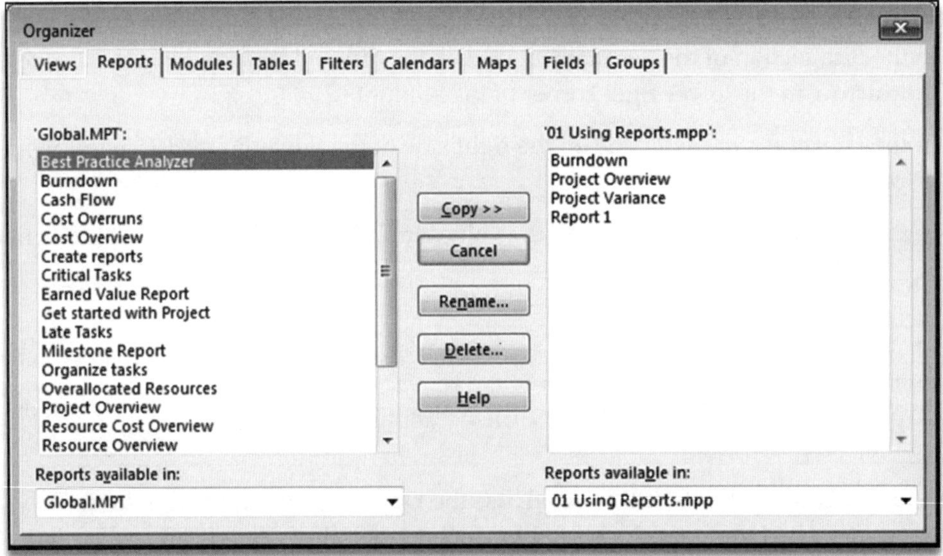

Figure 11 - 72: Organizer dialog

To copy a report from one file to another file, such as from the active project to the Global.mpt file, select the report in the list on the right side of the dialog and then click the *Copy* button. To delete a report, select the report and then click the *Delete* button. Project 2013 displays the confirmation dialog shown in Figure 11 - 73. In the confirmation dialog, click the *Yes* button to complete the deletion of the selected report. Click the *Close* button to close the *Organizer* dialog.

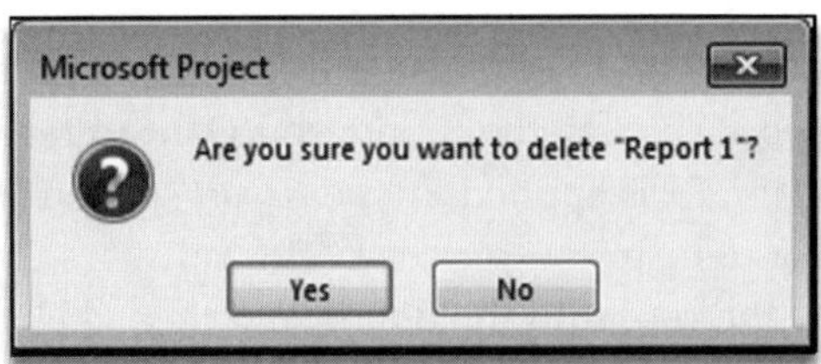

Figure 11 - 73: Confirmation dialog

Hands On Exercise

Exercise 11 - 11

Rename a report and delete a report in Project 2013.

1. Return to the **Using Reports 2013.mpp** sample file, if necessary.

2. Click the *Report* tab to display the *Report* ribbon.

3. In the *View Reports* section of the *Report* ribbon, click the *Custom* pick list button and select the *Overall Project Variance* report.

4. Click the *Design* tab to display the *Design* ribbon with the *Report Tools* applied, if necessary.

5. In the *Report* section of the *Design* ribbon, click the *Manage* pick list button and select the *Rename Report* item.

6. In the *Rename* dialog, change the name of the report to *Project Variance* in the *Name* field and then click the *OK* button.

Notice on the far left side of the report that Project 2013 displays the new name of the report.

7. In the *Report* section of the *Design* ribbon, click the *Manage* pick list button and select the *Organizer* item.

8. In the *Organizer* dialog, select the *Report 1* item in the list of reports on the right side of the dialog, and then click the *Delete* button.

9. In the confirmation dialog, click the *Yes* button to delete the unneeded report.

Information: My goal for you in completing Exercise 11 - 10 and Exercise 11 - 11 is to create a project variance report that you can use with your real projects. If you believe you can use the *Project Variance* report in your daily work with Project 2013, complete the next step in this Hands On Exercise. Completing the next step copies the new custom report to your Global.mpt file, making the new report available to every current and future project you manage. If you do not want to keep the custom *Project Variance* report, skip the next step in this Hands On Exercise.

10. In the list of reports on the right side of the dialog, select the *Project Variance* report, and then click the *Copy* button to copy the custom report to your Global.mpt file.

11. Click the *Close* button to close the *Organizer* dialog.

12. Save and close the **Using Reports 2013.mpp** sample file.

Using Visual Reports

Microsoft introduced visual reports as a new feature in Project 2007, and continues to offer improved visual report functionality in Project 2013. Visual reports allow you to see your project data in a *PivotChart* and *PivotTable* in Excel or in a *PivotDiagram* in Visio. The software creates the visual report by building a local OLAP (On Line Analytical Programming) cube directly on your computer's hard drive. The local OLAP cube provides a multidimensional summary of task and resource data in your project.

Information: You can use the Excel visual reports with Excel 2007, 2010, or 2013. To use the Visio visual reports, however, you must have the **Professional** version of Visio 2007, 2010, or 2013. If you use the Standard version of Visio, you do not see the Visio visual report templates at all in the *Visual Reports - Create Report* dialog.

To access visual reports, click the *Report* tab to display the *Report* ribbon. In the *Export* section of the *Report* ribbon, click the *Visual Reports* button. Project 2013 displays the *Visual Reports – Create Report* dialog shown in Figure 11 - 74.

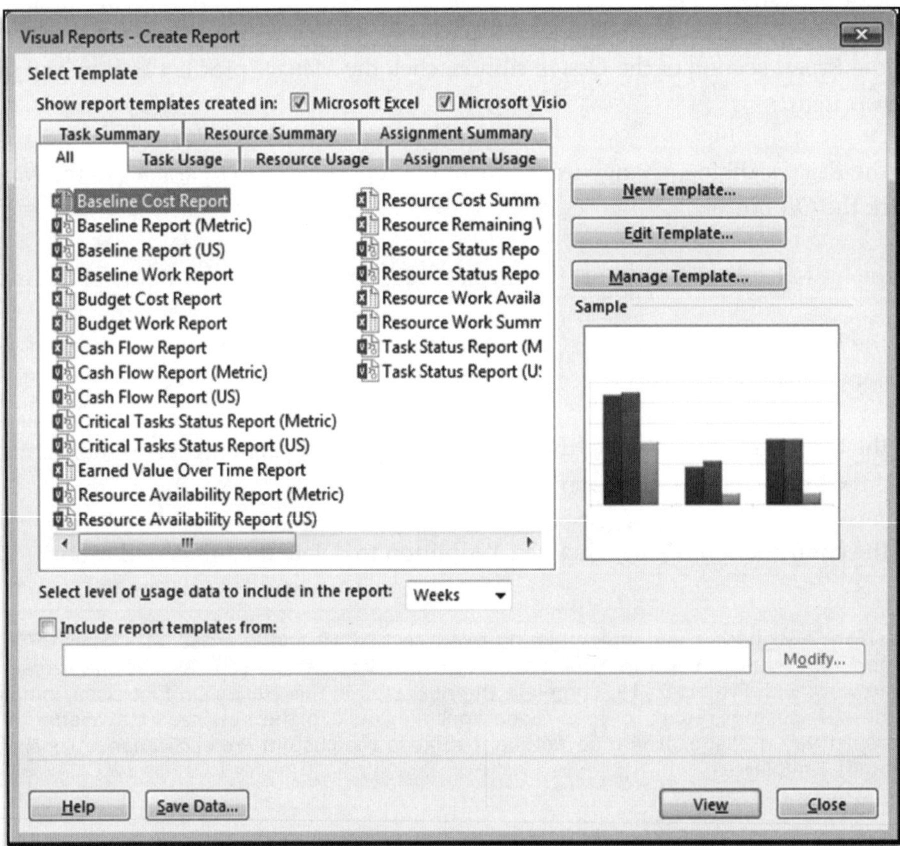

Figure 11 - 74: Visual Reports – Create Report dialog

The *Visual Reports – Create Report* dialog provides you with six categories of default visual reports. The *Task Usage, Resource Usage,* and *Assignment Usage* categories display timephased task, resource, and assignment data, respectively. The *Task Summary, Resource Summary,* and *Assignment Summary* categories display task, resource, and assignment data without timephased data. The next six tables describe the 16 default visual reports.

Information: Project 2013 offers two types of Visio visual reports: *Metric* and *US*. The differences between these two types of visual reports are minor. In the *Metric* visual reports for Visio, the software measures the *Ruler* bar in **millimeters** and the default paper size is **A4** (210 mm x 297 mm). In the *US* visual reports for Visio, the software measures the *Ruler* bar in **inches** and the default paper size is **Letter** (8.5 inches x 11 inches).

Task Summary		
Report Name	**Type**	**Description**
Critical Tasks Status	Visio	Diagram shows *Work, Remaining Work,* and *% Work Complete* for both critical and non-critical tasks at *Outline Level 1,* with a progress bar representing the *% Work Complete* for each summary task.

Table 11 - 1: Task Summary visual reports

Task Usage		
Report Name	**Type**	**Description**
Cash Flow	Excel	Combination column chart/line chart shows *Cost* (columns) and *Cumulative Cost* (line) over time.

Table 11 - 2: Task Usage visual reports

Resource Summary		
Report Name	**Type**	**Description**
Resource Remaining Work	Excel	Stacked column chart shows *Actual Work* and *Remaining Work*. By default, this report does not display any resources; therefore, you must add the *Resources* dimension to the *Axis Fields* drop area to use this report.

Table 11 - 3: Resource Summary visual reports

Resource Usage		
Report Name	**Type**	**Description**
Cash Flow	Visio	Diagram shows *Cost* and *Actual Cost* over time, broken down by resource type (*Work, Material,* and *Cost* resources). Diagram shows an orange triangle symbol when the *Cost* exceeds the *Baseline Cost*.
Resource Availability	Visio	Diagram shows *Work* and *Remaining Availability* for each resource, broken down by resource type (*Work, Material,* and *Cost* resources).
Resource Cost Summary	Excel	2-D pie chart shows project costs, filtered by the *Weekly Calendar* dimension. By default, this report does not display the resource types; therefore, you must add the *Type* dimension to the *Axis Fields* drop area to use this report.
Resource Work Availability	Excel	Column chart shows *Work Availability, Work,* and *Remaining Availability* for all resources over time.
Resource Work Summary	Excel	Column chart shows *Work Availability, Work, Remaining Availability,* and *Actual Work,* filtered by the *Weekly Calendar* dimension. By default, this report does not display any resources; therefore, you must add the *Resources* dimension to the *Axis Fields* drop area to use this report.

Table 11 - 4: Resource Usage visual reports

Assignment Summary		
Report Name	**Type**	**Description**
Resource Status	Visio	Diagram shows *Cost* and *Work* for each resource with color shading in each box representing *% Work Complete*. The shading gets lighter as the *% Work Complete* value nears *100%*, ranging from dark purple shading where the *% Work Complete* value is *0%* to white shading where the *% Work Complete* value is *100%*.
Task Status	Visio	Diagram displays *Cost* and *Work* for all tasks at *Outline Level 1*, and displays an orange progress bar representing *% Work Complete* for each task. Diagram shows a yellow "unhappy face" when *Work* exceeds *Baseline Work*, shows a yellow "neutral face" when *Work* is equal to *Baseline Work*, and shows a "happy face" when *Work* is less than *Baseline Work*.

Table 11 - 5: Assignment Summary visual reports

Assignment Usage		
Report Name	**Type**	**Description**
Baseline Cost	Excel	Column chart shows *Baseline Cost, Cost,* and *Actual Cost.* By default, this report does not display any tasks or resources; therefore, you must add the *Tasks* and/or *Resources* dimensions to the *Axis Fields* drop area to use this report.
Baseline	Visio	Diagram compares *Work* and *Cost* with *Baseline Work* and *Baseline Cost* over time for all tasks at *Outline Level 1.* Displays a red stoplight when *Work* exceeds *Baseline Work.* Displays a yellow flag when *Cost* exceeds *Baseline Cost.*
Baseline Work	Excel	Column chart shows *Baseline Work, Work,* and *Actual Work* for all tasks. By default, this report does not display any tasks; therefore, you must add the *Tasks* dimension to the *Axis Fields* drop area to use this report.
Budget Cost	Excel	Column chart shows *Budget Cost, Baseline Cost, Cost,* and *Actual Cost* over time.
Budget Work	Excel	Column chart shows *Budget Work, Baseline Work, Work,* and *Actual Work* over time.
Earned Value Over Time	Excel	Line chart shows *Earned Value, Planned Value,* and *Actual Cost* over time through the *Status Date* of the project.

Table 11 - 6: Assignment Usage visual reports

Viewing a Visual Report

To view a visual report, complete the following steps:

1. In the *Export* section of the *Reports* ribbon, click the *Visual Reports* button.

2. In the *Visual Reports – Create Report* dialog, select the tab containing the type of visual report you want to view.

3. On the selected report page of the dialog, select a visual report.

4. Click the *Select level of usage data to include in this report* pick list and select the data granularity you want to use in the report, as shown in Figure 11 - 75.

Information: Based on the size of your project, Project 2013 sets a recommended value in the *Select level of usage data to include in this report* pick list. For most projects, the recommended value is *Weeks*. For very large projects, the recommended value might be *Months, Quarters*, or even *Years*. Project 2013 then generates the data in the local OLAP cubes using the granularity you select and then transfers the data to the visual report.

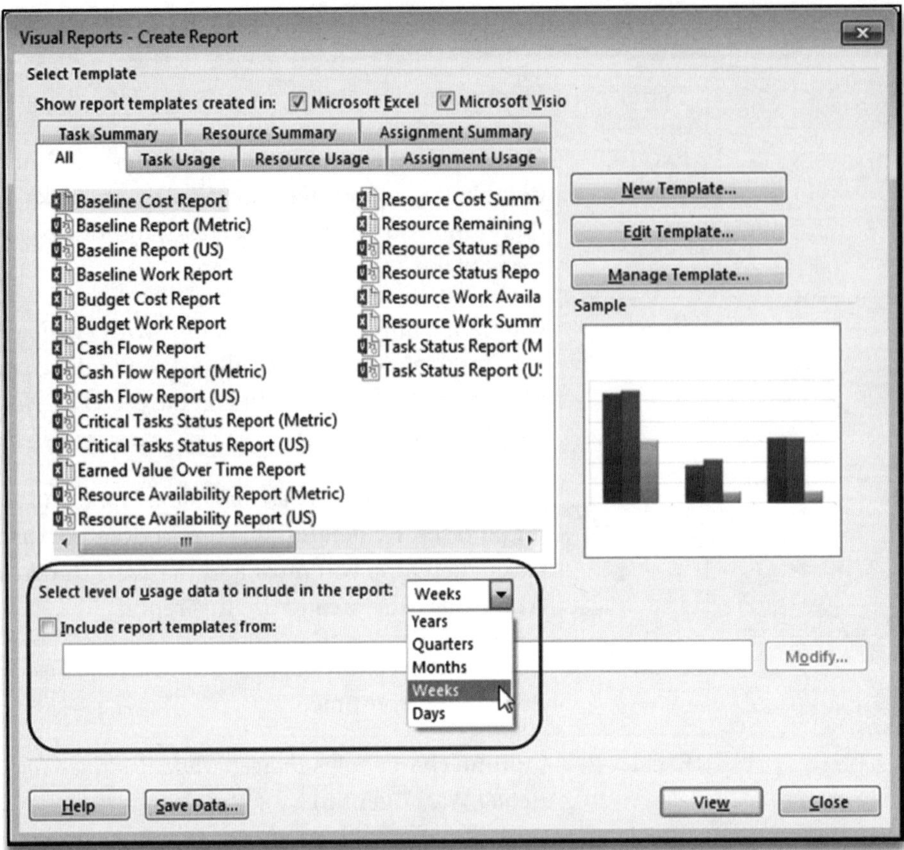

Figure 11 - 75: Visual Reports – Create Report dialog, select the granularity for the Baseline Cost Report

5. If you want to supplement the standard list of task and resource details included with the local OLAP cube, click the *Edit Template* button.

Project 2013 displays the *Visual Reports – Field Picker* dialog shown in Figure 11 - 76. In the *Selected Fields* list on the right side of the dialog, you see the default list of standard detail fields added to the local OLAP cube automatically. This list includes fields like *Cost, Baseline Cost,* and *Actual Cost.* If you want to supplement this list with additional standard fields, select one or more fields in the *Available Fields* list and click the *Add* button.

The *Available Custom Fields* list shows the list of custom fields available for inclusion in the local OLAP cube, and includes any custom fields you created in the project. For example, notice in Figure 11 - 76 that the list includes two custom fields I created in this project: the *Accountable Person Task (dimension)* field and the *Cost Center ID Task (dimension)* field. To add any custom field to the local OLAP cube, select one or more fields in the *Available Custom Fields* list and click the *Add* button. Click the *Edit Template* button when finished.

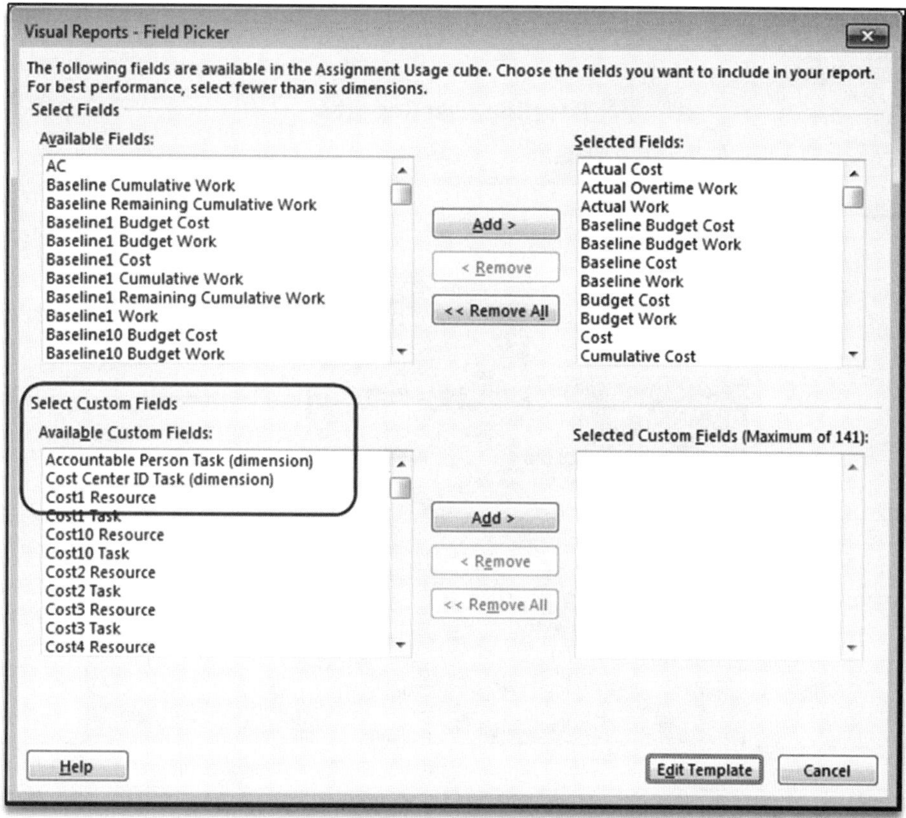

Figure 11 - 76: Visual Reports – Field Picker dialog

6. If you did not need to use step #5 and add custom fields to your visual report, click the *View* button in the *Visual Reports – Create Report* dialog to create the visual report.

Project 2013 displays a progress indicator at the bottom of the dialog in which it indicates that it is gathering data for the report, building the local OLAP cube, and then opening the visual report template for viewing. Figure 11 - 77 shows the completed *Baseline Cost* visual report in Excel. Notice that the legend at the top of the chart explains the meaning of each column color.

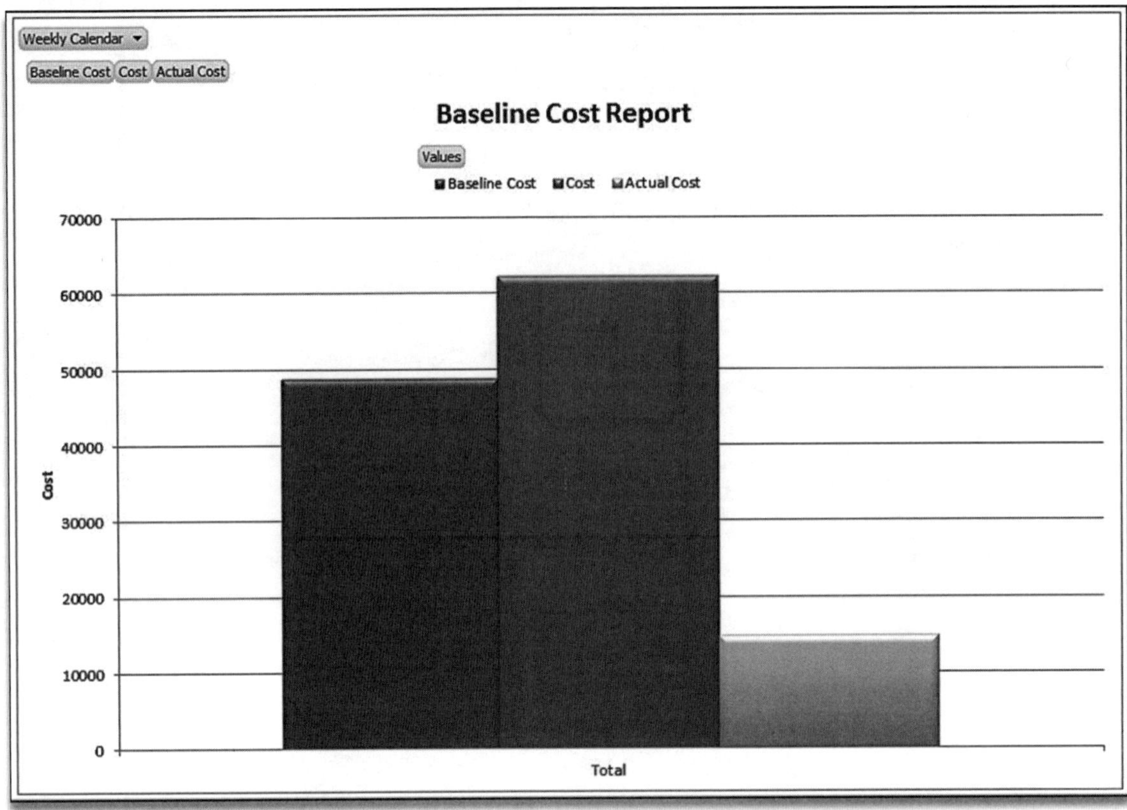

Figure 11 - 77: Baseline Cost visual report in Excel

Warning: The Excel application sets the default level of zoom to *125%* for each visual report. Depending on your monitor size and screen resolution, you may need to zoom out for every visual report you view. In Excel, click the *View* tab to display the *View* ribbon. In the *Zoom* section of the *View* ribbon, click the *Zoom* button. In the *Zoom* dialog, select a level of zoom, such as the *Fit selection* level, and then click the *OK* button. You can also set the level of zoom using the *Zoom Slider* in the lower right corner of the Excel application window.

The visual report in Excel consists of two parts: the graphical *PivotChart*, shown previously in Figure 11 - 77, and the *PivotTable* containing the underlying data. To view the *PivotTable* data, click right-most of the two worksheet tabs in the lower left corner of the application window. Figure 11 - 78 shows the *PivotTable* data on the *Assignment Usage* worksheet for the *Baseline Cost* visual report.

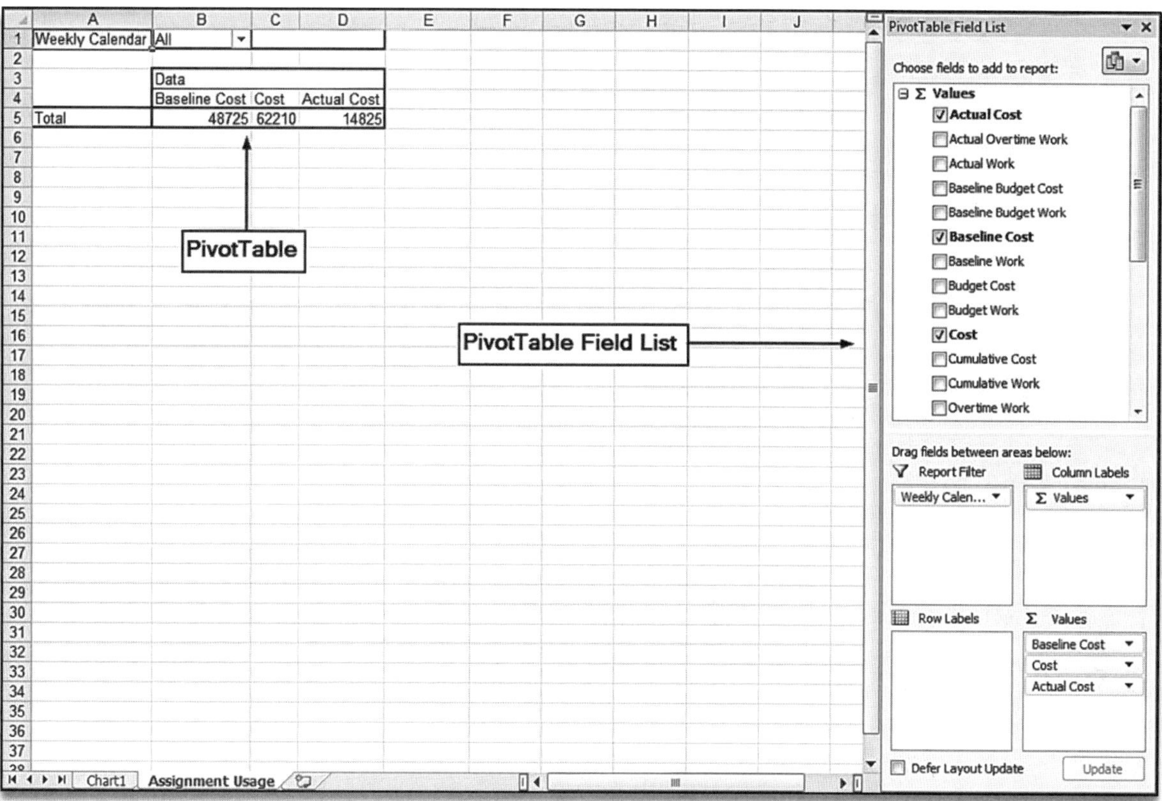

Figure 11 - 78: PivotTable data for the Baseline Cost visual report

Notice that the *Assignment Usage* worksheet shown previously in Figure 11 - 78 consists of two parts. The worksheet displays the *PivotTable* in the upper left corner of the page. The *PivotTable* includes data areas for row fields, column fields, project filter fields, and total fields. The worksheet displays the *PivotTable Field List* sidepane on the right side of the page. The top of the *PivotTable Field List* sidepane contains the list of fields that you can use in your report, while the bottom includes drop areas to which you can add the fields in your report.

Figure 11 - 79 shows the *Task Status* visual report in Visio. Notice that a visual report in Visio consists of the *PivotDiagram* and the *PivotDiagram* sidepane on the left side of the screen. If you work with Visio Professional 2007, the software displays a *PivotDiagram* toolbar at the top of the visual report page. If you work with Visio Professional 2010 or 2013, the software displays the *PivotDiagram* ribbon instead.

Warning: Because the Visio application sets the default zoom level to display the width of all the data shown in the *PivotDiagram*, you probably need to zoom in to see your visual report data clearly. In Visio, click the *View* tab to display the *View* ribbon. In the *Zoom* section of the *View* ribbon, click the *Zoom* button. In the *Zoom* dialog, select a level of zoom, such as *100%*, and then click the *OK* button. You can also set the level of zoom using the *Zoom Slider* in the lower right corner of the Visio application window.

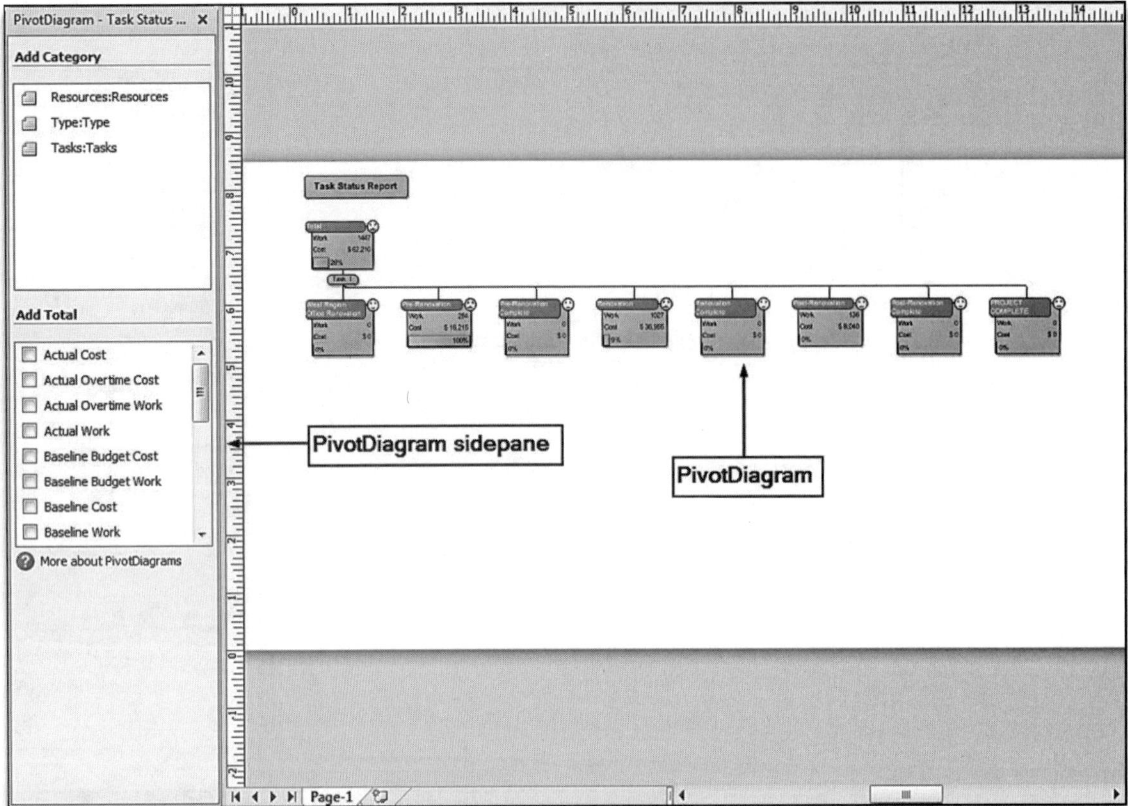

Figure 11 - 79: Task Status visual report

Hands On Exercise

Exercise 11 - 12

View visual reports in Project 2013.

1. Return to the **Training Advisor 11.mpp** sample file.
2. Click the *Report* tab to display the *Report* ribbon.
3. In the *Export* section of the *Report* ribbon, click the *Visual Reports* button.
4. In the *Visual Reports – Create Report* dialog, select the *Assignment Usage* tab.
5. On the *Assignment Usage* page of the dialog, select the *Baseline Work Report* item for Excel.
6. Click the *Select level of usage data to include in this report* pick list and select the *Days* level of data granularity.
7. Click the *View* button.

8. In the resulting Excel workbook, use the *Zoom Slider* tool to zoom the *PivotChart* so that you can see it completely (you may need to set the zoom level to approximately *80%* or so).

9. Examine the *PivotChart* shown on the *Chart1* worksheet.

10. Click the *Assignment Usage* tab to display the *Assignment Usage* worksheet.

11. Click anywhere in the *PivotTable* shown in the upper left corner of the worksheet.

12. Examine the project data shown in the *PivotTable* and in the *PivotTable Field List* sidepane on the right side of the worksheet.

13. Close and **do not** save the Excel workbook containing the visual report, but leave the Excel application running.

14. Return to the Project 2013 application window.

Warning: If you do not have the **Professional** version of Visio 2007, 2010, or 2013, then you must skip steps #15-21 in this Hands On Exercise.

15. In the *Visual Reports – Create Report* dialog, select the *Resource Usage* tab.

16. On the *Resource Usage* page of the dialog, select the *Cash Flow Report (US)* item for Visio, and then click the *View* button.

17. In your Visio application, click the *View* tab to display the *View* ribbon.

18. In the *Zoom* section of the *View* ribbon, click the *Zoom* button.

19. In the *Zoom* dialog, select the *100% (Actual Size)* option and then click the *OK* button.

20. Scroll through the Visio *PivotDiagram* and examine the data shown in each of the shapes in the Visio drawing.

21. Close and **do not** save the Visio diagram, and then exit the Visio application.

22. Return to your Project 2013 application window.

Customizing an Excel Visual Report

You can customize any Excel visual report by changing the data in the *PivotTable*. For example, you can use any of the following methods to customize the *PivotTable* data in the *Baseline Cost* visual report:

- In the *PivotTable Field List* sidepane, deselect any fields you do not want to display, and select the fields you do want to display. The software adds the newly selected field(s) to the appropriate area in the sidepane. For example, notice in Figure 11 - 80 that I **deselected** the *Actual Cost* field in the *PivotTable Field List* sidepane, removing this field from both the *PivotTable* and the *PivotChart* as a consequence. Though not visible in Figure 11 - 80, I also selected the *Tasks* field for inclusion in the Excel visual report.

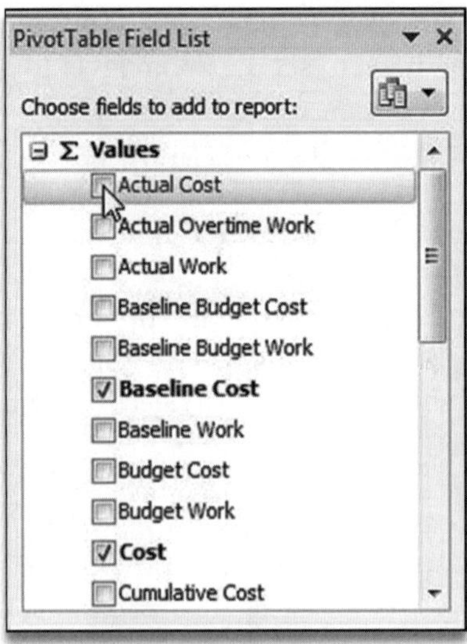

Figure 11 - 80: Deselect the Actual Cost field

- In the *PivotTable Field List* sidepane, drag and drop fields between the field list section at the top of the sidepane to the drop areas at the bottom of the sidepane. You can also drag and drop fields between the different drop areas at the bottom of the sidepane. For example, I dragged the *Weekly Calendar* field from the *Report Filter* drop area to the *Row Labels* drop area, as shown in Figure 11 - 81. You can see the *Tasks* field in the *Row Labels* area.

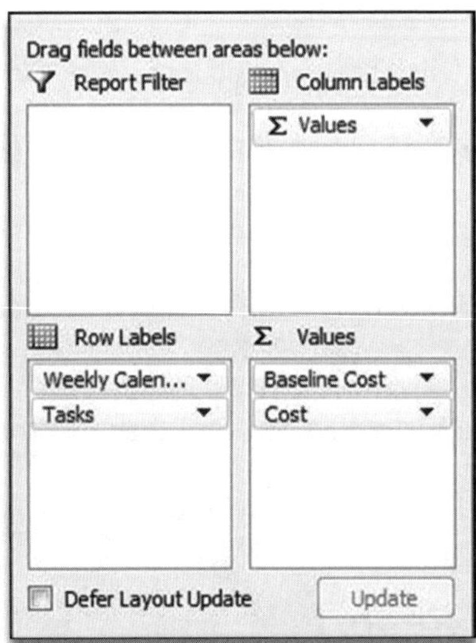

Figure 11 - 81: Move the Weekly Calendar field to the Row Labels area

- In the *PivotTable,* click the *Expand* (+) or *Collapse* (-) buttons in any section on the left side to show the level of details you want to see in the visual report. Notice in Figure 11 - 82 that I expanded the *Year* section to show *Quarters,* and I expanded the *West Region Office Renovation* task to show first-level tasks in the *Task 1* section.

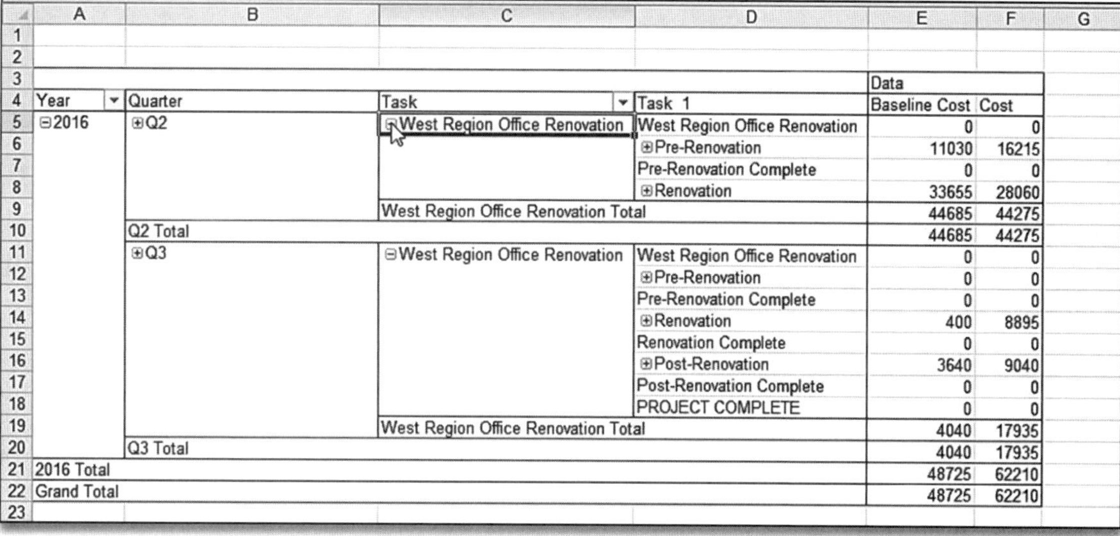

	A	B	C	D	E	F	G
1							
2							
3					Data		
4	Year	Quarter	Task	Task 1	Baseline Cost	Cost	
5	⊟2016	⊞Q2	⊟West Region Office Renovation	West Region Office Renovation	0	0	
6				⊞Pre-Renovation	11030	16215	
7				Pre-Renovation Complete	0	0	
8				⊞Renovation	33655	28060	
9			West Region Office Renovation Total		44685	44275	
10		Q2 Total			44685	44275	
11		⊞Q3	⊟West Region Office Renovation	West Region Office Renovation	0	0	
12				⊞Pre-Renovation	0	0	
13				Pre-Renovation Complete	0	0	
14				⊞Renovation	400	8895	
15				Renovation Complete	0	0	
16				⊞Post-Renovation	3640	9040	
17				Post-Renovation Complete	0	0	
18				PROJECT COMPLETE	0	0	
19			West Region Office Renovation Total		4040	17935	
20		Q3 Total			4040	17935	
21	2016 Total				48725	62210	
22	Grand Total				48725	62210	
23							

Figure 11 - 82: PivotTable with Year and Task sections expanded

- Select the details you want to see for any field in the *Row Labels* area by clicking the pick list arrow button in the column header for that field. For example, to edit the details for the *Task* field, click the *Task* pick list. The software displays the *Select field* dialog. Notice in the *Select field* dialog shown in Figure 11 - 83 that I expanded the Project Summary Task so that I can now see all first-level tasks, including summary tasks and milestone tasks. Using this dialog, I select the checkboxes for only the task items you want to see in the *PivotTable,* such as first-level summary tasks that represent phases of the project, and deselect the checkboxes for items you do not want to see, such as the first-level milestone tasks.

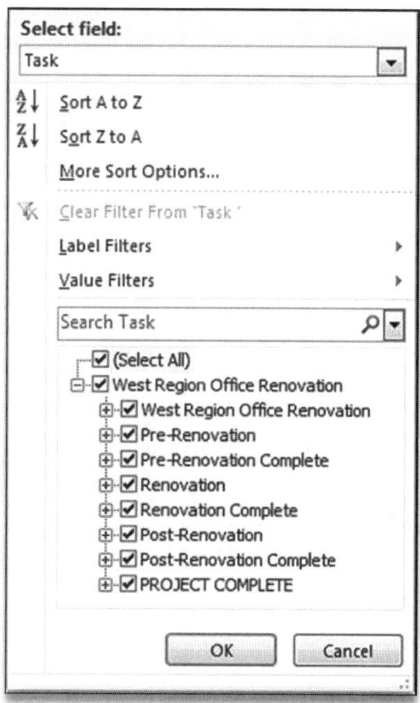

Figure 11 - 83: Select field dialog

Information: You can also use the *Select field* dialog to apply sorting or filtering to the data in the selected column of the *PivotTable*. Select the *Sort A to Z, Sort Z to A*, or *More Sort Options* item to apply sorting. Select the *Label Filters* or *Value Filters* items to apply filtering.

- Display properties fields in the *PivotTable*, if needed. If you add the *Task* field or the *Resource* field to the *Row Labels* area in a visual report, right-click the *Task* or *Resource* field. In the shortcut menu, select the *Show Properties in Report* menu item, and then use the fly out menu to select the additional details you want to see in the report, as shown in Figure 11 - 84.

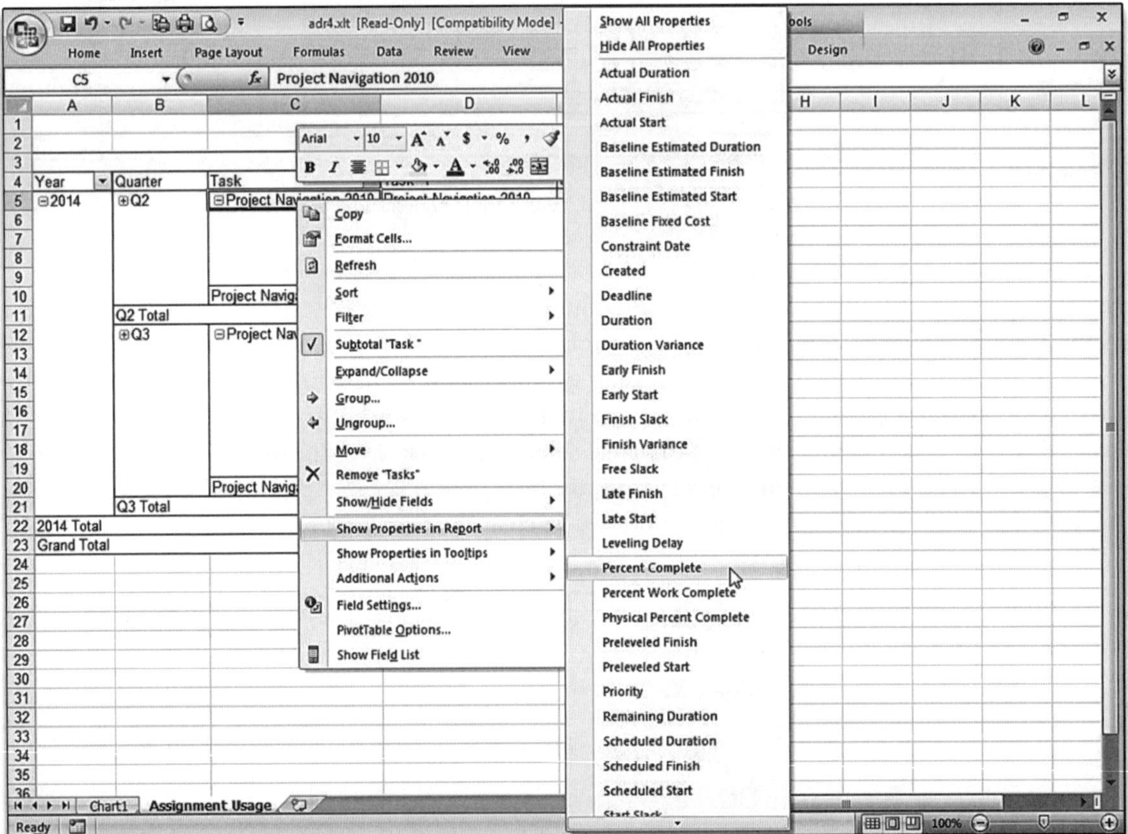

Figure 11 - 84: Add other details to the PivotTable

Information: For this example, I do not include any properties fields in the *PivotTable*. In your own projects, take a conservative approach with adding properties fields to your visual reports. Keep in mind that Excel limits how much number formatting you can apply to properties fields, or prevents number formatting entirely. Beyond this, adding properties fields to your *PivotTable* can negatively impact the appearance of your *PivotChart*.

- Apply numeric formatting to the numbers in the *PivotTable*. For example, in Figure 11 - 85, I applied the *Accounting Number Format* numeric formatting to the data shown in the *PivotTable*, and then I used the *Decrease Decimal* button to reduce to *zero* the number of digits to the right of the decimal.

	A	B	C	D	E	F	G
1							
2							
3					Data		
4	Year	Quarter	Task	Task 1	Baseline Cost	Cost	
5	⊟2016	⊞Q2	⊟West Region Office Renovation	⊞Pre-Renovation	$ 11,030	$ 16,215	
6				⊞Renovation	$ 33,655	$ 28,060	
7			West Region Office Renovation Total		$ 44,685	$ 44,275	
8		Q2 Total			$ 44,685	$ 44,275	
9		⊞Q3	⊟West Region Office Renovation	⊞Pre-Renovation	$ -	$ -	
10				⊞Renovation	$ 400	$ 8,895	
11				⊞Post-Renovation	$ 3,640	$ 9,040	
12			West Region Office Renovation Total		$ 4,040	$ 17,935	
13		Q3 Total			$ 4,040	$ 17,935	
14	2016 Total				$ 48,725	$ 62,210	
15	Grand Total				$ 48,725	$ 62,210	
16							

Figure 11 - 85: PivotTable with numeric formatting applied

When you make changes to the data shown in the *PivotTable,* Excel updates the changes immediately in the *PivotChart*. Figure 11 - 86 shows the updated *PivotChart* after making changes to the underlying data in the *PivotTable*. If you compare this updated *Baseline Cost* report with the original *Baseline Cost* report shown previously in Figure 11 - 77, you see dramatic changes in appearance after making only a few simple changes in the *PivotTable.*

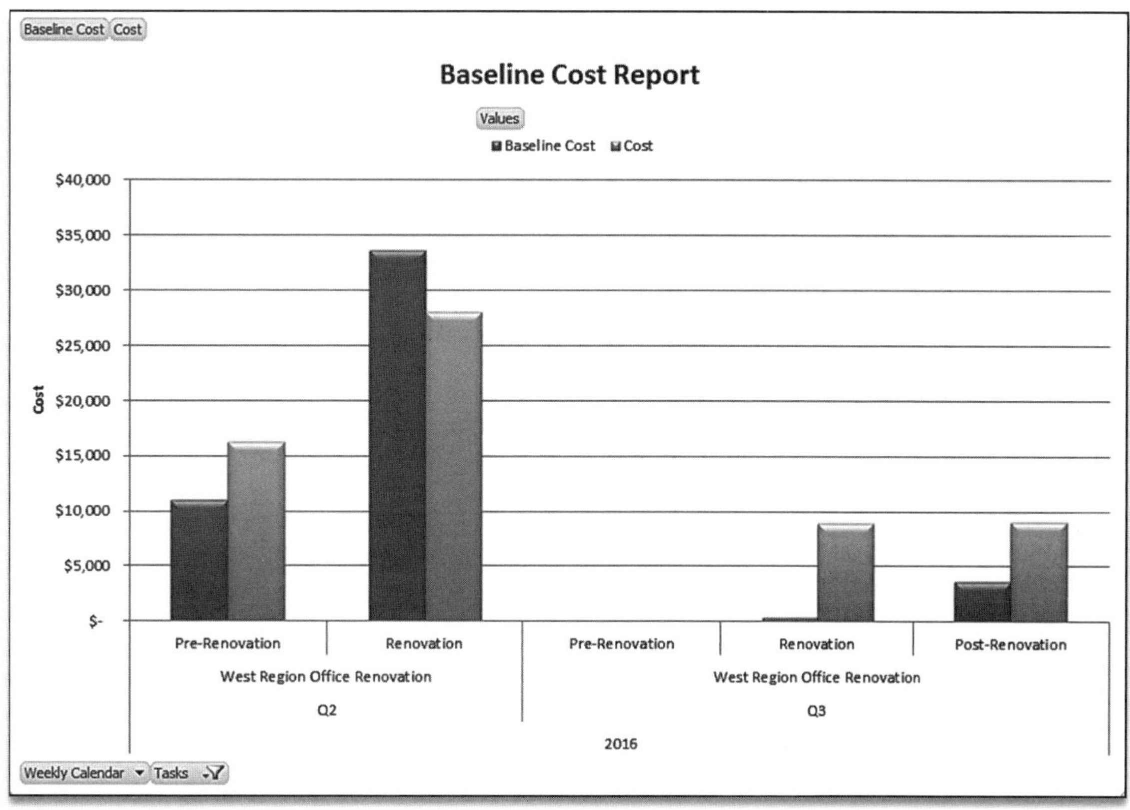

Figure 11 - 86: Updated Baseline Cost visual report

You can also modify the *PivotChart* by right-clicking anywhere in the chart area you want to change. For example, when you right-click in the *Plot Area* of the *PivotChart*, Excel displays the shortcut menu shown in Figure 11 - 87. Using the options on this shortcut menu, you can use any of the built-in chart formatting capabilities available in Excel, such as changing the chart type.

Information: In Excel 2007, 2010, and 2013 you can also double-click anywhere in the PivotChart. The software displays the appropriate *Format* dialog for the data you double-clicked. For example, if you double-click in the *Plot Area*, Excel displays the *Format Plot Area* dialog. In addition, Excel 2010 and 2013also display the contextual *Design* ribbon with the *PivotChart Tools* applied. Using the features in the *Format* dialog and on the *Design* ribbon, you can apply many different types of formatting to the PivotChart.

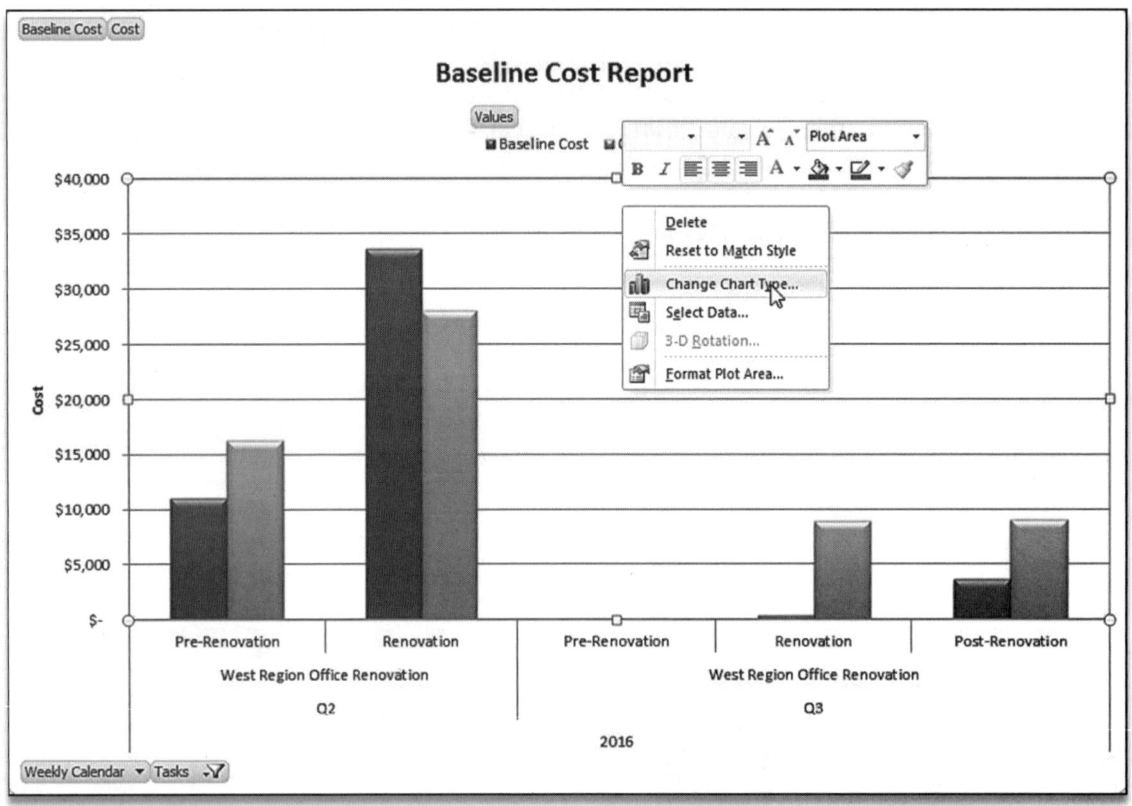

Figure 11 - 87: Right-click in the PivotChart to display the shortcut menu

If you select the *Change Chart Type* item on the shortcut menu, Excel displays the *Change Chart Type* dialog shown in Figure 11 - 88. Select an alternate chart type in this dialog and then click the *OK* button.

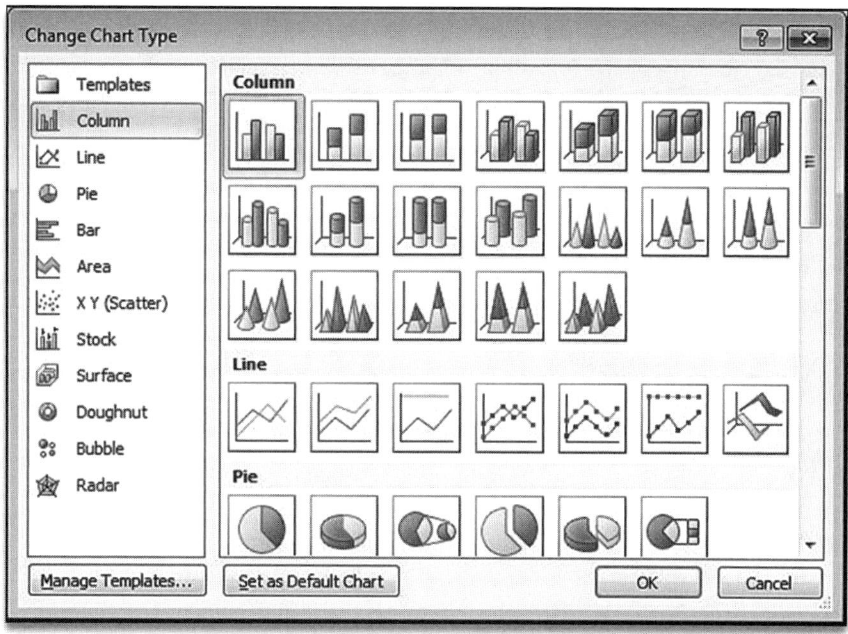

Figure 11 - 88: Change Chart Type dialog

Figure 11 - 89 shows the *PivotChart* after I applied the *Clustered Cylinder* chart type in the *Change Chart Type* dialog.

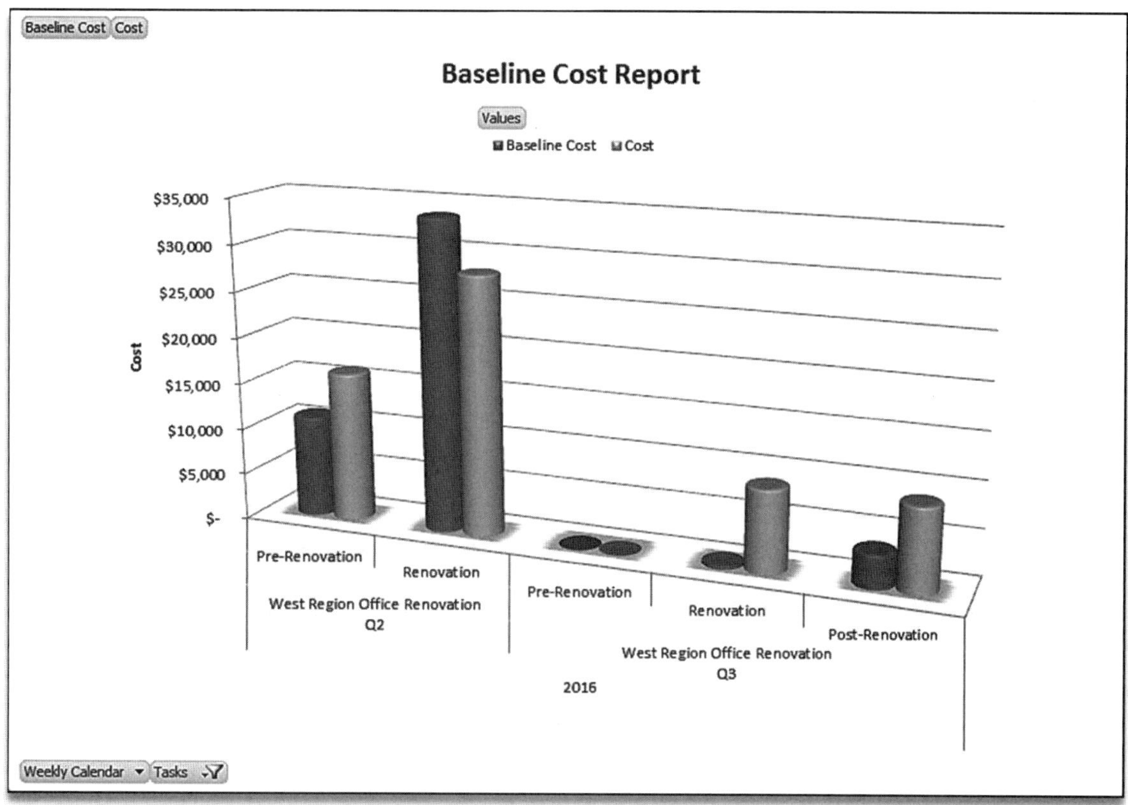

Figure 11 - 89: PivotChart formatted using the Clustered Cylinder chart type

After viewing and formatting an Excel visual report, you can print the visual report or save the visual report, as needed.

Information: Because this is not a course on Excel, I do not provide an exhaustive discussion about how to format either the PivotTable or the PivotChart in an Excel visual report.

Hands On Exercise

Exercise 11 - 13

Customize the *PivotTable* and *PivotChart* in an Excel visual report.

1. In the *Visual Reports – Create Report* dialog, select the *Assignment Usage* tab.
2. On the *Assignment Usage* page of the dialog, select the *Baseline Work Report* item, and then click the *View* button.
3. In your Excel application window, click the *Assignment Usage* worksheet tab to view the *PivotTable* data.
4. Click anywhere in the *PivotTable* to display the *PivotTable Field List* sidepane on the right side of the page.
5. In the *Choose fields to add to report* section of the *PivotTable Field List* sidepane, **deselect** the *Actual Work* item.
6. In the *Choose fields to add to report* section of the *PivotTable Field List* sidepane, **select** the *Tasks* item and then **deselect** the *Weekly Calendar* item.
7. In the *PivotTable*, expand the *Training Advisor Rollout* item in the *Task* section.
8. In the *PivotTable*, click the *Task* pick list.
9. In the *Select field* dialog, expand the *Training Advisor Rollout* item to view summary tasks and milestone tasks.
10. In the *Select field* dialog, **deselect** the *(Select All)* option and then select **only** the following items:
    - *INSTALLATION*
    - *TESTING*
    - *TRAINING*
11. Click the *OK* button to close the *Select field* dialog.

12. In the *PivotTable*, select all of the numbers in the *Baseline Work* and *Work* columns.

13. In the *Number* section of the *Home* ribbon, click the *Comma Style* button.

14. In the *Number* section of the *Home* ribbon, click the *Decrease Decimal* button **twice**.

15. Widen the *Work* column, as needed.

16. Click the *Chart1* worksheet tab to view new information shown in the *PivotChart*.

17. In the lower right corner of the Excel application window, use the *Zoom Slider* tool to zoom out until you can see the complete *PivotChart*.

18. Right-click anywhere in the *Plot Area* section of the *PivotChart* and select the *Change Chart Type* item on the shortcut menu.

19. In the *Change Chart Type* dialog, select the *3-D Clustered Column* item, and then click the *OK* button.

20. On the *Quick Access Toolbar* in your Excel application, click the *Save* button.

21. In the *Save As* dialog, navigate to the folder containing your sample files.

22. In the *Save As* dialog, click the *Save as type* pick list, and select the *Excel Workbook (*.xlsx)* file type.

23. In the *Save As* dialog, enter **Baseline Work Report.xlsx** in the *File name* field, and then click the *OK* button.

24. In your Excel application, click the *File* tab and then click the *Close* button to close the Excel visual report.

25. Leave your Excel application open, but return to your Project 2013 application window.

Customizing a Visio Visual Report

You can customize a Visio visual report by using any of the following methods:

Select one or more shapes in the *PivotDiagram* and then change the options in the *Add Category* section of the *PivotDiagram* sidepane. Notice in the *Task Status* visual report, shown previously in Figure 11 - 79, that the report displays only the first-level tasks representing the phases in the project. In this visual report, I want to show the second-level summary tasks for the *Renovation* phase to view the deliverables for that phase. To accomplish this, click the *Renovation* shape to select it in the *PivotDiagram*. In the *Add Category* section of the *PivotDiagram* sidepane, click the *Tasks* pick list, and then select the *Task 2* item, as shown in Figure 11 - 90. After completing these steps, Figure 11 - 91 shows the *Task Status* visual report after adding the second-level task shapes to the report. Notice that the *PivotDiagram* now shows the *Construction* and *Furnish* summary tasks, but it also shows the *Construction Complete* and *Furnish Complete* milestone tasks.

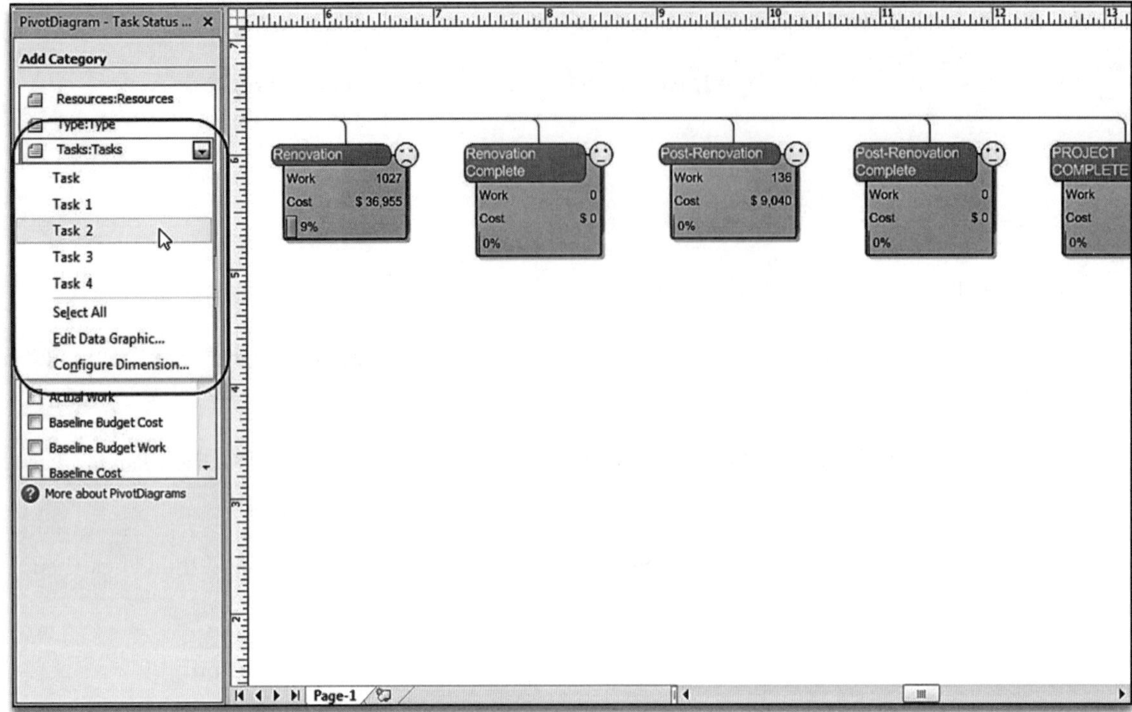

Figure 11 - 90: Tasks menu in the PivotDiagram sidepane

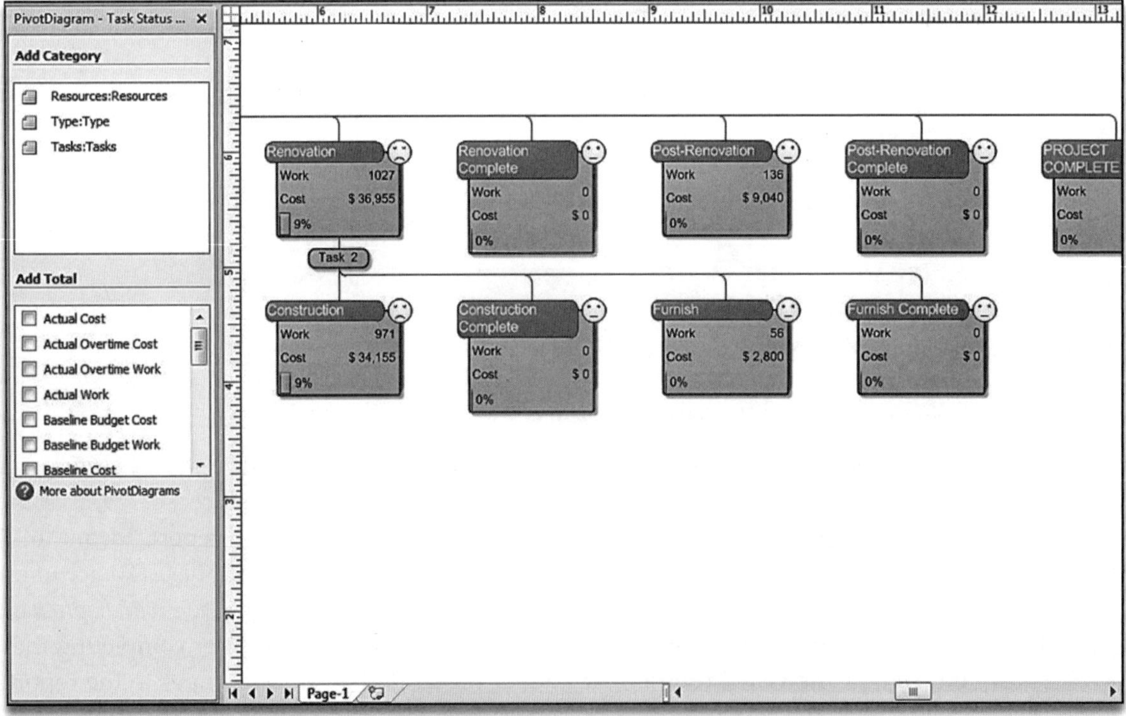

Figure 11 - 91: Task Status visual report with second-level summary tasks for the Renovation phase

- Change the fields displayed in the *PivotDiagram* by selecting or deselecting the fields in the *Add Total* section of the *PivotDiagram* sidepane. For example, Figure 11 - 92 shows the *Task Status* visual report after I selected the *Baseline Work* and *Baseline Cost* fields.

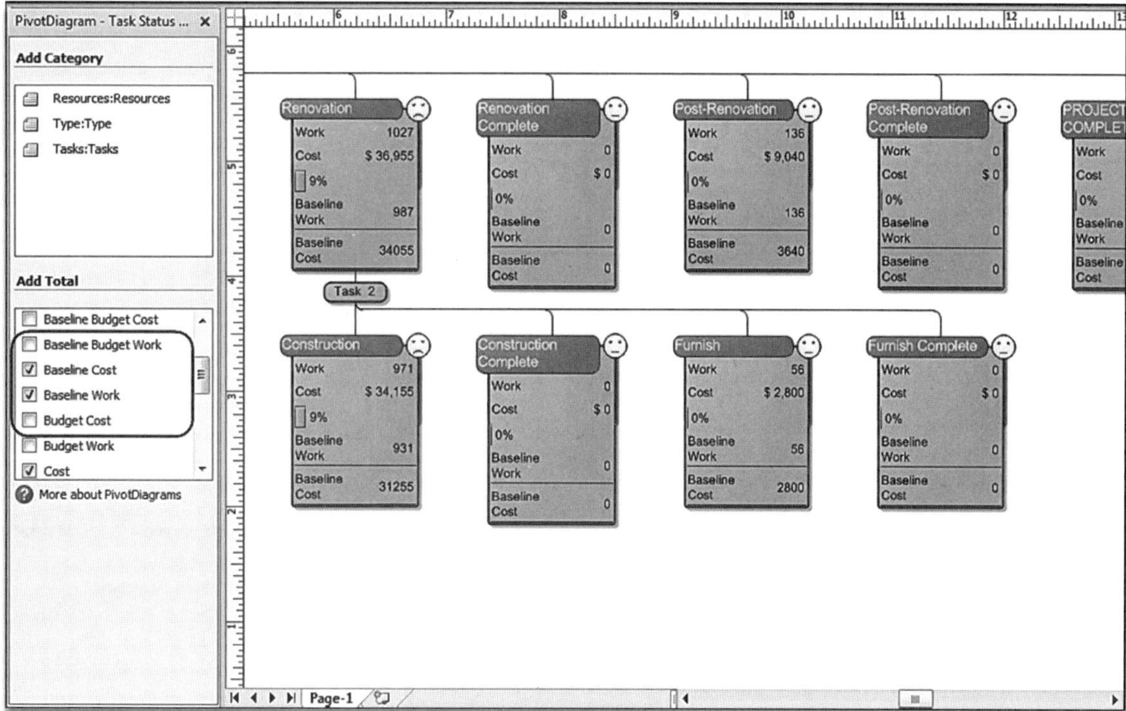

Figure 11 - 92: Task Status visual report after changing displayed fields

- Manually delete objects in the *PivotDiagram*. In the *Task Status* visual report shown previously in Figure 11 - 90 through Figure 11 - 92, I want to remove the shapes representing the Project Summary Task and all of the milestone tasks. To delete a shape in the *PivotDiagram*, click the shape to select it, and then press the **Delete** key on your computer keyboard.

- Rearrange the layout of shapes in the *PivotDiagram*. To change the layout of the shapes, click the *Re-Layout All* button in the *Layout* section of the *PivotDiagram* ribbon. You can also manually drag and drop shapes anywhere on the *PivotDiagram*. Figure 11 - 93 shows the *Task Status* visual report after changing the layout of the *PivotDiagram* shapes using the *Re-Layout All* button.

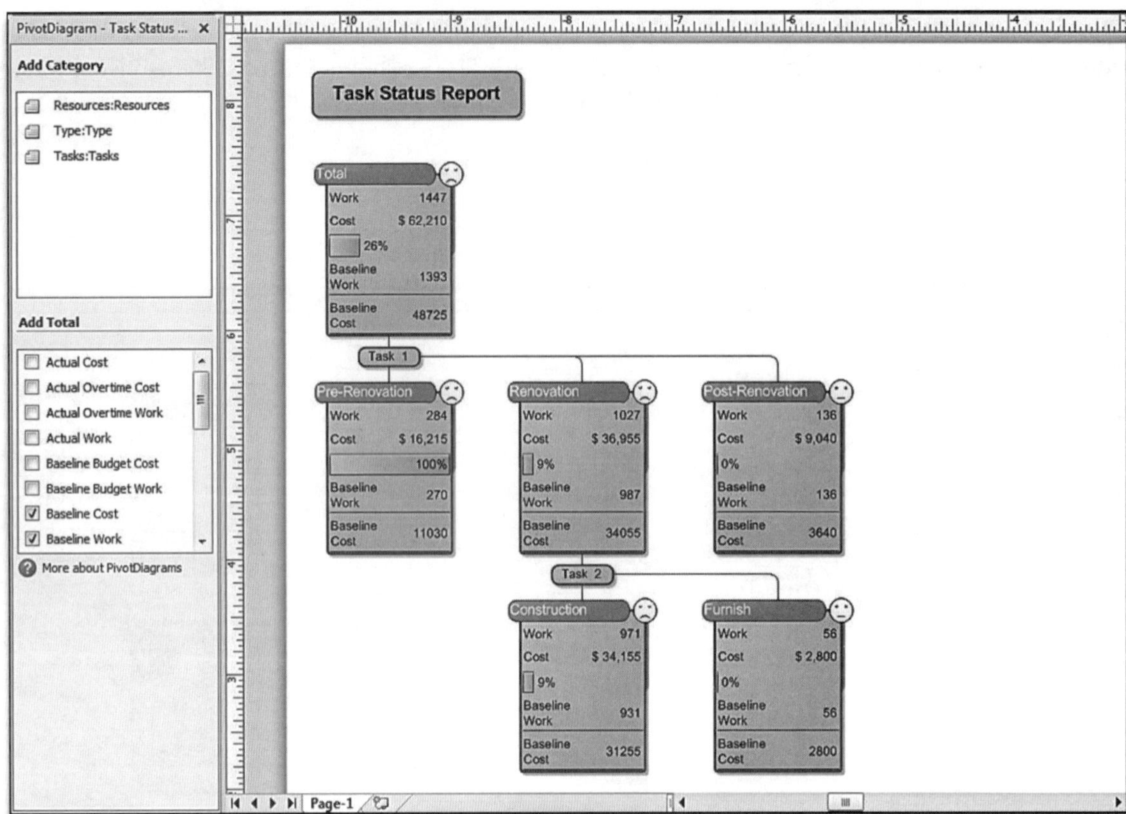

Figure 11 - 93: Task Status visual report after changing the layout

In addition to the preceding four procedures, you can also change the display order and formatting for additional fields you add to the shapes in the *PivotDiagram*. For example, in the *Task Status* visual report shown previously in Figure 11 - 93, I want to display the fields in the following order in each shape: *Work, Baseline Work, Cost,* and *Baseline Cost*. In addition, I want to format the *Baseline Cost* field using the *Currency* number formatting. To address these two needs, complete the following steps in the *Task Status* visual report in Visio:

1. In the *Add Category* section of the *PivotDiagram* sidepane, click the *Tasks* pick list button, and then select the *Edit Data Graphic* item. Visio displays the *Edit Data Graphic* dialog shown in Figure 11 - 94. This dialog contains all of the information needed by Visio to create all of the *Task* shapes in the *PivotDiagram*. Notice that the first item in the *Data Field* column is an IF statement. The software uses this IF statement to display a happy face, neutral face, or sad face symbol in the upper right corner of each shape to indicate whether the task is under budget, on budget, or over budget on work. Notice also that the third and fourth lines in the *Data Field* column show the *Work* and *Cost* fields, respectively.

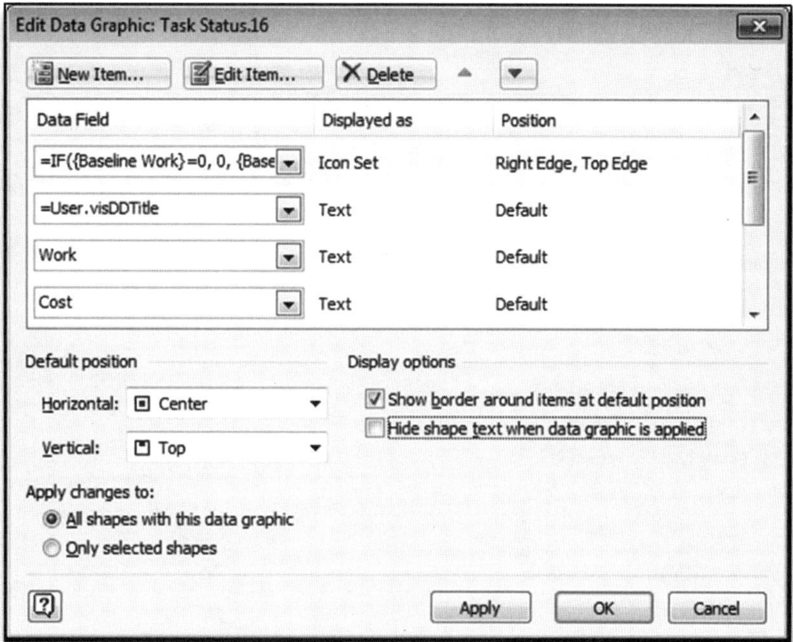

Figure 11 - 94: Edit Data Graphic dialog

2. Scroll down in the *Edit Graphic* dialog and select the row for the *Baseline Work* field.

3. With the *Baseline Work* field selected, click the *Move Up* button (up arrow button at the top of the dialog) until you see the *Baseline Work* field displayed immediately **below** the *Work* field.

4. Scroll down in the *Edit Graphic* dialog again and select the row for the *Baseline Cost* field.

5. With the *Baseline Cost* field selected, click the *Move Up* button (up arrow button at the top of the dialog) until you see the *Baseline Cost* field displayed immediately **below** the *Cost* field.

6. With the *Baseline Cost* field still selected, click the *Edit Item* button at the top of the dialog. Visio displays the *Edit Item* dialog shown in Figure 11 - 95. The *Edit Item* dialog displays all of the formatting information used by Visio to format the *Baseline Cost* field.

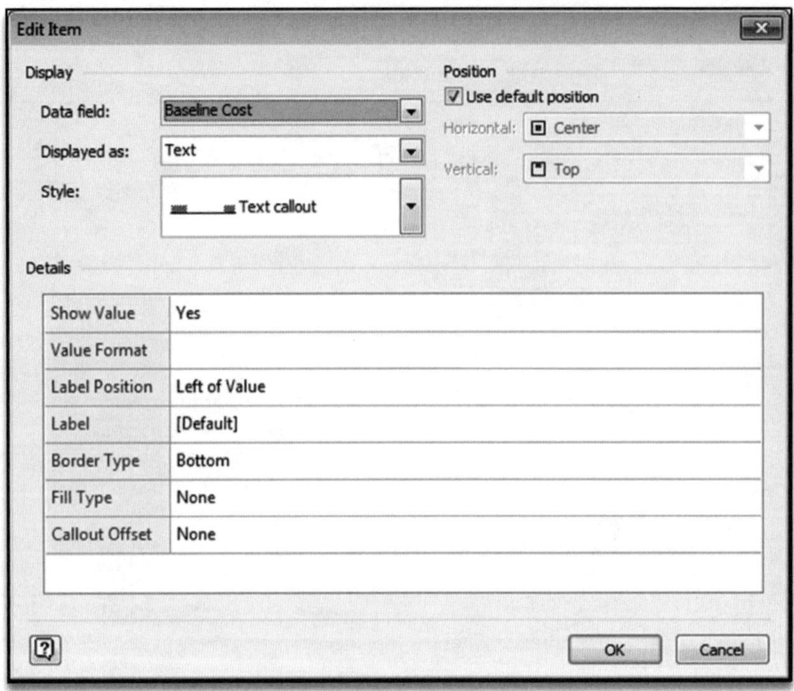

Figure 11 - 95: Edit Item dialog

7. In the *Edit Item* dialog, click anywhere in the white part of the *Value Format* line. The dialog displays a *Select Value* button (...) at the right end of the line.
8. Click the *Select Value* button at the right end of the *Value Format* line. Visio displays the *Data Format* dialog shown in Figure 11 - 96.

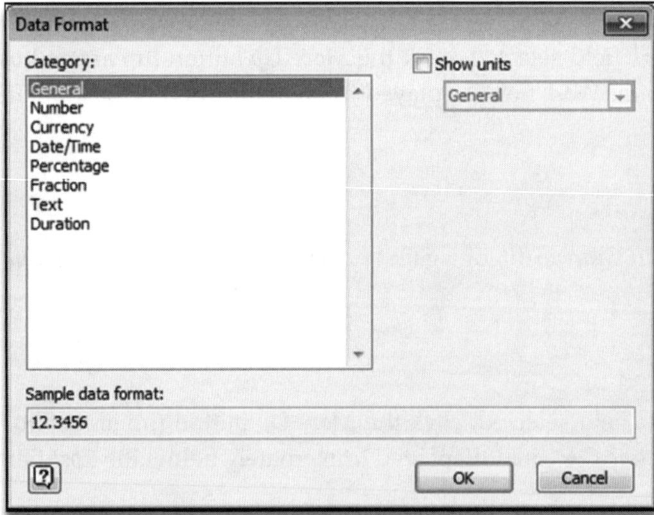

Figure 11 - 96: Data Format dialog

9. In the *Category* section of the *Data Format* dialog, select the *Currency* item.
10. In the upper right corner of the dialog, set the *Decimal places* value to *0* and then click the *OK* button.

11. Click the *OK* button to close the *Edit Item* dialog, and then click the *OK* button to close the *Edit Data Graphic* dialog. Figure 11 - 97 shows the *Task Status* visual report with the new formatting applied to the *Task* shapes.

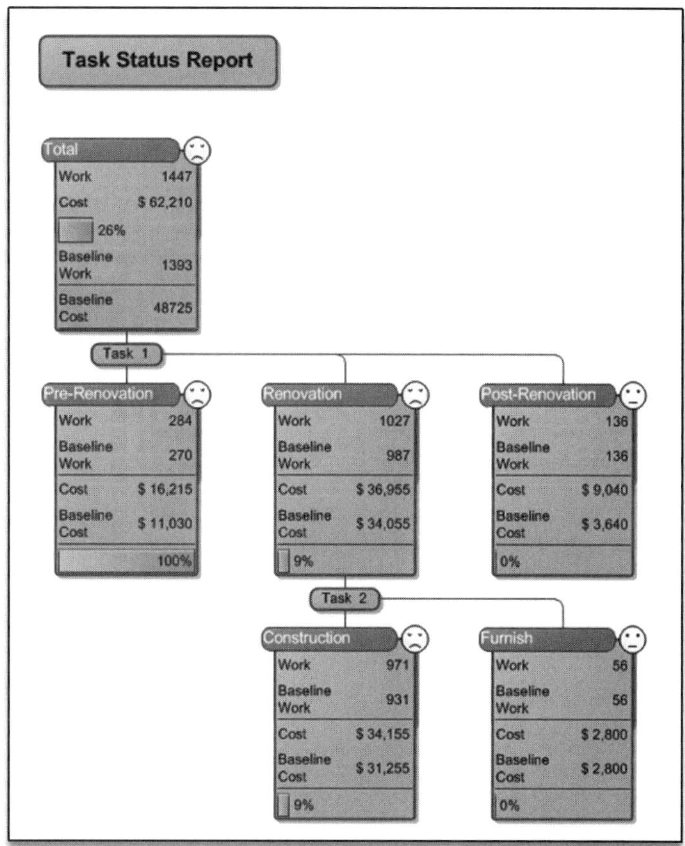

Figure 11 - 97: Task shapes with new formatting applied

Information: Using the preceding set of steps to format the *Task* shapes does not apply formatting to the *Total* shape in the upper left corner of the report. To format the *Total* shape, right-click anywhere in the shape, select the *Data* item on the shortcut menu, and then select the *Edit Data Graphic* item on the flyout menu. Visio displays the *Edit Data Graphic* dialog shown previously in Figure 11 - 94. Use steps #2-11 documented previously to format the *Total* shape.

After viewing and formatting a Visio visual report, you can print the visual report or save the visual report, as needed.

Information: Because this is not a course on Visio, I do not provide an exhaustive discussion about how to format a *PivotDiagram*.

Hands On Exercise

Exercise 11 - 14

Customize the *PivotDiagram* in a Visio visual report.

1. In the *Visual Reports – Create Report* dialog, select the *Resource Usage* tab.
2. On the *Resource Usage* page of the dialog, select the *Cash Flow Report (US)* item for Visio, and then click the *View* button.
3. In your Visio application, click the *View* tab to display the *View* ribbon.
4. In the *Zoom* section of the *View* ribbon, click the *Zoom* button.
5. In the *Zoom* dialog, select the *100% (Actual Size)* option and then click the *OK* button.
6. Scroll to the upper left corner the Visio *PivotDiagram* and examine the data shown in the shapes for the first quarter of the year.
7. In the *Add Total* section of the *PivotDiagram* sidepane, select the *Baseline Cost* field.

Notice that Visio does not apply the *Currency* formatting to the *Baseline Cost* field in the shapes shown in the *Cash Flow* visual report.

8. In the *Add Category* section of the *PivotDiagram* sidepane, click the *Type* pick list, and then select the *Edit Data Graphic* item.
9. Scroll down in the *Edit Graphic* dialog and select the row for the *Baseline Cost* field.
10. With the *Baseline Cost* field selected, click the *Move Up* button (up arrow button at the top of the dialog) until you see the *Baseline Cost* field displayed **above** the *Cost* field.
11. With the *Baseline Cost* field still selected, click the *Edit Item* button at the top of the dialog.
12. In the *Details* section of the *Edit Item* dialog, click anywhere in the white part of the *Value Format* line. The dialog displays a *Select Value* button (**...**) at the right end of the line.
13. Click the *Select Value* button at the right end of the *Value Format* line.
14. In the *Category* section of the *Data Format* dialog, select the *Currency* item.
15. In the upper right corner of the dialog, set the *Decimal places* value to *0* and then click the *OK* button.
16. Click the *OK* button to close the *Edit Item* dialog, and then click the *OK* button to close the *Edit Data Graphic* dialog.

Notice that Visio now displays the *Baseline Cost* field at the top of each shape in the third row of the *Cash Flow* visual report. Notice also that the software formats the *Baseline Cost* field using the *Currency* formatting you specified in the *Data Format* dialog.

17. On the *Quick Access Toolbar* in your Visio application, click the *Save* button.
18. In the *Save As* dialog, navigate to the folder containing your sample files.
19. In the *Save As* dialog, enter **Cash Flow Report.vsd** in the *File name* field, and then click the *OK* button.
20. Click the *File* tab and then click the *Close* button to close the Visio visual report.
21. Close your Visio application and return to your Project 2013 application window.

Saving Local OLAP Cube Data

After you view the visual report and return to Project 2013, you can save the local OLAP cube data by clicking the *Save Data* button at the bottom of the *Visual Reports – Create Report* dialog. The software displays the *Visual Reports – Save Reporting Data* dialog shown in Figure 11 - 98.

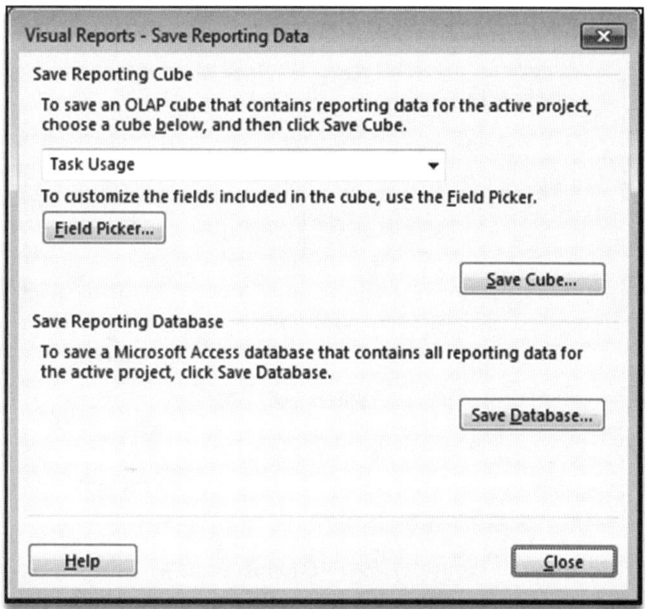

Figure 11 - 98: Visual Reports – Save Reporting Data dialog

In the *Save Reporting Cube* section of the dialog, click the pick list, and then select the local OLAP cube you want to save. The pick list includes the following OLAP cubes: *Task Usage, Resource Usage, Assignment Usage, Task Summary, Resource Summary,* and *Assignment Summary*. For example, I want to save the local OLAP cube data used to generate the *Baseline Cost* visual report for Excel. Therefore, I must select the *Assignment Usage* item on the pick list.

Click the *Field Picker* button to select any additional fields that you want to include when you save the local OLAP cube. Project 2013 displays the *Visual Reports – Field Picker* dialog shown previously in Figure 11 - 76. In this dialog, select the standard and custom fields you want to include in the local OLAP cube, and then click the *OK* button.

Click the *Save Cube* button when you are ready to save the local OLAP cube. In the *Save As* dialog, select a folder in which to save the cube file, enter a name for the cube file in the *File name* field, and then click the *Save* button. The software saves a file with the **.cub** file extension.

In the *Save Reporting Database* section of the dialog, you can click the *Save Database* button to save all of the local OLAP cube information in a Microsoft Access Database (***.mdb**) file. In the *Save As* dialog, select a folder in which to save the database file, enter a name for the database file in the *File name* field, and then click the *Save* button Click the *Close* button when you complete the operation.

Creating Visual Report Templates

Project 2013 allows you to create your own custom visual report templates or to edit any of the default visual report templates. The process is very similar whether creating or editing a visual report template. To create a new visual report template, click the *New Template* button in the *Visual Reports – Create Report* dialog. The software displays the *Visual Reports – New Template* dialog shown in Figure 11 - 99.

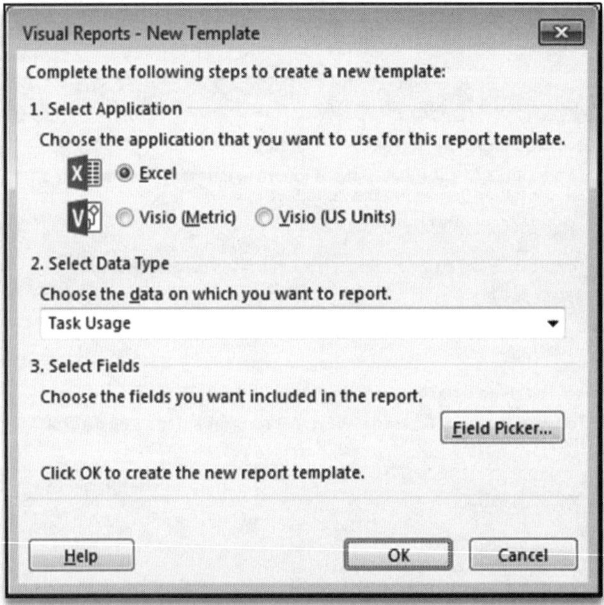

Figure 11 - 99: Visual Reports – New Template dialog

In the *Select Application* section of the dialog, select the *Excel*, the *Visio (Metric)*, or the *Visio (US Units)* option. In the *Select Data Type* section, click the pick list and select one of the following types of data: *Task Usage, Resource Usage, Assignment Usage, Task Summary, Resource Summary*, or *Assignment Summary*. In the *Select Fields* section, click the *Field Picker* button to select any additional standard or custom fields to include in the report template in the *Visual Reports – Field Picker* dialog, shown previously in Figure 11 - 76.

Information: In the *Visual Reports - Field Picker* dialog, the *Available Fields* list contains several fields denoted as dimension fields. Dimensions are project fields containing values at which the software totals fact data, such as work and availability. For example, the *Type* field represents the three types of resources available in Project 2013: *Work, Material*, and *Cost* resources.

Warning: Be cautious when selecting dimensions for your new visual report template. Including more than five dimension fields can seriously degrade the performance of your visual report.

In the *Visual Reports – New Template* dialog, click the *OK* button. If you selected the *Excel* option in the *Select application* section of the dialog, the software launches Excel and creates a new workbook with three worksheet tabs. The *Sheet1* worksheet contains an empty *PivotTable* shown in Figure 11 - 100. The software leaves the *Sheet2* and *Sheet3* worksheets blank.

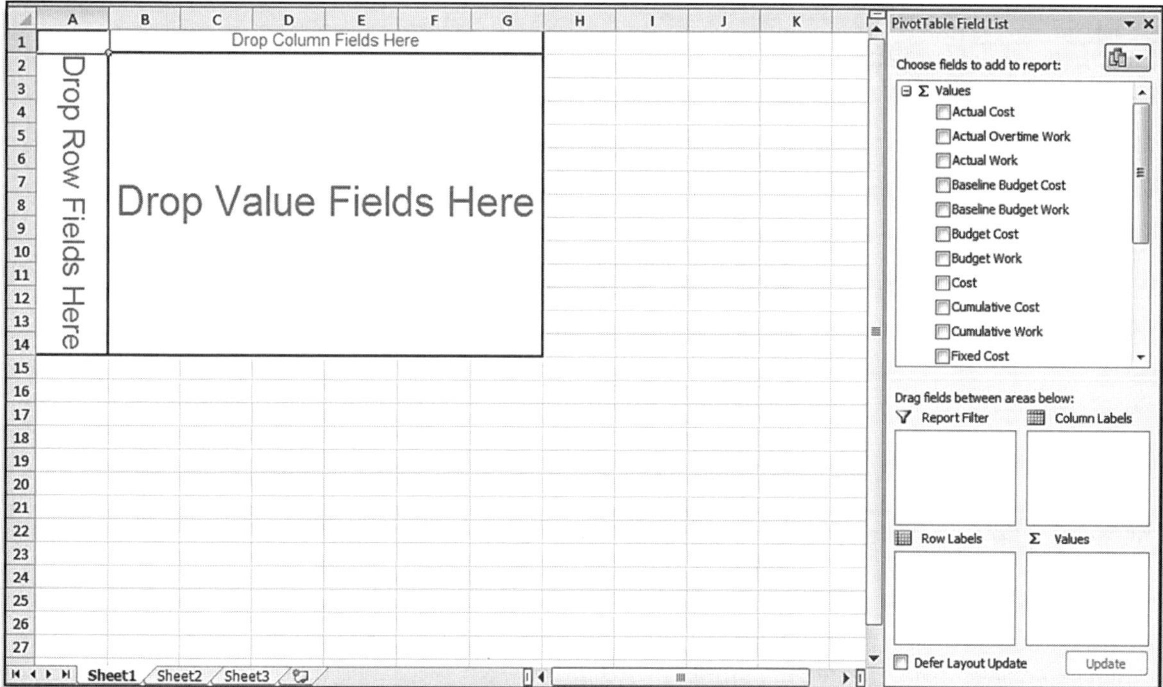

Figure 11 - 100: Sheet1 worksheet with empty PivotTable

Right-click the *Sheet1* worksheet tab and select the *Rename* option on the shortcut menu to rename the worksheet consistent with the type of visual report you want to create. Because I want to create a *Work Flow* report similar to the *Cash Flow* report, I rename the tab *Task Usage*. Right-click the *Sheet2* worksheet tab and select the *Delete* item to delete the worksheet. Repeat this action to delete the *Sheet3* worksheet.

Populate the *PivotTable* by selecting fields in the *Choose fields to add to report* section of the *PivotTable Field List* sidepane. Drag and drop the fields into the *Report Filter, Column Labels, Row Labels,* and *Values* areas at the bottom of the sidepane, as needed. To populate the *PivotTable* for the *Work Flow* report shown in Figure 11 - 101, I did the following:

- I selected the *Tasks* field and then dragged it from the *Row Labels* area to the *Report Filter* area.
- I selected the *Weekly Calendar* field and then dragged it from the *Column Labels* area to the *Row Labels* area.
- I selected the *Work* and *Cumulative Work* fields and the software added them to the *Values* area.
- I dragged the *Σ Values* field from the *Row Labels* drop area to the *Column Labels* drop area.
- I expanded the *Year* field in the *PivotTable* to show *Quarters*.

- I applied the *Accounting Number Format* numeric formatting to the numeric data in the *PivotTable*, and then used the *Decrease Decimal* button to reduce the number of digits to zero showing to the right of the decimal.
- I widened the *Work* and *Cumulative Work* columns in the *PivotTable*.

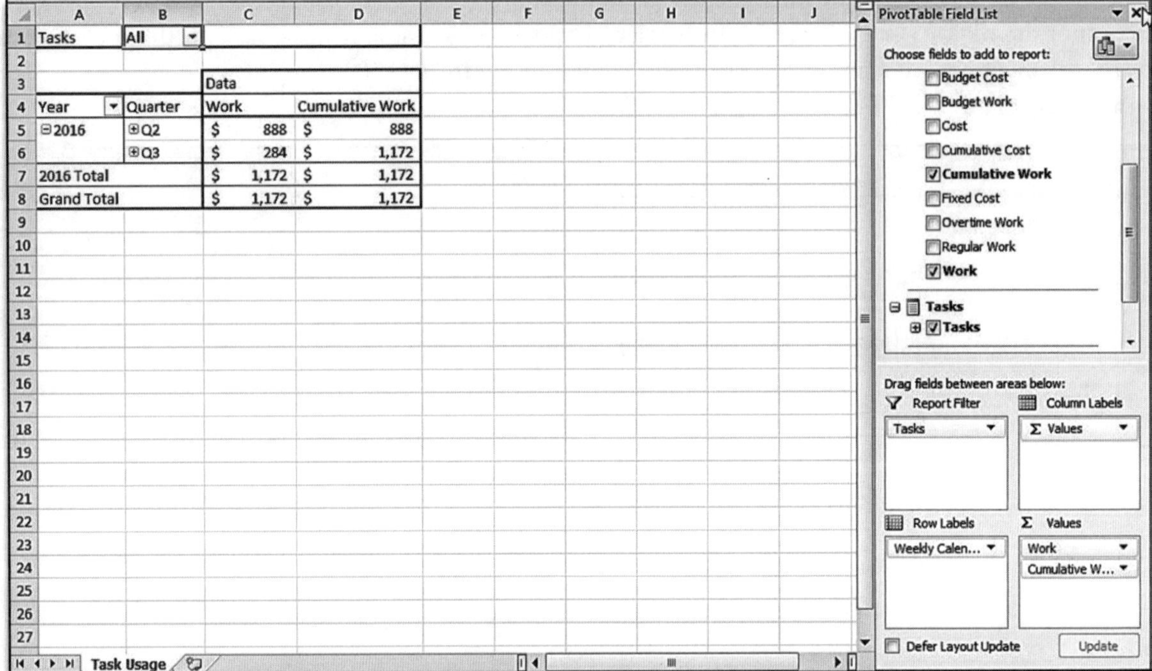

Figure 11 - 101: Task Usage page with populated PivotTable

Right-click the *Task Usage* tab at the bottom of the worksheet and select the *Insert* item on the shortcut menu. Excel displays the *Insert* dialog shown in Figure 11 - 102.

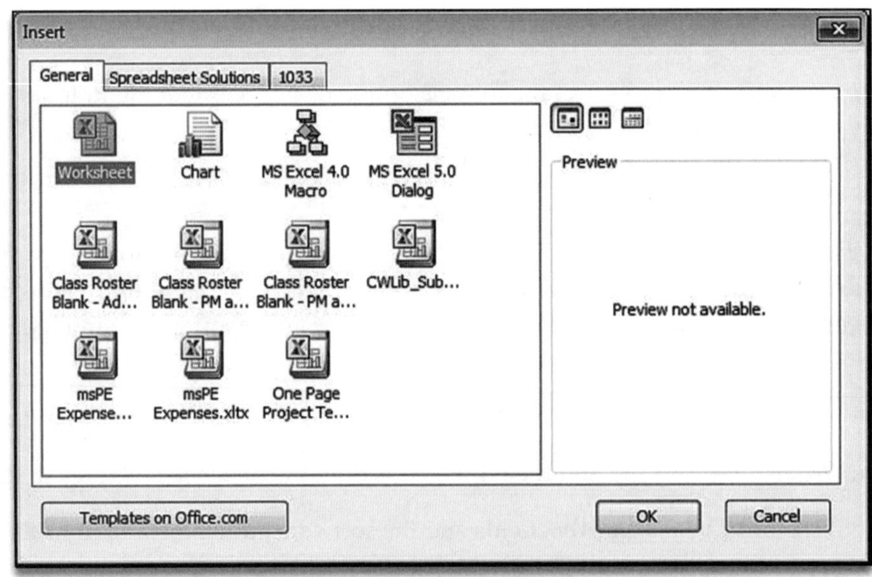

Figure 11 - 102: Insert dialog

In the *Insert* dialog, select the *Chart* icon, and then click the *OK* button. Excel generates a new worksheet labeled *Chart1* and displays a column chart based on the fields in the *PivotTable*. Figure 11 - 103 shows the resulting *PivotChart*. Close the *PivotTable Field List* sidepane to begin customizing the *PivotChart*.

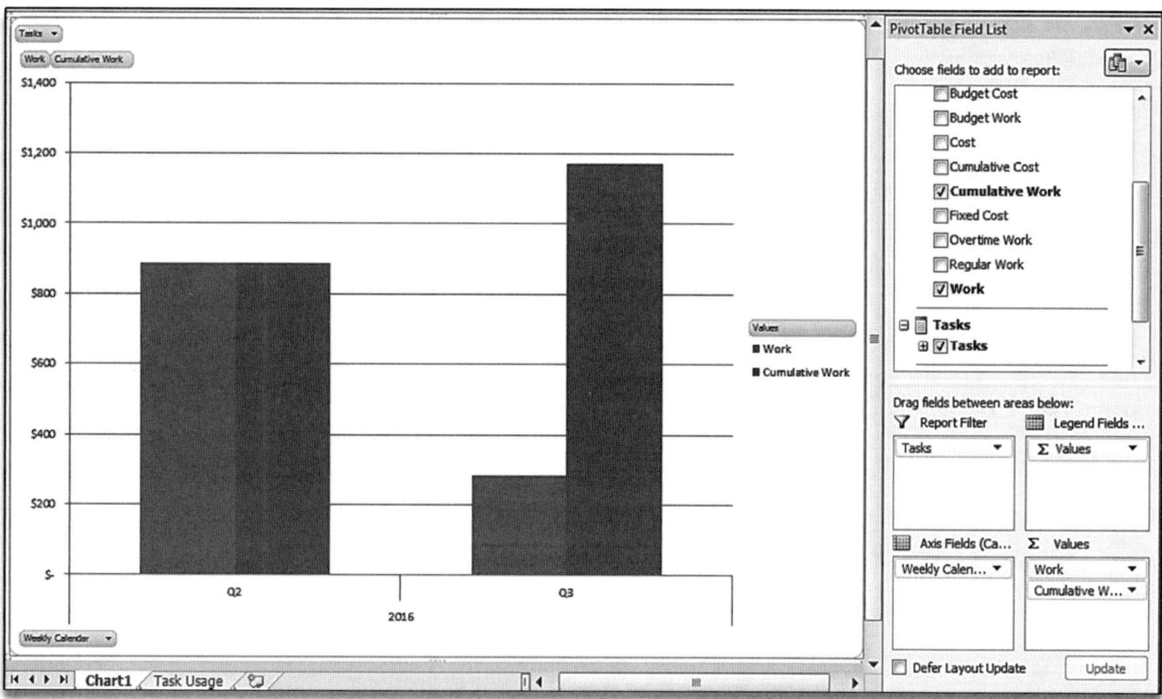

Figure 11 - 103: Generic PivotChart based on PivotTable data

Click anywhere in the *PivotChart* to select it and then click the *Layout* tab to display the contextual *Layout* ribbon with the *PivotChart Tools* applied. Using the options in the *Layout* ribbon, select your settings for one or more of the following:

- Chart Title
- Axis Titles
- Legend
- Data Labels
- Axes
- Gridlines

Click the *Design* tab to display the contextual *Design* ribbon with the *PivotChart Tools* applied. Using the options in the *Chart Styles* carousel, select chart formatting that meets your requirements. Figure 11 - 104 shows my completed *PivotChart*, and I am now ready to save the visual report as a new template.

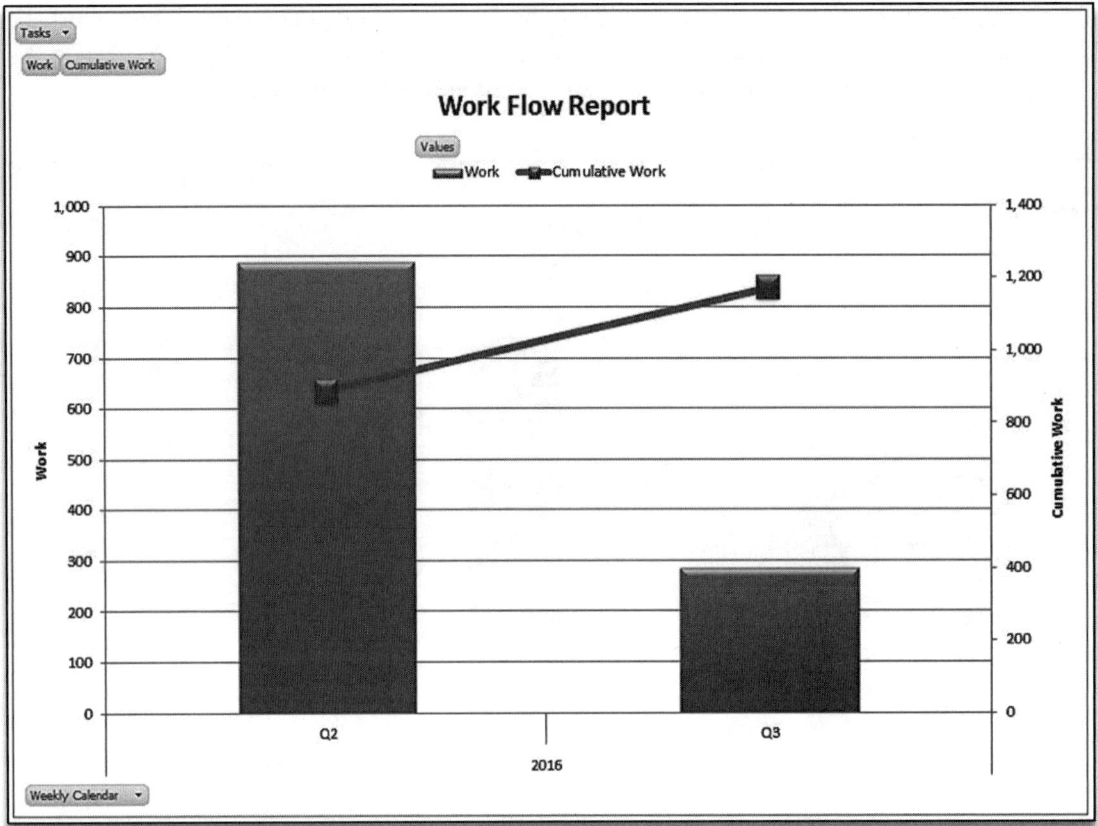

Figure 11 - 104: PivotChart for custom visual report template

When you finish formatting the *PivotChart,* click the *Task Usage* worksheet tab to display the *PivotTable.* Click anywhere in the *PivotTable* to select it and then click the *Options* tab to display the contextual *Options* ribbon with the *PivotTable Tools* applied. In the *Show* section of the *Options* ribbon, click the *Field List* button to redisplay the *PivotTable Field List* sidepane on the right side of the page. Click the *Chart1* worksheet tab to return to the *PivotChart.*

To save the new visual report template in Excel, click the *File* tab and then click the *Save As* button in the *Backstage.* In the *Save As* dialog, click the *Save as type* pick list and select the *Excel template (*.xltx)* option. The *Save As* dialog navigates to your default *Templates* folder, as shown in Figure 11 - 105. In the *File name* field, enter a template name using the name you want to appear in the *Visual Reports – Create Report* dialog, such as the *Work Flow Report.*

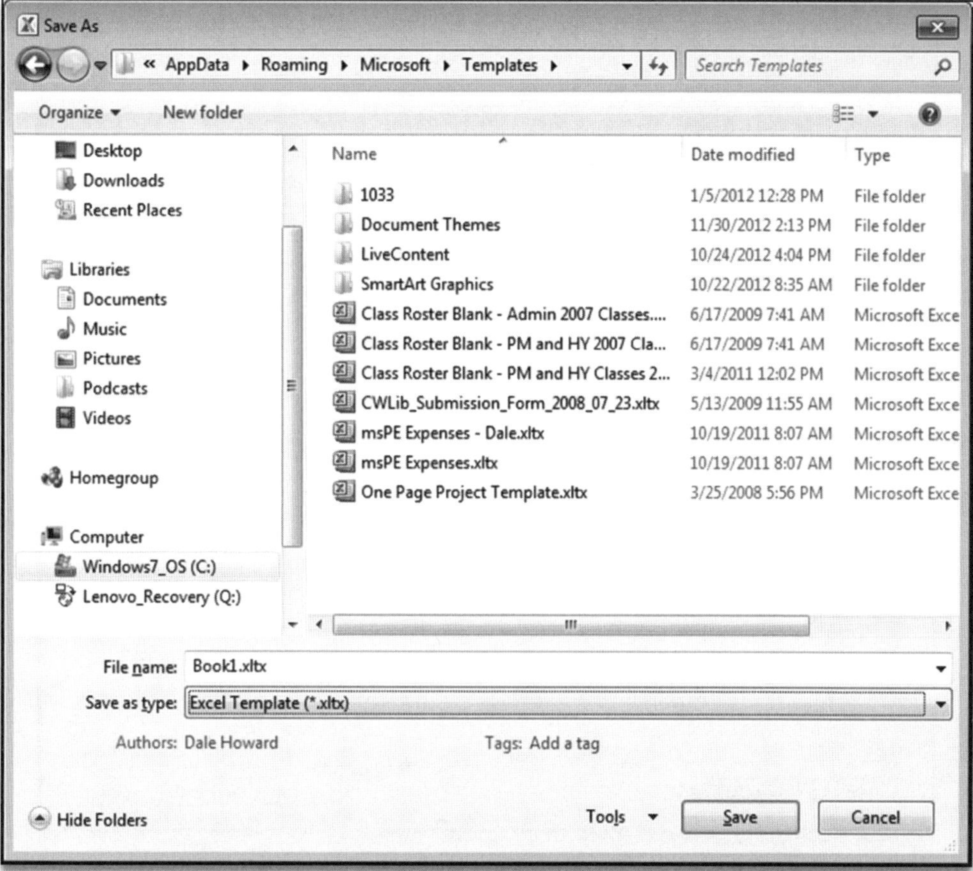

Figure 11 - 105: Save As dialog navigates to the default Templates folder

In the *Save As* dialog, click the *Save* button when finished to save your new visual report template. Excel displays the warning dialog shown in Figure 11 - 106 about how to handle external data in the workbook. Click the *Yes* button to save the new visual report template. Close the new Excel visual report template.

Figure 11 - 106: External data warning dialog

When you return to Project 2013, your new visual report template appears on the appropriate tab in the *Visual Reports – Create Report* dialog. Figure 11 - 107 shows my new *Work Flow Report* template on the *Task Usage* tab in the *Visual Reports – Create Report* dialog.

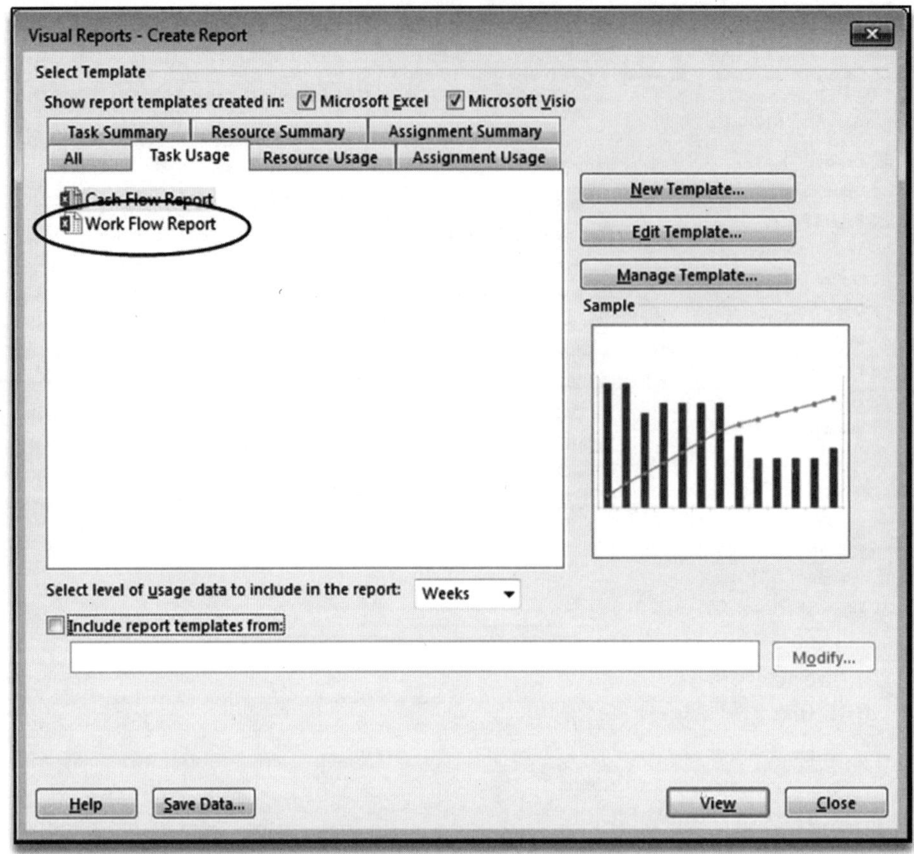

Figure 11 - 107: Work Flow Report appears on the Task Usage tab in the Visual Reports – Create Report dialog

Information: All visual report templates saved in the default templates folder appear automatically in the *Visual Reports - Create Report* dialog. If you save your visual report templates in any other folder, however, you **cannot** see them in the *Visual Reports - Create Report* dialog unless you select the *Include report templates from* option, click the *Modify* button, and then navigate to the folder containing your custom visual report templates.

Hands On Exercise

Exercise 11 - 15

Create a new visual report template for Excel.

1. In the *Visual Reports – Create Report* dialog in Project 2013, click the *New Template* button.
2. In the *Select Application* section of the *Visual Reports – New Template* dialog, select the *Excel* option.

3. In the *Select Data Type* section of the dialog, select the *Task Summary* option, and then click the *OK* button.
4. In your Excel application window, use the **Shift** key to select the *Sheet2* and *Sheet3* worksheet tabs as a group.
5. Right-click the selected worksheet tabs and then select the *Delete* item on the shortcut menu to remove these extra worksheets.
6. Right-click the *Sheet1* worksheet tab, click the *Rename* item on the shortcut menu, and name the worksheet *Task Summary*.
7. Drag the following fields to the following areas in the *PivotTable Field List* sidepane:

Field Name	Drop Area
Tasks	Report Filter
Actual Work	Values
Remaining Work	Values
Σ Values	Row Labels

8. In the *PivotTable*, select the numbers in the *Total* column.
9. In the *Number* section of the *Home* ribbon, click the *Comma Style* button.
10. In the *Number* section of the *Home* ribbon, click the *Decrease Decimal* button **twice**.
11. Widen the *Total* column as needed.
12. Right-click the *Task Summary* worksheet tab and select the *Insert* item on the shortcut menu.
13. In the *Insert* dialog, select the *Chart* item, and then click the *OK* button.
14. Close the *PivotTable Field List* sidepane.

Exercise 11 - 16

Customize the *PivotChart* of a new visual report template.

1. Click the *Design* tab to display the contextual *Design* ribbon with the *PivotChart Tools* applied.
2. In the *Type* section of the *Design* ribbon, click the *Change Chart Type* button.
3. In *Pie* section of the *Change Chart Type* dialog, select the *Exploded pie in 3-D* option (fifth item in the *Pie* section) and then click the *OK* button.
4. Right-click in the *Total* chart title and select the *Edit Text* item on the shortcut menu.
5. Rename the title as *Actual Work vs. Remaining Work* and then click anywhere outside of the title.
6. Click the *Layout* tab to display the contextual *Layout* ribbon with the *PivotChart Tools* applied.

7. In the *Labels* section of the *Layout* ribbon, click the *Legend* pick list button, and then select the *Show Legend at Top* item to display the legend below the title.
8. Right-click in either slice of the pie chart and select the *3-D Rotation* item on the shortcut menu.
9. In the *Format Chart Area* dialog, set the *X Rotation* to *90 degrees*, set the *Y Rotation* to *30 degrees*, and then click the *Close* button.
10. Right-click in either slice of the pie chart and select the *Add Data Labels* item on the shortcut menu.
11. Right-click in either of the *Data Labels* in the pie chart, and do the following in the floating *Mini Toolbar* at the top of the shortcut menu:
    - Click the *Bold* button.
    - Select the *14 points* item in the *Size* field.
    - Click on the *Font color* pick list button and choose the *White* color.
12. Click the *File* tab and then click the *Save As* button in the *Backstage*.
13. In the *Save As* dialog, click the *Save as type* pick list and select the *Excel template (*.xltx)* option.
14. In the *File name* field, enter the name **Actual and Remaining Work Report.xltx**, and then click the *Save* button.
15. When the software warns you in a dialog about external data, click the *Yes* button.
16. Click the *File* tab and then click the *Close* button to close the Excel visual report.
17. Close your Excel application and return to your Project 2013 application window.
18. In the *Visual Reports – Create Report* dialog in Project 2013, click the *Task Summary* tab.

You should now see your new *Actual and Remaining Work Report* file on the *Task Summary* page of the dialog.

19. Click the *Close* button to close the *Visual Reports – Create Report* dialog.
20. Save and close your **Training Advisor 11.mpp** project file.

Managing Your Visual Report Templates

To manage your visual report templates, select any visual report template in the *Visual Reports – Create Report* dialog and then click the *Manage Template* button. The software launches the Windows Explorer application, navigates to your default templates folder, and selects the template you want to manage, as shown in Figure 11 - 108. Using the Windows Explorer software, you can rename or delete visual report templates, as needed.

Warning: I recommend that you **do not** rename or delete any of the default visual report templates. Instead, feel free to rename or delete any custom visual report templates you create.

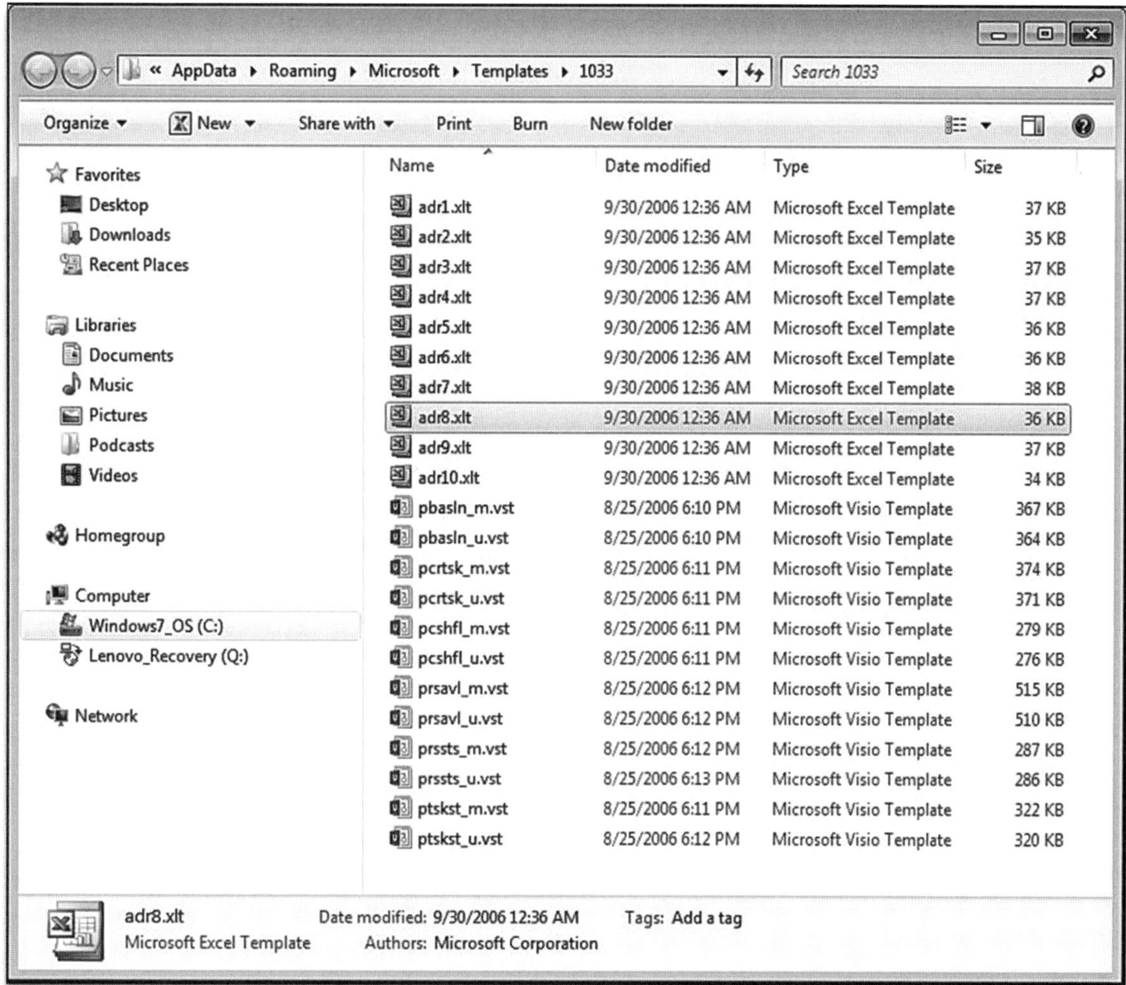

Figure 11 - 108: Templates folder

Module 12

Project Closure

Learning Objectives

After completing this module, you will be able to:

- Understand and use project closure methodologies
- Close a completed project in Project 2013
- Save a completed project as a project template
- Compare a completed project with the original project using the Compare Projects tool

Inside Module 12

Using Project Closure Methodologies

The final stage of every project is the closing stage, and your project closure process should include the following aspects:

- Update and complete all documents associated with the project, including the Project 2013 project file.
- Analyze the project management process using a Lessons Learned (aka "Post Mortem") meeting. You should primarily focus on project successes and effectiveness, but remember to look at project issues and failures, unforeseen risks, project variance and change requests as well as communication problems.

Best Practice: Do not play the "blame game" at your Lessons Learned meeting. Instead, MsProjectExperts recommends that you use this meeting to improve your project management skills so that your next project receives the benefits gained at the meeting. Stress to your project team members that the Lessons Learned meeting helps them to function better as project team members.

- Distribute a Lessons Learned report to all parties interested in your project, including project team members.
- Save all project documents in an archived project repository for future reference.
- Release project team members to work on other projects.
- If your organization maintains a resource skills database, update the database to reflect new skills and increased proficiency gains your resources realized while working on your project.

Best Practice: In addition to the closure process you use at the end of the project, the Project Management Institute (PMI) also recommends that you consider running a closure process at the end of every phase.

Closing a Project

To close a Project 2013 project file, complete the following steps:

1. Cancel unnecessary tasks.
2. Enter actual progress for tasks completed during the final reporting period.
3. Set to 100% complete all remaining milestone tasks.
4. If necessary or desired, save the completed project as a project template.
5. If possible, compare the original project with the completed project using the *Compare Projects* tool.

With the exception of #2, I discuss each step separately. I do not discuss how to enter progress for tasks since I documented this previously in Module 08, *Project Execution*.

Cancelling Unnecessary Tasks

During the task planning process, you undoubtedly included tasks in the project that you did not need to complete the project. MSProjectExperts recommends that you **do not delete** any baselined task, since deleting the task destroys baseline data and generates negative variance whose cause you cannot determine in your project. Instead, **cancel** the unnecessary task so that you can maintain the historical record of baselined tasks in the project and analyze the negative variance caused by cancelling the task.

For example, consider the task shown in Figure 12 - 1. The project sponsor elected to cancel the *Phase I Review* task after learning that the task was not necessary to complete the project work. Therefore, you need to cancel this task in the project.

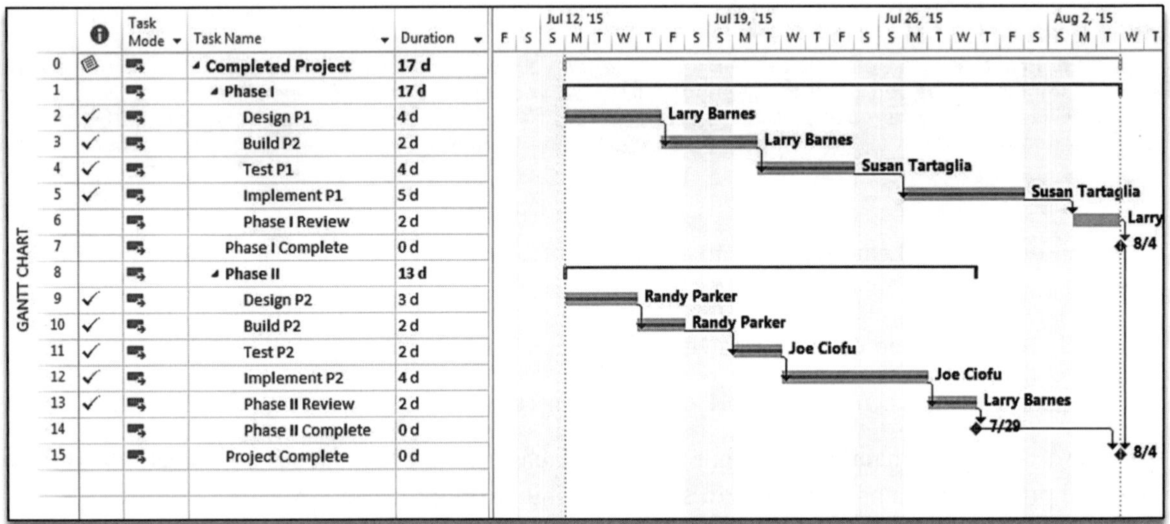

Figure 12 - 1: Project with an unnecessary task

Project 2013 offers two different ways to cancel unnecessary tasks. If you use the **Standard** version of the software, you should use the custom process I recommend in this book. If you use the **Professional** version of the software, you can cancel a task using the *Inactivate Task* feature.

Cancelling a Task Using Project Standard 2013

To cancel an unnecessary task using the **Standard** version of Project 2013, I recommend you use the following process:

1. Click the *View* tab to display the *View* ribbon.
2. In the *Task Views* section of the *View* ribbon, click the *Gantt Chart* pick list button and select the *Gantt Chart* view.
3. In the *Data* section of the *View* ribbon, click the *Tables* pick list and select the *Work* table.
4. Drag the split bar to the right to expose the *Remaining Work* column.
5. For the cancelled task, enter *0 hours* in the *Remaining Work* column.

When you set the *Remaining Work* value to *0 hours,* Project 2013 recalculates the *Duration* to *0 days,* and displays the task using the milestone symbol as shown in Figure 12 - 2.

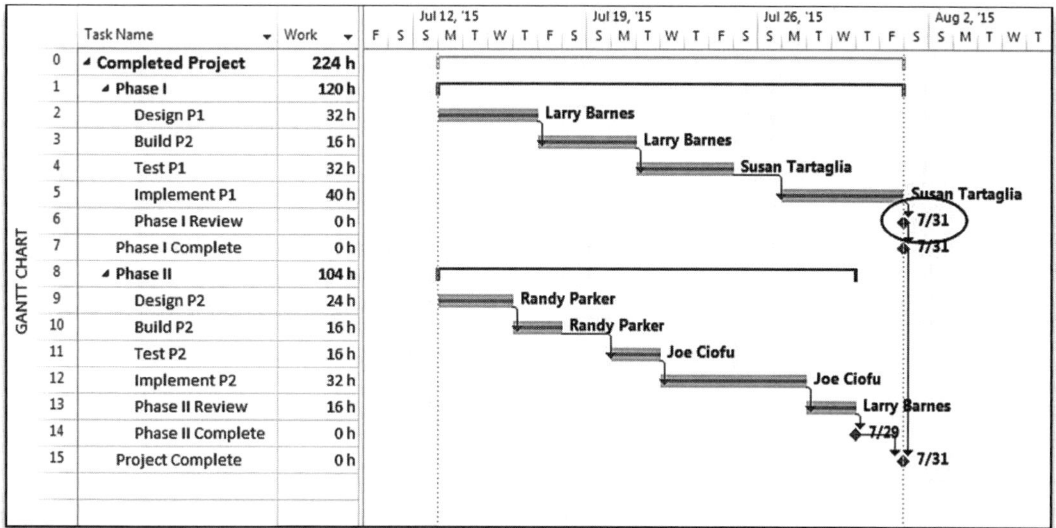

Figure 12 - 2: Cancelled task displayed as a milestone

6. In the *Data* section of the *View* ribbon, click the *Tables* pick list and select the *Entry* table.

7. Drag the split bar to the right edge of the *Duration* column.

8. Click the *Task* tab to display the *Task* ribbon.

9. In the *Schedule* section of the *Task* ribbon, click the *100% Complete* button.

Information: Although the preceding step may seem illogical, you must mark the cancelled task as *100% complete*. Before Project 2013 can mark the entire project as completed, you must mark every task as *100% complete*, including cancelled tasks.

10. In the *Properties* section of the *Task* ribbon, click the *Task Notes* button.

11. On the *Notes* page of the *Task Information* dialog, click the *Bulleted List* button, and then enter a note documenting the reason for cancelling the task.

12. Click the *OK* button when finished.

13. In the Gantt chart, double-click the milestone symbol (the black diamond) for the cancelled task. Project 2013 displays the *Format Bar* dialog shown in Figure 12 - 3.

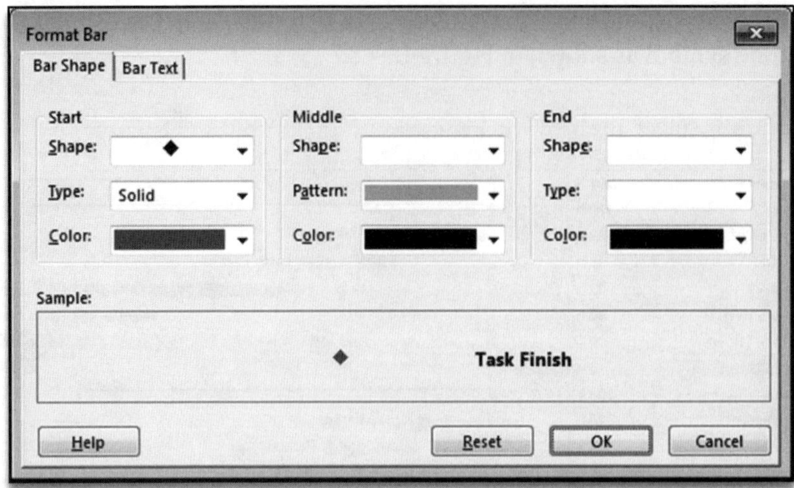

Figure 12 - 3: Format Bar dialog

14. In the *Start* section of the *Format Bar* dialog, click the *Shape* pick list, and then select a symbol to use in the Gantt chart for the cancelled task. For example, you might pick the solid circle near the bottom of the list.

15. In the *Start* section of the *Format Bar* dialog, click the *Color* pick list, and then select a color for the cancelled task symbol. For example, you might pick the *Green* color in the *Standard Colors* section of the list.

16. In the *Format Bar* dialog, select the *Bar Text* tab.

17. On the *Bar Text* page of the *Format Bar* dialog, select the *Task Finish* value in the *Right* field and press the **Backspace** key on your computer keyboard to delete the value and then press the **Enter** key.

18. Click the *OK* button. Project 2013 displays a unique symbol for the cancelled task, as shown in Figure 12 - 4.

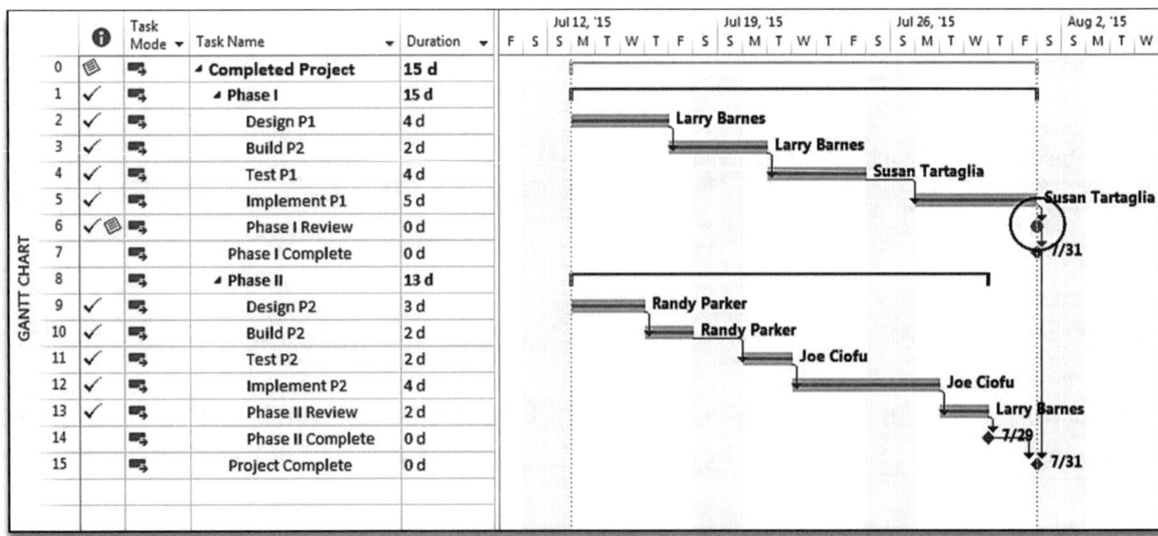

Figure 12 - 4: New symbol for a cancelled task with cell background formatting

To display the word *Cancelled* to the right of the special Gantt bar in the Gantt chart, complete the following additional steps:

1. Right-click the *Duration* column header and select the *Insert Column* item on the shortcut menu.

2. In the list of available fields, select the *Text1* field (or select the first unused custom *Text* field if the *Text1* field is already in use).

3. In the *Text1* column, select the cell for the cancelled task, type the word *Cancelled,* and then press the **Enter** key on your computer keyboard.

4. Right-click the *Text1* column header and select the *Hide Column* item on the shortcut menu.

5. In the Gantt chart, double-click the special symbol you selected for the cancelled task.

6. In the *Format Bar* dialog, select the *Bar Text* tab, if necessary.

7. Click the *Right* field to select it, click the pick list arrow button, and select the *Text1* field (or the custom *Text* field you selected in step #2 above).

8. Click the *OK* button. Project 2013 displays the word *Cancelled* to the right of the unique symbol for the cancelled task, as shown in Figure 12 - 5

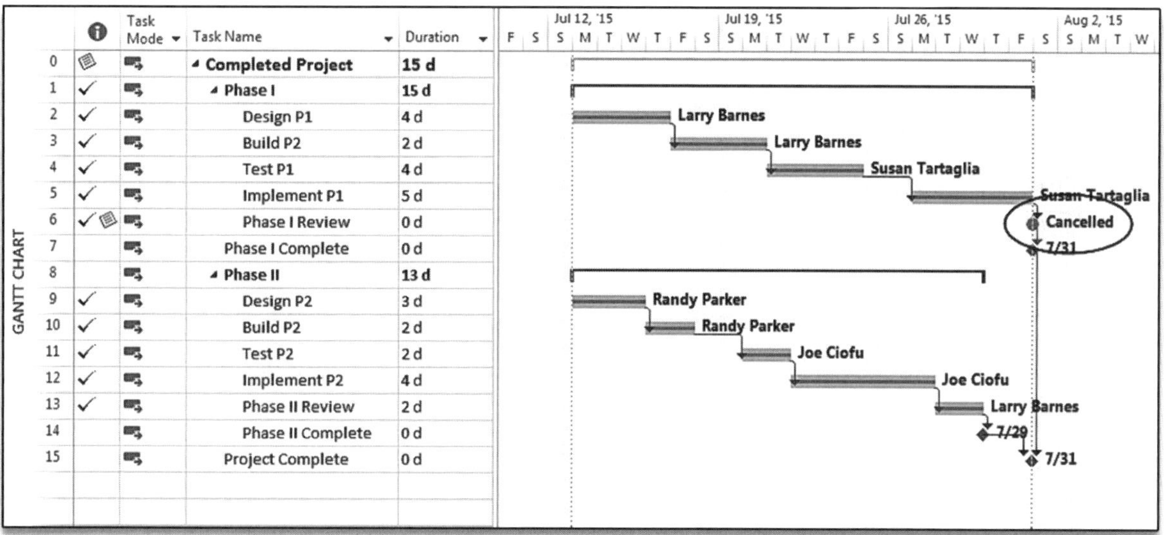

Figure 12 - 5: New symbol for a cancelled task includes the word Cancelled

Information: In addition to completing the preceding sets of steps to cancel an unneeded task, you might also want to format the cancelled task using cell background formatting. Use a unique cell background color to indicate all cancelled tasks in your project.

Cancelling a Task Using Project Professional 2013

To cancel an unnecessary task using the **Professional** version of Project 2013, complete the following steps:

1. Click the *Task* tab to display the *Task* ribbon.

2. Select the task you want to cancel.

3. In the *Schedule* section of the *Task* ribbon, click the *Inactivate* button. Figure 12 - 6 shows the *Inactivate* button on the *Task* ribbon, along with its floating tooltip.

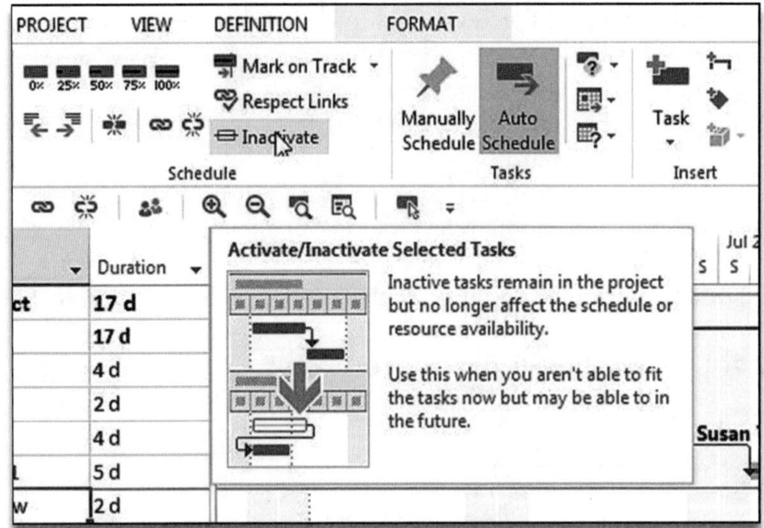

Figure 12 - 6: Inactivate button and tooltip

4. In the *Properties* section of the *Task* ribbon, click the *Task Notes* button.

5. On the *Notes* page of the *Task Information* dialog, click the *Bulleted List* button, and then enter a note documenting the reason for cancelling the task.

6. Click the *OK* button when finished. Figure 12 - 7 shows the original project shown previously in Figure 12 - 1, but after cancelling the *Phase I Review* task using the *Inactivate* button.

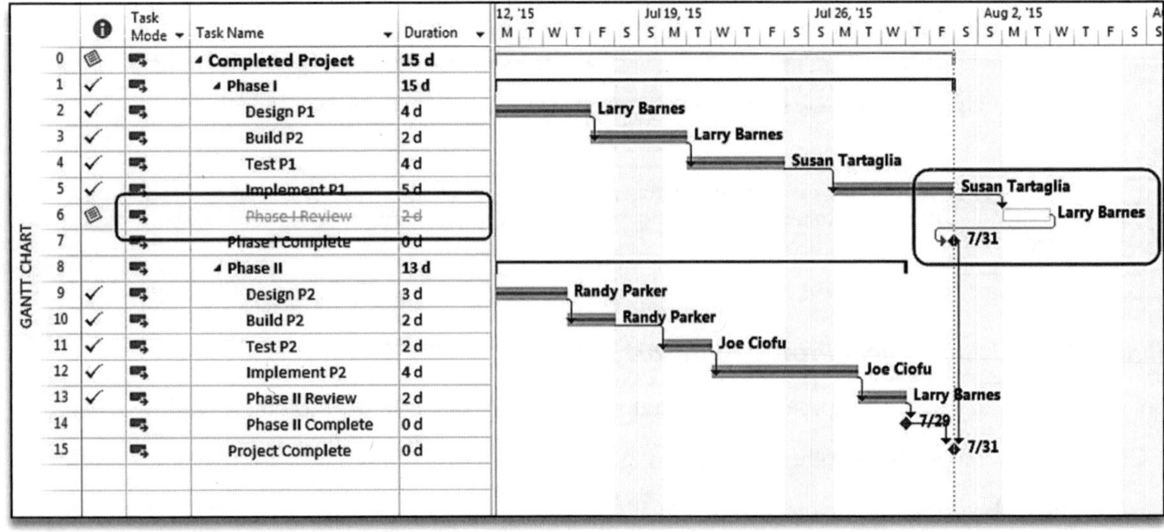

Figure 12 - 7: Phase I Review task set to Inactive status

When you cancel a task using the *Inactivate* button, Project 2013 does the following:

- The software formats the text of the *Inactive* task using the strikethrough font effect and the gray font color.
- The software formats the Gantt bar of the *Inactive* task using a hollow (unfilled) pattern.
- The software treats the *Inactive* task as if it has *0h* of remaining work. This means the *Inactive* task no longer affects resource availability for resources assigned to the task.
- Although the software continues to show link lines for the *Inactive* task, the software schedules successor tasks as if they are **not linked** to the *Inactive* task. Instead, the software treats the successor of the cancelled task as if it is linked to the predecessor of the cancelled task. This behavior is a new feature in Project 2013.

Figure 12 - 8 shows the *Inactive* task with the *Work* table applied in the *Gantt Chart* view. Notice that the software shows **-16h** of work variance in the *Variance* column for the *Phase I* summary task and for the Project Summary Task, caused by inactivating a task with *16h* of *Work* assigned to it.

GANTT CHART

	Task Name	Work	Baseline	Variance	Actual	Remaining	% W. Comp.
0	**Completed Project**	**224 h**	**240 h**	**-16 h**	**224 h**	**0 h**	**100%**
1	**Phase I**	**120 h**	**136 h**	**-16 h**	**120 h**	**0 h**	**100%**
2	Design P1	32 h	32 h	0 h	32 h	0 h	100%
3	Build P2	16 h	16 h	0 h	16 h	0 h	100%
4	Test P1	32 h	32 h	0 h	32 h	0 h	100%
5	Implement P1	40 h	40 h	0 h	40 h	0 h	100%
6	~~Phase I Review~~	~~16 h~~	~~16 h~~	~~0 h~~	~~0 h~~	~~16 h~~	~~0%~~
7	Phase I Complete	0 h	0 h	0 h	0 h	0 h	0%
8	**Phase II**	**104 h**	**104 h**	**0 h**	**104 h**	**0 h**	**100%**
9	Design P2	24 h	24 h	0 h	24 h	0 h	100%
10	Build P2	16 h	16 h	0 h	16 h	0 h	100%
11	Test P2	16 h	16 h	0 h	16 h	0 h	100%
12	Implement P2	32 h	32 h	0 h	32 h	0 h	100%
13	Phase II Review	16 h	16 h	0 h	16 h	0 h	100%
14	Phase II Complete	0 h	0 h	0 h	0 h	0 h	0%
15	Project Complete	0 h	0 h	0 h	0 h	0 h	0%

Figure 12 - 8: Work table shows cancelled tasks

Remember that when you set a task to *Inactive* status, Project 2013 treats the successor of the cancelled task as if it is linked to the predecessor of the cancelled task. Because of this, you may want to link successor tasks for the *Inactive* task to the nearest *Active* predecessor task to reset the project schedule from that point forward. This step is optional, however, based on the scheduling needs of the project for the successors of the cancelled task.

You do not need to mark the *Inactive* task to 100% complete, since Project 2013 treats the *Inactive* task as if it does not exist. If fact, if you try to mark the *Inactive* task as 100% complete, the software will not let you do it.

Warning: Project 2013 does not allow you to cancel a completed task or an in-progress task by setting it to *Inactive* status. To cancel the uncompleted work in an in-progress task, apply the task *Work* table and then set the *Remaining Work* value to *0h* for the task.

Marking Milestones as Complete

To mark a milestone as complete, use the following process:

1. Click the *Task* tab to display the *Task* ribbon.
2. Select the milestone task.
3. In the *Schedule* section of the *Task* ribbon, click the *100% Complete* button.

Project 2013 marks the milestone task as *100%* complete by entering a date in the *Actual Start* and *Actual Finish* fields and by displaying a completed task indicator (blue check mark) in the *Indicators* column for the task. When you set every task to *100%* complete in the project plan, the software automatically marks the Project Summary Task (Row 0) as *100%* complete.

Hands On Exercise

Exercise 12 - 1

The current date is **Monday, April 18, 2016**. Project team members completed work on the Training Advisor Rollout project during the previous week. The *Provide Training Advisor Classes* task finished one day earlier than expected. The project sponsor decided to cancel the *Provide End User Support* task due to a budget cutback for the project.

Steps for Project 2013 STANDARD Users Only

1. Open the **Training Advisor 12.mpp** sample file.
2. Click the *Task* tab to display the *Task* ribbon.
3. Select task ID #38, the *Provide Training Advisor Classes* task, and then click the *Scroll to Task* button in the *Editing* section of the *Task* ribbon.
4. Right-click the *Select All* button and select the *Work* table in the shortcut menu.
5. Drag the split bar to the right side so that you can see the *Remaining Work* column.
6. For task ID #38, the *Provide Training Advisor Classes* task, **increase** the value in the *Actual Work* column to *216h* and then set the *Remaining Work* value to *0h*.
7. For task ID #39, the *Provide End User Support* task, set the *Remaining Work* value to *0h* to cancel this unneeded task.

8. If you see a *Planning Wizard* dialog about a scheduling conflict, select the *Continue* option, and then click the *OK* button.
9. Right-click the *Select All* button and select the *Entry* table in the shortcut menu.
10. Drag the split bar back to the right edge of the *Duration* column.

Notice in the Gantt chart that Project 2013 shows the cancelled task using a milestone symbol (a black diamond).

11. Select task ID #39, the *Provide End User Support* task, and then click the *Task Notes* button in the *Properties* section of the *Task* ribbon.
12. On the *Notes* page of the *Task Information* dialog, click at the right end of the previous note and then press the **Enter** key on your computer keyboard to add a new line of notes text.
13. On the *Notes* page of the *Task Information* dialog, add the following task note:

    4/18/16 – Task cancelled at request of project sponsor due to budget cuts.

14. Click the *OK* button to close the *Task Information* dialog.
15. In the Gantt chart, double-click the milestone symbol for the *Provide End User Support* task (the black diamond symbol).
16. In the *Start* section of the *Format Bar* dialog, click the *Shape* pick list and select a symbol other than the diamond to use in the Gantt chart for the cancelled task.
17. In the *Start* section of the *Format Bar* dialog, click the *Color* pick list and select a color for the cancelled task symbol.
18. Click the *OK* button to close the *Format Bar* dialog.

Notice that the software displays a unique symbol for the cancelled task.

19. Save but **do not** close the **Training Advisor 12.mpp** sample file.

Steps for Project 2013 PROFESSIONAL Users Only

1. Open the **Training Advisor 12.mpp** sample file.
2. Click the *Task* tab to display the *Task* ribbon.
3. Select task ID #38, the *Provide Training Advisor Classes* task, and then click the *Scroll to Task* button in the *Editing* section of the *Task* ribbon.
4. Right-click the *Select All* button and select the *Work* table in the shortcut menu.
5. Drag the split bar to the right side so that you can see the *Remaining Work* column.
6. For task ID #38, the *Provide Training Advisor Classes* task, **increase** the value in the *Actual Work* column to *216h* and then set the *Remaining Work* value to *0h*.
7. Right-click the *Select All* button and select the *Entry* table on the shortcut menu.
8. Drag the split bar back to the right edge of the *Duration* column.

9. Select task ID #39, the *Provide End User Support* task, and then click the *Scroll to Task* button in the *Editing* section of the *Task* ribbon.
10. Click the gray row header for task ID #39 to select the entire task row.
11. In the *Font* section of the *Task* ribbon, click the *Background Color* pick list button, and then select the *No Color* item to remove the cell background color.
12. Leave task ID #39, the *Provide End User Support* task, still selected.
13. In the *Schedule* section of the *Task* ribbon, click the *Inactivate* button.
14. If you see a *Planning Wizard* dialog about a scheduling conflict, select the *Continue* option, and then click the *OK* button.
15. Click anywhere outside of the selected task row.

Notice how Project 2013 displays the cancelled task using the gray strikethrough font and the hollow Gantt bar shape.

16. Select task ID #38, the *Provide Training Advisor Classes* task, press and hold the **Control** key on your computer keyboard, and then select task ID# 40, the *Training Complete* milestone task.
17. In the *Schedule* section of the *Task* ribbon, click the *Link the Selected Tasks* button.
18. Save but **do not** close the **Training Advisor 12.mpp** sample file.

Exercise 12 - 2

Mark all remaining tasks as 100% complete to complete the Training Advisor Rollout project.

1. Return to the **Training Advisor 12.mpp** sample file.
2. Click the *Expand* indicator (white arrow) to the left of the *Project Status Meeting* recurring task to expand all of the meeting instances.
3. Select task IDs #14 and #15 and click the *100% Complete* button in the *Schedule* section of the *Task* ribbon.
4. Click the *Collapse* indicator (black triangle) to the left of the *Project Status Meeting* recurring task to collapse the meeting instances.
5. Select task IDs #40 and #41, the last two milestone tasks, and then in the *Schedule* section of the *Task* ribbon, click the *100% Complete* button.
6. Examine the *Indicators* column for the Project Summary Task (Row 0) and notice the blue checkmark in this column, indicating the project is totally complete.

Notice that Project 2013 displays a blue checkmark indicator in the *Indicators* column to the left of the Project Summary Task (Row 0), indicating that all work in the project is complete.

7. Press **Control + Home** and then press **Alt + Home** on your computer keyboard to scroll back to the beginning of the project.
8. Save but **do not** close the **Training Advisor 12.mpp** sample file.

Saving a Completed Project as a Template

If you need to create one or more future projects based on the completed project, then you should save the completed project as a project template. Before saving the project as a template, however, you need to "clean up" the project to prepare it for use as a template. To "clean up" a complete project for use as a template, complete the following steps:

1. Open the project and save it using a **new name**, such as by appending the words *Saved for Template* to the end of the file name. This prevents you from accidentally saving the "cleaned up" project over your final completed project.
2. Click the *Task* tab to display the *Task* ribbon.
3. Click the *Select All* button to select all tasks in the project.
4. In the *Properties* section of the *Task* ribbon, click the *Information* button.
5. In the *Multiple Task Information* dialog, click the *General* tab, and then enter or select *0%* in the *Percent complete* field.
6. In the *Multiple Task Information* dialog, click the *Advanced* tab.
7. On the *Advanced* tab of the dialog, manually type an *NA* value in the *Deadline* field.
8. On the *Advanced* tab of the dialog, click the *Constraint type* pick list, and then select the *As Soon As Possible* item.
9. On the *Advanced* tab of the dialog, click the *Calendar* pick list, and then select the *None* option.
10. Click the *OK* button to close the *Multiple Task Information* dialog.
11. Click the *Select All* button to select all tasks in the project again, if necessary.
12. In the *Editing* section of the *Task* ribbon, click the *Clear* pick list button, and then select the *Notes* item.

Information: Project templates should not contain constraints, *Deadline* dates, or task calendars. Users of the project template should set constraints, *Deadline* dates, and task calendars on an "as needed" basis for each new project created from the project template. Furthermore, project templates should not contain notes that document the history of completing the project. Instead, add notes to tasks in the project template to guide the project manager on how to plan the project properly.

13. In the *Editing* section of the *Task* ribbon, click the *Clear* pick list button, and then select the *Clear Formatting* item.
14. In the *Tasks* section of the *Task* ribbon, set the *Task Mode* value to either *Manually Schedule* or *Auto Schedule* for all tasks as needed.
15. Set all *Inactive* tasks to *Active* status by selecting the tasks and unclicking the *Inactivate* button in the *Schedule* section of the *Task* ribbon (Project **Professional** 2013 users only).

Information: In a large project, the fastest way to identify all *Inactive* tasks is to apply the default group named *Active v. Inactive*. To apply this group, click the *View* tab to display the *View* ribbon, click the *Group By* pick list, and then select the *Active v. Inactive* group. The group containing *Inactive* tasks appears at the top of the project. You can select all of the *Inactive* tasks as a block and then unclick the *Inactivate* button on the *Task* ribbon to reset all of them to *Active* status. When finished, return to the *View* ribbon and click the *Group By* pick list again, and then select the *[No Group]* group.

16. Select all tasks **except for** the Project Summary Task (Row 0) and then click the *Resource* tab to display the *Resource* ribbon.

17. In the *Assignments* section of the *Resource* ribbon, click the *Assign Resources* button.

18. In the *Assign Resources* dialog, select all resources, click the *Remove* button, and then click the *Close* button.

Information: If you use generic resources in your organization, instead of completing the preceding step, you may want to replace your named resources with their corresponding generic resources. For example, replace a human resource named *Mickey Cobb* with a generic resource named *SQL Server DBA*.

19. In the *View* section of the *Resource* ribbon, click the *Team Planner* pick list button, and then select the *Resource Sheet* view.

20. Click the *Select All* button to select all resources and then press the **Delete** key on your computer keyboard to delete all of the resources on the project team.

Information: The preceding step is an optional step if you build a completely new project team each time you create a new project. If you use a dedicated project team, skip the preceding step. If you want to create a template that includes generic resources, use a more selective approach to avoid deleting the generic resources from your plan.

21. Click the *Task* tab to display the *Task* ribbon.

22. In the *View* section of the *Task* ribbon, click the *Gantt Chart* pick list button and select the *Gantt Chart* view.

23. Reset the *Gantt Chart* view to its default settings by clicking the *Gantt Chart* pick list button again and then selecting the *Reset to Default* item on the list. In the confirmation dialog, click the *Yes* button.

In addition to the preceding steps, you may also need to remove task splits caused by entering *Actual Work* hours on a daily basis in the timephased grid of the *Resource Usage* view. Whenever you enter *0h* on the *Actual Work* line of the timephased grid for any time period during the life of a task, Project 2013 automatically creates a task split to show no work performed during that time period. For example, notice that there is a task split resulting from the entry of daily progress on the *Design P2* task shown in Figure 12 - 9.

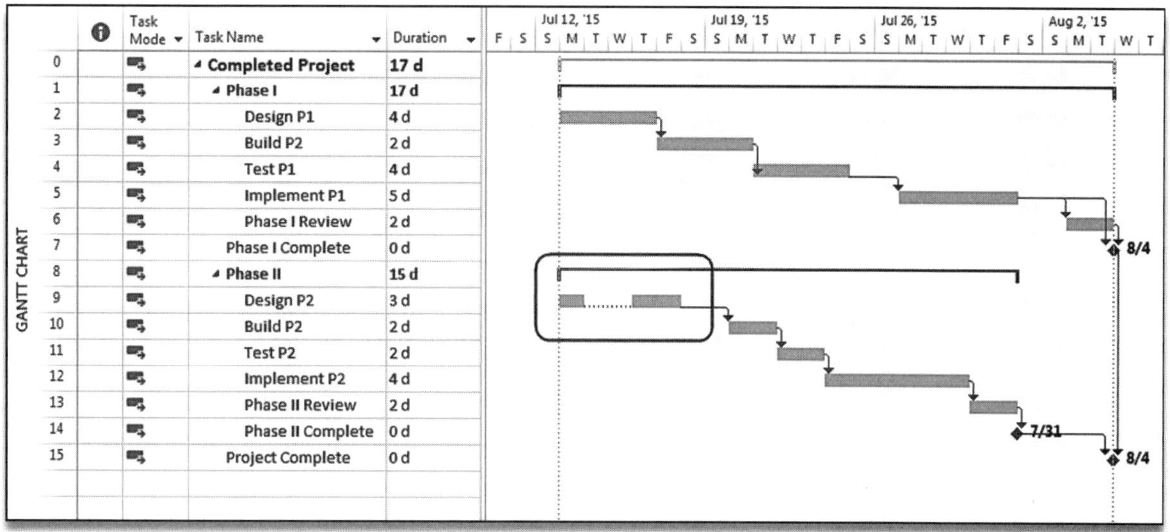

Figure 12 - 9: Task splits resulting from daily Actual Work entries

To remove a task split, float your mouse pointer over the right-most portion of the Gantt bar for the split task, click and hold to "grab" the Gantt bar portion, and then drag the Gantt bar portion to the left until it rejoins the left-most split portion. When you release the mouse button, Project 2013 rejoins the split portions of the Gantt bar. If a task contains multiple splits, repeat this process for every split section until you reassemble a complete, unbroken Gantt bar for the task.

Information: Since the completed project contains the final *Duration* value of every task, which might include a fraction such as *6.5 days*, you may want to set the fractions to whole numbers. For example, you might want to change a *Duration* value of *6.5 days* to either *6 days* or *7 days*.

After "cleaning up" your project, you are ready to save the project as a project template by completing the following steps:

1. Click the *File* tab and then click the *Save As* tab in the *Backstage*.
2. On the *Save As* page in the *Backstage*, click the *Browse* button. Project 2013 displays the *Save As* dialog.
3. In the *Save As* dialog, enter a name for the template in the *File name* field.
4. In the *Save As* dialog, click the *Save as type* pick list, and then select the *Project Template (*.mpt)* item as shown in Figure 12 - 10.

Information: After you select the *Project Template (*.mpt)* item on the *Save as type* pick list, Project 2013 navigates automatically to your default *Templates* folder.

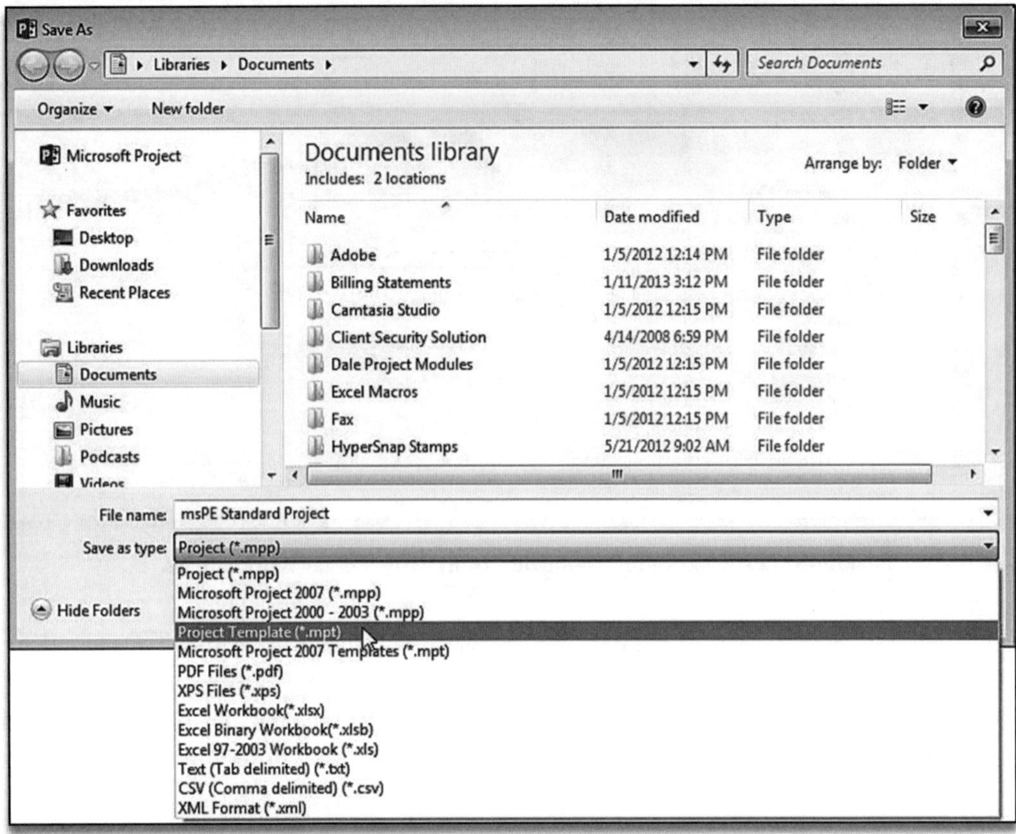

Figure 12 - 10: Save As dialog when saving a project template

5. Click the *Save* button. Project 2013 displays the *Save As Template* dialog shown in Figure 12 - 11.

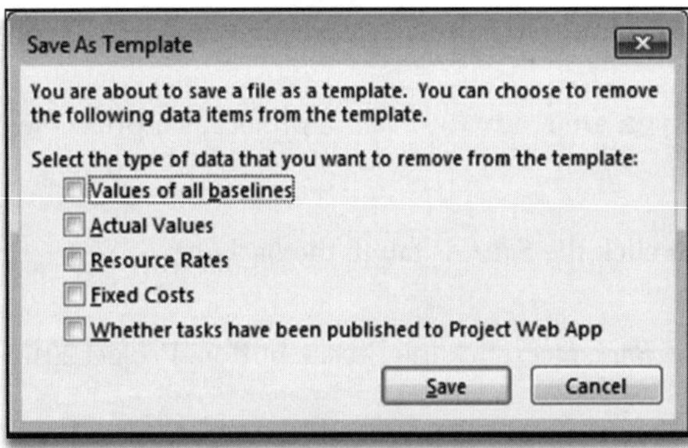

Figure 12 - 11: Save As Template dialog

6. In the *Save As Template* dialog, select **at least** the first two checkboxes, and then click the *OK* button.

You do not need to select the *Resource Rates* option if you already deleted all resources from the project team, or if you opt not to clear actual resources from your project, as might be the case with a dedicated project team using consistent resource rates. You should select the *Fixed Costs* option if you added extra task costs in the *Fixed Cost* column as part of entering actual progress on tasks. Do not select the *Fixed Costs* option if your fixed cost amounts represent planned task costs in the project. Select the final option, *Whether tasks have been published to Project Web App*, only if you use Project Server 2013 and the "cleaned up" project as an enterprise project.

7. Click the *File* tab and then click the *Close* tab in the *Backstage* to close the new project template.
8. If prompted to save the changes in a confirmation dialog, click the *Yes* button to save the latest changes to the project template file.

Creating a New Project from the Completed Template

To create a new project from the project template, complete the following steps:

1. Click the *File* tab and then click the *New* tab in the *Backstage*. Project 2013 displays the *New* page.
2. On the *New* page in the *Backstage*, click the *PERSONAL* link at the top of the page. The software displays personal templates as shown in Figure 12 - 12.

Warning: If you do not see a *PERSONAL* link at the top of the *New* page, click the *Options* tab in the *Backstage*. In the *Project Options* dialog, click the *Save* tab. In the *Default personal templates location* field in the *Save templates* section of the dialog, manually enter the path for your default *Templates* folder based on the example below, or use the *Browse* button to navigate to your default *Templates* folder.

C:\Users\YourWindowsUserID\AppData\Roaming\Microsoft\Templates

Click the *OK* button when finished. Click the *File* tab and then click the *New* tab in the *Backstage*. You should now see a *PERSONAL* link at the top of the *New* page.

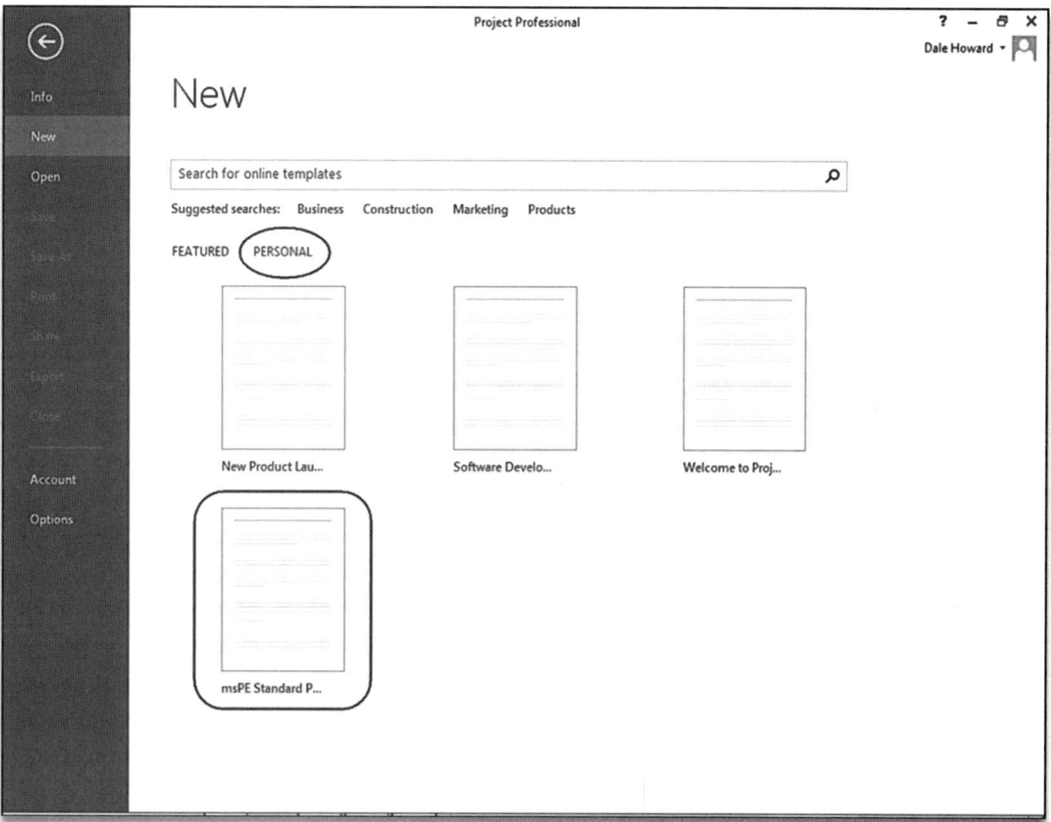

Figure 12 - 12: New page in the Backstage

3. On the *New* page in the *Backstage*, select the icon for the template you want to use. Project 2013 displays a preview dialog for the new saved template, similar to the one shown in Figure 12 - 13.

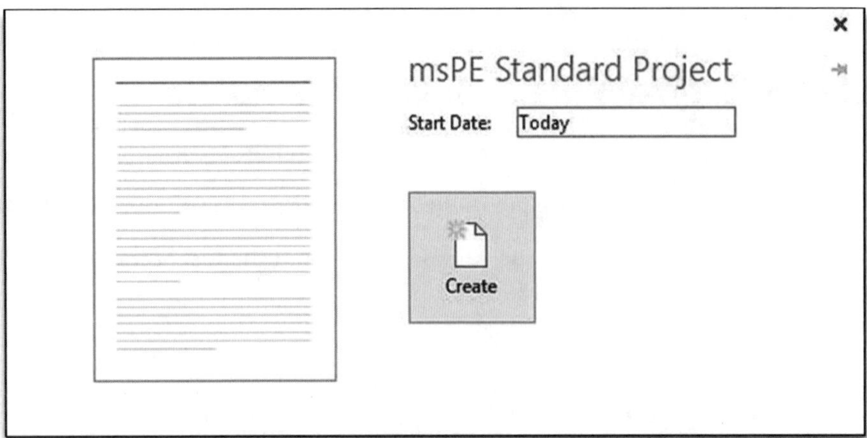

Figure 12 - 13: Preview dialog for the new saved template

4. In the preview dialog, enter a date in the *Start Date* field and then click the *Create* button. The software creates the new project as a copy of the template you selected

Hands On Exercise

Exercise 12 - 3

Clean up the tasks in the Training Advisor Rollout project to prepare to save it as a project template.

1. Return to the **Training Advisor 12.mpp** sample file.
2. Click the *File* tab and then click the *Save As* tab in the *Backstage.*
3. In the *Recent Folders* section of the *Save As* page, click the name of the folder containing your sample files.
4. In the *Save As* dialog, enter the new name **Training Advisor Project – Saved for Template.mpp** in the *File name* field, and then click the *Save* button.

Warning: **Do not skip** the preceding step in this exercise. You **must** save the sample project file using a new name to protect the original sample file for use later in this module.

5. Click the *Task* tab to display the *Task* ribbon, if necessary.
6. Click the *Select All* button to select all tasks in the project.
7. In the *Properties* section of the *Task* ribbon, click the *Information* button.

8. In the *Multiple Task Information* dialog, select the *General* tab and enter *0%* in the *Percent complete* field.
9. In the *Multiple Task Information* dialog, select the *Advanced* tab.
10. On the *Advanced* tab of the dialog, complete the following steps:
    - Manually enter an *NA* value in the *Deadline* field.
    - Click the *Constraint type* pick list and select the *As Soon As Possible* item on the list.
    - Click the *Calendar* pick list and select the *None* option.
11. Click the *OK* button to close the *Multiple Task Information* dialog.
12. Click the *Select All* button to select all tasks in the project again, if necessary.
13. In the *Editing* section of the *Task* ribbon, click the *Clear* pick list button, and then select the *Notes* item on the list.
14. In the *Editing* section of the *Task* ribbon, click the *Clear* pick list button again, and then select the *Clear Formatting* item on the list.

Notice that using the *Clear Formatting* command **does not** remove the cell background formatting applied to the milestone tasks. This is because you used the *Text Styles* feature to apply cell background formatting to all milestone tasks automatically.

15. Select task ID #39, the *Provide End User Support* task, and then unclick the *Inactivate* button in the *Schedule* section of the *Task* ribbon.
16. Click the *View* tab to display the *View* ribbon.
17. Select task ID #20, the *Load and Configure Software* task, and then click the *Scroll to Task* button in the *Editing* section of the *Task* ribbon.
18. Float your mouse pointer over the right-most portion of the Gantt bar for the split task, click and hold to "grab" the Gantt bar portion, and then drag the Gantt bar portion to the left until it rejoins the left-most split portion.

Ignore the trailing split (...) section at the right end of the Gantt bar, caused by the *Expense Cost* resource assigned to this task.

19. Select task ID #31, the *Create Training Module 01* task, and then click the *Scroll to Task* button again.
20. Remove the task split in the Gantt bar for this task using the same technique you used in step #18.
21. Right-click task ID #1, the *Project Status Meeting* recurring task, and select the *Delete Task* item on the shortcut menu.
22. In the *Planning Wizard* dialog, leave the *Continue* option selected, and then click the *OK* button.
23. In the confirmation dialog, click the *Yes* button to delete the recurring task and all of its subtasks.
24. In the *View* section of the *Task* ribbon, click the *Gantt Chart* pick list button, and then select the *Reset to Default* item on the list.
25. When prompted in a confirmation dialog, click the *Yes* button.

26. Widen the *Task Name* column as needed and then dock the split bar on the right edge of the *Duration* column.
27. Press **Control + Home** and then press **Alt + Home** on your computer keyboard to scroll back to the beginning of the project.
28. Save but **do not** close the **Training Advisor Project – Saved for Template.mpp** sample file.

Exercise 12 - 4

Clean up the resources in the Training Advisor Rollout project to prepare to save it as a project template.

1. Select all tasks in the project **except for** the Project Summary Task (Row 0).
2. Click the *Resource* tab to display the *Resource* ribbon.
3. In the *Assignments* section of the *Resource* ribbon, click the *Assign Resources* button to display the *Assign Resources* dialog.
4. In the *Assign Resources* dialog, scroll to the top of the resource list, and select all resource names from *Bob Jared* to *Terry Uland*.
5. In the *Assign Resources* dialog, click the *Remove* button.
6. When prompted in a warning dialog about removing actual values, click the *Yes* button.
7. Click the *Close* button to close the *Assign Resources* dialog.
8. In the *View* section of the *Resource* ribbon, click the *Team Planner* pick list button, and then select the *Resource Sheet* view.
9. Click the *Select All* button to select all resources on the project team, and then press the **Delete** key on your computer keyboard to delete them.
10. Click the *Task* tab to display the *Task* ribbon.
11. In the *View* section of the *Task* ribbon, click the *Gantt Chart* button to reapply the *Gantt Chart* view.
12. Save but **do not** close the **Training Advisor Project – Saved for Template.mpp** sample file.

Exercise 12 - 5

Save the "cleaned up" Training Advisor Rollout project file as a project template.

1. Return to the Training **Advisor Project – Saved for Template.mpp** sample file.
2. Click the *File* tab and then click the *Save As* tab in the *Backstage*.
3. On the *Save As* page in the *Backstage*, click the *Browse* button.
4. In the *Save As* dialog, enter the name **Enterprise Software Rollout** in the *File name* field.
5. In the *Save As* dialog, click the *Save as type* pick list, and then select the *Project Template (*.mpt)* file type.
6. Click the *Save* button.

7. In the *Save As Template* dialog, select all of the options, and then click the *Save* button.
8. Click the *File* tab and then click the *Close* tab to close the **Enterprise Software Rollout.mpt** project template file.
9. If prompted to save changes in a confirmation dialog, click the *Yes* button.

Using the Compare Projects Tool

Project 2013 offers a *Compare Projects* tool that you can use to study the differences between two projects. This tool is particularly useful for studying the changes between the original project and its completed counterpart or with other versions you save along the way. To use the *Compare Projects* tool for this purpose you **must** save a copy of your original baselined project before you begin entering progress in your production project. To use the *Compare Projects* tool, complete the following steps:

1. Open the earlier version of your project, such as the copy of the project you saved after baselining the project.
2. Open the later version of your project, such as the final completed version of the project.
3. Click the *Report* tab to display the *Report* ribbon.
4. In the *Project* section of the *Report* ribbon, click the *Compare Projects* button. Project 2013 displays the *Compare Project Versions* dialog shown in Figure 12 - 14.

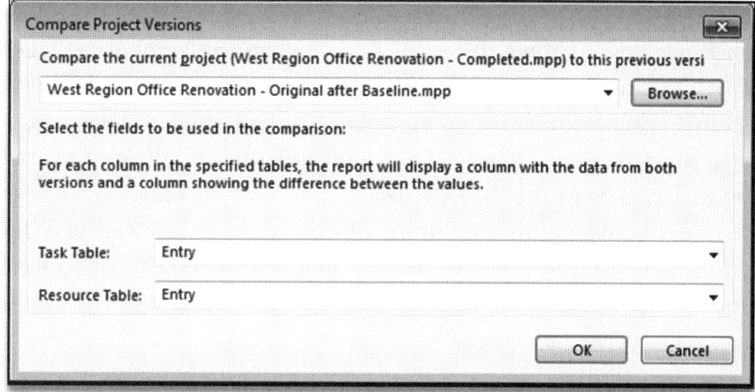

Figure 12 - 14: Compare Project Versions dialog

5. Click the pick list at the top of the dialog and select the earlier version, if necessary.
6. Click the *Task Table* pick list and select the table containing the task data you want to compare.
7. Click the *Resource Table* pick list and select the table containing the resource data you want to compare.
8. Click the *OK* button.

The software finds the differences between the two selected projects, and then displays the *Comparison Report* view shown in Figure 12 - 15. Notice that the *Comparison Report* view consists of a combination of three project windows, a *Legend* window, and the *Compare Projects* ribbon.

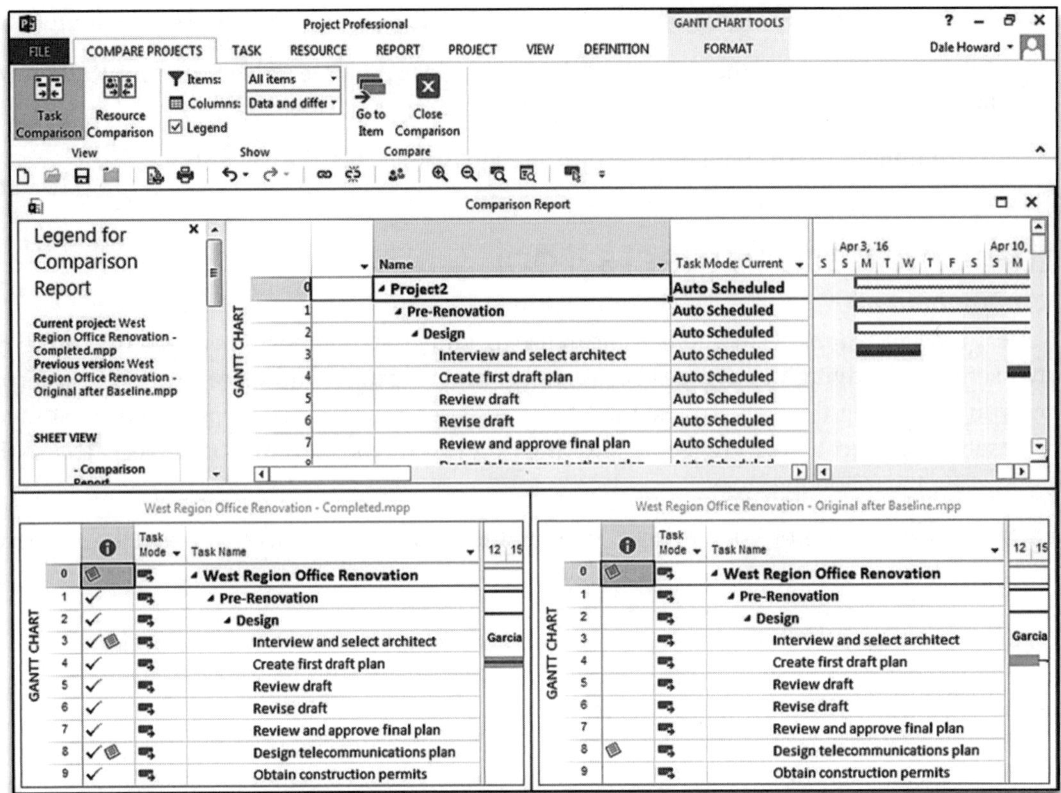

Figure 12 - 15: Comparison Report for two projects

By default, the *Comparison Report* view shows the results of task comparisons first. The bottom two panes show you the two projects compared using the *Compare Projects* tool. In the *Comparison Report* pane at the top, you see a special comparison project that contains the task comparison results between these two projects. Because I selected the task *Entry* table for comparison, the comparison project includes the differences between all columns in the task *Entry* table, including differences in the *Task Mode, Duration, Start, Finish, Predecessors,* and *Resource Names* columns. To see the comparison between other columns of data in your selected task table, scroll to the right in the table shown in the comparison project. If you selected the task *Entry* table for comparison, then the comparison project includes columns such as *Task Mode: Diff* or *Duration: Diff* to show you the differences.

To understand all of the symbols shown in the comparison project, refer to the *Legend for Comparison Report* pane in the upper left corner of the *Comparison Report* view. The *Legend for Comparison Report* pane contains two sections. Refer to the information in the *Sheet View* section to understand the indicators shown in the *Indicators* column of the comparison project. For example, the *Sheet View* section explains that the purple question mark symbol indicates that a task has a different name in each of the projects being compared. Refer to the *Gantt Chart* section to understand the Gantt bars shown in the *Gantt Chart* portion of the comparison project.

To compare the resource information between the two projects, click the *Resource Comparison* button in the *View* section of the *Compare Projects* ribbon. The software displays a similar *Comparison Report* view, except with the *Resource Sheet* view in all three project windows. Again, the *Legend for Comparison Report* pane helps you to understand the indicators shown in the *Indicators* column in the comparison project. Click the *Task Comparison* button to return to the *Comparison Report* view for tasks.

Click the *Items* pick list in the *Show* section of the *Compare Projects* ribbon to choose the exact type of comparison data you want to see in the *Comparison Report* view. For example, to see only the tasks with differences between the two projects, select the *All Differences* item on the *Items* pick list. Click the *Columns* pick list in the *Show* section of the *Compare Projects* ribbon to choose the sets of columns you want to see in the *Comparison Report* view. By default, the software selects the *Dates and Differences* item on the *Columns* pick list. This means that you see a set of three columns for every column in the selected task table, such as the *Task Mode: Current*, *Task Mode: Previous*, and *Task Mode: Diff* columns.

If you understand the indicators shown in the comparison project, deselect the *Legend* checkbox in the *Show* section of the *Compare Projects* ribbon. Project 2013 closes the *Legend for Comparison Report* pane and expands the width of the comparison project in the top pane.

To focus your analysis on an individual task in the *Comparison Report* view, select the task in any of the three project panes and then click the *Go to Item* button in the *Compare* section of the *Compare Projects* ribbon. The software selects the task in all three project panes as shown in Figure 12 - 16. Notice that I selected the *Install smoke and CO2 detectors* task in the comparison project pane and clicked the *Go to Item* button to view this task in all three project panes. Notice the purple question mark indicator for this task in the *Indicators* column of the comparison project, which indicates that I renamed the task.

To close the bottom two project panes, click the *Close Comparison* button. The software leaves open the comparison project pane and the *Legend for Comparison Report* pane. You can also save the comparison project for further analysis.

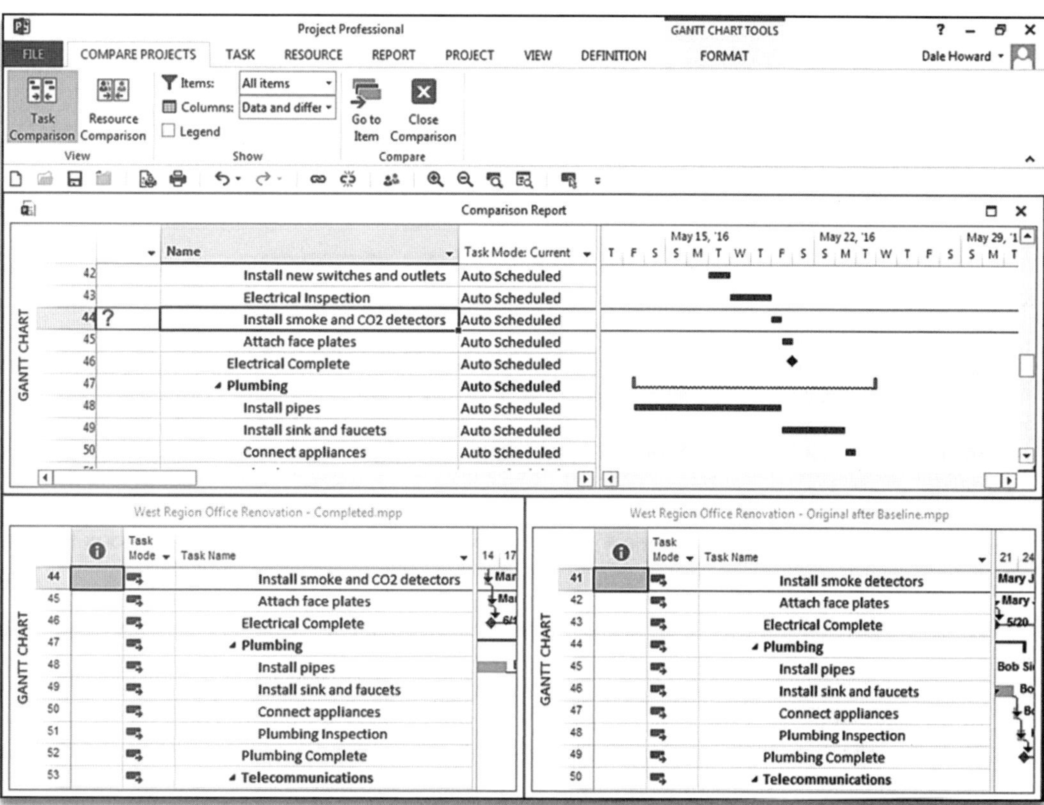

Figure 12 - 16: Go to Item for selected task

Hands On Exercise

Exercise 12 - 6

Use the *Compare Projects* tool to compare the baselined and completed versions of the Training Advisor Rollout project.

1. Open the **Training Advisor Original.mpp** sample file.
2. Open the **Training Advisor 12.mpp** sample file.
3. Click the *Report* tab to display the *Report* ribbon.
4. In the *Project* section of the *Report* ribbon, click the *Compare Projects* button.
5. In the *Compare Project Versions* dialog, make sure the pick list at the top displays the **Training Advisor Original.mpp** sample file.
6. In the *Compare Project Versions* dialog, leave all other default settings in place, and then click the *OK* button.
7. In the bottom two project panes, close the *Timeline* pane for each project.
8. In the *Comparison Report* pane at the top, drag the split bar all the way to the right side to view more columns in the table. You may need to scroll to the right to see all of the columns.
9. Examine each set of columns in the *Comparison Report* pane and look for differences for the tasks in each project. Widen columns, if necessary, to examine the information in each column.
10. Scroll down through the task list and examine the indicators shown in the *Indicators* column in the *Comparison Report* pane. Determine the meaning of the indicators using the *Legend for Comparison Report* pane.

Notice the new tasks added to the project during the execution stage, and notice the renamed task.

11. In the *Comparison Report* pane (the top pane), select task ID #40, the *Provide Training Advisor Classes* task, and then click the *Go to Item* button in the *Compare* section of the *Compare Projects* ribbon.
12. In the bottom two project panes, determine the original name of the task along with its new name.
13. In the *Show* section of the *Compare Projects* ribbon, **deselect** the *Legend* checkbox to close the *Legend for Comparison Report* sidepane.
14. In the *Show* section of the *Compare Projects* ribbon, click the *Items* pick list, and then select the *All Differences* item on the list.
15. In the *Show* section of the *Compare Projects* ribbon, click the *Columns* pick list, and then select the *Differences columns only* item on the list.
16. In the *Comparison Report* pane, examine each of the columns that show differences.

17. Click the *Close Comparison* button in the *Compare* section of the *Compare Projects* ribbon.
18. Close the **Comparison Report** project file without saving it.
19. Save and close the **Training Advisor 12.mpp** sample file.
20. Save and close the **Training Advisor Original.mpp** sample file.

Module 13

Digging Deeper into Project 2013

Learning Objectives

After completing this module, you will be able to:

- Work with task pane Office Apps
- Understand how to define all types of custom fields
- Create a shared resource pool file and attach sharing projects to the file
- Create and use a master project
- Export project data to a Microsoft Excel workbook

Inside Module 13

Using Task Pane Office Apps

Introduced as a new feature in Office 2013, Office Apps are simply web pages loaded in a pane inside an Office 2013 application. In Project 2013, you can only use task pane Office Apps to help you work with a project file. Before you can use an Office App, you must first connect to it by completing the following steps:

1. Click the *Project* tab to display the *Project* ribbon.

2. In the *Apps* section of the *Project* ribbon, click the *Apps for Office* button. Project 2013 displays a menu similar to the one shown in Figure 13 - 1. If you connected to any Office Apps recently, you see the app listed in the *Recently Used Apps* section at the top of the menu. Otherwise, you see a *No apps have been used recently* message at the top of the menu. Notice in Figure 13 - 1 that I used the *SharkPro SharePoint Insite for Project* app recently.

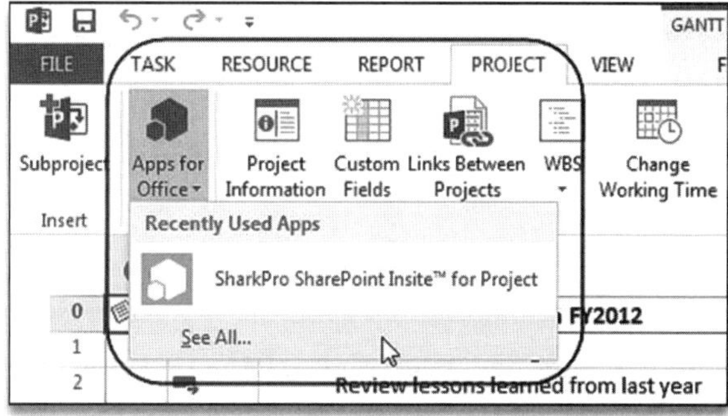

Figure 13 - 1: Apps for Office menu

3. If you recently used an Office App and want to use it again, click the name of the Office App in the *Recently Used Apps* section at the top of the menu. Otherwise, click the *See All* item at the bottom of the menu. The software displays the *Apps for Office* dialog with the *MY APPS* page selected by default, as shown in Figure 13 - 2. As the name implies, the *MY APPS* page shows Office Apps you used previously in Project 2013.

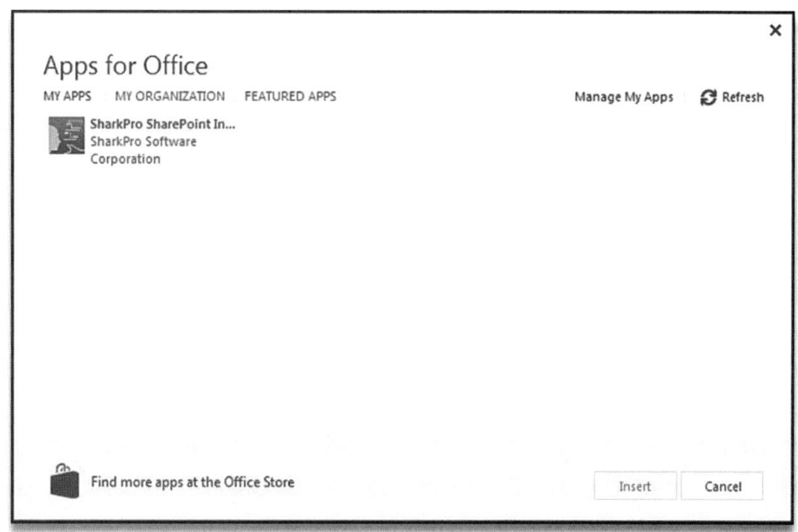

Figure 13 - 2: Apps for Office dialog, MY APPS page

4. In the upper left corner of the *Apps for Office* dialog, click the *FEATURED APPS* link to see Office Apps featured by Microsoft. The *FEATURED APPS* page normally displays a few of the Office Apps available for Project 2013, including both free and commercial apps. For example, notice that the *FEATURED APPS* page shown in Figure 13 - 3 shows two commercial apps and one free app.

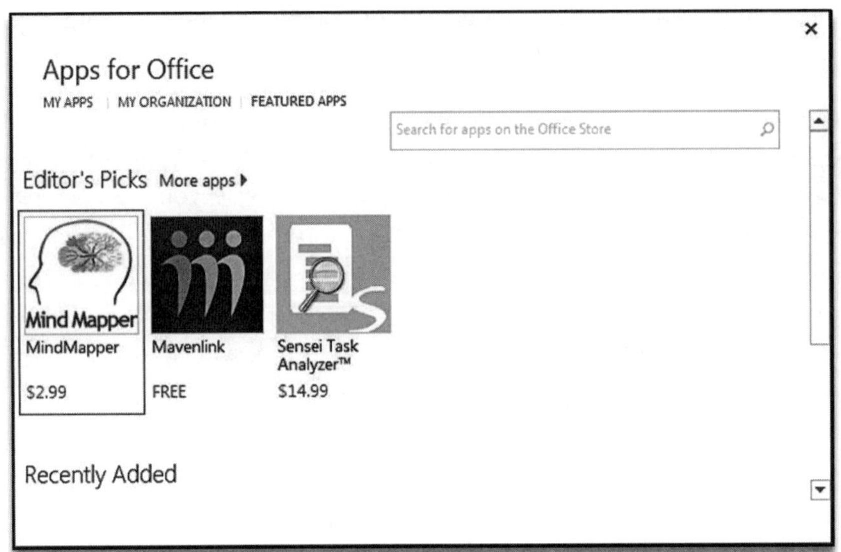

Figure 13 - 3: Apps for Office dialog, FEATURED APPS page

Information: Notice that the *Apps for Office* dialog shown previously in Figure 13 - 3 includes a third tab: the *MY ORGANIZATION* tab. You only need to use the *MY ORGANIZATION* page of the dialog if your organization creates Office Apps for you to use, and lists them in your organization's apps catalog.

5. To see all of the currently available Office Apps, click the *Find more apps at the Office Store* link in the lower left corner of the *MY APPS* page in the dialog, or click the *More apps* link in the upper left corner of the *FEATURED APPS* page. Project 2013 launches your Internet Explorer software and navigates to the *Office Store* website.

Information: If the *MY APPS* page contains no recently used Office Apps, click the *Office Store* button to navigate to the *Office Store* website.

6. Click the *Apps for Office and SharePoint* link at the top of the page and select *Apps for Project* to display the *Apps for Project* page shown in Figure 13 - 4. Notice that the available Office Apps listed on this page include both free and commercial apps, including apps for both Project 2013 and SharePoint 2013. Microsoft displays SharePoint apps on this page because you can use Project 2013 in conjunction with SharePoint when you sync a project with a *Tasks* list in SharePoint, and when you use Project 2013 with Project Server 2013.

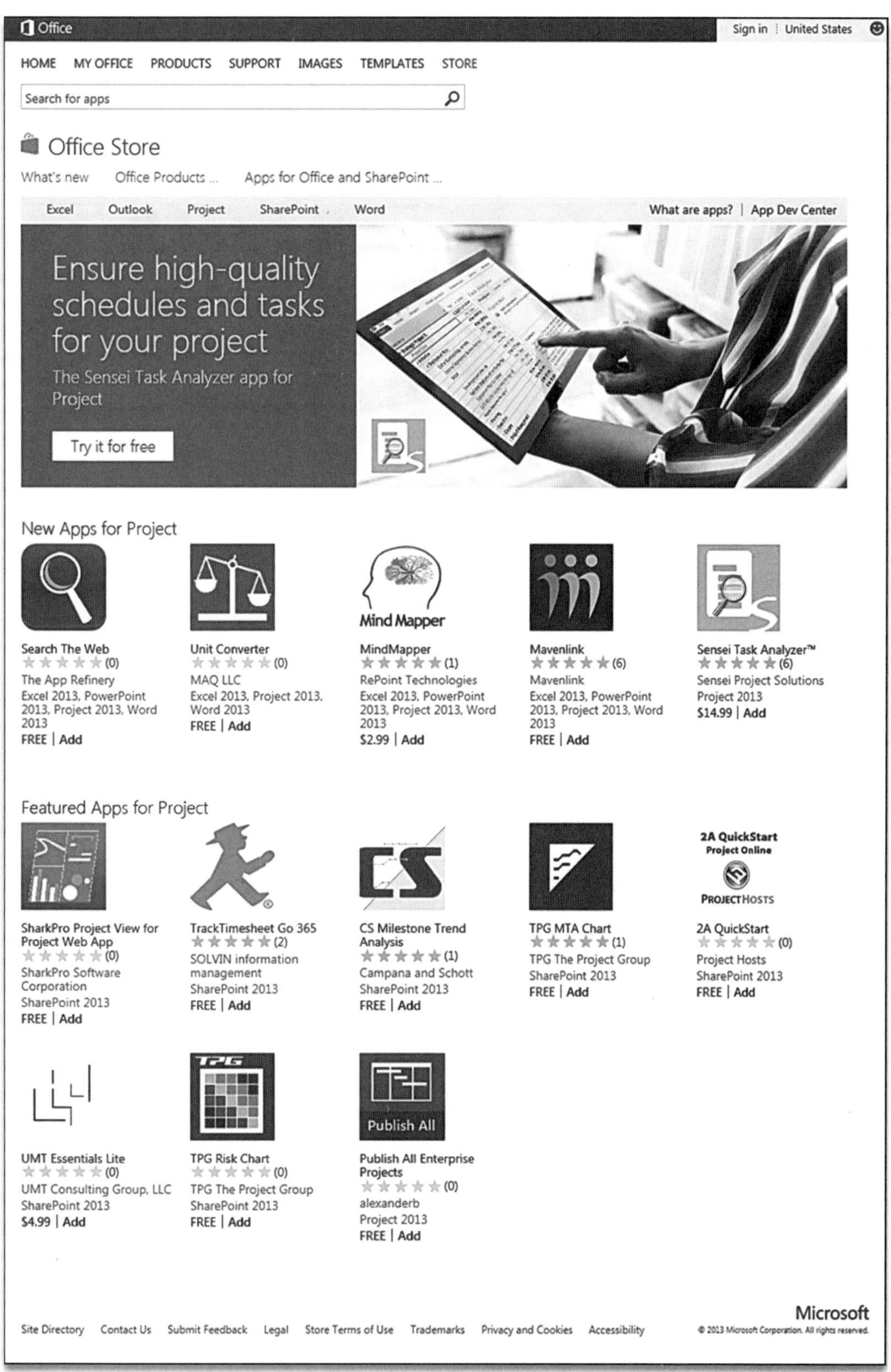

Figure 13 - 4: Apps for Project page of the Office Store website

7. On the *Apps for Project 2013* page, click the icon for the Office App you want to use. The software navigates to the *Home* page of the selected Office App in the *Office Store* website, as shown in Figure 13 - 5. Notice that I want to install the Office App called *Search the Web.*

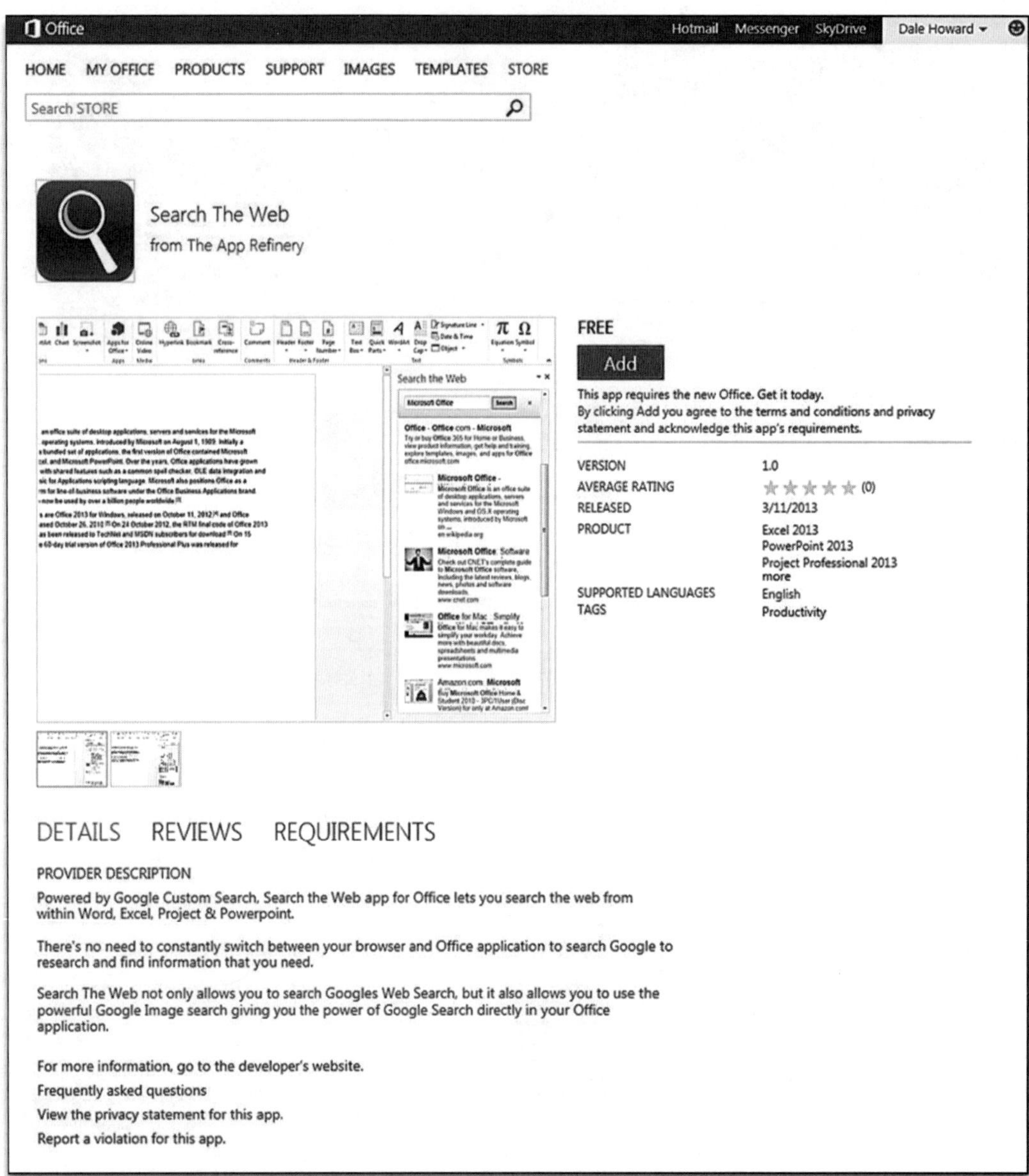

Figure 13 - 5: Home page of the selected Office App in the Office Store

8. Click the *Add* button to connect to the selected Office App. The software displays a confirmation page similar to the one shown in Figure 13 - 6.

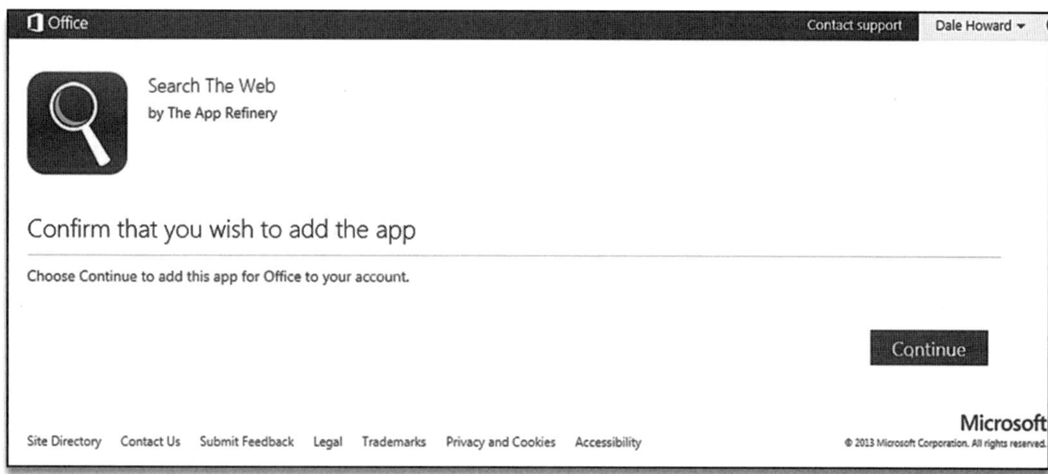

Figure 13 - 6: Confirmation page to add an Office App

9. On the confirmation page, click the *Continue* button. The software completes the process of connecting your selected Office App to Project 2013 and then displays a page with additional information about using the Office App, such as the page shown in Figure 13 - 7.

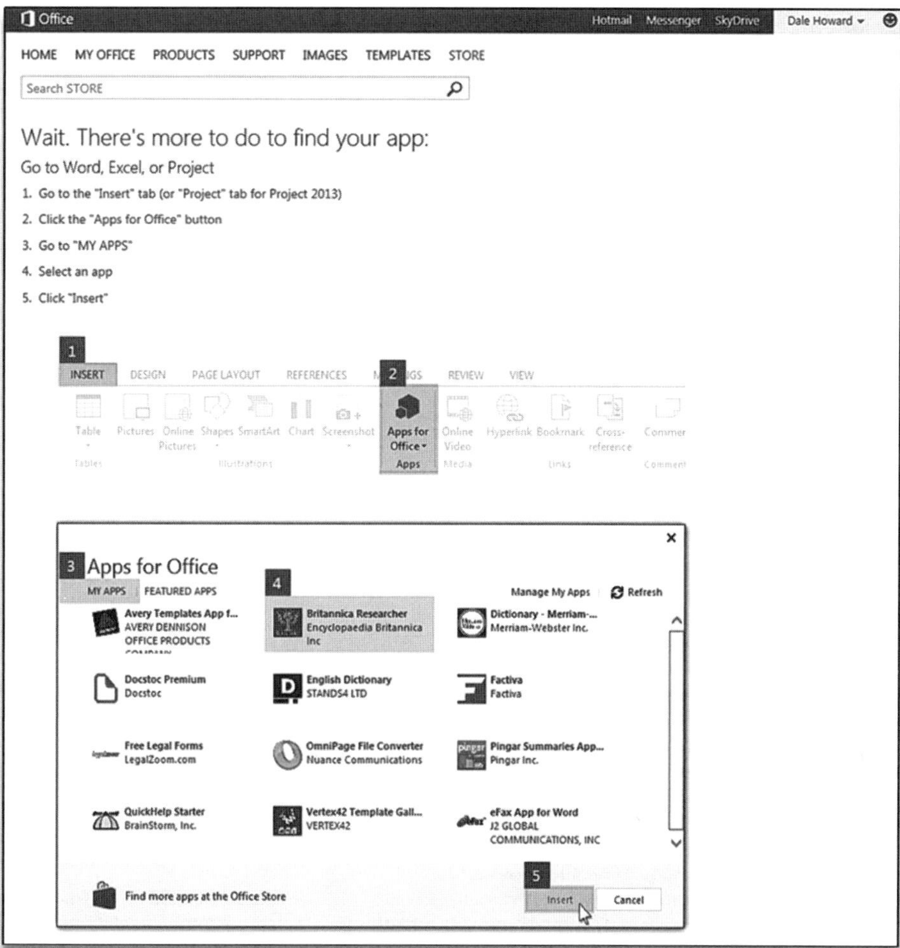

Figure 13 - 7: Additional information about how to use the Office App

10. Close your Internet Explorer application and then return to Project 2013.

11. In the *Apps* section of the *Project* ribbon, click the *Apps for Office* button again, and click the *See All* link again.

12. On the *MY APPS* page of the *Apps for Office* dialog, you should now see the new Office App to which you just connected. If you do not see your Office App, click the *Refresh* button in the upper right corner of the dialog.

13. In the *Apps for Office* dialog, select the name of the Office App to which you just connected and then click the *Insert* button. Project 2013 displays the new Office App in a task pane on the right side of the application window, such as the free *Search the Web* Office App shown in Figure 13 - 8.

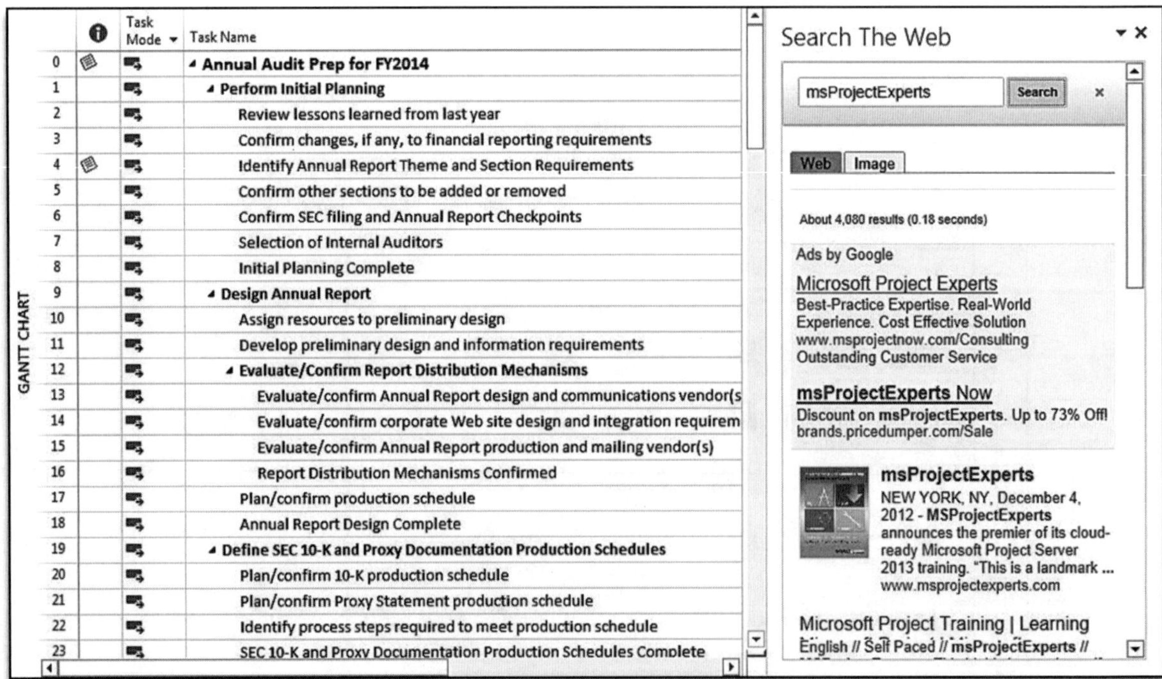

Figure 13 - 8: Office App displayed in a task pane

Once you display the Office App in a task pane, you can use the Office App in conjunction with your project file. In addition, after you use the Office App for the first time, you can see and select the Office App in the *Recently Used Apps* section of the *Apps for Office* menu. For example, notice that the *Apps for Office* menu now shows four Office Apps in the *Recently Used Apps* section, as shown in Figure 13 - 9.

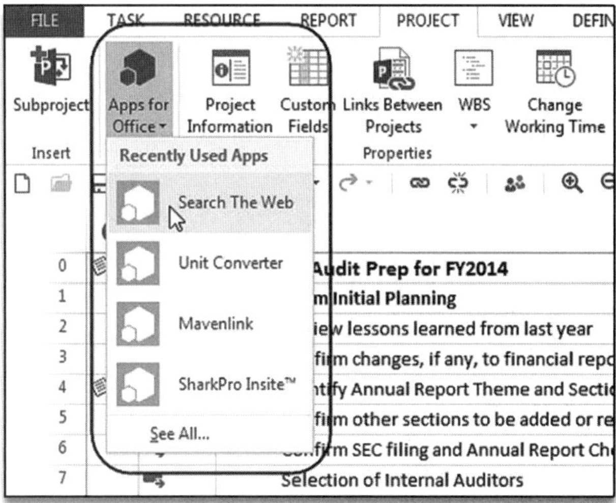

Figure 13 - 9: Updated Apps for Office menu

Hiding and Unhiding an Office App

To hide an Office App so that you no longer see it on the *Apps for Office* menu in Project 2013, complete the following steps:

1. In the *Apps* section of the *Project* ribbon, click the *Apps for Office* button and then select the *See All* item on the menu.

2. Click the *MY APPS* link in the upper left corner of the *Apps for Office* dialog shown previously in Figure 13 - 3.

3. In the upper right corner of the *MY APPS* page of the *Apps for Office* dialog, click the *Manage My Apps* link. The software launches your Internet Explorer software and displays the *My Apps for Office and SharePoint* page with the *Visible* tab selected, as shown in Figure 13 - 10. This page shows all of the Office Apps to which you previously connected, along with their status and the date on which you originally connected to the Office App.

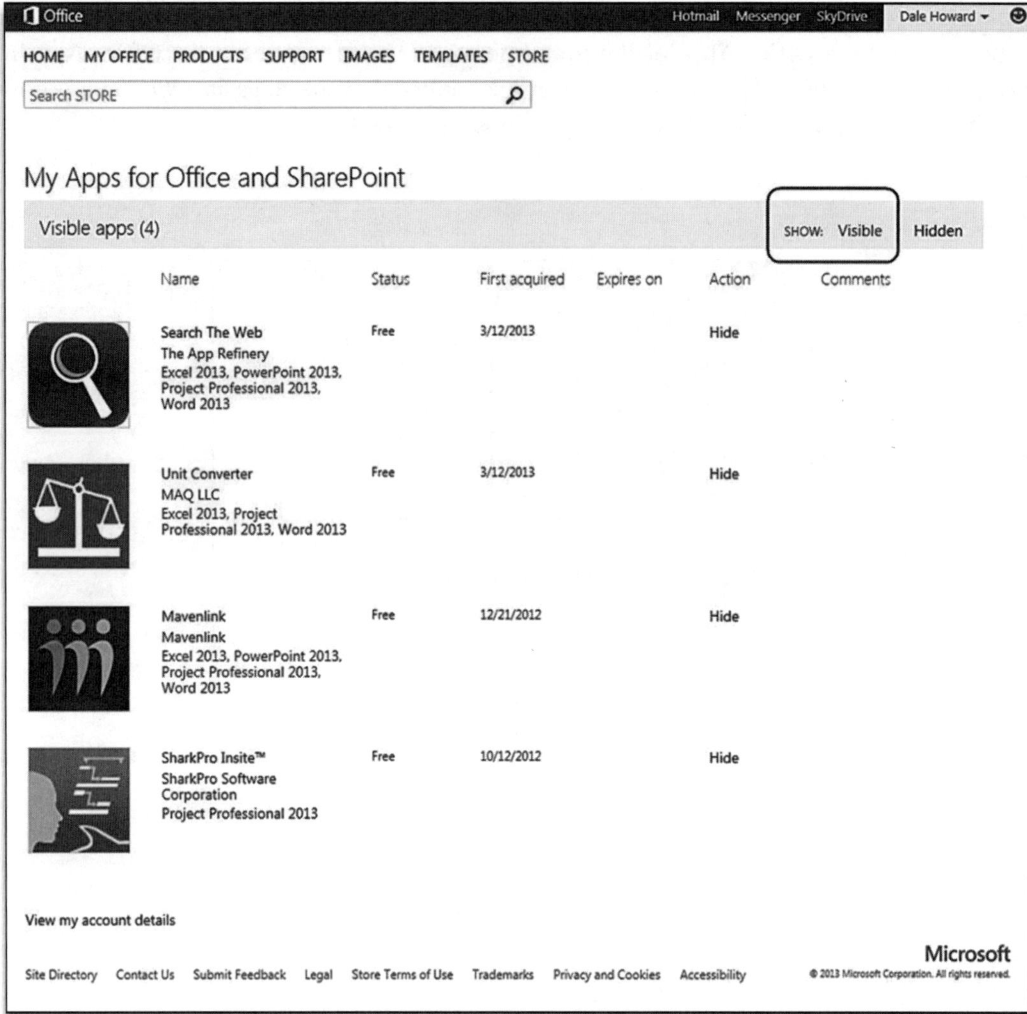

Figure 13 - 10: My Apps for Office and SharePoint page, Visible tab selected

4. In the *Action* column to the right of the Office App you want to hide, click the *Hide* link. After hiding two of my Office Apps, the *My Apps for Office and SharePoint* page refreshes as shown in Figure 13 - 11. Notice that the page shows that I currently have only visible apps.

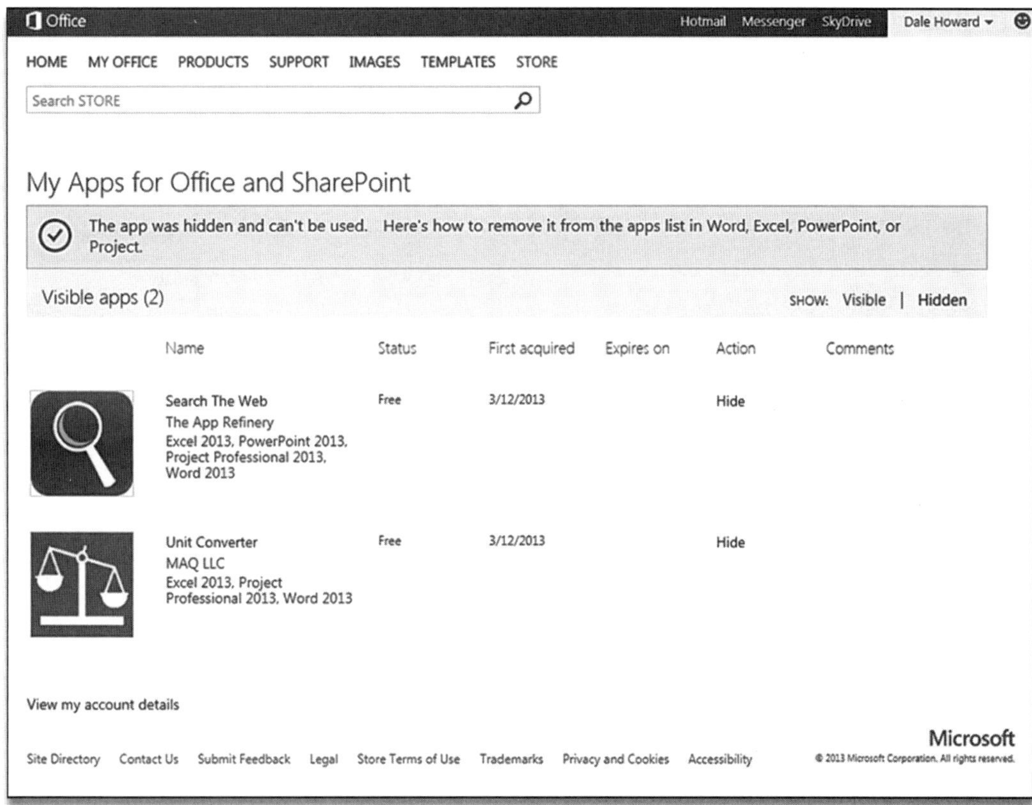

Figure 13 - 11: My Apps for Office and SharePoint page after hiding two Office Apps

5. After hiding Office Apps, return to the *Apps for Office* dialog in Project 2013 and click the *Refresh* link in the upper right corner of the dialog. The software no longer displays the hidden Office App in the *Apps for Office* dialog, and hides the Office App in the *Recently Used Apps* section of the *Apps for Office* menu.

Warning: Because of an unfixed bug in the release (RTM) version of Project 2013, when you hide an Office App, the software does not hide the Office App on the *Apps for Office* pick list. Instead, the software displays a *Failed to load app details* link on the *Apps for Office* pick list for each hidden Office App.

To unhide a hidden Office App, complete the following steps:

1. In the *Apps* section of the *Project* ribbon, click the *Apps for Office* button and then select the *See All* item on the menu.

2. In the *Apps for Office* dialog, click the *Manage My Apps* link in the upper right corner of the dialog. The software launches the Internet Explorer software and displays the *My Apps for Office And SharePoint* page with the *Visible* tab selected, as shown previously in Figure 13 - 11.

3. Click the *Hidden* tab at the top of the *My Apps for Office And SharePoint* page. The software displays the *Hidden* page shown in Figure 13 - 12. Notice that I previously hid two Office Apps.

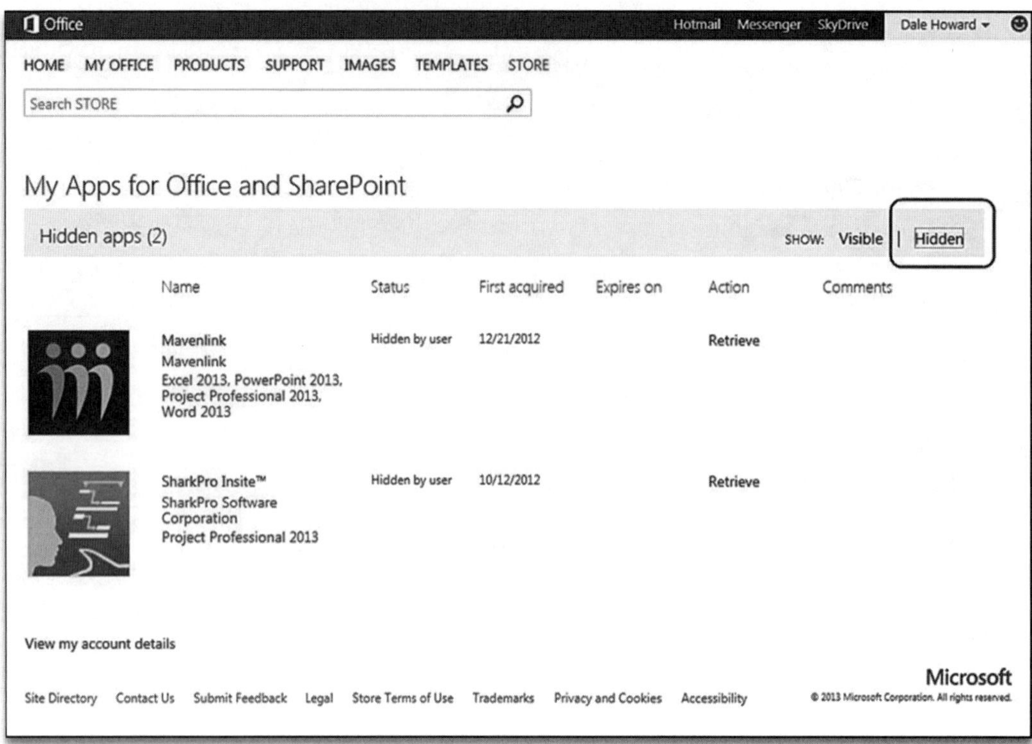

Figure 13 - 12: My Apps for Office and SharePoint, Hidden tab selected

4. In the *Action* column to the right of the Office App you want to unhide, click the *Retrieve* link. The *My Apps for Office and SharePoint* page refreshes as shown in Figure 13 - 13 with the *Hidden* tab selected. After unhiding both of the hidden Office Apps, notice that the page indicates that I currently have no hidden Office Apps.

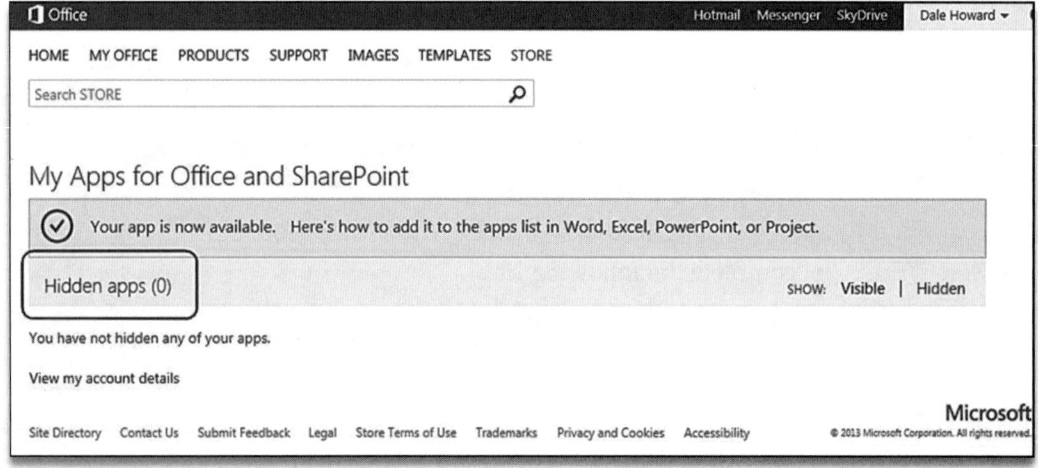

Figure 13 - 13: My Apps for Office And SharePoint page after unhiding an Office App

5. After unhiding the Office App, return to the *Apps for Office* dialog and click the *Refresh* link in the upper right corner of the dialog. The software redisplays Office App in both the *Apps for Office* dialog and the *Recently Used Apps* section of the *Apps for Office* menu.

Warning: Because of an unfixed bug in the release (RTM) version of Project 2013, if you hide all of your Office Apps, Project 2013 no longer displays a *Manage My Apps* link on the *MY APPS* page of the *Apps for Office* dialog shown previously in Figure 13 - 2. To return to the *My Apps for Office And SharePoint* website, click the *Office Store* button on the *MY APPS* page of the *Apps for Office* dialog. The software launches your Internet Explorer and navigates you to the *Office Store* website. On the home page of the *Office Store* website, click the *MY OFFICE* link in the upper left corner of the page. In the *Sign in to Office.com* dialog, log in with your Microsoft account. On the *MY OFFICE* page of the *Office Store* website, click the *My Apps* link in the upper right corner of the page to return to the *My Apps for Office And SharePoint* page of the *Office Store* website.

Controlling the Auto Launch Behavior of Office Apps

Using the *Trust Center* dialog, you can control whether Project 2013 launches Office Apps automatically whenever you launch Project 2013 and open a file used with one of your Office Apps. In fact, using this dialog, you actually control how **all** Office 2013 applications interact with their respective Office Apps. For example, suppose you navigate to the *Office Store and Apps* website and connect to one Office App for Project 2013 and connect to another Office App for Excel 2013. Using the *Trust Center* dialog in Project 2013, you can set up these two Office Apps so that they launch automatically whenever you launch their respective Office application and open a file used with the respective Office App.

Information: When you set up trusted Office Apps in the *Trust Center* dialog in Project 2013, the Office 2013 system enters the same information in the *Trust Center* dialog of **every** other application in the Office 2013 suite of tools, including applications such as Word 2013, Excel 2013, and PowerPoint 2013. When you remove a trusted catalog in the *Trust Center* dialog in Project 2013, the Office 2013 system removes the trusted catalog from the *Trust Center* dialog of **every** other application in the Office 2013 suite.

To set up Office Apps to launch with their respective Office 2013 applications automatically, complete the following steps:

1. Click the *File* tab and then click the *Options* tab in the *Backstage*.

2. In the *Project Options* dialog, click the *Trust Center* tab and then click the *Trust Center Settings* button.

3. In the *Trust Center* dialog, click the *Trusted App Catalogs* tab to display the *Trusted App Catalogs* page shown in Figure 13 - 14.

The *Trusted App Catalogs* page of the *Trust Center* dialog contains two sections of options that allow you to control how Office Apps interact with Project 2013 and with other members of the Office 2013 suite of applications. These sections include:

- Use the options in the *Trusted App Catalogs* section of the dialog to determine whether your Office Apps launch automatically when you open a project that uses the Office App.

- Use the *Trusted Catalogs Table* section of the dialog to add the URL of each website from which you access your Office Apps. For example, you may want to add the URL of the *Office Store* website.

In the *Trusted App Catalogs* section at the top of the *Trust Center* dialog shown in Figure 13 - 14, notice that the dialog offers two options. You can select only the *Don't allow apps from the Office Store to start* option to prevent Office Apps from the *Office Store and Apps* website from auto launching when you launch Project 2013. With this option selected, the software can auto launch Office Apps from other trusted catalogs, but does not auto launch Office Apps from the *Office Store* website. Alternately, you can select the *Don't allow any apps to start* option to prevent the software from auto launching all Office Apps, regardless of their location.

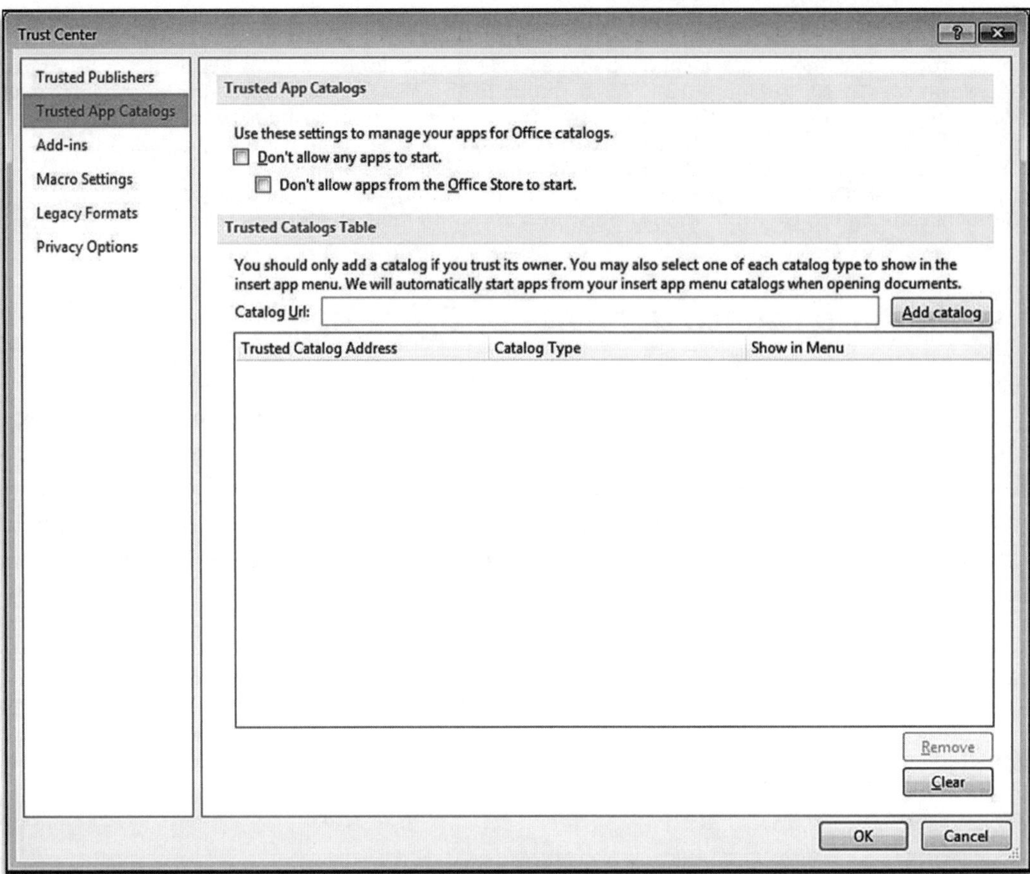

Figure 13 - 14: Trust Center dialog, Trusted App Catalogs page

4. In the *Catalog Url* field, enter the URL of the source of the Office App. For example, the URL of the *Office Store* website is **https://office.microsoft.com/en-us/store**.

5. Click the *Add Catalog* button. The software refreshes the *Trust Center* dialog to show the new Office Apps catalog in the *Trusted Catalogs Table* section, as shown in Figure 13 - 15.

Warning: Project 2013 does not allow you to add a URL beginning with **http://** in the *Catalog URL* field, displaying a *Manage App Catalogs* error dialog if you attempt to do so. The error dialog states that the URLs you enter must begin with **https://**, indicating the catalog is in a secure Internet zone.

6. Select the *Show in Menu* checkbox to the right of the URL for the new trusted catalog if you want the catalog to appear in the *Apps for Office* dialog. When you select the *Show in Menu* checkbox, Project 2013 displays a *MY ORGANIZATION* tab in the *Apps for Office* dialog, shown previously in Figure 13 - 2.

7. To remove an existing trusted catalog, select the URL in the *Trust Catalogs Table* section of the dialog and then click the *Remove* button.

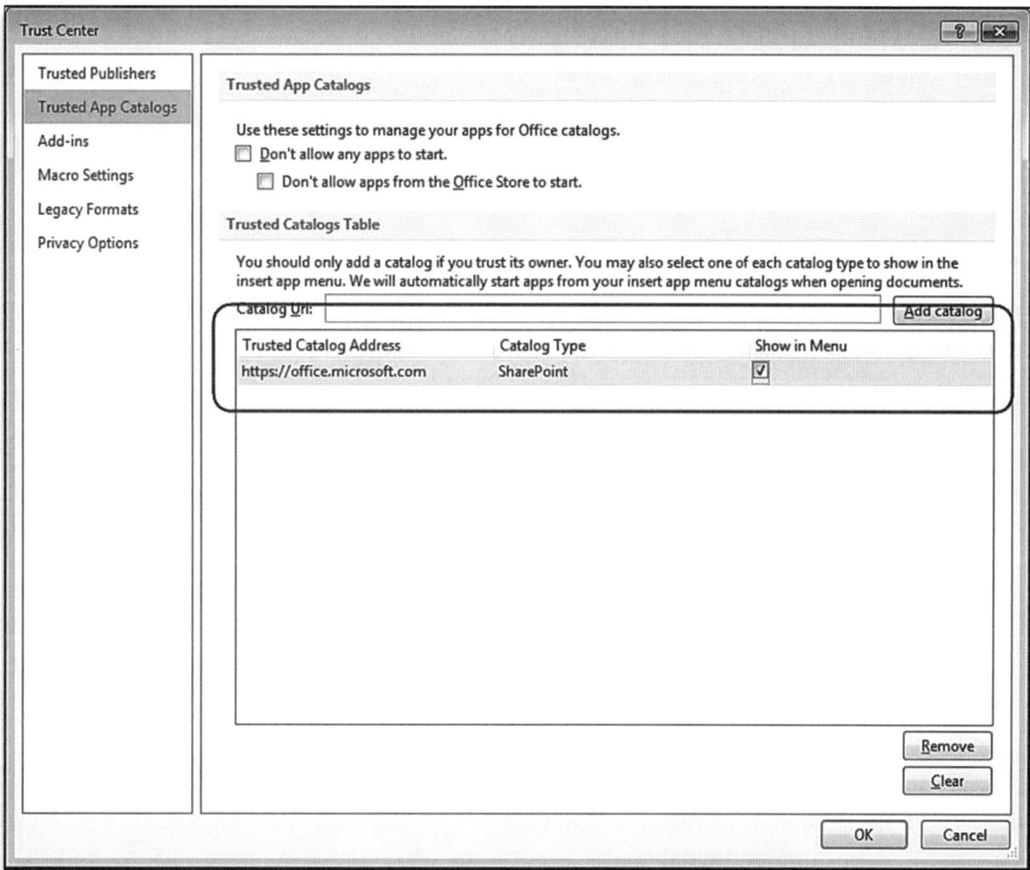

Figure 13 - 15: New catalog added on the Trusted App Catalogs page

8. Click the *OK* button. If you select the *Show in Menu* checkbox for a new trusted app catalog, the software displays the *Manage App Catalogs* dialog shown in Figure 13 - 16.

Figure 13 - 16: Manage App Catalogs dialog

9. Click the *OK* button to close the *Manage App Catalogs* dialog and then click the *OK* button to close the *Project Options* dialog.

10. Exit Project 2013 and then relaunch the application so that the software can apply the changes made in the *Trust Center* dialog.

Understanding Custom Fields

In addition to the default fields included with Project 2013, the software offers you a number of custom fields to capture additional project information about tasks and resources. Table 13 - 1 lists the custom fields available in Project 2013.

Field Type	Number Available	Data Type
Cost	30 (10 task, 10 resource, and 10 assignment fields)	Cost data formatted in your selected default currency format
Date	30 (10 task, 10 resource, and 10 assignment fields)	Date data formatted using the option specified in the *Project Options* dialog
Duration	30 (10 task, 10 resource, and 10 assignment fields)	Duration data formatted in days
Finish	30 (10 task, 10 resource, and 10 assignment fields)	Date data formatted using the option specified in the *Project Options* dialog
Flag	60 (20 task, 20 resource , and 20 assignment fields)	*Yes* or *No* values only
Number	60 (20 task, 20 resource , and 20 assignment fields)	Unformatted number data
Outline Code	30 (10 task, 10 resource, and 10 assignment outline codes)	Outline data formatted using an outline code definition
Start	30 (10 task, 10 resource, and 10 assignment fields)	Date data formatted using the option specified in the *Project Options* dialog
Text	90 (30 task, 30 resource , and 30 assignment fields)	Unformatted text data

Table 13 - 1: Custom fields available in Project 2013

Best Practice: To become truly knowledgeable about Project 2013, MSProjectExperts recommends that you learn as much as you can about both default and custom fields. Gaining more knowledge about fields also increases your knowledge about views, tables, filters, groups, and reports.

Defining Custom Fields

Before you define any custom fields, you must understand tracking and reporting needs of your organization. Based on this knowledge, you can define custom fields for use in the tracking and reporting process. To define a custom field, open a project, and then click the *Custom Fields* button in the *Properties* section of the *Project* ribbon. The software displays the *Custom Fields* dialog shown in Figure 13 - 17.

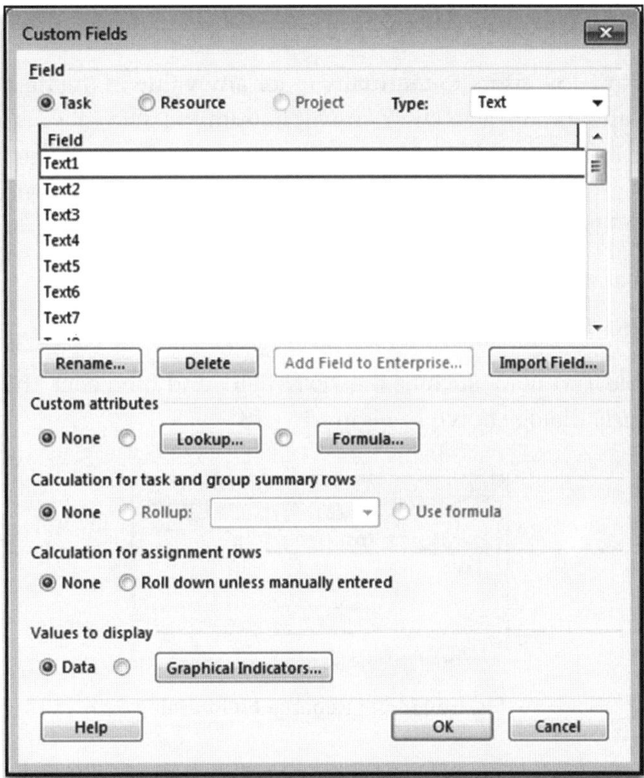

Figure 13 - 17: Custom Fields dialog

Notice in Figure 13 - 17 that each custom field has its own set of custom attributes, including lookup tables, formulas, and graphical indicators. In addition, notice that the options in the *Calculation for task and group summary rows* section allow you to determine the rollup behavior of custom fields containing a formula. Finally, notice that the options in the *Calculation for assignment rows* section allow you to determine whether task or resource information "rolls down" to assignment rows. Using the *Custom Fields* dialog, you can create any of the following types of custom fields:

- Free entry fields that allow the user to manually enter any value.
- Fields that require the user to select a value from a lookup table of allowable values.
- Fields containing a formula that automatically calculates a value using data in other fields.
- Fields that display graphical indicators instead of data.

Warning: The *Custom Fields* dialog shown in Figure 13 - 17 is for the **Professional** version of Project 2013. Because this version of the software is meant to connect to Project Server 2013, you see one item in this dialog that is specific to Project Server: the *Project* option at the top of the dialog. If your organization is not using Project Server 2013, then you **cannot** create custom *Project* fields. Furthermore, if your organization is using Project Server 2013, only your Project Server administrator can create custom *Project* fields.

Defining a Free Entry Custom Field

Use a free entry custom field to allow users to manually enter any value in the field, as defined by the field type. This means that the software allows a user to enter any alphanumeric data in a *Text* field, but permits the user to only enter numeric cost data in a *Cost* field. Assume that as a part of your organization's project management methodologies, you must assign a cost center number to each task in every project. To define a custom field to capture this information, complete the following steps in the *Custom Fields* dialog:

1. Select the *Task* option at the top of the dialog.
2. Click the *Type* pick list and select the *Text* field type.
3. Select the first available *Text* field, such as the *Text1* field, and then click the *Rename* button. The software displays the *Rename Field* dialog shown in Figure 13 - 18.

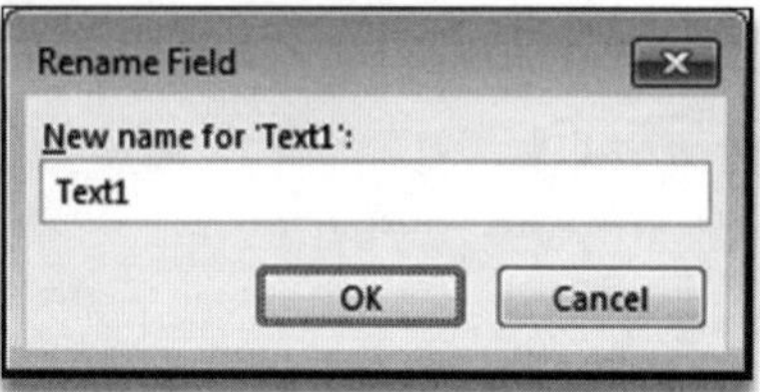

Figure 13 - 18: Rename Field dialog

4. Enter the text *Cost Center* in the *Rename Field* dialog and click the *OK* button. Figure 13 - 19 shows the *Custom Fields* dialog after renaming the new *Cost Center* field.

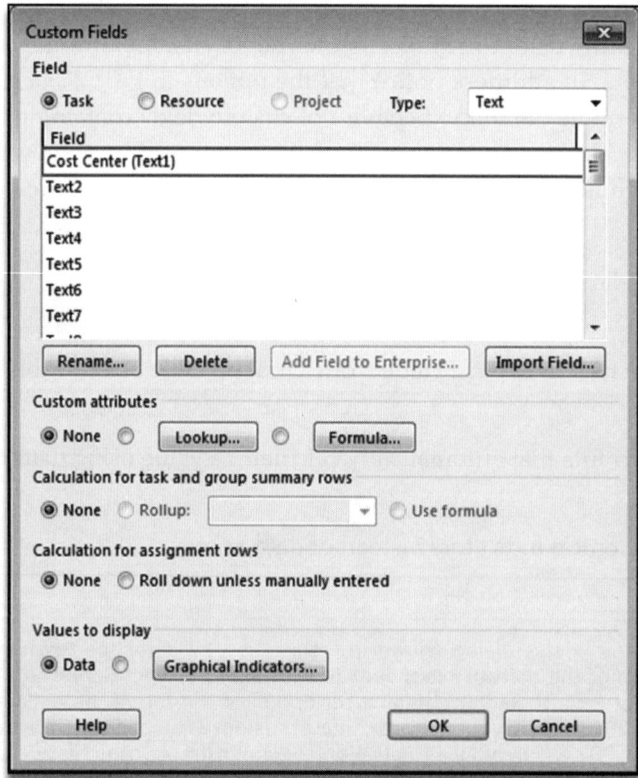

Figure 13 - 19: Custom Fields dialog shows the custom Cost Center field

Hands On Exercise

Exercise 13 - 1

As a part of your organization's change control methodologies, you need to type the name of a subject matter expert (SME) for each summary task in a project.

1. Open the **Using Custom Fields 2013.mpp** sample file.
2. Click the *Project* tab to display the *Project* ribbon.
3. In the *Properties* section of the *Project* ribbon, click the *Custom Fields* button.
4. Select the *Task* option at the top of the dialog, if necessary.
5. Click the *Type* pick list and select the *Text* field type, if necessary.
6. Select the *Text1* field and then click the *Rename* button.
7. Manually enter **SME** in the *Rename Field* dialog and click the *OK* button.
8. Click the *OK* button to close the *Custom Fields* dialog.
9. Save but **do not** close the **Using Custom Fields 2013.mpp** sample file.

Defining a Custom Field with a Lookup Table

You use lookup tables to control the values users enter into a custom field by allowing your users to select a valid value from a list rather than forcing them to manually type values into the field. Assume that as a part of your organization's project management methodologies, you must categorize the potential risk of date slippage as high, medium, or low for each task in every project. Assume also that the default risk on every task is low unless you specify otherwise. To create a custom task *Text* field containing a lookup table, complete the following steps in the *Custom Fields* dialog:

1. Select the *Task* option at the top of the dialog.
2. Click the *Type* pick list and select the *Text* field type.
3. Select the first available *Text* field, such as the *Text2* field, and then click the *Rename* button.
4. Enter the text *Risk* in the *Rename Field* dialog and click the *OK* button.
5. With the *Risk* field still selected in the list at the top, click the *Lookup* button in the *Custom attributes* section of the dialog. The software displays the *Edit Lookup Table* dialog for the new custom *Risk* field with a blank lookup table, as shown in Figure 13 - 20.

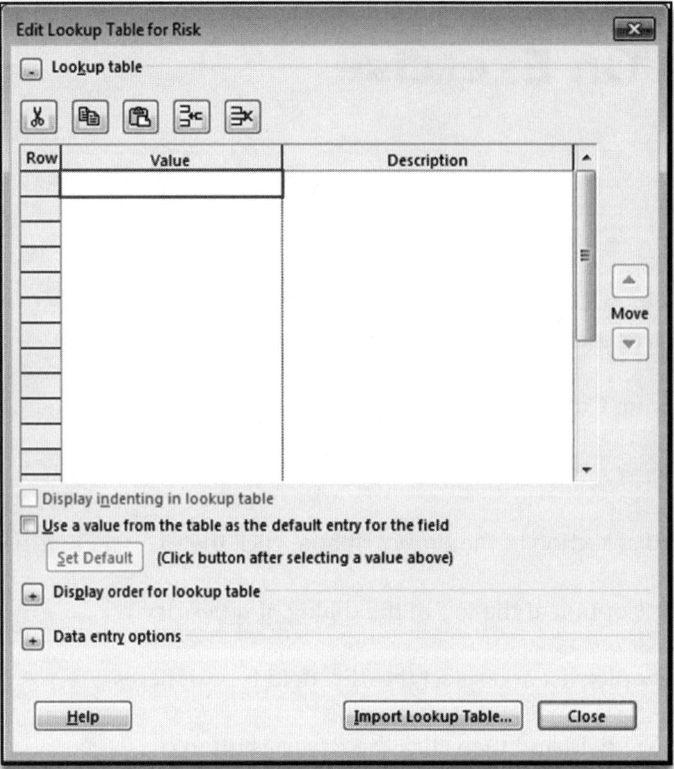

Figure 13 - 20: Edit Lookup Table dialog

6. Enter values in the *Value* and *Description* columns as shown in Table 13 - 2.

Value	Description
High	Very likely to slip
Medium	Somewhat likely to slip
Low	Not likely to slip

Table 13 - 2: Values for the Risk lookup table

Information: If you manually entered lookup table values in another Office application, such as in an Excel workbook or in a table in a Word document, you can copy the values in the other Office application, and then paste the values into the lookup table using the *Paste Row* button at the top of the *Edit Lookup Table* dialog.

7. Select the *Use a value from the table as the default entry for the field* option.
8. Select the *Low* value and click the *Set Default* button to set this value as the default value for every task. Project 2013 formats the *Low* item with blue text to indicate that it is the default value in the lookup table.

The *Edit Lookup Table* dialog contains two additional sections at the bottom of the dialog that the software collapses by default. Click the *Expand* button to the left of the *Display order for lookup table* and *Data entry options* sections. Figure 13 - 21 shows the *Edit Lookup Table* dialog with the options expanded in these two sections.

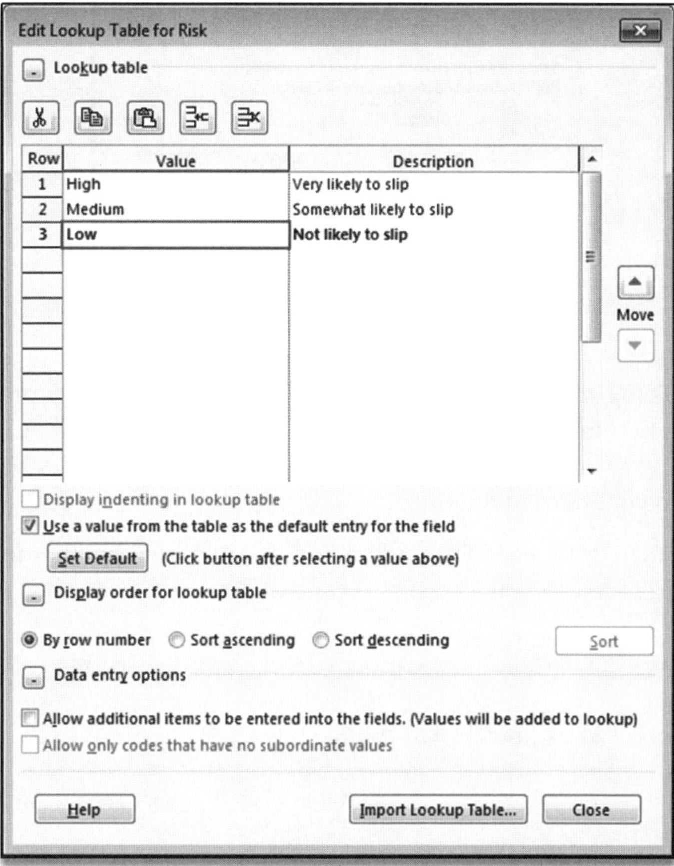

Figure 13 - 21: Edit Lookup Table dialog with all options expanded

Select an option in the *Display order for lookup table* section to determine how the software sorts the items in the list. If you select the *Sort ascending* or *Sort descending* option, Project 2013 activates the *Sort* button. Click the *Sort* button to sort the items in the list using the sort order you specify. Otherwise, leave the *By row number* option selected and the software sorts the items in the order you enter them.

The software uses your selected option in the *Data entry options* section of the dialog to validate values entered in your new *Risk* field. By selecting the *Allow additional items to be entered into the fields* option, you allow a user to type additional values into the lookup table when you display this custom field in any task table. The *Data entry options* section also contains the *Allow only codes that have no subordinate values* option, which the software uses only for hierarchical outline code files. I discuss custom outline codes later in this module.

Warning: If you select the *Allow additional items to be entered into the fields* option, you defeat one of the purposes of using a lookup table, which is to limit the values entered in the field to only the values in the lookup table. Select this option only if you cannot create a lookup table with all possible allowable values.

When you define a new field, you have the option to import a lookup table from an existing field. To do this, click the *Import Lookup Table* button at the bottom of the dialog. Project 2013 displays the *Import Lookup Table* dialog shown in Figure 13 - 22.

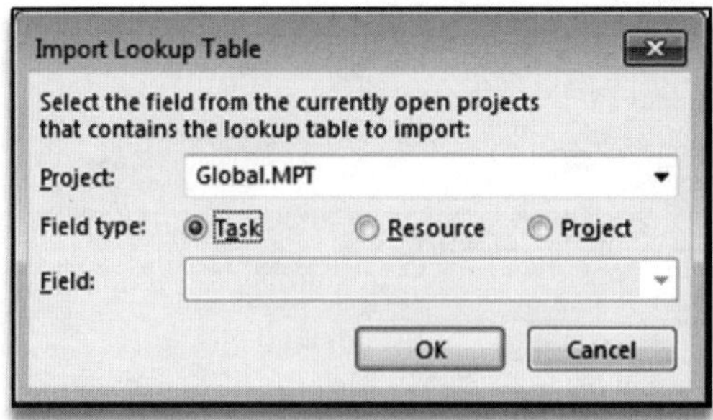

Figure 13 - 22: Import Lookup Table dialog

In the *Import Lookup Table* dialog, click the *Project* pick list button and select any project file you currently have open. Select the *Field type* option for the type of field containing the lookup table. Click the *Field* pick list button and select the field containing the lookup table you want to import. Click the *OK* button to complete importing the existing lookup table into your current field.

In the case of the *Risk* field, there is no need to import a lookup table from another field, so click the *Close* button in the *Edit Lookup Table* dialog to return to the *Custom Fields* dialog.

Hands On Exercise

Exercise 13 - 2

As a part of your organization's change control methodologies, you need to track the change request information for each task you add, modify, or cancel.

1. Return to the **Using Custom Fields 2013.mpp** sample file, if necessary.
2. In the *Properties* section of the *Project* ribbon, click the *Custom Fields* button.
3. Select the *Task* option at the top of the dialog, if necessary.
4. Click the *Type* pick list and select the *Text* field type, if necessary.
5. Select the *Text2* field and then click the *Rename* button.
6. Manually enter **CR Type** in the *Rename Field* dialog and click the *OK* button.
7. With the *CR Type* field still selected, click the *Lookup* button in the *Custom attributes* section of the dialog.
8. In the *Edit Lookup Table* dialog for the *CR Type* field, enter the following values:
    - New Task
    - Cancelled Task
    - Additional Resources
    - Increased Duration

9. Click the *Expand* button to expand the options in the *Display order for lookup table* section and then select the *Sort ascending* option.
10. Click the *Sort* button to sort the list of items in the lookup table.
11. Click the *Close* button to close the *Edit Lookup Table* dialog.
12. Click the *OK* button to close the *Custom Fields* dialog.
13. Save but **do not** close the **Using Custom Fields 2013.mpp** sample file

Defining a Custom Field with a Formula

Using a custom field with a formula provides a very flexible way to influence the output of views in Project 2013. By using a formula in a custom field, you can perform compound financial calculations such as net present value or build business-specific key performance indicators (KPIs). You can also provide data conditioned to a specific business interpretation using graphical indicators to accompany the formula in the custom field.

Assume that as part of your organization's project management methodologies, you must show the percentage of cost variance for every task in each project. This requires using a custom *Number* field containing a formula. To define this custom field, complete the following steps in the *Custom Fields* dialog:

1. Select the *Task* option at the top of the dialog.
2. Click the *Type* pick list and select the *Number* fields.
3. Select the first available *Number* field, such as the *Number1* field, and then click the *Rename* button.
4. Enter the text *Pct Cost Var* in the *Rename Field* dialog and click the *OK* button.
5. With the *Pct Cost Var* field still selected, click the *Formula* button. The software displays the *Formula* dialog for the *Pct Cost Var* field, as shown in Figure 13 - 23.

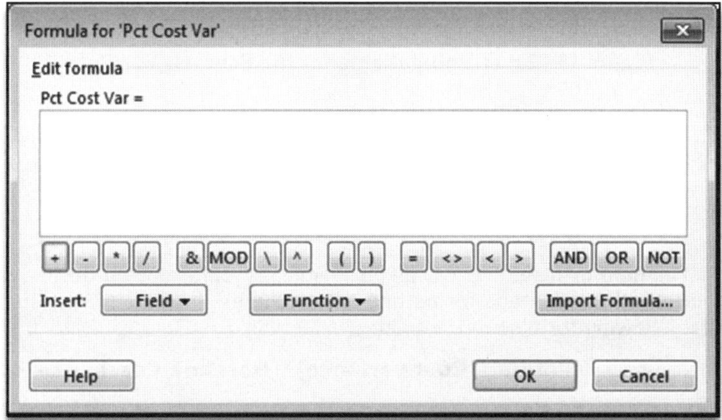

Figure 13 - 23: Formula dialog for the Pct Cost Var field

The *Formula* dialog provides graphical tools for building formulas. You can use the *Field, Function,* and various operand buttons to build your formula or you can type your formula manually. The software displays the resulting formula in the text area of the dialog.

6. Using the *Field* pick list button and operand buttons, create the following formula to calculate the percent of cost variance:

[Cost Variance] / [Baseline Cost]

Notice that the formula for the percentage of cost over budget is simply the cost variance divided by the baseline cost. If the current cost for a task is $5,000 when the baseline cost is only $4,500, then the cost variance is $500, using the formula Cost Variance = Cost – Baseline Cost. Applying the percentage of cost over budget formula, the task is 10% over budget ($500 ÷ $5,000).

Information: If you created a formula in another field, you can import it into the current field by clicking the *Import Formula* button. The formula can be in a field in the active project, or in another project, but the project containing the formula must be open before you can import it.

7. Click the *OK* button.

The software displays the warning dialog shown in Figure 13 - 24. The warning dialog indicates that upon acceptance, the software deletes any pre-existing values in the *Pct Cost Var* field because a formula now calculates all values in the field.

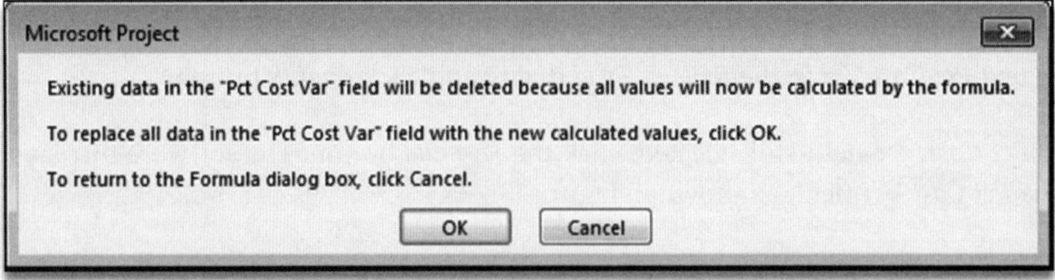

Figure 13 - 24: Warning dialog for the Pct Cost Var field

8. Click the *OK* button to close the warning dialog and return to the *Custom Fields* dialog.

Information: Project 2013 displays all values in a custom *Number* field as unformatted numbers. This means that the *Pct Cost Var* field displays the calculated values as unformatted decimal numbers. To display the *Pct Cost Var* field values with percentage formatting that includes the percent sign, select any available *Text* field and then enter the following formula in the field:

Format([Cost Variance]/[Baseline Cost],"0%")

The preceding formula formats the number as a percentage rounded to the nearest whole number.

Figure 13 - 25 shows the *Custom Fields* dialog with the new custom field containing the formula.

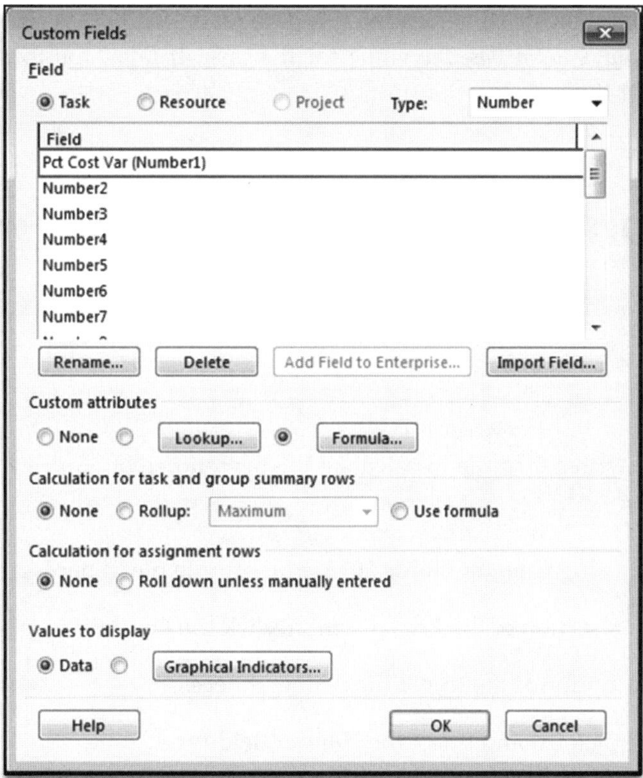

Figure 13 - 25: Custom Fields dialog shows the new Pct Cost Var field

When you define a custom field containing a formula, you must determine how the software uses the formula for summary tasks and group summary rows by selecting options in the *Calculation for task and group summary rows* section of the dialog. If you want Project 2013 to apply the formula directly to both summary tasks and group summary rows, select the *Use formula* option. For the *Pct Cost Var* field, I do want to use the formula, so I select the *Use formula* option to apply the formula to all summary tasks and subtasks in the project.

If you want to apply the formula in a different manner, select the *Rollup* option and then select a rollup value from the pick list. *Rollup* options apply to all custom fields except *Text* fields and *Outline Code* fields.

In addition to specifying how the software uses the formula for summary tasks and group summary rows, you should also specify how Project 2013 calculates the formula on assignment rows. Remember that you see assignments in either the *Task Usage* or *Resource Usage* views. To specify how the software calculates the formula for assignment rows, select either option in the *Calculation for assignment rows* section of the *Custom Fields* dialog. If you leave the default *None* option selected, the software does not calculate the formula on assignment rows. If you select the *Roll down unless manually entered* option, the software rolls down the value from the task to the assignment in the *Task Usage* view.

Testing for an NA Date Value

When there is no date in a *Date* field, such as the *Baseline Estimated Start* field, Project 2013 displays an *NA* value in that field. The software stores the *NA* value internally as the largest possible number the *Date* field can hold. To test for an *NA* value in any *Date* field, use the ProjDateValue("NA") function with an IIF statement in your formula. For example, using a custom *Text* field, I can test whether a date exists in the *Baseline Estimated Start* field by using the following formula:

```
IIf([Baseline Estimated Start] = ProjDateValue("NA"), "No Baseline", [Baseline Estimated Start])
```

Notice that the preceding formula tests to determine if a date exists in the *Baseline Estimated Start* field for each task. If true, the formula displays a *No Baseline* value for the task. If false, the formula displays the date in the *Baseline Estimated Start* field for the task.

Hands On Exercise

Exercise 13 - 3

Create a custom field with a formula to calculate the percentage of work variance for every task in a project.

1. Return to the **Using Custom Fields 2013.mpp** sample file, if necessary.
2. In the *Properties* section of the *Project* ribbon, click the *Custom Fields* button.
3. Select the *Task* option at the top of the dialog, if necessary.
4. Click the *Type* pick list and select the *Number* field type.
5. Select the *Number1* field and then click the *Rename* button.
6. Manually enter **Pct Work Var** in the *Rename Field* dialog and click the *OK* button.
7. With the *Pct Work Var* field still selected, click the *Formula* button.
8. Using the *Field* pick list button and operand buttons, create the following formula to calculate the percent of work variance:

   [Work Variance] / [Baseline Work]

9. Click the *OK* button to close the *Formula* dialog.
10. When prompted, click the *OK* button to close the warning dialog.
11. Select the *Use formula* option in the *Calculation for task and group summary rows* section.
12. Select the *Roll down unless manually entered* option in the *Calculation for assignment rows* section.
13. Click the *OK* button to close the *Custom Fields* dialog.
14. Save but **do not** close the **Using Custom Fields 2013.mpp** sample file

Defining a Custom Field with Graphical Indicators

Graphical indicators lend a powerful and eye-pleasing impact to views in Project 2013. Many users find graphical indicators easier to understand than the raw numerical data. For example, almost anyone can figure out that a red stoplight indicator is not a good thing; while a green "smiley face" indicator is a sign of something very good indeed! It is easiest to apply graphical indicators to a field that already contains lookup table values or a formula.

Assume that as a part of your organization's project management methodologies, you must use stoplight indicators to display the data in the *Pct Cost Var* field. Assume your organization's criteria for displaying stoplight indicators in the *Pct Cost Var* field are as follows:

- If the percentage of cost variance is less than 0% (the task is under budget), display a green happy face indicator.
- If the percentage of cost variance is greater than or equal to 0% but less than 10%, display a green stoplight indicator.
- If the percentage of cost variance is greater than or equal to 10% but less than 20%, display a yellow stoplight.
- If the percentage of cost variance is greater than or equal to 20%, display a red stoplight icon.

To define graphical indicators in the *Pct Cost Var* field, complete the following steps in the *Custom Fields* dialog:

1. In the top half of the dialog, select the *Pct Cost Var* field.
2. In the *Values to display* section of the *Custom Fields* dialog, click the *Graphical Indicators* button. Project 2013 displays the *Graphical Indicators* dialog for the *Pct Cost Var* field, as shown in Figure 13 - 26.

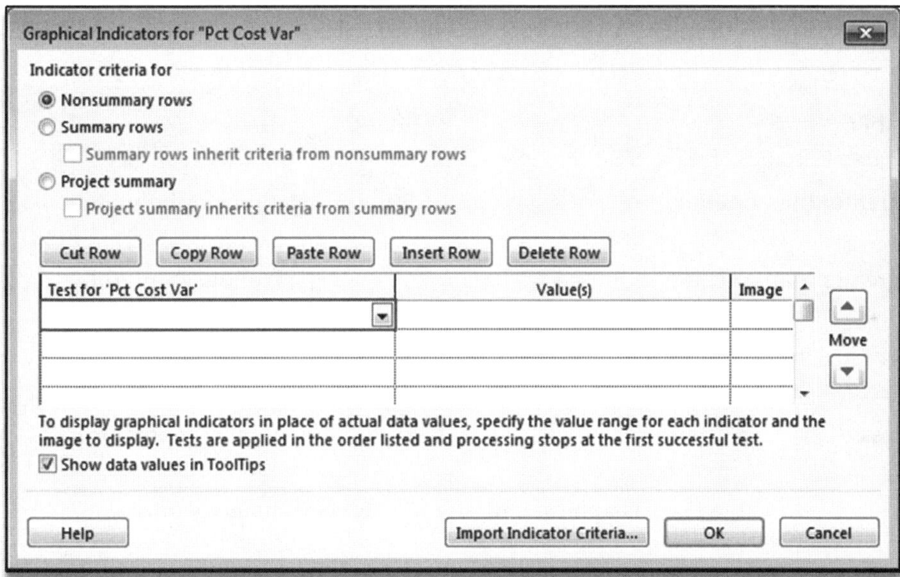

Figure 13 - 26: Graphical Indicators dialog for the Pct Cost Var field

Notice the three options in the *Indicator criteria for* section of the *Graphical Indicators* dialog. These options reveal that the software accepts graphical indicator criteria for three types of tasks: *Nonsummary rows* (subtasks), *Summary rows* (summary tasks), and *Project summary* (the Project Summary Task). Because of this, you can set completely different criteria for each of the three types of rows, or you can define the criteria for non-summary rows and then specify that summary rows inherit criteria from the non-summary rows.

Information: In Figure 13 - 26, notice the *Show data values in ToolTips* option located in the lower left corner of the *Graphical Indicators* dialog. When you select this option, the software displays the underlying value in the field as a tooltip when you float the mouse pointer over any graphical indicator.

Information: If you previously created graphical indicators in a field, you can import them into the current field by clicking the *Import Indicator Criteria* button. The indicator criteria can be in a field in the active project or in another project, but the project containing the indicator criteria must be open before you can import them.

To set the criteria used to determine the graphical indicator for each task, you must specify multiple tests using the available pick lists in the grid. The pick list in the *Test for* column offers a set of twelve standard mathematical and Boolean tests. The final test on the list, the *Is any value* test, returns a positive result in all cases. This test is useful as a "catch all" test to include at the bottom of the criteria list, as it will display an indicator to represent any value not otherwise defined.

The tests you select in the *Test for* column apply to the values you select or enter in the *Value(s)* column. In the *Value(s)* column, you can select any standard or custom field, or you can enter a literal value.

In the *Image* column, select a graphical indicator for each test. Project 2013 offers 65 graphical indicators, including stoplights, flags, solid colored squares, plus and minus signs, diamonds, arrows, semaphores, light bulbs, emoticons, and miscellaneous symbols.

3. Select the *Nonsummary rows* option.

4. Select or enter values in the *Test For, Value(s),* and *Image* columns using the data shown in Table 13 - 3.

Test For	Value(s)	Image
Is greater than or equal to	.20	Red stoplight
Is greater than or equal to	.10	Yellow stoplight
Is greater than or equal to	0	Green stoplight
Is less than	0	Green happy face

Table 13 - 3: Graphical indicator tests for Nonsummary rows

5. Select the *Summary rows* option in the *Indicator criteria for* section of the dialog.

6. Select the *Summary rows inherit criteria from nonsummary rows* option. Project 2013 displays the warning dialog shown in Figure 13 - 27.

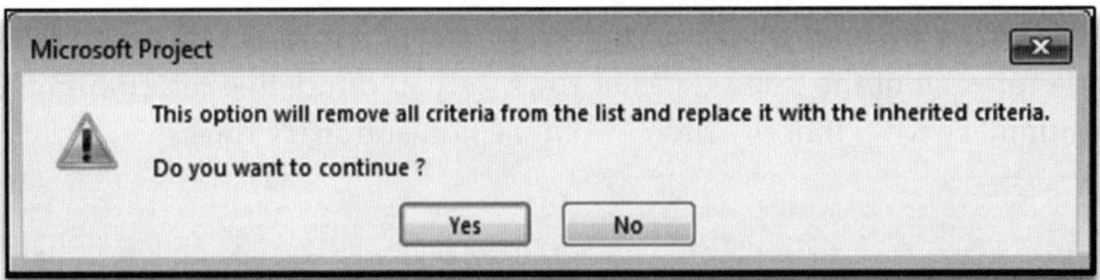

Figure 13 - 27: Warning dialog

7. Click the *Yes* button to close the warning dialog. Project 2013 redisplays the *Graphical Indicators* dialog, but with the indicator criteria grayed out, as shown in Figure 13 - 28.

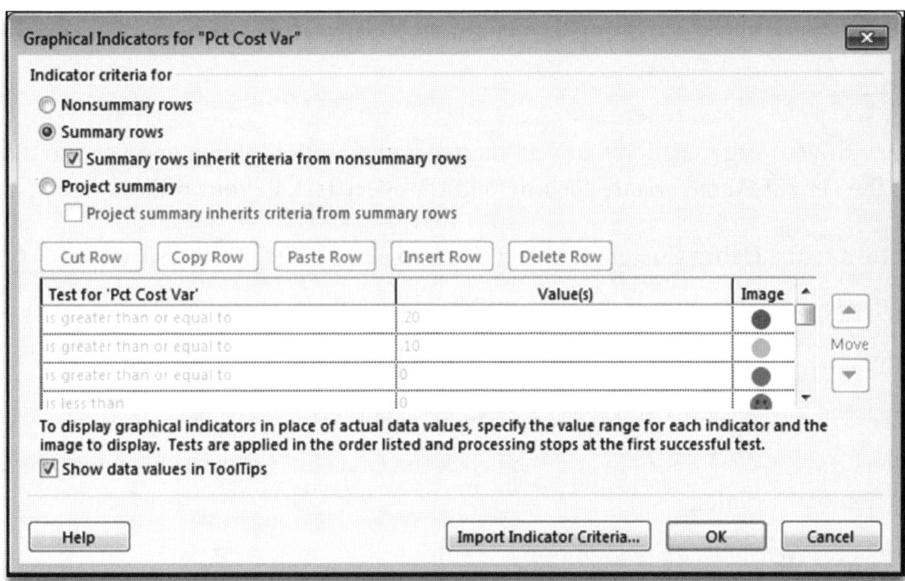

Figure 13 - 28: Graphical Indicators dialog shows inherited criteria for summary rows

8. Select the *Project summary* option in the *Indicator criteria for* section of the dialog.

9. Select the *Project summary inherits criteria from summary rows* option. Project 2013 displays the same warning dialog shown previously in Figure 13 - 27.

10. Click the *Yes* button to close the warning dialog.

11. Click the *OK* button to close the *Graphical Indicators* dialog and return to the *Custom Fields* dialog.

How does Project 2013 determine which graphical indicator to display for each task? The software processes the graphical indicator test criteria from the top down. If the first test results in a "False" condition, the software processes the second test, and continues processing each test in the list until a test results in a "True" condition. The software displays the graphical indicator for the first test that results in a "True" condition and then stops processing the list of tests. If none of the tests results in a "True" condition, the software does not display a graphical indicator for that task. You should keep this in mind while structuring your tests and, at the same time, use it to your advantage.

Information: Project 2013 displays a blank graphical indicator for any task in which a formula generates an error, such as when the software generates a division by zero error.

Hands On Exercise

Exercise 13 - 4

To comply with your organization's project management methodology, you need to display graphical indicators in the *Percent Work Variance* custom field for every task in your project.

1. Return to the **Using Custom Fields 2013.mpp** sample file, if necessary.
2. In the *Properties* section of the *Project* ribbon, click the *Custom Fields* button.
3. Select the *Task* option at the top of the dialog, if necessary.
4. Click the *Type* pick list and select the *Number* field type.
5. Select the *Pct Work Var* field and then click the *Graphical Indicators* button in the *Values to display* section of the dialog.
6. Select the *Nonsummary rows* option.
7. Select or enter values in the *Test For, Value(s),* and *Image* columns using the data shown in Table 13 - 4:

Test	Value(s)	Image
Is greater than or equal to	.50	Red unhappy face
Is greater than or equal to	.20	Red stoplight
Is greater than or equal to	.05	Yellow stoplight
Is greater than or equal to	0	Green stoplight
Is less than	0	Green happy face

Table 13 - 4: Graphical indicator tests for the Pct Work Var field

8. Select the *Summary rows* option in the *Indicator criteria for* section of the dialog.
9. Select the *Summary rows inherit criteria from nonsummary rows* option.
10. When prompted, click the *Yes* button in the warning dialog.
11. Select the *Project summary* option in the *Indicator criteria for* section of the dialog.
12. Select the *Project summary inherits criteria from summary rows* option.
13. When prompted, click the *Yes* button in the warning dialog.
14. Click the *OK* button to close the *Graphical Indicators* dialog.
15. Click the *OK* button to close the *Custom Fields* dialog.
16. Save but **do not** close the **Using Custom Fields 2013.mpp** sample file.

Defining a Custom Outline Code

Although similar to a custom field with a lookup table, custom outline codes differ significantly in the following ways:

- Outline codes can accommodate either a flat value list or a hierarchical outline structure.
- Outline codes cannot contain formulas or display graphical indicators.
- When defining a custom outline code, you must define a code mask that matches your outline code structure.

Assume that as a part of your organization's resource management information, you track each resource's primary job skill. To create a custom resource outline code for this purpose, complete the following steps in the *Custom Fields* dialog:

1. Select the *Resource* option at the top of the dialog.
2. Click the *Type* pick list and select the *Outline Code* item. Figure 13 - 29 shows the custom resource *Outline Codes* available in the *Custom Fields* dialog. Notice that Project 2013 selects the *Lookup* option by default for all *Outline Code* fields. This is because each *Outline Code* field contains a hierarchical lookup table.

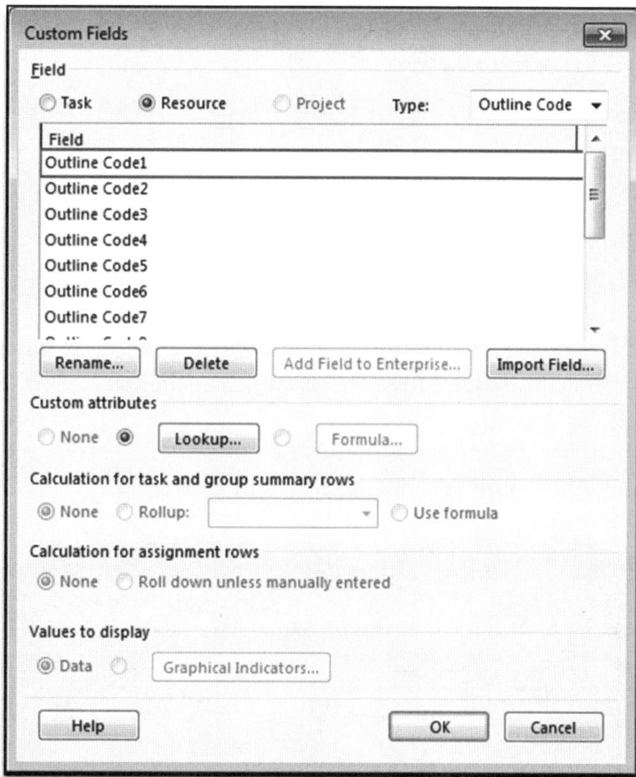

Figure 13 - 29: Custom Outline Codes available in the Custom Fields dialog

3. Select the first available *Outline Code* field, such as *Outline Code1*, and then click the *Rename* button.
4. Enter the text *Primary Skill* in the *Rename Field* dialog and click the *OK* button.

5. With the *Primary Skill* field selected, click the *Lookup* button. Project 2013 displays the *Edit Lookup Table* dialog for the *Primary Skill* outline code, as shown in Figure 13 - 30.

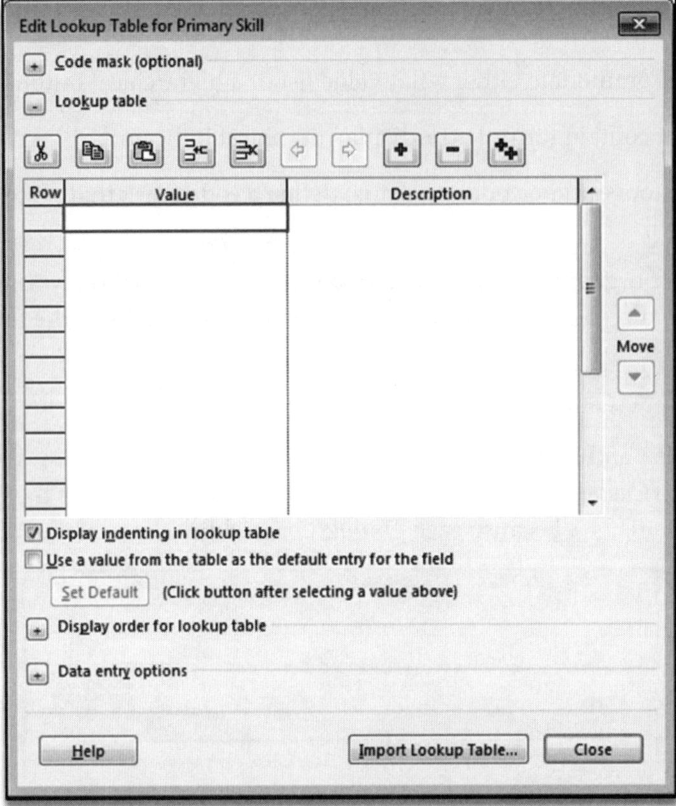

Figure 13 - 30: Edit Lookup Table dialog

6. To define the hierarchical outline structure for the lookup table, click the *Expand* button to expand the *Code mask (optional)* section at the top of the *Edit Lookup Table* dialog.

7. In the *Code mask (optional)* section, click the *Edit Mask* button. The software displays the *Code Mask Definition* dialog for the *Primary Skill* outline code, as shown in Figure 13 - 31.

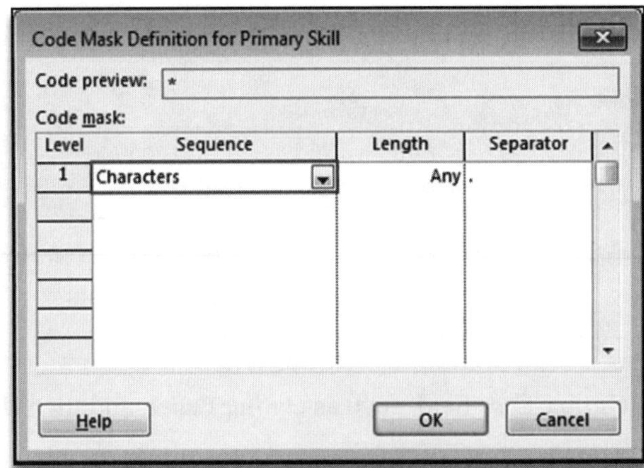

Figure 13 - 31: Code Mask Definition dialog

To define the outline code mask, you must specify values in the *Sequence, Length,* and *Separator* columns for each level of the outline code. In the *Sequence* column, you may select options for numbers, uppercase letters, lowercase letters, or characters. When you select a *Sequence* value, the values for each code segment must adhere to the type of data specified in the *Sequence* column. Selecting the *Characters* option gives you the most flexibility, as you may use any character to define your values.

In the *Length* column, you have the choice of limiting the segment to a number value on the list (between *1* and *10*) or to any number you type into the field. You may also choose the *Any* selection from the pick list to allow any number of defined characters for the outline code segment.

In the *Separator* column, you select the character used as the separator between outline code segments. You can use a period, dash, plus sign, or a forward slash as the separator for each code segment. The software also allows you to enter other special characters, such as those found on the number keys on your keyboard.

8. For the *Primary Skill* outline code, define a two-level code mask, set the *Sequence* value to *Characters,* set the *Length* value to *Any,* and set the *Separator* value as the *Period,* as shown in Figure 13 - 32.

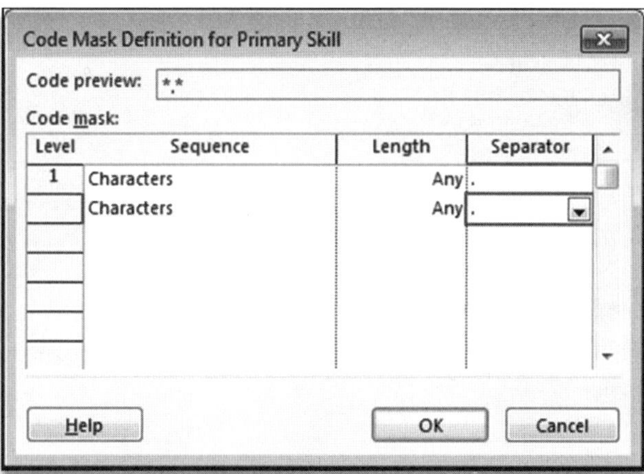

Figure 13 - 32: Completed Code Mask for the Primary Skill outline code

9. Click the *OK* button in the *Code Mask Definition* dialog and return to the *Edit Lookup Table* dialog.

10. Enter your outline code information in the *Value* column.

11. Enter an optional description for each outline code segment in the *Description* column.

12. For each item in the lookup table, use the *Indent* and *Outdent* buttons as necessary to build the outline code structure.

Figure 13 - 33 shows the completed outline code structure for the resource *Primary Skill* outline code. Notice that I indented the four skill items below the *Construction* and *Professional* rows.

Warning: If you see text formatted in red anywhere in the *Value* column, this means that your outline code does not conform to the code mask you created. To correct the errors, you must either edit the code mask or change the indenting of red items in the outline code.

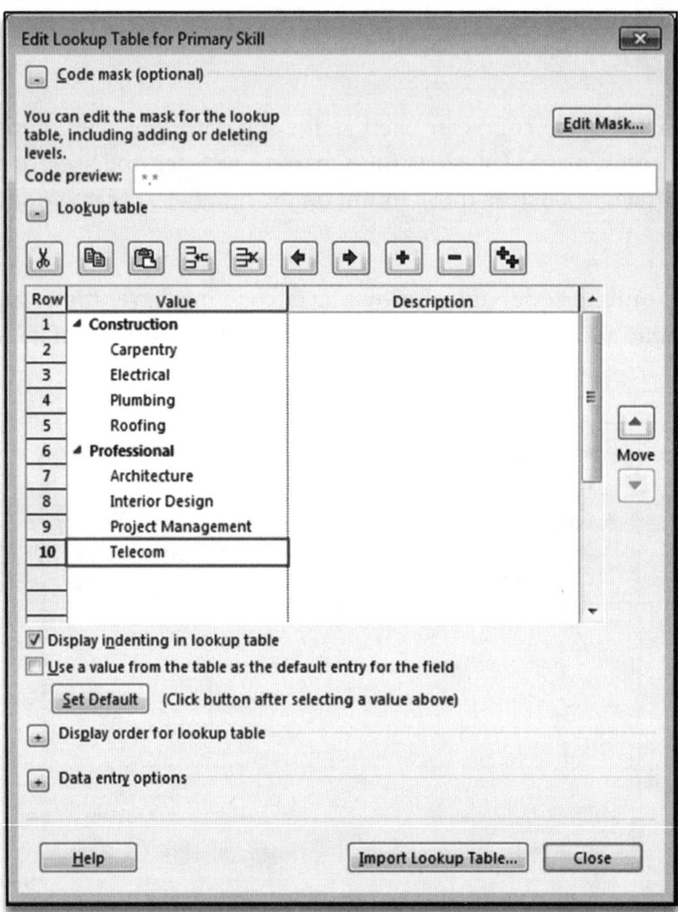

Figure 13 - 33: Completed outline code in the Edit Lookup Table dialog

13. Collapse the *Code mask (optional)* section at the top of the dialog.
14. Expand the *Data entry options* section at the bottom of the dialog. Figure 13 - 34 shows the *Edit Lookup Table* dialog with the *Data entry options* section expanded.

The *Data entry options* section of the dialog offers you two additional options for defining the code mask:

- Select the *Allow additional items to be entered into the fields* option to allow a user to type additional values into the lookup table when you display this custom outline code in any table.
- Select the *Allow only codes that have no subordinate values* option to force the user to select an outline code value that has no child values, such as the skills shown at the second level of indent in Figure 13 - 34.

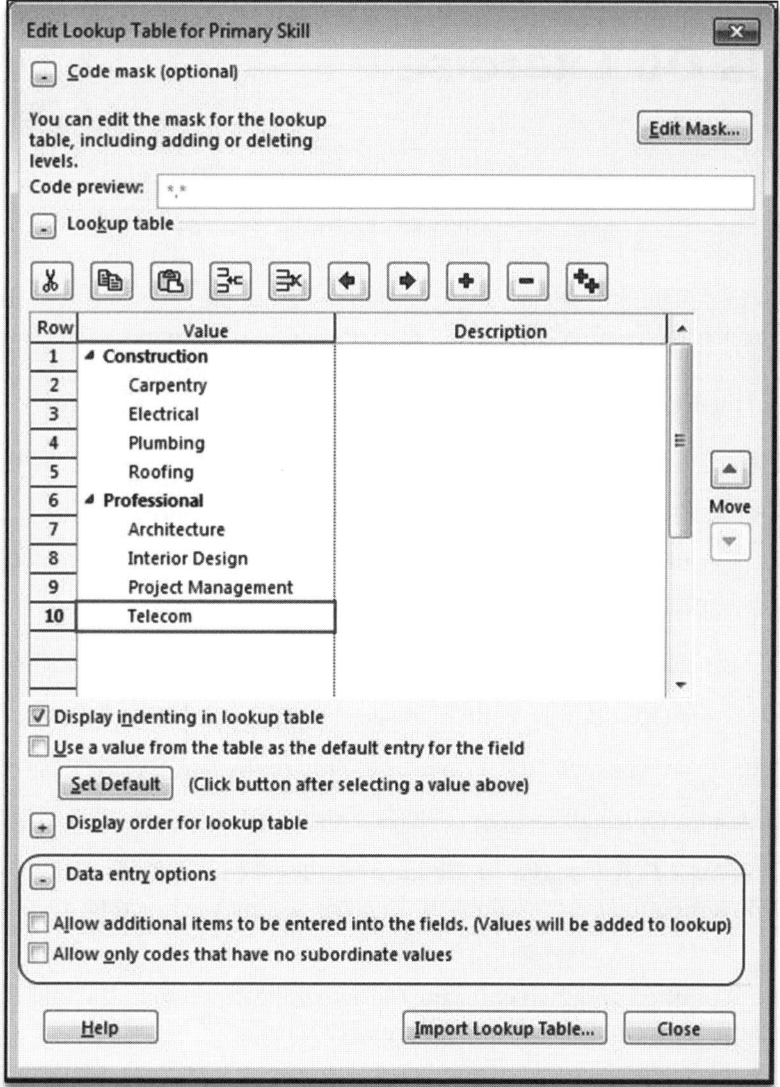

Figure 13 - 34: Edit Lookup Table with Data Entry Options section expanded

The *Edit Lookup Table* dialog also contains an option to specify a default value in the lookup table, and contains a section to control the display order of items in the lookup table. Because I discussed these options for lookup tables previously in this module, I do not discuss them again in this section.

Information: If you previously created a lookup table in another custom outline code field, you can import the lookup table into the current outline code field by clicking the *Import Lookup Table* button. The lookup table can be in an outline code in the active project, or in another project, but the project containing the lookup table must be open before you can import it.

15. Click the *Close* button to close the *Edit Lookup Table* dialog and return to the *Custom Fields* dialog.

Deleting a Custom Field

To delete a custom field or outline code, select the field or outline code in the *Custom Fields* dialog and click the *Delete* button. This action completely removes the custom field or custom outline code from the project.

Hands On Exercise

Exercise 13 - 5

As a part of your organization's project management methodology, you need to define a custom resource outline code to track each resource's geographical location in the organization.

1. Return to the **Using Custom Fields 2013.mpp** sample file, if necessary.
2. In the *Properties* section of the *Project* ribbon, click the *Custom Fields* button.
3. Select the *Resource* option at the top of the dialog.
4. Click the *Type* pick list and select the *Outline Code* item.
5. Select the *Outline Code1* field and then click the *Rename* button.
6. Manually enter **Region Office** in the *Rename Field* dialog and then click the *OK* button.
7. With the *Region Office* outline code field selected, click the *Lookup* button.
8. Expand the *Code mask (optional)* section at the top of the *Edit Lookup Table* dialog.
9. In the *Code mask (optional)* section, click the *Edit Mask* button.
10. In the *Code Mask Definition* dialog, define a **two-level** code mask, setting the *Sequence* values to *Characters*, setting the *Length* values to *Any*, and setting the *Separator* values as the *Period* for each level.
11. Click the *OK* button and then enter the following information in the *Edit Lookup Table* dialog using the *Indent* and *Outdent* buttons for hierarchal order:

    Midwest

        Chicago

        Columbus

        Nashville

    Northeast

        New York City

    South

        Tampa

    West

        Rancho Mirage

        Seattle

12. Expand the *Data entry options* section and select the *Allow only codes that have no subordinate values* option.

13. Click the *Close* button to close the *Edit Lookup Table* dialog.
14. Click the *OK* button to close the *Custom Fields* dialog.
15. Save but **do not** close the **Using Custom Fields 2013.mpp** sample file.

Exercise 13 - 6

Display the new custom fields in task and resource views.

1. Apply the *Gantt Chart* view in the **Using Custom Fields 2013.mpp** sample file, if necessary.
2. Right-click the *Task Mode* column header and select the *Hide Column* item in the shortcut menu.
3. Right-click the *Task Name* column header and select the *Insert Column* item in the shortcut menu.
4. In the pick list of available fields, select the *Pct Work Var* custom field.
5. Double-click the right edge of the *Pct Work Var* column header to "best fit" the column width.

Notice how Project 2013 displays a graphical indicator in the *Pct Work Var* column for every task **except** milestones. This is because the formula generates a division by zero error for each milestone task. If you float your mouse pointer over the blank cells in the *Pct Work Var* column, you can see the *#ERROR* value in the tooltip.

Information: If you do not see graphical indicators in the *Pct Work Var* column, press the **F9** function key on your computer keyboard to recalculate the project.

6. Right-click the *Pct Work Var* column header and select the *Field Settings* item on the shortcut menu.
7. In the *Field Settings* dialog, set the *Align title* and *Align data* values to *Centered*, and then click the *OK* button.
8. For task ID #12, the *Create Final Product Specs* task, increase the *Duration* value to *10 days*.

Notice how Project 2013 displays a red "unhappy face" graphical indicator for the *Create Final Product Specs* task.

9. Right-click the *Duration* column header and select the *Insert Column* item in the shortcut menu.
10. In the pick list of available fields, select the *CR Type* custom field.
11. For task ID #12, the *Create Final Product Specs* task, click the pick list in the *CR Type* cell, and then select the *Increased Duration* item.
12. Double-click the right edge of the *CR Type* column header to "best fit" the column width.
13. Click the *View* tab to display the *View* ribbon.
14. In the *Resource Views* section of the *View* ribbon, click the *Resource Sheet* button.
15. Right-click the *Type* column header and select the *Insert Column* item on the shortcut menu.
16. In the list of available fields, select the *Region Office* outline code field.

17. For each resource in the project team, select any value in the *Region Office* outline code field, as desired.

Notice how Project 2013 displays the values you selected in the *Region Office* column for each resource.

18. Double-click the right edge of the *Region Office* column to "best fit" the column width.
19. Save and close the **Using Custom Fields 2013.mpp** sample file.

Creating and Using a Master Project

In Project 2013, a **master project** is a single project that contains inserted projects known as **subprojects**. Some people also refer to a master project as a **consolidated project**. Using a master project, you can perform actions such as:

- Set cross-project dependencies on tasks in the subprojects.
- View the Critical Path for all subprojects.
- Analyze work, cost, and variance information across all of the subprojects.
- Analyze resource allocation and availability information across all of the subprojects.

Before you can create and work with a master project, however, you must create a **shared resource pool** file containing a list of all of the resources who work in projects. The process you must follow to create and work with a master project is as follows:

1. Create the shared resource pool file.
2. Connect each subproject to the shared resource pool file.
3. Create the master project.
4. Work with task and resource information in the master project.

I discuss each of these steps as subtopics in this topical section, and provide additional information about issues you may face when using a master project with a shared resource pool file.

Creating a Shared Resource Pool File

As I stated earlier, a **shared resource pool** file is a Project 2013 file containing a list of resources that work in projects. If your master project contains only projects you manage, the shared resource pool file should contain the list of resources that work in your own projects. If your master project contains projects managed by you and by other project managers, then the shared resource pool file must contain a list of all resources working in all of the projects.

There are several ways to create a shared resource pool file. For example, you can open a new blank project, apply the *Resource Sheet* view, and then type the names of all of the resources, along with their standard and custom resource information. If necessary, refer back to Module 06, *Project Resource Planning*, and review the information on how to populate the *Resource Sheet* view of a project. Another approach is to open a new blank project, apply the *Resource Sheet* view and then copy and paste the names of all of the resources from the projects you manage. After you create your shared resource pool file using either of these methods, save the file in the folder where you save your projects, and give it a name that allows you to easily recognize its function. For example, I might name my file *DAH Shared Resource Pool*, prefixing the file name with my three letter initials.

Information: If you use the second approach to create your shared resource pool file, confirm that you do not have any duplicate names in the list of resources. If you have duplicate names, be sure to remove them before you connect projects to the shared resource pool file.

Connecting Projects to a Shared Resource Pool File

After you create and save the shared resource pool file, you are ready to connect projects to the file to share the resources in the file. When you connect a project to a shared resource pool file, Project 2013 shares all of the resources in the shared resource pool file with the connecting project. Project 2013 users commonly refer to each connected project as a **sharing project**, by the way. To connect a project to a shared resource pool file, complete the following steps:

1. Open the shared resource pool file in *Read/Write* mode.
2. Open a project file.
3. Click the *Resource* tab to display the *Resource* ribbon.
4. In the *Assignments* section of the *Resource* ribbon, click the *Resource Pool* pick list button, and then select the *Share Resources* item. The software displays the *Share Resources* dialog.
5. In the *Share Resources* dialog, select the *Use resources* option in the top half of the dialog. Since you already opened the shared resource pool file, the software selects this file in the *From* field automatically, as shown in Figure 13 - 35. If you have multiple projects open, click the *From* pick list and select the shared resource pool file, if necessary.

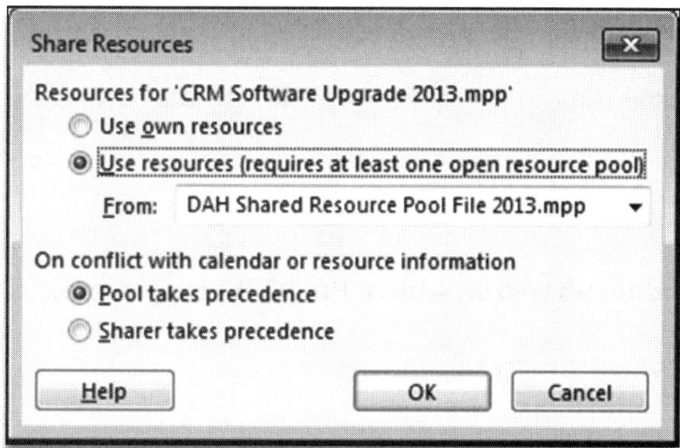

Figure 13 - 35: Share Resources dialog, select the Use resources option

6. In the *Share Resources* dialog, leave the *Pool takes precedence* option selected and then click the *OK* button.
7. Save and close the project.
8. Save the shared resource pool file.
9. Repeat steps #2-8 for every project you want to include in the master project.
10. After you connect every sharing project to the shared resource pool file, save and close the shared resource pool file.

Hands On Exercise

Exercise 13 - 7

Connect three projects to a shared resource pool file.

1. Open the **New Product Shared Resource Pool 2013.mpp** sample file.

Notice that the shared resource pool file contains a list of ten resources.

2. Open the **New Product 1.mpp** sample file.
3. Click the *Resource* tab to display the *Resource* ribbon.
4. In the *Assignments* section of the *Resource* ribbon, click the *Resource Pool* pick list button, and then select the *Share Resources* item.
5. In the *Share Resources* dialog, select the *Use resources* option in the top half of the dialog.

Since you already opened the shared resource pool file, notice that the software selects this file in the *From* field.

6. In the *Share Resources* dialog, leave the *Pool takes precedence* option selected, and then click the *OK* button.
7. Save and close the **New Product 1.mpp** sample file.
8. Save the **New Product Shared Resource Pool 2013.mpp** sample file.
9. Open the **New Product 2.mpp** sample file.
10. Repeat steps #4-6 to connect this project to the shared resource pool file.
11. Save and close the **New Product 2.mpp** sample file.
12. Save the **New Product Shared Resource Pool 2013.mpp** sample file.
13. Open the **New Product 3.mpp** sample file.
14. Repeat steps #4-6 to connect this project to the shared resource pool file.

Notice the burning man indicator on task ID #2, the *Create Product3 Specs* task, indicating that this task has an overallocated resource assigned to it.

15. Save and close the **New Product 3.mpp** sample file.
16. Save and close the **New Product Shared Resource Pool 2013.mpp** sample file.

Creating a Master Project

To create a master project, complete the following steps:

1. Create a new blank project.
2. Click the *Project* tab to display the *Project* ribbon.
3. In the *Properties* section of the *Project* ribbon, click the *Project Information* button.
4. In the *Project Information* dialog, set the *Start date* value to the date of the earliest starting project, and then click the *OK* button.
5. In the *Insert* section of the *Project* ribbon, click the *Subproject* button. Project 2013 displays the *Insert Project* dialog as shown in Figure 13 - 36.

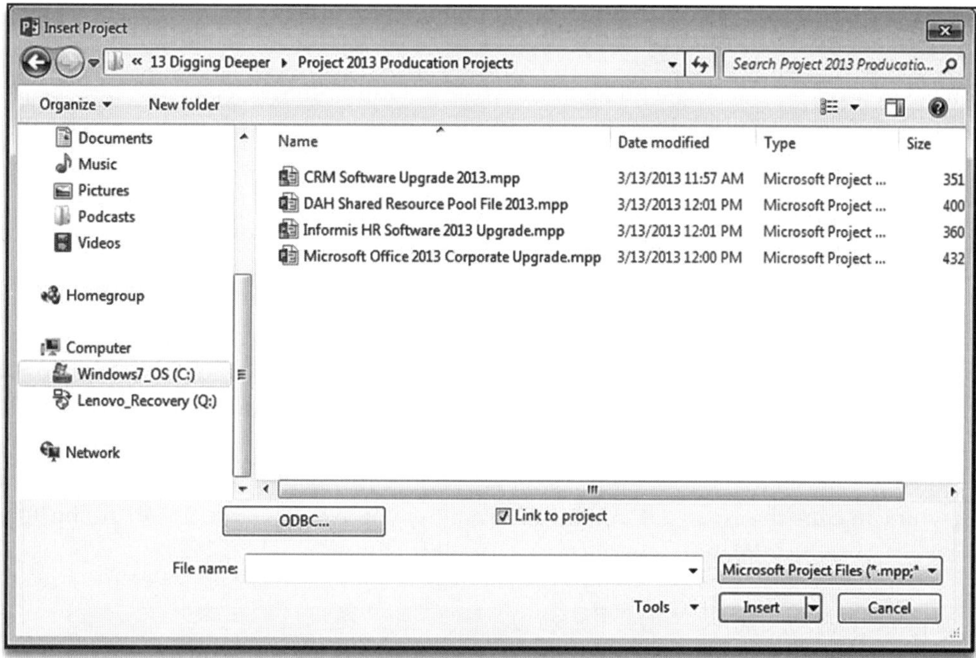

Figure 13 - 36: Insert Project dialog

6. In the *Insert Project* dialog, navigate to the folder containing a project you want to insert into your new master project.
7. Using either the **Control** key or the **Shift** key on your computer keyboard, select two or more projects and then click the *Insert* button. Project 2013 creates a master project with each subproject collapsed, such as the one with three subprojects shown in Figure 13 - 37.

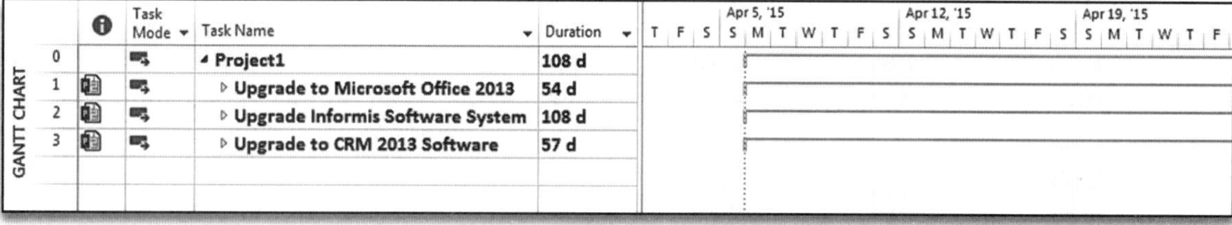

Figure 13 - 37: Three subprojects in a master project with task details collapsed

8. Click the *Expand* symbol (white arrow symbol) to the left of the **last** subproject name to expand the tasks in the subproject. The software displays the *Open Resource Pool Information* dialog shown in Figure 13 - 38.

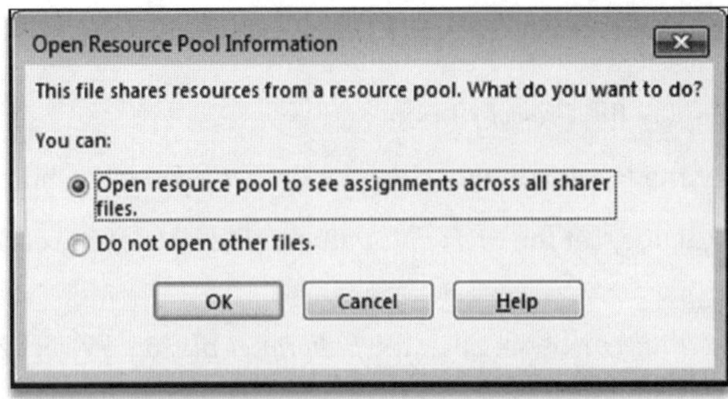

Figure 13 - 38: Open Resource Pool Information dialog

9. In the *Open Resource Pool Information* dialog, leave the default option selected to open the shared resource pool file, and then click the *OK* button. The software opens the shared resource pool file in *Read-Only* mode.

10. Click the *Expand* symbol (little white arrow symbol) to the left of every other subproject to expand the subtasks in every project.

To save your master project, click the *Save* button in the *Quick Access Toolbar*. In the *Save As* dialog, navigate to the folder where you want to save the project, enter a name for the master project, and then click the *Save* button. After saving your master project initially, every time you save schedule changes to a master project file, Project 2013 displays the dialog shown in Figure 13 - 39, prompting you to save each subproject. Most of the time, you should simply click the *Yes to All* button to quickly close the dialog. If you are absolutely certain you made no changes to your subprojects, you can click the *No to All* button. Alternately, you can click the *Yes* or *No* button for each project as the software displays this dialog for every project individually.

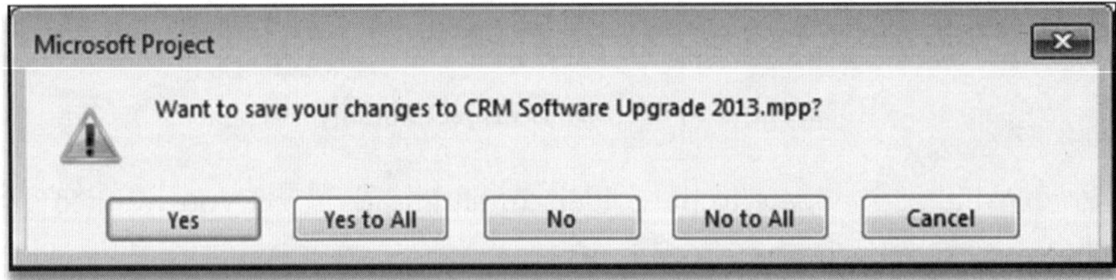

Figure 13 - 39: Dialog prompts you to save each subproject

After closing the dialog shown previously in Figure 13 - 39, the software displays the dialog shown in Figure 13 - 40, prompting you to save the changes to the shared resource pool file. If you made changes to the schedule of any of the subprojects in the master project, you should click the *OK* button and allow the software to update the shared resource pool file with the latest resource assignment information. If you are certain that you made no changes to the schedule in any subproject, you can click the *Cancel* button to cancel the update of the shared resource pool file. When you click the *OK* button in the dialog shown in Figure 13 - 40, Project 2013 changes the shared resource pool file from *Read-Only* to *Read/Write* mode, saves the file, and then changes the file from *Read/Write* to *Read-Only* mode again, all in the blink of an eye!

Figure 13 - 40: Dialog prompts you to update the shared resource pool file

Hands On Exercise

Exercise 13 - 8

Create a new master project consisting of three subprojects.

1. Click the *File* tab and then click the *New* tab in the *Backstage*, if necessary.
2. On the *New* page in the *Backstage*, click the *Blank Project* icon to create a new blank project.
3. Click the *Project Information* button in the *Properties* section of the *Project* ribbon.
4. In the *Project Information* dialog, set the *Start date* value to **January 4, 2016**, and then click the *OK* button.
5. In the *Insert* section of the *Project* ribbon, click the *Subproject* button.
6. In the *Insert Project* dialog, use the **Shift** key on your computer keyboard to select the following projects:
    - **New Product 1.mpp**
    - **New Product 2.mpp**
    - **New Product 3.mpp**
7. Click the *Insert* button to insert the three projects as subprojects of a new master project.
8. Double-click the right edge of the *Task Name* column header to "best fit" the contents of the column.
9. Drag and drop the subprojects into the following order: *Develop Product 1*, *Develop Product 2*, and *Develop Product 3*.

Information: You can "drag and drop" a subproject by selecting the row ID number of the project, releasing the mouse button, clicking and holding on the row ID number, and then dragging the subproject to its new location. This is the exact same method you use to drag a task to a different location in a project.

10. Click the *Expand* symbol (little white arrow symbol) to the left of the **last** subproject to expand the subtasks in that project.
11. When the software displays the *Open Resource Pool Information* dialog, click the *OK* button to open the shared resource pool file.
12. Click the *Expand* symbol for the other two subprojects to expand the subtasks in each project.
13. Double-click the right edge of the *Task Name* column header to "best fit" the contents of the column again.
14. Drag the split bar to the right edge of the *Duration* column.
15. Using the *Save* button in your *Quick Access Toolbar,* save the master project file in the folder containing your sample files, using the name **New Product Development Program.mpp** for the project file.
16. When prompted in a dialog to save the changes to each subproject, click the *Yes to All* button.
17. When prompted in a dialog to update the shared resource pool file, click the *OK* button.
18. Click and hold the right edge of the *Task Name* column header and manually widen the column as needed, then drag the split bar again to the right edge of the *Duration* column.

Notice the burning man indicator for tasks in the *Develop Product 1* project and the *Develop Product 3* project, indicating that an overallocated resource is assigned to tasks in these projects.

19. Leave the **New Product Development Program.mpp** master project file open for the next exercise.

Setting External Dependencies

When you set a task dependency between tasks in two or more different projects, you are setting what is known as an **external dependency** or a **cross-project dependency**. You can use a master project to set external dependencies by completing the following steps:

1. Expand all subtasks in all of the subprojects of the master project.
2. Using the **Control** key on your computer keyboard, select the predecessor task in one subproject, and then select the successor task in another subproject.
3. Click the *Task* tab to display the *Task* ribbon.
4. In the *Schedule* section of the *Task* ribbon, click the *Link Tasks* button.
5. Double-click the link line between the two linked tasks and edit the task dependency in the *Task Dependency* dialog, if necessary.
6. Save the master project.
7. When prompted in a dialog to save changes to each of the subprojects, click the *Yes to All* button.
8. When prompted in a dialog to update the shared resource pool file, click the *OK* button.

Hands On Exercise

Exercise 13 - 9

Create cross-project dependencies between subprojects of a master project.

1. Return to the **New Product Development Program.mpp** master project file, if necessary.

2. Click the *Task* tab to display the *Task* ribbon.

3. In your master project, select the *Design Product1* task in the *Develop Product 1* project.

4. Press and hold the **Control** key on your computer keyboard, select the *Design Product2* task in the *Develop Product 2* project and the *Design Product3* task in the *Develop Product 3* project.

5. Release the **Control** key and then click the *Link the Selected Tasks* button in the *Schedule* section of the *Task* ribbon.

6. Click the *Save* button in the *Quick Access Toolbar* to save the master project.

7. When prompted in a dialog to save changes to each of the subprojects, click the *Yes to All* button.

8. When prompted in a dialog to update the shared resource pool file, click the *OK* button.

9. Leave the **New Product Development Program.mpp** master project file open for the next exercise.

Viewing the Critical Path in a Master Project

You can view the Critical Path in a master project by completing the following steps, documented previously in Module 08, *Project Execution*:

1. Display the *Gantt Chart* view, if necessary.

2. Click the *Format* tab to display the *Format* ribbon.

3. In the *Bar Styles* section of the *Format* ribbon, select the *Critical Tasks* checkbox.

Remember that Project 2013 displays Critical tasks using red Gantt bars and displays non-Critical tasks using blue Gantt bars.

Hands On Exercise

Exercise 13 - 10

View the Critical Path in a master project.

1. Return to the **New Product Development Program.mpp** master project file, if necessary.

2. Click the *Format* tab to display the *Format* ribbon.

3. Select the *Critical Tasks* checkbox in the *Bar Styles* section of the *Format* ribbon.

4. Examine the path shown by the red Gantt bars in the project.

Notice how the Critical Path includes tasks in all three subprojects, but does not include every task in every subproject.

5. Click the *Save* button in the *Quick Access Toolbar* to save the master project.

6. When prompted in a dialog to save changes to each of the subprojects, click the *Yes to All* button.

7. When prompted in a dialog to update the shared resource pool file, click the *OK* button.

8. Leave the **New Product Development Program.mpp** master project file open for the next exercise.

Viewing Resource Assignment Information across Multiple Projects

You can also use a master project to view resource assignment information across all of the projects in a master project. To perform this kind of resource analysis, click the *View* tab and then click the *Resource Usage* button in the *Resources Views* section of the *View* ribbon. Project 2013 displays the *Resource Usage* view shown in Figure 13 - 41.

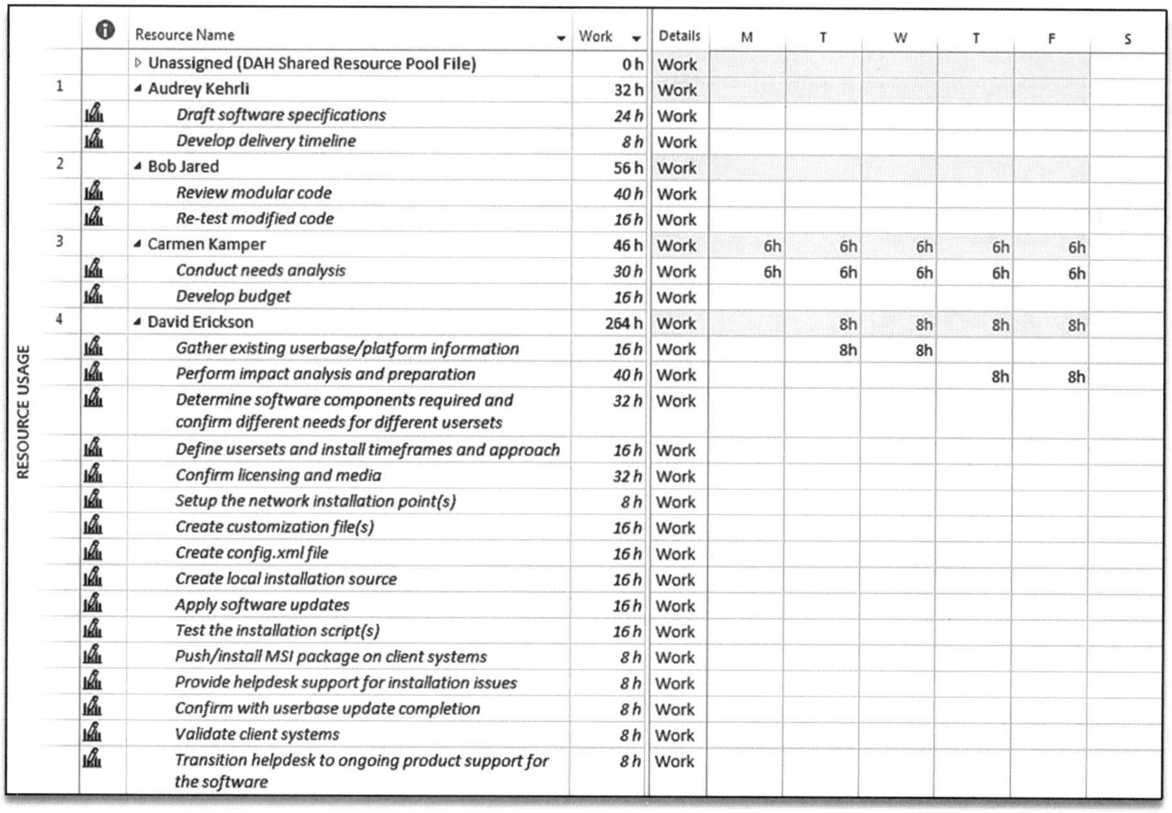

RESOURCE USAGE

	Indicators	Resource Name	Work	Details	M	T	W	T	F	S
		▷ Unassigned (DAH Shared Resource Pool File)	0 h	Work						
1		◢ Audrey Kehrli	32 h	Work						
		Draft software specifications	*24 h*	Work						
		Develop delivery timeline	*8 h*	Work						
2		◢ Bob Jared	56 h	Work						
		Review modular code	*40 h*	Work						
		Re-test modified code	*16 h*	Work						
3		◢ Carmen Kamper	46 h	Work	6h	6h	6h	6h	6h	
		Conduct needs analysis	*30 h*	Work	6h	6h	6h	6h	6h	
		Develop budget	*16 h*	Work						
4		◢ David Erickson	264 h	Work		8h	8h	8h	8h	
		Gather existing userbase/platform information	*16 h*	Work		8h	8h			
		Perform impact analysis and preparation	*40 h*	Work				8h	8h	
		Determine software components required and confirm different needs for different usersets	*32 h*	Work						
		Define usersets and install timeframes and approach	*16 h*	Work						
		Confirm licensing and media	*32 h*	Work						
		Setup the network installation point(s)	*8 h*	Work						
		Create customization file(s)	*16 h*	Work						
		Create config.xml file	*16 h*	Work						
		Create local installation source	*16 h*	Work						
		Apply software updates	*16 h*	Work						
		Test the installation script(s)	*16 h*	Work						
		Push/install MSI package on client systems	*8 h*	Work						
		Provide helpdesk support for installation issues	*8 h*	Work						
		Confirm with userbase update completion	*8 h*	Work						
		Validate client systems	*8 h*	Work						
		Transition helpdesk to ongoing product support for the software	*8 h*	Work						

Figure 13 - 41: Resource Usage view in a master project

Displayed for a master project, the *Resource Usage* view shows you the task assignments for every resource in every subproject of the master project. Using the task assignment information in the master project, you can locate cross-project resource overallocations and determine resource availability in the future. To enhance the *Resource Usage* view in a master project, complete the following steps:

1. Right-click the *Resource Name* column header and select the *Insert Column* item on the shortcut menu.

2. In the pick list of available columns, select the *Project* column.

3. Decrease the column width of the *Project* column, if desirable.

4. Click the *View* tab to display the *View* ribbon.

5. Click the *Group By* pick list in the *Data* section of the *View* ribbon and select the *Assignments Keeping Outline Structure* group.

By inserting the *Project* column, you can identify the project in which you assigned tasks to each resource. By applying the *Assignments Keeping Outline Structure* group, you can see the Work Breakdown Structure (WBS) for every task assigned to each resource. Figure 13 - 42 shows the *Resource Usage* view with the *Project* column inserted to the left of the *Resource Name* column and with the *Assignments Keeping Outline Structure* group applied.

RESOURCE USAGE

	Project	Resource Name	Work	Details	T	W
		Name: Audrey Kehrli	**32 h**	Work		
		1 Analysis/Software Requirements	**32 h**	Work		
	CRM Software Upgrade 2013	*Draft software specifications*	*24 h*	Work		
	CRM Software Upgrade 2013	*Develop delivery timeline*	*8 h*	Work		
		Name: Bob Jared	**56 h**	Work		
		4 Testing	**56 h**	Work		
	CRM Software Upgrade 2013	*Review modular code*	*40 h*	Work		
	CRM Software Upgrade 2013	*Re-test modified code*	*16 h*	Work		
		Name: Carmen Kamper	**46 h**	Work	6h	6h
		1 Analysis/Software Requirements	**46 h**	Work	6h	6h
	CRM Software Upgrade 2013	*Conduct needs analysis*	*30 h*	Work	6h	6h
	CRM Software Upgrade 2013	*Develop budget*	*16 h*	Work		
		Name: David Erickson	**264 h**	Work	8h	8h
		1 Plan the Software Deployment	**136 h**	Work	8h	8h
	Microsoft Office 2013 Corporate Upgrade	*Gather existing userbase/platform information*	*16 h*	Work	8h	8h
	Microsoft Office 2013 Corporate Upgrade	*Perform impact analysis and preparation*	*40 h*	Work		
	Microsoft Office 2013 Corporate Upgrade	*Determine software components required and confirm different needs for different usersets*	*32 h*	Work		
	Microsoft Office 2013 Corporate Upgrade	*Define usersets and install timeframes and approach*	*16 h*	Work		
	Microsoft Office 2013 Corporate Upgrade	*Confirm licensing and media*	*32 h*	Work		
		3 Software Installation	**112 h**	Work		
		3.3 Create network installation point(s)	**88 h**	Work		
	Microsoft Office 2013 Corporate Upgrade	*Setup the network installation point(s)*	*8 h*	Work		
	Microsoft Office 2013 Corporate Upgrade	*Test the installation script(s)*	*16 h*	Work		
		3.3.2 Setup push scripts or coordinated deployr	**64 h**	Work		
	Microsoft Office 2013 Corporate Upgrade	*Create customization file(s)*	*16 h*	Work		
	Microsoft Office 2013 Corporate Upgrade	*Create config.xml file*	*16 h*	Work		
	Microsoft Office 2013 Corporate Upgrade	*Create local installation source*	*16 h*	Work		

Figure 13 - 42: Resource Usage view modified to show the project and the WBS for each task assignment

Hands On Exercise

Exercise 13 - 11

Locate and resolve resource cross-project overallocations in a master project.

1. Return to the **New Product Development Program.mpp** master project file, if necessary.
2. Click the *View* tab to display the *View* ribbon.
3. In the *Resources Views* section of the *View* ribbon, click the *Resource Usage* button to display the *Resource Usage* view.
4. Double-click the right edge of the *Resource Name* column header to "best fit" the column width.
5. Drag the split bar to the right edge of the *Work* column.
6. For the *Unassigned* resource, click the *Collapse* indicator (black triangle symbol) to collapse the task assignments for unassigned tasks (they are all milestone tasks).

Notice that two resources, *Carole Madison* and *Russ Powell*, are overallocated (as indicated by their names formatted in red).

7. Click the *Resource* tab to display the *Resource* ribbon.
8. In the *Level* section of the *Resource* ribbon, successively click the *Go to Next Overallocation* button to locate the time periods during which *Carole Madison* and *Russ Powell* are overallocated.

Notice that *Carole Madison* is assigned to work 16 hours per day on January 4-5, 2016. Because the two tasks assigned to her are in different projects, her overallocation represents a cross-project overallocation. Notice that *Russ Powell* is assigned to work 16 hours per day on February 3-9, 2016. Because the two tasks assigned to him are in different projects, his overallocation also represents a cross-project overallocation.

9. When you see the dialog that indicates the software cannot find any more overallocations in the project, click the *OK* button to close the dialog.
10. Select *Carole Madison* and then click the *Level Resource* button in the *Level* section of the *Resource* ribbon
11. In the *Level Resource* dialog, click the *Level Now* button to level her overallocation.
12. Select *Russ Powell* and then click the *Level Resource* button in the *Level* section of the *Resource* ribbon.
13. In the *Level Resource* dialog, click the *Level Now* button to level his overallocation.
14. Click the *Save* button in your *Quick Access Toolbar* to save the changes to your master project.
15. When prompted in a dialog to save changes to each of the subprojects, click the *Yes to All* button.
16. When prompted in a dialog to update the shared resource pool file, click the *OK* button.
17. Leave the **New Product Development Program.mpp** master project file open for the next exercise.

Exercise 13 - 12

Analyze task and resource assignment data in a master project.

1. Return to the **New Product Development Program.mpp** master project file, if necessary.
2. Click the *View* tab to display the *View* ribbon.
3. Right-click the *Resource Name* column header and select the *Insert Column* item on the shortcut menu.
4. In the pick list of available columns, select the *Project* column.
5. In the *Data* section of the *View* ribbon, click the *Group By* pick list, and then select the *Assignments Keeping Outline Structure* group.
6. Double-click the right edge of the *Project* column header to "best fit" the column width.
7. Drag the split bar to the right edge of the *Work* column.

Notice that by adding the *Project* column and by applying the *Assignments Keeping Outline Structure* group in the *Resource Usage* view, you can now see the project in which each task is located and you can also see the WBS for every task.

8. In the *Zoom* section of the *View* ribbon, click the *Timescale* pick list, and select the *Weeks* item.

9. Scroll the timephased grid to the week of **January 3, 2016**.

Notice that you can now see the assigned work for each resource on a weekly basis across all three sub-projects in the master project.

10. In the *Task Views* section of the *View* ribbon, click the *Task Usage* button to display the *Task Usage* view.

11. Right-click the *Select All* button and select the *Work* table on the shortcut menu.

12. Double-click the right edge of the *Task Name* column header to "best fit" the column width.

13. Drag the split bar to the right side of the *Work* column.

14. Click the *Collapse* symbol (little black triangle) to the left of the *Develop Product 1, Develop Product 2,* and *Develop Product 3* projects to collapse all of the subtasks.

15. In the *Zoom* section of the *View* ribbon, click the *Timescale* pick list, and select the *Weeks* item.

16. Scroll the timephased grid to the week of **January 3, 2016**.

Notice that you can now see the total work on a weekly basis for all three subprojects in the master project.

17. Click the *Save* button on your *Quick Access Toolbar* to save the changes to your master project.

18. When prompted in a dialog to save changes to each of the subprojects, click the *Yes to All* button.

19. If prompted in a dialog to update the shared resource pool file, click the *OK* button.

20. Close the **New Product Development Program.mpp** master project file.

21. Close the **New Product Shared Resource Pool 2013.mpp** sample file.

Exporting a Project 2013 File to Excel

Project 2013 allows you to export project data to a variety of file formats readable by other applications. These include the PDF and XPS formats, several Excel workbook formats, two text file formats, and the XML file format. To export a Project 2013 file to an Excel workbook, complete the following steps:

1. Click the *File* tab and then click the *Export* tab in the *Backstage*. Project 2013 displays the *Export* page of the *Backstage*.
2. On the *Export* page, click the *Save Project as File* tab. The software displays the *Export* page with the *Save Project as File* section displayed, as shown in Figure 13 - 43.

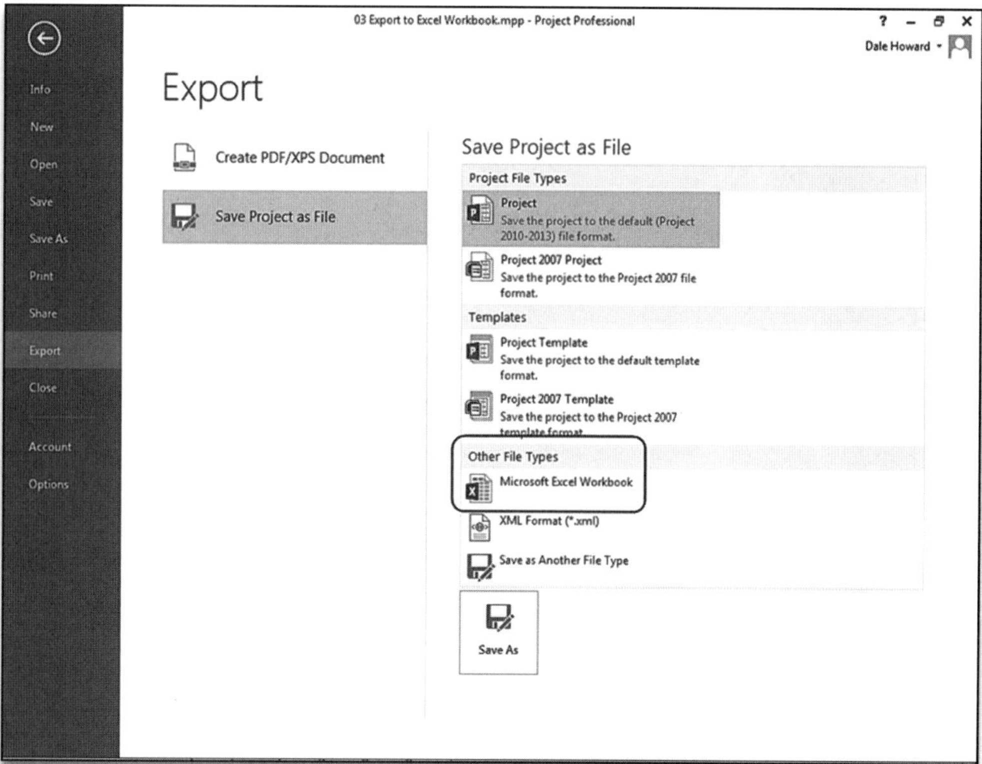

Figure 13 - 43: Export page in the Backstage

3. In the *Save Project as File* section of the *Export* page, select the *Microsoft Excel Workbook* file type in *the Other File Types* list and click the *Save As* button. The software displays the *Save As* dialog with the *Excel Workbook (*.xlsx)* option selected in the *Save as type* field, as shown in Figure 13 - 44.
4. In the *Save As* dialog, navigate to the location where you want to save your project file as an Excel workbook.

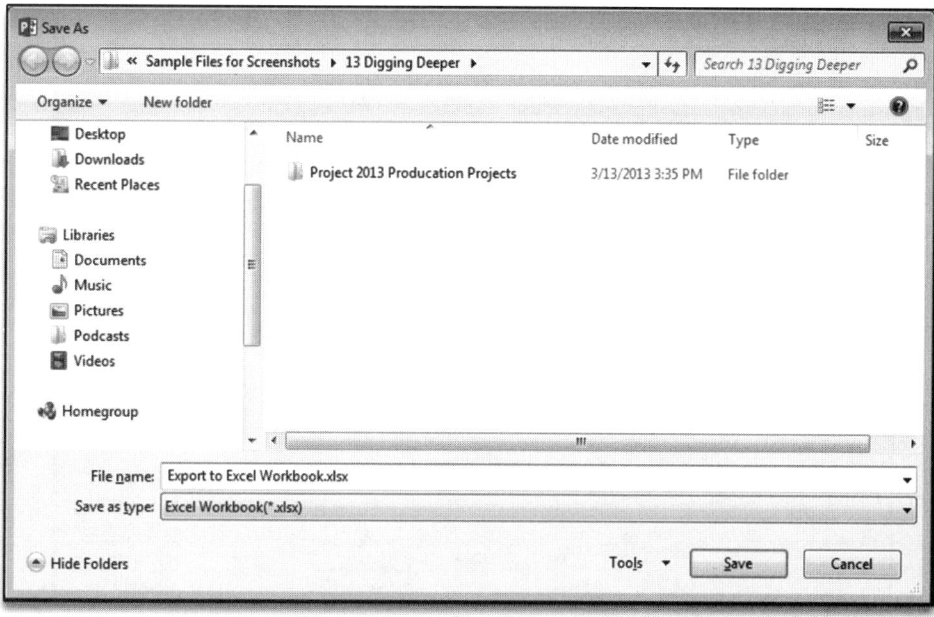

Figure 13 - 44: Save a project as an Excel workbook

5. Click the *Save* button. Project 2013 displays the *Welcome* page of the *Export Wizard* dialog, as shown in Figure 13 - 45.

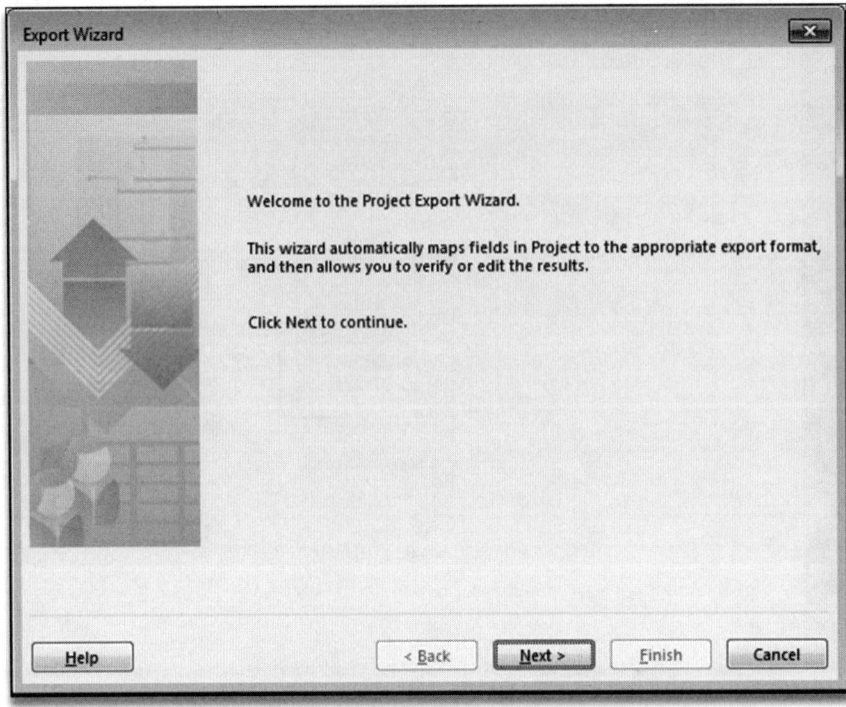

Figure 13 - 45: Export Wizard dialog, Welcome page

6. In the *Export Wizard* dialog, click the *Next* button. Project 2013 displays the *Data* page of the *Export Wizard* dialog shown in Figure 13 - 46.

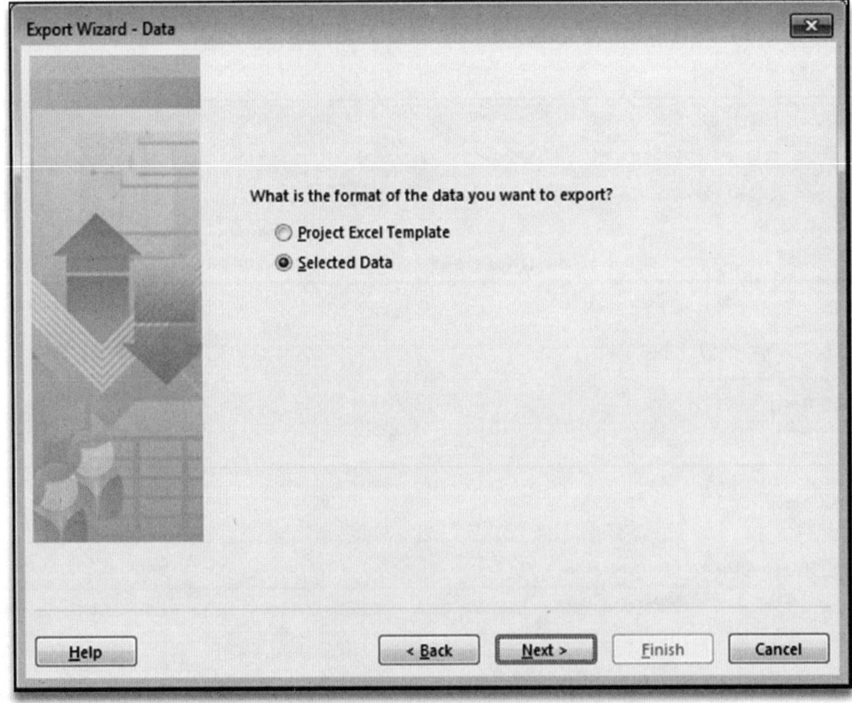

Figure 13 - 46: Export Wizard dialog, Data page

The *Data* page of the *Export* Wizard dialog offers you two options to determine what data you want to export:

- Select the *Project Excel Template* option to export a standardized set of task, resource, and assignment fields to an Excel workbook. The software creates a separate worksheet for each type of data.

- Select the *Selected Data* option if you want to choose which task, resource, and assignment fields to export to an Excel workbook. The software creates a separate worksheet for each type of data you select.

If you select the *Project Excel Template* option, click the *Finish* button to complete the export process. Using the *Project Excel* template, Project 2013 exports key data about project tasks, resources, and assignments into an Excel workbook. The resulting workbook contains three worksheets, labeled *Task_Table, Resource_Table,* and *Assignment_Table*. Each worksheet contains the type of data indicated in the name of the worksheet, meaning that you see the exported task data in the *Task_Table* worksheet.

Warning: Because of an unfixed bug in the release (RTM) version of Project 2013, the software displays the false error dialog shown in Figure 13 - 47 after you click the *Finish* button in the *Export Wizard* dialog. To complete the export operation, click the *OK* button in the error dialog to allow the software to export the project file to the Excel workbook.

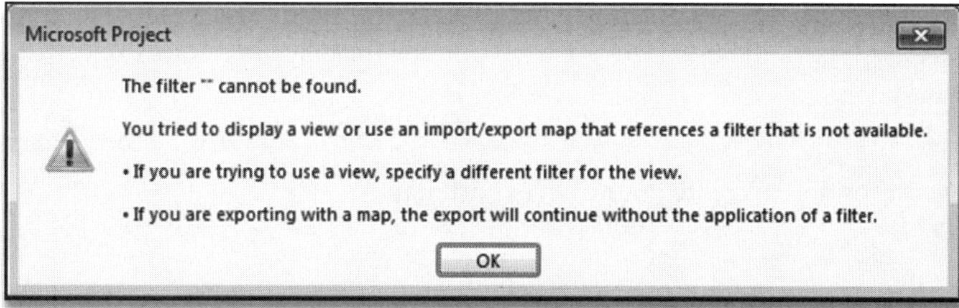

Figure 13 - 47: False error dialog

For example, Figure 13 - 48 shows the *Task_Table* worksheet for a Project 2013 file exported to an Excel workbook using the *Project Excel Template* option. Notice that this worksheet contains many of the relevant task columns required in Project 2013, including the *Name, Duration, Start,* and *Finish* columns.

	A	B	C	D	E	F	G
1	ID	Active	Task Mode	Name	Duration	Start	Finish
2	0	Yes	Auto Scheduled	Annual Audit Prep for FY2014	41.5 d	April 6, 2015 8:00 AM	June 3, 2015 12:00
3	1	Yes	Auto Scheduled	Perform Initial Planning	6 d	April 6, 2015 8:00 AM	April 13, 2015 5:00
4	2	Yes	Auto Scheduled	Review lessons learned from last year	1 d	April 6, 2015 8:00 AM	April 6, 2015 5:00 P
5	3	Yes	Auto Scheduled	Confirm changes, if any, to financial reporting requirements	1 d	April 7, 2015 8:00 AM	April 7, 2015 5:00 P
6	4	Yes	Auto Scheduled	Identify Annual Report Theme and Section Requirements	1 d	April 8, 2015 8:00 AM	April 8, 2015 5:00 P
7	5	Yes	Auto Scheduled	Confirm other sections to be added or removed	1 d	April 9, 2015 8:00 AM	April 9, 2015 5:00 P
8	6	Yes	Auto Scheduled	Confirm SEC filing and Annual Report Checkpoints	1 d	April 10, 2015 8:00 AM	April 10, 2015 5:00
9	7	Yes	Auto Scheduled	Selection of Internal Auditors	1 d	April 13, 2015 8:00 AM	April 13, 2015 5:00
10	8	Yes	Auto Scheduled	Initial Planning Complete	0 d	April 13, 2015 5:00 PM	April 13, 2015 5:00
11	9	Yes	Auto Scheduled	Design Annual Report	6 d	April 14, 2015 8:00 AM	April 21, 2015 5:00
12	10	Yes	Auto Scheduled	Assign resources to preliminary design	1 d	April 14, 2015 8:00 AM	April 14, 2015 5:00
13	11	Yes	Auto Scheduled	Develop preliminary design and information requirements	1 d	April 15, 2015 8:00 AM	April 15, 2015 5:00
14	12	Yes	Auto Scheduled	Evaluate/Confirm Report Distribution Mechanisms	3 d	April 16, 2015 8:00 AM	April 20, 2015 5:00
15	13	Yes	Auto Scheduled	Evaluate/confirm Annual Report design and communications vendor(s)	1 d	April 16, 2015 8:00 AM	April 16, 2015 5:00
16	14	Yes	Auto Scheduled	Evaluate/confirm corporate Web site design and integration requirements	1 d	April 17, 2015 8:00 AM	April 17, 2015 5:00
17	15	Yes	Auto Scheduled	Evaluate/confirm Annual Report production and mailing vendor(s)	1 d	April 20, 2015 8:00 AM	April 20, 2015 5:00
18	16	Yes	Auto Scheduled	Report Distribution Mechanisms Confirmed	0 d	April 20, 2015 5:00 PM	April 20, 2015 5:00
19	17	Yes	Auto Scheduled	Plan/confirm production schedule	1 d	April 21, 2015 8:00 AM	April 21, 2015 5:00
20	18	Yes	Auto Scheduled	Annual Report Design Complete	0 d	April 21, 2015 5:00 PM	April 21, 2015 5:00
21	19	Yes	Auto Scheduled	Define SEC 10-K and Proxy Documentation Production Schedules	3 d	April 22, 2015 8:00 AM	April 24, 2015 5:00
22	20	Yes	Auto Scheduled	Plan/confirm 10-K production schedule	1 d	April 22, 2015 8:00 AM	April 22, 2015 5:00
23	21	Yes	Auto Scheduled	Plan/confirm Proxy Statement production schedule	1 d	April 23, 2015 8:00 AM	April 23, 2015 5:00
24	22	Yes	Auto Scheduled	Identify process steps required to meet production schedule	1 d	April 24, 2015 8:00 AM	April 24, 2015 5:00
25	23	Yes	Auto Scheduled	SEC 10-K and Proxy Documentation Production Schedules Complete	0 d	April 24, 2015 5:00 PM	April 24, 2015 5:00
26	24	Yes	Auto Scheduled	Develop Annual Report	21 d	April 27, 2015 8:00 AM	May 26, 2015 5:00 P
27	25	Yes	Auto Scheduled	Develop Theme production components	7 d	April 27, 2015 8:00 AM	May 5, 2015 5:00 PM
28	26	Yes	Auto Scheduled	Schedule and hold Theme development sessions	1 d	April 27, 2015 8:00 AM	April 27, 2015 5:00
29	27	Yes	Auto Scheduled	Gather Theme statistics/validate Theme messages	1 d	April 28, 2015 8:00 AM	April 28, 2015 5:00
30	28	Yes	Auto Scheduled	Interview Theme Stakeholders	1 d	April 29, 2015 8:00 AM	April 29, 2015 5:00
31	29	Yes	Auto Scheduled	Develop initial Theme section writeups	1 d	April 30, 2015 8:00 AM	April 30, 2015 5:00
32	30	Yes	Auto Scheduled	Schedule Theme Photo and Web Site Design Sessions	1 d	May 1, 2015 8:00 AM	May 1, 2015 5:00 PM

Task_Table / Resource_Table / Assignment_Table

Figure 13 - 48: Task_Table worksheet in the Excel workbook

7. If you choose the *Selected Data* option on the *Data* page of the *Export Wizard* dialog, click the *Next* button. Project 2013 displays the *Map* page of the *Export Wizard* dialog shown in Figure 13 - 49.

The *Map* page of the *Export Wizard* dialog offers you two options for mapping your Project 2013 fields to columns of data in the Excel workbook:

- Select the *New map* option to create your own export map.
- Select the *Use existing map* option to select a default map or a custom map you created during a previous data export session.

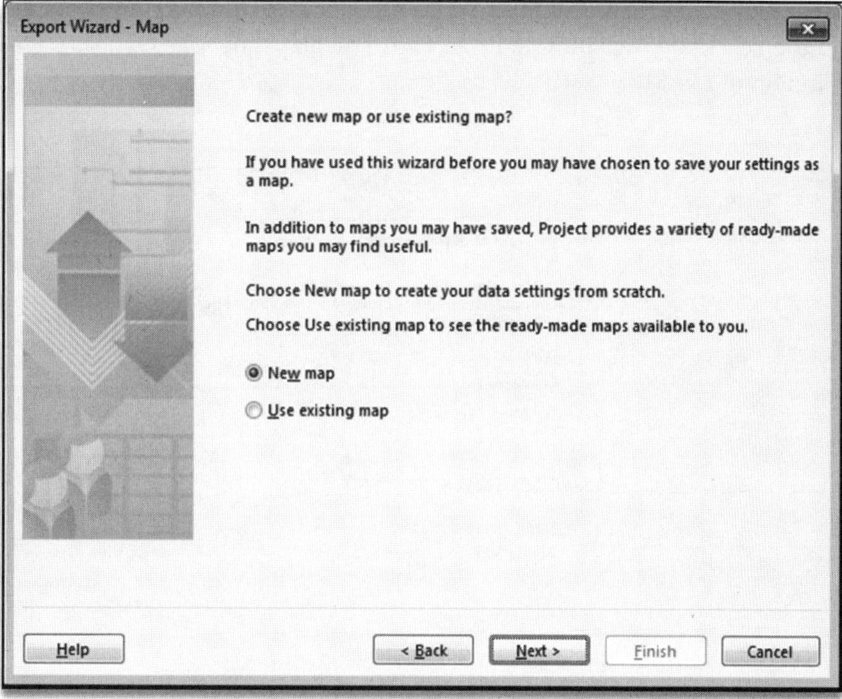

Figure 13 - 49: Export Wizard dialog, Map page

8. If you select the *Use existing map* option and click the *Next* button, the software displays the *Map Selection* page of the *Export Wizard* dialog shown in Figure 13 - 50. Each of the maps listed in the dialog contains a pre-defined list of Project 2013 fields to export. For example, the *"Who Does What" report* map exports resource and task assignment information. Select a map from this page and then click the *Finish* button.

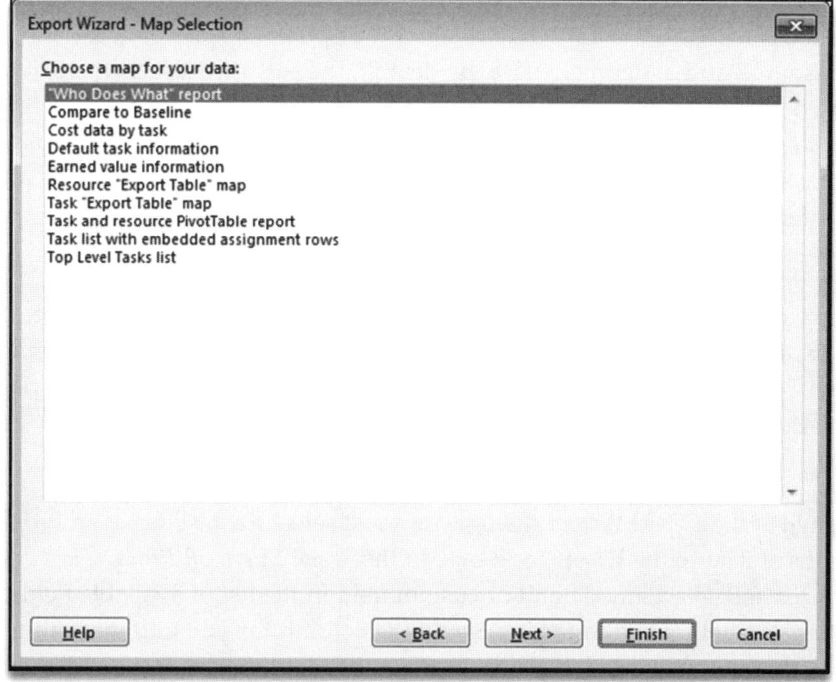

Figure 13 - 50: Export Wizard dialog, Map Selection page

9. If you do not want to use a predefined map, select the *New map* option on the *Map* page of the *Export Wizard* dialog, and then click the *Next* button. Project 2013 displays the *Map Options* page of the *Export Wizard* dialog shown in Figure 13 - 51.

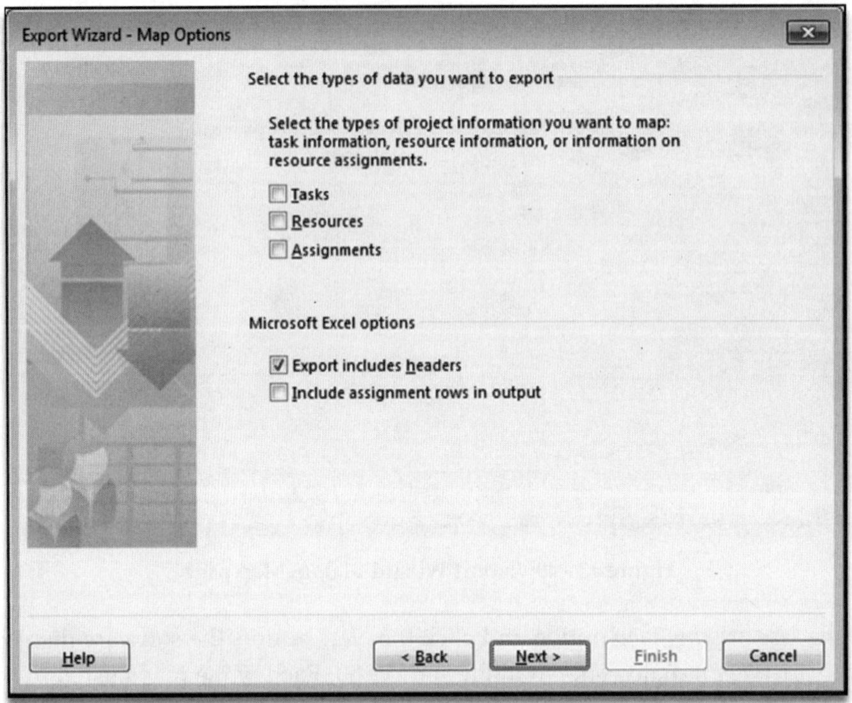

Figure 13 - 51: Export Wizard dialog, Map Options page

On the *Map Options* page of the *Export Wizard* dialog, select the options for the project data types you want to export, including task, resource, and assignment data. By default, the software selects the *Export includes headers* option so that the exported Excel workbook displays column headers for each data column. If you select the *Include assignment rows in output* option, Project 2013 includes assignment rows such as those displayed in the *Task Usage* and *Resource Usage* views. Keep in mind that the software **does not** automatically outline and indent the assignment rows in the exported Excel workbook.

10. After you select your options on the *Map Options* page of the *Export Wizard* dialog, click the *Next* button. Project 2013 displays the appropriate pages in the *Export Wizard* based on the options you selected on the previous page. For example, if you selected the *Task* option on the *Map Options* page, the software displays the *Task Mapping* page of the *Export Wizard* dialog shown in Figure 13 - 52.

In the *Task Mapping* page of the *Export Wizard* dialog, you must select the task fields in Project 2013 that the software exports as columns of data to the Excel workbook. In the *From: Microsoft Project Field* column, click the *(Click here to map a field)* pick list and select any default or custom field in the list of available fields. After you select the field, the software enters the field name in the *To: Excel Field* column for you automatically, but you can edit the name in the *To: Excel Field* column as needed. Select as many project fields as you need in successive rows in the *From: Microsoft Project Field* column.

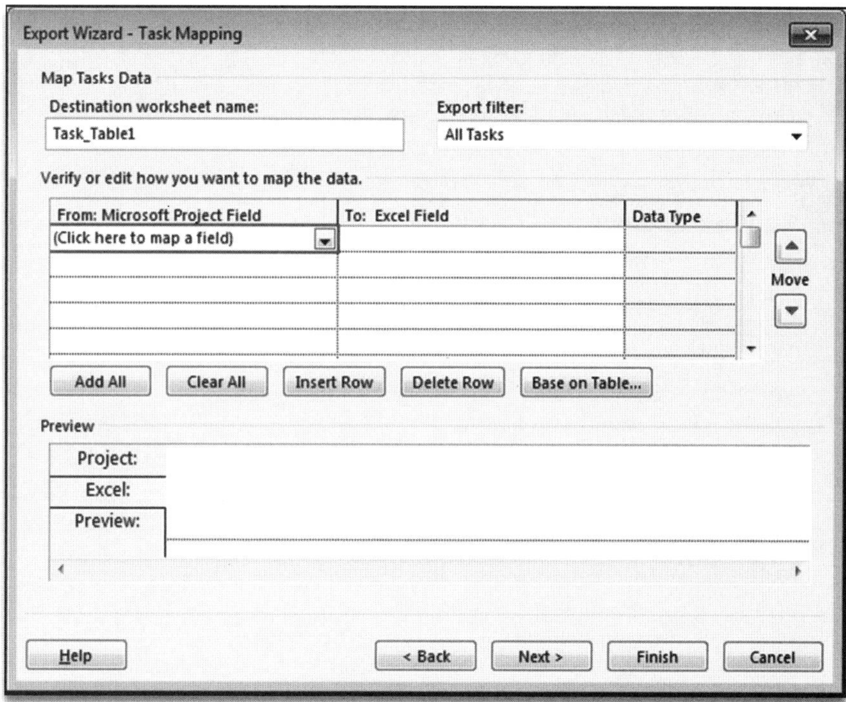

Figure 13 - 52: Export Wizard dialog, Task Mapping page

Manually selecting a list of fields to export can be a time consuming process. The fastest way to generate the list of fields is to use the list of fields included in a default or custom table in your project.

11. To quickly generate the list of fields using the fields in a default or custom table, click the *Base on Table* button on the *Task Mapping* page of the *Export Wizard* dialog. Project 2013 displays the *Select Base Table for Field Mapping* dialog shown in Figure 13 - 53. This dialog contains all of the default task tables, plus any custom task tables you created previously.

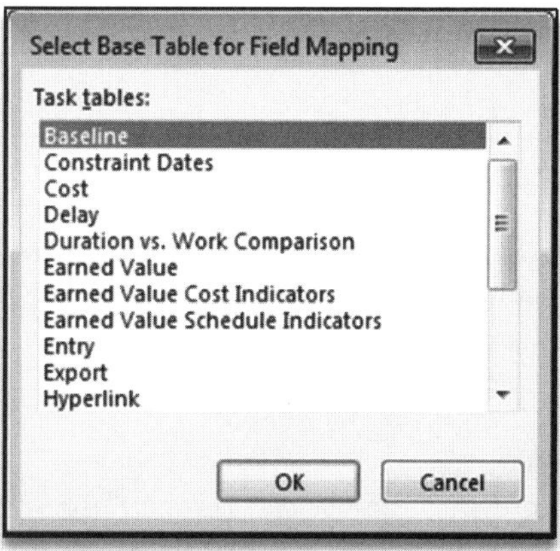

Figure 13 - 53: Select Base Table for Field Mapping dialog

12. Select a table in the *Select Base Table for Field Mapping* dialog and then click the *OK* button. Project 2013 generates the list of fields from the table you select. For example, Figure 13 - 54 shows the list of fields after selecting the *Work* table. After importing a list of fields from a table, you can also manually supplement the list of fields as needed.

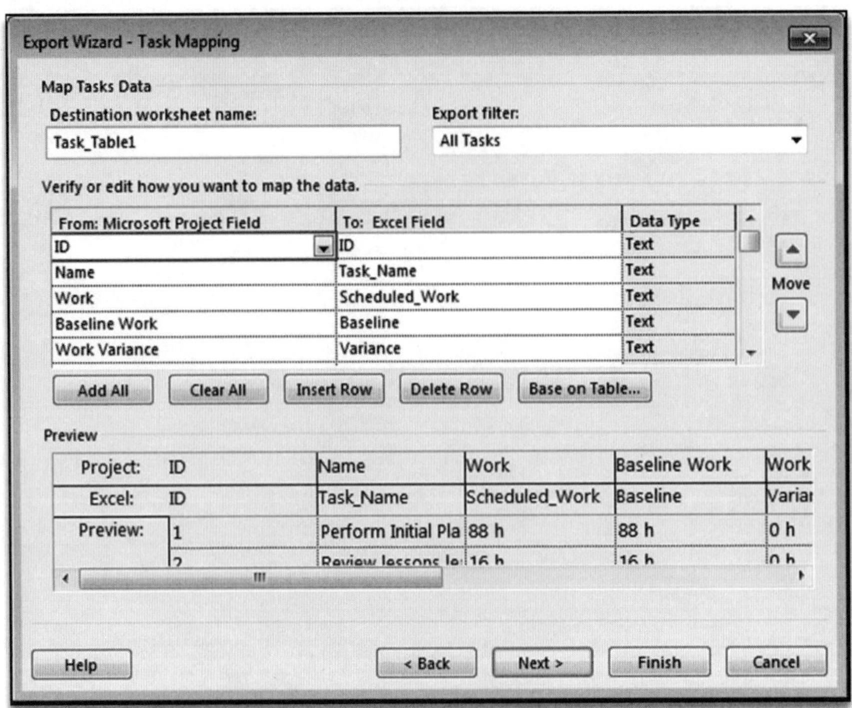

Figure 13 - 54: Export Wizard dialog, Task Mapping page with fields from task Work table

Best Practice: If you manually create an Excel workbook containing task data, and you intend to import the task data into a new project, MsProjectExperts recommends that you include the *Outline Level* column in the worksheet containing task data. Project 2013 needs the data in this column to display the Work Breakdown Structure (WBS) of summary tasks and subtasks when it imports the data from the Excel workbook. In addition, MsProjectExperts recommends that you name the columns in Excel using exactly the same names used in Project 2013, as doing so makes the import process much easier. This means that in your Excel workbook, you should use the *Name* column to refer to the *Task Name* column in Project 2013. The reason for this is because the real name of the *Task Name* column is actually *Name*. *Task Name* is simply the label or "nickname" for this column in Project 2013.

13. On the *Task Mapping* page of the *Export Wizard* dialog, optionally enter a name in the *Destination worksheet name* field for the Excel worksheet. You can also click the *Export filter* pick list and select a default or custom filter to filter the exported task list.

Information: For the sake of brevity, I do not discuss the *Resource Mapping* and *Assignment Mapping* pages in the *Export Wizard* dialog. Keep in mind, however, that you use these two pages exactly the same as you use the *Task Mapping* page.

14. Click the *Next* button when you complete your selections. Project 2013 displays the *End of Map Definition* page of the *Export Wizard* dialog shown in Figure 13 - 55.

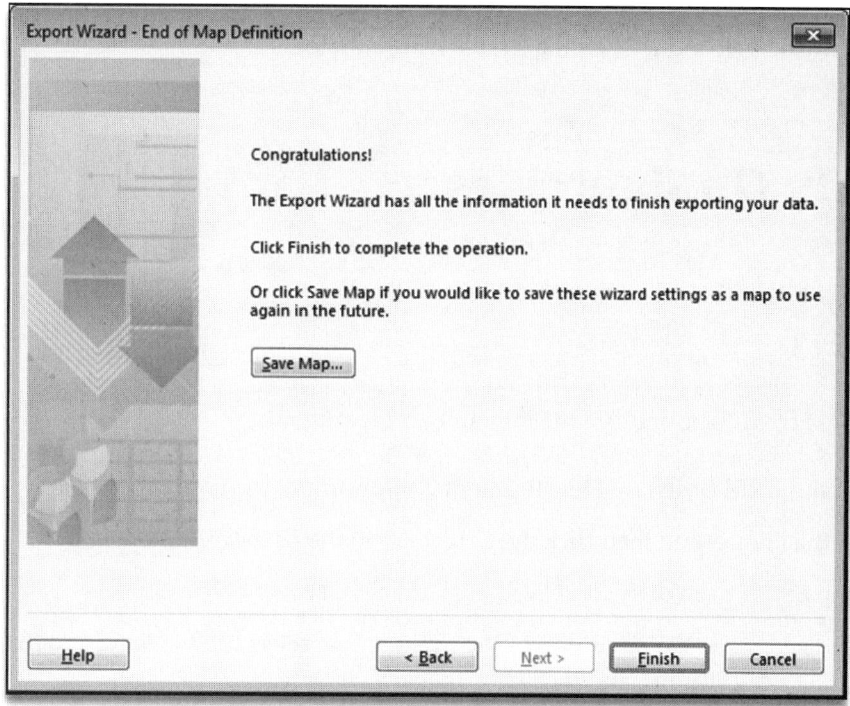

Figure 13 - 55: Export Wizard, End of Map Definition page

On the *End of Map Definition* page in *Export Wizard* dialog, click the *Save Map* button if you want to save your export map for future use. Project 2013 displays the *Save Map* dialog shown in Figure 13 - 56. Enter a name for the new map in the *Map name* field and then click the *Save* button.

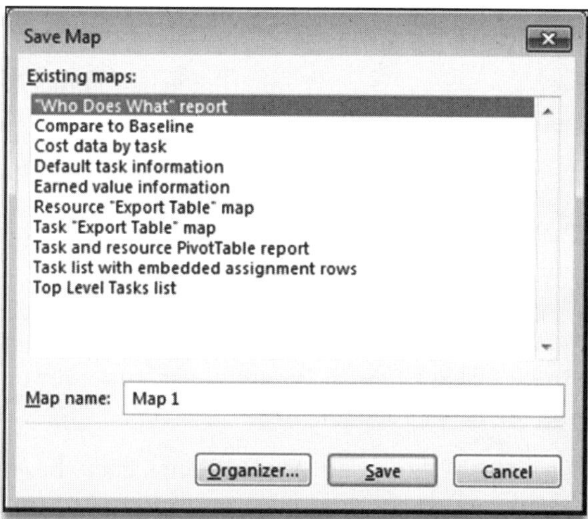

Figure 13 - 56: Save Map dialog

Information: When you save an export map using the *Save Map* dialog, Project 2013 stores the new map in the Global.mpt file and **not** in the active project. This means you can immediately use the new map in all current and future projects. You can use stored maps to export project data to an Excel workbook or to import data from an Excel workbook into a project file.

15. Click the *Finish* button on the *End of Map Definition* page in *Export Wizard* dialog to export the selected data to an Excel workbook and to close the *Export Wizard* dialog.

Hands On Exercise

Exercise 13 - 13

Export cost data from a Project 2013 file into an Excel workbook.

1. Open the **CRM Software Development 2013.mpp** sample file.
2. Click the *File* tab and then click the *Export* tab in the *Backstage*.
3. On the *Export* page of the *Backstage*, click the *Save Project as File* tab.
4. In the *Save Project as File* section of the *Export* page, select the *Microsoft Excel Workbook* file type in *the Other File Types* list, and then click the *Save As* button.
5. In the *Save As* dialog, click the *Save* button to launch the *Export Wizard*.
6. On the *Welcome* page of the *Export Wizard* dialog, click the *Next* button.
7. On the *Data* page of the *Export Wizard* dialog, choose the *Selected Data* option, and then click the *Next* button.
8. On the *Map* page of the *Export Wizard* dialog, select the *New map* option, and then click the *Next* button.
9. On the *Map Options* page of the *Export Wizard* dialog, select the *Tasks* option, and then click the *Next* button.
10. On the *Task Mapping* page of the *Export Wizard* dialog, click the *Base on Table* button.
11. In the *Select Base Table for Field Mapping* dialog, select the *Cost* table, and then click the *OK* button.
12. On the *Task Mapping* page of the *Export Wizard* dialog, select the *Name* cell in the *From: Microsoft Project Field* column, and then click the *Insert Row* button.
13. Click the pick list in the *From: Microsoft Project Field* column for the new blank row and select the *Outline Level* field on the list of available fields.
14. On the *Task Mapping* page of the *Export Wizard* dialog, click the *Next* button.
15. On the *End of Map Definition* page of the *Export Wizard* dialog, click the *Finish* button.
16. Launch your Excel application and navigate to the folder containing your student sample files.
17. Open the **CRM Software Development 2013.xlsx** workbook.
18. Double-click the right edge of each column header to auto fit the width of each worksheet column, as needed.
19. Examine the project data exported to the Excel workbook.

20. Save and close the **CRM Software Development 2013.xlsx** workbook and then exit the Excel application.

21. Return to your Project 2013 application window.

22. Save and close the **CRM Software Development 2013.mpp** sample file.

Working with VBA

Visual Basic for Applications (VBA) is a programming language included with the applications in the Office 2013 suite. Microsoft based the VBA programming language on early versions of the Visual Basic programming language, but modified and extended it to work with each program in the Office family. Project 2013 includes a full implementation of VBA that allows you to programmatically do everything you can manually do with the software, and offers the possibility of automating procedures that are not possible to do manually.

A **macro** is each program that you write in Project 2013 VBA. You can create a macro by recording it or by writing it. Many people use a combination of these two methods, recording what you can record, and then writing everything else.

Information: This module presents only a brief overview of Project 2013 VBA. For an in-depth treatment of the Project 2013 VBA programming language, see *VBA Programming for Project '98 through 2010 with an Introduction to VSTO*, by Rod Gill (ISBN 978-1-934240-21-2). This book is part of our *EPM Learning* series of books, available at http://www.projectserverbooks.com or your favorite bookseller.

Displaying the Developer Ribbon

Before you begin working with macros and the VBA programming language, I recommend you display the *Developer* ribbon in Project 2013. Using this ribbon, you can quickly locate the buttons you need to record, write, view, and run macros. To display the *Developer* ribbon, complete the following steps:

1. Right-click any ribbon tab and select the *Customize the Ribbon* item on the shortcut menu. Project 2013 displays the *Project Options* dialog with the *Customize Ribbon* tab selected.

2. In the list of ribbons shown on the right side of the dialog, select the option checkbox for the *Developer* ribbon, and then click the *OK* button.

Project 2013 displays the *Developer* ribbon shown in Figure 13 - 57. Notice that the *Developer* ribbon appears to the immediate left of the *Format* ribbon, and includes sections labeled *Code*, *Manage*, and *Add-Ins*. To record and write macros, you use the four buttons in the *Code* section. To rename, delete, or copy macros, you use the *Organizer* button in the *Manage* section of the *Developer* ribbon. You use the *COM Add-Ins* button in the *Add-Ins* section to manage Add-Ins you load into Project 2013.

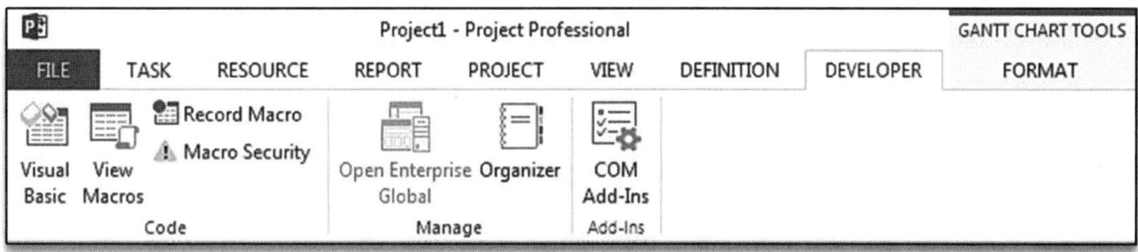

Figure 13 - 57: Developer ribbon

Information: Notice that the *Developer* ribbon shown previously in Figure 13 - 57 includes a button named *Open Enterprise Global* in the *Manage* section of the ribbon. This button is only available in the **Professional** version of Project 2013, and you can only use this button with Project Server 2013. If your organization does not use Project Server 2013, the software disables this button.

Warning: If you choose not to display the *Developer* ribbon in Project 2013, then you must access all macro-related commands using the *Macros* pick list button in the *Macros* section at the far right end of the *View* ribbon. In the remainder of Module 13, I refer to all macro-related commands using the buttons on the *Developer* ribbon.

Hands On Exercise

Exercise 13 - 14

Display the *Developer* ribbon in Project 2013.

1. Right-click any ribbon tab and then select the *Customize the Ribbon* item on the shortcut menu.

2. In the list of ribbons shown on the right side of the *Project Options* dialog, select the option checkbox for the *Developer* ribbon, and then click the *OK* button.

3. Examine the sections and buttons shown in the *Developer* ribbon.

Recording a Macro

If you perform a series of tasks repeatedly in Project 2013, you can record a macro to repeat the steps for you programmatically. To record a macro, complete the following steps:

1. In the *Code* section of the *Developer* ribbon, click the *Record Macro* button. Project 2013 displays the *Record Macro* dialog shown in Figure 13 - 58.

2. In the *Macro name* field, enter a meaningful name for the macro.

Warning: Project 2013 **does not** allow you to use spaces when naming a macro. To work around this limitation, I prefer to capitalize the first letter of each word in the macro name and to substitute the underscore character for the space character when I enter the names of macros I record.

3. Click the *Store macro in* pick list and select a location for the macro.

You can store the macro in the active project or in the Global.mpt file. If you store the macro in the active project, you can only run the macro when you have the project open. If you store the macro in the Global.mpt file, you can run the macro with any open project.

Figure 13 - 58: Record Macro dialog

4. Enter an optional description in the *Description* field to describe the function of your macro. Notice that the software automatically includes your name and the date you recorded the macro.

5. Leave the default options selected in the *Row references* and *Column references* sections of the dialog.

6. Click the *OK* button.

7. Manually complete the actions you want to record.

8. To stop recording the macro, click the *Stop Recording* button in the *Code* section of the *Developer* ribbon.

Viewing Your Recorded Macro VBA Code

After you record a new macro, you may want to view and even edit the resulting VBA code. To view and edit the VBA code, complete the following steps:

1. In the *Code* section of the *Developer* ribbon, click the *View Macros* button. Project 2013 displays the *Macros* dialog shown in Figure 13 - 59. Notice that the *Macros* dialog lists only one macro currently. Based on the name of this macro, *Create_Simple_Project,* you might guess that I use this macro to create a simple project for demonstration purposes.

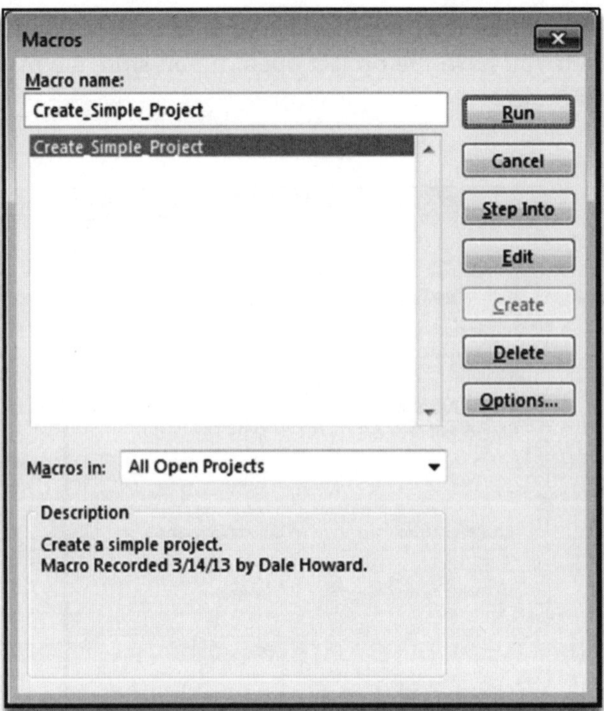

Figure 13 - 59: Macros dialog

2. In the *Macros* dialog, select the name of the newly recorded macro, and then click the *Edit* button.

Project 2013 opens a new window and displays the *Visual Basic Editor* in the window. The *Visual Basic Editor* includes three panes by default: the *Code* pane on the right side, the *Project Explorer* pane in the upper left corner, and the *Properties* pane in the lower left corner of the window, as shown in Figure 13 - 60.

The *Code* pane shows all of the VBA code created as you record a macro. Notice in Figure 13 - 60 that my macro contains approximately 35 lines of code to create a simple project according to my specifications.

In the *Project Explorer* pane shown in Figure 13 - 60, notice that Project 2013 stored my macro in a module named *Module1*. Modules are containers in which the software stores all recorded and written VBA code. To rename a module, select the module in the *Project Explorer* pane and then enter the new module name in the *Name* field in the *Properties* pane. For example, I might rename my new module as *Demos* to indicate that I intend to record and write new macros to use with various demonstrations that I give regularly to clients.

You can also use the Visual Basic Editor to edit your VBA code. When you finish making changes to your macro code, click the *Save* button and then close the *Visual Basic Editor* window.

Information: If you record a macro saved in a project, clicking the *Save* button saves the project. If you record a macro saved in the Global.mpt file, clicking the *Save* button saves the Global.mpt file instead of the project file. This is the only way you can manually save the Global.mpt file.

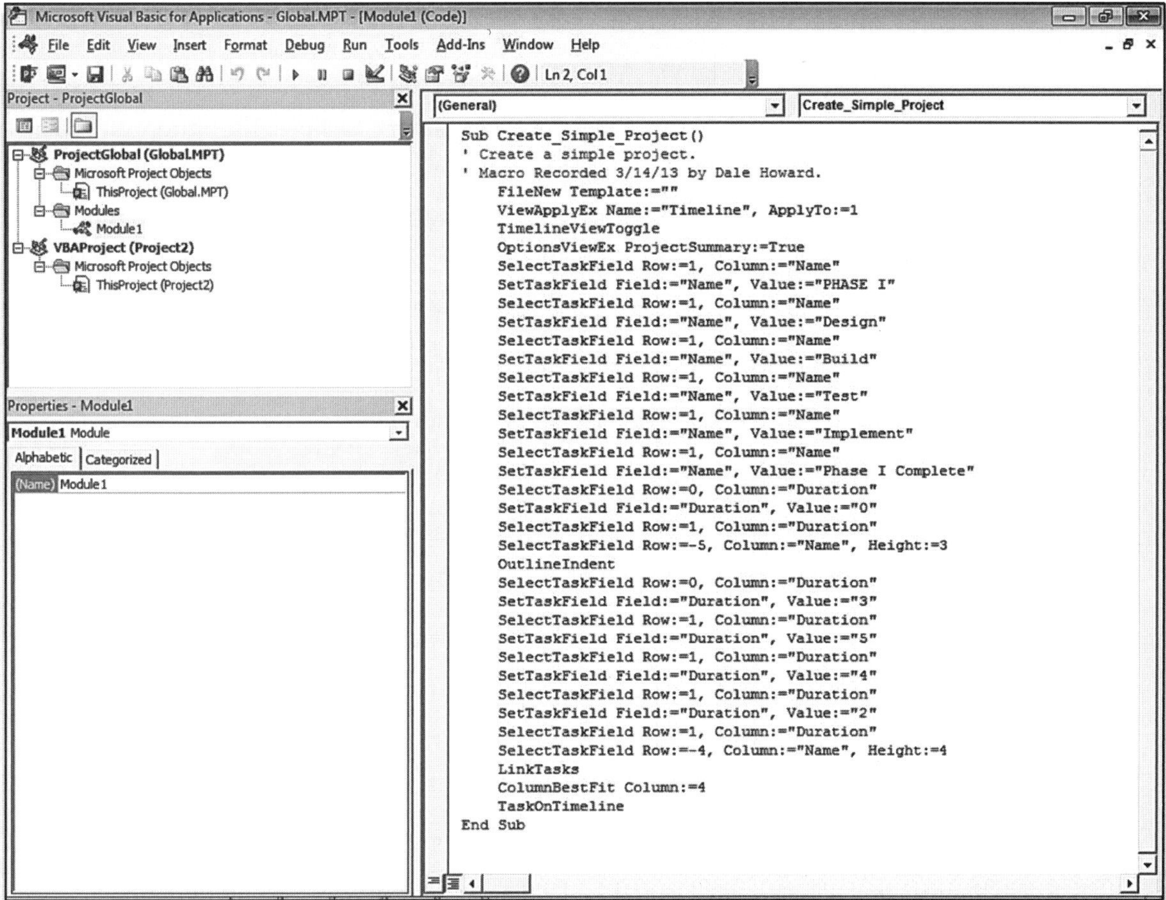

Figure 13 - 60: Visual Basic Editor window

Hands On Exercise

Exercise 13 - 15

Record a macro to automatically format the *Gantt Chart* view in a particular manner.

1. Open the **PMP Training Program Development 2013.mpp** sample file.
2. In the *Code* section of the *Developer* ribbon, click the *Record Macro* button.
3. In the *Record Macro* dialog, enter the following information:

Macro name	Format_Gantt_Chart
Store macro in	Global File
Description	Use this macro to format the Gantt Chart view.

4. Click the *OK* button to begin recording.
5. Click the *View* tab to display the *View* ribbon.
6. In the *Task Views* section of the *View* ribbon, click the *Gantt Chart* pick list button, and then select the *Gantt Chart* view.
7. In the *Zoom* section of the *View* ribbon, click the *Timescale* pick list and select the *Days* level of zoom.
8. Right-click the *Task Mode* column header and select the *Hide Column* item on the shortcut menu.
9. Select the task name shown for the Project Summary Task (Row 0).
10. Drag the split bar to the right edge of the *Duration* column.
11. Click the *Format* tab to display the contextual *Format* ribbon with the *Gantt Chart Tools* applied.
12. In the *Format* section of the *Format* ribbon, click the *Text Styles* button.
13. In the *Text Styles* dialog, click the *Item to Change* pick list, and select the *Summary Tasks* item.
14. In the *Font style* section of the dialog, select the *Bold Italic* item.
15. Click the *Background Color* pick list and select the *Orange, Lighter 60%* color in the *Theme Colors* section of the menu.
16. In the *Text Styles* dialog, click the *Item to Change* pick list, and select the *Milestone Tasks* item.
17. In the *Font style* section of the dialog, select the *Italic* item.
18. Click the *Background Color* pick list and select the *Green, Lighter 60%* color in the *Theme Colors* section of the menu.
19. Click the *OK* button to close the *Text Styles* dialog.
20. In the *Format* section of the *Format* ribbon, click the *Layout* button.
21. In the *Links* section of the *Layout* dialog, select the second item.
22. In the *Bars* section of the *Layout* dialog, click the *Date format* pick list, and then select the *Jan 28* item.
23. Click the *OK* button to close the *Layout* dialog.
24. In the *Bar Styles* section of the *Format* ribbon, select the *Critical Tasks* checkbox.
25. In the *Show/Hide* section of the *Format* ribbon, select the *Outline Number* checkbox.
26. Click the *Developer* tab to display the *Developer* ribbon again.
27. In the *Code* section of the *Developer* ribbon, click the *Stop Recording* button.
28. Click the *File* tab and then click the *Close* tab in the *Backstage.*
29. When prompted, click the *No* button so that you **do not save** the sample file.
30. If the software returns to the *Backstage*, press the **Escape** key on your computer keyboard to return to the main Project 2013 user interface.

Exercise 13 - 16

View the recorded VBA code in your new macro.

1. In the *Code* section of the *Developer* ribbon, click the *View Macros* button.
2. In the *Macros* dialog, select the *Format_Gantt_Chart* macro, and then click the *Edit* button.
3. In the *Visual Basic Editor* window, review the VBA code that you just recorded in Exercise 13 - 15.
4. In the *Visual Basic Editor* window, click the *Save* button to save the Global.mpt file.
5. Close the *Visual Basic Editor* window.

Running a Macro

Like Project 2010, Project 2013 **does not** include any default macros. This means that you can only run macros that you record, write, or obtain from another source. To run a macro, complete the following steps:

1. In the *Code* section of the *Developer* ribbon, click the *View Macros* button.
2. In the *Macros* dialog, select any macro, and then click the *Run* button.

Hands On Exercise

Exercise 13 - 17

Run the *Format_Gantt_Chart* macro.

1. Open the **PMP Training Program Development 2013.mpp** sample file again.
2. In the *Code* section of the *Developer* ribbon, click the *View Macros* button.
3. In the *Macros* dialog, select the *Format_Gantt_Chart* macro, and then click the *Run* button.

Notice how rapidly the macro formatted the *Gantt Chart* view of the project.

4. Save and close the **PMP Training Program Development 2013.mpp** sample file.
5. If interested, open any of your own production projects and try the *Format_Gantt_Chart* macro with them.
6. Close your own projects and **do not save them** unless you approve of the formatting applied to the *Gantt Chart* view of your own projects.

Index

A

B

P

X

Other Great books from MSProjectExperts:

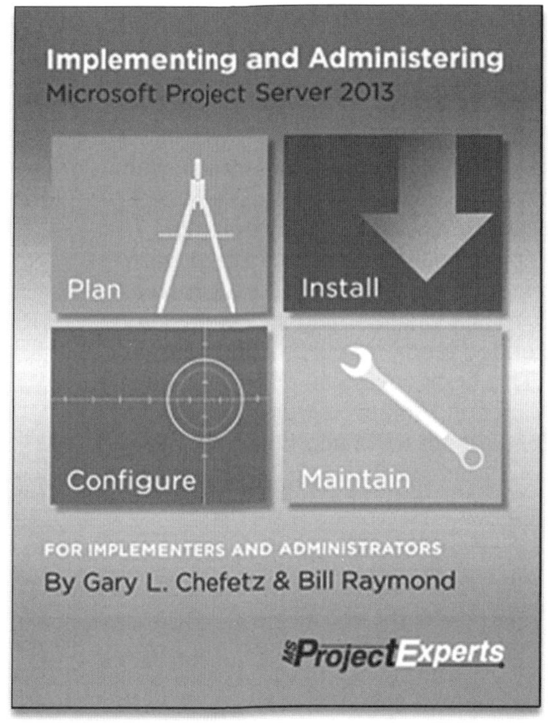

Implementing and Administering Microsoft Project Server 2013

ISBN 978-1-934240-25-0

Implementing and Administering Microsoft Project Server 2013, the essential reference guide for installing, configuring, and deploying Project Server 2013 now covers Project Online. This book begins with the organizational strategies you need to succeed with a PPM deployment and follows through with an implementation plan and step-by-step instructions for installing, configuring and deploying the SharePoint 2013 and Project Server 2013 platform to your organization. Loaded with best practices, warnings and tips from Project Server gurus Gary Chefetz and Bill Raymond, *Implementing and Administering Microsoft Project Server 2013* sets the gold standard for PPM implementations using Project Server.

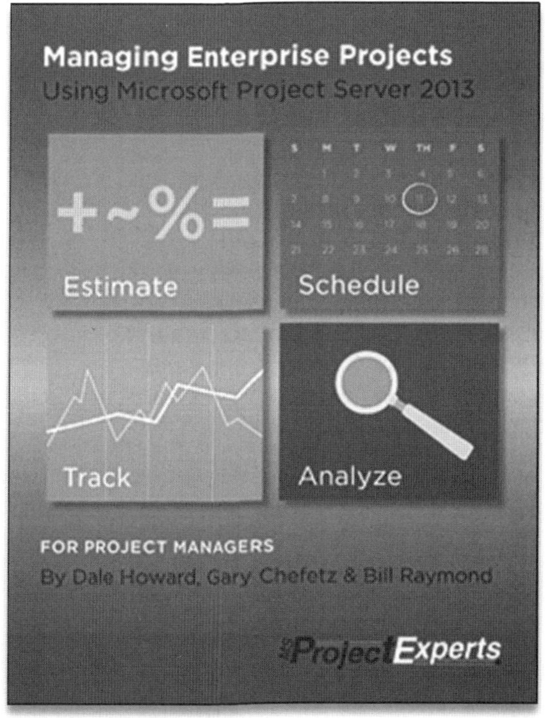

Managing Enterprise Projects Using Microsoft Project Server 2013

ISBN 978-1-934240-28-1

Managing Enterprise Projects Using Microsoft Project Server 2013 is an unprecedented learning guide and reference for project managers who use the Microsoft PPM platform. Our goal for this book is to provide a combination of training and reference manual, as well as a vital learning tool to help you build on your knowledge of the stand-alone application by mastering the Microsoft enterprise project management environment. Follow our best practices to success and heed our warnings to avoid the pitfalls.

Prepare for Microsoft Exam 74-344

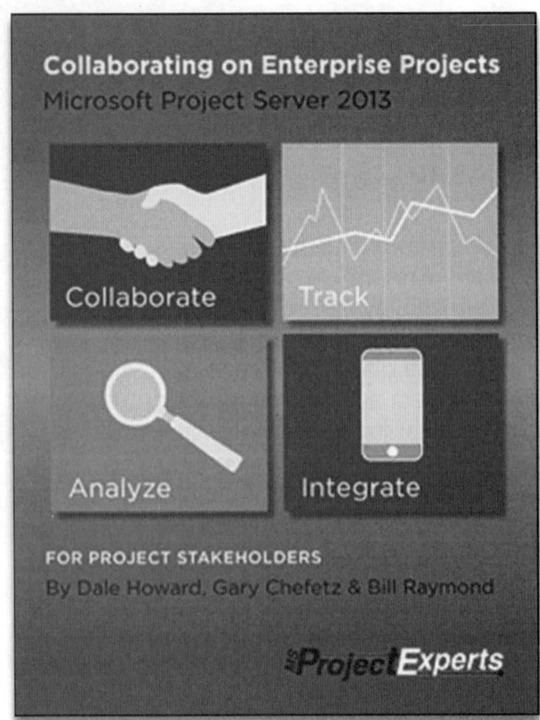

Collaborating on Enterprise Projects Microsoft Project Server 2013

ISBN 978-1-934240-29-8

This is the only book written specifically for managers and team members who use the Microsoft PPM platform, including SharePoint and Project Server 2013. Loaded with best practices, tips and tricks, and warnings, *Collaborating on Enterprise Projects Microsoft Project Server 2013* is a vital learning tool to help you educate your extended team, resource managers and senior staff. This book covers all of the collaborative features in Microsoft Project Server 2013, including SharePoint features for PPM and business intelligence tools.

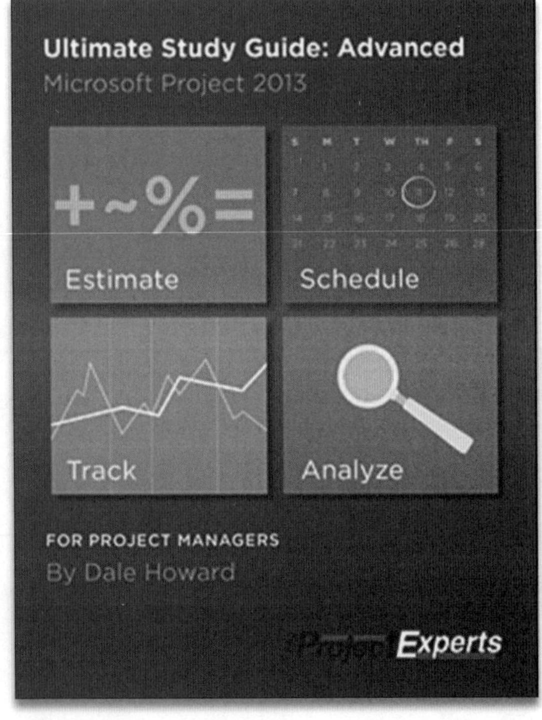

Ultimate Study Guide: Advanced Microsoft Project 2013

ISBN 978-1-934240-30-4

This book teaches you advanced techniques for using Microsoft Project 2013. You gain in-depth knowledge about standard and custom fields, calendars, scheduling, costing, critical path analysis, and exchanging project data with other applications. You learn advanced leveling techniques, how to create a shared resource pool, and how to record and write VBA macros for your project. After reading this book, you will be much more effective using Microsoft Project 2013.